The Political Science Concept Inventory

"I wish political science was as advanced as medical science, Doc . . . you got more words that nobody knows the meaning of . . ."

"Grin and Bear It" by George Lichty
Courtesy of Field Newspaper Syndicate

The Political Science Concept Inventory

Ralph M. Goldman
Philip G. Schoner
DeVere E. Pentony

Clio Books
Santa Barbara, California
Oxford, England

Library of Congress Cataloging in Publication Data

Goldman, Ralph Morris, 1920-
   The political science concept inventory.

   Bibliography: p.
   Includes index.
   1. Political science—Terminology. 2. Political science—Study and teaching (Higher) I. Schoner, Philip G., joint author. II. Pentony, DeVere Edwin, 1924- joint author. III. Title.
JA61.G64   320'.01'4   79-12722
ISBN 0-87436-295-4

American Bibliographical Center—Clio Press
Riviera Campus, 2040 A.P.S., Box 4397
Santa Barbara, California 93103

Clio Press, Ltd.
Woodside House, Hinksey Hill
Oxford, OX1 5BE, England

Manufactured in the United States of America

Contents

Tables and Figures vii

Acknowledgments ix

Chapter 1   The Vocabulary of a Discipline 1
    The Major Assessment Profile (MAP) Project   1
    Academic Disciplines as Language Communities 2
    Uses of Language in an Academic Discipline 3
    Sources of Terms and Concepts 4

Chapter 2   The Judging Panel and Evaluation Procedure 9
    Panel Representativeness 9
    Devising an Evaluation Procedure 12

Chapter 3   Characteristics of Political Science Concepts 17
    Consensus and Disagreement in Panel Ratings 17
    Reproducibility of Ratings 20
    The MAP Nomenclature Typology 21

Chapter 4   Using the Political Science Concept Inventory 27
    Scope of the Major: The Curriculum Guide 27
    Coordinating Scope of Particular Subfields and Courses   29
    The Introductory Course 30
    Computer-Assisted Instruction   32
    Examination Preparation 32
    Diagnosing Student Progress 33
    Reference Sources 34
    Substantive Content Comparisons 35

Chapter 5   Courses in American Government and International
      Relations: Two Applications 37
    American Government 37
    Ratings of American Government Concepts by ETS Committee 39

Tables and Figures

Tables

1	Subfield Training, Interests, and Activities of MAP Panelists	11
2	Distribution of MAP Inventory Terms by Category of Ascribed Importance and by Panelist	13
3	Distribution of Terms According to Mean of Ratings Assigned by MAP Panelists	18
4	Degrees of Disagreement among MAP Panelists According to Standard Deviation for Each Term	19
5	Panelists' Success in Reliability Test Using One Hundred Duplicate Concept Judgments	21
6	Distribution of Terms in Nomenclature Typology	24
7	Distribution of Inventory Terms by Panel Means and Nomenclature Types	25
8	Diagnostic Matrix Showing Student Improvement in Political Science Test Scores	34
9	Distribution of Nine-Member Panel Ratings of 1,236 International Relations Concepts According to Means and Standard Deviations	56
10	Statistical Characteristics of Each Panelist's Set of Concept Ratings	58
11	Degrees of Association (Gamma) in Concept Ratings of Pairs of IRIL Panelists	59

Figures

1–3		59-60

Acknowledgments

The Major Assessment Profile (MAP) Project was funded (1974–1976) by the New Program Development and Evaluation Division, Office of the Chancellor, The California State University and Colleges. The project was completed under the general administrative direction of DeVere E. Pentony, Dean of the School of Behavioral and Social Sciences, San Francisco State University. Professor Ralph M. Goldman, Department of Political Science, was the principal investigator, ably assisted by Philip G. Schoner, who served as senior research associate.

We extend our appreciation to Dean David Provost and Dr. John Smart of the New Program Division for their continued support of the MAP project and for their encouragement while we completed a task more difficult than we had initially anticipated. We also acknowledge, with sincere gratitude, the contribution of the inventory judging panel including John Sloane, Wayne Bradley, and Martin Hauser of San Francisco State University; Bernard Hennessy, California State University, Hayward; Max Franc and Lyman Heine, California State University, Fresno; John Wold, California State University, Stanislaus; and Jonathan Yinger, California State College, Fullerton, all of whom served loyally and patiently as volunteers.

We are, of course, responsible for whatever shortcomings there may be in this inquiry.

1

The Vocabulary of a Discipline

The Major Assessment Profile (MAP) Project

The MAP Project, of which this Political Science Concept Inventory is a part, was organized to outline an evaluation process and to create a set of prototype test instruments for use in political science curricula. The Major Assessment Profile, when completed, is expected to be a collection of coordinated tests designed to measure the learning outcomes of undergraduate instruction in the field. The goals of the project are:

> —to develop procedures to assist in the establishment of curricular objectives for undergraduate majors in political science;
> —to design a prototype Major Assessment Profile for the discipline;
> —to develop a diagnostic reporting system to evaluate student learning strengths and weaknesses;
> —to facilitate feedback processes to assist political science faculties in evaluating the results of their instruction.

The use of MAP measurements and the compilation of those data are intended to be the basis of curricula evaluation and modification. The instruments to be developed by the MAP Project for those purposes include (1) a survey of instructional objectives using the Delphi technique, (2) a Major Assessment Profile in Political Science, and (3) the Political Science Concept Inventory published in this volume.

The Political Science Concept Inventory lists 21,927 terms cited in forty-six political science dictionaries, encyclopedias, textbooks, master indexes, and similar sources.[1] A panel composed of ten political scientists rated each term on the basis of its importance for the undergraduate curriculum. The MAP panel was asked to judge whether students should know the term well, simply be aware of it, or need not know it. The terms were also classified by the Project staff according to the nomenclature typology described in Chapter 3.

The user will find the Inventory applicable to a variety of curriculum needs—it was designed to provide faculties a tool for curriculum development, and to provide students an aid to learning. The Inventory can also be used to assist the authors of books and monographs in political science in preparing their indexes. The designers of on-line data base systems may also find the Inventory useful as a controlled vocabulary for interrogating and accessing magnetic tape files. See Chapter 4 for a discussion of uses.

Academic Disciplines as Language Communities

Academic disciplines are organized to examine observable facts and events. Those who are committed to this examination identify and name the phenomena they observe, question their characteristics, propose and test generalizations about relationships among the phenomena, and make value judgments based on their conclusions. All of these activities involve the use of symbols, written and spoken language. Consequently, each discipline acquires a specialized idiom, or jargon, customarily employed in intradisciplinary communication. Thus, academic disciplines tend to become language communities bound together by common interests, values, concepts, and special conventions of terminology and method.

There are more than 3,000 languages. Anthropologists and linguists can verify the many ways language reflects the cultural activities and traditions of communities. Of course, learning a language does not ensure understanding the concerns, experience, and culture of a people—but information about the language (philology, etymology, and linguistics) of a community is a key to knowledge about that community. Thus, the first step toward understanding either a people or an academic discipline is to compile a lexicon of the words relevant to that particular culture or discipline—including word forms, pronunciations, functions, meanings, syntax, and idioms.

A dictionary, therefore, becomes a history book, a reference book, and an aid to communication indispensable for understanding and knowledge. The most advanced societies have vocabularies comprising several hundred thousand terms, many with more than one meaning or definition. The complexity of life in English-speaking societies is reflected in the 450,000 words listed in *Webster's Third New International Dictionary* (1969). Of course, such ponderous tomes leave the uninitiated wondering where to begin. To overcome that handicap, language specialists often produce a list of basic terms most frequently used and most essential to the newcomer, for example, the list of 800 Basic English terms. Similarly, the Political Science Concept Inventory is intended to introduce the undergraduate student to the basic terminology of this discipline.

The analogy is not overdrawn. Certainly a stranger who wanders into a professional meeting of chemists will recognize that the technical jargon employed there is distinctly different from that spoken in a meeting of political scientists, although he will also recognize that English is the language of both. The ability to communicate in a common technical language is "fundamental not only for effective teaching but for the

development of theoretically sound and systematic approaches to solving complex . . . problems."[2]

The publication of technical dictionaries is traditional in most disciplines, especially in those with substantial technologies. And, there has been increasing evidence of the need for such a dictionary in political science in recent years. Clement E. Vose examined ten recent books that were called dictionaries by their authors and editors.[3] He found that the largest volume contained 4,080 entries and the smallest listed 52. He concluded that the "books are not comprehensive in the sense of exhausting their subject and capturing all possible terminology." Vose added, ". . . they are really books that could have been case in other forms than dictionaries, but their authors simply found it attractive to do their work in this format rather than as one-act plays or videotape quiz shows." He concluded that political scientists "do not yet have a dictionary of professional quality."

The publication of these dictionaries suggests that political science is on the threshold of joining other disciplines by developing a separately identifiable language. However, a disciplinary language community requires more than a group of adherents to technical jargon and traditional terminology. The development of specialized. language and the use of language skills are essential to communication and learning within any discipline and must be common to all members of the discipline.

Uses of Language in an Academic Discipline

Language is used to orient people to the general concerns of the discipline by affixing labels, providing a way to state problems and questions related to matters of concern. Language is also used to formulate hypotheses and to make theoretical statements involving two or more events or phenomena. Hypotheses seek to explain relationships with sufficient validity and reliability to be understandable, predictable, and controllable, thereby facilitating the economical collection of information about a particular topic.

Language is also used in definition—and definition is particularly important in political science because the meanings of terms used in that discipline are still widely debated. The study of politics has not yet fully developed into a predominantly empirical science. Definition is still inadequately used to fix meanings and clarify the usage of terms employed to make conceptual statements. However, definition is essential to intradisciplinary communication and understanding. There are many ways to define a term. The dictionary defines words in terms of historical usages and meanings and through convention, stipulation, and by example. Extensional definitions arise from lists of referents subsumed within the meaning of a term. Intensional definitions identify the distinguishing sets of characteristics of referents that are within the meaning of the term. Scientists rely upon operational definitions resulting from observation, measurement, and tests of phenomena, events, and relationships suggested by the term.

4

The search for evidence to support or refute a hypothesis involves the use of language—and so do the collection, summarization, and reporting of evidence. Evidence is used to test hypotheses; when they are confirmed or refuted the results become validated generalizations. Generalizations are statements about relationships universally applicable to a class of phenomena. When hypotheses are proven by empirical or logical tests, they become lawlike generalizations or conclusions.

Language is also important in valuation. A valuation ranks or orders alternatives so as to express explicit preferences and priorities. The process is used to distinguish individual likes and dislikes as orders of preference. The subjunctive terms *ought* and *should* are often used to articulate preferences. For example, "John should do x rather than y" is a value statement.

Finally, language is used to specify goals and purposes. Goal statements describe a desired future state of affairs and communicate plans for the future.

Sources of Terms and Concepts

There is no complete, single, and widely accepted guide to the vocabulary of political science. The available dictionaries are of debatable quality, and none contains more than 4,080 terms. *The Political Science Thesaurus,* compiled by Carl Beck and his colleagues at the University of Pittsburgh, was not published when the MAP Project began.[4] Accordingly, the essential vocabulary of political science was yet to be compiled. Our search was complicated by the fact that political science relies upon the natural language community for so much of its terminology.

The MAP Project staff began by exploring social, behavioral, and political science bibliographies and reference works, e.g., Frederick Holler, *The Information Sources of Political Science,*[5] for annotated citations of dictionaries, encyclopedias, reference works, textbooks, and indexes that might serve as sources of vocabulary relevant to political science and its subfields. We assumed that bibliographers would be the most knowledgeable source of information about reference works in the field. The principal objective of our search was to be comprehensive, yet to give ample attention to the specialized terminologies of the various political science subfields.

The Bibliography of Sources (beginning on page   ) lists and briefly describes the sources used to compile the Inventory. The descriptions include the number of terms that were excluded from the Inventory, if any. Most of the terms excluded were place names widely available for reference purposes. Some of the source references were not immediately available so the initial compilation was collected in two rounds. Subsequently, the staff merged and consolidated the lists of terms collected in the two rounds to produce a list of 54,000 terms taken from forty-six sources.[6]

This raw inventory included some duplications, terms with variant spellings, terms with more than one format (e.g., U.N., United Nations, United Nations Organization), and abbreviations. These problems required careful editing by the Project staff, which was accomplished manually and by computer, and the Inventory was eventually

reduced to 21,827 terms.[7] The editors then randomly selected and added one hundred items to be used in testing the Inventory for reliability and reproducibility as described in Chapter 2.

The resulting list of terms was keypunched onto computer cards and duplicated for distribution to the MAP panel of ten political scientists for evaluation. The panel members separately judged the importance of each term for the undergraduate curriculum, i.e., whether the undergraduate should know the term well, merely be aware of it, or need not know it. The three members of the MAP Project staff reserved one of the decks of inventory card for use in classifying the terms in accordance with the nomenclature typology described in Chapter 3.

Notes

1. The 21,927 terms initially listed included some duplications and a few miscellaneous and unclassified terms. Those terms were deleted from the Inventory and the final list was reduced accordingly. The statistical analyses, however, were based on a total of 21,927 terms. See Appendixes A and B for the actual total. An evaluation of the sources from which the terms were compiled starts on page 00.

2. Jack C. Plano and Roy Olton, *The International Relations Dictionary* (New York: Holt, Rinehart & Winston, 1969), p. v.

3. Clement E. Vose, "Political Dictionaries: A Bibliographic Essay," *American Political Science Review* 68 (December 1974), pp. 1696–1705.

4. Carl Beck, et al., *Political Science Thesaurus* (Washington, D.C.: American Political Science Association, 1975). The *Thesaurus* contains 5,721 main entry terms, and with synonyms and related terms there are 30,000 in all. It was intended primarily to facilitate development of an on-line information retrieval system.

5. Frederick Holler, *The Information Sources of Political Science* (Santa Barbara, Calif.: ABC-Clio, 1971).

6. No attempt was made to evaluate the reference sources before the compilation of terms. A more systematic procedure would have been to create an authoritative panel to evaluate the source bibliographies and prescreen the citations taken from them. Fewer sources would have been used, the keypunching formats would have been standardized, and there would have been fewer duplications in the initial listing.

7. The editing process and the formatting rules are described in detail in the MAP Project files, but some of the rules merit brief mention here. Terms originally listed

as abbreviations are fully spelled out in the Inventory, followed by the abbreviation in parentheses. "United States" and "US" appear as "U.S."; "United Nations" and "UN" are listed "U.N." Plural terms appear in the singular except for nationality and ethnic groups. Personal names are listed last name first followed by a comma and the full first and middle names or middle initial, if available. See Appendixes A and B for a more complete description of the formatting and spelling conventions used. The staff retained a permanent record of all the sources in which each term appeared, including the source of duplicate terms consolidated into the master list.

2

The Judging Panel and Evaluation Procedure

Teaching is essentially authoritative; what the student is to learn is determined by others in positions of authority. The learning process, especially the curriculum planning phase, is usually accompanied by disagreement and debate, but often neither the instructor nor the learner has much independent choice in determining what material must be mastered. This is particularly true of the more structured disciplines, which have confirmed and validated bodies of knowledge, and where collective and traditional judgments about what should be taught are more compelling. The "hard sciences," medicine, and military studies are among the most structured disciplines. Political science, on the other hand, remains diffuse and poorly defined, as is confirmed by the findings of this Concept Inventory.

Panel Representativeness

What the leaders of a discipline or the members of an academic department consider important determines the concepts, technical vocabulary, topics, facts, and issues to which the student will be exposed. In political science, which is relatively unstructured, they disagree about basic content. One instructor's cherished concept is frequently another's jargon. A concept inventory reflects the diverse pedagogical interests and values of the discipline; therefore the panel of judges selected to evaluate its terms should be diverse and representative of the discipline.

There are approximately 9,000 college and university faculty teaching political science and government in the United States. The American Political Science Association (APSA), the principal professional organization of the field, has more than 13,000 members. Many of the members of the Association are not instructors; many of the 9,000 instructors are not members of the Association. As a consequence, the selection

10

of a representative panel to evaluate the Concept Inventory was especially difficult. The MAP Project staff selected ten panelists from a roster of volunteers, all teachers of political science and government in the California State University system. The staff selected these volunteers on the basis of their diversity of training, subfield interests, professional activities, age, and teaching experience. The resulting distribution of interests was compared with the classified interests of the 13,000 members listed in the *Biographical Directory* of the APSA in an attempt to correlate the composition of the panel to that of the discipline as a whole.[1]

The *Biographical Directory* identifies eight general subfields in political science:
>   (1) Foreign and cross-national political institutions and behaviors;
>   (2) International law, organization, and politics;
>   (3) Methodology;
>   (4) Political stability, instability, and change;
>   (5) Political theory;
>   (6) Public policy;
>   (7) Public administration;
>   (8) U.S. political institutions, processes, and behavior.

Political science, like other disciplines, frequently changes its subfield organization. In the case of panel members, some doctoral subfield work was academically required rather than of strictly personal interest. Still, the Project analysis found (see *Table 1*) that the panel was diversified in its subfield concerns, with modest over-representation of international politics and political stability-instability, and modest under-representation of public administration and political theory. This diversity ensured that inventory judgments would reflect the entire range of usage in the discipline.

As another check on the representativeness of the panel, they were asked to react to the following ten statements drawn from the 1963 Somit and Tanenhaus survey of the entire discipline:[2]

>   (1) Political scientists in the United States are unhappy about the state of their discipline.
>   (2) Political scientists cannot be said to have any generally agreed-upon body of methods and techniques.
>   (3) Communication between political scientists tends to be hampered by the inadequacy of their basic concepts.
>   (4) Efforts to formulate, refine, and clarify concepts and to obtain agreement on the labels to be attached to concepts often result in little more than hairsplitting and jargon.
>   (5) The involvement of political scientists in nonscholarly activities has tended to impede the development of the discipline.
>   (6) Given the present state of political science, efforts to develop a general theory of politics are premature.
>   (7) A high proportion of political scientists actually think of themselves as scientists only in a broad and figurative sense.

Table 1. Subfield Training, Interests, and Activities of MAP Panelists

APSA *Biographical Directory* Subfields (Variable)	No. of Names in APSA *Directory* (1)		Doctoral Training (2)	No. Panelists with some Interest (3)	Index of Interest* (4)	No. Panelists with some Activity (5)	Index of Activity** (6)
Cross-National	6,569	(22%)	5	9	14	6	6
International Law	2,875	(10%)	7	7	12	5	8
Methodology	1,962	(7%)	1	6	7	4	5
Political Stability	1,290	(4%)	1	9	15	7	6
Theory	2,422	(8%)	4	6	8	1	2
Public Policy	2,647	(9%)	0	7	8	3	3
Public Administration	3,000	(10%)	4	3	4	2	3
U.S. Institutions	8,757	(30%)	6	10	14	7	11

Data are based on responses to background questionnaire, which included questions on much, some, or little interest and activity.

* For index of interest, 2 = much present interest; 1 = some present interest; and 0 = little present interest

**For index of activity, 2 = much present activity; 1 = some present activity; and 0 = little present activity.

    (8) Doctoral programs in political science stress techniques rather than broad understanding and cultivation.

    (9) Much of the work being done in political behavior is only marginally related to political science.

    (10) There has developed an inner group in the American Political Science Association which, in large part, controls the key panel assignments at the annual association meetings.

The responses were recorded on a scale of five intervals:

        Agree ———:———:———:———:———: Disagree

Again, the panel demonstrated a well-diversified range of attitudes. Using an ordinary chi-square test for the independence of the two distributions, the Project staff was able to identify issues on which the panel's distribution was similar to that of the Somit-Tanenhaus sample, as well as those issues that revealed the greatest differences.

On one issue (statement 7), which seems as relevant today as in 1963, the MAP

12

panel's distribution showed the strongest similarity to that of the earlier study. Weaker similarities were discovered for statements 6, 8, 9, and 10. The greatest differences were found for statements 1, 2, 3, 4, and 5. These differences may be explained by changes that have occurred in the profession since 1963, e.g., an acceptance of the behavioral approach.

In sum, the MAP panel was not a scientific sample but it was representative of the views of the entire profession. Consequently, the Project staff is confident that the panel's evaluations of the 21,927 terms in the Concept Inventory are valid.[3]

Devising an Evaluation Procedure

The Project staff next considered how the panelists could rate the instructional importance they attached to each of the 21,927 terms. We elected to record the panelists' observations on the relative degree of importance of particular inventory terms. If the panel indicated that undergraduate students should "know a concept well," the concept was considered more important than one which the student need merely "be aware of." If the panel judged that students "need not know" a concept for undergraduate work, it was assumed that the concept was less important.

The use of a more common seven-interval scale would have provided a degree of refinement appropriate for judgments involving a large number of panelists and a small number of terms. We found, however, that the panel's judgments did not require that degree of sensitivity. In the pretests, the panelists tended to place their judgments at the poles (i.e., ranking terms as either important or unimportant). The MAP Project staff concluded that the seven-interval scale was unnecessarily burdensome and chose instead a three-interval scale that would accelerate the judging process given the large number of terms.

The MAP panel was asked: "Here are several thousand terms and concepts compiled from many political science sources. How well do you think the undergraduate major in political science should know each of these terms? Should the major know the term well, simply be aware of it, or is it a term that the major need not know?" The panelists were urged to use whatever subjective criteria they considered appropriate in determining the relative importance of each term.

The panel members were provided a deck of computer cards (21,927 in all), each card containing a term. Each panelist separated the cards into stacks representing the three categories of importance. This procedure permitted the panelists to work at their own pace, and it facilitated machine scoring of the results. The use of cards ensured that few terms would be missed; and when omissions occurred, the loss was easily rectified by providing replacement cards to the panelists. Consequently, every term in the Concept Inventory was rated; the task required from twelve to forty-eight hours for each panelist to complete.

When the ten panelists completed judging the inventory, the Project staff summarized and analyzed the results. The verbal evaluations were first quantified:

The Political Science Concept Inventory

"Should know well" terms were assigned number 1; "should be aware of," 2; and "need not know," 3. A term that received a rating of 1 from all ten panelists left little doubt that it was an important concept. Conversely, when the ten panelists agreed that the term belonged in the "need not know" category, the term was undoubtedly not essential in undergraduate instruction. The average importance of each term was then calculated by determining the mean score for each term. The standard deviation was also used to measure the panelists' disagreement regarding each term.[4]

On completion of the statistical summarization, the Project staff analyzed the ratings of the 21,927 terms. We found that the distribution of terms among the three categories varied as shown in *Table 2*. Panelist 8 rated 26.3 percent of the terms in the should-know-well category, 15.7 percent in the should-be-aware-of group, and 58.0 percent in the need-not-know class. Panelist 10 apparently expected less, and put 1.6, 27.8, and 70.5 percent of the terms in the respective categories. These two panelists represented the extreme maximal and minimal expectations concerning the scope of student learning. The other eight panelists rated the terms somewhere between the maximal-minimal extremes. Panelists who devoted the largest proportion of their time to teaching tended to have maximal expectations about how many concepts students should learn, while others who spent substantial time in administration or research tended to be minimalists.

Finally, the Project staff analyzed the degree of association between individual pairs of panelists in their rating patterns. The results indicated that there were no disciplinary cliques or coalitions that consistently voted together. This analysis verified that this small panel was indeed diversified in its professional characteristics.

Table 2. Distribution of MAP Inventory Terms by Category of Ascribed Importance and by Panelist

Panelist	Should Know Well		Should Be Aware Of		Need Not Know	
	Number	Percent	Number	Percent	Number	Percent
1	2,974	13.6	10,528	48.0	8,425	38.4
2	1,591	7.3	7,703	35.1	12,633	57.6
3	700	3.2	874	4.0	20,353	92.8
4	1,280	5.8	6,174	28.2	14,473	66.0
5	502	2.3	9,394	42.8	12,031	54.9
6	2,366	10.8	4,564	20.8	14,997	68.4
7	1,629	7.4	7,820	35.7	12,478	56.9
8	5,766	26.3	3,435	15.7	12,726	58.0
9	1,305	6.0	6,280	28.6	14,342	65.4
10	361	1.6	6,099	27.8	15,467	70.5
Total	18,474	8.4	62,871	28.7	137,925	62.9

Notes

1. *Biographical Directory* (Washington, D.C.: American Political Science Association, 1973).
2. Albert Somit and Joseph Tanenhaus, *American Political Science: A Profile of the Discipline* (New York: Atherton Press, 1964), pp. 10–19.
3. For a detailed analysis of the characteristics of the MAP panel, see Philip G. Schoner, "The Idiom of Political Science: A Concept Inventory" (Master's Thesis, San Francisco State University, 1977), pp. 68–113.
4. Future concept inventories should re-examine the options for statistical summarization. A weighted version of Thurstone's equal-appearing scale offers certain advantages in that it could produce arithmetic means to reflect the degree of ambiguity in certain distributions. For example, a distribution of panel ratings which includes ten twos is, intuitively, less ambiguous than one that includes five threes and five ones.

3

Characteristics of Political Science Concepts

The Project staff proceeded to analyze the statistical results of the panel ratings to determine:

    (a) The characteristics of the panel's collective ratings.

    (b) The distribution of judgments concerning the importance of each concept.

    (c) The relationship between the distribution of judgments and the classification of terms by nomenclature typology.

    (d) The reliability of the panelists' evaluations.

Consensus and Disagreement in Panel Ratings

The arithmetic mean of the ten judgments on each term of the Inventory was calculated and the resulting distribution of inventory terms is shown in *Table 3*. If all panelists placed a particular term in the should-know-well category, the panel mean would be 1.0, indicating the highest possible importance had been attributed to the term. If all the panelists placed the term in the need-not-know category, the mean would be 3.0, indicating the lowest possible importance. *Table 3* shows the distribution of the number of terms along a scale, by tenths, from 1.0 to 3.0

The most striking feature of the table is the very small number of terms and concepts about which the panelists fully agreed. Eleven terms (0.1 percent of the total inventory) were considered most important for undergraduate knowledge of political science. When the panel mean reached 1.7, however, the number of important terms began to be substantial; i.e., the panel means from 1.0 to 1.7 included 1,075 terms considered important for the undergraduates.

The next 8,399 terms, 38.3 percent of the full inventory, fall into the should-be-aware-of group, and 12,453 terms, approximately 57 percent of the total, were rated in

Table 3. DISTRIBUTION OF TERMS ACCORDING TO MEAN OF RATINGS ASSIGNED BY MAP PANELISTS*

Mean of Ratings by Panelists (by tenths)	Number of Terms (cumulative totals in parentheses)		Percent of Terms (cumulative totals in parentheses)	
1.0	11	(11)	0.1	(0.1)
1.1	19	(30)	0.1	(0.2)
1.2	43	(73)	0.3	(0.5)
1.3	58	(131)	0.3	(0.8)
1.4	113	(244)	0.5	(1.3)
1.5	204	(448)	0.9	(2.2)
1.6	273	(721)	1.2	(3.4)
1.7	354	(1,075)	1.6	(5.0)
1.8	460	(1,535)	2.1	(7.1)
1.9	623	(2,158)	2.8	(9.9)
2.0	798	(2,958)	3.6	(13.5)
2.1	1,024	(3,980)	4.7	(18.2)
2.2	1,115	(5,095)	5.1	(23.3)
2.3	1,307	(6,402)	6.0	(29.3)
2.4	1,467	(7,869)	6.7	(36.0)
2.5	1,605	(9,474)	7.3	(43.3)
2.6	1,726	(11,200)	7.9	(51.2)
2.7	1,896	(13,096)	8.6	(59.8)
2.8	2,162	(15,258)	9.9	(69.7)
2.9	2,805	(18,063)	12.8	(82.5)
3.0	3,864	(21,927)	17.6	(100.1)**

* Metric equivalents were 1 for should-know-well, 2 for should-be-aware-of, and 3 for need-not-know.

** Total not equal to 100 percent due to rounding.

the need-not-know category. The panel could not agree on the terms that should make up all of the vocabulary taught to undergraduate political science majors. There was, however, enough agreement to suggest to designers of any undergraduate political science curriculum that there are 1,075 terms, concepts, and topics that should become familiar to their undergraduate students.

The picture alters somewhat as we examine the standard deviations in relation to the panel means. The standard deviation describes the degree of disagreement among the panelists regarding the importance of the terms. For example, Term A and Term B may have panel means of 1.4, while A has a standard deviation of 0.42 and B has a standard

Table 4. DEGREES OF DISAGREEMENT AMONG MAP PANELISTS ACCORDING TO STANDARD DEVIATION FOR EACH TERM

Panel Means	1 0.00–0.10*	2 0.31–0.40	3 0.41–0.50	4 0.51–0.60	5 0.61–0.70	6 0.71–0.80	7 0.81–0.90	8 0.91–1.00	Row Total	Cumulative Total
Should-Know-Well										
A 1.0–1.1	11	19	0	0	0	0	0	0	30	30
	0.1	0.1	0.0	0.0	0.0	0.0	0.0	0.0	0.1	
B 1.2–1.3	0	0	63	0	38	0	0	0	101	131
	0.0	0.0	0.3	0.0	0.2	0.0	0.0	0.0	0.5	
C 1.4–1.5	0	0	135	0	163	0	19	0	317	448
	0.0	0.0	0.6	0.0	0.7	0.0	0.1	0.0	1.4	
D 1.6–1.7	0	0	139	0	314	96	74	4	627	1,075
	0.0	0.0	0.6	0.0	1.4	0.4	0.3	0.0	2.9	
Should-Be-Aware-Of										
E 1.8–1.9	0	31	66	218	438	160	143	27	1,083	2,158
	0.0	0.1	0.3	1.0	2.0	0.7	0.7	0.1	4.9	
F 2.0–2.1	11	73	165	396	747	192	206	32	1,822	3,980
	0.1	0.3	0.8	1.8	3.4	0.9	0.9	0.1	8.3	
G 2.2–2.3	0	0	585	0	1,130	589	116	2	2,422	6,402
	0.0	0.0	2.7	0.0	5.2	2.7	0.5	0.0	11.0	
H 2.4–2.5	0	0	1,454	0	1,364	0	242	12	3,072	9,474
	0.0	0.0	6.6	0.0	6.2	0.0	1.1	0.1	14.0	
Need-Not-Know										
I 2.6–2.7	0	0	2,527	0	1,073	0	22	0	3,622	13,096
	0.0	0.0	11.5	0.0	4.9	0.0	0.1	0.0	16.5	
J 2.8–2.9	0	2,805	1,905	0	257	0	0	0	4,967	18,063
	0.0	12.8	8.7	0.0	1.2	0.0	0.0	0.0	22.7	
K 3.0	3,864	0	0	0	0	0	0	0	3,864	21,927
	17.6	0.0	0.0	0.0	0.0	0.0	0.0	0.0	17.6	
Column Total	3,886	2,928	7,039	614	5,524	1,037	822	77	21,927	
	17.7	13.4	32.1	2.8	25.2	4.7	3.7	0.4	100.0	
Cumulative Total	3,886	6,814	13,853	14,467	19,991	21,028	21,850	21,927		

*Columns 0.11–0.20 and 0.21–0.30 are omitted because all cells consist of zeros.

deviation of 0.81. This suggests that the panelists disagree more about the importance of Term B than they do about Term A. *Table 4* relates the panel means of the 21,927 inventory terms to their respective standard deviations.

The ten-member panel agreed that eleven concepts (panel mean 1.0–1.9) should be part of every undergraduate major's instruction, and that 3,864 of the terms (panel mean 3.0) need not be. Disagreement among the panelists increases as the panel means increase and with standard deviations greater than 0.51. The greatest proportion of disagreement occurs with panel means of 1.8–1.9 and 2.0–2.1. For example, see panel mean 2.0–2.1, and note the substantial agreement shown for 249 terms with standard deviations of 0.50 or less (columns 1–3). On the other hand, 1,573 terms with standard deviations of 0.51 or greater (columns 4–8) resulted in strong disagreement. There is increasing agreement (low standard deviation) concerning the terms rated "need-not-know" as the panel means increase (see rows I–K).

Table 4 is a useful guide to terms that should be included in or excluded from undergraduate political science curricula. The table is also useful in determining those terms that need to be taught comprehensively and intensively. For example, a political science department may require its students to know the 1,075 terms in the should-know-well category, but since it is impossible to cover all of them in depth, the department may wish to teach concepts intensively which evoke the most agreement (e.g., the 367 in rows A–D, columns 1–4, in *Table 4*). Curricula may also be designed so that students are required to study terms in the should-know-well category that have high standard deviations (0.61 or greater).

The ten MAP panelists rated 18,484 terms (8.43 percent of the 219,270 judgments made) in the should-know-well category; 62,864 (28.67 percent) were rated as should-be-aware-of; and 137,925 (62.90 percent) were judged unnecessary for undergraduate political science majors. Thus, the MAP panel considered the Concept Inventory to be too inclusive for basic undergraduate instruction. The panelists judged one out of three terms to be essential, so the 7,000 to 7,500 should-know-well and should-be-aware-of terms are considered to be most useful in curriculum development.

Reproducibility of Ratings

The range of disagreement and inconsistency resulted because the terms were rated on the basis of their importance in *undergraduate* instruction. Many of the terms rated in the should-be-aware-of and need-not-know categories may be important for *graduate* instruction and should be separately evaluated for use at that level. Nonetheless, the curriculum planner may question the reliability and reproducibility of the panel's evaluations. *Table 5* indicates that they are very reliable.

One hundred Concept Inventory terms were selected randomly and duplicated in the master list to test the reliability of each panelist's evaluations. The MAP panel was not informed that duplicates were scattered throughout the computer card decks used

Table 5. PANELISTS' SUCCESS IN RELIABILITY TEST USING ONE HUNDRED DUPLICATE CONCEPT JUDGMENTS

Panelist	Number of Judgments Exactly Reproduced	Gamma
1	85	.980
2	84	.969
3	92	.907
4	84	.928
5	84	.932
6	87	.931
7	79	.904
8	80	.781
9	80	.933
10	81	.868

in the rating. The panel mean of each of the one hundred original items was compared to the panel mean on each of the one hundred duplicate terms in terms of a Pearson correlation analysis. The resulting correlation coefficient was $r = .890$, significant at the .00001 level. We concluded that if the panel repeated its evaluation of the 21,927 terms, the correlation between the panel's ratings on any two trials would fall between .848 and .930 ninety-five percent of the time. This is an impressive indication of collective reliability.

We arrived at a similar conclusion after examining the individual panelists. The sample of one hundred terms was rated twice by each of the panelists to obtain an index of his ability to exactly reproduce his own judgments. Each panelist's ratings of the two samples were compared and the results are shown in *Table 5*. If a panelist had judged the sample terms exactly the same, the result would be a Gamma of 1.000. Eight of ten panelists did better than .900 and the average was .913.

The MAP Nomenclature Typology

The problems, relationships, and concerns of political scientists can be found and identified only by analyzing the written works and the talk of political scientists. The cost of preparing a comprehensive bibliography and census would be prohibitive and the result ultimately redundant. The procedure discussed here is manageable, feasible, and adequate for most purposes even if it misses a few terms that some political scientists would consider relevant.

The MAP Project chose to classify the important categories in the vocabulary of political science by developing the MAP nomenclature typology. The terms were objectively classified this way: (1) to identify the main concepts in political science by

examining the discipline's referents; and (2) to aid in the preparation of political science curricula and examinations.

22

The typologies were developed as extensional definitions, i.e., by listing the terms for referents subsumed under each category. For example, "Groups" includes the names of groups as well as of organizations, associations, and movements suggested by the definition.

The typology evolved through trial and error. Three members of the MAP Project staff began by sorting out the readily classified terms, e.g., personal names, place names, publications, legal cases, slogans, and colloquialisms. The three staff members agreed nearly one hundred percent on the classification of these types of terms.

While making these obvious classifications, the Project staff studied the common characteristics of the other terms, including the names of groups or positions within groups, and the names of political events, processes, and policies. Other terms referred to systems of belief, methods of inquiry, research techniques, and theories. After several rounds, the staff evolved ten categories suited for the nomenclature typology.

Extensional definitions were used as the criteria for placing each term in only one category, even though it was recognized that many terms might be typed in two or more. The staff tried to place terms into categories where they were most frequently found. The typology is a guide for the user's convenience rather than a system of mutually exclusive sets.

SYSTEMS OF BELIEF, INQUIRY, AND EMPIRICAL THEORY

Names of ideologies, philosophies, theologies, and similar normative theories, e.g., democracy, socialism, Christianity.

Epistemological, methodological, and similar knowledge terms, e.g., empiricism, agnosticism.

Names of statistical and analytical techniques, e.g., correlational analysis, policy analysis.

States of mind, e.g., anxiety.

Empirical abstractions, concepts, and analytical terms usually used in identifying and observing behavioral processes, relationships, conditions, and patterns in politics, e.g., attitude, socialization, deference.

GROUPS AND ORGANIZATIONS

Names of organizations, groups, agencies, associations, factions, movements, alliances, organized funds, foundations, and similar collectivities of persons who share attributes, interact with one another, and maintain these interactions over time, e.g., Democratic Party, United Nations, NATO.

Generic names for various types of groupings, e.g., corporation, political party, society, system (as an organization), nationality and ethnic groupings.

The Political Science Concept Inventory

Events, Policies, and Processes

Names and other identifying terms referring to events, occurrences, incidents, outcomes of actions or events, states of affairs, conditions, proceedings, meetings, and activities, e.g., World War II, Geneva Conference.

Generic terms that refer to such events and other phenomena, e.g., war, famine, election, judicial review.

Names or phrases used to identify political proposals, policies (including tax and economic policies), statutes, laws, constitutions, treaties, doctrines, agreements, programs (unless "program" is part of an agency name), declarations, and rules aimed at producing some preferred outcome and usually implying some procedure for implementation, e.g., Truman Doctrine, instant registration, United Nations Charter.

The labels given to political maxims and principles of action, e.g., "one man, one vote."

Statuses and Roles

Names, both specific and generic, given to offices, organizational positions, roles, occupations, and statuses, e.g., president, chairman, politician, ruler.

Place Names

Specific place and location names, e.g., Atlantic Ocean.
Generic geographical and locational terms, e.g., land, ocean.

Persons

Proper names or nicknames of individuals, e.g., Thomas Jefferson, "Old Tippecanoe."

Legal Cases

Names of specific court cases; e.g., *Jones* v. *US*.
General series or categories of cases, e.g., civil rights cases, class-action suits.

Colloquialisms and Slogans

Slang terms or phrases, slogans, campaign phrases, and popular statements, e.g., "Don't tread on me."

MATERIEL

Proper names or generic terms for politically significant edifices, equipment, symbols, diseases, and other things, e.g., flags, bombs, capitals.

PUBLICATIONS

Titles of books, documents, periodicals, and other published works, e.g., *The Republic* (Plato).
Generic terms for types of publications, e.g., proceedings, reports, briefs.

The distribution of terms and concepts by nomenclature classification is shown in *Table 6*.

Table 6. DISTRIBUTION OF TERMS IN NOMENCLATURE TYPOLOGY

Type of Term	Number	Percent of Total
Systems of Belief, Inquiry, and Empirical Theory	2,671	12.1
Groups and Organizations	4,255	19.4
Statuses and Roles	1,621	7.3
Events, Policies, and Processes	6,800	31.1
Legal Cases	320	1.5
Persons	3,586	16.6
Place Names	1,042	4.8
Publications	423	2.0
Materiel	563	2.7
Colloquialisms and Slogans	570	2.6
Miscellaneous, Unclassified	76	.3
	21,927	100.4*

*Rounded to include Miscellaneous, Unclassified and to match row totals in *Table 7*.

The distribution suggests that political scientists tend to use terms associated with historical events, public policies, and political and social processes most of the time (31.0 percent of the terms). The next largest class comprised groups (19.4 percent of the total), followed by persons, i.e., political leaders and individuals who have written about politics (16.4 percent), and matters of belief, inquiry, and empirical theory, which made up the fourth largest category of terms (12.2 percent). The distribution

Table 7. DISTRIBUTION OF INVENTORY TERMS BY PANEL MEANS AND NOMENCLATURE TYPES

Nomenclature Typology	Panel Means							
	1		2		3		4	
	1.00–1.80* (should-know-well)		1.81–2.60 (should-be-aware-of)		2.61–3.00 (need-not-know)		Row Total	
A Belief, Inquiry, Theory	585	2.6%	1,357	6.2%	729	3.3%	2,671	12.1%
B Events, Policies, Processes	517	2.4	3,659	16.7	2,624	12.0	6,800	31.1
C Groups, Organizations	284	1.2	1,920	8.8	2,051	9.4	4,255	19.4
D Statuses, Roles	58	0.3	769	3.4	794	3.6	1,621	7.3
E Persons	50	0.3	745	3.5	2,791	12.8	3,586	16.6
F Place Names	16	0.1	625	2.9	401	1.8	1,042	4.8
G Publications	11	0.0	166	0.9	246	1.1	423	2.0
H Materiel	6	0.0	201	1.1	356	1.6	563	2.7
I Legal Cases	5	0.0	52	0.3	263	1.2	320	1.5
J Colloquialisms, Slogans	3	0.0	152	0.7	415	1.9	570	2.6
Column Total	1,535	6.9	9,646	44.5	10,670	48.7	21,851	100.0**

* In order to create intervals of even twentieths, dividing point between should-know-well and should-be-aware-of categories were set at panel mean of 1.80 instead of 1.70 as in other tables. Equal intervals permit better use of this table for structuring a stratified sample procedure for selecting terms for test items.

**Omitted from this distribution are seventy-six unclassified terms. Percentages are based upon the inventory total of 21,927. Percentages total more than one hundred percent due to rounding.

tends to verify the observation that political science has yet to develop the full range of conceptual interests.

Yet *Table 7* indicates that at least ten political science instructors think that the most important terms for the undergraduate major in this field are to be found under the belief, inquiry, and theory classifications. The relationship between nomenclature typology and importance attributed to the topics was measured by the panel means as shown in *Table 7*.

The ten panelists substantially agreed (see panel means 1.00–1.80) that the 585 terms classified under belief, inquiry, and empirical theory were most important (should-know-well) in undergraduate instruction. A closer examination of the 585 terms, however, reveals that most of them are related to normative theories and a lesser

proportion to empirical concepts—political theory and philosophy is thus of mixed content.

The next largest categories of should-know-well terms in *Table 7* were classified under events, policies, and political processes (517) and groups and organizations (284). Obviously, political scientists are concerned with political history and the problems of organizing society; this observation is confirmed in the should-be-aware-of column, where the events, policies, and processes typology comprises 16.7 percent of all the terms in the Concept Inventory. The next largest number of terms that the panel considered students should be aware of is found in row C, column 2 (groups and organizations). The terms classified under persons (mainly non-American political leaders, scholars, and leading members of the political science profession; see row E, column 3) included 2,791 "need-not-know."

Table 7 can be used to identify items to be included in comprehensive examinations for the undergraduate political science major. The table can be used in conjunction with *Table 11* to develop procedures for sampling the vocabulary for use in constructing test questions and compiling test banks. For example, the 1,535 should-know-well terms, column 1, *Table 7*, should probably appear three times as frequently as those in column 2 in comprehensive examinations. Similarly, test items from the need-not-know classification should appear in the same proportion as they appear in the curriculum. This procedure should also include test items selected in the proportions indicated by the standard deviation distribution shown in *Table 4*.

4

Using the Political Science Concept Inventory

Experienced instructors will appreciate how the Political Science Concept Inventory may serve as a comprehensive and objective tool for developing general political science curricula for majors, designing specific courses, preparing comprehensive examinations, and other instructional purposes. The Inventory is not intended to eliminate controversies over the relative importance of particular concepts; such controversies are vital parts of instruction and academic growth. Nor should the Inventory restrict the discipline's terrain. It can help and encourage the faculty as they design the curriculum for the major. The Inventory may also provide a convenient guide for students trying to find their way through the "foreign language" they encounter in their political science classrooms. This chapter is intended to serve as a kind of "instructor's manual" providing detailed examples for faculty and student application of Inventory materials.

Scope of the Major: The Curriculum Guide

The many dictionaries, encyclopedias, and glossaries used to develop the Inventory are testimony that its terms constitute an authoritative glossary of the discipline. The substantial agreement among the Panel regarding the important concepts and terms for instruction in undergraduate political science courses also indicates that the Inventory can provide the basis for a comprehensive curriculum guide to a department's major. The Inventory objectively summarizes otherwise subjective judgments and thus lends itself to the development of a core of recommended undergraduate curriculum topics.

Although the curriculum for an undergraduate major is the responsibility of the entire political science faculty, it is rarely the product of a systematic joint effort. For example, most departments try to infer what courses will cover by examining a colleague's training and interests; a searching discussion of the instructor's course

content as it relates to instructional goals of the department is usually perceived as bordering upon infringement of academic freedom. The Political Science Concept Inventory, on the other hand, can facilitate and encourage faculty sharing of responsibility for designing the curriculum for the major without undermining academic freedom or the sanctity of the classroom. The Inventory will enable the faculty to make collective judgments about curriculum content by discussion or by voting which item in the Inventory should be covered, while allowing individuals sufficient freedom to pursue their own interests.

The following procedure illustrates how to employ the Concept Inventory for the construction of a guide for the undergraduate curriculum. The procedure can be administered by a faculty group of any size.

(1) After examining *Table 4* and Appendix A the faculty determines the number of concepts the undergraduates should know well and be aware of. In this illustration, the total is 2,000, which includes 1,635 terms rated 1.0 to 1.9 with standard deviations of 0.70 or less (see *Table 4*), and allows a limited number of specialized terms each faculty member should have the opportunity to add.

(2) Keypunch the 2,000 terms on cards in machine-readable form and in several sets to speed the process of evaluation, perhaps one set for each political science subfield taught in the department. Cards are advantageous for hand-sorting concepts into different stacks. Printouts of the 2,000 terms will be needed for hand-tallying the results of the sorts if electronic data processing (EDP) procedures are not used.

(3) Decide how to divide political science into its component subfields. Use the list of 2,000 terms to prepare a list of terms for each subfield. In this illustration, we assume seven: political philosophy; research methodology; comparative government; international relations; American politics; political behavior; public policy.

Next, either subfield panels or the entire faculty reviews each term for its relevance to each subfield. The terms are sorted first on the basis of a yes or no response to the question: "Is the term relevant to this particular subfield of political science?" Note that the sorting and tallying process becomes more complicated and time-consuming if each of the subfield sorts is done by the faculty at large. On the other hand, individual members can sit on several subfield panels and confront a less laborious procedure than if he or she sorted the 2,000 terms seven times as a member of a faculty-at-large panel.

Eliminate terms which fail to receive a majority of "yes" votes. Some terms will, of course, appear on more than one subfield list.

If EDP procedures are used, code the identity of each panelist and his rating of each term for subsequent tallying and analysis. Keypunch the results to make a machine-readable record.

If EDP procedures are not used, the results can be tallied by hand on

printout sheets. Note the ratings of each subfield panelist on a printout of the 2,000 terms. A separate printout should be used for each sub-field.

(4) Sort the terms retained in each subfield according to the importance (know well, be aware of, need not know) of each term for under-graduate instruction in the subfield. If EDP procedures are used, each term is coded to identify the sorter and the importance rating assigned to it by that sorter. The results are then entered in machine-readable form. If EDP procedures are not used, the results can be tallied on printouts by hand. Political science departments may wish to weight the ratings of subfield specialists by a factor of two or three.

The results of the two sortings are: classification of each of the concepts by subfield; and the faculty's rating of the level of instructional importance within subfields. This information provides a conceptual and topical guide to the recommended content of course offerings in each subfield, and, as we shall see below, the test domain for comprehensive examinations that take into account the subfield specialization of particular students.

This procedure can also be used to design general studies or interdisciplinary courses. Certain concepts such as "empiricism" are important for undergraduates to know in more than one academic field. If several academic disciplines developed inventories and cross-tabulated their important concepts, the resulting list of common terms would be recognized as essential for the particular interdisciplinary or general studies curriculum.

Coordinating Scope of Particular Subfields and Courses

The departmental curriculum guide for each subfield, as compiled above, will sum-marize the concepts that the faculty in each subfield wishes its undergraduate students to know well. The curriculum guide can then serve as the basis for a division of instructional labor among the faculty and for further discussion regarding the instruc-tional objectives for the subfield. If shared with the students, it should become something of a learning contract between the subfield faculty and students specializ-ing in the subfield.

The departmental and subfield curriculum guides can also be used in the prepara-tion of specific courses. Ordinarily, new or revised courses are approved simply because they are requested by a member of the department faculty. Such requests are rarely denied if submitted by a well-respected scholar. The Inventory and the cur-riculum guides may compel a greater degree of coordination of new and revised courses with those already established in the department. The guides can also provide a basis for comparing what the faculty wishes to teach with what an instructor wishes to have adopted or revised in a particular course.

In preparing or proposing courses, individual faculty members can take "mini

inventories" of the concepts and topics to be covered. Comparisons can then be made between the mini inventories and the departmental or subfield curriculum guide developed above. Conceptual or topical areas not adequately covered in the specific course should then be added or augmented. Concepts or topics that are overemphasized should be adjusted. Together, the courses in a particular subfield should cover the areas recommended in the subfield curriculum guide. Departments can then include in course syllabi the concepts, terms, and other technical language that the student will be expected to learn.

The Introductory Course

Political scientists have for some time debated what should be included in the courses that introduce the discipline. Some argue that the content should be based on subfields, e.g., elementary surveys of political philosophy or theory, international relations, and comparative government. Others, who assume that political scientists have a special responsibility to provide civic education, insist that since many students take only the introductory course it should concentrate on American government and politics. An increasing number of instructors make a similar case for focusing on international relations in light of growing worldwide interdependence. The Inventory and the curriculum guides would enable each department to design introductory courses in its own way. For those departments that decide to concentrate entirely on American government or international relations, the equivalent of introductory-course curriculum guides is already available in Chapter 5.

Several criteria should be applied in developing the introductory political science course. At the outset, faculty should use Appendix A to introduce the students to the technical language of political science. By the end of the introductory course, students should be expected to comprehend a specified number of the most important terms: 50, 100, 200, or whatever number is determined by the preparation of the departmental curriculum guide. These terms can be analyzed for their general importance and frequency of usage and for their degree of complexity. The introductory vocabulary can also be surveyed for particular subfield relevance.

Teachers usually have the option of presenting technical terms with two objectives in mind. One is to provide the student with as comprehensive a survey of specialized language as possible in the time allowed. The other is to teach a few basic concepts thoroughly in order to familiarize the student with the logic and empirical issues pertinent to conceptual analysis and understanding. The Inventory can be used to avoid making this an either/or problem of instruction. The 10,000 terms in Appendix A provide the beginner with a convenient and authoritative overview of the vocabulary of political science. Class assignments, as suggested below, can be both broad and in-depth.

Breadth. As already suggested, the instructor can introduce students to the scope of the political science discipline simply by calling their attention to the Political Science

Concept Inventory. Like Basic English with its 800 words, the Inventory identifies the basic building blocks for progressing from elementary to more complex communication in this field.

If the instructor wishes to give the students a good sense of the scope of the discipline, he or she can ask students to study a sample of the terms in Appendix A. Assignment instructions may read:

> This assignment is designed to give you a sample of the specialized language of the political science discipline. The reference work to be used is Ralph M. Goldman *et al., The Political Science Concept Inventory,* available in the social science library (reference desk) or library reserve. Appendix A of this book lists 10,000 political science terms, each with a rating (Panel mean) from 1.0 to 3.0. Appendix A is divided into ten "nomenclature types" (names of theories, personal names, place names, names of events and processes, etc.). Select twenty-five terms with ratings from 1.0 to 1.5, another fifteen terms with ratings from 1.6 to 2.4, and a third set of ten terms with ratings from 2.5 to 3.0, that is, fifty terms in all. Try to choose terms from at least five of the ten nomenclature categories. Next, using the sources indicated by the source code numbers next to each term, write a brief definition for each term.

The instructor may wish to vary the number of terms to be selected. Individual students may be assigned 25 to 50 terms. Student teams could probably handle 200 to 300, depending on the size of the teams. On the other hand, the instructor may wish to make the selection and give the class the same set of concepts to better compare the quality of work.

Depth. In order to familiarize the students with the conceptual and definitional issues of the discipline, the instructor may wish to assign a concept definition exercise. The student is required to gather various definitions of the term from three or more sources, preferably sources besides those in Appendix A. The students should be asked to identify the points of agreement and disagreement among these definitions.

The assignment could call for definition and analysis of a single concept, several concepts, or a cluster of related concepts such as Third World, neocolonialism, and modernization. The instructor may wish to assign specific concepts to each student or allow each student to select his or her own terms. Here again students may work individually or as teams.

A variation of this assignment requires selection of terms with standard deviation scores taken into consideration. The larger the standard deviation of a term in Appendix A, the greater the disagreement among the Panel members regarding its importance for undergraduate learning. Large standard deviations are also likely to reflect professional disagreements about the meanings and applications of specific terms. In this assignment, students explore the reasons for these professional disagreements in order to understand some of the linguistic controversies in the discipline.

Nomenclature Typology. An innovative approach to an introductory survey of the political science discipline is to employ the nomenclature typology of this Inventory as

an organizing framework. The nomenclature typology indicates the different kinds of referents to which the terminology of political science alludes. These include the names of: theories, methodological techniques, ideologies, persons, places, events, policies, political processes, and significant political books. The most significant names of systems of belief, inquiry, and empirical theory could be used for lectures and discussions pertaining to normative and empirical political theory. A sampling of the 3,586 personal names could be the basis for lectures and discussions of political leadership and political biography. The substantial ground covered by political history could be sampled by choosing terms from the typology referring to historical events, political policies, and political processes. This method could also be applied to the design of more advanced courses.

Above all, the Concept Inventory and the curriculum guides derived from it should be employed as instruments of faculty consensus and coordination. These tools enable a faculty to discuss and plan the curriculum, whether for the major or the introductory course or the subfield, as a collective enterprise.

Computer-Assisted Instruction

The computer terminal is a familiar tool of contemporary language instruction. Lists like the ones in this Inventory lend themselves readily to computer programming for the purposes of individualized exercises in definition and syntactical analyses. The curriculum guides for the major, each of the department's subfields, the introductory course, the American government course, and the introductory international relations course can be stored on computer tapes. Definitions, glossaries, and objective examinations can be developed for these terms. The usual step-by-step exercises for individualized instruction can then be based upon these computer-stored materials. Different sets of exercises can be related to specific courses. It would also be possible to design a course entirely devoted to technical language, e.g., "Political Science 1, Basic Vocabulary." This computer-assisted approach is feasible at institutions with interactive computer terminals and would be particularly desirable for departments with large enrollments.

Examination Preparation

Tests that measure competency of undergraduate students in fields such as history, physics, and political science have been of growing interest to colleges and universities in recent years. The College Board and the Educational Testing Service have performed pioneer work in testing. More recently, the SOCRATES Project of The California State University and Colleges has collected extensive banks of test items for use in comprehensive examinations in selected undergraduate disciplines. The experience of these organizations and projects confirms the usefulness of comprehensive

field examinations as means of evaluating students' learning competencies and for bringing together faculty to plan common instructional goals. The Inventory can be an important aid in test design and development.

A number of problems are likely to arise when preparing comprehensive examinations. Since the scope and content of a major vary widely according to size of the faculty, nature of the institution, professional preference of instructors, etc., it is often difficult to draw boundaries around the domain of information from which questions will be drawn. It is not always sufficient to bring together a committee of instructors with specialities in different subfields and assume that the test items they create will validly delimit the test domain for the discipline. There are the inevitable disagreements between those who favor an interdisciplinary approach and those who prefer narrowly drawn boundaries. Another problem is deciding whether examinations should be designed by the senior faculty, whose members are often familiar with the more traditional literature, or by the junior staff, which is often more familiar with contemporary literature. Regardless of the issue, the Inventory provides a means by which any representative group of political science instructors can establish the domain of a comprehensive test or series of tests for the undergraduate major or particular subfields within the major.

Specifically, the departmental or subfield curriculum guides can also be used for constructing a comprehensive bank of test items, classified by subfield and possibly by course. This bank can be used to prepare semiannual or annual examinations for students completing the major. The items in each examination should of course be a representative sample of all the subfields offered by the department and the different levels of importance of concepts and topics within subfields. The faculty can, with the curriculum guides, construct examinations that enable students to answer only those questions in subfields actually studied according to student records.

A problem often arises because of the differences between the curriculum content covered on a particular campus and the content of standard examinations produced by such off-campus organizations as the Educational Testing Service. The Inventory can facilitate communication between off-campus test banks and campus test-users by permitting the campus faculty to identify the Inventory terms, concepts, and topics covered in its courses when ordering examination questions from the off-campus source. Simple coding procedures would enable the off-campus supplier to respond to the departmental request by randomly selecting items from its test banks that correspond to the Inventory list. A substantial body of computer experience would facilitate the selection of such items through a system of key words.

Diagnosing Student Progress

Examination scores can be used on a pass/fail basis, for testing completion of prerequisites, for advanced placement, or as a measure of student progress toward the instructional goals of the curriculum. Achievement may be measured against the norm of a

Table 8. Diagnostic Matrix Showing Student Improvement in Political Science Test Scores

Number of Questions Correct	Number of Political Science Units Completed			Row Total
	0	1 to 10	11 to 44	
0 to 10	0	1	0	1 5.0
11 to 15	1	1	0	2 10.0
16 to 20	3	2	3	8 40.0
21 to 25	0	0	3	3 15.0
26 to 32	0	3	3	6 30.0
	4 20.0	7 35.0	9 45.0	20 100.0

group or against some fixed standard of excellence. The purpose of diagnostic examinations is primarily to reveal areas of strength and weakness in the cognitive aspects of learning. The student whose work is thus evaluated does not pass or fail but simply discovers how he or she compares to the norm or standard.

A short but comprehensive examination, based upon concepts and topics suggested by the Inventory, was administered to a small group of twenty political science majors who had completed different numbers of units of course work: no course work at all; one to ten units completed; eleven to forty-four completed. The examination made up of thirty-two questions was scored simply for number of correct responses. *Table 8* reports the results. As students took more courses, the frequency of correct responses increased. This outcome is not surprising, but what makes it significant is that the questions were based on a sample of the Inventory as the authoritative universe of topics that a political science undergraduate major should know well.

The results of diagnostic examinations can be used not only to counsel students regarding their progress and areas of strength or weakness but also to evaluate the quality and scope of instruction. While most instructors resist "teaching the exam," most are likely to welcome some collective specification of the domain of the curriculum and its examinations.

Reference Sources

The Political Science Concept Inventory was derived from forty-six sources, each assigned a code number. Usually, the more important the term for the content of the

discipline, the more numerous the reference sources in which it was found. Many of the sources include bibliographical citations that will lead the student to significant textbooks, journals, and other literature that treat the term more fully.

Substantive Content Comparisons

Political Science departments and individual instructors often evaluate textbooks or an instructor's course syllabus. The Inventory is useful for such evaluations. Instructors can compare topics outlined in a syllabus with a selected part of the Inventory, e.g., a subfield curriculum guide. They can also compare the Inventory with tables of contents or indexes in textbooks. Students can use the Inventory to judge whether they are being taught the important political science concepts, and can plan their programs of study along the lines suggested by the Inventory.

There are undoubtedly other pedagogical and scholarly uses to which the Political Science Concept Inventory can be put. The authors welcome suggestions for possible inclusion in later editions of this book.

5

Courses in American Government and International Relations: Two Applications

The Political Science Concept Inventory was used in two experiments to identify the scope of the content of (a) a comprehensive course in American Government, and (b) an introductory course in International Relations. The procedures and results of these experiments are reported below. Two concept lists were among the results: one for American Government and the other for International Relations. These lists can be used not only as guidelines for the substantive content of these courses but also for the preparation of examinations.

American Government

The American Government concept experiment compared the judgments of two groups of political scientists: the ten-member MAP panel of California State University political scientists and a five-member committee of political science consultants to the Educational Testing Service of Princeton, New Jersey. The ETS group was a committee of examiners preparing a CLEP (College Level Examination Program) examination in American Government.*

* The Educational Testing Service is in no way responsible for this experiment or its findings. The members of the ETS committee participated voluntarily and informally with the courteous cooperation of ETS staff.
* The California State University and Colleges faculty panel included: M. A. Al-saadi, California State Polytechnic University at Pomona; Darril Hudson, CSU at Hayward; Shaw W. Khan, California State Polytechnic University at Pomona; Brij Khare, CSU at San Bernardino; Paul Magnelia, CSU at Stanislaus; Wayne Martin, CSC at Dominguez Hills; Stephen Newlin, CSU at Chico; William Nighswonger, CSC at Sonoma; and Louis Terrell, CSU at San Diego. The authors wish to express their appreciation for the excellent cooperation they received from the panel members.

The MAP panel rated the roster of 21,927 terms and concepts drawn from forty-six political science dictionaries, encyclopedias, textbooks, master indexes, and similar sources. Each term was rated as one that undergraduates in political science should know well (scored as 1), be aware of (2), or need not know (3). The ratings of the ten panelists produced panel means ranging from 1.00 to 3.00. This 1.00–3.00 scale was then divided into three roughly equal dimensions: 1.00–1.79, 1.80–2.59, and 2.60–3.00. The number of terms and concepts that fell into each of these three categories of panel means was as follows:

Panel Mean (Importance)	Number of Terms
1.00–1.79 (should-know-well)	1,075
1.80–2.59 (should-be-aware-of)	8,399
2.60–3.00 (need-not-know)	12,453
	21,927

The 1,075 most important terms were submitted for ratings to the Educational Testing Service committee of examiners, five political science faculty members from various regions of the United States who specialized in the teaching of American Government. The ETS group was asked to rate each of the 1,075 terms and concepts as "relevant" or "not relevant" for an American Government CLEP examination. A vote of "relevant" by five committee members was a unanimous judgment that a term or concept should be included in a comprehensive course and an examination in American Government. At the other extreme, one or zero votes were an indication that the topic should be excluded as "not relevant." In other words, topics covered by terms and concepts with five or four votes may be considered "required" for any comprehensive course or examination in American Government. Topics scored three or two may be considered "optional."

The terms are listed below by the number of ETS committee votes. The number following each term is its MAP panel mean rating.

38

Ratings of American Government Concepts by ETS Committee

Alphabetized within each vote level.

Five Votes

American Government Concept	Mean		Mean
ALIENATION	1.3	DECLARATION OF	
AMERICAN REVOLUTION	1.3	INDEPENDENCE	1.2
APATHY	1.5	DELEGATION OF POWERS	1.3
ATTITUDE	1.4	DEMOCRACY	1.0
AUTHORITY	1.4	DEMOCRATIC	1.5
BILL OF RIGHTS	1.2	DEMOCRATIC PARTY	1.5
BROWN VS. BOARD OF		DESEGREGATION	1.4
EDUCATION OF		DUE PROCESS	1.5
TOPEKA (1954)	1.2	DUE PROCESS CLAUSE	1.3
BUREAUCRACY	1.3	DUE PROCESS OF LAW	1.5
CHECKS-AND-BALANCES	1.1	ELECTORAL BEHAVIOR	1.2
CIVIL LIBERTIES	1.1	ELITES	1.3
CIVIL RIGHTS	1.2	EQUALITY	1.4
CONGRESS (U.S.)	1.4	EQUAL PROTECTION CLAUSE	1.4
CONGRESSIONAL		EXECUTIVE AGREEMENT	1.5
COMMITTEES	1.5	EXECUTIVE BRANCH	1.5
CONSENT OF THE GOVERNED	1.5	EXECUTIVE OFFICE OF THE	
CONSTITUTION (U.S.)	1.4	PRESIDENT	1.5
CONSTITUTIONAL		FEDERALISM	1.3
GOVERNMENT	1.4	FEDERAL SYSTEM	1.4
CONSTITUTIONAL POWER	1.5	FIFTH AMENDMENT	1.5
DECISION MAKING	1.4	FIRST AMENDMENT	1.4
DECISION-MAKING PROCESS	1.5	FOURTEENTH AMENDMENT	1.3

Several concepts in this list appear twice (e.g., egalitarianism, hierarchy, Monroe Doctrine, and multiparty system) because they were duplicated in the ratings of the MAP Panel for the purpose of reliability testing. They were retained in the rating procedure of the ETS Panel.

Library of

Davidson College

Five Votes

AMERICAN GOVERNMENT CONCEPT	MEAN		MEAN
FREEDOM OF ASSEMBLY	1.4	POLITICAL ELITE	1.4
FREEDOM OF RELIGION	1.3	POLITICAL GROUPS	1.5
FREEDOM OF SPEECH	1.2	POLITICAL LEADERSHIP	1.5
FREEDOM OF THE PRESS	1.3	POLITICAL PARTICIPATION	1.3
GROUP PRESSURE	1.4	POLITICAL PARTIES	1.0
HOUSE OF		POLITICAL RECRUITMENT	1.4
REPRESENTATIVES (U.S.)	1.1	POLITICAL	
IDEOLOGY	1.2	REPRESENTATION	1.2
INTERSTATE COMMERCE		POLITICS	1.0
CLAUSE	1.4	POPULAR DEMOCRACY	1.3
JUDICIAL BRANCH	1.5	POWER ELITE	1.4
JUDICIAL REVIEW	1.1	POWERS OF CONGRESS	1.4
JUDICIAL SYSTEM	1.4	POWER STRUCTURE	1.4
JURISDICTION	1.5	PRESIDENCY	1.4
LAW	1.5	PRESIDENT (U.S.)	1.4
LEGITIMACY	1.5	PRESIDENTIAL GOVERNMENT	1.5
LIBERAL	1.4	PRESIDENTIAL POWERS	1.5
LIBERALISM	1.0	PRESSURE GROUP	1.4
LIBERTY	1.5	REPRESENTATIVE	
LOBBYING	1.4	DEMOCRACY	1.5
LOBBYISTS	1.5	REPRESENTATIVE	
MAJORITY	1.5	GOVERNMENT	1.5
MAJORITY OPINION	1.5	REPUBLICAN FORM OF	
MAJORITY PARTY	1.4	GOVERNMENT	1.4
MAJORITY RULE,		REPUBLICAN PARTY	1.4
DEMOCRATIC THEORY	1.2	SEPARATION OF POWERS	1.4
MARBURY VS. MADISON		TWO-PARTY SYSTEM	1.5
(1808)	1.3	UNCONSTITUTIONAL	1.5
MASS MEDIA	1.4	UNCONSTITUTIONALITY	1.4
MEDIA	1.4	U.S. CONSTITUTION	1.4
MINORITY RIGHTS	1.4	U.S. SUPREME COURT	1.5
PARTY LEADERSHIP	1.5	VETO	1.5
PARTY SYSTEM	1.5	VETO (U.S. PRESIDENTIAL)	1.5
PASSAGE OF A BILL INTO LAW	1.5	VOTE	1.5
PATRONAGE SYSTEM	1.5	VOTING BEHAVIOR	1.3
PLURALISTIC SOCIETY	1.5	WAR POWERS OF THE	
POLITICAL ATTITUDES	1.5	PRESIDENT	1.4
POLITICAL CULTURE	1.4		

Four Votes

AMERICAN GOVERNMENT CONCEPT	MEAN		MEAN
ACCOUNTABILITY	1.4	PUNISHMENT	1.5
ADJUDICATION	1.5	CULTURE PATTERNS	1.7
ADVICE AND CONSENT	1.5	DECENTRALIZATION	1.5
AMENDING PROCESS,		DE FACTO SEGREGATION	1.7
U.S. CONSTITUTION	1.6	DEMOCRAT	1.7
AMERICAN BILL OF RIGHTS	1.3	DEMOCRATIC IDEOLOGY	1.3
ANALYSIS	1.7	DOCTRINE OF IMPLIED	
ATTITUDINAL CHANGES	1.3	POWERS	1.6
BARGAINING	1.7	ELECTORAL DISTRICT	1.6
BICAMERALISM	1.5	ELECTORAL PROCESSES	1.7
BILL	1.6	ELECTORATE	1.6
BRANCHES OF GOVERNMENT	1.6	ELITISM	1.7
BUDGET	1.7	EMERGENCY POWERS	1.7
BUDGETARY PROCESS	1.5	EGALITARIANISM	1.5
BURDEN OF PROOF	1.7	EGALITARIANISM	1.7
CABINET	1.7	EQUAL RIGHTS AMENDMENT	1.7
CAPITAL PUNISHMENT	1.7	EXECUTIVE	1.7
CHIEF EXECUTIVE	1.7	EXECUTIVE DEPARTMENT	1.7
CHIEF JUSTICE OF THE		EXECUTIVE-LEGISLATIVE	
SUPREME COURT	1.6	RELATIONSHIPS	1.6
CITIZEN	1.7	EXECUTIVE ORDER	1.5
CIVIL RIGHTS MOVEMENT	1.7	EXECUTIVE POWER	1.6
CLASS	1.6	EXECUTIVE PRIVILEGE	1.6
CLEAR AND PRESENT		FACT	1.7
DANGER DOCTRINE	1.5	FAIR TRIAL	1.7
COALITION	1.4	FEDERAL COURTS	1.7
COMMITTEE SYSTEM	1.7	FEDERAL DISTRICT COURTS	1.6
COMMON LAW	1.4	FEDERAL GOVERNMENT	1.7
CONSENSUS	1.6	FEDERALIST, THE	1.5
CONSERVATISM	1.6	FILIBUSTER	1.6
CONSERVATIVE	1.5	FOURTH AMENDMENT	1.7
CONSTITUENCY	1.6	FREEDOM	1.6
CONSTITUTION	1.6	FREE ENTERPRISE	1.6
CONSTITUTIONAL		GENERALIZATION	1.7
CONVENTION	1.7	GOVERNMENT	1.6
COURT OPINION	1.7	GRADUATED INCOME TAX	1.5
COURTS, FEDERAL	1.6	GRAND JURY	1.5
CRUEL AND UNUSUAL		GRANTS-IN-AID	1.7

Four Votes

American Government Concept	Mean		Mean
HIERARCHY	1.5	MINORITY	1.6
HIERARCHY	1.7	MINORITY REPRESENTATION	1.6
HYPOTHESIS(ES)	1.1	NATION	1.5
IMPEACHMENT	1.6	NATIONS	1.6
IMPLIED POWERS	1.3	NATIONAL BUDGET	1.5
INCUMBENT	1.7	NATIONAL INTEREST	1.2
INDICTMENT	1.7	NATIONAL POWER,	
INSTITUTION	1.7	ELEMENTS OF	1.5
INTERESTS	1.6	NECESSARY AND PROPER	
JEFFERSONIAN DEMOCRACY	1.4	CLAUSE OF THE	
JUDICIAL BEHAVIOR	1.5	CONSTITUTION	1.7
JUDICIAL LAW MAKING	1.6	NOMINATING CONVENTION	1.6
JUDICIAL POWER	1.6	NOMINATION	1.6
JUDICIAL SELF-RESTRAINT	1.6	OBJECTIVITY	1.5
JUDICIARY	1.7	ONE-MAN-ONE-VOTE	1.4
JURY SYSTEM	1.7	PARTICIPATORY	
JUSTICE	1.3	DEMOCRACY	1.2
LABOR UNION	1.6	PARTY	1.3
LAW-MAKING POWER	1.7	PARTY LOYALTY	1.7
LEADERSHIP	1.7	PLURALISM	1.4
LEFT, THE	1.7	POCKET VETO	1.6
LEGISLATION	1.6	POLICY	1.6
LEGISLATIVE BEHAVIOR	1.6	POLICY FORMULATION	1.7
LEGISLATIVE POWERS,		POLICYMAKING	1.6
CONGRESS	1.6	POLITICAL ACTION	1.6
LEGISLATIVE PROCESS	1.6	POLITICAL ACTOR	1.3
LEGISLATURE	1.7	POLITICAL ALIENATION	1.2
LOBBY	1.7	POLITICAL APATHY	1.6
LOGROLLING	1.7	POLITICAL	
MACHINE POLITICS	1.3	COMMUNICATION	1.5
MACHINERY OF		POLITICAL CONFLICT	1.5
GOVERNMENT	1.6	POLITICAL IDEOLOGY	1.4
MAJORITY FLOOR LEADER	1.7	POLITICAL INFLUENCE	1.3
MAJORITY GOVERNMENT	1.5	POLITICAL INSTITUTIONS	1.3
MAJORITY LEADER	1.6	POLITICAL INTEGRATION	1.4
MIDDLE CLASS	1.5	POLITICAL LEGITIMACY	1.5
MILITARY-INDUSTRIAL		POLITICAL MOVEMENTS	1.7
COMPLEX	1.5	POLITICAL ORDER	1.7

The Political Science Concept Inventory

Four Votes

American Government Concept	Mean		Mean
POLITICAL ORGANIZATIONS	1.5	PERSON TO COUNSEL	1.6
POLITICAL PHILOSOPHY	1.3	RIGHT OF ASSOCIATION	1.7
POLITICAL POWER	1.4	RIGHT OF PETITION	1.7
POLITICAL PRESSURE	1.6	RULE OF THE MAJORITY	1.6
POLITICAL PROCESSES	1.2	SEGREGATION	1.5
POLITICAL PROTEST	1.7	SENATE OF THE	
POLITICAL ROLES	1.3	UNITED STATES	1.7
POLITICAL STRUCTURES	1.6	SOVEREIGNTY	1.5
POLITICAL SUBCULTURES	1.5	STATE	1.6
POLITICAL VALUES	1.1	STATES' RIGHTS	1.5
POLITICIAN	1.6	SUPREME COURT OF	
POLITICIZATION	1.2	THE UNITED STATES	1.6
POPULAR CONSENT	1.7	THIRD PARTIES	1.5
POPULAR SOVEREIGNTY,		TRIAL BY JURY	1.6
DEMOCRATIC THEORY	1.6	UNICAMERAL SYSTEM	1.5
POWER	1.0	VALUES	1.3
POWERS OF THE PRESIDENT	1.6	VERIFICATION	1.6
PRESIDENT AND CONGRESS	1.6	VETO POWER	1.6
PRESIDENTIAL ELECTIONS	1.6	VOTER	1.6
PRESIDENTIAL SYSTEM	1.6	VOTER REGISTRATION	1.7
PRESIDENTIAL VETO	1.6	VOTING	1.6
PROCESS	1.7	VOTING PROCEDURE	1.7
PUBLIC	1.6	VOTING TURNOUT	1.7
PUBLIC OPINION	1.4	WOMEN, EQUALITY OF	1.7
RANDOM SAMPLE	1.3	WRIT OF HABEAS CORPUS	1.4
REPRESENTATION	1.6	WRITTEN CONSTITUTION	1.7
RIGHT OF ACCUSED			

Three Votes

	Mean		Mean
A-BOMB	1.7	ACT OF WAR	1.7
ABSENTEE VOTING	1.7	ADMINISTRATIVE PROCESS	1.6
ABSOLUTE MAJORITY	1.7	AGGREGATION OF	
ABSOLUTISM	1.6	INTERESTS	1.7

Three Votes

American Government Concept	Mean		Mean
AGGRESSION	1.3	CENTRALIZED	
AGRARIAN REFORM	1.7	GOVERNMENT	1.7
ALLIANCE	1.7	CHAUVINISM	1.7
ALLIANCE FOR PROGRESS		CHILDHOOD	
(1961)	1.7	SOCIALIZATION	1.5
AMERICAN CIVIL WAR	1.5	CITIZENSHIP	1.6
AMERICAN FEDERATION		CITY COUNCIL	1.6
OF LABOR	1.7	CITY GOVERNMENT	1.6
AMERICAN FOREIGN POLICY	1.7	CITY GOVERNMENT,	
ANGLO-AMERICAN SYSTEM		COMMISSION PLAN	1.6
OF LAW	1.7	CITY GOVERNMENT,	
ANTIBALLISTIC MISSILE		COUNCIL MANAGER	
SYSTEM (ABM)	1.7	PLAN	1.5
ANTI-SEMITISM	1.6	CITY GOVERNMENT, MAYOR-	
APOLITICAL	1.7	ADMINISTRATOR PLAN	1.5
APPEASEMENT	1.7	CITY GOVERNMENT, MAYOR-	
APPORTIONMENT	1.7	COUNCIL PLAN	1.5
ARMS CONTROL	1.6	CITY GOVERNMENT,	
ARMS REDUCTION	1.7	STRONG MAYOR PLAN	1.5
ARTICLES OF		CITY GOVERNMENT,	
CONFEDERATION	1.7	WEAK MAYOR PLAN	1.6
ASSIMILATION	1.7	CITY MANAGER	1.5
ATTITUDE SURVEYS	1.7	CITY MANAGER	
BALANCE OF PAYMENTS	1.6	GOVERNMENT	1.7
BALANCE OF POWER	1.2	CITY MANAGER PLAN	1.4
BALANCE OF TRADE	1.6	CITY PLANNING	1.7
BALLOT	1.5	CIVIL-MILITARY RELATIONS	1.7
BANDWAGON EFFECT	1.7	CIVIL RIGHTS ACT OF 1964	1.7
BARGAINING THEORY	1.6	CIVIL RIGHTS MOVEMENT	1.7
BEHAVIOR	1.6	CIVIL SERVICE	1.7
BILL OF ATTAINDER	1.6	CIVIL SERVICE SYSTEM	1.6
BIPOLARITY	1.7	CIVIL WAR	1.3
CAPITALISM	1.0	CLASSICAL ECONOMICS	1.7
CASE LAW	1.7	CLOSED PRIMARY	1.5
CAUCUS	1.6	CLOTURE RULE	1.7
CENSURE MOTION	1.7	COERCION	1.7
CENTRALIZATION	1.6	COLD WAR	1.4

Three Votes

AMERICAN GOVERNMENT CONCEPT	MEAN		MEAN
COLLECTIVE SECURITY	1.6	DEMOCRATIZATION	1.5
COLONIAL GOVERNMENTS	1.7	DEPARTMENT OF DEFENSE,	
COMMITTEE OF CONGRESS	1.7	U.S. (DOD)	1.7
COMMITTEE OF WAYS		DEPARTMENT OF JUSTICE	1.7
AND MEANS	1.7	DEPARTMENT OF STATE (U.S.)	1.6
COMMITTEE ON RULES	1.7	DEPRESSION, ECONOMIC	1.7
COMMUNICATION MEDIA	1.7	DETERRENCE	1.6
COMMUNICATION,		DICTATORSHIP	1.6
POLITICAL	1.7	DIRECT DEMOCRACY	1.7
COMMUNIST PARTY	1.3	DIRECT PRIMARY	1.6
COMMUNITY	1.7	DIVISION OF POWERS	1.6
COMMUNITY POWER		DOUBLE JEOPARDY	1.7
STRUCTURE	1.6	DRED SCOTT VS. SANFORD	
COMPETITION	1.7	(1857)	1.6
CONCEPT	1.2	EIGHTEENTH AMENDMENT	1.7
CONCURRENT RESOLUTION	1.7	ELECTION PROPAGANDA	1.7
CONFEDERATION	1.6	ELITIST THEORY	1.4
CONFLICT	1.4	EMANCIPATION	
CONFLICT RESOLUTION	1.4	PROCLAMATION	1.7
CONSENSUS-BUILDING	1.7	EMINENT DOMAIN	1.6
CONSTITUTIONALITY	1.6	ETHNOCENTRISM	1.6
CONSTITUTIONAL LAW	1.6	EXECUTIVE PROCESS	1.6
COST-BENEFIT ANALYSIS	1.6	EXPLANATION IN SOCIAL	
COUNCIL MANAGER PLAN	1.7	SCIENCES	1.4
COUNTERCULTURE	1.7	EX POST FACTO LAW	1.6
COUNTERVAILING POWER	1.7	EXTREMISM	1.6
COUNTY MANAGER PLAN	1.7	FACT AND VALUE	1.2
COUP D'ETAT	1.6	FEDERAL COURTS OF APPEAL	1.7
CUBAN MISSILE CRISIS	1.6	FEDERALIST PAPERS, THE	1.7
CULTURE	1.6	FEDERAL RESERVE SYSTEM	1.7
DECISION MAKERS	1.6	FIRST STRIKE CAPACITY	1.7
DECLARATION OF WAR	1.7	FORD, PRESIDENT GERALD R.	1.7
DEFENSIVE WEAPONS	1.7	FOREIGN POLICY	1.6
DE JURE	1.6	FREE ENTERPRISE SYSTEM	1.5
DELEGATION	1.7	FREE TRADE	1.7
DELIBERATIVE BODY	1.7	FREE WORLD	1.7
DEMAND AND SUPPLY	1.6	GALLUP POLL	1.6

Three Votes

AMERICAN GOVERNMENT CONCEPT	MEAN		MEAN
GERRYMANDER	1.5	INTEGRATION	1.6
GOVERNMENT REGULATION		INTEGRATION AND GOAL	
OF BUSINESS	1.6	ATTAINMENT	1.7
GOVERNOR	1.7	INTEREST ARTICULATION	1.7
GRADUALISM	1.7	INTERNATIONAL ALLIANCES	1.7
GRAND OLD PARTY (GOP)	1.7	INTERNATIONAL	
GRASS ROOTS	1.7	BARGAINING	1.7
GROSS NATIONAL		INTERNATIONAL CRISIS	1.7
PRODUCT (GNP)	1.7	INTERNATIONAL SECURITY	1.7
GREAT POWERS	1.6	INTERSTATE COMMERCE	1.5
GROUP BASIS OF POLITICS	1.6	INTERSTATE COMMERCE	
GROUP INFLUENCE	1.6	COMMISSION (ICC)	1.7
GROUP NORMS	1.7	INVESTIGATING COMMITTEES	
GROUP RELATIONS	1.6	OF CONGRESS	1.7
GROUP REPRESENTATION	1.6	INVESTIGATIVE POWER	1.7
GROUPS AND		IRON CURTAIN	1.7
ORGANIZATIONS	1.7	ISOLATIONISM	1.5
GUERRILLA WARFARE	1.7	ITEM VETO	1.5
HAMILTON, ALEXANDER	1.7	JUDICIAL ACTIVISM	1.5
HAMILTONIANISM	1.7	JUDICIAL PROCEDURE	1.7
HAVE AND HAVE-NOT		KEYNESIANISM	1.6
NATIONS	1.7	KING, DR. MARTIN	
HOME RULE	1.7	LUTHER, JR.	1.6
HOUSE UN-AMERICAN		LABOR-MANAGEMENT	
ACTIVITIES COMMITTEE		RELATIONS ACT OF 1947	
(HUAC); ALSO DIES		(TAFT-HARTLEY LAW)	1.7
COMMITTEE	1.7	LAME DUCK CONGRESS	1.7
HUMAN AND CIVIL RIGHTS	1.7	LAME DUCK SESSION	1.7
HUMAN RIGHTS	1.4	LEGISLATURE	
IF-THEN STATEMENT	1.7	APPORTIONMENT	1.7
IMMUNITY	1.7	LEGISLATIVE POWER	1.7
INDIVIDUAL INFLUENCES		LEGISLATIVE	
IN POLITICS	1.7	REAPPORTIONMENT	1.7
INDIVIDUAL POLITICAL		LIBERAL DEMOCRAT	1.7
EFFICACY	1.7	LINCOLN, PRESIDENT	
INITIATIVE	1.6	ABRAHAM	1.4
INJUNCTION	1.7	LOBBY REGULATION	1.7
INSURRECTION	1.6	LOCAL GOVERNMENT	1.5

The Political Science Concept Inventory

Three Votes

American Government Concept	Mean		Mean	

47

American Government Concept	Mean		Mean
LOCAL POLITICS	1.6	CORPORATIONS (MNC)	1.4
LOCKE, JOHN	1.3	MUNICIPAL GOVERNMENT	1.6
LONG BALLOT	1.6	NATIONAL DEBT	1.6
LOUISIANA PURCHASE	1.7	NATIONAL DEFENSE	1.7
LOWER CLASS	1.7	NATIONALITY	1.7
LOYALTY OATH	1.7	NATIONALIZATION	1.4
MAGNA CARTA	1.4	NATIONAL LIBERATION	
MAJORITARIANISM	1.5	WARS	1.7
MANIFEST DESTINY	1.6	NATIONAL RIGHTS	1.7
MARSHALL PLAN		NEGOTIATION	1.4
(EUROPEAN RECOVERY		NEUTRALISM	1.7
PROGRAM)	1.5	NEUTRALITY	1.4
MASS COMMUNICATIONS	1.7	NEW DEAL	1.6
MASS PARTICIPATION	1.7	NEW DEAL LEGISLATION	1.7
MASS PUBLIC, PUBLIC		NEW FEDERALISM	1.7
OPINION	1.5	NEW LEFT	1.5
MAYOR-COUNCIL FORM		NIXON, PRESIDENT RICHARD	1.5
OF GOVERNMENT	1.7	NONPARTISAN	1.7
MERIT SYSTEM	1.6	NONPARTISANSHIP	1.6
METROPOLITAN	1.7	NONVIOLENCE	1.7
METROPOLITAN		NORMS	1.7
GOVERNMENT	1.7	NORTH ATLANTIC TREATY	
MILITARY DICTATORSHIP	1.5	ORGANIZATION (NATO)	1.3
MILITARY GOVERNMENT	1.7	NUCLEAR DETERRENT	1.4
MINORITIES, NATIONAL		NUCLEAR WEAPONS	1.4
AND RACIAL	1.7	NULLIFICATION	1.7
MINORITY GOVERNMENT	1.7	NUREMBERG WAR	
MINORITY OPINION	1.7	CRIMES TRIALS	1.7
MINORITY PARTY	1.6	ONE-PARTY STATE	1.5
MODERN SOCIETY	1.7	ONE-PARTY SYSTEM	1.1
MONARCHY	1.6	OPEN PRIMARY	1.5
MONOPOLY	1.5	OPINION	1.7
MONROE DOCTRINE	1.3	OPINION ELITES, PUBLIC	
MONROE DOCTRINE	1.5	OPINION	1.6
MOTIVATION	1.6	OPINION LEADER	1.4
MULTILATERAL	1.7	ORGANIZATION BEHAVIOR	1.7
MULTILATERAL TREATY	1.7	PARTICIPATION (OF CITIZENS	
MULTINATIONAL		IN GOVERNMENT)	1.7

Three Votes

AMERICAN GOVERNMENT CONCEPT	MEAN		MEAN
PARTISANSHIP	1.6	PRIMARY GROUP	
PARTY CONVENTION	1.7	PRESIDENTIAL PRIMARY	1.5
PARTY DISCIPLINE	1.4	PROGRESSIVE MOVEMENT	1.7
PARTY PRIMARY	1.7	PROLETARIAT	1.7
		PROPAGANDA	1.7
VOTER ALIGNMENTS	1.6	PROPORTIONAL	1.6
PARTY UNITY	1.7	REPRESENTATION (PR)	1.4
PATRIOTISM	1.7	PUBLIC ADMINISTRATION	1.7
PEACE CORPS (U.S.)	1.7	PUBLIC LAW	1.7
PEACEFUL COEXISTENCE	1.6	PUBLIC OPINION POLLS	1.6
PERSONAL LIBERTY	1.6	PUBLIC OPINION SURVEYS	1.6
PLANNED ECONOMY	1.7	PUBLIC POLICY	1.7
POLICY MAKER	1.6	QUANTITATIVE METHODS	1.2
POLICY OF CONTAINMENT	1.6	RADICALISM	1.5
POLITICAL	1.3	RECALL	1.5
POLITICAL ANALYSIS	1.5	REFERENCE GROUP	1.6
POLITICAL AUTHORITY	1.6	REFERENDUM	1.5
POLITICAL BEHAVIOR	1.2	REGIONALISM	1.5
POLITICAL CHANGE	1.2	REGRESSIVE TAX	1.7
POLITICAL EDUCATION	1.7	RESPONSIBILITY, POLITICAL	1.6
POLITICAL EFFICACY	1.6	REVOLUTION	1.2
POLITICAL ETHICS	1.7	REVOLUTIONARY	
POLITICAL INSTABILITY	1.6	IDEOLOGY	1.7
POLITICAL INVOLVEMENT	1.7	REVOLUTIONARY WAR	1.7
POLITICAL MOBILIZATION	1.6	RIGHT OF SELF-	
POLITICAL OBLIGATION	1.6	DETERMINATION OF	
POLITICAL SCIENTISTS	1.5	NATIONS	1.7
POLITICAL STYLE	1.7	ROLE	1.6
POLITICAL SYSTEMS	1.0	ROLL-CALL VOTE	1.7
POLITY	1.2	ROOSEVELT, PRESIDENT	
POLLUTION,		FRANKLIN D.	1.6
ENVIRONMENTAL	1.7	RULE OF LAW, DEMOCRATIC	
POPULAR REFERENDUM	1.7	THEORY	1.7
POPULIST	1.6	RULING CLASS	1.7
POSTINDUSTRIAL SOCIETY	1.6	SAMPLING TECHNIQUES	1.2
POWER POLITICS	1.3	SCIENTIFIC METHOD	1.1
PRAGMATISM	1.3	SECURITY COUNCIL OF	

Three Votes

AMERICAN GOVERNMENT CONCEPT	MEAN		MEAN
THE UNITED NATIONS	1.6	TREATY OF VERSAILLES	
SELF-GOVERNMENT	1.6	(1919)	1.7
SEPARATION OF CHURCH		TYRANNY	1.7
AND STATE	1.7	TYRANNY OF THE	
SOCIAL CLASS	1.7	MAJORITY	1.6
SOCIAL CONTRACT,		TWENTY-THIRD	
THEORY OF	1.4	AMENDMENT	1.7
SOCIALIST PARTY	1.7	TWO-STEP FLOW, MASS	
SOCIALIZATION	1.5	MEDIA	1.7
SOCIALIZING AGENTS	1.6	UN CHARTER	1.7
SOCIAL SCIENCE	1.6	UNICAMERAL LEGISLATURE	1.6
SOCIAL SCIENCES	1.5	UN SECURITY COUNCIL	1.6
SOVEREIGN STATE	1.7	UNITARY GOVERNMENT	1.7
SOVIET BLOC	1.7	URBANIZATION	1.7
SPOILS SYSTEM	1.6	URBAN POLITICS	1.6
STALIN, JOSEPH	1.6	VALUE JUDGMENT	1.5
STATE AND LOCAL		VIETNAM	1.7
GOVERNMENT	1.7	VIETNAM, WAR IN	1.5
STATUS	1.7	VIETNAM CONFLICT	1.7
STEREOTYPE	1.7	VIETNAMIZATION	1.7
STRATEGIC ARMS		VOTE OF CENSURE	1.6
LIMITATION TALKS		VOTE OF CONFIDENCE	1.6
(SALT)	1.6	VOTE OF NO CONFIDENCE	1.7
STRICT INTERPRETATION		VOTER'S APATHY	1.7
OF THE CONSTITUTION	1.5	WASHINGTON,	
SUFFRAGE	1.7	PRESIDENT GEORGE	1.7
SUPERPOWER	1.7	WATERGATE	1.5
THERMONUCLEAR WAR	1.7	WAYS AND MEANS	
THIRD REICH	1.7	COMMITTEE	1.5
THIRD WORLD	1.7	WELFARE STATE	1.7
THIRTEENTH AMENDMENT	1.6	WOMEN'S LIBERATION	
TOTALITARIANISM,		MOVEMENT	1.7
FASCIST THEORY	1.6	WORLD WAR II	1.6
TOTALITARIAN		WRIT OF CERTIORARI	1.7
GOVERNMENT	1.7	ZIONISM	1.7
TOTALITARIAN STATE	1.7		
TREATY	1.7		

Two Votes

AMERICAN GOVERNMENT CONCEPT	MEAN		MEAN
ABSOLUTE MONARCHY	1.6	CIVIL DISOBEDIENCE	1.4
ANALOGY	1.4	CIVIL LAW (JUS CIVILE)	1.5
ANALYTICAL METHOD	1.7	CLASS CONFLICT	1.5
ANARCHIST	1.7	CLASSICAL THEORY	1.5
ANOMIE	1.6	CLASSLESS SOCIETY	1.6
A PRIORI	1.5	CLASS STRUGGLE	1.6
ARISTOCRACY	1.3	COALITION FORMATION	1.6
ARMS RACE	1.4	COALITION GOVERNMENT	1.4
ATHENIAN DEMOCRACY	1.7	COEXISTENCE, PEACEFUL	1.4
AUTHORITARIANISM	1.3	COLONIALISM	1.3
AUTHORITARIAN		COMMON MARKET	1.7
PERSONALITIES	1.3	COMMONS, HOUSE OF	1.6
AUTHORITARIAN SYSTEMS	1.4	COMMUNISM	1.0
AUTOCRACY	1.2	COMMUNIST PARTY,	
AXIOM	1.7	SOVIET UNION (CPSU)	1.5
BALANCE OF TERROR	1.6	COMPACT THEORY	1.6
BEHAVIOR, COLLECTIVE	1.4	COMPARATIVE ANALYSIS	1.4
BEHAVIORALISM	1.3	COMPARATIVE	
BEHAVIORISM	1.4	GOVERNMENT	1.6
BELLIGERENCY	1.6	COMPARATIVE POLITICS	1.4
BIASED SAMPLE	1.5	CONCEPTUALIZATION	1.6
BOLSHEVIK REVOLUTION	1.5	CONSTITUTIONAL	
BOLSHEVIKS	1.6	MONARCHY	1.6
BOLSHEVISM	1.6	CULTURAL REVOLUTION,	
BOURGEOISIE	1.5	CHINA (PRC)	1.7
CABINET GOVERNMENT	1.6	DATA	1.6
CABINET SYSTEM	1.3	DECISION-MAKING	
CAUSAL EXPLANATION	1.3	APPROACH	1.5
CAUSALITY	1.7	DECISION THEORY	1.5
CAUSATION	1.6	DEDUCTIVE REASONING	1.5
CAUSE AND EFFECT	1.3	DE GAULLE, GENERAL	
CHARISMA	1.4	CHARLES ANDRE	
CHARISMATIC LEADERSHIP	1.5	JOSEPH MARIE	1.7
CHARTER OF THE		DEMOCRATIC SOCIALISM	1.5
UNITED NATIONS	1.4	DESPOTISM	1.6
CHINA, COMMUNIST	1.6	DEVELOPING NATIONS	1.7
CHINA, PRC (POLITICAL		DEVELOPMENT, SOCIAL	
SYSTEM)	1.7	AND ECONOMIC	1.6

Two Votes

AMERICAN GOVERNMENT CONCEPT	MEAN		MEAN
DIVINE RIGHT OF KINGS	1.7	INTEGRATION, FUNCTION	
EFFICACY	1.7	OF SOCIAL SYSTEMS	1.6
EMPIRICAL	1.5	INTEREST AGGREGATION	1.5
EMPIRICAL STATEMENT	1.5	INTERNATIONAL BEHAVIOR	1.7
EMPIRICAL THEORY	1.2	INTERNATIONAL	
EMPIRICISM	1.2	COMMUNIST MOVEMENT	1.7
END-MEANS ANALYSIS	1.6	INTERNATIONAL	
ENGELS, FRIEDRICH	1.7	COMMUNITY	1.7
EUROPEAN COMMON		INTERNATIONAL CONFLICTS	1.7
MARKET	1.7	INTERNATIONALISM	1.6
EUROPEAN ECONOMIC		INTERNATIONAL LAW	1.4
COMMUNITY (EEC)	1.6	INTERNATIONAL MONETARY	
EUROPEAN INTEGRATION	1.7	FUND (IMF)	1.7
EXPERIMENTAL METHOD	1.6	INTERNATIONAL ORDER	1.7
FASCISM	1.2	INTERNATIONAL	
FEUDALISM	1.5	ORGANIZATION	1.5
FIELD RESEARCH	1.7	INTERNATIONAL SYSTEM	1.5
FRANKLIN, BENJAMIN	1.7	INTERVENING VARIABLE	1.5
FRUSTRATION-AGGRESSION	1.6	IRON LAW OF OLIGARCHY	1.5
FUNCTIONAL		LABOR THEORY OF VALUE	1.5
ORGANIZATION	1.7	LAISSEZ-FAIRE	1.3
GAME THEORY	1.6	LEAGUE OF NATIONS (LN)	1.4
GENERAL ASSEMBLY (UN)	1.7	LEARNING THEORY	1.6
GENERAL WILL	1.6	LIMITED GOVERNMENT	1.5
GENEVA ACCORDS (1954)	1.7	MACROECONOMICS	1.7
GREAT BRITAIN	1.7	MACRO-MICRO ANALYSIS	1.5
GREEK CITY-STATES	1.7	MACRO-POLITICS	1.5
HISTORICAL APPROACH	1.7	MAOISM, COMMUNIST	
HISTORICAL MATERIALISM	1.6	DOCTRINE	1.5
HITLER, ADOLPH	1.4	MARXISM, COMMUNIST	
HOUSE OF COMMONS		DOCTRINE	1.3
(BRITISH)	1.4	MARXISTS	1.6
IMPERIALISM	1.1	MARX, KARL	1.4
IMPERIALISM AND		MASS SOCIETY	1.4
COLONIALISM,		MATERIALISM	1.6
COMMUNIST THEORY	1.5	MEANS-TO-END ANALYSIS	1.7
INDUSTRIAL REVOLUTION	1.3	MERHANTILISM	1.6
INPUT-OUTPUT ANALYSIS	1.5	METHODOLOGY	1.4

Two Votes

AMERICAN GOVERNMENT CONCEPT	MEAN		MEAN
METHODS IN POLITICAL SCIENCE	1.3	PARLIAMENT	1.4
MILL, JOHN STUART	1.7	PARLIAMENT, BRITISH	1.7
MODEL	1.4	PARLIAMENTARIANISM	1.6
MONOPOLY CAPITALISM	1.5	PARLIAMENTARY ELECTIONS	1.6
MORGENTHAU, HANS J.	1.5	PARLIAMENTARY GOVERNMENT	1.3
MULTIPARTY SYSTEM	1.1	PARLIAMENTARY PROCEDURE	1.7
MULTIPARTY SYSTEM	1.3	PARLIAMENTARY PROCESSES	1.4
NAPOLEONIC CODE	1.6	PARLIAMENTARY REGIME	1.7
NATIONAL CHARACTER	1.7	PARLIAMENTARY SYSTEM	1.2
NATIONALISM	1.1	PEER GROUP	1.5
NATIONAL SELF-DETERMINATION	1.5	POLICY ANALYSIS	1.5
NATIONAL SOCIALISM	1.3	POLICY PROCESSES	1.6
NAZI	1.6	POLITICAL COMMUNITY	1.4
NAZISM	1.6	POLITICAL DECISION	1.6
NEOCOLONIALISM	1.5	POLITICAL DEVELOPMENT	1.6
NON-ZERO-SUM GAMES	1.6	POLITICAL ECOLOGY	1.5
NORM	1.4	POLITICAL ECONOMY	1.6
NORMAL DISTRIBUTION	1.7	POLITICAL MORALITY	1.5
NORMATIVE	1.5	POLITICAL PARTIES, COMPARATIVE ANALYSIS	1.5
NORMATIVE ARGUMENT	1.3	POLITICAL SCIENCE	1.1
NORMATIVE STATEMENT	1.2	POLITICAL SCIENCE, SUBFIELDS OF	1.4
NUCLEAR ARMS RACE	1.6	POLITICAL SCIENCE, THE PROFESSION	1.5
NUCLEAR DISARMAMENT	1.6	POLITICAL SOCIALIZATION THEORY	1.5
NUCLEAR WARFARE	1.5	POLITICAL STRATIFICATION	1.4
OLIGARCHY	1.2	POLITICAL THEORY	1.2
ONE-PARTY RULE	1.5	PREAMBLE TO THE CONSTITUTION	1.7
OPERATIONAL DEFINITION	1.6	PRESCRIPTIVE THEORY	1.6
OPERATIONALIZATION	1.7	PRIME MINISTER	1.6
OPINION RESEARCH	1.6	PROBABILITY	1.4
OPPOSITION, RULE OF (BRITAIN)	1.6		
ORGANIC THEORY OF THE STATE	1.5		
ORGANIZATIONAL GOAL	1.5		
ORGANIZATION THEORY	1.4		
PACIFISM	1.5		

Two Votes

AMERICAN GOVERNMENT CONCEPT	MEAN		MEAN	
				53
PSYCHOLOGY AND DECISION MAKING	1.6	THEORY	1.6	
		THEORY OF GAMES	1.6	
PUBLIC OPINION RESEARCH	1.6	TOTALITARIANISM	1.4	
QUANTITATIVE APPROACHES	1.3	TYPOLOGY	1.5	
		UNCONVENTIONAL WARFARE	1.7	
REALISM	1.7			
RELIABILITY	1.5	UNDERDEVELOPED COUNTRIES	1.7	
RESEARCH DESIGN	1.4			
ROLE THEORY	1.6	UNDERDEVELOPMENT	1.5	
ROUSSEAU, JEAN JACQUES	1.7	UN GENERAL ASSEMBLY	1.5	
RUSSIAN REVOLUTION OF 1917	1.4	UN SECRETARIAT	1.6	
SANCTIONS (COLLECTIVE SECURITY)	1.6	UNION OF SOVIET SOCIALIST REPUBLICS (USSR)	1.5	
SECONDARY GROUP	1.6	UNITARY STATE	1.6	
SOCIAL CHANGE	1.4	UNITED NATIONS (UN)	1.2	
SOCIALISM	1.0	UTILITARIANISM	1.5	
SOCIALISM AND NATIONALISM	1.7	VALIDITY	1.6	
		VALUE THEORY	1.5	
SOVIET COMMUNISM	1.6	VARIABLE	1.3	
SOVIET UNION	1.6	VERIFIABILITY	1.6	
STALINISM, COMMUNIST DOCTRINE	1.6	VETO, SECURITY COUNCIL	1.5	
STIMULUS-RESPONSE	1.6	VIET CONG	1.7	
SURPLUS VALUE, COMMUNIST THEORY	1.7	WEBER, MAX	1.6	
		WITHERING AWAY OF THE STATE	1.6	
SURVEY RESEARCH	1.4	ZERO-SUM GAMES	1.6	
THEORIES OF NONVIOLENCE	1.7			

One Vote

AMERICAN GOVERNMENT CONCEPT	MEAN
GEOPOLITICS	1.7

International Relations

The International Relations concept experiment was conducted as the International Relations Innovative Learning (IRIL) Project and its results were later compared with the judgments of the MAP panel. The IRIL terms were drawn from eighteen widely used introductory international relations textbooks.[1] After proper nouns and terms dealing with research methodology were removed, approximately 2,400 international relations terms were identified.

The Project staff edited the roster to eliminate duplications, combine singular and plural forms of the same terms, standardize format, and remove obviously irrelevant terms. The result was a roster of 1,236 terms which was submitted to the IRIL judges.

A panel of nine political scientists specializing in international relations was drawn from the faculty of The California State University and Colleges, a system consisting of nineteen campuses. The IRIL panel was not specifically designed to be representative of the political science profession, international relations specialists, or the CSUC system's faculty. As it turned out, however, the nine IRIL judges, like the MAP panel, proved to be sufficiently diverse in age, training, and background to produce a substantial distribution of judgments for the concept evaluations.*

The panelists were asked to rate each of the 1,236 concepts according to their judgment of its "importance for a core international relations curriculum." A scale of 1 to 4 was used for rating importance: 1 for the "essential" terms the student should "know well"; 2 for those "important, but not essential"; 3 for "marginal" but "useful for core knowledge testing purposes"; and 4 for those of "minor importance or irrelevant for the foundation or introductory level student." Thus, the highest total a concept could receive was 9, the lowest, 36. The highest mean score for the entire panel was 1.00 and the lowest 4.00.[2]

Summarizing the IRIL Panel's Ratings

The Project staff wanted to determine which concepts the IRIL panel considered most important for a newcomer to the field of international relations, to what extent the experts disagreed in their judgments about the importance of the terms, and whether their disagreements followed any distinctive pattern.

The staff chose the mean as the measure of central tendency because it provided a straightforward way of ranking the 1,236 terms in a roster of 1.00 to 4.00. The standard deviation was chosen as the best way to comment on the amount of disagreement among the panelists, i.e., the degree of dispersion of the ratings from the panel's average rating. A standard deviation is "the square root of the arithmetic mean of squared deviations from the mean."[3] Strictly speaking, the standard deviation requires data measured in interval units as well as cases that distribute in a normal curve. The panel ratings were more ordinal than interval and more skewed than normal in distribution. Nevertheless, standard deviation does make it relatively simple to distin-

The Political Science Concept Inventory

guish terms about which the panel substantially disagreed from those about which the panel substantially agreed. Thus, a standard deviation of 1.50 for one concept compared with 0.50 for another indicates much more disagreement on the first concept than the second.

Furthermore, with four possible ratings and nine panelists, the standard deviations may range from 0.00 to a maximum disagreement of 1.58. Standard deviations of 0.00 are produced when all panelists assign the same rating, whether the rating is 1, 2, 3, or 4. The maximum standard deviation of 1.58 may be produced as the consequence of two types of distribution of disagreement: when four panelists rate the concept as essential (1) and the other five consider the concept irrelevant (4); or vice versa.[4]

The international relations roster (p. 000) lists the 1,236 concepts by means 1.00 to 4.00. Concepts with the same panel means are ranked according to standard deviation, i.e., from greatest consensus (small standard deviation) to greatest disagreement (large standard deviation).

Table 9 shows the distribution of the ratings of the 1,236 terms and lists them by mean and standard deviation.

Table 9 provides the instructor of the introductory or core course in international relations with a map leading to the most important concepts for the course. How many terms and topics should be included in the scope of the course will depend on the instructor's goals. The instructor may wish to cover only the fourteen most important concepts (mean: 1:00) since these reflect the highest degree of consensus about importance (standard deviation: 0.00 to 0.25). These fourteen include well-known candidates: balance of power; international politics; international relations; national interest; nation-state system; nationalism; neocolonialism; politics; population/overpopulation; power; state; superpower; theory; third world. Other instructors will move toward the lower right-hand corner of *Table 9*, adding concepts of declining consensus.

In general, then, concepts falling in cells located in the upper left, i.e., terms rated high in importance and evoking little disagreement among the panelists, are likely to be a "must" for inclusion in any core course in international relations. Those terms falling in cells in the lower left corner, i.e., terms about whose unimportance there was great agreement, may be entirely disregarded in a core course. Terms in the middle right of *Table 9* are those about which there was much disagreement. Some instructors may wish to exclude these more controversial terms from the core course in order to avoid confusing or overburdening students. Others may wish to include them in order to demonstrate the conceptual ambiguities of the field. Terms in the middle left cells are those that the IRIL panel agreed are modestly important for the core course.

Table 9 reveals some "natural" boundaries in the distribution of concepts according to importance and panel consensus. The row totals show the number of terms in each mean level and rise in successive steps (74, 100, 148, etc.), reaching the highest row total of 250 at the mean rating of 1.76–2.00. A sharp decline follows the ratings that exceed 2.01–2.25. This distribution suggests that 2.00 is the point at which to begin making decisions about including or excluding concepts from the core course.

Table 9. Distribution of Nine-Member Panel Ratings of 1,236 International Relations Concepts According to Means and Standard Deviations

		Standard Deviation of Panel's Ratings						Row Totals	Cumulative Totals
		0.00–0.25	0.26–0.50	0.51–0.75	0.76–1.00	1.01–1.25	1.16–1.50		
Mean of Panel's Ratings	1.00–1.25	14	51	9	0	0	0	74	74
	1.26–1.50	0	34	51	15	0	0	100	174
	1.51–1.75	0	15	65	57	11	0	148	322
	1.76–2.00	0	2	31	156	60	1	250	572
	2.01–2.25	0	1	27	65	50	7	150	722
	2.26–2.50	0	10	28	76	57	11	182	904
	2.51–2.75	0	14	13	43	43	5	118	1,022
	2.76–3.00	6	6	30	47	19	3	111	1,133
	3.01–3.25	0	11	16	16	1	2	46	1,179
	3.26–3.50	0	24	4	5	3	0	36	1,215
	3.51–3.75	0	8	1	1	0	0	10	1,225
	3.76–4.00	10	1	0	0	0	0	11	1,236
	Column Totals	30	177	275	481	244	29	—	—
	Cumulative Totals	30	207	482	963	1,207	1,236	—	—

The column totals show the number of terms in each level of standard deviation. Here, too, the totals rise (30, 177, 275, etc.) to a standard deviation of 0.76–1.00 (481) and fall off sharply when the standard deviation exceeds 1.01. This suggests that a standard deviation of 1.00 is a good level at which to make decisions about including or excluding concepts from the core course.

The peak row (means up to 2.00) and the peak column (standard deviations up to 1.00) meet in the cell with the largest concentration of cases in the entire distribution: 156. The concepts represented by the numbers upward and leftward from this cell, as marked off by the lines framing that corner of the table, were judged important for the introductory core curriculum in international relations by the IRIL panel. The total number of concepts in this corner is 500. In short, the 500 concepts (omitting the seventy-two with standard deviations larger than 1.00) from "balance of power" to "weaponry" in the international relations roster (p. 000) are the ones upon which a core curriculum should be built.

The average judgment of the importance of each of the 1,236 terms by the nine panelists matches the judgments by the authors of the eighteen textbooks rather closely. We presumed that if a term is rated important by a panel of nine international relations instructors, this evaluation should coincide with that of the text writers as evidenced by what the latter included in their indexes. Therefore, if a term appeared in all eighteen text indexes, it was counted important; if it appeared in only one index, unimportant. In other words, the number of times a term appeared in the eighteen indexes served as a validation of the IRIL panel's collective rating for that term.

Using Pearson's correlation coefficient as the measure of degree of association between the panel's mean rating for each term and the number of indexes in which the term was mentioned, we found a substantial degree of association: -.483, significant at the .001 level. (The correlation is negative because a *low* mean and a *high* number of index appearances were the indicators of importance compared.)

Characteristics of the Panelists

The panelists generally exhibit similar patterns of judgment. Some expect beginning students to become familiar with a large proportion of the 1,236 concepts . Others think the proportion studied should be small (see *Table 10*).

The panelists rated each concept from 1 to 4, a spread of three rating intervals. Thus, if a panelist's 1,236 ratings were distributed in a normal curve, the mean of his ratings would be 2.50, i.e., $[(4.00 - 1.00)/2] + 1.00$. The overall mean rating for all nine panelists, however, was 2.16, slightly in the direction of maximal expectations regarding the number of the 1,236 concepts that their students should know. More specifically, panelist 3, with a mean rating of 1.61, clearly held maximal expectations; he believed, compared with the others, that the introductory course should incorporate the greatest proportion of the terms inventoried. On the other hand, panelist 6, with a

Table 10. STATISTICAL CHARACTERISTICS OF EACH PANELIST'S SET OF CONCEPT RATINGS
(N = ca. 1,236)

IRIL Panelist	Panelist's Mean*	Deviation of Panelist's Mean from Panel's (2.16)	Standard Deviation
1	2.32	+0.16	0.89
2	2.02	−0.14	0.91
3	1.60	−0.56	0.92
4	2.06	−0.10	0.97
5	2.42	+0.26	1.09
6	2.78	+0.62	0.81
7	1.94	−0.22	1.16
8	2.09	−0.07	0.98
9	1.71	−0.45	0.90

* Some panelists failed to rate all 1,236 concepts. Computations in this table are based upon the actual number of ratings made by each panelist. This procedure resulted in a grand mean for the entire panel (2.16) that differs slightly from the mean of the nine scores in this column (2.10). Rounding is also a factor in the difference.

mean rating of 2.78, expected his students to know the fewest number of terms. Six of the panelists (those with minuses preceding their deviations from the overall panel mean) leaned in the direction of maximal expectations, i.e., they tended to rank terms as "essential" and "important" for the beginning student. Three panelists (those with pluses preceding their deviation figures) had minimal expectations.

The standard deviation shows the degree to which a panelist placed a large number of concepts in one category of importance (1, 2, 3, or 4) or spread the concepts widely among all four. Panelist 6 had the lowest standard deviation in the panel (.81), and is the same one who judged the largest number of concepts "marginal" or "irrelevant" for the core course. On the other hand, panelists 7 and 5, with standard deviations of 1.16 and 1.09 respectively, had the most dispersed judgments.

To examine whether the overall rating patterns of the panelists reveal subgroups or voting blocs within the panel, the staff used the technique often applied in the analysis of bloc voting.[5] The statistic Gamma was computed as a measure of the degree of association between the rating patterns of every pair of panelists. The resulting matrix of association is reported in *Table 11*.

When the degree of association is set at Gamma = .328, the panel appears *(Figure 1)* to be well integrated. However, by raising the degree of association standard from .328 to Gamma = .365, panelists 3 and 4 emerge as a separate coalition *(Figure 2)*; their respective concept rating patterns show a relationship with each other (Gamma = .396) that is stronger than their associations with any of the other panelists. Note, too, that panelist 5 has no associations with other panelists at this level.

The coalition of panelists 3 and 4 persists until the requirement for strength of

The Political Science Concept Inventory

Table 11. Degrees of Association (Gamma) in Concept Ratings of Pairs of IRIL Panelists
(N = 1,236)*

Panelist	1	2	3	4	5	6	7	8	9
1	1.000	.392	.323	.363	.323	.191	.382	.242	.407
2		1.000	.258	.345	.131	.124	.242	.135	.311
3			1.000	.396	.293	.362	.355	.360	.325
4				1.000	.237	.331	.352	.282	.313
5					1.000	.229	.209	.330	.337
6						1.000	.534	.498	.408
7							1.000	.364	.429
8								1.000	.467
9									1.000

* Missing data, i.e., unrated concepts, are excluded from the computations.

association is raised above Gamma = .396. At this level, only the central bloc consisting of panelists 1, 6, 7, 8, and 9 persists, as shown in *Figure 3*.

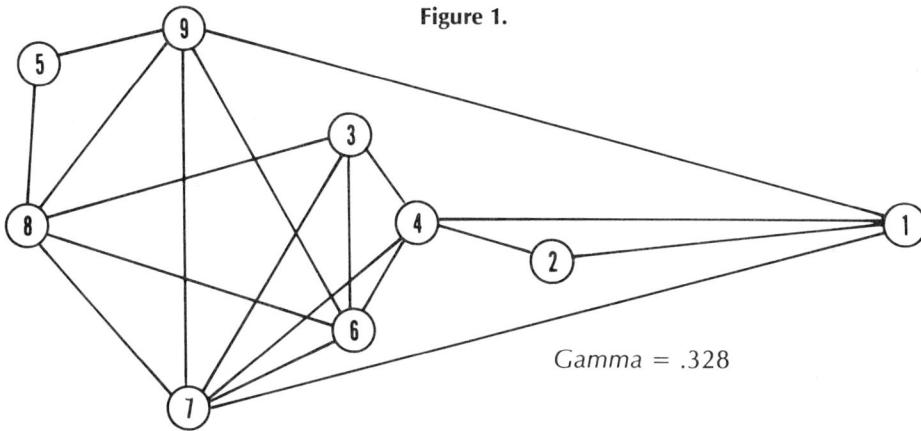

Figure 1.

Gamma = .328

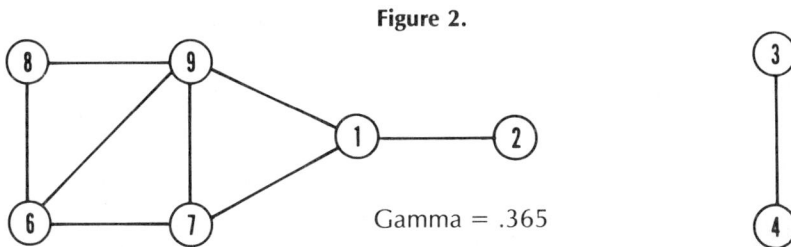

Figure 2.

Gamma = .365

Figure 3.

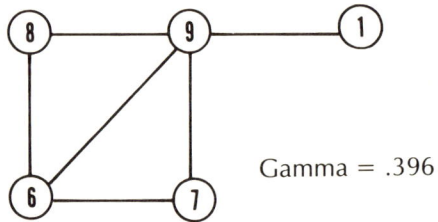

Gamma = .396

In an academic field in which intellectual factionalism is often exhibited by instructors and researchers alike, the IRIL panel, according to this bloc analysis, appears to be diverse without being polarized. The patterns of preference revealed by their respective concept ratings show a relatively well integrated group.

The international relations concepts are listed below according to degree of importance (mean), and alphabetically within each mean level. The degree of consensus (standard deviation) appears alongside the mean.

Ratings of International Relations Concepts by IRIL Panel

Alphabetized within each mean level.

INTERNATIONAL RELATIONS CONCEPT	MEAN	SD
BALANCE OF POWER	1.00	0
INTERNATIONAL POLITICS	1.00	0
INTERNATIONAL RELATIONS	1.00	0
NATIONAL INTEREST	1.00	0
NATIONALISM	1.00	0
NATION-STATE SYSTEM	1.00	0
NEOCOLONIALISM	1.00	0
POLITICS	1.00	0
POPULATION/OVERPOPULATION	1.00	0
POWER	1.00	0
STATE	1.00	0
SUPERPOWER	1.00	0
THEORY	1.00	0
THIRD WORLD	1.00	0
CAPABILITIES	1.11	.31
COEXISTENCE	1.11	.31
COLD WAR	1.11	.31
COMMUNISM	1.11	.31
CONFLICT	1.11	.31
CONTAINMENT	1.11	.31
DECISION MAKING	1.11	.31
DETENTE	1.11	.31
DIPLOMACY	1.11	.31
FOREIGN AID	1.11	.31

International Relations Concept	Mean	SD
FOREIGN POLICY	1.11	.31
IDEOLOGY	1.11	.31
IMPERIALISM	1.11	.31
INTERNATIONAL ORGANIZATION	1.11	.31
NATIONAL SECURITY	1.11	.31
NATIONAL SOVEREIGNTY	1.11	.31
REVOLUTIONS	1.11	.31
SOVEREIGNTY	1.11	.31
WAR	1.11	.31
BIPOLARITY	1.13	.33
NEOIMPERIALISM	1.13	.33
NUCLEAR ARMS RACE	1.13	.33
NUCLEAR DETERRENT	1.13	.33
DEVELOPED COUNTRIES	1.14	.35
POWER, BALANCE OF POWER	1.14	.35
STATE SYSTEM	1.14	.35
ECONOMIC FACTORS	1.17	.37
IMAGE	1.17	.37
STATE, UNDERDEVELOPED	1.17	.37
ALLIANCE	1.22	.42
COLLECTIVE SECURITY	1.22	.63
CONFLICT RESOLUTION	1.22	.42
COUP D'ETAT	1.22	.63
DEVELOPING NATIONS	1.22	.63
DISARMAMENT	1.22	.63
ECONOMIC DEVELOPMENT	1.22	.42
ELITES	1.22	.42
EUROPEAN INTEGRATION	1.22	.42
INTERNATIONAL LAW	1.22	.63
INTERNATIONAL SYSTEMS	1.22	.42
INTERVENTION	1.22	.42
MODERNIZATION	1.22	.42
MULTINATIONAL CORPORATIONS	1.22	.42
NEGOTIATION	1.22	.42
NONALIGNMENT	1.22	.63
PROPAGANDA	1.22	.42
SOVEREIGN STATE	1.22	.63
SPHERE OF INFLUENCE	1.22	.42
THEORY OF INTERNATIONAL POLITICS	1.22	.42
AGGRESSION	1.25	.43

The Political Science Concept Inventory

International Relations Concept	Mean	SD	
			63
BEHAVIORAL APPROACH	1.25	.43	
DETERRENCE THEORY	1.25	.43	
DEVELOPMENT	1.25	.43	
DIPLOMATIC BARGAINING	1.25	.43	
EAST-WEST CONFLICT	1.25	.43	
EXPLOITATION	1.25	.66	
INTERDEPENDENCE	1.25	.43	
NATURAL RESOURCES	1.25	.66	
SUMMIT CONFERENCE	1.25	.43	
WAR POTENTIAL	1.25	.43	
GROSS NATIONAL PRODUCT (GNP)	1.29	.45	
INDUSTRIALIZATION	1.29	.45	
INTERNATIONAL ECONOMY	1.29	.45	
METHODOLOGY	1.29	.70	
MILITARY EXPENDITURE	1.29	.45	
NORTH-SOUTH SPLIT	1.29	.45	
POLYCENTRIC INTERNATIONAL SYSTEM	1.29	.45	
VARIABLE	1.29	.45	
ACTORS, INTERNATIONAL	1.33	.47	
ARMS CONTROL	1.33	.47	
BALANCE OF TERROR	1.33	.67	
CAPITALISM	1.33	.47	
COLONIAL-ANTICOLONIAL STRUGGLE	1.33	.67	
COLONIALISM	1.33	.67	
COUPS	1.33	.75	
DATA BASE FOR INTERNATIONAL POLITICAL ANALYSIS	1.33	.47	
GOAL FORMATION	1.33	.75	
INFLUENCE	1.33	.67	
INTERNAL WAR	1.33	.47	
INTERNATIONAL ACTOR	1.33	.67	
MULTIPOLARITY	1.33	.67	
NATIONALIZATION	1.33	.47	
NATIONAL LIBERATION WARS	1.33	.67	
NUCLEAR PARITY	1.33	.47	
NUCLEAR STRATEGY	1.33	.47	
NUCLEAR WAR	1.33	.67	
SECURITY	1.33	.47	
THERMONUCLEAR WAR	1.33	.47	
TOTAL WAR	1.33	.47	
TREATIES	1.33	.67	

International Relations Concept	Mean	SD
ATOMIC WEAPONS	1.38	.99
DISARMAMENT, ARMS CONTROL AND INSPECTION	1.38	.70
GROSS NATIONAL PRODUCT (GNP)	1.38	.70
MARXISM	1.38	.48
MILITARY COUPS	1.38	.48
MUTUAL DETERRENCE	1.38	.48
NUCLEAR NONPROLIFERATION	1.38	.70
PEACE	1.38	.70
PEACEFUL COEXISTENCE	1.38	.48
ROLE	1.38	.70
SYSTEMIC LEVEL OF ANALYSIS	1.38	.48
SOCIALIZATION	1.38	.99
AGGRESSOR NATION	1.43	.73
ARMED CONFLICT	1.43	.73
DEVELOPED STATES	1.43	.73
MILITARY FACTORS	1.43	.73
MISSILE WEAPONS	1.43	.49
ADJUDICATION	1.44	.83
ANTICOLONIALISM	1.44	.68
ARBITRATION	1.44	.83
BALANCE OF TRADE	1.44	.68
BELIEF SYSTEMS	1.44	.68
COMMUNICATION	1.44	.68
ECONOMIC AID	1.44	.68
EMBARGO	1.44	.96
ESPIONAGE	1.44	.68
GENOCIDE	1.44	.68
GOALS	1.44	.50
INTERNATIONAL TREATIES	1.44	.83
NATION	1.44	.83
POLITICAL SOCIALIZATION	1.44	.68
REVOLUTION OF RISING EXPECTATIONS	1.44	.68
SANCTIONS	1.44	.83
SECURITY SYSTEM	1.44	.50
SYSTEMIC MODELS	1.44	.50
TRANSNATIONAL CORPORATIONS	1.44	.68
ALIGNMENT	1.50	.71
AUTHORITY	1.50	1.00
BALANCER	1.50	.71
CONFLICT CONTROL	1.50	.71

64

The Political Science Concept Inventory

International Relations Concept	Mean	SD
CONTAINMENT POLICIES	1.50	.76
CULTURE	1.50	.71
ECONOMIC AGREEMENTS	1.50	.50
ENERGY RESOURCES	1.50	.50
ETHICS AND THE STATESMAN	1.50	.76
FOREIGN INVESTMENT	1.50	.50
GEOGRAPHY	1.50	.76
GOVERNMENT	1.50	.71
IDEOLOGICAL CONFLICT	1.50	.71
IMMUNITY, DIPLOMATIC	1.50	.71
INTERACTION	1.50	.76
INTERNATIONAL DISPUTES	1.50	.71
INTERNATIONAL INTEGRATION	1.50	.71
INTERNATIONAL INTERDEPENDENCE	1.50	.71
INTERNATIONAL TRANSACTIONS	1.50	.50
JUST WAR	1.50	.71
MILITARY AID	1.50	.87
MILITARY-INDUSTRIAL COMPLEX	1.50	.71
NUCLEAR CAPACITY	1.50	.71
NUCLEAR POWER	1.50	.71
NUCLEAR TEST BAN	1.50	.71
POLITICAL CULTURE	1.50	.71
POLITICAL SYSTEM	1.50	.50
PSYCHOLOGICAL FACTORS	1.50	.50
PUBLIC OPINION	1.50	.71
RETALIATION	1.50	.71
SUPRANATIONAL INSTITUTIONS	1.50	.71
SUPRANATIONALISM	1.50	.71
SYSTEM THEORY	1.50	1.00
TRANSNATIONAL	1.50	.71
ANTICOMMUNISM	1.56	.83
ANTIIMPERIALISM	1.56	.68
ARMS RACE	1.56	.96
BARGAINING	1.56	.68
BLOCS	1.56	.83
CIVIL WARS	1.56	.68
COLONIAL SYSTEMS	1.56	.83
CONCILIATION	1.56	.68
CONVENTIONAL WAR CAPABILITY	1.56	.68
DE FACTO GOVERNMENT	1.56	.83

International Relations Concept	Mean	SD
ECONOMIC IMPERIALISM	1.56	.68
ESCALATION	1.56	.68
FUNCTIONALISM	1.56	.50
GUERRILLA WARFARE	1.56	.83
INTERCONTINENTAL BALLISTIC MISSILES (ICBM)	1.56	.68
INTERFERENCE, DIPLOMATIC INTERGOVERNMENTAL	1.56	.68
INTERNATIONAL ENVIRONMENT	1.56	.68
INTERNATIONAL INSTITUTIONS	1.56	.83
LIMITED WAR	1.56	.83
NATIONAL RESOURCES	1.56	.68
NATIONAL SELF-DETERMINATION	1.56	.83
NATIONAL UNIFICATION	1.56	.68
NEUTRALITY	1.56	.83
NUCLEAR WEAPONS	1.56	.68
RACISM	1.56	.68
RESOURCES	1.56	.96
RULE OF LAW (CONDUCT)	1.56	.68
SIMULATION	1.56	.68
STRATEGY	1.56	.83
THERMONUCLEAR WEAPONS	1.56	.68
WORLD GOVERNMENT	1.56	.96
DETERMINISM	1.57	.49
ECOLOGY	1.57	.90
ENVIRONMENT	1.57	.73
EQUALITY OF STATES	1.57	.73
EXPORT	1.57	.90
INTEGRATION, ECONOMIC	1.57	.49
NATIONAL OBJECTIVES	1.57	.49
NEUTRALISM	1.57	.73
NORMS	1.57	.73
NUCLEAR PROLIFERATION	1.57	1.05
POLARITY	1.57	.49
POLICY INFLUENCERS	1.57	.73
RATIONALITY OF POLICY MAKERS AND DETERRENCE	1.57	1.05
WORLD ORDER	1.57	.90
WORLD POLITICS	1.57	.73
WORLD TRADE	1.57	.49
ENEMY	1.60	.80
INTERNATIONAL POWER	1.60	.80
NUCLEAR CLUB	1.60	.80

66

The Political Science Concept Inventory

INTERNATIONAL RELATIONS CONCEPT	MEAN	SD	
ALLIES	1.63	.86	**67**
CHANGE IN INTERNATIONAL POLITICAL ENVIRONMENT	1.63	.99	
CREDIBILITY	1.63	.48	
DIPLOMATIC NEGOTIATIONS	1.63	.70	
EQUILIBRIUM	1.63	.70	
HUMAN RESOURCES	1.63	.86	
INTERNATIONAL COMMUNITY	1.63	1.11	
INTERNATIONALISM	1.63	.70	
INTERNATIONAL ORDER	1.63	.70	
INTERNATIONAL POLITICAL SYSTEM	1.63	.86	
INTERNATIONAL POLITICAL SYSTEM, CONTEMPORARY	1.63	.70	
LEGITIMACY	1.63	.70	
MOBILIZATION	1.63	.70	
NONNUCLEAR STATES	1.63	.70	
NORMATIVE AND ANALYTIC THINKING	1.63	.86	
NORMATIVE STATEMENTS	1.63	.86	
WESTERN NATIONS	1.63	.70	
SECURITY ORGANIZATIONS, REGIONAL	1.63	.99	
STATE CLASSIFICATORY SCHEMES, RICH/POOR	1.63	.86	
STATE CLASSIFICATORY SCHEMES, STATUS QUO/REVISIONIST	1.63	.86	
SYSTEMS	1.63	.99	
WORLD POPULATION	1.63	.99	
AID	1.67	.82	
ARMS LIMITATION	1.67	.82	
ATOMIC DETERRENCE	1.67	1.11	
ATOMIC ENERGY, CONTROL	1.67	.82	
ATTRIBUTES OF A GREAT POWER	1.67	1.05	
BARGAINING PATTERNS	1.67	.75	
BILATERAL AGREEMENTS	1.67	1.05	
CRISIS MANAGEMENT	1.67	.82	
CUSTOM AS A SOURCE OF INTERNATIONAL LAW	1.67	.82	
DECOLONIZATION	1.67	.82	
DELIVERY SYSTEMS	1.67	.67	
DIPLOMAT	1.67	.75	
EAST-WEST TRADE	1.67	.75	
ECONOMIC BOYCOTT	1.67	.82	
ECONOMIC INTEGRATION	1.67	.67	
EUROPEAN UNITY	1.67	.75	
FREE TRADE	1.67	.82	
GAME THEORY	1.67	.82	

International Relations Concept	Mean	SD
GLOBALIZATION	1.67	.75
HUMAN RIGHTS	1.67	.67
MASSIVE RETALIATION	1.67	.67
MILITARY FORCE	1.67	.75
NATIONAL IDENTITY	1.67	.67
NATIONAL POWER	1.67	.94
NUCLEAR BALANCING	1.67	.75
OVERPOPULATION	1.67	.94
PAYOFFS	1.67	.47
PERSONAL DIPLOMACY	1.67	.67
POLICYMAKING	1.67	1.05
RECOGNITION	1.67	.82
REGIONAL INTEGRATION	1.67	.82
REGIONALISM	1.67	.82
SATELLITES	1.67	.67
SELF-DETERMINATION	1.67	.82
STEREOTYPES	1.67	.67
TECHNOLOGY	1.67	1.05
ATTITUDES	1.71	.45
CONFLICT OF INTERESTS	1.71	.70
DECISION MAKING, ADMINISTRATIVE DECISIONS	1.71	.45
EMERGING NATIONS	1.71	.88
EXPANSIONISM	1.71	.70
GEOPOLITICS	1.71	.70
GLOBALISM	1.71	1.16
INSTRUMENTS OF STATECRAFT	1.71	.70
LESS DEVELOPED NATIONS	1.71	.70
MILITARY FACTORS, NUCLEAR CAPABILITY	1.71	.45
MILITARY PRESSURE	1.71	.70
PARITY	1.71	.70
POWER POLITICS	1.71	.88
SECURITY COMMUNITY	1.71	.45
STATESMEN	1.71	.45
STABLE BALANCE OF POWER	1.71	.70
WORLD COMMUNITY	1.71	.70
WARFARE	1.71	1.03
ATOMS FOR PEACE	1.75	.66
AUTHORITARIAN STATES	1.75	1.09
CAPITAL	1.75	.66
COALITION	1.75	.66

The Political Science Concept Inventory

INTERNATIONAL RELATIONS CONCEPT	MEAN	SD	
CONVENTIONAL FORCES	1.75	.83	**69**
CRIMES, WAR	1.75	.83	
DECISION MAKING, CRISIS DECISIONS	1.75	.43	
DECISION MAKING, GENERAL FOREIGN POLICY DECISIONS	1.75	.43	
INFORMATION	1.75	.83	
INTEREST GROUPS	1.75	.83	
LAISSEZ-FAIRE	1.75	.66	
NATIONAL LEADERSHIP	1.75	.83	
NUCLEAR BLACKMAIL	1.75	.66	
NUCLEAR ENERGY	1.75	.97	
NUCLEAR ERA	1.75	.66	
NUCLEAR TESTING	1.75	.97	
PATRIOTISM	1.75	.66	
SECOND STRIKE	1.75	.83	
SOCIALISM	1.75	.66	
STATECRAFT	1.75	.83	
THEORY OF GAMES	1.75	.83	
APARTHEID	1.78	.79	
ARMAMENTS	1.78	1.03	
BALANCING PROCESS	1.78	1.03	
BALANCE OF PAYMENTS	1.78	.92	
BELLIGERENT	1.78	1.23	
BRINKMANSHIP	1.78	.79	
COERCION	1.78	.79	
DIALECTICAL AND HISTORICAL MATERIALISM	1.78	.79	
ECONOMIC INTERDEPENDENCE	1.78	.79	
ETHNOCENTRIC ATTITUDES	1.78	.63	
EXTRATERRITORIALITY	1.78	.79	
FEEDBACK	1.78	.79	
FOREIGN ASSETS	1.78	.79	
INDEPENDENCE MOVEMENTS	1.78	1.03	
INFORMATIONAL FLOW	1.78	.79	
MOST-FAVORED-NATION CLAUSE	1.78	.92	
NATIONAL PRESTIGE	1.78	.79	
PEACEKEEPING	1.78	.79	
POLICYMAKERS	1.78	1.03	
PROTRACTED WARFARE	1.78	1.03	
PSYCHOLOGICAL WARFARE	1.78	.79	
REARMAMENT	1.78	.92	
REGIONAL ALLIANCES	1.78	.92	

INTERNATIONAL RELATIONS CONCEPT	MEAN	SD
REGIONAL ORGANIZATIONS	1.78	.79
REVOLUTIONARY WARFARE	1.78	.79
STATUS QUO	1.78	1.03
STRATEGIC AREAS	1.78	.79
SYSTEM ANALYSIS	1.78	.92
SYSTEMIC CHANGE	1.78	.79
TECHNICAL ASSISTANCE	1.78	.79
TERRITORIALITY	1.78	.42
TERRITORY	1.78	.79
TRADE	1.78	1.23
TRIPOLARITY	1.78	.92
VETO POWER	1.78	.92
WEAPONS	1.78	.79
WORLD FEDERALISM	1.78	.79
FEAR	1.80	1.17
MILITARY INSTRUMENTS	1.80	.75
PROPOSITION	1.80	1.17
SUPER STATES-SUPER POWERS	1.80	1.17
ECONOMIC ALLOCATIONS	1.83	.90
HETEROGENEITY	1.83	.69
MILITARY MOBILITY	1.83	.69
NATION-STATE DOMINANCE	1.83	1.07
POLITICAL IMPERIALISM	1.83	.69
POLITICAL SYSTEM, OPEN AND CLOSED	1.83	.90
POWER, FORMS OF	1.83	.37
SOCIALIST	1.83	.90
WEST	1.83	1.21
AIR POWER	1.86	.99
ARMED FORCES	1.86	1.12
COMMUNITY	1.86	.83
DECISION MAKING, PSYCHOLOGICAL FACTORS	1.86	.83
DEMOGRAPHIC REVOLUTION	1.86	1.12
ECOLOGICAL CRISIS	1.86	1.12
ECONOMIC WARFARE	1.86	.64
HEGEMONY	1.86	.83
INFLUENCES, INTERESTS	1.86	.83
INTELLECTUALS, INFLUENCE	1.86	.83
INTERNATIONAL RIVALRY	1.86	.99
KEYNESIAN REVOLUTION	1.86	.99
LEVEL OF ANALYSIS	1.86	1.12

The Political Science Concept Inventory

International Relations Concept	Mean	SD	
MILITARY	1.86	1.12	**71**
NATION-STATE LEVEL OF ANALYSIS	1.86	1.12	
NATURAL LAW	1.86	1.12	
NUCLEAR DISENGAGEMENT	1.86	.83	
PERCEPTUAL DISTORTION	1.86	1.12	
SCIENTIFIC KNOWLEDGE	1.86	1.12	
SOCIAL CHANGE	1.86	.99	
STABILITY IN INTERNATIONAL SYSTEMS	1.86	.83	
STATESMEN	1.86	.99	
STRUGGLE FOR POWER	1.86	.99	
UNDERDEVELOPED COUNTRIES	1.86	.64	
BLOC VOTING	1.88	.93	
BUREAUCRACIES	1.88	.93	
COMPULSORY JURISDICTION	1.88	.93	
CONFRONTATIONS	1.88	.60	
CONQUEST	1.88	.78	
CONVENTIONAL WEAPONS	1.88	.78	
COOPERATION	1.88	.93	
COUNTER-INSURGENCY	1.88	.78	
CULTURAL IMPERIALISM	1.88	.60	
DECISIONAL PROCESS	1.88	.93	
DECISION MAKING, NATIONAL DECISION MAKING	1.88	.78	
DEFENSE STRATEGY	1.88	.93	
DOMESTIC JURISDICTION	1.88	.93	
ECONOMIC PRESSURE	1.88	.60	
ECONOMIC PRODUCTIVITY	1.88	.78	
ECONOMIC SYSTEMS	1.88	.93	
FAIT ACCOMPLI	1.88	.78	
FIRST STRIKE	1.88	.78	
FUNCTIONAL COLLABORATION BETWEEN NATIONS	1.88	.78	
GOVERNMENTAL ELITE SECTOR	1.88	.93	
IDEOLOGICAL GOALS	1.88	.60	
IMPORTS	1.88	.78	
INDUSTRIAL SOCIETIES	1.88	.93	
INFLATION	1.88	.93	
INSECURITY	1.88	.93	
INTEGRATION	1.88	.93	
INTERACTION, INTERNATIONAL	1.88	1.05	
INTERNATIONAL LAW, ADJUDICATION	1.88	.78	
MAINTENANCE OF THE INTERNATIONAL SYSTEM	1.88	.78	

INTERNATIONAL RELATIONS CONCEPT	MEAN	SD
NONVIOLENCE	1.88	.93
PLURALISM	1.88	1.05
POLYETHNIC STATE	1.88	.78
POWER VACUUMS	1.88	.78
PRESTIGE	1.88	.78
RESTRAINT	1.88	.78
REVOLUTIONARY POWER	1.88	1.05
STRATEGIC DOCTRINE	1.88	.78
STRATEGIC NUCLEAR POWER	1.88	1.05
TARIFFS	1.88	.78
TECHNOLOGICAL CHANGES	1.88	.78
UNDERDEVELOPED AREAS	1.88	.78
UNDERDEVELOPED NATIONS	1.88	.93
ACTS OF STATE	1.89	.99
APPEASEMENT	1.89	1.10
BILATERAL ARRANGEMENTS	1.89	1.10
BLOCKADES	1.89	.99
BLUFFING AS A STRATEGY	1.89	.74
CONSENSUS	1.89	.87
DISTRIBUTION OF POWER	1.89	.87
FASCISM	1.89	1.10
INTERNAL CONFLICT	1.89	1.20
INTERNATIONAL STABILITY	1.89	.99
INTRAREGIONAL CONFLICTS	1.89	.74
MILITARY MOBILIZATION	1.89	.74
MODERNIZED SOCIETIES	1.89	.87
MULTILATERAL FORCE	1.89	.74
MULTIPOLAR PATTERN	1.89	.74
NATIONALITY	1.89	.87
NATIONAL LOYALTY	1.89	.87
NATIONAL UNITY	1.89	.99
REALPOLITIK POLICY	1.89	.99
SCARCITY IN WORLD ENVIRONMENT	1.89	.99
STANDARD OF LIVING	1.89	.74
STATE, DEVELOPED	1.89	.87
SYSTEM INTERACTION	1.89	.87
SYSTEMIC TRANSFORMATION	1.89	.99
THREATS	1.89	.99
UNITING FOR PEACE RESOLUTION	1.89	1.10
ACTION	2.00	1.41

The Political Science Concept Inventory

INTERNATIONAL RELATIONS CONCEPT	MEAN	SD
AUTOCRACY	2.00	1.07
BARGAINING SETTING	2.00	1.00
BUFFERS	2.00	.82
COLLECTIVE ACTION	2.00	.87
COLONIES	2.00	.87
CONSTITUTIONALISM	2.00	.87
CORPORATIONS	2.00	.71
CREDIBILITY GAPS	2.00	1.07
DEFERENCE	2.00	.82
DEMARCATION	2.00	1.07
DEMOCRACY	2.00	1.05
DEMOCRACY/DICTATORSHIP	2.00	.82
DEPENDENCIES	2.00	.87
DEPRESSION, ECONOMIC	2.00	.87
DIPLOMATIC IMMUNITY IN INTERNATIONAL LAW	2.00	.87
DOMESTIC POLITICS	2.00	.82
DOMINANCE IN FOREIGN POLICY DECISION MAKING	2.00	.87
ECOLOGICAL VALUES	2.00	.82
ECONOMIC DEPENDENCIES	2.00	.82
ECONOMIC FORCE	2.00	.63
ECONOMIC POWER	2.00	1.00
ECONOMICS	2.00	1.15
ENVIRONMENTAL QUALITY	2.00	.82
EXECUTIVE BRANCH OF GOVERNMENT	2.00	1.12
EXPLANATORY HYPOTHESIS	2.00	.82
FALLOUT, RADIOACTIVE	2.00	.94
FEDERATIONS	2.00	.87
FLEXIBLE RESPONSE	2.00	.67
FOREIGN AFFAIRS	2.00	1.22
FRONTIERS	2.00	.87
FRUSTRATION-AGGRESSION THEORY	2.00	.82
FUNCTIONAL DIFFERENTIATION	2.00	.53
GLOBAL PROBLEMS	2.00	1.15
GREAT POWER	2.00	1.00
HISTORICAL SETTING	2.00	1.05
IDEALISM	2.00	1.00
IDENTIFICATION OF ENEMY	2.00	.82
IMAGE AND REALITY	2.00	1.00
IMMIGRATION	2.00	.82
IMPERIALIST RIVALRIES	2.00	.89

International Relations Concept	Mean	SD
INCOME INEQUALITY, NATIONAL	2.00	1.07
INDEPENDENCE, ECONOMIC	2.00	.76
INDUSTRIAL REGIONS	2.00	1.07
INFLUENCERS, BUREAUCRATIC	2.00	.76
INFLUENCERS, MASS	2.00	1.00
INFLUENCERS, PARTISAN	2.00	1.00
INSPECTION, NUCLEAR WEAPONS	2.00	.71
INTEGRATION, SOCIOECONOMIC	2.00	.82
INTERGOVERNMENTAL ORGANIZATIONS, REGIONAL	2.00	.71
INTERMEDIATE RANGE BALLISTIC MISSILES (IRBM)	2.00	.82
INTERNATIONAL CARTELS	2.00	1.05
INTERNATIONAL ENVIRONMENT, FLOW OF IDEAS	2.00	.58
INTERNATIONAL ENVIRONMENT, INTERNATIONAL	2.00	.58
INTERNATIONAL ENVIRONMENT, INTERNATIONAL LAW	2.00	1.15
INTERNATIONAL INSTABILITY	2.00	.76
INTERNATIONAL LAW, AS A DECENTRALIZED SYSTEM	2.00	.76
INTERNATIONAL MORALITY	2.00	1.15
MANDATE SYSTEM	2.00	1.05
MARKET (INTERNATIONAL CURRENCY MARKET)	2.00	.82
MARKET, INTERNATIONAL	2.00	.89
MEDIATION	2.00	.82
MIDDLE RANGE POWERS	2.00	.76
MILITARY FACTORS, GUERRILLA WARFARE	2.00	.58
MORAL PRINCIPLES	2.00	1.07
MULTINATIONAL FORCE	2.00	.71
NATIONAL CHARACTER	2.00	.94
NATIONAL LIBERATION	2.00	.93
NATIONALS	2.00	1.12
NEGATIVE FEEDBACK	2.00	.67
NEW STATES	2.00	1.12
OBJECTIVES	2.00	1.15
OPERATIONAL DEFINITIONS	2.00	.76
PATTERNS	2.00	.82
PEACEFUL SETTLEMENT	2.00	.67
PEACE RESEARCH	2.00	.93
POLICY INFLUENCERS, INTEREST	2.00	.82
POLICY INFLUENCERS, MASS	2.00	.82
POLICY-INFLUENCE SYSTEM	2.00	.89
POLLUTANTS, MIGRATORY	2.00	1.00
PREVENTIVE DIPLOMACY	2.00	.87

The Political Science Concept Inventory

International Relations Concept	Mean	SD
PROBLEM SOLVING	2.00	1.15
PROLETARIAT	2.00	1.00
PROTECTORATE	2.00	.82
PUBLIC SECTOR	2.00	1.00
REALISM	2.00	.94
REGIME	2.00	.53
REWARD	2.00	.87
SCENARIOS	2.00	.93
SEPTIPOLARITY	2.00	1.00
STATE, THEORY OF	2.00	1.12
STATE CLASSIFICATORY SCHEMES, GREAT POWER/SMALL POWER	2.00	1.20
STATE CLASSIFICATORY SCHEMES, REGIONAL/SUPRAREGIONAL	2.00	1.12
STATE DECISIONS	2.00	.89
STATE POWER	2.00	1.07
STATESMANSHIP	2.00	1.05
STATES OF ECONOMIC GROWTH	2.00	.82
STRATEGIC FORCE	2.00	1.15
STRATIFICATION, INTERNATIONAL	2.00	1.12
SUBVERSION	2.00	.67
SURPRISE ATTACK AND DETERRENCE	2.00	.93
THEORIZING	2.00	1.15
TOTALITARIANISM	2.00	.82
TRADITIONAL SOCIETIES	2.00	.87
TRUSTEESHIP SYSTEM	2.00	1.05
WAR PRODUCTION	2.00	.76
WEALTH	2.00	.82
WEAPONRY	2.00	.82
ANTIBALLISTIC MISSILE DEFENSE SYSTEM	2.11	1.10
ASYLUM, RIGHT OF	2.11	1.20
BOUNDARY MAINTENANCE	2.11	.99
CLASS CONFLICT	2.11	.99
DECISION THEORY	2.11	.87
DIPLOMATIC MISSION	2.11	1.10
HOSTILITY	2.11	.99
MARKET ECONOMY	2.11	.99
MILITARISM	2.11	.87
NONGOVERNMENTAL ORGANIZATION (NGO)	2.11	1.10
OIL INTERESTS	2.11	1.10

International Relations Concept	Mean	SD
PAN-AFRICANISM	2.11	.87
POLITICAL DECISIONS	2.11	1.10
REGIONAL ASSOCIATIONS	2.11	1.10
RETALIATORY FORCES	2.11	1.10
STRATEGIC BOMBING	2.11	.74
TECHNOLOGICAL INNOVATIONS	2.11	.87
UNCOMMITTED NATIONS	2.11	1.29
ZIONIST	2.11	.74
COLLECTIVE ENFORCEMENT	2.13	.93
COUNTERGUERRILLA WARFARE	2.13	1.05
DIPLOMATIC TECHNIQUES	2.13	.93
DOMESTIC AFFAIRS	2.13	1.17
FEDERALISM	2.13	.93
IDEALISTS	2.13	.93
INTELLIGENTSIA	2.13	.93
INTERNATIONAL LAW, ENFORCEMENT	2.13	.78
ISOLATION	2.13	.60
MILITARY TECHNOLOGY	2.13	.93
MONOPOLY	2.13	1.05
NEUTRALIST STATES	2.13	.93
NUCLEAR FREE ZONES	2.13	.60
SUBVERSIVE WARFARE, GUERRILLA TACTICS IN	2.13	.60
SYSTEM DETERMINED BEHAVIOR	2.13	.78
TACTICS	2.13	.78
TERROR IN REVOLUTIONARY WARFARE	2.13	.78
TESTS, NUCLEAR WEAPONS	2.13	.60
TRANSNATIONAL IMAGES	2.13	.78
WESTERN CIVILIZATION	2.13	1.05
WHITE MAN'S BURDEN	2.13	.78
VIOLENCE	2.13	1.17
ASSURED DESTRUCTION	2.14	.83
COUNTERFORCE ATTACK	2.14	.99
COUNTERFORCE STRATEGY	2.14	.99
DEMAND	2.14	1.36
ECOLOGICAL PERSPECTIVE	2.14	1.12
ECONOMIC NATIONALISM	2.14	.83
FUNCTIONAL ORGANIZATION	2.14	.64
GRADUATED DETERRENCE	2.14	.83
INTELLIGENCE	2.14	1.12
INTERESTS	2.14	1.12

The Political Science Concept Inventory

International Relations Concept	Mean	SD
INTERNATIONAL POLITICAL SYSTEM, TRANSITIONAL	2.14	1.12
LIVING SPACE IDEA	2.14	1.25
MANPOWER	2.14	.83
MILITARY DEPENDENCIES	2.14	.64
POLICY INFLUENCERS, BUREAUCRATIC	2.14	.99
POLITICAL COHESION	2.14	.64
POWER POTENTIAL	2.14	.64
STATE CLASSIFICATORY SCHEMES, HOSTILITY/FRIENDSHIP	2.14	1.12
TECHNOCRATIC PERSPECTIVE	2.14	.64
BARGAINING TACTICS, COERCION	2.17	.90
BLACKMAIL	2.17	1.34
BLOCS, AMERICAN	2.17	.90
BLOCS, SOVIET	2.17	.90
COMPETITION	2.17	1.07
IDEOLOGICAL FRAGMENTATION IN THE INTERNATIONAL SYSTEM	2.17	.90
IMAGE, OPEN AND CLOSED	2.17	.69
INTERGOVERNMENTAL ORGANIZATIONS, GLOBAL	2.17	1.07
INTERNATIONAL LAW, AS A SETTING	2.17	.69
NATIONAL SECURITY, AS AN ISSUE AREA	2.17	.90
PSYCHOLOGICAL OPERATIONS	2.17	.90
SCIENTIFIC PERSPECTIVE	2.17	1.07
SEPARATION OF POWERS	2.17	.69
SPILLOVER	2.17	.69
SUPPLY AND DEMAND	2.17	.90
WORLD FEDERALISTS	2.17	1.07
ASSOCIATIONS OF POLITICAL SYSTEMS	2.20	1.17
DEFEAT	2.20	.75
DOMINANCE IN FOREIGN POLICY DECISION MAKING, OF POLICY INFLUENCER	2.20	1.17
DOMINANCE IN FOREIGN POLICY DECISION MAKING, PLURALIZED	2.20	1.17
ECONOMY	2.20	1.17
FACE SAVING	2.20	.75
MONEY SUPPLY	2.20	1.17
NATIONAL WELFARE	2.20	.75
POLICY-INFLUENCE SYSTEM, PLURALIZED	2.20	.75
NUCLEAR REACTIONS	2.20	.98
POLICY-INFLUENCE SYSTEM, PLURALIZED	2.20	.75
SATISFICING	2.20	.75

INTERNATIONAL RELATIONS CONCEPT	MEAN	SD
STRESS	2.20	.75
AUTONOMY	2.22	1.03
BIOLOGICAL WARFARE	2.22	.79
COOPTATION	2.22	1.03
DEMOCRATIC-CENTRALISM	2.22	.79
DEMOCRATIC STATES	2.22	.92
DEVALUATION	2.22	.79
DICTATORSHIPS	2.22	1.23
DISENGAGEMENT	2.22	.92
GAMES, NONZERO SUM	2.22	.79
GAMES, ZERO SUM	2.22	.79
INSURGENCY CAPABILITIES	2.22	.79
INTERBLOC RELATIONS	2.22	.92
LOANS	2.22	1.03
MAOISM	2.22	.63
NONBELLIGERENT	2.22	1.03
PEACEFUL CHANGE	2.22	.79
PROTOCOL, DIPLOMATIC	2.22	.92
RESPONSIVENESS	2.22	1.03
SABOTAGE	2.22	1.03
SANCTUARIES	2.22	1.13
SECRET DIPLOMACY	2.22	.79
TAKEOFF INTO ECONOMIC GROWTH	2.22	.92
TECHNOLOGICAL LEADERSHIP	2.22	.79
TECHNIQUES OF STATECRAFT	2.22	1.03
TENSIONS, INTERNATIONAL	2.22	1.03
TRANSACTIONS	2.22	.79
TRUST TERRITORIES	2.22	1.03
UNCONDITIONAL SURRENDER	2.22	1.13
WAR REPARATIONS	2.22	.79
ARROGANCE	2.25	.83
BOYCOTTS	2.25	1.09
COLONIZATION	2.25	1.30
COMPARATIVE ADVANTAGE	2.25	.66
CONTENT ANALYSIS	2.25	.83
COUNTERREVOLUTIONS	2.25	.83
CYBERNETICS	2.25	.66
DIPLOMATIC STRATEGY	2.25	1.20
DOMESTIC LAW	2.25	1.09
DOMESTIC OPINION	2.25	.83

The Political Science Concept Inventory

International Relations Concept	Mean	SD	
ECONOMIC INDEPENDENCE	2.25	1.09	**79**
GOOD OFFICES	2.25	.66	
INTERNATIONAL ECONOMY, INTERNATIONAL TRADE	2.25	.83	
INTERNATIONAL LAW, LEGISLATION	2.25	.66	
INTERNATIONAL REGULATION	2.25	1.09	
INTERNATIONAL TRANSACTIONS	2.25	.97	
ISOLATION POLICY	2.25	.97	
LAW, WORLD	2.25	1.30	
PAN-ASIANISM	2.25	.83	
PEACE CONFERENCES	2.25	.83	
PREVENTIVE INTERVENTION	2.25	.83	
PSYCHOLOGICAL PENETRATION	2.25	1.09	
SCIENTIFIC REVOLUTION	2.25	1.09	
SECONDARY POWERS	2.25	1.09	
SOCIAL MOBILIZATION	2.25	.97	
SOCIETY	2.25	1.09	
SPILLOVER EFFECT	2.25	.43	
SUBVERSIVE WARFARE	2.25	.66	
SYSTEM STRATIFICATION	2.25	.83	
TOTAL MILITARY VICTORY	2.25	.83	
WORLD INTEREST	2.25	1.30	
WORLD OPINION	2.25	1.30	
AFFLUENCE	2.29	1.03	
AUTARKY	2.29	.88	
CHECKS AND BALANCES	2.29	.88	
GEOGRAPHIC PERSPECTIVE	2.29	1.16	
GRADUATED ESCALATION	2.29	.70	
HOMOGENEITY	2.29	.45	
IMBALANCE OF POWER	2.29	.88	
INDIVIDUALISM	2.29	1.03	
INDUSTRIALISM	2.29	1.28	
INTEGRATION, INSTITUTIONAL	2.29	.88	
INTERACTION, COLLECTIVE PROBLEM SOLVING	2.29	1.03	
INTERGOVERNMENTAL ORGANIZATIONS, PURPOSES OF	2.29	1.03	
INTERNATIONAL ENVIRONMENT, ECOLOGICAL FACTORS	2.29	.88	
INTERNATIONAL POLITICAL SYSTEM, CLASSICAL SYSTEM	2.29	1.03	
IRREDENTISM	2.29	1.03	
MOBILE LAND FORCES	2.29	.70	
MODEL OF INTERNATIONAL INFLUENCE	2.29	.88	
MULTISTATE SYSTEM	2.29	1.28	

INTERNATIONAL RELATIONS CONCEPT	MEAN	SD
NUCLEAR SHARING	2.29	.88
POLITICAL COMMUNITY	2.29	.70
POVERTY	2.29	.88
PROPHECY, SELF-FULFILLING	2.29	1.03
STATE CLASSIFICATORY SCHEMES, EAST/WEST/NEUTRAL	2.29	1.28
STATE GOALS	2.29	1.03
AGGRANDIZEMENT	2.33	1.25
ARMY	2.33	1.11
BARGAINING TACTICS	2.33	1.11
BARGAINING TACTICS, THREATS	2.33	.75
CAPITAL ENDOWMENT	2.33	.94
CLIMATE	2.33	1.11
COMPELLENCE THREAT	2.33	.94
CULTURAL EXCHANGE	2.33	.82
DEMILITARIZATION OF OUTER SPACE	2.33	.94
ECONOMIC INTERPENETRATION	2.33	.47
ENFORCEABLE AGREEMENT	2.33	.82
EXPONENTIAL TRENDS	2.33	1.11
FAMILY OF NATIONS	2.33	1.25
GROWTH	2.33	1.11
INTERNATIONAL ENVIRONMENT, FLOW OF PEOPLE	2.33	.75
LIBERATION	2.33	1.05
LIFE EXPECTANCY	2.33	1.05
MARKET (INTERNATIONAL TRADE MARKET)	2.33	.75
MISSILE GAP	2.33	1.25
MOTIVATION	2.33	.94
PACIFISM	2.33	1.15
PAN-ISLAMISM	2.33	.82
POLICY-INFLUENCE SYSTEM, DOMINANT DECISION MAKER	2.33	.47
POWER GAP	2.33	.47
PROBLEM SOLVING, TACTICS	2.33	1.25
PROLETARIAN REVOLUTION	2.33	.94
REALISTS	2.33	1.15
REVOLUTIONARY STATE SYSTEM	2.33	.94
SALIENCE, DETERMINANTS OF	2.33	1.11
STATE CLASSIFICATORY SCHEMES, INTERVENTIONIST/NONINTERVENTIONIST	2.33	1.11
SYSTEM STRUCTURE	2.33	.82
VALUES	2.33	1.05

The Political Science Concept Inventory

INTERNATIONAL RELATIONS CONCEPT	MEAN	SD
VULNERABILITY	2.33	1.05
XENOPHOBIA	2.33	.94
CAPITALISTIC DEVELOPMENT	2.38	.70
CIVIL DISOBEDIENCE	2.38	.70
CLASS SYSTEM	2.38	.99
COUNTERFORCE CAPABILITY	2.38	.86
DOCTRINES	2.38	.70
ECONOMIC INFRASTRUCTURE	2.38	.99
GREAT-MAN THEORY	2.38	.99
INTERNATIONAL ECONOMY, INTERNATIONAL CURRENCY	2.38	.99
INTERNATIONAL POLITICAL SYSTEMS	2.38	.99
INTERNATIONAL TECHNICAL COOPERATION	2.38	.70
JUDICIAL SETTLEMENT	2.38	.86
JUSTICE	2.38	.99
LAND POWERS	2.38	.99
MERCANTILISM	2.38	.99
NATIONAL HONOR	2.38	.70
NATIONAL POLITICAL SYSTEMS	2.38	.97
PAN-EUROPEANISM	2.38	.70
POLITICAL ASYLUM	2.38	.86
SEAPOWER	2.38	.99
SOCIAL FERMENT IN UNDERDEVELOPED NATIONS	2.38	.99
TACIT NEGOTIATIONS	2.38	.70
TACTICAL DIPLOMACY	2.38	.70
TECHNOLOGICAL VARIABLES	2.38	.86
UNIVERSALISM	2.38	.70
ASSISTANCE	2.50	1.12
AUTHORITARIAN PERSONALITY	2.50	1.00
BARGAINING TACTICS, PROMISES	2.50	.96
BLOCS, SINO-SOVIET	2.50	.87
BOURGEOISIE	2.50	.76
CAPITAL, OBTAINING	2.50	.96
COMINTERN	2.50	1.12
COMMERCE AND NAVIGATION	2.50	.96
COMMUNICATION AGENCIES	2.50	.76
CONTROLLED RESPONSE	2.50	.87
COUNTERCITY ATTACK	2.50	.96
COUNTERELITE	2.50	.76
CULTURE, UNIFYING	2.50	.87
DOMINANT NATION	2.50	.87

International Relations Concept	Mean	SD
82		
EQUALITY	2.50	1.12
EXTANT INCENTIVES	2.50	1.50
FOSSIL FUELS	2.50	1.12
GEOGRAPHIC KNOWLEDGE	2.50	.96
GLOBAL PRIMACY	2.50	1.12
HETEROGENEOUS RIVALRY	2.50	.87
HUMAN NATURE	2.50	1.26
INTERFERENCE, DIPLOMATIC	2.50	.87
INTERNATIONAL FORCES	2.50	.96
INTERNATIONAL GOVERNMENT	2.50	1.26
NATIONAL STATE	2.50	1.50
NUCLEAR STABILITY	2.50	1.12
NUCLEAR STALEMATE	2.50	1.00
PERMEABILITY	2.50	.71
POLICY	2.50	1.26
PRETHEORY	2.50	.87
PROTECTION	2.50	.96
REGULATIVE MECHANISMS	2.50	.96
REIFICATION	2.50	.96
RELIGION	2.50	.96
REVANCHISM	2.50	.96
SMALL NATIONS	2.50	1.00
STRATIFICATION	2.50	1.12
TRANSNATIONAL NORMS	2.50	1.00
UNEQUAL TREATY SYSTEM	2.50	1.12
URBANIZATION	2.50	.87
VALUE OF A SECOND STRIKE	2.50	.96
VANGUARD OF THE PROLETARIAT	2.50	1.12
WESTERN STRATEGY	2.50	1.12
DIVIDE AND RULE	2.56	1.07
GAS WARFARE	2.56	.50
HOTLINE	2.56	.83
INFILTRATION	2.56	.68
MIGRATION	2.56	.83
OVERKILL	2.56	.83
SECULARISM	2.56	.83
SOCIAL DEMOCRACY	2.56	.83
COLOR BAR	2.57	1.18
CONSTANT SUM GAME	2.57	.73
ECONOMIC TRANSFORMATION	2.57	.73

The Political Science Concept Inventory

INTERNATIONAL RELATIONS CONCEPT	MEAN	SD
GEOGRAPHICAL BASE	2.57	.90
INTERACTION, ROUTINE	2.57	1.18
INTERGROUP CONFLICT VS. INTERGROUP WAR	2.57	.90
INTERNATIONAL RESTRAINTS	2.57	1.05
LOYALTY	2.57	1.18
NATIONAL POLITICAL COMMUNITY	2.57	.49
NEUTRALIZATION	2.57	.90
PENETRATION	2.57	.73
POLITICAL STYLE	2.57	1.18
POWER EQUALIZATION	2.57	.49
SECURITY DILEMMA	2.57	.90
SURVIVAL	2.57	.90
TERRITORIAL CLAIMS AND DETERRENCE	2.57	1.05
WORLD FEDERATION, PLANS	2.57	1.05
CONSERVATISM	2.60	1.02
CULTURE, TECHNOLOGICAL	2.60	1.02
CULTURE AND STATE SYSTEM	2.60	1.02
GUNPOWDER REVOLUTION	2.60	1.20
INDIRECT CONTAINMENT	2.60	.49
INTEGRATION, POLICY INFLUENCER	2.60	1.02
INTERNATIONALIZATION	2.60	1.36
NAVIES	2.60	1.20
OPERATIONAL MILIEU	2.60	1.20
PAYOFFS, PAYOFF MATRICES	2.60	.49
PERMANENT REVOLUTION	2.60	1.02
PERSPECTIVES IN POLITICAL ANALYSIS	2.60	.80
PROBLEM SOLVING, COLLECTIVE	2.60	1.20
PRODUCTION CURVE	2.60	1.20
REGULATIVE INSTRUMENTS	2.60	1.02
WORLD AFFAIRS	2.60	1.02
ACTOR ANALYSIS	2.63	.99
ALIENATION	2.63	.70
CLASSES AND NATIONALISM	2.63	.86
COLLABORATION	2.63	.86
INTERNATIONAL SOCIETY	2.63	.99
POLITICAL PHILOSOPHY	2.63	.70
POLITICAL PLURALISM	2.63	.99
PRAGMATISM	2.63	.86
REFUGEES	2.63	1.22
SOCIAL INEQUALITY	2.63	.99

INTERNATIONAL RELATIONS CONCEPT	MEAN	SD
WORLD LAW	2.63	1.22
BARGAINING PATTERNS	2.67	.94
BIPOLYCENTRIC SYSTEM	2.67	1.11
BOMBING	2.67	.94
CONSERVATIVE STATES	2.67	1.11
DISCONTINUITIES IN THE INTERNATIONAL SYSTEM	2.67	.94
DOMESTIC QUESTIONS	2.67	.47
ENVIRONMENTAL RELATIONSHIPS	2.67	.47
ENVIRONMENTAL SUPPLY	2.67	.47
GRANTS	2.67	1.11
INTERBLOC POLICY	2.67	.75
LIBERALISM	2.67	1.15
MATERIALISM	2.67	.94
MIDDLE CLASSES	2.67	.47
NATIONAL SOCIALISM	2.67	1.15
POWER POSITION	2.67	.94
PROBLEM SOLVING, SETTING	2.67	.94
PROTESTANT ETHIC	2.67	.94
RACE RELATIONS	2.67	.94
REGULATIVE STRATEGIES	2.67	.94
SELF-HELP, LEGAL PRINCIPLE OF	2.67	1.15
SOCIAL DIFFERENTIATION	2.67	1.05
SYNTHETIC MATERIALS	2.67	.94
TOTALITARIAN GOVERNMENT	2.67	1.15
TOTALITARIAN STATES	2.67	1.15
BRAIN WASHING	2.71	1.03
COGNITION	2.71	.88
COMMUNICATION MEDIA	2.71	.45
CRUSADES	2.71	1.28
DEATH RATES	2.71	.70
DECISION MAKING, GREAT-MAN THEORY	2.71	.45
DEFENSIVE EXPANSIONISM	2.71	.88
ECOSYSTEM	2.71	.70
INTERACTION, COMPETITIVE BARGAINING	2.71	1.03
INTERNATIONAL OBJECTIVES	2.71	.88
NONMILITARY TECHNOLOGY	2.71	1.03
POLITICAL ACTION	2.71	1.16
POLITICAL TRANSFORMATION	2.71	1.16
RELATIVISM	2.71	1.03
REVOLUTIONARY FORCE	2.71	.88
TRIP-WIRE FUNCTION AND DETERRENCE	2.71	.70

84

The Political Science Concept Inventory

INTERNATIONAL RELATIONS CONCEPT	MEAN	SD
ACQUISITIVE SOCIETY	2.75	.43
ADAPTATION	2.75	1.09
CATALYTIC WAR	2.75	.83
CLANDESTINE WEAPON PROBLEM	2.75	.97
COLLECTIVISM	2.75	.43
CULTURAL DIVERSITY	2.75	.66
DEMOGRAPHIC HYPOTHESIS	2.75	1.09
DOMINATION POLICY	2.75	1.09
INDEPENDENT NATIONAL DETERRENTS	2.75	.66
MASS ARMY	2.75	.97
MERCENARIES	2.75	.43
NONINVOLVEMENT POLICY	2.75	.97
ONE-PARTY RULE	2.75	1.20
POLITY	2.75	.97
PROBLEM SOLVING	2.75	1.30
PSYCHOLOGICAL REVOLUTION	2.75	1.09
PSYCHOMILIEU	2.75	1.09
REPUTATION AS DETERRENCE	2.75	.97
SOCIETY OF NATIONS	2.75	.83
SUBSISTENCE, AGRICULTURE	2.75	.83
UNDERSEA LONG-RANGE MISSILE SYSTEM	2.75	.66
UNIFYING CULTURE	2.75	.83
VALUE OF PEACE	2.75	.83
WESTERN POLICY	2.75	.97
WORLD ISLAND	2.75	1.30
WORLD VIEW	2.75	1.09
DOLLAR DIPLOMACY	2.78	.92
GUNBOAT DIPLOMACY	2.78	1.03
MASS EXTERMINATION	2.78	1.13
OPEN SKIES PLAN	2.78	.92
RADIATION EFFECT OF NUCLEAR EXPLOSION	2.78	.92
WAR CRIMES TRIALS	2.78	.79
WAR CRIMINALS	2.78	.79
CULTURE, WORLD SOCIAL	2.80	.40
DEMONSTRATION EFFECT	2.80	.98
ECONOMIC PATTERNS OF A NATION	2.80	.40
EXPORT INCENTIVES	2.80	.40
GROUPS	2.80	.98
MACHINE GUN REVOLUTION IN WARFARE	2.80	1.17
PARLIAMENT	2.80	.98
POTENTIAL	2.80	.98

INTERNATIONAL RELATIONS CONCEPT	MEAN	SD
POWER, NEED FOR	2.80	.75
PRINCIPLE OF COMPENSATION	2.80	.98
PUNISHMENT, DIPLOMATIC	2.80	.75
SALIENCE, DETERMINANTS OF, ECONOMIC RELATIONSHIPS	2.80	.75
SALIENCE, DETERMINANTS OF, GEOGRAPHICAL LOCATION	2.80	.75
SALIENCE, DETERMINANTS OF, HISTORICAL TIES	2.80	.75
SOCIALIST CONSTRUCTION	2.80	.98
AUTHORITARIAN TRENDS	2.83	.90
BARGAINING TACTICS, ARGUMENTS	2.83	.69
BLAST EFFECT OF NUCLEAR EXPLOSION	2.83	.90
BUREAUCRATIC INERTIA	2.83	.69
CONCENTRIC CIRCLES OF LOYALTY	2.83	.69
DYSFUNCTIONAL POWER	2.83	.90
EXPEDIENCY	2.83	.90
EXTRAREGIONAL CONFLICT	2.83	.69
FREE WORLD	2.83	.90
INCREASING SUM GAME	2.83	.50
INDIRECT STRATEGIES	2.83	.90
METHOD OF STRATEGIC STUDIES	2.83	1.07
MODEL OF REALITY	2.83	.37
PLURALISTIC REGIME	2.83	1.07
POLITICAL PARTIES IN UNDERDEVELOPED NATIONS	2.83	1.07
PUNISHMENT	2.83	.69
SPACE RACE	2.83	.37
ABSOLUTE MONARCHS	2.86	1.25
BLACKLISTING	2.86	.99
CLASSICAL LIBERALISM	2.86	.83
DEFLATION	2.86	.64
DISUNITY, FACTORS OF	2.86	.64
INTERNATIONAL CIVIL SERVICE TRADITION	2.86	.99
LAND REFORM	2.86	.64
MASS DEMOCRACY	2.86	1.12
MILITARY POWER AND DEMOCRACY	2.86	1.25
PRIMITIVE SOCIETY	2.86	.83
PROTEST MOVEMENT	2.86	.83
WORLD DOMINATION	2.86	1.25
INTEGRATED SOCIAL SYSTEM	2.88	.78
MORES	2.88	.93
SOCIOCULTURAL ASSIMILATION	2.88	.60
STRATEGIC FALLOUT	2.88	.78

The Political Science Concept Inventory

INTERNATIONAL RELATIONS CONCEPT	MEAN	SD	
THERMAL EFFECT OF NUCLEAR EXPLOSION	2.88	.78	**87**
TRIBALISM	2.88	.93	
FEUDALISM	2.89	1.10	
HOMEOSTASIS	2.89	.87	
MORALE	2.89	.57	
PASSIVE RESISTANCE	2.89	.99	
PRISONERS OF WAR	2.89	.99	
WEIGHTED VOTING	2.89	.74	
BARGAINING PATTERNS, FREEZING	3.00	.63	
CENSORSHIP	3.00	.71	
CIVIL DEFENSE	3.00	1.00	
COLLABORATORS	3.00	1.07	
COLLECTIVIZATION	3.00	.58	
COMMERCIAL REVOLUTION	3.00	.89	
COMMUNICATIONS AREAS	3.00	0	
DESERT-MOUNTAIN BARRIER	3.00	.63	
DOOMSDAY MACHINE	3.00	.63	
EAST-WEST INTERNATIONAL CONTINUUM	3.00	1.07	
EDUCATIONAL NEEDS	3.00	.82	
EXCHANGE CONTROLS	3.00	.71	
FRAGMENTATION	3.00	.82	
HOSTAGES	3.00	.67	
ILLUSION OF PERMANENCE	3.00	1.22	
IMBALANCES	3.00	.58	
IMPORT SURCHARGE	3.00	0	
INDUSTRIALIZED DEMOCRACY AND FOREIGN POLICY	3.00	0	
INTERNATIONAL POTENTIAL	3.00	1.41	
LEADERSHIP GROUP	3.00	.89	
LEVEE EN MASSE	3.00	.82	
LEVIATHAN	3.00	1.26	
LIBERAL DEMOCRACY	3.00	1.05	
LOW-LEVEL EQUILIBRIUM TRAP	3.00	1.41	
MARKETING AREAS	3.00	0	
MAXIMALIST	3.00	1.07	
NATIONALISTIC UNIVERSALISM	3.00	.89	
PEASANTRY	3.00	.93	
PERSONIFICATION OF STATES	3.00	1.07	
PROSPERITY	3.00	.58	
PROTESTANTISM	3.00	1.00	
SAVING	3.00	1.10	

INTERNATIONAL RELATIONS CONCEPT	MEAN	SD
SIGNAL-TO-NOISE RATIO	3.00	.63
SOCIAL SOLIDARITY	3.00	1.00
SOCIOPOLITICAL STRUCTURE	3.00	.50
SOFT FOREIGN POLICY	3.00	.71
STATE PERSONIFICATION	3.00	.82
TARGET STATE	3.00	.93
TECHNOLOGICAL TRENDS	3.00	1.00
TRIBES	3.00	1.00
UTILITARIANISM	3.00	.58
VALUE OF A JUST STRIKE	3.00	0
WARRIOR CLASSES	3.00	.82
WARRIOR SOCIETIES	3.00	0
WORLD PARTIES	3.00	1.22
WORLD REVOLUTION	3.00	.63
X-RAY DEFENSE SYSTEM	3.00	.58
ASSASSINATION, POLITICAL	3.13	.60
DUMPING	3.13	.93
FALLOUT SHELTERS	3.13	.78
LEND-LEASE	3.13	.93
SEARCH AND DESTROY	3.13	.78
DYNASTIC STATE	3.14	1.12
JOINT VENTURES	3.14	.64
POLITICAL TYPE	3.14	.83
STATESMEN'S DILEMMA	3.14	.99
TRANSNATIONALISTS	3.14	.99
WEATHER CONTROL	3.14	.35
WELFARE POLITICS	3.14	.83
CULTURAL DISTANCE	3.17	.69
DISTURBANCE STRATEGIES	3.17	.69
DOLLAR GAP	3.17	.69
MORTALITY	3.17	.69
MOSLEM NATIONALISM	3.17	.69
OVERLOADING	3.17	.69
POLITICAL AND ADMINISTRATIVE ISSUES	3.17	.90
POPULISM	3.17	.69
POWER TRANSITION	3.17	.69
WORLD CONDOMINIUM	3.17	.69
BIOSPHERE	3.20	.75
GROUP MEMBERSHIP	3.20	.75
NAVAL REARMAMENT	3.20	.75

The Political Science Concept Inventory

International Relations Concept	Mean	SD	
POLITICAL POTENTIAL	3.20	.40	**89**
PROGRAM POLICY	3.20	.75	
REVOLUTION, FASCIST	3.20	.40	
SUPERIORITY OF POWER	3.20	.40	
UNIVERSAL CONQUEST	3.20	.75	
WELFARE	3.20	.40	
WORLD POWER	3.20	.83	
BRIBES	3.25	.43	
CONTRACTIONIST POLICIES	3.25	.43	
DATAGRAMS	3.25	.83	
DECLARATION	3.25	1.30	
ENTITY ATTRIBUTES	3.25	.83	
EXPANSION OF EUROPE	3.25	.83	
FIFTH COLUMNS	3.25	.83	
NEGATIVE POWER	3.25	.83	
OPPORTUNISM	3.25	.83	
PROPERTY, PRIVATE	3.25	.43	
RURAL UNDEREMPLOYMENT	3.25	.43	
SUBMARINE	3.25	.43	
WAR GUILT	3.25	.43	
FRONT GROUPS	3.29	.70	
GAME OF CHICKEN	3.29	.45	
POISON GAS	3.29	.45	
CONFISCATION EFFECT	3.33	.47	
DECLARATION POLICY	3.33	1.11	
DILEMMA OF THE VICTORS, INHERITANCE	3.33	.47	
NOBILITY	3.33	1.11	
ORGANIZATIONAL PURPOSE	3.33	1.11	
POLICE	3.33	.94	
PROJECTILES	3.33	.75	
PSYCHOLOGICAL STATES AND BEHAVIORS	3.33	.47	
RADAR	3.33	.47	
RULE OF THE STRONG	3.33	.47	
SEMANTICS	3.33	.47	
STRATEGIC HAMLETS	3.33	.67	
CAPITAL TO OUTPUT RATIO	3.40	.49	
INTERNATIONAL OPERATIONS	3.40	.49	
MOSLEM WARS	3.40	.49	
WORLD SOCIETIES	3.40	.80	
REFORMATION	3.43	.49	

INTERNATIONAL RELATIONS CONCEPT	MEAN	SD
SOCIAL CONTRACT	3.44	.68
ANIMISM	3.50	.50
ANONYMOUS DELIVERY	3.50	.50
CONSERVATION COALITION	3.50	.87
DISRUPTION	3.50	.50
EDUCATIONAL SYSTEM	3.50	.50
MILIEU	3.50	.50
MULTIDIMENSIONAL COMMUNITIES	3.50	.50
OPTIONAL CLAUSE	3.50	.76
POSITIVE POWER	3.50	.50
POTENTIALITY	3.50	.50
POWER OF ANALYSIS	3.50	.50
REDISTRIBUTION	3.50	.76
SYNCRETIC POLITICS	3.50	.50
WORLD MEDIA	3.50	.50
WORLD STATE	3.50	.50
CULTURAL DEFENSE	3.60	.49
RENAISSANCE	3.60	.80
NIHILISM	3.63	.70
BLOCKBUSTERS	3.67	.47
ENGINEERING PERSPECTIVE	3.67	.47
ETHNOCENTRIC TRIBALISM	3.67	.47
FABIANISM	3.67	.47
TANK WARFARE	3.71	.45
INHIBITION	3.75	.43
LOAD	3.75	.43
POSITIVE VALENCE	3.80	.40
AGE COHORT ANALYSIS	4.00	0
ATHEISM	4.00	0
COMMUNITIES OF CUSTOM	4.00	0
ENDANGERED SPECIES	4.00	0
HELICOPTERS IN COUNTERREVOLUTIONARY WARFARE	4.00	0
HUB POWER	4.00	0
INTERNATIONAL TECHNIQUES	4.00	0
INTERSPECIFIC AGGRESSION	4.00	0
NEGATIVE VALENCE	4.00	0
UNCOMMITTED REALM	4.00	0

Notes

1. Elton Atwater, Kent Foster, and J. S. Prybyla, *World Tensions: Conflict and Accommodation* (New York: Appleton-Century-Crofts, 1967); W. A. Axline and J. A. Stegenga, *The Global Community* (New York: Dodd, Mead, 1972); W. D. Coplin, *Introduction to International Politics* (Chicago: Markham, 1971); I. E. Duchacek, *Nations and Men: International Politics Today* (New York: Holt, Rinehart & Winston, 1966); W. Friedmann, *An Introduction to World Politics*, 4th ed. (New York: St. Martin's, 1960); K. J. Holsti, *International Politics* (Englewood Cliffs: Prentice-Hall, 1967); D. C. Jordan, *World Politics in Our Time* (Lexington, Mass.: D. C. Heath, 1970); George Modelski, *Principles of World Politics* (New York: Free Press, 1972); H. J. Morgenthau, *Politics Among Nations* (New York: Knopf, 1967); A. F. K. Organski, *World Politics* (New York: Knopf, 1960); D. J. Puchala, *International Politics Today* (New York: Dodd, Mead, 1971); Richard Rosencrance, *International Relations—Peace or War?* (New York: McGraw-Hill, 1973); J. Spanier, *Games Nations Play* (London: Nelson, 1972); H. J. Spiro, *World Politics* (Homewood, Ill.: Dorsey, 1966); Harold Sprout and Margaret Sprout, *Foundations of International Politics* (Princeton: Van Nostrand, 1962); Harold Sprout and Margaret Sprout, *Toward a Politics of the Planet Earth* (New York: Van Nostrand Reinhold, 1971); J. G. Stoessinger, *The Might of Nations*, 4th ed. (New York: Random House, 1973); and Vernon Van Dyke, *International Politics* (New York: Appleton-Century-Crofts, 1957).

2. After the judging began it became clear that a card-sort procedure for classifying the 1,236 terms would have been preferable to the typed list that was used. Because it was difficult to follow the typed lines some judges overlooked a number of concepts. These instances were treated as missing data. The reported means are the means of the judgments actually rendered.

3. H. M. Blalock, *Social Statistics* (New York: McGraw-Hill, 1972), p. 80.

4. With ranked data, some of the intervals between 0.00 and 1.58 are not produced as a possible standard deviation value.

5. L. Anderson, M. W. Waters, Jr., and A. R. Wilcox, *Legislative Roll-Call Analysis* (Evanston: Northwestern University Press, 1966), pp. 61–75.

Bibliography of Concept Inventory Sources

The Inventory of political science terms and concepts includes terms found in political science dictionaries, textbook indexes, encyclopedias, journal indexes, bibliographies, catalogs, and similar works. The sources were chosen for their authoritativeness, general availability, and relevance to the political science discipline generally or to one or more of its subfields.

Concepts and terms were listed as they appeared in the various sources, although names of places and persons were omitted in certain cases.

In reporting the concept sources here, three types are indicated: (1) those sources from which concepts have been listed, (2) those potential sources examined but not used, and (3) those unavailable for inclusion at time of inventory. In addition to a bibliographic citation, each item includes a brief description of the source, the number of terms listed from it, and a source code number (beginning with number 11) in parentheses at beginning of citation to identify it.

Key to Sources by Code Number

(11)   Plano, Jack C., and Robert E. Riggs
(12)   Goldman, Ralph M.
(13)   Dunner, Joseph, ed.
(14)   Haas, Michael, and Henry S. Kariel
(15)   Hyneman, Charles S.
(16)   Smith, Edward C., and Arnold J. Zurcher
(17)   *ABC POL SCI*
(18)   Dahl, Robert A.
(19)   Bowle, John
(20)   Coker, Francis William
(21)   *International Political Science Abstracts*

(22)   Harmon, Robert B.
(23)   Van Dyke, Vernon
(24)   Roucek, Joseph S.
(25)   Dawson, Richard E.
(26)   White, Wilbur W.
(27)   Haensch, Gunther
(28)   Plano, Jack C., and Milton Greenberg
(29)   United Nations Educational, Scientific and Cultural Organization
(30)   Plano, Jack C., and Roy Olton
(31)   Hyamson, A. M.
(32)   Burns, Edward McNall
(33)   *International Bibliography of Political Science* [1952–]
(34)   Beck, Carl, and J. Thomas McKechnie
(35)   de Grazia, Alfred, ed.
(36)   Sabine, George H.
(37)   McCarthy, Eugene J.
(38)   Somit, Albert, and Joseph Tanenhaus
(39)   Sperber, Hans, and Travis Trittschush
(40)   Meyer, Jon K.
(41)   *American Political Science Review*
(42)   *American Government '73–'74 Encyclopedia*
(43)   Roberts, Geoffrey K.
(44)   Laqueur, Walter Ze'ev
(45)   Ebenstein, William
(46)   *Peace Research Abstracts Journal*
(47)   U.S. Civil Service Commission
(48)   Elliot, Florence
(49)   Safire, William
(50)   Cranston, Maurice, and Sanford A. Lakoff
(51)   *Worldmark Encyclopedia of Nations*
(52)   Holt, Solomon
(53)   *Philosopher's Index*
(54)   Heimanson, Rudolph
(55)   Tallman, Marjorie
(56)   SOCRATES Project

To prevent computer transpositions, e.g., 10 for 01, code numbers begin with 11.

Type 1—Concepts Listed

(17) *ABC POL SCI* (Advance Bibliography of Contents: Political Science and Government). Santa Barbara, Calif.: ABC-Clio, 1969.

Publishes the table of contents from over 300 international periodicals in political science and related fields. The indexes contain subject, biographical, geographical, and law entries, a list of court decisions and case notes, and author entries. Subject index of *ABC POL SCI*, cumulated for vol. 5, nos. 1–8, December 1973, was used as a source of concepts; 877 terms were included from this source. None of the items in the subject index were excluded.

(42) *American Government '73–'74 Encyclopedia.* Guilford, Conn.: Dushkin, 1972.

Represents an attempt by forty-one scholars to list and define the topics of most importance to the study of American government; 2,083 terms were taken from this source. Only geographical names were excluded.

(41) *American Political Science Review* 67 (December 1973).

We included ninety-seven names of past presidents of the American Political Science Association as listed in this issue.

(34) Beck, Carl, and J. Thomas McKechnie. *Political Elites, A Select Computer Bibliography.* Cambridge, Mass.: M.I.T. Press, 1968.

Divided into three parts: (1) a KWOC (key word out of context) title listing, (2) a listing of the full citation for the titles, and (3) a bibliography of authors' names. The KWOC listing of titles was used as a source. The keywords, with the exception of geographical names, were included in the Concept Inventory; 2,164 terms were taken from this source.

(19)   Bowle, John. *Western Political Thought.* New York: Barnes & Noble, 1961.

Describes the evolution of Western political thought in a historical context and analyzes the text of the most important writers from antiquity to the industrial revolution; 444 terms from the index of this source were included. Only species names of animals (three terms) were excluded.

(32)   Burns, Edward McNall. *Ideas in Conflict: Political Theories of the Contemporary World.* New York: W. W. Norton, 1960.

Presents a summary of political ideas set forth during the nineteenth and twentieth centuries. Arranged in four chapters which cover ideas of democracy, collectivism, conservatism, and world order. Index was used as source, from which 1,258 terms were taken. Only geographical names were excluded.

(20)   Coker, Francis William. *Recent Political Thought.* New York: Appleton-Century-Crofts, 1934.

Descriptive review of dominant political ideas expressed in theoretical writings or active social movements during the nineteenth and twentieth centuries; 711 terms from the combined name and subject index were included. None were excluded.

(50)   Cranston, Maurice, and Sanford A. Lakoff. *A Glossary of Political Ideas.* New York: Basic Books, 1968.

This American edition of a work originally prepared by British scholars contains fifty-five abstract terms denoting political concepts or doctrines. Attempts to offer a definition of a term show what the ambiguities are. When used in conjunction with the *Encyclopedia of Philosophy,* this glossary is an excellent introduction to the problems of political terminology and thought. All fifty-five terms were used.

(18)   Dahl, Robert A. *Modern Political Analysis.* Englewood Cliffs, N.J.: Prentice-Hall, 1970.

Describes basic concepts, ideas, and analytical approaches for the analysis of politics; 250 terms were taken from the subject index. None were excluded.

The Political Science Concept Inventory

(25)   Dawson, Richard E. "Political Socialization." *Political Science Annual* 1 (1966): 1–34.

Since the study of political socialization is a relatively new development, the author's essay and bibliography are especially valuable. They provide a summary of existing definitions, concepts, and writings on political socialization. Index was used as source, yielding 453 terms. Only geographical names were excluded.

(35)   de Grazia, Alfred, ed. *Universal Reference System. Political Science, Government and Public Policy Series.* Princeton: Princeton Research, 1968–.

The series contains ten volumes and three supplemental volumes. The cumulative index for the 1972 supplemental volume was used as a source of terms for the Concept Inventory; 1,348 terms were taken. Geographical names were excluded.

(13)   Dunner, Joseph, ed. *Dictionary of Political Science.* Totowa, N.J.: Littlefield, Adams, 1970.

Attempt by 95 political scientists—eighty-one from the U.S. and Canada, four from Europe, four from South America, three from the Middle East, two from the Far East, and one from Africa—to clarify the terminology of political science and provide descriptive information about old and new nations and former and contemporary statesmen and politicians; 2,704 terms were taken from this source and none were excluded.

(45)   Ebenstein, William. *Great Political Thinkers: Plato to the Present.* New York: Holt, Rinehart & Winston, 1960.

Carefully selected portions from the original writings of political thinkers. All 233 terms in the subject index were used.

(48)   Elliot, Florence. *A Dictionary of Politics.* Harmondsworth, Middlesex: Penguin Books, 1969.

Includes entries for individual states, political parties, organizations, living politicians and statesmen, and some political terms; 380 terms were used. Only geographical names were excluded.

98

(12)   Goldman, Ralph M. *Behavioral Perspectives on American Politics*. Homewood, Ill.: Dorsey Press, 1973.

American politics textbook. At the end of each chapter, author offers comprehensive list, with definitions, of behavioral and institutional concepts and provides a list of other important terms defined in the text; 343 terms were drawn from this source. None were excluded.

(14)   Haas, Michael, and Henry S. Kariel, eds. *Approaches to the Study of Political Science*. Scranton, Penn.: Chandler, 1970.

Compendium of articles by leading political scientists on various aspects and methods of studying political science. Subject index was used as a source of concepts; 1,017 terms were used. None were excluded.

(27)   Haensch, Gunther. *A Dictionary of International Relations and Politics, Systematic and Alphabetical in Four Languages: German, English/American, French, Spanish*. New York: Elsevier, 1965.

Terms are arranged in subject categories such as names of states, the state, international law, diplomacy, international negotiations, treaties and organizations, war, disarmament, history, etc. No definitions are given, and equivalent terms are listed only in foreign languages. No Russian terms are included. The English alphabetical index was used as source; 5,013 terms were taken. Only names of geographical places were excluded.

(22)   Harmon, Robert B. *Political Science: A Bibliographic Guide to the Literature*. Metuchen, N.J.: Scarecrow, 1965. Supplement, 1968.

This guidebook lists reference and general works in each of the subfields of political science, as well as general research material. Contains brief introductory notes to the numerous subchapters, but provides only a few annotations to the titles. Approximately 2,000 titles are listed in the base volume. There are separate author and subject indexes. The subject index was used as source; 120 terms were taken. Geographical names in the index were excluded.

(54)   Heimanson, Rudolph. *Dictionary of Political Science and Law*. Dobbs Ferry, N.Y.: Oceana, 1967.

The vocabulary of political science frequently coincides with legal terminology. This dictionary is an attempt to provide legal authority for the definition of American political terms. From this source 503 terms were drawn. None were excluded.

(52) Holt, Solomon. *The Dictionary of American Government.* New York: McFadden-Bartell, 1964.

A dictionary containing over 1,000 entries for political terms, legal acts, Supreme Court decisions, executive departments, or other organizational units of the U.S. government. From this source 1,471 terms were drawn. None were excluded.

(31) Hyamson, A. M. *A Dictionary of International Affairs.* Washington, D.C.: Public Affairs Press, 1947.

Entries refer to countries, ethnic groups, international conferences, organizations, conventions, etc. Useful mainly for concise information on historical development in international relations. Publication date precludes coverage of practically all post–World War II events. From this source 375 terms were taken. Geographical names were excluded.

(15) Hyneman, Charles S. *The Study of Politics: The Present State of American Political Science.* Urbana: University of Illinois Press, 1959.

Critical analysis of the scholarly activities of political scientists and the intellectual conflicts within American political science. All 356 terms in the index were taken.

(33) *International Bibliography of Political Science* [1952–]. Chicago: Aldine, 1952–.

Prepared by the International Committee for Social Science Documentation in cooperation with the International Political Science Association. Extensive, but selective, bibliography of articles, books, serials, monographs, *Festschriften*, government and international official documents (including mimeographed items) in many languages; 4,000 to 5,000 items per year. Covers 1,000 to 1,400 periodicals and other publications issued during a given year, with one- to two-year delay. An annotated list of books, articles, reports and other

publications of scientific character. Coverage is multilingual and worldwide. A separate author and subject index. Subject index of vol. 20, 1971, was used as source for 482 terms.

100

(21)   *International Political Science Abstracts.* Oxford: Basil Blackwell, 1950–.

Prepared by the International Political Science Association in cooperation with the International Committee for Social Sciences Documentation and with the financial assistance of UNESCO. Abstracts in English or French of articles in about 150 periodicals in political science and other social sciences, published in all parts of the world, classified in seven major categories: (1) political science, (2) political theory, (3) government and public administration, (4) governmental process, (5) public opinion, parties, groups, and elections, (6) international relations, and (7) area studies. Subject index in each issue; cumulative subject and author indexes in issue no. 4 of each volume. The cumulative subject index of vol. 23, no. 6, 1973, was used as source for 1,475 items.

(44)   Laqueur, Walter Ze'ev. *A Dictionary of Politics.* New York: Free Press, 1971.

Lists important terms, with definitions, to the study of contemporary politics. Of these, 1,157 were included. Geographical names were excluded.

(37)   McCarthy, Eugene J. *Dictionary of American Politics.* New York: Macmillan, 1968.

Senator McCarthy includes terms relating to the structure and form of the U.S. government as well as to political processes. Emphasis is on the most frequently used terminology, with definitions reflecting contemporary rather than historical usage. From this source 1,129 terms were taken. Only geographical names were excluded.

(40)   Meyer, Jon K. *Bibliography on the Urban Crisis.* Chevy Chase, Md.: National Institute of Mental Health, 1969.

A bibliography of books and articles dealing with the behavioral, psychological, and sociological aspects of urban life in the U.S. Entries are arranged under ten sections focusing on racially motivated social disorders, nonracial

social disorders, etc. Within each section the most recent (1968) items are listed first, followed by chronologically arranged entries dating back to the nineteenth century. Separate author and subject index. From this source 1,595 terms were taken. Only geographical names were excluded.

(46)   *Peace Research Abstracts Journal*. Clarkson, Ont.: Canadian Peace Research Institute, 1964–.

Abstracts, books, and articles published since 1945. Arranged under ten main headings, with numerous subdivisions. Separate author and subject indexes are provided. All 479 terms in the primary code index of vol. 10, 1973, were used.

(53)   *Philosopher's Index*. Bowling Green, Ohio: Bowling Green University, 1967–.

An author and KWOC index to philosophical articles in more than 140 periodicals published in English and other European languages. Apart from the bibliographic information, a brief abstract of the article is given. The subject index of the 1972 cumulative index was used as a source of concepts. Authors' names were listed in the index by last name only (e.g., Locke, Hegel, Hume) and were included among the 1,632 terms drawn from this source.

(28)   Plano, Jack C., and Milton Greenberg. *American Political Dictionary*. New York: Holt, Rinehart & Winston, 1967.

More than 1,100 terms relevant to a basic understanding of American governmental institutions, processes, and problems. Entries are arranged in chapters: U.S. Constitution; civil liberties; parties; pressure groups; legislative, executive, and judicial processes; foreign policy; etc. Separate index was used as source; 2,017 terms were chosen. Only geographical names were excluded.

(30)   Plano, Jack C., and Roy Olton. *International Relations Dictionary*. New York: Holt, Rinehart & Winston, 1969.

Lists terms (complete with definitions and discussion of significance) important to study of international relations; 893 terms were taken from this source. Only geographical names were excluded.

102

(11) Plano, Jack C., and Robert E. Riggs. *Dictionary of Political Analysis*. Hinsdale, Ill.: Dryden Press, 1973.

Attempts to define the major analytic terms of political science. Terms stress a behavioral approach to political analysis; 412 terms were drawn from this source. None were excluded.

(43) Roberts, Geoffrey K. *A Dictionary of Political Analysis*. London: Longman Group, 1971.

Defines terms relating to social science methodology, the discipline of political science and its distinctive subject matter, forms of political organization, and major belief systems and ideologies. Of these, 475 were included. None were excluded.

(24) Roucek, Joseph S., ed. *Contemporary Political Ideologies*. Totowa, N.J.: Littlefield, Adams, 1961.

Panoramic survey of twentieth-century ideologies, notably marxism, neo-marxism, socialism, nationalism, zionism, pan-Asiatic or pan-African ideas, new democracies, etc. Index was used as source; 353 terms were used. None were excluded.

(36) Sabine, George H. *History of Political Theory*. New York: Holt, Rinehart & Winston, 1961.

First written in 1937 and still the standard work for a critical treatment of the history of political ideas. Index was used as source; 941 terms were chosen. None were excluded.

(49) Safire, William. *The New Language of Politics*. New York: Random House, 1968.

By a former reporter and practicing public relations man, to make the words that "worked" for politicians readily available. Emphasizes modern catchwords, slogans, and rhetorical phrases which produce political results. All entries consist of a brief definition followed by a frequently detailed description of the usage employed by politicians for the purpose of leading or misleading the public. All 1,242 entries in this source were included.

(16) Smith, Edward C., and Arnold J. Zurcher. *Dictionary of American Politics.* 2d ed. New York: Barnes & Noble, 1968.

This dictionary has been frequently revised since it first appeared in 1888 and now contains over 3,800 entries for American political terms, slogans, nicknames, governmental units, legal acts, Supreme Court decisions, and political ideas. Weak on conceptual terms of social science. Stresses American politics and history. From this source 2,857 terms were extracted.

103

(56) SOCRATES Project

A keyword index created by a project of The California State University and Colleges in which test items are keyed to particular courses. Three hundred thirty-four terms were selected from the SOCRATES listing for Course 07030 in United States History A and B.

(38) Somit, Albert, and Joseph Tanenhaus. *American Political Science: A Profile of the Discipline.* New York: Atherton Press, 1964.

An attempt to identify major trends in American political science. On page 66, authors report results of a survey in which respondents were asked to list names of American political scientists who made the most significant contributions to the discipline before and after 1945. The names of the 33 political scientists who were mentioned most often in this study were included.

(39) Sperber, Hans, and Travis Trittschush. *American Political Terms.* Detroit: Wayne State University Press, 1962.

Attempt by two philologists to establish historical background for usage of political terms. Arranged alphabetically, the entries contain a brief definition followed by first usage, with reference to time and source. Of these, 1,057 terms were selected. Only geographical names were excluded.

(55) Tallman, Marjorie. *Dictionary of American Government.* Totowa, N.J.: Littlefield, Adams, 1963.

Brief definitions of American political terms, governmental and judicial units, important legal acts, as well as sociological and economic terms frequently used in political literature. From this source 1,568 terms were chosen. None were excluded.

(29)   United Nations Educational, Scientific and Cultural Organization, *Contemporary Political Science: A Survey of Methods, Research and Teaching, Publication* (UNESCO no. 426), 1950.

104

Leading scholars describe the state of worldwide study of political science. Includes separate sections concerning the study of political institutions, parties and groups, international relations, and organization of teaching and research. Subject index was used as source for the 91 terms included. Only geographical names were excluded.

(47)   U.S. Civil Service Commission. *Personnel Literature Index* 32, nos. 1–12 (1970).

Annotated index to selected books, pamphlets, periodicals, unpublished dissertations, and other material of interest in personnel administration. The subject index of vol. 32, 1970, was used; 582 terms were drawn from this source. None of the terms were excluded.

(23)   Van Dyke, Vernon. *Political Science: A Philosophical Analysis*. Stanford: Stanford University Press, 1960.

A descriptive analysis of political inquiry; 285 terms were taken from the index. Names of geographical places were excluded.

(26)   White, Wilbur W. *White's Political Dictionary*. Cleveland: World Publishing, 1947.

Emphasizes terms used in international relations; 3,695 terms were taken. Only geographical names were excluded.

(51)   *Worldmark Encyclopedia of Nations*. New York: Worldmark Press, 1967.

Authoritative information on the geographical, historical, political, social, and economic status of 141 countries and the U.N. system. Three hundred sixty-four terms were drawn from the index. Only geographical names were excluded.

Type 2—Rejected Sources

The following were examined as possible sources of concepts for the Concept Inventory but were not used for reasons indicated.

Adams, James Truslow. *Dictionary of American History*. New York: Charles Scribner's Sons, 1951.

Contains nearly 6,500 signed articles on specific aspects of American history. Because these terms covered a spectrum much broader than the political aspects of American history, this source was not included in the Inventory.

Back, Harry; Horst Circullies; and Gunter Marquard. *Polec, Dictionary of Politics and Economics*. Berlin: W. de Gruyter, 1964.

This source claims to have 16,000 terms in English, French, and German. It was not used because it is heavily laden with terms from economics and modern technology such as "atomic science" and "space travel." Most terms were in French and German and of primary relevance to users in those nations. Each term was translated to the corresponding expression in the other two languages.

Black, Henry C. *Black's Law Dictionary*. St. Paul, Minn.: West Publishing, 1968.

A comprehensive book of definitions of the terms, phrases, and maxims used in American and English jurisprudence. Also includes numerous words taken from Roman law and European law, as well as the principal vocabulary of international law. Because of its extensive scope and heavy concentration in technical legal terms, it was not used.

Catalog of the Foreign Relations Library. New York: Council on Foreign Relations, 1969.

106

A photographic reproduction of catalog cards relating to approximately 55,000 volumes in this collection. Covers all phases of international relations since 1918 and includes books, pamphlets, government documents, and international organizations material, but no periodicals or documents of the League of Nations and the U.N. Entries are by author and subject, with some title entries. This source was too massive for the Project staff to use.

Current World Leaders. Pasadena, 1975–.

Published three times a year, the almanac lists major government leaders, chief delegates to the U.N., ambassadors from foreign countries to the U.S., members of international organizations, etc. Also includes a calendar of forthcoming political or other events, last-minute news, and necrologies. Examined as a possible source for biographical names but was considered too comprehensive for the purposes of the Inventory.

Deutsch, Karl Wolfgang, and Richard L. Merritt. *Nationalism and National Development, an Interdisciplinary Bibliography.* Cambridge, Mass.: M.I.T. Press, 1970.

An unannotated bibliography of about 5,000 titles of books, scholarly articles, and pamphlets published between 1935 and 1977. Bibliography is divided into eleven sections and contains listings of special bibliographies and works on nationalism. There is a separate author index and computer-produced KWIC (keyword in context) index of titles. Because the keywords in the title index were not distinguishable from the titles as a whole, this source was not included in the Inventory.

Dissertation Abstracts International: Abstracts of Dissertations Available on Microfilm, or as Xerographic Reproductions. Ann Arbor, Mich.: University Microfilms, 1938–.

A monthly compilation of abstracts of doctoral dissertations submitted by more than 250 institutions in the U.S. and abroad. Abstracts are arranged by discipline. A keyword and author index is included. Since more than 150,000 dissertations have been listed and abstracted in 29 volumes published so far, researchers can use a new computer-based retrieval service, Datrix. This was not used as a source of concepts because the items in the index relevant to political science were not distinguishable from the rest.

Gray, Charles; Leslie Gray; and Glenn Gregory. *A Bibliography of Peace Research Indexed by Key Words*. Eugene, Oreg.: General Research Analysis Methods, 1968.

A KWIC index to over 1,300 titles published between 1957 and 1967. Entries are arranged alphabetically by author's name or title word. Title words or keywords were not readily distinguishable from the titles.

Harmon, Robert B. *Sources and Problems of Bibliography in Political Science*. San Jose, Calif.: Dibco Press, 1966.

An unannotated list of current and retrospective bibliographies, indexes, and abstracts in the various subfields of political science of about sixty pages. Lists sources of bibliographies by author, organization, and agency. Useful primarily as a reference work but not as a source of concepts.

Heady, Ferrel, and Sybil L. Stokes. *Comparative Public Administration*. New York: Institute of Public Administration, 1961.

Annotated bibliography of books and articles on modern bureaucracies, administrative relationships, personnel management, fiscal administration, administrative control, etc. An excellent source book in a subfield of political science, but not subject indexed.

Holler, Frederick. *The Information Sources of Political Science*. Santa Barbara, Calif.: ABC-Clio, 1971.

Complete citations and descriptions of basic political science reference literature. In addition to describing information retrieval systems and general reference works, it lists and describes the basic reference works which relate to the major subfields of political science. It was used extensively as a source of bibliographic information but not of terms or concepts in the preparation of the Inventory.

Index to Legal Periodicals. New York: H. W. Wilson, 1908–.

An author and subject index to articles in legal periodicals published in the U.S., Canada, United Kingdom, Australia, and New Zealand. Yearbooks and annual reviews were also indexed. Includes table of cases and a separate book review index. The subject index includes a large number of terms not relevant to political science, and source was not used.

International Who's Who. London: Allen & Unicorn, 1935–.

Provides biographical information on government leaders, politicians, and other personalities who have achieved international fame. The volume for 1972–73 contains over 12,000 names, but the names most appropriate to the study of political science were not distinguishable from the rest.

International Yearbook and Statesman's Who's Who. London: Burke's Peerage, 1953–.

Annual source of basic biographical information about personalities prominent in government, administration, diplomacy, international organizations, law, and other fields. The volume for 1973 contains approximately 9,000 names. Other volumes contain a like number of names. Because each volume is contemporary, none provides a comprehensive list of names appropriate to the study of political science.

Irish, Marian D. *Political Science: Advance of the Discipline.* Englewood Cliffs, N.J.: Prentice-Hall, 1968.

The state of the discipline and its changes during the past thirty years are surveyed by a number of prominent scholars. Extensive bibliographic citations are given. Does not contain a subject index, and appropriate terms were not readily identifiable.

Mason, John Brown. *Research Resources: Annotated Guide to the Social Sciences.* Vol. 1. *International Relations and Recent History.* Santa Barbara, Calif.: ABC-Clio, 1965.

A guide to indexes, abstracts, periodicals, books, national and trade bibliographies, U.S. government publications, and newspapers dealing with international relations. Approximately 1,300 items are listed and briefly annotated. Only reference tools such as bibliographies, handbooks, directories, dictionaries, etc., are listed in the book section. Of special value is an annotated directory to over five hundred periodicals arranged according to geographical or subject coverage. Also of interest is a list of biographical publications arranged by region or country. No reference sources are listed for international law, and documentary collections are not included. Primarily a reference guide and not useful for inventory.

Wilson, Robert S., ed. *Public Affairs Information Service Bulletin, 58th Annual Cumulation.* New York: Public Affairs Information Service, 1973.

Indexed by subject of articles appearing in periodicals relating to public affairs; contains approximately 20,000 terms. Because of the large number of terms not relevant to the study of political science, this source was not used.

Wynar, Lubomyr R. *Guide to Reference Materials in Political Science.* Vol. 1, Denver, Colo.: Bibliographic Institute, 1966; Vol. 2, Rochester, N.Y.: Libraries Unlimited, 1968.

This two-volume set provides extensive title listings, brief chapter introductions, and some annotations. The classified arrangement covers general social science material as well as all the subfields of political science. Reference and general works are listed. Includes author index, subject index, and list of periodicals in political science. The index lists primarily authors and to a somewhat lesser extent titles, and therefore it was not used.

The Political Science Concept Inventory

CAPITALISM   1.0   .00
  (1) 03
COMMUNISM   1.0   .00
  (22) 03 04 06 07 11 16 17 18 19 20
  21 22 23 24 25 26 27 29 30 32 33 34
DEMOCRACY   1.0   .00
  (25) 02 03 04 05 06 07 08 10 11 12
  16 17 18 19 20 22 23 24 26 27 29 30
  32 33 34
EMPIRICAL METHOD   1.0   .00
  (5) 04 23 24 30 43
LIBERALISM   1.0   .00
  (18) 03 04 06 07 10 11 15 16 17 18
  21 22 23 25 30 32 33 34
POLITICAL SYSTEMS   1.0   .00
  (7) 01 04 08 11 15 23 33
POLITICAL THEORY, CLASSICAL   1.0   .00
  (1) 04
POWER   1.0   .00
  (17) 01 03 05 07 08 11 13 16 17 19
  20 23 24 25 26 30 33
SOCIALISM   1.0   .00
  (1) 33
BEHAVIORAL APPROACH   1.1   .31
  (1) 33
BEHAVIORAL SCIENCES   1.1   .31
  (3) 01 07 25
CHECKS-AND-BALANCES   1.1   .31
  (10) 02 03 06 16 18 25 27 32 34 45
DEPENDENT VARIABLE   1.1   .31
  (1) 01
HYPOTHESIS(ES)   1.1   .31
  (7) 01 03 05 13 19 24 33
IMPERIALISM   1.1   .31
  (20) 06 07 10 11 12 16 17 19 20 21
  22 23 24 25 26 29 30 32 33 34 46
INDUCTIVE REASONING   1.1   .31
  (1) 03
NATIONALISM   1.1   .31
  (22) 03 06 07 10 11 12 15 16 17 18
  19 20 22 23 24 25 26 27 29 30 32 33
NORMATIVE THEORY   1.1   .31
  (2) 04 33
ONE-PARTY SYSTEM   1.1   .31
  (3) 03 17 20
PARADIGMS, AND CONCEPTUAL   1.1   .31
  SCHEMES
  (3) 01 04 33
POLITICAL SCIENCE   1.1   .31
  (14) 01 03 04 05 06 08 12 16 18 19
  23 26 27 33
POLITICAL VALUES   1.1   .31
  (2) 11 15
SCIENTIFIC METHOD   1.1   .31
  (7) 01 05 11 19 22 25 33
SYSTEMS ANALYSIS   1.1   .31
  (6) 01 04 11 23 25 33
ANARCHISM   1.2   .42
  (14) 03 06 10 11 12 16 17 18 22 23
  25 27 32 34
ANARCHY   1.2   .42
  (8) 03 06 07 16 17 27 30 33

CONCEPT   1.2   .42
  (6) 01 05 13 24 30 33
CONFLICT THEORY   1.2   .42
  (2) 23 25
ELECTORAL BEHAVIOR   1.2   .63
  (5) 11 15 23 24 30
EMPIRICAL THEORY   1.2   .42
  (3) 04 05 08
EMPIRICISM   1.2   .42
  (7) 01 03 04 13 19 26 33
FACT AND VALUE   1.2   .63
  (1) 26
FASCISM   1.2   .42
  (22) 03 06 07 10 11 12 16 17 18 19
  20 21 22 23 24 25 26 27 29 33 34 35
FUNCTIONAL ANALYSIS   1.2   .42
  (3) 04 11 24
IDEOLOGY   1.2   .63
  (20) 01 03 04 05 07 08 11 13 16 17
  18 19 20 23 24 25 26 27 30 33
INDEPENDENT VARIABLE   1.2   .63
  (1) 01
INTERNATIONAL RELATIONS   1.2   .42
  (12) 03 04 05 07 11 12 16 17 19 23
  25 33
LENINISM, COMMUNIST DOCTRINE   1.2   .42
  (6) 03 17 20 21 26 34
MAJORITY RULE, DEMOCRATIC THEORY   1.2   .42
  (5) 06 16 18 19 20
MARXIAN SOCIALISM   1.2   .42
  (1) 20
MARXISM-LENINISM   1.2   .42
  (2) 17 34
NATION-STATE SYSTEM   1.2   .42
  (4) 11 12 16 24
NORMATIVE STATEMENT   1.2   .42
  (1) 33
PARLIAMENTARY SYSTEM   1.2   .63
  (6) 06 16 17 18 19 27
POLITICAL ALIENATION   1.2   .42
  (2) 11 23
POLITICAL BEHAVIOR   1.2   .42
  (6) 01 03 04 11 23 33
POLITICAL CHANGE   1.2   .42
  (4) 01 07 11 15
POLITICAL PROCESSES   1.2   .42
  (3) 01 04 25
POLITICAL THEORY   1.2   .63
  (13) 01 03 04 05 06 11 12 16 19 23
  25 33 43
POLITICIZATION   1.2   .42
  (3) 02 24 33
QUANTITATIVE METHODS   1.2   .42
  (2) 19 23
SAMPLING TECHNIQUES   1.2   .42
  (3) 01 23 24
SYSTEMS THEORY   1.2   .42
  (1) 43
AGGREGATE ANALYSIS   1.3   .48
  (1) 23
ALIENATION   1.3   .67
  (10) 03 06 07 11 18 23 24 25 30 33

ATTITUDINAL CHANGES	1.3	.67
(1) 04		
AUTHORITARIAN PERSONALITIES	1.3	.48
(2) 04 08		
AUTHORITARIANISM	1.3	.48
(13) 07 10 11 12 15 18 19 22 23 24		
25 30 32		
BEHAVIORALISM	1.3	.67
(7) 01 03 04 11 13 24 33		
CABINET SYSTEM	1.3	.67
(4) 02 18 19 22		
CASE STUDY METHOD	1.3	.48
(1) 37		
CAUSAL EXPLANATION	1.3	.67
(2) 04 11		
CAUSE AND EFFECT	1.3	.48
(2) 05 13		
COLONIALISM	1.3	.48
(10) 03 07 11 17 20 23 25 26 33 34		
46		
CONCEPTUAL FRAMEWORK	1.3	.48
(3) 24 30 33		
DELEGATION OF POWERS	1.3	.67
(6) 03 06 16 17 18 32		
DEMOCRATIC IDEOLOGY	1.3	.67
(1) 08		
FEDERALISM	1.3	.67
(17) 02 03 06 07 11 12 16 17 18 19		
23 24 25 26 27 30 32		
FUNCTIONALISM	1.3	.48
(5) 01 03 04 20 25		
INTERNATIONAL POLITICS	1.3	.48
(6) 04 11 12 17 23 33		
LAISSEZ FAIRE	1.3	.48
(11) 02 03 06 16 18 20 22 25 26 27		
32 46		
LOGICAL EMPIRICISM	1.3	.48
(1) 43		
MACHIAVELLIANISM	1.3	.48
(3) 17 22 24		
MARXISM, COMMUNIST DOCTRINE	1.3	.48
(17) 03 06 07 11 16 17 19 20 21 22		
23 24 25 26 27 33 34		
MATERIALISTIC INTERPRETATION OF	1.3	.67
HISTORY		
(3) 17 22 26		
METHODS IN POLITICAL SCIENCE	1.3	.67
(1) 19		
NATIONAL SOCIALISM	1.3	.48
(9) 03 06 17 19 21 23 26 32 34		
NORMATIVE ARGUMENT	1.3	.48
(1) 08		
PARADIGM	1.3	.67
(1) 43		
POLITICAL INFLUENCE	1.3	.67
(2) 08 11		
POLITICAL PHILOSOPHY	1.3	.67
(2) 01 43		
POPULAR DEMOCRACY	1.3	.48
(1) 19		
POWER POLITICS	1.3	.67
(4) 06 16 17 22		

PRAGMATISM	1.3	.48
(6) 03 17 19 22 24 33		
QUANTITATIVE APPROACHES	1.3	.67
(2) 24 33		
RANDOM SAMPLE	1.3	.48
(2) 01 33		
VALUES	1.3	.67
(8) 05 07 11 13 20 23 25 33		
VARIABLE	1.3	.48
(4) 01 13 24 33		
VOTING BEHAVIOR	1.3	.67
(11) 01 04 06 11 15 18 23 24 30 32		
33		
ANALOGY	1.4	.51
(3) 01 17 33		
ATTITUDE	1.4	.69
(7) 01 02 03 07 17 24 30		
AUTHORITARIAN SYSTEMS	1.4	.51
(1) 04		
BEHAVIOR, COLLECTIVE	1.4	.69
(1) 04		
BEHAVIORISM	1.4	.69
(2) 19 22		
CAUSAL MODELS	1.4	.69
(1) 04		
CHARISMA	1.4	.51
(6) 01 11 18 24 25 33		
COMPARATIVE ANALYSIS	1.4	.51
(2) 11 33		
COMPARATIVE POLITICS	1.4	.51
(1) 33		
CONFLICT	1.4	.69
(9) 01 02 04 07 08 17 24 30 33		
CONFLICT RESOLUTION	1.4	.51
(1) 36		
CONTENT ANALYSIS	1.4	.51
(6) 01 03 04 05 23 33		
CULTURAL RELATIVISM	1.4	.51
(1) 15		
DECISION MAKING	1.4	.69
(1) 07		
DIALECTICAL MATERIALISM,	1.4	.69
COMMUNIST THEORY		
(7) 03 17 19 20 22 26 34		
DIALECTICAL METHOD	1.4	.51
(2) 19 30		
ELITIST THEORY	1.4	.69
(1) 01		
EQUALITY	1.4	.69
(9) 06 10 11 16 19 23 24 26 30		
EXPLANATION IN SOCIAL SCIENCES	1.4	.69
(3) 01 13 23		
IDEAL TYPE ANALYSIS	1.4	.51
(3) 01 15 33		
JEFFERSONIAN DEMOCRACY	1.4	.51
(4) 03 06 16 18		
LOGICAL POSITIVISM	1.4	.51
(2) 08 22		
METHODOLOGY	1.4	.69
(8) 01 04 05 07 19 24 25 33		
MODEL	1.4	.69
(2) 01 24		

MULTIVARIATE ANALYSIS	1.4	.51
(3) 01 23 25		
NORM	1.4	.69
(2) 01 33		
NULL HYPOTHESIS	1.4	.51
(1) 01		
ORGANIZATION THEORY	1.4	.51
(5) 01 04 07 11 33		
PARLIAMENTARY PROCESSES	1.4	.69
(1) 25		
PARTY DISCIPLINE	1.4	.51
(3) 16 17 19		
PLURALISM	1.4	.69
(17) 01 03 06 10 11 16 18 19 22 23		
24 25 26 30 32 33 34		
POLITICAL CULTURE	1.4	.51
(7) 01 04 07 11 15 23 33		
POLITICAL IDEOLOGY	1.4	.69
(3) 11 15 23		
POLITICAL INTEGRATION	1.4	.69
(4) 01 11 15 33		
POLITICAL POWER	1.4	.69
(4) 06 07 08 12		
POLITICAL RECRUITMENT	1.4	.51
(3) 01 07 25		
POLITICAL SCIENCE, SUBFIELDS OF	1.4	.69
(1) 04		
POLITICAL STRATIFICATION	1.4	.69
(1) 07		
POWER STRUCTURE	1.4	.51
(2) 03 18		
PROBABILITY	1.4	.51
(3) 01 24 25		
PUBLIC OPINION	1.4	.69
(1) 01		
RESEARCH DESIGN	1.4	.69
(1) 01		
SOCIAL CHANGE	1.4	.69
(5) 07 11 15 25 26		
SOCIAL CONTRACT, THEORY OF	1.4	.51
(10) 03 05 12 16 17 19 23 25 32 35		
STRUCTURAL-FUNCTIONALISM	1.4	.51
(2) 01 04		
SURVEY RESEARCH	1.4	.51
(3) 01 19 23		
TOTALITARIANISM	1.4	.69
(16) 03 04 11 12 18 19 20 21 22 23		
24 25 26 32 33 34		
AGGREGATE DATA	1.5	.52
(1) 01		
ANALYTIC STATEMENT	1.5	.70
(1) 01		
APATHY	1.5	.70
(2) 25 33		
BIASED SAMPLE	1.5	.52
(1) 01		
BICAMERALISM	1.5	.52
(7) 03 04 11 18 23 25 32		
BUDGETARY PROCESS	1.5	.70
(7) 04 11 17 23 24 25 27		
CHILDHOOD SOCIALIZATION	1.5	.70
(1) 15		
CLASS CONFLICT	1.5	.52
(1) 17		
CLASSICAL THEORY	1.5	.70
(1) 04		
COMMUNICATION THEORY	1.5	.70
(5) 01 04 05 11 33		
CYBERNETICS	1.5	.52
(8) 01 04 07 11 22 23 25 43		
DECENTRALIZATION	1.5	.70
(9) 03 06 11 16 17 18 19 24 33		
DECISION THEORY	1.5	.70
(6) 01 03 04 07 23 25		
DECISION-MAKING APPROACH	1.5	.70
(1) 01		
DECISION-MAKING PROCESS	1.5	.70
(1) 23		
DEDUCTIVE REASONING	1.5	.70
(2) 03 19		
DEMOCRATIC SOCIALISM	1.5	.84
(4) 18 20 22 32		
DOCUMENTATION	1.5	.70
(1) 19		
EGALITARIANISM	1.5	.52
(4) 16 20 24 25		
EMPIRICAL	1.5	.84
(1) 43		
EMPIRICAL STATEMENT	1.5	.84
(1) 02		
FASCIST THEORY	1.5	.70
(1) 20		
FEUDALISM	1.5	.70
(10) 03 04 08 16 17 22 24 25 26 33		
GENERAL SYSTEMS THEORY	1.5	.52
(4) 01 03 04 11		
HIERARCHY	1.5	.70
(4) 04 24 33 34		
HISTORICAL INEVITABILITY, COMMUNIST THEORY	1.5	.70
(1) 20		
IMPERIALISM AND COLONIALISM, COMMUNIST THEORY	1.5	.70
(1) 20		
INPUT-OUTPUT ANALYSIS	1.5	.52
(2) 04 33		
INTEREST AGGREGATION	1.5	.52
(1) 33		
INTERNATIONAL INTEGRATION	1.5	.70
(1) 11		
INTERNATIONAL SYSTEM	1.5	.84
(1) 11		
INTERVENING VARIABLE	1.5	.52
(1) 01		
IRON LAW OF OLIGARCHY	1.5	.70
(4) 03 18 22 33		
ISOLATIONISM	1.5	.70
(14) 02 03 08 11 16 17 18 20 22 24		
25 27 32 34 46		
JUDICIAL BEHAVIOR	1.5	.70
(4) 03 04 07 11		
LABOR THEORY OF VALUE	1.5	.70
(2) 10 26		

LEGITIMACY 1.5 .84
(12) 01 02 08 11 16 17 23 24 25 26 30 33
MACRO-MICRO ANALYSIS 1.5 .52
(1) 01
MACRO-POLITICS 1.5 .70
(1) 33
MAJORITARIANISM 1.5 .84
(2) 20 25
MAJORITY OPINION 1.5 .70
(1) 44
MAOISM, COMMUNIST DOCTRINE 1.5 .70
(3) 11 20 25
MICRO ANALYSIS 1.5 .70
(1) 01
MODELS, CAUSAL 1.5 .52
(1) 04
MODERNIZATION 1.5 .70
(7) 01 04 11 20 24 25 33
MODERNIZATION, AND 1.5 .70
STRUCTURAL-FUNCTIONALISM
(1) 04
MONOPOLY CAPITALISM 1.5 .52
(1) 34
MULTIPLE CORRELATION 1.5 .52
(1) 01
NATIONAL COMMUNISM (TITOISM) 1.5 .70
(3) 03 20 34
NATIONAL POWER, ELEMENTS OF 1.5 .84
(1) 20
NEO-COLONIALISM 1.5 .52
(2) 03 20
NORMATIVE 1.5 .84
(2) 01 13
OBJECTIVITY 1.5 .84
(2) 04 13
ORGANIC THEORY OF THE STATE 1.5 .52
(1) 03
ORGANIZATIONAL GOAL 1.5 .70
(1) 11
PACIFISM 1.5 .52
(12) 03 06 11 16 17 19 21 22 25 27 30 33
PARTY SYSTEM 1.5 .84
(5) 04 11 20 32 33
POLICY ANALYSIS 1.5 .52
(3) 01 11 33
POLITICAL ANALYSIS 1.5 .70
(1) 33
POLITICAL ATTITUDES 1.5 .70
(2) 07 11
POLITICAL COMMUNICATION 1.5 .70
(4) 01 11 23 33
POLITICAL CONFLICT 1.5 .70
(1) 15
POLITICAL ECOLOGY 1.5 .70
(1) 01
POLITICAL LEGITIMACY 1.5 .70
(1) 08
POLITICAL MORALITY 1.5 .52
(1) 45

POLITICAL PARTIES, COMPARATIVE 1.5 .70
ANALYSIS
(1) 04
POLITICAL SOCIALIZATION THEORY 1.5 .84
(6) 01 04 07 15 23 33
PROBABILITY STATEMENT 1.5 .70
(1) 01
RADICALISM 1.5 .52
(10) 07 11 16 17 19 23 24 26 30 33
RANK ORDER 1.5 .52
(2) 01 24
REGIONALISM 1.5 .52
(10) 03 06 07 11 16 17 20 24 25 33
RELIABILITY 1.5 .84
(1) 01
SMALL GROUP THEORY 1.5 .70
(3) 01 04 15
SOCIAL SCIENCES 1.5 .70
(1) 41
SOCIALIZATION 1.5 .70
(8) 01 02 07 15 17 24 25 30
SOVEREIGNTY 1.5 .52
(17) 03 06 09 10 11 12 16 17 18 19 20 22 23 25 26 27 33
STATISTICAL ANALYSIS 1.5 .52
(2) 24 33
STRUCTURAL ANALYSIS, SYSTEMS 1.5 .70
THEORY
(1) 04
STRUCTURAL-FUNCTIONAL THEORY 1.5 .70
(1) 25
THEORY OF DIALECTICAL MATERIALISM 1.5 .70
(1) 25
TYPOLOGY 1.5 .52
(7) 01 19 23 24 25 30 33
UTILITARIANISM 1.5 .52
(10) 03 10 11 12 16 17 19 22 26 33
VALUE JUDGMENT 1.5 .70
(1) 33
VALUE THEORY 1.5 .70
(1) 04
ABSOLUTISM 1.6 .69
(11) 06 11 17 18 19 20 22 24 26 32 33
ADMINISTRATIVE PROCESS 1.6 .69
(1) 04
ANOMIE 1.6 .69
(6) 07 11 22 25 30 33
ANTI-SEMITISM 1.6 .51
(13) 03 06 16 17 21 22 23 24 25 26 30 33 46
BARGAINING THEORY 1.6 .69
(1) 33
BEHAVIOR 1.6 .84
(5) 04 19 23 24 30
BIVARIATE ANALYSIS 1.6 .51
(1) 01
BOLSHEVISM 1.6 .51
(11) 03 06 16 17 21 23 24 25 27 33 34
CASE STUDY 1.6 .69
(3) 01 19 33

CAUSAL ANALYSIS	1.6	.69
(2) 23 30		
CAUSATION	1.6	.84
(1) 43		
CHI-SQUARE TEST	1.6	.51
(1) 33		
CLASS STRUGGLE	1.6	.69
(9) 03 06 10 16 17 19 20 22 26		
CLOSED SYSTEM	1.6	.51
(1) 01		
COALITION FORMATION	1.6	.51
(1) 11		
COMMUNITY POWER STRUCTURE	1.6	.69
(1) 23		
COMPACT THEORY	1.6	.84
(1) 16		
COMPARATIVE GOVERNMENT	1.6	.69
(6) 03 04 07 12 19 33		
COMPARATIVE METHOD	1.6	.84
(2) 19 26		
CONCEPTUALIZATION	1.6	.69
(2) 04 30		
CONFLICT BEHAVIOR	1.6	.84
(2) 02 11		
CONFLICT MANAGEMENT	1.6	.84
(1) 11		
CONSENSUS	1.6	.84
(9) 01 04 11 18 23 24 25 30 33		
CONSERVATISM	1.6	.84
(15) 03 06 10 11 12 16 17 18 19 22		
24 26 30 32 33		
CORRELATION	1.6	.84
(4) 01 03 30 33		
COST-BENEFIT ANALYSIS	1.6	.51
(1) 01		
CULTURE	1.6	.84
(7) 01 03 07 11 19 24 30		
DATA	1.6	.84
(3) 01 24 30		
DATA COLLECTION	1.6	.69
(2) 04 07		
DECISION-MAKING ANALYSIS	1.6	.69
(2) 01 33		
DEMAND AND SUPPLY	1.6	.69
(1) 03		
DESPOTISM	1.6	.51
(8) 03 06 16 17 22 24 29 32		
DEVELOPMENT THEORY	1.6	.69
(1) 04		
DEVELOPMENT, SOCIAL AND	1.6	.84
ECONOMIC		
(1) 41		
END-MEANS ANALYSIS	1.6	.51
(3) 01 04 05		
ETHNOCENTRISM	1.6	.69
(4) 11 20 22 33		
EXECUTIVE PROCESS	1.6	.84
(1) 25		
EXECUTIVE-LEGISLATIVE	1.6	.84
RELATIONSHIPS		
(1) 04		
EXPERIMENTAL METHOD	1.6	.69
(4) 01 19 24 30		
EXTREMISM	1.6	.84
(5) 11 17 24 25 30		
FRAME OF REFERENCE	1.6	.69
(1) 13		
FREE ENTERPRISE	1.6	.69
(1) 45		
FREEDOM	1.6	.69
(9) 11 16 19 22 24 25 26 27 30		
FRUSTRATION-AGGRESSION	1.6	.69
(1) 30		
FUNCTION	1.6	.84
(7) 01 04 11 13 17 24 33		
FUNCTIONAL CONCEPT	1.6	.84
(2) 04 19		
GAME THEORY	1.6	.69
(10) 01 02 03 04 07 11 13 22 25 33		
GENERAL WILL	1.6	.69
(4) 03 06 11 26		
GROUP BASIS OF POLITICS	1.6	.84
(1) 33		
GROUP INFLUENCE	1.6	.69
(1) 15		
GROUP RELATIONS	1.6	.84
(1) 37		
HISTORICAL MATERIALISM	1.6	.69
(3) 03 17 22		
HISTORICAL METHOD	1.6	.51
(3) 10 19 26		
INDUCTIVE STATISTICS	1.6	.69
(1) 01		
INFERENCE	1.6	.84
(1) 01		
INTEGRATION	1.6	.84
(10) 01 03 04 11 16 17 24 30 33 34		
INTEGRATION, FUNCTION OF SOCIAL	1.6	.84
SYSTEMS		
(1) 04		
INTERNATIONALISM	1.6	.69
(9) 11 12 16 17 19 22 24 27 32		
JUDICIAL LAW MAKING	1.6	.69
(1) 44		
KEYNESIANISM	1.6	.51
(1) 20		
LATENT FUNCTION	1.6	.51
(2) 01 33		
LEARNING THEORY	1.6	.69
(1) 01		
LEGISLATIVE BEHAVIOR	1.6	.69
(2) 04 11		
LEGISLATIVE PROCESS	1.6	.69
(2) 11 32		
LOCAL POLITICS	1.6	.84
(1) 11		
MATERIALISM	1.6	.69
(6) 02 17 19 22 24 26		
MEDIAN	1.6	.69
(1) 01		
MERCANTILISM	1.6	.51
(6) 06 16 17 20 25 27 46		
MODE OF ANALYSIS	1.6	.69
(1) 04		
MODELS AND MODELING	1.6	.69
(6) 04 07 13 23 30 36		

MOTIVATION	1.6	.69
(1) 43		
NATIONAL POLITICAL SYSTEMS	1.6	.69
(1) 20		
NAZISM	1.6	.69
(7) 08 16 17 19 22 24 32		
NON-ZERO-SUM GAME	1.6	.51
(1) 02		
OPERATIONAL DEFINITION	1.6	.84
(2) 01 02		
OPINION RESEARCH	1.6	.69
(1) 03		
PARLIAMENTARIANISM	1.6	.84
(2) 17 24		
PARTY SYSTEMS AND VOTER ALIGNMENTS	1.6	.69
(1) 04		
PHILOSOPHY OF SCIENCE	1.6	.51
(3) 01 07 25		
POLICY PROCESSES	1.6	.69
(1) 04		
POLITICAL APATHY	1.6	.51
(2) 08 11		
POLITICAL AUTHORITY	1.6	.69
(3) 08 12 15		
POLITICAL DEVELOPMENT	1.6	.69
(7) 01 04 07 11 15 23 33		
POLITICAL ECONOMY	1.6	.69
(5) 07 12 16 19 33		
POLITICAL EFFICACY	1.6	.69
(4) 07 11 15 25		
POLITICAL PRESSURE	1.6	.69
(1) 36		
POLITICAL STRUCTURES	1.6	.69
(1) 15		
POPULAR SOVEREIGNTY, DEMOCRATIC THEORY	1.6	.84
(9) 02 03 06 16 18 20 22 29 32		
PRESCRIPTIVE THEORY	1.6	.69
(2) 01 04		
PRESIDENTIAL SYSTEM	1.6	.69
(3) 11 17 23		
PROPAGANDA	1.6	.84
(17) 02 03 06 07 11 12 16 18 19 20 23 24 25 27 29 30 33		
PSYCHOLOGY, AND DECISION-MAKING	1.6	.51
(1) 04		
PUBLIC OPINION RESEARCH	1.6	.69
(1) 11		
QUANTIFICATION	1.6	.69
(3) 01 11 25		
QUANTITATIVE DATA	1.6	.69
(1) 04		
REALIST-IDEALIST DICHOTOMY	1.6	.51
(1) 20		
RESPONSIBILITY, POLITICAL	1.6	.69
(1) 06		
ROLE	1.6	.69
(7) 01 02 15 24 25 30 33		
ROLE THEORY	1.6	.69
(1) 04		
SELF-GOVERNMENT	1.6	.69
(5) 06 16 17 24 29 46		
SOCIAL SCIENCE	1.6	.84
(1) 01		
SOCIALIZING AGENTS	1.6	.69
(2) 15 17		
SOVIET COMMUNISM	1.6	.69
(1) 22		
STALINISM, COMMUNIST DOCTRINE	1.6	.69
(6) 16 17 20 22 24 34		
STATISTICAL CORRELATIONS	1.6	.51
(1) 25		
STIMULUS-RESPONSE	1.6	.51
(2) 01 30		
STRATIFIED RANDOM SAMPLE	1.6	.84
(1) 02		
SYSTEMS THEORY, AND STRUCTURAL-FUNCTIONALISM	1.6	.69
(1) 04		
THEORY	1.6	.84
(7) 01 03 04 13 24 30 33		
THEORY OF GAMES	1.6	.69
(3) 03 22 23		
TOTALITARIANISM, FASCIST THEORY	1.6	.69
(1) 20		
URBAN POLITICS	1.6	.69
(1) 04		
VALIDITY	1.6	.84
(3) 01 06 30		
VERIFIABILITY	1.6	.84
(1) 13		
VERIFICATION	1.6	.96
(5) 01 03 17 24 33		
WORLD COMMUNISM	1.6	.84
(1) 34		
ZERO-SUM GAMES	1.6	.51
(2) 02 33		
AGGREGATION OF INTERESTS	1.7	.82
(1) 01		
ANALYSIS	1.7	.82
(1) 43		
ANALYTICAL METHOD	1.7	.82
(1) 19		
APOLITICAL	1.7	.67
(2) 08 24		
APPLIED SOCIAL SCIENCE	1.7	.67
(1) 04		
ASSIMILATION	1.7	.67
(2) 06 30		
ATHENIAN DEMOCRACY	1.7	.67
(1) 08		
ATTITUDE SCALING	1.7	.48
(1) 33		
AUTOMATIC DATA PROCESSING	1.7	.48
(1) 37		
AXIOM	1.7	.67
(1) 43		
BANDWAGON EFFECT	1.7	.48
(8) 01 02 03 06 16 27 29 33		
CAUSALITY	1.7	.82
(3) 01 03 19		
CHAUVINISM	1.7	.67
(6) 06 16 17 20 22 27		
CIVIL-MILITARY RELATIONS	1.7	.82
(5) 03 07 25 33 37		

CLASSICAL ECONOMICS	1.7	.48
(1) 26		
CLASSIFICATION	1.7	.82
(8) 01 06 08 13 16 24 25 33		
COEFFICIENT OF CORRELATION	1.7	.67
(2) 01 33		
COERCION	1.7	.67
(7) 01 06 08 11 24 25 33		
COMMITTEE SYSTEM	1.7	.67
(1) 42		
COMMUNICATION, POLITICAL	1.7	.82
(1) 01		
COMPETITION	1.7	.67
(5) 06 11 16 24 30		
COMPUTER SIMULATION	1.7	.48
(2) 01 03		
CONSENSUS-BUILDING	1.7	.67
(1) 24		
COUNTERVAILING POWER	1.7	.67
(1) 22		
CROSS-CULTURAL ANALYSIS	1.7	.67
(4) 01 15 24 30		
CULTURE PATTERNS	1.7	.82
(2) 04 25		
DEVIANT BEHAVIOR	1.7	.67
(2) 04 07		
DIRECT DEMOCRACY	1.7	.82
(6) 17 18 22 27 32 33		
DIVINE RIGHT OF KINGS	1.7	.48
(10) 03 06 16 17 18 22 24 26 30 32		
DYSFUNCTION	1.7	.67
(2) 04 24		
EFFICACY	1.7	.82
(1) 24		
ELECTORAL PROCESSES	1.7	.67
(1) 12		
ELITISM	1.7	.82
(1) 43		
EMPIRICISM, POSITIVIST	1.7	.67
(1) 04		
EQUALITARIANISM	1.7	.82
(1) 24		
EQUILIBRIUM	1.7	.67
(4) 01 24 25 33		
EXISTENTIALISM	1.7	.67
(3) 22 25 30		
FACT	1.7	.94
(6) 01 08 13 17 24 26		
FACTOR ANALYSIS	1.7	.67
(5) 01 04 23 30 33		
FIELD RESEARCH	1.7	.82
(1) 23		
FUNCTIONAL ORGANIZATION	1.7	.82
(1) 03		
GENERALIZATION	1.7	.82
(5) 01 05 13 16 33		
GEOPOLITICS	1.7	.82
(10) 03 16 17 19 20 21 22 25 26 33		
GRADUALISM	1.7	.48
(2) 06 22		
GROUP NORMS	1.7	.82
(1) 15		
GUTTMAN SCALE	1.7	.67
(1) 01		
HAMILTONIANISM	1.7	.67
(1) 22		
HEIRARCHY	1.7	.94
(1) 24		
HISTORICAL APPROACH	1.7	.67
(3) 01 24 30		
IDEALIST-REALIST DICHOTOMY	1.7	.82
(1) 20		
IF-THEN STATEMENT	1.7	.94
(1) 01		
INDIVIDUAL INFLUENCES IN POLITICS	1.7	.82
(1) 08		
INDIVIDUAL POLITICAL EFFICACY	1.7	.67
(1) 08		
INFERENTIAL STATISTICS	1.7	.82
(1) 01		
INFRASTRUCTURE	1.7	.67
(1) 39		
INTEGRATION, AND GOAL ATTAINMENT	1.7	.82
(1) 04		
INTEREST ARTICULATION	1.7	.82
(1) 33		
INTERNATIONAL BEHAVIOR	1.7	.94
(1) 04		
INTERNATIONAL SECURITY	1.7	.82
(1) 17		
MACROECONOMICS	1.7	.67
(1) 25		
MARXIST METHOD	1.7	.67
(1) 19		
MASS COMMUNICATIONS	1.7	.67
(4) 03 11 19 23		
MASS PARTICIPATION	1.7	.67
(1) 15		
MEANS TO END ANALYSIS	1.7	.82
(1) 05		
METATHEORIES, AND PARADIGMS	1.7	.94
(1) 04		
MIDDLE RANGE THEORY	1.7	.67
(1) 01		
MINORITY OPINION	1.7	.67
(1) 42		
MOB BEHAVIOR	1.7	.67
(2) 25 30		
NATIONAL CHARACTER	1.7	.48
(5) 01 11 12 15 19		
NEUTRALISM	1.7	.82
(9) 03 17 18 20 22 23 27 32 33		
NEW FEDERALISM	1.7	.48
(1) 32		
NOMINAL SCALE	1.7	.67
(1) 01		
NORMAL DISTRIBUTION	1.7	.67
(1) 01		
NORMS	1.7	.82
(2) 24 30		
OPERATIONALIZATION	1.7	.82
(1) 33		
OPINION	1.7	.94
(7) 01 06 17 24 26 30 33		

ORDINAL SCALE	1.7	.67
(1) 01		
ORGANIZATION BEHAVIOR	1.7	.94
(3) 01 04 25		
PARTICIPATION (OF CITIZENS IN GOVERNMENT)	1.7	.94
(10) 02 05 11 15 19 24 25 30 32 33		
PARTY LOYALTY	1.7	.67
(1) 39		
PATRIOTISM	1.7	.82
(7) 10 15 16 17 27 29 30		
POLITICAL EDUCATION	1.7	.67
(3) 11 15 17		
POLITICAL ETHICS	1.7	.82
(1) 12		
POLITICAL INVOLVEMENT	1.7	.67
(1) 15		
POLITICAL STYLE	1.7	.82
(1) 11		
POLYCENTRISM	1.7	.67
(2) 20 34		
POWER THEORY	1.7	.67
(1) 04		
PRIMITIVE POLITICAL SYSTEMS	1.7	.67
(1) 03		
PROCESS	1.7	.94
(1) 01		
PUBLIC ADMINISTRATION	1.7	.67
(10) 03 04 07 11 12 16 18 19 23 33		
PUBLIC POLICY	1.7	.67
(6) 01 03 05 07 11 25		
REALISM	1.7	.82
(6) 03 11 16 19 22 30		
REALPOLITIK	1.7	.67
(4) 16 17 22 25		
REGRESSIONAL ANALYSIS	1.7	.67
(1) 25		
REVISIONISM	1.7	.67
(7) 16 17 20 22 24 26 34		
REVOLUTIONARY IDEOLOGY	1.7	.82
(1) 11		
RULE OF LAW, DEMOCRATIC THEORY	1.7	.94
(5) 03 11 17 20 33		
SIMULATION	1.7	.67
(6) 01 03 04 11 24 33		
SIMULATION AND GAMES	1.7	.67
(1) 07		
SOCIAL AND BEHAVIORAL SCIENCES	1.7	.67
(1) 37		
SOCIAL CONFLICT	1.7	.82
(1) 11		
SOCIAL SYSTEMS	1.7	.82
(3) 01 04 08		
SOCIALISM AND NATIONALISM	1.7	.67
(1) 35		
SOCIOLOGY AND POLITICAL THEORY	1.7	.82
(1) 22		
STATISTICAL METHODS	1.7	.48
(2) 19 23		
STATUS	1.7	.82
(4) 06 24 30 33		
STEREOTYPE	1.7	.67
(7) 01 03 20 22 25 30 33		
SURPLUS VALUE, COMMUNIST THEORY	1.7	.67
(4) 10 20 22 26		
THEORIES OF NON-VIOLENCE	1.7	.48
(1) 22		
TWO-STEP FLOW, MASS MEDIA	1.7	.67
(1) 15		
TYRANNY	1.7	.67
(9) 03 06 16 17 22 23 24 26 27		
URBANIZATION	1.7	.82
(6) 04 11 15 24 25 30		
VOTER'S APATHY	1.7	.67
(1) 44		
ZIONISM	1.7	.48
(11) 03 06 07 11 16 17 21 22 25 33 34		
ABOLITIONISM	1.8	.42
(1) 46		
ANALYTIC POLITICAL PHILOSOPHY	1.8	.78
(4) 01 03 13 30		
ANTI-COLONIALISM	1.8	.63
(2) 17 36		
ANTICOMMUNISM	1.8	.42
(2) 17 20		
APPLIED STATISTICS	1.8	.78
(1) 01		
ARTICULATION OF INTERESTS	1.8	.78
(1) 01		
CALVINISM	1.8	.78
(3) 19 22 26		
CASE METHOD	1.8	.91
(4) 03 04 06 17		
CENTRAL TENDENCY MEASUREMENT	1.8	.91
(1) 01		
CHANGE, ORGANIZATIONAL	1.8	.78
(1) 37		
CHANGE, RESISTANCE TO	1.8	.91
(1) 37		
CHURCH-STATE RELATIONS	1.8	.63
(1) 25		
CLASS CONSCIOUSNESS	1.8	.63
(3) 11 17 25		
COLLECTIVISM	1.8	.63
(12) 06 10 16 17 18 22 24 26 27 32 33 34		
COLONIAL SYSTEM	1.8	.63
(1) 06		
COMMUNCIATIONS THEORY	1.8	.78
(1) 01		
CONSENSUS THEORY	1.8	.78
(3) 11 15 20		
CONSTITUTIONALISM	1.8	.91
(12) 02 03 06 07 12 17 18 20 24 26 32 33		
CONTRACT THEORY OF GOVERNMENT	1.8	.78
(7) 06 09 18 26 32 33 44		
CROSS PRESSURE	1.8	.78
(1) 11		
CROSS-NATIONAL RESEARCH	1.8	.91
(1) 23		
CULTURAL IMPERIALISM	1.8	.42
(1) 20		

DEMOCRATIC CENTRALISM, COMMUNIST THEORY (1) 20	1.8	.78
DESCRIPTIVE STATISTICS (1) 01	1.8	.78
DETERMINISM (3) 01 19 33	1.8	.63
DETERMINIST THEORIES (1) 33	1.8	.63
DETERRENCE THEORIES (1) 03	1.8	.91
DIPLOMACY (12) 03 04 06 11 12 16 18 20 23 24 25 27	1.8	.78
DISTRIBUTION OF POWERS (2) 08 18	1.8	.78
DOMINO THEORY (2) 25 32	1.8	.63
EARLY SOCIALIZING EXPERIENCES (1) 15	1.8	.78
ECONOMIC DEVELOPMENT MODELS (1) 11	1.8	.63
ECONOMIC IMPERIALISM (2) 16 20	1.8	.63
ELITISM, FASCIST THEORY (3) 20 22 24	1.8	.63
EPISTEMOLOGY (4) 04 11 23 25	1.8	.78
ETHICS (11) 03 04 07 11 19 23 24 25 26 30 32	1.8	.78
ETHNIC POLITICS (2) 07 13	1.8	.78
EXPERIMENT (4) 01 24 30 33	1.8	1.03
FABIAN SOCIALISM (4) 03 10 22 26	1.8	.63
FEEDBACK (5) 01 02 03 04 33	1.8	.78
FIELD THEORY (4) 01 04 22 33	1.8	.78
FOREIGN RELATIONS (1) 44	1.8	.78
GENERAL THEORY (2) 01 33	1.8	.78
GOALS, POLITICAL (1) 04	1.8	.78
GROUP DYNAMICS (1) 15	1.8	.91
GROUP IDENTIFICATIONS (1) 15	1.8	.78
HIERARCHY AND POLYARCHY (1) 04	1.8	.91
HOMOGENEOUS POLITICAL CULTURE (1) 15	1.8	.91
IDENTIFICATION WITH POLITICAL PARTIES (1) 15	1.8	.78
INDICATORS (1) 11	1.8	.91
INDIVIDUALISM (15) 03 06 09 10 11 16 17 18 19 20 22 23 24 26 27	1.8	.91

INFORMATION THEORY (1) 43	1.8	.78
INPUT (2) 01 33	1.8	.78
INSTITUTIONALIZATION (1) 24	1.8	.91
INTERNATIONAL COMMUNICATIONS (1) 11	1.8	.91
JACKSONIAN DEMOCRACY (6) 03 06 16 18 22 32	1.8	.63
LEGAL SYSTEMS (1) 36	1.8	.78
LOGICAL STATEMENT (1) 01	1.8	.91
MAJORITARIAN DEMOCRACY (2) 22 25	1.8	1.03
MATRIX (1) 24	1.8	.63
MCCARTHYISM (5) 03 18 24 32 34	1.8	.63
METHOD OF VOTING (1) 17	1.8	.78
MILITARISM (12) 03 06 08 10 11 16 17 20 22 24 27 33	1.8	.78
MILITARY-INDUSTRIAL RELATIONS (1) 07	1.8	.63
MODE (3) 01 24 33	1.8	.91
MODERN TOTALITARIANISM (1) 08	1.8	.91
MYTH IN POLITICAL THEORY (1) 10	1.8	.78
MYTHS AND SYMBOLS (1) 07	1.8	.78
NATIONAL BEHAVIOR (1) 11	1.8	.78
NON-RECOGNITION (1) 17	1.8	.63
NON-VIOLENCE, THEORIES OF (1) 22	1.8	.63
NONALIGNMENT (NEUTRALISM) (1) 20	1.8	.63
OPINIONS AND PERSONALITY (1) 04	1.8	.91
ORGANIZATIONAL CHANGE (1) 04	1.8	.78
ORGANIZATIONAL CONFLICT (1) 37	1.8	.91
PATTERNS OF CULTURE (1) 08	1.8	.63
PATTERNS OF POWER (1) 20	1.8	.78
PEACEFUL CHANGE (4) 01 03 08 16	1.8	.78
PHENOMENOLOGY (1) 43	1.8	.63
POLICY FORMATION (1) 36	1.8	.78
POLICY SCIENCES (2) 01 05	1.8	.78
POLITICAL INFORMATION (2) 08 15	1.8	.78

POLITICAL LEARNING	1.8	.78
(1) 15		
POLITICAL ORTHODOXY	1.8	.63
(1) 29		
POLITICAL PSYCHOLOGY	1.8	.63
(2) 23 33		
POLITICAL SOCIOLOGY	1.8	.63
(7) 01 07 11 12 19 23 33		
POLITICAL SYMBOLISM	1.8	.63
(2) 15 23		
POLITICAL THOUGHT	1.8	.91
(6) 07 08 11 12 23 33		
POPULISM	1.8	.63
(4) 08 23 32 33		
POSITIVISM	1.8	.63
(5) 11 13 19 22 26		
POSTADOLESCENT SOCIALIZATION	1.8	.78
(1) 15		
PREDICTIVE POLITICAL KNOWLEDGE	1.8	.78
(1) 08		
PREMISE	1.8	.78
(2) 01 17		
PRESSURE POLITICS	1.8	.91
(2) 16 22		
PRIMARY RELATIONSHIPS	1.8	.63
(1) 15		
PROBLEM SOLVING	1.8	.78
(1) 25		
PROOF	1.8	1.03
(1) 43		
PROTECTIONISM	1.8	.63
(3) 20 22 25		
QUANTITATIVE ANALYSIS OF JUDICIAL BEHAVIOR	1.8	.63
(1) 04		
RATIONALISM	1.8	.63
(7) 01 03 08 09 13 22 26		
REASONABLE DOUBT	1.8	.63
. (1) 02		
REPLICATION	1.8	.78
(3) 01 24 33		
SAMPLE SURVEY	1.8	.78
(1) 25		
SCIENTIFIC EVIDENCE	1.8	.78
(1) 32		
SCIENTIFIC RESEARCH	1.8	.63
(1) 11		
SIMULATION STUDIES	1.8	.63
(1) 36		
SIMULATION TECHNIQUES	1.8	.63
(1) 23		
SOCIAL ATTITUDES	1.8	.63
(1) 15		
SOCIAL INDICATORS	1.8	.42
(1) 07		
SOCIAL INTEGRATION	1.8	.78
(1) 25		
SOCIAL MOBILITY	1.8	.78
(5) 01 07 11 15 25		
SOCIAL STRATIFICATION	1.8	.78
(3) 01 15 25		
SOCIAL STRUCTURE	1.8	.78
(4) 11 23 25 33		
STATE CAPITALISM	1.8	.78
(2) 17 33		
STATISTICAL DATA	1.8	.63
(1) 04		
STRUCTURAL ANALYSIS	1.8	.78
(4) 04 23 24 30		
SUBSYSTEM	1.8	.78
(2) 01 24		
SYSTEM	1.8	.78
(6) 01 04 08 24 25 30		
SYSTEMS THEORY, AND COMPARATIVE GOVERNMENT	1.8	.63
(1) 04		
THEORIES OF PASSIVE RESISTANCE	1.8	.42
(1) 22		
THEORY OF CONTRACT	1.8	.78
(1) 09		
TRANSNATIONAL POLITICS	1.8	.78
(1) 11		
TROTSKYISM, COMMUNIST DOCTRINE	1.8	.63
(4) 03 17 20 21		
UTOPIANISM	1.8	.78
(3) 03 22 33		
WEST-EAST RELATIONS	1.8	.91
(2) 11 23		
WORLD FEDERALISM	1.8	.42
(1) 11		
ADJUDICATIVE PROCESSES	1.9	.87
(1) 25		
ADMINISTRATIVE STRUCTURES	1.9	.87
(1) 04		
AGE OF ENLIGHTENMENT	1.9	.56
(1) 17		
AGE OF REASON	1.9	.56
(1) 17		
AGGREGATION	1.9	.87
(1) 33		
ANTI-DEMOCRATIC THEORY	1.9	.99
(1) 10		
ANTI-IMPERIALISM	1.9	.56
(1) 36		
AREA STUDIES	1.9	.73
(3) 04 25 33		
ARISTOTELIANISM	1.9	.99
(1) 43		
BEHAVIOR PATTERN	1.9	.73
(1) 01		
BIOLOGICAL BASIS OF HUMAN CONFLICT	1.9	.73
(1) 36		
BROAD-GAUGE THEORY (METATHEORY)	1.9	.87
(1) 04		
BUSINESS-GOVERNMENT RELATIONS	1.9	.73
(2) 25 32		
CIVILIZATION	1.9	.99
(2) 03 24		
COGNITION	1.9	.87
(4) 02 24 25 30		
COLLECTIVE LEADERSHIP	1.9	.73
(2) 11 34		
COMMUNICATION FLOW	1.9	.73
(1) 11		

COMPARATIVE ADMINISTRATION	1.9	.73
(1) 07		
COMPLEX SYSTEMS	1.9	.87
(1) 15		
COMPUTER ANALYSIS	1.9	.73
(1) 23		
CONDITIONED REFLEX	1.9	.87
(1) 22		
COOPTATION	1.9	.73
(3) 02 17 24		
COORDINATES	1.9	.73
(1) 30		
COPERNICAN THEORY	1.9	.73
(1) 22		
COUNTERVAILING THEORY OF	1.9	.73
PRESSURE POLITICS		
(3) 18 20 22		
CROSS-NATIONAL DIFFERENCES	1.9	.87
(1) 36		
CROSS-SECTIONAL ANALYSIS	1.9	.73
(2) 01 33		
CULTURAL HOMOGENEITY	1.9	.73
(1) 15		
CULTURAL PATTERNS	1.9	.73
(1) 25		
DEFINITION	1.9	.99
(5) 02 13 17 24 33		
DEMOGRAPHY	1.9	.73
(5) 07 19 24 25 33		
DEVELOPMENT	1.9	.73
(5) 01 04 11 24 30		
DISEQUILIBRIUM	1.9	.87
(1) 01		
DISTRIBUTIVE JUSTICE	1.9	.73
(1) 43		
DOCUMENTARY EVIDENCE	1.9	.87
(1) 16		
ECONOMIC MODELS	1.9	.56
(1) 11		
ECONOMICS	1.9	.73
(7) 04 07 08 19 20 25 30		
ENTROPY	1.9	.73
(1) 43		
EUROPEAN UNITY	1.9	.73
(2) 11 19		
EXPLANATION	1.9	.99
(1) 01		
FABIANISM	1.9	.73
(1) 33		
FEEDBACK LOOP	1.9	.87
(1) 33		
FIELD EXPERIMENT	1.9	.73
(1) 01		
GEOGRAPHICAL FACTORS	1.9	.73
(1) 36		
GOAL ATTAINMENT	1.9	.87
(2) 04 33		
GOVERN	1.9	.99
(2) 17 24		
GROUP THEORY	1.9	.87
(3) 01 04 33		
HEARTLAND THEORY, GEOPOLITICS	1.9	.87
(4) 03 16 20 22		

HEGELIANISM	1.9	.73
(1) 22		
HOBSON'S THEORY OF IMPERIALISM	1.9	.73
(1) 20		
HOMEOSTATIS	1.9	.99
(2) 01 24		
INSTITUTIONAL APPROACH	1.9	.73
(2) 01 19		
INTERDEPENDENCE	1.9	.87
(1) 03		
INTERDISCIPLINARY	1.9	.56
(1) 24		
INTERGOVERNMENTAL RELATIONS	1.9	.87
(1) 37		
INTERNATIONAL MONETARY RELATIONS	1.9	.99
(1) 11		
INTERNATIONAL REGIONALISM	1.9	.73
(2) 04 18		
INTERVAL SCALE	1.9	.73
(1) 01		
INTRAGROUP RELATIONS	1.9	.56
(2) 25 30		
INTUITIVE METHOD	1.9	.73
(1) 19		
JINGOISM	1.9	.56
(5) 06 16 17 27 29		
JUDICIAL SETTLEMENT (ADJUDICATION)	1.9	.56
(2) 17 20		
JURISPRUDENCE	1.9	.87
(9) 04 06 12 16 19 24 25 26 27		
LAW (SCIENTIFIC LAW)	1.9	.87
(1) 33		
LEGITIMATION	1.9	.87
(4) 16 17 24 30		
LEVEL OF ANALYSIS	1.9	.99
(1) 01		
LOGIC	1.9	.87
(3) 24 25 26		
LOGICAL METHOD	1.9	.87
(3) 01 19 24		
LONGITUDINAL ANALYSIS	1.9	.73
(3) 01 24 30		
LOOSE BIPOLAR SYSTEM	1.9	.73
(1) 03		
LOWER LEVEL THEORY	1.9	.73
(1) 01		
MARKETING SYSTEM	1.9	.87
(1) 25		
MEAN	1.9	.99
(2) 01 25		
MEASUREMENT	1.9	.87
(6) 01 03 07 11 24 30		
MICRO-POLITICS	1.9	.87
(1) 33		
MICROECONOMICS	1.9	.73
(1) 25		
MIDDLE-GAUGE THEORIES	1.9	.73
(1) 04		
MILITARISM, FASCIST THEORY	1.9	.56
(1) 20		
MILITARY INFLUENCES IN POLITICS	1.9	.73
(1) 23		

MOBILITY 1.9 .87
(3) 15 24 30
MODELS, REFERENCE 1.9 .73
(1) 04
MOTIVATION RESEARCH 1.9 .56
(1) 36
MULTIDIMENSIONALITY 1.9 .56
(2) 24 30
NATIONAL AND STATE RELATIONS 1.9 .87
(1) 12
NORMATIVE METHOD 1.9 .87
(1) 19
OUTPUTS 1.9 .87
(3) 01 04 33
PARAMETERS 1.9 .73
(3) 01 24 33
PARTIAL CORRELATION 1.9 .87
(1) 01
PARTICIPANT OBSERVATION 1.9 .87
(2) 01 33
PARTY LINE 1.9 .56
(6) 02 06 16 17 27 29
PERCEPTION 1.9 .99
(1) 01
POLARIZATION 1.9 .73
(2) 25 33
POLITICAL AWARENESS 1.9 .56
(1) 11
POLITICAL FACTORS 1.9 .87
(1) 36
POLITICAL FORECASTING 1.9 .73
(1) 11
POLITICAL GEOGRAPHY 1.9 .56
(1) 03
POLITICAL HISTORY 1.9 .87
(1) 33
POLITICAL INDOCTRINATION 1.9 .73
(1) 15
POLITICAL JUSTICE 1.9 .73
(1) 11
POLITICAL KNOWLEDGE 1.9 .87
(1) 15
POLITICAL PERSONALITY 1.9 .87
(1) 01
POLITICAL PRINCIPLES 1.9 .87
(1) 19
PROJECTION OF HISTORICAL TRENDS 1.9 .73
(1) 25
PROLETARIAN INTERNATIONALISM 1.9 .56
(1) 17
PUBLIC POLICY STUDIES 1.9 .87
(1) 07
RATIONALIZATION 1.9 .87
(3) 03 16 30
REALIST APPROACH 1.9 .87
(1) 01
REIFICATION 1.9 .73
(2) 13 33
RELATIONS AMONG THREE BRANCHES 1.9 .99
OF U.S. GOVERNMENT
(1) 25
RELATIVISM 1.9 .56
(2) 03 22

RELIGIOUS FREEDOM 1.9 .73
(5) 11 16 17 22 32
SCALE ANALYSIS 1.9 .56
(3) 01 23 24
SECTIONALISM 1.9 .73
(5) 06 16 18 24 27 46
SITUATIONAL ANALYSIS 1.9 .56
(4) 02 20 24 30
SOCIAL ENGINEERING 1.9 .73
(3) 01 04 22
SOCIAL SYSTEMS, AND 1.9 .87
STRUCTURAL-FUNCTIONALISM
(1) 04
SOCIALIST DEMOCRACY 1.9 .73
(1) 03
SOCIOLOGY OF POLITICS 1.9 .73
(1) 01
STATE SOCIALISM 1.9 .73
(3) 16 17 29
STATISTICS 1.9 .73
(1) 01
SUPRANATIONALISM 1.9 .87
(1) 20
SYNDICALISM 1.9 .56
(15) 03 07 10 12 16 17 19 20 21 22
26 29 30 32 33
SYSTEMS THEORY IN INTERNATIONAL 1.9 .56
POLITICS
(4) 03 04 07 13
TAUTOLOGY 1.9 .73
(1) 01
TRADITIONALISM 1.9 .73
(8) 03 04 11 15 17 19 24 25
UNDEMOCRATIC 1.9 .87
(1) 17
URBANISM 1.9 .87
(4) 04 19 24 30
VERTICAL INTEGRATION 1.9 .56
(1) 45
VOTER PARTICIPATION 1.9 .73
(1) 32
WORLD REVOLUTION (TROTSKYISM) 1.9 .56
(3) 16 17 20
ABSTRACTION 2.0 .94
(1) 13
AGENTS OF SOCIALIZATION 2.0 .94
(1) 15
AGRARIAN SOCIALISM 2.0 .66
(1) 19
ANALYZE 2.0 .94
(3) 24 25 30
ANTHROPOLOGY 2.0 .66
(7) 01 04 07 19 22 24 25
ANTI-CLERICALISM 2.0 .66
(1) 38
AUTARKY 2.0 .66
(4) 16 17 20 21
BIASES 2.0 .81
(1) 24
CAESARISM 2.0 .66
(4) 03 17 22 29
CAPABILITY ANALYSIS 2.0 .66
(2) 01 20

CASTROISM	2.0	.47
(2) 17 24		
CATEGORICAL-IMPERATIVE	2.0	.66
(1) 43		
CHRISTIANITY	2.0	.81
(6) 03 09 11 22 26 30		
CIVIL LAW SYSTEM	2.0	.66
(1) 44		
COATTAIL THEORY	2.0	.47
(1) 45		
COLLECTIVE DECISIONS	2.0	.81
(1) 11		
COMMON GOOD	2.0	.81
(1) 03		
CONCILIATION	2.0	.66
(7) 03 06 16 18 20 27 32		
CONDITIONING	2.0	.81
(1) 30		
CONFLICT REDUCTION	2.0	.81
(1) 36		
CONVERGENCE THEORY	2.0	.81
(2) 11 24		
COOPERATIVE FEDERALISM	2.0	.81
(2) 18 32		
CORRELATIVE METHOD	2.0	.94
(2) 10 24		
COST EFFECTIVENESS	2.0	.66
(1) 37		
CREATIVE FEDERALISM	2.0	.94
(1) 39		
CREDIBILITY	2.0	.66
(1) 30		
CREDIBILITY GAP	2.0	.66
(1) 39		
CROWD PSYCHOLOGY	2.0	.66
(3) 10 24 30		
CULTURAL HETEROGENEITY	2.0	.66
(1) 15		
CULTURAL PLURALISM THEORY	2.0	1.05
(3) 01 22 42		
DARWINISM	2.0	.66
(2) 03 22		
DEDUCTION	2.0	.81
(3) 01 13 17		
DEDUCTION-THEOREM	2.0	.94
(1) 43		
DEMOCRATIC COLLECTIVISM	2.0	.81
(1) 22		
DEMOCRATIC POWER	2.0	.94
(1) 42		
DEMOGRAPHIC	2.0	.47
(2) 24 30		
DEPENDENCE	2.0	.81
(2) 11 24		
DEPRIVATION	2.0	.81
(2) 17 30		
DEPTH INTERVIEW	2.0	.81
(2) 25 33		
DEPTH POLLING	2.0	.81
(1) 39		
DEPTH QUESTIONNAIRES	2.0	.81
(1) 25		

DIPLOMATIC RELATIONS	2.0	.47
(1) 41		
DIVISION OF LABOR	2.0	.66
(1) 26		
DOGMATISM	2.0	.66
(1) 17		
ECLECTIC APPROACH	2.0	.81
(2) 01 33		
ECOLOGY	2.0	.66
(6) 07 19 24 25 30 32		
ECONOMIC INTEGRATION	2.0	.66
(2) 17 20		
ECONOMIC INTERDEPENDENCE	2.0	.66
(1) 45		
ECONOMIC INTERPRETATION OF	2.0	.81
HISTORY, COMMUNIST THEORY		
(1) 20		
ECONOMIC SYSTEMS	2.0	.81
(2) 08 25		
EQUALITY OF STATES, DOCTRINE OF	2.0	.81
(1) 03		
EVIDENCE	2.0	1.05
(4) 06 17 24 32		
EXPERIMENTAL STUDY	2.0	.94
(1) 36		
FALSIFIABILITY	2.0	.94
(1) 43		
FIELD STUDY	2.0	.81
(1) 01		
FREE WILL	2.0	.81
(1) 01		
GENERATIONAL CONFLICT	2.0	.81
(1) 15		
GREEK CIVILIZATION	2.0	.66
(1) 22		
HEGEMONY	2.0	.66
(5) 06 16 17 20 33		
HEURISTIC DEVICE	2.0	.66
(1) 01		
HISTORICISM	2.0	.66
(3) 04 11 22		
HISTORICO-SOCIOLOGICAL METHOD	2.0	.94
(1) 19		
HUMAN NATURE	2.0	.94
(2) 22 25		
IDEALISM	2.0	.81
(7) 04 06 16 19 22 26 27		
IMPLICATION AND FACT	2.0	.94
(1) 26		
INDIVIDUALISM, ECONOMIC	2.0	.81
(1) 35		
INDOCTRINATION	2.0	.66
(4) 03 15 16 17		
INEQUALITY	2.0	.81
(1) 30		
INTEGRATION, AND INTERNATION	2.0	.94
RELATIONS		
(1) 04		
INTER-AMERICAN RELATIONS	2.0	.81
(1) 32		
INTER-GOVERNMENTAL RELATIONS	2.0	.81
(2) 03 07		

INTERACTION	2.0	.94
(5) 01 02 04 24 30		
INTERGROUP RELATIONS	2.0	.66
(1) 37		
INTERNAL RELATIONS	2.0	.94
(1) 43		
INTERNATIONAL COOPERATION	2.0	.94
(1) 11		
INTERNATIONAL ECONOMICS	2.0	.81
(1) 20		
INTERNATIONALIZATION	2.0	.81
(2) 16 17		
INTERSTATE RELATIONS	2.0	.81
(1) 12		
INTERVIEWING AND OBSERVATION	2.0	.81
(3) 04 11 24		
INTERVIEWS AND QUESTIONNAIRES	2.0	.81
(1) 23		
IRREDENTISM	2.0	.66
(7) 06 16 17 20 21 22 33		
KANTIAN IMPERATIVE	2.0	.47
(1) 22		
LEGAL REALISM	2.0	.66
(1) 22		
LINKAGE	2.0	.66
(1) 24		
LONGITUDINAL STUDIES	2.0	.81
(1) 33		
MASS MEDIA, TWO-STEP FLOW	2.0	.66
(1) 15		
MESSIANISM	2.0	.66
(2) 03 23		
METHODOLOGICAL CONCEPTS	2.0	.94
(2) 24 25		
MILITANCY	2.0	.81
(1) 30		
MODAL PERSONALITY	2.0	.81
(2) 01 15		
MORAL PHILOSOPHY	2.0	.81
(1) 19		
MORAL RELATIVISM	2.0	.94
(1) 04		
MYTH	2.0	.94
(7) 03 10 24 25 26 30 33		
NEO-FASCISM	2.0	.47
(3) 11 17 24		
NEO-FUNCTIONALISM	2.0	.81
(1) 01		
NEUTRAL	2.0	.66
(5) 16 17 24 25 27		
ONTOLOGY	2.0	.94
(1) 43		
OPPRESSION	2.0	.81
(2) 17 30		
ORDINAL	2.0	.66
(1) 43		
ORGANIC CONCEPTION OF THE STATE	2.0	.81
(1) 35		
PARTY IDENTIFIERS	2.0	.81
(1) 02		
PATTERN MAINTENANCE	2.0	.94
(2) 04 33		

PEACE RESEARCH	2.0	.66
(3) 01 07 11		
PERONISM	2.0	.47
(4) 03 11 17 24		
PHENOMENON	2.0	.81
(2) 24 30		
PHILOSOPHY	2.0	.81
(7) 04 07 11 13 19 24 30		
PHILOSOPHY OF LAW	2.0	.66
(2) 11 19		
POLITICAL ALTERNATIVES	2.0	.94
(1) 08		
POLITICAL COERCION	2.0	.81
(1) 08		
POLITICAL CRITICISM	2.0	.81
(1) 11		
POLITICAL MATURATION	2.0	.66
(1) 15		
POLITICAL MILITANCY	2.0	.66
(1) 11		
POLITICAL SKILLS	2.0	.66
(1) 08		
POWER PATTERNS	2.0	.66
(1) 20		
POWERLESSNESS	2.0	.66
(2) 17 30		
PREJUDICE	2.0	.81
(4) 03 06 17 30		
PRESCRIPTION-PRESCRIPTIVE	2.0	.94
(6) 06 13 16 17 20 24		
PRINCIPLE(S)	2.0	.81
(2) 13 24 43		
PROGRESSIVISM	2.0	.66
(1) 24		
PROPOSITION	2.0	.81
(1) 01		
PROTESTANTISM	2.0	.66
(4) 11 22 25 30		
PUBLIC PHILOSOPHY	2.0	.66
(1) 22		
PURITANISM	2.0	.66
(3) 03 09 22		
QUESTIONNAIRE	2.0	.47
(5) 01 17 23 25 33		
RACIAL PREJUDICE	2.0	.81
(1) 17		
RATIONALITY	2.0	.66
(8) 01 02 03 07 11 13 24 25		
REPUBLICANISM	2.0	.81
(2) 17 26		
RIGHT-WING RADICALISM	2.0	.66
(1) 11		
ROLL-CALL ANALYSIS	2.0	.66
(3) 04 11 33		
SCALOGRAM ANALYSIS	2.0	.81
(1) 04		
SOCIAL COHESION	2.0	.66
(1) 20		
SOCIAL MATRIX	2.0	.81
(1) 01		
SOCIAL PLURALISM	2.0	.81
(1) 01		

SOCIAL PROBLEMS	2.0	.94
(1) 11		
SOCIAL PSYCHOLOGY	2.0	.47
(4) 15 19 24 30		
SOCIAL STABILITY	2.0	.81
(1) 15		
SOCIAL STATUS	2.0	.81
(1) 07		
SOCIO-ECONOMIC STATUS (SES)	2.0	.81
(3) 24 30 33		
STATISM, FASCIST THEORY	2.0	.47
(3) 16 20 33		
STATISTICAL SIGNIFICANCE	2.0	.66
(1) 01		
STRATIFICATION	2.0	.94
(4) 01 02 24 30		
STRUCTURALISM	2.0	.81
(1) 43		
SUBJECTIVITY	2.0	.81
(1) 43		
SUBSET	2.0	.66
(1) 01		
SUBSISTENCE ECONOMY	2.0	.47
(1) 03		
TAX THEORIES	2.0	.94
(1) 42		
TRADE UNIONISM	2.0	.66
(1) 03		
UTOPIAN	2.0	.66
(1) 40		
VALUE SYSTEM	2.0	.94
(1) 33		
VARIABLE ANALYSIS	2.0	.81
(1) 05		
VARIANCE ANALYSIS	2.0	.66
(1) 11		
ACTIVISM	2.1	.73
(3) 11 25 32		
ADAPTATION	2.1	.87
(3) 04 25 33		
ADMINISTRATIVE SCIENCES	2.1	.87
(1) 23		
ADULT POLITICAL LEARNING	2.1	.87
(1) 15		
AGNOSTICISM	2.1	.73
(1) 22		
ANALYTIC THEORIES	2.1	.87
(1) 04		
ANTHROPOLOGICAL METHOD	2.1	.87
(3) 19 24 30		
ANTICIPATORY POLITICAL SOCIALIZATION	2.1	.56
(1) 15		
ANTIMILITARISM	2.1	.73
(1) 17		
ARTICULATION	2.1	.87
(1) 43		
ATHEISM	2.1	.73
(1) 26		
AUTARCHY	2.1	.73
(4) 03 06 16 33		
BIOPOLITICS	2.1	.73
(1) 07		
BLACK BOX TECHNIQUE	2.1	.87
(1) 33		
BLACK POLITICS	2.1	.56
(1) 07		
CAUDILLISM	2.1	.31
(2) 20 24		
COATTAIL EFFECT	2.1	.56
(4) 02 29 32 39		
COEFFICIENT OF REPRODUCIBILITY	2.1	.87
(1) 01		
COGNITIVE STRUCTURE	2.1	.87
(2) 01 04		
COHESION	2.1	.87
(3) 17 24 33		
COMMERCE	2.1	.73
(3) 06 17 18		
COMPARATIVE LAW	2.1	.87
(3) 16 17 19		
COMPETITIVE SYSTEM	2.1	.73
(3) 06 24 30		
CONTINGENCY	2.1	.73
(1) 43		
CONTINUUM	2.1	.73
(1) 01		
CORRELATES	2.1	.87
(2) 24 30		
CRITICAL METHOD	2.1	.73
(1) 19		
CULTURAL ANTHROPOLOGY	2.1	.73
(2) 15 19		
CULTURAL FACTORS	2.1	.73
(1) 36		
CULTURAL VARIATIONS	2.1	.73
(1) 15		
CZARISM	2.1	.31
(2) 03 17		
DECISIONAL ELEMENTS	2.1	.87
(1) 02		
DEVELOPMENT STUDIES	2.1	.73
(3) 04 11 33		
DISTRIBUTION OF INCOME	2.1	.56
(1) 08		
ECLECTICISM	2.1	.73
(1) 19		
ECONOMIC THEORY	2.1	.73
(2) 07 25		
EMPIRICAL ARGUMENT	2.1	.99
(1) 08		
ENVIRONMENTALISM	2.1	.73
(1) 22		
EVOLUTION	2.1	.87
(7) 03 10 19 22 24 26 30		
EXCHANGE THEORY	2.1	.73
(2) 01 11		
FORMAL LOGIC	2.1	.73
(1) 43		
FRAMEWORK	2.1	.99
(2) 17 24		
FREE ECONOMY	2.1	.73
(1) 16		
FREE ELECTIONS	2.1	.87
(1) 17		

GAULLISM	2.1	.56
(3) 11 20 24		
GEO-POLITICAL METHOD	2.1	.87
(1) 19		
GREATEST HAPPINESS PRINCIPLE	2.1	.87
(1) 26		
HETEROGENEOUS POLITICAL CULTURE	2.1	.87
(1) 15		
HIGHER-LAW DOCTRINE	2.1	.73
(2) 06 44		
HISTORICISM, CONTEMPORARY	2.1	.73
(1) 04		
HISTORY	2.1	.87
(9) 04 07 11 13 19 24 25 26 30		
IMPARTIALITY	2.1	.73
(2) 04 16		
IMPLICATION	2.1	.87
(1) 43		
INDUCTION	2.1	.87
(4) 01 13 30 43		
INDUSTRIAL RELATIONS	2.1	.73
(1) 37		
INFLUENCE	2.1	.99
(6) 03 05 23 24 30 33		
INTER-PARTY COMPETITION	2.1	.87
(2) 03 24		
INTERNATIONAL	2.1	.99
(5) 16 17 24 26 30		
INTERNATIONAL ECONOMIC RELATIONS	2.1	.87
(1) 11		
INTERSTATE	2.1	.56
(1) 24		
INTOLERANCE	2.1	.73
(2) 03 30		
IRRATIONAL FACTORS	2.1	.56
(1) 36		
IRRATIONALITY	2.1	.87
(1) 24		
ISM	2.1	.73
(1) 39		
JACKSONIANISM	2.1	.73
(1) 43		
JACOBINISM	2.1	.56
(4) 17 19 22 25		
JURIDICAL METHOD	2.1	.73
(4) 16 19 24 27		
KNOWLEDGE	2.1	.99
(5) 01 13 17 25 26		
LINGUISTIC ANALYSIS	2.1	.87
(1) 43		
LINGUISTICS	2.1	.87
(1) 25		
LOGICAL THEORY	2.1	.99
(1) 43		
LOYALTY	2.1	.87
(3) 22 24 30		
MACROTHEORIES	2.1	.73
(1) 04		
MANIFEST FUNCTION	2.1	.73
(2) 01 33		
MATHEMATICAL MODELS	2.1	.56
(3) 01 04 08		
MEASURES OF ASSOCIATION	2.1	.99
(1) 01		
METAPHOR	2.1	.73
(1) 43		
METHODS OF STUDY	2.1	.87
(1) 36		
MONETARY SYSTEM	2.1	.73
(1) 27		
MORES	2.1	.99
(1) 30		
NARROW-GAUGE THEORY	2.1	.73
(1) 04		
NATIONAL DEMOCRACY	2.1	.87
(2) 03 29		
NATIONALISTIC FACTORS	2.1	.99
(1) 36		
NATURAL SELECTION	2.1	.73
(1) 22		
NEEDS	2.1	.99
(2) 24 30		
NIHILISM	2.1	.73
(5) 06 07 10 17 22		
NORMATIVE CONCEPTION	2.1	.87
(1) 19		
NORMATIVE DOCTRINE	2.1	.73
(1) 05		
NORMATIVE ETHICS	2.1	.87
(1) 43		
OPERATIONS RESEARCH	2.1	.73
(3) 01 25 33		
ORGANIZATIONAL STYLES	2.1	.73
(1) 04		
PAN-AMERICANISM	2.1	.56
(7) 06 16 17 21 22 29 32		
PARTY ORTHODOXY	2.1	.56
(1) 29		
PERCEIVED ALTERNATIVES	2.1	.99
(1) 02		
PERSONALIZATION OF POWER	2.1	.87
(1) 17		
PERSUASION	2.1	.73
(3) 24 25 30		
POLITICAL ANTHROPOLOGY	2.1	.31
(3) 01 11 33		
POLITICAL IDEAS	2.1	.73
(3) 04 11 23		
POLITICAL LANGUAGE	2.1	.73
(1) 11		
POLITICAL LOYALTY	2.1	.56
(1) 15		
POLITICAL STABILITY, THEORY	2.1	.87
(2) 11 23		
POLITICAL STATISTICS	2.1	.56
(1) 12		
POSITIVIST BEHAVIORALISM	2.1	.73
(1) 04		
POSITIVIST EMPIRICISM	2.1	.56
(1) 04		
POST-CHILDHOOD POLITICAL LEARNING	2.1	.87
(1) 15		
PRESSURE, SOCIAL	2.1	.56
(1) 06		

PRESTIGE	2.1	.73	TRADITIONAL APPROACH	2.1	.87
(2) 03 17			(1) 01		
PROGRESS	2.1	.87	TRICKLE-DOWN THEORY	2.1	.56
(1) 40			(1) 39		
PSYCHOLOGY OF LEARNING	2.1	.56	UNIVERSE	2.1	.73
(1) 37			(2) 01 24		
PSYCHOLOGY, OF PERSONALITY	2.1	.56	VALIDATION	2.1	.99
(1) 04			(2) 01 33		
RANDOM	2.1	.87	VARIANCE	2.1	.73
(1) 01			(1) 17		
REALITY	2.1	.87	WELFARE CAPITALISM	2.1	.87
(1) 43			(1) 45		
REASON	2.1	.99	WELTENSCHAUUNG	2.1	.73
(4) 04 11 13 17			(1) 16		
REASONING	2.1	.99	WESTERN CIVILIZATION	2.1	.87
(1) 11			(2) 04 07		
REGRESSION TECHNIQUES	2.1	.73	WHIGGISM	2.1	.31
(2) 01 25			(1) 26		
RELIGIOUS FACTORS	2.1	.87	WILSONIAN DEMOCRACY	2.1	.56
(1) 36			(1) 16		
RESEARCH	2.1	.87	WORLD VIEW	2.1	.73
(1) 01			(1) 39		
RESISTANCE TO CHANGE	2.1	.73	AGRARIANISM	2.2	.78
(1) 37			(3) 16 24 29		
RESPONSIBILITY	2.1	.87	ALLEGIANCE	2.2	.63
(5) 17 19 24 30 33			(5) 06 16 17 24 33		
ROLE PLAYING	2.1	.56	AMERICANISM	2.2	.91
(1) 37			(4) 16 17 29 30		
RURAL-URBAN MIGRATION	2.1	.73	ANALYTIC	2.2	.91
(1) 15			(1) 43		
SCIENCE AND GOVERNMENT	2.1	.87	ANTIFASCISM	2.2	.63
(1) 23			(2) 03 17		
SET THEORY	2.1	.56	ANXIETY	2.2	.78
(2) 01 25			(4) 11 17 25 30		
SIGNIFICANCE	2.1	.87	ARAB NATIONALISM	2.2	.42
(3) 13 24 30			(1) 03		
SINO-SOVIET RELATIONSHIPS	2.1	.56	ARYANISM	2.2	.63
(2) 24 25			(2) 22 26		
SOCIAL DARWINISM	2.1	.73	AXIOMATIC	2.2	.63
(4) 03 11 22 25			(1) 43		
SOCIAL JUSTICE	2.1	.73	BILATERALISM	2.2	.78
(3) 11 17 19			(1) 32		
SOCIAL PROCESSES	2.1	.87	BONAPARTISM	2.2	.63
(1) 15			(1) 03		
SOCIO-POLITICAL	2.1	.73	BRAINWASH	2.2	.63
(1) 24			(7) 03 09 10 17 20 25 39		
SPECIALIZATION OF FUNCTION	2.1	.73	CALCULUS	2.2	.63
(1) 08			(1) 43		
STATE AND LOCAL RELATIONS	2.1	.56	CATEGORY	2.2	.78
(1) 12			(1) 43		
STEWARDSHIP THEORY	2.1	.56	CATHOLIC POLITICAL THEORY	2.2	.63
(2) 06 29			(1) 22		
STOICISM	2.1	.73	CHARACTERISTICS	2.2	.78
(1) 26			(2) 24 30		
SUPEREGO	2.1	.56	CHRISTIAN SOCIALISM	2.2	.63
(2) 22 25			(4) 03 19 22 25		
TECHNOLOGY	2.1	.73	CIRCULATION OF ELITES	2.2	.91
(7) 03 04 07 11 20 23 24			(1) 22		
TELEOLOGICAL EXPLANATION	2.1	.73	CIVIC EDUCATION	2.2	.78
(1) 33			(3) 11 15 17		
THEORY OF STATE, GENERAL	2.1	.87	COMMUNICATION	2.2	.91
(1) 17			(9) 02 03 06 07 11 17 20 24 30		

COMMUNICATION TECHNIQUES	2.2	.91
(1) 37		
COMMUNIST TERMINOLOGY	2.2	.63
(1) 39		
COMPARATIVE CONSTITUTIONAL LAW	2.2	.63
(2) 11 17		
CONFORMITY	2.2	.78
(4) 04 24 25 30		
CONGRESSIONAL ETHICS	2.2	.63
(1) 32		
CONSPIRACY THEORIES	2.2	.42
(1) 33		
CONSTITUTIONAL HISTORY	2.2	.78
(2) 17 19		
CONTEXTUAL ANALYSIS	2.2	.63
(2) 01 04		
CRIMINOLOGY	2.2	.78
(5) 03 07 19 25 30		
CRITICAL DISTINCTIONS IN POLITICS	2.2	.91
(1) 08		
CULTURAL TRANSMISSION	2.2	.63
(1) 15		
CUMULATIVE SCALE	2.2	.78
(1) 01		
DEISM	2.2	.63
(1) 43		
DELPHI METHOD	2.2	.78
(1) 33		
DENOTATION	2.2	.91
(1) 43		
DESCRIPTION	2.2	.91
(5) 01 05 13 24 43		
DESPOTIC ABSOLUTISM	2.2	.78
(1) 17		
DETERMINANTS	2.2	.91
(2) 24 30		
DILEMMA	2.2	.78
(2) 24 30		
DISTRIBUTION	2.2	.78
(3) 17 24 30		
DISTRIBUTION OF PROPERTY	2.2	.42
(1) 08		
DISTRIBUTIVE SYSTEM	2.2	.78
(1) 25		
ECOLOGICAL ANALYSIS	2.2	.78
(4) 01 04 24 30		
ECONOMIC DETERMINISM	2.2	.42
(8) 03 06 10 16 18 22 26 32		
ECONOMIC FACTORS	2.2	.63
(1) 36		
ECONOMIC NATIONALISM	2.2	.63
(6) 03 06 16 18 20 22		
ELITES, CIRCULATION OF	2.2	.91
(1) 22		
ENVIRONMENT AND SYSTEM CHANGES	2.2	.78
(1) 04		
EXCHANGE	2.2	.78
(3) 01 24 25		
EXCHANGE RATE	2.2	.42
(1) 16		
EXPLICATION	2.2	.91
(1) 24		
FACTOR	2.2	.78
(2) 24 30		
FALSIFICATION	2.2	.78
(1) 43		
FINANCE CAPITALISM	2.2	.78
(1) 22		
FUTURE-DESCRIPTIVE STATEMENT	2.2	.78
(1) 02		
GESTALT	2.2	.63
(1) 43		
GROWTH	2.2	.78
(2) 24 30		
HINDUISM	2.2	.63
(4) 03 22 24 25		
HUMANITARIANISM	2.2	.78
(3) 03 22 45		
IDEAL	2.2	.91
(1) 43		
IDENTIFICATION	2.2	.91
(3) 15 24 30		
IMAGE	2.2	.91
(3) 24 30 33		
INCONSISTENCY	2.2	.78
(1) 43		
INDETERMINACY	2.2	.78
(1) 43		
INDEX OF INTERCODER RELIABILITY	2.2	.78
(1) 01		
INDUSTRIAL DEMOCRACY	2.2	.42
(2) 03 11		
INDUSTRIALISM	2.2	.78
(4) 19 24 26 30		
INFORMATION	2.2	1.03
(10) 01 04 06 11 16 18 23 24 32 42		
INTER-PERSONAL RELATIONS	2.2	.91
(1) 07		
INTERSUBJECTIVITY	2.2	.78
(1) 01		
INVESTITURE	2.2	.42
(3) 02 17 33		
JAPANESE EMPEROR CONCEPT	2.2	.63
(1) 03		
LEARNING	2.2	.91
(2) 02 30		
LOADED QUESTION (IN POLLING)	2.2	.78
(1) 03		
LOCALISM	2.2	.78
(1) 45		
LOGICAL IMPOSSIBILITY	2.2	.91
(1) 43		
MANAGEMENT SCIENCE	2.2	.63
(2) 01 04		
MANAGEMENT THEORY	2.2	.63
(1) 04		
MECHANISTIC CONCEPTION	2.2	.63
(1) 19		
MEDIEVAL	2.2	.78
(1) 43		
METROPOLITICS	2.2	.78
(3) 03 24 30		
MOTIVE	2.2	.91
(1) 43		

MYTHOLOGY	2.2	.91
(1) 43		
NATIVISM	2.2	.63
(2) 06 27 46		
NEW CONSERVATISM	2.2	.78
(1) 22		
NONPARAMETRIC STATISTICS	2.2	.91
(1) 01		
OCCUPATIONAL MOBILITY	2.2	.63
(1) 37		
OLIGARCHIC	2.2	.91
(2) 17 24		
ORTHODOXY	2.2	.78
(1) 24		
PAN-AFRICANISM	2.2	.63
(5) 03 11 16 17 25		
PAN-ARABISM	2.2	.42
(3) 03 17 22		
PARTISAN LOYALTIES	2.2	.63
(1) 15		
PARTY COMPETITION	2.2	.78
(1) 03		
PHENOMENALISM	2.2	.63
(1) 43		
PHILOSOPHY OF THE STATE	2.2	.78
(1) 19		
PLATONISM	2.2	.78
(1) 43		
POLITICAL CLEAVAGES	2.2	.63
(1) 11		
POLITICAL EXPLANATION	2.2	.78
(1) 15		
POLITICAL METHOD	2.2	.91
(1) 19		
POLITICAL SELF	2.2	.78
(1) 15		
POLITICKING	2.2	.78
(1) 42		
PREDICTION	2.2	.91
(6) 01 02 13 24 30 33		
PRISONERS DILEMMA	2.2	.63
(2) 11 33		
PROCESS ANALYSIS	2.2	.78
(1) 11		
PROFESSIONALISM	2.2	.78
(1) 24		
PROGRESSIVE	2.2	.78
(6) 06 16 17 24 27 29		
PSYCHOANALYSIS	2.2	.42
(4) 19 22 24 30		
PSYCHOANALYTIC METHOD	2.2	.63
(4) 15 19 30 35		
PSYCHOLOGICAL FACTORS	2.2	.63
(1) 36		
PSYCHOLOGY	2.2	.63
(6) 04 07 19 24 25 30		
PSYCHOMETRIC	2.2	.63
(1) 24		
PUBLIC PURPOSE	2.2	.78
(2) 06 18		
PUNISHMENT	2.2	.63
(3) 17 24 30		
RACISM	2.2	.63
(8) 03 07 11 16 17 19 22 30		
REGULARITIES IN PHENOMENA	2.2	.78
(1) 05		
RELEVANT EVIDENCE	2.2	.78
(1) 32		
RELIGIOUS TOLERATION	2.2	.63
(1) 17		
RESPONSIBILITY, LEGAL	2.2	.78
(1) 06		
REVOLUTIONARY PURPOSE	2.2	.78
(1) 19		
REVOLUTIONARY SYNDICALISM	2.2	.42
(1) 11		
RIGHT	2.2	.78
(7) 06 11 16 17 19 24 34		
ROMAN CATHOLICISM	2.2	.78
(1) 25		
RUGGED INDIVIDUALISM	2.2	.78
(3) 16 27 29		
SELF-INTEREST	2.2	.78
(1) 26		
SEMANTICS	2.2	.63
(2) 04 30		
SMALL GROUP POLITICS	2.2	.78
(1) 33		
SOCIAL ADAPTATION	2.2	.91
(1) 19		
SOCIAL CONTROL	2.2	.63
(2) 01 06		
SOCIAL HISTORY	2.2	.78
(1) 19		
SOCIAL THEORY	2.2	.78
(5) 04 07 11 15 19		
SOCIOLOGICAL METHOD	2.2	.78
(1) 19		
SOCIOLOGY OF KNOWLEDGE	2.2	.63
(1) 07		
SPHERE OF INTEREST	2.2	.63
(1) 16		
STABILITY	2.2	.78
(3) 01 11 24		
STATE SOVEREIGNTY	2.2	.63
(4) 06 16 18 32		
STATISTIC	2.2	.63
(1) 30		
STRATEGY	2.2	.91
(6) 01 02 03 11 24 30		
STRUCTURES, INFLUENCE OF FORMAL	2.2	.78
(1) 04		
SUBCONSCIOUS MIND	2.2	.63
(1) 22		
SYMBOLIC INTERACTION THEORY	2.2	.78
(1) 15		
SYMBOLISM	2.2	.78
(2) 24 30		
SYNTHESIS	2.2	.78
(4) 01 04 24 30		
TAOISM	2.2	.78
(1) 03		
TAXONOMY	2.2	.91
(2) 01 24		

TECHNOCRACY	2.2	.42	CENTRALISM	2.3	.67
(10) 06 07 11 16 17 22 23 24 25 33			(1) 38		
TELEOLOGY	2.2	.78	CHANCE	2.3	.82
(1) 13			(1) 01		
TENDENCY STATEMENT	2.2	.91	CHANGE	2.3	.94
(1) 01			(3) 01 24 30		
THEORETICAL ANALYSIS	2.2	.78	CODING	2.3	.67
(1) 36			(2) 01 17		
THEORY OF PROGRESS	2.2	.91	COHERENCE	2.3	.82
(1) 10			(1) 43		
THINKING	2.2	.91	COHORT	2.3	.67
(1) 43			(1) 01		
THREAT THEORY	2.2	.91	COHORT ANALYSIS	2.3	.67
(1) 04			(3) 11 23 33		
TITOISM, COMMUNIST DOCTRINE	2.2	.42	COLLECTIVE GOODS	2.3	.67
(4) 03 17 20 34			(2) 01 11		
TRADITION	2.2	.78	COMMON SENSE	2.3	.67
(6) 03 11 24 25 30 33			(3) 06 32 43		
TRIBALISM	2.2	.78	COMMUNITY OF INTEREST	2.3	.82
(4) 07 11 23 24			(1) 45		
URBANISM, IN EMERGENT NATIONS	2.2	.63	COMMUNITY PARTICIPATION	2.3	.82
(1) 04			(1) 11		
UTILITY	2.2	.91	CONFLICT, ORGANIZATIONAL	2.3	.82
(3) 24 25 33			(1) 37		
VALUE CONSENSUS	2.2	.91	CONFUCIANISM	2.3	.48
(1) 20			(3) 03 19 24		
WORLD OPINION	2.2	.63	CONSOLIDATION	2.3	.67
(1) 39			(6) 03 06 11 18 24 29		
XENOPHOBIA	2.2	.42	COOPERATION	2.3	.94
(6) 16 17 20 22 27 33			(1) 01		
YANKEE IMPERIALISM	2.2	.63	CULTURAL TRANSFORMATION	2.3	.82
(1) 03			(1) 15		
ALTRUISM	2.3	.67	CYBERNATION	2.3	.67
(1) 22			(1) 36		
AMBIVALENCE	2.3	.82	DEFERENCE	2.3	.82
(1) 24			(2) 24 30		
AMERICAN WAY OF LIFE	2.3	.82	DESCRIPTIVE THEORIES	2.3	.82
(1) 39			(1) 04		
ANCESTOR WORSHIP	2.3	.67	DEVIANCY	2.3	.82
(1) 03			(2) 24 30		
APTITUDE TESTS	2.3	.67	DIAGNOSIS	2.3	.82
(1) 25			(2) 24 30		
ASYMMETRY	2.3	.82	DICHOTOMOUS CLASSIFICAITON	2.3	.67
(3) 01 04 43			(1) 01		
ATTRIBUTE	2.3	.67	DUAL FEDERALISM	2.3	.48
(1) 43			(3) 06 18 32		
AXIOMS, POLITICAL	2.3	.67	ECONOMIC DEMOCRACY	2.3	.67
(1) 39			(1) 22		
BELIEF	2.3	.94	EGO-INVOLVEMENT	2.3	.48
(3) 02 11 24			(1) 02		
BICULTURAL	2.3	.82	ERROR	2.3	.82
(1) 24			(1) 43		
BIGOTRY	2.3	.82	ETHNOLOGY	2.3	.48
(1) 30			(1) 19		
BLACK STUDIES	2.3	.67	EXCHANGE BEHAVIOR	2.3	.67
(1) 43			(1) 02		
BUDDHISM	2.3	.67	FEEDBACK CHANNEL	2.3	.67
(5) 03 11 22 24 25			(1) 33		
CATHARSIS	2.3	.82	FEEDBACK PHENOMENA	2.3	.67
(1) 30			(1) 25		
CATHOLICISM	2.3	.67	FIDELISMO	2.3	.67
(6) 03 11 19 22 24 26			(1) 03		

FINITE	2.3	.82	INTERPERSONAL RELATIONSHIPS	2.3	.82
(1) 43			(2) 15 30		
FORMATION OF PERSONALITY	2.3	.82	INTERVALS	2.3	.82
(1) 15			(1) 17		
FRACTIONALISM	2.3	.82	INTERVENTIONISM	2.3	.67
(2) 11 17			(3) 16 17 25		
FUHRERPRINZIP	2.3	.48	INTUITION	2.3	.67
(3) 16 22 34			(1) 01		
FUTURISM	2.3	.82	IRRATIONAL	2.3	.82
(1) 22			(1) 24		
GANDHISM	2.3	.48	JOB SATISFACTION	2.3	.82
(1) 11			(1) 37		
GENERALIZATION METHOD OF	2.3	.67	JUDAISM	2.3	.67
POLITICAL LEARNING			(3) 03 22 25		
(1) 15			KREMLINOLOGY	2.3	.67
GEOGRAPHIC DETERMINISM	2.3	.48	(1) 34		
(1) 06			LANGUAGE	2.3	.82
GOOD FAITH	2.3	.82	(5) 07 11 19 24 30		
(1) 17			LEGAL HISTORY	2.3	.82
HERO-WORSHIP	2.3	.82	(1) 12		
(1) 26			LIBERAL EDUCATION	2.3	.82
HEURISTICS	2.3	.82	(1) 43		
(1) 43			LIBERTARIANISM	2.3	.82
HIGHEST GOOD	2.3	.82	(1) 43		
(1) 03			LOCAL FEDERALISM	2.3	.48
HISTORIOGRAPHY	2.3	.82	(1) 03		
(3) 11 25 30			LOYAL	2.3	.94
HOMEGENEITY	2.3	.82	(1) 30		
(1) 24			LYSENKOISM	2.3	.67
HUMAN RELATIONS	2.3	.82	(1) 03		
(1) 37			MALTHUSIANISM	2.3	.67
HUMANISM	2.3	.82	(2) 20 22		
(4) 03 11 19 22			MANAGEMENT OF PUBLIC AFFAIRS	2.3	.82
ID	2.3	.67	(1) 03		
(1) 22			MATHEMATICAL ANALYSIS	2.3	.67
IDEA	2.3	.82	(2) 33 43		
(4) 03 04 05 24			MAXIMIZATION	2.3	.67
IDEAL SOCIETY	2.3	.82	(1) 43		
(1) 36			MESSAGE FLOWS	2.3	.67
IDENTITY	2.3	.82	(1) 04		
(2) 24 30			METAPHYSICS	2.3	.67
ILLEGITIMACY	2.3	.82	(1) 22		
(2) 24 30			MOBILITY, OCCUPATIONAL	2.3	.48
IMMOBILISM	2.3	.67	(1) 37		
(2) 03 24			MODERN REPUBLICANISM	2.3	.67
INDEX NUMBERS	2.3	.67	(2) 27 39		
(1) 33			MOHAMMEDANISM	2.3	.48
INFALLIBILITY OF THE POPE	2.3	.67	(1) 16		
(1) 17			MONARCHISM	2.3	.82
INFANT INDUSTRY (PROTECTIONISM)	2.3	.48	(2) 17 22		
(3) 06 16 20 45			MONOTHEISM	2.3	.67
INFORMING FUNCTION OF CONGRESS	2.3	.48	(1) 43		
(1) 44			MORAL	2.3	.94
INSTABILITY	2.3	.67	(2) 24 30		
(2) 24 30			MORAL TURPITUDE	2.3	.82
INSTITUTIONAL METHOD	2.3	.67	(1) 45		
(1) 19			MORALE	2.3	.82
INSTRUMENTALISM	2.3	.82	(3) 03 19 30		
(2) 19 22			NATIONAL CONSCIOUSNESS	2.3	.48
INTEGRATIVE	2.3	.82	(1) 17		
(2) 24 30			NATIONAL DECISIONS	2.3	.82
INTELLIGENCE	2.3	.82	(1) 36		
(4) 18 20 24 30					

NATIONAL LOYALTY	2.3	.82
(1) 15		
NATIVE AMERICAN STUDIES	2.3	.67
(1) 07		
NATURAL MONOPOLY	2.3	.82
(2) 06 18		
NEHRUISM	2.3	.82
(1) 24		
NEO-LIBERALISM	2.3	.82
(2) 19 24		
NEO-MALTHUSIANISM	2.3	.82
(2) 20 22		
NEO-POSITIVISM	2.3	.82
(1) 22		
NONDIRECTED INTERVIEW	2.3	.67
(1) 01		
NORMATIVE-JURIDICAL METHOD	2.3	.82
(1) 19		
OBEDIENCE	2.3	.94
(1) 24		
OPERATIVE IDEALS	2.3	.82
(1) 19		
ORGANIZATION AND ADMINISTRATIVE RELATIONSHIPS	2.3	.82
(1) 12		
PAN-ISLAMISM	2.3	.48
(3) 03 16 17		
PAN-SLAVISM	2.3	.48
(3) 16 17 22		
PARTICULARISM	2.3	.94
(2) 06 17		
PATTERN	2.3	.94
(2) 01 24		
PECKING ORDER	2.3	.82
(1) 39		
PERSONALITY	2.3	.94
(8) 01 02 04 15 23 24 25 30		
PHILOSOPHY OF HISTORY	2.3	.67
(2) 11 19		
POLICY APPROACH	2.3	.82
(2) 03 33		
POLITICAL CHARACTER	2.3	.67
(1) 15		
POLITICAL CRITERIA	2.3	.67
(1) 08		
POLITICAL PREDISPOSITIONS	2.3	.67
(1) 15		
POLYARCHAL DEMOCRACY	2.3	.82
(1) 22		
PREDESTINATION	2.3	.67
(1) 43		
PROBABILISM	2.3	.82
(1) 43		
PSYCHIATRY	2.3	.67
(6) 07 15 19 24 25 30		
PSYCHOLOGICAL METHOD	2.3	.82
(1) 19		
PSYCHOLOGICAL TESTING	2.3	.67
(1) 36		
PSYCHOSIS	2.3	.67
(1) 30		
PURE THEORY	2.3	.67
(1) 22		
QUALITY	2.3	.82
(1) 43		
RATIO SCALE	2.3	.82
(1) 01		
REDUCTIONISM	2.3	.67
(1) 01		
REDUCTIONIST THEORIES	2.3	.48
(1) 33		
REDUNDANCY	2.3	.67
(1) 02		
REFORMISM	2.3	.67
(4) 03 11 17 25		
RIGHT DEVIATIONISM	2.3	.48
(1) 17		
RIMLAND THEORY, GEOPOLITICS	2.3	.48
(1) 20		
ROMANTICISM	2.3	.67
(2) 09 22		
SAMPLE	2.3	.67
(2) 24 33		
SCEPTICISM	2.3	.82
(1) 43		
SCIENCE	2.3	.94
(10) 01 04 05 07 11 13 19 24 26 30		
SCIENCE, PURE	2.3	.67
(1) 04		
SCIENTISM	2.3	.67
(1) 22		
SEA POWER THEORY, GEOPOLITICS	2.3	.67
(2) 17 20		
SECULARISM	2.3	.67
(2) 22 24		
SHARED ATTITUDE	2.3	.67
(1) 02		
SOCIAL FACTORS	2.3	.82
(1) 36		
SOCIAL PROGRESS	2.3	.82
(1) 11		
SOCIAL RESPONSIBILITY	2.3	.67
(1) 36		
SOCIAL SCIENCE, UNIFIED	2.3	.67
(1) 05		
SOCIALIST REALISM	2.3	.67
(1) 25		
SOCIO-PSYCHOLOGICAL	2.3	.67
(1) 30		
SOCIOCULTURAL	2.3	.82
(1) 24		
SOCIOECONOMIC	2.3	.67
(1) 24		
SOCIOLOGICAL JURISPRUDENCE	2.3	.67
(2) 04 22		
SPANISH-AMERICAN CULTURE	2.3	.67
(1) 25		
STATE CENTRALIZATION	2.3	.82
(1) 06		
STRUCTURE	2.3	.82
(1) 36		
STRUCTURES, CONCEPT OF	2.3	.82
(6) 01 04 11 24 30 33		
SUZERAINTY	2.3	.67
(3) 06 16 17		

SYLLOGISTIC	2.3	.67
(1) 43		
SYMBOL	2.3	.82
(6) 02 03 06 24 30 33		
SYNTAX	2.3	.82
(1) 43		
SYSTEM, AS A QUALITY OF SCIENTIFIC	2.3	.94
KNOWLEDGE		
(1) 13		
TENSION REDUCTION	2.3	.82
(1) 36		
TESTABILITY	2.3	.82
(1) 43		
THEORY OF SOCIALIST EVOLUTION	2.3	.67
(1) 22		
TOLERANCE	2.3	.82
(3) 03 24 30		
TRUTH	2.3	.82
(1) 35		
UNIVERSALISM	2.3	.82
(2) 20 22		
VALUATIONAL STATEMENT	2.3	.82
(1) 02		
VALUE	2.3	.94
(6) 01 03 19 24 26 30		
VOTE INDICATOR	2.3	.67
(1) 17		
WHIG THEORY OF GOVERNMENT	2.3	.67
(1) 09		
ZEN-BUDDHISM	2.3	.67
(1) 43		
ACTION THEORY	2.4	.69
(3) 01 25 33		
AFFILIATION	2.4	.69
(3) 16 17 24		
ALGEBRA	2.4	.84
(1) 43		
AMERICAN DREAM	2.4	.84
(1) 39		
AMERICAN YOUTH CULTURE	2.4	.84
(1) 15		
ANALYTICAL JURISPRUDENCE	2.4	.69
(1) 44		
ANALYTICAL THEORY OF LAW	2.4	.84
(1) 10		
BORDERLINE	2.4	.69
(1) 30		
CAVEAT	2.4	.69
(2) 06 24		
CHRISTIAN ANARCHISM	2.4	.69
(1) 10		
CLERICALISM	2.4	.69
(1) 17		
COMMUNALISM	2.4	.69
(2) 03 24		
COMPARABILITY	2.4	.84
(2) 24 30		
COMPREHENSION	2.4	.84
(1) 43		
CONCLUSIONS	2.4	.69
(2) 17 24		
CONSCIENCE	2.4	.69
(2) 25 30		
CONVERSION PROCESS	2.4	.69
(2) 01 33		
CREED	2.4	.84
(2) 29 30		
CRITICAL RANGE	2.4	.69
(1) 33		
CRITICISM	2.4	.69
(2) 24 30		
CULTURAL COOPERATION	2.4	.69
(1) 11		
CYNICISM	2.4	.51
(1) 22		
DENOTING	2.4	.84
(1) 43		
DEPENDENCY	2.4	.84
(4) 06 16 24 30		
DEPTH-PSYCHOLOGY	2.4	.69
(1) 43		
DEVIATIONISM	2.4	.84
(1) 17		
DICHOTOMIES	2.4	.69
(1) 24		
DIRECTED INTERVIEW	2.4	.51
(1) 01		
DISTRIBUTION OF RIGHTS AND DUTIES	2.4	.84
(1) 12		
DISTRUST	2.4	.84
(1) 24		
DURESS	2.4	.84
(1) 16		
ECLECTIC FUNCTIONALISM	2.4	.84
(2) 01 04		
ECONOMIC METHOD	2.4	.51
(1) 19		
EFFECTIVE	2.4	.96
(3) 16 17 24		
EGO	2.4	.51
(2) 22 30		
EGO-DEFENSES	2.4	.51
(1) 04		
EGOISM	2.4	.69
(2) 22 26		
ELECTORAL CHANGE	2.4	.69
(1) 11		
EMOTION	2.4	.84
(1) 43		
ETHNOGRAPHY	2.4	.51
(1) 43		
EUROPEAN FEDERALISM	2.4	.69
(2) 17 19		
EVALUATION	2.4	.69
(1) 24		
EXTENSIONAL DEFINITION	2.4	.84
(1) 02		
FALLACY	2.4	.84
(1) 43		
FANATICISM	2.4	.69
(1) 17		
FORMALIZATION	2.4	.84
(1) 02		
FORMATION OF SOCIETY	2.4	.84
(1) 08		

FRONTIER DEMOCRACY	2.4	.51
(1) 46		
FUNNEL OF CAUSALITY	2.4	.51
(1) 33		
FUTUROLOGY	2.4	.84
(1) 36		
GENERALIZED OTHER	2.4	.51
(1) 15		
GENETIC THEORY	2.4	.69
(2) 04 25		
GEOGRAPHIC MOBILITY	2.4	.51
(1) 15		
GEOGRAPHY	2.4	.84
(1) 19		
GERONTOLOGY	2.4	.69
(1) 07		
GOD	2.4	.69
(1) 30		
GROUP MIND	2.4	.84
(1) 06		
GROUP PERSONALITY	2.4	.84
(1) 19		
GROUP STANDARDS	2.4	.69
(1) 15		
GUILD SYSTEM	2.4	.69
(1) 45		
GUILT	2.4	.69
(1) 30		
HALF-TRUTH	2.4	.69
(1) 39		
HUMAN ELEMENT	2.4	.84
(1) 39		
HUMANITIES	2.4	.69
(1) 43		
IMAGE STUDIES	2.4	.84
(1) 36		
IMAGERY	2.4	.84
(1) 24		
IMAGINATION	2.4	.84
(1) 43		
INDETERMINISM	2.4	.84
(2) 01 22		
INSTRUMENTALIST VIEW OF THE STATE	2.4	.69
(1) 35		
INTEGRATION, AND CONFLICT	2.4	.84
(1) 04		
INTELLECTUAL CONSTRUCTS	2.4	.69
(2) 04 25		
INTENSIONAL DEFINITION	2.4	.84
(1) 02		
INTERGENERATIONAL CONTINUITY	2.4	.84
(1) 15		
INTERNAL COMMUNICATION	2.4	.84
(1) 03		
INTERPRETATION	2.4	.84
(2) 17 24		
INTERRELATIONS	2.4	.84
(1) 24		
INTERVIEWER-RESPONDENT	2.4	.69
(3) 24 30 37		
INTERVIEWING	2.4	.84
(1) 37		

INVESTIGATION	2.4	.69
(2) 17 27		
JACOBIN DEMOCRACY	2.4	.51
(1) 22		
JARGON	2.4	.69
(1) 05		
JURIMETRICS	2.4	.51
(1) 24		
LABORATORY APPROACH	2.4	.69
(1) 01		
LATENT OPINION	2.4	.51
(1) 01		
LIBERAL ARTS	2.4	.84
(1) 05		
LIBERAL CONSERVATISM	2.4	.84
(1) 22		
LOCAL POWER	2.4	.69
(1) 11		
MANAGERIAL ECONOMICS	2.4	.84
(1) 04		
MEANING	2.4	.96
(2) 24 30		
MEASURE	2.4	.84
(2) 16 24		
MEMORY	2.4	.96
(1) 43		
MESSAGE	2.4	.84
(1) 06		
METATHEORIES, IN INTERNATIONAL RELATIONS	2.4	.51
(1) 04		
MODEL METHOD	2.4	.84
(1) 23		
MORALITY	2.4	.84
(4) 03 07 11 30		
MYSTICISM	2.4	.84
(2) 22 25		
NATURAL SCIENCE	2.4	.84
(1) 19		
NEO-HEGELIANISM	2.4	.51
(2) 03 22		
NEO-PLATONISM	2.4	.69
(1) 22		
NEOPOSITIVISM	2.4	.84
(1) 43		
NEW CHINESE MAN (MAOISM)	2.4	.69
(1) 20		
NEW LIBERALISM	2.4	.84
(1) 25		
NOMINALISM	2.4	.69
(1) 22		
NONPOLITICAL PARTICIPATION	2.4	.69
(1) 15		
NULL SET	2.4	.84
(1) 01		
NUMERICAL INDICES AND INDICATORS	2.4	.84
(1) 25		
OBJECTIVE	2.4	.69
(1) 43		
OBJECTIVE POLITICAL EVALUATION	2.4	.69
(1) 08		
OFFICIAL RELIGION	2.4	.51
(1) 17		

OPPORTUNITY	2.4	.84
(3) 17 24 30		
ORIGINAL SIN	2.4	.84
(2) 09 22		
OUGHT	2.4	.96
(1) 43		
OUT OF CONTEXT	2.4	.69
(1) 39		
PANEL STUDY	2.4	.51
(2) 01 33		
PARADOX	2.4	.69
(1) 24		
PARTIAL THEORY	2.4	.96
(1) 33		
PAST	2.4	.96
(1) 43		
PER CAPITA	2.4	.69
(3) 06 16 27		
PERCEIVE	2.4	.84
(1) 30		
PERSONALITY TRAITS	2.4	.84
(1) 15		
PHILOSOPHICAL RADICALISM	2.4	.51
(1) 26		
PHOBIA	2.4	.69
(1) 16		
POLITICAL CURRENCIES	2.4	.69
(1) 02		
POSITIVISM (LEGAL THEORY)	2.4	.51
(1) 20		
POSITIVISTIC HUMANISM	2.4	.69
(1) 19		
POSSIBILITY	2.4	.69
(1) 43		
POST-FREUDIAN PSYCHOLOGY	2.4	.51
(1) 08		
POWER PROCESS	2.4	.84
(1) 25		
PREDICTABILITY OF LAW	2.4	.69
(1) 44		
PREFERENCE	2.4	.69
(2) 24 43		
PROBLEM-ANALYSIS QUESTIONNAIRE	2.4	.69
(1) 04		
PRODUCT MOMENT	2.4	.69
(1) 01		
PSYCHOCULTURAL THEORY OF SOCIALIZATION	2.4	.69
(1) 15		
PSYCHOLOGICAL MASS COERCION	2.4	.69
(1) 03		
PSYCHOLOGICAL PROCESSES	2.4	.69
(1) 15		
PSYCHOPATHOLOGY	2.4	.69
(2) 24 30		
PUBLIC CHARACTER	2.4	.69
(1) 17		
PURPOSE	2.4	.84
(2) 13 17		
Q-SORT	2.4	.69
(1) 30		
QUANTITY	2.4	.84
(1) 43		
RATIONAL	2.4	.69
(1) 43		
RATIONALE	2.4	.51
(1) 13		
REDUCTIO AD ABSURDUM	2.4	.69
(1) 43		
REINFORCEMENT	2.4	.84
(1) 30		
RELATED DISCIPLINES	2.4	.69
(1) 19		
RELATIONS BETWEEN GOVERNMENTS	2.4	.84
(1) 25		
RELATIONSHIP	2.4	.69
(3) 15 24 30		
RELATIVE	2.4	.69
(1) 43		
RELATIVITY	2.4	.69
(1) 43		
RELIGIOUS INTOLERANCE	2.4	.51
(1) 41		
RESOCIALIZATION	2.4	.69
(1) 15		
RETROACTIVE	2.4	.51
(1) 16		
REVANCHISM	2.4	.51
(2) 16 34		
SACRED	2.4	.84
(1) 24		
SCHOLASTICISM	2.4	.69
(2) 19 22		
SCIENTIFIC FREEDOM	2.4	.69
(1) 03		
SELF-IMAGE	2.4	.69
(2) 24 30		
SENSITIVITY TRAINING	2.4	.69
(1) 37		
SETTING, AND SYSTEMS THEORY	2.4	.69
(1) 04		
SHINTOISM	2.4	.51
(3) 03 16 25		
SIZE, GEOGRAPHIC POWER FACTOR	2.4	.51
(1) 20		
SOCIAL DEVELOPMENT	2.4	.69
(2) 07 11		
SOCIAL INNOVATION	2.4	.84
(1) 04		
SOCIAL TRENDS	2.4	.69
(1) 10		
SOURCES OF INTERNATIONAL LAW	2.4	.69
(2) 17 20		
STATE RELIGION	2.4	.51
(1) 17		
STATEMENT	2.4	.69
(1) 17		
STEADY STATE	2.4	.51
(1) 01		
STRATEGY THEORY	2.4	.84
(1) 04		
SUBJECTIVE	2.4	.69
(2) 24 30		
SYSTEMATIC THEORY	2.4	.84
(1) 22		

TERMINOLOGY, DEFINITIONS   2.4   .69
(3) 19 23 24
TESTIMONY   2.4   .69
(2) 06 30
THEISM   2.4   .69
(1) 43
THEOLOGY   2.4   .69
(1) 43
THOMISM   2.4   .69
(1) 22
TIME AND MOTION STUDY   2.4   .69
(1) 37
TIME SERIES ANALYSIS   2.4   .69
(1) 01
TOLERATION   2.4   .84
(3) 03 17 26
TOPOGRAPHY, GEOGRAPHIC POWER   2.4   .69
  FACTOR
(1) 20
TRANSITION   2.4   .69
(2) 24 30
TREND   2.4   .84
(2) 24 30
UN-AMERICAN   2.4   .69
(1) 39
UNIONISM   2.4   .69
(2) 24 30
UNIVERSALITY OF PHENOMENA   2.4   .84
(1) 05
URBAN SYSTEM   2.4   .69
(1) 43
UTOPIA AND POLITICS   2.4   .51
(10) 06 12 16 18 23 24 27 30 32 40
VALID   2.4   .84
(1) 17
VERTICAL FEDERALISM   2.4   .51
(1) 18
VITAL INTERESTS   2.4   .84
(1) 16
WHOLESALE PRICE INDEX   2.4   .69
(1) 02
ABSOLUTE   2.5   .52
(3) 03 17 24
ADMINISTRATIVE JURISPRUDENCE   2.5   .52
(1) 11
ADOLESCENCE   2.5   .70
(4) 11 15 25 30
ANALYTICAL SCHOOL   2.5   .84
(1) 22
ARCHAEOLOGY   2.5   .70
(1) 07
ARCHETYPE   2.5   .84
(1) 43
ARITHMETIC   2.5   .84
(1) 43
ART   2.5   .70
(4) 11 24 30 36
ASPIRATIONS   2.5   .70
(2) 24 30
BAD TENDENCY TEST   2.5   .70
(3) 03 18 32
BASIC ORIENTATIONS   2.5   .84
(1) 15

BENEFIT THEORY   2.5   .70
(3) 06 16 18
BIOGRAPHICAL METHOD   2.5   .70
(3) 12 19 24
CATALYST   2.5   .70
(1) 30
CERTAINTY   2.5   .70
(1) 43
CHARACTER   2.5   .70
(2) 24 30
CHRONOLOGY   2.5   .52
(1) 25
CIRCULARITY   2.5   .70
(1) 43
COGNITIVE RATIONALISM   2.5   .52
(1) 04
COMMUNITARIAN SOCIALISM   2.5   .52
(1) 22
COMPARATIVE   2.5   .70
(2) 24 30
CONSTITUTIVE SYSTEMS   2.5   .70
(1) 04
CONSUMER PRICE INDEX   2.5   .70
(1) 02
CONTEXT   2.5   .84
(1) 24
CONTROL-THEORY   2.5   .70
(1) 43
CONTROLLED DIRECT OBSERVATATION   2.5   .70
(1) 25
CONVERGENCE   2.5   .52
(1) 43
COOPERATIVE RESEARCH   2.5   .70
(1) 19
CORPORATISM   2.5   .70
(2) 11 19
COSMOPOLITANISM   2.5   .52
(4) 06 17 22 34
COUNTRY STUDIES   2.5   .70
(1) 33
DEBUREAUCRATIZATION   2.5   .70
(1) 24
DEMOGRAPHIC CYCLE   2.5   .70
(1) 20
DENSITY   2.5   .84
(1) 30
DERIVATIONS   2.5   .52
(1) 22
DESCRIBING   2.5   .84
(1) 43
DISPLACEMENT AND PROJECTION   2.5   .84
(1) 25
DISSONANCE   2.5   .70
(1) 43
DIVIDED SOVEREIGNTY   2.5   .70
(1) 06
DOCTRINAIRE   2.5   .52
(4) 06 16 27 29
DOGMATIC METHOD   2.5   .70
(1) 19
ECOLOGY, POLITICAL   2.5   .52
(1) 01

EMPATHY	2.5	.70
(1) 03		
ENLIGHTENED ABSOLUTISM	2.5	.70
(1) 17		
ENQUIRY	2.5	.84
(1) 17		
EPISTEMIC-LOGIC	2.5	.70
(1) 43		
EQUAL DISTRIBUTION THEORY	2.5	.70
(1) 42		
EQUITABLE	2.5	.84
(1) 17		
ESPERANTO	2.5	.52
(1) 43		
ESSENCE	2.5	.70
(1) 24		
EUPHEMISM, POLITICAL	2.5	.70
(1) 39		
EXACT SCIENCES	2.5	.70
(1) 19		
EXCLUDED MIDDLE	2.5	.70
(1) 43		
EXCLUSION	2.5	.70
(3) 06 16 24		
EXCLUSIVE POWER	2.5	.70
(5) 03 06 16 18 32		
EXPERTISE	2.5	.70
(1) 24		
FATALISM	2.5	.70
(1) 30		
FEAR	2.5	.70
(2) 24 30		
FICTION	2.5	.70
(3) 24 26 30		
FIGURATIVE LANGUAGE	2.5	.70
(1) 43		
FLEMISH NATIONALISM	2.5	.52
(1) 19		
FORCES OF CHANGE	2.5	.70
(1) 04		
FRAGMENTATION	2.5	.70
(2) 11 24		
FRUSTRATION	2.5	.70
(1) 30		
GENERALITY	2.5	.70
(1) 43		
GENETICS	2.5	.70
(1) 07		
GEOGRAPHIC POWER FACTORS	2.5	.70
(1) 20		
GERIATRICS	2.5	.52
(1) 07		
GESTALT PSYCHOLOGY	2.5	.52
(1) 01		
GOOD	2.5	.84
(1) 43		
GROUNDED THEORY	2.5	.84
(1) 33		
HATE	2.5	.70
(1) 30		
HEDONISM	2.5	.52
(1) 43		
HISTORICAL JURISPRUDENCE	2.5	.52
(1) 44		
HISTORICO-JURIDICAL METHOD	2.5	.70
(1) 19		
HOLISM	2.5	.70
(1) 01		
IDENTIFIABILITY	2.5	.70
(1) 43		
IDENTIFICATION METHOD OF POLITICAL	2.5	.52
LEARNING		
(1) 15		
IMPERATIVES	2.5	.70
(1) 43		
INCONGRUITY	2.5	.52
(1) 43		
INDIVIDUATION	2.5	.70
(1) 43		
INFALLIBILITY	2.5	.70
(1) 35		
INFORMATION COST	2.5	.70
(1) 02		
INSANITY	2.5	.70
(2) 25 30		
INSECURITY	2.5	.70
(2) 06 30		
INSTINCTS	2.5	.70
(2) 22 30		
INTEGRAL NATIONALISM	2.5	.70
(2) 20 22		
INTELLECTUALISM	2.5	.84
(2) 03 24		
INTER-GENERATION	2.5	.70
(1) 24		
INTERNAL FACTORS	2.5	.84
(1) 36		
INTERPELLATE	2.5	.70
(3) 16 17 33		
INTERPERSONAL COMMUNICATION	2.5	.70
(1) 25		
INTIMACY	2.5	.70
(1) 30		
INVALIDATION	2.5	.70
(2) 17 44		
IRRATIONALISM	2.5	.70
(2) 03 26		
ISOMORPHISM	2.5	.52
(1) 01		
KINSHIP	2.5	.70
(3) 15 24 25		
KNOWING	2.5	.84
(1) 43		
LABORATORY TRAINING	2.5	.84
(1) 04		
LEFT DEVIATIONISM	2.5	.52
(1) 17		
LOVE OF LIBERTY	2.5	.70
(1) 17		
MACHTPOLITIK (POWER POLITICS)	2.5	.70
(1) 22		
MASOCHISM	2.5	.70
(1) 22		
MATHEMATICAL METHODS	2.5	.70
(3) 23 24 36		

MENTAL HEALTH	2.5	.70
(3) 07 11 18		
META-CONCEPTS	2.5	.84
(1) 04		
METAETHICS	2.5	.70
(1) 43		
METHOD	2.5	.70
(3) 11 13 24		
MODEL STUDIES	2.5	.70
(1) 36		
MODERNITY	2.5	.52
(1) 24		
MONISM	2.5	.70
(4) 03 19 22 33		
MONOLITH	2.5	.52
(1) 24		
MOTIVATION, MOTIVES	2.5	.70
(5) 13 19 24 30 33		
MULTILINGUAL	2.5	.70
(1) 30		
MUNICIPAL SOCIALISM	2.5	.52
(2) 06 19		
NATIONAL REGIONALISM	2.5	.70
(1) 18		
NATURE	2.5	.70
(5) 11 24 26 30 43		
NEO-MERCANTILISM	2.5	.70
(2) 16 20		
NEO-MILITARISM	2.5	.52
(1) 24		
OBSERVER-MODEL	2.5	.70
(1) 30		
OEDIPUS COMPLEX	2.5	.52
(1) 22		
ONTOLOGICAL PROOF	2.5	.70
(1) 43		
OPERATIONAL TEST IN POLITICS	2.5	.84
(1) 08		
ORDER, THEORY OF	2.5	.84
(1) 23		
ORDERING	2.5	.70
(2) 13 33		
PAN-GERMANISM	2.5	.52
(3) 16 17 22		
PANTHEISM	2.5	.52
(1) 43		
PAYOFF FUNCTION	2.5	.84
(1) 02		
PENOLOGY	2.5	.70
(1) 07		
PERCEIVING	2.5	.52
(1) 43		
PERCENTAGE	2.5	.70
(1) 17		
PERSONALISMO	2.5	.52
(5) 03 11 19 20 22		
PERSONNEL RESEARCH	2.5	.70
(1) 37		
PHILOSOPHICO-LEGAL METHOD	2.5	.70
(1) 19		
POLITICAL ACRONYMS	2.5	.52
(1) 39		

POLITICAL INVECTIVE	2.5	.52
(1) 39		
POLITICAL MEMORY	2.5	.70
(1) 15		
POLITICO-JURIDICAL THEORY	2.5	.52
(1) 04		
PRE-SOCRATIC PHILOSOPHY	2.5	.52
(1) 35		
PREDICATION	2.5	.84
(1) 43		
PRESIDENTIAL BUG	2.5	.70
(1) 39		
PRIMARY POLITICAL LOYALTIES	2.5	.52
(1) 15		
PROFESSIONALIZATION	2.5	.52
(1) 24		
PROJECTION, AND SIMULATION	2.5	.52
(1) 04		
PROJECTIVE METHODS	2.5	.52
(1) 01		
PROOF-THEORY	2.5	.84
(1) 43		
PROPOSITIONAL LOGIC	2.5	.70
(1) 43		
PROTOTYPE	2.5	.70
(1) 45		
PSYCHOPATHY	2.5	.52
(1) 43		
PUBLIC GOODS	2.5	.70
(1) 11		
PUBLIC WEAL	2.5	.70
(1) 17		
RECTITUDE	2.5	.52
(1) 24		
REDISTRIBUTION	2.5	.52
(1) 33		
REFERENCE POINTS	2.5	.52
(1) 15		
REGIMENTATION	2.5	.52
(1) 45		
RELIGION	2.5	.84
(11) 03 05 07 10 11 19 22 23 24 26 30		
RENT, CLASSIC THEORY OF	2.5	.70
(1) 26		
REVERENCE FOR LIFE	2.5	.70
(1) 22		
SADISM	2.5	.70
(1) 22		
SALIENCY	2.5	.70
(2) 24 33		
SCHIZOPHRENIA	2.5	.70
(1) 30		
SECONDARY RELATIONSHIPS	2.5	.70
(1) 15		
SECTARIANISM	2.5	.70
(2) 17 24		
SECULAR	2.5	.70
(1) 30		
SELF-DECEPTION	2.5	.70
(1) 43		
SEPARATISM	2.5	.52
(5) 03 16 17 30 33		

SIGNIFICANT OTHER	2.5	.70	ANGLOPHOBIA	2.6	.51
(1) 15			(2) 06 16		
SKEPTICISM	2.5	.70	ANTHROPOLOGIST	2.6	.69
(2) 22 26			(2) 22 30		
SLOGAN	2.5	.70	ANTI-JAPANESE	2.6	.69
(2) 16 17			(1) 30		
SOCIAL ADJUSTMENT	2.5	.84	ANTI-NEGRO	2.6	.69
(2) 15 25			(1) 30		
SOCIAL CONVENTION	2.5	.70	ANTIPOSITIVISM	2.6	.51
(1) 06			(1) 43		
SOCIAL ECONOMY	2.5	.70	APHORISM	2.6	.69
(1) 19			(1) 43		
SOCIAL LEARNING	2.5	.84	ASCETICISM	2.6	.69
(1) 15			(1) 22		
SOCIOLOGICO-JURIDICAL METHOD	2.5	.52	ASSERTION	2.6	.69
(1) 19			(1) 43		
SOCIOLOGY, HISTORICAL	2.5	.70	ASTRONAUTICS	2.6	.51
(1) 04			(1) 03		
SPAN OF CONTROL	2.5	.70	BEING	2.6	.69
(1) 18			(1) 43		
SPECIALIZATION	2.5	.70	BELLICOSE	2.6	.69
(1) 45			(1) 17		
STATE-ISM	2.5	.52	BILINGUALISM	2.6	.69
(1) 45			(1) 43		
STRATA	2.5	.70	BIOLOGY	2.6	.69
(1) 24			(1) 43		
SYNDROME	2.5	.84	BOOLEAN ALGEBRA	2.6	.69
(1) 30			(1) 43		
TESTS FOR FACTUAL KNOWLEDGE	2.5	.52	BRAINSTORMING	2.6	.69
(1) 25			(1) 37		
THEME	2.5	.70	CATHOLIC-LIBERAL UNIONISM	2.6	.51
(2) 24 30			(1) 19		
THERAPY	2.5	.70	CHILD REARING PRACTICES	2.6	.51
(1) 30			(1) 15		
THRESHOLD	2.5	.70	CHRISTIAN TOTALITARIANISM	2.6	.51
(1) 24			(1) 22		
TRANSCENDENTAL	2.5	.70	CLIENTELISM	2.6	.69
(1) 43			(1) 11		
TSARISM	2.5	.52	CLINICAL METHOD	2.6	.69
(1) 17			(2) 19 30		
UNCERTAINTY PRINCIPLE	2.5	.70	COLLECTIVE DECISION RULE	2.6	.51
(3) 02 24 43			(1) 02		
UNIFUNCTIONALISM	2.5	.70	COLONELISM	2.6	.69
(1) 04			(1) 03		
VITAL STATISTICS	2.5	.70	COMBINATORY-LOGIC	2.6	.69
(2) 06 16			(1) 43		
VOLUNTARISM	2.5	.70	COMPATIBILITY	2.6	.69
(1) 43			(1) 17		
WEBERIAN	2.5	.70	CONCENTRATION, THEORY OF	2.6	.51
(1) 24			(1) 38		
WORLD DATA	2.5	.84	CONCESSION THEORY	2.6	.69
(1) 36			(1) 06		
ADMINISTRATIVE ETHICS	2.6	.69	CONFIDENCE	2.6	.51
(1) 12			(1) 30		
AGGRESSIVENESS	2.6	.69	CONSERVATIVE COLLECTIVISM	2.6	.51
(1) 35			(1) 22		
ALGORITHM	2.6	.84	CONSISTENCY	2.6	.69
(1) 43			(2) 24 30		
AMBIGUITY	2.6	.51	CONTINUING ASSESSMENT	2.6	.51
(1) 43			(1) 16		
ANCIENT	2.6	.69	CONTRADICTION	2.6	.51
(1) 43			(1) 43		

CONTROL	2.6	.51
(4) 17 24 25 30		
CRITIQUE	2.6	.51
(2) 24 30		
CROWISM	2.6	.69
(1) 30		
DETECTION METHODS	2.6	.51
(1) 36		
DEVELOPMENTAL PROFILE	2.6	.51
(1) 15		
DIFFERENTIATION	2.6	.51
(2) 24 30		
DISCOURSE, LEVELS OF	2.6	.69
(1) 13		
DISPLACEMENT	2.6	.69
(1) 30		
DOMINATION	2.6	.51
(3) 06 24 25		
DUALISM	2.6	.69
(2) 17 19		
ECONOMETRICS	2.6	.51
(1) 25		
ECONOMIC MATURITY	2.6	.51
(1) 29		
ECONOMIC SCIENCE	2.6	.69
(1) 26		
EDUCATION	2.6	.69
(13) 02 06 07 11 15 19 22 23 24 25		
26 27 30		
ELECTORAL EQUILIBRIUM	2.6	.69
(1) 11		
ESCHATOLOGY	2.6	.51
(1) 43		
ETHNOHISTORICAL	2.6	.51
(1) 24		
EVIL	2.6	.69
(1) 43		
EXPECTATION	2.6	.69
(1) 43		
FALSE	2.6	.84
(1) 43		
FALSIFY	2.6	.69
(1) 17		
FORECAST	2.6	.69
(4) 01 11 23 30		
FORMALISM	2.6	.51
(1) 43		
FRICTION	2.6	.69
(2) 17 30		
GENETIC SERIES	2.6	.69
(1) 25		
GEOMETRY	2.6	.69
(1) 43		
GRAMMAR	2.6	.84
(1) 11		
GUILD SOCIALISM	2.6	.51
(6) 06 10 16 21 22 33		
HABITS	2.6	.69
(1) 30		
HAPPINESS	2.6	.69
(1) 43		
HUMOR	2.6	.69
(1) 30		
HUMOR, SELF-DEPRECATING	2.6	.69
(1) 39		
HYLOMORPHISM	2.6	.69
(1) 43		
HYPNOSIS	2.6	.69
(1) 30		
IDEOLOGICAL PSYCHOLOGY	2.6	.51
(1) 19		
IGNORANCE	2.6	.69
(1) 43		
ILLUSION	2.6	.51
(2) 24 30		
IMPORTANCE	2.6	.69
(1) 43		
INCARNATION	2.6	.69
(1) 43		
INDIAN STUDIES	2.6	.69
(1) 07		
INDIFFERENCE	2.6	.69
(1) 30		
INDUSTRIAL PSYCHOLOGY	2.6	.69
(1) 37		
INFINITE	2.6	.69
(1) 43		
INFINITE REGRESS	2.6	.51
(1) 43		
INFINITY	2.6	.69
(1) 43		
INFORMATION AND MANAGEMENT	2.6	.69
SCIENCE		
(1) 04		
INHIBITIONS	2.6	.69
(1) 30		
INTENTION	2.6	.69
(1) 43		
INTER-GROUP	2.6	.69
(2) 24 30		
INTERCODER RELIABILITY INDEX	2.6	.69
(1) 01		
INTERNATIONAL ETHICS	2.6	.51
(3) 16 17 19		
INTERROGATIVE LOGIC	2.6	.51
(1) 43		
INTIMIDATION	2.6	.51
(1) 06		
INTRINSIC	2.6	.69
(1) 43		
INVARIANCE	2.6	.69
(1) 43		
IRONY	2.6	.69
(1) 43		
IRRECONCILABLE	2.6	.69
(3) 06 16 29		
IRRELEVANT	2.6	.69
(1) 17		
KULTUR	2.6	.69
(1) 16		
KULTURKAMPF	2.6	.69
(2) 17 22		
LADDER OF VALUES	2.6	.51
(1) 33		
LATENT THEORY, ERA OF	2.6	.69
(1) 04		

LAW OF CONTRADICTION	2.6	.69
(2) 24 26		
LAW OF DIMINISHING ADMINISTRATIVE	2.6	.69
RETURNS		
(1) 03		
LENINIST NORMS	2.6	.51
(1) 34		
LIBIDO	2.6	.51
(1) 22		
LUTHERANISM	2.6	.51
(2) 17 22		
MATURING	2.6	.69
(1) 24		
METALOGIC	2.6	.69
(1) 43		
METAPHILOSOPHY	2.6	.69
(1) 43		
MIND	2.6	.69
(2) 24 30		
MISCALCULATION	2.6	.69
(1) 39		
MODAL LOGIC	2.6	.69
(1) 43		
MODALITY	2.6	.84
(1) 43		
MODERN	2.6	.69
(2) 24 30		
MODERNISM	2.6	.51
(2) 17 24		
MOOD	2.6	.69
(1) 30		
MORBID	2.6	.69
(1) 30		
MULTIPLE	2.6	.69
(1) 24		
MYTHOLOGICAL METHOD	2.6	.69
(1) 19		
NATIONAL SYNDICALISM	2.6	.51
(1) 17		
NATURAL EXPERIMENT	2.6	.69
(1) 01		
NATURALIST CONCEPTION OF LAW	2.6	.51
(2) 19 22		
NATURALISTIC FALLACY	2.6	.84
(1) 43		
NEGATIVE	2.6	.69
(1) 43		
NEO-ORTHODOXY	2.6	.51
(1) 22		
NEO-THOMISM	2.6	.69
(2) 19 22		
NEUROSES	2.6	.51
(1) 43		
NEWTONIANISM	2.6	.69
(1) 03		
NOMENCLATURE	2.6	.69
(1) 43		
NOMOTHETIC EXPLANATION	2.6	.69
(1) 01		
NORDICISM	2.6	.51
(1) 22		
NUMBER	2.6	.69
(1) 43		
NUMERICAL DECISION RULE	2.6	.69
(1) 02		
OBJECTIVISM	2.6	.51
(1) 43		
OFFICIAL CHANNELS	2.6	.51
(1) 17		
OPPORTUNISM	2.6	.51
(3) 06 16 17		
OPTIMISM	2.6	.51
(1) 43		
ORIENTATION	2.6	.69
(2) 24 30		
PARAPSYCHOLOGY	2.6	.51
(1) 43		
PEOPLE'S CAPITALISM	2.6	.51
(1) 22		
PERMISSIVENESS	2.6	.69
(1) 30		
PERSONAL STATEMENT	2.6	.69
(1) 17		
PHILOSOPHICAL METHOD	2.6	.51
(1) 19		
PLEASURE	2.6	.69
(1) 43		
POLITICAL THEOLOGY	2.6	.51
(1) 11		
POSTWAR	2.6	.51
(1) 24		
PREDICATE-LOGIC	2.6	.69
(1) 43		
PRESIDENTIAL FEVER	2.6	.51
(1) 29		
PRESUPPOSITION	2.6	.51
(1) 43		
PRIMARY SOURCE OF LAW	2.6	.51
(1) 44		
PRISMATIC	2.6	.51
(1) 24		
PROPENSITIES	2.6	.51
(1) 24		
PROPORTION	2.6	.51
(1) 43		
PSYCHO-SOCIOLOGICAL METHOD	2.6	.69
(1) 19		
PSYCHODYNAMICS	2.6	.51
(1) 30		
PSYCHOLOGICAL DOCTRINES	2.6	.69
(1) 10		
PSYCHOSOCIAL	2.6	.51
(1) 30		
PSYCHOTHERAPY	2.6	.51
(1) 30		
PURE THEORY OF LAW	2.6	.51
(2) 03 22		
QUANTITATIVE SEMANTICS	2.6	.51
(1) 19		
QUANTUM THEORY	2.6	.51
(1) 43		
RACIAL FACTORS	2.6	.51
(1) 36		
RATIONAL FACTORS	2.6	.69
(1) 36		

RE-EDUCATION 2.6 .51
(1) 17
RECORDING OF DIRECT OBSERVATIONS 2.6 .51
(1) 25
RECORDING OF INTERVIEWS 2.6 .51
(1) 25
REGIONAL STUDIES 2.6 .51
(1) 33
REHABILITATION 2.6 .51
(5) 06 16 24 25 30
RELEVANCE 2.6 .69
(1) 24
REPUTATION 2.6 .51
(1) 24
ROUTINIZATION 2.6 .69
(1) 24
SELF-KNOWLEDGE 2.6 .51
(1) 43
SEMANTIC DIFFERENTIAL 2.6 .51
(2) 01 33
SENSE 2.6 .69
(1) 43
SENSE DATA 2.6 .51
(1) 43
SEQUENTIAL DEVELOPMENT 2.6 .51
(1) 15
SEXUAL BEHAVIOR 2.6 .51
(1) 11
SIMPLICITY 2.6 .69
(1) 43
SKILL 2.6 .69
(1) 43
SOCIAL 2.6 .51
(1) 43
SOCIAL ANTHROPOLOGY 2.6 .51
(1) 15
SOCIAL PHILOSOPHY 2.6 .51
(1) 19
SOCIOMETRY 2.6 .69
(1) 01
SOLIPSISM 2.6 .51
(1) 43
SPECULATIVE 2.6 .51
(1) 43
STATUS INCONSISTENCY 2.6 .69
(1) 11
STRESS 2.6 .69
(3) 24 30 33
SUBJECTIVISM 2.6 .51
(1) 43
SYNTHETIC CONCEPT 2.6 .69
(2) 03 19
TECHNOSTRUCTURE 2.6 .69
(1) 25
TENDENCY 2.6 .69
(2) 24 30
TIME FACTOR 2.6 .69
(1) 25
TRIBAL IDENTIFICATION 2.6 .51
(1) 15
TRUST 2.6 .51
(7) 02 06 16 17 18 27 32

TRUTH TABLE 2.6 .69
(1) 43
TUDOR ABSOLUTISM 2.6 .51
(1) 26
UNCONSCIOUS 2.6 .69
(2) 26 30
UNIDIMENSIONALISM 2.6 .69
(1) 24
UNITARY DEMOCRACIES 2.6 .51
(1) 08
UNIVERSAL 2.6 .69
(1) 43
UNIVERSAL SET 2.6 .69
(1) 01
UNKNOWN 2.6 .69
(1) 30
UNSTANDARDIZED INTERVIEW 2.6 .84
(1) 01
VALUATION 2.6 .69
(2) 06 18
VERB 2.6 .84
(1) 43
VIGILANTISM 2.6 .51
(1) 45
WALLOON NATIONALISM 2.6 .51
(3) 19 21 34
WAY OF LIFE 2.6 .69
(1) 03
WISDOM 2.6 .69
(2) 24 30
POLITICAL PARTIES 1.0 .00
(16) 02 03 04 07 11 12 15 17 18 19
23 25 26 27 32 33 46
HOUSE OF REPRESENTATIVES (U.S.) 1.1 .31
(11) 02 06 11 16 17 18 19 25 27 32
34
AUTOCRACY 1.2 .42
(8) 03 04 06 16 17 22 23 33
OLIGARCHY 1.2 .63
(13) 02 03 06 16 17 18 22 23 24 26
27 32 33
PARTICIPATORY DEMOCRACY 1.2 .63
(1) 32
POLITY 1.2 .63
(6) 01 03 04 16 24 33
UNITED NATIONS (UN) 1.2 .42
(19) 03 04 06 07 08 11 12 16 17 19
20 21 22 24 25 27 32 34 41 46
ARISTOCRACY 1.3 .67
(15) 03 04 06 10 16 17 18 22 24 25
26 27 30 32 33
BUREAUCRACY 1.3 .67
(19) 02 03 04 06 07 11 12 16 17 18
19 22 23 24 25 26 27 30 33
COMMUNIST PARTY 1.3 .48
(8) 11 16 17 19 22 23 25 26
DICTATORSHIP OF THE PROLETARIAT, 1.3 .48
COMMUNIST THEORY
(8) 03 10 11 16 17 19 20 22 23
ELITES 1.3 .67
(1) 36

NORTH ATLANTIC TREATY ORGANIZATION (NATO)	1.3	.48
(13) 03 07 11 12 17 18 20 22 23 25 27 32 34 46		
PARLIAMENTARY GOVERNMENT	1.3	.67
(3) 03 20 32		
PARTY	1.3	.67
(8) 06 16 17 24 26 27 30 33		
POLITICAL INSTITUTIONS	1.3	.48
(2) 15 19		
COALITION	1.4	.51
(11) 02 06 11 16 17 18 24 29 30 32 33		
COALITION GOVERNMENT	1.4	.51
(4) 03 16 17 20		
CONGRESS (U.S.)	1.4	.69
(15) 04 06 07 11 16 17 19 20 22 24 25 27 30 32 34		
CONSTITUTIONAL GOVERNMENT	1.4	.51
(2) 17 22		
FEDERAL SYSTEM	1.4	.69
(1) 17		
HOUSE OF COMMONS, BRITAIN	1.4	.69
(9) 03 06 11 16 17 20 22 25 34		
LEAGUE OF NATIONS (LN)	1.4	.51
(2) 17 34 46		
MAJORITY PARTY	1.4	.69
(1) 17		
MASS MEDIA	1.4	.69
(10) 02 03 07 11 15 18 20 25 27 33		
MASS SOCIETY	1.4	.69
(2) 23 33		
MEDIA	1.4	.69
(3) 03 24 30		
MULTINATIONAL CORPORATIONS (MNC)	1.4	.51
(3) 11 23 25		
PARLIAMENT	1.4	.69
(13) 03 07 09 11 16 19 20 22 23 24 25 26 27		
POLITICAL COMMUNITY	1.4	.69
(7) 01 03 11 12 15 20 33		
POLITICAL ELITE	1.4	.84
(3) 11 15 33		
POWER ELITE	1.4	.51
(2) 01 22		
PRESIDENCY	1.4	.69
(7) 07 16 17 19 24 25 27		
PRESSURE GROUP	1.4	.69
(15) 01 02 03 04 06 11 16 17 18 19 23 25 27 32 33		
REPUBLICAN FORM OF GOVERNMENT	1.4	.51
(3) 03 06 18		
REPUBLICAN PARTY	1.4	.51
(12) 02 04 06 08 16 18 19 22 25 27 32 34 46		
BOURGEOISIE	1.5	.52
(6) 03 06 16 17 24 30		
CHINESE COMMUNIST PARTY (CCP)	1.5	.52
(2) 20 34		
COMMUNIST PARTY, SOVIET UNION (CPSU)	1.5	.52
(3) 20 24 34		
CONGRESSIONAL COMMITTEES	1.5	.52
(3) 16 32 34 46		
DEMOCRATIC PARTY	1.5	.70
(14) 02 03 04 06 08 11 16 18 19 22 25 27 32 34 46		
EXECUTIVE BRANCH	1.5	.70
(3) 02 27 32		
EXECUTIVE OFFICE OF THE PRESIDENT	1.5	.70
(7) 06 16 18 20 27 32 34		
GRAND JURY	1.5	.52
(8) 02 03 06 16 18 25 27 32		
INTERNATIONAL ORGANIZATION	1.5	.52
(9) 07 11 12 16 19 20 23 25 32		
JUDICIAL BRANCH	1.5	.70
(1) 32		
LIMITED GOVERNMENT	1.5	.70
(3) 03 18 32		
LOCAL GOVERNMENT	1.5	.70
(12) 03 06 07 11 12 16 17 19 23 25 32 33		
MAJORITY	1.5	.84
(10) 06 16 17 24 25 26 27 30 32 33		
MAJORITY GOVERNMENT	1.5	.70
(1) 17		
MASS PUBLIC, PUBLIC OPINION	1.5	.70
(1) 20		
MIDDLE CLASS	1.5	.70
(6) 11 16 17 23 26 30		
MILITARY DICTATORSHIP	1.5	.70
(1) 17		
MILITARY-INDUSTRIAL COMPLEX	1.5	.52
(2) 25 32		
MODERNIZING SOCIETIES	1.5	.70
(3) 04 15 24		
MONOPOLY	1.5	.52
(8) 03 06 16 18 22 25 27 29 46		
NATION	1.5	.84
(13) 03 06 11 15 16 17 18 19 20 23 24 30 33		
NEW LEFT	1.5	.52
(3) 11 25 34		
ONE-PARTY RULE	1.5	.70
(1) 39		
ONE-PARTY STATE	1.5	.70
(1) 17		
PEER GROUP	1.5	.70
(1) 33		
PLURALISTIC SOCIETY	1.5	.70
(1) 27		
POLITICAL GROUPS	1.5	.70
(4) 08 11 12 33		
POLITICAL ORGANIZATIONS	1.5	.70
(1) 15		
POLITICAL SCIENCE, THE PROFESSION	1.5	.70
(1) 07		
POLITICAL SUBCULTURES	1.5	.70
(1) 15		
PRESIDENTIAL GOVERNMENT	1.5	.52
(5) 03 06 16 18 32		
PRIMARY GROUP	1.5	.70
(4) 01 02 15 33		
REPRESENTATIVE DEMOCRACY	1.5	.84
(1) 17		

REPRESENTATIVE GOVERNMENT 1.5 .84
   (8) 06 11 16 18 20 22 27 32
THIRD PARTIES 1.5 .70
   (6) 02 06 16 18 27 29 46
U.N. GENERAL ASSEMBLY 1.5 .52
   (3) 03 18 20
U.S. SUPREME COURT 1.5 .70
   (1) 42
WAYS AND MEANS COMMITTEE 1.5 .52
   (5) 06 16 18 27 32
ABSOLUTE MONARCHY 1.6 .51
   (2) 16 17
AMERICAN POLITICAL SCIENCE 1.6 .51
   ASSOCIATION (APSA)
   (6) 05 06 11 16 19 32
BOLSHEVIKS 1.6 .51
   (7) 10 16 17 22 24 25 34
BRANCHES OF GOVERNMENT 1.6 .84
   (1) 16
CABINET GOVERNMENT 1.6 .96
   (4) 03 11 16 33
CITY COUNCIL 1.6 .51
   (5) 03 17 18 27 32
CLASS 1.6 .69
   (8) 01 03 06 19 23 24 26 30
CLASSLESS SOCIETY 1.6 .51
   (4) 17 22 24 26
COMMONS, HOUSE OF 1.6 .69
   (1) 22
CONFEDERATION 1.6 .69
   (10) 02 03 06 16 17 18 20 21 27 33
CONSTITUENCY 1.6 .69
   (1) 04
CONSTITUTIONAL MONARCHY 1.6 .69
   (3) 17 18 20
COURTS, FEDERAL 1.6 .69
   (1) 42
DEPARTMENT OF STATE (U.S.) 1.6 .51
   (1) 20 32
DICTATORSHIP 1.6 .69
   (16) 03 06 08 10 11 12 16 17 19 20
   22 23 24 26 27 33
ELECTORATE 1.6 .84
   (8) 02 03 06 16 17 24 27 30
EUROPEAN ECONOMIC COMMUNITY 1.6 .69
   (EEC)
   (10) 03 07 11 17 20 23 24 25 27 34
FEDERAL DISTRICT COURTS 1.6 .69
   (1) 16
GOVERNMENT 1.6 .96
   (15) 03 04 06 08 11 12 16 17 18 19
   20 24 26 30 33
GREAT POWERS 1.6 .69
   (2) 16 17
INTERESTS 1.6 .84
   (1) 01
LABOR UNION 1.6 .69
   (2) 45 46
MARXISTS 1.6 .69
   (4) 17 22 24 25
MILITARY IN LATIN AMERICAN POLITICS 1.6 .51
   (1) 03

MINORITY 1.6 .69
   (8) 02 06 16 17 30 33 44 45
MINORITY PARTY 1.6 .69
   (2) 16 17
MONARCHY 1.6 .51
   (15) 03 04 06 10 11 16 17 18 20 22
   23 24 26 27 33
MULTI-NATIONAL STATE 1.6 .51
   (2) 16 17
MUNICIPAL GOVERNMENT 1.6 .69
   (5) 03 04 12 19 32
NATIONS 1.6 .96
   (1) 36
OPINION ELITES, PUBLIC OPINION 1.6 .69
   (1) 20
POPULISTS 1.6 .69
   (1) 39 45 46
POST-INDUSTRIAL SOCIETY 1.6 .69
   (1) 11
PRESIDENT « CONGRESS 1.6 .69
   (9) 04 06 11 16 17 18 20 24 30
PUBLIC 1.6 .84
   (3) 16 24 30
REFERENCE GROUP 1.6 .69
   (4) 01 02 15 25
SECONDARY GROUP 1.6 .69
   (3) 01 15 33
SECURITY COUNCIL OF THE UNITED 1.6 .69
   NATIONS
   (1) 38
STATE 1.6 .84
   (17) 03 06 08 10 11 12 16 17 18 19
   20 23 24 25 26 30 33
SUPREME COURT OF THE UNITED 1.6 .69
   STATES
   (12) 04 06 07 11 16 18 19 22 25 27
   32 34
U.N. SECRETARIAT 1.6 .51
   (5) 03 17 18 20 32
U.N. SECURITY COUNCIL 1.6 .69
   (3) 03 20 25
UNICAMERAL LEGISLATURE 1.6 .69
   (2) 17 27
UNITARY STATE 1.6 .69
   (6) 03 06 17 18 27 33
ABSOLUTE MAJORITY 1.7 .67
   (7) 06 16 17 18 27 32 33
ALLIANCE 1.7 .67
   (13) 02 03 06 07 11 16 17 18 20 23
   24 27 33
ALLIANCE FOR PROGRESS (1961) 1.7 .48
   (11) 03 07 11 17 18 20 25 27 32 34
   46
AMERICAN FEDERATION OF LABOR 1.7 .48
   (4) 06 16 38 46
CABINET 1.7 .82
   (1) 06
CENTRALIZED GOVERNMENT 1.7 .82
   (1) 39
CHINA, PRC (POLITICAL SYSTEM) 1.7 .48
   (3) 03 20 34
CITY-MANAGER GOVERNMENT 1.7 .67
   (1) 42

CIVIL RIGHTS MOVEMENT	1.7	.67
(2) 32 34		
CIVIL RIGHTS MOVEMENT	1.7	.82
(2) 32 34		
COLONIAL GOVERNMENTS	1.7	.67
(1) 19 46		
COMMITTEE OF CONGRESS	1.7	.82
(1) 45		
COMMITTEE OF WAYS AND MEANS	1.7	.67
(2) 03 17		
COMMITTEE ON RULES	1.7	.67
(5) 03 06 16 18 27 28		
COMMON MARKET	1.7	.67
(9) 03 07 17 18 20 23 25 27 34		
COMMUNICATION MEDIA	1.7	.67
(1) 15		
COMMUNITY	1.7	.82
(7) 01 04 17 24 26 30 33		
COUNTER-CULTURE	1.7	.67
(2) 11 25		
DELEGATION	1.7	.67
(7) 06 16 17 24 27 33 37		
DELIBERATIVE BODY	1.7	.82
(1) 16		
DEPARTMENT OF DEFENSE (U.S.) (DOD)	1.7	.67
(1) 20 32		
DEPARTMENT OF JUSTICE	1.7	.67
(1) 08		
DEVELOPING NATIONS	1.7	.67
(6) 04 07 11 15 17 24		
EUROPEAN COMMON MARKET	1.7	.67
(1) 23		
EXECUTIVE DEPARTMENT	1.7	.82
(4) 06 16 19 32		
FEDERAL COURTS	1.7	.94
(1) 42		
FEDERAL COURTS OF APPEALS	1.7	.67
(1) 42		
FEDERAL GOVERNMENT	1.7	.82
(4) 08 17 20 27		
FEDERAL RESERVE SYSTEM	1.7	.67
(8) 06 07 16 18 22 27 32 34 46		
FREE WORLD	1.7	.48
(2) 03 17		
GENERAL ASSEMBLY (UN)	1.7	.67
(1) 41		
GRAND OLD PARTY (GOP)	1.7	.67
(6) 06 16 17 27 29 34		
GREEK CITY-STATES	1.7	.67
(1) 08		
GROUPS AND ORGANIZATIONS	1.7	.82
(1) 19		
HAVE AND HAVE-NOT NATIONS	1.7	.82
(1) 39		
HOUSE UN-AMERICAN ACTIVITIES COMMITTEE (HUAC; ALSO DIES COMMITTEE)	1.7	.67
(1) 13 26 32 42 45		
INSTITUTION	1.7	.82
(6) 01 13 24 29 30 33		
INTERNATIONAL ALLIANCES	1.7	.94
(1) 23		
INTERNATIONAL COMMUNIST MOVEMENT	1.7	.82
(1) 11		
INTERNATIONAL COMMUNITY	1.7	.67
(1) 23		
INTERNATIONAL MONETARY FUND (IMF)	1.7	.67
(13) 03 07 11 17 18 19 20 21 23 25 27 32 45		
INTERSTATE COMMERCE COMMISSION (ICC)	1.7	.48
(10) 03 06 16 17 18 19 22 25 27 32 34		
INVESTIGATING COMMITTEES OF CONGRESS	1.7	.67
(1) 45		
JUDICIARY	1.7	.94
(8) 04 06 11 16 18 24 27 33		
LEFT, THE	1.7	.67
(1) 42		
LEGISLATURE	1.7	.94
(11) 04 06 07 11 16 17 24 25 27 32 33		
LIBERAL DEMOCRAT	1.7	.67
(1) 17		
LOBBY	1.7	.82
(10) 06 16 17 23 24 27 29 32 33 34		
LOWER-CLASS	1.7	.82
(1) 30		
MAYOR-COUNCIL FORM OF GOVERNMENT	1.7	.82
(3) 03 25 32		
METROPOLITAN GOVERNMENT	1.7	.82
(1) 11		
MILITARY GOVERNMENT	1.7	.67
(1) 03		
MINORITIES, NATIONAL AND RACIAL	1.7	.82
(8) 07 11 19 21 23 24 26 30		
MINORITY GOVERNMENT	1.7	.67
(2) 11 17		
MODERN SOCIETY	1.7	.82
(2) 01 15		
MULTILATERAL	1.7	.48
(2) 16 17		
OLIGOPOLY	1.7	.82
(3) 18 22 25		
PARLIAMENT, BRITISH	1.7	.82
(1) 22		
PARLIAMENTARY REGIME	1.7	.82
(1) 17		
PARTY CONVENTION	1.7	.67
(2) 06 17		
PEACE CORPS (U.S.)	1.7	.48
(8) 03 17 18 20 25 27 32 34 46		
POLITICAL MOVEMENTS	1.7	.67
(2) 11 25		
POLITICAL ORDER	1.7	.67
(1) 11		
PROGRESSIVE MOVEMENT	1.7	.67
(2) 22 25 46		
PROLETARIAT	1.7	.67
(8) 03 06 16 17 22 26 27 34		
RULING CLASS	1.7	.67
(1) 33		

SENATE OF THE UNITED STATES	1.7	.82
(14) 02 04 06 11 16 17 18 19 22 24 25 27 32 34		
SOCIAL CLASS	1.7	.82
(6) 01 11 15 23 26 33		
SOCIALIST PARTY	1.7	.48
(1) 42 46		
SOVEREIGN STATE	1.7	.67
(1) 17		
SOVIET BLOC	1.7	.48
(1) 36		
STATE AND LOCAL GOVERNMENT	1.7	.67
(1) 12		
SUPERPOWER	1.7	.48
(1) 16		
THIRD REICH	1.7	.48
(4) 16 17 22 34 46		
TOTALITARIAN GOVERNMENT	1.7	.82
(1) 44		
TOTALITARIAN STATE	1.7	.82
(7) 06 08 10 16 17 24 27		
UNDERDEVELOPED COUNTRIES	1.7	.48
(4) 04 12 23 26		
UNITARY GOVERNMENT	1.7	.67
(2) 16 20		
UTOPIAN SOCIALISTS	1.7	.48
(2) 10 22		
VIET CONG	1.7	.48
(4) 07 24 25 34		
WELFARE STATE	1.7	.67
(12) 03 04 11 17 18 22 23 25 27 32 33 34		
WOMEN'S LIBERATION MOVEMENT	1.7	.48
(1) 32		
AFFLUENT SOCIETY	1.8	.78
(1) 39		
AMERICANS FOR DEMOCRATIC ACTION (ADA)	1.8	.42
(3) 16 32 34		
ATLANTIC COMMUNITY	1.8	.78
(2) 08 20		
AXIS	1.8	.63
(2) 34 46		
AXIS POWERS	1.8	.63
(3) 17 21 22		
BICAMERAL LEGISLATURE	1.8	.63
(6) 02 06 16 17 27 33		
BLACK MUSLIMS	1.8	.63
(3) 03 25 34		
BLACK PANTHER PARTY	1.8	.63
(1) 25		
BOURGEOIS	1.8	.42
(3) 03 17 24		
BRITISH EMPIRE	1.8	.42
(1) 16		
CABINETS, PRESIDENTIAL	1.8	.78
(1) 46		
CENTRAL INTELLIGENCE AGENCY (CIA)	1.8	.42
(9) 03 07 11 18 20 25 27 32 34 46		
COMINTERN (ALSO, COMMUNIST INTERNATIONAL)	1.8	.42
(1) 03		
COMMUNIST INTERNATIONAL (COMINTERN)	1.8	.63
(8) 03 16 21 22 23 24 26 34		
COMMUNIST PARTY (USA)	1.8	.42
(1) 45		
CONFEDERACY	1.8	.63
(1) 16 46		
CONSTITUTIONAL DEMOCRACY	1.8	.91
(1) 18		
COURT OF APPEALS	1.8	.42
(7) 04 11 17 18 25 27 32		
DE FACTO GOVERNMENT	1.8	.63
(2) 17 19		
DEPARTMENT OF HOUSING AND URBAN DEVELOPMENT (HUD)	1.8	.63
(1) 32 42		
ETHNIC GROUPS	1.8	.78
(2) 15 25		
FACTION	1.8	.78
(8) 02 06 16 17 24 25 27 33		
FOREIGN SERVICE (U.S.)	1.8	.63
(8) 03 06 16 18 20 25 27 32		
INDUSTRIAL SOCIETY	1.8	.91
(2) 26 33		
INTERNATIONAL LABOR ORGANIZATION (ILO)	1.8	.42
(14) 03 06 07 11 16 17 18 19 20 21 23 25 27 32		
IRISH REPUBLICAN ARMY (IRA)	1.8	.63
(2) 25 34		
JURY	1.8	.78
(10) 02 03 04 06 16 18 25 26 27 30		
LABOR PARTY	1.8	.63
(8) 11 16 17 19 20 22 25 34		
LEFT AND RIGHT	1.8	.78
(1) 34		
LEFT WING	1.8	.78
(2) 26 27		
LEGISLATIVE BRANCH	1.8	.91
(2) 27 32		
LEGISLATIVE COMMITTEE	1.8	.78
(1) 16		
LIMITED MONARCHY	1.8	.78
(1) 42		
LOWER CHAMBER	1.8	.42
(3) 16 17 27		
LOWER MIDDLE CLASS	1.8	.78
(1) 17		
MENSHEVIKS	1.8	.42
(7) 10 16 17 22 25 26 34		
MERITOCRACY	1.8	.63
(1) 24		
MILITARY JUNTA	1.8	.63
(1) 17		
MIXED ECONOMY	1.8	.63
(3) 18 19 20		
MODEL CITIES	1.8	.42
(1) 32		
MODERN POLITICAL PARTIES	1.8	.63
(1) 04		
NAZI MOVEMENT	1.8	.78
(1) 25		

OPEN SOCIETY	1.8	.63
(1) 39		
ORGANIZED INTEREST	1.8	.78
(1) 02		
ORGANIZED LABOR	1.8	.63
(2) 03 32		
PALESTINE LIBERATION ORGANIZATION	1.8	.42
(PLO)		
(1) 34		
PARTY ORGANIZATION	1.8	.63
(1) 42		
PATRIARCHY	1.8	.42
(1) 16		
PEOPLE'S DEMOCRACIES	1.8	.78
(1) 23		
PEOPLE'S DEMOCRACY	1.8	.78
(4) 03 17 23 34		
PEOPLE'S REPUBLIC OF CHINA (PRC)	1.8	.63
(2) 03 17		
PLURALITY	1.8	.78
(7) 02 06 16 18 27 32 33		
POLICE STATE	1.8	.78
(2) 16 17		
POLITICAL MACHINE	1.8	.63
3) 03 18 32 46		
POLITICAL OPPOSITION	1.8	.63
(2) 11 23		
POLITICAL REFERENCE GROUP	1.8	.63
(1) 15		
POLITIES	1.8	.91
(1) 24		
POPULAR GOVERNMENT	1.8	.78
(1) 08		
POPULIST MOVEMENT	1.8	.63
(1) 22		
PRIMITIVE SOCIETIES	1.8	.63
(3) 15 24 30		
RADICAL RIGHT	1.8	.42
(1) 25		
REGULATORY AGENCIES	1.8	.78
(3) 07 11 32		
REPUBLIC	1.8	.91
(12) 03 04 06 16 17 18 19 20 24 27		
32 33		
REPUBLICAN	1.8	.78
(4) 16 17 24 29		
REVOLUTIONARY MOVEMENT	1.8	.78
(1) 11		
SECRETARIAT OF THE UNITED NATIONS	1.8	.63
(1) 17		
SENATE	1.8	.78
(1) 38		
SIMPLE MAJORITY	1.8	.42
(4) 02 17 27 32		
SOCIAL DEMOCRACY	1.8	.91
(2) 17 29		
SOCIAL DEMOCRATS	1.8	.63
(1) 17		
SOUTHEAST ASIA TREATY	1.8	.42
ORGANIZATION (SEATO)		
(8) 03 17 18 20 25 27 32 34 38 46		
TRADITIONAL SOCIETY	1.8	.78
(3) 01 15 20		

U.S. AGENCY FOR INTERNATIONAL	1.8	.42
DEVELOPMENT (AID)		
(1) 34		
VIET MINH	1.8	.42
(5) 03 21 24 25 34		
VIETNAM, REPUBLIC OF (SOUTH	1.8	.63
VIETNAM)		
(3) 03 07 11		
WHIG PARTY	1.8	.63
(6) 06 18 19 25 27 32 46		
WORLD COMMUNITY	1.8	.78
(1) 35		
WORLD GOVERNMENT	1.8	.63
(4) 03 17 20 25		
ADMINISTRATIVE ORGANIZATION	1.9	.87
(1) 12		
ADMINISTRATIVE TRIBUNAL	1.9	.73
(2) 03 33		
AGENCY FOR INTERNATIONAL	1.9	.56
DEVELOPMENT (AID)		
(1) 32		
ALLIES	1.9	.73
(3) 16 22 24		
AMERICAN CIVIL LIBERTIES UNION	1.9	.56
(ACLU)		
(5) 03 16 25 32 34		
ANTIFEDERALISTS	1.9	.56
(1) 45		
APPEALS COURTS	1.9	.73
(2) 04 32		
APPELLATE COURT	1.9	.56
(3) 02 27 32		
APPELLATE COURT SYSTEM	1.9	.56
(1) 25		
APPROPRIATIONS COMMITTEE	1.9	.87
(1) 32		
ASSOCIATIONAL GROUP	1.9	.73
(1) 01		
ATOMIC ENERGY COMMISSION (AEC)	1.9	.56
(2) 32 46		
ATTENTIVE PUBLIC	1.9	.87
(1) 18		
BALANCED TICKET	1.9	.73
(1) 02		
BOARD OF COUNTY SUPERVISORS	1.9	.87
(1) 42		
BODY POLITIC	1.9	.56
(1) 16		
BRITISH CABINET	1.9	.73
(1) 22		
BRITISH LABOR PARTY	1.9	.31
(4) 03 10 22 26		
BUREAU OF THE BUDGET (U.S.)	1.9	.56
(10) 03 06 11 16 19 25 27 32 34 45		
CENTER PARTIES	1.9	.56
(3) 03 11 22		
CHINA, REPUBLIC OF	1.9	.73
(1) 03		
CIRCUIT COURT OF APPEALS	1.9	.56
(2) 06 16		
CITY-STATES, GREEK	1.9	.56
(5) 08 16 17 26 32		

CLOSED (AND OPEN) SHOP	1.9	.31
(2) 06 29		
COLLECTIVE	1.9	.73
(2) 24 30		
COLLECTIVE FARM	1.9	.56
(2) 16 20		
COMMITTEE OF THE WHOLE HOUSE	1.9	.73
(8) 02 03 06 16 17 18 27 32		
COMMITTEE ON COMMITTEES	1.9	.73
(3) 03 32 34		
COMMUNES, CHINA (PRC)	1.9	.56
(1) 20		
CONGRESSIONAL CAUCUS	1.9	.56
(1) 06		
CONGRESSIONAL GOVERNMENT	1.9	.73
(2) 04 08		
CONSERVATIVE PARTY	1.9	.56
(1) 03		
CONSTITUTIONAL MAJORITY	1.9	.73
(1) 27		
CONTINENTAL CONGRESS	1.9	.56
(5) 02 06 16 18 32		
CONTROL GROUP	1.9	.87
(1) 01		
COURT SYSTEM	1.9	.87
(2) 25 32		
DEMOCRATIC SOCIETIES	1.9	.73
(1) 06		
DEPARTMENT OF AGRICULTURE	1.9	.56
(2) 27 32		
DEPARTMENT OF HEALTH, EDUCATION, AND WELFARE (HEW)	1.9	.56
(1) 27		
DEPARTMENT OF LABOR	1.9	.56
(1) 27		
DEPARTMENT OF THE NAVY	1.9	.56
(3) 16 17 32		
DEPARTMENT OF THE TREASURY	1.9	.56
(1) 27 32		
DEPARTMENT OF WAR (ALSO, WAR DEPARTMENT)	1.9	.56
(1) 27		
DISTRICT COURTS, FEDERAL	1.9	.56
(4) 02 03 16 18		
ECONOMY	1.9	.73
(7) 11 16 19 23 24 26 30		
ELECTORAL COLLEGE	1.9	.56
(9) 02 06 16 18 25 27 32 33 34		
EMPIRE	1.9	.99
(7) 11 16 17 24 26 30 33		
FEDERAL	1.9	.87
(5) 16 17 24 29 30		
FEDERAL BUREAU OF INVESTIGATION (FBI)	1.9	.56
(10) 03 06 07 08 16 18 22 27 32 34		
FEDERAL REPUBLIC OF GERMANY	1.9	.56
(2) 03 17		
FEDERATION	1.9	.87
(1) 33		
FIFTH COLUMN	1.9	.56
(7) 03 06 16 17 20 21 29		
FIFTH REPUBLIC OF FRANCE	1.9	.73
(4) 03 20 25 34		

FIRST CONTINENTAL CONGRESS	1.9	.56
(1) 18 46		
GOVERNMENT COALITION	1.9	.73
(2) 11 17		
GOVERNMENT ORGANIZATION	1.9	.87
(1) 32		
HETEROGENOUS SOCIETY	1.9	.87
(1) 15		
HOUSE OF REPRESENTATIVES COMMITTEES	1.9	.73
(1) 42		
INSTITUTIONAL GROUP	1.9	.87
(1) 01		
INTER-STATE COMMERCE COMMISSION	1.9	.56
(1) 38		
INTERNATIONAL COMMISSIONS	1.9	.73
(1) 11		
INTERNATIONAL POLICE FORCE, UNITED NATIONS	1.9	.73
(3) 03 17 20		
JOINT CHIEFS OF STAFF (JCS)	1.9	.56
(5) 18 20 27 32 34		
JOINT COMMITTEE	1.9	.31
(6) 02 16 17 18 27 32		
KANGAROO COURT	1.9	.31
(1) 16		
KU KLUX KLAN	1.9	.56
(10) 02 03 06 11 16 25 27 30 32 34 46		
LABOR MOVEMENT	1.9	.87
(3) 11 19 32		
LEGISLATIVE BODY	1.9	.73
(2) 17 27		
LORDS, HOUSE OF	1.9	.56
(1) 22		
LOWER HOUSE	1.9	.73
(1) 16		
LOYAL OPPOSITION	1.9	.73
(2) 02 27		
MAFIA	1.9	.56
(2) 16 25		
MASSES	1.9	.87
(2) 20 25		
MILITARY ALLIANCES	1.9	.73
(1) 36		
MINORITY GROUPS	1.9	.73
(1) 37		
MULTI-RACIAL SOCIETY	1.9	.73
(1) 17		
MUNICIPALITY	1.9	.87
(3) 16 17 27		
NATIONAL ASSOCIATION FOR THE ADVANCEMENT OF COLORED PEOPLE (NAACP)	1.9	.56
(1) 18		
NATIONAL LABOR RELATIONS BOARD (NLRB)	1.9	.56
(9) 06 07 16 18 22 24 25 27 32		
NATIONAL SECURITY COUNCIL (NSC)	1.9	.56
(7) 11 18 20 25 27 32 34		
NON-ALIGNED NATIONS	1.9	.31
(2) 07 17		

NON-SELF-GOVERNING TERRITORIES	1.9	.56
(2) 17 41		
NUCLEAR POWER	1.9	.56
(2) 17 25		
OFFICE OF ECONOMIC OPPORTUNITY (OEO)	1.9	.56
(2) 25 32		
OFFICE OF MANAGEMENT AND BUDGET (OMB)	1.9	.31
(1) 32		
OPPOSITION	1.9	.87
(8} 02 11 16 17 19 23 24 33		
ORGANIZATION	1.9	.99
(10) 01 02 03 06 11 16 18 24 30 33		
ORGANIZATION OF AMERICAN STATES (OAS)	1.9	.31
(11) 03 07 11 12 17 18 20 23 25 27 32		
ORGANIZATION OF PETROLEUM EXPORTING COUNTRIES (OPEC)	1.9	.56
(1) 38		
PALESTINIANS	1.9	.56
(1) 11		
PARTY GOVERNMENT, BRITAIN	1.9	.87
(2) 20 22		
PEACE MOVEMENT	1.9	.73
(1) 16		
PLANNED SOCIETY	1.9	.73
(1) 22		
PLUTOCRACY	1.9	.56
(5) 03 06 16 17 33		
POLITICAL ASSOCIATION	1.9	.73
(1) 08		
POSITIVISTS	1.9	.56
(1) 22		
PRAESIDIUM OF THE SUPREME SOVIET (USSR)	1.9	.56
(1) 19		
PROTECTORATE	1.9	.73
(7) 03 06 16 17 24 26 33		
PUPPET GOVERNMENT	1.9	.56
(2) 16 17		
RACE	1.9	.73
(8) 03 06 11 16 17 24 26 30		
RED GUARD, CHINA (PRC)	1.9	.56
(3) 20 22 34		
REGIONAL ORGANIZATIONS	1.9	.73
(4) 03 11 17 20		
REGULATORY COMMISSIONS	1.9	.87
(3) 02 03 16		
RESPONSIBLE GOVERNMENT	1.9	.99
(1) 16		
RIGHT WING	1.9	.56
(2) 24 27		
RIGHT-WING MOVEMENTS	1.9	.56
(1) 36		
SECOND CONTINENTAL CONGRESS	1.9	.56
(1) 18 46		
SENATE COMMITTEES	1.9	.73
(1) 42		
SOCIAL INSTITUTIONS	1.9	.73
(1) 11		

SOCIETY	1.9	.87
(7) 01 06 11 24 26 30 33		
SOLID SOUTH	1.9	.56
(6) 04 06 16 27 29 32 46		
SPECIAL INTERESTS	1.9	.73
(1) 39		
SUBCULTURE	1.9	.73
(3) 15 24 30		
SURVEY RESEARCH CENTER	1.9	.56
(1) 05		
TENNESSEE VALLEY AUTHORITY (TVA)	1.9	.31
(10) 06 16 18 19 22 24 25 27 32 34 46		
TORIES	1.9	.73
(6) 03 06 16 24 29 34		
TRANSITIONAL SOCIETY	1.9	.87
(3) 01 20 24		
U.N. EDUCATIONAL, SCIENTIFIC, AND CULTURAL ORGANIZATION (UNESCO)	1.9	.56
(1) 38		
U.N. INTERNATIONAL COURT OF JUSTICE	1.9	.31
(2) 03 18		
U.S. REGULATORY COMMISSIONS	1.9	.73
(1) 32		
UNDERGROUND MOVEMENT	1.9	.73
(3) 16 17 24		
VIETNAM, DEMOCRATIC REPUBLIC OF (NORTH VIETNAM)	1.9	.56
(3) 03 07 11		
WEIMAR REPUBLIC	1.9	.56
(4) 07 11 16 22 25		
WESTERN POWERS	1.9	.73
(3) 11 16 17		
WHIG	1.9	.73
(4) 03 16 22 29		
WORLD BANK	1.9	.56
(6) 07 16 18 25 27 32		
WORLD ORGANIZATION	1.9	.56
(1) 19		
AD HOC COMMITTEE	2.0	.66
(2) 03 17		
AFRIKANERS	2.0	.47
(1) 24		
AMERICAN COMMUNIST PARTY	2.0	.47
(1) 42		
AMERICAN FARM BUREAU FEDERATION	2.0	.66
(1) 03		
AMERICAN FEDERATION OF LABOR-CONGRESS OF INDUSTRIAL ORG. (AFL-CIO)	2.0	.81
(1) 42		
AMERICAN INSTITUTE OF PUBLIC OPINION (GALLUP)	2.0	.66
(2) 03 19		
ANCIEN REGIME	2.0	.66
(1) 22		
ARAB LEAGUE	2.0	.66
(7) 11 16 17 20 21 23 34		
ARYAN	2.0	.66
(4) 03 16 21 22		
ATLANTIC ALLIANCE	2.0	.66
(2) 23 25		

BIG BUSINESS   2.0   .81
  (3) 16 22 46
BOARD OF SUPERVISORS   2.0   .81
  (1) 42
BROOKINGS INSTITUTION   2.0   .47
  (WASHINGTON, D.C.)
  (2) 16 19
BUREAU OF INDIAN AFFAIRS   2.0   .47
  (4) 18 25 27 32
BUREAU OF INTERNAL REVENUE   2.0   .66
  (1) 16
BUREAU OF THE CENSUS (U.S.)   2.0   .66
  (5) 16 19 27 32 42
CENTRAL COMMITTEE, CHINA (PRC)   2.0   .47
  (1) 20
CENTRAL GOVERNMENT   2.0   .94
  (3) 17 19 23
CHAMBER OF DEPUTIES (FRANCE)   2.0   .66
  (6) 03 16 17 22 25 34 41
CHINA LOBBY   2.0   .00
  (1) 39
CHRISTIAN DEMOCRAT   2.0   .66
  (1) 17
CHRISTIAN DEMOCRATIC PARTY   2.0   .47
  (8) 11 16 17 19 22 25 33 34
CHURCH OF ENGLAND   2.0   .47
  (1) 16
CITIES   2.0   .81
  (1) 04
CITY   2.0   .81
  (1) 43
CIVIL RIGHTS COMMISSION, FEDERAL   2.0   .66
  (1) 42
CLOSED SHOP   2.0   .47
  (6) 06 16 18 27 29 32
COLONY   2.0   .66
  (8) 06 16 17 20 24 27 30 33
COMMITTEE   2.0   .81
  (9) 06 11 16 17 24 25 27 30 33
COMMON CAUSE   2.0   .47
  (1) 32
COMMONWEALTH COUNTRIES   2.0   .00
  (1) 19
COMMUNIST THIRD INTERNATIONAL   2.0   .47
  (1) 25
COMPLEX ORGANIZATIONS   2.0   .94
  (3) 04 24 30
COMPLEX SOCIETIES   2.0   .81
  (1) 15
CONFEDERATE STATES OF AMERICA   2.0   .66
  (1) 06
CONGRESS OF RACIAL EQUALITY   2.0   .47
  (CORE)
  (4) 03 30 32 34
CONSTITUENT ASSEMBLY   2.0   .47
  (1) 16
CONSTITUTIONAL COURTS   2.0   .47
  (7) 03 06 11 17 18 27 32
COST OF LIVING COUNCIL (COLC)   2.0   .66
  (1) 32
COUNCIL OF THE ORGANIZATION OF   2.0   .66
  AMERICAN STATES
  (1) 17

COURTS OF APPEALS, FEDERAL   2.0   .47
  (1) 42
COURTS, STATE   2.0   .81
  (1) 42
DEFENSE INTELLIGENCE AGENCY (DIA)   2.0   .81
  (2) 18 32
DEFENSIVE ALLIANCE   2.0   .81
  (1) 17
DEPARTMENT OF AIR FORCE   2.0   .66
  (1) 27
DEPARTMENT OF INTERIOR   2.0   .47
  (1) 42
DEPARTMENT OF THE ARMY   2.0   .66
  (1) 32
DEPARTMENT OF TRANSPORTATION   2.0   .66
  (DOT)
  (1) 18 32
DIPLOMATIC CORPS   2.0   .66
  (4) 06 16 17 27
ELECTION BOARD   2.0   .66
  (1) 06
EMBASSY   2.0   .66
  (5) 06 16 17 27 32
EMERGENT NATIONS   2.0   .66
  (1) 04
EUROPEAN RECOVERY PROGRAM (ERP)   2.0   .47
  (6) 16 17 18 20 32 34
EXECUTIVE BODY   2.0   .94
  (1) 17
FARM PRESSURE GROUPS   2.0   .47
  (1) 18
FEDERAL AUTHORITY   2.0   .81
  (1) 17
FEDERAL CABINET   2.0   .81
  (1) 17
FEDERAL CIVIL RIGHTS COMMISSION   2.0   .66
  (1) 42
FEDERAL COMMUNICATIONS   2.0   .66
  COMMISSION (FCC)
  (8) 03 06 07 16 18 22 27 32
FEDERAL TRADE COMMISSION (FTC)   2.0   .66
  (11) 03 06 07 16 18 19 22 25 27 32
  34
FOOD AND DRUG ADMINISTRATION   2.0   .47
  (FDA)
  (9) 03 06 07 16 18 25 27 32 34
FOREIGN RELATIONS COMMITTEE (U.S.   2.0   .47
  SENATE)
  (2) 08 17
FOURTH BRANCH OF GOVERNMENT   2.0   .66
  (1) 44
GENERAL ACCOUNTING OFFICE (GAO)   2.0   .66
  (7) 06 16 18 24 25 27 32
GOVERNMENT CORPORATION   2.0   .81
  (4) 03 06 18 27
GOVERNMENT ENTERPRISE   2.0   .81
  (1) 16
GROUP   2.0   .94
  (10) 01 02 03 04 15 17 19 24 30 33
HOUSE OF LORDS, BRITAIN   2.0   .66
  (8) 03 11 16 17 20 22 25 34
HUNG JURY   2.0   .47
  (1) 42

INDEPENDENT (NON-PARTY) VOTERS	2.0	.66
(2) 25 26		
INDEPENDENT AGENCIES AND	2.0	.66
REGULATORY COMMISSIONS		
(5) 16 18 27 32 34		
INDEPENDENTS	2.0	.81
(1) 39		
INDUSTRIAL WORKERS OF THE WORLD	2.0	.66
(IWW)		
(5) 06 10 16 21 25 46		
INNER SIX (EUROPEAN ECONOMIC	2.0	.66
COMMUNITY)		
(1) 20		
INSTITUTIONALIZED GROUP	2.0	.81
(2) 01 02		
INSTITUTIONALIZED PRESIDENCY	2.0	.81
(1) 32		
INTERLOCKING DIRECTORATES	2.0	.66
(2) 06 18		
INTERNATIONAL COURT OF JUSTICE	2.0	.66
(ICJ)		
(11) 03 07 11 16 17 18 20 23 25 27		
32		
INTERNATIONAL NON-GOVERNMENTAL	2.0	.94
ORGANIZATIONS		
(1) 36		
INTERNATIONAL TRIBUNAL	2.0	.81
(1) 17		
INVESTIGATING COMMITTEE	2.0	.66
(3) 17 18 32		
ISLAM	2.0	.66
(6) 03 11 22 24 25 30		
JOHN BIRCH SOCIETY	2.0	.66
(5) 03 25 27 32 34		
JOINT CONGRESSIONAL COMMITTEES	2.0	.66
(1) 42		
JUDICIARY COMMITTEE	2.0	.66
(1) 42		
JUNTA	2.0	.66
(2) 16 29 34		
KGB (KOMITET GOSUDARSTEVENNOI	2.0	.66
BEZOPASNOSTI) (U.S.S.R.)		
(1) 34		
KITCHEN CABINET	2.0	.47
(4) 06 16 27 29		
KNOW-NOTHING PARTY (NATIVE	2.0	.66
AMERICAN PARTY)		
(6) 03 06 16 29 32 45 46		
KUOMINTANG	2.0	.66
(6) 03 16 21 24 25 34		
LA FOLLETTE PROGRESSIVE MOVEMENT	2.0	.81
(1) 22		
LABOUR PARTY, BRITAIN	2.0	.47
(1) 20 38		
LEAGUE OF WOMEN VOTERS	2.0	.66
(4) 03 06 16 32		
MEXICAN-AMERICANS	2.0	.47
(2) 07 25 46		
MIDDLE MANAGEMENT	2.0	.47
(1) 37		
MILITARY	2.0	.81
(1) 43		

MILITARY ESTABLISHMENT	2.0	.94
(1) 42		
MILITARY REGIMES	2.0	.66
(1) 11		
MINOR PARTIES	2.0	.66
(4) 02 03 06 18		
MOB	2.0	.81
(1) 24 30		
MOSCOW-PEKING AXIS	2.0	.66
(1) 03		
MUNICIPAL COURTS	2.0	.47
(2) 27 32		
NAPOLEONIC EMPIRE	2.0	.66
(1) 17		
NATIONAL ADVISORY COMMISSION ON	2.0	.66
CIVIL DISORDER		
(1) 25		
NATIONAL BANK	2.0	.66
(3) 02 06 16		
NATIONALITIES	2.0	.81
(1) 11		
NEUTRAL STATE	2.0	.66
(1) 17		
NEW ENGLAND TOWN MEETING	2.0	.66
(2) 03 08		
NON-COMMUNIST LEFT	2.0	.66
(1) 45		
NON-GOVERNMENTAL ORGANIZATION	2.0	.81
(NGO)		
(3) 17 20 23		
NUCLEAR STRIKING FORCE	2.0	.66
(1) 17		
OCCUPATIONAL GROUPS	2.0	.81
(1) 15		
PALESTINE REFUGEES	2.0	.47
(1) 41		
PARTY CELL	2.0	.66
(1) 17		
PEOPLE'S COMMISSARIAT OF INTERNAL	2.0	.66
AFFAIRS (USSR) (N.K.V.D.)		
(1) 16		
PERSONALITY CULT	2.0	.47
(2) 17 34		
PILGRIMS	2.0	.47
(1) 46		
POLICY PLANNING STAFF	2.0	.66
(1) 42		
POLIS	2.0	.66
(1) 08		
POLITBURO, SOVIET UNION	2.0	.66
(7) 16 17 20 22 24 25 34		
POLITICAL INTEREST	2.0	.66
(1) 15		
POPULAR ASSEMBLY	2.0	.81
(1) 06		
POST OFFICE DEPARTMENT	2.0	.66
(5) 06 16 17 18 26 27 37		
PRESS	2.0	.94
(8) 03 11 19 23 24 25 27 30		
PUBLIC CORPORATIONS AND	2.0	.66
ENTERPRISES		
(3) 06 11 19		

PUBLIC ENTERPRISE	2.0	.66
(2) 11 23		
PURITANS	2.0	.66
(1) 46		
QUORUM	2.0	.66
(9) 02 03 06 16 17 18 27 32 33		
RACE AND POLITICS	2.0	.47
(1) 23		
REFORM MOVEMENTS	2.0	.47
(2) 12 17		
REVOLUTIONARY GOVERNMENT	2.0	.81
(1) 17		
RIGHT-WING PARTIES	2.0	.66
(1) 17		
ROMAN EMPIRE	2.0	.66
(4) 04 07 22 25		
ROPER POLL	2.0	.66
(2) 04 32		
SCHOOL BOARDS	2.0	.66
(2) 04 11		
SOCIAL ORDER	2.0	.66
(2) 11 17		
SOCIAL SCIENTISTS	2.0	.81
(1) 11		
SOUTHERN CHRISTIAN LEADERSHIP CONFERENCE (SCLC)	2.0	.47
(4) 25 30 32 34		
SOVIET	2.0	.66
(7) 10 11 16 19 24 26 34		
SPLINTER PARTIES	2.0	.47
(2) 16 17		
STATE SUPREME COURT	2.0	.47
(1) 27		
STOICS	2.0	.66
(1) 43		
STUDENTS FOR A DEMOCRATIC SOCIETY (SDS)	2.0	.47
(1) 32		
SUBCOMMITTEE	2.0	.66
(1) 42		
TEMPERANCE MOVEMENT	2.0	.47
(3) 06 16 19 46		
THIRD-PARTY MOVEMENT	2.0	.66
(2) 39 45		
TORY	2.0	.66
(1) 38		
TRADE UNION	2.0	.66
(6) 11 15 16 17 19 22		
TROTSKYITE	2.0	.47
(3) 16 17 38		
U.N. ATOMIC ENERGY COMMISSION	2.0	.00
(1) 03		
U.N. HUMAN RIGHTS COMMISSION	2.0	.66
(1) 03		
U.S. FEDERAL RESERVE SYSTEM	2.0	.47
(1) 25		
U.S. INFORMATION AGENCY (USIA)	2.0	.00
(5) 18 20 25 27 32		
UNCOMMITTED NATIONS	2.0	.81
(1) 39		
UNITED WORLD FEDERALISTS	2.0	.47
(1) 20		
VATICAN	2.0	.66
(6) 03 07 11 17 19 25		
VESTED INTERESTS	2.0	.81
(2) 03 16		
VETERANS ADMINISTRATION (VA)	2.0	.66
(7) 03 06 16 18 27 32 34		
VOLUNTARY ASSOCIATION	2.0	.81
(5) 03 06 07 25 26		
WARSAW PACT TREATY ORGANIZATION (WTO)	2.0	.66
(6) 07 17 20 25 34 36		
WHITE HOUSE STAFF	2.0	.81
(1) 42		
WORKING CLASS	2.0	.81
(4) 03 06 11 26		
WORLD BANK AND INTERNATIONAL MONETARY FUND	2.0	.81
(1) 36		
WORLD COURT (INTERNATIONAL COURT OF JUSTICE)	2.0	.66
(9) 06 16 18 20 22 23 25 27 32		
WORLD ORDER	2.0	.81
(1) 17		
ADMINISTRATIVE AGENCIES	2.1	.87
(1) 04		
ALLIED POWERS	2.1	.56
(2) 16 17		
AMERICAN INDEPENDENT PARTY	2.1	.56
(1) 25		
AMERICAN MEDICAL ASSOCIATION (AMA)	2.1	.73
(5) 08 18 19 25 27		
ANTI-DEFAMATION LEAGUE OF BNAI BRITH	2.1	.56
(1) 03		
ARMY	2.1	.73
(6) 06 11 17 23 24 25		
ASSEMBLY	2.1	.87
(5) 03 06 16 17 24		
ASSOCIATION	2.1	.99
(1) 17		
BELLIGERENT POWERS	2.1	.56
(1) 16		
BIG GOVERNMENT	2.1	.73
(1) 39		
BIRCHERS	2.1	.73
(1) 03		
BLOC	2.1	.56
(7) 06 16 18 27 30 32 33		
BORDER STATE	2.1	.56
(3) 06 16 27		
BRITISH COMMONWEALTH OF NATIONS	2.1	.73
(5) 07 11 16 25 34		
BRITISH CONSERVATIVE PARTY	2.1	.56
(2) 03 22		
BRITISH LIBERAL PARTY	2.1	.31
(1) 03		
BROWN SHIRTS	2.1	.56
(1) 16		
BUFFER STATE	2.1	.31
(4) 06 16 17 20		

BUNDESRAT (FEDERAL COUNCIL),   2.1   .31
  GERMANY
  (5) 03 16 17 20 24
CAMPAIGN COMMITTEES   2.1   .73
  (1) 32
CARNEGIE ENDOWMENT FOR   2.1   .73
  INTERNATIONAL PEACE
  (3) 17 19 32
CARTEL   2.1   .56
  (4) 06 16 19 20
CENTRAL COMMITTEE   2.1   .73
  (2) 17 27
CENTRAL COMMITTEE, COMMUNIST   2.1   .56
  PARTY, SOVIET UNION
  (3) 03 20 25
CENTRAL TREATY ORGANIZATION   2.1   .56
  (CENTO)
  (1) 20
CIRCUIT COURT   2.1   .73
  (6) 03 06 16 18 27 32
CIVIL RIGHTS ORGANIZATIONS   2.1   .73
  (1) 18
COLONIES   2.1   .73
  (1) 24
COMINFORM (ALSO, INFORMATION   2.1   .56
  BUREAU OF COMMUNIST PARTIES
  AND WORKERS)
  (1) 03
COMMITTEE OF THE WHOLE   2.1   .73
  (1) 42
COMMITTEE ON POLITICAL EDUCATION   2.1   .73
  (COPE)
  (1) 32
COMMONWEALTH   2.1   .56
  (8) 03 06 16 19 24 26 33 34
COMMUNE (FRANCE)   2.1   .56
  (10) 03 10 11 16 17 19 20 25 32 34
CONCURRENT MAJORITY   2.1   .73
  (3) 18 32 33
CONFERENCE COMMITTEE   2.1   .73
  (6) 02 03 16 18 27 32
CONGRESS OF INDUSTRIAL   2.1   .56
  ORGANIZATIONS
  (5) 06 16 27 32 34
CONGRESSIONAL CAMPAIGN   2.1   .56
  COMMITTEE
  (4) 02 06 18 32
CONGRESSIONAL INVESTIGATING   2.1   .73
  COMMITTEE
  (1) 42
CONSERVATIVE COALITION   2.1   .56
  (1) 32
CONSOLIDATED CITY-COUNTY   2.1   .56
  GOVERNMENT
  (1) 03
CONSTITUTIONAL DICTATORSHIP   2.1   .87
  (2) 03 20
CORPORATE STATE   2.1   .73
  (5) 17 21 22 26 32
COUNCIL OF ECONOMIC ADVISERS   2.1   .87
  (CEA)
  (6) 03 07 18 19 27 32

COUNCIL OF MINISTERS (USSR)   2.1   .56
  (5) 11 16 17 19 20
COUNTY GOVERNMENT   2.1   .73
  (2) 03 32
COURT OF ARBITRATION   2.1   .56
  (1) 17
DEFENSE INDUSTRY   2.1   .73
  (1) 25
DEMOCRATIC REPUBLIC OF VIETNAM   2.1   .56
  (NORTH VIETNAM)
  (1) 03
DEPARTMENT OF COMMERCE   2.1   .56
  (1) 16 32
DEPENDENT TERRITORY   2.1   .56
  (1) 20
DIPLOMATIC SERVICE   2.1   .31
  (1) 42
DISTRICT COURT, STATE   2.1   .56
  (1) 42
DIXIECRAT   2.1   .56
  (1) 39
DOVES   2.1   .56
  (1) 34
EASTERN ESTABLISHMENT   2.1   .56
  (1) 39
ECONOMIC CLASS   2.1   .73
  (1) 27
ENVIRONMENTAL PROTECTION AGENCY   2.1   .56
  (EPA)
  (3) 07 17 32
ETHNIC MINORITIES   2.1   .73
  (1) 03
EUROPEAN ATOMIC ENERGY   2.1   .31
  COMMUNITY (EURATOM)
  (6) 03 17 20 23 25 34 38
EUROPEANS   2.1   .73
  (1) 30
EXECUTIVE AGENCIES   2.1   .87
  (2) 04 32
EXPORT-IMPORT BANK OF   2.1   .56
  WASHINGTON
  (6) 06 16 18 20 27 34 42
EXTREMIST PARTY   2.1   .73
  (4) 17 24 29 30
FACT-FINDING COMMITTEE   2.1   .56
  (1) 17
FAIR EMPLOYMENT PRACTICES   2.1   .56
  COMMISSION (FEPC)
  (1) 27
FARM BLOC   2.1   .73
  (5) 06 16 18 29 32
FEDERAL ASSEMBLY   2.1   .73
  (1) 17
FEDERAL CLAIMS COURT   2.1   .73
  (1) 18
FEDERAL HOUSING ADMINISTRATION   2.1   .56
  (FHA)
  (5) 03 06 16 27 32
FEDERAL LAW-ENFORCEMENT   2.1   .56
  AGENCIES
  (1) 42
FEDERAL POWER COMMISSION (FPC)   2.1   .56
  (1) 32

FEDERAL RESERVE BOARD	2.1	.56
(3) 06 08 16		
FEDERAL STATE	2.1	.87
(3) 16 17 21		
FEDERAL SYSTEM, SOVIET UNION	2.1	.73
(1) 20		
FEDERALIST PARTY	2.1	.73
(5) 06 16 18 25 27		
FORMAL ORGANIZATION	2.1	.87
(1) 02		
GAULLIST PARTY IN FRANCE	2.1	.56
(1) 25		
GERMAN SOCIAL DEMOCRATS	2.1	.56
(1) 26		
GERMANY	2.1	.31
(1) 11		
GESTAPO	2.1	.31
(4) 03 16 21 34		
GOVERNING BODY	2.1	.73
(1) 17		
GOVERNMENT AGENCIES	2.1	.73
(2) 17 25		
GOVERNMENT-IN-EXILE	2.1	.56
(2) 16 17		
GRANGER MOVEMENT	2.1	.56
(1) 45		
GROUND FORCES	2.1	.56
(1) 17		
GROUPS	2.1	.99
(1) 36		
HOLY ROMAN EMPIRE	2.1	.56
(2) 16 17		
HOUSE FOREIGN AFFAIRS COMMITTEE, CONGRESS	2.1	.73
(1) 20		
HUGUENOTS	2.1	.56
(3) 03 17 26 46		
INCORPORATED AND UNINCORPORATED AREAS	2.1	.87
(4) 06 16 18 24		
INDEPENDENT EXECUTIVE AGENCIES	2.1	.73
(1) 42		
INTERNAL REVENUE SERVICE	2.1	.56
(4) 16 18 27 32		
INTERNATIONAL ATOMIC ENERGY AGENCY (IAEA)	2.1	.31
(5) 11 17 20 23 27		
INTERNATIONAL INTERGOVERNMENTAL ORGANIZATIONS	2.1	.87
(1) 36		
INTERNATIONAL WORKERS OF THE WORLD	2.1	.73
(1) 25		
JEFFERSONIAN REPUBLICANS	2.1	.73
(1) 32		
LABOR	2.1	.87
(3) 07 24 30		
LAND, AIR AND SEA FORCES	2.1	.87
(1) 17		
LEAGUE OF ARAB STATES	2.1	.56
(3) 17 20 34		
LEFT	2.1	.87
(7) 06 11 16 17 19 24 34		
LEFT-WING OPPOSITION	2.1	.56
(1) 17		
LEFT-WING PARTIES	2.1	.73
(1) 17		
LEFT-WING SOCIALIST	2.1	.56
(1) 17		
LEGAL GOVERNMENTS	2.1	.87
(1) 05		
LEGISLATIVE ASSEMBLY	2.1	.73
(1) 17		
LIBERAL-LEFT	2.1	.73
(1) 24		
LITTLE HOOVER COMMISSIONS	2.1	.73
(1) 42		
LOCAL SOVIETS	2.1	.87
(1) 11		
MANHATTAN PROJECT	2.1	.56
(1) 34		
MAU MAU	2.1	.56
(2) 03 34		
METROPOLITAN SYSTEMS, AND SUBURBIA	2.1	.87
(1) 04		
MINISTRY OF JUSTICE	2.1	.73
(1) 44		
MOVEMENT	2.1	.99
(4) 17 24 30 33		
MULTI-NUCLEAR FORCE	2.1	.56
(1) 17		
MUNITIONS INDUSTRY	2.1	.87
(1) 16		
NATIONAL AERONAUTICS AND SPACE ADMINISTRATION (NASA)	2.1	.73
(1) 18 27 32 34 42		
NATIONAL ASSEMBLY, FRANCE	2.1	.56
(4) 11 16 17 20		
NATIONAL ASSOCIATION OF MANUFACTURERS (NAM)	2.1	.73
(3) 16 27 32		
NATIONAL GOVERNMENT	2.1	.87
(5) 06 16 19 25 34		
NATIONAL LEAGUE OF WOMEN VOTERS	2.1	.73
(1) 16		
NATIONAL PARTY	2.1	.73
(1) 34		
NATIONAL RECOVERY ADMINISTRATION (NRA)	2.1	.56
(5) 02 06 16 27 32		
PAN-AMERICAN UNION	2.1	.56
(10) 03 06 11 17 18 20 21 27 32 34 46		
PARLIAMENTARY PARTY, BRITAIN	2.1	.99
(1) 20		
PEOPLE'S LIBERATION ARMY (PLA)	2.1	.56
(1) 34		
PERMANENT COMMITTEE	2.1	.73
(2) 17 32		
PERSONNEL ADMINISTRATION	2.1	.73
(2) 12 16		
PETTY BOURGEOISIE	2.1	.56
(1) 17		
POLYARCHY	2.1	.73
(4) 04 08 17 24		

POPULIST PARTY	2.1	.56
(5) 06 16 19 27 29		
PRESIDIUM OF THE COUNCIL OF MINISTERS, U.S.S.R.	2.1	.73
(1) 20		
PRESIDIUM OF THE SUPREME SOVIET, SOVIET UNION	2.1	.56
(6) 03 16 17 19 20 22		
PROGRESSIVE PARTY	2.1	.56
(7) 03 06 11 16 19 27 32		
PROVINCIAL GOVERNMENT	2.1	.31
(1) 17		
PUBLIC INSTITUTION	2.1	.73
(1) 17		
PUPPET STATE	2.1	.56
(1) 16		
QUASI-JUDICIAL AGENCY	2.1	.56
(1) 42		
RADICAL REPUBLICANS	2.1	.56
(2) 08 32 46		
RAND CORPORATION (U.S.)	2.1	.56
(3) 19 25 32		
RANK-AND-FILE	2.1	.31
(4) 02 16 29 39		
RED ARMY	2.1	.56
(1) 16		
REGIONAL SYSTEMS	2.1	.87
(1) 11		
RELOCATION CENTERS	2.1	.73
(3) 16 32 45 46		
REPUBLICAN-SOUTHERN DEMOCRATIC COALITION	2.1	.56
(1) 02		
ROMAN CATHOLIC CHURCH	2.1	.73
(4) 03 04 25 34		
ROOSEVELT COURT, THE	2.1	.56
(1) 04		
RUSSIAN COMMUNISTS	2.1	.73
(1) 10		
SECRET SERVICE	2.1	.56
(7) 06 16 17 18 27 32 34		
SECRETARIAT OF THE CENTRAL COMMITTEE, U.S.S.R.	2.1	.31
(1) 20		
SMALL CLAIMS COURT	2.1	.56
(4) 06 16 18 32		
SOCIAL DEMOCRATIC PARTY OF GERMANY (SPD)	2.1	.56
(10) 03 10 11 16 17 19 22 25 32 34		
SOCIAL GROUPS	2.1	.73
(3) 15 19 25		
SOCIALIST POLITICAL PARTIES	2.1	.56
(10) 03 06 10 11 16 17 18 19 25 32		
SOUTH AFRICA, REPUBLIC OF	2.1	.31
(3) 03 07 11		
SOVIET REPUBLICS	2.1	.73
(1) 16		
SPECIALIZED AGENCY, UNITED NATIONS	2.1	.87
(4) 03 17 18 20		
STAFF AND LINE	2.1	.73
(1) 18		
STANDING COMMITTEE	2.1	.56
(1) 42		
STATE COURTS	2.1	.56
(1) 32		
STATE GOVERNMENTS	2.1	.73
(3) 07 12 18		
STATE LEGISLATURE	2.1	.73
(3) 11 12 18		
STRATEGIC AIR COMMAND (SAC)	2.1	.31
(1) 03		
STUDENT NONVIOLENT COORDINATING COMMITTEE (SNCC)	2.1	.31
(3) 03 30 32 34		
SUBGROUPS	2.1	.73
(1) 15		
SUPRANATIONAL ORGANIZATION	2.1	.73
(2) 03 17		
SUPREME SOVIET OF THE USSR	2.1	.56
(9) 03 11 16 17 19 20 25 34 38		
TAMMANY HALL	2.1	.56
(7) 04 06 07 11 16 27 32		
THEOCRACY	2.1	.73
(7) 03 06 16 17 18 32 33		
TORIES (LOYALISTS)	2.1	.31
(1) 46		
TORY PARTY	2.1	.73
(1) 19		
TRUSTEESHIP COUNCIL, UNITED NATIONS	2.1	.31
(8) 03 16 17 18 20 21 27 32		
TRUSTS	2.1	.73
(1) 46		
U.N. EMERGENCY FORCE (UNEF)	2.1	.73
(3) 03 17 20		
U.N. FOOD AND AGRICULTURAL ORGANIZATION	2.1	.31
(1) 19		
U.N. SPECIALIZED AGENCIES	2.1	.56
(2) 20 27		
U.N. TRUSTEESHIP COUNCIL	2.1	.31
(2) 03 20		
U.S. FEDERAL BUREAU OF INVESTIGATION	2.1	.56
(1) 25		
UNDERGROUND RAILWAY	2.1	.73
(2) 06 16 46		
UNITED AUTO WORKERS (UAW)	2.1	.31
(1) 25		
VOLUNTEERS IN SERVICE TO AMERICA (VISTA)	2.1	.56
(3) 18 32 34		
WEATHERMAN	2.1	.31
(1) 25		
WESTERN ALLIES	2.1	.73
(1) 22		
WESTERN BLOC	2.1	.56
(1) 23		
WORLD POWER	2.1	.99
(1) 17		
YELLOW PERIL	2.1	.56
(3) 06 16 21 46		

YOUNG COMMUNIST LEAGUE, SOVIET UNION	2.1	.56
(1) 20		
ADVISORY COMMISSION	2.2	.63
(2) 06 16		
AFRO-AMERICANS	2.2	.63
(3) 25 30 43		
AGRARIAN PARTY	2.2	.63
(1) 19		
AMERICAN EXPEDITIONARY FORCE (AEF)	2.2	.78
(2) 06 16		
AMERICAN LEGION	2.2	.42
(5) 03 06 16 27 34		
ANGLO-AMERICAN ALLIANCE	2.2	.63
(1) 22		
ANGLOS	2.2	.78
(1) 30		
ANOMIC GROUP	2.2	.91
(1) 01		
APPARATCHIK	2.2	.63
(2) 03 24		
ARABS	2.2	.42
(4) 03 07 11 22		
ARMED SERVICES OF THE UNITED STATES	2.2	.78
(1) 45		
ARMY INTELLIGENCE (G2)	2.2	.78
(1) 18		
ASIAN AMERICANS	2.2	.63
(1) 07		
ASSOCIATED PRESS	2.2	.63
(1) 45		
ATOMIC ENERGY COMMISSION (UN)	2.2	.63
(1) 41		
AUSTRO-HUNGARIAN EMPIRE	2.2	.63
(1) 22		
BAATH PARTY (ARAB SOCIALIST RESURRECTION PARTY)	2.2	.63
(2) 03 34		
BLACK AMERICANS	2.2	.78
(1) 46		
BLACKS	2.2	.78
(3) 24 30 43		
BLUE RIBBON PANEL	2.2	.63
(1) 39		
BOARD OF EDUCATION	2.2	.78
(3) 03 18 27		
BRAIN TRUST	2.2	.63
(6) 02 06 16 22 27 29		
BRITISH WHIGS	2.2	.42
(1) 29		
BUDGET BUREAU	2.2	.91
(4) 08 16 18 32		
BUNDESTAG (FEDERAL DIET), GERMANY	2.2	.42
(5) 03 17 20 24 34		
CAPITAL DEVELOPMENT FUND, UNITED NATIONS	2.2	.42
(1) 20		
CAREER SERVICE	2.2	.78
(5) 06 16 18 24 30		
CARETAKER GOVERNMENT	2.2	.63
(2) 03 16		

CATHOLIC CHURCH	2.2	.63
(2) 11 22		
CELL	2.2	.78
(3) 03 16 33		
CENTRAL ADMINISTRATION	2.2	.91
(1) 16		
CENTRAL POWERS	2.2	.63
(2) 16 17		
CHICANO	2.2	.63
(2) 07 25		
CIRCUIT COURT, STATE	2.2	.78
(1) 42		
CITY COURT	2.2	.91
(1) 06		
CIVIL SERVICE COMMISSION	2.2	.78
(6) 03 07 18 26 27 32 37		
CLIQUE	2.2	.63
(2) 17 24		
COLLEGE OF CARDINALS	2.2	.63
(2) 17 26		
COLONIAL	2.2	.78
(3) 17 24 30		
COMMITTEE OF CORRESPONDENCE	2.2	.42
(2) 02 06		
COMMONWEALTH OF NATIONS	2.2	.63
(2) 07 20		
CONCERT OF EUROPE	2.2	.63
(6) 03 16 17 20 22 25		
CONFERENCE COMMITTEE OF CONGRESS	2.2	.78
(1) 45		
CONGRESS PARTY	2.2	.42
(6) 11 16 17 19 25 34		
CONSERVATIVE PARTY, BRITISH	2.2	.42
(9) 03 11 16 17 19 20 22 25 34		
COUNCIL OF EUROPE	2.2	.78
(7) 07 11 12 17 20 23 34		
COUNCIL OF MINISTERS, EUROPEAN COMMUNITY	2.2	.78
(1) 20		
COUNCIL OF MUTUAL ECONOMIC ASSISTANCE (COMECON)	2.2	.63
(1) 03		
COUNCIL OF THE LEAGUE OF NATIONS	2.2	.78
(1) 16		
COUNTERFORCE	2.2	.78
(1) 03		
COUNTY COURT	2.2	.78
(6) 03 06 16 18 27 32		
COURT OF CLAIMS	2.2	.78
(5) 06 16 18 27 32		
COURT OF JUSTICE	2.2	.78
(1) 17		
CUSTOMS UNION	2.2	.78
(4) 06 16 21 32		
DEMOCRATIC SOCIALIST PARTY	2.2	.42
(1) 19		
DEPARTMENT OF FINANCE	2.2	.63
(1) 17		
DEPENDENT STATE	2.2	.63
(2) 03 17		
DEPRESSED CLASSES	2.2	.63
(1) 16		

DIVIDED COURT	2.2	.42
(1) 44		
DRAFT BOARD	2.2	.63
(2) 16 34		
ECONOMIC UNION	2.2	.63
(2) 11 20		
ECUMENICAL COUNCIL	2.2	.78
(1) 17		
ELECTIVE MONARCHY	2.2	.63
(1) 17		
ESTABLISHED CHURCH	2.2	.63
(3) 03 16 22		
ESTABLISHMENT	2.2	.91
(4) 02 07 17 24		
EXPEDITIONARY FORCE	2.2	.63
(2) 16 17		
FASCIST PARTY	2.2	.63
(2) 16 22		
FEDERAL EXECUTIVE DEPARTMENTS	2.2	.91
(1) 42		
FEDERAL UNION	2.2	.78
(1) 21		
FEDERATION OF RHODESIA AND NYASALAND	2.2	.42
(1) 03		
FIRST SOCIALIST INTERNATIONAL	2.2	.63
(1) 08		
FORCED LABOR CAMPS	2.2	.42
(3) 03 16 34		
FORD FOUNDATION	2.2	.42
(1) 41		
FOREIGN AFFAIRS COMMITTEE	2.2	.42
(1) 17		
FOREIGN OFFICE	2.2	.63
(3) 16 17 20		
FOUNDING FATHERS	2.2	.78
(2) 06 16		
FOUR-POWER ADMINISTRATION OF BERLIN	2.2	.63
(1) 17		
FOURTH REPUBLIC (FRANCE)	2.2	.63
(1) 03 08		
FREE TRADE AREA	2.2	.91
(2) 17 20		
FRENCH COMMUNIST PARTY	2.2	.42
(1) 03		
FRENCH NATIONAL ASSEMBLY	2.2	.42
(1) 03		
FUSION TICKET	2.2	.63
(1) 27		
GARRISON STATE	2.2	.42
(1) 35		
GENERAL MOTORS CORPORATION	2.2	.63
(2) 22 25		
GENERAL SERVICES ADMINISTRATION (GSA)	2.2	.63
(3) 18 27 32		
GERMAN DEMOCRATIC REPUBLIC (GDR) (DDR)	2.2	.42
(4) 03 11 24 34		
GERMAN-ITALIAN ALLIANCE	2.2	.42
(1) 16		
GOVERNMENT PRINTING OFFICE (GPO)	2.2	.63
(3) 16 27 32		
GOVERNMENT-OWNED CORPORATION	2.2	.63
(1) 06		
GREENBACK PARTY	2.2	.63
(5) 06 08 16 22 32		
GUIDED DEMOCRACY	2.2	.63
(2) 03 20		
HITLER YOUTH	2.2	.63
(2) 16 26		
HOUSE OF WINDSOR	2.2	.63
(1) 16		
HUMAN RIGHTS COMMISSIONS	2.2	.63
(1) 25		
IMPERIAL DYNASTY	2.2	.63
(1) 17		
INTERNATIONAL BANK FOR RECONSTRUCTION AND DEVELOPMENT (IBRD,IBRAD)	2.2	.78
(1) 17 41		
INTERNATIONAL DEVELOPMENT AGENCY	2.2	.42
(1) 38		
INTERNATIONAL POLICE	2.2	.78
(1) 06		
INTERNATIONAL POLITICAL PARTY	2.2	.91
(1) 17		
INTERNATIONAL REFUGEE ORGANIZATION (IRO)	2.2	.78
(3) 17 20 27		
INTERNATIONAL TRADE ORGANIZATION (ITO)	2.2	.63
(4) 03 17 20 32		
INTERNMENT CAMP	2.2	.63
(3) 16 17 32		
IRELAND, REPUBLIC OF (EIRE)	2.2	.63
(4) 03 07 10 11		
ITALIAN COMMUNISTS	2.2	.42
(1) 03		
JAPANESE-AMERICANS	2.2	.78
(1) 46		
JESUITS	2.2	.63
(3) 09 24 26		
JEWS	2.2	.78
(7) 09 11 22 24 25 26 30		
JOINT COMMISSION	2.2	.78
(1) 06		
JOINT ECONOMIC COMMITTEES	2.2	.63
(1) 16		
KERNER COMMISSION	2.2	.63
(1) 32		
KIBBUTZ	2.2	.42
(3) 03 24 25		
KNESSET	2.2	.63
(3) 03 17 24		
LABOR FORCE	2.2	.78
(1) 37		
LAND FORCES	2.2	.63
(1) 17		
LANDED GENTRY	2.2	.63
(1) 17 24		
LEFT-WING GOVERNMENT	2.2	.63
(1) 17		

LIBERAL-REPUBLICANS	2.2	.63
(1) 45		
LINE ORGANIZATION	2.2	.63
(1) 06		
LOCAL SOVEREIGNTY (SELF GOVERNMENT)	2.2	.78
(1) 29		
LONDON SCHOOL OF ECONOMICS AND POLITICAL SCIENCE	2.2	.78
(1) 19		
LOYALIST	2.2	.78
(2) 06 16		
MACHINE	2.2	.91
(5) 06 16 24 27 29		
MATRIARCHY	2.2	.78
(1) 30		
MEDIEVAL SOCIETY	2.2	.78
(3) 07 24 25		
MEXICAN	2.2	.78
(1) 43		
MILITARY COURTS	2.2	.63
(2) 03 17		
MINISTRY	2.2	.91
(4) 06 16 17 24		
MIXED ENTERPRISE	2.2	.91
(1) 11		
MOSLEM	2.2	.78
(3) 16 22 24		
MULTI-PARTITE	2.2	.78
(1) 16		
MUNICIPAL CORPORATION	2.2	.63
(2) 06 18		
MUSLIM PEOPLE AND RELIGION	2.2	.63
(1) 25		
NARROW MAJORITY	2.2	.78
(1) 17		
NATIONAL FARMERS UNION	2.2	.63
(1) 32		
NATIONAL LIBERATION FRONT (NLF)	2.2	.63
(3) 17 20 25		
NATIONAL REPUBLICAN PARTY	2.2	.78
(3) 06 29 32		
NATIONAL SOCIALIST GERMAN WORKERS PARTY	2.2	.78
(1) 22		
NAVAL FORCES	2.2	.78
(1) 17		
NEW SOUTH	2.2	.42
(1) 45 46		
NINE OLD MEN	2.2	.42
(1) 39		
NOBILITY	2.2	.78
(3) 16 17 24		
NONASSOCIATIONAL GROUP	2.2	.91
(1) 01		
OFFICE OF CIVIL AND DEFENSE MOBILIZATION (OCDM)	2.2	.63
(1) 27 42		
OFFICE OF DEFENSE MOBILIZATION	2.2	.63
(1) 42		
OIL CORPORATIONS	2.2	.78
(1) 25		
ORGANIZATION AND METHODS	2.2	.91
(1) 37		
ORGANIZATION FOR EUROPEAN ECONOMIC COOPERATION (OEEC)	2.2	.63
(7) 12 17 18 25 27 32 34		
ORGANIZATION OF AFRICAN UNITY (OAU)	2.2	.42
(7) 11 20 23 25 34 38 41		
PATHET-LAO	2.2	.42
(2) 03 25		
PEASANTRY	2.2	.63
(5) 07 19 23 24 26		
PEOPLE'S COURT	2.2	.63
(2) 03 16		
POLICE	2.2	.63
(10) 03 06 07 11 16 23 24 25 27 30		
POLITICAL FORCES	2.2	.91
(1) 11		
POLITICAL OPINION POLL	2.2	.78
(1) 32		
POPULAR FRONT GOVERNMENT	2.2	.42
(1) 17		
PROBATE COURT	2.2	.63
(4) 03 16 18 32		
PROPAGANDA MACHINE	2.2	.42
(1) 17		
PROPERTIED CLASSES	2.2	.63
(1) 17		
PROVISIONAL GOVERNMENT	2.2	.42
(3) 06 16 17		
PUBLIC AUDIENCE	2.2	.78
(1) 17		
PUBLIC BROADCASTING SYSTEM (PBS)	2.2	.42
(1) 32		
PUBLIC UTILITY COMMISSIONS	2.2	.42
(1) 42		
REGIME	2.2	.78
(4) 16 24 30 33		
REGIONAL FEDERATIONS	2.2	.63
(1) 36		
REGIONAL GOVERNMENT	2.2	.63
(1) 19		
REPUBLICAN PARTY, JEFFERSONIAN	2.2	.63
(1) 06		
RIGHT-LEFT	2.2	.78
(1) 04		
ROMAN REPUBLIC	2.2	.63
(1) 25		
SCHOOLS OF PHILOSOPHY	2.2	.63
(1) 26		
SECRETARIAT (INTERNATIONAL ORGANIZATION)	2.2	.63
(7) 06 16 17 18 20 24 27		
SLATE	2.2	.63
(4) 06 16 27 29		
SMALL BUSINESS ADMINISTRATION (SBA)	2.2	.42
(4) 07 18 27 32		
SOCIAL MOVEMENTS	2.2	.63
(2) 07 11		
SOCIALIST WORKERS PARTY	2.2	.63
(3) 18 25 32		

SPECIALIZED AGENCIES	2.2	.78
(1) 38		
SPLINTER GROUP	2.2	.63
(1) 39		
STANDING JOINT COMMITTEES	2.2	.63
(1) 32		
STATE CENTRAL COMMITTEE	2.2	.63
(3) 03 06 18		
STATE COURT OF APPEALS	2.2	.63
(1) 18		
STATE MILITIA	2.2	.42
(1) 27		
STEERING COMMITTEE	2.2	.63
(7) 03 06 16 17 18 27 32		
STUDENT MOVEMENT	2.2	.63
(1) 11		
TEAMSTER UNION	2.2	.63
(1) 27		
TRANSNATIONAL SOCIETY	2.2	.78
(1) 01		
TREASURY DEPARTMENT	2.2	.63
(1) 42		
TRUSTEESHIP COUNCIL	2.2	.42
(1) 36		
U.N. CHILDRENS INTERNATIONAL EMERGENCY FUND (UNICEF)	2.2	.42
(4) 03 17 20 32		
U.N. DISARMAMENT COMMISSION	2.2	.42
(1) 20		
U.N. FORCE IN CYPRUS (UNFICYP)	2.2	.42
(1) 20		
U.N. ORGANIZATION (UNO)	2.2	.78
(2) 17 23		
U.S. OF EUROPE	2.2	.78
(4) 16 17 21 22		
U.S. POSTAL SERVICE	2.2	.63
(2) 18 32		
U.S. VETERANS ADMINISTRATION (VA)	2.2	.63
(1) 03		
UNION MOVEMENT	2.2	.78
(1) 38		
UNITED ARAB REPUBLIC (UAR)	2.2	.42
(5) 03 07 11 25 34		
VICHY GOVERNMENT	2.2	.42
(7) 03 11 16 19 24 25 34		
VOICE OF AMERICA	2.2	.63
(4) 20 27 32 34		
WAR HAWK	2.2	.63
(1) 06		
WHITE POWER STRUCTURE	2.2	.42
(1) 39		
WORLD FEDERATION OF TRADE UNIONS (WFTU)	2.2	.63
(1) 17		
WORLD HEALTH ORGANIZATION (WHO)	2.2	.42
(9) 03 17 18 20 22 23 25 27 32		
WORLD STATE	2.2	.78
(2) 11 17		
ZIONIST	2.2	.63
(1) 17		
ADMINISTRATIVE COURT	2.3	.67
(4) 06 11 16 32		
AFRO-ASIAN BLOC	2.3	.48
(1) 03		
AGRICULTURAL ADJUSTMENT ADMINISTRATION (AAA)	2.3	.67
(4) 06 16 27 32		
AIR FORCE ACADEMY	2.3	.67
(1) 42		
AMALGAMATED SECURITY-COMMUNITY	2.3	.94
(1) 03		
AMERICAN BAR ASSOCIATION (ABA)	2.3	.67
(7) 07 11 19 24 25 27 32		
ANTITRUST DIVISION	2.3	.67
(2) 18 42		
ARIANS	2.3	.82
(1) 03		
ARMED FORCES	2.3	.67
(2) 11 25		
ATLANTIC FREE TRADE AREA	2.3	.67
(1) 25		
ATOMIC ENERGY AUTHORITY OF UNITED NATIONS	2.3	.48
(1) 25		
ATOMIC ENERGY COMMITTEE	2.3	.67
(1) 42		
AZTECS	2.3	.67
(1) 22		
BANTU	2.3	.82
(4) 03 15 24 25		
BAO DAI	2.3	.67
(2) 03 34		
BAR ASSOCIATION	2.3	.67
(1) 11		
BEDOUINS	2.3	.48
(1) 03		
BETTER BUSINESS BUREAUS	2.3	.67
(1) 32		
BIG FIVE	2.3	.67
(1) 16		
BIG FOUR	2.3	.67
(1) 16		
BIG THREE	2.3	.48
(2) 16 46		
BLACK SHIRTS	2.3	.48
(2) 16 17		
BLUE RIBBON JURY	2.3	.67
(5) 03 16 18 32 45		
BOARD OF REGENTS	2.3	.67
(1) 16		
BRITISH BROADCASTING CORPORATION (B.B.C.)	2.3	.48
(2) 16 19		
BRITISH CROWN COLONIES	2.3	.48
(1) 03		
BRITISH TORIES	2.3	.48
(1) 29		
BROTHERHOOD OF TEAMSTERS	2.3	.48
(1) 25		
BULL MOOSE PARTY	2.3	.48
(7) 03 06 16 18 27 29 32		
BUREAU OF LABOR STATISTICS (BLS)	2.3	.48
(4) 06 16 27 32		
BUREAU OF LAND MANAGEMENT	2.3	.48
(2) 18 32		

CABAL 2.3 .67
(1) 16
CADRE 2.3 .67
(3) 17 24 34
CANTONS, SWITZERLAND 2.3 .48
(1) 11
CARNEGIE CORPORATION 2.3 .67
(1) 19
CATEGORIC GROUP 2.3 .94
(1) 01
CATHOLIC PARTY 2.3 .48
(1) 19
CAUCASIAN 2.3 .67
(2) 22 30
CAUCUSING GROUP, UNITED NATIONS 2.3 .67
(1) 20
CHARTER COLONY 2.3 .48
(2) 06 18
CHRISTIAN DEMOCRATIC UNION (CDU) 2.3 .48
(5) 03 17 22 24 34
CHRISTIANS 2.3 .67
(5) 11 22 24 25 30
CIVIL AERONAUTICS ADMINISTRATION 2.3 .67
(CAA)
(2) 06 16
CIVIL AERONAUTICS BOARD (CAB) 2.3 .48
(6) 03 06 16 18 27 32
CIVIL RIGHTS DIVISION 2.3 .82
(1) 18
CIVILIAN CONSERVATION CORPS (CCC) 2.3 .48
(5) 06 16 17 27 32
COMMISSION OF INQUIRY (ENQUIRY) 2.3 .67
(3) 06 11 16
COMMUNIST FRONT ORGANIZATIONS 2.3 .67
(2) 03 42
COMMUNIST PARTY OF FRANCE 2.3 .48
(1) 03
COMSOMOL 2.3 .67
(1) 16
CONSEIL D'ETAT (FRANCE) 2.3 .67
(1) 03 19
CONSTITUTIONAL STATE 2.3 .82
(1) 17
CONSULAR SERVICE 2.3 .48
(2) 16 32
COUNCIL OF MINISTERS, ITALY 2.3 .67
(1) 20
COUNTY 2.3 .67
(10) 03 06 07 16 17 18 19 24 27 32
COUNTY BOARD 2.3 .67
(2) 18 27
COURT 2.3 .82
(9) 03 04 06 16 17 19 24 26 30
COURT OF CRIMINAL APPEAL 2.3 .82
(1) 16
CREDENTIALS COMMITTEE 2.3 .82
(4) 06 16 18 32
CUSTOMS TARIFFS UNION 2.3 .67
(1) 16
DAUGHTERS OF THE AMERICAN 2.3 .48
REVOLUTION (DAR)
(1) 16

DE GAULLIST 2.3 .67
(1) 16
DEMOCRATIC NATIONAL COMMITTEE 2.3 .67
(1) 22
DEPARTEMENT (FRANCE) 2.3 .48
(1) 03 16
DEPARTMENT OF COMMERCE AND 2.3 .67
LABOR
(1) 42
DEVELOPMENT LOAN FUND 2.3 .82
(3) 18 27 34
EAST INDIA COMPANY 2.3 .67
(3) 03 25 26
EUROPEAN 2.3 .67
(1) 43
EUROPEAN COMMUNITY 2.3 .82
(3) 11 20 34
EUROPEAN FREE TRADE ASSOCIATION 2.3 .48
(EFTA)
(8) 03 11 17 20 23 25 27 34
EUROPEAN PARLIAMENT 2.3 .67
(5) 11 17 20 23 34
EXECUTIVE COMMITTEE 2.3 .82
(1) 17
FABIAN SOCIETY 2.3 .48
(7) 03 16 19 22 24 25 34
FANNY MAY (FANNIE MAE - ALSO, 2.3 .48
FEDERAL NATIONAL MORTGAGE
ASSOCIATION)
(1) 32 42
FARMERS UNION 2.3 .67
(2) 27 34
FEDERAL AVIATION ADMINISTRATION 2.3 .67
(FAA)
(4) 03 18 27 32
FEDERAL DIET 2.3 .67
(1) 17
FEDERAL LEVEL 2.3 .67
(1) 17
FEDERAL MEDIATION AND 2.3 .48
CONCILIATION SERVICE (FMCS)
(4) 08 18 27 32
FEDERATION OF NIGERIA 2.3 .48
(1) 03
FINANCE COMMITTEE 2.3 .67
(3) 06 17 27
FOOD AND AGRICULTURE 2.3 .48
ORGANIZATION (FAO)
(10) 03 16 17 18 20 23 25 27 32 34
FOURTH ESTATE 2.3 .67
(3) 03 06 16
FRENCH PARLIAMENT 2.3 .67
(1) 03
GENERATION 2.3 .67
(1) 24
GET-OUT-THE-VOTE MOVEMENT 2.3 .67
(1) 16
GHANA, REPUBLIC OF 2.3 .48
(3) 03 07 11
GOSPLAN COMMISSION (USSR) 2.3 .48
(3) 16 19 34
GUINEA, REPUBLIC OF 2.3 .67
(3) 03 07 11 36

HAGUE ARBITRATION TRIBUNAL	2.3	.48
(1) 22		
HITLER-JUGEND	2.3	.67
(1) 16		
HOLDING COMPANY	2.3	.48
(3) 06 16 18		
HOOVER COMMISSION	2.3	.82
(6) 18 19 22 27 32 34		
HOUSE INTERNAL SECURITY COMMITTEE	2.3	.67
(1) 32		
HOUSE OF BURGESSES	2.3	.67
(1) 46		
HOUSE OF DEPUTIES	2.3	.67
(1) 17		
HOUSE OF HAPSBURG	2.3	.48
(1) 25		
HOUSE OF PEERS	2.3	.82
(1) 16		
HOUSE OF ROMANOV	2.3	.67
(1) 16		
HOWARD UNIVERSITY	2.3	.67
(1) 32		
HUKS	2.3	.67
(1) 25		
IMMIGRATION AND NATURALIZATION SERVICE	2.3	.48
(3) 18 27 32		
IMPORT BANK OF WASHINGTON	2.3	.67
(1) 03		
INCAS	2.3	.48
(3) 03 22 24		
INTERNATIONAL POLITICAL SCIENCE ASSOCIATION	2.3	.67
(1) 19		
INTERNATIONAL SOCIETY	2.3	.82
(2) 03 17		
INVISIBLE GOVERNMENT	2.3	.48
(3) 06 16 29		
IRISH FREE STATE	2.3	.48
(1) 34		
JOB CORPS	2.3	.67
(3) 18 25 32		
JOINT COMMITTEE ON ATOMIC ENERGY	2.3	.67
(2) 18 27		
JUNKERS	2.3	.67
(5) 16 17 22 24 25		
KEFAUVER INVESTIGATING COMMITTEE	2.3	.67
(1) 42		
KING CAUCUS	2.3	.48
(2) 18 29		
KINGDOM	2.3	.67
(2) 17 24		
KNIGHTS OF LABOR	2.3	.48
(3) 03 06 16 46		
KOMSOMOL	2.3	.48
(4) 03 16 24 34		
KULAKS	2.3	.67
(3) 16 22 34		
LABOUR GOVERNMENT	2.3	.48
(1) 17		
LAND BANK	2.3	.82
(1) 16		

LAND GRANT COLLEGES	2.3	.48
(5) 06 16 18 25 32		
LATIN AMERICAN FREE TRADE ASSOCIATION (LAFTA)	2.3	.67
(5) 11 17 20 25 34		
LEGISLATIVE COUNCIL	2.3	.67
(3) 16 18 19		
LIBERAL PARTY	2.3	.82
(1) 38		
LIBERAL PARTY, BRITAIN	2.3	.48
(1) 20		
LINE AGENCY	2.3	.67
(1) 03		
LINE DEPARTMENTS IN THE CITY GOVERNMENT	2.3	.67
(1) 45		
LONG PARLIAMENT	2.3	.67
(1) 26		
LUFTWAFFE	2.3	.67
(1) 16		
LUNATIC FRINGE	2.3	.67
(3) 06 27 29		
MANPOWER	2.3	.82
(3) 16 24 30		
MARSHALL MISSION TO CHINA	2.3	.48
(1) 03		
MASS	2.3	.82
(3) 03 24 30		
MEMBER STATE	2.3	.67
(1) 17		
MEMBERSHIP	2.3	.82
(3) 17 20 24		
MEXICAN FARM LABOR	2.3	.48
(1) 46		
MIXED CAUCUS	2.3	.67
(1) 06		
MIXED GOVERNMENT	2.3	.82
(2) 08 10		
MODERATE PARTY	2.3	.67
(1) 17		
MONOLITHIC STATE	2.3	.67
(1) 42		
MOSLEM LEAGUE	2.3	.67
(3) 16 19 34		
MOTHER COUNTRY	2.3	.67
(1) 17		
MOTHERLAND	2.3	.82
(1) 17		
MUNICIPAL COUNCIL	2.3	.67
(1) 17		
MUSLIM	2.3	.67
(2) 24 30		
NATIONAL ARCHIVES	2.3	.48
(1) 06		
NATIONAL CHURCH	2.3	.82
(1) 26		
NATIONAL COMMISSION ON CAUSES AND PREVENTION OF VIOLENCE	2.3	.67
(1) 32		
NATIONAL CONGRESS	2.3	.67
(1) 17		
NATIONAL COUNCIL OF CHURCHES	2.3	.48
(2) 11 25		

NATIONAL EDUCATION ASSOCIATION	2.3	.48
(1) 32		
NATIONAL INSTITUTES OF HEALTH (NIH)	2.3	.67
(2) 25 32		
NATIONAL LEAGUE OF CITIES (NLC)	2.3	.82
(2) 07 32		
NATIONAL MILITARY ESTABLISHMENT	2.3	.82
(1) 42		
NATIONAL OPINION RESEARCH CENTER (U.S.)	2.3	.67
(2) 19 32		
NATIONAL SCIENCE FOUNDATION (NSF)	2.3	.48
(2) 27 32		
NATIONAL SOCIALIST PARTY	2.3	.48
(3) 10 16 19		
NATIONAL URBAN LEAGUE	2.3	.48
(1) 32		
NATIONALIZED ENTERPRISE	2.3	.94
(3) 16 17 23		
NAVY	2.3	.67
(5) 11 17 24 25 30		
NEGRO	2.3	.82
(7) 04 07 11 22 24 25 30		
NEIGHBORING STATE	2.3	.48
(1) 17		
NEW RIGHT	2.3	.82
(1) 34		
NOMINATIONS COMMITTEE	2.3	.67
(1) 17		
NON-COMMITTED COUNTRIES	2.3	.67
(1) 17		
NON-HIERARCHIC PRIMARY GROUP	2.3	.67
(1) 15		
NON-MEMBER STATE	2.3	.48
(1) 17		
NORTH ATLANTIC ALLIANCE	2.3	.67
(1) 11		
OFFICE OF CONSUMER AFFAIRS	2.3	.67
(1) 32		
OFFICE OF STRATEGIC SERVICES (OSS)	2.3	.48
(1) 16		
OLD-AGE, SURVIVORS, DISABILITY INSURANCE (OASDI)	2.3	.67
(2) 18 32		
OTTOMAN EMPIRE	2.3	.48
(2) 16 25		
OVERSEAS CHINESE	2.3	.67
(2) 03 20		
PAN-AFRICAN CONGRESS	2.3	.67
(1) 34		
PAN-ARABIC MOVEMENT	2.3	.67
(2) 16 17		
PARIS COMMUNE	2.3	.67
(5) 03 19 22 25 26		
PARLIAMENTARY COMMITTEE	2.3	.67
(2) 11 17		
PARLIAMENTARY GROUP	2.3	.67
(1) 17		
PARTY IN POWER	2.3	.48
(1) 17		
PEACE GROUPS	2.3	.67
(1) 36		

PEOPLE'S LOBBY	2.3	.48
(1) 06		
PEOPLE'S PARTY	2.3	.67
(4) 06 11 29 32		
PERMANENT COURT OF INTERNATIONAL JUSTICE (HAGUE)	2.3	.48
(7) 06 16 17 19 21 25 27		
PETIT JURY	2.3	.67
(3) 16 18 27		
POLICY COMMITTEE	2.3	.67
(3) 18 27 32		
POLITBURO, CHINA (PRC)	2.3	.67
(1) 20		
POLITICAL REGIME	2.3	.67
(1) 17		
POPULAR FRONT	2.3	.48
(7) 03 16 17 20 21 22 34		
POPULATION	2.3	.82
(12) 01 03 06 11 12 19 20 24 26 30 32 33		
PRESIDENT'S COMMITTEE ON CIVIL RIGHTS	2.3	.67
(1) 19		
PUBLIC SCHOOL SYSTEM	2.3	.67
(1) 42		
PUBLIC UTILITIES	2.3	.67
(8) 03 06 11 16 18 25 27 32		
RADICAL DEMOCRACY	2.3	.48
(1) 06		
RADICAL PARTY	2.3	.67
(2) 17 19		
RADIO FREE EUROPE	2.3	.48
(1) 03		
RED CHINESE COMMUNES	2.3	.48
(1) 03		
RED CHINESE PEOPLES REPUBLIC	2.3	.67
(1) 03		
RED CROSS	2.3	.48
(1) 42		
REGIONAL ECONOMIC COMMISSIONS	2.3	.48
(1) 41		
REGIONAL ECONOMIC ORGANIZATIONS	2.3	.48
(1) 20		
REPUBLICAN CONFERENCE	2.3	.67
(1) 02		
REPUBLICAN POLICY COMMITTEE	2.3	.67
(1) 02		
REVISIONIST SOCIALISTS	2.3	.67
(1) 10		
RIGHT-WING COALITION	2.3	.67
(1) 17		
ROME-BERLIN AXIS	2.3	.48
(4) 16 17 21 22		
SCIENTIFIC MANAGEMENT MOVEMENT	2.3	.82
(3) 01 04 45		
SECOND INTERNATIONAL	2.3	.48
(5) 06 10 16 22 34		
SELECT COMMITTEE	2.3	.67
(5) 02 03 18 27 32		
SHADOW CABINET	2.3	.48
(4) 17 27 30 34		
SINGLE-MEMBER CONSTITUENCIES	2.3	.67
(2) 17 32		

SLAVS	2.3	.48
(1) 25		
SOCIAL SECURITY ADMINISTRATION	2.3	.67
(SSA)		
(2) 27 32		
SOCIALIST INTERNATIONAL	2.3	.48
(1) 17		
SOCIALIST REVOLUTIONARIES	2.3	.48
(1) 11		
SOUTHERN PACIFIC RAILROAD	2.3	.67
(1) 46		
SOVIET PEOPLES COURTS	2.3	.67
(1) 03		
STATE CHURCH	2.3	.67
(1) 16		
STATE DEPARTMENT	2.3	.67
(1) 38		
STATE EXECUTIVE DEPARTMENTS	2.3	.67
(1) 42		
STATES' RIGHTS PARTY	2.3	.67
(2) 29 32		
STERLING BLOC	2.3	.48
(1) 16		
SUDAN, REPUBLIC OF (JAMHURYAT	2.3	.48
EL-SUDAN)		
(2) 03 07		
SUPERIOR COURT-CIRCUIT COURT	2.3	.67
(2) 18 42		
SUPREME HEADQUARTERS ALLIED	2.3	.48
POWERS EUROPE (SHAPE)		
(1) 17		
TECHNOCRAT	2.3	.67
(1) 39		
THIRD INTERNATIONAL	2.3	.48
(6) 06 10 16 21 26 34		
TOWN COUNCIL	2.3	.67
(1) 17		
TUPAMAROS	2.3	.67
(1) 25		
U.N. ECONOMIC AND SOCIAL COUNCIL	2.3	.48
(ECOSOC)		
(3) 03 18 20		
U.N. RELIEF AND REHABILITATION	2.3	.48
ADMINISTRATION (UNRRA)		
(9) 03 16 17 19 20 21 32 36 38 41		
U.N. SPECIAL FUND	2.3	.48
(1) 17		
U.N. TRUCE SUPERVISION	2.3	.48
ORGANIZATION		
(1) 03		
U.S. CENSUS BUREAU	2.3	.48
(1) 16		
U.S. CIVIL SERVICE COMMISSION (CSC)	2.3	.48
(2) 03 27		
U.S. FEDERAL HOUSING	2.3	.48
ADMINISTRATION		
(1) 25		
U.S. OF MEXICO	2.3	.67
(1) 17		
UNIFIED COURT SYSTEM	2.3	.67
(1) 18		
UNION	2.3	.82
(7) 06 16 17 24 27 30 32		

UNION SHOP	2.3	.48
(4) 06 18 27 32		
UNITED FRONT	2.3	.67
(2) 03 16		
UNIVERSAL POSTAL UNION (UPU)	2.3	.48
(7) 03 06 16 17 20 27 32		
UNTOUCHABLES	2.3	.48
(4) 11 16 17 22		
UPPER CHAMBER	2.3	.48
(2) 06 19		
UPPER HOUSE	2.3	.48
(4) 10 16 17 27		
WASHINGTON, D.C. COURTS	2.3	.48
(1) 42		
WEST POINT	2.3	.48
(3) 16 25 32		
WESTERN EUROPEAN UNION (WEU)	2.3	.67
(1) 20		
WESTERN SOCIETY	2.3	.82
(1) 11		
WORK PROJECTS ADMINISTRATION	2.3	.67
(WPA)		
(2) 06 14		
WORLD COUNCIL OF CHURCHES (WCC)	2.3	.48
(1) 17		
YOUNG REPUBLICAN	2.3	.67
(1) 29		
ADMINISTRATIVE DEPARTMENT	2.4	.69
(1) 17		
AFRICANS	2.4	.69
(1) 43		
AFRO-ASIANS	2.4	.51
(1) 24		
AGRICULTURAL EXTENSION SERVICE	2.4	.69
(2) 06 32		
ALIANZA POPULAR REVOLUCIONARIA	2.4	.51
AMERICANA (APRA)		
(3) 03 24 34		
ALLIED CONTROL COUNCIL FOR	2.4	.69
GERMANY		
(3) 03 16 17		
AMERICAN ACADEMY OF POLITICAL	2.4	.84
AND SOCIAL SCIENCE		
(1) 32		
AMERICAN FEDERATION OF TEACHERS	2.4	.69
(1) 25		
AMERICAN FIRST COMMITTEE	2.4	.69
(2) 16 29		
AMERICAN INDIAN	2.4	.69
(3) 07 25 32		
AMERICANS FOR CONSTITUTIONAL	2.4	.69
ACTION (ACA)		
(1) 32		
ANTI-PARTY GROUP	2.4	.84
(2) 03 34		
APPELLATE TRIBUNAL	2.4	.51
(1) 17		
ARAB FEDERATION	2.4	.51
(1) 38		
ARAB STATES	2.4	.51
(1) 11		
ARMED SERVICES COMMITTEE	2.4	.69
(1) 42		

ARMY WAR COLLEGE	2.4	.84
(2) 06 16		
ATLANTIC UNION	2.4	.69
(2) 07 17		
BAATH	2.4	.69
(1) 38		
BANKING AND CURRENCY COMMITTEE	2.4	.69
(1) 42		
BIG LABOR	2.4	.69
(1) 45		
BOARD OF GOVERNORS OF FEDERAL RESERVE SYSTEM	2.4	.69
(1) 42		
BOARD OF TRUSTEES	2.4	.69
(1) 17		
BOERS	2.4	.51
(1) 22		
BROOK FARM	2.4	.69
(1) 03		
BRUSSELS TREATY ORGANIZATION	2.4	.51
(2) 03 17		
BUREAU OF LABOR STANDARDS	2.4	.51
(1) 42		
BUREAU OF PATENTS	2.4	.51
(1) 42		
BUREAU OF STANDARDS	2.4	.51
(2) 16 27		
BUSINESS	2.4	.69
(9) 03 06 07 11 16 17 18 24 30		
BUSINESS CORPORATION	2.4	.51
(1) 11		
CANTON (FRANCE)	2.4	.51
(3) 03 11 16 17		
CAPTIVE NATIONS	2.4	.51
(1) 27		
CATHOLIC ACTION LEAGUE	2.4	.69
(1) 17		
CATHOLIC CENTER PARTY	2.4	.51
(1) 16		
CHAMBER	2.4	.69
(5) 06 16 17 24 27		
CHAMBER OF COMMERCE OF UNITED STATES	2.4	.69
(1) 45		
CHINESE	2.4	.84
(1) 43		
CHRISTIAN SOCIALIST PARTY	2.4	.51
(3) 10 11 22		
CIVIL SERVICE, INTERNATIONAL	2.4	.51
(1) 37		
CIVILIAN REVIEW BOARDS	2.4	.69
(1) 25		
CLAN	2.4	.51
(1) 24		
COAST GUARD, UNITED STATES	2.4	.51
(1) 32		
COLONIAL OFFICE	2.4	.51
(1) 16		
COMBINATION IN RESTRAINT OF TRADE	2.4	.51
(2) 06 16		
COMMISSION ON CIVIL RIGHTS	2.4	.69
(3) 11 27 32		
COMMISSION ON THE STATUS OF WOMEN	2.4	.69
(1) 17		
COMMISSIONS, UNITED STATES REGULATORY	2.4	.84
(1) 32		
COMMONWEAL	2.4	.69
(1) 17		
COMPANY UNION	2.4	.51
(3) 06 27 32		
CONCILIATION SERVICE	2.4	.84
(1) 16		
CONFESSIONAL PARTIES	2.4	.69
(2) 24 33		
CONSTITUTIONAL COMMISSION	2.4	.51
(2) 03 18		
COOPERATIVE	2.4	.51
(1) 17		
COPYRIGHT OFFICE	2.4	.69
(1) 32		
CORPS OF ENGINEERS	2.4	.69
(2) 18 32		
COUNCIL OF STATE, FRANCE	2.4	.51
(1) 20		
COUNCIL OF THE REPUBLIC (FRANCE)	2.4	.69
(1) 03 17		
COUNCIL OF THE UNION (U.S.S.R.)	2.4	.69
(1) 16		
CREDIT UNIONS	2.4	.84
(1) 37		
CRIME SYNDICATES	2.4	.69
(1) 36		
CROWN COLONY	2.4	.51
(2) 16 17		
DECEMBRISTS	2.4	.51
(1) 03		
DEMOCRATIC-REPUBLICAN PARTY	2.4	.69
(3) 02 16 45		
DEPARTMENT OF NATIONAL DEFENSE	2.4	.69
(1) 17		
DIET	2.4	.69
(2) 17 24		
DISADVANTAGED	2.4	.69
(1) 30		
DISARMAMENT COMMISSION, UNITED NATIONS	2.4	.51
(2) 17 20		
DISTRICT OF COLUMBIA COMMITTEE	2.4	.69
(1) 42		
DIVIDED NATIONS	2.4	.51
(1) 11		
DIXIECRAT PARTY	2.4	.51
(6) 03 18 27 29 32 34		
DOMESTIC RELATIONS COURT	2.4	.51
(1) 06		
DUMA	2.4	.69
(2) 16 22		
DYNASTY	2.4	.51
(3) 17 29 33		
EAST AFRICAN COMMUNITY	2.4	.51
(3) 11 20 25		
ECHELONS	2.4	.69
(1) 24		

ECONOMIC ARISTOCRACY	2.4	.69
(1) 10		
EDUCATION AND LABOR COMMITTEE	2.4	.51
(1) 42		
EDUCATIONAL INSTITUTIONS	2.4	.69
(1) 15		
ENTENTE CORDIALE	2.4	.51
(4) 03 16 17 21		
EQUAL EMPLOYMENT OPPORTUNITY	2.4	.69
COMMISSION		
(3) 18 25 32		
ESTATES GENERAL (FRANCE)	2.4	.51
(1) 03		
EUROPEAN COAL AND STEEL	2.4	.51
COMMUNITY (ECSC)		
(9) 03 04 11 12 17 19 20 25 34		
EUROPEAN DEFENCE COMMUNITY	2.4	.51
(EDC)		
(1) 38		
EUROPEAN SOCIALIST AND SOCIAL	2.4	.51
DEMOCRATIC PARTIES		
(1) 03		
EUROPEAN UNION	2.4	.84
(1) 36		
FARMER-LABOR PARTY	2.4	.69
(4) 06 16 27 32		
FASCIST ORGANIZATIONS, U.S.	2.4	.69
(1) 42		
FEDAYEEN (ALSO, FIDAIYUN)	2.4	.69
(1) 25		
FEDERAL COUNCIL	2.4	.69
(2) 16 17		
FEDERAL EMPLOYEES	2.4	.69
(1) 37		
FEDERAL OFFICE OF EDUCATION	2.4	.51
(1) 42		
FEDERAL PUBLIC HOUSING AUTHORITY	2.4	.69
(2) 06 16		
FEDERATION OF THE WEST INDIES	2.4	.51
(1) 38		
FIRST BANK OF THE UNITED STATES	2.4	.84
(1) 16 46		
FIRST INTERNATIONAL	2.4	.69
(5) 06 08 10 16 22		
FIRST REPUBLIC (FRANCE)	2.4	.51
(1) 03		
FOLK	2.4	.69
(2) 26 30		
FREE SOCIETY	2.4	.96
(1) 10		
FREEDOM RIDERS	2.4	.51
(1) 39		
FREEMASON	2.4	.51
(1) 17		
FREEMASONRY	2.4	.51
(3) 03 17 22		
FRIENDS, AMERICAN	2.4	.69
(3) 03 15 30		
GARRISON	2.4	.51
(1) 24		
GENERAL ASSEMBLY COMMITTEES	2.4	.51
(1) 36		
GENERAL COURT	2.4	.69
(1) 45		
GENERAL STAFF	2.4	.69
(1) 06		
GERMAN CONFEDERATION	2.4	.51
(1) 17		
GOVERNMENT BODIES	2.4	.84
(1) 17		
GOVERNMENT OPERATIONS COMMITTEE	2.4	.51
(1) 42		
GRANGE	2.4	.69
(1) 46		
GROUND, AIR AND NAVAL FORCES	2.4	.69
(1) 17		
GUGGENHEIM FOUNDATION	2.4	.69
(1) 19		
HAGUE TRIBUNAL	2.4	.51
(1) 16		
HARD-CORE	2.4	.69
(1) 30		
HESSIANS	2.4	.51
(2) 29 30		
HOME OFFICE	2.4	.51
(3) 03 16 17		
HOUSE OF DELEGATES	2.4	.69
(1) 16		
HOUSE OF HOHENZOLLERN	2.4	.69
(1) 16		
HOUSING AGENCIES	2.4	.51
(1) 42		
IBO TRIBE	2.4	.51
(2) 25 34		
INDESTRUCTIBLE UNION	2.4	.69
(1) 42		
INDIAN NATIONAL CONGRESS	2.4	.69
(4) 03 06 16 22		
INDIAN OFFICE	2.4	.69
(1) 16		
INDIANS	2.4	.69
(1) 37 43		
INDUSTRY	2.4	.69
(3) 24 25 30		
INTELLIGENTSIA	2.4	.69
(5) 24 25 26 33 34		
INTERNATIONAL POSTAL UNION (IPU)	2.4	.51
(1) 21		
INTERNATIONAL TRADE CENTER OF	2.4	.69
GATT		
(1) 41		
INTERPOL	2.4	.51
(2) 17 32		
IRISH-AMERICANS	2.4	.69
(1) 25		
ITALIAN CHRISTIAN DEMOCRATS	2.4	.51
(1) 03		
ITALIAN SOCIALISTS	2.4	.51
(1) 03		
ITALIAN-AMERICANS	2.4	.69
(1) 25		
JAPANESE DIET	2.4	.51
(1) 03		

JOINT COMMITTEE ON THE ECONOMIC 2.4 .51
REPORT
(1) 18
JUDICIAL COUNCIL 2.4 .69
(2) 06 18
JUSTICE OF THE PEACE COURT 2.4 .51
(1) 42
KENT STATE UNIVERSITY 2.4 .69
(2) 11 25
LEGISLATIVE COURT 2.4 .69
(5) 06 16 18 27 32
LEGISLATIVE REFERENCE SERVICE 2.4 .51
(3) 16 18 27
LEVELLERS 2.4 .69
(4) 03 09 26 29
LIBRARY OF CONGRESS 2.4 .51
(5) 06 16 18 27 32
LITTLE ENTENTE 2.4 .51
(4) 16 17 21 34
LOYALTY REVIEW BOARD 2.4 .69
(1) 45
MARINE CORPS (U.S.) 2.4 .69
(2) 06 42
MEDIUM 2.4 .84
(1) 43
MILITARY ACADEMIES 2.4 .69
(1) 42
MILITARY AUTHORITIES 2.4 .69
(1) 17
MILITIA 2.4 .51
(5) 03 06 16 17 27
MILITIA (NATIONAL GUARD) 2.4 .51
(1) 18
MIXED COMMISSION 2.4 .69
(2) 16 17
MOHAMMEDAN 2.4 .69
(1) 16
MORMONS 2.4 .51
(1) 46
NATIONAL ACADEMY OF SCIENCE (NAS) 2.4 .69
(1) 32
NATIONAL COMMITTEE 2.4 .69
(6) 03 06 16 18 27 32
NATIONAL COURT OF APPEALS 2.4 .51
(1) 07
NATIONAL DEMOCRATIC PARTY (NPD), 2.4 .51
GERMANY
(1) 34
NATIONAL GUARD 2.4 .51
(4) 16 18 27 34
NATIONAL SECURITY AGENCY (NSA) 2.4 .69
(4) 03 18 27 32
NATIONAL-REPUBLICANS 2.4 .69
(1) 45
NEGATIVE REFERENCE GROUPS 2.4 .69
(1) 15
NEIGHBORHOOD YOUTH CORPS (NYC) 2.4 .51
(1) 32
NON-GOVERNMENTAL 2.4 .84
(1) 24
NON-GOVERNMENTAL ENTITIES 2.4 .51
(2) 11 24

NON-SIGNATORY GOVERNMENTS 2.4 .51
(1) 17
OCCUPATION FORCES 2.4 .51
(1) 17
OFFICE OF EDUCATION (OE) 2.4 .51
(4) 06 16 18 27
OFFICE OF EMERGENCY PLANNING 2.4 .51
(OEP)
(4) 03 18 27 32
OFFICE OF THE TREASURER OF THE 2.4 .51
U.S.
(1) 42
ONE-CHAMBER 2.4 .69
(1) 17
ONE-PARTY PRESS 2.4 .51
(1) 39
ORGANIZATION OF CENTRAL AMERICAN 2.4 .69
STATES (ODECA)
(2) 17 20
ORTHODOX SOCIALISTS 2.4 .69
(1) 10
OUT PARTY 2.4 .51
(1) 39
PACKED CAUCUS 2.4 .69
(1) 06
PALACE GUARD 2.4 .51
(4) 16 17 27 29
PARTICIPATING GOVERNMENTS 2.4 .69
(1) 17
PARTICIPATING STATES 2.4 .69
(1) 17
PARTISAN MOVEMENT 2.4 .51
(1) 17
PARTY COMMITTEE 2.4 .51
(2) 06 32
PARTY ORGAN 2.4 .69
(1) 06
PEACE BLOC 2.4 .69
(1) 39
PEACE OBSERVATION COMMITTEE 2.4 .69
(1) 45
PENAL ADMINISTRATION 2.4 .69
(1) 06
PERMANENT MISSION 2.4 .69
(1) 17
PLANNING BOARD 2.4 .69
(1) 17
PLENARY ASSEMBLY 2.4 .51
(1) 17
POOR 2.4 .69
(1) 30
POPULAR CHAMBER 2.4 .51
(1) 17
PORT AUTHORITY 2.4 .69
(3) 06 16 32
POST TRADITIONAL SOCIETY 2.4 .51
(1) 07
PRECINCT CAUCUS 2.4 .69
(1) 03
PRESIDENTIAL LOBBY 2.4 .51
(2) 03 18
PRISONER-OF-WAR CAMP 2.4 .51
(1) 17

PROFESSIONAL ORGANIZATIONS (2) 17 25	2.4	.51
PROHIBITION PARTY (4) 06 16 18 32	2.4	.51
PROTECTED STATE (1) 17	2.4	.51
PUBLIC HEALTH SERVICE (PHS) (6) 06 16 18 25 27 32	2.4	.51
PUBLIC UTILITIES COMMISSION (1) 27	2.4	.51
PUBLIC WORKS COMMITTEE (1) 42	2.4	.51
QUADRIPARTITE ADMINISTRATION OF BERLIN (1) 17	2.4	.51
REICH (2) 16 24	2.4	.69
REICHSTAG (4) 03 16 22 34	2.4	.51
RELIGIOUS GROUPS (2) 15 25	2.4	.69
REPRESENTATIVE REGIME (1) 17	2.4	.69
RESERVE OFFICERS TRAINING CORPS (ROTC) (2) 06 25	2.4	.51
RESISTANCE MOVEMENT (2) 16 17	2.4	.51
RIGHT-WING OPPOSITION (1) 17	2.4	.51
ROCKEFELLER FOUNDATION (1) 19	2.4	.51
RURAL ELECTRIFICATION ADMINISTRATION (REA) (6) 06 16 18 22 27 32	2.4	.51
RURAL GOVERNMENT (2) 03 19	2.4	.84
RUSSIAN AUTOCRACY UNDER TSARDOM (1) 10	2.4	.51
RUSSIAN SOCIALIST FEDERAL SOVIET REPUBLIC (RSFSR) (1) 34	2.4	.51
SCHOOL (6) 11 12 15 24 25 30	2.4	.69
SECURITIES AND EXCHANGE COMMISSION (SEC) (8) 06 07 16 18 22 25 27 32	2.4	.51
SELECTIVE SERVICE SYSTEM (8) 06 07 16 18 25 27 32 34	2.4	.51
SENATORIAL CAMPAIGN COMMITTEE (1) 18	2.4	.69
SHARE-THE-WEALTH MOVEMENT (3) 06 16 45	2.4	.51
SIGNATORY GOVERNMENTS (1) 17	2.4	.51
SINN FEIN (1) 16	2.4	.51
SMITHSONIAN INSTITUTION (5) 06 16 27 30 32	2.4	.51
SOCIAL SCIENCE RESEARCH COUNCIL (U.S.) (2) 13 19	2.4	.69
SOCIALIST LABOR PARTY (3) 06 18 32	2.4	.51
SOPHISTS (2) 22 26	2.4	.69
SPECIAL UN FUND FOR ECONOMIC DEVELOPMENT (SUNFED) (1) 20	2.4	.51
STORM TROOPERS (2) 06 16	2.4	.51
STRATEGIC AIR FORCE (1) 17	2.4	.51
STUDENT GOVERNMENT (2) 15 25	2.4	.69
SUDETEN GERMANS (2) 03 34	2.4	.51
SUPREME COMMANDER FOR THE ALLIED POWERS (SCAP) (2) 03 16	2.4	.51
SWISS CONFEDERATION (1) 17	2.4	.51
TASK FORCE (1) 39	2.4	.69
TASS (1) 16	2.4	.51
THINK TANK (1) 39	2.4	.69
THIRD ESTATE (1) 17	2.4	.51
TOWN GOVERNMENT (1) 42	2.4	.84
TRANSCONTINENTAL RAILROAD (1) 46	2.4	.69
TRIAL COURT (1) 06	2.4	.69
TRIBUTARY STATE (2) 06 16	2.4	.51
U.N. CAPITAL DEVELOPMENT FUND (UNCDF) (1) 20	2.4	.51
U.N. DEVELOPMENT PROGRAM (UNDP) (1) 20	2.4	.51
U.N. OPERATION IN THE CONGO (ONYC) (2) 03 20	2.4	.51
U.N. REGIONAL COMMISSIONS (1) 20	2.4	.51
U.S. ARMS CONTROL AND DISARMAMENT AGENCY (ACDA) (3) 18 32 34	2.4	.51
U.S. FEDERAL COMMUNICATIONS COMMISSION (1) 25	2.4	.51
U.S. FEDERAL POWER COMMISSION (1) 25	2.4	.51
U.S. HOUSING AUTHORITY (1) 06	2.4	.51
U.S. NAVAL ACADEMY (1) 16	2.4	.51
U.S. OF INDONESIA (1) 16	2.4	.51
U.S. OFFICE OF EDUCATION (USOE) (2) 06 16	2.4	.51
UNHOLY ALLIANCE (1) 39	2.4	.69

UNION OF CENTRAL AFRICAN STATES (UEAC)	2.4	.51
(1) 20		
UNITED ARAB STATES (U.A.S.)	2.4	.51
(1) 38		
UNRECOGNIZED STATES	2.4	.51
(1) 17		
URBAN RENEWAL ADMINISTRATION	2.4	.51
(1) 27		
VETERANS OF FOREIGN WARS OF THE U.S. (VFW)	2.4	.51
(2) 27 34		
WALLOONS	2.4	.51
(1) 38		
WATCHDOG COMMITTEE	2.4	.51
(2) 18 32		
WEHRMACHT	2.4	.51
(1) 16		
WELFARE ADMINISTRATION	2.4	.69
(1) 18		
WHITE CITIZENS COUNCILS	2.4	.51
(1) 34		
WORLD ASSOCIATION OF WORLD FEDERALISTS	2.4	.51
(1) 17		
WORLD BANK GROUP (IRBD,IDA,IFC)	2.4	.69
(2) 18 20		
WORLD CONFEDERATION OF LABOUR	2.4	.69
(1) 23		
YOUNG DEMOCRAT	2.4	.69
(1) 29		
YOUTH ORGANIZATIONS	2.4	.84
(2) 11 15		
ACADEMIES (NAVY, ARMY, AIR FORCE)	2.5	.52
(1) 27		
ACADEMY OF POLITICAL SCIENCE	2.5	.70
(2) 16 32		
ADMINISTRATIVE COUNCIL	2.5	.70
(1) 17		
ADVISORY BODY	2.5	.52
(1) 17		
AGENCY SHOP	2.5	.70
(1) 32		
AGRICULTURAL BLOC	2.5	.52
(1) 06		
AIR DEFENSE COMMAND	2.5	.52
(1) 03		
ALL-AMERICAN CITIES	2.5	.70
(1) 03		
ALL-UNION PARTY CONGRESS, SOVIET UNION	2.5	.52
(1) 20		
ALLIED HIGH COMMISSION	2.5	.70
(1) 17		
ALPHABETICAL AGENCY	2.5	.70
(2) 06 16		
AMERICAN FIRST PARTY	2.5	.70
(1) 45		
AMERICAN MUNICIPAL ASSOCIATION	2.5	.70
(3) 03 19 32		
AMERICAN SOCIETY FOR PUBLIC ADMINISTRATION (ASPA)	2.5	.70
(2) 19 32		
ANGLICANS	2.5	.70
(2) 22 26		
ANGLO-AMERICAN	2.5	.52
(2) 24 30		
ANGLO-RUSSIAN ALLIANCES	2.5	.52
(2) 16 21		
ARABIC	2.5	.70
(1) 43		
ARCHDIOCESE	2.5	.70
(1) 17		
ASIANS	2.5	.70
(1) 43		
ASSOCIATED STATES, EUROPEAN ECONOMIC COMMUNITY	2.5	.70
(1) 20		
AUDIT OFFICE	2.5	.70
(2) 17 23		
BALKAN FEDERATION	2.5	.52
(3) 03 21 34		
BALTIC ENTENTE	2.5	.52
(2) 16 21		
BANTUSTANS	2.5	.70
(1) 11		
BARBARY PIRATES	2.5	.70
(2) 06 16		
BILL-DRAFTING OFFICE	2.5	.70
(1) 16		
BOROUGH	2.5	.52
(6) 03 06 16 17 18 32		
BRAZZAVILLE BLOC	2.5	.52
(4) 03 17 34 38		
BRITISH HIGH COURT OF JUSTICE	2.5	.52
(1) 03		
BUND	2.5	.52
(2) 05 16		
BUREAU	2.5	.52
(6) 06 16 17 18 24 27		
BUREAU OF CUSTOMS	2.5	.52
(2) 16 32		
BUREAU OF ECONOMIC AFFAIRS	2.5	.52
(1) 42		
BUREAU OF ENGRAVING AND PRINTING	2.5	.52
(2) 16 32		
BUREAU OF EUROPEAN AFFAIRS	2.5	.52
(1) 42		
BUREAU OF FAR EASTERN AFFAIRS	2.5	.52
(1) 42		
BUREAU OF NARCOTICS	2.5	.52
(2) 16 32		
BUREAU OF NARCOTICS AND DANGEROUS DRUGS (BNDD)	2.5	.52
(1) 32		
BUREAU OF NEAR EASTERN AND SOUTH ASIAN AFFAIRS	2.5	.52
(1) 42		
BUREAU OF OLD AGE AND SURVIVORS INSURANCE	2.5	.52
(1) 42		
BUREAU OF PRISONS	2.5	.52
(1) 42		
BUREAU OF PUBLIC ASSISTANCE	2.5	.52
(1) 42		

BUREAU OF RECLAMATION	2.5	.70
(3) 16 18 32		
BUREAU OF THE MINT	2.5	.52
(1) 42		
CANVASSING BOARDS	2.5	.70
(3) 06 18 32		
CENTRAL AFRICAN REPUBLIC (CAR)	2.5	.52
(1) 07		
CENTRAL AMERICAN COMMON MARKET	2.5	.52
(CACM)		
(3) 07 20 25		
CHANCELLERY	2.5	.70
(1) 16		
CHANCERY	2.5	.70
(3) 16 17 18		
CHARTIST MOVEMENT	2.5	.52
(2) 06 16		
CHINESE COMMUNIST YOUTH LEAGUE	2.5	.52
(1) 03		
CHRISTIAN SOCIAL PARTY	2.5	.70
(3) 16 17 19		
CHRISTIAN TRADE UNIONS	2.5	.52
(1) 17		
CLAY WHIG	2.5	.52
(1) 29		
COAST GUARD ACADEMY	2.5	.52
(1) 27		
COCHIN CHINESE REPUBLIC	2.5	.52
(1) .16		
COLONIAL COURTS	2.5	.52
(1) 03		
COLOSSUS OF THE NORTH	2.5	.52
(1) 16		
COMMISSION (BOARD)	2.5	.70
(9) 03 06 11 16 17 18 19 24 30		
COMMISSION GOVERNMENT	2.5	.70
(1) 42		
COMMISSIONS (GOVERNMENTAL)	2.5	.70
(1) 19		
COMMITTEE OF PUBLIC SAFETY	2.5	.52
(1) 17		
COMMITTEE ON DECOLONIZATION	2.5	.52
(COMMITTEE OF 24)		
(1) 20		
COMMODITY CREDIT CORPORATION	2.5	.52
(CCC)		
(7) 03 06 16 18 22 27 32		
COMMUNIST YOUTH LEAGUE, CHINA	2.5	.52
(PRC)		
(1) 20		
CONCLAVE	2.5	.70
(2) 16 17		
CONFEDERATION GENERALE DU	2.5	.52
TRAVAIL (CGT)		
(5) 03 10 16 19 34		
CONGRESSIONAL RESEARCH SERVICE	2.5	.52
(1) 32		
CONSTITUTIONAL COUNCIL, FRANCE	2.5	.52
(3) 11 17 20		
CONSULAR OFFICERS	2.5	.52
(1) 03		
CONSULTATIVE ASSEMBLY	2.5	.70
(2) 17 34		

CONSUMERS COOPERATIVE	2.5	.70
(1) 03		
CONTINENTAL ARMY UNITED STATES	2.5	.70
(CONUS)		
(1) 32		
CORONER'S JURY	2.5	.70
(1) 42		
CORPORATION	2.5	.70
(8) 03 06 11 16 18 24 25 27		
COUNCIL OF FOREIGN MINISTERS	2.5	.52
(2) 17 19		
COUNCIL OF NATIONALITIES	2.5	.70
(1) 16		
COUNCIL OF STATE	2.5	.70
(4) 11 16 17 23		
COUNCIL ON FOREIGN RELATIONS	2.5	.52
(U.S.)		
(2) 16 19		
COUNTY BOROUGH	2.5	.52
(1) 03		
COUNTY COMMITTEE	2.5	.70
(1) 03		
COURT OF CUSTOMS AND PATENT	2.5	.70
APPEALS		
(4) 06 16 18 27 32		
CRAFT UNION (TRADE UNION)	2.5	.52
(3) 06 16 45		
CUSTOMS	2.5	.70
(2) 06 16		
CUSTOMS SERVICE	2.5	.70
(1) 45		
DEMOCRATIC STUDY GROUP	2.5	.70
(2) 02 32		
DEPARTMENT	2.5	.52
(8) 03 06 16 17 18 19 24 32		
DISPLACED PERSONS (DPS)	2.5	.52
(3) 16 17 27		
DOMESTIC CORPORATION	2.5	.52
(1) 06		
ECONOMIC COOPERATION	2.5	.70
ADMINISTRATION (ECA)		
(1) 17 38		
ELECTORAL COMMISSION	2.5	.70
(2) 06 16		
EMIGRE GOVERNMENT	2.5	.52
(1) 16		
EMPIRE, THE	2.5	.84
(1) 16		
EMPLOYMENT SERVICE	2.5	.70
(1) 32		
ENEMY STATE	2.5	.52
(1) 17		
ENTENTE	2.5	.70
(3) 06 16 27		
ENTERPRISE	2.5	.84
(2) 19 24		
ESKIMOS	2.5	.52
(1) 22		
EUROPEAN MOVEMENT	2.5	.70
(1) 17		
EXECUTIONERS	2.5	.70
(1) 30		

EXECUTIVE COUNCIL	2.5	.70
(2) 06 17		
FALANGISTS	2.5	.52
(1) 38		
FARM BUREAU FEDERATION	2.5	.52
(1) 42		
FARMERS ALLIANCE	2.5	.52
(1) 06		
FASCIST YOUTH ORGANIZATION	2.5	.52
(1) 16		
FEDERAL COURTS, TERRITORIAL	2.5	.52
(1) 18		
FEDERAL DEPOSIT INSURANCE	2.5	.52
CORPORATION (FDIC)		
(6) 06 16 18 22 27 32		
FEDERAL HIGHWAY ADMINISTRATION	2.5	.52
(FHWA)		
(1) 32		
FEDERAL HOME LOAN BANK BOARD	2.5	.52
(FHLBB)		
(4) 06 16 32 42		
FEDERAL MARITIME COMMISSION (FMC)	2.5	.52
(1) 18		
FEDERAL NATIONAL MORTGAGE	2.5	.52
ASSOCIATION (FNMA)		
(3) 16 27 32		
FEDERAL SAVINGS AND LOAN	2.5	.52
INSURANCE CORPORATION		
(3) 06 16 32		
FEDERATION OF MALAYA	2.5	.52
(1) 03		
FIELD SERVICE	2.5	.70
(1) 18		
FORD CORPORATION	2.5	.52
(1) 25		
FOREIGN POLICY ASSOCIATION (U.S.)	2.5	.52
(3) 16 19 32		
FOURTH INTERNATIONAL	2.5	.52
(1) 34		
FREE FRENCH	2.5	.52
(3) 16 17 21		
FREEDMEN'S BUREAU	2.5	.70
(1) 46		
FRENCH	2.5	.70
(1) 43		
FRENCH CIVIL SERVICE	2.5	.52
(1) 03		
FRENCH COMMUNITY	2.5	.70
(2) 03 34		
FRENCH EMPIRE	2.5	.52
(1) 21		
FRENCH NATIONALIZED INDUSTRIES	2.5	.70
(1) 03		
FRENCH ROYALISTS	2.5	.70
(1) 10		
FRONT	2.5	.70
(1) 24		
FRONT DE LIBERATION NATIONALE	2.5	.70
(FLN)		
(4) 03 17 25 34		
GENERAL ELECTRIC COMPANY	2.5	.70
(1) 04		
GENERAL LAND OFFICE	2.5	.70
(1) 16		
GENTILE	2.5	.70
(1) 43		
GERMAN COMMUNIST PARTY	2.5	.52
(1) 17		
GERMAN TRADE UNIONS	2.5	.52
(1) 03		
GOLD BLOC	2.5	.70
(1) 21		
GOVERNMENT FORCES	2.5	.70
(1) 17		
GRAVE YARD COMMITTEE	2.5	.70
(1) 45		
HOLY ALLIANCE	2.5	.52
(5) 03 06 16 17 29		
HOUSE OF ASSEMBLY	2.5	.70
(2) 16 17		
HOUSE OF SAVOY	2.5	.70
(1) 16		
HOUSE, THE	2.5	.70
(1) 16		
I. G. FARBENINDUSTRIE (IGFIG)	2.5	.70
(GERMAN CHEMICAL TRUST)		
(2) 16 22		
IMPERIAL CITY	2.5	.70
(1) 17		
INCORPORATED VILLAGE	2.5	.52
(1) 27		
INDOCHINESE	2.5	.52
(1) 43		
INNER CLUB	2.5	.70
(1) 39		
INTERNATIONAL CIVIL AVIATION	2.5	.52
ORGANIZATION (ICAO)		
(4) 17 20 27 32		
INTERNATIONAL COOPERATION	2.5	.70
ADMINISTRATION (ICA)		
(3) 17 27 34 38		
INTERNATIONAL RED CROSS	2.5	.52
(3) 03 17 21		
INTRAPARTY	2.5	.70
(1) 24		
INVESTMENT BANK	2.5	.52
(1) 45		
IRREGULAR TROOPS	2.5	.52
(1) 17		
ITALIAN LIBERAL PARTY	2.5	.52
(1) 03		
JAPANESE	2.5	.70
(1) 43		
JOINT MARITIME COMMISSION	2.5	.70
(1) 17		
JUVENILE COURT	2.5	.52
(3) 06 16 25		
KING'S COUNCIL	2.5	.52
(1) 09		
KURDS	2.5	.52
(4) 03 11 21 25		
LAND POWER	2.5	.52
(1) 17		
LANDING FORCES	2.5	.52
(1) 17		

LAW ENFORCEMENT ASSISTANCE ADMINISTRATION	2.5	.70	OUTER SEVEN (EFTA)	2.5	.52
(2) 07 32			(2) 20 38		
LEAGUE	2.5	.70	PARTY OF THE PEOPLE	2.5	.70
(3) 06 17 24			(1) 39		
LEGATION	2.5	.52	PATENT OFFICE	2.5	.52
(5) 06 16 17 27 32			(4) 06 16 18 32		
LEGISLATIVE REFERENCE BUREAU	2.5	.52	PEOPLE'S COMMISSARIAT OF STATE SECURITY (USSR) (N.K.G.B.)	2.5	.52
(2) 03 06			(1) 34		
LINCOLN BRIGADE	2.5	.52	PEOPLE'S COMMUNES	2.5	.52
(1) 16			(1) 34		
LUBLIN GOVERNMENT	2.5	.52	PERMANENT SECRETARIAT	2.5	.70
(2) 16 34			(1) 17		
MANUFACTURING INDUSTRIES	2.5	.70	POLICE REGIME	2.5	.70
(1) 25			(1) 17		
MEDITERRANEAN COUNTRIES	2.5	.52	POLITICAL CLUB	2.5	.52
(2) 07 11			(1) 16		
MICRO STATES	2.5	.52	POLITICAL GENERATIONS	2.5	.70
(1) 11			(1) 11		
MOSLEM BROTHERHOOD	2.5	.70	POLITIES, NON-WESTERN	2.5	.70
(1) 34			(1) 04		
MOUVEMENT REPUBLICAIN POPULAIRE (MRP)	2.5	.52	PORT OF NEW YORK AUTHORITY	2.5	.70
(6) 03 16 17 19 24 34			(2) 03 18		
MUGWUMP	2.5	.52	PREHISTORIC SOCIETY	2.5	.70
(5) 06 16 22 27 29			(1) 25		
MUSCOVITES	2.5	.52	PRIVATE ORGANIZATION	2.5	.52
(1) 34			(1) 17		
NATIONAL BUREAU OF STANDARDS	2.5	.52	PRIVY COUNCIL	2.5	.52
(4) 06 18 27 32			(5) 03 06 16 17 34		
NATIONAL COMMITTEE ON THE CAUSES AND PREVENTION OF VIOLENCE	2.5	.52	PROTESTANT POLITICAL PARTIES	2.5	.52
(1) 32			(1) 19		
NATIONAL ECONOMIC COUNCIL	2.5	.52	PUBLIC AFFAIRS, SCHOOLS OF	2.5	.52
(2) 10 22			(1) 04		
NATIONAL LABOR PARTY	2.5	.70	PUBLIC INDUSTRY	2.5	.52
(1) 16			(1) 16		
NATIONAL MUNICIPAL LEAGUE (U.S.)	2.5	.52	PUBLIC SCHOOL	2.5	.52
(4) 03 18 19 32			(1) 06		
NETHERLANDS, KINGDOM OF THE	2.5	.52	PUERTO RICANS	2.5	.70
(3) 03 07 11			(1) 37		
NIGERIA, FEDERATION OF	2.5	.52	QUAKERS	2.5	.52
(3) 03 07 11			(4) 19 22 25 26		
NON-MEMBER GOVERNMENT	2.5	.52	QUASI-PUBLIC CORPORATION	2.5	.52
(1) 17			(1) 06		
NORTH ATLANTIC COUNCIL	2.5	.52	RACIAL GROUPINGS	2.5	.70
(1) 17			(1) 15		
OCTOBRISTS	2.5	.52	RADICAL-SOCIALISTS	2.5	.52
(2) 16 22			(3) 03 17 34		
OFFICE OF ALIEN PROPERTY	2.5	.70	RECHTSTAAT	2.5	.52
(1) 42			(2) 19 22		
OFFICE OF PRICE ADMINISTRATION (OPA)	2.5	.52	RECONSTRUCTION FINANCE CORPORATION (RFC)	2.5	.52
(3) 06 16 19			(5) 03 06 16 22 32		
OFFICE OF PRICE STABILIZATION	2.5	.52	REIGNING DYNASTY	2.5	.52
(1) 45			(1) 17		
OLD GUARD	2.5	.52	RELIGIOUS ORGANIZATIONS	2.5	.52
(5) 02 06 16 27 29			(2) 11 15		
ORGANIZATION FOR ECONOMIC COOPERATION AND DEVELOPMENT (OECD)	2.5	.52	REPARATIONS COMMISSION	2.5	.52
			(1) 16		
			RIGHT-WING GOVERNMENT	2.5	.52
			(1) 17		
(1) 36			ROME, BERLIN, TOKYO TRIANGLE	2.5	.52
			(1) 16		

ROYAL DYNASTY	2.5	.52
(1) 17		
ROYAL INSTITUTE OF INTERNATIONAL AFFAIRS (BRITAIN)	2.5	.70
(1) 19		
RUMP PARLIAMENT	2.5	.52
(1) 17		
RURAL COMMUNE	2.5	.52
(1) 17		
RURAL LOCAL GOVERNMENT	2.5	.52
(1) 12		
SACRED COLLEGE OF CARDINALS	2.5	.52
(1) 17		
SAMURAI	2.5	.52
(1) 16		
SAN FRANCISCO CONFERENCE (UNCIO)	2.5	.70
(4) 16 20 21 32		
SECOND EMPIRE OF FRANCE	2.5	.52
(3) 03 16 17		
SECOND NATIONAL BANK OF THE U.S.	2.5	.84
(1) 16 46		
SECOND REICH	2.5	.52
(1) 16		
SECOND REPUBLIC OF FRANCE	2.5	.52
(2) 03 16		
SECONDARY INSTITUTIONS	2.5	.70
(1) 15		
SECT	2.5	.70
(3) 24 25 29		
SELECTIVE SERVICE ADMINISTRATION	2.5	.52
(1) 42		
SEMIOFFICIAL	2.5	.70
(1) 17		
SEMITES	2.5	.52
(1) 09		
SENATE, FRANCE	2.5	.52
(1) 20		
SERBIANS	2.5	.52
(1) 22		
SERVICE INDUSTRY	2.5	.52
(1) 25		
SETTLEMENT HOUSES	2.5	.52
(1) 45 46		
SIGNATORY STATES	2.5	.52
(1) 17		
SINGLE CHAMBER	2.5	.52
(1) 17		
SIXTH COLUMNISTS	2.5	.70
(1) 29		
SOCIAL AGENCIES	2.5	.70
(1) 45		
SOCIOLOGY, THE PROFESSION	2.5	.52
(12) 04 07 11 12 15 19 22 23 24 25 26 30		
SOVIET OF NATIONALITIES	2.5	.52
(4) 03 16 17 19		
STAFF	2.5	.70
(3) 06 17 24		
STANDING ARMY	2.5	.52
(1) 06		
STATE BANKS	2.5	.52
(1) 16		
STATE CIRCUIT COURT	2.5	.52
(1) 42		
STATE DISTRICT COURT	2.5	.70
(1) 42		
STATE POLICE	2.5	.52
(2) 06 16		
STRICT MARXISTS	2.5	.52
(1) 22		
SUBGROUPS, LEGISLATIVE	2.5	.70
(1) 04		
SUBVERSIVE ORGANIZATIONS	2.5	.52
(1) 32		
SUCCESSION STATES	2.5	.52
(1) 38		
SUPREME COMMAND	2.5	.52
(1) 17		
TACTICAL AIR COMMAND	2.5	.52
(1) 03		
TAX COURT OF THE UNITED STATES	2.5	.70
(5) 06 16 18 27 32		
THIRD HOUSE OF CONGRESS	2.5	.52
(1) 06 16 18 42		
THIRD HOUSE OF LEGISLATURE	2.5	.52
(1) 44		
TOGO REPUBLIC	2.5	.52
(4) 03 07 11 17 36		
TREASURY	2.5	.70
(1) 24		
TRIBUNAL	2.5	.52
(3) 06 16 27		
TRUSTEE STATE	2.5	.52
(1) 17		
TWENTIETH PARTY CONGRESS	2.5	.52
(2) 22 34		
U.S. AIR FORCE ACADEMY	2.5	.52
(1) 42		
U.S. ARMY SPECIAL FORCES	2.5	.52
(1) 03		
U.S. COAST AND GEODETIC SURVEY	2.5	.52
(1) 32		
U.S. CONCILIATION SERVICE	2.5	.52
(1) 06		
U.S. COURT OF MILITARY APPEALS	2.5	.52
(1) 32		
U.S. MILITARY ACADEMY	2.5	.52
(3) 16 25 33		
UNIVERSAL POSTAL UNION CONGRESS	2.5	.52
(8) 03 06 16 17 20 27 32 41		
UNIVERSITY OF CALIFORNIA	2.5	.70
(1) 25		
UNIVERSITY OF CHICAGO	2.5	.70
(2) 04 19		
URBAN MUNICIPALITY	2.5	.52
(1) 17		
VASSAL STATE	2.5	.52
(3) 06 16 17		
VETERANS ORGANIZATIONS	2.5	.70
(1) 18		
VETO GROUPS	2.5	.70
(2) 22 33		
WAR DEMOCRATS	2.5	.52
(2) 06 32		

WAR DEPARTMENT (ALSO, DEPARTMENT OF WAR) (1) 42	2.5	.70
WAR PRODUCTION BOARD (U.S.) (4) 06 16 19 25	2.5	.52
WAR RELOCATION AUTHORITY (1) 16	2.5	.84
WHITE MAN'S GOVERNMENT (1) 29	2.5	.52
WORKS PROGRESS ADMINISTRATION (WPA) (5) 06 16 17 19 32	2.5	.70
YOUNG PIONEERS, CHINA (PRC) (1) 20	2.5	.52
YOUTH CORPS (1) 32	2.5	.52
YOUTH GROUPS (1) 15	2.5	.84
YOUTH INTERNATIONAL PARTY (YIPPIES) (1) 11	2.5	.70
ZOLLVEREIN (4) 06 16 17 21	2.5	.70
ABORIGINES (2) 24 25	2.6	.51
ACADEMY OF PLATO (1) 26	2.6	.51
AFRICAN DEVELOPMENT BANK (1) 20	2.6	.51
AIR FORCE (1) 17	2.6	.51
AIR FORCE INTELLIGENCE (1) 18	2.6	.51
ALL-INDIA NATIONALIST CONGRESS (1) 16	2.6	.51
ALL-UNION COMMUNIST PARTY OF RUSSIA (1) 10	2.6	.51
ALLIED COUNCIL FOR JAPAN (2) 03 16	2.6	.69
ALLIED MILITARY GOVERNMENT (AMG) (1) 16	2.6	.51
AMERICAN ANARCHISTS (1) 10	2.6	.51
AMERICAN LABOR PARTY (ALP) (3) 06 16 32	2.6	.51
AMERICAN LIBERTY LEAGUE (1) 06	2.6	.51
AMERICAN NATIONAL PARTY (1) 06	2.6	.69
AMERICAN NATIONAL RED CROSS (1) 06	2.6	.51
AMERICAN SOCIETY OF INTERNATIONAL LAW (1) 07	2.6	.69
ANABAPTISTS (1) 26	2.6	.69
ANDEAN GROUP (2) 07 11	2.6	.51
ANGLO-EGYPTIAN ALLIANCE (1) 16	2.6	.51
ANGLO-TURKISH ALLIANCE (1) 21	2.6	.51
ANTI-SALOON LEAGUE OF AMERICA (2) 06 16	2.6	.51
ANTIMASONIC PARTY (4) 03 06 29 32	2.6	.51
ARAB DEVELOPMENT BANK (1) 17	2.6	.69
ARAB REPUBLICS, FEDERATION OF (1) 07	2.6	.51
ARAB SOCIALIST UNION (1) 25	2.6	.51
ARAB UNION (1) 38	2.6	.51
ASHANTI (2) 03 24	2.6	.51
ASSOCIATION OF SOUTHEAST ASIAN NATIONS (ASEAN) (2) 20 34	2.6	.51
ASSYRIANS (2) 09 22	2.6	.51
AUTONOMOUS REPUBLICS (1) 03	2.6	.69
BALKAN LEAGUE (1) 16	2.6	.51
BALKAN UNION (1) 21	2.6	.51
BANK FOR INTERNATIONAL SETTLEMENTS (4) 06 16 17 21	2.6	.51
BANK OF ENGLAND (3) 16 19 22	2.6	.51
BAPTISTS (2) 22 26	2.6	.69
BENEVOLENT AND PROTECTIVE ORDER OF ELKS (1) 08	2.6	.51
BILL DRAFTING SERVICES (1) 45	2.6	.51
BOARD OF COMMISSIONERS (COUNTY) (1) 18	2.6	.51
BOARD OF HEALTH (1) 03	2.6	.51
BOARD OF IMMIGRATION APPEALS (1) 18	2.6	.51
BOARD OF PAROLE (1) 42	2.6	.51
BOARD OF TRADE (1) 16	2.6	.51
BRITISH (1) 43	2.6	.69
BRITISH IMPERIAL WAR CABINET (1) 41	2.6	.51
BUREAU OF INSULAR AFFAIRS (1) 16	2.6	.51
BUREAU OF INTER-AMERICAN AFFAIRS (1) 42	2.6	.51
BUREAU OF INTERNATIONAL ORGANIZATION AFFAIRS (1) 42	2.6	.51
BUREAU OF MINES (5) 06 16 18 27 32	2.6	.51
BUREAU OF PUBLIC AFFAIRS (1) 42	2.6	.51

BUREAU OF PUBLIC ROADS	2.6	.51
(2) 18 27		
BUSINESS ASSOCIATIONS	2.6	.51
(2) 15 18		
CARIBBEAN FREE TRADE ASSOCIATION	2.6	.51
(CARIFTA)		
(2) 38 41		
CATHOLIC	2.6	.69
(2) 24 30		
CENTRAL AFRICAN FEDERATION	2.6	.51
(1) 34		
CITIZENS COMMITTEE	2.6	.51
(1) 39		
CIVIL DEFENSE ADMINISTRATION,	2.6	.51
FEDERAL		
(1) 42		
CLUB	2.6	.51
(3) 06 17 24		
COAST AND GEODETIC SURVEY	2.6	.51
(4) 06 16 18 32		
COLORED	2.6	.69
(1) 30		
COLUMBIA UNIVERSITY	2.6	.69
(3) 11 19 25		
COMMERCIAL BANK	2.6	.51
(1) 45		
COMMITTEE ON CREDENTIALS	2.6	.51
(1) 16		
COMMITTEE ON FAIR EMPLOYMENT	2.6	.51
PRACTICES		
(1) 16		
COMMUNIST ECONOMIC ORGANIZATION	2.6	.51
EAST EUROPE		
(1) 25		
CONFLUENT SOCIETY	2.6	.69
(1) 03		
CONSOLIDATED EDISON COMPANY	2.6	.51
(1) 11		
CONSOLIDATED SCHOOLS	2.6	.51
(1) 45		
CONSORTIUM	2.6	.69
(3) 16 17 30		
CONSTITUTIONAL COMMITTEE	2.6	.51
(1) 17		
CONSTRUCTION INDUSTRY	2.6	.69
(1) 25		
CONSUMER ADVISORY COUNCIL	2.6	.51
(1) 32		
CONTESTING DELEGATION	2.6	.69
(1) 06		
CONTRACTING GOVERNMENTS	2.6	.69
(1) 17		
CORPORATE BODY	2.6	.51
(3) 17 24 30		
COUNCIL FOR MUTUAL ECONOMIC	2.6	.51
ASSISTANCE		
(3) 11 17 34		
COUNCIL FOR NUCLEAR DISARMAMENT	2.6	.51
(CND)		
(1) 34		
COUNCIL OF NICAEA	2.6	.69
(1) 09 26		

COUNCIL OF REPRESENTATIVES	2.6	.51
(1) 17		
COUNCIL OF STATE GOVERNMENTS	2.6	.51
(U.S.)		
(7) 06 16 18 19 27 32 42		
COUNCIL OF TRENT	2.6	.51
(1) 17		
COURT OF COMMON PLEAS	2.6	.69
(1) 16		
COURT OF JUSTICE, EUROPEAN	2.6	.51
COMMUNITY		
(1) 17 20 23 25		
COURT OF RECORD	2.6	.51
(1) 06		
CREDIT MOBILIER	2.6	.51
(1) 06		
CREOLE	2.6	.51
(1) 24		
CUSTOMS COURT	2.6	.69
(4) 06 18 27 32		
DEMOCRATIC POLICY COMMITTEE	2.6	.51
(1) 02		
DEMOCRATIC-FARMER LABOR PARTY	2.6	.51
(1) 32		
DEPOSIT BANK	2.6	.69
(1) 06		
DIPLOMATIC CIRCLES	2.6	.51
(1) 17		
ECCLESIASTICAL COURTS	2.6	.51
(1) 03		
ECONOMIC DEVELOPMENT	2.6	.51
ADMINISTRATION		
(2) 25 32		
EGYPTIAN-BRITISH ALLIANCE	2.6	.51
(1) 16		
EMPLOYERS UNION	2.6	.51
(1) 17		
EN BLOC	2.6	.51
(1) 16		
ENGLISH	2.6	.69
(1) 43		
ENGLISH-SPEAKING UNION	2.6	.51
(1) 16		
EOKA (CYPRUS)	2.6	.51
(1) 34		
EPICUREAN SCHOOL	2.6	.51
(2) 22 26		
EPICUREANS	2.6	.51
(2) 09 22		
EUROPEAN PAYMENTS UNION	2.6	.51
(2) 17 34		
EXECUTIVE BOARD	2.6	.51
(1) 17		
EXEMPT CLASS	2.6	.69
(1) 06		
EXTRA-LEGAL PARTY	2.6	.69
(1) 03		
FABIAN RESEARCH DEPARTMENT	2.6	.51
(1) 22		
FACULTY	2.6	.69
(2) 19 24		
FALANGE PARTY	2.6	.51
(6) 16 17 21 24 25 34		

FAMILY	2.6	.69
(7) 07 11 15 24 25 26 30		
FAMILY OF NATIONS	2.6	.51
(3) 06 16 17		
FEDERAL CIVIL DEFENSE ADMINISTRATION	2.6	.69
(1) 03		
FEDERAL CONSTITUTIONAL COURT	2.6	.51
(2) 11 17		
FEDERAL EXECUTIVE BOARDS	2.6	.69
(1) 37		
FEDERAL FARM MORTGAGE CORPORATION	2.6	.69
(2) 16 32		
FEDERAL LAND BANK	2.6	.51
(2) 06 16		
FEDERAL SECURITY AGENCY	2.6	.51
(1) 06		
FEDERAL TELECOMMUNICATIONS SYSTEM (FTS)	2.6	.51
(1) 32		
FEDERATION OF ARAB EMIRATES	2.6	.51
(1) 38		
FEDERATION OF ARAB REPUBLICS	2.6	.51
(2) 07 11		
FEDERATION OF SOUTH ARABIA	2.6	.51
(1) 38		
FINANCE DEPARTMENT	2.6	.69
(1) 16		
FIRST REICH	2.6	.51
(1) 16		
FLOATING VOTE	2.6	.69
(1) 19		
FOREIGN LEGION	2.6	.51
(2) 16 17		
FORMS OF STATE	2.6	.84
(1) 35		
FRENCH COMMITTEE OF NATIONAL LIBERATION	2.6	.69
(2) 16 34		
FRENCH RESISTANCE MOVEMENT	2.6	.51
(1) 03		
FRENCH SOCIALIST PARTY	2.6	.51
(2) 03 10		
FRIENDSHIP CLIQUES	2.6	.69
(1) 15		
GARDEN CITY MOVEMENT	2.6	.51
(1) 06		
GENERAL COMMITTEE	2.6	.69
(1) 17		
GENERAL POST OFFICE	2.6	.69
(3) 17 27 32		
GENERAL ZIONISTS	2.6	.69
(1) 03		
GERMAN COLONIES	2.6	.51
(1) 21		
GERMANS	2.6	.69
(1) 43		
GOLD DEMOCRATS	2.6	.51
(1) 06		
GOOD-GOVERNMENT ASSOCIATION	2.6	.69
(1) 06		
HAGANAH	2.6	.51
(3) 03 16 34		
HARVARD GRADUATE SCHOOL OF BUSINESS ADMINISTRATION	2.6	.69
(1) 19		
HEADQUARTERS	2.6	.69
(2) 17 29		
HEALTH DEPARTMENT	2.6	.69
(1) 27		
HIGH COURT OF JUSTICE	2.6	.51
(2) 03 16		
HINDUS	2.6	.69
(5) 16 22 24 25 30		
HOME LOAN BANKS	2.6	.51
(1) 16		
HOME OWNERS LOAN CORPORATION (HOLC)	2.6	.69
(3) 06 16 32		
HOME STATE	2.6	.69
(1) 17		
HOUSE ADMINISTRATION COMMITTEE	2.6	.51
(1) 42		
HOUSING AND HOME FINANCE AGENCY (HHFA)	2.6	.51
(1) 27		
HUMAN RESOURCES DEVELOPMENT DIVISION OF ECA	2.6	.51
(1) 41		
IMPACT PANEL	2.6	.69
(1) 01		
INDEPENDENT ESTABLISHMENT	2.6	.69
(2) 06 16		
INDEPENDENT WORKERS OF THE WORLD	2.6	.69
(1) 21		
INDUSTRIAL RELATIONS COURT	2.6	.69
(1) 06		
INDUSTRIAL UNION	2.6	.51
(1) 16		
INNER-PARTY	2.6	.51
(1) 24		
INSIDERS	2.6	.69
(1) 24		
INTER-AMERICAN DEVELOPMENT BANK (IDB)	2.6	.69
(6) 03 17 18 20 25 32		
INTERDEPARTMENTAL COMMITTEE	2.6	.69
(1) 02		
INTERIM COMMITTEE	2.6	.69
(1) 17		
INTERNATIONAL BROTHERHOOD OF AUTO WORKERS (IAW)	2.6	.69
(1) 17		
INTERNATIONAL CHAMBER OF COMMERCE	2.6	.51
(1) 17		
INTERNATIONAL CIVIL SERVICE	2.6	.69
(2) 03 23		
INTERNATIONAL COMMITTEE OF THE RED CROSS	2.6	.51
(2) 11 17		

INTERNATIONAL DEVELOPMENT ASSOCIATION (IDA)   2.6   .51
(6) 03 17 18 20 25 32
INTERNATIONAL DISARMAMENT ORGANIZATION (IDO)   2.6   .51
(1) 20
INTERNATIONAL FEDERATION OF CHRISTIAN TRADE UNIONS   2.6   .51
(1) 17
INTERNATIONAL LONGSHOREMENS ASSOCIATION (ILA)   2.6   .51
(1) 17
INTERNATIONAL MILITARY TRIBUNAL   2.6   .51
(2) 17 22
INTERNATIONAL OLYMPIC COMMITTEE   2.6   .51
(1) 17
INTERNATIONAL TELECOMMUNICATION UNION (ITU)   2.6   .51
(7) 03 16 17 20 25 27 32
INTERNATIONAL WORKINGMENS ASSOCIATION   2.6   .69
(1) 10
INTERSERVICE   2.6   .69
(1) 24
INTERSESSIONAL COMMITTEE   2.6   .51
(1) 17
INTERSTATE AND FOREIGN COMMERCE COMMITTEE   2.6   .51
(1) 42
IRISH MAFIA   2.6   .69
(1) 39
ITALIAN MONARCHISTS   2.6   .51
(1) 03
ITALIAN RADICAL PARTY   2.6   .51
(1) 03
JEWISH AGENCY FOR ISRAEL   2.6   .69
(5) 03 16 17 34 38
JEWISH NATIONAL HOME   2.6   .51
(1) 16
JOHNS HOPKINS UNIVERSITY   2.6   .69
(1) 04
JOINT-STOCK ASSOCIATION   2.6   .51
(1) 06
KOREAN   2.6   .69
(1) 43
LABOR FRONT   2.6   .69
(2) 16 26
LABOR REFORM PARTY   2.6   .51
(1) 06
LANDER   2.6   .51
(1) 11
LATIN   2.6   .69
(1) 43
LAUNDRY TICKET   2.6   .51
(1) 39
LEGAL-AID BUREAUS   2.6   .51
(1) 45
LIAISON COMMITTEE   2.6   .51
(1) 17
LIAISON OFFICE   2.6   .69
(1) 17
LIBERAL DEMOCRATIC PARTY   2.6   .51
(1) 17

LOCAL COUNCIL   2.6   .69
(3) 17 19 23
LUBLIN COMMITTEE   2.6   .51
(1) 34
MAGISTRATE COURTS   2.6   .51
(2) 27 32
MAGYAR   2.6   .51
(1) 16
MANAGED MASSES   2.6   .69
(1) 29
MANPOWER ADMINISTRATION   2.6   .69
(1) 32
MAQUIS   2.6   .69
(3) 03 16 34
MARINES   2.6   .69
(1) 30
MEMBER BANK   2.6   .69
(1) 06
METROPOLITAN URBAN COUNTY   2.6   .69
(1) 18
MICHIGAN, UNIVERSITY OF   2.6   .51
(1) 04
MIDDLE-OF-THE-ROAD POPULISTS   2.6   .69
(1) 06
MILITARY RESERVES   2.6   .51
(1) 18
MINISTERIAL DEPARTMENTS   2.6   .69
(1) 11
MULTICENTERED SOCIETIES   2.6   .69
(1) 03
MUTUAL SECURITY AGENCY   2.6   .69
(1) 38
NAPOLEON'S GRAND ARMY   2.6   .69
(1) 17
NATION OF SHOPKEEPERS   2.6   .51
(1) 39
NATIONAL ASSOCIATION OF BROADCASTERS (NAB)   2.6   .51
(1) 32
NATIONAL GRANGE   2.6   .51
(5) 03 18 27 32 34
NATIONAL MEDIATION BOARD   2.6   .51
(4) 06 16 18 32
NATIONAL PARK SERVICE   2.6   .51
(4) 06 18 27 32
NATIONAL PEOPLE'S CONGRESS (NPC), CHINA (PRC)   2.6   .69
(3) 03 17 20
NATIONAL RESOURCES PLANNING BOARD (U.S.)   2.6   .69
(5) 06 16 19 22 32
NATIONALIZED INDUSTRIES OF FRANCE   2.6   .69
(1) 03
NATIVE COUNTRY   2.6   .51
(1) 17
NAVAL WAR COLLEGE   2.6   .51
(1) 16
NEGRO-AMERICANS   2.6   .69
(1) 30
NEIGHBORHOOD ASSOCIATIONS   2.6   .51
(1) 45
NEW STATES   2.6   .51
(1) 11

NEW TOWN	2.6	.51
(1) 32		
NISEI	2.6	.51
(2) 16 25		
NON-PARTICIPATING GOVERNMENTS	2.6	.51
(1) 17		
NONPARTISAN BOARD (OR	2.6	.69
COMMISSION OR COMMITTEE)		
(1) 03		
NORTH ATLANTIC FREE TRADE AREA	2.6	.51
(1) 25		
OCCUPATION POWER	2.6	.51
(1) 17		
OFFICE OF CENSORSHIP	2.6	.51
(2) 06 16		
OFFICE OF INDIAN AFFAIRS	2.6	.69
(1) 06		
OFFICE OF NAVAL INTELLIGENCE (ONI)	2.6	.51
(1) 18		
OFFICE OF NAVAL RESEARCH (ONR)	2.6	.51
(1) 42		
OFFICE OF PRODUCTION MANAGEMENT	2.6	.69
(OPM)		
(2) 06 16		
OFFICE OF THE DIRECTOR-GENERAL	2.6	.69
(1) 17		
OFFICE OF UNITED NATIONS POLITICAL	2.6	.51
AFFAIRS		
(1) 42		
OKIES	2.6	.51
(1) 16		
ORGANIZING COMMITTEE	2.6	.69
(1) 17		
ORIGINAL MEMBERSHIP, UNITED	2.6	.51
NATIONS		
(1) 20		
PAIR	2.6	.69
(3) 16 18 27		
PANCHAYAT	2.6	.69
(1) 03		
PANEL	2.6	.51
(3) 17 18 24		
PAROCHIAL SCHOOL	2.6	.51
(1) 06		
PARTY CIRCLE	2.6	.69
(2) 06 16		
PEACE DEMOCRAT	2.6	.69
(2) 06 29		
PEACE-LOVING PEOPLES	2.6	.51
(1) 17		
PEOPLE	2.6	.84
(3) 11 26 30		
PEOPLE'S ASSEMBLY	2.6	.51
(1) 17		
PEOPLE'S COUNCIL	2.6	.69
(1) 17		
PERMANENT COUNCIL	2.6	.69
(1) 17		
PERSONNEL DEPARTMENTS	2.6	.69
(1) 37		
PETROGRAD SOVIET	2.6	.51
(1) 22		
PHILOSOPHES	2.6	.69
(1) 22		
POPULAR REPUBLICAN MOVEMENT	2.6	.51
(1) 22		
POPULIST PEOPLES PARTY	2.6	.69
(1) 32		
POSTAL SERVICE, UNITED STATES	2.6	.51
(2) 07 32		
POWER ECONOMY	2.6	.69
(1) 03		
PRESIDENT'S COMMISSION ON	2.6	.51
CAMPUS UNREST		
(1) 32		
PRESIDENT'S COMMISSION ON	2.6	.51
INTERGOVERNMENTAL RELATIONS		
(1) 04		
PRICE FIXING MONOPOLY	2.6	.69
(1) 18		
PRISONS AND PENOLOGY	2.6	.69
(1) 07		
PROCEDURAL COMMITTEE	2.6	.51
(1) 17		
PRODUCERS COOPERATIVE	2.6	.51
(1) 03		
PROPRIETARY COLONY	2.6	.51
(2) 03 18		
PUBLIC EMPLOYEE ASSOCIATION	2.6	.51
(1) 03		
PUBLIC SERVICE COMMISSION	2.6	.51
(2) 06 18		
PUBLIC WORKS ADMINISTRATION (PWA)	2.6	.51
(3) 06 16 32		
QUADRUPLE ALLIANCE	2.6	.69
(1) 16		
RAZA UNIDA PARTY	2.6	.69
(1) 11		
REGIONAL AGENCIES	2.6	.69
(1) 17		
REGIONAL MILITARY ORGANIZATIONS	2.6	.51
(1) 20		
REICHSRAT	2.6	.51
(1) 16		
RELATIVE MAJORITY	2.6	.51
(1) 17		
RESISTANCE	2.6	.51
(3) 22 24 30		
RIGGED MARKET	2.6	.51
(1) 45		
RIKSDAG (SWEDEN)	2.6	.51
(3) 17 19 24		
ROYAL COMMISSION OF ENQUIRY	2.6	.51
(BRITAIN)		
(1) 19		
ROYAL COMMISSION, BRITAIN	2.6	.51
(5) 03 11 19 20 34		
RURAL PARTY	2.6	.51
(1) 11		
RUSSIANS	2.6	.69
(1) 43		
SAINT LAWRENCE SEAWAY PROJECT	2.6	.51
(1) 42		
SAXONS	2.6	.51
(2) 09 22		

SCOTTISH NATIONAL PARTY 2.6 .51
(1) 11
SECOND CHAMBER 2.6 .51
(3) 06 16 17
SECRET SOCIETIES 2.6 .51
(2) 11 17
SENATE, ITALY 2.6 .51
(1) 20
SET 2.6 .51
(3) 01 17 30
SINGLE LIST 2.6 .51
(1) 17
SOCIAL DEMOCRATIC PARTY OF 2.6 .51
RUSSIA
(1) 10
SOCIAL STATE 2.6 .51
(2) 11 17
SOUTH ARABIAN FEDERATION 2.6 .51
(1) 34
SPECIAL MAJORITY 2.6 .69
(1) 02
STAR CHAMBER 2.6 .51
(3) 06 16 29
STATELESS SOCIETIES 2.6 .51
(2) 04 15
SUBSIDIARY BODY 2.6 .51
(1) 17
SUBVERSIVE ACTIVITIES CONTROL 2.6 .51
BOARD
(4) 18 27 32 34
SUPERSTATE 2.6 .51
(2) 16 17
SUPERVISORY BODY 2.6 .51
(1) 17
SUPREME COURT OF JUSTICE 2.6 .51
(1) 17
SWISS 2.6 .51
(1) 43
SYNDICAT 2.6 .51
(1) 03
TARIFF COMMISSION (UNITED STATES) 2.6 .51
(1) 45
TELECOMMUNICATIONS UNION 2.6 .51
(1) 16
THIRD COMMITTEE 2.6 .51
(1) 17
THIRD REPUBLIC (FRANCE) 2.6 .51
(3) 03 16 34
TOWN BOARD 2.6 .69
(1) 27
TOWNSHIP BOARD 2.6 .69
(1) 42
TRADE DELEGATION 2.6 .51
(1) 17
TRADE UNION CONGRESS (TUC) 2.6 .51
(3) 16 34 38
TRAFFIC COURT 2.6 .51
(1) 06
TREATY-BREAKING STATE 2.6 .51
(1) 17
TRIUMVIRATE 2.6 .51
(1) 17

TROOPS 2.6 .51
(1) 30
TRUCE COMMISSION 2.6 .51
(1) 17
TRUCIAL STATES 2.6 .51
(1) 34
TWO-OCEAN NAVY 2.6 .51
(1) 16
U.N. DEVELOPMENT ORGANIZATION 2.6 .51
(UNIDO)
(1) 41
U.N. INTERNATIONAL LAW COMMISSION 2.6 .51
(1) 25
U.N. PREPARATORY COMMISSION 2.6 .69
(1) 03
U.N. TECHNICAL ASSISTANCE BOARD 2.6 .51
(1) 03
U.S. MARITIME COMMISSION 2.6 .51
(2) 06 45
UNION OF AFRICAN STATES 2.6 .51
(1) 17
URBAN MASS TRANSPORTATION 2.6 .51
ADMINISTRATION
(1) 32
VANGUARD 2.6 .51
(1) 30
VICTORIOUS POWER 2.6 .51
(1) 17
VIRGINIA DYNASTY 2.6 .69
(1) 06
VOLK 2.6 .51
(1) 26
VOLUNTEER CORPS 2.6 .69
(1) 17
WAR CABINET 2.6 .51
(2) 06 17
WAR OFFICE 2.6 .51
(1) 17
WAR PARTY 2.6 .51
(1) 39
WEDNESDAY CLUB 2.6 .69
(1) 39
WOMEN'S AIR FORCE (WAFS) 2.6 .51
(1) 42
WOMEN'S ARMY CORPS (WACS) 2.6 .51
(1) 42
WORKINGMEN'S PARTY 2.6 .51
(1) 46
WORLD PARLIAMENT ASSOCIATION 2.6 .51
(1) 17
YOUTH LEAGUE, CHINA (PRC) 2.6 .51
(1) 20
ZAIBATSU 2.6 .51
(2) 03 24
ZENGAKUREN 2.6 .51
(1) 03
JUSTICE 1.3 .67
(10) 03 06 11 16 19 23 24 26 27 30
POLITICAL ACTOR 1.3 .67
(2) 01 33
POLITICAL ROLES 1.3 .48
(2) 08 15

AUTHORITY	1.4	.69
(9) 01 03 06 08 11 15 17 24 33		
LIBERAL	1.4	.69
(9) 02 06 15 16 17 24 27 29 30		
OPINION LEADER	1.4	.69
(3) 02 15 33		
PRESIDENT	1.4	.69
(1) 42		
PRESIDENT OF THE UNITED STATES	1.4	.69
(2) 03 32		
CHARISMATIC LEADERSHIP	1.5	.52
(11) 01 02 03 11 18 20 22 24 25 30 33		
CITY MANAGER	1.5	.52
(3) 19 25 27		
CONSERVATIVE	1.5	.84
(9) 02 06 15 16 17 22 24 27 29		
LOBBYISTS	1.5	.70
(6) 02 16 17 18 24 27		
PARTY LEADERSHIP	1.5	.70
(1) 17		
POLITICAL LEADERSHIP	1.5	.70
(4) 08 11 15 23		
POLITICAL SCIENTISTS	1.5	.52
(1) 37		
CHIEF JUSTICE OF THE SUPREME COURT	1.6	.69
(5) 03 06 16 18 25		
CITIZENSHIP	1.6	.69
(12) 02 03 15 16 17 18 19 24 25 26 30 32		
DECISION MAKERS	1.6	.84
(1) 20		
MAJORITY LEADER	1.6	.51
(3) 27 32 34		
NAZI	1.6	.69
(10) 02 07 10 16 17 21 22 24 27 34		
POLICY-MAKER	1.6	.69
(1) 26		
POLITICIAN	1.6	.84
(8) 03 11 16 17 24 27 29 30		
PRIME MINISTER	1.6	.51
(10) 03 06 11 16 17 18 19 20 25 27		
VOTER	1.6	.84
(4) 06 17 24 30		
ANARCHIST	1.7	.67
(1) 17		
CHIEF EXECUTIVE	1.7	.82
(2) 16 17		
CITIZEN	1.7	.67
(13) 06 08 15 16 17 18 20 23 24 27 29 30 33		
DEMOCRAT	1.7	.82
(1) 24		
EXECUTIVE	1.7	.94
(8) 03 06 07 16 17 24 30 33		
GOVERNOR	1.7	.82
(11) 03 06 11 12 16 17 24 25 27 30 33		
GRASS ROOTS	1.7	.67
(6) 02 06 16 24 27 29		
INCUMBENT	1.7	.67
(4) 02 17 18 27		
LEADERSHIP	1.7	.94
(13) 01 02 03 04 11 17 19 23 24 25 26 30 33		
MAJORITY FLOOR LEADER	1.7	.67
(2) 16 18		
NATIONALITY	1.7	.82
(7) 06 16 17 19 20 27 30		
NONPARTISAN	1.7	.67
(2) 27 39		
ADMINISTRATOR	1.8	.78
(3) 16 24 25		
AUTHORITARIAN	1.8	.78
(5) 03 06 16 17 24		
BUREAUCRAT	1.8	.78
(4) 16 17 24 27		
CANDIDATE	1.8	.78
(5) 06 16 17 24 33		
CHIEF OF STATE	1.8	.63
(5) 17 18 25 27 32		
COMMANDER-IN-CHIEF	1.8	.63
(5) 06 16 18 20 27		
COUNTY MANAGER	1.8	.78
(4) 03 06 16 18		
DELEGATE	1.8	.78
(6) 06 16 17 27 32 33		
DICTATOR	1.8	.78
(3) 17 24 29		
INSURGENT	1.8	.63
(1) 38		
MAYOR	1.8	.78
(9) 06 16 17 18 24 25 27 30 32		
MEMBER OF CONGRESS (MC)	1.8	.63
(1) 16		
OMBUDSMAN	1.8	.63
(4) 07 11 32 33		
PARTISAN	1.8	.63
(4) 03 16 17 24		
PARTY WHIP	1.8	.63
(1) 17		
PHILOSOPHER-KING	1.8	.91
(1) 26		
POLL WATCHER	1.8	.42
(3) 16 18 32		
POLLSTER	1.8	.63
(1) 39		
SECRETARY OF DEFENSE	1.8	.78
(3) 11 17 27 42		
SPEAKER OF THE HOUSE	1.8	.78
(4) 17 18 27 32		
TOTALITARIAN	1.8	.78
(1) 38		
U.N. SECRETARY-GENERAL	1.8	.63
(4) 16 17 18 20		
U.S. ATTORNEY GENERAL	1.8	.63
(2) 32 42		
WHIP	1.8	.63
(10) 02 03 06 16 17 18 24 27 30 32		
ACTOR	1.9	.99
(1) 02		
ALIEN	1.9	.73
(9) 03 06 16 17 18 20 27 32 33		
ANTICOMMUNIST	1.9	.73
(2) 17 30		

ARBITRATOR	1.9	.73
(1) 17		
CONGRESSMAN	1.9	.73
(6) 06 16 17 24 27 30		
CONSTITUENT	1.9	.56
(4) 16 17 18 20		
COUNTER-REVOLUTIONARY	1.9	.31
(1) 45		
CZAR	1.9	.56
(4) 06 16 17 29		
DISTRICT ATTORNEY	1.9	.56
(5) 03 06 16 18 27		
DUAL CITIZENNSHIP	1.9	.31
(1) 18		
FEDERAL JUDGES	1.9	.87
(1) 42		
FIFTH COLUMNIST	1.9	.56
(1) 44		
FILIBUSTERERS	1.9	.73
(1) 46		
FRIEND OF THE COURT (AMICUS	1.9	.73
CURIAE)		
(2) 18 32		
HEADS OF STATE	1.9	.56
(1) 11 33 36		
INFLUENTIALS	1.9	.87
(2) 24 30		
LAME DUCK	1.9	.73
(5) 16 18 27 29 32		
LEADER OF THE OPPOSITION	1.9	.56
(1) 17		
LEGISLATIVE LEADERSHIP	1.9	.73
(1) 03		
LEGISLATOR	1.9	.87
(3) 17 24 30		
LIEUTENANT GOVERNOR	1.9	.73
(5) 03 06 16 18 27		
LINE AND STAFF	1.9	.87
(1) 18		
MAJORITY WHIP	1.9	.56
(1) 42		
MAN, ECONOMIC	1.9	.73
(1) 04		
MEMBER OF PARLIAMENT (M.P.)	1.9	.56
(3) 03 16 17		
MIGRANT WORKERS	1.9	.56
(1) 25		
MILITANT	1.9	.87
(3) 17 24 30		
MINISTER WITHOUT PORTFOLIO	1.9	.56
(1) 17		
MINORITY FLOOR LEADER	1.9	.56
(1) 42		
MINORITY LEADER	1.9	.73
(3) 27 32 34		
MINORITY WHIP	1.9	.56
(1) 42		
MUCKRAKERS	1.9	.31
(5) 06 16 27 29 32 46		
NATIONAL CHAIRMAN- POLITICAL PARTY	1.9	.73
(4) 06 16 18 32		
NEGOTIATOR	1.9	.56
(2) 08 17		
NON-VOTERS	1.9	.73
(2) 02 17		
POLITICAL ACTIVISTS	1.9	.73
(2) 11 15		
POLITICAL AGITATOR	1.9	.73
(1) 17		
POWER-SEEKERS AND LEADERS	1.9	.73
(1) 08		
PRESIDENT PRO TEMPORE	1.9	.56
(5) 03 06 18 27 32		
REPRESENTATIVE	1.9	.87
(8) 06 16 17 18 24 27 30 32		
SOUTHERN DEMOCRAT	1.9	.56
(1) 27		
VICE PRESIDENCY	1.9	.73
(1) 39		
WOMEN IN POLITICS	1.9	.73
(1) 23		
ABOLITIONIST	2.0	.47
(6) 03 06 16 17 22 30		
AGGRESSOR	2.0	.81
(3) 16 17 30		
AGITATOR	2.0	.47
(4) 08 16 24 30		
AMICUS CURIAE	2.0	.66
(5) 02 03 06 18 32		
ARISTOCRAT	2.0	.81
(1) 17		
ATTORNEY GENERAL	2.0	.66
(9) 03 06 08 16 17 18 27 32 34		
AUTHORITATIVE SOURCES	2.0	.81
(1) 39		
BOSS	2.0	.81
(9) 02 03 06 16 18 24 27 30 32		
CABINET MINISTERS	2.0	.66
(1) 36		
CHANCELLOR	2.0	.47
(6) 06 11 16 17 20 24		
CHIEF OF STAFF	2.0	.47
(1) 42		
DEMAGOGUE	2.0	.66
(1) 33		
DESPOT	2.0	.66
(2) 16 17		
DIRECTOR OF THE BUDGET	2.0	.66
(1) 42		
DUAL NATIONALITY	2.0	.47
(5) 03 16 17 18 20		
EMIGRANT	2.0	.66
(2) 17 25		
EX OFFICIO	2.0	.66
(5) 06 16 17 18 27		
FLOOR LEADER	2.0	.47
(5) 02 03 06 16 32		
FOREIGN SERVICE OFFICER (FSO)	2.0	.66
(1) 20		
INDEPENDENT VOTER	2.0	.66
(1) 42		
JACOBIN	2.0	.66
(6) 06 17 22 24 26 29		
LEGAL SOVEREIGN	2.0	.94
(2) 06 10		

MANAGEMENT	2.0	.81
(3) 24 25 30		
MAYORALITY	2.0	.66
(2) 17 30		
MERCENARIES	2.0	.47
(2) 06 16		
MIDDLE-INCOME	2.0	.47
(1) 30		
MIDDLE-OF-THE-ROAD	2.0	.47
(2) 02 17		
MINORITY PRESIDENT	2.0	.66
(2) 03 18		
MONARCH	2.0	.81
(4) 17 19 20 24		
NATIONAL	2.0	.94
(1) 44		
NATURALIZED CITIZEN	2.0	.47
(1) 27		
PARLIAMENTARIAN	2.0	.66
(2) 02 27		
PARTY BOSS	2.0	.81
(2) 17 18		
PEER	2.0	.66
(7) 06 15 16 17 24 27 30		
POLITICAL EXECUTIVES	2.0	.81
(1) 37		
POLITICAL PRISONER	2.0	.47
(3) 06 16 17		
PREMIER	2.0	.66
(5) 03 16 17 20 27		
PRESIDENTIAL APPOINTMENT	2.0	.47
(1) 32		
PROLETARIAN	2.0	.47
(3) 03 17 24		
PROXY	2.0	.66
(1) 45		
PUBLIC DEFENDER	2.0	.66
(6) 03 06 16 18 27 32		
RADICAL	2.0	.81
(8) 06 16 17 18 24 27 30 32		
RANKING MINORITY MEMBER	2.0	.47
(2) 06 18		
REACTIONARY	2.0	.66
(9) 06 16 17 18 25 27 30 32 34		
REVISIONISTS	2.0	.66
(1) 22		
REVOLUTIONARY	2.0	.66
(1) 40		
SECRETARY OF HOUSING AND URBAN DEVELOPMENT	2.0	.47
(1) 42		
SECRETARY OF STATE	2.0	.81
(7) 03 17 18 20 25 27 34		
SECRETARY OF THE INTERIOR	2.0	.47
(2) 17 27		
SECRETARY-GENERAL	2.0	.66
(2) 17 41		
SWING VOTER	2.0	.66
(1) 39		
WASP	2.0	.66
(1) 39		
WRITE-IN CANDIDATES	2.0	.66
(2) 03 32		

AGENT PROVOCATEUR	2.1	.56
(5) 03 06 16 17 45		
ASSESSOR	2.1	.73
(4) 03 06 18 27		
BLACK ABOLITIONIST	2.1	.56
(2) 28 46		
CARPETBAGGER	2.1	.56
(4) 03 06 16 27		
CHANCELLOR OF THE EXCHEQUER	2.1	.56
(2) 16 17		
CITIZENRY	2.1	.87
(1) 17		
CITY COMMISSIONERS	2.1	.87
(1) 27		
CIVILIAN	2.1	.73
(3) 06 16 24		
COMMITTED DELEGATES	2.1	.56
(1) 42		
COMMITTEE CHAIRMAN	2.1	.73
(1) 18		
COMMON MAN	2.1	.87
(1) 44		
CONSCIENTIOUS OBJECTOR	2.1	.73
(5) 03 06 16 18 27		
CONSTITUTIONAL OFFICERS	2.1	.56
(2) 18 27		
CONSUL	2.1	.73
(9) 06 16 17 18 20 24 27 32 42		
CONSUL GENERAL	2.1	.73
(3) 06 16 17		
COUNCILMAN	2.1	.73
(3) 06 16 24		
COUNCILMAN-AT-LARGE	2.1	.73
(1) 42		
DARK-HORSE CANDIDATE	2.1	.73
(7) 03 06 16 27 29 32 39		
DEMONSTRATORS	2.1	.73
(2) 17 30		
DEPENDENT	2.1	.99
(2) 01 30		
DEVIANT	2.1	.87
(2) 24 30		
ETHNIC	2.1	.73
(4) 16 17 24 30		
EXECUTIVES	2.1	.99
(1) 37		
EXILE	2.1	.73
(3) 16 17 24		
IMMIGRANT	2.1	.73
(4) 17 24 25 30		
INDENTURED LABOR	2.1	.73
(1) 46		
INDIVIDUAL	2.1	.99
(2) 17 24		
INDIVIDUALS, IN GROUPS	2.1	.87
(1) 04		
ISOLATIONISTS	2.1	.73
(1) 38		
JURIST	2.1	.73
(1) 16		
KING	2.1	.87
(4) 16 17 24 25		

KREMLINOLOGIST	2.1	.56
(1) 39		
LEGALISTS	2.1	.73
(1) 30		
LEGISLATIVE COUNSEL	2.1	.73
(1) 27		
MAJOR WAR CRIMINALS	2.1	.73
(1) 17		
MAN, SOCIAL	2.1	.56
(1) 04		
MILITARY INTELLIGENCE	2.1	.56
(1) 06		
MINISTERS-PARLIAMENT MEMBERS	2.1	.73
(1) 11		
MINUTEMAN	2.1	.56
(3) 03 06 16		
MODERATE	2.1	.73
(1) 17		
NON-BELLIGERENT	2.1	.31
(1) 44		
PARTY OFFICIALS	2.1	.87
(1) 17		
PERMANENT MEMBER	2.1	.56
(1) 17		
POWER BROKERS	2.1	.56
(1) 39		
PRECINCT CAPTAIN	2.1	.73
(2) 02 27		
PREMIERSHIP	2.1	.56
(1) 17		
PRESIDENTIAL CANDIDATE	2.1	.56
(1) 17		
PRO TEM	2.1	.56
(1) 16		
PRO TEMPORE	2.1	.56
(2) 16 32		
PROSECUTING ATTORNEY	2.1	.73
(2) 16 18		
PUBLIC AUTHORITIES	2.1	.73
(1) 03		
RANKING MEMBER	2.1	.56
(4) 06 16 18 27		
REPRESENTATIVE AT LARGE	2.1	.73
(1) 45		
RUNNING MATE	2.1	.56
(1) 29		
SECRETARY OF HEALTH, EDUCATION AND WELFARE	2.1	.56
(2) 17 27		
SENATOR	2.1	.56
(7) 06 16 17 18 24 27 30		
SOCIAL ROLES	2.1	.87
(2) 11 15		
SPEAKER	2.1	.87
(4) 03 06 16 24		
STATES' RIGHTS DEMOCRAT	2.1	.56
(1) 29		
SUBVERSIVE	2.1	.56
(1) 44		
UNCLE TOM	2.1	.56
(3) 29 30 34		
WETBACKS	2.1	.56
(1) 45		
YOUNG TURKS	2.1	.73
(4) 02 16 17 32		
ACTIVIST	2.2	.78
(4) 11 17 25 30		
ASSOCIATE JUSTICE	2.2	.78
(1) 16		
ATTACHE	2.2	.78
(8) 06 16 17 18 20 27 32 42		
BACKBENCHERS	2.2	.42
(1) 24		
BIGOT	2.2	.78
(1) 39		
CAREER DIPLOMAT	2.2	.63
(1) 45		
CHIEF ADMINISTRATIVE OFFICER	2.2	.91
(1) 03		
CHIEF LEGISLATOR	2.2	.63
(2) 18 20		
CHIEF MAGISTRATE	2.2	.63
(1) 16		
CITIZENSHIP DUAL NATURE	2.2	.42
(1) 18		
CIVIC	2.2	.78
(3) 17 24 30		
CIVIL	2.2	.91
(3) 16 24 30		
CONSTITUTION-MAKER	2.2	.78
(1) 24		
DEPUTY	2.2	.78
(4) 06 16 17 24		
DIPLOMAT	2.2	.78
(6) 11 16 17 20 24 27		
DOUBLE CITIZENSHIP	2.2	.63
(1) 16		
ELECTOR	2.2	.78
(1) 16		
ENTREPRENEUR	2.2	.63
(3) 04 24 30		
FEDERAL PRESIDENT	2.2	.78
(1) 17		
FEUDAL LORD	2.2	.63
(1) 17		
FOREIGN MINISTER	2.2	.63
(4) 11 16 17 20		
FOREIGN SERVICE, CONSUL	2.2	.63
(1) 18		
FRONT RUNNER	2.2	.63
(2) 02 27		
GOVERNMENT EMPLOYEES	2.2	.78
(1) 37		
HYPHENATED AMERICANS	2.2	.63
(1) 45		
INDEPENDENT	2.2	.78
(1) 45		
JUSTICE OF THE PEACE	2.2	.63
(5) 03 06 16 18 27		
JUSTICES	2.2	.78
(1) 24		
LAWMAKERS	2.2	.91
(2) 17 24		
LEFTIST	2.2	.78
(5) 03 11 17 18 32		

LORD CHANCELLOR	2.2	.63
(3) 03 16 17		
MINISTER	2.2	.91
(6) 06 16 17 24 27 30		
MINISTER PLENIPOTENTIARY	2.2	.63
(2) 17 27		
MONARCHIST	2.2	.63
(1) 17		
NATIONAL ORIGINS	2.2	.63
(3) 06 16 27		
NON-QUOTA IMMIGRANT	2.2	.63
(1) 45		
NONCOMBATANT	2.2	.42
(1) 45		
OBSTRUCTIONIST	2.2	.63
(1) 16		
OFFICE-HOLDERS	2.2	.78
(1) 24		
OPPONENT	2.2	.78
(2) 17 30		
PARLIAMENTARY LEADER OF A PARTY	2.2	.78
(1) 17		
PEASANT	2.2	.78
(4) 11 24 25 30		
PEERAGE	2.2	.42
(2) 16 17		
PERSONA NON GRATA	2.2	.63
(6) 03 06 16 18 27 32		
PHILOSOPHER	2.2	.78
(2) 24 43		
PLAINTIFF	2.2	.63
(3) 02 16 27		
POLITICAL ROLE OF THE	2.2	.63
SECRETARY-GENERAL		
(1) 41		
POLITICAL STRATA	2.2	.91
(1) 08		
PRESIDENT OF THE REPUBLIC, FRANCE	2.2	.78
(2) 11 20		
PRESIDENT-ELECT	2.2	.42
(3) 17 18 32		
PRESIDENTIAL ELECTORS	2.2	.42
(2) 03 06		
PRISONER OF WAR	2.2	.63
(5) 03 06 11 16 17		
PROTESTANT	2.2	.78
(4) 22 24 25 30		
PUBLIC OFFICE	2.2	.78
(2) 16 17		
PURITAN	2.2	.78
(3) 17 22 29		
RAPPORTEUR	2.2	.63
(3) 03 16 17		
SCIENTIST	2.2	.78
(3) 11 24 30		
SECRETARY OF COMMERCE	2.2	.63
(2) 17 27		
SECRETARY OF LABOR	2.2	.63
(2) 17 27		
SECRETARY OF THE TREASURY	2.2	.78
(2) 17 27		
SEGREGATIONIST	2.2	.63
(1) 30		

SHERIFF	2.2	.63
(6) 03 06 16 18 27 30		
SLUMLORD	2.2	.42
(1) 30		
SOVEREIGN	2.2	.78
(3) 06 17 29		
STATESMANSHIP	2.2	.63
(1) 24		
TERRORIST	2.2	.63
(1) 38		
TYRANT	2.2	.63
(3) 08 17 24		
VETERANS	2.2	.78
(3) 04 07 24		
VICE PRESIDENT	2.2	.78
(9) 03 06 16 17 18 24 25 27 32		
ADJUTANT GENERAL	2.3	.67
(1) 06		
AMBASSADOR	2.3	.67
(7) 06 16 17 18 20 27 32		
ARISTOTELIANS	2.3	.82
(1) 43		
ASSEMBLYMAN	2.3	.67
(2) 06 16		
AT LARGE (CONGRESSMAN AT LARGE)	2.3	.67
(5) 06 18 27 32 45		
AUTHORITIES	2.3	.67
(1) 24		
AVERAGE MAN	2.3	.67
(1) 39		
BLUE COLLAR	2.3	.48
(1) 37		
BOOKBURNERS	2.3	.67
(1) 39		
BOSTON BRAHMINS	2.3	.67
(1) 22		
CAUDILLO	2.3	.67
(4) 03 16 17 24		
CHAIR	2.3	.67
(2) 17 24		
CHARACTER ASSASSIN	2.3	.67
(2) 29 39		
CHARGE D'AFFAIRES	2.3	.67
(7) 06 16 17 18 20 27 32		
CHIEF OF NAVAL OPERATIONS	2.3	.67
(1) 42		
CHIEF OF PROTOCOL	2.3	.67
(1) 17		
CHINA WATCHERS	2.3	.48
(1) 39		
CITY ATTORNEY	2.3	.67
(1) 27		
CLIENT	2.3	.82
(2) 24 30		
COLLABORATOR	2.3	.48
(2) 16 24		
COMBATANT	2.3	.67
(2) 16 17		
COMMISSAR	2.3	.48
(1) 16		
COMMISSIONER OF INTERNAL REVENUE	2.3	.67
(1) 42		

COMPTROLLER GENERAL OF THE UNITED STATES	2.3	.67
(4) 06 16 18 32		
COMPTROLLER, STATE	2.3	.67
(1) 42		
CONGRESSMAN AT LARGE	2.3	.67
(4) 06 16 18 32		
CONTROLLER	2.3	.82
(3) 06 24 27		
CULTURAL ATTACHE	2.3	.67
(2) 16 17		
DEFENDANT	2.3	.67
(3) 02 16 27		
DEMOCRAT WITH A SMALL D	2.3	.67
(1) 29		
DISSENTERS	2.3	.67
(2) 09 24		
DISTRICT JUDGE	2.3	.67
(1) 16		
DRAFT DODGER	2.3	.67
(1) 16		
ECONOMISTS	2.3	.67
(1) 37		
ELDER STATESMAN	2.3	.67
(1) 16		
EMIRATE	2.3	.48
(1) 17		
ENEMY	2.3	.82
(3) 06 16 30		
ENEMY ALIEN	2.3	.67
(5) 03 06 16 17 20		
EXPATRIATE	2.3	.48
(1) 44		
FEDERAL CHANCELLOR	2.3	.67
(2) 03 17		
FEDERAL REGISTRAR	2.3	.67
(1) 18		
FOREIGN SECRETARY, BRITAIN	2.3	.48
(2) 17 20		
GOVERNED	2.3	.82
(1) 24		
HABITUAL OFFENDER	2.3	.67
(2) 06 27		
HAWKS	2.3	.67
(1) 34		
HEIR APPARENT	2.3	.67
(3) 16 17 29		
ILLITERATES	2.3	.67
(1) 30		
INDENTURED SERVANT	2.3	.67
(1) 32		
INDUSTRIALIST	2.3	.82
(1) 24		
INSTRUCTED DELEGATE	2.3	.82
(1) 29		
INTERN	2.3	.67
(1) 17		
INTERNSHIP	2.3	.67
(1) 37		
JOB	2.3	.94
(3) 09 30 32		
JUDGE	2.3	.94
(8) 04 06 11 16 17 24 30 32		

JUVENILE DELINQUENT	2.3	.82
(1) 44		
LANDLORD	2.3	.82
(2) 24 30		
LEADER	2.3	.94
(4) 06 17 24 30		
LEADER OF THE PARLIAMENTARY GROUP	2.3	.48
(1) 17		
LEGISLATIVE LIAISON OFFICER	2.3	.67
(1) 03		
LITIGANTS	2.3	.67
(1) 02		
MANAGEMENT ANALYSTS	2.3	.67
(1) 37		
MANDARIN	2.3	.67
(1) 17		
MEDIATORS	2.3	.67
(2) 17 30		
MIGRANTS	2.3	.67
(1) 30		
MILITARY ATTACHE	2.3	.48
(2) 11 17		
MONARCH BY DIVINE RIGHT	2.3	.82
(1) 17		
NATIONALS	2.3	.82
(1) 45		
NATURAL-BORN CITIZEN	2.3	.48
(2) 18 32		
NON-COMBATANT	2.3	.48
(1) 17		
OCCUPATION	2.3	.67
(5) 07 16 17 24 30		
ORIENTAL DESPOTISM	2.3	.67
(1) 03		
PAPACY	2.3	.48
(6) 04 09 16 17 26 34		
PARTY FAITHFUL	2.3	.48
(1) 39		
PEON	2.3	.82
(1) 24		
PERMANENT DELEGATE	2.3	.67
(1) 17		
PERMANENT REPRESENTATIVE	2.3	.67
(1) 17		
PERSONNEL	2.3	.94
(5) 06 17 19 24 30		
POLICEMAN	2.3	.82
(1) 15		
PRESIDENTIAL TIMBER	2.3	.67
(1) 27		
PROSECUTOR	2.3	.82
(1) 27		
PROSECUTOR, PUBLIC	2.3	.48
(1) 16		
PUBLIC PROSECUTOR	2.3	.48
(1) 16		
RULER	2.3	.67
(2) 17 24		
SECOND CLASS CITIZEN	2.3	.67
(1) 39		
SECRETARY OF AGRICULTURE	2.3	.67
(1) 27		

SECRETARY OF THE ARMY	2.3	.67
(1) 42		
SECRETARY OF THE NAVY	2.3	.67
(1) 17		
SECRETARY OF WAR	2.3	.67
(1) 17		
SOLICITOR GENERAL	2.3	.67
(5) 03 06 16 18 27		
STATE'S EVIDENCE	2.3	.48
(2) 06 16		
TSAR	2.3	.48
(2) 16 17		
U.S. MARSHAL	2.3	.67
(1) 27		
UNDERSECRETARY OF STATE	2.3	.67
(1) 17		
UNDESIRABLE ALIEN	2.3	.48
(1) 17		
VASSAL	2.3	.67
(2) 17 29		
WARD HEELER	2.3	.82
(3) 06 27 45		
WARLORDS	2.3	.48
(1) 03		
WHITE COLLAR WORKER	2.3	.67
(1) 16		
ADULT	2.4	.69
(3) 15 25 30		
ADVANCE MAN	2.4	.69
(1) 39		
ANTICOLONIALIST	2.4	.69
(1) 17		
ANTIFASCIST	2.4	.51
(2) 17 24		
APPRENTICESHIP	2.4	.69
(1) 24		
ARBITER	2.4	.51
(1) 24		
ASSASSIN	2.4	.69
(2) 17 30		
ASSISTANT TO THE PRESIDENT	2.4	.84
(1) 27		
AUDITOR	2.4	.69
(6) 03 06 16 17 18 27		
BAILIFF	2.4	.69
(2) 06 16		
BROKER	2.4	.69
(1) 24		
CENSOR	2.4	.69
(1) 17		
CENTRIST	2.4	.69
(1) 39		
CHAIRMAN	2.4	.69
(3) 06 17 24		
COLLECTOR OF INTERNAL REVENUE	2.4	.69
(2) 06 16		
COMMISSIONERS, FEDERAL	2.4	.84
(1) 42		
COMMUNICATOR	2.4	.69
(1) 02		
COMPTROLLER	2.4	.69
(4) 06 16 18 27		
COUNTY ATTORNEY (DISTRICT ATTORNEY)	2.4	.51
(2) 18 27		
COUNTY CLERK	2.4	.69
(3) 06 16 18		
COUNTY TREASURER	2.4	.69
(1) 42		
COURT REFEREE	2.4	.69
(1) 18		
COURT REPORTER	2.4	.51
(1) 42		
CZARINA	2.4	.69
(1) 17		
DALAI LAMA	2.4	.51
(2) 03 17		
DESERTER	2.4	.84
(2) 16 17		
DISLOYAL	2.4	.69
(2) 24 30		
DOUBLE NATIONALITY	2.4	.51
(1) 16		
EMPEROR	2.4	.69
(3) 16 17 24		
EXCHANGE STUDENTS	2.4	.69
(1) 19		
FEDERAL MARSHAL	2.4	.69
(1) 42		
FELLOW TRAVELER	2.4	.51
(1) 39		
FIFTH AMENDMENT COMMUNIST	2.4	.51
(1) 38		
FOREIGN SERVICE ATTACHE	2.4	.51
(1) 18		
FOREIGN SERVICE, CHARGE D,AFFAIRES	2.4	.51
(1) 18		
FREEDMEN	2.4	.69
(1) 06 16 30 46		
FREEDOM FIGHTER	2.4	.51
(1) 39		
FREEMAN	2.4	.69
(3) 02 06 17		
GANGSTER	2.4	.69
(1) 16		
GENERAL SECRETARY, SOVIET UNION	2.4	.51
(1) 20		
GENERALIST	2.4	.69
(1) 03		
GHOSTWRITER	2.4	.69
(1) 39		
GOVERNMENT SERVICE AS A CAREER	2.4	.69
(1) 37		
HEARING EXAMINER	2.4	.69
(1) 18		
HEIR PRESUMPTIVE	2.4	.69
(2) 16 17		
HOLY FATHER	2.4	.69
(1) 17		
HONKIES	2.4	.69
(1) 30		
ILLIBERAL	2.4	.69
(3) 03 24 29		

INDIVIDUALS IN INTERNATIONAL ORDER	2.4	.84
(1) 23		
INTELLECTUAL	2.4	.84
(3) 03 24 30		
JEWISH	2.4	.69
(1) 43		
JOBLESS	2.4	.69
(1) 30		
LABORER	2.4	.84
(2) 25 30		
LAW ENFORCEMENT PERSONNEL	2.4	.69
(1) 37		
LEGAL PERSONALITY	2.4	.84
(1) 06		
MAVERICK	2.4	.69
(2) 03 45		
MEMBER	2.4	.84
(1) 24		
MEMBERSHIP (UN)	2.4	.51
(1) 41		
MERCHANT	2.4	.84
(1) 30		
MISSIONARIES	2.4	.69
(3) 09 24 25		
MUNICIPAL OFFICER	2.4	.69
(1) 17		
NEO-NAZI	2.4	.51
(2) 11 17		
NEUTRALIST	2.4	.51
(1) 39		
NOMINAL CANDIDATE	2.4	.69
(1) 29		
NON-MEMBER	2.4	.69
(1) 17		
OFFENDER	2.4	.51
(1) 30		
OTHER-DIRECTED TYPES	2.4	.69
(1) 22		
PARAPROFESSIONALS	2.4	.51
(1) 37		
PARTICIPANT	2.4	.69
(3) 17 24 30		
PATRIARCH	2.4	.51
(3) 16 17 24		
PERENNIAL CANDIDATE	2.4	.69
(1) 39		
PERMANENT STAFF	2.4	.69
(1) 17		
PETITIONERS	2.4	.51
(1) 30		
PLANNERS	2.4	.96
(2) 24 30		
PLENIPOTENTIARY	2.4	.51
(4) 06 16 17 27		
POLICEMAN OF THE WORLD	2.4	.69
(1) 39		
POLITICAL REFUGEE	2.4	.51
(2) 16 17		
PRESIDENT OF THE SENATE	2.4	.51
(1) 27		
PRESS SECRETARY	2.4	.51
(1) 17		

PRIVATEER	2.4	.51
(3) 06 16 17		
PROFESSIONAL DIPLOMAT	2.4	.51
(1) 17		
PROGRAMMERS	2.4	.69
(1) 37		
PUBLIC EMPLOYEE	2.4	.69
(1) 16		
QUANTIFIER	2.4	.69
(1) 43		
REFUGEE	2.4	.69
(11) 03 06 07 11 16 17 19 20 25 27		
30		
RELIABLE SOURCE	2.4	.69
(1) 17		
RESIDENT ALIEN	2.4	.51
(1) 44		
RIGHT-WING DEVIATIONIST	2.4	.51
(1) 17		
RIGHTIST	2.4	.69
(5) 03 18 24 30 32		
RULED	2.4	.84
(1) 24		
SCAB	2.4	.69
(2) 29 32		
SCANDINAVIANS	2.4	.51
(1) 43		
SECRETARY OF STATE IN STATES	2.4	.69
(1) 42		
SECRETARY OF THE AIR FORCE	2.4	.69
(1) 42		
SECRETARY OF TRANSPORTATION	2.4	.51
(1) 42		
SECURITY RISK	2.4	.51
(3) 03 18 32		
SENATE-VICE PRESIDENT	2.4	.69
(1) 18		
SENIOR CITIZEN	2.4	.69
(1) 39		
SENIOR SENATOR	2.4	.69
(1) 27		
SERGEANT-AT-ARMS	2.4	.69
(3) 06 16 27		
SINECURE	2.4	.51
(3) 03 06 16		
SLAVE	2.4	.51
(4) 24 29 30 34		
STATE ATTORNEY GENERAL	2.4	.51
(1) 42		
STATE COMPTROLLER	2.4	.69
(1) 42		
STATE TREASURER	2.4	.69
(1) 18		
STAY-AT-HOME VOTER	2.4	.69
(2) 06 39		
STRAW MAN	2.4	.51
(1) 39		
SUFFRAGETTE	2.4	.51
(6) 02 06 16 17 22 27		
SUPERMEN	2.4	.69
(1) 24		
SUPREME AUTHORITY	2.4	.69
(1) 17		

TREASURER OF THE UNITED STATES	2.4	.51
(4) 06 16 27 42		
U.S. REPRESENTATIVE TO THE UNITED NATIONS	2.4	.51
(1) 42		
VIGILANTES	2.4	.69
(1) 16		
WHIPPING BOY	2.4	.69
(1) 27		
YOUTH AND POLITICS	2.4	.84
(1) 23		
ABSENTEE SENATOR	2.5	.70
(1) 39		
ACTING PRESIDENT	2.5	.70
(1) 42		
AGRARIAN	2.5	.70
(1) 06		
AIR TRAFFIC CONTROLLERS	2.5	.70
(1) 37		
ALDERMAN	2.5	.52
(5) 06 16 18 27 32		
ANTEDILUVIAN	2.5	.52
(1) 29		
ANTI-MONOPOLIST	2.5	.52
(1) 29		
ATTORNEY AT LAW	2.5	.52
(1) 27		
BARRISTER	2.5	.52
(1) 16		
BLOCKADE RUNNER	2.5	.52
(2) 06 16		
BOURBON	2.5	.52
(3) 06 16 29		
BRAHMIN	2.5	.52
(3) 03 16 29		
CASUALTIES	2.5	.70
(1) 17		
CLERK OF THE COURT	2.5	.52
(1) 42		
CO-SIGNATORY	2.5	.52
(1) 17		
COLLECTOR OF TAXES	2.5	.70
(1) 06		
COMPETENT AUTHORITY	2.5	.70
(1) 17		
COMPLAINANT	2.5	.52
(1) 17		
COMSYMP	2.5	.52
(1) 39		
CONSORT	2.5	.52
(1) 16		
CONSULAR AGENT	2.5	.70
(2) 06 16		
CONSULTANTS	2.5	.70
(2) 25 30		
CONSUMER	2.5	.70
(1) 30		
COP	2.5	.84
(1) 30		
CORONER	2.5	.70
(5) 03 06 16 18 27		
COUNSEL	2.5	.70
(2) 17 24		
COUNTY ASSESSOR	2.5	.52
(1) 42		
COUNTY PROSECUTOR (DISTRICT ATTORNEY)	2.5	.52
(1) 18		
CZARDOM	2.5	.52
(1) 17		
DEAN OF THE DIPLOMATIC CORPS	2.5	.70
(2) 16 17		
DEPUTY SHERIFF	2.5	.70
(2) 06 16		
DIE-HARD	2.5	.70
(2) 06 16		
DIPLOMATIC COURIER	2.5	.52
(1) 17		
DO-GOODER	2.5	.70
(1) 39		
DRAFTEE	2.5	.70
(1) 42		
EMIR	2.5	.52
(1) 17		
EMPLOYEES	2.5	.70
(2) 24 30		
EMPRESS	2.5	.70
(1) 17		
ENVOY	2.5	.52
(2) 06 16		
ENVOY EXTRAORDINARY AND MINISTER PLENIPOTENTIARY	2.5	.70
(1) 17		
EXCHEQUER	2.5	.70
(1) 16		
EXECUTIVE AGENT	2.5	.70
(1) 06		
EXPERT	2.5	.70
(3) 11 17 24		
FEDERAL MINISTER	2.5	.52
(1) 17		
FIRST SECRETARY OF THE PARTY	2.5	.52
(2) 03 17		
FLAMING LIBERAL	2.5	.52
(1) 39		
FOREIGN WORKERS	2.5	.52
(1) 11		
FUGITIVE FROM JUSTICE	2.5	.52
(1) 45		
FULL MEMBER	2.5	.70
(1) 17		
FUTURISTS	2.5	.70
(1) 22		
GATEKEEPERS	2.5	.70
(2) 24 33		
GAULEITER	2.5	.70
(1) 16		
GENERALISSIMO	2.5	.70
(1) 24		
GOVERNMENT MEMBERS	2.5	.70
(1) 11		
GUARD	2.5	.70
(1) 30		
GUBERNATORIAL	2.5	.52
(1) 24		

HALF-BREED	2.5	.52	MINISTER-PRESIDENT	2.5	.70
(3) 06 16 29			(1) 17		
HAND-PICKED	2.5	.52	MUTINEER	2.5	.70
(1) 39			(1) 17		
HERETICS	2.5	.70	NATIVE	2.5	.70
(1) 24			(1) 30		
HIGH AUTHORITY	2.5	.70	NEO-FREUDIANS	2.5	.52
(1) 17			(1) 22		
HIGH COMMISSIONER	2.5	.52	NEW SOVIET MAN	2.5	.52
(4) 03 06 16 17			(1) 20		
HIGHEST AUTHORITY	2.5	.52	NON-RESIDENT	2.5	.52
(1) 39			(1) 17		
HIPPIE	2.5	.70	NON-WHITE	2.5	.70
(1) 30			(1) 30		
HOME SECRETARY	2.5	.52	OFFICE	2.5	.70
(1) 17			(1) 45		
HOSTAGE	2.5	.52	OFFICER	2.5	.70
(2) 16 17			(3) 17 24 30		
INFERIOR MAGISTRATES	2.5	.70	OLD LIBERAL	2.5	.52
(1) 26			(1) 25		
INFERIOR OFFICER	2.5	.70	PAPAL LEGATE AND NUNCIO	2.5	.52
(1) 06			(4) 03 16 17 20		
INTERSTATE CITIZENSHIP	2.5	.52	PARTIES TO A DISPUTE	2.5	.52
(2) 03 16			(1) 17		
JOB CORPS PERSONNEL	2.5	.52	PARTY CHIEFS	2.5	.52
(1) 37			(1) 17		
JOHN Q. PUBLIC	2.5	.70	PARTY ELDERS	2.5	.52
(1) 39			(1) 39		
JOURNEYMAN	2.5	.70	PATRIOT	2.5	.52
(1) 32			(2) 17 24		
JUDGE ADVOCATE	2.5	.52	PEACENIK	2.5	.70
(1) 06			(1) 39		
KINGMAKER	2.5	.52	PEKINGOLOGIST	2.5	.52
(1) 39			(1) 39		
LACKEY	2.5	.70	PERSON	2.5	.84
(1) 29			(1) 16		
LEGAL ADVISOR	2.5	.52	PERSONA GRATA	2.5	.52
(1) 17			(3) 16 17 20		
LIAISON OFFICER	2.5	.70	PERSUASIVE AUTHORITY	2.5	.70
(1) 16			(1) 44		
LITTLE LADIES IN TENNIS SHOES	2.5	.70	POLITICAL ANIMAL	2.5	.52
(1) 39			(1) 39		
LORD	2.5	.70	POPE	2.5	.70
(2) 17 24			(4) 16 17 25 26		
MALCONTENT	2.5	.70	POSTMASTER-GENERAL	2.5	.52
(1) 29			(5) 16 17 18 27 32		
MAN	2.5	.70	PREFERRED POSITION CONCEPT	2.5	.70
(4) 04 12 24 30			(1) 44		
MAN OF THE PEOPLE	2.5	.52	PRESIDENT'S PRESS SECRETARY	2.5	.52
(1) 39			(1) 27		
MAN ON HORSEBACK	2.5	.52	PROBATE JUDGE	2.5	.52
(1) 29			(1) 16		
MANAGER	2.5	.70	PROFESSIONAL	2.5	.70
(4) 06 24 29 30			(1) 39		
MARGINAL MAN	2.5	.52	PROFESSIONAL REVOLUTIONARIES	2.5	.70
(1) 43			(1) 35		
MIDNIGHT JUDGES	2.5	.52	PROFESSOR	2.5	.84
(2) 06 16			(1) 24		
MILITARY GOVERNOR	2.5	.52	PSYCHOLOGISTS	2.5	.70
(1) 17			(1) 37		
MINISTER (DIPLOMAT)	2.5	.52	PUBLICISTS	2.5	.84
(1) 20			(2) 16 30		

PUPPET	2.5	.70
(1) 29		
QUISLING (FIFTH COLUMN)	2.5	.52
(5) 03 06 16 20 27		
RANK	2.5	.70
(2) 06 24		
REDNECK	2.5	.70
(1) 39		
REGENCY	2.5	.52
(1) 16		
ROVING AMBASSADOR	2.5	.52
(1) 17		
ROYAL GOVERNOR	2.5	.52
(1) 18		
SCEPTIC	2.5	.70
(1) 43		
SHAH	2.5	.52
(1) 17		
SPEECHWRITER	2.5	.70
(1) 39		
SPY	2.5	.70
(2) 16 17		
STATELESS PERSONS	2.5	.52
(2) 11 17		
STATESMEN	2.5	.84
(5) 03 06 17 24 27		
SUPERPATRIOTS	2.5	.52
(1) 39		
SUPREME ALLIED COMMANDER	2.5	.52
ATLANTIC (SACLANT)		
(1) 17		
SURGEON GENERAL	2.5	.70
(1) 42		
TECHNICAL ADVISER	2.5	.70
(1) 17		
THEOLOGIAN	2.5	.70
(1) 43		
TITULAR LEADER	2.5	.70
(1) 39		
UGLY AMERICANS	2.5	.70
(1) 39		
UNEMPLOYED	2.5	.70
(1) 30		
VOTE-GETT(ER, -ING)	2.5	.70
(1) 29		
WARMONGERS	2.5	.52
(1) 17		
WATCHDOG OF THE TREASURY	2.5	.52
(3) 06 16 29		
WELL-INFORMED SOURCE	2.5	.52
(1) 17		
YES MAN	2.5	.52
(1) 29		
YOUTH	2.5	.84
(5) 07 11 24 25 30		
ACCUSED	2.6	.51
(1) 30		
ACQUIRED NATIONALITY	2.6	.51
(1) 17		
ADMINISTRATOR OF GENERAL	2.6	.51
SERVICES		
(1) 42		

AGENT	2.6	.51
(2) 17 24		
AGRICULTURAL ATTACHE	2.6	.51
(1) 17		
AIR ATTACHE	2.6	.51
(1) 17		
ALIEN PROPERTY CUSTODIAN	2.6	.69
(2) 06 16		
ANGRY YOUNG MEN	2.6	.69
(1) 39		
ARCHBISHOP	2.6	.69
(1) 17		
ASSISTANT PRESIDENT	2.6	.69
(1) 44		
ASSISTANT SECRETARY-GENERAL	2.6	.69
(1) 17		
ATTORNEY	2.6	.51
(1) 24		
BAGMAN	2.6	.51
(1) 29		
BEATNIK	2.6	.69
(1) 39		
BLACK REPUBLICAN	2.6	.51
(3) 06 16 29		
BLEEDING HEARTS	2.6	.51
(1) 39		
BLOCK CAPTAIN	2.6	.51
(1) 42		
BONDSMAN	2.6	.51
(1) 06		
BROTHERHOOD	2.6	.69
(2) 24 30		
CARDINAL	2.6	.69
(1) 17		
CHEAP LABOR	2.6	.51
(1) 46		
CHIEF	2.6	.69
(1) 24		
CITIZEN OF THE WORLD	2.6	.51
(1) 39		
CODE AUTHORITY	2.6	.51
(2) 06 16		
COLLECTOR OF THE CUSTOMS	2.6	.51
(1) 06		
COMMISSIONED OFFICER	2.6	.51
(1) 06		
COMMISSIONER	2.6	.51
(4) 03 06 11 30		
COMPTROLLER OF THE CURRENCY	2.6	.69
(5) 06 16 18 32 42		
CONFEREE	2.6	.51
(2) 17 27		
CONSTABLE	2.6	.51
(2) 06 16		
CONTRACT LABOR	2.6	.51
(2) 06 16		
CONVICT	2.6	.69
(2) 06 16		
COUNCILLOR	2.6	.51
(1) 24		
COUNTY AGENT	2.6	.69
(1) 18		

COUNTY SURVEYOR 2.6 .51
(1) 27
CROWN PRINCE 2.6 .51
(1) 17
CRYPTO-COMMUNIST 2.6 .51
(1) 38
DEFENDER 2.6 .69
(2) 24 30
DEMOS 2.6 .69
(1) 08
DEPRIVED 2.6 .69
(1) 30
DIPLOMATIC AGENT 2.6 .69
(4) 03 06 16 17
DIPLOMATIC CAREER 2.6 .51
(1) 17
DISADVANTAGED YOUTH 2.6 .69
(1) 37
DISTRICT LEADER 2.6 .69
(1) 06
DOLLAR-A-YEAR MAN 2.6 .51
(2) 06 16
DOMESTIC 2.6 .51
(3) 16 17 24
DULY AUTHORIZED REPRESENTATIVE 2.6 .51
(1) 17
EDUCATOR 2.6 .69
(1) 30
EMINENCE GRISE 2.6 .51
(2) 08 17
EVERYMAN 2.6 .69
(1) 39
FAT CAT 2.6 .51
(4) 06 16 27 29
FATHERS OF THE CHURCH 2.6 .69
(1) 26
FAVORITE SON 2.6 .51
(7) 03 06 16 18 27 29 32
FELLOWSHIPS 2.6 .51
(1) 41
FENCE STRADDLER 2.6 .51
(1) 29
FEUDAL KINGSHIP 2.6 .51
(1) 09
FIGUREHEAD 2.6 .51
(1) 29
FIRST LADY 2.6 .51
(1) 39
FIVE PERCENTER 2.6 .51
(1) 39
FOLLOWERS 2.6 .84
(2) 17 24
FOREIGN AGENT 2.6 .51
(1) 17
FOREIGN SERVICE AMBASSADOR 2.6 .51
(1) 18
GENERAL 2.6 .69
(3) 06 24 26
GENIUS 2.6 .69
(1) 43
GRAND MUFTI 2.6 .69
(1) 16

GUARDIAN 2.6 .51
(2) 17 24
HACK 2.6 .51
(1) 29
HANDSHAKER 2.6 .69
(1) 29
HATCHETMAN 2.6 .69
(1) 39
HEAD 2.6 .69
(2) 17 24
HERO 2.6 .69
(1) 24
HIGH COMMISSIONER FOR REFUGEES, 2.6 .51
UNITED NATIONS
(2) 17 20
HIGH CONTRACTING PARTIES 2.6 .51
(1) 17
HIS HONOR 2.6 .69
(1) 06
HOLD-OVER 2.6 .51
(3) 06 16 29
HOMOSEXUALS 2.6 .69
(3) 07 25 37
HOODLUMS 2.6 .69
(1) 30
HOST 2.6 .69
(1) 17
HUMAN 2.6 .69
(2) 24 30
HURRAH BOYS 2.6 .69
(1) 29
INCITERS OF WAR 2.6 .69
(1) 17
INDISPENSABLE MAN 2.6 .51
(1) 16
INDUCTEE 2.6 .51
(1) 16
INFLUENCE PEDDLER 2.6 .51
(1) 39
INTELLECTUALS AND POLITICS 2.6 .69
(3) 07 11 23
INVESTIGATORS 2.6 .51
(1) 37
JUDGE ADVOCATE GENERAL (JAG) 2.6 .51
(1) 32
JUDGE OF ELECTIONS 2.6 .51
(1) 06
JUDGE OF PROBATE 2.6 .51
(1) 27
JUVENILE 2.6 .69
(1) 30
KAMIKAZE 2.6 .51
(1) 16
KEYNOTE SPEAKER 2.6 .51
(2) 03 29
KINGFISH 2.6 .51
(1) 39
LABOR LEADER 2.6 .51
(1) 06
LABOR REFORMER 2.6 .51
(1) 06
LABOR SPIES 2.6 .51
(1) 45

LAND-GRABBER	2.6	.69
(1) 06		
LECTURER	2.6	.51
(1) 17		
LONELIEST JOB IN THE WORLD	2.6	.69
(1) 39		
LONG HAIR	2.6	.69
(1) 29		
LORD CHAMBERLAIN	2.6	.51
(1) 17		
MAGISTRATE	2.6	.69
(5) 06 16 18 26 27		
MAN IN THE STREET	2.6	.51
(1) 29		
MARTYR	2.6	.69
(1) 30		
MATERIAL WITNESS	2.6	.51
(1) 44		
MESTIZO	2.6	.69
(1) 46		
MINISTER OF FOREIGN AFFAIRS, FRANCE	2.6	.51
(2) 11 20		
MINOR	2.6	.69
(1) 16		
MODERATOR	2.6	.69
(1) 03		
MOSSBACK	2.6	.51
(1) 29		
NONCOMISSIONED OFFICERS	2.6	.51
(1) 42		
NONPROFESSIONALS	2.6	.69
(1) 37		
NOTARY PUBLIC	2.6	.51
(3) 06 16 27		
OFFICIAL	2.6	.69
(3) 17 24 30		
OLD CHINA HANDS	2.6	.51
(1) 39		
OLD PRO	2.6	.69
(1) 39		
PARIAH	2.6	.51
(3) 17 24 29		
PARLIAMENTARY DEPUTY	2.6	.51
(1) 17		
PATROLMAN	2.6	.51
(1) 45		
PEACE CORPS EMPLOYEES	2.6	.69
(1) 37		
PIONEERS	2.6	.51
(1) 30		
POLITICAL GENERAL	2.6	.84
(1) 29		
POPULAR	2.6	.69
(4) 16 17 24 30		
PREDECESSOR	2.6	.69
(1) 17		
PRESIDENT OF THE REPUBLIC, ITALY	2.6	.51
(1) 20		
PRESIDENT-DESIGNATE	2.6	.51
(1) 32		
PRESIDENT-MAKER	2.6	.51
(1) 29		
PRETENDER TO THE THRONE	2.6	.51
(2) 16 17		
PRIESTHOOD	2.6	.69
(1) 24		
PRIME-MOVER	2.6	.51
(1) 43		
PRINCE OF WALES	2.6	.51
(2) 16 17		
PRIVATE INDIVIDUALS	2.6	.51
(1) 36		
PROPHETS OF GLOOM AND DOOM	2.6	.69
(1) 39		
PROSECUTED PERSONS	2.6	.51
(1) 17		
RACIST	2.6	.51
(2) 17 30		
REBEL	2.6	.51
(4) 16 17 29 30		
REGISTRAR	2.6	.51
(1) 17		
REPORTER	2.6	.69
(1) 17		
SCALAWAG	2.6	.51
(3) 06 16 29		
SECRETARY	2.6	.69
(5) 06 16 17 18 24		
SEMI-OFFICIAL SOURCE	2.6	.51
(1) 17		
SENIOR OFFICIALS	2.6	.69
(1) 17		
SHARE CROPPER	2.6	.51
(1) 45		
SHEIK	2.6	.51
(1) 17		
SOLICITOR	2.6	.69
(3) 03 06 16		
SPOILS (-MEN, PARTY, SYSTEM)	2.6	.51
(8) 03 04 06 16 18 27 29 32		
SQUATTER	2.6	.51
(2) 06 16		
STAFF MEMBER	2.6	.51
(1) 17		
STANDARD BEARER	2.6	.51
(1) 39		
STATE'S ATTORNEY	2.6	.51
(2) 06 16		
STUDENT	2.6	.69
(6) 11 15 19 23 24 30		
SUPERINTENDENT OF PUBLIC INSTRUCTION	2.6	.51
(3) 03 18 27		
SUPERINTENDENT OF SCHOOLS	2.6	.51
(1) 18		
SUPREME COURT REPORTER	2.6	.69
(1) 18		
SURROGATE	2.6	.51
(2) 06 16		
TITLE OF NOBILITY	2.6	.51
(1) 17		
TOWN CLERK	2.6	.69
(1) 42		
TRANS-EMPIRICAL THEORISTS	2.6	.69
(1) 08		

TREASURER	2.6	.69
(5) 03 06 16 17 27		
UNEMPLOYABLES	2.6	.51
(1) 30		
VAGRANT	2.6	.69
(1) 45		
VETO MAYOR	2.6	.69
(1) 06		
VICTORIAN	2.6	.51
(1) 24		
WAR REBELS	2.6	.51
(1) 16		
WHITEY	2.6	.51
(1) 30		
WINDSOR, DUKE OF	2.6	.51
(2) 16 34		
WITNESS	2.6	.69
(4) 06 17 18 30		
WORKERS	2.6	.69
(4) 11 24 25 30		
YANKEE	2.6	.51
(2) 06 30		
POLITICS	1.0	.00
(17) 01 03 04 06 08 11 12 13 16 17		
19 23 24 26 27 30 33		
CIVIL LIBERTIES	1.1	.31
(11) 03 06 11 16 18 20 25 26 27 32		
34		
JUDICIAL REVIEW	1.1	.31
(14) 03 06 07 10 11 16 17 18 19 23		
25 27 32 33		
MULTI-PARTY SYSTEM	1.1	.31
(1) 42		
BALANCE OF POWER	1.2	.42
(13) 03 06 08 09 11 16 17 18 19 20		
22 25 29		
BILL OF RIGHTS	1.2	.42
(11) 03 06 16 17 18 22 25 27 32 34		
46		
CIVIL RIGHTS	1.2	.42
(15) 02 03 06 11 16 17 18 19 23 25		
27 29 30 33 34		
FREEDOM OF SPEECH	1.2	.42
(7) 03 06 10 16 17 18 32 46		
NATIONAL INTEREST	1.2	.42
(4) 02 03 18 20		
POLITICAL REPRESENTATION	1.2	.42
(1) 23		
POLITICAL SCIENCE, DEVELOPMENT OF	1.2	.42
(1) 04		
REVOLUTION	1.2	.42
(17) 06 07 10 11 12 16 17 19 20 22		
23 24 25 26 27 30 33		
AGGRESSION	1.3	.48
(9) 03 06 11 16 17 18 20 23 30		
AMERICAN BILL OF RIGHTS	1.3	.48
(1) 42		
AMERICAN REVOLUTION	1.3	.48
(4) 22 25 26 46		
CIVIL WAR	1.3	.48
(9) 03 06 08 11 16 17 20 25 33 46		
DUE PROCESS CLAUSE	1.3	.67
(1) 45		

FOURTEENTH AMENDMENT	1.3	.48
(4) 06 18 27 34 46		
FREEDOM OF RELIGION	1.3	.48
(6) 03 06 16 18 22 32 46		
FREEDOM OF THE PRESS	1.3	.48
(1) 03 11 16 17 18 32 46		
IMPLIED POWERS	1.3	.48
(8) 03 06 16 17 18 20 27 32 46		
INDUSTRIAL REVOLUTION	1.3	.48
(7) 06 09 16 17 22 25 32 46		
MACHINE POLITICS	1.3	.48
(3) 03 32 33		
MONROE DOCTRINE	1.3	.48
(11) 03 06 16 17 18 20 21 25 26 27		
32 46		
MULTIPARTY SYSTEM	1.3	.67
(8) 03 06 16 18 20 24 32 33		
NATURAL LAW (JUS NATURALE)	1.3	.48
(15) 03 06 09 10 11 16 17 18 19 20		
22 23 25 26 27		
POLITICAL	1.3	.48
(4) 16 17 24 30		
POLITICAL PARTICIPATION	1.3	.67
(4) 07 11 15 23		
ACCOUNTABILITY	1.4	.69
(5) 17 18 20 25 29		
ARMS RACE	1.4	.51
(2) 03 11		
CHARTER OF THE UNITED NATIONS	1.4	.51
(3) 17 18 20 41		
CITY MANAGER PLAN	1.4	.51
(1) 16		
CIVIL DISOBEDIENCE	1.4	.51
(10) 03 06 07 11 16 18 22 23 25 33		
COEXISTENCE, PEACEFUL	1.4	.51
(4) 23 24 26 36		
COLD WAR	1.4	.51
(11) 03 07 11 16 17 20 22 23 25 27		
32 46		
COMMON LAW	1.4	.69
(12) 02 03 06 16 17 18 19 22 25 26		
27 32		
CONSTITUTION, UNITED STATES	1.4	.69
(4) 06 16 32 45		
DESEGREGATION	1.4	.51
(4) 03 24 30 32 46		
EQUAL PROTECTION CLAUSE	1.4	.51
(7) 02 03 06 16 18 27 32		
FIRST AMENDMENT	1.4	.69
(4) 18 22 27 34		
FREEDOM OF ASSEMBLY	1.4	.51
(1) 32		
GROUP PRESSURE	1.4	.69
(1) 06		
HUMAN RIGHTS	1.4	.69
(4) 03 11 17 20		
INTERNATIONAL LAW	1.4	.69
(13) 06 09 11 12 16 17 18 19 20 22		
23 25 26		
INTERSTATE COMMERCE CLAUSE	1.4	.69
(1) 42		
JUDICIAL SYSTEM	1.4	.51
(1) 32		

LIMITED WAR	1.4	.51
(4) 03 18 20 27		
LOBBYING	1.4	.69
(3) 03 07 24		
MAGNA CARTA	1.4	.51
(9) 02 03 06 16 18 22 25 26 32		
MINORITY RIGHTS	1.4	.69
(1) 18		
NATIONALIZATION	1.4	.51
(9) 06 10 11 17 18 19 20 24 33		
NEGOTIATION	1.4	.51
(4) 06 17 20 24		
NEUTRALITY	1.4	.51
(10) 03 06 16 17 18 20 23 30 32 33 46		
NUCLEAR DETERRENT	1.4	.51
(2) 03 17		
ONE MAN, ONE VOTE	1.4	.51
(1) 32		
POWERS OF CONGRESS	1.4	.69
(1) 42		
PROLETARIAN REVOLUTION	1.4	.69
(1) 26		
PROPORTIONAL REPRESENTATION (PR)	1.4	.51
(15) 03 06 10 11 16 17 18 19 20 22 26 27 32 33 34		
RUSSIAN REVOLUTION OF 1917	1.4	.69
(3) 08 25 26		
SEPARATION OF POWERS	1.4	.69
(15) 02 03 06 12 16 17 18 19 22 23 26 27 32 33 34 46		
U.S. CONSTITUTION	1.4	.69
(1) 45		
UNCONSTITUTIONALITY	1.4	.51
(1) 42		
WAR POWERS OF THE PRESIDENT	1.4	.51
(8) 03 06 11 16 18 20 27 32		
WRIT OF HABEAS CORPUS	1.4	.51
(8) 02 03 05 16 18 27 32 42		
A PRIORI	1.5	.52
(3) 01 03 43		
ADJUDICATION	1.5	.70
(5) 06 16 17 20 27		
ADVICE AND CONSENT	1.5	.52
(2) 18 32		
AMERICAN CIVIL WAR	1.5	.70
(1) 17		
ARAB-ISRAELI CONFLICTS	1.5	.70
(3) 07 34 46		
BALLOT	1.5	.70
(9) 03 06 16 17 24 26 27 32 33		
BOLSHEVIK REVOLUTION	1.5	.52
(1) 22		
CITY GOVERNMENT, COUNCIL-MANAGER PLAN	1.5	.52
(1) 18		
CITY GOVERNMENT, MAYOR-ADMINISTRATOR PLAN	1.5	.52
(1) 18		
CITY GOVERNMENT, MAYOR-COUNCIL PLAN	1.5	.52
(1) 18		
CITY GOVERNMENT, STRONG MAYOR PLAN	1.5	.52
(1) 18		
CIVIL LAW (JUS CIVILE)	1.5	.52
(8) 03 06 16 18 19 20 25 32		
CLEAR AND PRESENT DANGER DOCTRINE	1.5	.52
(2) 18 22		
CLOSED PRIMARY	1.5	.52
(6) 03 06 16 18 32 34		
CONSENT OF THE GOVERNED	1.5	.70
(2) 16 29		
CONSTITUTIONAL POWER	1.5	.70
(1) 17		
CRUEL AND UNUSUAL PUNISHMENT	1.5	.52
(5) 03 06 16 18 32		
DEMOCRATIC	1.5	.84
(1) 30		
DEMOCRATIZATION	1.5	.70
(2) 17 24		
DUE PROCESS	1.5	.70
(1) 02		
DUE PROCESS OF LAW	1.5	.70
(9) 02 03 06 16 18 27 32 33 34		
EXECUTIVE AGREEMENT	1.5	.52
(9) 02 03 06 16 18 20 27 32 34		
EXECUTIVE ORDER	1.5	.70
(6) 02 03 16 18 27 32		
FIFTH AMENDMENT	1.5	.52
(5) 06 18 24 27 34		
FREE ENTERPRISE SYSTEM	1.5	.70
(6) 02 03 18 22 27 29		
GERRYMANDER	1.5	.52
(12) 02 03 06 16 17 18 25 27 32 33 34 45		
GRADUATED INCOME TAX	1.5	.52
(1) 27		
INTERSTATE COMMERCE	1.5	.70
(4) 06 16 18 27 46		
ITEM VETO	1.5	.52
(6) 03 06 16 18 27 32		
JUDICIAL ACTIVISM	1.5	.70
(3) 02 11 32		
JURISDICTION	1.5	.70
(8) 03 06 16 17 19 20 27 32		
LAW	1.5	.70
(16) 01 02 03 06 11 12 13 16 17 18 19 23 24 25 26 30		
LIBERTY	1.5	.70
(13) 02 06 10 12 16 17 19 22 23 25 26 27 30		
MARSHALL PLAN (EUROPEAN RECOVERY PROGRAM)	1.5	.52
(1) 45 46		
MONROE DOCTRINE	1.5	.52
(1) 46		
NATIONAL BUDGET	1.5	.70
(1) 42		
NATIONAL SELF-DETERMINATION	1.5	.70
(3) 06 11 20		
NUCLEAR WARFARE	1.5	.70
(1) 17		

OPEN PRIMARY	1.5	.52
(6) 03 06 16 18 32 34		
PASSAGE OF A BILL INTO LAW	1.5	.70
(1) 17		
PATRONAGE SYSTEM	1.5	.70
(1) 04		
PRESIDENTIAL POWERS	1.5	.70
(1) 32		
RECALL	1.5	.52
(11) 02 03 06 16 17 18 19 22 27 29 32 46		
REFERENDUM	1.5	.52
(13) 02 03 06 11 16 17 18 19 22 25 27 32 33 46		
SEGREGATION	1.5	.52
(14) 02 03 06 07 17 18 23 24 25 27 29 30 32 34 46		
STATES' RIGHTS	1.5	.52
(1) 44 46		
STRICT INTERPRETATION OF THE CONSTITUTION	1.5	.52
(1) 45		
TWO-PARTY SYSTEM	1.5	.70
(8) 03 06 16 18 27 30 32 33		
UNCONSTITUTIONAL	1.5	.52
(6) 06 16 17 27 29 30		
UNDERDEVELOPMENT	1.5	.52
(4) 03 11 20 24		
UNICAMERAL SYSTEM	1.5	.70
(7) 03 04 06 16 17 32 44		
VETO	1.5	.52
(1) 38		
VETO (U.S. PRESIDENTIAL)	1.5	.52
(11) 02 03 06 16 17 18 20 25 27 32 33		
VETO, SECURITY COUNCIL	1.5	.52
(2) 18 20		
VIET NAM, WAR IN	1.5	.70
(1) 46		
VOTE	1.5	.70
(4) 16 17 24 30		
WATERGATE	1.5	.52
(1) 07		
AMENDING PROCESS, U.S. CONSTITUTION	1.6	.51
(1) 42		
ARMS CONTROL	1.6	.51
(7) 03 07 11 18 20 25 27		
BALANCE OF PAYMENTS	1.6	.69
(8) 03 11 16 18 20 25 27 32		
BALANCE OF TERROR	1.6	.51
(4) 03 17 20 34		
BALANCE OF TRADE	1.6	.69
(3) 06 16 20		
BELLIGERENCY	1.6	.51
(5) 03 06 16 17 20		
BILL	1.6	.69
(9) 02 03 06 16 17 18 27 30 32		
BILL OF ATTAINDER	1.6	.51
(7) 02 03 06 16 18 21 32		
CAUCUS	1.6	.51
(11) 02 03 06 16 17 18 24 27 32 33 34		
CENTRALIZATION	1.6	.69
(11) 03 06 16 18 19 24 25 27 29 32 33		
CITY GOVERNMENT, COMMISSION PLAN	1.6	.51
(1) 18		
CITY GOVERNMENT, WEAK MAYOR PLAN	1.6	.69
(1) 18		
CIVIL SERVICE SYSTEM	1.6	.69
(1) 42		
COLLECTIVE SECURITY	1.6	.69
(11) 03 06 16 18 19 20 21 23 27 32 34		
CONSTITUTION	1.6	.84
(1) 03 46		
CONSTITUTIONAL LAW	1.6	.69
(10) 03 05 11 16 17 18 19 23 32 33		
CONSTITUTIONALITY	1.6	.69
(4) 03 17 19 23		
COUP D'ETAT	1.6	.51
(8) 03 06 11 16 17 20 25 33		
CUBAN MISSILE CRISIS	1.6	.51
(4) 04 25 32 34 46		
DE JURE	1.6	.69
(4) 06 16 17 27		
DETERRENCE	1.6	.69
(7) 04 07 11 18 20 24 25		
DIALECTIC	1.6	.69
(4) 03 17 26 43		
DIRECT PRIMARY	1.6	.51
(9) 02 03 06 16 18 19 22 32 34		
DIVISION OF POWERS	1.6	.69
(2) 06 16		
DOCTRINE OF IMPLIED POWERS	1.6	.51
(1) 03		
EMINENT DOMAIN	1.6	.51
(6) 03 06 16 18 27 32		
EX POST FACTO LAW	1.6	.51
(8) 02 03 06 16 17 18 27 32		
EXECUTIVE POWER	1.6	.84
(1) 44		
EXECUTIVE PRIVILEGE	1.6	.69
(2) 27 32		
FILIBUSTER	1.6	.51
(9) 02 03 06 16 18 27 32 34 38		
FOREIGN POLICY	1.6	.69
(12) 03 04 06 07 11 12 16 19 20 23 25 27		
GALLUP POLL	1.6	.69
(3) 03 19 32		
GOVERNMENT REGULATION OF BUSINESS	1.6	.69
(2) 25 32		
GROUP REPRESENTATION	1.6	.69
(1) 06		
IMPEACHMENT	1.6	.69
(9) 03 06 11 16 17 18 27 32 33		
INITIATIVE	1.6	.51
(14) 02 03 06 16 17 18 19 22 24 27 29 30 32 33 46		
INSURRECTION	1.6	.69
(7) 06 16 17 24 27 30 33		

JUDICIAL POWER 1.6 .69
(4) 06 17 19 23
JUDICIAL SELF-RESTRAINT 1.6 .51
(1) 02
LAW, NATURAL 1.6 .84
(1) 22
LEGISLATION 1.6 .84
(9) 06 11 16 17 19 24 27 30 32
LEGISLATIVE POWERS, CONGRESS 1.6 .84
(1) 20
LONG BALLOT 1.6 .51
(1) 18 27
MANIFEST DESTINY 1.6 .51
(5) 06 16 22 25 29 46
MERIT SYSTEM 1.6 .84
(6) 03 06 16 18 27 32
MINORITY REPRESENTATION 1.6 .69
(3) 06 10 16
NAPOLEONIC CODE 1.6 .51
(2) 16 26
NATION-BUILDING 1.6 .69
(2) 15 24
NATIONAL DEBT 1.6 .69
(6) 16 17 18 25 27 32
NATURAL LAW, DEMOCRATIC THEORY 1.6 .69
(1) 20
NEW DEAL 1.6 .69
(12) 03 04 06 10 11 16 19 21 22 25
29 34 46
NOMINATING CONVENTION 1.6 .69
(2) 16 33
NOMINATION 1.6 .69
(6) 03 06 16 18 27 32
NONPARTISANSHIP 1.6 .51
(1) 03
NUCLEAR ARMS RACE 1.6 .69
(1) 41
NUCLEAR DISARMAMENT 1.6 .51
(1) 17
OPPOSITION, ROLE OF (BRITAIN) 1.6 .51
(1) 20
PARLIAMENTARY ELECTIONS 1.6 .69
(1) 17
PARTISANSHIP 1.6 .69
(1) 24
PEACEFUL CO-EXISTENCE 1.6 .51
(6) 03 17 20 22 23 34
PERSONAL LIBERTY 1.6 .84
(3) 03 06 16
POCKET VETO 1.6 .51
(8) 02 03 06 16 18 27 29 32
POLICY 1.6 .84
(8) 03 11 13 16 17 24 30 33
POLICY OF CONTAINMENT 1.6 .51
(1) 17
POLICY-MAKING 1.6 .69
(5) 03 04 11 24 26
POLITICAL ACTION 1.6 .84
(2) 01 08
POLITICAL DECISION 1.6 .69
(2) 08 23
POLITICAL INSTABILITY 1.6 .69
(1) 15

POLITICAL MOBILIZATION 1.6 .69
(1) 15
POLITICAL OBLIGATION 1.6 .69
(2) 11 23
POWERS OF THE PRESIDENT 1.6 .69
(1) 32
PRESIDENTIAL ELECTIONS 1.6 .69
(3) 17 18 32
PRESIDENTIAL VETO 1.6 .69
(1) 34
PUBLIC OPINION POLLS 1.6 .69
(3) 11 25 32
PUBLIC OPINION SURVEYS 1.6 .69
(1) 36
REPRESENTATION 1.6 .84
(11) 02 03 06 10 11 17 23 24 25 26
33
RIGHT OF ACCUSED PERSON TO 1.6 .51
COUNSEL
(1) 18 32
RULE OF THE MAJORITY 1.6 .84
(1) 16
SANCTIONS (COLLECTIVE SECURITY) 1.6 .69
(1) 20
SPOILS SYSTEM 1.6 .51
(1) 46
STRATEGIC ARMS LIMITATION TALKS 1.6 .69
(SALT)
(1) 32
THIRTEENTH AMENDMENT 1.6 .51
(3) 06 18 27 46
TRIAL BY JURY 1.6 .51
(2) 32 45
TYRANNY OF THE MAJORITY 1.6 .51
(1) 44
VETO POWER 1.6 .69
(2) 04 17
VOTE OF CENSURE 1.6 .51
(1) 17
VOTE OF CONFIDENCE 1.6 .51
(2) 16 17
VOTING 1.6 .69
(1) 44
WITHERING AWAY OF THE STATE 1.6 .51
(2) 03 16
WORLD WAR II 1.6 .69
(8) 06 11 16 22 23 25 26 34 46
ABSENTEE VOTING 1.7 .67
(7) 03 06 16 17 18 27 32
ACT OF WAR 1.7 .67
(1) 03
AGRARIAN REFORM 1.7 .82
(4) 07 11 17 23
AMERICAN FOREIGN POLICY 1.7 .82
(2) 20 27
ANGLO-AMERICAN SYSTEM OF LAW 1.7 .82
(1) 44
APPEASEMENT 1.7 .48
(11) 03 06 16 17 18 20 22 27 32 34
46
APPORTIONMENT 1.7 .67
(7) 02 03 06 16 18 27 33

ARMS REDUCTION	1.7	.48
(1) 36		
ARTICLES OF CONFEDERATION	1.7	.48
(8) 02 03 06 16 18 27 32 46		
ATTITUDE SURVEYS	1.7	.82
(1) 37		
BACTERIOLOGICAL WARFARE	1.7	.48
(1) 17		
BARGAINING	1.7	.82
(6) 06 08 11 17 24 25		
BIOLOGICAL WARFARE	1.7	.48
(2) 17 25		
BIPOLARITY	1.7	.67
(4) 03 04 20 33		
BUDGET	1.7	.67
(11) 03 06 16 17 18 19 20 24 25 32 33		
BURDEN OF PROOF	1.7	.67
(2) 17 32		
CAPITAL PUNISHMENT	1.7	.48
(6) 03 17 18 25 27 32		
CASE LAW	1.7	.67
(1) 44		
CENSURE MOTION	1.7	.67
(1) 03		
CITY PLANNING	1.7	.82
(4) 06 11 16 32		
CIVIL RIGHTS ACT OF 1964	1.7	.67
(1) 18 46		
CIVIL SERVICE	1.7	.67
(12) 03 06 07 11 16 18 19 23 24 25 27 32		
CLOTURE RULE	1.7	.48
(1) 18 42		
CONCURRENT RESOLUTION	1.7	.48
(7) 02 03 06 16 18 27 32		
CONSTITUTIONAL CONVENTION	1.7	.48
(10) 02 03 06 08 11 18 25 26 27 46		
COUNCIL-MANAGER PLAN	1.7	.67
(1) 44		
COUNTY-MANAGER PLAN	1.7	.67
(1) 03		
COURT OPINION	1.7	.67
(1) 02		
CULTURAL REVOLUTION, CHINA (PRC)	1.7	.67
(5) 11 20 25 34 39		
DE FACTO SEGREGATION	1.7	.67
(1) 18		
DECLARATION OF WAR	1.7	.48
(5) 06 16 17 18 20 26		
DEPRESSION, ECONOMIC	1.7	.67
(1) 04		
DOUBLE JEOPARDY	1.7	.67
(6) 03 06 16 18 27 32		
EIGHTEENTH AMENDMENT	1.7	.48
(5) 06 16 18 24 27 46		
ELECTION PROPAGANDA	1.7	.67
(1) 17		
EMANCIPATION PROCLAMATION	1.7	.48
(5) 06 16 17 24 30 46		
EMERGENCY POWERS	1.7	.67
(5) 06 11 16 18 19		
EQUAL RIGHTS AMENDMENT (ERA)	1.7	.48
(2) 03 32		
EUROPEAN INTEGRATION	1.7	.48
(2) 11 17		
FAIR TRIAL	1.7	.82
(1) 18		
FIRST STRIKE CAPACITY	1.7	.67
(2) 03 20		
FOURTH AMENDMENT	1.7	.82
(1) 18		
FREE TRADE	1.7	.48
(8) 06 16 18 20 21 25 27 32		
GENEVA ACCORDS (1954)	1.7	.48
(1) 38 46		
GRANTS-IN-AID	1.7	.67
(1) 39		
GROSS NATIONAL PRODUCT (GNP)	1.7	.67
(7) 02 03 18 20 25 27 32		
GUERRILLA WARFARE	1.7	.48
(8) 06 11 16 17 20 25 29 30		
HOME RULE	1.7	.48
(9) 03 06 16 18 22 27 29 32 38		
HUMAN AND CIVIL RIGHTS	1.7	.82
(1) 07		
IMMUNITY	1.7	.48
(6) 03 06 16 17 18 32		
INDICTMENT	1.7	.67
(6) 06 16 18 27 30 32		
INJUNCTION	1.7	.48
(7) 02 03 06 16 18 27 32		
INTERNATIONAL BARGAINING	1.7	.82
(1) 11		
INTERNATIONAL CONFLICTS	1.7	.94
(2) 11 23		
INTERNATIONAL CRISES	1.7	.94
(2) 03 04		
INTERNATIONAL ORDER	1.7	.94
(1) 11		
INVESTIGATIVE POWER	1.7	.82
(3) 06 16 32		
JUDICIAL PROCEDURE	1.7	.67
(1) 17		
JURY SYSTEM	1.7	.67
(1) 32		
LABOR-MANAGEMENT RELATIONS ACT OF 1947 (TAFT-HARTLEY LAW)	1.7	.67
(6) 16 18 27 32 34 45		
LAME DUCK CONGRESS	1.7	.48
(1) 42		
LAME DUCK SESSION	1.7	.48
(1) 06		
LAW-MAKING POWER	1.7	.82
(2) 17 24		
LEGISLATIVE APPORTIONMENT	1.7	.67
(1) 32		
LEGISLATIVE POWER	1.7	.67
(4) 11 17 19 23		
LEGISLATIVE REAPPORTIONMENT	1.7	.67
(2) 03 32		
LOBBY REGULATION	1.7	.67
(1) 45		
LOGROLLING	1.7	.82
(6) 02 06 16 18 29 32 45		

LOUISIANA PURCHASE	1.7	.48
(2) 06 16 46		
LOYALTY OATH	1.7	.48
(4) 03 18 32 34		
MULTILATERAL TREATY	1.7	.48
(1) 18		
NATIONAL DEFENSE	1.7	.82
(1) 17		
NATIONAL LIBERATION WARS	1.7	.67
(1) 03		
NATURAL RIGHTS	1.7	.67
(7) 06 10 16 18 22 26 32		
NECESSARY AND PROPER CLAUSE OF	1.7	.48
THE CONSTITUTION		
(1) 45		
NEW DEAL LEGISLATION	1.7	.67
(1) 32		
NON-VIOLENCE	1.7	.67
(7) 06 11 17 19 22 25 30		
NULLIFICATION	1.7	.48
(7) 06 16 18 22 27 29 32		
NUREMBERG WAR CRIMES TRIALS	1.7	.67
(9) 03 11 16 17 19 20 25 27 34		
PARLIAMENTARY PROCEDURE	1.7	.82
(4) 06 16 19 27		
PARTY PRIMARY	1.7	.82
(2) 03 32		
PARTY UNITY	1.7	.67
(1) 39		
PLANNED ECONOMY	1.7	.67
(2) 16 26		
POLICY FORMULATION	1.7	.82
(1) 37		
POLITICAL PROTEST	1.7	.67
(2) 07 25		
POLLUTION, ENVIRONMENTAL	1.7	.67
(5) 04 07 11 25 32		
POPULAR CONSENT	1.7	.82
(1) 32		
POPULAR REFERENDUM	1.7	.67
(1) 17		
POST-BEHAVIORAL REVOLUTION	1.7	.67
(2) 01 04		
PREAMBLE TO THE CONSTITUTION	1.7	.67
(1) 32 46		
PRESIDENTIAL PRIMARY	1.7	.67
(7) 03 06 16 18 32 34 42		
PUBLIC LAW	1.7	.82
(8) 02 03 04 06 11 16 17 19		
REGRESSIVE TAX	1.7	.48
(4) 06 16 18 27		
REVOLUTIONARY WAR	1.7	.82
(1) 16		
RIGHT OF ASSOCIATION	1.7	.67
(1) 06		
RIGHT OF PETITION	1.7	.67
(3) 16 17 18		
RIGHT OF SELF-DETERMINATION OF	1.7	.67
NATIONS		
(1) 17		
ROLL-CALL VOTE	1.7	.48
(1) 17		
SANCTIONS (INTERNATIONAL LAW)	1.7	.67
(1) 20		
SEPARATION OF CHURCH AND STATE	1.7	.67
(5) 03 17 18 27 32 35 42		
SUFFRAGE	1.7	.67
(1) 32		
THERMONUCLEAR WAR	1.7	.48
(1) 03		
TREATY	1.7	.82
(12) 02 03 06 07 11 16 17 18 20 25		
27 33		
TREATY OF VERSAILLES (1919)	1.7	.48
(7) 03 06 16 17 19 21 22		
TWENTY-THIRD AMENDMENT	1.7	.48
(1) 18		
UNCONVENTIONAL WARFARE	1.7	.48
(1) 03		
VIET-NAM CONFLICT	1.7	.67
(1) 41		
VIETNAMIZATION	1.7	.67
(1) 32		
VOTE OF NO-CONFIDENCE	1.7	.48
(1) 17		
VOTER REGISTRATION	1.7	.48
(4) 02 18 32 34		
VOTING PROCEDURE	1.7	.82
(1) 17		
VOTING TURNOUT	1.7	.67
(1) 03		
WOMEN, EQUALITY OF	1.7	.48
(1) 35		
WRIT OF CERTIORARI	1.7	.67
(6) 02 03 06 18 27 32		
WRITTEN CONSTITUTION	1.7	.48
(3) 06 16 26		
A POSTERIORI	1.8	.63
(2) 01 43		
ABUSE OF POWER	1.8	.63
(1) 17		
ACCIDENTAL WAR	1.8	.63
(2) 03 20		
ACT OF CONGRESS	1.8	.63
(2) 06 32		
AMENDMENT PROCESS	1.8	.78
(3) 03 20 32		
AMERICAN CONSTITUTIONAL	1.8	.78
CONVENTION		
(1) 08		
APARTHEID	1.8	.42
(9) 03 07 11 17 23 24 25 32 34		
ARMS CONTROL AND DISARMAMENT	1.8	.63
(2) 20 32		
ATLANTIC CHARTER	1.8	.63
(10) 03 06 16 17 20 21 27 32 34 46		
CAMPAIGN FINANCE	1.8	.63
(1) 32		
CASUS BELLI	1.8	.63
(5) 03 06 16 17 20		
CEASE AND DESIST ORDER	1.8	.63
(1) 42		
CENSORSHIP	1.8	.78
(7) 03 06 16 17 18 19 25		

CITY CHARTER 1.8 .63
  (4) 03 16 18 32
CLASS WAR 1.8 .63
  (2) 17 21
COLLECTIVE BARGAINING 1.8 .42
  (6) 06 16 18 27 29 32
COLONIZATION 1.8 .42
  (5) 06 16 17 29 33
COMMISSION-MANAGER PLAN 1.8 .78
  (1) 06
COMMUNITY POWER 1.8 .63
  (3) 04 07 11
COMPULSORY VOTING 1.8 .63
  (3) 03 06 16
CONCENTRATION (OF ECONOMIC 1.8 .78
  POWER)
  (3) 03 06 24
CONFIRMATION 1.8 .63
  (6) 02 06 16 18 24 27
CONFLICT OF INTEREST 1.8 .78
  (3) 17 23 27
CONSTITUTIONAL LAW 1.8 .78
  (1) 06
CONSTITUTIONAL AMENDMENT 1.8 .78
  (3) 06 18 32
CONTAINMENT POLICY 1.8 .63
  (6) 03 17 18 20 32 34
CONTEMPT OF CONGRESS 1.8 .63
  (3) 03 18 32
COUNTER-REVOLUTION 1.8 .63
  (5) 06 16 17 19 25 43
CRUEL AND UNUSUAL PUNISHMENTS 1.8 .63
  PROHIBITED
  (1) 45
CURRENCY DEVALUATION 1.8 .63
  (1) 18
DE FACTO 1.8 .63
  (4) 06 16 17 27
DE JURE RECOGNITION 1.8 .63
  (6) 03 17 18 20 32 34
DEFENDANT'S RIGHTS 1.8 .91
  (1) 32
DEFENSE SPENDING 1.8 .78
  (1) 11
DEFENSIVE WAR 1.8 .63
  (1) 17
DELEGATION OF AUTHORITY 1.8 .78
  (1) 18
DELEGATION OF LEGISLATIVE POWER 1.8 .78
  (3) 03 06 33
DETERRENT 1.8 .63
  (1) 39
DIRECT ELECTIONS 1.8 .78
  (1) 44
DISARMAMENT AND ARMS CONTROL 1.8 .63
  (2) 20 23
DISENGAGEMENT 1.8 .42
  (4) 03 17 20 22
EAST-WEST RELATIONS 1.8 .78
  (3) 11 23 24
ECONOMIC GROWTH 1.8 .78
  (2) 11 20

ECONOMIC POLICY 1.8 .78
  (2) 11 17
EISENHOWER DOCTRINE 1.8 .63
  (3) 03 32 34 46
ELECTION 1.8 .78
  (14) 03 04 06 07 11 12 16 17 19 24
  26 30 32 33
ELECTION RETURNS 1.8 .78
  (1) 17
EMERGENCY POWERS OF THE 1.8 .63
  PRESIDENT
  (2) 03 32
ENGLISH CONSTITUTION 1.8 .63
  (2) 04 26
EQUAL PROTECTION OF THE LAW 1.8 .63
  (1) 46
EXCISE TAX 1.8 .42
  (5) 06 16 18 27 32
EXECUTIVE BUDGET 1.8 .63
  (2) 03 18
EXECUTIVE CLEMENCY 1.8 .63
  (1) 44
EXTRATERRITORIALITY 1.8 .42
  (8) 03 06 16 17 19 20 27 32
FIFTEENTH AMENDMENT 1.8 .78
  (4) 06 18 25 27
FOREIGN AFFAIRS 1.8 .78
  (2) 07 17
FULL EMPLOYMENT 1.8 .63
  (2) 02 22
FUNDAMENTAL RIGHTS 1.8 .91
  (1) 17
GENERAL ELECTIONS 1.8 .78
  (2) 18 27
GOVERNMENT EXPENDITURES 1.8 .78
  (1) 32
GOVERNMENT REVENUE 1.8 .91
  (1) 42
GOVERNMENT SUBSIDY 1.8 .78
  (1) 25
GRADUATED TAX 1.8 .63
  (1) 42
HIGH CRIMES AND MISDEMEANORS 1.8 .63
  (3) 06 18 32
HOUSE RULES 1.8 .63
  (1) 42
IDEOLOGICAL WARFARE 1.8 .78
  (2) 18 20
INCOME DISTRIBUTION 1.8 .63
  (2) 11 25
INCUMBENCY 1.8 .91
  (2) 02 25
INDEPENDENCE 1.8 .91
  (4) 11 16 17 24
INTERNATIONAL CONTROL OF ATOMIC 1.8 .63
  WEAPONS
  (1) 32
INTERNATIONAL TRADE 1.8 .78
  (5) 04 07 11 18 25
INTERNATIONAL TREATIES AND 1.8 .91
  AGREEMENTS
  (1) 03

INVASION OF PRIVACY	1.8	.63
(1) 25		
JUDICIAL INTERPRETATION	1.8	.78
(2) 02 32		
JUDICIAL LEGISLATION	1.8	.91
(1) 33		
JUDICIAL PRECEDENT	1.8	.78
(1) 44		
JURY TRIAL	1.8	.78
(2) 16 32		
JUS CIVILE	1.8	.63
(1) 20		
KOREAN WAR	1.8	.63
(5) 03 04 17 22 25 46		
LAME DUCK AMENDMENT	1.8	.63
(3) 03 16 34		
LAW ENFORCEMENT	1.8	.91
(1) 18		
LAW OF NATURE	1.8	.63
(2) 17 26		
LEGAL AUTHORITY	1.8	.78
(1) 01		
LEGISLATIVE INVESTIGATION	1.8	.91
(1) 03		
LIBEL AND SLANDER	1.8	.63
(7) 02 03 06 16 18 25 32		
LOCAL LEGISLATION	1.8	.78
(2) 06 16		
LONG MARCH	1.8	.42
(1) 34		
MACHIAVELLIAN DIPLOMACY	1.8	.63
(2) 16 20		
MANHOOD SUFFRAGE	1.8	.63
(4) 06 16 17 29 46		
MAYOR-ADMINISTRATOR PLAN	1.8	.78
(1) 18		
MAYOR-MANAGER FORM	1.8	.78
(1) 32		
MEDIATION	1.8	.78
(8) 03 06 11 16 17 20 27 32		
MIDDLE EAST CONFLICT	1.8	.63
(2) 11 32		
MISDEMEANOR	1.8	.78
(6) 02 03 06 16 18 27		
MISSOURI COMPROMISE	1.8	.63
(2) 06 16 46		
MOBILIZATION	1.8	.63
(9) 06 16 17 18 20 24 27 30 33		
MONETARY POLICY	1.8	.63
(5) 11 17 18 20 32		
MOST-FAVORED-NATION CLAUSE	1.8	.63
(8) 03 06 16 17 18 20 21 32		
MOTION OF CENSURE	1.8	.63
(1) 17		
MULTILATERAL TRADE	1.8	.63
(1) 20		
MUNICIPAL ELECTIONS	1.8	.63
(1) 17		
NATIONAL PRIMARY	1.8	.63
(1) 32		
NATIONAL SECURITY	1.8	.78
(1) 07		
NATURAL RESOURCES, CONSERVATION OF	1.8	.78
(1) 32		
NATURALIZATION	1.8	.63
(7) 03 06 16 18 20 27 32		
NATURE, STATE OF	1.8	.63
(1) 26		
NEGATIVE INCOME TAX	1.8	.63
(2) 25 32		
NON-ALIGNMENT	1.8	.42
(7) 03 11 18 20 23 24 32		
NON-INTERVENTION	1.8	.42
(4) 16 17 21 29		
NONPARTISAN PRIMARY	1.8	.42
(1) 03		
NUCLEAR CONFLICT	1.8	.78
(1) 04		
NUCLEAR PROLIFERATION	1.8	.78
(2) 20 32		
OFF-YEAR ELECTION	1.8	.78
(4) 02 16 29 39		
OVERTHROW OF A REGIME	1.8	.63
(1) 17		
PARDONING POWER	1.8	.42
(1) 17		
PATRONAGE	1.8	.78
(10) 03 06 11 16 18 24 27 29 32 33		
PEACE	1.8	.91
(8) 06 11 16 17 19 23 24 30		
PEACE-KEEPING	1.8	.63
(1) 11		
PHILADELPHIA CONVENTION OF 1787	1.8	.78
(2) 03 18		
PLEBISCITE	1.8	.63
(9) 03 06 16 17 20 21 29 32 33		
POLICE POWER	1.8	.78
(7) 03 06 11 16 18 27 32		
POLICY OF RAPPROCHMENT	1.8	.78
(1) 17		
POLITICAL PATRONAGE	1.8	.42
(2) 25 32		
POLL	1.8	.78
(8) 03 06 16 17 18 24 27 33		
POLL TAX	1.8	.42
(6) 03 06 16 18 27 32		
POWER BASE	1.8	.78
(1) 39		
PRACTICAL POLITICS	1.8	.91
(1) 25		
PREEMPTIVE STRIKE	1.8	.63
(1) 20		
PREFERENCE POLL	1.8	.78
(1) 39		
PRIVATE ENTERPRISE	1.8	.78
(2) 16 27		
PRIVILEGES AND IMMUNITIES	1.8	.42
(3) 16 18 32		
PROCEDURAL DUE PROCESS OF LAW	1.8	.78
(1) 45		
PROTEST	1.8	.63
(4) 11 17 24 30		
PROTEST VOTE	1.8	.63
(1) 06		

PUBLIC DEBT	1.8	.63
(7) 06 16 18 25 27 29 32		
PUBLIC INTEREST	1.8	.78
(3) 06 07 11		
PUBLIC RELATIONS (P.R.)	1.8	.63
(5) 03 16 25 27 32		
RAPPROCHEMENT	1.8	.63
(3) 16 17 20		
REAPPORTIONMENT	1.8	.78
(6) 03 06 16 27 33 34		
REAPPORTIONMENT, LEGISLATIVE	1.8	.63
(1) 32		
RECALL ELECTIONS	1.8	.63
(2) 18 33		
REGIONAL INTEGRATION	1.8	.78
(1) 11		
RESERVED POWERS	1.8	.78
(5) 03 16 18 27 32		
REVENUE-SHARING	1.8	.78
(3) 07 25 32		
REVOLUTION OF RISING EXPECTATIONS	1.8	.63
(1) 20		
RIGHTS OF ACCUSED PERSONS	1.8	.63
(1) 32		
ROMAN LAW	1.8	.42
(6) 09 19 22 25 26 32		
RULE-MAKING POWER	1.8	.91
(3) 03 06 18		
SCHOOL DESEGREGATION	1.8	.78
(1) 02		
SECESSION	1.8	.63
(6) 06 11 16 17 29 33 46		
SECRET BALLOT	1.8	.63
(4) 17 29 32 33		
SELF-DETERMINATION	1.8	.78
(1) 39		
SENIORITY	1.8	.63
(4) 02 24 25 32		
SENIORITY RULE	1.8	.63
(7) 03 06 16 18 32 34 45		
SEPARATE BUT EQUAL DOCTRINE	1.8	.42
(4) 03 18 32 34		
SHORT BALLOT	1.8	.63
(7) 03 16 18 19 22 27 32		
SINO-SOVIET CONFLICT	1.8	.42
(1) 34		
SIXTEENTH AMENDMENT	1.8	.42
(2) 06 18 46		
TAKING THE FIFTH AMENDMENT	1.8	.42
(1) 03		
TARIFF	1.8	.42
(9) 03 06 07 16 18 20 22 27 32		
TRUMAN DOCTRINE	1.8	.63
(10) 03 11 16 17 18 20 25 27 32 34 46		
TWENTY-FIRST AMENDMENT	1.8	.42
(2) 06 18		
TWENTY-SECOND AMENDMENT	1.8	.42
(1) 18		
UNCONDITIONAL SURRENDER	1.8	.42
(5) 03 06 16 17 20		
UNIVERSAL SUFFRAGE	1.8	.63
(3) 17 22 32		
URBAN PLANNING	1.8	.63
(1) 32		
VIOLENCE	1.8	.91
(8) 07 10 11 19 23 24 25 30		
VOTING METHODS	1.8	.78
(1) 23		
WAR CRIMES	1.8	.42
(1) 38		
WAR OF INDEPENDENCE	1.8	.63
(1) 17		
WAR OF LIBERATION	1.8	.63
(1) 03		
WAR OF NATIONAL LIBERATION	1.8	.78
(3) 17 20 39		
WEAK-MAYOR PLAN	1.8	.78
(3) 06 18 32		
WEIMAR CONSTITUTION	1.8	.42
(2) 03 22		
WHITE SUPREMACY	1.8	.42
(1) 25 46		
WOMEN'S SUFFRAGE, NINETEENTH AMENDMENT	1.8	.42
(5) 06 16 17 25 32		
WORLD WAR I	1.8	.63
(7) 06 11 16 22 23 25 26 46		
WRIT OF MANDAMUS	1.8	.78
(1) 32		
ABOLITION	1.9	.56
(2) 17 45		
ACADEMIC FREEDOM	1.9	.73
(5) 03 11 18 25 32		
ACT	1.9	.73
(3) 16 17 30		
ACT (STATUTE)	1.9	.87
(1) 18		
ADMINISTRATION	1.9	.73
(15) 03 04 06 11 12 16 17 18 19 23 25 27 30 32 33		
ADMINISTRATION OF JUSTICE	1.9	.73
(1) 44		
ADMINISTRATIVE BEHAVIOR	1.9	.73
(2) 01 04		
ADMINISTRATIVE DECENTRALIZATION	1.9	.99
(2) 11 23		
ADMINISTRATIVE LAW	1.9	.87
(8) 03 06 11 16 18 19 25 33		
ADMINISTRATIVE REORGANIZATION	1.9	.73
(4) 03 06 16 18		
ADMINISTRATIVE SYSTEMS	1.9	.73
(1) 04		
ALIEN AND SEDITION ACTS OF 1798	1.9	.31
(5) 03 06 18 32 46		
AMENDMENT	1.9	.56
(8) 06 16 17 18 27 30 44 45		
AMNESTY	1.9	.56
(9) 03 06 16 17 18 25 27 30 32		
ARMAGEDDON	1.9	.56
(1) 06		
ARMS EMBARGO	1.9	.31
(1) 16		
BALANCED BUDGET	1.9	.73
(1) 32		

BERLIN AIRLIFT   1.9   .31
(3) 03 17 34

BERLIN BLOCKADE   1.9   .31
(2) 34 46

BILATERAL TREATY   1.9   .56
(1) 18

BILL REFERRAL   1.9   .56
(1) 02

BIPARTISANSHIP   1.9   .73
(3) 18 20 32

BLACK POWER   1.9   .56
(2) 25 34

BOSTON TEA PARTY   1.9   .56
(3) 03 06 16

BOURGEOIS REVOLUTION   1.9   .56
(1) 26

BRINKMANSHIP   1.9   .31
(1) 03

BUSINESS CYCLE   1.9   .73
(4) 03 16 18 25

CAMPAIGN   1.9   .73
(10) 02 03 06 07 16 24 27 29 32 33

CASTE SYSTEM   1.9   .56
(8) 01 11 16 19 22 24 30 33

CAUCUS, CONGRESSIONAL   1.9   .31
(1) 18

CAUCUS, NOMINATING   1.9   .31
(1) 18

CEASE-FIRE   1.9   .56
(1) 17

CENSUS   1.9   .73
(7) 03 06 16 18 25 30 32

CIVIL CODE   1.9   .56
(2) 06 16

CIVIL DISORDERS   1.9   .73
(1) 42

CLEMENCY   1.9   .73
(1) 17

COLLECTIVE RESPONSIBILITY   1.9   .73
(1) 20

COMMERCE CLAUSE   1.9   .87
(3) 16 27 34

COMMUNITY DEVELOPMENT   1.9   .73
(2) 11 25

COMPARATIVE ADVANTAGE (TRADE   1.9   .73
THEORY)
(1) 20

COMPROMISE   1.9   .73
(6) 06 16 17 24 27 30

CONSENT, POPULAR   1.9   .73
(1) 32

CONSTITUTION, BRITAIN   1.9   .73
(1) 20

CONSTITUTIONAL CONVENTION OF 1787   1.9   .56
(3) 16 18 32

CONSTITUTIONAL REVISION   1.9   .73
(1) 17

CONTESTED ELECTION   1.9   .73
(3) 06 16 18

COUP   1.9   .73
(3) 17 24 30

COURT LEGISLATION   1.9   .73
(1) 44

CRIMINAL LAW   1.9   .73
(6) 03 06 16 18 25 32

CROSS-FILING   1.9   .73
(4) 03 27 32 42

DE FACTO RECOGNITION   1.9   .73
(6) 03 17 18 20 32 34

DE FACTO WAR   1.9   .56
(1) 03

DEATH PENALTY   1.9   .73
(3) 06 17 32

DECISION   1.9   .99
(6) 06 16 17 24 30 33

DEMAND   1.9   .87
(2) 17 24

DEPORTATION   1.9   .56
(8) 03 06 07 16 17 18 27 32

DETENTE   1.9   .73
(3) 03 17 20

DEVALUATION   1.9   .56
(1) 16

DEVIATION   1.9   .73
(1) 30

DIPLOMATIC IMMUNITY   1.9   .56
(4) 03 06 18 32

DIRECT LEGISLATION   1.9   .73
(6) 03 06 12 16 18 32

DIRECT NOMINATION   1.9   .73
(1) 06

DISARMAMENT   1.9   .73
(14) 03 06 07 08 11 16 17 18 19 21
24 25 27 32

DISFRANCHISE   1.9   .56
(1) 18

DISFRANCHISEMENT   1.9   .56
(1) 42

DISSENT   1.9   .73
(4) 07 24 30 34

DOCTRINE OF HOT PURSUIT   1.9   .56
(1) 16

DOMESTIC POLICY   1.9   .73
(1) 17

ECONOMIC DEVELOPMENT   1.9   .73
(1) 36

ECONOMIC POWER   1.9   .73
(1) 11

ELECTION CAMPAIGN   1.9   .87
(1) 17

ELECTORAL LAW (SYSTEM)   1.9   .87
(3) 11 17 19

ELECTORAL PROCEDURE   1.9   .87
(1) 17

EMBARGO   1.9   .56
(7) 06 16 17 20 25 32 33

ENFORCEMENT   1.9   .87
(3) 06 20 30

EQUAL JUSTICE UNDER LAW   1.9   .87
(1) 42

ESCALATION   1.9   .87
(5) 04 20 30 33 34

EXECUTIVE SESSION   1.9   .73
(6) 02 06 16 18 27 32

EXPANSIONIST POLICY   1.9   .56
(6) 03 06 11 17 22 29

EXPRESS POWERS 1.9 .73
(2) 06 17
EXTRADITION 1.9 .56
(8) 06 16 17 18 20 25 27 32
EXTRAORDINARY SESSION 1.9 .73
(2) 06 32
FEDERAL BUDGET 1.9 .56
(1) 32
FELONY 1.9 .56
(5) 03 06 16 18 27
FEMALE SUFFRAGE 1.9 .31
(1) 17
FORCE 1.9 .87
(5) 10 12 17 24 30
FOREIGN SERVICE EXAMINATION 1.9 .56
(1) 20
FREEDOM FROM ARBITRARY ARREST 1.9 .73
AND DETENTION
(1) 17
FREEDOM FROM SELF-INCRIMINATION 1.9 .73
(1) 45
FREEDOM OF ASSOCIATION 1.9 .87
(5) 03 06 17 18 32
FUNCTIONAL REPRESENTATION 1.9 .87
(4) 06 16 18 33
GENERAL LAWS 1.9 .87
(1) 18
GENOCIDE 1.9 .56
(7) 07 16 17 19 20 25 30
GOVERNMENT DEBT 1.9 .73
(1) 32
GOVERNMENT PROGRAMS 1.9 .73
(1) 04
GOVERNMENT REGULATION 1.9 .99
(1) 42
GRAFT 1.9 .73
(3) 06 16 27
GRANDFATHER CLAUSE 1.9 .56
(4) 06 16 18 32
GUARANTEED ANNUAL INCOME 1.9 .56
(3) 22 25 32
HATCH ACTS 1.9 .73
(6) 06 16 18 27 32 34
HAWTHORNE EXPERIMENT 1.9 .73
(1) 04
HOMESTEAD ACT OF 1862 1.9 .56
(4) 03 06 18 32 46
INDUSTRIALIZATION 1.9 .87
(6) 04 07 15 22 24 25
INFLATION AND DEFLATION 1.9 .73
(11) 03 06 16 18 20 21 22 25 27 29 32
INFORMATION RETRIEVAL 1.9 .73
(2) 04 25
INITIATIVE AND REFERENDUM 1.9 .73
(1) 32
INJUSTICE 1.9 .73
(1) 30
INSURGENCY 1.9 .73
(4) 06 07 16 20
INTERNATIONAL AGREEMENTS 1.9 .87
(2) 06 25

INTERNATIONAL TARIFF 1.9 .73
(1) 18
INTERNATIONAL TENSION 1.9 .99
(1) 19
INTERSTATE COMMERCE ACT OF 1887 1.9 .73
(2) 18 19 46
ITEMIZED APPROPRIATIONS 1.9 .56
(1) 06
JIM CROW 1.9 .56
(4) 03 27 29 32 46
JUDICIAL DECISIONS 1.9 .87
(1) 17
JUDICIAL SUPREMACY 1.9 .56
(1) 44
JUS SOLI (LAW OF THE LAND) 1.9 .73
(7) 03 06 16 17 18 20 32
JUST WAR 1.9 .56
(1) 17
LABOR MARKET 1.9 .73
(1) 11
LAWMAKING, CONGRESSIONAL 1.9 .99
(1) 42
LEGISLATE 1.9 .87
(1) 17
LEGISLATIVE AUTHORITY 1.9 .56
(1) 17
LEGISLATIVE CAUCUS 1.9 .56
(2) 03 32
LEGISLATIVE OVERSIGHT 1.9 .73
(1) 32
LEGISLATIVE PROCEDURE 1.9 .73
(1) 17
LIBERATION MOVEMENTS 1.9 .73
(1) 11
LIN PIAO STRATEGY (WARS OF 1.9 .73
NATIONAL LIBERATION)
(1) 20
LINE OF SUCCESSION 1.9 .56
(2) 06 16
MALAPPORTIONMENT IN LEGISLATURE 1.9 .73
(1) 04
MARTIAL LAW 1.9 .56
(8) 03 06 16 17 18 20 27 32
MASSIVE RETALIATION 1.9 .56
(3) 03 20 34
MEDIATE 1.9 .73
(1) 17
MEDICARE 1.9 .56
(1) 18
METHODS OF VOTING IN CONGRESS 1.9 .56
(1) 45
MILITARY AID 1.9 .73
(1) 11
MISSILE GAP 1.9 .31
(1) 03
MORAL LAW 1.9 .99
(1) 03
MOTION OF NO-CONFIDENCE 1.9 .73
(1) 17
MULTILATERAL FORCE (MLF) PROPOSAL 1.9 .56
(3) 11 20 34 38
MUNICIPAL HOME RULE 1.9 .56
(2) 03 04

NATIONAL INDEPENDENCE   1.9   .87
  (1) 15
NEPOTISM   1.9   .31
  (8) 03 16 17 18 27 28 29 33
NO CONFIDENCE   1.9   .73
  (1) 16
NON-PROLIFERATION TREATY   1.9   .31
  (1) 11
NONPARTISAN BALLOT   1.9   .73
  (3) 03 32 42
NONPARTISAN ELECTION   1.9   .56
  (3) 03 06 18
NUCLEAR TEST BAN   1.9   .73
  (1) 17
NUCLEAR TEST BAN TREATY (1963)   1.9   .56
  (4) 17 20 32 34
NUCLEAR WEAPONS BAN   1.9   .73
  (1) 36
OFFENSIVE WAR   1.9   .56
  (1) 17
OPEN DOOR POLICY   1.9   .56
  (8) 03 06 16 17 21 27 29 32 46
OPEN SYSTEM   1.9   .99
  (1) 01
OVERPOPULATION   1.9   .87
  (2) 19 25
OVERTHROW OF A GOVERNMENT   1.9   .73
  (1) 17
PALACE REVOLUTION   1.9   .56
  (2) 17 33
PARDONS AND REPRIEVES   1.9   .56
  (1) 42
PARITY   1.9   .56
  (4) 02 06 16 18
PARLIAMENTARY DEBATE   1.9   .56
  (1) 17
PASSIVE RESISTANCE   1.9   .56
  (5) 06 16 17 22 32
PEACE TREATY   1.9   .73
  (1) 17
PEACE-KEEPING OPERATIONS OF THE   1.9   .73
  UN
  (1) 41
PLANNING-PROGRAMMING-BUDGETING   1.9   .87
  SYSTEM (PPBS)
  (3) 11 25 33
PLATFORM PLANK   1.9   .87
  (1) 17
POLARIZE   1.9   .73
  (1) 39
POLITICAL CAMPAIGN   1.9   .73
  (3) 07 25 32
POLITICAL CONVENTION   1.9   .73
  (1) 32
POLITICAL DISOBEDIENCE   1.9   .73
  (1) 23
POLLS (OF PUBLIC OPINION)   1.9   .87
  (4) 19 23 30 32
POPULATION EXPLOSION   1.9   .56
  (3) 03 04 34
POWER OF APPOINTMENT   1.9   .56
  (1) 17

POWER OF THE PURSE, CONGRESS   1.9   .73
  (3) 18 20 32
POWER TO TAX   1.9   .73
  (1) 39
PRECEDENT   1.9   .56
  (5) 06 16 17 18 33
PREFERENTIAL PRIMARIES   1.9   .73
  (1) 18
PRESIDENTIAL SUCCESSION   1.9   .56
  (5) 06 16 18 27 32
PRIMARY ELECTIONS   1.9   .73
  (7) 02 06 18 27 32 33 34
PRIVATE PROPERTY   1.9   .56
  (2) 10 16
PROGRESSIVE TAX   1.9   .56
  (5) 06 16 18 27 32
PROPERTY RIGHTS   1.9   .56
  (1) 11
PUBLIC BILL   1.9   .56
  (4) 06 16 18 27
PUBLIC FINANCE   1.9   .73
  (4) 06 07 16 32
PUBLIC ORDER   1.9   .87
  (1) 11
PUBLIC UTILITY REGULATION   1.9   .73
  (1) 42
PUBLIC WELFARE   1.9   .73
  (1) 03
RAISON D'ETAT   1.9   .73
  (1) 03
RATIFICATION OF CONSTITUTIONAL   1.9   .56
  AMENDMENTS
  (1) 18
RECESSION   1.9   .73
  (5) 16 18 20 27 32
RECOGNITION OF A GOVERNMENT   1.9   .56
  (1) 17
RECRUITMENT   1.9   .73
  (7) 01 06 15 17 24 30 33
REDISTRICTING   1.9   .73
  (7) 06 16 17 18 27 32 33
RENAISSANCE   1.9   .73
  (5) 08 09 22 24 25
RIGHT OF WOMEN TO VOTE   1.9   .56
  (1) 17
RIGHT TO BENEFIT OF COUNSEL   1.9   .73
  (1) 45
RIGHT TO COUNSEL   1.9   .73
  (2) 03 18 44
RIGHTS OF MAN   1.9   .87
  (3) 16 17 19
RULES   1.9   .87
  (3) 02 13 24
RUN-OFF PRIMARY   1.9   .56
  (1) 02
SALES TAX   1.9   .56
  (5) 06 16 18 27 32
SANCTIONS   1.9   .87
  (9) 02 03 11 16 18 19 20 21 32
SCIENTIFIC REVOLUTION   1.9   .87
  (1) 22
SEARCH AND SEIZURE   1.9   .56
  (6) 03 16 18 24 30 32

SELF-INCRIMINATION 1.9 .73
(4) 03 06 18 32
SLAVERY 1.9 .73
(12) 06 07 08 16 17 18 22 24 26 29
30 32 46
SLAVERY QUESTION 1.9 .73
(1) 46
SOCIAL SECURITY 1.9 .56
(8) 03 16 18 19 23 25 27 32
SPANISH CIVIL WAR 1.9 .31
(5) 16 17 21 22 34 46
SPANISH-AMERICAN WAR 1.9 .56
(3) 06 16 17 46
SPLIT-TICKET VOTING 1.9 .56
(1) 42
STATE OF THE UNION MESSAGE 1.9 .73
(8) 02 03 16 18 27 32 34 39
STATES, RIGHTS AND DUTIES OF 1.9 .73
(1) 41
STATES' RIGHTS DOCTRINE 1.9 .56
(9) 02 03 06 16 18 25 27 32 34
STRICT CONSTRUCTION 1.9 .73
(1) 06
STRONG-MAYOR PLAN 1.9 .73
(3) 06 18 32
SUFFRAGE, UNIVERSAL 1.9 .73
(1) 46
SUMMIT DIPLOMACY 1.9 .73
(2) 18 20
SUMMITRY AS AN INSTRUMENT OF 1.9 .56
DIPLOMACY
(2) 03 17 39
TAXATION AND REVENUE 1.9 .87
(1) 07
TAXING POWER 1.9 .87
(1) 16
TIGHT MONEY POLICY 1.9 .73
(1) 18
TREASON 1.9 .56
(8) 03 06 16 18 27 30 32 33
TREATY POWER OF THE PRESIDENT 1.9 .56
(4) 17 20 23 32
UNIVERSAL DISARMAMENT 1.9 .73
(1) 17
VIENNA CONGRESS (1814-15) 1.9 .73
(1) 03
WAR 1.9 .73
(15) 03 06 07 10 11 16 19 20 22 23
24 26 27 30 33
WAR BETWEEN THE STATES 1.9 .73
(1) 16
WAR CRIME TRIALS 1.9 .56
(1) 36
WAR OF AGGRESSION 1.9 .73
(1) 17
WAR OF ATTRITION 1.9 .73
(2) 16 17
WAR POWERS, CONGRESS 1.9 .87
(1) 20
WARFARE 1.9 .87
(4) 04 17 24 30
WEAPONS CONTROL 1.9 .73
(1) 32

WELFARE LEGISLATION 1.9 .73
(1) 42
YALTA CONFERENCE 1.9 .56
(1) 38 46
AD HOC 2.0 .66
(1) 16
ADMINISTRATIVE RULE OR REGULATION 2.0 .81
(1) 18
ADMISSIBILITY 2.0 .81
(1) 17
AMERICANIZATION 2.0 .81
(1) 30
ANTI-COMMUNIST LEGISLATION 2.0 .66
(1) 42
APPEAL 2.0 .81
(1) 32
APPROPRIATION BILL 2.0 .66
(1) 27
ARBITRATION 2.0 .66
(10) 03 06 16 17 18 19 20 25 27 32
ARREST 2.0 .94
(3) 06 11 17
ARREST WARRANT 2.0 .66
(1) 18
ATOMIC ESPIONAGE 2.0 .66
(1) 17
ATOMIC WEAPONS CONTROL 2.0 .66
(1) 32
BACKLASH 2.0 .66
(1) 30
BAIL SYSTEM 2.0 .66
(1) 32
BALLOT BOX STUFFING 2.0 .66
(1) 16
BATTLE OF WATERLOO 2.0 .66
(1) 17
BILATERAL 2.0 .66
(1) 45
BILATERAL AGREEMENTS 2.0 .47
(1) 38
BILATERAL TRADE 2.0 .66
(1) 20
BIPARTISAN FOREIGN POLICY 2.0 .66
(1) 34
BLANKET PRIMARY 2.0 .81
(1) 03
BLOC VOTING 2.0 .66
(3) 03 32 33
BLOCKADE 2.0 .47
(5) 03 06 16 17 20
BOSSISM 2.0 .81
(3) 25 30 33
CANON LAW 2.0 .66
(7) 03 06 16 17 19 25 26
CAPABILITIES 2.0 .94
(1) 04
CENSURE 2.0 .81
(7) 03 06 16 18 27 30 32
CHANGE OF VENUE 2.0 .47
(2) 18 32
CHARTER, CITY 2.0 .66
(1) 32

CHEMICAL WARFARE	2.0	.47
(3) 06 17 25		
CIRCUMSTANTIAL EVIDENCE	2.0	.47
(1) 32		
CITIZENSHIP, LOSS OF	2.0	.66
(1) 42		
CITY-COUNTY CONSOLIDATION	2.0	.81
(1) 03		
CIVIL DEFENSE	2.0	.47
(1) 36		
CIVIL RIGHTS ACT OF 1960	2.0	.47
(2) 04 18 46		
CIVIL SERVICE EXAMINATIONS	2.0	.66
(1) 18		
CIVIL WAR AMENDMENTS	2.0	.66
(1) 27		
CIVILIAN CONTROL	2.0	.66
(3) 03 18 20		
CLOSURE RULE	2.0	.66
(1) 45		
CODE NAPOLEON	2.0	.47
(2) 06 16		
CODIFICATION	2.0	.47
(3) 03 17 20		
COMMERCE POWER	2.0	.94
(2) 18 32		
COMMUNITY ACTION PROGRAM	2.0	.66
(4) 11 18 25 32		
COMPROMISE OF 1850	2.0	.66
(1) 06 46		
COMPULSORY ARBITRATION	2.0	.66
(5) 06 16 17 18 32		
COMPULSORY MILITARY SERVICE	2.0	.66
(1) 06		
CONCURRING OPINION	2.0	.66
(5) 03 06 16 18 27		
CONFRONTATION	2.0	.81
(5) 04 17 25 30 34		
CONGRESSIONAL IMMUNITY	2.0	.47
(1) 27		
CONGRESSIONAL INVESTIGATIONS	2.0	.66
(3) 16 32 34		
CONGRESSIONAL RULES	2.0	.66
(1) 42		
CONSCIENTIOUS OBJECTION	2.0	.66
(4) 11 25 32 43		
CONSCRIPTION	2.0	.66
(5) 06 16 25 27 32		
CONSENT	2.0	.94
(2) 24 26		
CONSTITUTIONAL GUARANTEES	2.0	.66
(1) 17		
CONSTITUTIONAL LIMITATIONS	2.0	.81
(2) 03 06		
CONSTITUTIONAL REFORM	2.0	.66
(1) 17		
CONSTITUTIONAL REVIEW	2.0	.81
(1) 11		
CONSTITUTIONAL RULES	2.0	.81
(1) 17		
CONTROLS	2.0	.94
(1) 43		
COST-OF-LIVING ESCALATOR	2.0	.66
(1) 45		
COUNTERINTELLIGENCE	2.0	.47
(2) 17 20		
COURT JURISDICTION	2.0	.66
(1) 42		
COURT-MARTIAL	2.0	.66
(6) 06 16 17 18 25 32		
COVENANT OF THE LEAGUE OF NATIONS	2.0	.66
(5) 06 16 17 19 20		
CRISIS	2.0	.94
(6) 03 04 11 24 30 33		
CRITERIA	2.0	.81
(1) 24		
CUBAN INVASION, 1961	2.0	.66
(1) 46		
CULTURAL EXCHANGE	2.0	.47
(2) 17 20		
CUSTOMS DUTY	2.0	.66
(3) 20 32 41		
D-DAY	2.0	.66
(2) 16 17		
DECIDING VOTE	2.0	.66
(1) 17		
DECLARATION OF NEUTRALITY	2.0	.66
(2) 16 17		
DECLARATION OF WAR, CONGRESS	2.0	.66
(1) 20		
DECOLONIZATION	2.0	.81
(4) 11 17 23 30		
DEFENSE	2.0	.81
(3) 11 24 30		
DEFICIT FINANCING	2.0	.81
(4) 06 16 18 22		
DEMOBILIZATION	2.0	.47
(4) 06 16 17 27		
DENUCLEARIZATION	2.0	.66
(1) 20		
DEPLETION ALLOWANCE	2.0	.66
(2) 25 32		
DEPRESSION	2.0	.66
(9) 04 06 16 17 18 20 24 27 32		
DIPLOMATIC ASYLUM	2.0	.47
(1) 23		
DIPLOMATIC PRIVILEGES AND IMMUNITIES	2.0	.47
(3) 16 17 20		
DIRECT TAX	2.0	.66
(3) 06 16 18		
DISCRIMINATION	2.0	.81
(7) 03 07 16 17 24 25 30		
DISSENTING OPINION	2.0	.66
(4) 06 16 17 18		
DOMESTIC JURISDICTION	2.0	.81
(3) 03 17 20		
DUTIES OF CITIZENS	2.0	.81
(1) 42		
ECONOMIC BLOCKADE	2.0	.66
(1) 17		
ECONOMIC COOPERATION	2.0	.66
(1) 17		

ECONOMIC DEMAND   2.0   .81
  (1) 25
ECONOMIC DEPRESSION   2.0   .66
  (2) 16 25
ECONOMIC PLANNING   2.0   .81
  (6) 06 10 11 18 19 23
ECONOMIC STABILIZATION POLICIES   2.0   .94
  (1) 32
ELECTIONS AT LARGE   2.0   .66
  (1) 18
ELECTRONIC SURVEILLANCE   2.0   .47
  (1) 32
ENFRANCHISEMENT   2.0   .81
  (3) 03 06 16
ENVIRONMENTAL PROBLEMS   2.0   .66
  (1) 41
EQUAL OPPORTUNITY IN EMPLOYMENT   2.0   .66
  (1) 37
ESPIONAGE   2.0   .66
  (5) 03 07 16 17 25
EXCESS PROFITS TAX   2.0   .66
  (5) 06 16 18 27 32
EXPRESS POWERS OF CONGRESS   2.0   .81
  (1) 16
FAIL-SAFE   2.0   .81
  (1) 39
FAIR DEAL   2.0   .66
  (5) 03 04 27 29 34
FAIT ACCOMPLI   2.0   .47
  (4) 06 16 17 20
FARM PRICE SUPPORTS   2.0   .66
  (1) 32
FEDERAL AID   2.0   .66
  (1) 16
FEDERAL APPOINTMENTS   2.0   .66
  (1) 42
FEDERAL LAW   2.0   .66
  (1) 44
FEDERAL QUESTION   2.0   .81
  (1) 02
FIRST READING   2.0   .66
  (1) 27
FISCAL PLANNING   2.0   .66
  (1) 25
FOREIGN AID PROGRAM   2.0   .66
  (1) 42
FOREIGN ECONOMIC POLICY   2.0   .66
  (1) 11
FOREIGN TRADE   2.0   .66
  (1) 11
FREEDOM FROM DOUBLE JEOPARDY   2.0   .66
  (1) 45
FREEDOM OF BELIEF   2.0   .66
  (1) 17
FREEDOM OF EXPRESSION   2.0   .81
  (4) 03 11 22 32
FREEDOM OF THE SEAS   2.0   .47
  (3) 16 17 21 46
FREEDOM OF WORSHIP   2.0   .94
  (1) 17
FRENCH REVOLUTION OF 1789   2.0   .81
  (6) 03 09 17 22 25 26

GENERAL AGREEMENT ON TARIFFS   2.0   .81
  AND TRADE (GATT)
  (9) 03 07 11 17 18 20 25 27 32
GENERAL DEBATE, UNITED NATIONS   2.0   .47
  (1) 20
GENERAL MOBILIZATION   2.0   .81
  (1) 17
GENERAL STRIKE   2.0   .66
  (5) 06 10 16 22 26
GENERAL WELFARE   2.0   .81
  (1) 16
GENERAL WELFARE CLAUSE   2.0   .94
  (1) 06
GENOCIDE CONVENTION, UNITED   2.0   .66
  NATIONS
  (1) 20
GEOGRAPHICAL REPRESENTATION   2.0   .81
  (1) 03
GOLD STANDARD   2.0   .66
  (7) 06 16 18 20 21 25 32
GOOD NEIGHBOR POLICY   2.0   .47
  (1) 46
GOOD NEIGHBOR POLICY TOWARD   2.0   .66
  LATIN AMERICA
  (8) 03 17 20 25 27 29 32 34
GOVERNMENT INTERVENTION IN   2.0   .94
  BUSINESS
  (1) 08
GOVERNMENT OWNERSHIP   2.0   .66
  (3) 07 16 22
GREAT DEPRESSION   2.0   .66
  (1) 46
GRESHAM'S LAW   2.0   .66
  (1) 06
GUILT BY ASSOCIATION   2.0   .66
  (3) 03 18 34
GUT ISSUE   2.0   .66
  (1) 39
HEARING , JUDICIAL   2.0   .66
  (5) 03 06 16 17 18
HIGHER LAW   2.0   .94
  (2) 22 29
HITLER-STALIN PACT   2.0   .47
  (1) 34
HOUSE CONGRESSIONAL RESOLUTION   2.0   .66
  (H CON RES)
  (1) 16
HOUSE JOINT RESOLUTION (H J RES)   2.0   .66
  (1) 16
IMMIGRATION LAWS   2.0   .66
  (2) 16 27
IMMIGRATION QUOTAS   2.0   .47
  (1) 32
INADMISSIBILITY   2.0   .47
  (1) 17
INALIENABLE INDIVIDUAL RIGHTS   2.0   .66
  (3) 17 29 30
INCOME TAX   2.0   .66
  (6) 06 16 18 22 27 32
INFRASTRUCTURE DEVELOPMENT   2.0   .81
  (1) 20
INTERSTATE COMPACTS   2.0   .81
  (5) 03 06 16 18 25

INTERVENTION	2.0	.81
(9) 03 06 11 16 17 20 23 24 25		
INTOLERABLE ACTS	2.0	.47
(1) 03 46		
INVADE	2.0	.81
(1) 17		
ISOLATION	2.0	.94
(4) 06 17 24 25		
JOHN DOE WARRANT	2.0	.66
(1) 16		
JUS GENTIUM	2.0	.81
(4) 03 06 20 26		
JUS NATURALE	2.0	.66
(1) 20		
JUSTICIABLE AND NON-JUSTICIABLE	2.0	.81
DISPUTES		
(6) 03 16 17 18 20 32		
LABOR DISPUTES	2.0	.81
(1) 36		
LABOR RELATIONS	2.0	.81
(1) 11		
LANDSLIDE	2.0	.66
(4) 06 16 27 29		
LAW OF OUTER SPACE	2.0	.47
(1) 17		
LAW OF THE SEA	2.0	.66
(3) 03 17 20		
LIBERATION	2.0	.81
(3) 16 24 30		
LIBERTIES	2.0	.81
(1) 24		
LIMITED VOTING	2.0	.66
(2) 03 06		
LITIGATION	2.0	.81
(1) 24		
LOOSE INTERPRETATION OF THE	2.0	.66
CONSTITUTION		
(1) 45		
MARCH REVOLUTION OF 1917	2.0	.81
(1) 22		
MEDICAID	2.0	.66
(1) 32		
MESSAGE ON THE STATE OF THE	2.0	.66
UNION		
(1) 16		
METROPOLITAN ANNEXATION	2.0	.66
(1) 18		
METROPOLITAN CITY-COUNTY	2.0	.81
CONSOLIDATION		
(1) 18		
MILITARY CONSCRIPTION	2.0	.66
(1) 07		
MILITARY SANCTIONS	2.0	.81
(1) 17		
MISUSE OF POWER	2.0	.94
(1) 17		
MOB-LYNCHING	2.0	.66
(1) 30		
MORATORIUM	2.0	.81
(2) 06 16		
MULTIPOLARITY	2.0	.66
(1) 33		
MUNICH CONFERENCE	2.0	.66
(1) 46		
MUNICIPAL LAW	2.0	.47
(2) 16 17		
MY LAI INCIDENT	2.0	.47
(1) 25		
NAPOLEONIC WARS	2.0	.66
(1) 17		
NATIONAL HEALTH INSURANCE	2.0	.66
(2) 18 32		
NATIONAL INCOME	2.0	.81
(2) 06 32		
NAZI-SOVIET PACT OF 1939	2.0	.47
(3) 03 22 34 46		
NEGRO SUFFRAGE	2.0	.66
(2) 06 16		
NET INCOME	2.0	.66
(1) 16		
NOMINATE	2.0	.81
(3) 16 17 24		
NON-VOTING	2.0	.66
(3) 03 17 19		
NUCLEAR TESTING	2.0	.66
(1) 08		
OBLIGATORY ARBITRATION	2.0	.66
(1) 16		
OPEN CONVENTION	2.0	.66
(1) 39		
ORDER	2.0	.94
(7) 02 06 11 17 24 25 30		
ORIGINAL JURISDICTION OF COURTS	2.0	.66
(6) 02 03 06 16 18 27		
OVERHEATED ECONOMY	2.0	.66
(1) 39		
PACIFICATION	2.0	.66
(1) 17		
PACKING OF THE U.S. SUPREME COURT	2.0	.47
(1) 03		
PARLIAMENTARY CONTROL	2.0	.81
(1) 11		
PARTY PLATFORM	2.0	.66
(3) 02 03 32		
PARTY-LIST SYSTEM	2.0	.66
(1) 17		
PAX BRITANNICA	2.0	.66
(2) 03 22		
PAX ROMANA	2.0	.66
(3) 03 17 22		
PEACE NEGOTIATIONS	2.0	.47
(1) 17		
PEACE-FEELERS	2.0	.66
(1) 17		
PERJURY	2.0	.66
(1) 16		
PERMANENT REGISTRATION	2.0	.81
(4) 06 16 18 32		
PERMANENT REVOLUTION	2.0	.66
(4) 03 22 26 34		
PLATFORM	2.0	.81
(1) 06		
PLURALITY VOTING	2.0	.66
(1) 03		

POGROM	2.0	.47	RESIDUAL POWERS	2.0	.47
(3) 16 17 21			(2) 03 16		
POLICE ACTION	2.0	.47	REUNIFICATION OF GERMANY	2.0	.47
(1) 39			(1) 17		
POLITICAL ASSASSINATION	2.0	.47	RIGHT TO LIFE	2.0	.47
(1) 11			(1) 17		
POLITICAL CONTROL	2.0	.81	RIGHT TO OWN PROPERTY	2.0	.66
(1) 23			(1) 17		
POLITICAL DISPUTE	2.0	.94	RIGHT TO WORK	2.0	.47
(1) 17			(2) 17 29		
POLITICAL QUESTION	2.0	.66	ROLL CALL	2.0	.66
(2) 06 18			(9) 02 06 16 17 18 24 25 27 32		
POLITICAL RIGHTS	2.0	.81	SECULARIZATION	2.0	.81
(2) 03 18			(1) 43		
POPULAR ELECTION OF SENATORS	2.0	.66	SEDITION	2.0	.66
(1) 45			(6) 17 18 27 30 32 33		
POPULAR INITIATIVE	2.0	.66	SELF-DEFENSE	2.0	.66
(1) 17			(3) 11 16 17 43		
POVERTY PROGRAM	2.0	.81	SELF-DETERMINATION OF NATIONS	2.0	.66
(1) 32			(12) 03 06 07 11 16 17 19 20 22 23		
PREVENTIVE WAR	2.0	.66	27 30		
(4) 03 16 17 20			SESSIONS OF CONGRESS	2.0	.66
PRICE CONTROLS	2.0	.66	(1) 42		
(3) 10 25 32			SHERMAN ANTITRUST ACT OF 1890	2.0	.47
PRICE STABILIZATION	2.0	.47	(9) 06 16 18 19 22 25 27 32 34 46		
(1) 16			SIT-DOWN STRIKE	2.0	.47
PRIMARY	2.0	.66	(6) 06 16 27 29 30 32		
(1) 16			SOCIAL SECURITY ACT	2.0	.66
PROCEDURAL LAW	2.0	.81	(1) 46		
(1) 02			SOCIAL SECURITY ACT OF 1935	2.0	.47
PROCEDURAL RULES	2.0	.66	(5) 08 16 18 22 27		
(1) 17			SOCIAL WELFARE	2.0	.81
PRODUCTIVITY	2.0	.81	(2) 11 19		
(2) 03 25			SOVEREIGN RIGHT	2.0	.66
PROHIBITION OF CRUEL PUNISHMENT,	2.0	.81	(1) 17		
EIGHTH AMENDMENT			SOVIET-NAZI PACT OF	2.0	.00
(1) 25			NON-AGGRESSION		
PROPERTY TAX	2.0	.47	(1) 03		
(3) 18 25 32			SPECIFIC POWERS-DELEGATED	2.0	.81
PROTESTANT REVOLUTION	2.0	.66	POWERS		
(1) 22			(1) 18		
PROXY VOTING	2.0	.47	STARE DECISIS	2.0	.81
(3) 02 27 33			(6) 03 06 16 18 27 32		
PSYCHOLOGICAL WARFARE	2.0	.47	STATE AND REVOLUTION	2.0	.81
(5) 03 17 19 20 25			(1) 35		
PUBLIC OWNERSHIP	2.0	.66	STATE OF WAR	2.0	.66
(2) 10 16			(2) 03 17		
PUBLIC POWER	2.0	.94	STATUTE OF LIMITATIONS	2.0	.47
(1) 18			(6) 03 06 16 18 27 32		
QUASI-LEGISLATIVE POWERS	2.0	.81	STATUTORY LAW	2.0	.66
(4) 06 17 18 32			(1) 44		
QUOTA SYSTEM	2.0	.47	SUBVERSION	2.0	.66
(2) 03 32			(7) 11 17 24 25 27 29 32		
RECIPROCITY	2.0	.47	SUMMIT CONFERENCE	2.0	.66
(5) 03 06 16 17 20			(2) 17 20		
REFORMATION	2.0	.66	TACTICAL NUCLEAR WAR	2.0	.66
(6) 03 09 17 22 25 26			(1) 36		
REGULATION	2.0	.81	TAXATION	2.0	.94
(1) 43			(7) 04 10 11 16 19 25 32		
REPRESSION	2.0	.81	TAXES	2.0	.94
(1) 30			(1) 42		
RESIDENCE REQUIREMENT	2.0	.47	TECHNICAL ASSISTANCE	2.0	.66
(1) 03			(3) 17 20 23		

TENTH AMENDMENT	2.0	.47
(3) 06 18 27		
TICKET SPLITTING	2.0	.47
(1) 44		
TONKIN GULF RESOLUTION	2.0	.66
(2) 32 34		
TOWN MEETING	2.0	.66
(1) 46		
TREATY POWER, CONGRESS	2.0	.66
(1) 20		
TREATY RATIFICATION	2.0	.66
(1) 20		
TRUST BUSTING	2.0	.66
(4) 06 16 27 34 46		
TWENTIETH AMENDMENT	2.0	.47
(2) 06 18		
TWENTY-FOURTH AMENDMENT	2.0	.47
(1) 18		
TWO-TERM TRADITION	2.0	.66
(1) 44		
TWO-THIRDS VOTE	2.0	.66
(1) 45		
UNANIMITY RULE	2.0	.81
(4) 06 16 17 20		
UNDECLARED WAR	2.0	.66
(1) 16		
UNITING FOR PEACE RESOLUTION, UNITED NATIONS	2.0	.81
(4) 03 18 20 41		
UNIVERSAL DECLARATION OF HUMAN RIGHTS	2.0	.66
(6) 03 19 20 22 32 41		
UNWRITTEN CONSTITUTION	2.0	.81
(3) 06 16 18		
URBAN AFFAIRS	2.0	.66
(1) 07		
VOTER QUALIFICATIONS	2.0	.66
(2) 32 44		
VOTING RIGHTS ACT OF 1965	2.0	.81
(2) 18 32		
WAGE CONTROLS	2.0	.66
(1) 32		
WAR ON POVERTY	2.0	.66
(3) 18 32 34		
WASHINGTON'S FAREWELL ADDRESS	2.0	.66
(2) 06 16		
WELFARE PROGRAMS IN THE UNITED STATES	2.0	.81
(2) 27 32		
WHITE BACKLASH	2.0	.47
(1) 34		
WORLD DISARMAMENT CONFERENCE	2.0	.47
(1) 20		
WRIT	2.0	.66
(5) 02 06 17 18 27		
ABDICATION	2.1	.56
(5) 06 16 17 33 34		
ACCEPTANCE SPEECH	2.1	.73
(2) 06 17		
ACQUITTAL	2.1	.56
(3) 03 06 27		
ACT OF AGGRESSION	2.1	.73
(1) 17		

AD VALOREM DUTY	2.1	.56
(7) 06 16 18 20 27 32 45		
ADJOURNMENT MOTION	2.1	.73
(1) 03		
ADMINISTRATIVE JURISDICTION	2.1	.73
(1) 23		
AGRICULTURAL PRICE SUPPORTS	2.1	.73
(1) 32		
AIR WARFARE	2.1	.73
(1) 17		
ALIGNMENT	2.1	.73
(1) 24		
AMERICAN SYSTEM	2.1	.73
(3) 06 29 46		
ANTITRUST	2.1	.73
(3) 06 27 32		
ANTITRUST ACTIONS	2.1	.73
(1) 25		
ANTITRUST ACTS	2.1	.31
(4) 03 16 18 32		
APPROPRIATION	2.1	.73
(5) 06 18 27 32 34		
APPROVAL OF BILLS	2.1	.87
(1) 06		
ARBITRARY ARREST	2.1	.73
(1) 17		
ARMS TRAFFIC	2.1	.56
(1) 36		
ARTICLES OF WAR	2.1	.56
(2) 06 16		
ASSASSINATION	2.1	.73
(8) 06 11 16 17 25 29 30 42		
ASSASSINATIONS OF PRESIDENTS	2.1	.73
(1) 46		
ATOMIC AGE	2.1	.73
(2) 17 24		
ATOMIC HOLOCAUST	2.1	.73
(1) 39		
ATTAINDER	2.1	.87
(1) 06		
ATTICA PRISON REVOLT	2.1	.56
(1) 25		
AUSTRALIAN BALLOT	2.1	.73
(6) 03 06 16 18 27 32		
AUTHORIZATION	2.1	.56
(1) 24		
AUTOMATION	2.1	.87
(3) 03 07 25		
AUTONOMY	2.1	.73
(5) 06 16 17 24 33		
BALFOUR DECLARATION (1926)	2.1	.56
(5) 03 16 17 21 34		
BANDUNG (ASIAN-AFRICAN) CONFERENCE	2.1	.56
(3) 03 17 34		
BANKRUPTCY	2.1	.56
(5) 03 06 16 18 27		
BARUCH PLAN	2.1	.56
(1) 20		
BAY OF PIGS FIASCO	2.1	.56
(1) 39		
BIRTH CONTROL	2.1	.73
(3) 03 22 25		

BLUE LAWS   2.1   .31
   (4) 06 16 18 27
BOUNDARY DISPUTE   2.1   .31
   (1) 17
BOYCOTT   2.1   .56
   (8) 06 10 16 18 20 27 30 32
BREACH OF CONTRACT   2.1   .31
   (1) 27
BREACH OF THE PEACE   2.1   .31
   (2) 06 16
BREZHNEV DOCTRINE   2.1   .56
   (2) 11 34
BRIBE   2.1   .73
   (2) 06 16
BROAD CONSTRUCTION   2.1   .73
   (1) 16
BRUSHFIRE WARS   2.1   .56
   (1) 39
BURR CONSPIRACY   2.1   .56
   (1) 06
BUSING OF SCHOOL CHILDREN   2.1   .73
   (1) 25
BY-ELECTION   2.1   .73
   (4) 06 16 17 27
CALCULATED RISK   2.1   .73
   (1) 39
CAMPAIGN FUND   2.1   .56
   (3) 06 16 29
CAPITALIST ENCIRCLEMENT   2.1   .56
   (2) 19 26
CHALLENGE, JURY   2.1   .56
   (1) 18
CHARTER REVISION   2.1   .56
   (1) 03
CHICANO POLITICS   2.1   .73
   (1) 07
CHILD LABOR LAWS   2.1   .31
   (2) 16 27
CHINESE EXCLUSION ACTS   2.1   .73
   (3) 06 16 25
CHOICE   2.1   .99
   (2) 17 24
CIVIL JURISDICTION   2.1   .73
   (1) 17
CIVIL RIGHTS ACT OF 1957   2.1   .56
   (1) 18 46
CIVIL RIGHTS ACT OF 1968   2.1   .56
   (1) 46
CIVIL RIGHTS ACTS OF 1866   2.1   .56
   (1) 18 46
CIVIL SERVICE REFORM   2.1   .87
   (1) 45
CIVIL SUIT   2.1   .56
   (1) 02
CIVILIAN REVIEW   2.1   .56
   (1) 39
CLASS ACTION   2.1   .56
   (1) 32
CODE OF HAMMURABI   2.1   .73
   (2) 03 09
CODE OF MILITARY JUSTICE   2.1   .31
   (1) 32

COMPULSORY EDUCATION   2.1   .56
   (1) 45
COMPULSORY JURISDICTION   2.1   .87
   (1) 20
COMPULSORY SCHOOL ATTENDANCE   2.1   .56
   (1) 06
CONCURRENT JURISDICTION   2.1   .56
   (4) 06 17 18 32
CONDITIONAL SURRENDER   2.1   .56
   (1) 17
CONGRESSIONAL CALENDAR   2.1   .56
   (1) 32
CONGRESSIONAL LAWMAKING   2.1   .99
   (1) 42
CONGRESSIONAL PRIVILEGE   2.1   .73
   (1) 42
CONSENT CALENDAR   2.1   .73
   (3) 02 16 18
CONSEQUENCES   2.1   .87
   (2) 03 30
CONSTITUTIONAL JURISDICTION   2.1   .73
   (1) 23
CONSULAR IMMUNITY   2.1   .73
   (1) 06
CONTEMPT OF COURT   2.1   .73
   (3) 03 18 32
COUNCIL-MANAGER FORM   2.1   .87
   (4) 03 06 18 32
COUNTERESPIONAGE   2.1   .31
   (1) 17
COURT JURISDICTION, FEDERAL   2.1   .73
   (1) 42
CREEPING SOCIALISM   2.1   .56
   (2) 03 29
CRIME AGAINST HUMANITY   2.1   .73
   (1) 17
CROSS-OF-GOLD SPEECH   2.1   .56
   (2) 06 16
CULT OF PERSONALITY, SOVIET UNION   2.1   .31
   (3) 17 20 39
CUMULATIVE VOTING   2.1   .73
   (4) 03 06 16 18
CUSTOM AND USAGE   2.1   .87
   (1) 42
CUSTOMARY LAW   2.1   .87
   (4) 03 06 20 23
DE JURE WAR   2.1   .73
   (1) 03
DEBATE   2.1   .73
   (4) 06 16 17 24
DECREE   2.1   .87
   (1) 16
DELIBERATE SPEED   2.1   .56
   (1) 39
DEMAGOGUERY   2.1   .73
   (2) 17 38
DEMILITARIZATION   2.1   .56
   (2) 06 17
DEMOCRATIC CONFERENCE   2.1   .73
   (1) 02
DENAZIFICATION   2.1   .31
   (1) 03

DEPOLITICIZATION	2.1	.73
(1) 33		
DEPOSE	2.1	.73
(1) 16		
DESTALINIZATION	2.1	.56
(5) 03 17 24 25 34		
DIPLOMATIC PROTECTION	2.1	.56
(2) 16 17		
DIRECT ELECTION OF SENATORS	2.1	.56
(1) 45		
DISCHARGE RULE IN HOUSE OF	2.1	.73
REPRESENTATIVES		
(1) 45		
DISCRIMINATION, SOCIAL	2.1	.73
(1) 06		
DISOBEDIENCE	2.1	.99
(1) 30		
DISORGANIZATION	2.1	.87
(2) 29 30		
DIVISION OF GERMANY	2.1	.56
(1) 17		
DOCTRINE OF STATE IMMUNITY	2.1	.56
(1) 03		
DOMESTIC VIOLENCE	2.1	.73
(2) 06 16		
DOUBLE TAXATION	2.1	.73
(4) 16 17 18 32		
EIGHTEEN YEAR OLD VOTE,	2.1	.73
TWENTY-SIXTH AMENDMENT		
(1) 25		
EIGHTH AMENDMENT	2.1	.73
(1) 18		
ELECTORAL COUNT	2.1	.73
(1) 16		
ELECTORAL REFORM	2.1	.56
(1) 17		
ELECTORAL VOTE	2.1	.73
(1) 16		
ENABLING ACT	2.1	.56
(6) 03 06 16 17 18 27		
ENGLISH LAW	2.1	.56
(1) 25		
ENUMERATED POWERS (DELEGATED	2.1	.87
POWERS)		
(4) 06 16 18 32		
EQUAL TIME	2.1	.73
(1) 39		
ETHNICITY	2.1	.73
(1) 25		
EUROPEAN UNIFICATION	2.1	.56
(1) 11		
EXCHANGE OF PRISONERS	2.1	.56
(2) 16 17		
EXCLUSIVE JURISDICTION	2.1	.73
(1) 17		
EXPATRIATION	2.1	.56
(7) 03 06 16 18 20 27 32		
EXPORT TAX	2.1	.56
(1) 06		
EXTRADITABLE OFFENSES	2.1	.56
(1) 17		
FACTIONALISM	2.1	.73
(2) 11 24		
FALSE IMPRISONMENT	2.1	.56
(1) 06		
FEDERAL AID TO EDUCATION	2.1	.56
(1) 18		
FEDERAL COURT JURISDICTION	2.1	.73
(1) 42		
FEDERAL RESERVE ACT	2.1	.73
(1) 22		
FEDERALIST PERIOD	2.1	.73
(1) 46		
FIAT	2.1	.73
(2) 16 29		
FILING FOR OFFICE	2.1	.56
(1) 45		
FISCAL POLICY	2.1	.87
(3) 03 18 32		
FOOD FOR PEACE PROGRAM	2.1	.73
(1) 20		
FOOD STAMP PLAN	2.1	.56
(2) 06 16		
FOREIGN EXCHANGE	2.1	.56
(1) 20		
FRANKING PRIVILEGE	2.1	.56
(6) 03 06 16 18 27 32		
FREEDOM OF INFORMATION	2.1	.73
(1) 03		
FREEDOM OF INFORMATION ACT	2.1	.56
(1) 32		
FRENCH AND INDIAN WAR	2.1	.73
(1) 03 46		
FUNCTIONAL CONSOLIDATION, LOCAL	2.1	.73
GOVERNMENT		
(1) 18		
FUNDAMENTAL FREEDOMS	2.1	.99
(1) 17		
GENERAL CONSCRIPTION	2.1	.56
(1) 17		
GERMAN-RUSSIAN NON-AGGRESSION	2.1	.31
PACT		
(1) 16		
GETTYSBURG ADDRESS	2.1	.56
(1) 06		
GLORIOUS REVOLUTION	2.1	.56
(1) 17		
GOLD EXCHANGE STANDARD	2.1	.73
(1) 20		
GOOD OFFICES	2.1	.56
(6) 06 16 17 18 20 27		
GOVERNMENT CONTRACTS	2.1	.73
(1) 37		
GOVERNMENT CRISIS	2.1	.73
(1) 17		
GREAT PURGE	2.1	.56
(1) 34		
GREAT SOCIETY	2.1	.56
(2) 25 34		
GRIEVANCE	2.1	.73
(2) 06 30		
GUARANTEED ANNUAL WAGE	2.1	.56
(1) 45		
HARD CURRENCY	2.1	.73
(1) 20		

HARD MONEY	2.1	.73
(3) 06 16 27		
HEADSTART	2.1	.56
(1) 32		
HEARING, ADMINISTRATIVE	2.1	.73
(1) 18		
HEARING, LEGISLATIVE	2.1	.87
(1) 18		
HEARINGS	2.1	.87
(4) 02 27 32 34		
HEMISPHERIC SECURITY	2.1	.73
(1) 45		
HOSTILITIES	2.1	.73
(2) 03 16		
HOT PURSUIT	2.1	.73
(5) 03 16 17 20 45		
HUNDRED FLOWERS CAMPAIGN	2.1	.73
(1) 34		
ILLEGAL	2.1	.87
(1) 17		
IMMIGRATION	2.1	.73
(9) 03 06 07 11 16 17 18 20 32		
IMPRISONMENT	2.1	.87
(1) 06		
INAUGURATION	2.1	.56
(4) 06 16 27 34		
INCORPORATION	2.1	.73
(4) 03 06 17 27		
INDETERMINATE SENTENCE	2.1	.73
(4) 03 06 16 18		
INDIRECT ELECTION	2.1	.73
(4) 16 17 32 33		
INHERENT POWERS	2.1	.73
(5) 03 06 18 20 32		
INSPECTION (DISARMAMENT)	2.1	.56
(1) 20		
INVASION	2.1	.73
(2) 16 17		
IUS GENTIUM	2.1	.56
(1) 03		
JOINT RESOLUTION, CONGRESS	2.1	.56
(8) 02 03 06 16 18 20 27 32		
JOINT SESSION	2.1	.56
(4) 16 18 27 32		
JUDGMENT	2.1	.87
(5) 04 06 16 24 30		
JUNKET	2.1	.73
(4) 06 16 27 29		
JURISDICTIONAL DISPUTE	2.1	.56
(1) 16		
JUS BELLI	2.1	.73
(1) 16		
JUS SANGUINIS (LAW OF THE BLOOD)	2.1	.87
(7) 03 06 16 17 18 20 32		
JUST COMPENSATION	2.1	.73
(3) 06 16 18		
JUVENILE DELINQUENCY	2.1	.73
(2) 03 25		
KASHMIR QUESTION	2.1	.56
(1) 41		
KILL IN COMMITTEE	2.1	.73
(1) 45		
LABOR DISPUTES, MEDIATION OF	2.1	.73
(1) 32		
LABOR LEGISLATION	2.1	.73
(6) 06 10 16 19 26 27		
LACK OF CONFIDENCE	2.1	.73
(1) 16		
LAND GRANT	2.1	.56
(2) 06 32		
LAND REFORM	2.1	.73
(4) 07 11 17 20		
LAND WARFARE	2.1	.73
(2) 17 39		
LAW OF NATIONS (JUS GENTIUM)	2.1	.56
(4) 09 16 17 20		
LAWS OF WAR (RULES OF WARFARE)	2.1	.73
(2) 16 20		
LEGAL AID	2.1	.73
(2) 06 32		
LEGALITY	2.1	.87
(3) 16 19 24		
LEGISLATIVE JUNKETS	2.1	.56
(1) 45		
LEGISLATIVE REORGANIZATION ACT OF 1946	2.1	.73
(3) 03 18 32		
LEGISLATIVE SUPREMACY	2.1	.56
(2) 06 22		
LIBEL	2.1	.73
(1) 45		
LIFE TENURE	2.1	.56
(1) 27		
LIMITATION OF ARMAMENTS	2.1	.73
(3) 06 16 17		
LOBBYING ACT	2.1	.73
(1) 32		
LOCAL OPTION	2.1	.73
(4) 06 16 18 27		
LOCALIZATION OF A CONFLICT	2.1	.56
(1) 17		
LOCKOUT	2.1	.56
(4) 06 18 27 32		
LOW-INCOME	2.1	.73
(1) 30		
LOYALTY-SECURITY PROGRAMS	2.1	.56
(2) 18 32		
LYNCH LAW	2.1	.73
(2) 06 29		
LYNCHING	2.1	.73
(3) 16 30 45		
MAINTENANCE OF PEACE	2.1	.99
(1) 17		
MAJORITY SOVEREIGNTY	2.1	.87
(1) 22		
MANAGERIAL REVOLUTION	2.1	.56
(1) 22		
MANDATE	2.1	.73
(8) 02 03 06 16 17 18 27 33		
MASTER RACE DOCTRINE	2.1	.56
(1) 16		
MCCARRAN INTERNAL SECURITY ACT OF 1950	2.1	.73
(4) 03 18 32 34		

MEASURES SHORT OF WAR	2.1	.73
(2) 03 20		
MEXICAN WAR	2.1	.73
(1) 06 46		
MILITARY JUSTICE	2.1	.73
(1) 32		
MILITARY OCCUPATION	2.1	.56
(2) 16 19		
MILITARY SPENDING	2.1	.73
(1) 11		
MINIMUM WAGE LAW	2.1	.56
(5) 06 16 18 27 32		
MINIMUM WAGE LEGISLATION	2.1	.56
(1) 42		
MISCONDUCT IN OFFICE	2.1	.56
(1) 06		
MONETARY REFORM	2.1	.73
(1) 17		
MONEY BILL	2.1	.73
(2) 16 27		
MORGENTHAU PLAN	2.1	.73
(3) 03 17 21		
MOSCOW TRIALS OF 1936	2.1	.87
(3) 16 22 34		
MOTION	2.1	.99
(5) 03 06 16 17 27 43		
MOTION FOR ADJOURNMENT	2.1	.73
(1) 17		
MOTION-PICTURE CENSORSHIP	2.1	.87
(1) 06		
MUNICH AGREEMENT	2.1	.56
(1) 38		
MUNICH CONFERENCE (1938)	2.1	.56
(1) 20		
MUNICIPAL ADMINISTRATION	2.1	.56
(1) 03		
NATIONAL LABOR RELATIONS ACT	2.1	.56
(WAGNER ACT) OF 1935		
(6) 08 16 18 25 27 34		
NATIONAL ORIGINS QUOTA SYSTEM	2.1	.73
(2) 18 32		
NEGOTIATE	2.1	.73
(1) 16		
NEUTRALIZATION	2.1	.73
(2) 06 17		
NEW FRONTIER	2.1	.56
(3) 34 38 39		
NIXON DOCTRINE	2.1	.56
(1) 11		
NO KNOCK SEARCH PROVISION	2.1	.56
(1) 32		
NON-COMPLIANCE	2.1	.56
(1) 17		
NUCLEAR TRIGGER	2.1	.56
(1) 39		
NULLIFICATION	2.1	.56
(1) 46		
NUREMBERG LAWS	2.1	.73
(3) 16 21 34		
OCTOBER REVOLUTION	2.1	.56
(3) 16 17 22		
OFFSHORE OIL CONTROVERSY	2.1	.56
(1) 03		

OIL-DEPLETION ALLOWANCE	2.1	.56
(1) 32		
OPEN HOUSING	2.1	.56
(1) 32		
OPEN SHOP	2.1	.73
(5) 06 16 18 27 32		
ORAL AGREEMENT	2.1	.73
(1) 17		
ORIENTALS , EXCLUSION OF	2.1	.56
(2) 06 27		
OVERKILL	2.1	.56
(1) 03		
PARLIAMENTARY LAW	2.1	.56
(1) 16		
PARTITION	2.1	.87
(4) 16 17 24 25		
PARTY AFFILIATION TESTS	2.1	.73
(1) 06		
PARTY CONFERENCE	2.1	.56
(1) 45		
PARTY CONGRESS	2.1	.73
(1) 17		
PARTY-COLUMN BALLOT	2.1	.56
(5) 06 16 18 27 32		
PEOPLE'S REVOLUTION	2.1	.73
(1) 22		
PEREMPTORY CHALLENGE	2.1	.56
(1) 18		
PERFORMANCE EVALUATION	2.1	.73
(1) 37		
PIGEONHOLE	2.1	.73
(7) 02 06 16 17 18 27 32		
PLANNING	2.1	.87
(10) 03 06 11 18 19 22 25 27 30 33		
POINT OF ORDER	2.1	.73
(4) 06 16 17 27		
POLICY OF APPEASEMENT	2.1	.56
(1) 17		
POLICY OF ENCIRCLEMENT	2.1	.56
(1) 17		
POLICY OF EXPANSION	2.1	.56
(1) 17		
POLITICAL NECESSITY	2.1	.73
(1) 29		
POLITICAL REWARDS	2.1	.56
(1) 08		
POPULATION CONTROL	2.1	.56
(1) 36		
POPULATION GROWTH	2.1	.73
(1) 11		
POWER OF DECISION	2.1	.73
(1) 17		
PRAGMATIC	2.1	.87
(2) 17 24		
PRE-TRIAL DETENTION	2.1	.56
(1) 32		
PRESIDENT'S ECONOMIC REPORT	2.1	.73
(1) 02		
PRESIDENTIAL IMMUNITY	2.1	.56
(1) 44		
PRETRIAL SETTLEMENT	2.1	.56
(1) 02		

PREVENTION OF WAR 2.1 .73
(1) 17
PRICE FIXING 2.1 .73
(2) 06 16
PRICE SUPPORT PROGRAM 2.1 .31
(1) 42
PRICE SYSTEM 2.1 .73
(1) 11
PRICE-FIXING 2.1 .73
(1) 45
PRIVACY 2.1 .87
(3) 07 11 25
PRIVATE BILL 2.1 .56
(5) 06 16 18 27 32
PRIVATE CALENDAR 2.1 .73
(4) 02 06 16 18
PRIVILEGED QUESTION 2.1 .56
(3) 06 16 27
PROFIT 2.1 .87
(3) 19 25 30
PROHIBITION OF EX-POST-FACTO LAWS 2.1 .73
(1) 17
PROPORTIONAL TAXATION 2.1 .31
(1) 16
PROTECTIVE TARIFF 2.1 .73
(1) 16
PROTOCOL 2.1 .73
(5) 06 16 17 27 32
PUBLIC EXPENDITURE 2.1 .73
(2) 11 23
PUBLIC SAFETY 2.1 .73
(1) 16
PUBLICITY 2.1 .73
(1) 03
PUMP PRIMING 2.1 .73
(5) 06 16 18 27 29
PURGE 2.1 .56
(1) 39
PURSE STRINGS 2.1 .56
(2) 29 32
QUASI-JUDICIAL POWERS 2.1 .73
(3) 06 18 32
RACIAL PERSECUTION 2.1 .87
(1) 17
RATE OF EXCHANGE 2.1 .56
(1) 16
RATIFICATION 2.1 .56
(4) 06 16 17 24
RATIFICATION OF A TREATY 2.1 .73
(3) 03 18 20
RE-ELECTION 2.1 .56
(1) 17
RECIPROCAL TRADE 2.1 .87
(1) 27
RECOGNITION OF A STATE 2.1 .56
(1) 17
RECOGNITION OF FOREIGN 2.1 .56
GOVERNMENTS
(1) 42
RECOGNITION OF STATES 2.1 .56
(1) 36
RECONSTRUCTION 2.1 .56
(5) 06 08 16 27 30

RECOURSE (AGAINST GOVERNMENT 2.1 .73
ACTION)
(1) 19
RED-BAITING 2.1 .31
(1) 45
REFORM 2.1 .87
(2) 24 30
REGISTRATION OF VOTERS 2.1 .56
(1) 34
REGULATION (CONTROL) 2.1 .87
(3) 06 11 33
REPEAL OF LAWS 2.1 .56
(1) 42
RESEARCH AND DEVELOPMENT (R AND 2.1 .56
D)
(2) 20 25
REVENUE 2.1 .87
(3) 06 16 27
REVOLUTION OF 1688 2.1 .56
(1) 09
RIGHT OF APPEAL 2.1 .73
(1) 45
RIGHT OF ASSEMBLY 2.1 .56
(1) 16
RIGHT OF ASSEMBLY AND PETITION 2.1 .73
(1) 45
RIGHT OF ASYLUM 2.1 .56
(2) 16 17
RIGHT OF NEUTRALITY 2.1 .73
(1) 17
RIGHT OF PARDON 2.1 .56
(1) 17
RIGHT OF PRIMOGENITURE 2.1 .31
(1) 17
RIGHT TO BEAR ARMS 2.1 .31
(3) 18 32 45
ROOSEVELT COROLLARY OF THE 2.1 .31
MONROE DOCTRINE
(4) 03 16 32 46
RULE 2.1 .99
(1) 43
RULE OF REASON 2.1 .73
(5) 03 06 16 18 32
RULES OF WARFARE 2.1 .56
(1) 20
RUN-OFF BALLOT 2.1 .56
(1) 17
RUNOFF PRIMARY 2.1 .56
(9) 02 03 06 16 17 18 27 32 34
SALES AND USE TAX 2.1 .56
(1) 18
SEARCH WARRANT 2.1 .73
(3) 06 18 32
SECRET TREATIES 2.1 .56
(2) 16 17
SELECTIVE SERVICE 2.1 .73
(1) 46
SENATE JOINT RESOLUTION (S J RES) 2.1 .56
(1) 16
SENATORIAL COURTESY 2.1 .56
(8) 03 06 16 18 27 29 32 34
SERFDOM 2.1 .73
(1) 25

SEVENTEENTH AMENDMENT	2.1	.56
(3) 06 18 30		
SEVENTH AMENDMENT	2.1	.56
(2) 18 30		
SHAYS' REBELLION	2.1	.56
(1) 03 06 18 46		
SINGLE TAX	2.1	.73
(5) 06 10 16 22 32		
SIT-IN	2.1	.56
(1) 39		
SIX DAY WAR	2.1	.56
(1) 41		
SIXTH AMENDMENT	2.1	.56
(1) 18		
SLANDER	2.1	.56
(4) 03 16 18 32		
SLAVE TRADE	2.1	.31
(3) 06 16 17		
SOCIALIZED MEDICINE	2.1	.56
(3) 02 06 16		
SPECIAL DRAWING RIGHTS (SDR)	2.1	.73
(INTERNATIONAL MONETARY UNITS)		
(1) 20		
SPLIT DECISIONS, JUDICIAL	2.1	.56
(1) 04		
SPLIT TICKET	2.1	.56
(5) 06 16 18 27 32		
STATE OF EMERGENCY	2.1	.56
(1) 17		
STATE OF NATURE	2.1	.87
(4) 06 16 18 26		
STATUS QUO	2.1	.56
(3) 16 17 18		
STATUTE-MAKING POWER	2.1	.73
(1) 03		
STRAIGHT-TICKET VOTING	2.1	.56
(6) 06 16 18 27 32 42		
STRATEGIC BOMBING	2.1	.56
(1) 03		
STRAW VOTE	2.1	.31
(5) 03 06 16 27 29		
STRIKE	2.1	.56
(1) 32		
STRIKES	2.1	.56
(1) 37		
STUDENT PROTESTS	2.1	.56
(1) 25		
SUBPOENA	2.1	.56
(6) 03 06 16 18 27 32		
SUBSIDY	2.1	.56
(7) 03 06 16 18 20 27 30		
SUBSTANTIVE DUE PROCESS	2.1	.73
(2) 03 18		
SUBSTANTIVE LAW	2.1	.73
(3) 02 06 16		
SUBVERSIVE ACTIVITY	2.1	.73
(1) 45		
SUPREME COURT APPEAL	2.1	.56
(1) 18		
SUPREME COURT PACKING PLAN	2.1	.56
(2) 03 18		
SUPREME LAW	2.1	.73
(1) 44		
SURVEY	2.1	.73
(3) 24 30 33		
SURVIVAL OF THE FITTEST	2.1	.56
(1) 35		
SUSPENSION OF DIPLOMATIC	2.1	.56
RELATIONS		
(1) 17		
TAX	2.1	.87
(4) 06 16 18 27		
TAX BASE	2.1	.56
(1) 06		
TAX EXEMPTION	2.1	.56
(4) 06 16 18 45		
TAX LOOPHOLE	2.1	.31
(1) 32		
TECHNOLOGICAL CHANGE AND	2.1	.87
POLITICS		
(3) 03 11 37		
TENURE	2.1	.73
(4) 06 16 18 24		
TERRORISM	2.1	.56
(8) 07 11 16 17 22 24 29 30		
TEST BAN TREATY	2.1	.31
(1) 38		
THIRD-TERM TRADITION	2.1	.31
(2) 06 16		
TOKYO WAR CRIMES TRIALS	2.1	.73
(1) 20		
TREATY OF VERSAILLES	2.1	.31
(1) 46		
TREATY ON THE NONPROLIFERATION	2.1	.87
OF NUCLEAR WEAPONS		
(1) 41		
TRIAL	2.1	.87
(5) 02 06 16 18 24		
TWELFTH AMENDMENT	2.1	.56
(2) 06 18		
TWO-THIRDS RULE	2.1	.73
(3) 06 16 42		
U.N. CHARTER REVISION	2.1	.73
(1) 03		
U-2 INCIDENT	2.1	.56
(2) 03 34 46		
ULTIMATUM	2.1	.73
(4) 11 16 17 20		
UNANIMOUS OPINION	2.1	.73
(1) 44		
UNEMPLOYMENT	2.1	.73
(3) 22 24 30		
UNILATERAL DISARMAMENT	2.1	.56
(1) 20		
UNIT RULE	2.1	.56
(6) 02 06 16 18 27 32		
UNIT VETO SYSTEM	2.1	.73
(1) 03		
UNREASONABLE SEARCHES AND	2.1	.73
SEIZURES		
(1) 06		
UNWRITTEN LAW	2.1	.56
(3) 06 16 32		
VALUE ADDED TAX	2.1	.56
(1) 32		

VEST POCKET VOTE	2.1	.87
(1) 29		
VIOLATION OF NEUTRALITY	2.1	.56
(1) 17		
VOICE VOTE	2.1	.87
(2) 16 27		
VOTE BY SECRET BALLOT	2.1	.73
(1) 17		
WAR ATROCITIES	2.1	.56
(1) 17		
WAR DEBTS	2.1	.56
(2) 16 21		
WAR OF SECESSION	2.1	.73
(1) 17		
WAR OF 1812	2.1	.73
(1) 06 46		
WAR PREVENTION	2.1	.73
(1) 17		
WAR PROPAGANDA	2.1	.56
(1) 17		
WEALTH	2.1	.87
(1) 24		
WEIGHTED VOTING	2.1	.87
(1) 20		
WELFARE	2.1	.99
(5) 06 11 24 25 30		
WIRETAPPING	2.1	.73
(4) 03 06 18 32		
WITH ALL DELIBERATE SPEED	2.1	.87
(1) 39		
WITHINPUTS	2.1	.87
(1) 01		
WORLD DEPRESSION	2.1	.56
(1) 17		
WRITE-IN	2.1	.73
(1) 39		
YALTA AGREEMENTS	2.1	.73
(4) 03 11 20 34		
ABSTENTION	2.2	.78
(3) 11 17 33		
ACCLAMATION	2.2	.78
(2) 06 16		
ACCUMULATION (OF CAPITAL)	2.2	.78
(1) 03		
ACHIEVEMENT	2.2	.91
(2) 25 30		
ADMINISTRATIVE LEGISLATION	2.2	.78
(1) 16		
ADMINISTRATIVE PROCEDURE	2.2	.78
(3) 03 11 18		
ADMINISTRATIVE TRUSTEESHIP	2.2	.63
(1) 19		
ADMISSION OF ALIENS	2.2	.63
(1) 44		
ADVISORY OPINION	2.2	.63
(6) 02 06 16 17 18 20		
AFFLUENCE	2.2	.63
(2) 24 30		
AID TO DEPENDENT CHILDREN (ADC)	2.2	.78
(4) 18 25 27 32		
AIR PIRACY	2.2	.63
(1) 11		
AIRLIFT	2.2	.63
(1) 17		
ALGERIAN CONFLICT	2.2	.42
(1) 17		
ALLIED INVASION	2.2	.63
(1) 17		
AMENDING PROCESS, STATE CONSTITUTIONS	2.2	.63
(1) 42		
ANNAPOLIS CONVENTION, 1786	2.2	.78
(6) 03 06 16 18 32 46		
ANNEXATION	2.2	.42
(9) 03 06 16 17 18 20 25 29 33		
ANSCHLUSS	2.2	.78
(7) 03 06 16 17 21 22 34		
ANTI-COMINTERN PACT	2.2	.63
(4) 16 17 21 34		
ANZUS TREATY	2.2	.42
(7) 03 11 17 18 20 32 34		
APPOINTMENT	2.2	.78
(4) 06 16 17 24		
ARAB-ISRAEL WAR, 1948-49	2.2	.42
(1) 03		
ARBITRATION, LABOR	2.2	.63
(1) 18		
ARMISTICE	2.2	.63
(6) 03 06 16 17 20 45		
ASCRIPTION	2.2	.78
(1) 01		
ASSESSED VALUATION	2.2	.42
(1) 18		
ATOMS FOR PEACE PLAN	2.2	.63
(1) 20		
ATROCITIES	2.2	.78
(1) 16		
AUTONOMOUS	2.2	.78
(1) 17		
BAGHDAD PACT	2.2	.63
(5) 03 20 25 27 34		
BATTLE OF BRITAIN	2.2	.63
(3) 16 17 34		
BEGGING-THE-QUESTION	2.2	.91
(1) 43		
BIG STICK DIPLOMACY	2.2	.42
(1) 46		
BILATERAL AID	2.2	.63
(3) 16 17 20		
BIPARTISAN	2.2	.42
(1) 39		
BLACK CAPITALISM	2.2	.63
(2) 07 25		
BLACK MARKET	2.2	.63
(3) 06 17 27		
BLITZKRIEG	2.2	.42
(3) 16 17 22		
BOSTON MASSACRE	2.2	.63
(1) 06		
BOXER REBELLION	2.2	.42
(4) 03 16 17 22		
BRACERO PROGRAM	2.2	.63
(1) 46		
BRETTON WOODS AGREEMENT (1944)	2.2	.42
(6) 03 16 18 19 20 21		

BY-LAW   2.2 .78
  (1) 06
CAMPAIGN CONTRIBUTIONS   2.2 .63
  (1) 32
CAPITAL FLIGHT   2.2 .42
  (1) 20
CHALLENGE, VOTING   2.2 .63
  (1) 18
CHILD LABOR   2.2 .63
  (4) 06 18 25 32
CHILD LABOR AMENDMENT   2.2 .42
  (1) 06
CHINESE REVOLUTION OF 1911   2.2 .42
  (2) 03 34
CHINESE-JAPANESE WAR   2.2 .42
  (1) 34
CIVIL RIGHTS ACT OF 1875   2.2 .42
  (1) 18 46
CIVIL SUPREMACY   2.2 .78
  (1) 03
CLASS LEGISLATION   2.2 .42
  (1) 44
CLOSED SESSION   2.2 .42
  (1) 17
CODE CIVIL   2.2 .42
  (1) 16
COLLUSION   2.2 .78
  (1) 45
COMMISSION PLAN OF CITY   2.2 .78
  GOVERNMENT
  (1) 45
COMMUTATION   2.2 .63
  (1) 06
COMPACT   2.2 .63
  (1) 06
CONCURRENT POWER   2.2 .63
  (5) 03 06 16 18 32
CONFIRMATION OF APPOINTMENTS,   2.2 .63
  CONGRESS
  (1) 20
CONFLICT OF LAWS   2.2 .78
  (3) 06 17 20
CONGO CRISIS   2.2 .42
  (1) 17
CONGRESS OF VIENNA   2.2 .63
  (2) 16 17
CONGRESS PROCEEDINGS   2.2 .91
  (1) 17
CONGRESSIONAL AMENDMENT   2.2 .78
  (1) 32
CONGRESSIONAL REORGANIZATION   2.2 .63
  ACTS
  (1) 32
CONSERVATION OF NATURAL   2.2 .63
  RESOURCES
  (1) 42
CONSPIRACY   2.2 .63
  (7) 03 06 17 18 25 30 33
CONSTITUENT POWER   2.2 .91
  (2) 06 18
CONSTITUTIONAL CONGRESS   2.2 .78
  (1) 17

CONSTITUTIONAL CONSTRUCTION   2.2 .78
  (2) 18 32
CONSTITUTIONAL ORDER   2.2 .91
  (1) 17
CONSTITUTIONAL REFERENDUM   2.2 .42
  (2) 18 32
CONSUMER PROTECTION   2.2 .63
  (2) 07 32
CONTEMPT   2.2 .78
  (1) 06
CONTROLLED ECONOMY   2.2 .63
  (1) 19
CONVENTION SYSTEM   2.2 .91
  (1) 42
CONVENTIONAL WAR   2.2 .63
  (1) 36
CORONATION   2.2 .63
  (1) 17
CORPORATION INCOME TAX   2.2 .63
  (4) 06 16 18 32
CORRUPT PRACTICES ACT, FEDERAL   2.2 .78
  (1) 42
CORRUPT PRACTICES LAWS (U.S.)   2.2 .63
  (7) 03 06 16 18 19 27 32
CORRUPTION   2.2 .63
  (6) 07 11 23 24 25 33
COST   2.2 .91
  (3) 17 24 30
COUNTER-COUP   2.2 .63
  (1) 24
COUNTERINSURGENCY   2.2 .42
  (2) 18 20
COURTESY OF THE SENATE   2.2 .63
  (2) 06 29
CRIME   2.2 .78
  (4) 16 22 25 30
CRIMINAL CODE   2.2 .63
  (1) 16
CUSTOM   2.2 .78
  (3) 11 17 33
DEBT CEILING   2.2 .78
  (2) 06 27
DECLARATORY JUDGMENT   2.2 .78
  (5) 03 06 16 18 27
DEFAMATION OF CHARACTER   2.2 .78
  (1) 32
DEFICIT   2.2 .63
  (2) 02 06
DEFLATION   2.2 .63
  (5) 03 06 16 18 20 32
DELINEATION OF LEGISLATIVE   2.2 .78
  DISTRICTS
  (1) 25
DELINQUENT TAXES   2.2 .42
  (1) 06
DEMOCRATIC CONVENTION OF 1968   2.2 .78
  (1) 25
DEPRIVATION OF LIBERTY   2.2 .78
  (1) 17
DEVELOPMENT AID   2.2 .63
  (1) 23
DIALOGUE   2.2 .78
  (1) 30

DILATORY MOTION	2.2	.78
(2) 06 18		
DIPLOMATIC CHANNELS	2.2	.63
(1) 17		
DIPLOMATIC MISSION	2.2	.42
(2) 16 17		
DISARMAMENT AND PEACE	2.2	.42
CONFERENCES, 1920-1930		
(1) 46		
DISBARMENT	2.2	.63
(1) 06		
DISCHARGE PETITION	2.2	.78
(3) 03 18 32		
DISINTEGRATION	2.2	.78
(1) 30		
DISPUTED ELECTION	2.2	.63
(2) 06 16		
DISSOLUTION	2.2	.78
(7) 03 16 17 24 29 30 33		
DIVERSIFICATION OF INDUSTRY	2.2	.63
(1) 45		
DOLLAR DIPLOMACY	2.2	.63
(9) 03 06 16 18 20 27 29 32 34 45		
DOMESTIC AFFAIRS	2.2	.63
(4) 17 27 29 32		
DRUG REGULATION	2.2	.63
(1) 32		
ECONOMIC SANCTIONS	2.2	.42
(2) 11 17		
ECONOMIC WAR	2.2	.63
(3) 06 16 17		
EFFICIENCY	2.2	.91
(1) 24		
ELASTIC DEMAND	2.2	.78
(1) 45		
ELECT	2.2	.91
(2) 17 24		
ELECTION PETITIONS	2.2	.63
(1) 18		
ELECTORAL PRIMARIES	2.2	.63
(1) 25		
ELECTORAL QUOTA	2.2	.63
(2) 06 33		
EMPLOYMENT TAX (SOCIAL SECURITY	2.2	.63
ACT)		
(1) 45		
EQUAL-TIME PROVISION	2.2	.63
(2) 27 32		
EQUITY	2.2	.78
(7) 03 06 16 17 18 27 32		
EXECUTION	2.2	.91
(3) 06 17 32		
EXPEL	2.2	.78
(1) 17		
FACT-FINDING TRIP	2.2	.63
(1) 39		
FEDERAL ACT	2.2	.91
(1) 17		
FEDERAL DEBT	2.2	.63
(1) 02		
FEDERAL POLICE POWER	2.2	.78
(1) 44		

FEUDAL CONTRACT	2.2	.78
(1) 09		
FILING FEE	2.2	.63
(2) 06 18		
FISCAL YEAR	2.2	.42
(4) 06 16 18 27		
FIVE-TO-FOUR DECISION	2.2	.78
(3) 06 16 18		
FLOOR DEBATE	2.2	.42
(1) 02		
FOREIGN AID	2.2	.42
(11) 04 07 11 12 17 18 20 23 25 27		
32		
FOREIGN COMMERCE	2.2	.63
(2) 16 18		
FREE ACCESS	2.2	.63
(1) 17		
FREE COMPETITION	2.2	.78
(1) 16		
FREEDOM OF COMMERCE AND	2.2	.42
NAVIGATION		
(1) 17		
FREEDOM OF CONSCIENCE	2.2	.78
(1) 17		
FREEDOM OF DEBATE	2.2	.78
(2) 06 18		
FREEDOM OF THOUGHT	2.2	.78
(1) 17		
FRIENDLY NEUTRALITY	2.2	.42
(1) 17		
FRONTLASH	2.2	.78
(1) 39		
FULL FAITH AND CREDIT	2.2	.78
(1) 03		
FUNCTIONAL CONSOLIDATION	2.2	.78
(1) 03		
FUNCTIONAL CONSOLIDATION,	2.2	.78
ADMINISTRATIVE		
(1) 18		
FUNDAMENTAL LAW	2.2	.78
(2) 06 16		
GAG RULE	2.2	.63
(4) 06 16 27 29		
GENERAL PROPERTY TAX	2.2	.63
(3) 06 16 18		
GENEVA SUMMIT CONFERENCE (1955)	2.2	.78
(1) 34		
GLOBAL WAR	2.2	.78
(1) 16		
GOVERNANCE	2.2	.91
(3) 06 16 24		
GOVERNMENT BILL	2.2	.42
(2) 16 17		
GOVERNORS CONFERENCE	2.2	.63
(3) 03 06 27		
GREAT COMPROMISE	2.2	.63
(2) 18 32		
GROSS INCOME	2.2	.78
(2) 06 16		
HEALTH INSURANCE	2.2	.63
(2) 11 18		
HIGH SEAS, JURISDICTION	2.2	.63
(4) 06 16 17 20		

HITLER PUTSCH	2.2	.63
(1) 17		
HONEYMOON PERIOD	2.2	.78
(1) 39		
HOUSE RESOLUTION (H R)	2.2	.78
(1) 16		
IMMUNITIES OF A DIPLOMAT	2.2	.63
(1) 17		
IMPLEMENTATION	2.2	.78
(2) 11 24		
IMPORT DUTY	2.2	.63
(2) 06 16		
IMPORT TAXES	2.2	.63
(1) 42		
IN-SERVICE TRAINING	2.2	.78
(2) 06 16		
INCOME MAINTENANCE	2.2	.42
(1) 32		
INDIRECT INITIATIVE	2.2	.78
(2) 06 18		
INDUSTRIAL DEVELOPMENT	2.2	.63
(1) 41		
INFLATION	2.2	.78
(1) 38		
INTERNAL REVENUE	2.2	.78
(2) 06 16		
INTERNAL SECURITY ACT OF 1950	2.2	.42
(3) 18 32 34		
INTERNATIONAL CRIMES	2.2	.78
(2) 16 17		
INTERNATIONAL LAW OF THE SEA	2.2	.78
(1) 17		
INTERNATIONAL OFFENSE	2.2	.63
(1) 17		
INTERNATIONAL SETTLEMENT	2.2	.78
(1) 16		
INVOLUNTARY SERVITUDE	2.2	.42
(4) 03 06 18 32		
JAY TREATY	2.2	.78
(2) 06 16 46		
JIM CROW LAWS	2.2	.63
(5) 06 16 18 27 34		
JOB DESCRIPTION	2.2	.91
(1) 17		
JOB EVALUATION	2.2	.91
(1) 37		
JUDICIAL DOCTRINE	2.2	.63
(1) 44		
JUDICIAL VETO	2.2	.42
(1) 42		
JULY 4, 1776	2.2	.91
(1) 03		
JURY DUTY	2.2	.63
(1) 44		
JUSTICIABILITY	2.2	.63
(1) 43		
JUSTIFICATION	2.2	.91
(1) 43		
KEYNOTE SPEECH	2.2	.63
(3) 06 16 27		
LAW AND ORDER	2.2	.63
(1) 39		

LEGAL	2.2	.91
(1) 30		
LEGAL NEUTRALITY	2.2	.63
(1) 25		
LEGISLATIVE REFORM	2.2	.63
(1) 07		
LET A HUNDRED FLOWERS BLOOM	2.2	.63
(1) 03		
LEWIS AND CLARK EXPEDITION	2.2	.78
(1) 46		
LICENSE	2.2	.78
(5) 06 16 17 18 27		
LIEN	2.2	.78
(2) 06 27		
LIST SYSTEM OF VOTING	2.2	.63
(6) 03 06 16 20 33 44		
LITERACY TEST	2.2	.63
(7) 02 03 06 16 18 27 34		
LOCAL FINANCE	2.2	.78
(1) 11		
LOCAL LAW	2.2	.91
(1) 44		
LOW-RENT HOUSING	2.2	.63
(1) 45		
LUMP-SUM APPROPRIATION	2.2	.63
(1) 06		
MADISON AVENUE TECHNIQUES	2.2	.78
(1) 39		
MANAGED NEWS	2.2	.63
(1) 39		
MANDATES SYSTEM, LEAGUE OF	2.2	.63
NATIONS		
(3) 17 20 21		
MASS EXECUTIONS	2.2	.63
(1) 17		
MAYFLOWER COMPACT	2.2	.42
(6) 03 06 16 26 27 32		
MEDIATION AND CONCILIATION, LABOR	2.2	.63
(1) 18		
MEDICAL CARE	2.2	.91
(3) 11 24 30		
MEDICAL INSURACE	2.2	.78
(1) 32		
MEDICARE LAW	2.2	.78
(1) 42		
MERIT	2.2	.91
(1) 24		
METROPOLITAN CITY-COUNTY	2.2	.42
SEPARATION		
(1) 18		
MIDDLE AGES	2.2	.63
(1) 22		
MIGRATION	2.2	.63
(6) 06 16 20 24 25 30		
MILITARY INTEGRATION OF WESTERN	2.2	.63
EUROPE		
(1) 17		
MILITARY LAW	2.2	.63
(5) 03 06 16 18 32		
MILITARY NECESSITY	2.2	.63
(1) 16		
MILITARY PACT	2.2	.63
(1) 17		

MILITARY TREATY 2.2 .63
(1) 17
MINISTERIAL RESPONSIBILITY 2.2 .78
(3) 11 16 17
MOB VIOLENCE 2.2 .78
(1) 03
MODIFICATION OF THE CONSTITUTION 2.2 .78
(1) 17
MOTION OF CONFIDENCE 2.2 .78
(1) 17
MUTUAL AID 2.2 .78
(2) 16 22
NATIONAL CONVENTION (OF PARTIES IN 2.2 .91
U.S.A.)
(7) 03 06 16 17 18 32 34
NATIONAL LAW 2.2 .91
(1) 17
NATIONAL SUPREMACY 2.2 .63
(4) 06 18 27 32
NEGATIVE VOTE 2.2 .63
(1) 17
NEGOTIATED PEACE 2.2 .63
(1) 16
NEWS BAN 2.2 .63
(1) 17
NEWS BLACKOUT 2.2 .63
(1) 17
NINETEENTH AMENDMENT 2.2 .63
(1) 18
NON-AGGRESSION PACT 2.2 .42
(4) 03 16 17 21
NON-BELLIGERENCY 2.2 .42
(2) 03 17
NON-INTERFERENCE 2.2 .42
(2) 10 29
NORMALCY 2.2 .63
(4) 06 16 27 29
NORTH ATLANTIC PACT 2.2 .78
(1) 42
NORTHWEST ORDINANCE (1787) 2.2 .78
(4) 03 06 16 18 46
OBLIGATION TO VOTE 2.2 .42
(1) 17
OBSCENITY 2.2 .63
(1) 07
OMNIBUS CRIME CONTROL ACT OF 2.2 .78
1970
(1) 32
OPEN BALLOT 2.2 .63
(1) 32
OPEN DIPLOMACY 2.2 .42
(3) 16 17 20
ORDINANCE 2.2 .78
(6) 03 06 11 16 18 27
ORDINARY DIPLOMATIC CHANNELS 2.2 .42
(1) 17
ORGANIC LAW 2.2 .78
(2) 06 17
ORGANIZATIONAL PROBLEMS 2.2 .78
(1) 04
OUT-OF-COURT SETTLEMENT 2.2 .63
(1) 02

OVERRULING 2.2 .78
(1) 44
PACT 2.2 .78
(5) 06 16 17 27 33
PAIRING 2.2 .78
(2) 06 32
PARIS PEACE CONFERENCE 2.2 .63
(3) 06 16 34
PARIS PEACE TALKS, 1968-1971 2.2 .63
(1) 46
PARTITION OF PALESTINE 2.2 .63
(1) 03
PAX AMERICANA 2.2 .42
(1) 22
PAY-AS-YOU-GO TAXATION 2.2 .63
(2) 16 29
PEACE CONFERENCE 2.2 .63
(3) 06 16 17
PEACEFUL USES OF ATOMIC ENERGY 2.2 .63
(1) 36
PEACEFUL USES OF OUTER SPACE 2.2 .63
(1) 32
PEACETIME BLOCKADE 2.2 .42
(1) 17
PEASANT REVOLTS 2.2 .78
(1) 26
PENDLETON CIVIL SERVICE ACT OF 2.2 .78
1883
(5) 03 06 16 18 32 46
PERIODIC REGISTRATION 2.2 .91
(3) 06 18 32
PERMISSIVE POWERS OF CONGRESS 2.2 .63
(2) 06 16
PERSONALITY DEVELOPMENT 2.2 .91
(1) 15
PETITION 2.2 .63
(6) 02 03 06 17 24 32
PIGEONHOLING A BILL 2.2 .63
(1) 42
PLANNING AND LAND USE 2.2 .63
(1) 07
PLENARY MEETING 2.2 .63
(1) 17
POLICE BRUTALITY 2.2 .63
(1) 39
POLITICAL JURISPRUDENCE 2.2 .78
(1) 04
POLITICAL LIFE 2.2 .78
(1) 15
POLITICAL OFFENSES 2.2 .63
(3) 06 16 17
PORK BARREL LEGISLATION 2.2 .63
(2) 18 32
POSITIVE LAW 2.2 .63
(4) 06 16 19 22
PREFERENTIAL VOTING 2.2 .63
(3) 03 06 16
PRESIDENT'S ANNUAL MESSAGE 2.2 .63
(1) 16
PRESIDENTIAL ASSASSINATION 2.2 .63
(1) 42
PRESIDENTIAL PRESS CONFERENCE 2.2 .63
(2) 27 32

PRESIDENTIAL PROCLAMATIONS	2.2	.63
(1) 42		
PRESIDENTIAL TERM	2.2	.42
(1) 44		
PRESUMPTION OF INNOCENCE	2.2	.42
(1) 32		
PRIMARY BOYCOTT	2.2	.42
(1) 18		
PROBATION AND PAROLE	2.2	.42
(6) 03 06 07 16 18 27		
PROCEDURAL RIGHTS	2.2	.78
(4) 03 06 18 32		
PROCEDURE	2.2	.78
(2) 17 24		
PROFIT-SHARING	2.2	.63
(1) 37		
PROGRAMMED INSTRUCTION	2.2	.63
(1) 37		
PROHIBITION	2.2	.63
(7) 03 06 16 18 27 32 34		
PROHIBITION OF ATOMIC WEAPONS	2.2	.63
(1) 17		
PROPOSED BUDGET	2.2	.63
(1) 17		
PROSECUTION	2.2	.78
(3) 02 06 27		
PUBLIC ACTS	2.2	.78
(1) 11		
PUBLIC ASSISTANCE	2.2	.42
(1) 27		
PUBLIC HOUSING	2.2	.63
(1) 32		
PUBLIC SERVICE	2.2	.78
(2) 23 25		
PURITAN REVOLUTION	2.2	.78
(1) 26		
PUTSCH	2.2	.42
(3) 16 17 33		
QUARANTINE	2.2	.63
(2) 06 16		
QUASI-LEGISLATIVE	2.2	.78
(1) 18		
QUESTION HOUR, BRITAIN	2.2	.42
(2) 16 20		
QUOTA	2.2	.63
(4) 06 16 20 27		
QUOTED OUT OF CONTEXT	2.2	.63
(1) 39		
RACE RELATIONS	2.2	.78
(3) 07 11 25		
RACE RIOTS	2.2	.63
(1) 36		
RATIFICATION CLAUSE	2.2	.78
(1) 17		
READINGS OF A BILL	2.2	.78
(4) 18 27 30 32		
REBELLION	2.2	.78
(6) 11 16 17 27 30 33		
RECIPROCAL TARIFF	2.2	.63
(1) 32		
RECOGNITION	2.2	.42
(11) 03 06 11 16 17 18 20 27 30 32 34		
RECONSTRUCTION ACTS	2.2	.42
(1) 32		
RECONSTRUCTION PERIOD	2.2	.63
(1) 25		
RECONSTRUCTION, RADICAL	2.2	.63
(1) 46		
RECRUITING	2.2	.63
(1) 45		
RED HUNT (MENACE, SCARE)	2.2	.42
(1) 29		
RED REVOLUTION	2.2	.63
(1) 16		
REDRESS OF GRIEVANCES	2.2	.63
(2) 06 16		
REGIONAL DEVELOPMENT	2.2	.63
(1) 03		
REGIONAL ECONOMIC PLANNING	2.2	.63
(1) 11		
REGIONAL PACTS	2.2	.78
(1) 21		
REGIONAL PLANNING	2.2	.78
(3) 11 16 23		
REGISTRATION	2.2	.78
(7) 03 06 16 17 18 27 32		
REPATRIATION	2.2	.63
(3) 06 16 17		
REPEAL	2.2	.63
(2) 06 17		
RESPONSIBLE PARTY SYSTEM	2.2	.78
(1) 18		
RESTRAINT OF TRADE	2.2	.42
(3) 06 16 18		
RIGHT OF ACCESS	2.2	.63
(1) 17		
RIGHT TO BENEFIT OF COUNSEL	2.2	.63
(1) 45		
RIGHT TO PEACEABLE ASSEMBLY	2.2	.63
(1) 03		
RIGHT TO STRIKE	2.2	.63
(1) 17		
RIGHTS OF CHILDREN	2.2	.63
(1) 41		
RULES OF THE GAME	2.2	.78
(1) 22		
RUSSO-JAPANESE WAR	2.2	.42
(3) 03 16 22 46		
SECRECY IN GOVERNMENT	2.2	.63
(1) 07		
SECRET DIPLOMACY	2.2	.42
(2) 16 17		
SEIZURE OF POWER	2.2	.78
(1) 17		
SELECTION OF JUDGES	2.2	.78
(1) 44		
SENATE RESOLUTION (S RES)	2.2	.42
(1) 16		
SENATE RULES	2.2	.63
(1) 42		
SEVERANCE OF DIPLOMATIC RELATIONS	2.2	.63
(1) 17		
SEX DISCRIMINATION	2.2	.63
(2) 11 32		

SHORT-TERM BORROWING 2.2 .42
(1) 45
SOURCES OF THE LAW 2.2 .63
(1) 44
SOVEREIGN EQUALITY 2.2 .78
(1) 17
SPACE LAW 2.2 .63
(3) 11 17 25
SPECIAL ELECTION 2.2 .78
(1) 18
SPHERE OF INFLUENCE 2.2 .63
(6) 03 06 11 16 17 20
SPLIT DECISION 2.2 .63
(1) 42
STATE CONSTITUTION 2.2 .78
(1) 45
STATE OF PEACE 2.2 .91
(1) 17
STATUS OF WOMEN 2.2 .78
(1) 32
STATUTE LAW 2.2 .78
(2) 03 16
STATUTES 2.2 .91
(1) 44
STRATEGIC INTELLIGENCE 2.2 .63
(1) 03
SUBSISTENCE LEVEL 2.2 .42
(1) 45
SUBSTANTIVE DECISION, SECURITY 2.2 .63
COUNCIL
(1) 20
SUBSTANTIVE RIGHTS 2.2 .63
(4) 03 06 18 32
SUPPLEMENTARY APPROPRIATION 2.2 .63
(3) 06 18 32
SUPREMACY CLAUSE 2.2 .78
(2) 18 32
SURTAX 2.2 .63
(4) 02 06 16 27
TARIFF AGREEMENT 2.2 .78
(1) 17
TARIFF PROTECTION 2.2 .42
(1) 03
TAX INCENTIVES 2.2 .63
(1) 25
TAX POWER OF THE STATES 2.2 .78
(1) 45
TAX REFORM 2.2 .63
(1) 32
TERMS AND CONDITIONS OF 2.2 .63
APPOINTMENT
(1) 17
TERRITORIAL SOVEREIGNTY 2.2 .42
(1) 17
THIRD AMENDMENT 2.2 .63
(1) 18
THIRD PARTY ARBITRATION 2.2 .63
(1) 36
THREAT OF WAR 2.2 .63
(1) 17
THREE-MILE LIMIT 2.2 .42
(4) 03 06 16 17

THREE-PARTY SYSTEM 2.2 .63
(1) 17
TOWN MEETING 2.2 .78
(6) 06 16 18 22 27 32
TRADE BARRIERS, STATE 2.2 .78
(1) 45
TREATY LAW 2.2 .78
(1) 17
TREATY OF EXTRADITION 2.2 .63
(1) 17
TREATY OF GHENT 2.2 .63
(1) 16 46
TRIAL BALLOON 2.2 .63
(2) 16 27
TWENTY-FIFTH AMENDMENT 2.2 .78
(1) 42
TWENTY-SIXTH AMENDMENT 2.2 .78
(1) 42
UNANIMOUS CONSENT 2.2 .78
(5) 02 03 06 16 18
UNANIMOUS DECISION 2.2 .63
(1) 44
UNDERDOG EFFECT 2.2 .78
(3) 01 29 33
UNEMPLOYMENT INSURANCE 2.2 .63
(5) 06 16 18 27 32
UNIFICATION 2.2 .78
(3) 18 24 25
UNIVERSAL MILITARY TRAINING 2.2 .42
(1) 45
URBAN RENEWAL 2.2 .78
(4) 03 18 25 32
USURP 2.2 .78
(1) 17
USURPATION 2.2 .63
(3) 06 17 19
USURY 2.2 .63
(2) 06 18
UTOPIAN EXPERIMENTS 2.2 .63
(1) 46
VANDENBERG TRADITION OF 2.2 .63
BIPARTISAN FOREIGN POLICY
(1) 03
VETO ITEM 2.2 .78
(1) 18
VIOLATION OF INTERNATIONAL LAW 2.2 .78
(1) 17
VIRGINIA PLAN 2.2 .63
(5) 03 06 18 27 32
VISA 2.2 .63
(7) 06 16 17 18 20 27 32
VOTE BY ACCLAMATION 2.2 .78
(1) 17
VOTE BY PROXY 2.2 .78
(1) 17
VOTE FRAUD 2.2 .78
(1) 39
VOTING PAIR 2.2 .78
(1) 02
WAGE AND HOUR REGULATIONS 2.2 .78
(1) 18
WARRANT 2.2 .78
(2) 06 27

WARTIME TREATMENT OF JAPANESE-AMERICANS (1) 32	2.2	.63
WEAPONS TECHNOLOGY (1) 36	2.2	.63
WHISKEY REBELLION (1) 46	2.2	.63
WITHHOLDING TAX (4) 16 18 27 32	2.2	.63
WOMEN'S RIGHTS (1) 46	2.2	.78
WORKMEN, COMPENSATION (4) 06 18 27 32	2.2	.78
YELLOW JOURNALISM (1) 45 46	2.2	.63
ZONING (8) 03 06 07 16 18 27 30 32	2.2	.78
ABORTION (3) 07 11 25	2.3	.67
ACCESSIBILITY (1) 25	2.3	.82
ADMINISTRATIVE AUTHORITY (1) 17	2.3	.67
ADMINISTRATIVE DEVELOPMENT (1) 11	2.3	.82
ADMINISTRATIVE JUSTICE (1) 11	2.3	.82
ADMIRALTY LAW (4) 16 20 27 32	2.3	.82
ADMISSION OF NEW STATES (2) 03 18	2.3	.67
ADMISSION OF STATES TO THE UNION (3) 03 06 16	2.3	.67
ADVOCATE (1) 17	2.3	.67
AGGRANDIZEMENT (2) 03 16	2.3	.67
AGING (2) 11 32	2.3	.67
AGREEMENT (10) 03 06 16 17 20 24 25 30 34 41	2.3	.82
AIR POLLUTION (2) 11 32	2.3	.82
AIR SUPREMACY (1) 17	2.3	.67
ALBANY PLAN OF UNION (3) 03 06 46	2.3	.82
ALL-OUT WAR (1) 39	2.3	.67
ALLOCATION (2) 24 33	2.3	.67
AMERICAN WAR OF INDEPENDENCE (1) 17	2.3	.82
ANTI-DISCRIMINATION (1) 30	2.3	.82
ANTI-HITLER PLOT (1) 34	2.3	.67
APPELLATE JURISDICTION (5) 03 06 16 18 27	2.3	.48
ARMED ATTACK (1) 17	2.3	.48
ARMED NEUTRALITY (2) 06 29	2.3	.48
ARMISTICE OF 1940, FRENCH (1) 21	2.3	.67
ARTICLE 51 (UN CHARTER) (1) 20	2.3	.67
ATOMIZATION (1) 03	2.3	.94
AUSTERITY (1) 39	2.3	.67
AUTHORIZATION BILL (1) 27	2.3	.82
BATTLE OF MIDWAY (1) 03	2.3	.67
BATTLE OF SAN JUAN HILL (1) 22	2.3	.67
BEHAVIOR TESTS (1) 25	2.3	.82
BENEVOLENT NEUTRALITY (1) 17	2.3	.67
BIENNIAL SESSION (2) 06 18	2.3	.67
BIPARTY SYSTEM (2) 06 17	2.3	.82
BLACKMAIL, POLITICAL (1) 06	2.3	.67
BLANKET INJUNCTION (1) 16	2.3	.48
BOER WAR (3) 17 22 25	2.3	.48
BORDER WAR (1) 06	2.3	.48
BREACH OF A TREATY (1) 17	2.3	.48
BRICKER AMENDMENT PROPOSAL (6) 03 18 20 32 34 42	2.3	.67
BUDGET SESSION (1) 42	2.3	.67
CAMPAIGN ORATORY (1) 39	2.3	.67
CAMPAIGN PROMISES (1) 39	2.3	.48
CAPITALIST REVOLUTION (1) 22	2.3	.82
CAUSE (1) 43	2.3	.94
CESSATION OF HOSTILITIES (2) 16 17	2.3	.67
CHARTER (6) 03 06 16 17 18 27	2.3	.67
CITATION (1) 24	2.3	.67
CITY-COUNTY SEPARATION (2) 03 18	2.3	.48
CIVIL SERVICE REFORM ACT (2) 29 32	2.3	.67
CLAYTON ANTI-TRUST ACT (1914) (7) 03 06 16 18 22 27 32	2.3	.48
CLEAVAGE (3) 01 24 33	2.3	.82
CLOSED SESSION OF CONGRESS (1) 45	2.3	.48
CODE OF THE UNITED STATES (2) 18 27 32	2.3	.67

COLOMBO PLAN   2.3   .48
  (5) 03 11 17 20 34
COLORADO RIVER COMPACT   2.3   .67
  (3) 03 06 18
COMMISSION PLAN   2.3   .82
  (3) 03 06 18
COMMODITY AGREEMENT   2.3   .67
  (1) 20
COMMON-LAW MARRIAGE   2.3   .82
  (1) 16
COMMUNITY PROPERTY SYSTEM   2.3   .48
  (1) 45
COMPENSATION   2.3   .48
  (4) 06 16 17 30
COMPLY   2.3   .82
  (1) 17
CONDEMNATION PROCEEDINGS   2.3   .67
  (1) 42
CONFISCATION   2.3   .67
  (4) 06 16 24 27
CONNECTICUT COMPROMISE   2.3   .67
  (5) 06 16 18 27 32
CONSERVATION   2.3   .67
  (8) 06 11 16 18 25 27 30 32
CONSTITUTION, FRANCE   2.3   .82
  (1) 20
CONSULAR FUNCTIONS   2.3   .67
  (1) 11
CONSULAR PRIVILEGES AND   2.3   .67
  IMMUNITIES
  (2) 06 16
CONSUMER LEGISLATION   2.3   .48
  (1) 42 46
CONTRACT CLAUSE IN THE   2.3   .67
  CONSTITUTION
  (1) 45
CONTRIBUTORY NEGLIGENCE   2.3   .82
  (1) 06
CONTROLLED DISARMAMENT   2.3   .67
  (1) 17
CONVENTION   2.3   .82
  (9) 06 16 17 18 24 27 29 30 32
CONVERTIBILITY   2.3   .48
  (2) 03 20
COOPERATIVE MOVEMENT   2.3   .67
  (2) 19 35
COPYRIGHT   2.3   .67
  (5) 06 16 18 27 32
CORDON SANITAIRE   2.3   .67
  (1) 16
CORPORAL PUNISHMENT   2.3   .67
  (1) 06
CORPUS JURIS   2.3   .82
  (2) 03 22
COST-OF-LIVING ALLOWANCE   2.3   .67
  (2) 17 32
COUNTER-PROPOSALS   2.3   .67
  (1) 17
COUNTING OF VOTES   2.3   .82
  (1) 17
COURT DECISION   2.3   .67
  (1) 44

CRIMEA CONFERENCE   2.3   .82
  (3) 16 17 21
CRIMEAN WAR   2.3   .48
  (1) 17
CRIMINAL JURISDICTION   2.3   .67
  (2) 16 17
CRISIS AREAS   2.3   .67
  (1) 36
CRUSADES   2.3   .67
  (3) 16 22 25
CUTTING OF BUDGET APPROPRIATIONS   2.3   .67
  (1) 17
DARK AGES   2.3   .67
  (1) 22
DEBT, IMPRISONMENT FOR   2.3   .67
  (1) 45
DECLARATION OF RECIPROCITY   2.3   .67
  (1) 17
DECREE LAW   2.3   .82
  (2) 16 17
DEFOLIATE   2.3   .48
  (1) 39
DELIBERATE   2.3   .82
  (1) 30
DENIAL OF JUSTICE   2.3   .67
  (2) 03 17
DEPORTATION OF COMMUNISTS   2.3   .67
  (1) 18
DEPOSITION   2.3   .67
  (1) 45
DETECTION OF UNDERGROUND   2.3   .67
  NUCLEAR EXPLOSIONS
  (1) 17
DIPLOMATIC EXCHANGE   2.3   .67
  (1) 17
DIPLOMATIC REPRESENTATION   2.3   .48
  (1) 17
DIRECT INITIATIVE   2.3   .82
  (2) 06 18
DISABILITY INSURANCE   2.3   .67
  (1) 32
DISARMAMENT INSPECTION   2.3   .48
  (1) 36
DISCIPLINE IN THE HOUSE OF   2.3   .48
  REPRESENTATIVES
  (1) 45
DISCIPLINE IN THE SENATE   2.3   .48
  (1) 45
DISCRETIONARY   2.3   .67
  (2) 16 17
DISMISSAL FROM OFFICE   2.3   .67
  (2) 06 17
DISORDERLY CONDUCT   2.3   .67
  (1) 06
DISQUALIFICATION   2.3   .48
  (1) 06
DISTRICTING   2.3   .82
  (1) 32
DOCTRINE OF EQUALITY OF STATES   2.3   .82
  (1) 03
DOMESTIC JURISDICTION CLAUSE,   2.3   .82
  UNITED NATIONS
  (1) 20

DRAFT CARD BURNING	2.3	.67	EXCHANGE OF VIEWS	2.3	.67
(1) 32			(1) 17		
DRAFT REGISTRATION	2.3	.67	EXCISE	2.3	.82
(1) 16			(1) 45		
DREYFUS AFFAIR	2.3	.48	EXECUTIVE DISCRETION	2.3	.67
(4) 03 16 17 22			(1) 06		
DUMBARTON OAKS CONFERENCE,	2.3	.48	EXPROPRIATION (NATIONALIZATION)	2.3	.67
UNITED NATIONS			(7) 06 16 17 18 19 20 25		
(6) 03 16 20 21 32 34			EXPULSION OF MEMBERS	2.3	.67
DUTIES	2.3	.94	(1) 45		
(1) 24			EXTORTION	2.3	.67
EARMARKED REVENUES	2.3	.67	(1) 45		
(3) 03 16 18			EXTRA-CONSTITUTIONAL	2.3	.48
ECONOMIC AID	2.3	.48	(3) 03 06 45		
(1) 36			EXTRALEGAL	2.3	.67
ECONOMIC LAW	2.3	.82	(2) 06 16		
(1) 23			FAIR EMPLOYMENT PRACTICES LAWS	2.3	.67
ECONOMIC PENETRATION	2.3	.48	(2) 03 18		
(1) 16			FAIR TRADE LAWS	2.3	.67
EDUCATION GRANT	2.3	.67	(2) 32 42		
(1) 17			FEDERAL COMMUNICATIONS ACT OF	2.3	.82
EFFECT	2.3	.94	1934		
(3) 02 17 24			(2) 18 32		
EFFECTIVE DATE OF APPOINTMENT	2.3	.67	FEDERAL CORRUPT PRACTICES ACT	2.3	.67
(1) 17			(1) 42		
EFFECTIVENESS	2.3	.94	FEDERAL RESERVE NOTES	2.3	.67
(1) 24			(1) 06 18 45		
ELASTIC CLAUSE (NECESSARY AND	2.3	.82	FEDERAL SERVICE ENTRANCE	2.3	.67
PROPER CLAUSE)			EXAMINATION		
(5) 06 16 18 27 32			(2) 03 18		
ELECTION DAY	2.3	.67	FINAL SOLUTION	2.3	.48
(1) 17			(1) 39		
ELECTIONEERING	2.3	.67	FINDINGS	2.3	.67
(1) 45			(2) 06 24		
ELECTORAL FRAUD	2.3	.67	FINNISH-RUSSIAN WAR	2.3	.48
(1) 17			(1) 34		
ELECTRIC VOTING	2.3	.67	FISCAL ADMINISTRATION	2.3	.82
(2) 06 16			(1) 12		
ELEVENTH AMENDMENT	2.3	.67	FISCAL INTEGRITY	2.3	.82
(2) 06 18			(1) 39		
EMANCIPATION	2.3	.67	FIXED-TERM APPOINTMENT	2.3	.48
(2) 06 45			(1) 17		
EMERGENCY LAW	2.3	.48	FORCED LABOR	2.3	.67
(4) 06 16 17 33			(1) 45		
EMIGRATION	2.3	.67	FOREIGN INVESTMENT	2.3	.48
(4) 16 17 20 30			(2) 11 25		
EMOLUMENTS	2.3	.82	FOREIGN MILITARY ASSISTANCE	2.3	.48
(2) 06 16			(1) 36		
ENACTING CLAUSE	2.3	.67	FRANCHISE	2.3	.82
(3) 06 16 27			(5) 06 16 17 18 25		
ENCIRCLEMENT	2.3	.48	FREE SILVER	2.3	.67
(2) 16 17			(1) 06 46		
ENLIGHTENMENT	2.3	.82	FREE SPEECH MOVEMENT	2.3	.48
(6) 03 08 22 24 25 26			(1) 25		
ENOSIS (CYPRUS)	2.3	.48	FREEDOM MOVEMENT	2.3	.67
(2) 03 34			(1) 17		
EQUAL EMPLOYMENT OPPORTUNITIES	2.3	.67	FREEDOM OF CONTRACT	2.3	.67
(1) 46			(1) 06		
EQUIVALENCE	2.3	.67	FREEDOM OF ENTRY	2.3	.67
(1) 43			(1) 45		
ESCALATOR CLAUSE	2.3	.48	FREEDOM OF OPINION	2.3	.82
(4) 06 16 29 32			(2) 11 17		

FREQUENCY	2.3	.82
(1) 30		
FRINGE BENEFIT	2.3	.48
(1) 32		
FUGITIVE SLAVE LAWS	2.3	.67
(2) 02 06		
FULL FAITH AND CREDIT CLAUSE	2.3	.82
(7) 03 06 16 18 27 32 34		
FULL POWERS	2.3	.48
(2) 16 17		
GAS WARFARE	2.3	.67
(2) 16 17		
GASOLINE TAX	2.3	.67
(2) 06 16		
GENERAL FUND	2.3	.67
(3) 03 06 16		
GENTLEMEN'S AGREEMENT	2.3	.67
(1) 16 17 21 46		
GOAL	2.3	.82
(4) 01 04 30 43		
GOLD RESERVE SYSTEM	2.3	.67
(1) 32		
GOVERNMENT BY EXECUTIVE COMMITTEE	2.3	.67
(1) 17		
GRADUATED UNILATERAL DISARMAMENT	2.3	.67
(1) 36		
GREEN REVOLUTION	2.3	.67
(1) 25		
GUN CONTROL LEGISLATION	2.3	.48
(2) 32 42		
HAGUE CONVENTIONS	2.3	.67
(3) 16 17 21		
HAGUE PEACE CONFERENCES (1899, 1907)	2.3	.82
(4) 03 16 17 20		
HARE SYSTEM	2.3	.82
(8) 03 06 16 18 22 32 33 44		
HEAD TAX	2.3	.67
(2) 06 16		
HEALTH CARE	2.3	.67
(4) 07 11 19 30		
HEARING	2.3	.82
(1) 45		
HOLY WAR	2.3	.67
(1) 17		
HORSE-TRADING	2.3	.67
(1) 39		
HORSESHOE SEATING ARRANGEMENT	2.3	.67
(1) 17		
HOUSE-DIVIDED SPEECH	2.3	.67
(1) 06		
HOUSING ACT OF 1949	2.3	.67
(1) 18		
HOUSING LEGISLATION	2.3	.48
(1) 42		
HUNGARIAN REVOLUTION OF 1956	2.3	.48
(2) 03 22		
IMMIGRATION ACT OF 1965	2.3	.82
(1) 18		
IMMINENT THREAT	2.3	.67
(1) 17		
IMMUNIZATION	2.3	.82
(1) 45		
IMPORTANT QUESTION, UNITED NATIONS	2.3	.48
(1) 20		
INCENTIVE SYSTEM	2.3	.67
(2) 37 45		
INCOME	2.3	.82
(4) 11 24 25 30		
INCRIMINATION	2.3	.48
(1) 06		
INDEMNIFICATION	2.3	.48
(1) 06		
INDIRECT RULE	2.3	.48
(2) 03 34		
INDIRECT TAX	2.3	.48
(2) 06 16		
INEQUITIES	2.3	.82
(1) 30		
INFILTRATE	2.3	.67
(3) 16 17 30		
INFORMATION MANAGEMENT	2.3	.67
(1) 37		
INQUISITION	2.3	.67
(4) 03 09 16 22		
INTERIM AGREEMENT	2.3	.67
(1) 17		
INTERNAL IMPROVEMENTS	2.3	.82
(1) 16 29 46		
INTERNATIONAL ADMINISTRATION	2.3	.82
(1) 03		
INTERNATIONAL ECONOMIC LAW	2.3	.67
(1) 11		
INTERNATIONAL PUBLIC LAW	2.3	.48
(1) 17		
INTERNATIONAL TECHNICAL ASSISTANCE	2.3	.67
(1) 23		
INTERNATIONAL TRUSTEESHIP SYSTEM	2.3	.48
(1) 17		
INTERNECINE CONFLICT	2.3	.48
(1) 17		
INTERNMENT	2.3	.67
(2) 06 17		
INTERPOSITION	2.3	.67
(4) 18 27 29 32		
INTERVENE	2.3	.67
(1) 17		
INTRASTATE COMMERCE	2.3	.67
(4) 06 16 18 27		
INVALID BALLOT	2.3	.48
(1) 17		
ISSUES	2.3	.82
(3) 16 24 33		
IUS SOLI	2.3	.67
(1) 16		
JOB ANALYSIS	2.3	.82
(1) 37		
JUDGE MADE LAW (COMMON LAW)	2.3	.67
(3) 06 16 18		
JUDICIARY ACT OF 1789	2.3	.67
(2) 18 32		

KELLOGG-BRIAND PACT (TREATY FOR RENUNCIATION OF WAR) (6) 06 16 17 20 21 38	2.3	.48
KENNEDY ROUND TARIFF NEGOTIATIONS (5) 17 18 20 32 34	2.3	.82
KING COTTON (1) 29	2.3	.67
LABOR STANDARDS ACT OF 1938 (1) 32	2.3	.67
LABOR-MANAGEMENT RELATIONS (1) 37	2.3	.82
LAND TENURE (1) 25	2.3	.48
LAND VALUE TAX (1) 25	2.3	.48
LARCENY (1) 06	2.3	.82
LATIFUNDIA SYSTEM (LATIFUNDISMO) (2) 03 20	2.3	.82
LAW OF THE LAND (1) 32	2.3	.67
LAW OF TORTS (1) 25	2.3	.67
LAW-MAKING TREATY (2) 17 20	2.3	.67
LEAK (1) 27	2.3	.67
LEGAL ACTION (1) 36	2.3	.67
LEGAL FICTION (1) 06	2.3	.67
LICENSING (2) 03 20	2.3	.82
LIFE CYCLE (1) 15	2.3	.67
LIGHTNING WAR (1) 17	2.3	.67
LONG-TERM APPOINTMENT (1) 17	2.3	.67
LONG-TERM BORROWING (1) 45	2.3	.67
LOOSE CONSTRUCTION (4) 16 18 27 32	2.3	.82
MAIDEN SPEECH (1) 39	2.3	.48
MALNUTRITION (1) 41	2.3	.67
MANIPULATION OF ELECTIONS (1) 17	2.3	.67
MANSLAUGHTER (1) 16	2.3	.67
MANUFACTURING (1) 30	2.3	.94
MARGINAL (2) 24 30	2.3	.67
MARGINALITY (2) 11 30	2.3	.67
MARITIME LAW (3) 06 16 32	2.3	.67
MASS MEETING (2) 17 29	2.3	.67
MASS PRODUCTION (1) 45	2.3	.48
MATCHING FUNDS (1) 42	2.3	.48
MCCARTHY-ARMY HEARINGS (1) 02	2.3	.67
MEIJI, THE REIGN OF EMPEROR MUTSUHITO OF JAPAN (2) 24 25	2.3	.67
MILITARY AND STRATEGIC POLICIES (1) 07	2.3	.67
MILITARY POLICY (3) 12 17 20	2.3	.67
MINISTER POWERS (1) 06	2.3	.82
MISCEGENATION (1) 29	2.3	.67
MISFEASANCE (2) 16 17	2.3	.67
MOLOTOV-RIBBENTROP PACT (2) 03 34	2.3	.48
MONOPOLY LEGISLATION (1) 42	2.3	.67
MONOPOLY OF POLITICAL POWER (1) 25	2.3	.48
MORAL REARMAMENT (2) 22 34	2.3	.48
MUNICH ACCORD (4) 16 17 21 34	2.3	.67
MUNICIPAL OWNERSHIP (2) 06 16	2.3	.67
MURDER (2) 25 30	2.3	.82
NAT TURNER'S INSURRECTION (1) 06	2.3	.82
NATIONAL DEFENSE (PROTECTIONISM) (2) 17 20	2.3	.67
NATIONAL HONOR (1) 16	2.3	.82
NATIONAL INDUSTRIAL RECOVERY ACT (NIRA) (4) 06 16 22 32	2.3	.48
NAVAL BLOCKADE (1) 17	2.3	.48
NAVAL SUPREMACY (1) 17	2.3	.48
NAZIFICATION OF GERMANY (1) 17	2.3	.48
NEGLIGENCE (1) 06	2.3	.82
NEUTRALITY ACTS (2) 16 34	2.3	.48
NEW ECONOMIC POLICY OF THE U.S.S.R. (6) 03 10 16 24 25 34	2.3	.67
NEW JERSEY PLAN (4) 03 18 27 32	2.3	.67
NO-WIN POLICY (1) 39	2.3	.48
NON-EXTRADITION (1) 17	2.3	.67
NON-RETROACTIVE LAWS (1) 17	2.3	.67

NUREMBERG PRINCIPLES 2.3 .67
(1) 41
OATH OF ALLEGIANCE 2.3 .48
(2) 03 17
OATH OF OFFICE 2.3 .48
(2) 16 27
OBITER DICTUM (INCIDENTAL OPINION) 2.3 .67
(5) 02 06 16 18 32
OBLIGATION 2.3 .82
(1) 43
OBSERVANCE OF TREATIES 2.3 .67
(1) 17
OFFICE-BLOCK BALLOT 2.3 .82
(5) 03 06 16 18 32
OLD AGE AND SURVIVORS INSURANCE 2.3 .48
(OASI)
(1) 27
OMNIBUS BILL 2.3 .67
(4) 02 06 24 29
OPIUM WARS 2.3 .48
(2) 03 16
OPTIONAL CLAUSE 2.3 .67
(7) 03 06 16 17 18 20 21
ORDINARY SESSION 2.3 .48
(1) 17
ORGANIZATION DEVELOPMENT 2.3 .94
(1) 37
OUTCOME 2.3 .82
(1) 24
OUTER SPACE AND INTERNATIONAL 2.3 .67
LAW
(3) 17 23 25
OUTLAWRY OF WAR 2.3 .67
(3) 06 16 17
OVERSIGHT 2.3 .82
(1) 24
PACIFIC SETTLEMENT OF 2.3 .82
INTERNATIONAL DISPUTES
(4) 06 16 18 32
PALESTINE MANDATE 2.3 .67
(1) 03
PANACEA 2.3 .67
(1) 45
PARDON 2.3 .67
(6) 06 16 17 18 27 32
PARLIAMENTARY DIPLOMACY 2.3 .82
(2) 03 20
PARTY FINANCE 2.3 .48
(1) 06
PARTY RALLY 2.3 .67
(1) 17
PEACE OF WESTPHALIA 2.3 .48
(2) 17 25
PEACE OVERTURE 2.3 .67
(1) 17
PEACEFUL RELATIONS 2.3 .67
(1) 17
PERMANENT APPOINTMENT 2.3 .82
(1) 17
PERMANENT NEUTRALITY 2.3 .48
(1) 17
PICKETING 2.3 .67
(4) 06 18 27 32

PLENARY SESSION 2.3 .48
(4) 06 16 17 27
PLURAL VOTING 2.3 .67
(2) 06 16
POINT FOUR PROGRAM 2.3 .48
(4) 20 27 32 34
POLEMICS 2.3 .67
(3) 13 17 30
POLICY OF FAIT ACCOMPLI 2.3 .82
(1) 17
POLITICAL ACTIVITY 2.3 .82
(1) 37
POLITICAL CONSEQUENCES 2.3 .67
(1) 08
POLITICAL HONEYMOON 2.3 .67
(1) 02
POLITICAL LAW 2.3 .67
(1) 19
POLITICAL PRACTICES 2.3 .82
(1) 08
POLLUTION 2.3 .82
(1) 43
POPULATION POLICY 2.3 .67
(1) 17
PORK BARREL 2.3 .67
(4) 06 16 27 29
POSITIONS OF STRENGTH 2.3 .82
(1) 39
POTSDAM AGREEMENT 2.3 .48
(1) 38
POTSDAM CONFERENCE (1945) 2.3 .48
(5) 03 16 17 20 34
POVERTY 2.3 .67
(3) 07 11 30
PREFERENTIAL TRADE AGREEMENTS 2.3 .67
(1) 20 45
PREPARATIONS FOR WAR 2.3 .48
(1) 17
PRESIDENT'S ECONOMIC MESSAGE 2.3 .67
(2) 02 32
PRESIDENT'S OATH OF OFFICE 2.3 .67
(1) 27
PRESIDENTIAL DISABILITY 2.3 .48
(2) 03 32
PRESIDENTIAL MESSAGE 2.3 .48
(1) 44
PRESSURE 2.3 .67
(2) 24 30
PREVENTION OF SPREAD OF NUCLEAR 2.3 .48
WEAPONS
(1) 36
PREVENTIVE DIPLOMACY 2.3 .82
(1) 20
PREVENTIVE MEASURES 2.3 .67
(1) 17
PRICE SUPPORT 2.3 .67
(3) 03 18 27
PRICE WAR 2.3 .67
(1) 45
PRIMA FACIE EVIDENCE 2.3 .67
(1) 32
PRINCIPLE OF RECIPROCITY 2.3 .48
(1) 17

PRIOR RESTRAINT	2.3	.82
(1) 32		
PRIORITIES	2.3	.82
(2) 16 30		
PRIVATE LAW	2.3	.48
(5) 02 03 06 16 19		
PRIVATE MEMBER'S BILL	2.3	.67
(2) 16 17		
PRIVILEGE	2.3	.82
(5) 03 06 18 24 25		
PROCEDURAL MOTION	2.3	.67
(1) 17		
PROCEDURAL SYSTEMS	2.3	.67
(1) 25		
PROCLAMATION OF A STATE OF	2.3	.48
EMERGENCY		
(1) 17		
PROHIBITION OF LIQUOR, EIGHTEENTH	2.3	.67
AMENDMENT		
(1) 25		
PROJECT HEAD START	2.3	.48
(1) 42		
PROPERTY QUALIFICATIONS	2.3	.48
(4) 03 16 17 18		
PROTECTIVE CUSTODY	2.3	.67
(1) 16		
PROVISO	2.3	.48
(1) 17		
PUBLIC DOMAIN	2.3	.48
(4) 06 16 18 27		
PUBLIC ENTERPRISE AND PLANNING	2.3	.82
(1) 12		
PUBLIC INTERNATIONAL LAW	2.3	.67
(1) 16		
PUBLIC REVENUE	2.3	.82
(1) 16		
PUBLIC TRIAL	2.3	.48
(1) 44		
PURE FOOD AND DRUG ACTS	2.3	.67
(2) 16 32		
PYRRHIC VICTORY	2.3	.48
(1) 16		
QUALIFIED TO VOTE	2.3	.48
(1) 17		
QUASI-JUDICIAL	2.3	.82
(1) 18		
RACIAL DISCRIMINATION	2.3	.67
(3) 06 11 17		
RACIAL PROBLEM	2.3	.82
(1) 17		
RADICAL (REFORM)	2.3	.48
(1) 29		
RATIONING	2.3	.48
(2) 06 25		
REAL WAGES	2.3	.67
(1) 32		
REARMAMENT	2.3	.48
(2) 08 17		
REASON OF STATE	2.3	.82
(3) 10 16 17		
RECIPROCAL TRADE AGREEMENTS	2.3	.67
(1) 45		

RECOGNITION OF BELLIGERENCY	2.3	.48
(1) 17		
RECOUNT	2.3	.67
(1) 16		
RED TAPE	2.3	.82
(4) 06 16 17 27		
REFUGEE PROBLEM	2.3	.48
(2) 17 23		
REGULATION (RULE)	2.3	.82
(1) 33		
REGULATION OF BUSINESS	2.3	.67
(1) 32		
REGULATORY TAX	2.3	.82
(1) 18		
REICHSTAG FIRE	2.3	.48
(2) 16 17		
REIGN OF TERROR	2.3	.48
(2) 22 29		
RELIGIOUS TEST	2.3	.82
(3) 03 06 18		
RELIGIOUS WAR	2.3	.48
(1) 17		
REMEDIAL LEGISLATION	2.3	.48
(1) 44		
RENUNCIATION OF CITIZENSHIP	2.3	.48
(1) 32		
REPRIEVE	2.3	.67
(5) 06 16 17 18 32		
REQUEST FOR EXTRADITION	2.3	.48
(1) 17		
RESTRICTED SUFFRAGE	2.3	.67
(1) 17		
RESTRICTIVE COVENANT	2.3	.48
(2) 18 32		
RHINELAND REMILITARIZATION	2.3	.48
(1) 16		
RIGGED CONVENTION	2.3	.48
(1) 39		
RIGHT OF ENTRY	2.3	.67
(1) 45		
RIGHT OF SELF-DEFENSE	2.3	.67
(1) 17		
RIGHT OF VETO	2.3	.48
(1) 17		
RIGHT TO BE PRESUMED INNOCENT	2.3	.67
UNTIL PROVEN GUILTY		
(1) 17		
RIGHT TO WORK LAWS	2.3	.48
(1) 42		
RIOT	2.3	.82
(7) 06 07 11 16 17 25 30		
RITUAL	2.3	.67
(1) 24		
ROME TREATY, EEC (1957)	2.3	.82
(3) 17 20 34		
RULE OF PROCEDURE	2.3	.67
(1) 17		
RULE OF UNANIMITY	2.3	.48
(1) 16		
RULE 22 OF THE SENATE	2.3	.67
(1) 18		
RURAL ELECTRIFICATION	2.3	.67
(1) 18		

RUSS-JAPANESE WAR   2.3   .48
  (1) 17
RUSSO-FINNISH WAR   2.3   .48
  (2) 03 34
RUSSO-JAPANESE PACT   2.3   .48
  (1) 21
SANCTIONS (DISARMAMENT   2.3   .48
  ENFORCEMENT)
  (1) 20
SCARCITY   2.3   .82
  (2) 24 30
SCHOOL LUNCH PROGRAM   2.3   .48
  (1) 45
SCOPES EVOLUTION TRIAL   2.3   .48
  (1) 22
SCORCHED-EARTH POLICY   2.3   .48
  (1) 17
SECOND AMENDMENT   2.3   .67
  (1) 18
SECONDARY BOYCOTT   2.3   .48
  (3) 18 27 32
SECURITIES ACT OF 1933   2.3   .48
  (2) 18 32
SECURITIES EXCHANGE ACT OF 1934   2.3   .48
  (2) 06 18
SELECTIVE SERVICE ACT   2.3   .67
  (1) 42
SHOW-OF-HANDS VOTE   2.3   .67
  (1) 17
SINO-JAPANESE WAR   2.3   .48
  (3) 24 25 34
SLAVERY COMPROMISE   2.3   .48
  (1) 42
SLUM CLEARANCE   2.3   .67
  (6) 04 06 16 24 25 30
SOCIAL WELFARE LEGISLATION   2.3   .48
  (1) 22
SOUTHWEST AFRICA QUESTION   2.3   .48
  (2) 20 41
SPACE EXPLORATION AND USE   2.3   .67
  (3) 07 11 30
SPECIAL SESSION   2.3   .67
  (5) 06 16 18 27 32
STAGGERED TERM   2.3   .48
  (1) 42
STAMP ACT (1765)   2.3   .67
  (2) 03 06 46
STATE AID   2.3   .67
  (4) 03 06 16 18
STATE CONTROL   2.3   .82
  (1) 17
STATE OF HOSTILITIES   2.3   .67
  (1) 03
STATE OF SIEGE   2.3   .48
  (2) 03 17
STATUS QUO POLICY   2.3   .48
  (1) 20
STATUTE   2.3   .67
  (9) 02 06 16 17 18 20 24 27 30
STRAW POLL   2.3   .48
  (1) 39
STRUGGLE FOR POWER   2.3   .67
  (1) 17

STUDENT POWER   2.3   .67
  (1) 15
SUBSISTENCE FARMING   2.3   .48
  (1) 45
SUCCESSION   2.3   .67
  (3) 03 16 24
SUEZ CRISIS OF 1956   2.3   .48
  (1) 11 17 34 46
SUMMIT   2.3   .67
  (1) 30
SURPRISE ATTACK ON PEARL HARBOR   2.3   .48
  (1) 17
SUSPENSION OF RULES   2.3   .48
  (4) 06 16 18 32
TARIFF WAR   2.3   .48
  (1) 16
TAX SHARING   2.3   .94
  (2) 18 32
TEAPOT DOME SCANDAL   2.3   .48
  (3) 03 06 16
TECHNOLOGICAL DEVELOPMENTS   2.3   .67
  (3) 11 24 25
TEHERAN CONFERENCE   2.3   .67
  (5) 03 16 17 21 34
TERMS OF CONGRESS   2.3   .48
  (1) 42
TERRITORIAL ASYLUM   2.3   .67
  (1) 17
TERRITORIAL INTEGRITY   2.3   .48
  (2) 16 17
TERRITORIAL SUPREMACY   2.3   .48
  (1) 17
TEST BAN   2.3   .48
  (1) 36
TET OFFENSIVE IN 1968   2.3   .48
  (1) 25
THOUGHT CONTROL   2.3   .67
  (1) 16
THREE-FIFTHS COMPROMISE,   2.3   .67
  CONSTITUTIONAL CONVENTION
  (1) 06 16 18 32
TOKENISM   2.3   .67
  (1) 30
TORT   2.3   .67
  (5) 03 06 18 27 32
TOTAL WAR   2.3   .48
  (4) 04 17 20 27
TRADITIONAL ORDER   2.3   .82
  (1) 15
TREATIES OF WESTPHALIA   2.3   .67
  (1) 16
TREATY DENUNCIATION   2.3   .67
  (1) 20
TREATY OF ALLIANCE   2.3   .67
  (1) 17
TREATY OF BREST-LITOVSK   2.3   .48
  (1) 03
TREATY OF MUTUAL ASSISTANCE   2.3   .48
  (1) 19
TREATY OF PARIS   2.3   .67
  (3) 06 17 34
TRUCE (ARMISTICE)   2.3   .48
  (1) 20

TRUSTEESHIP 2.3 .48
  (3) 16 24 42
TURNOUT 2.3 .82
  (1) 39
TWO CHINAS PROPOSAL, UNITED 2.3 .48
NATIONS
  (4) 03 20 25 34
TYRANNICIDE 2.3 .67
  (3) 03 16 26
U.S. CENSUS 2.3 .48
  (1) 32
U.S. CODE ANNOTATED 2.3 .82
  (1) 44
UNANIMOUS 2.3 .82
  (1) 17
UNDISTRIBUTED PROFITS 2.3 .67
  (1) 45
UNEMPLOYMENT COMPENSATION 2.3 .67
  (1) 37
UNEQUAL TREATIES 2.3 .67
  (2) 03 20
UNFAIR LABOR PRACTICE 2.3 .67
  (2) 18 32
UNIFORM STATE LAWS 2.3 .82
  (2) 06 18
URBAN-RURAL REPRESENTATION 2.3 .48
  (1) 42
VOTE BY A SHOW OF HANDS 2.3 .82
  (1) 17
WAGE FLOOR 2.3 .82
  (1) 16
WAR OF EXTERMINATION 2.3 .67
  (1) 17
WAR ON TWO FRONTS 2.3 .67
  (1) 17
WARRANT, ARREST 2.3 .67
  (1) 42
WELFARE AND PUBLIC ASSISTANCE 2.3 .67
  (1) 07
WESTWARD MOVEMENT 2.3 .82
  (1) 46
WHITE PRIMARY 2.3 .82
  (7) 03 06 16 18 27 32 34
WILDCAT STRIKE 2.3 .48
  (1) 32
WORLD DOMINATION 2.3 .67
  (1) 17
WORLD UNITY 2.3 .82
  (1) 36
WORLD WAR III 2.3 .82
  (1) 22
ZONING LAWS 2.3 .48
  (1) 45
ABATEMENT 2.4 .51
  (2) 06 16
ABILITY TESTS 2.4 .69
  (1) 37
ABUSE OF OFFICE 2.4 .69
  (1) 17
ACCESS 2.4 .84
  (4) 01 17 30 33
ACT OF CHAPULTEPEC OF 1945 2.4 .51
  (5) 03 18 20 21 34

ACT OF STATE DOCTRINE 2.4 .84
  (1) 11
ACTION 2.4 .84
  (4) 06 25 30 32
ACTIVISM VERSUS SELF-RESTRAINT 2.4 .84
  (1) 18
ADJOURNMENT SINE DIE 2.4 .69
  (1) 27
ADMINISTRATIVE ACTS 2.4 .69
  (1) 19
ADMINISTRATIVE ORDER 2.4 .69
  (3) 06 16 18
ADOPTION 2.4 .69
  (1) 17
ADVISORY REFERENDUM 2.4 .69
  (1) 18
AID 2.4 .84
  (1) 27
ALASKA, PURCHASE OF 2.4 .51
  (1) 46
ALLEGATION 2.4 .84
  (1) 06
AMERICAN DEBT 2.4 .69
  (1) 21
ANTARCTIC TREATY OF 1959 2.4 .69
  (1) 20
ANTI-AMERICAN 2.4 .69
  (1) 29
ANTI-MONOPOLY LEGISLATION 2.4 .69
  (1) 42
APPOINT 2.4 .84
  (1) 17
ARBITRATION, INTERNATIONAL 2.4 .51
  (1) 18
ARMS PROCUREMENT 2.4 .51
  (1) 11
ARRAIGNMENT 2.4 .69
  (3) 06 18 27
ASSESSMENT 2.4 .69
  (5) 03 06 16 18 24
ASSUMPTION 2.4 .84
  (2) 01 03
ATTACK 2.4 .69
  (1) 17
AUSTRALIA-NEW ZEALAND-UNITED 2.4 .51
STATES DEFENSE TREATY (ANZUS)
  (2) 25 32
AUSTRO-PRUSSIAN WAR 2.4 .51
  (1) 17
BAIL 2.4 .69
  (5) 03 06 18 25 27
BALKAN WARS 2.4 .51
  (1) 16
BANK DEPOSIT INSURANCE 2.4 .69
  (1) 45
BANK HOLIDAY 2.4 .69
  (2) 06 16
BANKRUPTCY LAWS 2.4 .51
  (2) 03 45
BASIC LAW 2.4 .69
  (1) 17
BASTILLE DAY 2.4 .51
  (1) 16

BEER-HALL PUTSCH OF 1923	2.4	.51
(2) 16 22		
BILL DRAFTING	2.4	.69
(2) 06 18		
BILL READINGS	2.4	.51
(1) 42		
BLACK RECONSTRUCTION	2.4	.51
(1) 46		
BLANK VOTE	2.4	.69
(1) 17		
BLANKET BALLOT	2.4	.69
(3) 06 16 32		
BLOOD-AND-SOIL CONCEPT	2.4	.51
(1) 16		
BOMBING PAUSE	2.4	.51
(1) 39		
BONDAGE	2.4	.69
(1) 06		
BROKERED CONVENTION	2.4	.69
(1) 39		
CAIRO CONFERENCE OF 1943	2.4	.51
(3) 03 16 34		
CAMPAIGN TRAIL	2.4	.51
(1) 39		
CANVASS	2.4	.51
(4) 06 16 27 29		
CAPITULATION	2.4	.51
(6) 03 06 16 17 20 21		
CASTING VOTE	2.4	.69
(3) 06 16 17		
CATALYTIC WAR	2.4	.84
(1) 03		
CEDE	2.4	.69
(1) 17		
CHAOS	2.4	.69
(1) 30		
CHARGE TO THE JURY	2.4	.51
(2) 02 18		
CHECK-OFF SYSTEM	2.4	.69
(1) 45		
CITIZENSHIP TRAINING	2.4	.69
(1) 15		
CIVIL RIGHTS ACT OF 1870	2.4	.51
(1) 18		
CIVIL SERVICE ACT OF 1940	2.4	.69
(1) 18		
CIVIL SERVICE, REFORMS	2.4	.69
(1) 46		
CLAIM	2.4	.69
(3) 06 17 19		
CODE	2.4	.69
(6) 03 06 16 17 18 24		
COMBAT	2.4	.69
(2) 24 30		
COMMAND	2.4	.51
(3) 17 24 30		
COMMUNICATIONS, INTERNATIONAL	2.4	.84
(1) 23		
COMMUNITY BUILDING	2.4	.51
(1) 11		
COMPROMISE OF 1877	2.4	.51
(1) 08 46		

CONCESSION	2.4	.69
(2) 16 17		
CONCURRENT LEGISLATION	2.4	.51
(1) 17		
CONFER	2.4	.69
(1) 17		
CONGRESSIONAL JUNKETS	2.4	.51
(1) 42		
CONQUEST	2.4	.69
(2) 06 16		
CONSCRIPTION ACT	2.4	.69
(1) 22		
CONSTITUENT FUNCTION	2.4	.51
(1) 03		
CONSTITUTION OF SOVIET UNION	2.4	.69
(2) 16 20		
CONSTITUTIONAL CONVENTIONS, STATE	2.4	.69
(1) 42		
CONSTRUCT	2.4	.84
(1) 30		
CONSULTATION	2.4	.69
(2) 11 17		
CONTINENTAL SYSTEM	2.4	.69
(1) 17		
CONTINUITY OF THE STATE	2.4	.84
(1) 17		
CONTRACT CLAUSE	2.4	.84
(4) 03 06 18 32		
CONTRACTUAL RIGHTS	2.4	.69
(1) 06		
CORRECTION OF THE MINUTES	2.4	.51
(1) 17		
COST-PUSH	2.4	.51
(1) 39		
COUNTER-REFORMATION	2.4	.51
(4) 09 11 17 26		
COURT PACKING PROPOSALS	2.4	.69
(1) 16		
CRIMINAL COMMON LAW	2.4	.69
(1) 44		
CRITICAL	2.4	.69
(1) 30		
CULT OF THE INDIVIDUAL, SOVIET UNION	2.4	.69
(2) 03 20		
CULTURAL AGREEMENT	2.4	.69
(1) 17		
CZECH CRISIS	2.4	.51
(1) 17		
DEADLOCK	2.4	.69
(2) 06 17		
DECIDE	2.4	.96
(1) 17		
DECODE	2.4	.69
(1) 17		
DECONTROL	2.4	.69
(1) 24		
DEFAMATION	2.4	.69
(1) 45		
DEFERMENT	2.4	.69
(1) 37		
DEFICIENCY BILL	2.4	.84
(3) 06 16 32		

DELIBERATION   2.4   .84
  (1) 43
DELINQUENCY   2.4   .84
  (3) 06 16 30
DEMONSTRATION CITIES ACT   2.4   .69
  (2) 32 42
DENUNCIATION   2.4   .69
  (2) 06 16
DERELICTION   2.4   .69
  (2) 16 17
DETENTION   2.4   .69
  (2) 17 32
DETERMINATION OF THE AGGRESSOR   2.4   .69
  (1) 17
DEVELOPMENT DECADE   2.4   .84
  (1) 41
DEVELOPMENT LOANS   2.4   .69
  (1) 20
DILATORY POLICY   2.4   .69
  (1) 17
DIRECT ACTION   2.4   .69
  (5) 06 10 16 22 33
DIRECT EVIDENCE   2.4   .84
  (1) 32
DISAGREEMENT   2.4   .84
  (1) 43
DISARMAMENT PLANS   2.4   .51
  (1) 36
DISCHARGE CALENDAR   2.4   .69
  (1) 18
DISCIPLINARY POWER   2.4   .51
  (1) 17
DISCLOSURE   2.4   .69
  (1) 43
DISCLOSURE OF INFORMATION ACT   2.4   .69
  (1) 32
DISCONTENT   2.4   .69
  (2) 24 30
DISCUSSION   2.4   .84
  (2) 17 24
DISESTABLISHMENT   2.4   .51
  (1) 16
DISORDER   2.4   .51
  (1) 30
DISPENSING POWER   2.4   .69
  (1) 06
DISPUTE SETTLEMENT (PEACEFUL   2.4   .69
  SETTLEMENT)
  (1) 20
DISUNITY   2.4   .84
  (2) 24 30
DIVISION VOTE   2.4   .69
  (1) 27
DOCTRINE   2.4   .69
  (2) 17 24
DOCTRINE OF SUPREMACY OF   2.4   .84
  NATIONAL LAW
  (1) 17
DRAFT   2.4   .51
  (6) 06 16 17 27 30 32
DRUG ABUSE   2.4   .69
  (1) 37

DUAL SYSTEM OF GOVERNMENT   2.4   .51
  (1) 42
DUMPING   2.4   .69
  (4) 06 16 20 32
DURATION OF OFFICE   2.4   .69
  (1) 17
EARMARKED TAX   2.4   .69
  (1) 42
ECONOMIC ORDER   2.4   .69
  (1) 17
ECONOMY OF ABUNDANCE   2.4   .51
  (1) 45
EFFECTIVE BLOCKADE   2.4   .51
  (1) 17
EGYPTIAN REVOLUTION OF 1952   2.4   .51
  (1) 08
ELECTION PLEDGE   2.4   .69
  (1) 17
ELECTIONEERING CAMPAIGN   2.4   .69
  (3) 17 19 29
ELEMENTARY AND SECONDARY   2.4   .51
  EDUCATION ACT OF 1965
  (2) 18 42
ENACTMENT   2.4   .69
  (3) 06 16 17
ENCROACHMENT   2.4   .51
  (2) 10 17
ENERGY POLICY   2.4   .51
  (1) 07
EQUAL   2.4   .84
  (1) 24
EQUALIZATION OF ASSESSMENTS   2.4   .69
  (1) 06
EQUITY (EX AEQUO ET BONO)   2.4   .84
  (1) 20
ERA OF GOOD FEELING   2.4   .69
  (2) 06 29 46
ESPIONAGE ACT OF 1917   2.4   .69
  (5) 03 06 16 22 32 46
EXCHANGE OF NOTES   2.4   .51
  (1) 17
EXECUTE   2.4   .84
  (2) 16 17
EXHAUSTION OF LOCAL REMEDIES   2.4   .51
  (2) 17 24
EXPLOITATION OF MAN BY MAN   2.4   .69
  (1) 17
EXPULSION   2.4   .69
  (6) 06 16 17 18 20 32
FACTORY SYSTEM   2.4   .69
  (1) 32
FALLBACK POSITION   2.4   .51
  (1) 39
FAMINE   2.4   .69
  (1) 43
FEDERAL ELECTORAL ACT   2.4   .69
  (1) 17
FEDERAL TRADE COMMISSION ACT OF   2.4   .51
  1914
  (2) 18 19
FINANCE, INTERNATIONAL   2.4   .69
  (1) 41

FISHING ON THE HIGH SEAS   2.4   .51
  (1) 03
FISSION   2.4   .69
  (1) 24
FIVE YEAR PLANS   2.4   .69
  (5) 06 16 17 22 26
FLOOR FIGHT   2.4   .51
  (1) 39
FORCE DE FRAPPE   2.4   .51
  (1) 34
FOREIGN WARS   2.4   .69
  (1) 39
FOURTEEN POINTS   2.4   .51
  (6) 03 06 16 17 20 21
FRANCO-PRUSSIAN WAR   2.4   .51
  (2) 17 22
FRAUD   2.4   .69
  (2) 06 16
FREE SOIL   2.4   .51
  (1) 29
FREEDOM FROM ARREST   2.4   .84
  (1) 45
FREEDOM FROM FEAR   2.4   .84
  (1) 35
FREEDOM FROM SLAVERY AND   2.4   .69
  SERVITUDE
  (1) 17
FREEDOM OF ENTERPRISE   2.4   .84
  (1) 42
FREEDOM OF THE AIR   2.4   .69
  (2) 17 21
FULL EMPLOYMENT ACT   2.4   .69
  (1) 42
FUNDED DEBT   2.4   .69
  (2) 06 45
FUSION   2.4   .69
  (5) 06 16 24 29 32
G.I. BILL OF RIGHTS   2.4   .51
  (2) 16 34
GADSDEN PURCHASE   2.4   .51
  (2) 06 16
GAME   2.4   .84
  (3) 04 11 24
GENERAL ACT   2.4   .69
  (2) 16 17
GENERAL PROSPERITY AS POLITICAL   2.4   .51
  FACTOR
  (1) 08
GENEVA CONFERENCE   2.4   .69
  (2) 16 25
GENEVA CONFERENCE ON NUCLEAR   2.4   .51
  TESTING
  (1) 41
GIFT TAX   2.4   .51
  (4) 06 16 18 32
GOLD RESERVE ACT   2.4   .51
  (2) 06 16
GOLD RUSH   2.4   .51
  (1) 46
GOVERNMENT BY ASSASSINATION   2.4   .69
  (1) 29
GOVERNMENT BY COMMISSION   2.4   .51
  (1) 29

GRADUATED DETERRENCE STRATEGY   2.4   .69
  (1) 20
GRANDSTANDING   2.4   .84
  (2) 29 45
GRANGER LEGISLATION   2.4   .69
  (2) 06 16
GREAT DEBATES   2.4   .69
  (1) 39
GREEK-TURKISH AID   2.4   .69
  (1) 08
GUIDELINES   2.4   .69
  (1) 39
GUIDING PRINCIPLES   2.4   .69
  (1) 17
HARA-KIRI   2.4   .51
  (1) 16
HARTFORD CONVENTION   2.4   .69
  (3) 03 06 16
HAT IN THE RING   2.4   .69
  (3) 16 27 29
HAYMARKET SQUARE RIOTS   2.4   .69
  (1) 22
HEMISPHERIC DEFENSE   2.4   .51
  (1) 16
HEMISPHERIC SOLIDARITY   2.4   .51
  (1) 16
HIGHER EDUCATION   2.4   .69
  (1) 25
HIGHER EDUCATION ACT OF 1965   2.4   .69
  (2) 18 42
HIGHWAY BEAUTIFICATION ACT   2.4   .51
  (1) 32
HIJACKING   2.4   .51
  (1) 25
HISTORICITY   2.4   .84
  (1) 43
HOBSON'S CHOICE   2.4   .69
  (1) 39
HOMICIDE   2.4   .69
  (1) 30
HONOR   2.4   .69
  (1) 24
HOSTILE NEUTRALITY   2.4   .51
  (1) 44
HOT WAR   2.4   .69
  (1) 17
HOUSE ARREST   2.4   .51
  (1) 16
HOUSING AND URBAN DEVELOPMENT   2.4   .51
  ACT
  (1) 42
HUMAN RIGHTS DAY   2.4   .69
  (1) 17
IGNORANCE OF LAW   2.4   .51
  (1) 44
IMMIGRATION AND NATIONALITY ACT   2.4   .69
  OF 1952
  (2) 18 32
IMPACT   2.4   .69
  (1) 24
IMPANEL   2.4   .69
  (1) 45

IMPRESSMENT	2.4	.69
(2) 06 16 46		
IMPRISONMENT FOR DEBT	2.4	.51
(1) 45		
INCAPACITATION	2.4	.69
(1) 06		
INCENTIVE PAY	2.4	.69
(2) 16 37		
INCEST	2.4	.69
(1) 22		
INCIDENCE	2.4	.69
(1) 45		
INCIDENT	2.4	.69
(2) 16 30		
INDEMNITY	2.4	.51
(3) 06 16 17		
INDIAN WARS	2.4	.84
(1) 46		
INERTIA	2.4	.69
(1) 43		
INFORMAL	2.4	.84
(1) 24		
INHERITANCE TAX	2.4	.69
(3) 06 16 18		
INJUNCTION, LABOR	2.4	.51
(1) 18		
INNOVATION	2.4	.84
(1) 24		
INOPERATIVE	2.4	.69
(1) 17		
INQUEST	2.4	.51
(4) 06 16 18 26		
INTERGOVERNMENTAL AGREEMENT	2.4	.51
(1) 17		
INTERGOVERNMENTAL AGREEMENT	2.4	.51
(1) 17		
INTERGOVERNMENTAL TAX IMMUNITY	2.4	.51
(1) 18		
INTERNAL POLITICAL STRUGGLES	2.4	.69
(1) 36		
INTERNATIONAL ADMINISTRATIVE LAW	2.4	.69
(1) 17		
INTERNATIONAL CONCESSION	2.4	.69
(1) 16		
INTERNATIONAL COVENANTS ON	2.4	.51
HUMAN RIGHTS		
(1) 25		
INTERNATIONAL CUSTOMARY LAW	2.4	.51
(1) 17		
INTERNATIONAL LEGISLATION	2.4	.69
(3) 06 16 20		
INTERNATIONAL SUGAR AGREEMENT	2.4	.84
(1) 17		
INTERNATIONAL TREATY ON PEACEFUL	2.4	.51
USES OF OUTER SPACE		
(1) 32		
INTERVIEW	2.4	.84
(7) 01 17 19 24 25 30 33		
JAPANESE CONSTITUTION OF 1946	2.4	.69
(1) 16		
JAPANESE WAR CRIMES TRIALS	2.4	.51
(1) 03		
JAPANESE-AMERICAN SECURITY	2.4	.69
TREATY		
(2) 03 20		
JOINT BALLOT	2.4	.69
(1) 06		
JUDICIAL NOTICE	2.4	.69
(2) 02 32		
JUDICIAL SOVEREIGNTY	2.4	.51
(1) 17		
JUDICIAL SPOILS	2.4	.69
(1) 45		
JULY 14, 1789	2.4	.69
(1) 03		
JURISDICTIONAL STRIKE	2.4	.69
(2) 18 32		
JUVENILE CRIME	2.4	.51
(1) 25		
KANSAS-NEBRASKA ACT	2.4	.51
(3) 03 06 32		
KARMA	2.4	.69
(1) 43		
KENTUCKY AND VIRGINIA	2.4	.69
RESOLUTIONS		
(3) 03 06 32		
KICK UPSTAIRS	2.4	.69
(1) 29		
KICKBACK	2.4	.51
(1) 32		
LAG	2.4	.84
(1) 01		
LAKEWOOD PLAN	2.4	.84
(1) 03		
LAND DEVELOPMENT	2.4	.69
(1) 11		
LAND USE	2.4	.51
(1) 07		
LAW OF INTERNATIONAL RIVERS	2.4	.51
(1) 17		
LAW OF OCCUPATION	2.4	.69
(1) 17		
LAW OF RECIPROCITY	2.4	.69
(1) 17		
LAW REFORM	2.4	.84
(1) 44		
LAY ON THE TABLE	2.4	.69
(1) 16		
LAYOFF	2.4	.84
(1) 32		
LEGISLATIVE RECIPROCITY	2.4	.51
(1) 17		
LEND-LEASE PROGRAM	2.4	.51
(6) 16 17 20 25 32 34		
LETTER AND SPIRIT OF THE TREATY	2.4	.69
(1) 17		
LEVERAGE	2.4	.69
(1) 39		
LIDICE MASSACRE	2.4	.69
(3) 03 16 34		
LIMIT	2.4	.84
(1) 17		
LIQUIDATION	2.4	.69
(1) 03		

LIVING WAGE	2.4	.69
(1) 06		
LOOPHOLE	2.4	.69
(1) 27		
LOOSE MONEY POLICY	2.4	.69
(1) 18		
LOSE	2.4	.84
(1) 17		
LOSS OF CITIZENSHIP	2.4	.51
(1) 42		
LOSS OF NATIONALITY	2.4	.51
(1) 17		
LOTTERY	2.4	.69
(1) 06		
MALE SUFFRAGE	2.4	.51
(1) 17		
MALFEASANCE	2.4	.51
(2) 06 16		
MALPRACTICE	2.4	.51
(1) 06		
MANAGE	2.4	.96
(2) 24 30		
MANAGEMENT CONTROL	2.4	.84
(1) 37		
MANIPULATION	2.4	.96
(1) 24		
MANN ACT	2.4	.51
(1) 06		
MARRIAGE AND DIVORCE LAWS	2.4	.69
(1) 03		
MASSACHUSETTS BALLOT	2.4	.69
(1) 42		
MASSACRE	2.4	.84
(1) 30		
MEASURED RESPONSE	2.4	.69
(1) 39		
MEIJI CONSTITUTION	2.4	.69
(1) 03		
MEMBERS BILL	2.4	.69
(1) 17		
MEXICAN CESSION	2.4	.69
(1) 06		
MID-TERM	2.4	.51
(1) 24		
MILIEU	2.4	.69
(3) 01 24 30		
MILITARY ESTABLISHMENT, RESTRICTIONS OF	2.4	.84
(1) 42		
MILITARY SERVICE	2.4	.69
(4) 09 11 16 17		
MISSOURI COURT PLAN	2.4	.69
(3) 03 18 32		
MIXED CONSTITUTION	2.4	.84
(1) 03		
MODEL STATE CONSTITUTION	2.4	.69
(2) 03 18		
MODERATE POLICY	2.4	.69
(1) 17		
MODERATION	2.4	.69
(1) 24		
MONETARY AGREEMENT	2.4	.69
(1) 17		
MONEY, COINAGE OF	2.4	.69
(1) 42		
MOONLIGHTING	2.4	.69
(1) 37		
MORAL EQUIVALENT OF WAR	2.4	.51
(1) 22		
MOTION HAVING PRIORITY	2.4	.69
(1) 17		
MOTION TO LAY UPON THE TABLE	2.4	.51
(1) 02		
MOTION TO RECONSIDER	2.4	.51
(1) 02		
MUDSLINGING	2.4	.51
(3) 06 16 29		
MUNICIPAL LIABILITY	2.4	.69
(1) 45		
MUTINY	2.4	.69
(5) 06 16 17 24 32		
NATIONAL IDENTIFICATION	2.4	.84
(1) 15		
NATIONAL ORIGINS ACT	2.4	.69
(1) 45		
NAVAL POWER	2.4	.69
(1) 36		
NEGOTIATED DISENGAGEMENT	2.4	.69
(1) 36		
NEW ECONOMICS	2.4	.84
(1) 39		
NEW ORDER, NAZI	2.4	.69
(1) 21		
NEWS	2.4	.96
(2) 11 24		
NINTH AMENDMENT	2.4	.69
(2) 06 18		
NON-DISCRIMINATION	2.4	.51
(1) 30		
NON-RECOGNITION DOCTRINE	2.4	.69
(1) 16		
NON-TAX REVENUE	2.4	.51
(1) 45		
NOTICE AND HEARING	2.4	.69
(1) 16		
NTH NATION PROBLEM	2.4	.69
(1) 20		
NULL AND VOID	2.4	.69
(1) 17		
NUTRITION	2.4	.51
(1) 41		
OBLIGATION OF CONTRACTS	2.4	.69
(1) 06		
OCCUPATION IN TIME OF WAR	2.4	.51
(1) 17		
OFFICIAL CAPACITY	2.4	.69
(1) 17		
OLD AGE AND SECURITY INSURANCE	2.4	.51
(1) 45		
OPTIMALITY	2.4	.84
(1) 25		
OPTION	2.4	.69
(1) 17		
ORIENTAL IMMIGRATION	2.4	.51
(1) 42		

OUTER SPACE, JURISDICTION   2.4   .51
(1) 20

OUTLAWING OF THE ATOMIC BOMB   2.4   .69
(1) 17

OVERCENTRALIZATION   2.4   .84
(1) 24

OVERWHELMING MAJORITY   2.4   .51
(1) 17

PACIFIC BLOCKADE   2.4   .51
(3) 06 16 17

PACIFY   2.4   .69
(1) 17

PACT OF PARIS (KELLOGG-BRIAND   2.4   .51
PACT)
(2) 16 20

PARITY PRICE   2.4   .69
(1) 27

PARLIAMENTARY PRIVILEGE   2.4   .51
(1) 16

PARTIAL MOBILIZATION   2.4   .51
(1) 17

PARTIAL TEST BAN TREATY (1963)   2.4   .51
(1) 20

PASSIVE OBEDIENCE   2.4   .69
(2) 16 26

PAY ROLL TAX (SOCIAL SECURITY ACT)   2.4   .51
(4) 06 16 18 45

PAYOFF   2.4   .69
(1) 02

PEACE OFFENSIVE   2.4   .51
(1) 17

PELOPONNESIAN WAR   2.4   .69
(1) 26

PENALTY   2.4   .84
(1) 06

PEOPLE'S WAR   2.4   .69
(1) 11

PER CURIAM OPINION   2.4   .69
(1) 44

PERFORMANCE BUDGET   2.4   .69
(2) 03 18

PERMANENT APPROPRIATION   2.4   .69
(2) 06 16

PERQUISITES   2.4   .69
(3) 06 16 27

PERSONAL IMMUNITY   2.4   .51
(1) 17

PERSONAL INVIOLABILITY   2.4   .69
(1) 17

PERSONAL PROPERTY TAX   2.4   .69
(1) 18

PERSONALITY TESTS   2.4   .69
(1) 25

PETITION OF RIGHT   2.4   .51
(2) 03 06

PICKET   2.4   .69
(3) 16 29 30

PLATT AMENDMENT   2.4   .51
(3) 03 06 16 46

PLAUSIBILITY   2.4   .84
(1) 43

POINT OF LAW   2.4   .69
(1) 17

POLITICAL BARGAIN   2.4   .69
(1) 06

POLITICAL BARGAINING POSITION   2.4   .51
(1) 08

POLITICAL COMPLIANCE   2.4   .51
(1) 08

POLITICAL CRIME   2.4   .51
(1) 44

POLITICAL DEADLOCK   2.4   .51
(1) 08

POLITICAL DIFFERENCES   2.4   .84
(1) 08

POLITICAL RELATIONS   2.4   .84
(1) 19

POLITICAL TRAINING   2.4   .51
(1) 15

POLL PROCEDURE   2.4   .69
(1) 17

POPULATION PRESSURE   2.4   .69
(1) 16

POSITIVE INTERNATIONAL LAW   2.4   .51
(1) 17

PRE-EMPTION   2.4   .51
(1) 06

PRECONDITIONS   2.4   .69
(1) 30

PRESERVATION OF PEACE   2.4   .69
(1) 17

PRESIDENT TRUMAN'S TWELVE POINTS   2.4   .69
(1) 21

PRESIDENTIAL OATH   2.4   .51
(1) 42

PRESIDENTIAL PREFERENTIAL SYSTEM   2.4   .51
(1) 42

PRESIDENTIAL TRANSITIONS   2.4   .69
(1) 37

PREVENTIVE PRE-TRIAL DETENTION   2.4   .51
(1) 32

PREVIOUS QUESTION   2.4   .69
(6) 06 16 17 18 27 32

PRICE   2.4   .69
(3) 19 24 25

PRICE CEILING   2.4   .51
(2) 06 16

PRIMOGENITURE   2.4   .51
(3) 06 16 17

PRO FORMA AGREEMENT   2.4   .69
(1) 06

PROCEDURAL DECISIONS, SECURITY   2.4   .69
COUNCIL
(1) 20

PROCEDURAL MATTERS   2.4   .69
(1) 17

PRODUCTION   2.4   .69
(1) 43

PROGRAM   2.4   .69
(1) 24

PROGRESSIVE EDUCATION   2.4   .69
(1) 22

PROMULGATE   2.4   .51
(2) 16 17

PROPER CHANNELS   2.4   .69
(1) 17

PROTECTION	2.4	.51
(6) 06 16 21 24 29 30		
PROTEST DEMONSTRATION	2.4	.69
(1) 17		
PUBLIC HEALTH, SAFETY, AND MORALS	2.4	.69
(1) 27		
PUBLIC INTEGRITY	2.4	.69
(1) 35		
PUBLIC SPEAKING	2.4	.69
(1) 37		
PUBLIC TRANSPORTATION	2.4	.51
(1) 25		
PUBLIC WORKS	2.4	.51
(6) 06 12 16 18 25 27		
PUBLIC-INTEREST LAW	2.4	.69
(1) 32		
RATION	2.4	.51
(1) 16		
REACTION	2.4	.69
(4) 01 03 17 29		
REARMAMENT OF GERMANY	2.4	.51
(1) 17		
RECALL OF JUDICIAL DECISIONS	2.4	.51
(2) 06 22		
RECIDIVISM	2.4	.51
(1) 30		
RECIPROCITY CLAUSE	2.4	.51
(1) 17		
RECLAMATION	2.4	.51
(2) 06 16		
RECOGNIZANCE	2.4	.51
(2) 06 32		
RED CHINESE FIVE YEAR PLANS	2.4	.69
(1) 03		
REDUCTION OF MILITARY FORCES	2.4	.51
(1) 17		
REFERENCE TO A COMMITTEE	2.4	.69
(1) 17		
REFORM WITHIN THE PARTY	2.4	.69
(1) 29		
REGIONAL COMPACTS	2.4	.69
(1) 42		
REGIONAL POLICY	2.4	.69
(1) 11		
REGULATION OF LOBBYING ACT OF	2.4	.69
1946		
(3) 18 19 32		
REGULATION OF UNFAIR TRADE	2.4	.51
PRACTICES		
(1) 32		
RELAXATION OF TENSION	2.4	.69
(1) 17		
REMOVABLE FROM OFFICE	2.4	.51
(1) 17		
REMOVAL FROM OFFICE	2.4	.51
(1) 06		
REMOVAL POWER	2.4	.51
(1) 18		
RENT CONTROL	2.4	.51
(1) 45		
REPARATIONS	2.4	.51
(8) 03 06 16 17 19 20 21 25		
REPATRIATION OF PRISONERS OF WAR	2.4	.51
(1) 17		
REPEAL AMENDMENT	2.4	.51
(1) 16		
RESISTANCE TO TYRANNY	2.4	.69
(1) 35		
RETROACTIVE LAW	2.4	.51
(3) 06 16 17		
RETURNS	2.4	.51
(2) 06 16		
REVOLT	2.4	.69
(5) 06 16 17 24 30		
RIGHT OF PASSAGE	2.4	.51
(1) 17		
RIGHT OF VISIT AND SEARCH	2.4	.69
(1) 17		
RIGHT TO A FAIR TRIAL BY	2.4	.69
INDEPENDENT AND IMPARTIAL JURY		
(1) 17		
RISK	2.4	.69
(1) 03		
ROOSEVELT DOCTRINE	2.4	.51
(1) 06		
ROYAL SUCCESSION	2.4	.51
(1) 16		
RULE OF TERROR	2.4	.51
(1) 29		
RUN AHEAD OF THE TICKET	2.4	.69
(1) 29		
SANCTION OF LAW	2.4	.69
(4) 06 24 25 30		
SANCTITY OF TREATIES	2.4	.51
(1) 17		
SARAJEVO ASSASSINATIONS	2.4	.51
(2) 16 22		
SCAPE-GOATING	2.4	.51
(3) 24 30 45		
SCHISM	2.4	.69
(1) 24		
SECOND BALLOT SYSTEM	2.4	.69
(1) 33		
SECRECY	2.4	.69
(5) 07 11 17 24 30		
SECRET AGREEMENTS	2.4	.51
(1) 39		
SECURITY	2.4	.84
(5) 07 11 24 25 30		
SECURITY PACT	2.4	.51
(1) 17		
SEDITIOUS LIBEL	2.4	.51
(1) 16		
SEIZE	2.4	.51
(1) 17		
SELF-HELP	2.4	.69
(1) 16		
SELF-LIQUIDATING DEBT	2.4	.51
(1) 18		
SENATE CONGRESSIONAL RESOLUTION	2.4	.51
(S CON RES)		
(1) 16		
SENTENCE	2.4	.69
(3) 06 16 25		

SERVITUDE 2.4 .51
(3) 03 06 16
SETTLEMENT BY COMPROMISE 2.4 .69
(1) 17
SHARECROPPING 2.4 .51
(1) 46
SHOW TRIALS 2.4 .69
(2) 17 34
SINGLE TRANSFERABLE VOTE SYSTEM 2.4 .69
(2) 06 33
SLOW DOWN STRIKE 2.4 .51
(1) 45
SMEAR 2.4 .69
(1) 39
SMOOT-HAWLEY TARIFF ACT OF 1930 2.4 .51
(3) 16 18 20
SOCIAL ACTION 2.4 .69
(1) 05
SOCIAL WORK 2.4 .69
(1) 25
SOVIETIZATION 2.4 .69
(3) 17 24 34
SPECIAL FUND, UNITED NATIONS 2.4 .51
(2) 20 41
SPEECH OF ACCEPTANCE 2.4 .51
(2) 06 16
SQUARE DEAL 2.4 .69
(2) 06 29
STANDARD OF LIVING 2.4 .69
(1) 03
STATE CONSTITUTIONAL CONVENTIONS 2.4 .51
(1) 42
STATE INTERVENTION 2.4 .69
(2) 10 17
STATE LIABILITY 2.4 .51
(1) 16
STATE UNIFIED COURT SYSTEM 2.4 .51
(1) 18
STATUS QUO ANTE BELLUM 2.4 .51
(1) 06
STATUTORY CONSTRUCTION 2.4 .69
(2) 03 18
STOCKPILING OF ATOMIC WEAPONS 2.4 .51
(1) 17
STOCKPILING OF STRATEGIC 2.4 .51
MATERIALS
(1) 03
STYLE 2.4 .69
(2) 24 30
SUBJECT TO RATIFICATION 2.4 .51
(1) 17
SUBSIDIZE 2.4 .69
(1) 16
SURPLUS 2.4 .69
(2) 06 16
SURRENDER 2.4 .69
(1) 17
SUSPENSION OF HOSTILITIES 2.4 .51
(1) 16
TABLING 2.4 .69
(1) 27
TAX SHELTER 2.4 .51
(2) 25 32

TAXPAYER'S SUIT 2.4 .51
(4) 03 06 18 32
TECHNOLOGICAL UNEMPLOYMENT 2.4 .51
(1) 45
TECHNOLOGY TRANSFERS 2.4 .69
(1) 11
TENURE OF OFFICE ACT 2.4 .51
(2) 06 16
TERMINATION OF THE STATE OF WAR 2.4 .69
(1) 17
TERMS OF TRADE 2.4 .69
(1) 20
TERRITORIAL CESSION 2.4 .51
(1) 03
THIRD DEGREE 2.4 .51
(3) 06 16 27
THIRD PARTY CONCILIATION 2.4 .69
(1) 36
THREAT 2.4 .84
(4) 11 17 24 30
THREAT TO PEACE 2.4 .69
(1) 17
THREAT TO SECURITY 2.4 .51
(1) 17
TRADE 2.4 .69
(2) 06 24
TRADE NEGOTIATIONS 2.4 .51
(1) 17
TRADE OFF 2.4 .51
(1) 39
TRANSACTION 2.4 .69
(1) 02
TRANSPORTATION 2.4 .69
(1) 07
TREATMENT OF PRISONERS OF WAR 2.4 .51
(1) 17
TREATY OF GUADALUPE-HIDALGO 2.4 .69
(1) 16 46
TREATY OF NEUTRALITY 2.4 .51
(1) 17 38
TRUCE 2.4 .51
(5) 06 16 17 20 27
TRUTH IN PACKAGING LAW 2.4 .51
(2) 32 42
TRUTH-IN-LENDING ACT 2.4 .51
(2) 32 42
TV DEBATES 2.4 .69
(1) 03
U.N. FINANCING 2.4 .51
(1) 03
UNCONSTITUTIONAL CONDITIONS 2.4 .51
(1) 06
UNDERGROUND DETECTION METHODS 2.4 .69
(1) 36
UNEARNED INCOME 2.4 .69
(2) 06 16
UNENFORCED LAW 2.4 .69
(1) 44
UNFAIR COMPETITION 2.4 .69
(1) 16
UNIFORM LEGISLATION 2.4 .51
(1) 16

UNIFORMITY OF LAW   2.4   .84
  (1) 44
UNILATERAL ACT   2.4   .51
  (1) 17
UNILATERAL DECLARATION   2.4   .51
  (1) 17
UNIVERSAL MILITARY SERVICE   2.4   .51
  (1) 17
UNIVERSAL, EQUAL, DIRECT, AND SECRET SUFFRAGE   2.4   .69
  (1) 17
UNIVERSALITY   2.4   .69
  (1) 43
UNPROVOKED AGGRESSION   2.4   .51
  (1) 17
UNRESTRICTED SUBMARINE WARFARE   2.4   .51
  (1) 17
USE TAX   2.4   .51
  (4) 06 18 27 32
VERDICT   2.4   .69
  (3) 06 16 30
VETERANS PREFERENCE   2.4   .69
  (3) 06 16 18
VIRGINIA AND KENTUCKY RESOLUTIONS   2.4   .69
  (1) 45 46
VOLSTEAD ACT   2.4   .69
  (2) 06 16
VOTES CAST   2.4   .69
  (1) 17
VOTING FOR A LIST BY SIMPLE MAJORITY   2.4   .69
  (1) 17
WAGNER ACT   2.4   .69
  (6) 16 18 22 27 32 34
WAGNER-CONNERY LABOR RELATIONS ACT OF 1935   2.4   .84
  (2) 42 45
WAR BONDS   2.4   .51
  (1) 16
WAR GUILT   2.4   .69
  (2) 06 16
WAR OF CONQUEST   2.4   .69
  (1) 17
WAR PROFITS TAX   2.4   .51
  (1) 06
WELFARE BENEFITS   2.4   .69
  (1) 04
WORLD POPULATION, UNITED NATIONS CONFERENCE   2.4   .69
  (1) 41
WRIT OF ERROR   2.4   .69
  (1) 06
WRIT OF QUO WARRANTO   2.4   .84
  (1) 06
YELLOW DOG CONTRACT   2.4   .51
  (1) 42
ZONING ORDINANCES   2.4   .51
  (1) 42
ABSENTEEISM   2.5   .52
  (2) 29 32
ACCESSION   2.5   .52
  (3) 06 16 17

AD HOC CONFERENCE   2.5   .70
  (1) 20
ADDICTION   2.5   .70
  (1) 25
ADJOURNMENT   2.5   .52
  (6) 06 16 17 18 27 32
ADMIRALTY JURISDICTION   2.5   .70
  (4) 03 06 18 20
ADMISSION OF NEW MEMBERS   2.5   .52
  (1) 17
ADMISSIONS TAX   2.5   .70
  (1) 06
AFFIRMATIVE VOTE   2.5   .52
  (1) 17
AGITATION   2.5   .52
  (2) 06 17
AGRICULTURAL CREDIT   2.5   .70
  (1) 06
AID TO THE TOTALLY AND PERMANENTLY DISABLED   2.5   .70
  (1) 18
AIR QUALITY ACTS   2.5   .70
  (1) 32
ALGIERS CONFERENCE OF AFRO-ASIAN STATES   2.5   .52
  (1) 34
ALIEN REGISTRATION ACT OF 1940   2.5   .52
  (1) 18
AMITY   2.5   .70
  (1) 16
ANTARCTIC CLAIMS   2.5   .70
  (1) 03
ANTI-GOVERNMENT   2.5   .70
  (1) 17
APERTURA A SINISTRA (OPENING TO THE LEFT)   2.5   .52
  (1) 17
APOCALYPSE   2.5   .70
  (1) 11
APPALACHIAN REGIONAL PROGRAM   2.5   .52
  (1) 32
APPOINTED   2.5   .70
  (1) 24
APPROVAL   2.5   .70
  (2) 17 24
ARMS TRANSFERS   2.5   .52
  (1) 11
ARTICLE NINE, JAPANESE CONSTITUTION   2.5   .70
  (2) 03 20
ATMOSPHERIC DETECTION METHODS   2.5   .52
  (1) 36
ATOMIC ENERGY ACTS (1946 AND 1954)   2.5   .52
  (1) 38
ATTACHMENT   2.5   .84
  (1) 06
AUSTERITY PROGRAM   2.5   .52
  (1) 17
AWARD (LEGAL JUDGMENT)   2.5   .70
  (4) 06 16 17 20
BALANCED FORCES POLICY (U.S.)   2.5   .52
  (2) 17 20

BANK DEPOSITS GUARANTEE	2.5	.70
(1) 06		
BANKING ACT OF 1933	2.5	.52
(1) 32		
BARTER	2.5	.52
(2) 16 20		
BELGRADE CONFERENCE	2.5	.52
(1) 34		
BENEFIT PAYMENT	2.5	.70
(2) 06 16		
BILATERAL SECURITY PACT	2.5	.52
(1) 20		
BLITZ	2.5	.70
(1) 39		
BOOTLEG	2.5	.52
(3) 06 16 27		
BREACH OF PRIVILEGE	2.5	.52
(1) 06		
BRITISH NORTH AMERICA ACT (1867)	2.5	.52
(1) 03		
BUDGET AND ACCOUNTING ACT OF 1921	2.5	.70
(3) 16 18 32		
BUILDING CODE	2.5	.52
(3) 06 16 27		
BUSINESS COMPETITION	2.5	.52
(1) 36		
CALENDAR WEDNESDAY	2.5	.52
(5) 02 06 16 18 32		
CAPITAL GAINS TAX	2.5	.52
(3) 06 16 32		
CARTHAGINIAN PEACE	2.5	.52
(1) 16		
CASABLANCA CONFERENCE	2.5	.70
(3) 03 16 34		
CASH-AND-CARRY PRINCIPLE	2.5	.52
(4) 03 06 16 45		
CEILING PRICE	2.5	.52
(1) 16		
CHEAP MONEY	2.5	.70
(1) 45		
CHECKERS SPEECH	2.5	.52
(1) 39		
CIVICS COURSES	2.5	.52
(1) 15		
CIVIL RIGHTS ACT OF 1871	2.5	.52
(1) 18		
COASTAL DEFENSE	2.5	.52
(1) 17		
COBELLIGERENCY	2.5	.52
(1) 17		
COLLECTIVE AGREEMENTS	2.5	.52
(1) 45		
COLLECTIVE GUARANTEE	2.5	.52
(1) 17		
COLLECTIVE RECOGNITION	2.5	.52
(1) 03		
COLONIAL LAW	2.5	.52
(1) 19		
COLOR LINE	2.5	.52
(1) 29		
COMITY	2.5	.52
(5) 03 06 16 18 20		
COMMITTEE MEETINGS	2.5	.70
(1) 17		
COMMUNIST CONTROL ACT (1954)	2.5	.52
(3) 18 32 34		
COMMUTE	2.5	.70
(1) 16		
COMPARISON	2.5	.84
(4) 11 24 25 30		
COMPENSATORY SPENDING	2.5	.52
(1) 18		
CONCESSION SPEECH	2.5	.52
(1) 39		
CONCORDAT	2.5	.70
(7) 03 06 16 17 21 25 34		
CONFERENCE	2.5	.70
(7) 06 17 18 24 25 27 30		
CONFERENCE OF GOVERNORS	2.5	.52
(1) 42		
CONGRESS OF BERLIN	2.5	.52
(2) 16 17		
CONNALLY AMENDMENT	2.5	.52
(6) 03 16 18 20 27 32		
CONSCRIPTION OF LABOR	2.5	.52
(1) 45		
CONSTITUTION (BONN), GERMANY	2.5	.52
(1) 20		
CONSTITUTION OF ATHENS	2.5	.70
(1) 26		
CONSTRAINTS	2.5	.70
(2) 24 33		
CONSULAR JURISDICTION	2.5	.52
(1) 03		
CONSUMER CREDIT PROTECTION ACT	2.5	.52
(1) 32		
CONSUMPTION TAX	2.5	.52
(1) 16		
CONTRACT, FEUDAL	2.5	.70
(1) 09		
CONVERSION	2.5	.70
(1) 16		
COOPERATIVE ECONOMY	2.5	.52
(1) 26		
COORDINATION	2.5	.84
(2) 17 24		
CORPORATE REVOLUTION	2.5	.70
(1) 45		
CORRUPTIBILITY	2.5	.70
(1) 43		
COUNTERFEIT	2.5	.70
(3) 06 16 42		
COVENANT	2.5	.70
(4) 06 16 17 30		
CRIMINAL	2.5	.70
(2) 06 30		
CRIMINAL CASE	2.5	.70
(1) 27		
CRUSADE	2.5	.52
(2) 29 30		
CULPABILITY	2.5	.52
(1) 43		
CURFEW	2.5	.52
(2) 20 30		

CYPRUS QUESTION   2.5   .52
(1) 41
DATE OF APPOINTMENT   2.5   .52
(1) 17
DAY OF INFAMY   2.5   .70
(1) 39
DEBT SERVICE   2.5   .84
(1) 06
DECIPHER   2.5   .70
(1) 17
DECLARATION   2.5   .70
(3) 06 16 17
DECLARATION ON OUTER SPACE (1963)   2.5   .70
(1) 20
DECLARATION REGARDING   2.5   .70
NON-SELF-GOVERNING TERRITORIES
(1) 20
DEFAULT   2.5   .70
(2) 17 24
DEFEAT   2.5   .70
(3) 17 24 30
DEFEAT OF THE SPANISH ARMADA   2.5   .52
(1) 17
DEFENSIVE CAMPAIGN   2.5   .52
(1) 29
DEFICIENCY APPROPRIATION   2.5   .70
(1) 18
DEMAND   2.5   .70
(2) 17 24
DEMAND-PULL   2.5   .70
(1) 39
DEMONSTRATION   2.5   .70
(2) 17 30
DENIAL   2.5   .70
(2) 17 30
DENUNCIATION OF TREATIES   2.5   .70
(1) 20
DEPLOYMENT   2.5   .70
(1) 24
DEPOSIT OF THE INSTRUMENT OF   2.5   .52
RATIFICATION
(1) 17
DEPRESSIONS   2.5   .70
(1) 46
DERIVATIVE RIGHT   2.5   .52
(1) 03
DESTRUCTION   2.5   .84
(2) 29 30
DEVELOP   2.5   .84
(3) 04 15 17
DEVOLUTION   2.5   .84
(3) 06 16 33
DILATORY EFFECT   2.5   .70
(1) 17
DISABILITY   2.5   .70
(2) 06 30
DISALLOWANCE   2.5   .70
(1) 06
DISCIPLINE   2.5   .70
(4) 06 24 30 37
DISCOVERY   2.5   .52
(1) 43

DISCRETION   2.5   .70
(1) 16
DIVERSITY   2.5   .70
(1) 43
DIVISIVE   2.5   .52
(1) 24
DOCTRINE OF CONTINUOUS VOYAGE   2.5   .70
(3) 16 17 20
DRAFT CLASSIFICATIONS   2.5   .70
(1) 42
DRAGO DOCTRINE   2.5   .52
(4) 03 06 16 20
DRANG NACH OSTEN   2.5   .70
(1) 16
DULY APPOINTED   2.5   .52
(1) 17
DUNKIRK, EVACUATION OF   2.5   .52
(1) 34
DUTY   2.5   .84
(3) 06 16 27
ECONOMIC MEASURES   2.5   .52
(1) 25
ECONOMIC OPPORTUNITY ACT OF 1964   2.5   .52
(3) 18 25 32 42
ECONOMIC STAGES OF MANKIND   2.5   .84
(1) 45
ECONOMIC VALUE   2.5   .70
(1) 25
ECONOMY OF SCARCITY   2.5   .52
(1) 16
EDICT   2.5   .52
(1) 16
EFFICIENCY RATING   2.5   .70
(1) 16
ELECTION BY ACCLAMATION   2.5   .52
(1) 17
ELECTIONS, FILING   2.5   .52
(1) 18
ELIGIBILITY   2.5   .52
(4) 06 16 17 27
EMBARGO ACT OF 1807   2.5   .70
(1) 46
EMPLOYEES COMPENSATION   2.5   .52
(1) 37
EMPLOYMENT ACT OF 1946   2.5   .70
(2) 18 27
ENFORCEMENT ACTION   2.5   .70
(1) 17
ENTANGLING ALLIANCE   2.5   .52
(3) 06 16 24
ENVIRONMENTAL QUALITY   2.5   .52
(1) 32
EQUALIZATION   2.5   .52
(2) 03 18
ESCAPE CLAUSE   2.5   .52
(5) 03 16 17 18 20
ESTATE TAX   2.5   .70
(3) 06 18 32
ESTIMATES   2.5   .70
(2) 06 16
EUTHENASIA   2.5   .52
(1) 25

EVACUATION	2.5	.52
(2) 17 30		
EVACUATION OF DUNKIRK	2.5	.52
(1) 17		
EXPEDIENCY	2.5	.52
(1) 16		
EXPUNGE	2.5	.70
(2) 06 16		
FAIR LABOR STANDARDS ACT OF 1938	2.5	.52
(7) 03 06 16 18 22 27 32		
FEBRUARY REVOLUTION	2.5	.52
(1) 17		
FEDERAL ELECTION CAMPAIGN ACT	2.5	.70
(1) 32		
FEDERAL REGULATION OF LOBBYING	2.5	.52
ACT OF 1946 (U.S.)		
(1) 19		
FINANCE	2.5	.70
(4) 07 19 24 30		
FINANCES (UN)	2.5	.52
(1) 41		
FIRESIDE CHAT	2.5	.52
(5) 06 16 27 29 34		
FIVE FREEDOMS	2.5	.52
(1) 16		
FLEXIBLE CONSTITUTION	2.5	.52
(2) 06 16		
FLEXIBLE TARIFF	2.5	.52
(2) 06 16		
FOLKWAYS	2.5	.52
(1) 24		
FORFEITURE	2.5	.52
(1) 45		
FORM	2.5	.84
(2) 17 24		
FORMULAE	2.5	.70
(1) 24		
FRANCHISE TAX	2.5	.52
(1) 16		
FRANCO-GERMAN ARMISTICE	2.5	.70
(1) 16		
FREEDOM OF NAVIGATION ON RIVERS	2.5	.52
(1) 17		
FREEPORT DOCTRINE	2.5	.70
(1) 06		
FRENCH ARMISTICE OF 1940	2.5	.70
(1) 21		
FULTON SPEECH	2.5	.70
(1) 34		
FUNDING	2.5	.70
(1) 06		
FUTURE	2.5	.70
(3) 24 25 30		
GALVESTON PLAN	2.5	.70
(1) 06		
GAME OF CONFLICT	2.5	.70
(1) 11		
GARNISHMENT	2.5	.52
(1) 37		
GENERAL ASSISTANCE	2.5	.70
(1) 27		
GENERAL CONFERENCE	2.5	.70
(1) 17		
GENEVA SPIRIT	2.5	.70
(1) 17		
GEOLOGICAL SURVEY	2.5	.70
(1) 06		
GERMANIC LAW	2.5	.52
(1) 26		
GOOD-WILL MISSION	2.5	.52
(1) 17		
GOVERNMENT BY CRONY	2.5	.52
(1) 29		
GOVERNMENT BY INJUNCTION	2.5	.52
(1) 06		
GRANT	2.5	.70
(2) 06 17		
GREAT SCHISM	2.5	.52
(1) 26		
GRECO-TURKISH WAR	2.5	.52
(1) 16		
GROSS MISCONDUCT	2.5	.52
(1) 17		
GROSS SALARY	2.5	.70
(1) 17		
GROUND INSPECTION	2.5	.70
(1) 17		
HABIT	2.5	.70
(1) 43		
HABSBURG RESTORATION	2.5	.70
(1) 21		
HAGUE CONFERENCE	2.5	.52
(2) 17 19		
HALLSTEIN DOCTRINE	2.5	.52
(3) 03 17 34		
HAVANA CHARTER	2.5	.52
(1) 38		
HAVANA CONFERENCE	2.5	.52
(1) 16		
HAWLEY-SMOOT ACT OF 1932	2.5	.52
(4) 03 06 16 22		
HAWLEY-SMOOT TARIFF OF 1930	2.5	.52
(1) 45		
HAY-PAUNCEFOTE TREATY	2.5	.52
(3) 03 06 16		
HEALTH INSURANCE PLAN (NATIONAL)	2.5	.52
(1) 45		
HOLDING APPOINTMENT FOR LIFE	2.5	.52
(1) 17		
HOLOCAUST	2.5	.52
(1) 34		
HONEST GRAFT	2.5	.52
(3) 06 16 27		
HOOVER MORATORIUM	2.5	.70
(2) 16 21		
HUNDRED DAYS	2.5	.70
(1) 17		
HYDE PARK DECLARATION	2.5	.70
(1) 03		
IDENTICAL PRICING	2.5	.70
(1) 45		
IMITATION	2.5	.70
(2) 15 30		
IMMIGRATION REFORM ACT	2.5	.70
(1) 42		

IMMORTALITY	2.5	.70
(1) 43		
IMPLEMENTATION AGREEMENT	2.5	.52
(1) 17		
IMPORT	2.5	.52
(2) 25 27		
IMPOST	2.5	.70
(2) 06 16		
IMPROVEMENT OF RELATIONS	2.5	.70
(1) 17		
IMPUGN	2.5	.70
(1) 45		
IN ABSENTIA	2.5	.52
(1) 16		
INACTIVE STATUS	2.5	.52
(1) 17		
INCENTIVE AWARDS	2.5	.52
(1) 37		
INCOMPLETE RATIFICATION	2.5	.70
(1) 17		
INDEXING	2.5	.52
(1) 43		
INDIVIDUALITY	2.5	.84
(1) 43		
INDUSTRY-WIDE BARGAINING	2.5	.70
(1) 45		
INNOCENT PASSAGE	2.5	.52
(4) 03 16 17 20		
INSOLVENCY	2.5	.52
(2) 06 45		
INSPECTION LAWS	2.5	.52
(2) 06 16		
INSTRUCTIONS	2.5	.70
(4) 06 16 17 24		
INSULARITY	2.5	.52
(1) 17		
INTELLIGENCE TESTS	2.5	.70
(1) 22		
INTER-AMERICAN DEFENSE TREATY	2.5	.70
(1) 42		
INTERDEPARTMENTAL CONFERENCE	2.5	.70
(1) 17		
INTEREST	2.5	.70
(1) 33		
INTERFERENCE	2.5	.52
(1) 17		
INTERIM REPORT	2.5	.52
(1) 17		
INTERLOCUTORY HEARING	2.5	.70
(1) 18		
INTERNAL AUDITS	2.5	.70
(1) 37		
INTERNAL SECURITY INVESTIGATIONS	2.5	.70
(1) 46		
INTERNATIONAL ANARCHY	2.5	.70
(1) 22		
INTERNATIONAL COPYRIGHT	2.5`	.52
(1) 06		
INTERNATIONAL COURTESY	2.5	.70
(1) 17		
INTERNATIONAL CUSTOMS	2.5	.52
(1) 17		
INTERPRET	2.5	.70
(1) 17		
INTERREGNUM	2.5	.52
(3) 17 24 27		
INTERROGATION	2.5	.52
(1) 43		
INTERSTATE RENDITION	2.5	.70
(2) 03 18		
INTERSTATE TRANSPORTATION	2.5	.70
(1) 03		
INTERZONAL AGREEMENT	2.5	.52
(1) 17		
INTIMIDATE	2.5	.70
(1) 45		
INTRODUCE	2.5	.70
(1) 17		
INVIOLABILITY	2.5	.52
(2) 16 17		
IRRIGATION	2.5	.52
(1) 06		
IUS	2.5	.70
(1) 17		
JOB DESIGN	2.5	.84
(1) 37		
JUDGING	2.5	.70
(1) 43		
JUDICIAL NULLIFICATION	2.5	.52
(1) 44		
JUDICIAL PROCEEDINGS	2.5	.70
(1) 17		
JUDICIAL SELF-LIMITATION	2.5	.52
(1) 44		
JUS IN BELLO	2.5	.70
(1) 17		
KANSAS PLAN	2.5	.70
(1) 06		
KILLING	2.5	.70
(1) 43		
LABOR UNION LEGISLATION	2.5	.52
(1) 42		
LABOR-MANAGEMENT REPORTING AND DISCLOSURE ACT (1959)	2.5	.70
(2) 18 32		
LAND POOR	2.5	.52
(1) 45		
LANDRUM-GRIFFIN ACT 1959	2.5	.70
(4) 03 18 32 34		
LATERAN ACCORD	2.5	.52
(3) 16 17 21		
LAW OF THE JUNGLE	2.5	.70
(1) 17		
LAW OF THE SEA CONFERENCE	2.5	.52
(1) 41		
LEAVE WITHOUT PAY	2.5	.70
(1) 17		
LEGALITY, SOCIALIST	2.5	.70
(1) 23		
LEISURE	2.5	.70
(1) 43		
LEND-LEASE ACT, MARCH 11, 1941	2.5	.52
(4) 03 06 16 21		
LENGTH OF SERVICE	2.5	.70
(1) 17		

LEVEE EN MASSE	2.5	.52
(2) 16 17		
LEVY	2.5	.52
(2) 16 27		
LIBERATION OF CAPTIVE PEOPLES	2.5	.52
(1) 39		
LIFE	2.5	.70
(1) 24		
LINDBERGH LAW	2.5	.70
(1) 42		
LITERACY	2.5	.70
(1) 25		
LOAN FLOTATION	2.5	.70
(1) 16		
LONG SESSION	2.5	.70
(2) 06 16		
LONG-TERM	2.5	.70
(1) 17		
LOOTING	2.5	.70
(2) 17 30		
LOYALTY PROGRAM	2.5	.70
(1) 37		
LOYALTY, PRINCIPLE OF	2.5	.70
(1) 22		
MAINTENANCE	2.5	.70
(1) 24		
MANAGERIAL OBSOLESCENCE	2.5	.70
(1) 37		
MANDATORY	2.5	.70
(1) 16		
MANDATORY POWER	2.5	.52
(1) 17		
MARCH ON WASHINGTON	2.5	.70
(1) 39		
MAY FIRST	2.5	.52
(1) 16		
MCCARRAN-WALTER IMMIGRATION AND	2.5	.52
NATIONALITY ACT		
(1) 42		
MEKONG RIVER PROJECT	2.5	.70
(1) 41		
MERGER	2.5	.52
(2) 18 24		
MERGER OF POWERS	2.5	.70
(1) 17		
MODEL METROPOLITAN CHARTER	2.5	.70
(1) 04		
MODUS VIVENDI	2.5	.52
(4) 06 16 17 27		
MONETARY CONFERENCE	2.5	.52
(1) 17		
MONNET PLAN	2.5	.70
(2) 03 19		
MONTEVIDEO CONFERENCE	2.5	.70
(1) 16		
MORRILL ACT OF 1862	2.5	.70
(4) 06 16 18 32		
MULTIPLE ELECTION	2.5	.70
(1) 33		
NAME	2.5	.70
(2) 17 30		

NATIONAL DEFENSE EDUCATION ACT	2.5	.52
OF 1958 (NDEA)		
(2) 18 32		
NATIONAL HEALTH SERVICE ACT	2.5	.70
(BRITAIN)		
(1) 19		
NATIONAL HOLIDAY	2.5	.70
(2) 16 17		
NATIONAL INSURANCE	2.5	.70
(1) 16		
NATIONAL SECURITY ACTS, 1947 AND	2.5	.70
1949		
(2) 18 32		
NATIONAL STYLE	2.5	.52
(1) 20		
NAVAL OPERATIONS	2.5	.70
(1) 11		
NAVAL WARFARE	2.5	.52
(1) 17		
NECESSITY	2.5	.70
(1) 43		
NEGOTIATED CONTRACT	2.5	.52
(1) 27		
NEGOTIATED SAFEGUARDS	2.5	.52
(1) 36		
NEGRO SUPREMACY	2.5	.70
(1) 29		
NET SALARY	2.5	.84
(1) 17		
NONCONFORMTIY	2.5	.70
(1) 24		
NORMANDY, INVASION OF	2.5	.52
(1) 46		
NUCLEAR WEAPONS BAN ON OCEAN	2.5	.84
FLOOR		
(1) 36		
NUMBERS GAME	2.5	.70
(1) 39		
OATH	2.5	.70
(3) 06 17 27		
OATH OF INAUGURATION	2.5	.70
(1) 45		
OBJECTION	2.5	.70
(1) 17		
OBLIGATION TO EXTRADITE	2.5	.70
(1) 17		
OBSERVATION	2.5	.70
(4) 01 24 25 33		
OFFICE-COLUMN BALLOT	2.5	.70
(1) 27		
OLD AGE ASSISTANCE	2.5	.52
(2) 03 18		
ONE WORLD	2.5	.52
(1) 39		
OPENING ADDRESS	2.5	.52
(1) 17		
OPINION, AS EVIDENCE	2.5	.70
(1) 32		
OPTIONAL REFERENDUM	2.5	.70
(1) 18		
OUTER SPACE TREATY	2.5	.52
(1) 20		

OVERREACT   2.5   .70
 (1) 39
OVERRIDE   2.5   .70
 (1) 17
OVERRULING, INDIRECT   2.5   .70
 (1) 44
OWNERSHIP   2.5   .70
 (2) 24 25
PACKAGE DEAL   2.5   .52
 (1) 45
PAN-EUROPEAN   2.5   .52
 (3) 03 16 17
PANAMA CANAL ZONE AGREEMENT   2.5   .52
 (1) 42
PANMUNJON TRUCE   2.5   .52
 (1) 03
PARLIAMENTARY INVESTIGATIONS   2.5   .52
 (1) 11
PAROLE   2.5   .52
 (6) 03 06 16 17 18 27
PAX   2.5   .70
 (1) 24
PAY SCALE   2.5   .70
 (1) 17
PEACE OFFER   2.5   .52
 (1) 17
PEACEFUL OCCUPATION   2.5   .52
 (1) 17
PEACEFUL SPACE EXPLORATION   2.5   .52
 (1) 36
PENAL   2.5   .70
 (1) 16
PENAL LAW   2.5   .70
 (1) 19
PERFORMANCE   2.5   .84
 (1) 24
PETTY OFFENSE   2.5   .52
 (1) 27
PHILANTHROPY   2.5   .52
 (1) 25
PIRACY   2.5   .52
 (3) 06 16 17
PLANK   2.5   .52
 (5) 06 16 17 27 29
PLANTATION SYSTEM   2.5   .70
 (1) 46
POCKETBOOK ISSUE   2.5   .52
 (1) 39
POLICY OF EXPEDIENCY   2.5   .70
 (1) 17
POLITICAL BUILD-UP   2.5   .52
 (1) 02
POLITICAL DISCOURSE   2.5   .52
 (1) 11
POLITICS OF PREVENTION   2.5   .70
 (1) 22
POSITION CLASSIFICATION   2.5   .70
 (2) 03 18
POST-AUDIT   2.5   .70
 (2) 06 18
POWER GRAB   2.5   .52
 (1) 39

PRAGUE COUP D'ETAT OF 1948   2.5   .52
 (1) 03
PRAYER   2.5   .84
 (1) 43
PRE-AUDIT   2.5   .70
 (3) 03 06 18
PREAMBLE   2.5   .52
 (6) 02 06 16 17 18 32
PREFERRED POSITION TEST   2.5   .70
 (1) 32
PRELIMINARY HEARING   2.5   .52
 (1) 18
PREPRIMARY CONVENTION   2.5   .70
 (2) 06 16
PRESS CONFERENCE   2.5   .70
 (1) 17
PREVENTION   2.5   .70
 (1) 30
PRICE CONTROL ACT   2.5   .52
 (1) 16
PRICES AND INCOMES POLICY   2.5   .70
 (1) 34
PRIVATE AUDIENCE   2.5   .52
 (1) 17
PRIVATE INTERNATIONAL LAW   2.5   .52
 (3) 06 16 20
PROBATE   2.5   .52
 (2) 06 27
PROBATION   2.5   .52
 (1) 42
PROBATIONARY PERIOD   2.5   .52
 (1) 17
PROBLEM   2.5   .84
 (3) 17 24 30
PROGRAM OF THE GOVERNMENT   2.5   .70
 (1) 17
PROPAGANDA FOR WAR   2.5   .52
 (1) 17
PROPOSAL   2.5   .52
 (2) 17 30
PROPOSED AMENDMENTS   2.5   .52
 (1) 42
PROPRIETARY FUNCTIONS OF CITIES   2.5   .52
 (1) 45
PROTECTION OF NATIONALS ABROAD   2.5   .52
 (1) 17
PUBLIC INTEREST, CONVENIENCE AND   2.5   .70
 NECESSITY
 (1) 39
PUBLIC PERSONNEL ADMINISTRATION   2.5   .52
 (1) 11
PUBLIC RELIEF   2.5   .52
 (1) 19
PUBLIC SERVICE TRAINING   2.5   .70
 (1) 05
PUBLIC USE   2.5   .70
 (1) 45
PUEBLO INCIDENT   2.5   .52
 (1) 25
PUNISHABLE BY DEATH   2.5   .70
 (1) 17
PURE FOOD, DRUG AND COSMETIC ACT   2.5   .52
 (1) 42

QUESTION OF CONFIDENCE	2.5	.70
(1) 17		
RACIAL QUESTION	2.5	.52
(1) 04		
RAILROAD LAND GRANTS	2.5	.52
(1) 32		
RAPACKI PLAN	2.5	.52
(4) 03 17 20 34		
RATE-MAKING	2.5	.70
(2) 18 45		
REAPPOINTMENT	2.5	.52
(2) 06 17		
REBATE	2.5	.52
(2) 06 16		
REBUTTAL	2.5	.52
(1) 45		
RECESS	2.5	.52
(4) 06 17 27 32		
RECESS APPOINTEMNT	2.5	.52
(5) 03 06 16 18 32		
RECIPROCAL TARIFF ACT	2.5	.70
(1) 42		
RECIPROCAL TRADE ACT	2.5	.70
(1) 03		
RECIPROCITY TREATY	2.5	.70
(1) 17		
RECONCILIATION	2.5	.52
(2) 29 30		
RECORD VOTE	2.5	.52
(5) 06 17 18 27 32		
RED SCARE	2.5	.52
(1) 16		
REDISCOUNT	2.5	.52
(2) 06 18		
REDISTRIBUTION (OF ELECTORAL	2.5	.52
DISTRICTS)		
(1) 17		
REDUCTION OF STAFF	2.5	.70
(1) 17		
REFER TO COMMITTEE	2.5	.52
(3) 17 18 32		
REGICIDE	2.5	.52
(1) 16		
REGIONAL ARRANGEMENTS	2.5	.70
(2) 16 17		
REGISTRATION FORM	2.5	.52
(1) 17		
REJECT	2.5	.70
(1) 17		
REMOVAL	2.5	.52
(1) 37		
RENUCIATION OF ATOMIC WEAPONS	2.5	.52
(1) 17		
REOCCUPATION OF THE RHINELAND	2.5	.52
(1) 17		
REPRESENT	2.5	.70
(2) 17 24		
REPRIMAND	2.5	.52
(1) 06		
REPRISALS	2.5	.52
(6) 03 06 11 16 17 20		
RESIDUARY POWERS	2.5	.70
(3) 06 18 32		

RESOLUTION	2.5	.52
(7) 06 16 17 24 27 32 34		
RESTRAINING ORDER	2.5	.52
(1) 16		
RETALIATION	2.5	.52
(2) 03 30		
RETROACTIVE LEGISLATION	2.5	.52
(1) 45		
REVERSE BIGOTRY	2.5	.52
(1) 39		
REVIEW	2.5	.70
(3) 06 17 24		
REVISED STATUTES	2.5	.70
(1) 06		
REVISION OF A TREATY	2.5	.52
(1) 17		
REVOLVING FUND	2.5	.52
(5) 03 06 16 18 27		
RIGHT OF EXPULSION	2.5	.70
(1) 16		
RIGHT OF SELF-PRESERVATION	2.5	.70
(1) 17		
RIGHT TO AN ADEQUATE STANDARD OF	2.5	.70
LIVING		
(1) 17		
RIGHT TO KNOW	2.5	.52
(1) 39		
RIGHT TO SPEAK	2.5	.70
(1) 17		
RIO TREATY OF 1947	2.5	.52
(2) 18 42		
RUHR OCCUPATION	2.5	.52
(1) 16		
RULING CASE LAW	2.5	.52
(1) 12		
RUMOR	2.5	.70
(1) 30		
RUMP SESSION	2.5	.52
(1) 39		
RUN (ON BANKS)	2.5	.70
(2) 03 24		
RUN SCARED	2.5	.70
(1) 39		
RUNOFF	2.5	.52
(1) 16		
SABOTAGE	2.5	.52
(7) 06 10 16 17 20 30 32		
SAFE STREETS ACT	2.5	.52
(1) 32		
SALVATION	2.5	.70
(1) 43		
SAVINGS BONDS AND STAMPS	2.5	.52
(1) 06		
SCENARIO	2.5	.70
(1) 39		
SCHUMAN PLAN	2.5	.52
(2) 03 17		
SEAT	2.5	.52
(2) 17 24		
SECOND CIVIL RIGHTS ACT	2.5	.70
(1) 32		
SECONDARY PICKETING	2.5	.52
(1) 32		

SECRET CLAUSE   2.5   .52
  (1) 17
SECRET PROTOCOL   2.5   .52
  (1) 17
SECRET SESSION   2.5   .52
  (3) 06 16 17
SEDITION ACT OF 1918   2.5   .52
  (1) 03
SELECTIVE TRAINING AND SERVICE ACT   2.5   .52
  (1) 16
SELF-CRITICISM IN THE U.S.S.R.   2.5   .52
  (2) 03 17
SELF-PRESERVATION   2.5   .70
  (2) 17 26
SENATE SPECIAL POWERS   2.5   .70
  (1) 42
SENTENCING   2.5   .70
  (1) 25
SERMON ON THE MOUNT   2.5   .70
  (1) 22
SEVERANCE PAY   2.5   .52
  (1) 32
SHORT SESSION   2.5   .52
  (2) 06 16
SHORTER WORKWEEK   2.5   .70
  (1) 37
SMITH ACT   2.5   .52
  (1) 42
SMUGGLING   2.5   .70
  (2) 06 16
SOAK THE RICH   2.5   .52
  (1) 29
SOCIAL LEGISLATION   2.5   .52
  (3) 06 16 19
SOCIAL POLICY   2.5   .52
  (4) 11 17 19 23
SOLID-WASTE DISPOSAL   2.5   .70
  (1) 32
SOUTHERN RHODESIA QUESTION   2.5   .52
  (1) 41
SOVIET REPARATIONS IN GERMANY   2.5   .52
  (1) 03
SPACE JURISDICTION   2.5   .52
  (1) 03
SPECIAL ASSESSMENT   2.5   .52
  (4) 03 06 16 18
SPECIAL LEGISLATION   2.5   .52
  (2) 06 16
STANDARDIZED EXAMINATION   2.5   .70
  (1) 16
STANDARDIZED INTERVIEW   2.5   .52
  (2) 01 25
STANDARDS   2.5   .70
  (1) 30
STAR-CHAMBER PROCEEDING   2.5   .52
  (1) 06
STATE OF BLOCKADE   2.5   .70
  (1) 17
STATE SUCCESSION   2.5   .52
  (2) 06 11
STATELESSNESS   2.5   .52
  (5) 03 06 16 17 20

STATUS OF INDIANS   2.5   .52
  (1) 16
STATUS QUO ANTE   2.5   .52
  (1) 16
STERILIZATION   2.5   .70
  (1) 30
STOP AND FRISK PROVISION   2.5   .52
  (1) 32
STUMPING   2.5   .52
  (1) 42
SUBJECT TO LOCAL JURISDICTION   2.5   .52
  (1) 17
SUBJUGATION   2.5   .52
  (2) 06 17
SUBVERSIVE ACTIVITIES CONTROL ACT,   2.5   .52
  1950
  (1) 38
SUCCESSION TO THE THRONE   2.5   .52
  (1) 17
SUMMONS   2.5   .70
  (6) 03 06 17 18 27 32
SUSPENDED SENTENCE   2.5   .52
  (1) 45
SWING TO THE LEFT   2.5   .52
  (1) 17
SYMPATHY STRIKE   2.5   .52
  (2) 06 32
SYSTEMS AND PROCEDURES   2.5   .52
  (1) 37
TACIT CONSENT   2.5   .52
  (1) 17
TARIFF NEGOTIATIONS   2.5   .52
  (1) 17
TAX AVOIDANCE   2.5   .52
  (1) 06
TAX EVASION   2.5   .52
  (2) 06 32
TAX IMMUNITY   2.5   .52
  (1) 03
TENANT FARMING   2.5   .52
  (1) 46
TENDER OF GOOD OFFICES   2.5   .70
  (1) 16
TERM OF OFFICE   2.5   .52
  (1) 17
TERRITORIAL CLAIM   2.5   .52
  (2) 11 17
TEST   2.5   .70
  (2) 24 30
THIRTY YEARS WAR   2.5   .52
  (2) 17 25
TORT LAW   2.5   .70
  (1) 18
TOTAL VICTORY   2.5   .52
  (1) 17
TOWN PLANNING   2.5   .52
  (2) 11 25
TREATY COMMITMENTS   2.5   .52
  (1) 17
TREATY OF ARBITRATION   2.5   .52
  (1) 17
TROIKA PROPOSAL, UNITED NATIONS   2.5   .52
  (4) 03 20 34 39

TRUCE AGREEMENT	2.5	.52
(1) 17		
TRUCE NEGOTIATIONS	2.5	.52
(1) 17		
TRUE BILL	2.5	.70
(2) 18 27		
TRUSTEESHIP AGREEMENT	2.5	.52
(1) 17		
TUTELAGE	2.5	.52
(1) 16		
ULTRA VIRES ACTION	2.5	.70
(2) 16 17		
UNCONDITIONAL NEUTRALITY	2.5	.52
(1) 17		
UNDISTRIBUTED PROFITS TAX	2.5	.52
(2) 06 16		
UNIFORM CODE OF MILITARY JUSTICE	2.5	.70
(2) 18 32		
UNILATERAL DECLARATION OF INDEPENDENCE (U.D.I.)	2.5	.52
(1) 38		
UNIVERSAL MEMBERSHIP	2.5	.70
(1) 36		
UNLAWFUL	2.5	.52
(1) 17		
UPRISING	2.5	.52
(1) 17		
UPSET	2.5	.70
(1) 17		
V-J DAY	2.5	.52
(1) 16		
VICTORY	2.5	.70
(1) 30		
VIRGINIA RESOLUTIONS	2.5	.70
(1) 06		
VISIT AND SEARCH	2.5	.70
(3) 06 16 17		
VOLUNTARY CONTRIBUTIONS	2.5	.70
(1) 17		
VOTE BY SITTING AND STANDING	2.5	.84
(1) 17		
VULNERABILITY	2.5	.70
(1) 24		
WAGING PEACE	2.5	.70
(1) 39		
WAIVE	2.5	.70
(1) 17		
WAIVER	2.5	.70
(1) 06		
WAR AIMS	2.5	.70
(1) 17		
WAR FOR THE UNIFICATION OF ITALY	2.5	.52
(1) 17		
WAR OF ROSES	2.5	.52
(1) 03		
WAR STRATEGEM	2.5	.52
(1) 17		
WARFARE ON LAND	2.5	.70
(1) 17		
WASHINGTON CONFERENCE OF 1921-1922	2.5	.70
(3) 16 21 25		
WATER CONSERVATION, U.S.A.	2.5	.70
(3) 03 18 32		
WHISKEY INSURRECTION (1794)	2.5	.70
(4) 02 03 06 44		
WHITE MAN'S WAR	2.5	.70
(1) 39		
WORK RELIEF	2.5	.70
(2) 06 16		
WORLD FOOD PROGRAM	2.5	.52
(1) 41		
YEAS AND NAYS	2.5	.70
(3) 06 17 27		
ABROGATION	2.6	.51
(3) 06 16 17		
ABUSE OF INTERNATIONAL LAW	2.6	.51
(1) 17		
ABYSSINIAN WAR	2.6	.51
(1) 17		
ACCORD	2.6	.51
(2) 06 27		
ACCUSATION	2.6	.51
(1) 30		
ACTIVITIES	2.6	.69
(2) 25 30		
ADMISSION (INTERNATIONAL ORGANIZATION)	2.6	.51
(1) 20		
AFFIRMATION	2.6	.69
(2) 06 16		
AFRICAN RE-COLONIZATION	2.6	.51
(1) 46		
AFRO-ASIAN CONFERENCE	2.6	.51
(1) 17		
AFRO-ASIAN MOVEMENT	2.6	.51
(1) 11		
AGRICULTURAL ADJUSTMENT ACTS (OF 1933)	2.6	.51
(1) 18		
AGRICULTURAL CONSERVATION PROGRAM	2.6	.51
(1) 03		
AIR JURISDICTION	2.6	.51
(2) 06 16		
ALLOTMENT	2.6	.69
(1) 45		
AMERICAN-GERMAN PEACE TREATY	2.6	.69
(1) 16		
ANNUAL MESSAGE	2.6	.51
(1) 16		
ANTI-LYNCHING BILL	2.6	.51
(4) 06 16 30 45		
ANTI-POVERTY ACT	2.6	.69
(2) 34 42		
ANTI-PREJUDICE	2.6	.69
(1) 30		
ANTIESPIONAGE ACT	2.6	.51
(1) 45		
APPORTIONMENT ACT OF 1929	2.6	.69
(1) 18		
APPRAISAL	2.6	.69
(3) 06 16 24		
ARGUMENTATION	2.6	.69
(1) 43		

ARMISTICE DAY	2.6	.51
(1) 16		
ARYAN DECREES	2.6	.69
(1) 21		
ASSUMPTION OF OFFICE	2.6	.51
(1) 17		
ASSUMPTION OF RISK	2.6	.69
(1) 06		
ATTRIBUTIONS	2.6	.69
(1) 24		
BALTIC PACT	2.6	.51
(1) 21		
BALTIMORE CONVENTION	2.6	.51
(1) 22		
BAN	2.6	.51
(1) 17		
BAR	2.6	.51
(5) 06 16 17 24 27		
BATTLE OF JUTLAND	2.6	.51
(1) 17		
BERLIN CONFERENCE	2.6	.51
(2) 03 21		
BETWEEN SESSIONS	2.6	.51
(1) 17		
BIMETALLISM	2.6	.51
(2) 06 16		
BIRTH REGISTRATION	2.6	.69
(2) 06 27		
BLAME	2.6	.69
(1) 43		
BLOCKED CURRENCY	2.6	.51
(2) 06 16		
BOGOTA CHARTER	2.6	.51
(1) 17		
BOGOTA CONFERENCE	2.6	.51
(1) 38		
BONA FIDE	2.6	.51
(1) 16		
BOOM	2.6	.51
(4) 06 16 27 29		
BOROUGH PLAN	2.6	.51
(1) 45		
BORROWING POWER	2.6	.51
(2) 06 18		
BOXER INDEMNITY	2.6	.51
(2) 06 21		
BROWNOUT	2.6	.51
(1) 16		
BRUSSELS CONFERENCE	2.6	.51
(1) 16		
BRUTALITY	2.6	.69
(1) 30		
BUILDING PERMIT	2.6	.51
(2) 06 16		
BUNDLE OF COMPROMISES	2.6	.69
(1) 42		
CAIRO DECLARATION	2.6	.51
(1) 38		
CALL TO ORDER	2.6	.51
(1) 17		
CAPITAL BUDGET	2.6	.51
(1) 42		

CAPITATION	2.6	.69
(1) 16		
CAPTIVITY	2.6	.51
(1) 17		
CENTRALIZED PURCHASING	2.6	.51
(2) 06 18		
CESSION	2.6	.51
(5) 06 16 17 20 33		
CHACO WAR	2.6	.51
(4) 03 16 21 34		
CHAIN VOTING	2.6	.51
(2) 03 16		
CHALLENGE	2.6	.69
(4) 06 16 24 30		
CHARTER OF PUNTA DEL ESTE	2.6	.51
(1) 03		
CHARTER OF RIGHTS	2.6	.51
(1) 22		
CHINESE-RUSSIAN AGREEMENTS OF	2.6	.51
1945		
(1) 16		
CITIZENSHIP, EXPATRIATION	2.6	.51
(1) 18		
CIVIC TRAINING	2.6	.51
(1) 15		
CLARIFICATION	2.6	.84
(1) 43		
CLASSIFICATION OF CITIES	2.6	.51
(1) 45		
CLEAN AIR AMENDMENTS	2.6	.51
(1) 32		
CODE OF FAIR COMPETITION	2.6	.51
(1) 16		
COINAGE	2.6	.51
(2) 06 16		
COLLECTIVE NATURALIZATION	2.6	.51
(1) 18		
COLLUSIVE BIDDING	2.6	.51
(2) 06 16		
COLUMBIA RIVER COMPACT	2.6	.51
(2) 06 18		
COMBINE	2.6	.51
(1) 16		
COMMERCIAL AGREEMENT	2.6	.51
(1) 17		
COMMERCIAL REVOLUTION	2.6	.69
(1) 22		
COMMERCIAL TREATY	2.6	.51
(2) 06 16		
COMMITMENT	2.6	.51
(4) 06 16 24 30		
COMMON PLEAS	2.6	.51
(1) 06		
COMMUNAL ELECTIONS	2.6	.51
(1) 17		
COMPANION BILLS	2.6	.69
(1) 06		
COMPETENCY	2.6	.51
(4) 16 17 24 32		
CONCENTRATED EMPLOYMENT	2.6	.69
PROGRAM (CEP)		
(1) 32		

CONCORDAT OF 1929	2.6	.51
(2) 16 22		
CONDITION	2.6	.51
(1) 30		
CONSTRUCTION	2.6	.84
(1) 06		
CONSULT	2.6	.69
(1) 17		
CONSUMER AFFAIRS	2.6	.51
(1) 25		
CONTINUE	2.6	.84
(2) 17 24		
CONTINUOUS VOYAGE DOCTRINE	2.6	.69
(3) 06 16 20		
CONVENE	2.6	.51
(1) 17		
CONVOCATION	2.6	.51
(1) 17		
COOLING-OFF PERIOD	2.6	.69
(3) 06 18 32		
COST REDUCTION	2.6	.69
(1) 37		
COST-PLUS CONTRACT	2.6	.51
(3) 06 16 27		
COUNSELING	2.6	.84
(1) 37		
COUNTERPART FUNDS	2.6	.51
(1) 20		
CREATION OF A POST	2.6	.69
(1) 17		
CREDIT	2.6	.69
(3) 03 25 30		
CRIME AGAINST PEACE	2.6	.51
(1) 17		
CRIME PREVENTION PROGRAMS	2.6	.51
(1) 45		
CRITICAL PERIOD	2.6	.51
(1) 06		
CUSTODY	2.6	.69
(2) 06 16		
DAWES PLAN	2.6	.51
(4) 06 16 17 21		
DECISIS	2.6	.69
(1) 24		
DECLARATION OF ELIMINATION OF	2.6	.51
DISCRIMINATION AGAINST WOMEN		
(1) 41		
DECLARATION OF INTENTION	2.6	.69
(2) 16 17		
DEED	2.6	.69
(1) 45		
DEFENSE ASSISTANCE PACT	2.6	.51
(1) 32		
DELIMITATION	2.6	.51
(1) 17		
DESIGNATE	2.6	.51
(2) 17 24		
DESTROYER-BASE DEAL	2.6	.51
(1) 45		
DIPLOMATIC LAW	2.6	.51
(2) 17 19		
DIPLOMATIC LEVEL	2.6	.51
(1) 17		
DISAPPROVAL	2.6	.69
(1) 17		
DISCIPLINARY ACTION	2.6	.69
(1) 17		
DISCOURSE	2.6	.69
(1) 43		
DISPUTE	2.6	.69
(3) 17 24 30		
DISSOLVE	2.6	.69
(1) 17		
DIVERSIONARY MOVE	2.6	.51
(1) 17		
DIVEST	2.6	.51
(1) 45		
DOCTRINE OF SUABILITY	2.6	.51
(1) 03		
DOCTRINE OF VESTED RIGHTS	2.6	.51
(1) 03		
DOLE	2.6	.69
(3) 06 16 27		
DOLLAR GAP	2.6	.51
(1) 38		
DORR'S REBELLION, RHODE ISLAND	2.6	.51
(5) 03 06 08 18 29		
DRAFTED	2.6	.69
(1) 45		
DRAWING OF LOTS	2.6	.69
(1) 17		
DRUG ABUSE PREVENTION	2.6	.69
(1) 32		
DUAL OFFICEHOLDING	2.6	.51
(1) 06		
EARNED INCOME	2.6	.51
(3) 06 16 25		
EASTERN QUESTION	2.6	.51
(2) 16 17		
EAVESDROPPING	2.6	.69
(1) 37		
ECONOMIC ADMINISTRATION	2.6	.51
(1) 11		
ECONOMIC MANAGEMENT	2.6	.51
(1) 11		
ECONOMIC MIRACLE	2.6	.51
(1) 17		
EDUCATION ACT OF 1965	2.6	.51
(1) 32		
ELASTIC CURRENCY	2.6	.51
(1) 06		
ELECTION ADDRESS	2.6	.51
(1) 17		
ELECTIONEER	2.6	.51
(1) 39		
EMBEZZLEMENT	2.6	.69
(1) 06		
EMPLOYEES--PARTICIPATION IN	2.6	.69
MANAGEMENT		
(1) 37		
EMPOWER	2.6	.69
(1) 17		
ENFORCEMENT ACT	2.6	.51
(2) 06 32		
ENGAGE	2.6	.69
(1) 17		

ENLISTMENT   2.6   .51
   (2) 06 16
ENVIRONMENTAL POLICY ACT   2.6   .51
   (2) 23 32
EQUILIBRATION   2.6   .69
   (1) 24
ESCROW   2.6   .69
   (1) 45
EVENT   2.6   .69
   (2) 17 24
EX PARTE   2.6   .51
   (5) 03 06 16 18 27
EXAMINATION   2.6   .69
   (3) 05 17 24
EXCHANGE OF INSTRUMENTS OF   2.6   .51
   RATIFICATIONS
   (1) 17
EXCHANGE OF TERRITORY   2.6   .51
   (1) 17
EXECUTIVE CALENDAR   2.6   .69
   (2) 18 32
EXECUTIVE WAR   2.6   .69
   (1) 34
EXEMPTION   2.6   .69
   (2) 06 32
EXERCISE   2.6   .69
   (2) 17 24
EXPENSE BUDGET   2.6   .69
   (1) 42
EXPLORATION   2.6   .69
   (1) 24
EXPLORATORY   2.6   .69
   (1) 24
EXPORT BOUNTY (SUBSIDY)   2.6   .51
   (1) 20
EXTEMPORE   2.6   .51
   (1) 17
EXTENSION   2.6   .69
   (1) 24
EXTENSION OF A CONFLICT   2.6   .51
   (1) 17
EXTERNAL SOVEREIGNTY   2.6   .51
   (1) 17
EXTRA SESSION   2.6   .69
   (1) 16
FACE-TO-FACE TALK   2.6   .69
   (1) 17
FAITH AND CREDIT   2.6   .51
   (1) 06
FALKLAND ISLANDS CONTROVERSY   2.6   .51
   (1) 03
FAMILY ASSISTANCE PLAN (FAP)   2.6   .51
   (1) 32
FAMILY PLANNING   2.6   .51
   (1) 11
FEDERAL COMMON LAW   2.6   .69
   (1) 44
FEDERAL RELIEF   2.6   .69
   (1) 16
FEDERAL SUPPLEMENT   2.6   .51
   (1) 18

FEDERAL-LOCAL COOPERATION IN LAW   2.6   .51
   ENFORCEMENT
   (1) 45
FEE   2.6   .51
   (2) 06 17
FERTILE CRESCENT PLAN   2.6   .51
   (2) 03 21
FINAL BALLOT   2.6   .51
   (1) 17
FINAL COMMUNIQUE   2.6   .51
   (1) 17
FISHING AGREEMENT   2.6   .51
   (1) 17
FIVE PRINCIPLES OF PEACEFUL   2.6   .51
   CO-EXISTENCE
   (1) 34
FIVE-FIVE-THREE RATIO   2.6   .51
   (1) 16
FLOATING DEBT   2.6   .69
   (2) 06 16
FLOOD CONTROL   2.6   .51
   (2) 06 32
FLOOR WAGE   2.6   .69
   (1) 16
FOREIGN VALUATION   2.6   .51
   (1) 06
FORMAL   2.6   .69
   (1) 24
FORMOSA RESOLUTION   2.6   .51
   (2) 32 34
FREE   2.6   .69
   (2) 24 30
FREEHOLDERS CHARTER   2.6   .69
   (1) 06
FRONT PORCH CAMPAIGN   2.6   .51
   (3) 06 16 29
FULBRIGHT ACT   2.6   .51
   (1) 20
FULBRIGHT-CONNALLY RESOLUTION   2.6   .51
   (1) 42
FUND   2.6   .69
   (1) 17
GAIN   2.6   .69
   (1) 24
GIFT   2.6   .69
   (1) 17
GLASSBORO SUMMIT   2.6   .51
   (1) 34
GREENBACKISM   2.6   .51
   (1) 03
GROOM FOR OFFICE   2.6   .51
   (1) 06
GROUNDSWELL   2.6   .51
   (1) 29
GROUP INSURANCE   2.6   .51
   (1) 45
GROUP LIBEL LAWS   2.6   .51
   (1) 03
GUARANTEE CLAUSE   2.6   .51
   (1) 18
GUARANTEES   2.6   .51
   (1) 19

GUIDING RULES	2.6	.69
(1) 17		
HANDS-OFF POLICY	2.6	.51
(1) 16		
HAVANA DECLARATION	2.6	.51
(2) 21 34		
HEAR	2.6	.69
(1) 24		
HELLENISTIC ERA	2.6	.51
(1) 35		
HEREDITY	2.6	.69
(2) 10 17		
HIGH-LEVEL CONFERENCE	2.6	.51
(1) 17		
HOARDING	2.6	.69
(1) 45		
HOMAGE	2.6	.51
(1) 17		
HOME AFFAIRS	2.6	.69
(1) 17		
HOUSE OF REPRESENTATIVES SPECIAL	2.6	.69
POWERS		
(1) 42		
HUNGER BLOCKADE	2.6	.69
(1) 17		
HURRAH CAMPAIGN	2.6	.69
(1) 29		
ILLICIT	2.6	.51
(1) 17		
IN FORMA PAUPERIS	2.6	.51
(1) 18		
INDEFINITE APPOINTMENT	2.6	.51
(1) 17		
INDENTURE	2.6	.51
(1) 16		
INDIANA BALLOT	2.6	.69
(3) 06 16 18		
INDICATIONS	2.6	.69
(1) 24		
INDUSTRIALIZATION OF FARMING	2.6	.51
(1) 45		
INEFFECTIVE BLOCKADE	2.6	.51
(1) 17		
INEVITABILITY	2.6	.69
(1) 43		
INFORMAL TALKS	2.6	.51
(1) 17		
INFRINGEMENT	2.6	.51
(1) 45		
INITIAL	2.6	.69
(3) 16 17 24		
INITIALED	2.6	.69
(1) 45		
INQUIRY	2.6	.69
(4) 01 17 20 24		
INSPECT	2.6	.69
(1) 25		
INSPECTION	2.6	.69
(2) 03 11		
INSULATION	2.6	.51
(1) 24		
INTELLECTUAL REVOLUTION	2.6	.69
(1) 22		
INTER-AMERICAN CONFERENCE	2.6	.51
(2) 03 17		
INTER-AMERICAN COOPERATION	2.6	.51
(1) 45		
INTERCESSION	2.6	.69
(1) 17		
INTERIM	2.6	.69
(1) 06		
INTERNATIONAL CRIMINAL LAW	2.6	.51
(1) 17		
INTERNATIONAL EXCHANGE PROGRAM	2.6	.51
(1) 03		
INTERNATIONAL LABOR CONFERENCE	2.6	.51
(1) 41		
INTERNATIONAL LABOR LAW	2.6	.51
(1) 17		
INTERNATIONAL WHEAT AGREEMENT	2.6	.69
(1) 17		
INTRODUCTION	2.6	.69
(1) 24		
INVISIBLE EXPORTS	2.6	.51
(1) 16		
INVOKE	2.6	.51
(1) 17		
IRAN, ANGLO-SOVIET TREATY WITH	2.6	.51
(1) 21		
ITALIAN CONSTITUTION	2.6	.51
(1) 03		
JACKSON DAY	2.6	.69
(1) 06		
JAPANESE CONSTITUTION, ARTICLE	2.6	.51
NINE		
(2) 03 20		
JIHAD (HOLY WAR)	2.6	.51
(2) 03 16		
JURISDICTION CLAUSE	2.6	.51
(1) 17		
LAND POLICIES	2.6	.51
(2) 10 12		
LAND RETIREMENT	2.6	.69
(1) 32		
LAUSANNE CONFERENCE	2.6	.69
(1) 16		
LAW OF LAND WARFARE	2.6	.51
(1) 17		
LAW OF NAVAL WARFARE	2.6	.51
(1) 17		
LAW OF PEACE	2.6	.51
(1) 17		
LAW OF WAGES	2.6	.51
(1) 26		
LAWLESSNESS	2.6	.51
(1) 30		
LEASE AGREEMENT	2.6	.69
(1) 17		
LECTURE	2.6	.51
(1) 17		
LEGAL FORCE OF JUDGMENT	2.6	.69
(1) 17		
LEGISLATIVE PERIOD	2.6	.69
(1) 17		
LIMITS	2.6	.69
(1) 24		

LIQUIDATE	2.6	.69
(1) 16		
LIQUOR REGULATION	2.6	.51
(1) 45		
LIQUOR TRAFFIC	2.6	.51
(1) 16		
LOCAL RELIEF	2.6	.51
(1) 45		
LOCAL REMEDIES	2.6	.51
(1) 17		
LOCARNO TREATIES	2.6	.51
(7) 06 11 16 17 21 22 38		
LONG HOT SUMMER	2.6	.69
(1) 34		
LONG-AND-SHORT HAUL	2.6	.69
(1) 06		
LONG-DISTANCE BLOCKADE	2.6	.69
(1) 17		
LYING	2.6	.69
(1) 43		
MANAGED CURRENCY	2.6	.51
(2) 16 18		
MANDATORY REFERENDUM	2.6	.51
(1) 06		
MANPOWER DEVELOPMENT AND TRAINING ACT	2.6	.69
(1) 32		
MANPOWER PLANNING	2.6	.69
(1) 37		
MARE NOSTRUM (OUR SEA)	2.6	.51
(1) 16		
MARITIME WARFARE	2.6	.51
(1) 17		
MARK-UP	2.6	.51
(1) 27		
MARRIAGE	2.6	.69
(3) 07 11 30		
MASSIVE RESISTANCE	2.6	.51
(1) 39		
MATTERS AFFECTING BOTH COUNTRIES	2.6	.51
(1) 17		
MCKINLEY TARIFF ACT	2.6	.51
(1) 06		
MENTAL TESTS	2.6	.69
(1) 37		
MERCY	2.6	.69
(1) 43		
MERGE	2.6	.69
(1) 17		
METRO FUNCTIONAL CONSOLIDATION	2.6	.69
(1) 18		
MIDDLE EAST PACT	2.6	.69
(2) 16 21		
MIDWAY, BATTLE OF	2.6	.51
(1) 03		
MILITARY INDEMNITY	2.6	.51
(1) 06		
MILLENIUM	2.6	.51
(1) 30		
MINISTERIAL ACT	2.6	.51
(1) 18		
MOBILE WARFARE	2.6	.51
(1) 17		
MOMENTUM	2.6	.69
(1) 30		
MORTGAGE MORATORIUM	2.6	.69
(1) 45		
MOTION TO DISMISS	2.6	.51
(1) 02		
MUGWUMPERY	2.6	.51
(1) 29		
NARCOTIC DRUGS CONTROL	2.6	.69
(1) 41		
NASSAU AGREEMENT, 1962	2.6	.51
(1) 34		
NATIONALIZATION OF THE SUEZ CANAL COMPANY	2.6	.51
(1) 17		
NAVAL DISARMAMENT CONFERENCES	2.6	.51
(1) 16		
NAVAL TREATY	2.6	.51
(1) 17		
NAVIGATION ACTS	2.6	.69
(2) 03 06 46		
NEGLECT	2.6	.51
(1) 17		
NEW ORDER	2.6	.51
(1) 39		
NEW ORDER IN EUROPE	2.6	.51
(2) 16 17		
NOBLE BIRTH	2.6	.51
(1) 17		
NOBLE EXPERIMENT	2.6	.69
(1) 29		
NON-RETROACTIVITY	2.6	.51
(1) 17		
NORRIS-LAGUARDIA (ANTI-INJUNCTION) ACT OF 1932	2.6	.69
(2) 18 32		
NORTH AFRICAN CAMPAIGNS	2.6	.51
(1) 17		
NUISANCE TAX	2.6	.51
(1) 16		
OCCUPATIONAL REPRESENTATION	2.6	.51
(2) 06 16		
OFFENSE	2.6	.51
(3) 06 17 30		
OFFENSIVE	2.6	.69
(1) 30		
ON-THE-JOB TRAINING (OJT)	2.6	.69
(1) 32		
OPEN SKIES PROPOSAL	2.6	.51
(2) 17 39		
OPPORTUNITY TO BE HEARD	2.6	.51
(1) 45		
OPUS DEI (WORK OF GOD)	2.6	.51
(1) 11		
ORDER OF BUSINESS	2.6	.69
(2) 06 16		
ORDER OF PRECEDENCE	2.6	.51
(1) 17		
ORDINARY BUDGET	2.6	.69
(1) 17		
ORGANIC ACT	2.6	.51
(1) 45		

OVERT ACT	2.6	.51
(1) 06		
PACIFIC SECURITY PACT	2.6	.51
(1) 38		
PACT OF CORFU	2.6	.51
(1) 16		
PARLIAMENT ACTS, 1911 AND 1949	2.6	.69
(1) 38		
PARLIAMENTARY RECESS	2.6	.69
(1) 17		
PART-TIME WORK	2.6	.69
(1) 37		
PARTITIONS OF POLAND	2.6	.51
(1) 16		
PASSION FOR ANONYMITY	2.6	.69
(1) 39		
PAX CHRISTI	2.6	.51
(1) 17		
PAY AS YOU GO	2.6	.51
(1) 39		
PEACE CONFERENCE OF 1919	2.6	.51
(1) 22		
PENSION	2.6	.51
(4) 06 16 17 27		
PEONAGE	2.6	.51
(5) 03 06 16 18 30		
PERFORMANCE CONTRACTING	2.6	.69
(1) 43		
PERFORMANCE TEST	2.6	.69
(1) 06		
PERMISSION	2.6	.69
(1) 17		
PINCKNEY TREATY	2.6	.69
(1) 06 46		
PLEDGE OF ALLEGIANCE	2.6	.69
(1) 27		
PLOT	2.6	.51
(3) 17 30 43		
PLOY	2.6	.51
(1) 39		
POLITICAL ATTACHMENTS	2.6	.69
(1) 15		
POLITICAL IMPACT	2.6	.51
(1) 39		
POLITICAL SUICIDE	2.6	.51
(1) 39		
POOR RELIEF	2.6	.51
(2) 06 16		
PREDICATE	2.6	.69
(1) 43		
PREFECTORAL SYSTEM	2.6	.51
(1) 11		
PRELIMINARY CANVASS	2.6	.69
(1) 06		
PREROGATIVE	2.6	.51
(3) 06 16 33		
PRESIDENTIAL INAUGURATION DAY	2.6	.51
(1) 03		
PRESIDENTIAL SHORT BALLOT	2.6	.51
(1) 06		
PRESIDENTIAL SUCCESSION ACT OF 1947	2.6	.69
(1) 18		
PRETRIAL CONFERENCE	2.6	.51
(1) 27		
PREVENT	2.6	.69
(3) 17 24 30		
PREVENTION OF SURPRISE ATTACKS	2.6	.51
(1) 17		
PREVENTIVE JUSTICE	2.6	.51
(1) 16		
PROBATIONARY APPOINTMENT	2.6	.51
(1) 17		
PROCLAMATION	2.6	.51
(3) 16 17 27		
PRODUCTION TAX	2.6	.69
(1) 06		
PROMULGATION	2.6	.51
(1) 17		
PROPRIETARY FUNCTION	2.6	.51
(1) 18		
PROTECTING POWER	2.6	.51
(1) 17		
PUBLIC LAW 480	2.6	.51
(1) 27		
PUBLICITY LAWS	2.6	.84
(2) 06 16		
QUALIFICATION	2.6	.51
(3) 03 06 30		
QUALITY CONTROL	2.6	.69
(1) 37		
QUARANTINE SPEECH	2.6	.51
(1) 16		
QUESTION	2.6	.69
(3) 06 17 24		
QUIET DIPLOMACY	2.6	.51
(1) 20		
RACE RELATIONS ACTS	2.6	.51
(1) 34		
RAID ON THE TREASURY	2.6	.51
(1) 06		
RAILROAD	2.6	.69
(4) 06 11 16 25		
RALLY	2.6	.51
(3) 06 16 29		
RE-ESTABLISHING OF FRIENDLY RELATIONS	2.6	.51
(1) 17		
READINESS TO REACH A COMPROMISE	2.6	.69
(1) 17		
REAL EVIDENCE	2.6	.69
(1) 32		
RECIPROCAL LEGISLATION	2.6	.51
(1) 06		
RECIPROCAL TRADE AGREEMENTS ACT OF 1934	2.6	.51
(5) 03 06 16 18 20		
RECOGNITION AS INSURGENTS	2.6	.51
(1) 17		
RECOGNITION, DIPLOMATIC, OF THE PEOPLE'S REPUBLIC OF CHINA	2.6	.51
(1) 03		
RECOMMIT	2.6	.51
(1) 16		
RECOMMITTAL	2.6	.51
(5) 06 16 18 27 32		

RECONSIDER 2.6 .51
(1) 16
RECONSIDERATION 2.6 .51
(1) 06
RECONVERSION OF ARMAMENTS 2.6 .69
(1) 17
REDUCTION OF ARMAMENTS 2.6 .51
(1) 17
REFORM ACT OF 1832 2.6 .51
(2) 22 26
REFORM BILL 2.6 .51
(1) 26
REFUTE 2.6 .69
(1) 17
REGIONAL AGREEMENT 2.6 .69
(1) 17
REGISTER 2.6 .69
(2) 06 17
REGISTRATION FEE 2.6 .51
(1) 17
REGISTRATION OF TREATIES 2.6 .51
(1) 17
REGULARLY APPOINTED 2.6 .51
(1) 17
REGULATORY 2.6 .51
(1) 24
REJECTION 2.6 .69
(2) 06 30
RELEASED-TIME PLAN 2.6 .51
(1) 42
REMOVE 2.6 .69
(2) 16 17
RENDEZVOUS WITH DESTINY 2.6 .69
(1) 39
REPARATIONS IN KIND 2.6 .51
(1) 16
REPORTED OUT 2.6 .51
(1) 45
REPUDIATION 2.6 .51
(2) 06 16
REPUDIATION OF OBLIGATIONS 2.6 .51
(1) 19
RES JUDICATA 2.6 .51
(1) 20
RESPECT FOR HUMAN RIGHTS 2.6 .51
(1) 17
RESPONSIBILITY OF STATES 2.6 .69
(1) 03
RESTRAINT 2.6 .51
(1) 25
RESTRICTIVE INTERPRETATION 2.6 .51
(1) 17
RESTRICTIVE PROVISIONS 2.6 .51
(1) 17
RETENTION 2.6 .51
(1) 43
RETRENCHMENT 2.6 .69
(3) 06 16 24
REVISE AND EXTEND 2.6 .69
(1) 27
REVOLT OF THE PALACE GUARD 2.6 .51
(1) 17

RIGHT OF CONQUEST 2.6 .51
(1) 17
RIGHT OF DISCOVERY 2.6 .51
(1) 06
RIGHT OF DISSOLUTION 2.6 .51
(1) 17
RIGHT OF DOMICILE 2.6 .51
(1) 17
RIGHT OF RESISTANCE 2.6 .51
(1) 16
RIGHT OF WAY 2.6 .69
(2) 06 16
RIGHT TO DECLARE WAR 2.6 .51
(1) 17
RIGHT TO PENSION 2.6 .51
(1) 17
RIGHT-TO-KNOW LAWS 2.6 .51
(1) 32
RIGID CONSTITUTION 2.6 .51
(1) 16
RIGID CONSTRUCTION 2.6 .51
(1) 06
RISORGIMENTO (POLITICAL MOVEMENT) 2.6 .51
(2) 16 17
RIVER AND HARBOR BILLS 2.6 .51
(1) 06
ROME TREATY, EURATOM (1957) 2.6 .51
(3) 17 20 34
ROTATION-IN-OFFICE 2.6 .51
(5) 02 06 16 26 29
ROUNDTABLE CONFERENCES 2.6 .51
(2) 16 17
ROYAL PREROGATIVE 2.6 .51
(1) 16
RULE OF THREE 2.6 .69
(1) 18
RURAL FREE DELIVERY (RFD) 2.6 .51
(2) 06 16
RUSSIAN CONSTITUTION 2.6 .51
(1) 26
RUSSO-JAPANESE AGREEMENTS 2.6 .51
(1) 21
SAAR AGREEMENT (SA) 2.6 .51
(1) 16
SAAR PLEBISCITE 2.6 .51
(1) 17
SAFE-CONDUCT 2.6 .51
(2) 16 17
SAFETY 2.6 .69
(1) 37
SALT TAX 2.6 .51
(1) 16
SALUTE 2.6 .51
(1) 17
SATYAGRAHA (GHANDIAN POLICY) 2.6 .51
(1) 22
SCANDALS 2.6 .51
(1) 11 46
SCORE 2.6 .69
(1) 30
SEASONAL EMPLOYMENT 2.6 .51
(1) 45

SECOND BANDUNG CONFERENCE	2.6	.51
(1) 34		
SECOND READING	2.6	.51
(1) 27		
SECURITY PROGRAM	2.6	.51
(2) 03 25		
SELF-LIQUIDATING PROJECT	2.6	.51
(1) 45		
SESSION	2.6	.51
(6) 06 16 17 18 27 32		
SEVEN YEARS WAR	2.6	.51
(1) 17		
SIDE PAYMENTS	2.6	.51
(1) 33		
SIEGE	2.6	.51
(1) 16		
SIN	2.6	.69
(1) 43		
SINAI CAMPAIGN	2.6	.51
(1) 03		
SINE DIE (WITHOUT A DAY -	2.6	.69
INDEFINITELY)		
(5) 03 06 16 18 32		
SISTER CITY MOVEMENT	2.6	.69
(1) 17		
SIX-YEAR PLAN	2.6	.51
(1) 17		
SLAVE REVOLTS	2.6	.51
(1) 46		
SLUMP	2.6	.69
(1) 38		
SLUSH FUND	2.6	.51
(4) 06 16 27 29		
SMITH ACT -ALIEN REGISTRATION ACT	2.6	.51
OF 1940		
(4) 18 22 32 34		
SOFT CURRENCY	2.6	.51
(1) 20		
SOIL BANK PLAN	2.6	.51
(1) 42		
SOLIDARITY	2.6	.51
(4) 10 17 24 30		
SOUND MONEY	2.6	.51
(1) 16		
SPACE PROGRAM	2.6	.51
(1) 11		
SPARTACIST INSURRECTION	2.6	.51
(3) 03 16 17		
SPLENDID ISOLATION	2.6	.51
(1) 03		
SPLIT SESSION	2.6	.51
(3) 03 06 16		
SQUATTER SOVEREIGNTY	2.6	.51
(5) 02 06 16 29 32		
STANDARDS OF PERFORMANCE	2.6	.69
(1) 37		
STANDING DIVISION	2.6	.69
(1) 32		
STANDING ORDERS OF THE HOUSE OF	2.6	.51
COMMONS		
(3) 06 16 17		
STANDING VOTE	2.6	.69
(1) 32		
STATE TRADE BARRIERS	2.6	.51
(1) 45		
STATUTES AT LARGE	2.6	.84
(1) 44		
STORMING OF THE BASTILLE	2.6	.51
(1) 17		
SUBJECT MATTER OF A DISPUTE	2.6	.51
(1) 17		
SUBMARINE WARFARE	2.6	.51
(2) 16 17		
SUING	2.6	.51
(1) 30		
SUPPORT	2.6	.69
(3) 24 30 33		
SURVIVAL	2.6	.51
(2) 24 30		
SUSPENSIVE VETO	2.6	.51
(3) 06 16 17		
TACTICS	2.6	.69
(4) 01 03 24 30		
TARIFF FOR REVENUE ONLY	2.6	.51
(2) 16 29		
TAX IMMUNITY-INTERGOVERNMENTAL	2.6	.51
(1) 18		
TAX INCIDENCE	2.6	.69
(1) 18		
TEACHER'S OATH	2.6	.51
(1) 06		
TEACHING	2.6	.69
(1) 43		
TELLER VOTE	2.6	.69
(3) 18 27 32		
TEMPERANCE	2.6	.51
(1) 43		
TERMS	2.6	.69
(1) 24		
TERRITORIAL CHANGE	2.6	.51
(1) 17		
TEST OATH	2.6	.51
(1) 06		
TESTIMONIAL DINNERS	2.6	.69
(1) 39		
THIRD READING	2.6	.51
(1) 27		
TICKET	2.6	.51
(3) 03 16 29		
TIDELANDS OIL ACT	2.6	.51
(1) 32		
TIDELANDS OIL CONTROVERSY	2.6	.51
(1) 45		
TIE-BREAK	2.6	.69
(1) 17		
TIME MANAGEMENT	2.6	.69
(1) 37		
TOWNSEND PLAN	2.6	.51
(4) 03 06 14 16		
TRADING-WITH-THE-ENEMY ACT	2.6	.51
(1) 06		
TREATY OF ASSISTANCE	2.6	.51
(1) 17		
TREATY OF FRIENDSHIP	2.6	.51
(1) 17		

TREATY OF INDEPENDENCE	2.6	.51
(1) 17		
TREATY OF PARIS (1783)	2.6	.51
(1) 46		
TREATY OF RAPALLO	2.6	.51
(3) 16 17 21		
TREATY OF VIENNA	2.6	.51
(1) 16		
TRIBAL WARFARE	2.6	.51
(1) 36		
TRIBUTE	2.6	.51
(2) 06 16		
TRIPARTITE PACT	2.6	.51
(2) 21 34		
TRUCE OFFER	2.6	.51
(1) 17		
U.S. FEDERAL AID HIGHWAY ACT OF 1956	2.6	.51
(1) 03		
UNITY	2.6	.69
(2) 11 24		
UNIVERSAL COPYRIGHT CONVENTION	2.6	.51
(1) 17		
UNIVERSITY SUFFRAGE	2.6	.69
(1) 16		
UPWARD BOUND	2.6	.51
(1) 42		
V-E DAY	2.6	.51
(1) 16		
VASSALAGE	2.6	.51
(2) 09 17		
VENEZUELA BOUNDARY DISPUTE	2.6	.51
(1) 06 46		
VETERANS BONUS	2.6	.69
(1) 16		
VICE	2.6	.69
(2) 06 24		
VIOLATION	2.6	.69
(2) 17 30		
VIRTUAL REPRESENTATION	2.6	.69
(1) 33		
VOCATIONAL EDUCATION	2.6	.51
(4) 06 24 30 37		
VOID FOR VAGUENESS DOCTRINE	2.6	.69
(1) 44		
VOLUNTARY SERVICE	2.6	.51
(1) 37		
WAGES AND HOURS ACT	2.6	.69
(1) 32		
WANT	2.6	.69
(1) 43		
WAR OF NERVES	2.6	.51
(1) 17		
WARFARE AT SEA	2.6	.69
(1) 17		
WARSAW RISING	2.6	.51
(1) 34		
WASHINGTON NAVAL TREATY	2.6	.69
(2) 20 21		
WATERSHED ELECTION	2.6	.69
(1) 39		
WEST IRIAN CONFLICT	2.6	.51
(1) 03		
WHITE SLAVE ACT	2.6	.51
(2) 06 29		
WHITEWASH	2.6	.51
(4) 06 27 29 30		
WILDERNESS ACT	2.6	.51
(1) 32		
WITCH HUNT	2.6	.51
(1) 27		
WORKER CONTROL	2.6	.51
(1) 11		
WORKERS PARTICIPATION	2.6	.51
(1) 11		
WORKING CONDITIONS	2.6	.69
(1) 37		
WORLD ECONOMIC CONFERENCE	2.6	.51
(3) 06 16 21		
WORLD ECONOMIC SURVEY	2.6	.51
(1) 41		
WRONG	2.6	.69
(1) 30		
BROWN VS. BOARD OF EDUCATION OF TOPEKA (1954)	1.2	.42
(7) 18 25 27 32 34 42 46		
MARBURY VS. MADISON (1803)	1.3	.48
(5) 03 06 18 27 32		
DRED SCOTT VS. SANFORD (1857)	1.6	.69
(7) 03 06 16 18 27 29 32 46		
MCCULLOCH VS. MARYLAND (1819)	1.8	.78
(5) 03 06 18 27 32		
MIRANDA VS. ARIZONA (1966)	2.0	.94
(2) 18 32		
SACCO-VANZETTI CASE	2.0	.47
(2) 03 06		
BAKER VS. CARR (1962)	2.1	.73
(4) 03 18 25 32		
BARRON VS. BALTIMORE (1833)	2.1	.87
(1) 42		
CIVIL RIGHTS CASES	2.1	.73
(3) 06 18 32		
JEHOVAH'S WITNESSES CASES	2.1	.73
(4) 18 22 25 32		
PLESSY VS. FERGUSON (1896)	2.1	.73
(3) 18 27 32		
GIBBONS VS. OGDEN (1824)	2.2	.78
(1) 42		
NEW YORK SCHOOL PRAYER CASE (1962)	2.2	.63
(1) 03		
FLAG SALUTE CASES	2.3	.48
(1) 42		
HISS CASE	2.3	.67
(1) 03		
CIVIL CASE	2.4	.69
(1) 45		
COMMUNIST PARTY CASES	2.4	.51
(1) 42		
GIDEON VS. WAINWRIGHT (1963)	2.4	.69
(2) 18 32		
POWERS (FRANCIS GARY) CASE	2.4	.51
(1) 03		
U.S. VS. CURTISS-WRIGHT CORPORATION (1936)	2.4	.51
(4) 18 20 27 32		

YOUNGSTOWN SHEET AND TUBE CO. 2.4 .51
  VS. SAWYER (1952)
  (3) 18 20 32
ABINGTON SCHOOL DISTRICT VS. 2.5 .70
  SCHEMPP (1963)
  (1) 32
CASE 2.5 .70
  (1) 44
COLGROVE VS. GREEN (1946) 2.5 .70
  (2) 18 32
CORFU CHANNEL CASE 2.5 .52
  (2) 03 16
EX PARTE MILLIGAN (1866) 2.5 .52
  (2) 18 32
GRANGER CASES 2.5 .70
  (1) 42
SCHECTER POULTRY CORP VS. U.S. 2.5 .52
  (1935)
  (4) 06 18 27 32
SHREVEPORT RATE CASE 2.5 .52
  (1) 06
SLAUGHTERHOUSE CASES 2.5 .52
  (4) 06 18 29 32
ADKINS VS. CHILDRENS HOSPITAL 2.6 .69
  (1923)
  (1) 42
ASHWANDER VS. TENNESSEE VALLEY 2.6 .69
  AUTHORITY (1936)
  (3) 03 18 32
BOARD OF EDUCATION VS. ALLEN 2.6 .51
  (1968)
  (1) 32
BOLLING VS. SHARPE (1954) 2.6 .51
  (2) 18 32
DARTMOUTH COLLEGE VS. WOODWARD 2.6 .69
  (1819)
  (1) 42
ESCOBEDO VS. ILLINOIS (1964) 2.6 .69
  (1) 42
GINSBERG VS. UNITED STATES (1966) 2.6 .51
  (1) 32
GITLOW VS. NEW YORK (1925) 2.6 .69
  (3) 18 22 32
HURTADO VS. CALIFORNIA (1884) 2.6 .51
  (2) 18 32
ILLINOIS EX REL. MCCOLLUM VS. 2.6 .51
  BOARD OF EDUCATION (1948)
  (1) 42
IN RE GAULT (1967) 2.6 .51
  (1) 32
MCCOLLUM VS. BOARD OF EDUCATION 2.6 .51
  (1948)
  (2) 18 32
MISSOURI VS. HOLLAND (1920) 2.6 .69
  (4) 03 18 20 32
NATIONAL LABOR RELATIONS BOARD 2.6 .51
  VS. J« L STEEL (1937)
  (1) 42
PRIZE CASES 2.6 .51
  (1) 06
RELEASED TIME CASES 2.6 .51
  (1) 32

ROTH VS. U.S. (1957) 2.6 .69
  (2) 18 32
SCHENCK VS. U.S. (1919) 2.6 .51
  (3) 18 22 27
SCOTTSBORO CASES 2.6 .51
  (2) 06 32
SMITH VS. ALLWRIGHT (1944) 2.6 .51
  (1) 18
WESBERRY VS. SANDERS (1964) 2.6 .51
  (2) 18 32
YATES VS. U.S. (1957) 2.6 .69
  (3) 18 22 32
MACHIAVELLI, NICCOLO 1.2 .42
  (12) 03 04 05 07 08 09 11 14 22 23
  25 26
LOCKE, JOHN 1.3 .67
  (12) 03 04 05 09 10 11 14 15 23 25
  26 32
HITLER, ADOLF 1.4 .51
  (11) 03 07 08 10 14 15 22 24 25 26
  34 46
LINCOLN, PRESIDENT ABRAHAM 1.4 .51
  (9) 03 07 08 11 14 22 25 30 32 46
MAO TSE-TUNG 1.4 .51
  (9) 03 07 11 14 22 23 24 25 34
MARX, KARL 1.4 .69
  (15) 03 04 05 07 08 10 11 13 14 22
  23 24 25 26 32
ARISTOTLE 1.5 .70
  (11) 03 04 05 08 09 11 14 15 22 23
  26
HOBBES, THOMAS 1.5 .70
  (1) 26
LENIN, NIKOLAI 1.5 .52
  (4) 03 10 14 26
LENIN, VLADIMIR ILICH ULYANOV 1.5 .70
  (5) 07 22 23 25 34
MORGENTHAU, HANS J. 1.5 .52
  (6) 04 05 13 22 25 28
NIXON, PRESIDENT RICHARD M. 1.5 .52
  (6) 07 11 23 25 32 34 46
SOCRATES 1.5 .52
  (7) 03 07 08 09 22 25 26
KING, DR. MARTIN LUTHER, JR. 1.6 .51
  (1) 03 11 23 25 30 32 34 46
PLATO 1.6 .84
  (13) 03 04 05 07 08 09 11 15 22 23
  24 25 26
ROOSEVELT, PRESIDENT FRANKLIN D. 1.6 .51
  (11) 03 07 08 10 11 14 22 23 25 32
  34 46
STALIN, JOSEPH 1.6 .69
  (11) 07 08 10 11 13 14 22 23 24 25
  26 46
WEBER, MAX 1.6 .51
  (11) 04 05 07 08 11 15 22 23 24 25
  26
CHURCHILL, SIR WINSTON LEONARD 1.7 .48
  SPENCER
  (2) 38 41 46
DE GAULLE, GENERAL CHARLES ANDRE 1.7 .67
  JOSEPH MARIE
  (1) 14 38 46

ENGELS, FRIEDRICH	1.7	.67
(10) 03 08 10 11 13 14 22 23 25 26		
FORD, PRESIDENT GERALD R.	1.7	.67
(0)		
FRANKLIN, BENJAMIN	1.7	.48
(3) 14 25 32 46		
HAMILTON, ALEXANDER	1.7	.67
(4) 03 22 25 32 46		
MILL, JOHN STUART	1.7	.67
(12) 03 04 05 07 10 11 13 22 23 25		
26 32		
MUSSOLINI, BENITO	1.7	.48
(10) 03 08 10 14 22 23 24 25 26 34		
46		
ROUSSEAU, JEAN JACQUES	1.7	.48
(1) 35		
WASHINGTON, PRESIDENT GEORGE	1.7	.48
(4) 03 25 32 46		
BENTHAM, JEREMY	1.8	.63
(10) 03 08 09 10 11 14 22 23 25 26		
BURKE, EDMUND	1.8	.42
(12) 03 05 07 09 10 11 22 23 24 25		
26 32		
CALHOUN, JOHN C.	1.8	.63
(4) 03 22 25 32 46		
EISENHOWER, PRESIDENT DWIGHT	1.8	.63
DAVID		
(8) 03 08 22 23 24 25 32 34 46		
HO CHI MINH	1.8	.63
(6) 03 07 11 23 25 34		
JACKSON, PRESIDENT ANDREW	1.8	.63
(1) 03 46		
JEFFERSON, PRESIDENT THOMAS	1.8	.63
(11) 03 07 08 10 11 15 22 23 25 26		
32 46		
JOHNSON, PRESIDENT LYNDON BAINES	1.8	.63
(8) 03 07 10 23 25 30 32 34 46		
KENNEDY, PRESIDENT JOHN F. (JFK)	1.8	.63
(8) 03 08 23 24 25 30 32 34 46		
KEYNES, JOHN MAYNARD	1.8	.63
(5) 03 10 22 25 32		
LIPSET, SEYMOUR MARTIN	1.8	.63
(5) 04 07 08 13 15		
MADISON, PRESIDENT JAMES	1.8	.63
(6) 03 08 22 23 25 32 46		
MARSHALL, JOHN	1.8	.63
(5) 03 07 22 25 32 46		
MONTESQUIEU, BARON CHARLES-LOUIS	1.8	.63
DE LA BREDE ET DE		
(7) 03 05 07 09 11 23 26 35		
NADER, RALPH	1.8	.42
(3) 07 25 32		
TROTSKY, LEON	1.8	.63
(9) 03 10 11 14 22 23 25 26 34		
TRUMAN, PRESIDENT HARRY S.	1.8	.63
(9) 03 07 08 14 23 24 25 32 34 46		
WILSON, PRESIDENT WOODROW	1.8	.42
(13) 03 04 05 07 08 10 11 14 22 25		
28 31 32 46		
AGNEW, SPIRO	1.9	.56
(1) 25		
BREZHNEV, LEONID ILYICH	1.9	.56
(4) 07 23 25 34		

CALVIN, JOHN	1.9	.31
(8) 03 05 09 22 23 25 26 35		
CHIANG KAI-SHEK	1.9	.31
(5) 03 07 23 25 34		
CHOU EN-LAI	1.9	.56
(4) 07 14 25 34		
DEUTSCH, KARL W.	1.9	.56
(8) 04 05 11 13 22 25 28 31		
FUHRER	1.9	.56
(2) 16 34		
GANDHI, MAHATMA	1.9	.56
(1) 25		
GOLDWATER, BARRY M.	1.9	.56
(4) 03 04 32 34		
HEGEL, GEORG WILHELM FRIEDRICH	1.9	.56
(10) 03 04 07 09 10 11 14 22 25 26		
HUME, DAVID	1.9	.56
(6) 03 05 09 11 22 26		
KHRUSHCHEV, NIKITA SERGEEVICH	1.9	.56
(10) 03 07 11 20 22 23 24 25 26 34		
MALCOLM X	1.9	.56
(3) 25 30 34		
MERTON, ROBERT K.	1.9	.56
(5) 04 07 13 15 23		
MONROE, PRESIDENT JAMES	1.9	.56
(4) 03 14 25 32 46		
MYRDAL, GUNNAR	1.9	.56
(1) 25		
NAPOLEON BONAPARTE	1.9	.73
(7) 03 08 14 22 24 25 26		
NAPOLEON I, EMPEROR	1.9	.73
(1) 14		
NIETZSCHE, FRIEDRICH	1.9	.73
(8) 03 04 10 11 14 22 25 26		
PAINE, THOMAS	1.9	.56
(6) 05 10 11 22 23 32 46		
ROOSEVELT, PRESIDENT THEODORE	1.9	.56
(8) 03 08 10 14 22 23 25 32 46		
SKINNER, B. F.	1.9	.56
(3) 07 11 25		
THOMAS AQUINAS	1.9	.56
(1) 26		
TOCQUEVILLE, (CHARLES) ALEXIS	1.9	.56
(HENRI CLEREL) DE		
(7) 03 08 10 11 15 22 23 25 32		
U THANT	1.9	.56
(2) 25 34		
WARREN, EARL	1.9	.56
(6) 03 07 24 25 32 34		
ADAMS, PRESIDENT JOHN	2.0	.66
(4) 03 22 32 46		
ADAMS, PRESIDENT JOHN QUINCY	2.0	.66
(4) 03 25 32 46		
ALEXANDER THE GREAT	2.0	.47
(3) 03 22 26		
ALLENDE, SALVADOR	2.0	.66
(1) 25		
ALMOND, GABRIEL A.	2.0	.81
(7) 04 05 11 15 23 28 31		
AQUINAS, SAINT THOMAS	2.0	.47
(4) 03 05 09 22		
BEARD, CHARLES A.	2.0	.66
(6) 05 10 13 22 28 31		

BRYAN, WILLIAM JENNINGS	2.0	.66
(3) 22 25 32 46		
CASTRO, DR. FIDEL RUIZ	2.0	.47
(1) 38		
CHAVEZ, CESAR	2.0	.66
(2) 07 25		
CHRIST	2.0	.81
(2) 11 30		
CLEVELAND, PRESIDENT GROVER	2.0	.66
(3) 03 32 46		
DAHL, ROBERT A.	2.0	.66
(8) 04 05 11 13 15 22 28 31		
DAVIS, JEFFERSON	2.0	.47
(1) 32		
DEBS, EUGENE VICTOR	2.0	.47
(5) 03 10 22 25 32 46		
DEWEY, JOHN	2.0	.66
(8) 03 08 13 14 22 23 25 26		
DU BOIS, W.E.B.	2.0	.47
(1) 25 46		
DULLES, JOHM FOSTER	2.0	.47
(4) 03 25 32 34		
EASTON, DAVID	2.0	.66
(9) 03 04 07 11 13 15 22 28 31		
FRANCO, GENERAL FRANCISCO	2.0	.47
(6) 03 07 14 22 25 34		
GANDHI, INDIRA	2.0	.47
(1) 38		
GRANT, PRESIDENT ULYSSES SIMPSON	2.0	.81
(2) 03 32 46		
HAMMARSKJOLD, DAG HJALMAR AGNE CARL	2.0	.66
(4) 03 07 25 34		
HOOVER, J. EDGAR	2.0	.66
(2) 25 34		
HOOVER, PRESIDENT HERBERT CLARK	2.0	.66
(7) 07 10 14 22 25 32 34 46		
JACKSON, HENRY (SCOOP)	2.0	.66
(1) 25		
JOHNSON, PRESIDENT ANDREW	2.0	.66
(5) 03 07 25 30 32 46		
KENNEDY, EDWARD MOORE	2.0	.66
(3) 25 32 34		
KERENSKY, ALEXANDER	2.0	.47
(3) 03 14 22		
KEY, V. O., JR.	2.0	.81
(7) 04 05 07 15 22 28 31		
KISSINGER, HENRY ALFRED	2.0	.66
(3) 07 25 32		
KOSYGIN, ALEKSEI NIKOLAEVICH	2.0	.47
(3) 03 25 34		
LLOYD GEORGE, DAVID	2.0	.47
(3) 03 10 34		
LUTHER, MARTIN	2.0	.94
(4) 05 14 22 25 43		
MACARTHUR, GENERAL DOUGLAS	2.0	.66
(5) 08 14 22 25 34		
MALTHUS, THOMAS ROBERT	2.0	.47
(4) 14 22 25 26		
MARCUSE, HERBERT	2.0	.47
(4) 07 11 23 25		
MCGOVERN, GEORGE S.	2.0	.47
(4) 07 11 25 32		
MCKINLEY, PRESIDENT WILLIAM	2.0	.47
(4) 03 22 25 32 46		
MCNAMARA, ROBERT STRANGE	2.0	.47
(4) 07 25 32 34		
MILLS, C. WRIGHT	2.0	.47
(4) 13 22 24 25		
NAPOLEON III	2.0	.66
(1) 22		
NASSER, GAMAL ABDUL	2.0	.47
(7) 03 11 14 23 24 25 34		
NEHRU, JAWAHARLAL	2.0	.66
(9) 03 07 11 14 22 23 24 25 34		
ROCKEFELLER, JOHN D.	2.0	.47
(1) 08 22 46		
RUSSELL, BERTRAND	2.0	.47
(4) 03 10 15 22		
SAINT AUGUSTINE	2.0	.66
(2) 23 25		
SINCLAIR, UPTON	2.0	.47
(1) 03 07 46		
SMITH, ADAM	2.0	.81
(7) 03 09 10 14 22 25 26		
STEVENSON, ADLAI EWING	2.0	.66
(3) 03 25 34		
TITO, JOSIP BROZ	2.0	.00
(7) 03 07 14 22 23 25 34		
VEBLEN, THORSTEIN	2.0	.47
(4) 07 14 25 26		
WEBSTER, DANIEL	2.0	.81
(3) 03 25 32 46		
ADAMS, HENRY	2.1	.56
(2) 07 22		
ARENDT, HANNAH	2.1	.73
(3) 04 07 25		
ARTHUR, PRESIDENT CHESTER ALAN	2.1	.73
(3) 03 32 46		
ATTLEE, CLEMENT RICHARD	2.1	.56
(1) 38		
BISMARCK, OTTO VON	2.1	.56
(5) 03 14 22 24 25		
BOLIVAR, SIMON	2.1	.56
(1) 03		
BOND, JULIAN	2.1	.73
(2) 25 30		
BRANDT, WILLY	2.1	.56
(6) 03 07 11 23 25 34		
BROWN, JOHN	2.1	.56
(2) 22 46		
BURGER, WARREN	2.1	.87
(3) 07 25 32		
BURR, AARON	2.1	.31
(1) 46		
CAESAR, GAIUS JULIUS	2.1	.56
(1) 08		
CHAMBERLAIN, NEVILLE	2.1	.56
(6) 03 07 14 22 25 34		
CLAUSEWITZ, KARL VON	2.1	.56
(7) 03 07 11 13 14 22 25		
CLAY, HENRY	2.1	.56
(3) 08 25 32 46		
CLEMENCEAU, GEORGES	2.1	.56
(2) 03 14		

COOLIDGE, PRESIDENT CALVIN	2.1	.56	
(5) 03 14 22 24 32 46			
DALEY, MAYOR RICHARD	2.1	.56	
(2) 07 25			
DARWIN, CHARLES	2.1	.56	
(7) 05 07 10 11 22 25 26			
DAVIS, ANGELA	2.1	.56	
(3) 07 15 25			
DIEM, NGO-DINH	2.1	.56	
(3) 03 25 34			
EICHMANN, ADOLF	2.1	.56	
(2) 03 34			
FREUD, SIGMUND	2.1	.73	
(8) 04 07 11 13 15 22 25 26			
GEORGE III OF ENGLAND	2.1	.73	
(2) 25 26			
GEORGE, DAVID LLOYD	2.1	.56	
(1) 25			
GEORGE, HENRY	2.1	.73	
(5) 10 14 22 25 26 46			
GIAP, VO NGUYEN, GENERAL	2.1	.73	
(2) 25 34			
GOMPERS, SAMUEL	2.1	.56	
(1) 32			
HARDING, PRESIDENT WARREN G.	2.1	.73	
(4) 03 22 25 32 46			
HEARST, WILLIAM RANDOLPH	2.1	.56	
(1) 32			
JESUS OF NAZARETH	2.1	.73	
(3) 03 09 22			
KAI-SHEK, CHIANG	2.1	.56	
(1) 25			
KANT, IMMANUEL	2.1	.73	
(8) 03 04 08 09 22 23 25 26			
KENNEDY, ROBERT F.	2.1	.56	
(3) 25 30 34			
KRUPP	2.1	.56	
(1) 16			
LASSWELL, HAROLD D.	2.1	.73	
(8) 04 05 08 13 22 25 28 31			
LEE, GENERAL ROBERT E.	2.1	.73	
(1) 46			
LIN PIAO	2.1	.56	
(1) 38			
LIPPMANN, WALTER	2.1	.31	
(6) 05 10 13 22 25 32			
LIU SHAO-CHI	2.1	.73	
(7) 03 07 11 14 23 25 34			
LUMUMBA, PATRICE	2.1	.56	
(2) 25 34			
MACMILLAN, PRIME MINISTER HAROLD	2.1	.73	
(3) 03 25 34			
MARSHALL, GENERAL GEORGE C.,	2.1	.56	
(1) 32 34 46			
MCCARTHY, EUGENE J.	2.1	.31	
(3) 03 25 34			
MEANY, GEORGE	2.1	.31	
(3) 03 07 25			
MERRIAM, CHARLES E.	2.1	.56	
(5) 05 15 22 28 31			
MORE, SIR THOMAS	2.1	.56	
(3) 22 23 26			
PARSONS, TALCOTT	2.1	.73	
(7) 04 07 11 13 15 23 25			
PERON, JUAN DOMINGO	2.1	.31	
(6) 07 14 23 24 25 34			
ROCKEFELLER, NELSON A.	2.1	.56	
(2) 23 34			
ROOSEVELT, ANNA ELEANOR	2.1	.73	
(2) 25 34			
SADAT, ANWAR	2.1	.56	
(3) 07 23 25			
SARTRE, JEAN-PAUL	2.1	.56	
(5) 08 11 22 23 25			
TAFT, PRESIDENT WILLIAM HOWARD	2.1	.56	
(6) 03 10 23 24 25 32 46			
TRUDEAU, PIERRE	2.1	.56	
(3) 07 25 34			
VOLTAIRE, FRANCOIS MARIE AROUET DE	2.1	.56	
(1) 35			
WALDHEIM, KURT	2.1	.56	
(1) 07			
WALLACE, GEORGE C.	2.1	.31	
(5) 07 11 23 25 34			
WASHINGTON, BOOKER T.	2.1	.56	
(1) 25 46			
ACHESON, DEAN	2.2	.63	
(4) 22 23 25 34			
ACTON, LORD	2.2	.78	
(2) 11 22			
ADAMS, SAMUEL	2.2	.63	
(1) 32			
ADENAUER, DR. KONRAD	2.2	.63	
(1) 38			
ARON, RAYMOND	2.2	.78	
(3) 11 14 23			
ATATURK	2.2	.63	
(1) 34			
BAKUNIN, MICHAEL	2.2	.42	
(6) 03 10 11 14 22 25			
BERRIGAN, PHILLIP	2.2	.78	
(1) 25			
BLACK, HUGO L.	2.2	.63	
(2) 03 25			
BUCHANAN, PRESIDENT JAMES A.	2.2	.63	
(2) 03 32 46			
CAMUS, ALBERT	2.2	.63	
(2) 03 08			
CARMICHAEL, STOKELY	2.2	.63	
(4) 07 11 30 34			
CHIANG KAI-SHEK, MME.	2.2	.63	
(1) 03			
COLUMBUS, CHRISTOPHER	2.2	.63	
(2) 03 08			
COMTE, AUGUSTE	2.2	.63	
(1) 26			
COPERNICUS, NICHOLAS	2.2	.78	
(3) 05 08 22			
DA VINCI, LEONARDO	2.2	.63	
(1) 22 35			
DESCARTES, RENE	2.2	.63	
(4) 09 11 23 26			
DURKHEIM, EMILE	2.2	.78	
(6) 04 07 10 11 22 25			

ECHEVERRIA, LUIS	2.2	.63
(1) 07		
EINSTEIN, ALBERT	2.2	.63
(2) 05 22		
EULAU, HEINZ	2.2	.63
(3) 15 28 31		
EVERS, CHARLES	2.2	.42
(1) 25		
FESTINGER, LEON	2.2	.78
(3) 04 13 15		
FRANKFURTER, FELIX	2.2	.63
(5) 03 04 10 22 25		
FULBRIGHT, J. WILLIAM	2.2	.63
(7) 03 11 14 20 25 32 34		
GALBRAITH, JOHN KENNETH	2.2	.63
(3) 14 22 25		
GOERING, HERMANN	2.2	.63
(3) 03 22 34		
GREELEY, HORACE	2.2	.63
(1) 03		
GROMYKO, ANDREI ANDREEVICH	2.2	.63
(2) 03 07		
HAILE SELASSIE 1, EMPEROR OF	2.2	.63
ETHIOPIA		
(1) 43		
HAYES, PRESIDENT RUTHERFORD B.	2.2	.78
(2) 03 25 46		
HENRY, PATRICK	2.2	.63
(1) 03		
HIROHITO, EMPEROR	2.2	.63
(2) 03 34		
HISS, ALGER	2.2	.63
(2) 25 34		
HUMPHREY, HUBERT HORATIO, JR.	2.2	.63
(5) 03 07 25 32 34		
JAVITS, JACOB K.	2.2	.63
(2) 03 32		
JAY, JOHN	2.2	.63
(2) 30 32		
JUNG, CARL GUSTAV	2.2	.63
(3) 07 11 22		
KY, NGUYEN CAO	2.2	.78
(1) 25		
LA FOLLETTE, ROBERT M.	2.2	.78
(3) 03 22 32		
LAFAYETTE, MARQUIS DE	2.2	.78
(1) 03		
LANE, ROBERT E.	2.2	.63
(5) 04 08 13 15 31		
LONG, HUEY PIERCE	2.2	.42
(3) 03 14 32		
LUXEMBURG, ROSA	2.2	.63
(7) 03 07 10 14 23 25 26		
MANNHEIM, KARL	2.2	.42
(7) 03 04 13 22 23 24 25		
MARSHALL, THURGOOD	2.2	.63
(4) 03 07 24 34		
MCLUHAN, MARSHALL	2.2	.42
(1) 25		
MEANY, WILLIAM GEORGE	2.2	.63
(1) 38		
MITCHELL, JOHN N.	2.2	.63
(1) 25		
MORRIS, GOUVENEUR	2.2	.78
(1) 22		
ORWELL, GEORGE	2.2	.78
(7) 04 07 08 11 14 22 25		
POLK, PRESIDENT JAMES K.	2.2	.78
(4) 03 25 29 32 46		
RICHELIEU, CARDINAL DE (ARMAND	2.2	.42
JEAN DUPLESSIS)		
(5) 03 08 09 25 26		
RIESMAN, DAVID	2.2	.63
(2) 15 22		
RIGGS, FRED W.	2.2	.63
(1) 04		
SAMUELSON, PAUL	2.2	.63
(2) 07 25		
SANTAYANA, GEORGE	2.2	.63
(1) 22		
SELASSIE, HAILE	2.2	.42
(1) 25		
SOLZHENITSYN, ALEXANDER I.	2.2	.63
(2) 07 34		
STEVENSON, ADLAI EWING, III	2.2	.78
(1) 32		
SUN YAT-SEN	2.2	.42
(4) 03 14 23 25		
THIEU, GENERAL NGUYEN VAN	2.2	.63
(3) 07 25 34		
THUCYDIDES	2.2	.42
(7) 04 07 09 11 22 23 26		
TOYNBEE, ARNOLD J.	2.2	.63
(5) 08 09 14 22 25		
TYLER, PRESIDENT JOHN	2.2	.78
(3) 03 25 32 46		
VAN BUREN, PRESIDENT MARTIN	2.2	.63
(3) 03 25 32 46		
VICTORIA, QUEEN	2.2	.63
(1) 25		
ALGER, HORATIO	2.3	.67
(1) 22		
ANTHONY, SUSAN BROWNELL	2.3	.67
(1) 32		
APTER, DAVID E.	2.3	.67
(2) 05 13		
BACON, SIR FRANCIS	2.3	.67
(6) 03 09 11 14 22 26		
BAGEHOT, WALTER	2.3	.67
(1) 10		
BARUCH, BERNARD MANNES	2.3	.67
(1) 34		
BATISTA, JUAN	2.3	.67
(1) 25		
BAYH, BIRCH EVANS, JR.	2.3	.67
(1) 32		
BEN-GURION, DAVID	2.3	.48
(1) 25		
BENTLEY, ARTHUR F.	2.3	.67
(6) 03 04 05 13 22 28		
BROOKE, EDWARD WILLIAM	2.3	.67
(1) 32		
BRYCE, LORD JAMES	2.3	.48
(9) 03 04 10 11 13 22 25 26 31		
BUDDHA, GAUTAMA	2.3	.48
(1) 03		

CARNEGIE, ANDREW	2.3	.48
(1) 46		
CHARLEMAGNE	2.3	.67
(2) 09 26		
CLEAVER, ELDRIDGE	2.3	.67
(1) 25		
CONVERSE, PHILIP E.	2.3	.67
(2) 04 15		
CROMWELL, OLIVER	2.3	.48
(3) 03 09 26		
DEBRAY, REGIS	2.3	.67
(1) 25		
DOUGLAS, WILLIAM O.	2.3	.67
(5) 03 22 23 25 34		
EAGLETON, THOMAS FRANCIS	2.3	.67
(1) 32		
ELIZABETH I OF ENGLAND	2.3	.67
(3) 08 14 26		
ELLSBERG, DANIEL	2.3	.67
(1) 25		
EMERSON, RALPH WALDO	2.3	.67
(2) 03 22		
EVERS, MEDGAR	2.3	.48
(1) 25		
FAISAL, KING	2.3	.67
(1) 34		
FRIEDMAN, MILTON	2.3	.82
(1) 07		
GALILEO	2.3	.82
(3) 09 22 26 43		
GARFIELD, PRESIDENT JAMES A.,	2.3	.67
(1) 46		
GARIBALDI, GIUSEPPE	2.3	.67
(3) 03 07 22		
GARRISON, WILLIAM LLOYD	2.3	.82
(3) 03 22 32 46		
GLADSTONE, WILLIAM E.	2.3	.48
(4) 03 22 25 26		
GOEBBELS, DR. JOSEPH	2.3	.67
(5) 03 22 25 26 34		
GOLDBERG, ARTHUR J.	2.3	.48
(3) 03 25 34		
HAND, LEARNED	2.3	.82
(3) 03 24 32		
HARRISON, PRESIDENT BENJAMIN	2.3	.67
(2) 03 32 46		
HIMMLER, HEINRICH	2.3	.67
(3) 03 22 34		
HUGHES, CHARLES EVANS	2.3	.82
(5) 03 07 22 25 32		
HULL, CORDELL	2.3	.48
(3) 03 32 34		
HUSSEIN I, KING OF JORDAN	2.3	.48
(1) 25		
IRON CHANCELLOR	2.3	.67
(1) 17		
KENNAN, GEORGE F.	2.3	.67
(5) 04 07 14 22 25		
KENYATTA, JOMO	2.3	.48
(2) 25 34		
LAIRD, MELVIN R.	2.3	.82
(1) 32		

LAZARSFELD, PAUL F.	2.3	.67
(4) 04 05 13 15		
LINDSAY, JOHN V.	2.3	.48
(1) 25		
LOUIS XIV OF FRANCE	2.3	.48
(1) 26		
LUBELL, SAMUEL	2.3	.48
(1) 05		
MAKARIOS III, ARCHIBISHOP	2.3	.67
(1) 34		
MAZZINI, GIUSEPPE	2.3	.67
(3) 03 11 22		
MCCARTHY, JOSEPH RAYMOND	2.3	.67
(4) 03 25 32 34		
MINDSZENTY, CARDINAL J.	2.3	.67
(2) 03 34		
MITSUBISHI	2.3	.67
(1) 16		
MUSKIE, EDMUND SIXTUS	2.3	.48
(3) 25 32 38		
NEHRU, PUNDIT MOTILAL	2.3	.67
(1) 25		
NIEBUHR, REINHOLD	2.3	.48
(3) 05 22 25		
PARETO, VILFREDO	2.3	.48
(5) 03 10 11 14 22		
PARK CHUNG HEE, GENERAL	2.3	.67
(2) 25 34		
PROXMIRE, WILLIAM	2.3	.67
(1) 32		
RAYBURN, SAMUEL T.	2.3	.48
(2) 32 34		
RHEE, DR. SYNGMAN	2.3	.48
(2) 03 34		
RICARDO, DAVID	2.3	.67
(6) 03 10 14 22 25 26		
ROBESPIERRE, MAXIMILEIN FRANCOIS MARIE ISADORE DE	2.3	.48
(4) 03 22 25 26		
SHAW, GEORGE BERNARD	2.3	.67
(5) 10 14 15 22 25		
SIMON, HERBERT A.	2.3	.67
(4) 05 07 13 28		
SPENCER, HERBERT	2.3	.48
(6) 03 10 14 22 25 26		
TAYLOR, PRESIDENT ZACHARY	2.3	.67
(1) 32 46		
THOREAU, HENRY DAVID	2.3	.67
(4) 07 10 22 25		
WIENER, NORBERT	2.3	.82
(2) 13 22		
WILLIAM THE CONQUEROR	2.3	.48
(1) 09		
WILSON, HAROLD W.	2.3	.48
(2) 25 34		
WITTGENSTEIN, LUDWIG JOSEF JOHANN	2.3	.67
(2) 07 22		
ZAPATA, EMILIANO	2.3	.67
(2) 14 23		
ADAMS, SHERMAN	2.4	.69
(1) 34		
ADORNO, THEODORE W.	2.4	.69
(1) 04		

AL-FATAH	2.4	.51	DUVALIER, FRANCOIS (PAPA DOC)	2.4	.51
(1) 34			(3) 07 25 34		
ALEMAN, IGUEL	2.4	.69	EASTLAND, JAMES O.	2.4	.51
(1) 14			(1) 32		
ALEXANDER II, TSAR OF RUSSIA	2.4	.69	ERASMUS, DESIDERIUS	2.4	.69
(2) 14 22			(4) 09 14 22 26		
ARISTOPHANES	2.4	.51	ERIKSON, ERIK H.	2.4	.51
(1) 26			(1) 15		
AUGUSTINE , SAINT , OF HIPPO	2.4	.69	EROS	2.4	.84
(6) 03 05 09 11 22 26			(1) 22		
BEER, SAMUEL	2.4	.69	ERVIN, SAMUEL JAMES, JR.	2.4	.69
(1) 13			(1) 32		
BERIA, LAVRENTI P.	2.4	.51	ETZIONI, AMITAI	2.4	.51
(5) 03 14 22 24 34			(1) 04		
BERRIGAN, DANIEL	2.4	.84	FILLMORE, PRESIDENT MILLARD	2.4	.69
(1) 25			(2) 03 32 46		
BEVAN, ANEURIN	2.4	.51	FORTAS, JUSTICE ABRAHAM	2.4	.51
(3) 14 24 34			(1) 25		
BLACKSTONE, SIR WILLIAM	2.4	.51	FRIEDRICH, CARL J.	2.4	.69
(5) 03 16 22 23 26			(5) 04 05 13 28 31		
BODIN, JEAN	2.4	.69	FROMM, ERICH	2.4	.51
(5) 05 09 10 23 26			(4) 13 15 22 37		
BRIAND, ARISTIDE	2.4	.51	GOMULKA, WLADYSLAW	2.4	.51
(4) 03 10 22 25			(4) 03 14 25 34		
BRZEZINSKI, ZBIGNIEW	2.4	.69	GROTIUS, HUGO	2.4	.51
(1) 04			(4) 09 11 25 26		
BUBER, MARTIN	2.4	.51	HADRIAN, ROMAN EMPEROR	2.4	.69
(2) 11 25			(2) 08 22		
BUCKLEY, WILLIAM F.	2.4	.69	HALLECK, CHARLES A.	2.4	.69
(1) 25			(1) 03		
BUKHARIN, NIKOLAI IVANOVICH	2.4	.51	HAMLET	2.4	.69
(6) 03 10 22 25 26 34			(1) 44		
BUNDY, MCGEORGE	2.4	.69	HARRISON, PRESIDENT WILLIAM HENRY	2.4	.69
(1) 25			(2) 03 32 46		
CATHERINE II, CATHERINE THE GREAT	2.4	.51	HATFIELD, SENATOR MARK O.	2.4	.51
(2) 03 09			(2) 25 32		
CLEMENS, SAMUEL	2.4	.69	HENRY VIII OF ENGLAND	2.4	.69
(1) 25			(2) 14 26		
CLIFFORD, CLARK	2.4	.51	HESS, RUDOLF	2.4	.69
(1) 34			(2) 22 34		
CONFUCIUS	2.4	.51	HINDENBURG, PAUL VON	2.4	.69
(3) 03 11 25			(3) 03 22 34		
CRANSTON, ALAN	2.4	.51	HOFSTADTER, RICHARD	2.4	.69
(1) 32			(1) 08		
DEWEY, THOMAS EDMUND	2.4	.51	HOLMES, OLIVER WENDELL, JR.	2.4	.69
(1) 34			(6) 03 10 22 25 26 32		
DIEFENBAKER, JOHN	2.4	.51	HUGO, VICTOR MARIE	2.4	.69
(1) 34			(1) 03		
DIRKSEN, EVERETT MCKINLEY	2.4	.51	HUTCHINS, ROBERT MAYNARD	2.4	.69
(1) 03			(1) 22		
DISRAELI, BENJAMIN	2.4	.69	IBN SAUD, KING ABDUL-AZIZ	2.4	.69
(3) 03 22 26			(2) 03 34		
DJILAS, MILOVAN	2.4	.51	IBSEN, HENRIK	2.4	.69
(5) 03 14 25 26 34			(1) 22		
DOSTOEVSKY, FEDOR MIKHAILOVICH	2.4	.69	IVAN THE TERRIBLE	2.4	.51
(3) 07 09 22			(1) 17		
DOUGLAS, STEPHEN A.	2.4	.51	JAMES, WILLIAM	2.4	.69
(2) 22 32			(3) 13 22 26		
DOUGLASS, FREDERICK	2.4	.51	JOAN OF ARC	2.4	.51
(3) 25 30 32 46			(1) 03		
DREYFUS, ALFRED	2.4	.69	JOHNSON, HIRAM W.	2.4	.51
(1) 14			(1) 22		

KAHN, H.	2.4	.69
(2) 11 23		
KEFAUVER, ESTES	2.4	.69
(4) 03 23 25 32		
KRISHNA MENON, V.	2.4	.51
(1) 34		
LA GUARDIA, FIORELLO HENRY	2.4	.69
(3) 03 08 32		
LASKI, HAROLD J.	2.4	.51
(8) 03 07 10 11 22 26 28 32		
LODGE, HENRY CABOT	2.4	.51
(2) 03 34		
LORENZ, KONRAD	2.4	.69
(1) 25		
MACIVER, ROBERT M.	2.4	.51
(3) 05 10 22		
MALENKOV, GEORGI M.	2.4	.51
(4) 03 14 22 34		
MANCHU DYNASTY	2.4	.51
(2) 03 16		
MASARYK, JAN	2.4	.51
(2) 03 34		
MEAD, MARGARET	2.4	.51
(3) 07 15 25		
MEIR, MRS. GOLDA	2.4	.51
(1) 34		
MENCKEN, HENRY L.	2.4	.51
(2) 10 22		
MILTON, JOHN	2.4	.51
(6) 03 05 09 10 22 26		
MOBUTU, GENERAL JOSEPH	2.4	.51
(2) 25 34		
MOSCA GAETANAO	2.4	.69
(3) 11 14 22		
MOSES	2.4	.69
(3) 03 29 30		
MOYNIHAN, DANIEL PATRICK	2.4	.51
(3) 07 25 30		
NAGY, IMRE	2.4	.51
(3) 03 14 34		
NEWTON, SIR ISAAC	2.4	.69
(3) 05 14 26		
NKRUMAH, DR. KWAME	2.4	.51
(9) 03 07 11 14 22 23 24 25 34		
OSWALD, LEE HARVEY	2.4	.51
(1) 30		
PENN, WILLIAM	2.4	.69
(1) 32		
PIERCE, PRESIDENT FRANKLIN	2.4	.69
(1) 03 32 46		
PODGORNY, NIKOLAI VIKTOROVICH	2.4	.51
(1) 38		
POPE JOHN XXIII	2.4	.69
(2) 26 34		
POPPER, KARL R.	2.4	.51
(3) 07 13 23		
QADDAFI, MOAMAR AL	2.4	.51
(2) 07 25		
REAGAN, RONALD W.	2.4	.51
(2) 25 34		
REHNQUIST, WILLIAM H.	2.4	.51
(1) 07		
SAXBE, WILLIAM B.	2.4	.69
(1) 32		
SCHUMPETER, JOSEPH A.	2.4	.51
(3) 07 14 22		
SCHWEITZER, ALBERT	2.4	.51
(2) 14 22		
SCOTT, HUGH D., JR.	2.4	.51
(2) 03 32		
SIHANOUK, PRINCE NORODOM	2.4	.51
(1) 25		
SMITH, ALFRED E.	2.4	.51
(1) 07		
SMUTS, JAN CHRISTIAN	2.4	.51
(2) 03 34		
SPAAK, PAUL-HENRI	2.4	.51
(3) 03 25 34		
STALIN, ALLILUEVA SVETLANA	2.4	.84
(1) 34		
STRAUSS, FRANZ JOSEPH	2.4	.51
(1) 34		
STRAUSS, LEO	2.4	.69
(5) 05 08 11 13 28		
TRUJILLO, RAFAEL	2.4	.51
(2) 25 34		
VANDENBERG, ARTHUR H.	2.4	.51
(1) 07		
WEBB, SIDNEY	2.4	.51
(4) 03 10 22 26		
WHITE, BYRON	2.4	.51
(1) 07		
WILLIAM OF ORANGE, PRINCE	2.4	.51
(1) 35		
WRIGHT, QUINCY	2.4	.69
(6) 04 05 11 13 28 31		
ALEXANDER III, TSAR OF RUSSIA	2.5	.70
(1) 22		
AMIN, IDI	2.5	.70
(1) 07		
ANDORRA	2.5	.52
(1) 03		
AYER, A. J.	2.5	.84
(1) 13		
AYUB KHAN, MOHAMMED	2.5	.52
(1) 03		
BABBITT, IRVING	2.5	.84
(3) 10 22 24		
BACON, ROGER	2.5	.70
(1) 26		
BAILEY, STEPHEN K.	2.5	.70
(4) 04 05 13 22		
BALDWIN, STANLEY	2.5	.70
(2) 22 34		
BALFOUR, ARTHUR JAMES	2.5	.52
(1) 14		
BANFIELD, EDWARD C.	2.5	.70
(1) 07		
BECKET, THOMAS	2.5	.70
(1) 35		
BELL, DANIEL	2.5	.70
(1) 13		
BEN BELLA, MOHAMMED	2.5	.70
(4) 03 25 34 38		

BENEDICT, RUTH	2.5	.84
(2) 15 22		
BERNODOTTE, COUNT FOLKE	2.5	.52
(1) 03		
BEVIN, ERNEST	2.5	.52
(2) 14 34		
BHUTTO, ZULFIKAR ALI	2.5	.52
(3) 07 25 34		
BORGIA, CESARE	2.5	.52
(2) 09 26		
BORMANN, MARTIN LUDWIG	2.5	.52
(1) 03		
BOSCH, JUAN	2.5	.52
(1) 34		
BOULDING, KENNETH	2.5	.52
(1) 04		
BOURGUIBA, HABIB BEN ALI	2.5	.52
(4) 03 07 25 34		
BOWLES, CHESTER,	2.5	.52
(1) 14		
BRANDEIS, LOUIS DEMBITZ	2.5	.52
(7) 03 10 22 25 32 34 35		
BRECHT, ARNOLD	2.5	.52
(3) 04 08 13		
BULGANIN, MARSHAL NIKOLAI	2.5	.70
ALEXANDROVICH		
(1) 38		
BUNCHE, RALPH JOHNSON	2.5	.52
(1) 38		
BURNS, JAMES M.	2.5	.52
(2) 05 28		
BYRNES, JAMES F.	2.5	.52
(2) 14 34		
CAMPBELL, ANGUS	2.5	.52
(2) 05 15		
CAPONE, AL	2.5	.52
(1) 25		
CARLYLE, THOMAS	2.5	.52
(5) 03 10 14 22 26		
CARR, EDWARD H.	2.5	.70
(2) 13 22		
CEAUSESCU, NICOLAE	2.5	.52
(2) 25 34		
CHARLES I OF ENGLAND	2.5	.70
(1) 26		
CHARLES II OF ENGLAND	2.5	.70
(2) 09 26		
CHURCH, FRANK	2.5	.52
(1) 32		
COLE, G.D.H.	2.5	.52
(5) 10 14 22 25 26		
COLEMAN, JAMES S.	2.5	.52
(3) 04 08 15		
COUSINS, NORMAN	2.5	.52
(1) 22		
DANTE ALIGHIERI	2.5	.52
(4) 03 09 22 26		
DARROW, CLARENCE	2.5	.52
(2) 10 25		
DAYAN, GENERAL MOSHE	2.5	.52
(3) 07 25 34		
DE GRAZIA, ALFRED	2.5	.52
(1) 05		
DEMOCRITUS	2.5	.70
(1) 43		
DIAZ ORDAZ, GUSTAVO	2.5	.70
(1) 34		
DIAZ, PORFIRIO	2.5	.52
(3) 03 14 24		
DICKENS, CHARLES	2.5	.70
(1) 11		
DOUGLAS-HOME, SIR ALEXANDER	2.5	.52
(ALEC) FREDERICK		
(1) 38		
DUCE	2.5	.52
(1) 16		
DULLES, ALLEN WELSH	2.5	.70
(1) 03		
EBAN, ABBA S.	2.5	.52
(1) 03		
FAINSOD, MERLE	2.5	.70
(1) 31		
FANON, FRANTZ	2.5	.70
(3) 07 11 25		
FAROUK, KING	2.5	.52
(1) 34		
GARRISON, JIM	2.5	.70
(1) 30		
GOETHE, JOHANN WOLFGANG VON	2.5	.70
(3) 09 22 25		
GOLDMAN, RALPH M.	2.5	.84
(1) 02		
GOODMAN, PAUL	2.5	.70
(1) 07		
GOODNOW, FRANK J.	2.5	.70
(4) 04 10 28 31		
GREGORY, DICK	2.5	.70
(1) 30		
GUEVARA, DR. ERNESTO (CHE)	2.5	.52
(3) 11 25 34		
HARRIMAN, WILLIAM AVERELL	2.5	.52
(1) 34		
HEIDEGGER, MARTIN	2.5	.52
(2) 22 26		
HERO OF APPOMATTOX	2.5	.70
(1) 06		
HIPPOCRATES	2.5	.52
(1) 43		
HOMER	2.5	.52
(1) 09		
HORNEY, KAREN	2.5	.70
(2) 13 22		
HUNTINGTON, SAMUEL	2.5	.70
(1) 04		
HUXLEY, ALDOUS	2.5	.70
(2) 08 22		
JAMES I OF ENGLAND	2.5	.52
(1) 26		
KAFKA, F.	2.5	.70
(1) 11		
KEMAL, MUSTAFA (ATATURK)	2.5	.52
(2) 03 34		
KIERKEGAARD, SOREN	2.5	.70
(1) 22		
KIESINGER, KURT GEORG	2.5	.52
(1) 34		

KNOX, JOHN	2.5	.70
(2) 22 26		
KOESTLER, ARTHUR	2.5	.70
(2) 22 26		
LAVAL, PIERRE	2.5	.70
(3) 03 22 34		
LIE, TRYGVE	2.5	.70
(2) 03 34		
LINDBERGH, CHARLES E.	2.5	.52
(1) 08		
LINDBLOM, CHARLES E.	2.5	.52
(4) 04 05 13 22		
LINDSAY, A.D.	2.5	.70
(5) 09 10 13 22 26		
LONG, RUSSELL B.	2.5	.52
(2) 03 32		
LYND, ROBERT	2.5	.84
(1) 04		
MACRIDIS, ROY C.	2.5	.84
(1) 13		
MAHAN, ALFRED THAYER	2.5	.70
(2) 22 26		
MALRAUX, ANDRE	2.5	.52
(2) 22 34		
MCCLOSKEY, PAUL	2.5	.52
(1) 25		
MEREDITH, JAMES	2.5	.52
(1) 30		
MICHELS, ROBERTO	2.5	.52
(8) 03 04 08 10 11 22 23 24		
MITTERAND, FRANCOIS	2.5	.52
(2) 25 34		
MOHAMMED	2.5	.52
(2) 22 24		
MORSE, WAYNE	2.5	.52
(2) 03 24		
MOSSADEGH, MOHAMMED	2.5	.52
(3) 03 24 34		
MUJIBUR, SHEIK, RAHMAN	2.5	.70
(1) 07		
MUMFORD, LEWIS	2.5	.52
(2) 22 25		
NICHOLAS I, CZAR	2.5	.52
(1) 25		
NYERERE, JULIUS KAMBARAGE	2.5	.52
(4) 07 23 25 34		
PARKINSON, C. NORTHCOTE	2.5	.52
(1) 13		
PAVLOV, IVAN	2.5	.70
(1) 22		
PERICLES	2.5	.52
(2) 22 26		
PIAGET, JEAN	2.5	.52
(2) 15 43		
POMPIDOU, GEORGES JEAN RAYMOND	2.5	.52
(5) 07 11 23 25 34		
PROTHRO, JAMES W.	2.5	.52
(3) 04 05 13		
PROUDHON, PIERRE JOSEPH	2.5	.52
(1) 26		
PYE, LUCIAN	2.5	.52
(3) 04 05 15		
QUISLING, VIDKUN	2.5	.52
(2) 22 34		
REUTHER, WALTER PHILIP	2.5	.52
(4) 03 25 32 34		
RIBBENTROP, JOACHIM VON	2.5	.52
(3) 03 22 34		
RIBICOFF, ABRAHAM ALEXANDER	2.5	.52
(2) 30 32		
RIKER, WILLIAM H.	2.5	.52
(2) 05 13		
RORSCHACH, HERMANN	2.5	.52
(1) 30		
ROSENAU, JAMES	2.5	.52
(1) 04		
ROSSITER, CLINTON	2.5	.70
(1) 05		
RUSK, DAVID DEAN	2.5	.52
(1) 38		
SALAZAR, DR. ANTONIO DE OLIVEIRA	2.5	.52
(1) 38		
SCHELLING, THOMAS C.	2.5	.52
(3) 04 11 13		
SEKOU TOURE, AHMED	2.5	.52
(1) 38		
SHAKESPEARE, WILLIAM	2.5	.52
(2) 07 30		
SHRIVER, SARGENT	2.5	.52
(1) 30		
SINGER, J. DAVID	2.5	.52
(1) 04		
SOPHOCLES	2.5	.70
(2) 08 26		
SOREL, GEORGES	2.5	.52
(7) 03 10 11 22 23 25 26		
SOROKIN, PITRIM A.	2.5	.70
(2) 11 14		
SPINOZA, BARUCH (BENEDICT DE)	2.5	.52
(3) 03 09 26		
SPROUT, HAROLD AND MARGARET	2.5	.70
(2) 05 13		
SPYKMAN, NICHOLAS J.	2.5	.70
(1) 22		
SUN KING	2.5	.52
(1) 17		
SYMINGTON, WILLIAM STUART	2.5	.52
(2) 03 32		
TAFT, ROBERT ALPHONSO	2.5	.52
(4) 03 25 32 34		
THURMOND, JAMES STROM	2.5	.52
(2) 03 32		
TRUMAN, DAVID B.	2.5	.52
(7) 04 05 13 15 22 28 31		
TSHOMBE, MOISE KAPENDE	2.5	.52
(2) 03 34		
TUBMAN, HARRIET	2.5	.70
(1) 46		
ULBRECHT, WALTER	2.5	.52
(5) 03 14 24 25 34		
VERBA, SIDNEY	2.5	.52
(3) 04 15 23		
VERWOERD, DR. HENDRIK FRENSCH	2.5	.52
(2) 14 34		

VORSTER, BALTHAZAR JOHANNES	2.5	.52
(1) 34		
WHITEHEAD, PROF. A. N.	2.5	.84
(2) 09 43		
ZHUKOV, GEORGI	2.5	.52
(4) 03 14 24 34		
ZOLA, EMILE EDOUARD CHARLES ANTOINE	2.5	.52
(1) 03		
AIKEN, GEORGE DAVID	2.6	.69
(1) 32		
AUSTIN, JOHN	2.6	.51
(3) 10 22 26		
BALZAC, HONORE DE	2.6	.69
(1) 07		
BARGHOORN, FREDERICK C.	2.6	.69
(1) 15		
BECKER, CARL	2.6	.69
(1) 13		
BENTSEN, LLOYD MILLARD, JR.	2.6	.51
(1) 32		
BETANCOURT, ROMULO	2.6	.51
(2) 03 34		
BIDAULT, GEORGES	2.6	.51
(2) 03 34		
BOUMEDIENNE, COLONEL HOUARI	2.6	.51
(1) 34		
BRADLEY, GENERAL OMAR	2.6	.51
(1) 22		
BRODIE, BERNARD	2.6	.51
(1) 13		
BUCKLEY, JAMES L.	2.6	.51
(1) 32		
BYRD, HARRY FLOOD, JR.	2.6	.51
(1) 32		
CANNON, JOSEPH G.	2.6	.51
(1) 25		
CARADON, LORD	2.6	.51
(1) 34		
CARDENAS, LAZARO	2.6	.51
(3) 03 14 34		
CARRANZA, VENUSTIANO	2.6	.51
(1) 14		
CATHERINE OF RUSSIA, EMPRESS	2.6	.51
(1) 09		
CATLIN, GEORGE E.G.	2.6	.51
(3) 04 05 13		
CATO	2.6	.51
(1) 43		
CHAMBERLAIN, JOSEPH	2.6	.51
(4) 14 22 23 25		
CHAUCER	2.6	.51
(1) 26		
CHOMSKY, N.	2.6	.69
(1) 11		
CLAY, CASSIUS	2.6	.51
(1) 30		
COOPER, JAMES FENIMORE	2.6	.69
(1) 03		
CORTES, HERNAN	2.6	.69
(1) 03		
CORWIN, EDWARD S.	2.6	.51
(1) 31		
COUGHLIN, CHARLES EDWARD	2.6	.69
(1) 03		
COUVE DE MURVILLE, MAURICE	2.6	.51
(1) 34		
CROCE, BENEDETTO	2.6	.69
(7) 07 09 10 11 14 22 26		
DALADIER, EDOUARD	2.6	.51
(2) 03 34		
DOOLITTLE, GENERAL JAMES H.	2.6	.51
(1) 22		
DOUGLAS, PAUL H.	2.6	.51
(2) 03 25		
DOWNS, ANTHONY	2.6	.69
(2) 04 05		
DUBCEK, ALEXANDER	2.6	.51
(3) 23 25 34		
DUVERGER, MAURICE	2.6	.51
(2) 04 24		
EDEN, SIR ROBERT ANTHONY	2.6	.51
(1) 38		
EISENSTADT, S. N.	2.6	.51
(2) 04 15		
ELIOT, T. S.	2.6	.69
(1) 10		
EPICURUS	2.6	.69
(1) 09		
FATHER OF HIS COUNTRY	2.6	.51
(1) 06		
FATHER OF THE CONSTITUTION	2.6	.51
(1) 42		
FAWKES, GUY	2.6	.51
(1) 22		
FONG, HIRAM LEONG	2.6	.51
(2) 03 32		
FRANK, JEROME D.	2.6	.51
(2) 07 22		
GARVEY, MARCUS	2.6	.51
(4) 14 22 25 30 46		
GASPERI, ALCIDE DE	2.6	.51
(2) 03 14		
GHEORGHIU-DEJ, GHEORGHE	2.6	.51
(2) 03 34		
GIBBON, EDWARD	2.6	.51
(3) 09 22 26		
GRUENING, ERNEST	2.6	.51
(1) 03		
GUETZKOW, HAROLD	2.6	.51
(2) 04 05		
HALIFAX, FIRST MARQUIS OF, GEORGE SAVILE	2.6	.51
(4) 03 09 11 26		
HARLAN, JOHN MARSHALL	2.6	.51
(2) 03 25		
HART, PHILIP ALOYSIUS	2.6	.51
(1) 32		
HAYDEN, THOMAS	2.6	.69
(1) 25		
HAYEK, FRIEDRICH A.	2.6	.51
(3) 05 11 22		
HEATH, EDWARD RICHARD GEORGE	2.6	.51
(1) 38		
HEISENBERG	2.6	.69
(1) 43		

HERO OF NEW ORLEANS   2.6   .51
(1) 06
HEYDRICH, REINHARD   2.6   .69
(1) 03
HICKENLOOPER, BOURKE BLAKEMORE   2.6   .51
(1) 03
HOFFMANN, STANLEY H.   2.6   .51
(2) 04 13
HRUSKA, ROMAN LEE   2.6   .51
(1) 32
HUSSERL, EDMUND   2.6   .51
(1) 22
HUXLEY, JULIAN   2.6   .69
(1) 13
ICKES, HAROLD   2.6   .51
(1) 14
INOUYE, DANIEL KEN   2.6   .51
(1) 32
JACKSON, ROBERT H.   2.6   .51
(2) 03 22
JAMES II OF ENGLAND   2.6   .51
(1) 26
JASPERS, KARL   2.6   .69
(1) 22 43
KASAVUBU, JOSEPH   2.6   .51
(1) 34
KAUTSKY, KARL   2.6   .51
(7) 03 10 11 14 22 25 26
KORNHAUSER, WILLIAM   2.6   .51
(2) 04 15
KROPOTKIN, PRINCE PETER   2.6   .51
(1) 22
LAO TSZE   2.6   .69
(1) 22
LAO TZU   2.6   .69
(1) 43
LAWRENCE, T. E.   2.6   .69
(1) 09
LEWIS, JOHN L.   2.6   .51
(2) 32 34
LILIENTHAL, DAVID E.   2.6   .51
(3) 05 22 32
LITVINOV, MAXIM   2.6   .51
(1) 34
MACAULAY, T.B.   2.6   .51
(1) 26
MACBETH   2.6   .51
(1) 43
MARCOS, FERDINAND E.   2.6   .51
(2) 25 34
MAYO, ELTON   2.6   .69
(1) 05
MCCLELLAN, GENERAL GEORGE C.   2.6   .51
(1) 46
MEEHAN, EUGENE J.   2.6   .69
(1) 07
MENDES-FRANCE, PIERRE   2.6   .51
(4) 03 14 24 34
MIKOYAN, ANASTAS   2.6   .51
(3) 03 14 34
MOLOTOV, VYACHESLAV M.   2.6   .51
(4) 03 14 22 34

MONTAIGNE, MICHEL DE   2.6   .51
(1) 22
MORGAN, PIERPONT   2.6   .51
(1) 22
MR. REPUBLICAN   2.6   .51
(1) 39
NAGUIB, GENERAL MOHAMMED   2.6   .51
(3) 03 22 34
OBOTE, DR. MILTON   2.6   .51
(3) 11 25 34
OCKHAM, WILLIAM OF   2.6   .51
(1) 09
OLD ABE   2.6   .69
(1) 06
ORTEGA Y GASSET, JOSE   2.6   .51
(3) 10 14 22
PAHLAVI, MOHAMMED REZA SHAH   2.6   .51
(1) 34
PAPADOPOULOS, GEORGE   2.6   .51
(1) 34
PAPANDREOU, GEORGE   2.6   .51
(1) 34
PERCY, CHARLES HARTING   2.6   .51
(1) 32
PETAIN, HENRI PHILIPPE   2.6   .51
(5) 03 22 24 25 34
PETER I, THE GREAT   2.6   .51
(1) 03
PLUTARCH   2.6   .51
(1) 09
POINCARE, HENRI   2.6   .51
(1) 26
POLSBY, NELSON   2.6   .51
(1) 04
POOL, ITHIEL DE SOLA   2.6   .51
(2) 04 05
POPE JOHN XXIII   2.6   .51
(1) 25
POPE PAUL VI   2.6   .51
(2) 25 34
POPE PAUL VI   2.6   .51
(1) 25
POUND, ROSCOE   2.6   .51
(3) 10 22 25
PROMETHEUS   2.6   .51
(2) 21 22
PROUST   2.6   .69
(1) 43
QUIXOTE, DON   2.6   .69
(1) 09
RANNEY, AUSTIN   2.6   .51
(1) 04
RHODES, CECIL   2.6   .51
(1) 14
ROI SOLEIL   2.6   .51
(1) 17
ROSENBERG, ALFRED   2.6   .51
(3) 22 26 34
ROSTOW, EUGENE   2.6   .69
(1) 04
SAGE OF MONTICELLO   2.6   .69
(1) 06

SAINT-SIMON, COUNT HENRI DE	2.6	.51
(8) 03 07 10 11 22 23 24 25		
SAN MARTIN, JOSE DE	2.6	.51
(1) 03		
SAUD, KING	2.6	.51
(1) 34		
SCHATTSCHNEIDER, ELMER E.	2.6	.51
(7) 04 05 07 13 22 28 31		
SCHOPENHAUER, ARTHUR	2.6	.51
(4) 03 22 26 43		
SMITH, IAN DOUGLAS	2.6	.51
(1) 34		
SNYDER, RICHARD C.	2.6	.51
(4) 04 05 13 28		
SPENGLER, OSWALD	2.6	.51
(6) 03 10 14 22 25 26		
STEFFENS, LINCOLN	2.6	.51
(2) 03 22		
STENNIS, JOHN CORNELIUS	2.6	.51
(1) 32		
STIMSON, HENRY L.	2.6	.51
(1) 25		
SUHARTO, GENERAL T. N. J.	2.6	.51
(2) 25 34		
SUKARNO, ACHMED	2.6	.51
(5) 03 04 07 25 34		
TALLEYRAND-PERIGORD, CHARLES	2.6	.51
MAURICE DE		
(1) 03		
TALMADGE, HERMAN EUGENE	2.6	.51
(1) 32		
TANEY, ROGER BROOKE	2.6	.51
(2) 03 32		
THOMAS, NORMAN	2.6	.51
(5) 03 10 22 25 32		
THRASYMACHUS	2.6	.69
(2) 08 26		
TOURE, SEKOU	2.6	.51
(5) 03 14 23 25 34		
TUBMAN, WILLIAM V. S.	2.6	.51
(1) 34		
TWAIN, MARK	2.6	.69
(1) 25		
WALDO, DWIGHT	2.6	.51
(3) 05 13 28		
WALLACE, HENRY AGARD	2.6	.51
(5) 03 14 22 25 32		
WEBB, BEATRICE	2.6	.51
(3) 03 10 22		
WELLES, SUMNER	2.6	.51
(1) 03		
WILHELM II	2.6	.51
(1) 22		
WILLIAMS, ROGER	2.6	.51
(4) 03 22 26 32 46		
WILLKIE, WENDELL L.	2.6	.51
(2) 03 34		
UNION OF SOVIET SOCIALIST	1.5	.52
REPUBLICS (USSR)		
(6) 07 11 16 23 25 36		
CHINA, COMMUNIST	1.6	.51
(1) 46		
ELECTORAL DISTRICT	1.6	.69
(1) 17		
SOVIET UNION	1.6	.69
(6) 03 04 08 16 20 27		
GREAT BRITAIN	1.7	.82
(2) 03 07		
IRON CURTAIN	1.7	.48
(6) 03 16 17 20 22 34		
METROPOLITAN	1.7	.67
(2) 24 30		
THIRD WORLD	1.7	.67
(5) 04 07 32 33 34		
VIETNAM	1.7	.48
(2) 04 11		
ASWAN DAM	1.8	.42
(2) 03 17		
BANGLADESH	1.8	.42
(3) 07 11 23		
CHINA, NATIONALIST	1.8	.63
(1) 46		
ELECTION DISTRICT	1.8	.78
(1) 06		
ENGLAND	1.8	.78
(2) 03 04		
LATIN AMERICA	1.8	.78
(4) 03 07 11 43		
WEST GERMANY	1.8	.63
(2) 07 11		
BAY OF PIGS	1.9	.31
(1) 46		
CANAL ZONE	1.9	.31
(3) 06 07 32		
CHINA	1.9	.73
(5) 03 04 07 11 30		
CHINA, NATIONALIST (TAIWAN)	1.9	.56
(1) 07		
CONGRESSIONAL DISTRICT	1.9	.56
(5) 06 16 18 27 32		
EUROPE	1.9	.73
(4) 04 07 11 17		
KREMLIN	1.9	.56
(4) 16 17 24 34		
MAGINOT LINE	1.9	.56
(3) 03 16 17		
METROPOLIS	1.9	.87
(3) 24 30 33		
METROPOLITAN AREA	1.9	.73
(7) 03 06 11 12 18 27 32		
NORTH VIETNAM	1.9	.31
(1) 11		
PEARL HARBOR	1.9	.56
(4) 03 06 16 24 46		
SATELLITE NATION	1.9	.56
(2) 16 27		
SOUTH VIETNAM	1.9	.56
(1) 11		
SOVIET SATELLITES	1.9	.31
(1) 03		
UNITED KINGDOM (UK)	1.9	.56
(4) 03 07 11 34		
ALGERIA	2.0	.47
(3) 03 07 11		

ARGENTINA	2.0	.47	SAFE DISTRICTS	2.0	.66
(3) 03 07 11			(1) 45		
AUSCHWITZ	2.0	.66	SOUTH KOREA	2.0	.47
(1) 34			(2) 07 11		
BERLIN WALL	2.0	.00	SWEDEN	2.0	.47
(3) 17 34 46			(3) 03 07 11		
CALIFORNIA	2.0	.47	SWITZERLAND	2.0	.47
(4) 06 07 11 25 46			(3) 03 07 11		
CAPITAL	2.0	.66	TAIWAN	2.0	.47
(6) 06 16 20 24 25 30			(1) 11		
CHILE	2.0	.47	U.N. TRUST TERRITORY	2.0	.47
(5) 03 04 07 11 43			(1) 03		
COLONIAL TERRITORIES	2.0	.81	UNITED STATES (U.S.)	2.0	.94
(1) 41			(1) 36		
CONTIGUITY	2.0	.81	WASHINGTON, D.C.	2.0	.66
(1) 17			(1) 18		
CZECHOSLOVAKIA	2.0	.47	WESTERN EUROPE	2.0	.81
(4) 03 07 11 43			(1) 11		
EAST BERLIN	2.0	.47	AMERICA	2.1	.87
(1) 11			(2) 11 43		
EAST EUROPE	2.0	.47	ANCIENT GREECE	2.1	.73
(1) 07			(1) 25		
EAST GERMANY	2.0	.47	ANCIENT ROME	2.1	.73
(1) 07			(1) 25		
EASTERN BLOC	2.0	.66	ANGOLA	2.1	.56
(3) 11 17 23			(3) 03 11 25		
FAR EAST	2.0	.81	ASIA	2.1	.56
(2) 03 22			(3) 04 07 11		
HIROSHIMA	2.0	.66	ATHENS	2.1	.73
(1) 03			(1) 26		
INDIGENOUS	2.0	.81	BERLIN	2.1	.56
(1) 30			(3) 03 07 11		
MARKET	2.0	.94	BIAFRA	2.1	.56
(3) 19 24 30			(2) 11 25		
MASON-DIXON LINE	2.0	.47	BOUNDARY	2.1	.73
(2) 06 16			(6) 03 06 07 08 17 20		
MEGALOPOLIS	2.0	.66	CAPITOL HILL	2.1	.56
(3) 25 30 32			(2) 16 32		
MIDDLE EAST	2.0	.66	CENTRAL AMERICA	2.1	.56
(3) 03 07 11			(3) 03 07 11		
NATIONALIST CHINA (TAIWAN)	2.0	.47	DEMILITARIZED ZONE	2.1	.73
(1) 07			(2) 16 17		
NATO COUNTRIES	2.0	.47	DISTRICT	2.1	.73
(1) 11			(2) 06 24		
NEW NATIONS	2.0	.81	EASTERN EUROPE	2.1	.56
(1) 15			(1) 11		
NORTHERN IRELAND	2.0	.66	ELECTION PRECINCT	2.1	.73
(2) 03 11			(1) 06		
NUCLEAR-FREE ZONE	2.0	.66	FIEF	2.1	.73
(2) 17 20			(1) 17		
PALESTINE	2.0	.47	FRANCE	2.1	.56
(1) 07			(4) 04 07 11 20		
PANAMA CANAL ZONE	2.0	.47	FRONTIER	2.1	.87
(3) 03 18 34			(1) 46		
POLITICAL ASYLUM	2.0	.47	GREECE	2.1	.73
(1) 33			(4) 03 04 07 11		
PRECINCT	2.0	.66	GUANTANAMO	2.1	.56
(7) 03 06 16 18 24 29 32			(1) 03		
RURAL DISTRICT	2.0	.66	HARPERS FERRY	2.1	.73
(1) 17			(1) 22		
RUSSIA	2.0	.66	INDOCHINA	2.1	.56
(1) 11			(2) 07 11		

INTERNAL WATERS	2.1	.73	ALBANIA	2.2	.42
(1) 03			(3) 03 07 11		
INTERNATIONAL TERRITORY	2.1	.56	BALTIC STATES	2.2	.42
(1) 17			(3) 03 16 36		
IRAN	2.1	.56	BAMBOO CURTAIN	2.2	.42
(3) 03 07 11			(1) 17		
LANDLOCKED COUNTRY	2.1	.31	BENELUX COUNTRIES	2.2	.42
(1) 17			(5) 03 17 20 25 34		
MANDATED AREA	2.1	.56	BOLIVIA	2.2	.42
(1) 17			(3) 03 07 11		
MARKETPLACE	2.1	.73	BRAZIL	2.2	.42
(1) 24			(3) 03 07 11		
MELTING POT	2.1	.56	BUCHENWALD	2.2	.63
(2) 06 30			(1) 22		
MICRONESIA	2.1	.56	BURMA	2.2	.42
(2) 07 11			(3) 03 07 11		
MUNICIPAL	2.1	.73	BYELORUSSIA	2.2	.63
(5) 06 16 17 24 27			(2) 03 17		
NATIONAL WATERS	2.1	.31	CAMBODIA	2.2	.42
(1) 17			(3) 03 07 11		
NEUTRAL ZONE	2.1	.31	CAMP DAVID	2.2	.42
(1) 17			(1) 39		
NORTH AMERICA	2.1	.87	CANADA	2.2	.63
(1) 36			(3) 03 07 11		
OPPOSITION BENCH	2.1	.56	CENTRAL ASIA	2.2	.42
(1) 16			(2) 07 11		
OVAL OFFICE	2.1	.56	CHICAGO	2.2	.63
(1) 39			(1) 11		
PANAMA CANAL	2.1	.56	CLOAKROOM	2.2	.63
(1) 07 46			(2) 17 27		
POSSESSIONS OF THE UNITED STATES	2.1	.31	CONGO (BRAZZAVILLE)	2.2	.42
(1) 45			(1) 07		
PUERTO RICO	2.1	.56	CONGO (KINSHASA)	2.2	.42
(6) 03 07 11 18 25 42			(1) 07		
RHODESIA	2.1	.31	CONTINENTAL SHELF	2.2	.78
(2) 07 11			(3) 11 23 25		
SATELLITE STATE	2.1	.56	CUBA	2.2	.42
(1) 17			(4) 03 06 07 11		
SAUDI ARABIA	2.1	.31	CYPRUS	2.2	.42
(3) 03 07 11			(4) 03 07 11 25		
SUBURBIA	2.1	.73	DACHAU	2.2	.63
(1) 24			(2) 22 34		
SUEZ CANAL	2.1	.56	DETROIT, MICHIGAN	2.2	.78
(2) 03 07			(2) 04 11		
TERRITORY	2.1	.73	DIEN-BIEN-PHU	2.2	.42
(7) 03 06 16 17 18 24 30			(1) 03		
U.S. OF AMERICA	2.1	.87	DISTRICT OF COLUMBIA	2.2	.63
(2) 11 32			(5) 11 16 18 27 32		
UGANDA	2.1	.31	DOWNING STREET	2.2	.63
(2) 07 11			(1) 16		
URBAN	2.1	.73	ECUADOR	2.2	.42
(2) 24 30			(3) 03 07 11		
VENEZUELA	2.1	.31	ERITREA	2.2	.63
(3) 03 07 11			(1) 36		
WEST BERLIN	2.1	.56	ETHIOPIA	2.2	.42
(1) 11			(3) 03 07 11		
WEST EUROPE	2.1	.73	FINLAND	2.2	.42
(1) 07			(1) 03		
WHITE RUSSIA	2.1	.31	FORMOSA (TAIWAN)	2.2	.42
(4) 16 17 21 34			(1) 03		
AFRICA	2.2	.78	GENEVA	2.2	.63
(3) 04 07 11			(1) 39		

GETTYSBURG	2.2	.78
(1) 46		
GUAM	2.2	.63
(2) 03 18		
HAITI	2.2	.63
(3) 03 07 11		
HARLEM	2.2	.63
(1) 25		
HOMESTEAD	2.2	.63
(3) 06 16 32		
HONG KONG	2.2	.63
(3) 07 11 25		
INDIA	2.2	.63
(6) 03 04 07 11 30 32		
INDIAN RESERVATION	2.2	.63
(2) 06 16		
IRAQ	2.2	.42
(3) 03 07 11		
ISRAEL, STATE OF (MENDINAT ISRAEL)	2.2	.42
(3) 03 07 11		
JAPAN	2.2	.78
(4) 03 04 07 11		
JORDAN	2.2	.63
(1) 36		
KENYA	2.2	.63
(3) 03 07 11		
KUWAIT	2.2	.63
(3) 03 07 17		
LAOS	2.2	.42
(3) 03 07 11		
LEBANON	2.2	.42
(3) 03 07 11		
LEBENSRAUM	2.2	.63
(5) 16 17 20 22 26		
LIBYA	2.2	.42
(3) 03 07 11		
LOCAL	2.2	.91
(2) 24 30		
MALAYA	2.2	.42
(2) 07 22		
MALAYSIA	2.2	.42
(2) 07 11		
MEXICO	2.2	.63
(3) 03 07 11		
MOROCCO	2.2	.63
(3) 03 07 11		
NATIONAL TERRITORY	2.2	.91
(1) 17		
NATURAL FRONTIER	2.2	.63
(1) 17		
NORTH KOREA	2.2	.63
(2) 07 11		
NORTHWEST TERRITORY	2.2	.63
(1) 46		
OCEANS	2.2	.78
(1) 07		
ODER-NIESSE LINE	2.2	.42
(4) 03 17 20 34		
OUTLET TO THE SEA	2.2	.42
(1) 17		
PORTUGAL	2.2	.42
(3) 03 07 11		
PRUSSIA	2.2	.42
(1) 25		
SCHOOL DISTRICTS	2.2	.63
(4) 03 16 18 27		
SIERRA LEONE	2.2	.42
(3) 03 07 11		
SINGLE-MEMBER DISTRICT	2.2	.63
(2) 03 06 16 18		
SOUTH EAST ASIA	2.2	.42
(1) 11		
SOUTHEAST ASIA	2.2	.42
(2) 07 11		
SPECIAL DISTRICT	2.2	.78
(1) 03		
TERRITORIAL JURISDICTION	2.2	.63
(1) 20		
THAILAND	2.2	.42
(3) 03 07 11		
TRUST TERRITORY, UNITED NATIONS	2.2	.63
(4) 03 16 17 20 45		
TRUSTEESHIP TERRITORIES	2.2	.42
(1) 38		
ULSTER	2.2	.63
(3) 07 11 34		
UNION OF ARAB REPUBLICS	2.2	.63
(1) 11		
UNION OF SOUTH AFRICA	2.2	.42
(1) 03		
URUGUAY	2.2	.42
(3) 03 07 11		
WESTERN HEMISPHERE	2.2	.63
(1) 22		
YALTA	2.2	.63
(1) 39		
YUGOSLAVIA	2.2	.42
(3) 03 07 11		
ZAIRE	2.2	.42
(2) 07 11		
ZAMBIA	2.2	.42
(2) 07 11		
ZANZIBAR-TANGANYIKA	2.2	.42
(1) 11		
AFGHANISTAN	2.3	.48
(2) 03 07		
ALSACE	2.3	.67
(1) 11		
ALSACE-LORRAINE	2.3	.48
(1) 03		
AMERICAS	2.3	.82
(1) 11		
ARABIAN PENINSULA	2.3	.48
(1) 11		
AUSTRALIA	2.3	.48
(3) 03 07 11		
AUSTRIA	2.3	.48
(3) 03 07 11		
BARBADOS	2.3	.67
(1) 07		
BARRIOS	2.3	.82
(1) 30		
BATAAN	2.3	.67
(2) 03 16		

BAVARIA, GERMANY	2.3	.48
(1) 11		
BELGIUM	2.3	.48
(3) 03 07 11		
BRITISH HONDURAS	2.3	.48
(1) 03		
BULGARIA	2.3	.48
(3) 03 07 11		
CHINA SEA	2.3	.48
(1) 11		
CO-PROSPERITY SPHERE, EAST ASIA	2.3	.48
(1) 21		
COSTA RICA	2.3	.48
(3) 03 07 11		
COTTON STATES	2.3	.67
(1) 06		
COUNTRY	2.3	.94
(3) 17 24 30		
DANZIG	2.3	.67
(1) 16		
DOMINICAN REPUBLIC	2.3	.48
(3) 03 07 11		
EGYPT	2.3	.48
(3) 07 11 29		
FREE PORT	2.3	.48
(4) 06 16 17 21		
GAZA STRIP	2.3	.48
(1) 03		
GEORGIA	2.3	.67
(1) 25		
GOVERNMENT BENCH	2.3	.48
(1) 17		
GUATEMALA	2.3	.48
(3) 07 11 25		
HAWAII	2.3	.48
(3) 03 11 25		
HUNGARY	2.3	.67
(3) 03 07 11		
ICELAND	2.3	.67
(3) 03 07 11		
ILLINOIS	2.3	.67
(1) 07		
INDIAN TERRITORY	2.3	.48
(1) 06		
INLAND WATERS	2.3	.48
(1) 17		
ITALY	2.3	.67
(5) 03 07 11 20 36		
JERUSALEM	2.3	.48
(1) 25		
LANDLOCKED SEA	2.3	.48
(1) 17		
LONDON	2.3	.67
(1) 11		
MALTA	2.3	.48
(4) 03 07 11 25		
MANCHURIA	2.3	.48
(1) 25		
MASSACHUSETTS BAY COLONY	2.3	.48
(1) 46		
MECCA	2.3	.48
(1) 16		
METROPOLITAN DISTRICT	2.3	.67
(1) 19		
METROPOLITAN REGION	2.3	.67
(1) 16		
MONGOLIA	2.3	.48
(3) 03 07 11		
MOZAMBIQUE	2.3	.48
(1) 07		
NEUTRAL WATERS	2.3	.48
(1) 17		
NEW YORK CITY (NYC)	2.3	.67
(2) 04 11		
PERSIAN GULF	2.3	.48
(2) 07 11		
PERSIAN GULF STATES	2.3	.48
(1) 34		
PERU	2.3	.48
(2) 07 11		
POLAND	2.3	.48
(3) 03 07 11		
POLISH CORRIDOR	2.3	.48
(3) 16 17 21		
POLLING PLACE	2.3	.67
(2) 16 17		
RHODESIA AND NYASALAND	2.3	.48
(1) 03		
ROME	2.3	.48
(1) 11		
ROTTEN BOROUGH	2.3	.48
(3) 06 16 29		
RUMANIA (ROUMANIA)	2.3	.48
(3) 03 07 11		
SAAR	2.3	.48
(1) 03		
SCANDINAVIA	2.3	.48
(2) 07 11		
SENEGAL	2.3	.48
(3) 03 07 11		
SINO-INDIAN BORDER	2.3	.48
(1) 03		
SLUMS	2.3	.67
(1) 25		
SMOKE-FILLED ROOM	2.3	.48
(4) 02 16 27 29		
SOUTH ASIA	2.3	.48
(2) 07 11		
SOUTHERN RHODESIA	2.3	.48
(1) 36		
SPAIN	2.3	.48
(4) 03 07 11 30		
SPARTA	2.3	.48
(1) 35		
SUB-SAHARA	2.3	.48
(1) 24		
SYRIA	2.3	.48
(3) 03 07 11		
TANGANYIKA	2.3	.48
(1) 03		
TANGANYIKA-ZANZIBAR	2.3	.48
(1) 11		
TANZANIA	2.3	.48
(2) 07 11		

TERRITORIAL SEA	2.3	.67
(2) 03 17		
TERRITORIAL WATERS	2.3	.48
(6) 03 06 16 17 20 32		
TIBET	2.3	.48
(2) 03 07		
TOWNSHIP	2.3	.82
(6) 03 06 16 18 27 32		
TRUST TERRITORY OF THE PACIFIC	2.3	.48
ISLANDS		
(1) 42		
TUNISIA	2.3	.48
(3) 03 07 11		
TURKEY	2.3	.48
(4) 03 07 09 11		
TWELVE-MILE LIMIT	2.3	.48
(1) 16		
UNINCORPORATED AREAS	2.3	.67
(1) 18		
VENUE	2.3	.82
(4) 02 06 18 32		
WALL STREET	2.3	.67
(5) 16 22 24 25 27		
WARD	2.3	.82
(6) 03 06 16 18 27 30		
WATTS, CALIFORNIA	2.3	.67
(1) 25		
YEMEN	2.3	.48
(5) 03 07 11 17 24		
ZANZIBAR	2.3	.48
(2) 03 07		
ADEN	2.4	.51
(1) 07		
AIR CORRIDOR	2.4	.69
(1) 17		
ANTARTICA	2.4	.51
(1) 07		
APPALACHIA	2.4	.51
(1) 32		
ARABIAN GULF	2.4	.51
(1) 11		
ASYLUM	2.4	.69
(4) 03 11 16 32		
BALKANS	2.4	.51
(2) 11 25		
BARBARY STATES	2.4	.69
(1) 16		
BENGAL AND BENGALIS	2.4	.51
(1) 25		
BERCHTESGADEN	2.4	.69
(1) 16		
BRITISH INDIA	2.4	.51
(1) 16		
BURUNDI	2.4	.51
(4) 03 11 17 24		
CAMEROON	2.4	.51
(3) 03 07 11		
CAPE CANAVERAL	2.4	.51
(1) 42		
CAPE KENNEDY	2.4	.51
(1) 42		
CAPITAL (CITY)	2.4	.69
(1) 44		

CARIBBEAN	2.4	.51
(2) 07 11		
CEYLON	2.4	.51
(3) 03 07 11		
CLOSED SEA	2.4	.51
(3) 06 16 17		
COLOMBIA	2.4	.51
(3) 03 07 11		
COLORADO	2.4	.51
(1) 06		
COMBAT AREA	2.4	.51
(2) 06 17		
COMMITTEE ROOM	2.4	.69
(1) 17		
CONGO	2.4	.51
(2) 03 11		
COUNTY SEAT	2.4	.51
(1) 27		
DAHOMEY	2.4	.51
(4) 03 07 11 17		
DELAWARE	2.4	.51
(1) 07		
DENMARK	2.4	.51
(3) 03 07 11		
DENVER, COLORADO	2.4	.51
(1) 11		
DUST BOWL	2.4	.69
(1) 16 46		
EAST AFRICA	2.4	.51
(2) 07 11		
EASTERN FRONT	2.4	.69
(1) 16		
EIRE	2.4	.51
(1) 07		
EL SALVADOR	2.4	.51
(2) 03 25		
EURASIA	2.4	.51
(1) 22		
FATHERLAND	2.4	.69
(1) 17		
FIELD	2.4	.84
(1) 24		
FRONT BENCH	2.4	.51
(1) 16		
FRONTIERS	2.4	.84
(1) 19		
GHETTOS	2.4	.51
(5) 17 24 25 30 34		
GIBRALTAR	2.4	.51
(2) 03 11		
GREENBELT COMMUNITIES	2.4	.51
(1) 16		
GUYANA	2.4	.51
(1) 07		
HIGH SEAS	2.4	.51
(1) 45		
HOLY SEE	2.4	.69
(2) 03 17		
HONDURAS	2.4	.51
(4) 03 07 11 25		
INDIAN SUB-CONTINENT	2.4	.51
(1) 11		

INTERNATIONAL RIVERS	2.4	.51
(2) 17 23		
INTERNATIONAL WATERWAYS	2.4	.51
(2) 16 17		
INTERSTATE HIGHWAYS	2.4	.69
(1) 27		
IOWA	2.4	.69
(1) 11		
IVORY TOWER	2.4	.69
(1) 45		
KANSAS	2.4	.69
(2) 07 11		
KASHMIR, INDIA	2.4	.51
(2) 03 11		
KATANGA	2.4	.51
(1) 34		
KENTUCKY	2.4	.69
(2) 11 25		
LAND DOMAIN	2.4	.69
(1) 17		
LATVIA	2.4	.51
(1) 03		
LITHUANIA	2.4	.51
(2) 03 43		
LITTLE ROCK, ARKANSAS	2.4	.51
(1) 03		
LOCATION, GEOGRAPHIC POWER FACTOR	2.4	.84
(1) 20		
LOS ANGLES	2.4	.69
(1) 11		
LOW COUNTRIES	2.4	.51
(1) 16		
LUXEMBOURG, GRAND DUCHY OF	2.4	.51
(3) 03 07 11 36		
MAINLAND	2.4	.69
(2) 17 24		
MALAWI	2.4	.51
(3) 03 07 11		
MALI, REPUBLIC OF	2.4	.51
(3) 03 07 11 38		
MAURITANIA	2.4	.51
(4) 03 07 11 36		
MESOPOTAMIA	2.4	.51
(2) 09 16		
NATURAL BOUNDARY	2.4	.51
(1) 17		
NEUTRALIZED ZONE	2.4	.51
(1) 17		
NEW YORK STATE	2.4	.69
(1) 11		
NON-WESTERN	2.4	.69
(1) 24		
NORTH SEA	2.4	.51
(1) 11		
OCCUPIED TERRITORY	2.4	.51
(1) 17		
PAN-AMERICAN HIGHWAY	2.4	.51
(1) 16		
PAPAL STATES	2.4	.51
(1) 17		
PIVOTAL STATES	2.4	.51
(4) 03 06 18 29		
POTSDAM	2.4	.51
(1) 25		
PRIVILEGED SANCTUARY	2.4	.51
(1) 39		
PUBLIC ACCOMMODATIONS	2.4	.51
(2) 18 32		
PUBLIC LAND	2.4	.51
(1) 16		
RUANDA URUNDI	2.4	.51
(1) 36		
RWANDA	2.4	.51
(2) 03 07		
SAINT LAWRENCE WATERWAY	2.4	.51
(1) 45		
SAMOA	2.4	.51
(1) 18 24		
SAMOA, AMERICAN	2.4	.51
(1) 42		
SANITARY CORDON	2.4	.51
(1) 17		
SCOTLAND	2.4	.51
(1) 11		
SINGAPORE	2.4	.51
(2) 07 11		
SLUM AREA	2.4	.69
(1) 45		
SRI LANKA	2.4	.51
(2) 07 11		
STRATEGIC TRUSTEESHIP TERRITORY	2.4	.69
(1) 18 20 38		
TRIESTE	2.4	.51
(1) 25		
TRINIDAD	2.4	.51
(1) 07		
ULTRA VIRES	2.4	.69
(1) 45		
UPPER VOLTA	2.4	.51
(3) 03 07 11		
URBAN DISTRICT	2.4	.69
(1) 17		
VATICAN CITY	2.4	.51
(3) 17 21 34		
WEST AFRICA	2.4	.51
(2) 07 11		
WESTERN FRONT	2.4	.69
(1) 16		
WISCONSIN	2.4	.51
(1) 07		
ABYSSINIA	2.5	.52
(1) 03		
AIR SPACE	2.5	.70
(2) 17 23		
ALASKA	2.5	.52
(2) 06 07		
AMERICAN SAMOA	2.5	.70
(2) 03 06		
ANCIENT EGYPT	2.5	.52
(1) 25		
ANNAPOLIS	2.5	.70
(1) 16		
ANTIETAM	2.5	.52
(2) 22 46		

ANTIGUA	2.5	.52
(2) 06 45		
ARAB WORLD	2.5	.52
(1) 25		
ARRONDISSEMENT (FRANCE)	2.5	.52
(2) 03 32		
ATLANTA (GEORGIA)	2.5	.70
(1) 11		
ATTICA	2.5	.70
(2) 25 26		
BAHAMA ISLANDS	2.5	.52
(1) 06		
BECHUANALAND	2.5	.52
(1) 03		
BELFAST, U.K.	2.5	.52
(1) 11		
BERMUDA	2.5	.52
(2) 06 07		
BORDER	2.5	.70
(3) 17 24 25		
BORNEO	2.5	.52
(1) 11		
BOTSWANA	2.5	.52
(1) 07		
BRUSSELS, BELGIUM	2.5	.52
(1) 11		
BYZANTINE	2.5	.52
(1) 43		
BYZANTINE EMPIRE	2.5	.52
(2) 22 25		
CARTHAGE	2.5	.52
(1) 26		
CHAD	2.5	.52
(4) 03 07 17 24		
CLOSED FRONTIER	2.5	.52
(1) 17		
COALING STATION	2.5	.52
(1) 16		
CONQUERED TERRITORY	2.5	.52
(1) 06		
CONTIGUOUS ZONE, JURISDICTION	2.5	.70
(2) 17 20		
CORREGIDOR	2.5	.70
(2) 03 16		
CROATIA	2.5	.52
(2) 11 16		
DEMARCATION LINE	2.5	.70
(1) 17		
DEWLINE (DEW, DISTANT EARLY WARNING)	2.5	.52
(1) 34		
DOMINION	2.5	.52
(7) 03 06 16 17 19 24 34		
EAST ASIA	2.5	.52
(2) 07 11		
EAST ASIA CO-PROSPERITY SPHERE	2.5	.52
(1) 21		
EAST OF SUEZ	2.5	.52
(1) 34		
ELK HILLS	2.5	.84
(1) 16		
ELYSEE PALACE	2.5	.52
(1) 16		
ENCLAVE	2.5	.52
(2) 16 17		
ESTONIA	2.5	.52
(1) 03		
FIJI	2.5	.52
(1) 11		
FOGGY BOTTOM	2.5	.70
(1) 39		
FORT KNOX	2.5	.52
(1) 42		
FORT SUMTER	2.5	.52
(1) 08		
FREE ZONE	2.5	.52
(2) 16 17		
FREEHOLD	2.5	.70
(1) 45		
GABON	2.5	.52
(3) 07 17 24		
GREATER EAST ASIA CO-PROSPERITY SPHERE	2.5	.52
(2) 03 16		
GUINEA-BISSAU	2.5	.52
(1) 11		
HIGHWAY	2.5	.70
(2) 19 27		
HUMAN ENVIRONMENT	2.5	.70
(1) 41		
HUSTINGS	2.5	.52
(2) 16 39		
ICE-FREE PORT	2.5	.52
(1) 17		
INDIAN OCEAN	2.5	.52
(2) 07 11		
INDIANA	2.5	.52
(1) 11		
INLAND SEA	2.5	.52
(1) 17		
INSULAR POSSESSIONS	2.5	.52
(1) 16		
INTER-OCEANIC CANAL	2.5	.52
(1) 17		
IVORY COAST	2.5	.52
(2) 03 07		
JAMAICA	2.5	.52
(2) 03 07		
KURDISTAN	2.5	.52
(1) 17		
LAND FRONTIER	2.5	.52
(1) 17		
LIBERIA	2.5	.52
(3) 03 07 11		
LOUISIANA	2.5	.52
(2) 07 11		
MADAGASCAR	2.5	.52
(2) 07 11		
MADRID	2.5	.52
(1) 11		
MALAGASY REPUBLIC	2.5	.52
(2) 03 07		
MASSACHUSETTS	2.5	.52
(1) 11		
MELANESIA	2.5	.52
(1) 25		

MELBOURNE, AUSTRALIA	2.5	.52
(1) 11		
MIDWEST	2.5	.84
(2) 24 30		
MISSOURI	2.5	.52
(1) 07		
MITTELEUROPA	2.5	.52
(1) 16		
MUSCAT AND OMAN	2.5	.52
(1) 17		
NAVAL BASE	2.5	.52
(3) 16 17 21		
NAVIGABLE WATERS	2.5	.52
(3) 06 16 18		
NEPAL	2.5	.52
(3) 03 07 11		
NEUTRAL ASYLUM	2.5	.52
(1) 17		
NEW DELHI	2.5	.52
(1) 03		
NICARAGUA	2.5	.52
(1) 03		
NIGER	2.5	.52
(. 3) 03 07 11		
NORTH AFRICA	2.5	.52
(2) 07 11		
NORTH CAROLINA	2.5	.52
(1) 04		
OFFSHORE ISLANDS	2.5	.52
(1) 03		
OKINAWA	2.5	.52
(1) 22		
OKLAHOMA	2.5	.52
(1) 07		
OPEN SEA	2.5	.52
(1) 16		
ORGANIZED TERRITORY	2.5	.70
(1) 06		
OVERSEAS POSSESSIONS	2.5	.52
(1) 17		
OVERSEAS TERRITORIES	2.5	.52
(1) 17		
PAKISTAN	2.5	.52
(3) 03 07 11		
PANAMA	2.5	.52
(3) 03 07 11		
PHILIPPINES	2.5	.52
(3) 03 07 11		
POLITICAL CAPITAL	2.5	.52
(1) 29		
QUEMOY (KINMEN) AND MATSU	2.5	.52
(2) 03 24		
RHINE	2.5	.52
(1) 11		
ROYAL COLONY	2.5	.70
(2) 06 18		
RURAL	2.5	.70
(1) 44		
RYUKU ISLANDS	2.5	.52
(1) 11		
SANTIAGO, CHILE	2.5	.52
(1) 11		

SILK-STOCKING DISTRICT	2.5	.52
(3) 06 29 39		
SOMALIA	2.5	.52
(2) 03 07		
SOUTH	2.5	.70
(2) 11 30		
SOUTH DAKOTA	2.5	.52
(1) 07		
SOUTHWEST AFRICA (NAMABIA)	2.5	.52
(1) 07		
ST. LAWRENCE SEAWAY	2.5	.52
(3) 03 06 16		
STANDARD METROPOLITAN	2.5	.70
STATISTICAL AREAS (U.S.A.)		
(1) 03		
STERLING AREA	2.5	.52
(1) 16		
STRAITS CLOSED TO WARSHIPS	2.5	.52
(1) 17		
SUBURBAN	2.5	.52
(1) 45		
SUBURBS	2.5	.52
(4) 04 24 25 30		
SWAZILAND	2.5	.52
(2) 07 24		
SWEAT SHOP	2.5	.52
(1) 16		
TEXAS	2.5	.52
(3) 03 07 11		
THEATRE OF WAR	2.5	.52
(1) 17		
TIGRIS-EUPHRATES VALLEY	2.5	.52
(1) 22		
TOKYO	2.5	.52
(1) 03		
TOWN	2.5	.84
(1) 44		
TOWN (U.S.A.)	2.5	.70
(9) 03 06 16 18 24 25 27 30 32		
U.N. STRATEGIC TRUST TERRITORIES	2.5	.52
(1) 03		
UNINCORPORATED TERRITORY	2.5	.52
(2) 06 16		
URBAN COUNTY	2.5	.52
(2) 03 18		
VERMONT	2.5	.52
(1) 07		
VIRGIN ISLANDS	2.5	.52
(2) 07 18		
WALES	2.5	.52
(1) 11		
WAR ZONE	2.5	.52
(1) 17		
WASHINGTON STATE	2.5	.52
(1) 11		
WEST BENGAL, INDIA	2.5	.52
(1) 11		
ZONE OF OCCUPATION	2.5	.52
(1) 17		
AFRICAN EMPIRE	2.6	.51
(1) 22		
ANGUILLA	2.6	.51
(1) 25		

ANTILLES	2.6	.51	IRISH BOUNDARY	2.6	.69
(1) 11			(1) 21		
ARCHIVES	2.6	.51	KAZAKHSTAN	2.6	.51
(3) 06 16 17			(1) 24		
ARIZONA	2.6	.51	KERALA	2.6	.51
(1) 06			(1) 03		
ARKANSAS	2.6	.51	KYOTO	2.6	.51
(2) 06 07			(1) 03		
ARLINGTON NATIONAL CEMETERY	2.6	.51	LANDLOCKED BAY	2.6	.51
(1) 42			(1) 17		
ARTIFICIAL BOUNDARY	2.6	.51	LIECHTENSTEIN	2.6	.51
(1) 17			(2) 07 11		
BAHRAIN	2.6	.69	LINE	2.6	.69
(1) 17			(1) 24		
BYZANTIUM	2.6	.51	LITTLE EUROPE	2.6	.51
(1) 03			(1) 17		
CAMPUS	2.6	.69	MACAO	2.6	.51
(1) 30			(1) 34		
CANBERRA, AUSTRALIA	2.6	.51	MARITIME PROVINCES	2.6	.51
(1) 11			(1) 16		
CHUNGKING	2.6	.69	MARTINIQUE	2.6	.51
(10) 03 11 22 23 24 25 26 27 29 30			(1) 25		
COCKPIT OF EUROPE	2.6	.51	MARYLAND	2.6	.51
(1) 16			(1) 11		
COMMON	2.6	.69	MEGALOPOLITAN	2.6	.69
(1) 24			(1) 45		
CONNECTICUT	2.6	.51	MICHIGAN	2.6	.51
(2) 06 25			(1) 11		
CURACAO	2.6	.51	MIDDLE COLONIES	2.6	.69
(1) 11			(1) 46		
DOMICILE	2.6	.51	MILITARY AREA	2.6	.69
(2) 06 16			(1) 11		
EAST	2.6	.69	MINNESOTA	2.6	.51
(1) 24			(1) 07		
ETHOPIA-SOMALI	2.6	.51	MONACO	2.6	.51
(1) 03			(1) 03		
EXTERNAL	2.6	.84	MURMANSK ROUTE	2.6	.51
(1) 43			(1) 16		
FLORIDA	2.6	.51	NAGASAKI	2.6	.51
(2) 11 25			(1) 03		
FOREIGN	2.6	.69	NATIONAL PARKS	2.6	.69
(1) 44			(1) 42		
FRANCO-GERMAN FRONTIER	2.6	.51	NATIVE STATES	2.6	.69
(1) 21			(1) 16		
FREE CITY	2.6	.51	NAVAL BASES, AMERICAN	2.6	.51
(2) 17 32			(1) 21		
GAME PRESERVE	2.6	.51	NEBRASKA	2.6	.51
(1) 16			(1) 07		
GENEVA FREE ZONES	2.6	.51	NEUTRALITY ZONE	2.6	.51
(1) 21			(1) 16		
GOLD COAST	2.6	.51	NEW GUINEA	2.6	.51
(2) 21 24			(1) 07		
GREENLAND	2.6	.51	NEW HAVEN	2.6	.51
(1) 03			(2) 04 11		
HIMALAYAS	2.6	.51	NEW WORLD	2.6	.51
(1) 22			(1) 17		
HOUSTON	2.6	.51	NEW ZEALAND	2.6	.51
(1) 11			(3) 03 07 11		
INDIANAPOLIS	2.6	.51	NO-MAN'S-LAND	2.6	.51
(1) 11			(1) 17		
INTERNATIONAL HIGHWAY	2.6	.51	NORDIC COUNTRIES	2.6	.51
(1) 16			(1) 11		

NORWAY	2.6	.51
(4) 03 04 07 11		
OREGON	2.6	.51
(1) 11		
PACIFIC ISLAND TRUST TERRITORY	2.6	.51
(1) 45		
PACIFIC ISLANDS	2.6	.51
(1) 42		
PARAGUAY	2.6	.51
(3) 03 07 11		
PARIS	2.6	.51
(1) 11		
PEIPING	2.6	.51
(1) 03		
PERIPHERAL STATE	2.6	.51
(1) 17		
PRESS GALLERY	2.6	.51
(3) 06 17 27		
PROTECTORATE, DEPENDENT	2.6	.51
TERRITORY		
(1) 20		
PROVINCE	2.6	.51
(5) 16 17 19 24 25		
QATAR	2.6	.51
(1) 17		
RIPARIAN	2.6	.51
(1) 16		
RURAL SLUMS	2.6	.51
(1) 45		
SALVADOR(EL)-HONDURAS	2.6	.51
(1) 11		
SATELLITE CITY	2.6	.51
(1) 04 06		
SEA FLOOR	2.6	.51
(1) 17		
SEABED	2.6	.51
(3) 11 17 41		
SIEGFRIED LINE	2.6	.51
(2) 16 17		
SOUTH EAST AFRICA	2.6	.51
(1) 11		
SOUTHEAST EUROPE	2.6	.51
(2) 07 11		
STRAITS	2.6	.51
(1) 16		
STRASBOURG	2.6	.51
(1) 09		
TENNESSEE	2.6	.51
(1) 11		
TERRITORIAL AIR	2.6	.51
(1) 03		
TORONTO	2.6	.51
(1) 11		
UNINCORPORATED VILLAGE	2.6	.51
(1) 27		
VOLGA BASIN	2.6	.69
(1) 22		
WAILING WALL	2.6	.51
(1) 16		
WORLD	2.6	.84
(1) 43		
WORLD-ISLAND	2.6	.69
(1) 22		
YENAN	2.6	.51
(1) 34		
ZONE OF OPERATIONS	2.6	.51
(1) 17		
DECLARATION OF INDEPENDENCE	1.2	.42
(11) 03 06 16 17 18 22 25 26 27 32		
42 46		
COMMUNIST MANIFESTO	1.4	.51
(9) 03 06 08 10 16 17 22 26 32		
FEDERALIST ,THE	1.5	.70
(1) 46		
AMERICAN POLITICAL SCIENCE REVIEW	1.6	.51
(2) 04 05		
FEDERALIST PAPERS, THE	1.7	.67
(8) 02 03 06 08 11 16 18 32		
U.N. CHARTER	1.7	.48
(4) 16 18 19 20		
DEMOCRACY IN AMERICA	1.8	.63
(1) 35		
MAJORITY REPORT	1.8	.42
(2) 17 27		
ON LIBERTY	1.8	.78
(1) 35		
PENTAGON PAPERS	1.8	.42
(3) 11 25 32		
DECLARATIONS OF HUMAN RIGHTS	1.9	.73
(1) 25		
EVOLUTIONARY SOCIALISM	1.9	.87
(1) 10		
INTERNATIONALE, THE	1.9	.56
(1) 16		
MINORITY REPORT	1.9	.31
(5) 06 16 17 27 45		
SOVIET CONSTITUTION	1.9	.56
(1) 34		
DAILY WORKER	2.0	.66
(1) 16		
ELECTORAL ROLL	2.0	.47
(1) 17		
IZVESTIA (NEWS)	2.0	.66
(3) 03 16 34		
KERNER REPORT	2.0	.66
(1) 42		
LITERATURE AND POLITICS	2.0	.81
(4) 11 23 24 30		
MESSAGE TO CONGRESS	2.0	.66
(1) 42		
REPUBLIC, THE	2.0	.94
(1) 35		
SAMPLE BALLOT	2.0	.66
(2) 06 16		
WARREN COMMISSION REPORT	2.0	.00
(3) 25 32 34		
AFFIDAVIT	2.1	.73
(3) 06 17 27		
ATTORNEY GENERAL'S LIST	2.1	.73
(2) 18 32		
CITY OF GOD	2.1	.56
(2) 17 26		
CLASSIFIED MATERIAL	2.1	.87
(1) 27		
CONGRESSIONAL QUARTERLY	2.1	.56
(1) 27		

CONSTITUTION, STATE   2.1   .73
   (2) 06 18
GOVERNMENT ORGANIZATION MANUAL   2.1   .73
   (1) 32
LEVIATHAN   2.1   .73
   (2) 05 26
NEW YORK TIMES   2.1   .73
   (2) 11 25
PERMANENT VISA   2.1   .56
   (1) 17
POLITICAL LITERATURE   2.1   .56
   (1) 39
PORNOGRAPHY   2.1   .73
   (2) 07 11
POSITION PAPER   2.1   .56
   (1) 39
AGENDA   2.2   .78
   (6) 02 06 16 17 18 24
BUDGET MESSAGE   2.2   .63
   (5) 02 16 18 27 32
CALENDAR   2.2   .63
   (6) 03 06 16 18 27 32
CERTIFICATE OF ELECTION   2.2   .63
   (2) 06 16
COMMUNITY STUDIES   2.2   .91
   (2) 24 33
CONGRESSIONAL RECORD   2.2   .42
   (5) 06 16 18 27 32
DECLARATION OF RIGHTS   2.2   .78
   (7) 03 16 17 18 19 22 32
DIPLOMATIC NOTE   2.2   .63
   (1) 17
DOCUMENT   2.2   .63
   (2) 06 30
ECONOMIC INTERPRETATION OF THE   2.2   .63
   CONSTITUTION
   (1) 18
ECONOMIC REPORT OF THE PRESIDENT   2.2   .63
   (3) 27 32 34
FEDERAL REGISTER   2.2   .42
   (5) 06 16 18 27 32
GOVERNMENT REPORTS   2.2   .63
   (1) 11
HOUSE CALENDAR   2.2   .42
   (1) 42
KORAN   2.2   .63
   (1) 16
MANIFESTO   2.2   .91
   (4) 17 27 30 33
ORGANIZATIONAL CHARTS   2.2   .63
   (1) 25
PRAVDA (THE TRUTH)   2.2   .63
   (5) 03 16 22 24 34
PRESIDENTIAL DRAFT   2.2   .63
   (1) 39
PUBLIC OPINION QUARTERLY   2.2   .78
   (1) 05
BRIEF   2.3   .82
   (2) 02 17
CONTRACT   2.3   .82
   (6) 03 06 17 25 27 32
DIPLOMATIC VISA   2.3   .48
   (1) 17

ENCYCLICAL   2.3   .67
   (1) 38
EXIT VISA   2.3   .48
   (1) 17
FALL OF THE THIRD REICH   2.3   .67
   (1) 17
GOVERNMENT DOCUMENTS   2.3   .67
   (1) 12
HOUSE JOURNAL   2.3   .48
   (1) 42
INSTRUMENT OF GOVERNMENT   2.3   .82
   (1) 26
LETTER OF RESIGNATION   2.3   .67
   (1) 17
NATIONAL ANTHEM   2.3   .82
   (2) 17 27
RIDER   2.3   .67
   (7) 06 16 17 18 27 29 32
SENATE JOURNAL   2.3   .67
   (1) 42
SPECIAL MESSAGE   2.3   .67
   (1) 02
UNION CALENDAR   2.3   .82
   (4) 02 06 16 18
WHITE PAPER   2.3   .67
   (2) 16 34
WILSON, WOODROW, ON CONGRESS   2.3   .67
   (1) 04
YEARBOOK OF THE UNITED NATIONS   2.3   .48
   (1) 41
AMERICAN DECLARATION OF RIGHTS   2.4   .69
   AND DUTIES OF MAN
   (1) 41
BIBLE   2.4   .84
   (1) 35
BONN CONSTITUTION, GERMANY   2.4   .51
   (2) 03 20
CALENDAR OF BILLS AND   2.4   .84
   RESOLUTIONS
   (2) 06 45
CITIZENSHIP PAPERS   2.4   .51
   (1) 17
CONTRACTS, GOVERNMENT   2.4   .51
   (1) 37
DRAFT RESOLUTION   2.4   .69
   (1) 17
ELECTORAL REGISTER   2.4   .69
   (1) 17
JOURNAL OF THE HOUSE OF   2.4   .51
   REPRESENTATIVES
   (1) 45
LEGISLATIVE STUDY   2.4   .69
   (1) 05
MEMORANDUM   2.4   .84
   (3) 02 17 18
MIDDLETOWN STUDIES   2.4   .51
   (2) 04 24
NATIONAL REVIEW   2.4   .51
   (1) 22
NEWSPAPER   2.4   .84
   (4) 04 12 24 30
PASSPORTS AND VISAS   2.4   .51
   (6) 16 17 18 20 27 32

PERSONNEL RECORDS	2.4	.69
(1) 37		
SHEPARD'S CITATIONS	2.4	.84
(1) 04		
SPIRIT OF THE LAWS	2.4	.69
(1) 35		
U.S. GOVERNMENT MANUAL	2.4	.69
(4) 06 16 18 32		
U.S. GOVERNMENT ORGANIZATION MANUAL	2.4	.69
(1) 42		
APPROVED AGENDA	2.5	.70
(1) 17		
BENNINGTON COLLEGE STUDY	2.5	.70
(1) 15		
BRANDEIS BRIEF	2.5	.52
(1) 42		
COMMUNIQUE	2.5	.52
(2) 16 17		
CONGRESSIONAL DIRECTORY	2.5	.52
(5) 06 16 18 27 32		
CREDENTIALS	2.5	.52
(3) 03 06 17		
DER STUERMER	2.5	.70
(1) 16		
DOCUMENTARY	2.5	.52
(1) 30		
DRAFT TREATY	2.5	.70
(1) 17		
EDITORIAL	2.5	.70
(1) 30		
ELMIRA (NEW YORK) STUDY	2.5	.70
(1) 05		
ENCYCLICAL LETTER	2.5	.52
(2) 16 17		
EXTENSION OF REMARKS	2.5	.70
(4) 06 16 18 32		
FEDERAL CODE ANNOTATED	2.5	.52
(1) 44		
INDEX OF PROHIBITED BOOKS	2.5	.70
(1) 35		
JOINT RETURN	2.5	.52
(1) 06		
JOURNAL	2.5	.52
(4) 06 11 16 27		
LETTER OF APPOINTMENT	2.5	.70
(1) 17		
LETTER OF MARQUE AND REPRISAL	2.5	.52
(1) 06		
LETTERS OF NATURALIZATION	2.5	.52
(1) 17		
MADISON'S JOURNAL	2.5	.70
(3) 06 18 32		
MAPS AND ATLASES	2.5	.70
(2) 25 41		
NEW REPUBLIC	2.5	.52
(1) 22		
NOBILITY, TITLES OF	2.5	.52
(1) 42		
PASSPORT	2.5	.52
(1) 42		
POLITICAL COMMENTARY	2.5	.70
(1) 07		
PROTOCOLS OF THE ELDERS OF ZION	2.5	.52
(3) 22 26 34		
SIGNATURE	2.5	.70
(1) 17		
STATISTICAL YEARBOOK	2.5	.70
(1) 17		
STATUTES AT LARGE OF THE UNITED STATES	2.5	.84
(4) 06 16 17 18		
TEXT	2.5	.70
(1) 16		
TREASURY NOTE	2.5	.52
(2) 06 16		
VERBATIM RECORD	2.5	.52
(1) 17		
WORKING PAPER	2.5	.52
(1) 17		
WRIT OF ASSISTANCE	2.5	.70
(1) 06		
XYZ PAPERS	2.5	.52
(1) 06		
ANTI-DUHRING	2.6	.69
(1) 26		
CALENDAR OF BUSINESS	2.6	.51
(1) 42		
CHINA WHITE PAPER	2.6	.51
(1) 03		
CLARK MEMORANDUM	2.6	.51
(1) 16		
COMMUNITAS	2.6	.69
(1) 30		
CONFESSION	2.6	.69
(3) 18 30 32		
DICTUM	2.6	.69
(1) 16		
DIE NEUE ZEIT	2.6	.69
(1) 22		
DIPLOMATIC PASSPORT	2.6	.51
(1) 17		
DOCKET	2.6	.69
(2) 06 16		
DOSSIER	2.6	.51
(1) 17		
DRAFT AGENDA	2.6	.69
(1) 17		
DRAFT CONSTITUTION	2.6	.69
(1) 17		
ELECTION CERTIFICATE	2.6	.51
(1) 06		
ELIGIBLE LIST	2.6	.69
(2) 06 16		
ENTRY VISA	2.6	.51
(1) 17		
FEDERAL DIGEST	2.6	.51
(1) 42		
FINAL REPORT	2.6	.69
(1) 17		
FOREIGN SERVICE LIST	2.6	.51
(1) 16		
GENESIS	2.6	.69
(1) 24		
HANSARD	2.6	.51
(2) 03 16		

IDENTICAL NOTES	2.6	.69
(1) 17		
INSTRUMENT	2.6	.69
(2) 17 24		
JEFFERSON'S MANUAL	2.6	.51
(1) 06		
LEAFLETS	2.6	.69
(1) 17		
LETTERS OF MARQUE AND REPRISAL	2.6	.51
(1) 42		
LITERATURE	2.6	.69
(1) 41		
MINUTES	2.6	.51
(4) 06 16 17 27		
NOVELS, POLITICAL	2.6	.69
(1) 23		
OFFICIAL REPORT	2.6	.51
(1) 17		
OLD TESTAMENT	2.6	.69
(1) 11		
OPINIONS OF THE ATTORNEY GENERAL	2.6	.51
(2) 12 16		
PRELIMINARY REPORT	2.6	.51
(1) 17		
PROVISIONAL AGENDA	2.6	.51
(1) 17		
PUBLICITY PAMPHLET	2.6	.51
(2) 06 16		
REFORM LITERATURE	2.6	.51
(1) 05		
REPORT	2.6	.69
(5) 06 17 18 24 30		
STAR SPANGLED BANNER, THE	2.6	.69
(3) 06 16 27		
SUMMA THEOLOGICA	2.6	.51
(1) 09		
TWO TREATISES OF GOVERNMENT	2.6	.51
(1) 35		
U.N. MONTHLY CHRONICLE	2.6	.69
(1) 41		
U.S. REPORTS	2.6	.51
(3) 06 16 18		
WINDS OF CHANGE	2.6	.51
(2) 34 39		
ZIMMERMAN NOTE	2.6	.51
(1) 16		
NUCLEAR WEAPONS	1.4	.51
(6) 03 07 17 22 23 25		
A-BOMB	1.7	.48
(1) 17		
ANTI-BALLISTIC MISSILE (ABM) SYSTEM	1.7	.82
(1) 20		
DEFENSIVE WEAPONS	1.7	.67
(1) 02		
ATOM BOMB	1.8	.63
(4) 03 17 21 46		
ATOMIC ENERGY	1.8	.63
(3) 11 19 46		
NATURAL RESOURCES	1.8	.78
(8) 06 07 11 16 19 20 25 27		
NUCLEAR ARMAMENTS	1.8	.78
(1) 17		
CONCENTRATION CAMPS	1.9	.73
(2) 25 34		
MILITARY RESOURCES	1.9	.99
(1) 17		
NATIONAL RESOURCES	1.9	.73
(1) 16		
TACTICAL NUCLEAR WEAPONS	1.9	.56
(1) 17		
THERMONUCLEAR WEAPONS	1.9	.56
(1) 17		
WHITE HOUSE	1.9	.73
(6) 06 16 17 27 32 34		
ARMS	2.0	.81
(2) 17 24		
ATOMIC WEAPONS	2.0	.66
(1) 11		
EXPORT	2.0	.94
(1) 06		
GUIDED MISSILES	2.0	.66
(1) 17		
MONEY	2.0	.94
(5) 06 16 23 24 30		
NUCLEAR STOCKPILE	2.0	.00
(1) 03		
OFFENSIVE WEAPONS	2.0	.66
(1) 02		
PENTAGON	2.0	.47
(6) 03 24 25 27 32 34		
VOTING MACHINE	2.0	.66
(4) 03 06 16 27		
WHITE HOUSE OFFICE	2.0	.81
(5) 06 18 27 32 34		
ARMAMENTS	2.1	.87
(1) 16		
CONSULATE	2.1	.56
(4) 06 16 17 32		
DOOMSDAY MACHINE	2.1	.73
(1) 39		
ENVIRONMENT	2.1	.87
(7) 01 04 11 24 30 32 33		
H-BOMB	2.1	.87
(1) 17		
HOT LINE	2.1	.56
(2) 20 34		
HYDROGEN BOMB	2.1	.56
(1) 17		
MASS DESTRUCTION WEAPONS	2.1	.73
(1) 17		
MIRV (MULTIPLE INDEPENDENT REENTRY VEHICLE)	2.1	.56
(1) 36		
OIL	2.1	.87
(3) 07 11 21		
POLITICAL RESOURCES	2.1	.87
(2) 08 33		
PROPERTY	2.1	.87
(8) 06 11 16 19 23 24 26 30		
SURFACE TO AIR MISSILES (SAM)	2.1	.56
(1) 29		
SWASTIKA	2.1	.56
(3) 16 17 24		
WEAPONS	2.1	.73
(3) 11 24 30		

AIR POWER	2.2	.78		CONVENTIONAL ARMS	2.3	.67
(1) 36				(2) 17 20		
BALLOT BOX	2.2	.78		CURRENCY	2.3	.67
(1) 42				(3) 06 16 27		
CITY HALL	2.2	.78		DIPLOMATIC POUCH	2.3	.48
(1) 39				(3) 16 17 32		
COMMUNITY PROPERTY	2.2	.42		FLAG	2.3	.82
(1) 42				(1) 17		
COMPUTER	2.2	.78		FLAG OF TRUCE	2.3	.67
(4) 07 11 24 33				(2) 16 17		
EAVESDROPPING DEVICES	2.2	.63		GOLD	2.3	.82
(1) 32				(1) 21		
FISSIONABLE MATERIAL	2.2	.63		IMPORTS	2.3	.67
(1) 17				(1) 41		
GREAT WALL, CHINESE	2.2	.63		LAND	2.3	.82
(2) 03 16				(4) 11 16 24 34		
HAMMER AND SICKLE	2.2	.63		MAINE, THE	2.3	.67
(2) 16 17				(1) 06		
HILL, THE	2.2	.63		MEANS	2.3	.94
(1) 39				(2) 13 24		
HOUSE	2.2	.78		MUNITIONS	2.3	.82
(2) 17 24				(2) 06 16		
INTERCONTINENTAL ROCKETS	2.2	.78		NUCLEAR	2.3	.67
(1) 17				(1) 24		
LEGAL TENDER	2.2	.63		NUCLEAR SUBMARINE	2.3	.67
(3) 06 18 27				(1) 17		
MACE	2.2	.78		POLLING BOOTH	2.3	.67
(2) 06 16				(1) 17		
MISSILES	2.2	.42		ROCKETS	2.3	.67
(1) 38				(1) 36		
MONETARY	2.2	.91		RUSSIAN SATELLITES	2.3	.48
(1) 16				(1) 17		
NATIONAL CURRENCY	2.2	.63		SPUTNIK	2.3	.82
(1) 17				(1) 03		
NOBEL PEACE PRIZE	2.2	.42		UNION JACK	2.3	.48
(3) 11 16 17				(1) 16		
NUCLEAR ENERGY	2.2	.63		UNION LABEL	2.3	.67
(1) 41				(1) 06		
OIL, MIDDLE EAST	2.2	.63		AMERICAN FLAG	2.4	.69
(1) 21				(1) 42		
PETROLEUM RESOURCES	2.2	.78		BOND	2.4	.69
(1) 41				(4) 06 16 18 27		
POLARIS SUBMARINE	2.2	.42		CAPITAL, U.S.	2.4	.69
(2) 03 34				(1) 42		
POLYGRAPHS	2.2	.42		CHINESE GREAT WALL	2.4	.51
(1) 37				(1) 03		
RAW MATERIALS	2.2	.63		COMMON CARRIER	2.4	.51
(3) 06 16 20				(3) 06 16 18		
REAL PROPERTY	2.2	.63		CONTRABAND	2.4	.69
(1) 16				(4) 06 16 17 20		
RESOURCES	2.2	.78		CROWN	2.4	.51
(1) 24				(4) 03 16 17 24		
SCALE	2.2	.78		DOLLAR	2.4	.69
(3) 01 24 30				(2) 06 16		
STRATEGIC ARMS	2.2	.78		FALLOUT	2.4	.51
(1) 11				(1) 24		
AIR BASE	2.3	.67		GOODS	2.4	.84
(1) 17				(1) 24		
BLACKLIST	2.3	.48		GREENBACK	2.4	.69
(6) 06 16 17 29 32 39				(1) 16		
CAPITOL	2.3	.48		JAIL	2.4	.69
(4) 06 16 24 34				(3) 06 27 30		

LANDMARK	2.4	.69
(1) 24		
LUSITANIA, THE	2.4	.69
(1) 06		
MECHANISM	2.4	.84
(1) 24		
NARCOTICS	2.4	.84
(2) 30 41		
NATIONAL FLAG	2.4	.69
(1) 17		
ORGANISM	2.4	.69
(1) 43		
PAPER MONEY	2.4	.69
(1) 06		
PARTY DESIGNATION	2.4	.69
(1) 27		
PERSONAL PROPERTY	2.4	.69
(3) 06 16 17		
PETROLEUM	2.4	.69
(2) 11 21		
POLITICAL PLUM	2.4	.69
(1) 39		
REAL ESTATE	2.4	.69
(1) 06		
ROCKETS CARRYING NUCLEAR WARHEADS	2.4	.69
(1) 17		
TELEVISION	2.4	.84
(5) 11 23 24 25 30		
TOWN HALL	2.4	.84
(1) 17		
UNCLE SAM	2.4	.69
(1) 16		
WAR POTENTIAL	2.4	.69
(2) 16 17		
WATER RESOURCES	2.4	.69
(1) 41		
ARSENAL	2.5	.52
(1) 06		
BASTILLE	2.5	.52
(3) 03 16 29		
BUCKINGHAM PALACE	2.5	.52
(1) 16		
CAMPAIGN BUTTONS	2.5	.52
(1) 39		
COBALT	2.5	.70
(1) 21		
COMMODITY	2.5	.52
(1) 43		
COMMUNICATIONS SATELLITE	2.5	.52
(1) 25		
CURRENCY, VARIETIES USED IN THE U.S.	2.5	.70
(1) 45		
EARTH	2.5	.84
(1) 43		
EARTH SATELLITE	2.5	.52
(1) 17		
ELEPHANT, REPUBLICAN	2.5	.52
(3) 16 29 39		
ENERGY	2.5	.70
(1) 41		

ERSATZ	2.5	.52
(1) 16		
ESTATE	2.5	.70
(1) 24		
EXTERMINATION CAMP	2.5	.70
(1) 17		
FACTORY	2.5	.84
(4) 04 11 24 30		
FLAG (UN)	2.5	.70
(1) 41		
FOOD	2.5	.70
(1) 41		
FREEDOM TRAIN	2.5	.52
(1) 45		
GREAT SEAL OF THE U.S.	2.5	.52
(1) 42		
LEAD	2.5	.84
(2) 21 24		
LORD PRIVY SEAL	2.5	.52
(2) 16 17		
MARIJUANA	2.5	.70
(1) 25		
OBJECT	2.5	.70
(2) 17 24		
PARTY EMBLEM	2.5	.52
(1) 06		
PRISON	2.5	.70
(5) 06 07 25 27 30		
RED STAR	2.5	.70
(1) 16		
SATELLITE	2.5	.52
(4) 03 24 29 34		
STARS AND STRIPES	2.5	.84
(2) 06 17		
STATUE OF LIBERTY	2.5	.84
(1) 42		
STOCKPILES	2.5	.52
(1) 17		
SUPERSONIC TRANSPORTS	2.5	.52
(1) 25		
TROJAN HORSE	2.5	.52
(2) 16 29		
U.S. CAPITOL	2.5	.70
(1) 32		
WATER POWER	2.5	.70
(1) 06		
AIRCRAFT	2.6	.69
(1) 17		
ALMSHOUSE	2.6	.69
(1) 06		
APPLICATIONS FOR POSITIONS	2.6	.69
(1) 37		
ARMORY	2.6	.51
(2) 06 16		
ARTIFACT	2.6	.51
(2) 24 25		
BAUXITE	2.6	.84
(1) 21		
BENCH	2.6	.51
(4) 03 06 16 27		
BOMBER	2.6	.51
(1) 30		

CAMPAIGN TRAIN	2.6	.51
(1) 39		
CANNABIS	2.6	.69
(1) 41		
COMMERCIAL PAPER	2.6	.51
(1) 45		
CONGRESSIONAL MEDAL OF HONOR	2.6	.51
(1) 06		
COPPER	2.6	.51
(2) 11 21		
CRITICAL MATERIAL	2.6	.51
(1) 06		
CUSTOMHOUSE	2.6	.69
(1) 06		
DAY-CARE CENTER	2.6	.69
(1) 32		
DEVICE	2.6	.84
(1) 24		
EMBLEM (UN)	2.6	.51
(1) 41		
FASCES	2.6	.69
(1) 17		
FLAG, AMERICAN	2.6	.51
(1) 42		
FORMS (PERSONNEL)	2.6	.69
(1) 37		
GALLERIES	2.6	.51
(2) 06 17		
GARBAGE-DISPOSAL PLANTS	2.6	.51
(1) 45		
GIVEAWAY	2.6	.69
(1) 39		
GRAPEVINE	2.6	.69
(1) 39		
GUILLOTINE	2.6	.51
(2) 16 29		
GUN	2.6	.69
(1) 30		
HOSPITAL SHIP	2.6	.51
(1) 17		
HOUSING	2.6	.51
(5) 07 11 16 25 30		
IMPEDIMENTS	2.6	.69
(1) 24		
INHERITANCE	2.6	.69
(2) 22 30		
LABELS	2.6	.69
(1) 39		
LIBERTY BELL	2.6	.69
(1) 42		
MAIL	2.6	.69
(1) 24		
MAN-OF-WAR	2.6	.69
(1) 17		
MEXICO PETROLEUM	2.6	.69
(1) 21		
MINERAL RESOURCES	2.6	.69
(1) 41		
MINT	2.6	.51
(2) 06 16		
MOLECULE	2.6	.69
(1) 43		
OCCUPATIONAL DISEASE	2.6	.69
(1) 06		
PART	2.6	.84
(1) 43		
PERMIT	2.6	.69
(3) 06 16 17		
POISON GAS	2.6	.51
(2) 16 17		
POSSESSION	2.6	.51
(2) 17 24		
RADIATION EFFECTS	2.6	.69
(1) 36		
REPUBLICAN ELEPHANT	2.6	.51
(1) 39		
RISING SUN	2.6	.69
(2) 16 17		
SECURITIES	2.6	.51
(1) 25		
TRICOLOR	2.6	.51
(1) 16		
WARSHIP	2.6	.51
(1) 17		
MACHINERY OF GOVERNMENT	1.6	.69
(1) 39		
ARROGANCE OF POWER	1.8	.78
(1) 39		
LIBERTE, EGALITE, FRATERNITE	1.8	.63
(1) 16		
CAVEAT EMPTOR	1.9	.56
(1) 18		
WHITE MANS BURDEN	2.0	.47
(3) 06 16 22		
ART OF THE POSSIBLE	2.1	.73
(1) 39		
BIG STICK	2.1	.56
(4) 06 16 27 29		
FEATHERBEDDING	2.1	.31
(3) 18 27 32		
FUCKING	2.1	.87
(1) 43		
GOVERNMENT OF LAWS AND NOT OF MEN	2.1	.87
(1) 16		
GREAT LEAP FORWARD, MAOIST	2.1	.56
(3) 03 20 34		
LIFE, LIBERTY OR PROPERTY	2.1	.87
(1) 42		
NO TAXATION WITHOUT REPRESENTATION	2.1	.56
(1) 03		
OF THE PEOPLE, BY THE PEOPLE, AND FOR THE PEOPLE	2.1	.56
(1) 16		
POLITICAL AXIOMS	2.1	.73
(1) 39		
POWER CORRUPTS	2.1	.56
(1) 39		
VOX POPULI (VOICE OF THE PEOPLE)	2.1	.87
(1) 02 16		
WAR TO END WARS	2.1	.87
(2) 06 16		
WE SHALL OVERCOME	2.1	.73
(1) 39		

WHO GETS WHAT, WHEN, AND HOW   2.1   .73
  (1) 39
BAN THE BOMB   2.2   .63
  (1) 39
BETTER RED THAN DEAD   2.2   .63
  (1) 39
BUYING AN ELECTION   2.2   .63
  (1) 39
GOVERNMENT OF THE PEOPLE, BY THE   2.2   .63
  PEOPLE, FOR THE PEOPLE
  (2) 17 29
HARD LINE   2.2   .63
  (1) 39
L'ETAT C'EST MOI   2.2   .63
  (1) 39
LIFE, LIBERTY AND THE PURSUIT OF   2.2   .78
  HAPPINESS
  (1) 42
OPEN COVENANTS OPENLY ARRIVED AT   2.2   .63
  (2) 06 16
POLITICAL EUPHEMISMS   2.2   .42
  (1) 39
QUID PRO QUO   2.2   .42
  (3) 03 18 20
TAXATION WITHOUT REPRESENTATION   2.2   .42
  (1) 16
ACROSS-THE-BOARD INCREASE   2.3   .82
  (1) 32
ANOTHER MUNICH   2.3   .82
  (1) 39
BANDWAGON   2.3   .67
  (1) 02
BIG LIE   2.3   .48
  (1) 39
BOONDOGGLE   2.3   .67
  (4) 06 16 27 29
BREAD AND BUTTER ISSUE   2.3   .48
  (2) 29 39
DIRTY POLITICS   2.3   .67
  (1) 39
DIVIDE AND RULE   2.3   .67
  (1) 16
FENCE MENDING   2.3   .67
  (1) 27
GUNS BEFORE BUTTER   2.3   .67
  (1) 39
LIVING SPACE   2.3   .82
  (1) 17
OFF THE RECORD   2.3   .67
  (1) 39
PAPER TIGER   2.3   .48
  (1) 39
PEACE IN OUR TIME   2.3   .67
  (1) 16 39
SYSTEM, THE   2.3   .82
  (1) 06
AYES AND NOES   2.4   .69
  (1) 16
BANDWAGON, TO GET ON   2.4   .51
  (1) 45
BELLWEATHER   2.4   .69
  (1) 29

BEYOND THE WELFARE STATE   2.4   .69
  (1) 35
BRAIN DRAIN   2.4   .51
  (1) 39
CARTE BLANCHE   2.4   .51
  (2) 16 17
E PLURIBUS UNUM   2.4   .69
  (4) 06 16 27 29
HEARTBEAT AWAY FROM THE   2.4   .51
  PRESIDENCY
  (1) 39
I DO NOT CHOOSE TO RUN   2.4   .69
  (1) 16
IF YOU CAN'T LICK 'EM, JOIN 'EM   2.4   .69
  (1) 39
IF YOU CAN'T STAND THE HEAT, GET   2.4   .69
  OUT OF THE KITCHEN
  (1) 39
JOHN BULL   2.4   .69
  (1) 16
KING CAN DO NO WRONG   2.4   .69
  (1) 16
LAST HURRAH   2.4   .69
  (1) 39
LOST CAUSE   2.4   .69
  (1) 29
MAINSTREAM   2.4   .69
  (1) 39
MAKE THE WORLD SAFE FOR   2.4   .69
  DEMOCRACY
  (1) 16
MUNICH, ANOTHER   2.4   .69
  (1) 39
ON THE FENCE   2.4   .69
  (1) 29 39 45
PEACE AT ANY PRICE   2.4   .84
  (1) 16
PEACE WITH HONOR   2.4   .69
  (1) 39
POWER BEHIND THE THRONE   2.4   .51
  (1) 29
RED HERRING   2.4   .51
  (1) 29
SUPREME COURT FOLLOWS THE   2.4   .69
  ELECTION RETURNS
  (1) 39
THE WORLD MUST BE MADE SAFE FOR   2.4   .69
  DEMOCRACY
  (1) 16
WE WILL BURY YOU   2.4   .69
  (1) 39
WHAT'S GOOD FOR GENERAL MOTORS   2.4   .69
  IS GOOD FOR THE COUNTRY
  (1) 39
YOU CAN'T FIGHT CITY HALL   2.4   .69
  (1) 39
ABOVE POLITICS   2.5   .52
  (1) 39
AID AND COMFORT TO THE ENEMY   2.5   .70
  (1) 06
AS MAINE GOES, SO GOES THE NATION 2.5   .52
  (1) 29

BACK TO NORMALCY   2.5   .70
(1) 16
BARNSTORM   2.5   .70
(1) 29
BOOM AND BUST   2.5   .52
(1) 39
BUCK STOPS HERE   2.5   .52
(1) 39
BULLET VOTE   2.5   .70
(1) 39
BUTTON-HOLE   2.5   .70
(1) 29
CEMETERY VOTE   2.5   .52
(1) 39
CLOSING RANKS   2.5   .52
(1) 39
CRADLE-TO-THE-GRAVE   2.5   .52
(1) 39
DON'T WASTE YOUR VOTE   2.5   .70
(1) 39
FINGER ON THE BUTTON   2.5   .70
(1) 39
FREE COINAGE OF SILVER   2.5   .52
(2) 06 22
GIVE ME LIBERTY OR GIVE ME DEATH   2.5   .70
(1) 16
GO-IT-ALONE   2.5   .70
(1) 39
HAPPY DAYS ARE HERE AGAIN   2.5   .70
(1) 39
HE KEPT US OUT OF WAR   2.5   .70
(1) 16
I AM THE LAW   2.5   .70
(1) 39
I HAVE A DREAM   2.5   .52
(1) 39
I'D RATHER BE RIGHT THAN BE   2.5   .70
PRESIDENT
(2) 16 39
KICK THE RASCALS OUT   2.5   .70
(1) 45
NEW FREEDOM   2.5   .70
(5) 06 22 29 39 45
NOTHING TO FEAR BUT FEAR ITSELF   2.5   .52
(1) 39
OLD GLORY   2.5   .70
(1) 17
PACKING THE GALLERIES   2.5   .52
(1) 39
SELLING CANDIDATES LIKE SOAP   2.5   .70
(1) 39
SHOO-IN   2.5   .70
(1) 39
SHOOT FROM THE HIP   2.5   .70
(1) 39
TO MAKE POLITICAL CAPITAL   2.5   .52
(1) 39
TO THE VICTORS BELONG THE SPOILS   2.5   .70
(1) 16 29
AMERICA FOR AMERICANS   2.6   .69
(2) 06 29
AX TO GRIND   2.6   .51
(1) 45

BLOODY SHIRT   2.6   .51
(2) 16 29
BRIDGE BUILDING   2.6   .51
(1) 39
BUSINESS AFFECTED WITH A PUBLIC   2.6   .51
INTEREST
(1) 45
CHOICE NOT AN ECHO   2.6   .51
(1) 39
CLEAN SWEEP   2.6   .51
(3) 06 16 29
CLOUT   2.6   .69
(1) 03
DEAD END, POLITICAL   2.6   .51
(1) 39
DEPARTMENT OF DIRTY TRICKS   2.6   .69
(1) 39
DONKEY, DEMOCRATIC   2.6   .51
(1) 39
EYEBALL TO EYEBALL   2.6   .69
(1) 39
EYEWASH   2.6   .69
(1) 29
FEEDING AT THE PUBLIC TROUGH   2.6   .51
(1) 39
FIFTY-FOUR FORTY OR FIGHT   2.6   .51
(3) 06 16 29
FISHING EXPEDITION   2.6   .51
(4) 06 16 27 29
FOOTBALL, POLITICAL   2.6   .51
(1) 39
FOR ROOSEVELT BEFORE CHICAGO   2.6   .69
(1) 39
GIVE 'EM HELL, HARRY   2.6   .69
(1) 39
GO FIGHT CITY HALL   2.6   .69
(1) 39
GOVERNMENT BY ALPHABET   2.6   .51
(1) 29
GREAT UNWASHED   2.6   .69
(1) 39
HAIRSPLITTING   2.6   .51
(1) 05
HOOPLA   2.6   .69
(1) 39
HOT POTATO   2.6   .51
(1) 16
I NEED HIM   2.6   .69
(1) 39
IMPERIUM IN IMPERIO (EMPIRE WITHIN   2.6   .51
AN EMPIRE)
(2) 16 26
JUST AND LASTING PEACE   2.6   .69
(1) 39
KING BY THE GRACE OF GOD   2.6   .69
(1) 17
LET'S TAKE A LOOK AT THE RECORD   2.6   .51
(1) 16
LILY WHITE   2.6   .51
(4) 06 16 27 29
POLITICAL FOOTBALL   2.6   .51
(1) 39

RED TERROR	2.6	.51	SHELL GAME	2.6	.51
(1) 16			(1) 29		
REMEMBER PEARL HARBOR	2.6	.51	SITTING ON THE FENCE	2.6	.51
(2) 06 16			(1) 39		
REMEMBER THE ALAMO	2.6	.51	STOPPING THE CLOCK	2.6	.51
(2) 06 16			(1) 42		
REMEMBER THE MAINE	2.6	.51	THROW AWAY YOUR VOTE	2.6	.51
(2) 06 16			(1) 39		
RICH RICHER, POOR POORER	2.6	.51	TRAITOR TO HIS CLASS	2.6	.51
(1) 29			(1) 39		
RUBBER STAMP, TO BE A	2.6	.51	UNION AS IT WAS AND THE	2.6	.69
(1) 45			CONSTITUTION AS IT IS		
RUM, ROMANISM, AND REBELLION	2.6	.51	(1) 29		
(1) 16			UNITED WE STAND, DIVIDED WE FALL	2.6	.51
SACRED COW	2.6	.69	(2) 16 39		
(1) 29					

A COUPON	821	B	ACADEMIC FREEDOM	202	A
A POSTERIORI	199	A	ACADEMIC SOCIALISTS	465	B
A PRIORI	195	A	ACADEMIE DE DROIT	478	B
A-BOMB	286	A	INTERNATIONAL		
ABATEMENT	233	A	ACADEMIE DIPLOMATIQUE	494	B
ABBAS, FERHAT	727	B	INTERNATIONALE		
ABBOTT, ROBERT S.	727	B	ACADEMIES (NAVY, ARMY, AIR	170	A
ABBOTT, WILBUR C.	727	B	FORCE)		
ABC POWERS	465	B	ACADEMY OF PLATO	175	A
ABDICATION	211	A	ACADEMY OF POLITICAL SCIENCE	170	A
ABDUCTION	621	B	ACADIANS	513	B
ABDUL RAHMAN, TUNKU	689	B	ACCEDE	621	B
ABDULLAH, KING	689	B	ACCEDING GOVERNMENTS	478	B
ABEL, I.W.	683	B	ACCEPTANCE SPEECH	211	A
ABELARD	728	B	ACCESS	233	A
ABELMAN VS. BOOTH (1859)	677	B	ACCESSIBILITY	225	A
ABELSON, ROBERT	728	B	ACCESSION	242	A
ABENDROTH, WOLFGANG	689	B	ACCIDENT	647	B
ABILITY TESTS	233	A	ACCIDENT INSURANCE	596	B
ABILITY THEORY	454	B	ACCIDENT, INDUSTRIAL	596	B
ABINGTON SCHOOL DISTRICT VS.	673	B	ACCIDENTAL WAR	199	A
SCHEMPP (1963)			ACCION DEMOCRACIES	513	B
ABINGTON SCHOOL DISTRICT VS.	261	A	ACCLAMATION	218	A
SCHEMPP (1963)			ACCOMMODATIONS	817	B
ABJURATION	621	B	ACCORD	251	A
ABOLITION	202	A	ACCOUNTABILITY	194	A
ABOLITIONISM	120	A	ACCOUNTANTS	547	B
ABOLITIONIST	182	A	ACCOUNTING ACT	647	B
ABOMINABLE NO-MAN	561	B	ACCOUNTING DEPARTMENT	513	B
ABORIGINES	175	A	ACCOUNTS, COMMITTEE ON	494	B
ABORTION	225	A	ACCREDIT	573	B
ABOVE POLITICS	290	A	ACCRETION	596	B
ABRAMS VS. UNITED STATES (1919)	673	B	ACCRETION, JURISDICTION	596	B
ABRAMS, PETER	728	B	ACCUMULATION (OF CAPITAL)	218	A
ABROGATION	251	A	ACCUSATION	251	A
ABSENTEE SENATOR	189	A	ACCUSED	191	A
ABSENTEE VOTING	197	A	ACHESON-LILIENTHAL REPORT	806	B
ABSENTEEISM	242	A	ACHESON, DEAN	264	A
ABSOLUTE	138	A	ACHIEVEMENT	218	A
ABSOLUTE CONTRABAND	819	B	ACQUAINTANCE GROUP	478	B
ABSOLUTE MAJORITY	146	A	ACQUIRED NATIONALITY	191	A
ABSOLUTE MONARCHY	146	A	ACQUIRED RIGHTS	621	B
ABSOLUTE MONEY	647	B	ACQUISITION	573	B
ABSOLUTISM	116	A	ACQUISITIVE PRESCRIPTION	596	B
ABSORPTION	596	B	ACQUITTAL	211	A
ABSTENTION	218	A	ACROSS-THE-BOARD INCREASE	290	A
ABSTRACTION	124	A	ACT	202	A
ABSTRACTIONIST	546	B	ACT (STATUTE)	202	A
ABUSE OF INTERNATIONAL LAW	251	A	ACT OF AGGRESSION	211	A
ABUSE OF OFFICE	233	A	ACT OF ALGECIRAS	621	B
ABUSE OF POWER	199	A	ACT OF CHAPULTEPEC OF 1945	233	A
ABUSES	621	B	ACT OF COMMITTAL	596	B
ABYSSINIA	279	A	ACT OF CONGRESS	199	A
ABYSSINIAN PACT	596	B	ACT OF HAVANA	596	B
ABYSSINIAN WAR	251	A	ACT OF INTERNATIONAL	647	B
ACADEMIC	546	B	DEVELOPMENT OF 1961		

ACT OF SETTLEMENT	573	B
ACT OF STATE DOCTRINE	233	A
ACT OF WAR	197	A
ACT-UTILITARIANISM	440	B
ACTH (CHEMICAL)	821	B
ACTING MINISTER	541	B
ACTING PRESIDENT	189	A
ACTING SECRETARY OF STATE	541	B
ACTION	233	A
ACTION COMMITTEE	478	B
ACTION FRANCAISE	465	B
ACTION THEORY	135	A
ACTIVISM	127	A
ACTIVISM VERSUS SELF-RESTRAINT	233	A
ACTIVIST	184	A
ACTIVITIES	251	A
ACTON, LORD	264	A
ACTOR	181	A
ACTUAL-ENTITY	824	B
ACTUAL-OCCASION	647	B
ACTUALISM	454	B
ACTUALITY	596	B
ACTUARY	547	B
AD HOC	206	A
AD HOC COMMITTEE	151	A
AD HOC CONFERENCE	242	A
AD REFERENDUM	573	B
AD VALOREM DUTY	211	A
ADAIR VS. UNITED STATES (1908)	672	B
ADAMANTINE	513	B
ADAMS-CLAY REPUBLICANS	465	B
ADAMS, BROOKS	701	B
ADAMS, HENRY	263	A
ADAMS, JANE	683	B
ADAMS, PRESIDENT JOHN	262	A
ADAMS, PRESIDENT JOHN QUINCY	262	A
ADAMS, SAMUEL	264	A
ADAMS, SHERMAN	266	A
ADAMSON ACT	621	B
ADAMSON VS. CALIFORNIA (1947)	671	B
ADAPTATION	127	A
ADAPTION	573	B
ADAPTIVENESS	433	B
ADDERLY VS. FLORIDA (1966)	673	B
ADDICTION	242	A
ADDITION	596	B
ADDITIONAL BALLOT	621	B
ADDRESS	597	A
ADELSON, JOSEPH	728	B
ADEN	278	A
ADENAUER, DR. KONRAD	264	A
ADEQUACY	440	B
ADHESION	647	B
ADJECTIVE LAW	621	B
ADJOURNMENT	242	A
ADJOURNMENT MOTION	211	A
ADJOURNMENT SINE DIE	233	A
ADJUDICATION	195	A
ADJUDICATIVE PROCESSES	122	A
ADJUSTED COMPENSATION	621	B
ADJUSTMENT	621	B
ADJUTANT	547	B
ADJUTANT GENERAL	185	A
ADKINS VS. CHILDRENS HOSPITAL (1923)	261	A
ADLER VS. BD OF EDUCATION OF N.Y. CITY (1952)	673	B
ADLER, ALFRED	683	B
ADLER, FRIEDRICH	728	B
ADLER, MORTIMER J.	683	B
ADLER, VICTOR	728	B
ADMINISTERED PRICES	573	B
ADMINISTERING STATE	478	B
ADMINISTRATION	202	A
ADMINISTRATION OF JUSTICE	202	A
ADMINISTRATION ON AGING	478	B
ADMINISTRATION RESEARCH	440	B
ADMINISTRATIVE ACTS	233	A
ADMINISTRATIVE AGENCIES	154	A
ADMINISTRATIVE AGREEMENT	597	B
ADMINISTRATIVE AND BUDGETARY COMMITTEE	465	B
ADMINISTRATIVE AUTHORITY	225	A
ADMINISTRATIVE BEHAVIOR	202	A
ADMINISTRATIVE COMMITTEE ON COORDINATION	465	B
ADMINISTRATIVE CONFERENCE	621	B
ADMINISTRATIVE CONTRACTS	573	B
ADMINISTRATIVE COUNCIL	170	A
ADMINISTRATIVE COUNTY	478	B
ADMINISTRATIVE COURT	161	A
ADMINISTRATIVE DECENTRALIZATION	202	A
ADMINISTRATIVE DEPARTMENT	165	A
ADMINISTRATIVE DEVELOPMENT	225	A
ADMINISTRATIVE ETHICS	141	A
ADMINISTRATIVE JURISDICTION	211	A
ADMINISTRATIVE JURISPRUDENCE	138	A
ADMINISTRATIVE JUSTICE	225	A
ADMINISTRATIVE LAW	202	A
ADMINISTRATIVE LEGISLATION	218	A
ADMINISTRATIVE OFFICE OF U.S. COURTS	465	B
ADMINISTRATIVE ORDER	233	A
ADMINISTRATIVE ORGANIZATION	149	A
ADMINISTRATIVE PROCEDURE	218	A
ADMINISTRATIVE PROCEDURE ACT OF 1946	621	B
ADMINISTRATIVE PROCESS	116	A
ADMINISTRATIVE REORGANIZATION	202	A
ADMINISTRATIVE REVENUES	573	B

ADMINISTRATIVE RULE OR REGULATION	206	A
ADMINISTRATIVE SCIENCES	127	A
ADMINISTRATIVE STRUCTURES	122	A
ADMINISTRATIVE SYSTEMS	202	A
ADMINISTRATIVE TRIBUNAL	149	A
ADMINISTRATIVE TRUSTEESHIP	218	A
ADMINISTRATOR	181	A
ADMINISTRATOR OF GENERAL SERVICES	191	A
ADMINISTRATOR OF VETERANS AFFAIRS	541	B
ADMIRAL	547	B
ADMIRALTY	479	B
ADMIRALTY JURISDICTION	242	A
ADMIRALTY LAW	225	A
ADMISSIBILITY	206	A
ADMISSION	573	B
ADMISSION (INTERNATIONAL ORGANIZATION)	251	A
ADMISSION OF ALIENS	218	A
ADMISSION OF NEW MEMBERS	242	A
ADMISSION OF NEW STATES	225	A
ADMISSION OF STATES TO THE UNION	225	A
ADMISSIONS TAX	242	A
ADMIT	621	B
ADMITTANCE	573	B
ADMONITION	621	B
ADMONITION OF IPUWER	811	B
ADMONITIONS OF PTAHOPT	811	B
ADOLESCENCE	138	A
ADOLESCENTS COURT	494	B
ADOPTION	233	A
ADORNO, THEODORE W.	266	A
ADOULA, CYRILLE	728	B
ADRIAN IV	728	B
ADULT	187	A
ADULT EDUCATION	597	B
ADULT POLITICAL LEARNING	127	A
ADULTERATION	597	B
ADULTHOOD	541	B
ADVANCE	621	B
ADVANCE MAN	187	A
ADVANCEMENT	647	B
ADVERTISEMENT	621	B
ADVICE	573	B
ADVICE AND CONSENT	195	A
ADVISORY BALLOT	573	B
ADVISORY BODY	170	A
ADVISORY COMM. ON APPLICATN OF SCIENCE AND TECH. TO DEVELOPING NATIONS	513	B
ADVISORY COMMISSION	158	A
ADVISORY COMMITTEE ON ADMINISTRATION AND BUDGET QUESTIONS	513	B
ADVISORY GROUP ON RESEARCH AND DEVELOPMENT (AGARD)	513	B
ADVISORY OPINION	218	A
ADVISORY RECALL	573	B
ADVISORY REFERENDUM	233	A
ADVOCATE	225	A
ADVOCATE-GENERAL	547	B
AEGIDIUS	728	B
AERIAL DOMAIN	792	B
AERIAL INCIDENT	621	B
AERONAUTICAL AND SPACE SCIENCE COMMITTEE	465	B
AEROPOLITICS	621	B
AESTHETICS	433	B
AETHELRED THE REDELESS	701	B
AETIUS	728	B
AFFAIRS	621	B
AFFARS ET ISSAS	621	B
AFFECTION	433	B
AFFIDAVIT	283	A
AFFILIATED ORGANIZATIONS	495	B
AFFILIATION	135	A
AFFIRMATION	251	A
AFFIRMATIVE VOTE	242	A
AFFIX	621	B
AFFLUENCE	218	A
AFFLUENT SOCIETY	148	A
AFFORD	573	B
AFGHANISTAN	276	A
AFLAQ, MICHEL	728	B
AFRICA	275	A
AFRICAN AND MALAGASY UNION	465	B
AFRICAN DEVELOPMENT BANK	175	A
AFRICAN EMPIRE	281	A
AFRICAN NATIONAL CONGRESS	621	B
AFRICAN POSTAL AND TELECOMMUNICATIONS UNION (APTU)	513	B
AFRICAN PROTECTORATES	465	B
AFRICAN RE-COLONIZATION	251	A
AFRICANS	165	A
AFRIKANERS	151	A
AFRO-AMERICANS	158	A
AFRO-ASIAN BLOC	161	A
AFRO-ASIAN CONFERENCE	251	A
AFRO-ASIAN MOVEMENT	251	A
AFRO-ASIAN PEOPLES SOLIDARITY COUNCIL (AAPSC)	479	B
AFRO-ASIAN PEOPLES SOLIDARITY ORGANIZATION (AAPSO)	479	B
AFRO-ASIANS	165	A
AGAIN AND AGAIN AND AGAIN	837	B
AGE	433	B

AGE OF ENLIGHTENMENT	122	A	AGRICULTURAL STABILIZATION AND	479	B
AGE OF REACTION	573	B	CONSERVATION SERVICE		
AGE OF REASON	122	A	AGRICULTURAL TRADE	597	B
AGE-HOMOGENOUS GROUPS	479	B	DEVELOPMENT AND ASSISTANCE		
AGENCY	465	B	ACT		
AGENCY FOR INTERNATIONAL	149	A	AGRICULTURAL WHEEL	513	B
DEVELOPMENT (AID)			AGRICULTURE	433	B
AGENCY SHOP	170	A	AGRONOMIST	561	B
AGENDA	284	A	AGROVILLE	796	B
AGENT	191	A	AGUASCALIENTES, MEXICO	787	B
AGENT PROVOCATEUR	183	A	AGUDAT ISRAEL	513	B
AGENTS OF SOCIALIZATION	124	A	AHAFO, GHANA	796	B
AGGER, ROBERT E.	728	B	AHIDJO, AHMADOU	728	B
AGGRANDIZEMENT	225	A	AI-SSU-CH'I	728	B
AGGRAVATION OF THE SITUATION	621	B	AID	233	A
AGGREGATE ANALYSIS	113	A	AID AND COMFORT TO THE ENEMY	290	A
AGGREGATE DATA	115	A	AID TO DEPENDENT CHILDREN (ADC)	218	A
AGGREGATION	122	A	AID TO THE BLIND	573	B
AGGREGATION OF INTERESTS	118	A	AID TO THE TOTALLY AND	242	A
AGGRESSION	194	A	PERMANENTLY DISABLED		
AGGRESSIVENESS	141	A	AIDE-MEMOIRE	806	B
AGGRESSOR	182	A	AIDIT	728	B
AGING	225	A	AIKEN ACT OF 1948	647	B
AGITATION	242	A	AIKEN, GEORGE DAVID	271	A
AGITATOR	182	A	AILLY, PETER D,	728	B
AGNEW, SPIRO	262	A	AIM	433	B
AGNOSTICISM	127	A	AIR ATTACHE	191	A
AGONIZING REAPPRAISAL	597	B	AIR BASE	287	A
AGRARIAN	189	A	AIR CORRIDOR	278	A
AGRARIAN LAW, IN HARRINGTON	448	B	AIR DEFENSE COMMAND	170	A
AGRARIAN PARTY	158	A	AIR DOMAIN	790	B
AGRARIAN REFORM	197	A	AIR FORCE	175	A
AGRARIAN SOCIALISM	124	A	AIR FORCE ACADEMY	161	A
AGRARIANISM	129	A	AIR FORCE INTELLIGENCE	175	A
AGREEMENT	225	A	AIR INCIDENT	573	B
AGREEMENT OF THE PEOPLE,	806	B	AIR JURISDICTION	251	A
LEVELLER MANIFESTO			AIR LAW	597	B
AGRICULTURAL ADJUSTMENT ACTS	251	A	AIR MINISTRY	465	B
(OF 1933)			AIR NAVIGATION COMMISSION	513	B
AGRICULTURAL ADJUSTMENT	161	A	AIR PIRACY	218	A
ADMINISTRATION (AAA)			AIR POLLUTION	225	A
AGRICULTURAL AND MECHANICAL	495	B	AIR POWER	287	A
COLLEGE			AIR QUALITY ACTS	242	A
AGRICULTURAL ATTACHE	191	A	AIR RAID WARDEN	547	B
AGRICULTURAL BLOC	170	A	AIR SPACE	279	A
AGRICULTURAL CONSERVATION	251	A	AIR SUBSIDIES	573	B
PROGRAM			AIR SUPREMACY	225	A
AGRICULTURAL CREDIT	242	A	AIR TRAFFIC CONTROLLERS	189	A
AGRICULTURAL EXPERIMENT	465	B	AIR TRANSPORT	817	B
STATIONS (UNITED STATES)			AIR TRANSPORT COMMITTEE	513	B
AGRICULTURAL EXTENSION SERVICE	165	A	AIR WARFARE	211	A
AGRICULTURAL MARKETING	465	B	AIR-MAIL SERVICE	573	B
SERVICE			AIR-RAID PRECAUTIONS	621	B
AGRICULTURAL PRICE SUPPORTS	211	A	AIRCRAFT	288	A
AGRICULTURAL PROTEST	597	B	AIRLIFT	218	A
AGRICULTURAL RESEARCH SERVICE	495	B	AIRPORT	787	B

AITKEN, MAX	728	B	ALGECIRAS CONFERENCE	597	B
AITUTAKI	796	B	ALGER, HORATIO	265	A
AJDUKIEWCZ	728	B	ALGERIA	273	A
AL-AZHAR	728	B	ALGERIAN CONFLICT	218	A
AL-FARABI	728	B	ALGERINE	513	B
AL-FATAH	267	A	ALGIERS CONFERENCE OF	242	A
AL-GHAZALI	728	B	AFRO-ASIAN STATES		
AL-SIGISTANI	728	B	ALGORITHM	141	A
ALABAMA AWARD	597	B	ALIANZA DEMOCRATICA	465	B
ALABAMA CLAIMS	597	B	ALIANZA POPULAR	165	A
ALAIN (E. CHARTIER)	728	B	REVOLUCIONARIA AMERICANA		
ALAIN-DE-LILLE	728	B	(APRA)		
ALARIC	728	B	ALIEN	181	A
ALARMIST	547	B	ALIEN AND SEDITION ACTS OF 1798	202	A
ALASKA	279	A	ALIEN ENEMY ACT	573	B
ALASKA HIGHWAY	790	B	ALIEN PROPERTY CUSTODIAN	191	A
ALASKA, PURCHASE OF	233	A	ALIEN REGISTRATION ACT OF 1940	242	A
ALASKAN BOUNDARY DISPUTE	573	B	ALIENATION	113	A
ALBANIA	275	A	ALIGNMENT	211	A
ALBANY CONGRESS OF 1754	597	B	ALKER, HAYWARD	689	B
ALBANY PLAN OF UNION	225	A	ALL AFRICAN PEOPLES	573	B
ALBANY REGENCY	465	B	CONFERENCE		
ALBERT THE GREAT	683	B	ALL THINGS TO ALL MEN	833	B
ALBERTS VS. CALIFORNIA (1957)	671	B	ALL-AMERICAN CITIES	170	A
ALBERTSON VS. SUBVERSIVE	672	B	ALL-AMERICAN HIGHWAY	819	B
ACTIVITIES CONTROL BOARD			ALL-GERMAN PARTY	495	B
(1965)			ALL-INDIA MOSLEM LEAGUE	479	B
ALBIGENSES	513	B	ALL-INDIA NATIONALIST CONGRESS	175	A
ALCAN HIGHWAY	787	B	ALL-OUT WAR	225	A
ALCATRAZ	787	B	ALL-PARTICIPATION CLAUSE	647	B
ALCIBIADES	701	B	ALL-PARTY GOVERNMENT	479	B
ALCIDAMAS	728	B	ALL-RUSSIAN CONGRESS OF	465	B
ALCMAEON	728	B	SOVIETS		
ALCOHOLIC EMPLOYEES	541	B	ALL-UNION COMMUNIST PARTY OF	175	A
ALCOHOLISM	819	B	RUSSIA		
ALDERMAN	189	A	ALL-UNION PARTY CONGRESS,	170	A
ALDOUS, JOHN	729	B	SOVIET UNION		
ALDRICH-VREELAND ACT	622	B	ALLEGATION	233	A
ALEKSANDROV, GEORGI	729	B	ALLEGIANCE	129	A
ALEMAN, IGUEL	267	A	ALLEN, JAMES BROWNING	701	B
ALEMBERT, JEAN D,	729	B	ALLENDE, SALVADOR	262	A
ALESSANDRI, RTURO	701	B	ALLIANCE	146	A
ALEXANDER	689	B	ALLIANCE FOR PROGRESS (1961)	146	A
ALEXANDER II, TSAR OF RUSSIA	267	A	ALLIED CONTROL COUNCIL FOR	165	A
ALEXANDER III, TSAR OF RUSSIA	268	A	GERMANY		
ALEXANDER THE GREAT	262	A	ALLIED COUNCIL FOR JAPAN	175	A
ALEXANDER VS. HOLMES COUNTY	673	B	ALLIED HIGH COMMISSION	170	A
BD OF EDUCATION (1969)			ALLIED INVASION	218	A
ALEXANDRETTA, SANJAK OF	729	B	ALLIED MILITARY GOVERNMENT	175	A
ALFARO, ELOY	729	B	(AMG)		
ALFONSO XTH, THE WISE	729	B	ALLIED POWERS	154	A
ALFORD, ROBERT	729	B	ALLIES	149	A
ALFRED, KING OF WESSEX	701	B	ALLOCATION	225	A
ALFVEN, HANNES	729	B	ALLOT, GORDON LLEWELLYN	729	B
ALGEBRA	135	A	ALLOTMENT	251	A
ALGEBRAIC-LOGIC	433	B	ALLOTMENT PLAN	597	B

ALLOWED TIME	573	B
ALLUVION	597	B
ALMIRANTE, GIORGIO	689	B
ALMOND, GABRIEL A.	262	A
ALMSHOUSE	288	A
ALPHABETICAL AGENCY	170	A
ALRIC, THE GOTH	729	B
ALSACE	276	A
ALSACE-LORRAINE	276	A
ALTBACH, PHILIP G.	729	B
ALTERATION	647	B
ALTERNATE	554	B
ALTERNATIVE	448	B
ALTERNATIVE VOTE SYSTEM	597	B
ALTHUSIUS, JOHANNES	701	B
ALTHUSSER, LOUIS	729	B
ALTING	495	B
ALTON LOCKE OF KINGSLEY	729	B
ALTRUISM	132	A
ALWAYS FALLING, NEVER FALLEN	842	B
AMALASNUTHA, QUEEN	729	B
AMALGAMATE	573	B
AMALGAMATED SECURITY-COMMUNITY	161	A
AMARNA TABLETS	824	B
AMATEUR	547	B
AMBASSADOR	185	A
AMBEDKAR, BHIMRAO RAMJI	701	B
AMBIGUITY	141	A
AMBIGUOUS POLICY	622	B
AMBIT	622	B
AMBITION	433	B
AMBIVALENCE	132	A
AMBROSE OF MILAN	729	B
AMBROSE, SAINT	729	B
AMEN CORNER	790	B
AMENDING PROCESS, STATE CONSTITUTIONS	218	A
AMENDING PROCESS, U.S. CONSTITUTION	196	A
AMENDMENT	202	A
AMENDMENT LIMITATION	622	B
AMENDMENT PROCESS	199	A
AMENDOLA, GIORGIO	729	B
AMENDOLA, GIOVANNI	729	B
AMER, FIELD MARSHAL ABDEL HAKIM	729	B
AMERICA	274	A
AMERICA FOR AMERICANS	291	A
AMERICAN ACADEMY OF POLITICAL AND SOCIAL SCIENCE	165	A
AMERICAN ANARCHISTS	175	A
AMERICAN ANTHROPOLOGICAL ASSOCIATION	479	B
AMERICAN ARBITRATION ASSOCIATION	465	B
AMERICAN BAR ASSOCIATION (ABA)	161	A
AMERICAN BATTLE MONUMENTS COMMISSION	465	B
AMERICAN BILL OF RIGHTS	194	A
AMERICAN BOYS	561	B
AMERICAN BROADCASTING STATION IN EUROPE (ABSIE)	513	B
AMERICAN CATO	729	B
AMERICAN CIVIL LIBERTIES UNION (ACLU)	149	A
AMERICAN CIVIL WAR	195	A
AMERICAN COLONIZATION SOCIETY	513	B
AMERICAN COMMONWEALTH, THE	479	B
AMERICAN COMMUNIST PARTY	151	A
AMERICAN CONSTITUTIONAL CONVENTION	199	A
AMERICAN DEBT	233	A
AMERICAN DECLARATION OF RIGHTS AND DUTIES OF MAN	284	A
AMERICAN DIGEST SYSTEM	811	B
AMERICAN DREAM	135	A
AMERICAN ECONOMIC ASSOCIATION	479	B
AMERICAN EMPIRE	465	B
AMERICAN EXPEDITIONARY FORCE (AEF)	158	A
AMERICAN FARM BUREAU FEDERATION	151	A
AMERICAN FEDERATION OF LABOR	146	A
AMERICAN FEDERATION OF LABOR-CONGRESS OF INDUSTRIAL ORG. (AFL-CIO)	151	A
AMERICAN FEDERATION OF TEACHERS	165	A
AMERICAN FIRST COMMITTEE	165	A
AMERICAN FIRST PARTY	170	A
AMERICAN FLAG	287	A
AMERICAN FOREIGN POLICY	197	A
AMERICAN INDEPENDENT PARTY	154	A
AMERICAN INDIAN	165	A
AMERICAN INSTITUTE OF PUBLIC OPINION (GALLUP)	151	A
AMERICAN JUDICATURE SOCIETY	495	B
AMERICAN KNIGHTS	479	B
AMERICAN LABOR PARTY (ALP)	175	A
AMERICAN LEGION	158	A
AMERICAN LEGISLATORS ASSOCIATION	495	B
AMERICAN LIBERTY LEAGUE	175	A
AMERICAN MEDICAL ASSOCIATION (AMA)	154	A
AMERICAN MERCURY, THE	811	B
AMERICAN MOLASSES COMPANY	513	B
AMERICAN MUNICIPAL ASSOCIATION	170	A
AMERICAN NATIONAL PARTY	175	A
AMERICAN NATIONAL RED CROSS	175	A
AMERICAN NAVAL AND AIR BASES	817	B

AMERICAN PARTY	479	B	ANALYTICAL JURISPRUDENCE	135	A
AMERICAN POLITICAL SCIENCE	146	A	ANALYTICAL METHOD	118	A
ASSOCIATION (APSA)			ANALYTICAL SCHOOL	138	A
AMERICAN POLITICAL SCIENCE	283	A	ANALYTICAL THEORY OF LAW	135	A
REVIEW			ANALYTICITY	454	B
AMERICAN PRINTING HOUSE FOR	513	B	ANALYZE	124	A
THE BLIND			ANANIAS CLUB	514	B
AMERICAN PROTECTIVE	495	B	ANARCHISM	113	A
ASSOCIATION			ANARCHIST	181	A
AMERICAN PSYCHOLOGICAL	479	B	ANARCHY	113	A
ASSOCIATION			ANATOLIA, TURKEY	790	B
AMERICAN PUBLIC WORKS	479	B	ANATONIC POLITIES	514	B
ASSOCIATION			ANAXAGORAS	689	B
AMERICAN REVOLUTION	194	A	ANAXIMANDER	701	B
AMERICAN SAMOA	279	A	ANAXIMENES	702	B
AMERICAN SECURITY COUNCIL	465	B	ANCESTOR WORSHIP	132	A
AMERICAN SOCIETY FOR PUBLIC	170	A	ANCHORAGE	790	B
ADMINISTRATION (ASPA)			ANCIEN REGIME	151	A
AMERICAN SOCIETY OF	175	A	ANCIENT	141	A
INTERNATIONAL LAW			ANCIENT EGYPT	279	A
AMERICAN SOCIOLOGICAL SOCIETY	465	B	ANCIENT GREECE	274	A
AMERICAN STATISTICAL	479	B	ANCIENT ROME	274	A
ASSOCIATION			ANCILLARY RESTRAINTS	647	B
AMERICAN SYSTEM	211	A	ANDEAN COMMON MARKET	465	B
AMERICAN WAR OF INDEPENDENCE	225	A	ANDEAN DEVELOPMENT	495	B
AMERICAN WAY OF LIFE	132	A	CORPORATION		
AMERICAN YOUTH CULTURE	135	A	ANDEAN GROUP	175	A
AMERICAN-GERMAN PEACE TREATY	251	A	ANDERS, EDWARD	729	B
AMERICANISM	129	A	ANDERSON, C. ARNOLD	729	B
AMERICANIZATION	206	A	ANDERSON, CLINTON PRESBA	702	B
AMERICANS FOR CONSTITUTIONAL	165	A	ANDERSON, WILLIAM	729	B
ACTION (ACA)			ANDHRA PRADESH (INDIA)	792	B
AMERICANS FOR DEMOCRATIC	148	A	ANDORRA	268	A
ACTION (ADA)			ANDREWS, STEPHEN PEARL	729	B
AMERICANS FOR INDIAN	513	B	ANFUSO, ILIPPO	730	B
OPPORTUNITY			ANGARY	647	B
AMERICAS	276	A	ANGEL	554	B
AMGOT	513	B	ANGELL, NORMAN	689	B
AMIABLE COMPOSITEUR	729	B	ANGELL, ROBERT	702	B
AMICUS CURIAE	182	A	ANGER	433	B
AMIN, IDI	268	A	ANGLE-WORM NOMINATION	842	B
AMITY	242	A	ANGLEY, EDWARD	730	B
AMMONIUS	729	B	ANGLICANS	170	A
AMNESTY	202	A	ANGLO-AMERICAN	170	A
AMPARO	622	B	ANGLO-AMERICAN ALLIANCE	158	A
AMRI, GENERAL HASSAN	729	B	ANGLO-AMERICAN SYSTEM OF LAW	197	A
AMRITSAR MASSACRE	573	B	ANGLO-EGYPTIAN ALLIANCE	175	A
AMTORG (SOVIET TRADE	479	B	ANGLO-FRENCH-TURKISH TREATY	597	B
ORGANIZATION)			ANGLO-GERMAN NAVAL TREATY	597	B
ANABAPTISTS	175	A	ANGLO-IRAQI ALLIANCE	479	B
ANALOGY	114	A	ANGLO-IRISH TREATY	597	B
ANALYSIS	118	A	ANGLO-JAPANESE ALLIANCE	465	B
ANALYTIC	129	A	ANGLO-RUSSIAN ALLIANCES	170	A
ANALYTIC POLITICAL PHILOSOPHY	120	A	ANGLO-SAXON CHRONICLE	811	B
ANALYTIC STATEMENT	115	A	ANGLO-SAXON WIDOWS	561	B
ANALYTIC THEORIES	127	A	ANGLO-SOVIET TREATY WITH IRAN	573	B

ANGLO-TURKISH ALLIANCE	175	A
ANGLOMANIA	454	B
ANGLOPHOBIA	141	A
ANGLOS	158	A
ANGOLA	274	A
ANGRY YOUNG MEN	191	A
ANGUILLA	281	A
ANGUISH	454	B
ANIMAL	819	B
ANKRAH, GENERAL J. A.	730	B
ANNA KOMNENA	730	B
ANNAPOLIS	279	A
ANNAPOLIS CONVENTION, 1786	218	A
ANNEX	573	B
ANNEXATION	218	A
ANNEXATIONISM	441	B
ANNEXATIONIST	547	B
ANNIVERSARY	648	B
ANNOINTED	554	B
ANNOTATED REPORTS SYSTEM	805	B
ANNOUNCEMENTS OF THE SECRETARIAT	622	B
ANNUAL (PARTY) CONFERENCE, BRITAIN	574	B
ANNUAL ASSEMBLY	574	B
ANNUAL MESSAGE	251	A
ANNUITY	597	B
ANOMIC GROUP	158	A
ANOMIE	116	A
ANONYMOUS	448	B
ANOTHER MUNICH	290	A
ANSCHLUSS	218	A
ANSEELE, EDOUARD	730	B
ANSELM	689	B
ANTARCTIC CLAIMS	242	A
ANTARCTIC TREATY OF 1959	233	A
ANTARTICA	278	A
ANTEDILUVIAN	189	A
ANTHEM	805	B
ANTHONY RULE	648	B
ANTHONY, SUSAN BROWNELL	265	A
ANTHROPOLOGICAL METHOD	127	A
ANTHROPOLOGIST	141	A
ANTHROPOLOGY	124	A
ANTI	574	B
ANTI-AMERICAN	233	A
ANTI-AUCTION	597	B
ANTI-BALLISTIC MISSILE (ABM) SYSTEM	286	A
ANTI-CHAIN STORE ACT	622	B
ANTI-CLERICALISM	124	A
ANTI-COLONIALISM	120	A
ANTI-COMINTERN PACT	218	A
ANTI-COMMUNIST LEGISLATION	206	A
ANTI-DEFAMATION LEAGUE OF BNAI BRITH	154	A
ANTI-DEMOCRATIC THEORY	122	A
ANTI-DISCRIMINATION	225	A
ANTI-DISCRIMINATION LAW OF NEW YORK STATE	648	B
ANTI-DUHRING	285	A
ANTI-GOVERNMENT	242	A
ANTI-HITLER PLOT	225	A
ANTI-IMPERIALISM	122	A
ANTI-IMPERIALIST LEAGUE	465	B
ANTI-JAPANESE	141	A
ANTI-KU KLUX KLAN ACT	622	B
ANTI-LECOMPTON DEMOCRAT	495	B
ANTI-LYNCHING BILL	251	A
ANTI-MONOPOLIST	189	A
ANTI-MONOPOLY LEGISLATION	233	A
ANTI-MONOPOLY PARTY	495	B
ANTI-NEBRASKA MEN	495	B
ANTI-NEGRO	141	A
ANTI-PARTY GROUP	165	A
ANTI-POVERTY ACT	251	A
ANTI-PREJUDICE	251	A
ANTI-PRICE DISCRIMINATION ACT	622	B
ANTI-RENT (PARTY)	479	B
ANTI-RENT WAR	574	B
ANTI-REVOLUTIONARY PARTY (NETHERLANDS)	495	B
ANTI-SALOON LEAGUE OF AMERICA	175	A
ANTI-SEMITISM	116	A
ANTICIPATION	441	B
ANTICIPATION WARRANT	622	B
ANTICIPATORY BORROWING	597	B
ANTICIPATORY POLITICAL SOCIALIZATION	127	A
ANTICOLONIALIST	187	A
ANTICOMMUNISM	120	A
ANTICOMMUNIST	181	A
ANTIESPIONAGE ACT	251	A
ANTIETAM	279	A
ANTIFASCISM	129	A
ANTIFASCIST	187	A
ANTIFEDERALISTS	149	A
ANTIGONUS II OF MACEDON	730	B
ANTIGUA	280	A
ANTILLES	282	A
ANTIMASONIC PARTY	175	A
ANTIMILITARISM	127	A
ANTIMONY	824	B
ANTIOCHUS EPIPHANES	730	B
ANTIPEONAGE ACT OF 1867	648	B
ANTIPHON, THE OLIGARCH	702	B
ANTIPHON, THE SOPHIST	702	B
ANTIPOSITIVISM	141	A
ANTIQUITY	597	B
ANTIRENTERS	495	B
ANTISNAPPER	514	B
ANTISTHENES, THE CYNIC	730	B

ANTITRUST	211	A	APPREHENSION	441	B
ANTITRUST ACTIONS	211	A	APPRENTICESHIP	187	A
ANTITRUST ACTS	211	A	APPRENTICESHIPS, MUNICIPAL	554	B
ANTITRUST DIVISION	161	A	APPROACH	433	B
ANTONESCU, GENERAL ION	730	B	APPROBATION	574	B
ANXIETY	129	A	APPROPRIATION	211	A
ANXIOUS SEAT	842	B	APPROPRIATION BILL	206	A
ANY OTHER BUSINESS (AOB)	842	B	APPROPRIATIONS COMMITTEE	149	A
ANZUS TREATY	218	A	APPROVAL	242	A
APACHE INDIANS	479	B	APPROVAL OF BILLS	211	A
APARTHEID	199	A	APPROVE	597	B
APATHY	115	A	APPROVED AGENDA	285	A
APEL, KARL-OTTO	730	B	APRISMO	433	B
APERTURA A SINISTRA (OPENING TO	242	A	APRISTA	465	B
THE LEFT)			APTER, DAVID E.	265	A
APHORISM	141	A	APTHEKER VS. SECRETARY OF	671	B
APOCALYPSE	242	A	STATE (1964)		
APOLITICAL	118	A	APTITUDE TESTS	132	A
APOLLO HALL	821	B	AQUEDUCT AT RAVENNA	825	B
APOLLONIAN	479	B	AQUINAS, SAINT THOMAS	262	A
APOLLONIAN PEOPLES	514	B	ARAB DEVELOPMENT BANK	175	A
APOLOGIZE	597	B	ARAB FEDERATION	165	A
APOSTLE OF HATE	835	B	ARAB HIGHER COMMITTEE	479	B
APOSTOLIC DELEGATE	541	B	ARAB LEAGUE	151	A
APPALACHIA	278	A	ARAB NATIONALISM	129	A
APPALACHIAN REGIONAL PROGRAM	242	A	ARAB PACT	597	B
APPARATCHIK	158	A	ARAB REPUBLICS, FEDERATION OF	175	A
APPARATUS	495	B	ARAB SOCIALIST UNION	175	A
APPEAL	206	A	ARAB SOUTH	796	B
APPEALS COURTS	149	A	ARAB STATES	165	A
APPEARANCE	622	B	ARAB UNION	175	A
APPEASEMENT	197	A	ARAB WORLD	280	A
APPELLATE COURT	149	A	ARAB-ISRAEL WAR, 1948-49	218	A
APPELLATE COURT SYSTEM	149	A	ARAB-ISRAELI CONFLICTS	195	A
APPELLATE JURISDICTION	225	A	ARABIAN GULF	278	A
APPELLATE TRIBUNAL	165	A	ARABIAN PENINSULA	276	A
APPEND	648	B	ARABIC	170	A
APPENDIX	806	B	ARABISM	441	B
APPERCEPTION	648	B	ARABS	158	A
APPLEBY, PAUL H.	689	B	ARBITER	187	A
APPLICABLE	433	B	ARBITRABLE	597	B
APPLICANT	541	B	ARBITRAL	597	B
APPLICATION	574	B	ARBITRARY ARREST	211	A
APPLICATION BLANKS	817	B	ARBITRATION	206	A
APPLICATIONS FOR POSITIONS	288	A	ARBITRATION, INTERNATIONAL	233	A
APPLIED SOCIAL SCIENCE	118	A	ARBITRATION, LABOR	218	A
APPLIED STATISTICS	120	A	ARBITRATOR	182	A
APPLY	622	B	ARBUS, DIANE	730	B
APPOINT	233	A	ARCADIA	796	B
APPOINTED	242	A	ARCADIA CONFERENCE	648	B
APPOINTMENT	218	A	ARCHAEOLOGY	138	A
APPORTIONMENT	197	A	ARCHBISHOP	191	A
APPORTIONMENT ACT OF 1929	251	A	ARCHBISHOPRIC	541	B
APPRAISAL	251	A	ARCHDIOCESE	170	A
APPRAISAL INTERVIEWS	574	B	ARCHDUCHESS	547	B
APPRECIATION	448	B	ARCHDUKE	541	B

ARZHAK, NIKOLAI   730   B
ARZHANOV, .A.   730   B
AS MAINE GOES, SO GOES THE   290   A
  NATION
AS-SAID, NURI   690   B
AS-SHAABI, QAHTAN   730   B
ASANUMA, INEJIRO   730   B
ASCENDANCY   622   B
ASCENT   648   B
ASCETICISM   141   A
ASCRIPTION   218   A
ASH, MAURICE   730   B
ASHANTI   175   A
ASHCRAFT VS. TENNESSEE (1944)   677   B
ASHES   825   B
ASHIDA, HITOSHI   702   B
ASHWANDER VS. TENNESSEE   261   A
  VALLEY AUTHORITY (1936)
ASIA   274   A
ASIA ADVISORY COMMITTEE   514   B
ASIAN AMERICANS   158   A
ASIAN AND PACIFIC COUNCIL   495   B
  (ASPAC)
ASIAN DEVELOPMENT BANK (ASDB)   479   B
ASIAN DRAMA   811   B
ASIAN PARLIAMENTARY UNION   495   B
ASIANS   170   A
ASIATIC PACT   622   B
ASKI-MARKS   825   B
ASOCIACION DE MAYO (ARGENTINA)   514   B
ASPIRATIONS   138   A
ASSAAD-MIKHAIL   730   B
ASSASSIN   187   A
ASSASSINATION   211   A
ASSASSINATIONS OF PRESIDENTS   211   A
ASSAULT   574   B
ASSAY   598   B
ASSAY OFFICE   495   B
ASSEMBLED EXAMINATION   598   B
ASSEMBLEE NATIONALE   495   B
ASSEMBLY   154   A
ASSEMBLYMAN   185   A
ASSERTION   141   A
ASSESSED VALUATION   218   A
ASSESSMENT   233   A
ASSESSMENT RATIO   598   B
ASSESSOR   183   A
ASSIGN   622   B
ASSIGNMENT   622   B
ASSIMILATION   118   A
ASSISTANCE   622   B
ASSISTANCE CLAUSE   622   B
ASSISTANCE PAYMENTS   514   B
  ADMINISTRATION
ASSISTANT PRESIDENT   191   A
ASSISTANT SECRETARY-GENERAL   191   A

ASSISTANT TO THE PRESIDENT   187   A
ASSIZE COURTS   479   B
ASSIZE OF WOODSTOCK   648   B
ASSIZES   495   B
ASSOCIATE JUSTICE   184   A
ASSOCIATE STATUS   547   B
ASSOCIATED POWERS   465   B
ASSOCIATED PRESS   158   A
ASSOCIATED STATES, EUROPEAN   170   A
  ECONOMIC COMMUNITY
ASSOCIATED WEALTH   561   B
ASSOCIATION   154   A
ASSOCIATION OF SOUTH-EAST ASIA   479   B
  (ASA)
ASSOCIATION OF SOUTHEAST   175   A
  ASIAN NATIONS (ASEAN)
ASSOCIATIONAL GROUP   149   A
ASSUME   598   B
ASSUMPTION   233   A
ASSUMPTION OF OFFICE   252   A
ASSUMPTION OF RISK   252   A
ASSUMPTION OF STATE DEBTS   574   B
ASSURING   454   B
ASSYRIAN CHRISTIANS   514   B
ASSYRIANS   175   A
ASTROLOGY   433   B
ASTRONAUTICS   141   A
ASTRONOMY   433   B
ASTROPHYSICAL OBSERVATORY   825   B
ASTURIAS, PRINCE OF THE   554   B
ASWAN DAM   273   A
ASYLUM   278   A
ASYMMETRY   132   A
AT LARGE (CONGRESSMAN AT   185   A
  LARGE)
ATASSI, EL, NOUREDDINE   730   B
ATATURK   264   A
ATHEISM   127   A
ATHENIAN DEMOCRACY   118   A
ATHENS   274   A
ATLANTA (GEORGIA)   280   A
ATLANTIC ALLIANCE   151   A
ATLANTIC CHARTER   199   A
ATLANTIC COMMUNITY   148   A
ATLANTIC FREE TRADE AREA   161   A
ATLANTIC INSTITUTE   514   B
ATLANTIC NUCLEAR FORCE (ANF)   466   B
ATLANTIC STATES MARINE   648   B
  FISHERIES COMPACT
ATLANTIC UNION   166   A
ATMOSPHERIC DETECTION   242   A
  METHODS
ATOM BOMB   286   A
ATOMIC AGE   211   A
ATOMIC ENERGY   286   A

ATOMIC ENERGY ACTS (1946 AND 1954)	242	A
ATOMIC ENERGY AUTHORITY OF UNITED NATIONS	161	A
ATOMIC ENERGY COMMISSION (AEC)	149	A
ATOMIC ENERGY COMMISSION (UN)	158	A
ATOMIC ENERGY COMMITTEE	161	A
ATOMIC ESPIONAGE	206	A
ATOMIC HOLOCAUST	211	A
ATOMIC WEAPONS	286	A
ATOMIC WEAPONS CONTROL	206	A
ATOMIZATION	225	A
ATOMS FOR PEACE PLAN	218	A
ATROCITIES	218	A
ATTACHE	184	A
ATTACHMENT	242	A
ATTACK	233	A
ATTAINDER	211	A
ATTEMPT	574	B
ATTENDANCE LIST	811	B
ATTENTAT	648	B
ATTENTISM	648	B
ATTENTIVE PUBLIC	149	A
ATTESTATION	622	B
ATTICA	280	A
ATTICA PRISON REVOLT	211	A
ATTITUDE	114	A
ATTITUDE SCALING	118	A
ATTITUDE SURVEYS	198	A
ATTITUDINAL CHANGES	114	A
ATTLEE, CLEMENT RICHARD	263	A
ATTORNEY	191	A
ATTORNEY AT LAW	189	A
ATTORNEY GENERAL	182	A
ATTORNEY GENERAL'S LIST	283	A
ATTRIBUTE	132	A
ATTRIBUTIONS	252	A
ATWOOD, HARRY F.	702	B
ATWOOD, MARGARET	730	B
AU H2O ∎ 1964	837	B
AUBERT, VILHELM	731	B
AUBREY, JOHN	731	B
AUBURN SYSTEM	648	B
AUCKLAND, NEW ZEALAND	792	B
AUDIENCE	466	B
AUDIT OFFICE	170	A
AUDITOR	187	A
AUGUSTINE , SAINT , OF HIPPO	267	A
AUGUSTINE OF CANTERBURY, SAINT	690	B
AUGUSTUS	683	B
AURIOL, VINCENT	731	B
AUROBINDO	690	B
AUSCHWITZ	274	A
AUSGLEICH	648	B
AUSPICES	574	B
AUSTERITY	225	A
AUSTERITY PROGRAM	242	A
AUSTIN, JOHN	271	A
AUSTINIAN THEORY	433	B
AUSTRALIA	276	A
AUSTRALIA-NEW ZEALAND-UNITED STATES DEFENSE TREATY (ANZUS)	233	A
AUSTRALIAN BALLOT	211	A
AUSTRIA	276	A
AUSTRIAN LEGION	514	B
AUSTRIAN STATE TREATY	574	B
AUSTRO-FASCISM	448	B
AUSTRO-HUNGARIAN EMPIRE	158	A
AUSTRO-PRUSSIAN WAR	233	A
AUTARCHY	127	A
AUTARKY	124	A
AUTHENTIC	454	B
AUTHENTICATED COPY	811	B
AUTHENTICATION	598	B
AUTHENTICITY	574	B
AUTHORITARIAN	181	A
AUTHORITARIAN PERSONALITIES	114	A
AUTHORITARIAN SYSTEMS	114	A
AUTHORITARIANISM	114	A
AUTHORITATIVE SOURCES	182	A
AUTHORITIES	185	A
AUTHORITY	181	A
AUTHORIZATION	211	A
AUTHORIZATION BILL	225	A
AUTOBIOGRAPHY	806	B
AUTOCHTHONOUS	433	B
AUTOCRACY	144	A
AUTOMATA	817	B
AUTOMATIC DATA PROCESSING	118	A
AUTOMATION	211	A
AUTOMOBILE ALLOWANCES	648	B
AUTOMOBILE INFORMATION DISCLOSURE ACT	598	B
AUTOMOBILE METAPHOR	842	B
AUTOMOBILES	817	B
AUTONOMOUS	218	A
AUTONOMOUS PLANNING	648	B
AUTONOMOUS REPUBLICS	175	A
AUTONOMY	211	A
AUXILIARY AGENCY	514	B
AUXILIARY BODY	514	B
AVAILABILITY	574	B
AVALANCHE	622	B
AVANGUARDIA (AVANT-GARDE)	514	B
AVANTI	842	B
AVELING, EDWARD	731	B
AVELING, ELEANOR MARX	731	B
AVENTINE BLOCK, THE	514	B
AVENUES	797	B
AVERAGE BEHAVIORS	441	B

AVERAGE MAN	185	A	BACKER	547	B
AVERROES	683	B	BACKGROUND	448	B
AVERROISM	433	B	BACKGROUND CONFERENCE	574	B
AVERSION	448	B	BACKGROUNDER	598	B
AVERY, SEWELL	702	B	BACKLASH	206	A
AVIATION	598	B	BACKSTAIRS	837	B
AVICENNA	792	B	BACKUP CANDIDATE	541	B
AVIGNON	787	B	BACKWARD	622	B
AVNOS	514	B	BACKWARD TERRITORY	790	B
AVOCATIONAL INTERESTS	454	B	BACON, ROGER	268	A
AVON, LORD (SIR ANTHONY EDEN)	702	B	BACON, SIR FRANCIS	265	A
AVULSION	648	B	BACON'S REBELLION	622	B
AWARD (LEGAL JUDGMENT)	242	A	BACTERIOLOGICAL WARFARE	198	A
AWARDS	821	B	BAD	433	B
AWARENESS	433	B	BAD TENDENCY TEST	138	A
AWOLOWO, CHIEF ABAFEMI	702	B	BADEN SYSTEM	648	B
AX TO GRIND	291	A	BADEN-WURTTEMBERG, GERMANY	797	B
AXE	622	B	BADGE	817	B
AXELROD, P. B.	731	B	BADGER STATE	792	B
AXIOLOGY	441	B	BADOGLIO, MARSHAL PIETRO	702	B
AXIOM	118	A	BAER, K.E. VON	731	B
AXIOM-OF-CHOICE	454	B	BAFFLEGAB	842	B
AXIOMATIC	129	A	BAGEHOT, WALTER	265	A
AXIOMS, POLITICAL	132	A	BAGGIT VS. BULLITT (1964)	673	B
AXIS	148	A	BAGHDAD PACT	218	A
AXIS POWERS	148	A	BAGHDAD RAILWAY	495	B
AYDELOTTE, WILLIAM O.	731	B	BAGMAN	191	A
AYDEMIR	731	B	BAGUIO CONFERENCE	622	B
AYER, A. J.	268	A	BAHAMA ISLANDS	280	A
AYES AND NOES	290	A	BAHAR, MALIKU'L-SHU'ARA'	731	B
AYRES, CLARENCE EDWIN	731	B	BAHR, EGO	731	B
AYUB KHAN, MOHAMMED	268	A	BAHRAIN	282	A
AZERBAIJAN, IRAN	787	B	BAIKAL, LAKE	797	B
AZIKIWE, R. BENJAMIN NNAMDI	702	B	BAIL	233	A
AZRAEL, JEREMY R.	731	B	BAIL SYSTEM	206	A
AZTECS	161	A	BAILEY MEMORANDUM	808	B
B COUPON	821	B	BAILEY VS. DREXEL FURNITURE CO.	672	B
B. Z. AM MITTAG	811	B	(1922)		
B.O.W. (GREAT BRITAIN)	479	B	BAILEY, A.	731	B
B'HOYS	842	B	BAILEY, STEPHEN K.	268	A
BAATH	166	A	BAILIFF	187	A
BAATH PARTY (ARAB SOCIALIST	158	A	BAILLARGER	731	B
RESURRECTION PARTY)			BAINVILLE, JACQUES	731	B
BABBITT, IRVING	268	A	BAIT(ER, ING)	833	B
BABEUF ,FRANCIS	702	B	BAKER ISLAND	797	B
BABY ACT, TO PLEAD THE	842	B	BAKER VS. CARR (1962)	260	A
BABYLONIANS	479	B	BAKR, MAJOR GENERAL AHMED	702	B
BACHKA, THE	797	B	BAKUNIN, MICHAEL	264	A
BACK COUNTRY	495	B	BALAGUER, JOAQUIN	683	B
BACK PAY	622	B	BALANCE	574	B
BACK SEAT	837	B	BALANCE OF PAYMENTS	196	A
BACK TO NORMALCY	291	A	BALANCE OF POWER	194	A
BACK, KURT	731	B	BALANCE OF TERROR	196	A
BACKBENCHERS	184	A	BALANCE OF TRADE	196	A
BACKBONE	562	B	BALANCED BUDGET	202	A
BACKDOOR SPENDING	574	B	BALANCED FORCES POLICY (U.S.)	242	A

BALANCED TICKET	149	A		BANFIELD, EDWARD C.	268	A
BALD EAGLE	833	B		BANGLADESH	273	A
BALDWIN-BUCKLEY	731	B		BANISH	623	B
BALDWIN, HANSON	690	B		BANISHMENT	598	B
BALDWIN, SIMEON E.	731	B		BANK	480	B
BALDWIN, STANLEY	268	A		BANK DEPOSIT INSURANCE	233	A
BALES, ROBERT F.	702	B		BANK DEPOSITS GUARANTEE	243	A
BALEWA, SIR ALHAJI ABUBAKAR	731	B		BANK EXAMINER	547	B
TAFAWA				BANK FOR INTERNATIONAL	175	A
BALFOUR DECLARATION (1926)	211	A		SETTLEMENTS		
BALFOUR, ARTHUR JAMES	268	A		BANK HOLIDAY	233	A
BALILLA	514	B		BANK MORATORIUM	574	B
BALKAN CRISIS OF 1908	623	B		BANK NOTE	817	B
BALKAN ENTENTE	466	B		BANK OF CANADA	480	B
BALKAN FEDERATION	170	A		BANK OF ENGLAND	175	A
BALKAN LEAGUE	175	A		BANK OF FRANCE	480	B
BALKAN PACT	574	B		BANK OF THE UNITED STATES	466	B
BALKAN UNION	175	A		BANK TAX	623	B
BALKAN WARS	233	A		BANK WORKERS	562	B
BALKANS	278	A		BANKER, HOWARD HENRY, JR.	731	B
BALL-BURTON-HATCH-HILL	623	B		BANKHEAD COTTON CONTROL ACT	648	B
RESOLUTION (B2H2)				BANKHEAD-JONES FARM TENANT	648	B
BALL, ABBE JOHN	731	B		ACT		
BALLINGER-PINCHOT CONTROVERSY	623	B		BANKING	623	B
BALLON DESSAI	648	B		BANKING ACT OF 1933	243	A
BALLOT	195	A		BANKING AND CURRENCY	166	A
BALLOT BOX	287	A		COMMITTEE		
BALLOT BOX STUFFING	206	A		BANKING SYSTEMS	574	B
BALLOT STUB	819	B		BANKRUPTCY	211	A
BALLS BLUFF	842	B		BANKRUPTCY LAWS	233	A
BALLYBEG	842	B		BANKS, JOSEPH	731	B
BALLYHOO	837	B		BANNER COUNTY	514	B
BALMES, J.	731	B		BANNER DISTRICT	495	B
BALONEY	837	B		BANNER STATE	797	B
BALONEY DOLLARS	835	B		BANTU	161	A
BALTIC ENTENTE	170	A		BANTUSTANS	170	A
BALTIC PACT	252	A		BAO DAI	161	A
BALTIC STATES	275	A		BAPTISTS	175	A
BALTIMORE CONVENTION	252	A		BAR	252	A
BALTIMORE HERALD	811	B		BAR ASSOCIATION	161	A
BALZAC, HONORE DE	271	A		BAR OF THE SENATE	790	B
BAMBIBIA	797	B		BARBADOS	276	A
BAMBOO CURTAIN	275	A		BARBARIAN CODES	574	B
BAN	252	A		BARBARY PIRATES	170	A
BAN THE BOMB	290	A		BARBARY STATES	278	A
BANAT	797	B		BARBER, JAMES DAVID	683	B
BANCOR	648	B		BARBEYRAC	731	B
BAND-BOX STATESMAN	562	B		BARBITUATES	819	B
BANDA, DR. HASTINGS KAMUZU	690	B		BARCLAY, WILLIAM	731	B
BANDARANAIKE, MRS. SIRIMAVO	702	B		BAREFOOT BOY FROM WALL	702	B
BANDITTI (BANDITS)	479	B		STREET		
BANDUNG (ASIAN-AFRICAN)	211	A		BARENBLATT VS. UNITED STATES	671	B
CONFERENCE				(1959)		
BANDWAGON	290	A		BARGAIN AND CORRUPTION	648	B
BANDWAGON EFFECT	118	A		BARGAINING	198	A
BANDWAGON, TO GET ON	290	A		BARGAINING THEORY	116	A

BARGHOORN, FREDERICK C.	271	A	BATTLE OF BRITAIN	218	A
BARIO (PHILLIPINES)	514	B	BATTLE OF JUTLAND	252	A
BARKER, ERNEST	690	B	BATTLE OF MIDWAY	225	A
BARLOW COMMISSION	514	B	BATTLE OF SADOWA	649	B
BARNARD, CHESTER I.	690	B	BATTLE OF SAN JUAN HILL	225	A
BARNBURNER	480	B	BATTLE OF THE BOOK	649	B
BARNETT HOUSE	825	B	BATTLE OF WATERLOO	206	A
BARNHART, EDWARD H.	731	B	BATTLES OF MARNE	574	B
BARNSTORM	291	A	BATTLING BOB	702	B
BARON	547	B	BAUDELAIRE	732	B
BARONESS	547	B	BAUDOUIN, KING	683	B
BARONET	547	B	BAUER, OTTO	732	B
BARONY	541	B	BAUER, RAY	732	B
BAROQUE	433	B	BAUMES LAW	649	B
BAROTSE TRIBE OF RHODESIA	514	B	BAUXITE	288	A
BARREL (BAR'L)	825	B	BAVARIA, GERMANY	277	A
BARREN IDEALITY	454	B	BAVARIAN PARTY	466	B
BARRES, MAURICE	732	B	BAX, E. BELFORT	732	B
BARRIENTOS-ORTUNO, GENERAL RENE	690	B	BAY OF PIGS	273	A
			BAY OF PIGS FIASCO	211	A
BARRIOS	276	A	BAYEUX TAPESTRY	821	B
BARRISTER	189	A	BAYH, BIRCH EVANS, JR.	265	A
BARRON VS. BALTIMORE (1833)	260	A	BAYLE	732	B
BARTER	243	A	BAYLE, PIERRE	732	B
BARTH, KARL	690	B	BAYNES, PROF. N. H.	732	B
BARTHOLOMEW, HARLAND	732	B	BAYONET	821	B
BARTKUS VS. ILLINOIS (1958)	677	B	BAYONNE PAWNSHOP SCANDAL	649	B
BARTLEY, ERNEST R.	732	B	BAYOU STATE	793	B
BARTON, ALLEN H.	732	B	BEALE, HOWARD K.	732	B
BARUCH PLAN	211	A	BEALL, J. GLENN, JR.	702	B
BARUCH, BERNARD MANNES	265	A	BEAN, LOUIS	732	B
BARZEL, R.	732	B	BEAR FLAG BATTALION	466	B
BASCOMB, JOHN	732	B	BEAR FLAG REVOLT	623	B
BASE	787	B	BEARD, CHARLES A.	262	A
BASE RATE	623	B	BEATNIK	191	A
BASE-DESTROYER AGREEMENT	574	B	BEAUMANOIR	732	B
BASHAW (PASHA - PERSON OF HIGH RANK)	562	B	BEAVERBROOK, LORD	683	B
			BEBEL AUGUST	732	B
BASIC	441	B	BECCARIA, CESARE	732	B
BASIC IDENTIFICATIONS	433	B	BECHHOFER, C. E.	732	B
BASIC LAW	233	A	BECHUANALAND	280	A
BASIC ORIENTATIONS	138	A	BECK, LEWIS WHITE	732	B
BASING POINT SYSTEM	598	B	BECKER, CARL	271	A
BASKET MEETING	648	B	BECKER, THEODORE	702	B
BASQUES	480	B	BECKET, THOMAS	268	A
BASSOW, NIKOLAI	732	B	BEDE, THE VENERABLE	683	B
BASTILLE	288	A	BEDOUINS	161	A
BASTILLE DAY	233	A	BEER-HALL PUTSCH OF 1923	234	A
BASUTO	793	B	BEER, SAMUEL	267	A
BATAAN	276	A	BEERSHOP POLITICIAN	562	B
BATES VS. LITTLE ROCK (1960)	677	B	BEETHOVEN, LUDWIG VON	690	B
BATES, E. S.	732	B	BEFORE APRIL 9TH MEN	842	B
BATISTA, JUAN	265	A	BEGGARS DEMOCRACY	495	B
BATLLE Y ORDONEZ, JOSE	702	B	BEGGING-THE-QUESTION	218	A
BATON ROUGE (LOUISIANA)	790	B	BEHAVIOR	116	A
BATTLE ACT OF 1951	649	B	BEHAVIOR PATTERN	122	A

BEHAVIOR TESTS	225	A	BENN, ANTHONY WEDGWOOD	702	B
BEHAVIOR, COLLECTIVE	114	A	BENN, ERNEST J. P.	733	B
BEHAVIORAL APPROACH	113	A	BENNE, KENNETH	690	B
BEHAVIORAL SCIENCES	113	A	BENNETT, WALLACE FOSTER	733	B
BEHAVIORALISM	114	A	BENNINGTON COLLEGE STUDY	285	A
BEHAVIORISM	114	A	BENNIS, WARREN	733	B
BEIGIN, MENACHEM	732	B	BENOIST, CHARLES	733	B
BEING	141	A	BENT, SILAS	702	B
BELAUNDE-TERRY, FERNANDO	702	B	BENTHAM, JEREMY	262	A
BELFAST GAZETTE	811	B	BENTLEY, ARTHUR F.	265	A
BELFAST, U.K.	280	A	BENTON VS. MARYLAND (1969)	677	B
BELFORT GAP	797	B	BENTSEN, LLOYD MILLARD, JR.	271	A
BELGIAN INSTITUTE OF	514	B	BERCHTESGADEN	278	A
ADMINISTRATIVE SCIENCES			BERCHTESGADEN AGREEMENT	575	B
BELGIAN NEUTRALITY DECLARATION	574	B	BERDAHL, CLARENCE A.	733	B
BELGIANS	480	B	BERDYAEV, NICHOLAS	690	B
BELGIUM	277	A	BERELSON, BERNARD	683	B
BELGO-LUXEMBOURG ECONOMIC	466	B	BERGER VS. NEW YORK (1967)	673	B
UNION			BERGMANN, GUSTAV	733	B
BELGRADE CONFERENCE	243	A	BERGSON, HENRI	690	B
BELIEF	132	A	BERIA, LAVRENTI P.	267	A
BELKNAP, GEORGE M.	732	B	BERING SEA ARBITRATION	575	B
BELL, DANIEL	268	A	BERKELEY, GEORGE	733	B
BELLAMY, EDWARD	702	B	BERLE, ADOLF A., JR.	690	B
BELLARMINE, ROBERT	690	B	BERLIN	274	A
BELLICOSE	141	A	BERLIN AIRLIFT	203	A
BELLIGERENCY	196	A	BERLIN BLOCKADE	203	A
BELLIGERENT POWERS	154	A	BERLIN CONFERENCE	252	A
BELLMARE	562	B	BERLIN DECREE	598	B
BELLMON, HENRY	732	B	BERLIN TO BAGHDAD RAILWAY	821	B
BELLOC, HILAIRE	702	B	BERLIN WALL	274	A
BELLWEATHER	290	A	BERMAN, DANIEL	690	B
BELPHEGOR	811	B	BERMUDA	280	A
BEN BARKA, MEHDI	732	B	BERNAYS, EDWARD L.	690	B
BEN BELLA, MOHAMMED	268	A	BERNE CONVENTION	623	B
BEN-GURION, DAVID	265	A	BERNHARDI, FRIEDRICH VON	703	B
BEN-ZVI, ITZHAK	732	B	BERNODOTTE, COUNT FOLKE	269	A
BENCH	288	A	BERNS, WALTER	733	B
BENDA, E.	733	B	BERNSTEIN, EDUARD	690	B
BENDIX, REINHARD	690	B	BERRIGAN, DANIEL	267	A
BENEDICT II	733	B	BERRIGAN, PHILLIP	264	A
BENEDICT IX, POPE	733	B	BERRY, BURTON	733	B
BENEDICT, BERTRAM	733	B	BERTALANFFY, LUDWIG VON	690	B
BENEDICT, RUTH	269	A	BERTH, EDOUARD	733	B
BENEFIT PAYMENT	243	A	BERTHELEMY, JOSEPH	733	B
BENEFIT PLANS	649	B	BERTILLON SYSTEM	454	B
BENEFIT THEORY	138	A	BESANT, ANNIE	733	B
BENELUX COUNTRIES	275	A	BESSARABIA	787	B
BENES, EDUARD	683	B	BESSON, W.	733	B
BENEVOLENCE	598	B	BEST MAN	547	B
BENEVOLENT AND PROTECTIVE	175	A	BETANCOURT, ROMULO	271	A
ORDER OF ELKS			BETH, LOREN P.	703	B
BENEVOLENT ASSIMILATION	623	B	BETTER BUSINESS BUREAUS	161	A
BENEVOLENT NEUTRALITY	225	A	BETTER RED THAN DEAD	290	A
BENGAL AND BENGALIS	278	A	BETTERMENT TAX	623	B
BENGUET	514	B	BETTS VS. BRADY (1942)	672	B

BETWEEN SESSIONS	252	A	BILATERAL	206	A
BETWEENITES	562	B	BILATERAL AGREEMENTS	206	A
BEVAN, ANEURIN	267	A	BILATERAL AID	218	A
BEVERIDGE COMMITTEE	466	B	BILATERAL SECURITY PACT	243	A
BEVERIDGE REPORT	805	B	BILATERAL TRADE	206	A
BEVERIDGE, ALBERT J.	683	B	BILATERAL TREATY	203	A
BEVERIDGE, SIR WILLIAM	703	B	BILATERALISM	129	A
BEVIN, ERNEST	269	A	BILBOSIM	835	B
BEY	554	B	BILINGUALISM	141	A
BEYLE, HERMAN C.	733	B	BILL	196	A
BEYOND THE WELFARE STATE	290	A	BILL DRAFTING	234	A
BEZA, THEODORE	733	B	BILL DRAFTING SERVICES	175	A
BHAVE, VINOBA	733	B	BILL OF ATTAINDER	196	A
BHUTAN	790	B	BILL OF RIGHTS	194	A
BHUTTO, ZULFIKAR ALI	269	A	BILL READINGS	234	A
BIAFRA	274	A	BILL REFERRAL	203	A
BIASED SAMPLE	115	A	BILL-DRAFTING OFFICE	170	A
BIASES	124	A	BILLBOARD REGULATION	598	B
BIBLE	284	A	BILLETING	598	B
BIBLE, ALAN	690	B	BILLION DOLLAR CONGRESS	842	B
BIBLIOTHEQUE DE DOCUMENTATION	811	B	BIMETALLISM	252	A
INTERNATIONALE			BINDING	623	B
CONTEMPORAINE			BINGA, JESSE	733	B
BICAMERAL LEGISLATURE	148	A	BIOCHEMISTRY	454	B
BICAMERALISM	115	A	BIOCYBERNETICS	454	B
BICULTURAL	132	A	BIOGRAPHICAL METHOD	138	A
BIDAULT, GEORGES	271	A	BIOGRAPHY	806	B
BIDDLE, FRANCIS	703	B	BIOLOGICAL BASIS OF HUMAN	122	A
BIENNIAL SESSION	225	A	CONFLICT		
BIENNIUM	433	B	BIOLOGICAL SURVEY	649	B
BIER	825	B	BIOLOGICAL WARFARE	198	A
BIERSTEDT, ROBERT	733	B	BIOLOGY	141	A
BIERUT, BOLESLAW	733	B	BIOMETRY	454	B
BIFACTIONAL	598	B	BIOPOLITICS	127	A
BIG BUG	842	B	BIOSOCIAL PROCESSES	433	B
BIG BUSINESS	152	A	BIPARTISAN	218	A
BIG DADDY	547	B	BIPARTISAN FOREIGN POLICY	206	A
BIG DEAL	837	B	BIPARTISANSHIP	203	A
BIG FIVE	161	A	BIPARTY SYSTEM	225	A
BIG FIX	837	B	BIPOLARITY	198	A
BIG FOUR	161	A	BIRCHERS	154	A
BIG GOVERNMENT	154	A	BIRD DOG	833	B
BIG GUN	842	B	BIRKENHEAD	733	B
BIG INCH	838	B	BIRMAN	514	B
BIG LABOR	166	A	BIROBIDJAN, U.S.S.R.	793	B
BIG LIE	290	A	BIRTH	649	B
BIG STICK	289	A	BIRTH CERTIFICATE	805	B
BIG STICK DIPLOMACY	218	A	BIRTH CONTROL	211	A
BIG TENT	842	B	BIRTH REGISTRATION	252	A
BIG THREE	161	A	BISHOPRIC	547	B
BIG-MAN	562	B	BISMARCK, OTTO VON	263	A
BIGGER BANG FOR A BUCK	833	B	BISSOLATI, LEONIDA	733	B
BIGOT	184	A	BISTATE AGENCY	495	B
BIGOTRY	132	A	BITUMINOUS COAL CONSERVATION	623	B
BIGWIG	554	B	ACTS		
BIHAR, INDIA	793	B	BITUMINOUS COAL DIVISION	514	B

BIVARIATE ANALYSIS	116	A	BLANQUI, LOUIS AUGUSTE	690	B
BIZEN	797	B	BLANQUISM	441	B
BIZONAL	793	B	BLAU, PETER	703	B
BLACK ABOLITIONIST	183	A	BLEEDING HEARTS	191	A
BLACK AMERICANS	158	A	BLEEDING KANSAS	598	B
BLACK AND TANS	480	B	BLIGHTED DISTRICT	790	B
BLACK BELT	555	B	BLIND	562	B
BLACK BOOK	825	B	BLIND PENSIONS	649	B
BLACK BOURSE	797	B	BLITZ	243	A
BLACK BOX TECHNIQUE	127	A	BLITZKRIEG	218	A
BLACK CAPITALISM	218	A	BLOATED BONDHOLDER	562	B
BLACK COCKADE	825	B	BLOC	154	A
BLACK CODES	575	B	BLOC VOTING	206	A
BLACK DEMOCRACY	480	B	BLOCK CAPTAIN	191	A
BLACK DRAGON	842	B	BLOCK PLAN	575	B
BLACK HAND	480	B	BLOCK-BUSTER	541	B
BLACK HAWK WAR	598	B	BLOCK, E.	734	B
BLACK HORSE CAVALRY	514	B	BLOCKADE	206	A
BLACK JACK	842	B	BLOCKADE RUNNER	189	A
BLACK KNOW NOTHING	514	B	BLOCKAGE (CONCEPT)	623	B
BLACK LAW	649	B	BLOCKED CREDIT	598	B
BLACK LINE (ER)	842	B	BLOCKED CURRENCY	252	A
BLACK MARKET	218	A	BLOCKS OF FIVE	623	B
BLACK MUSLIMS	148	A	BLOK, ALEXANDER	734	B
BLACK PANTHER PARTY	148	A	BLOOD PURGE	623	B
BLACK POLITICS	127	A	BLOOD-AND-SOIL CONCEPT	234	A
BLACK POWER	203	A	BLOODHOUND LAW	623	B
BLACK RECONSTRUCTION	234	A	BLOODSHED	575	B
BLACK REPUBLICAN	191	A	BLOODY BILL	623	B
BLACK SHIRTS	161	A	BLOODY CHASM	838	B
BLACK STAR STEAMSHIP LINE	515	B	BLOODY SATURDAY	575	B
BLACK STUDIES	132	A	BLOODY SHIRT	291	A
BLACK ZIONISM	448	B	BLOOPER	842	B
BLACK, C. F.	703	B	BLUCHER (BLUIKHER), VASILY K.	703	B
BLACK, DONALD J.	733	B	BLUE BOOK	808	B
BLACK, HUGO L.	264	A	BLUE COLLAR	185	A
BLACK, MAX	733	B	BLUE DIVISION	515	B
BLACKBIRDING	842	B	BLUE EAGLE	838	B
BLACKFOOT INDIANS	480	B	BLUE HELMETS	480	B
BLACKLEG	555	B	BLUE HEN STATE	793	B
BLACKLIST	287	A	BLUE LAWS	212	A
BLACKMAIL, POLITICAL	225	A	BLUE LEGION	515	B
BLACKMAILING LEGISLATION	598	B	BLUE LIGHTS	515	B
BLACKOUT	575	B	BLUE POINTS	825	B
BLACKS	158	A	BLUE RIBBON JURY	161	A
BLACKSTONE, SIR WILLIAM	267	A	BLUE RIBBON PANEL	158	A
BLAME	252	A	BLUE SKY LAW	575	B
BLANC, LOUIS	690	B	BLUEBACKED LOCOFOCO	496	B
BLAND-ALLISON ACT	598	B	BLUEGRASS STATE	793	B
BLAND, HUBERT	734	B	BLUEPRINTS	811	B
BLANK CHECK	835	B	BLUM, G. S.	734	B
BLANK VOTE	234	A	BLUM, LEON	690	B
BLANKET BALLOT	234	A	BLUMER, HERBERT A.	734	B
BLANKET CODE	598	B	BLUT UND BODEN	835	B
BLANKET INJUNCTION	225	A	BOARD	496	B
BLANKET PRIMARY	206	A	BOARD OF AUDITORS	496	B

BOARD OF COMMISSIONERS	466	B	BOMB	817	B
BOARD OF COMMISSIONERS (COUNTY)	175	A	BOMBER	288	A
			BOMBING PAUSE	234	B
BOARD OF CONTROL	480	B	BOMFOG	842	B
BOARD OF COUNTY SUPERVISORS	149	A	BONA FIDE	252	A
BOARD OF DIRECTORS	480	B	BONALD, LOUIS G.A.	734	B
BOARD OF ECONOMIC WARFARE	496	B	BONANZA STATE	797	B
BOARD OF EDUCATION	158	A	BONAPARTISM	129	A
BOARD OF EDUCATION VS. ALLEN (1968)	261	A	BONAVENTURE	703	B
			BOND	287	A
BOARD OF ESTIMATE	466	B	BOND, JULIAN	263	A
BOARD OF GOVERNORS	466	B	BONDAGE	234	A
BOARD OF GOVERNORS OF FEDERAL RESERVE SYSTEM	166	A	BONDING	598	B
			BONDSMAN	191	A
BOARD OF HEALTH	175	A	BONE AND SINEW	838	B
BOARD OF IMMIGRATION APPEALS	175	A	BONE TAKER	562	B
BOARD OF PARDON	466	B	BONELESS WONDER	562	B
BOARD OF PAROLE	175	A	BONHOFFER, CLAUSE	703	B
BOARD OF REGENTS	161	A	BONHOFFER, DIETRICH	683	B
BOARD OF REVIEW	466	B	BONN CONSTITUTION, GERMANY	284	A
BOARD OF STRATEGY AND PLANNING	515	B	BONNEVILLE POWER ADMINISTRATION	480	B
BOARD OF SUPERVISORS	152	A	BONOMI, IVANCE	734	B
BOARD OF TAX REVIEW	480	B	BONUS	598	B
BOARD OF TRADE	175	A	BONUS BILL	598	B
BOARD OF TRUSTEES	166	A	BOODLE	835	B
BOAS, FRANZ	703	B	BOODLE BOYS	547	B
BOBBY	541	B	BOOHOO	842	B
BOCK, A. E.	734	B	BOOK	805	B
BODENREFORM	623	B	BOOK OF THE STATES	805	B
BODIN, JEAN	267	A	BOOKBURNERS	185	A
BODY	496	B	BOOKKEEPING	623	B
BODY POLITIC	149	A	BOOLEAN ALGEBRA	141	A
BOER WAR	225	A	BOOM	252	A
BOERS	166	A	BOOM AND BUST	291	A
BOERSNER, DEMETRIO	734	B	BOOMERANG	835	B
BOETHIUS	703	B	BOOMLET	575	B
BOGGS, J. CALEB	734	B	BOONDOGGLE	290	A
BOGORAZ-DANIEL, LARISSA	734	B	BOOTLEG	243	A
BOGOTA CHARTER	252	A	BOOTY	817	B
BOGOTA CONFERENCE	252	A	BORAH, WILLIAM E.	683	B
BOGUS BABY	842	B	BORDER	280	A
BOILER PLATE CAMPAIGN	598	B	BORDER RUFFIAN	562	B
BOISGUILLEBERT, PIERRE	734	B	BORDER STATE	154	A
BOLINGBROKE, HENRY ST JOHN, VISCOUNT	703	B	BORDER WAR	225	A
			BORDERLINE	135	A
BOLIVAR, SIMON	263	A	BORGHESE, VALERIO	703	B
BOLIVIA	275	A	BORGIA, CESARE	269	A
BOLLING VS. SHARPE (1954)	261	A	BORING FROM WITHIN	835	B
BOLOGNA, LAW SCHOOL OF	515	B	BORING, EDWIN G.	734	B
BOLSHEVIK REVOLUTION	195	A	BORMANN, MARTIN LUDWIG	269	A
BOLSHEVIKS	146	A	BORNEO	280	A
BOLSHEVISM	116	A	BORODIN, MICHAEL	690	B
BOLT	598	B	BOROUGH	170	A
BOLTER	547	B	BOROUGH PLAN	252	A
BOLZANO	734	B	BORROWING POWER	252	A

BORUNDI	787	B	BRACE, CHARLES LORING	734	B
BOSANQUET, BERNARD	734	B	BRACERO PROGRAM	218	A
BOSCH, JUAN	269	A	BRACTON, HENRY	734	B
BOSCOMBE, WILTS	734	B	BRADLEY, FRANCIS HERBERT	734	B
BOSE, SUBHAS CHANDRA	703	B	BRADLEY, GENERAL OMAR	271	A
BOSNIAN CRISIS	598	B	BRAG HORSE	562	B
BOSS	182	A	BRAHMIN	189	A
BOSSISM	206	A	BRAILSFORD, H. N.	734	B
BOSSUET, BISHOP JACQUES BENIGNE	734	B	BRAIN	555	B
			BRAIN DRAIN	290	A
BOSTON BRAHMINS	185	A	BRAIN TRUST	158	A
BOSTON MASSACRE	218	A	BRAINSTORMING	141	A
BOSTON POLICE STRIKE	599	B	BRAINWASH	129	A
BOSTON TEA PARTY	203	A	BRAMHALL, BISHOP	735	B
BOSWELL	690	B	BRANCHES OF GOVERNMENT	146	A
BOTANIC GARDEN, UNITED STATES	793	B	BRANDEIS BRIEF	285	A
BOTSIO, KOJO	734	B	BRANDEIS, LOUIS DEMBITZ	269	A
BOTSWANA	280		BRANDENBURG VS. OHIO (1969)	674	B
BOTTLENECKS	838	B	BRANDT, WILLY	263	A
BOUCHER, JEAN	734	B	BRANNAN PLAN	599	B
BOUCKE, O. F.	734	B	BRANT, JOSEPH	703	B
BOUDIN, LOUIS B.	703	B	BRANTING, KARL	703	B
BOULAINVILLIERS, HENRI DE	703	B	BRASS BAND	480	B
BOULANGER, GENERAL GEORGES	690	B	BRASS COLLAR DEMOCRAT	496	B
BOULANGER, N. A.	703	B	BRAVE	448	B
BOULDING, KENNETH	269	A	BRAVO, LOPEZ	703	B
BOULE (LEGISLATIVE COUNCIL, ANCIENT GREECE)	515	B	BRAY, J. F.	703	B
			BRAYBROOKE, DAVID	683	B
BOULOGNE-BILLANCOURT, FRANCE	797	B	BRAZIL	275	A
BOUMEDIENNE, COLONEL HOUARI	271	A	BRAZILIAN CONGO	787	B
BOUNDARY	274	A	BRAZZAVILLE BLOC	170	A
BOUNDARY DISPUTE	212	A	BRAZZAVILLE CONFERENCE (1944)	599	B
BOUNDARY EXCHANGE	575	B	BREACH OF A TREATY	225	A
BOUNTY	575	B	BREACH OF CONTRACT	212	A
BOUNTY JUMPER	555	B	BREACH OF PRIVILEGE	243	A
BOURBON	189	A	BREACH OF THE PEACE	212	A
BOURGEOIS	148	A	BREAD AND BUTTER ISSUE	290	A
BOURGEOIS REVOLUTION	203	A	BREAK	649	B
BOURGEOIS, LEON	734	B	BREAKAWAY GROUP	466	B
BOURGEOISIE	145	A	BREAKDOWN	599	B
BOURGUIBA, HABIB BEN ALI	269	A	BREASTED, J. H.	703	B
BOW	623	B	BRECHT, ARNOLD	269	A
BOW GROUP	496	B	BREITER	703	B
BOWLBY, JOHN	734	B	BRENTANO, LUDO	703	B
BOWLES, CHESTER,	269	A	BRETT, OLIVER	703	B
BOWMAN, GUY	703	B	BRETTON WOODS AGREEMENT (1944)	218	A
BOWRA, PROF. C. M.	734	B			
BOXER INDEMNITY	252	A	BREZHNEV DOCTRINE	212	A
BOXER REBELLION	218	A	BREZHNEV, LEONID ILYICH	262	A
BOY	562	B	BRIAND MEMORANDUM	805	B
BOY ORATOR	703	B	BRIAND, ARISTIDE	267	A
BOY SCOUT	480	B	BRIBE	212	A
BOYCOTT	212	A	BRICKER AMENDMENT PROPOSAL	225	A
BOYS CLUB OF AMERICA INCORPORATED	496	B	BRICKNER, RICHARD	704	B
			BRICKS WITHOUT STRAW	833	B
BOYS IN THE BACKROOM	547	B	BRIDGE BUILDING	291	A

BRIDGES VS. CALIFORNIA (1941)	672	B	BROSIO, MANLIO	704	B
BRIEF	284	A	BROTHER JONATHAN	704	B
BRIGHAM, C. C.	704	B	BROTHERHOOD	191	A
BRIGHT, JOHN	704	B	BROTHERHOOD OF TEAMSTERS	161	A
BRINDLE (TAIL)	496	B	BROUSSE, P.	704	B
BRINKMANSHIP	203	A	BROUSSISTS	496	B
BRISBANE, AUSTRALIA	790	B	BROWN DERBY	819	B
BRITISH	175	A	BROWN DERBY SYMBOL	819	B
BRITISH ASSIZE COURTS	496	B	BROWN HOUSE	821	B
BRITISH BROADCASTING	161	A	BROWN SHIRTS	154	A
CORPORATION (B.B.C.)			BROWN VS. BOARD OF EDUCATION	260	A
BRITISH CABINET	149	A	OF TOPEKA (1954)		
BRITISH CARIBBEAN FEDERATION	623	B	BROWN VS. MARYLAND (1827)	671	B
ACT			BROWN VS. MISSISSIPPI (1936)	672	B
BRITISH CENTRAL CRIMINAL COURT	480	B	BROWN, GEORGE ALFRED	704	B
BRITISH COMMONWEALTH OF	154	A	BROWN, IVOR	704	B
NATIONS			BROWN, JOHN	263	A
BRITISH CONSERVATIVE PARTY	154	A	BROWN, LESTER R.	704	B
BRITISH CROWN COLONIES	161	A	BROWNE, ROBERT	704	B
BRITISH DEFENSE OF THE REALM	599	B	BROWNE, SIR THOMAS	704	B
ACT (DORA)			BROWNING, RUFUS P.	691	B
BRITISH EMPIRE	148	A	BROWNLOW, LOUIS	704	B
BRITISH HIGH COURT OF JUSTICE	170	A	BROWNOUT	252	A
BRITISH HONDURAS	277	A	BROZ, JOSIP	683	B
BRITISH IMPERIAL WAR CABINET	175	A	BRUNEI	480	B
BRITISH INDIA	278	A	BRUNER, JEROME S.	704	B
BRITISH LABOR PARTY	149	A	BRUNFAUT, GASTON	704	B
BRITISH LIBERAL PARTY	154	A	BRUNING, HEINRICH	691	B
BRITISH MEDICAL ASSOCIATION	480	B	BRUNNER, EMIL	704	B
BRITISH MUSEUM	817	B	BRUNO	704	B
BRITISH NORTH AMERICA ACT	243	A	BRUNSCHVIG, LEON	704	B
(1867)			BRUSHFIRE WARS	212	A
BRITISH TORIES	161	A	BRUSSELS CONFERENCE	252	A
BRITISH UNION OF FASCISTS	466	B	BRUSSELS LINE	793	B
BRITISH WHIGS	158	A	BRUSSELS TREATY ORGANIZATION	166	A
BROAD	555	B	BRUSSELS, BELGIUM	280	A
BROAD CONSTRUCTION	212	A	BRUTALITY	252	A
BROAD SEAL WAR	623	B	BRUTUS, STEPHEN JUNIUS	704	B
BROAD-GAUGE THEORY	122	A	BRYAN-CHAMORRA TREATY	599	B
(METATHEORY)			BRYAN, WILLIAM JENNINGS	263	A
BROCK, H. W.	704	B	BRYCE, LORD JAMES	265	A
BROCK, WILLIAM EMERSON III	704	B	BRZEZINSKI, ZBIGNIEW	267	A
BROCKWAY, FENNER	704	B	BUBER, MARTIN	267	A
BRODBECK, ARTHUR J.	691	B	BUCHAN, JOHN	691	B
BRODBECK, MAY	704	B	BUCHANA, JANES	704	B
BRODIE, BERNARD	271	A	BUCHANAN VS. WARLEY (1917)	674	B
BROEDERBOND	496	B	BUCHANAN, GEORGE	691	B
BROKER	187	A	BUCHANAN, PRESIDENT JAMES A.	264	A
BROKERED CONVENTION	234	A	BUCHANIER	555	B
BROMAGE, ARTHUR W.	704	B	BUCHENWALD	275	A
BRONOWSKI, JACOB	691	B	BUCHMAN, FRANK	691	B
BROOK FARM	166	A	BUCK STOPS HERE	291	A
BROOKE, EDWARD WILLIAM	265	A	BUCK VS. BELL (1927)	674	B
BROOKINGS INSTITUTION	152	A	BUCK, R.C.	704	B
(WASHINGTON, D.C.)			BUCKEYE STATE	790	B
BROOKS, ROBERT C.	704	B	BUCKINGHAM PALACE	288	A

BUCKLEY, JAMES L.	271	A		BURDICK, EUGENE	705	B
BUCKLEY, WILLIAM F.	267	A		BURDICK, QUENTIN NORTHROP	705	B
BUCKLIN PLAN	623	B		BUREAU	170	A
BUCKSHOT WAR	623	B		BUREAU OF ACCOUNTS	496	B
BUCKTAILS	480	B		BUREAU OF AERONAUTICS	515	B
BUDDHA, GAUTAMA	265	A		BUREAU OF AFRICAN AFFAIRS	466	B
BUDDHISM	132	A		BUREAU OF AGRICULTURAL	480	B
BUDGET	198	A		ECONOMICS (U.S.)		
BUDGET AND ACCOUNTING ACT OF	243	A		BUREAU OF ANIMAL HUSBANDRY	480	B
1921				BUREAU OF APPRENTICESHIP AND	496	B
BUDGET AND ACCOUNTING	575	B		TRAINING		
PROCEDURES ACT OF 1950				BUREAU OF CHIEF POSTAL	496	B
BUDGET BUREAU	158	A		INSPECTORS		
BUDGET MESSAGE	284	A		BUREAU OF CUSTOMS	170	A
BUDGET SESSION	225	A		BUREAU OF DAIRY INDUSTRY	496	B
BUDGETARY PROCESS	115	A		BUREAU OF DOMESTIC COMMERCE	496	B
BUENOS AIRES CONFERENCE	599	B		(BDC)		
BUFF AND BLUE	825	B		BUREAU OF ECONOMIC AFFAIRS	170	A
BUFFALO HUNT	649	B		BUREAU OF ECONOMIC RESEARCH	480	B
BUFFER STATE	154	A		BUREAU OF EMPLOYEES	480	B
BUGABOO	842	B		COMPENSATION		
BUGBEAR	842	B		BUREAU OF EMPLOYMENT	480	B
BUILDING	825	B		SECURITY		
BUILDING CODE	243	A		BUREAU OF ENGRAVING AND	170	A
BUILDING PERMIT	252	A		PRINTING		
BUKHARIN, NIKOLAI IVANOVICH	267	A		BUREAU OF ENTOMOLOGY AND	496	B
BUKOVSKY, VLADIMIR	735	B		PLANT QUARANTINE		
BULGANIN, MARSHAL NIKOLAI	269	A		BUREAU OF EUROPEAN AFFAIRS	170	A
ALEXANDROVICH				BUREAU OF FAR EASTERN AFFAIRS	170	A
BULGARIA	277	A		BUREAU OF FEDERAL CREDIT	496	B
BULL	835	B		UNIONS		
BULL MOOSE PARTY	161	A		BUREAU OF FOREIGN AND	480	B
BULLDOZE	835	B		DOMESTIC COMMERCE		
BULLER, CHARLES	704	B		BUREAU OF FOREIGN COMMERCE	481	B
BULLET VOTE	291	A		BUREAU OF GOVERNMENTAL	481	B
BULLIONIST	466	B		RESEARCH		
BULLITT, WILLIAM C.	705	B		BUREAU OF HUMAN NUTRITION AND	496	B
BULLWHACK (ING)	835	B		HOME ECONOMICS		
BULLY PULPIT	797	B		BUREAU OF HUMAN NUTRITION AND	481	B
BULTMANN	735	B		HOME ECONOMICS		
BUNCHE, RALPH JOHNSON	269	A		BUREAU OF INDIAN AFFAIRS	152	A
BUNCOMBE	838	B		BUREAU OF INSULAR AFFAIRS	175	A
BUND	170	A		BUREAU OF INTELLIGENCE AND	496	B
BUNDESRAT (FEDERAL COUNCIL),	155	A		RESEARCH		
GERMANY				BUREAU OF INTER-AMERICAN	175	A
BUNDESTAG (FEDERAL DIET),	158	A		AFFAIRS		
GERMANY				BUREAU OF INTERNAL REVENUE	152	A
BUNDLE OF COMPROMISES	252	A		BUREAU OF INTERNATIONAL	496	B
BUNDY, MCGEORGE	267	A		COMMERCE (BIC)		
BUNK	454	B		BUREAU OF INTERNATIONAL	175	A
BUNTING VS. OREGON (1917)	677	B		ORGANIZATION AFFAIRS		
BUNYORO	797	B		BUREAU OF LABOR STANDARDS	166	A
BURAKU	515	B		BUREAU OF LABOR STATISTICS	161	A
BURCHARD INCIDENT	623	B		(BLS)		
BURCKHARDT, J.	735	B		BUREAU OF LAND MANAGEMENT	161	A
BURDEN OF PROOF	198	A				

BUREAU OF MARINE INSPECTION AND NAVIGATION	515	B	BURNS, JOHN	735	B
			BURR CONSPIRACY	212	A
BUREAU OF MEDICAL SERVICES	515	B	BURR, AARON	263	A
BUREAU OF MINES	175	A	BURR, CLINTON S.	735	B
BUREAU OF MUNICIPAL RESEARCH (U.S.)	481	B	BURSTYN VS. WILSON (1925)	677	B
			BURTON, R.	735	B
BUREAU OF NARCOTICS	170	A	BURUNDI	278	A
BUREAU OF NARCOTICS AND DANGEROUS DRUGS (BNDD)	170	A	BURY, PROF. J. B.	735	B
			BUSHIDO (JAPANESE CODE OF CHIVALRY)	448	B
BUREAU OF NEAR EASTERN AND SOUTH ASIAN AFFAIRS	170	A	BUSHWHACK(ER, ING)	838	B
BUREAU OF OLD AGE AND SURVIVORS INSURANCE	170	A	BUSIA, DR. K. A.	735	B
			BUSINESS	166	A
BUREAU OF PATENTS	166	A	BUSINESS AFFECTED WITH A PUBLIC INTEREST	291	A
BUREAU OF PLANT INDUSTRY, SOILS AND AGRICULTURAL ENGINEERING	496	B	BUSINESS AGENT	547	B
			BUSINESS AND DEFENSE SERVICES ADMINISTRATION	515	B
BUREAU OF PRISONS	170	A	BUSINESS AS USUAL	833	B
BUREAU OF PRODUCT SAFETY	466	B	BUSINESS ASSOCIATIONS	176	A
BUREAU OF PUBLIC AFFAIRS	175	A	BUSINESS COMPETITION	243	A
BUREAU OF PUBLIC ASSISTANCE	170	A	BUSINESS CORPORATION	166	A
BUREAU OF PUBLIC DEBT	496	B	BUSINESS CYCLE	203	A
BUREAU OF PUBLIC ROADS	176	A	BUSINESS EDUCATION	448	B
BUREAU OF RECLAMATION	171	A	BUSINESS GAMES	624	B
BUREAU OF SECURITY AND CONSULAR AFFAIRS	466	B	BUSINESS MAN'S CAMPAIGN	649	B
			BUSINESS UNIONISM	575	B
BUREAU OF STANDARDS	166	A	BUSINESS-GOVERNMENT RELATIONS	122	A
BUREAU OF STATE HEALTH SERVICES	496	B	BUSING OF SCHOOL CHILDREN	212	A
BUREAU OF THE BUDGET (U.S.)	149	A	BUSTAMANTE, SIR WILLIAM ALEXANDER	735	B
BUREAU OF THE CENSUS (U.S.)	152	A			
BUREAU OF THE MINT	171	A	BUTHELEZI, CHIEF GATSHA	735	B
BUREAU OF VETERANS RE-EMPLOYMENT RIGHTS	496	B	BUTLER, BARON, RICHARD AUSTEN	735	B
			BUTLER, D.E.	705	B
BUREAUCRACY	144	A	BUTT-ENDER	562	B
BUREAUCRAT	181	A	BUTTERNUT	562	B
BURGER, WARREN	263	A	BUTTON-HOLE	291	A
BURGERMEISTER	541	B	BUYING AN ELECTION	290	A
BURGESS, JOHN W.	735	B	BUZZARD DOLLAR	843	B
BURKE, EDMUND	262	A	BY-ELECTION	212	A
BURKE, KENNETH	691	B	BY-LAW	219	A
BURLINGAME TREATY	623	B	BYELORUSSIA	275	A
BURMA	275	A	BYRD, HARRY FLOOD, JR.	271	A
BURMA HUMP	793	B	BYRD, ROBERT CARLYLE	691	B
BURMA ROAD	787	B	BYRNES, JAMES F.	269	A
BURMESE WAY TO SOCIALISM	448	B	BYRON, GEORGE GORDON, LORD	691	B
BURNET, GILBERT	691	B	BYZANTINE	280	A
BURNHAM, JAMES	705	B	BYZANTINE EMPIRE	280	A
BURNHAM, LINDON FORBES SAMPSON	735	B	BYZANTINE LAW	624	B
			BYZANTIUM	282	A
BURNING QUESTION	838	B	C COUPON	819	B
BURNS THESIS	448	B	C THREE C 3	843	B
BURNS, ALAN	735	B	CABAL	162	A
BURNS, CECIL D.	735	B	CABALLERO, LARGO	735	B
BURNS, EVELINE M.	691	B	CABET, HUGH	735	B
BURNS, JAMES M.	269	A			

CABINET	146	A
CABINET GOVERNMENT	146	A
CABINET MINISTERS	182	A
CABINET OF BARONS	515	B
CABINET OF MONOCLES	515	B
CABINET SYSTEM	114	A
CABINETS, PRESIDENTIAL	148	A
CABLE ACT OF 1922	649	B
CABOTAGE	649	B
CABRERA , LUIS	735	B
CACHIN, MARCEL	735	B
CADASTRAL SURVEY	649	B
CADMIUM	825	B
CADRE	162	A
CAESAR, GAIUS JULIUS	263	A
CAESARISM	124	A
CAETANO, PROFESSOR MARCELO JOSE DAS NEVES	705	B
CAGOULARDS	515	B
CAIRO CONFERENCE OF 1943	234	A
CAIRO DECLARATION	252	A
CAISSON	825	B
CALAMITY HOWLER	562	B
CALCULATED RISK	212	A
CALCULUS	129	A
CALDERON, GARCIA	735	B
CALENDAR	284	A
CALENDAR OF BILLS AND RESOLUTIONS	284	A
CALENDAR OF BUSINESS	285	A
CALENDAR WEDNESDAY	243	A
CALHOUN, JOHN C.	262	A
CALICO VOTE	515	B
CALIFORNIA	274	A
CALIFORNIA MISSIONS	817	B
CALIGULA	683	B
CALIPH (CALIF) (KHALIF)	541	B
CALIPHATE	547	B
CALL	599	B
CALL OF THE HOUSE	599	B
CALL OF THE STATES	575	B
CALL TO ORDER	252	A
CALLAGHAN, JAMES	705	B
CALLAGHAN, LEONARD JAMES	735	B
CALLES, PLUTARCO ELIAS	683	B
CALLICLES	735	B
CALLING-CARD	825	B
CALMUCK	515	B
CALVIN, JOHN	262	A
CALVINISM	120	A
CALVO DOCTRINE	575	B
CAMACHO, MANUEL AVILA	691	B
CAMBODIA	275	A
CAMBRIDGE, MASSACHUSETTS	787	B
CAMBYSES	735	B
CAMELOTS DU ROI	797	B
CAMEROON	278	A
CAMP	793	B
CAMP DAVID	275	A
CAMP FOLLOWER	547	B
CAMPAIGN	203	A
CAMPAIGN BUTTONS	288	A
CAMPAIGN COMMITTEES	155	A
CAMPAIGN CONTRIBUTIONS	219	A
CAMPAIGN FINANCE	199	A
CAMPAIGN FUND	212	A
CAMPAIGN ORATORY	225	A
CAMPAIGN PROMISES	225	A
CAMPAIGN SONGS	805	B
CAMPAIGN TEXTBOOK	805	B
CAMPAIGN TRAIL	234	A
CAMPAIGN TRAIN	289	A
CAMPBELL, ANGUS	269	A
CAMPBELL, NORMAN R.	735	B
CAMPUS	282	A
CAMUS, ALBERT	264	A
CAN	825	B
CAN'T WIN TECHNIQUE	838	B
CANADA	275	A
CANAL RING	496	B
CANAL ZONE	273	A
CANBERRA, AUSTRALIA	282	A
CANCELLATION	624	B
CANDIDATE	181	A
CANDIDATE'S DISEASE	649	B
CANDIDE	805	B
CANDLE-BOX RETURNS	649	B
CANNABIS	289	A
CANNON, HOWARD WALTER	705	B
CANNON, JOSEPH G.	271	A
CANNONISM	624	B
CANON LAW	206	A
CANOSSA	797	B
CANT	649	B
CANTON (FRANCE)	166	A
CANTON ISLAND	797	B
CANTONS, SWITZERLAND	162	A
CANTRIL, HADLEY	683	B
CANTWELL VS. CONNECTICUT (1940)	674	B
CANVAS CLUB	515	B
CANVASS	234	A
CANVASSING BOARDS	171	A
CAO DIA	466	B
CAPABILITIES	206	A
CAPABILITY ANALYSIS	124	A
CAPE CANAVERAL	278	A
CAPE KENNEDY	278	A
CAPITAL	274	A
CAPITAL (CITY)	278	A
CAPITAL BUDGET	252	A
CAPITAL DEVELOPMENT FUND, UNITED NATIONS	158	A

CAPITAL FLIGHT	219	A
CAPITAL GAINS TAX	243	A
CAPITAL LEVY	575	B
CAPITAL PUNISHMENT	198	A
CAPITAL SHIP	819	B
CAPITAL STOCK TAX	624	B
CAPITAL, U.S.	287	A
CAPITALISM	113	A
CAPITALIST ENCIRCLEMENT	212	A
CAPITALIST REVOLUTION	225	A
CAPITANT, R.	735	B
CAPITATION	252	A
CAPITOL	287	A
CAPITOL HILL	274	A
CAPITULATION	234	A
CAPONE, AL	269	A
CAPTAIN OF INDUSTRY	541	B
CAPTIVE	541	B
CAPTIVE CANDIDATE	548	B
CAPTIVE MINE	793	B
CAPTIVE NATIONS	166	A
CAPTIVITY	252	A
CARADON, LORD	271	A
CARBONARI	466	B
CARD METAPHORS	838	B
CARD-CARRYING	833	B
CARD-STACKING	833	B
CARDENAS, LAZARO	271	A
CARDINAL	191	A
CARDOZO, BENJAMIN N.	683	B
CARDWELL	735	B
CAREER DIPLOMAT	184	A
CAREER PLANNING	624	B
CAREER SERVICE	158	A
CAREER STAFFING	599	B
CARETAKER	541	B
CARETAKER GOVERNMENT	158	A
CAREY ACT	575	B
CARIBBEAN	278	A
CARIBBEAN COMMISSION	497	B
CARIBBEAN FEDERATION	466	B
CARIBBEAN FREE TRADE ASSOCIATION (CARIFTA)	176	A
CARITAS INTERNATIONALIS	481	B
CARLISM	441	B
CARLYLE, A.J.	705	B
CARLYLE, R. W.	736	B
CARLYLE, THOMAS	269	A
CARMICHAEL, STOKELY	264	A
CARNAP, RUDOLF	691	B
CARNEADES, THE CYNIC	705	B
CARNEGIE CORPORATION	162	A
CARNEGIE ENDOWMENT FOR INTERNATIONAL PEACE	155	A
CARNEGIE, ANDREW	266	A
CARNOT, SAID	705	B
CAROL, KING	683	B
CAROLINE, THE	821	B
CARPATHO-UKRAINE	787	B
CARPETBAGGER	183	A
CARR-SAUNDERS, A. M.	705	B
CARR, EDWARD H.	269	A
CARR, ROBERT	705	B
CARRANZA, VENUSTIANO	271	A
CARSON, SIR EDWARD	705	B
CARTE BLANCHE	290	A
CARTEL	155	A
CARTEL DES GAUCHES (LEFTIST COALITION)	466	B
CARTEL SHIP	821	B
CARTER, BYRUM E.	736	B
CARTHAGE	280	A
CARTHAGINIAN PEACE	243	A
CARTHAGO DELENDA EST	838	B
CARTWRIGHT, D.	736	B
CARVER, T. N.	705	B
CASABLANCA CONFERENCE	243	A
CASCON SYSTEM	649	B
CASE	261	A
CASE LAW	198	A
CASE METHOD	120	A
CASE STUDY	116	A
CASE STUDY METHOD	114	A
CASE, CLIFFORD P.	683	B
CASE, JACK	705	B
CASH-AND-CARRY PRINCIPLE	243	A
CASSEL, GUSTAV	705	B
CASSIODORUS	705	B
CASSIRER, ERNST	705	B
CASSON, STANLEY	705	B
CASTE SYSTEM	203	A
CASTILLO, RAMON	705	B
CASTING VOTE	234	A
CASTLE, BARBARA ANNE	691	B
CASTLE, W. E.	705	B
CASTRATION COMPLEX	441	B
CASTRO, DR. FIDEL RUIZ	263	A
CASTROISM	125	A
CASTRUCCIO CASTRACANI	705	B
CASUALTIES	189	A
CASUS BELLI	199	A
CASUS FOEDERIS	599	B
CATAFALQUE	821	B
CATALYST	138	A
CATALYTIC WAR	234	A
CATAMNESTIC	448	B
CATCHALL	838	B
CATCHWORD	838	B
CATECHOLAMINE	821	B
CATEGORIC GROUP	162	A
CATEGORICAL TONNAGE	624	B
CATEGORICAL-IMPERATIVE	125	A

CATEGORY	129	A
CATHARSIS	132	A
CATHERINE II, CATHERINE THE GREAT	267	A
CATHERINE OF RUSSIA, EMPRESS	271	A
CATHOLIC	176	A
CATHOLIC ACTION LEAGUE	166	A
CATHOLIC CENTER PARTY	166	A
CATHOLIC CHURCH	158	A
CATHOLIC PARTY	162	A
CATHOLIC POLITICAL THEORY	129	A
CATHOLIC UNION (BELGIUM)	481	B
CATHOLIC WORKER'S COLLEGE (GREAT BRITAIN)	497	B
CATHOLIC-LIBERAL UNIONISM	141	A
CATHOLICISM	132	A
CATLIN, GEORGE E.G.	271	A
CATO	271	A
CATTELL, J. M.	691	B
CAUCASIAN	162	A
CAUCUS	196	A
CAUCUS, CONGRESSIONAL	203	A
CAUCUS, NOMINATING	203	A
CAUCUSING GROUP, UNITED NATIONS	162	A
CAUDILLISM	127	A
CAUDILLO	185	A
CAUSAL ANALYSIS	117	A
CAUSAL EXPLANATION	114	A
CAUSAL MODELS	114	A
CAUSALITY	118	A
CAUSATION	117	A
CAUSE	225	A
CAUSE AND EFFECT	114	A
CAVALRY CABINET	497	B
CAVE IN	838	B
CAVEAT	135	A
CAVEAT EMPTOR	289	A
CAVEAT VENDITOR	833	B
CAVITE	797	B
CAVOUR, COUNT CAMILLO DI	683	B
CEASE AND DESIST ORDER	199	A
CEASE-FIRE	203	A
CEAUSESCU, NICOLAE	269	A
CECIL-REQUIN DRAFT TREATY	624	B
CECIL, LORD HUGH	705	B
CECIL, VISCOUNT ROBERT	736	B
CEDE	234	A
CEDENT STATE	497	B
CEILING PRICE	243	A
CELEBRITY	562	B
CELESTIAL EMPIRE	481	B
CELL	158	A
CELLER-KEFAUVER ANTIMERGER ACT (1950)	575	B
CELSUS	705	B

CEMETERY VOTE	291	A
CENSOR	187	A
CENSORSHIP	199	A
CENSURE	206	A
CENSURE MOTION	198	A
CENSUS	203	A
CENTENARY	441	B
CENTENNIAL STATE	497	B
CENTER	793	B
CENTER OF POPULATION	787	B
CENTER PARTIES	149	A
CENTRAL ADMINISTRATION	158	A
CENTRAL AFRICAN ECONOMIC AND CUSTOMS UNION (UDEAC)	466	B
CENTRAL AFRICAN FEDERATION	176	A
CENTRAL AFRICAN REPUBLIC (CAR)	171	A
CENTRAL AMERICA	274	A
CENTRAL AMERICAN COMMON MARKET (CACM)	171	A
CENTRAL AMERICAN COURT OF JUSTICE	497	B
CENTRAL ASIA	275	A
CENTRAL COMMISSION FOR THE NAVIGATION OF THE RHINE	481	B
CENTRAL COMMITTEE	155	A
CENTRAL COMMITTEE, CHINA (PRC)	152	A
CENTRAL COMMITTEE, COMMUNIST PARTY, SOVIET UNION	155	A
CENTRAL CRIMINAL COURT	497	B
CENTRAL EXECUTIVE COMMITTEE	497	B
CENTRAL GOVERNMENT	152	A
CENTRAL INTELLIGENCE AGENCY (CIA)	148	A
CENTRAL LAND BOARD (GREAT BRITAIN)	497	B
CENTRAL PACIFIC RAILROAD	497	B
CENTRAL PLANNING COMMISSION	466	B
CENTRAL POWERS	158	A
CENTRAL TENDENCY MEASUREMENT	120	A
CENTRAL TRADE UNION COUNCIL (TUC) (USSR)	466	B
CENTRAL TREATY ORGANIZATION (CENTO)	155	A
CENTRALISM	132	A
CENTRALIZATION	196	A
CENTRALIZED GOVERNMENT	146	A
CENTRALIZED PURCHASING	252	A
CENTRE D'ETUDES DE POLITIQUE ETRANGERE	481	B
CENTRE DES HAUTES ETUDES ADMINISTRATIVES (FRANCE)	481	B
CENTRE INTERNATIONAL DE SYNTHESE	515	B

CENTRE NATIONAL DE LA RECHERCHE SCIENTIFIQUE (FRANCE)	515	B
CENTRIST	187	A
CENTURY	649	B
CENTURY OF THE COMMON MAN	575	B
CERDA, PEDRO AGUIRRE	736	B
CEREMONY	575	B
CERNIK, O.	736	B
CERTAINTY	138	A
CERTIFICATE	806	B
CERTIFICATE OF AVAILABILITY	806	B
CERTIFICATE OF ELECTION	284	A
CERTIFICATE OF PUBLIC CONVENIENCE AND NECESSITY	808	B
CERTIFICATION	575	B
CERTIFICATION OF ELIGIBLES	624	B
CERTIFIED COPY	807	B
CERTITUDE	441	B
CERVANTES	705	B
CESSATION OF HOSTILITIES	225	A
CESSION	252	A
CESSIONARY STATE	466	B
CEYLON	278	A
CH'EN PO-TA	705	B
CH'OE-SUUN	736	B
CHABAN-DELMAS, JACQUES	736	B
CHACO WAR	252	A
CHAD	280	A
CHADWICK, EDWIN	736	B
CHAFEE, ZACHARIAH, JR.	736	B
CHAIN BANKING	599	B
CHAIN STORE ANTI-DISCRIMINATION LAW	599	B
CHAIN STORE TAX	624	B
CHAIN VOTING	252	A
CHAIR	185	A
CHAIRMAN	187	A
CHALASINSKI	736	B
CHALDEANS	515	B
CHALLENGE	252	A
CHALLENGE, JURY	212	A
CHALLENGE, VOTING	219	A
CHAMBER	166	A
CHAMBER OF COMMERCE OF UNITED STATES	166	A
CHAMBER OF COUNCILLORS	515	B
CHAMBER OF CULTURE	515	B
CHAMBER OF DEPUTIES (FRANCE)	152	A
CHAMBER OF FASCES AND CORPORATIONS	481	B
CHAMBER OF NATIONALITIES	467	B
CHAMBER OF NOBLES	467	B
CHAMBER OF REPRESENTATIVES	467	B
CHAMBER OF THE FEDERAL STATES	497	B
CHAMBERLAIN, HOUSTON STEWART	691	B
CHAMBERLAIN, JOSEPH	271	A
CHAMBERLAIN, LAWRENCE H.	736	B
CHAMBERLAIN, NEVILLE	263	A
CHAMIZAL BORDER SETTLEMENT	599	B
CHAMORRO	515	B
CHAMOUN, CAMILLE	736	B
CHAMPAGNE STATESMANSHIP	649	B
CHANCE	132	A
CHANCELLERY	171	A
CHANCELLOR	182	A
CHANCELLOR OF THE EXCHEQUER	183	A
CHANCERY	171	A
CHANCERY COURTS	467	B
CHANDLER ACT OF 1938	599	B
CHANDNI CHOWK, INDIA	797	B
CHANDRA	736	B
CHANG HSUEH-LIANG	691	B
CHANG TSO-LIN	691	B
CHANG, PI-SHIH	736	B
CHANGE	132	A
CHANGE OF VENUE	206	A
CHANGE, ORGANIZATIONAL	120	A
CHANGE, RESISTANCE TO	120	A
CHANNEL CAPACITY	455	B
CHANNEL COMMANDS	649	B
CHANNEL ISLANDS	790	B
CHANNELS	441	B
CHAOS	234	A
CHAPLINSKY VS. NEW HAMPSHIRE (1942)	674	B
CHARACTER	138	A
CHARACTER ASSASSIN	185	A
CHARACTERISTICS	129	A
CHARCOALS	825	B
CHARCOT, JEAN	736	B
CHARDIN, SIR JOHN	736	B
CHARGE	624	B
CHARGE D'AFFAIRES	185	A
CHARGE TO THE JURY	234	A
CHARISMA	114	A
CHARISMATIC LEADERSHIP	181	A
CHARITY	575	B
CHARLEMAGNE	266	A
CHARLES I OF ENGLAND	269	A
CHARLES II OF ENGLAND	269	A
CHARLES IV, EMPEROR	691	B
CHARLES MARTEL	706	B
CHARLES RIVER BRIDGE VS. WARREN BRIDGE (1937)	677	B
CHARLES THE GREAT	683	B
CHARLES V	691	B
CHARLIE	562	B
CHARLIE REGAN	706	B
CHARMONT, JOSEPH	706	B
CHARTER	225	A
CHARTER COLONY	162	A

CHARTER OF LABOR	811	B	CHICKEN IN EVERY POT	833	B
CHARTER OF PUNTA DEL ESTE	252	A	CHIEF	191	A
CHARTER OF RIGHTS	252	A	CHIEF ADMINISTRATIVE OFFICER	184	A
CHARTER OF THE UNITED NATIONS	194	A	CHIEF BURGOMASTER	562	B
CHARTER REVISION	212	A	CHIEF EXECUTIVE	181	A
CHARTER-OF-DEMOCRACY SPEECH	624	B	CHIEF JUSTICE OF THE SUPREME	181	A
CHARTER, CITY	206	A	COURT		
CHARTIST MOVEMENT	171	A	CHIEF LEGISLATOR	184	A
CHARTRES	790	B	CHIEF MAGISTRATE	184	A
CHASE, SAMUEL PORTLAND	706	B	CHIEF OF NAVAL OPERATIONS	185	A
CHASE, STUART	684	B	CHIEF OF PROTOCOL	185	A
CHATAUQUA MOVEMENT	575	B	CHIEF OF STAFF	182	A
CHATEAUBRIAND, FRANCOIS	706	B	CHIEF OF STATE	181	A
CHATTEL MORTGAGE	575	B	CHIEFS OF MISSION	541	B
CHAUCER	271	A	CHILD	548	B
CHAUVINISM	118	A	CHILD DISCIPLINE	433	B
CHAVEZ, CESAR	263	A	CHILD LABOR	219	A
CHEAP LABOR	191	A	CHILD LABOR AMENDMENT	219	A
CHEAP MONEY	243	A	CHILD LABOR LAWS	212	A
CHEATER	555	B	CHILD REARING PRACTICES	141	A
CHEBAB, GENERAL FUAD	706	B	CHILD WELFARE	599	B
CHECK-OFF SYSTEM	234	A	CHILD, IRVIN L.	706	B
CHECKERS SPEECH	243	A	CHILDE, PROF. GORDON	706	B
CHECKOFF	575	B	CHILDHOOD PLAY GROUPS	497	B
CHECKROOM	793	B	CHILDHOOD SOCIALIZATION	115	A
CHECKS-AND-BALANCES	113	A	CHILDREN	562	B
CHEESEPARING	838	B	CHILDREN'S BUREAU	467	B
CHEF DE CABINET	541	B	CHILDRENS ALLOWANCE	599	B
CHEKA	481	B	CHILDS, HARWOOD L.	706	B
CHEMICAL INDUSTRY	481	B	CHILDS, RICHARD S.	736	B
CHEMICAL WARFARE	207	A	CHILE	274	A
CHEMISTRY	448	B	CHILES, LAWTON MAINOR, JR.	706	B
CHEMISTS	555	B	CHILIASTIC	441	B
CHEMURGY	448	B	CHILPERIC, HANDICAPS OF	736	B
CHEN PO-TA	691	B	CHILTERN HUNDREDS	797	B
CHEQUERS	793	B	CHIN, ROBERT	736	B
CHERNOV, V.	706	B	CHINA	273	A
CHERNYSHEVSKY, N.	706	B	CHINA INCIDENT	599	B
CHEROKEE CASES	674	B	CHINA LOBBY	152	A
CHEROKEE OUTLET	821	B	CHINA SEA	277	A
CHEROKEE STRIP	793	B	CHINA WATCHERS	185	A
CHERVENKOV, V.	706	B	CHINA WHITE PAPER	285	A
CHESTERFIELD, LORD	706	B	CHINA, COMMUNIST	273	A
CHESTERTON, GILBERT K.	706	B	CHINA, NATIONALIST	273	A
CHETNIKS	497	B	CHINA, NATIONALIST (TAIWAN)	273	A
CHEYNEY, EDWARD P.	706	B	CHINA, PRC (POLITICAL SYSTEM)	146	A
CHI-SQUARE TEST	117	A	CHINA, REPUBLIC OF	149	A
CHIANG CHING	691	B	CHINESE	166	A
CHIANG KAI-SHEK	262	A	CHINESE CHANGCHUN RAILWAY	821	B
CHIANG KAI-SHEK, MME.	264	A	CHINESE COMMUNIST LEAGUE	467	B
CHIANG-LI-CH'UN	706	B	CHINESE COMMUNIST PARTY (CCP)	145	A
CHIANG, MENG-LIN	706	B	CHINESE COMMUNIST YOUTH	171	A
CHICAGO	275	A	LEAGUE		
CHICANO	158	A	CHINESE CONSTITUTION OF 1946	575	B
CHICANO POLITICS	212	A	CHINESE EASTERN RAILWAY	467	B
CHICHESTER-CLARK, MAJOR JAMES	706	B	CHINESE EXCLUSION ACTS	212	A

CHINESE GREAT WALL	287	A
CHINESE REVOLUTION OF 1911	219	A
CHINESE-JAPANESE WAR	219	A
CHINESE-RUSSIAN AGREEMENTS OF 1945	252	A
CHINOY, ELY	736	B
CHIP-IN-PORRIDGE POLITICIAN	562	B
CHIPLUNKAR, VISHNU KHRISHNA	736	B
CHISEL	624	B
CHISHOLM VS. GEORGIA (1793)	672	B
CHIVALRY	434	B
CHOATE, RUFUS	736	B
CHOCTAW (PEOPLE)	515	B
CHOFAR (RAM'S HORN)	825	B
CHOICE	212	A
CHOICE NOT AN ECHO	291	A
CHOLERA	821	B
CHOMSKY, N.	271	A
CHORNOVIL, VYACHESLAV	706	B
CHOSEN FREEHOLDER	548	B
CHOU EN-LAI	262	A
CHOW CHOW	838	B
CHRIMES, J. B.	706	B
CHRIST	263	A
CHRISTIAN ANARCHISM	135	A
CHRISTIAN DEMOCRAT	152	A
CHRISTIAN DEMOCRATIC PARTY	152	A
CHRISTIAN DEMOCRATIC UNION (CDU)	162	A
CHRISTIAN FRONT	497	B
CHRISTIAN HISTORICAL UNION	497	B
CHRISTIAN MOBILIZERS	515	B
CHRISTIAN SOCIAL PARTY	171	A
CHRISTIAN SOCIALISM	129	A
CHRISTIAN SOCIALIST PARTY	166	A
CHRISTIAN TOTALITARIANISM	141	A
CHRISTIAN TRADE UNIONS	171	A
CHRISTIANITY	125	A
CHRISTIANS	162	A
CHRISTIE, RICHARD	736	B
CHROME	825	B
CHRONIC CAMPAIGNER	555	B
CHRONICLES	811	B
CHRONOLOGY	138	A
CHRYSANTHEMUM	821	B
CHRYSIPPUS	736	B
CHU TEH, MARSHAL	706	B
CHUNGKING	282	A
CHURCH	467	B
CHURCH FATHERS	541	B
CHURCH OF ENGLAND	152	A
CHURCH OF FINLAND	515	B
CHURCH-BURNER	562	B
CHURCH-STATE RELATIONS	120	A
CHURCH, FRANK	269	A
CHURCHILL, SIR WINSTON LEONARD SPENCER	261	A
CIANO. GALEAZZO	691	B
CICERO, MARCUS TULLIUS	684	B
CIDERITE	516	B
CIENTIFICOS	516	B
CIGARETTE HOLDER SYMBOL	843	B
CINCINNATI, SOCIETY OF THE	497	B
CINCINNATUS OF THE WEST	706	B
CIPHER	822	B
CIRCLE	481	B
CIRCUIT COURT	155	A
CIRCUIT COURT OF APPEALS	149	A
CIRCUIT COURT, STATE	158	A
CIRCULARITY	138	A
CIRCULATION	649	B
CIRCULATION OF ELITES	129	A
CIRCUMLOCUTION	599	B
CIRCUMLOCUTION OFFICE (CIRCUMLOCUTIONIST)	838	B
CIRCUMSTANTIAL EVIDENCE	207	A
CITATION	225	A
CITIES	152	A
CITIZEN	181	A
CITIZEN KING	548	B
CITIZEN OF THE WORLD	191	A
CITIZENRY	183	A
CITIZENS COMMITTEE	176	A
CITIZENS TICKETS	481	B
CITIZENS UNION OF NEW YORK CITY	467	B
CITIZENSHIP	181	A
CITIZENSHIP DENATURALIZATION	575	B
CITIZENSHIP DUAL NATURE	184	A
CITIZENSHIP PAPERS	284	A
CITIZENSHIP TRAINING	234	A
CITIZENSHIP, EXPATRIATION	252	A
CITIZENSHIP, LOSS OF	207	A
CITY	152	A
CITY ATTORNEY	185	A
CITY CHARTER	200	A
CITY COMMISSIONERS	183	A
CITY COUNCIL	146	A
CITY COURT	158	A
CITY GOVERNMENT, COMMISSION PLAN	196	A
CITY GOVERNMENT, COUNCIL-MANAGER PLAN	195	A
CITY GOVERNMENT, MAYOR-ADMINISTRATOR PLAN	195	A
CITY GOVERNMENT, MAYOR-COUNCIL PLAN	195	A
CITY GOVERNMENT, STRONG MAYOR PLAN	195	A
CITY GOVERNMENT, WEAK MAYOR PLAN	196	A
CITY HALL	287	A

CITY MANAGER	181	A	CIVIL SERVICE REFORM	212	A
CITY MANAGER PLAN	194	A	CIVIL SERVICE REFORM ACT	225	A
CITY OF GOD	283	A	CIVIL SERVICE RETIREMENT PLANS	599	B
CITY OF GOLD	793	B	CIVIL SERVICE SYSTEM	196	A
CITY PLANNING	198	A	CIVIL SERVICE, INTERNATIONAL	166	A
CITY RECORD	808	B	CIVIL SERVICE, REFORMS	234	A
CITY-COUNTY CONSOLIDATION	207	A	CIVIL SUIT	212	A
CITY-COUNTY SEPARATION	225	A	CIVIL SUPREMACY	219	A
CITY-MANAGER GOVERNMENT	146	A	CIVIL WAR	194	A
CITY-STATES, GREEK	149	A	CIVIL WAR AMENDMENTS	207	A
CIVIC	184	A	CIVIL WORKS ADMINISTRATION (CWA)	497	B
CIVIC EDUCATION	129	A			
CIVIC TRAINING	252	A	CIVIL-MILITARY RELATIONS	118	A
CIVICS COURSES	243	A	CIVILIAN	183	A
CIVIL	184	A	CIVILIAN CONSERVATION CORPS (CCC)	162	A
CIVIL AERONAUTICS ADMINISTRATION (CAA)	162	A			
			CIVILIAN CONTROL	207	A
CIVIL AERONAUTICS BOARD (CAB)	162	A	CIVILIAN PRODUCT ADMINISTRATION (CPA)	516	B
CIVIL AFFAIRS OFFICER (U.S. ARMY OR NAVY)	548	B			
			CIVILIAN REVIEW	212	A
CIVIL CASE	260	A	CIVILIAN REVIEW BOARDS	166	A
CIVIL CODE	203	A	CIVILIZATION	122	A
CIVIL DEFENSE	207	A	CIVISM	448	B
CIVIL DEFENSE ADMINISTRATION, FEDERAL	176	A	CLAIM	234	A
			CLAN	166	A
CIVIL DEFENSE SERVICE	467	B	CLARENDON, EDWARD HYDE	706	B
CIVIL DISOBEDIENCE	194	A	CLARIFICATION	252	A
CIVIL DISORDERS	203	A	CLARK MEMORANDUM	285	A
CIVIL INTERN	562	B	CLARK, JOHN M.	706	B
CIVIL JURISDICTION	212	A	CLARKE PAPERS	811	B
CIVIL LAW (JUS CIVILE)	195	A	CLARKE, EDWIN L.	736	B
CIVIL LAW SYSTEM	125	A	CLARKE, WILLIAM	706	B
CIVIL LIBERTIES	194	A	CLASS	146	A
CIVIL LIST	807	B	CLASS ACTION	212	A
CIVIL PARTY	624	B	CLASS CONFLICT	115	A
CIVIL RIGHTS	194	A	CLASS CONSCIOUSNESS	120	A
CIVIL RIGHTS ACT OF 1870	234	A	CLASS LEGISLATION	219	A
CIVIL RIGHTS ACT OF 1871	243	A	CLASS STRUGGLE	117	A
CIVIL RIGHTS ACT OF 1875	219	A	CLASS WAR	200	A
CIVIL RIGHTS ACT OF 1957	212	A	CLASSICAL ECONOMICS	119	A
CIVIL RIGHTS ACT OF 1960	207	A	CLASSICAL THEORY	115	A
CIVIL RIGHTS ACT OF 1964	198	A	CLASSICISM	434	B
CIVIL RIGHTS ACT OF 1968	212	A	CLASSIFICATION	119	A
CIVIL RIGHTS ACTS OF 1866	212	A	CLASSIFICATION OF CITIES	252	A
CIVIL RIGHTS CASES	260	A	CLASSIFIED MATERIAL	283	A
CIVIL RIGHTS COMMISSION, FEDERAL	152	A	CLASSIFIED SERVICE	481	B
			CLASSIFIED TAX	576	B
CIVIL RIGHTS DIVISION	162	A	CLASSLESS SOCIETY	146	A
CIVIL RIGHTS MOVEMENT	147	A	CLAUSE	576	B
CIVIL RIGHTS MOVEMENT	147	A	CLAUSEWITZ, KARL VON	263	A
CIVIL RIGHTS ORGANIZATIONS	155	A	CLAY WHIG	171	A
CIVIL SERVICE	198	A	CLAY, CASSIUS	271	A
CIVIL SERVICE ACT OF 1940	234	A	CLAY, GENERAL LUCIUS	691	B
CIVIL SERVICE ASSEMBLY	497	B	CLAY, HENRY	263	A
CIVIL SERVICE COMMISSION	158	A	CLAYBANKS	562	B
CIVIL SERVICE EXAMINATIONS	207	A	CLAYTON ANTI-TRUST ACT (1914)	225	A

CLAYTON-BULWER TREATY	576	B
CLEAN AIR AMENDMENTS	252	A
CLEAN BILL	576	B
CLEAN SWEEP	291	A
CLEANTHES	736	B
CLEAR AND PRESENT DANGER DOCTRINE	195	A
CLEAR EVERYTHING WITH SIDNEY	843	B
CLEARANCE	576	B
CLEARING AGREEMENT	649	B
CLEARING UNIONS, INTERNATIONAL	516	B
CLEAVAGE	225	A
CLEAVER, ELDRIDGE	266	A
CLEISTHENES, CONSTITUTION OF	649	B
CLEMENCEAU, GEORGES	263	A
CLEMENCY	203	A
CLEMENS, SAMUEL	267	A
CLEMENT VI, POPE	737	B
CLEMENTIS, VLADO	737	B
CLERICALISM	135	A
CLERICIS LAICOS (LAY CLERGY)	555	B
CLERICO-FASCISM	434	B
CLERK	548	B
CLERK OF THE COURT	189	A
CLEVELAND, FREDERICK A.	706	B
CLEVELAND, PRESIDENT GROVER	263	A
CLIENT	185	A
CLIENTELISM	141	A
CLIFFORD, CLARK	267	A
CLIMATE	599	B
CLINE, HOWARD F.	737	B
CLINICAL METHOD	141	A
CLINTONIANS	497	B
CLIQUE	158	A
CLIVE, ROBERT	737	B
CLIVEDEN SET	516	B
CLOAKROOM	275	A
CLOSE LINKS	649	B
CLOSED (AND OPEN) SHOP	150	A
CLOSED AIR DOCTRINE	624	B
CLOSED FRONTIER	280	A
CLOSED PRIMARY	195	A
CLOSED SEA	278	A
CLOSED SEASON	624	B
CLOSED SESSION	219	A
CLOSED SESSION OF CONGRESS	225	A
CLOSED SHOP	152	A
CLOSED SYSTEM	117	A
CLOSING	624	B
CLOSING RANKS	291	A
CLOSURE RULE	207	A
CLOTH COAT	835	B
CLOTHING ALLOWANCE	599	B
CLOTURE RULE	198	A
CLOUD NO BIGGER THAN A MAN'S HAND	835	B
CLOUT	291	A
CLOVIS	691	B
CLOVIS II	691	B
CLUB	176	A
CLUBMEN	497	B
CLUES	599	B
CLUNIAC REFORMS	624	B
CO-PROSPERITY SPHERE, EAST ASIA	277	A
CO-SIGNATORY	189	A
COACH DRIVER THEORY	624	B
COACHING	624	B
COAL	819	B
COAL AND IRON POLICE	497	B
COAL AND STEEL POOL	467	B
COAL COMMITTEE (ECE)	481	B
COAL MINES ADMINISTRATION	481	B
COAL MINES COMMITTEE (ILO)	481	B
COAL MINING	599	B
COALING STATION	280	A
COALITION	145	A
COALITION FORMATION	117	A
COALITION GOVERNMENT	145	A
COAST AND GEODETIC SURVEY	176	A
COAST GUARD ACADEMY	171	A
COAST GUARD, UNITED STATES	166	A
COASTAL DEFENSE	243	A
COASTING TRADE	599	B
COAT OF ARMS	817	B
COATTAIL EFFECT	127	A
COATTAIL THEORY	125	A
COBALT	288	A
COBB, FRANK I.	707	B
COBBAN, ALFRED	692	B
COBELLIGERENCY	243	A
COCA LEAF	819	B
COCAINE	817	B
COCHIN CHINESE REPUBLIC	171	A
COCHRAN VS. LOUISIANA (1930)	672	B
COCKPIT OF EUROPE	282	A
COCKTAIL PARTY	624	B
CODE	234	A
CODE AUTHORITY	191	A
CODE CIVIL	219	A
CODE NAPOLEON	207	A
CODE OF FAIR COMPETITION	252	A
CODE OF FEDERAL REGULATIONS (CFR)	599	B
CODE OF HAMMURABI	212	A
CODE OF MILITARY JUSTICE	212	A
CODE OF THE UNITED STATES	225	A
CODFISH AND CABBAGE TICKET	497	B
CODFISH ARISTOCRACY	497	B
CODIFICATION	207	A
CODING	132	A
COEFFICIENT OF CORRELATION	119	A
COEFFICIENT OF REPRODUCIBILITY	127	A

COERCION	119	A	COLLEGE	481	B
COEXISTENCE, PEACEFUL	194	A	COLLEGE DE FRANCE	497	B
COFFEE HOUSE POLITICIAN	548	B	COLLEGE GRADUATES	548	B
COFFEE-KLATSCH CAMPAIGN	576	B	COLLEGE LIBRE DES SCIENCES	497	B
COFFIN HANDBILL	807	B	SOCIALES ET ECONOMIQUES		
COGNITION	122	A	COLLEGE OF CARDINALS	158	A
COGNITIVE RATIONALISM	138	A	COLLEGE OF COMMISSIONERS	498	B
COGNITIVE STRUCTURE	127	A	COLLIGATION	441	B
COGNITIVISM	441	B	COLLINGWOOD, R.G.	692	B
COHEN, MORRIS R.	692	B	COLLOQUY	576	B
COHENS VS. VIRGINIA (1821)	672	B	COLLUSION	219	A
COHERENCE	132	A	COLLUSIVE BIDDING	252	A
COHESION	127'	A	COLOGNE WHIG	555	B
COHORT	132	A	COLOMBIA	278	A
COHORT ANALYSIS	132	A	COLOMBO PLAN	226	A
COIMPERIUM	481	B	COLONEL BLIMP	692	B
COIN	817	B	COLONELISM	141	A
COINAGE	252	A	COLONIAL	158	A
COINS FINANCIAL SCHOOL	497	B	COLONIAL AGENT	541	B
COKE, SIR EDWARD	684	B	COLONIAL COURTS	171	A
COKER, FRANCIS W.	707	B	COLONIAL DEVELOPMENT	481	B
COLD WAR	194	A	CORPORATION (GREAT BRITAIN)		
COLD WATER	838	B	COLONIAL GOVERNMENTS	147	A
COLE, G.D.H.	269	A	COLONIAL LAW	243	A
COLE, GEORGE	692	B	COLONIAL OFFICE	166	A
COLE, R. TAYLOR	692	B	COLONIAL SYSTEM	120	A
COLEGIADO	497	B	COLONIAL TERRITORIES	274	A
COLEGROVE, KENNETH	707	B	COLONIALISM	114	A
COLEMAN VS. MILLER (1939)	674	B	COLONIES	155	A
COLEMAN, JAMES S.	269	A	COLONIZATION	200	A
COLERIDGE, S.T.	692	B	COLONNA, EGIDIUS	707	B
COLGROVE VS. GREEN (1946)	261	A	COLONY	152	A
COLINS, I.	707	B	COLOR	822	B
COLLABORATOR	185	A	COLOR LINE	243	A
COLLAPSE	624	B	COLOR METAPHORS	838	B
COLLECTION	624	B	COLORADO	278	A
COLLECTIVE	150	A	COLORADO RIVER COMPACT	226	A
COLLECTIVE AGREEMENTS	243	A	COLORATION	448	B
COLLECTIVE BARGAINING	200	A	COLORED	176	A
COLLECTIVE DECISION RULE	141	A	COLOSSUS OF THE NORTH	171	A
COLLECTIVE DECISIONS	125	A	COLUMBA, SAINT	707	B
COLLECTIVE EGOTISM	448	B	COLUMBANUS, SAINT	707	B
COLLECTIVE FARM	150	A	COLUMBIA RIVER COMPACT	252	A
COLLECTIVE GOODS	132	A	COLUMBIA UNIVERSITY	176	A
COLLECTIVE GUARANTEE	243	A	COLUMBIANS, INC.	498	B
COLLECTIVE LEADERSHIP	122	A	COLUMBUS DAY	576	B
COLLECTIVE NATURALIZATION	252	A	COLUMBUS, CHRISTOPHER	264	A
COLLECTIVE RECOGNITION	243	A	COMBAT	234	A
COLLECTIVE REPRESENTATION	576	B	COMBAT AREA	278	A
COLLECTIVE RESPONSIBILITY	203	A	COMBATANT	185	A
COLLECTIVE SECURITY	196	A	COMBINATION IN RESTRAINT OF	166	A
COLLECTIVISM	120	A	TRADE		
COLLECTOR OF INTERNAL REVENUE	187	A	COMBINATORY-LOGIC	141	A
COLLECTOR OF TAXES	189	A	COMBINE	252	A
COLLECTOR OF THE CUSTOMS	191	A	COMBINED FOOD BOARD	516	B
COLLECTOR VS. DAY (1871)	674	B			

COMBINED PRODUCTION AND RESOURCES BOARD	516	B
COMBINED RAW MATERALS BOARD	516	B
COME NOW, AND LET US REASON TOGETHER	835	B
COME-OUTER	843	B
COMEDIAN	562	B
COMEDY	650	B
COMICS	811	B
COMINFORM (ALSO, INFORMATION BUREAU OF COMMUNIST PARTIES AND WORKERS)	155	A
COMING MAN	563	B
COMINTERN (ALSO, COMMUNIST INTERNATIONAL)	148	A
COMITE DES FORGES	516	B
COMITY	243	A
COMITY CLAUSE	576	B
COMMAND	234	A
COMMAND PAPER	808	B
COMMANDER-IN-CHIEF	181	A
COMMEMORATION	624	B
COMMENDATION, FEUDAL	650	B
COMMENSURABILITY	624	B
COMMERCE	127	A
COMMERCE AND SLAVE TRADE COMPROMISE	599	B
COMMERCE CLAUSE	203	A
COMMERCE COURT	498	B
COMMERCE POWER	207	A
COMMERCIAL AGREEMENT	252	A
COMMERCIAL BANK	176	A
COMMERCIAL PAPER	289	A
COMMERCIAL REVOLUTION	252	A
COMMERCIAL TREATY	252	A
COMMISSAIRE DU GOUVERNEMENT	555	B
COMMISSAR	185	A
COMMISSARIAT	541	B
COMMISSARIAT FOR ADMINISTRATIVE REFORM (BELGIUM)	516	B
COMMISSARIAT FOR NATIONAL AFFAIRS (USSR)	481	B
COMMISSARY	481	B
COMMISSION (BOARD)	171	A
COMMISSION FOR CONVENTIONAL ARMAMENTS	498	B
COMMISSION FOR SOCIAL DEVELOPMENT	516	B
COMMISSION FOR TECHNICAL COOPERATION IN AFRICA	498	B
COMMISSION FOR UNIFICATION AND REHABILITATION OF KOREA	481	B
COMMISSION FORM	467	B
COMMISSION GOVERNMENT	171	A
COMMISSION OF FINE ARTS	516	B
COMMISSION OF INQUIRY (ENQUIRY)	162	A
COMMISSION ON CIVIL RIGHTS	166	A
COMMISSION ON INTERNATIONAL COMMODITY TRADE	516	B
COMMISSION ON NARCOTIC DRUGS	498	B
COMMISSION ON THE STATUS OF WOMEN	166	A
COMMISSION PLAN	226	A
COMMISSION PLAN OF CITY GOVERNMENT	219	A
COMMISSION-MANAGER PLAN	200	A
COMMISSIONED OFFICER	191	A
COMMISSIONER	191	A
COMMISSIONER OF EDUCATION	541	B
COMMISSIONER OF INTERNAL REVENUE	185	A
COMMISSIONERS, FEDERAL	187	A
COMMISSIONS (GOVERNMENTAL)	171	A
COMMISSIONS ON INTERSTATE COOPERATION	516	B
COMMISSIONS, UNITED STATES REGULATORY	166	A
COMMITMENT	252	A
COMMITTED	600	B
COMMITTED DELEGATES	183	A
COMMITTEE	152	A
COMMITTEE CHAIRMAN	183	A
COMMITTEE MEETINGS	243	A
COMMITTEE OF CONGRESS	147	A
COMMITTEE OF CORRESPONDENCE	158	A
COMMITTEE OF FORTY-EIGHT	516	B
COMMITTEE OF FOUR	498	B
COMMITTEE OF IMPERIAL DEFENSE	516	B
COMMITTEE OF MINISTERS	467	B
COMMITTEE OF PRESIDENTS	498	B
COMMITTEE OF PUBLIC SAFETY	171	A
COMMITTEE OF SUPPLY	516	B
COMMITTEE OF THE WHOLE	155	A
COMMITTEE OF THE WHOLE HOUSE	150	A
COMMITTEE OF UNION AND PROGRESS	516	B
COMMITTEE OF WAYS AND MEANS	147	A
COMMITTEE OF 24 (UN)	481	B
COMMITTEE ON ACCOUNT	516	B
COMMITTEE ON ADMINISTRATION MANAGEMENT (U.S.)	498	B
COMMITTEE ON AGRICULTURAL PROBLEMS	516	B
COMMITTEE ON COMMITTEES	150	A
COMMITTEE ON CONTRIBUTION (GA)	498	B
COMMITTEE ON CREDENTIALS	176	A
COMMITTEE ON DECOLONIZATION (COMMITTEE OF 24)	171	A
COMMITTEE ON ECONOMIC SECURITY	516	B

COMMITTEE ON FAIR EMPLOYMENT PRACTICES	176	A	COMMONWEALTH DEVELOPMENT CORPORATION	517	B
COMMITTEE ON GAS	498	B	COMMONWEALTH ECONOMY COMMITTEE	517	B
COMMITTEE ON INTELLECTUAL COOPERATION	516	B	COMMONWEALTH GRANTS COMMISSION (AUSTRALIA)	498	B
COMMITTEE ON POLITICAL EDUCATION (COPE)	155	A	COMMONWEALTH IMMIGRATION ACTS (U.K.)	576	B
COMMITTEE ON PRIVILEGES AND IMMUNITIES	481	B	COMMONWEALTH LEGAL ADVISORY SERVICE	517	B
COMMITTEE ON RECORDS OF WAR ADMINISTRATION (U.S.)	516	B	COMMONWEALTH OF NATIONS	158	A
COMMITTEE ON RULES	147	A	COMMONWEALTH SOCIETY	498	B
COMMITTEE ON STANDING ORDERS	516	B	COMMONWEALTH VS. DAVIS (1895)	677	B
COMMITTEE ON TECHNICAL ASSISTANCE	516	B	COMMONWEALTH VS. HUNT (1842)	677	B
			COMMUNAL ANOMIE	448	B
COMMITTEE ON THE ADMISSION OF NEW MEMBERS	516	B	COMMUNAL COUNCIL	482	B
			COMMUNAL ELECTIONS	252	A
COMMITTEE ON WATER PROBLEMS	516	B	COMMUNALISM	135	A
COMMITTEE ROOM	278	A	COMMUNCIATIONS THEORY	120	A
COMMITTEE SYSTEM	119	A	COMMUNE (FRANCE)	155	A
COMMITTEE TO DEFEND AMERICA BY AIDING THE ALLIES	498	B	COMMUNES, CHINA (PRC)	150	A
			COMMUNES, MEDIAEVAL	467	B
COMMODITY	288	A	COMMUNICATION	129	A
COMMODITY AGREEMENT	226	A	COMMUNICATION FLOW	122	A
COMMODITY CREDIT CORPORATION (CCC)	171	A	COMMUNICATION MEDIA	147	A
			COMMUNICATION TECHNIQUES	130	A
COMMODITY EXCHANGE ACT	576	B	COMMUNICATION THEORY	115	A
COMMODITY EXCHANGE ADMINISTRATION	517	B	COMMUNICATION, POLITICAL	119	A
			COMMUNICATIONS ACTS	600	B
COMMODITY STABILIZATION SERVICE	517	B	COMMUNICATIONS INDUSTRY	467	B
			COMMUNICATIONS SATELLITE	288	A
COMMODUS	707	B	COMMUNICATIONS, INTERNATIONAL	234	A
COMMON	282	A	COMMUNICATOR	187	A
COMMON ASSEMBLY	467	B	COMMUNIQUE	285	A
COMMON CARRIER	287	A	COMMUNISM	113	A
COMMON CAUSE	152	A	COMMUNIST CONTROL ACT (1954)	243	A
COMMON COUNCIL	482	B	COMMUNIST ECONOMIC ORGANIZATION EAST EUROPE	176	A
COMMON CRIMINAL LAW	576	B	COMMUNIST FRONT ORGANIZATIONS	162	A
COMMON GOOD	125	A			
COMMON HERD	555	B	COMMUNIST INTERNATIONAL (COMINTERN)	148	A
COMMON LAW	194	A			
COMMON MAN	183	A	COMMUNIST MANIFESTO	283	A
COMMON MARKET	147	A	COMMUNIST PARTY	144	A
COMMON ORGANIZATION OF AFRICA AND MALAGASY (OCAM)	498	B	COMMUNIST PARTY (USA)	148	A
			COMMUNIST PARTY CASES	260	A
COMMON PLEAS	252	A	COMMUNIST PARTY OF FRANCE	162	A
COMMON ROLL	482	B	COMMUNIST PARTY VS. SUBVERSIVE ACTIVITIES CONTROL BOARD (1956)	671	B
COMMON SENSE	132	A			
COMMON STEP	650	B			
COMMON-LAW MARRIAGE	226	A	COMMUNIST PARTY, SOVIET UNION (CPSU)	145	A
COMMONS, HOUSE OF	146	A			
COMMONWEAL	166	A	COMMUNIST TERMINOLOGY	130	A
COMMONWEAL ARMY	498	B	COMMUNIST THIRD INTERNATIONAL	152	A
COMMONWEALTH	155	A	COMMUNIST YOUTH LEAGUE, CHINA (PRC)	171	A
COMMONWEALTH CLUB	517	B			
COMMONWEALTH COUNTRIES	152	A			

COMMUNITARIAN SOCIALISM	138	A
COMMUNITARIANISM	441	B
COMMUNITAS	285	A
COMMUNITY	147	A
COMMUNITY ACTION PROGRAM	207	A
COMMUNITY BUILDING	234	A
COMMUNITY CHEST	482	B
COMMUNITY DEVELOPMENT	203	A
COMMUNITY DEVELOPMENT CORPORATIONS	467	B
COMMUNITY FACILITIES ADMINISTRATION	498	B
COMMUNITY OF INTEREST	132	A
COMMUNITY OF THE RESURRECTION	517	B
COMMUNITY PARTICIPATION	132	A
COMMUNITY PLANNING COUNCILS	467	B
COMMUNITY POWER	200	A
COMMUNITY POWER STRUCTURE	117	A
COMMUNITY PROPERTY	287	A
COMMUNITY PROPERTY SYSTEM	226	A
COMMUNITY RELATIONS SERVICE	517	B
COMMUNITY SERVICES ADMINISTRATION	498	B
COMMUNITY STUDIES	284	A
COMMUNITY THEATRE	498	B
COMMUNITY TRUSTS	517	B
COMMUTATION	219	A
COMMUTE	243	A
COMORO ISLANDS	797	B
COMPACT	219	A
COMPACT OF FIFTH AVENUE	650	B
COMPACT THEORY	117	A
COMPAIGNE REPUBLICAINE DE SECURITE (CRS)	517	B
COMPANION	563	B
COMPANION BILLS	252	A
COMPANIONS STAR OF INDIA (CSI)	517	B
COMPANY	517	B
COMPANY UNION	166	A
COMPARABILITY	135	A
COMPARATIVE	138	A
COMPARATIVE ADMINISTRATION	123	A
COMPARATIVE ADVANTAGE (TRADE THEORY)	203	A
COMPARATIVE ANALYSIS	114	A
COMPARATIVE CONSTITUTIONAL LAW	130	A
COMPARATIVE GOVERNMENT	117	A
COMPARATIVE LAW	127	A
COMPARATIVE METHOD	117	A
COMPARATIVE POLITICS	114	A
COMPARISON	243	A
COMPASSION	441	B
COMPASSIONATE SAMARITANE OF WILLIAM WALWYN	811	B
COMPATIBILITY	141	A
COMPEL	576	B
COMPENSATED DOLLAR	600	B
COMPENSATING DUTY	600	B
COMPENSATION	226	A
COMPENSATION INSURANCE	624	B
COMPENSATORY SPENDING	243	A
COMPENSATORY TIME OFF	624	B
COMPERE-MOREL	737	B
COMPETENCE	625	B
COMPETENCY	252	A
COMPETENT AUTHORITY	189	A
COMPETITION	119	A
COMPETITIVE SYSTEM	127	A
COMPIEGNE FOREST	797	B
COMPLAINANT	189	A
COMPLEMENTAL MOTION	625	B
COMPLEMENTARITY	576	B
COMPLEMENTARY AGREEMENT	625	B
COMPLETENESS	455	B
COMPLEX ORGANIZATIONS	152	A
COMPLEX SOCIETIES	152	A
COMPLEX SYSTEMS	123	A
COMPLEXITY	576	B
COMPLIED LAWS	576	B
COMPLIMENTARY VOTE	600	B
COMPLY	226	A
COMPONENT	822	B
COMPOSITION	441	B
COMPOSSIBILITY	448	B
COMPOUND DUTIES	625	B
COMPREHENSION	135	A
COMPROMIS DARBITRAGE	625	B
COMPROMISE	203	A
COMPROMISE OF 1850	207	A
COMPROMISE OF 1877	234	A
COMPROMISSORY CLAUSE	576	B
COMPTROLLER	187	A
COMPTROLLER GENERAL OF THE UNITED STATES	186	A
COMPTROLLER OF THE CURRENCY	191	A
COMPTROLLER, STATE	186	A
COMPULSORY ARBITRATION	207	A
COMPULSORY EDUCATION	212	A
COMPULSORY JURISDICTION	212	A
COMPULSORY LABOR SERVICE	498	B
COMPULSORY LOANS	625	B
COMPULSORY MILITARY SERVICE	207	A
COMPULSORY SCHOOL ATTENDANCE	212	A
COMPULSORY TESTIMONY ACT OF 1954	600	B
COMPULSORY VACCINATION	576	B
COMPULSORY VOTING	200	A
COMPUTABILITY	441	B
COMPUTER	287	A
COMPUTER ANALYSIS	123	A

COMPUTER SIMULATION	119	A
COMRADE X	548	B
COMSOMOL	162	A
COMSYMP	189	A
COMTE, AUGUSTE	264	A
CONANT, JAMES B.	684	B
CONCEIVABILITY	449	B
CONCENTRATED EMPLOYMENT PROGRAM (CEP)	252	A
CONCENTRATION (OF ECONOMIC POWER)	200	A
CONCENTRATION CAMPS	286	A
CONCENTRATION, THEORY OF	141	A
CONCEPT	113	A
CONCEPTION	576	B
CONCEPTUAL FRAMEWORK	114	A
CONCEPTUALIZATION	117	A
CONCERT OF EUROPE	158	A
CONCESSION	234	A
CONCESSION SPEECH	243	A
CONCESSION THEORY	141	A
CONCHY	563	B
CONCILIAR THEORY OF THE CHURCH	434	B
CONCILIATION	125	A
CONCILIATION COMMISSION	482	B
CONCILIATION SERVICE	166	A
CONCLAVE	171	A
CONCLUSIONS	135	A
CONCORD	600	B
CONCORDAT	243	A
CONCORDAT OF WORMS	576	B
CONCORDAT OF 1929	253	A
CONCRETE	825	B
CONCURRENT JURISDICTION	212	A
CONCURRENT LEGISLATION	234	A
CONCURRENT MAJORITY	155	A
CONCURRENT POWER	219	A
CONCURRENT RESOLUTION	198	A
CONCURRENT VOICE	625	B
CONCURRING OPINION	207	A
CONDE	650	B
CONDEMNATION	576	B
CONDEMNATION AS PRIZE	833	B
CONDEMNATION PROCEEDINGS	226	A
CONDILLAC, ETIENNE BONNOT DE	737	B
CONDITION	253	A
CONDITIONAL	576	B
CONDITIONAL CONTRABAND	822	B
CONDITIONAL SURRENDER	212	A
CONDITIONED REFLEX	123	A
CONDITIONING	125	A
CONDOLE	625	B
CONDOLLE, ALPHONSE DE	737	B
CONDOMINIUM	650	B
CONDORCET, M.J.A.N.	707	B
CONDOTTIERI	563	B
CONDUCT	576	B
CONDUCT EMPLOYEE	563	B
CONFEDERACY	148	A
CONFEDERATE STATES OF AMERICA	152	A
CONFEDERATION	146	A
CONFEDERATION FRANCAISE DEMOCRATIQUE DU TRAVAIL	482	B
CONFEDERATION FRANCAISE DES TRAVAILLEURS CHRETIENS	498	B
CONFEDERATION GENERALE DU TRAVAIL (CGT)	171	A
CONFER	234	A
CONFEREE	191	A
CONFERENCE	243	A
CONFERENCE COMMITTEE	155	A
CONFERENCE COMMITTEE OF CONGRESS	158	A
CONFERENCE OF AFRICAN INDEPENDENT STATES	498	B
CONFERENCE OF EUROPEAN STATISTICIANS	517	B
CONFERENCE OF EXPERTS	498	B
CONFERENCE OF GOVERNORS	243	A
CONFERENCE OF NEW EMERGING FORCES (CONEFO)	576	B
CONFERENCE OF NON-NUCLEAR WEAPON STATES OF GENEVA	576	B
CONFERENCE OF THE COMMITTEE ON DISARMAMENT (CCD)	600	B
CONFERENCE OF 18-NATION DISARMAMENT COMMISSION (ENDC)	482	B
CONFERENCE ON HUMAN ENVIRONMENT	576	B
CONFERENCE SERVICES PROVIDED BY UN	625	B
CONFERENCES	577	B
CONFESSION	285	A
CONFESSIONAL PARTIES	166	A
CONFESSIONALISM	441	B
CONFIDENCE	141	A
CONFIDENCE GAME	625	B
CONFIDENTIAL NOTE	807	B
CONFIRMATION	200	A
CONFIRMATION OF APPOINTMENTS, CONGRESS	219	A
CONFISCATION	226	A
CONFLICT	114	A
CONFLICT BEHAVIOR	117	A
CONFLICT INTERACTION	434	B
CONFLICT MANAGEMENT	117	A
CONFLICT OF INTEREST	200	A
CONFLICT OF LAWS	219	A
CONFLICT REDUCTION	125	A
CONFLICT RESOLUTION	114	A

CONFLICT THEORY	113	A		CONKLIN, E. G.	737	B
CONFLICT, ORGANIZATIONAL	132	A		CONNALLY AMENDMENT	243	A
CONFLUENT SOCIETY	176	A		CONNECTICUT	282	A
CONFORMITY	130	A		CONNECTICUT COMPROMISE	226	A
CONFRONTATION	207	A		CONNOLLY, JAMES	684	B
CONFUCIANISM	132	A		CONQUERED TERRITORY	280	A
CONFUCIUS	267	A		CONQUERORS	541	B
CONGO	278	A		CONQUEST	234	A
CONGO (BRAZZAVILLE)	275	A		CONQUISTADOR	541	B
CONGO (KINSHASA)	275	A		CONRAD OF GELNHAUSEN	737	B
CONGO (LEOPOLDVILLE)	790	B		CONRAD, JOSEPH	707	B
CONGO BASIN TREATIES	625	B		CONSCIENCE	135	A
CONGO CREED	455	B		CONSCIENCE DEMOCRAT	498	B
CONGO CRISIS	219	A		CONSCIENCE MONEY	600	B
CONGRATULATION	650	B		CONSCIENCE WHIGS	517	B
CONGRATULATORY LETTER	808	B		CONSCIENTIOUS OBJECTION	207	A
CONGRESS (U.S.)	145	A		CONSCIENTIOUS OBJECTOR	183	A
CONGRESS CARD	822	B		CONSCIOUSNESS	441	B
CONGRESS OF BERLIN	243	A		CONSCRIPTION	207	A
CONGRESS OF INDUSTRIAL	155	A		CONSCRIPTION ACT	234	A
ORGANIZATIONS				CONSCRIPTION OF LABOR	243	A
CONGRESS OF RACIAL EQUALITY	152	A		CONSECRATION	434	B
(CORE)				CONSECUTIVE INTERPRETATION	600	B
CONGRESS OF VIENNA	219	A		CONSEIL D'ETAT (FRANCE)	162	A
CONGRESS PARTY	158	A		CONSEIL DE L'ENTENTE	467	B
CONGRESS PROCEEDINGS	219	A		CONSENSUS	117	A
CONGRESSIONAL AMENDMENT	219	A		CONSENSUS THEORY	120	A
CONGRESSIONAL CALENDAR	212	A		CONSENSUS-BUILDING	119	A
CONGRESSIONAL CAMPAIGN	155	A		CONSENT	207	A
COMMITTEE				CONSENT CALENDAR	212	A
CONGRESSIONAL CAUCUS	150	A		CONSENT OF THE GOVERNED	195	A
CONGRESSIONAL COMMITTEES	145	A		CONSENT, POPULAR	203	A
CONGRESSIONAL DIRECTORY	285	A		CONSEQUENCES	212	A
CONGRESSIONAL DISTRICT	273	A		CONSEQUENTIALISM	455	B
CONGRESSIONAL ETHICS	130	A		CONSERVATION	226	A
CONGRESSIONAL GOVERNMENT	150	A		CONSERVATION OF NATURAL	219	A
CONGRESSIONAL IMMUNITY	207	A		RESOURCES		
CONGRESSIONAL INVESTIGATING	155	A		CONSERVATISM	117	A
COMMITTEE				CONSERVATIVE	181	A
CONGRESSIONAL INVESTIGATIONS	207	A		CONSERVATIVE COALITION	155	A
CONGRESSIONAL JUNKETS	234	A		CONSERVATIVE COLLECTIVISM	141	A
CONGRESSIONAL LAWMAKING	212	A		CONSERVATIVE PARTY	150	A
CONGRESSIONAL MEDAL OF HONOR	289	A		CONSERVATIVE PARTY, BRITISH	158	A
CONGRESSIONAL PRIVILEGE	212	A		CONSIDERATIONS	822	B
CONGRESSIONAL QUARTERLY	283	A		CONSISTENCY	141	A
CONGRESSIONAL RECORD	284	A		CONSISTENT	441	B
CONGRESSIONAL REORGANIZATION	219	A		CONSOLATO DEL MARO	555	B
ACTS				CONSOLIDATE	577	B
CONGRESSIONAL RESEARCH	171	A		CONSOLIDATED CITY-COUNTY	155	A
SERVICE				GOVERNMENT		
CONGRESSIONAL RULES	207	A		CONSOLIDATED EDISON COMPANY	176	A
CONGRESSIONAL TOWNSHIP	498	B		CONSOLIDATED FUND	600	B
SYSTEM				CONSOLIDATED LAWS	577	B
CONGRESSMAN	182	A		CONSOLIDATED SCHOOLS	176	A
CONGRESSMAN AT LARGE	186	A		CONSOLIDATION	132	A
CONJUNCTION	441	B		CONSORT	189	A

CONSORTIUM	176	A
CONSPIRACY	219	A
CONSPIRACY THEORIES	130	A
CONSTABLE	191	A
CONSTABULARY	467	B
CONSTANCE (LAKE)	797	B
CONSTANT	434	B
CONSTANT, B.	737	B
CONSTANTINE	684	B
CONSTANTINE XIII, KING	692	B
CONSTANTINOPLE AGREEMENT	600	B
CONSTITUENCY	146	A
CONSTITUENT	182	A
CONSTITUENT ASSEMBLY	152	A
CONSTITUENT FUNCTION	234	A
CONSTITUENT POWER	219	A
CONSTITUTE	600	B
CONSTITUTIO ATONIANA	650	B
CONSTITUTION	196	A
CONSTITUTION (BONN), GERMANY	243	A
CONSTITUTION DAY	600	B
CONSTITUTION DOES NOT FOLLOW THE FLAG	833	B
CONSTITUTION OF ATHENS	243	A
CONSTITUTION OF SOVIET UNION	234	A
CONSTITUTION OF THE ITALIAN REPUBLIC	577	B
CONSTITUTION-MAKER	184	A
CONSTITUTION, BRITAIN	203	A
CONSTITUTION, FRANCE	226	A
CONSTITUTION, STATE	284	A
CONSTITUTION, UNITED STATES	194	A
CONSTITUTIONAL DEMOCRACY	148	A
CONSTITUTIONAL LAW	200	A
CONSTITUTIONAL AMENDMENT	200	A
CONSTITUTIONAL COMMISSION	166	A
CONSTITUTIONAL COMMITTEE	176	A
CONSTITUTIONAL CONGRESS	219	A
CONSTITUTIONAL CONSTRUCTION	219	A
CONSTITUTIONAL CONVENTION	198	A
CONSTITUTIONAL CONVENTION OF 1787	203	A
CONSTITUTIONAL CONVENTIONS, STATE	234	A
CONSTITUTIONAL COUNCIL, FRANCE	171	A
CONSTITUTIONAL COURTS	152	A
CONSTITUTIONAL DEMOCRATS OF RUSSIA	482	B
CONSTITUTIONAL DICTATORSHIP	155	A
CONSTITUTIONAL GOVERNMENT	145	A
CONSTITUTIONAL GUARANTEES	207	A
CONSTITUTIONAL HISTORY	130	A
CONSTITUTIONAL JURISDICTION	212	A
CONSTITUTIONAL LAW	196	A
CONSTITUTIONAL LIMITATIONS	207	A
CONSTITUTIONAL MAJORITY	150	A
CONSTITUTIONAL MONARCHY	146	A
CONSTITUTIONAL OFFICERS	183	A
CONSTITUTIONAL ORDER	219	A
CONSTITUTIONAL POWER	195	A
CONSTITUTIONAL REFERENDUM	219	A
CONSTITUTIONAL REFORM	207	A
CONSTITUTIONAL REVIEW	207	A
CONSTITUTIONAL REVISION	203	A
CONSTITUTIONAL RULES	207	A
CONSTITUTIONAL STATE	162	A
CONSTITUTIONAL UNION PARTY	482	B
CONSTITUTIONALISM	120	A
CONSTITUTIONALITY	196	A
CONSTITUTIVE SYSTEMS	138	A
CONSTRAINTS	243	A
CONSTRUCT	234	A
CONSTRUCTION	253	A
CONSTRUCTION INDUSTRY	176	A
CONSTRUCTIVISM	449	B
CONSUL	183	A
CONSUL ELECTUS	555	B
CONSUL GENERAL	183	A
CONSUL MISSUS	555	B
CONSULAR AGENT	189	A
CONSULAR FUNCTIONS	226	A
CONSULAR IMMUNITY	212	A
CONSULAR JURISDICTION	243	A
CONSULAR OFFICERS	171	A
CONSULAR PRIVILEGES AND IMMUNITIES	226	A
CONSULAR SERVICE	162	A
CONSULATE	286	A
CONSULT	253	A
CONSULTANTS	189	A
CONSULTATION	234	A
CONSULTATIVE ASSEMBLY	171	A
CONSULTATIVE COMMITTEE	467	B
CONSULTATIVE COMMONWEALTH	498	B
CONSULTIVE COMMITTEE FOR POSTAL STUDIES (CCPS)	517	B
CONSUMER	189	A
CONSUMER ADVISORY COUNCIL	176	A
CONSUMER AFFAIRS	253	A
CONSUMER AND MARKETING SERVICE	498	B
CONSUMER CREDIT PROTECTION ACT	243	A
CONSUMER LEGISLATION	226	A
CONSUMER PRICE INDEX	138	A
CONSUMER PROTECTION	219	A
CONSUMERS ADVISORY BOARD	499	B
CONSUMERS COOPERATIVE	171	A
CONSUMERS UNION OF THE UNITED STATES	482	B
CONSUMPTION TAX	243	A
CONTACT	625	B

CONTACT MINES	825	B	CONTROL COMMISSION	517	B
CONTAGION	650	B	CONTROL GROUP	150	A
CONTAINMENT POLICY	200	A	CONTROL-THEORY	138	A
CONTEMPLATION	449	B	CONTROLLED DIRECT	138	A
CONTEMPORARY	577	B	OBSERVATATION		
CONTEMPT	219	A	CONTROLLED DISARMAMENT	226	A
CONTEMPT OF CONGRESS	200	A	CONTROLLED ECONOMY	219	A
CONTEMPT OF COURT	212	A	CONTROLLER	186	A
CONTENT	449	B	CONTROLS	207	A
CONTENT ANALYSIS	114	A	CONTROVERSY	577	B
CONTEST	577	B	CONURBATION	793	B
CONTESTED ELECTION	203	A	CONVENE	253	A
CONTESTING DELEGATION	176	A	CONVENING	625	B
CONTEXT	138	A	CONVENTION	226	A
CONTEXTUAL ANALYSIS	130	A	CONVENTION ON INTERNATIONAL	625	B
CONTIGUITY	274	A	CIVIL AVIATION (1944)		
CONTIGUOUS ZONE, JURISDICTION	280	A	CONVENTION SYSTEM	219	A
CONTINENTAL ARMY UNITED	171	A	CONVENTIONAL ARMS	287	A
STATES (CONUS)			CONVENTIONAL WAR	219	A
CONTINENTAL CONGRESS	150	A	CONVENTIONS AND AGREEMENTS	577	B
CONTINENTAL SHELF	275	A	(UN)		
CONTINENTAL SYSTEM	234	A	CONVERGENCE	138	A
CONTINENTALISM	441	B	CONVERGENCE THEORY	125	A
CONTINENTS	790	B	CONVERSATIONS	600	B
CONTINGENCY	127	A	CONVERSE, PHILIP E.	266	A
CONTINGENT EXPENSE	600	B	CONVERSION	243	A
CONTINGENT FUND	600	B	CONVERSION PROCESS	135	A
CONTINUE	253	A	CONVERTIBILITY	226	A
CONTINUING ASSESSMENT	141	A	CONVICT	191	A
CONTINUISMO (CONTINUISM)	434	B	CONVICT LABOR	548	B
CONTINUITIES	441	B	CONVOCATION	253	A
CONTINUITY OF THE STATE	234	A	CONVOKE	577	B
CONTINUOUS VOYAGE DOCTRINE	253	A	CONVOY	817	B
CONTINUUM	127	A	CONWAY CABAL	517	B
CONTRABAND	287	A	CONWAY, MARTIN	737	B
CONTRACT	284	A	COODY (MEMBER OF FEDERALIST	517	B
CONTRACT ADMINISTRATORS	555	B	FACTION)		
CONTRACT CLAUSE	234	A	COOK, MARLOW WEBSTER	737	B
CONTRACT CLAUSE IN THE	226	A	COOK, THOMAS I.	707	B
CONSTITUTION			COOKIE PUSHER	555	B
CONTRACT LABOR	191	A	COOLEY VS. BOARD OF WARDENS	672	B
CONTRACT THEORY OF	120	A	(1852)		
GOVERNMENT			COOLEY, CHARLES	692	B
CONTRACT, FEUDAL	243	A	COOLIDGE, PRESIDENT CALVIN	264	A
CONTRACTING GOVERNMENTS	176	A	COOLING-OFF PERIOD	253	A
CONTRACTOR PERSONNEL	555	B	COOLING-OFF TREATY	600	B
CONTRACTORS	555	B	COONMANDERING	838	B
CONTRACTS, GOVERNMENT	284	A	COONSKIN ON THE WALL	843	B
CONTRACTUAL RIGHTS	234	A	COOPER-CHURCH AMENDMENT	577	B
CONTRADICTION	141	A	COOPER, JAMES FENIMORE	271	A
CONTRAPUNTAL PHRASES	455	B	COOPER, JOHN SHERMAN	684	B
CONTRATONIC POLITIES	517	B	COOPERACION POPULAR	517	B
CONTRIBUTION	600	B	COOPERATION	132	A
CONTRIBUTORS	541	B	COOPERATIVE	166	A
CONTRIBUTORY NEGLIGENCE	226	A	COOPERATIVE ECONOMY	243	A
CONTROL	142	A	COOPERATIVE EXTENSION SERVICE	499	B

COOPERATIVE FEDERALISM	125	A
COOPERATIVE MOVEMENT	226	A
COOPERATIVE PROJECTS	650	B
COOPERATIVE RESEARCH	138	A
COOPTATION	123	A
COORDINATES	123	A
COORDINATION	243	A
COORIENTATION	449	B
COP	189	A
COPERNICAN THEORY	123	A
COPERNICUS, NICHOLAS	264	A
COPPAGE VS. KANSAS (1915)	674	B
COPPER	289	A
COPPERHEAD	482	B
COPRA	819	B
COPYRIGHT	226	A
COPYRIGHT OFFICE	166	A
CORBETT, J.	737	B
CORBETT, PERCY E.	737	B
CORBIN, JOHN	737	B
CORDIAL ATMOSPHERE	600	B
CORDON SANITAIRE	226	A
CORFU CHANNEL CASE	261	A
CORINTH	793	B
CORMIER, ERNEST	737	B
CORMORANT	563	B
CORN DODGER	563	B
CORN LAWS	577	B
CORN PONE	822	B
CORN PRODUCTS REFINING CO. VS. FTC (1945)	674	B
CORNCRACKER STATE	797	B
CORNER	600	B
CORNERSTONE	822	B
CORNERSTONE SPEECH	625	B
CORNET	825	B
CORONATION	219	A
CORONER	189	A
CORONER'S JURY	171	A
CORPORAL PUNISHMENT	226	A
CORPORAL'S GUARD	482	B
CORPORATE BODY	176	A
CORPORATE REVOLUTION	243	A
CORPORATE STATE	155	A
CORPORATION	171	A
CORPORATION INCOME TAX	219	A
CORPORATISM	138	A
CORPORATIVE CHAMBER	482	B
CORPORATIVE REPRESENTATION	577	B
CORPOREITY	455	B
CORPS	467	B
CORPS OF ENGINEERS	166	A
CORPUS JURIS	226	A
CORRADINI, ENRICO	737	B
CORRECTION	577	B
CORRECTION OF THE MINUTES	234	A
CORRECTIONAL WORKERS	555	B
CORREGIDOR	280	A
CORRELATES	127	A
CORRELATION	117	A
CORRELATIVE METHOD	125	A
CORRESPONDENCE	808	B
CORRESPONDENCE COURSES	808	B
CORRIGAN VS. BUCKLEY (1926)	674	B
CORRIGIBILITY	650	B
CORRUPT PRACTICES ACT, FEDERAL	219	A
CORRUPT PRACTICES LAWS (U.S.)	219	A
CORRUPTIBILITY	243	A
CORRUPTION	219	A
CORRUPTION OF BLOOD	625	B
CORTES, HERNAN	271	A
CORTICO	650	B
CORTINES, ADOLFO RUIZ	737	B
CORVEE	650	B
CORWIN, EDWARD S.	271	A
COSGRAVE, LIAM	707	B
COSMIC	434	B
COSMIC SPACE LAW	577	B
COSMOGENISIS	650	B
COSMOGONY	442	B
COSMOLOGICAL-PROOF	449	B
COSMOLOGY	434	B
COSMOPOLITAN	790	B
COSMOPOLITANISM	138	A
COSMOS	793	B
COSPAR	517	B
COSSACK	467	B
COST	219	A
COST EFFECTIVENESS	125	A
COST OF LIVING COUNCIL (COLC)	152	A
COST REDUCTION	253	A
COST-BENEFIT ANALYSIS	117	A
COST-OF-LIVING ALLOWANCE	226	A
COST-OF-LIVING ESCALATOR	207	A
COST-PLUS CONTRACT	253	A
COST-PUSH	234	A
COSTA E SILVA, MARSHAL ARTUR DA	692	B
COSTA RICA	277	A
COSTA, J.	737	B
COTERIE	467	B
COTTAGE SYSTEM	577	B
COTTON	822	B
COTTON IS KING	833	B
COTTON STATES	277	A
COTTON TICKET	499	B
COTTON WHIGS	482	B
COTTON, JOHN	707	B
COTTON, NORRIS	707	B
COTTONOCRACY	517	B
COTY, RENE	707	B
COUGHLIN, CHARLES EDWARD	271	A

COULD-HAVE	455	B
COUNCIL	482	B
COUNCIL FOR AFRICAN AND MALAGASY AFFAIRS	499	B
COUNCIL FOR MUTUAL ECONOMIC ASSISTANCE	176	A
COUNCIL FOR NUCLEAR DISARMAMENT (CND)	176	A
COUNCIL OF APPOINTMENT	517	B
COUNCIL OF ASSOCIATION	517	B
COUNCIL OF BASEL	499	B
COUNCIL OF CENSORS	517	B
COUNCIL OF COMMISSARS	482	B
COUNCIL OF CONSTANCE	482	B
COUNCIL OF ECONOMIC ADVISERS (CEA)	155	A
COUNCIL OF ELDERS	482	B
COUNCIL OF EUROPE	158	A
COUNCIL OF EUROPEAN INDUSTRIAL FEDERATIONS (CEIF)	499	B
COUNCIL OF FOREIGN AFFAIRS	467	B
COUNCIL OF FOREIGN MINISTERS	171	A
COUNCIL OF FOUR	517	B
COUNCIL OF LABOUR (USSR)	467	B
COUNCIL OF MINISTERS (USSR)	155	A
COUNCIL OF MINISTERS, EUROPEAN COMMUNITY	158	A
COUNCIL OF MINISTERS, ITALY	162	A
COUNCIL OF MUTUAL ECONOMIC ASSISTANCE (COMECON)	158	A
COUNCIL OF NATIONAL DEFENSE	517	B
COUNCIL OF NATIONALITIES	171	A
COUNCIL OF NICAEA	176	A
COUNCIL OF NOTABLES	499	B
COUNCIL OF PEOPLES COMMISSARS	467	B
COUNCIL OF PRODUCERS	518	B
COUNCIL OF REPRESENTATIVES	176	A
COUNCIL OF REVISION	499	B
COUNCIL OF SOCIAL ADVISERS	518	B
COUNCIL OF STATE	171	A
COUNCIL OF STATE GOVERNMENTS (U.S.)	176	A
COUNCIL OF STATE, FRANCE	166	A
COUNCIL OF TEN, VENICE	518	B
COUNCIL OF THE ENTENTE	707	B
COUNCIL OF THE KINGDOM	482	B
COUNCIL OF THE LEAGUE OF NATIONS	158	A
COUNCIL OF THE ORGANIZATION OF AMERICAN STATES	152	A
COUNCIL OF THE REPUBLIC (FRANCE)	166	A
COUNCIL OF THE UNION (U.S.S.R.)	166	A
COUNCIL OF TRENT	176	A
COUNCIL ON ENVIRONMENTAL QUALITY	468	B
COUNCIL ON FOREIGN RELATIONS (U.S.)	171	A
COUNCIL-MANAGER FORM	212	A
COUNCIL-MANAGER PLAN	198	A
COUNCILLOR	191	A
COUNCILMAN	183	A
COUNCILMAN-AT-LARGE	183	A
COUNSEIL	482	B
COUNSEL	189	A
COUNSELING	253	A
COUNSELOR	542	B
COUNT	555	B
COUNT PALATINE	737	B
COUNTDOWN	600	B
COUNTER	625	B
COUNTER-COUP	219	A
COUNTER-CULTURE	147	A
COUNTER-PROPOSALS	226	A
COUNTER-REFORMATION	234	A
COUNTER-REVOLUTION	200	A
COUNTER-REVOLUTIONARY	182	A
COUNTER-UTOPIANS	518	B
COUNTERESPIONAGE	212	A
COUNTERFACTUAL	455	B
COUNTERFEIT	243	A
COUNTERFORCE	158	A
COUNTERINSURGENCY	219	A
COUNTERINTELLIGENCE	207	A
COUNTERPART FUNDS	253	A
COUNTERSIGN	600	B
COUNTERSIGNATURE	822	B
COUNTERVAILING DUTY	625	B
COUNTERVAILING POWER	119	A
COUNTERVAILING THEORY OF PRESSURE POLITICS	123	A
COUNTESS	542	B
COUNTING	577	B
COUNTING BOARD	499	B
COUNTING HOUSE POLITICIAN	555	B
COUNTING OF VOTES	226	A
COUNTING OUT	625	B
COUNTRY	277	A
COUNTRY PARTY	499	B
COUNTRY STUDIES	138	A
COUNTY	162	A
COUNTY AGENT	191	A
COUNTY ASSESSOR	189	A
COUNTY ATTORNEY (DISTRICT ATTORNEY)	187	A
COUNTY AUDITOR	542	B
COUNTY BOARD	162	A
COUNTY BOROUGH	171	A
COUNTY CLERK	187	A
COUNTY COMMITTEE	171	A

COUNTY COUNCIL	468	B	COURTESY VISIT	577	B
COUNTY COURT	158	A	COURTIER	548	B
COUNTY ENGINEER	548	B	COURTS OF APPEALS, FEDERAL	152	A
COUNTY GOVERNMENT	155	A	COURTS, FEDERAL	146	A
COUNTY HEALTH OFFICER	542	B	COURTS, STATE	152	A
COUNTY MANAGER	181	A	COUSINS, NORMAN	269	A
COUNTY PROSECUTOR (DISTRICT	189	A	COUVE DE MURVILLE, MAURICE	271	A
ATTORNEY)			COVENANT	243	A
COUNTY SEAT	278	A	COVENANT OF THE LEAGUE OF	207	A
COUNTY SURVEYOR	192	A	NATIONS		
COUNTY TREASURER	187	A	COVER	600	B
COUNTY-MANAGER PLAN	198	A	COW-WADDLE	843	B
COUP	203	A	COWBOY	563	B
COUP D'ETAT	196	A	COWBOY PRESIDENT	707	B
COURAGE	434	B	COWDUNG CLUB	518	B
COURIER	548	B	COX VS. NEW HAMPSHIRE (1941)	674	B
COURNOT, ANTOINE AUGUSTIN	737	B	COX, HAROLD G.	737	B
COURONNEMENT DE LOUIS	650	B	COXEY'S ARMY	499	B
COURSE	650	B	COYLE VS. SMITH (1911)	677	B
COURSE OF LAW	625	B	CRACKDOWN	625	B
COURT	162	A	CRADLE OF LIBERTY	838	B
COURT DECISION	226	A	CRADLE-TO-THE-GRAVE	291	A
COURT EXECUTIVE OFFICERS	555	B	CRAFT	563	B
COURT JURISDICTION	207	A	CRAFT UNION (TRADE UNION)	171	A
COURT JURISDICTION, FEDERAL	212	A	CRAFTMANSHIP	455	B
COURT LEGISLATION	203	A	CRAM, RALPH ADAMS	737	B
COURT MOURNING	650	B	CRAMB, J. A.	737	B
COURT OF APPEALS	148	A	CRANACH	737	B
COURT OF ARBITRAL JUSTICE	482	B	CRANSTON, ALAN	267	A
COURT OF ARBITRATION	155	A	CRATES THE CYNIC	737	B
COURT OF CASSATION	468	B	CRAWFISH	843	B
COURT OF CHANCERY	468	B	CRAWFORD COUNTY SYSTEM	650	B
COURT OF CLAIMS	158	A	CREATION	600	B
COURT OF COMMON PLEAS	176	A	CREATION OF A POST	253	A
COURT OF CONFLICTS	499	B	CREATIVE FEDERALISM	125	A
COURT OF CRIMINAL APPEAL	162	A	CREATIVE PROCESSES	434	B
COURT OF CUSTOMS AND PATENT	171	A	CREATIVE THINKING	434	B
APPEALS			CREATIVITY	442	B
COURT OF JUSTICE	158	A	CREATOR	548	B
COURT OF JUSTICE, EUROPEAN	176	A	CREDENTIALS	285	A
COMMUNITY			CREDENTIALS COMMITTEE	162	A
COURT OF PETTY SESSION	482	B	CREDIBILITY	125	A
COURT OF QUARTER SESSIONS	518	B	CREDIBILITY GAP	125	A
COURT OF RECORD	176	A	CREDIT	253	A
COURT OF SESSIONS	499	B	CREDIT MOBILIER	176	A
COURT OF SOCIAL HONOR	518	B	CREDIT UNIONS	166	A
COURT OPINION	198	A	CREED	135	A
COURT PACKING PROPOSALS	234	A	CREEPING SOCIALISM	212	A
COURT REFEREE	187	A	CREOLE	176	A
COURT REPORTER	187	A	CREOLE CASE	674	B
COURT SYSTEM	150	A	CRESCENT	825	B
COURT-HOUSE GANG	482	B	CREVEA, ALTAMIRE,	737	B
COURT-MARTIAL	207	A	CRICK, BERNARD	738	B
COURTESY	577	B	CRIME	219	A
COURTESY OF THE SENATE	219	A	CRIME AGAINST HUMANITY	212	A
COURTESY TITLES	577	B	CRIME AGAINST PEACE	253	A

CRIME COMMISSION	482	B
CRIME CONTROL ACT	577	B
CRIME OF 73	650	B
CRIME PREVENTION PROGRAMS	253	A
CRIME SYNDICATES	166	A
CRIME WAVE	577	B
CRIMEA CONFERENCE	226	A
CRIMEAN WAR	226	A
CRIMINAL	243	A
CRIMINAL ANARCHY	577	B
CRIMINAL CASE	243	A
CRIMINAL CODE	219	A
CRIMINAL COMMON LAW	234	A
CRIMINAL IDENTIFICATION	625	B
CRIMINAL JURISDICTION	226	A
CRIMINAL LAW	203	A
CRIMINAL SYNDICALISM	434	B
CRIMINOLOGY	130	A
CRIPPS MISSION	482	B
CRIPPS, SIR RICHARD STAFFORD	707	B
CRISIS	207	A
CRISIS AREAS	226	A
CRISP, DOROTHY	738	B
CRITERIA	207	A
CRITICAL	234	A
CRITICAL DISTINCTIONS IN POLITICS	130	A
CRITICAL MATERIAL	289	A
CRITICAL METHOD	127	A
CRITICAL PERIOD	253	A
CRITICAL RANGE	135	A
CRITICISM	135	A
CRITIQUE	142	A
CRITTENDEN COMPROMISE	625	B
CROATIA	280	A
CROCE, BENEDETTO	271	A
CROIX DE FEU	822	B
CROLY, HERBERT	738	B
CROMWELL, OLIVER	266	A
CROMWELL, THOMAS	684	B
CROP LOAN ACT	625	B
CROSLAND, CHARLES ANTHONY RAVEN	738	B
CROSS	825	B
CROSS PICKETING	625	B
CROSS PRESSURE	120	A
CROSS THE AISLE	577	B
CROSS THE STREET	843	B
CROSS-CULTURAL ANALYSIS	119	A
CROSS-CUTTING	434	B
CROSS-FILING	203	A
CROSS-NATIONAL DIFFERENCES	123	A
CROSS-NATIONAL RESEARCH	120	A
CROSS-OF-GOLD SPEECH	212	A
CROSS-SECTIONAL ANALYSIS	123	A
CROSSER-DILL ACT	650	B
CROSSMAN, RICHARD HOWARD STAFFORD	738	B
CROTTY, WILLIAM J.	707	B
CROW	843	B
CROWD PSYCHOLOGY	125	A
CROWISM	142	A
CROWN	287	A
CROWN COLONY	166	A
CROWN PRINCE	192	A
CROZIER, M.	707	B
CRUEL AND UNUSUAL PUNISHMENT	195	A
CRUEL AND UNUSUAL PUNISHMENTS PROHIBITED	200	A
CRUISER	822	B
CRUNCH	625	B
CRUSADE	243	A
CRUSADES	226	A
CRUSIUS	738	B
CRUST-DIVER	563	B
CRYPTO-COMMUNIST	192	A
CRYSTAL NIGHT	625	B
CUARTELAZO	626	B
CUBA	275	A
CUBAN INVASION, 1961	207	A
CUBAN MISSILE CRISIS	196	A
CUBANS	468	B
CUBE LAW	455	B
CUBISM	455	B
CUE	434	B
CUFF LINKS CLUB (GANG)	499	B
CULPABILITY	243	A
CULT	434	B
CULT OF PERSONALITY, SOVIET UNION	212	A
CULT OF THE INDIVIDUAL, SOVIET UNION	234	A
CULTIVATION	650	B
CULTURAL AGREEMENT	234	A
CULTURAL ANTHROPOLOGY	127	A
CULTURAL ATTACHE	186	A
CULTURAL COOPERATION	135	A
CULTURAL EXCHANGE	207	A
CULTURAL FACTORS	127	A
CULTURAL HETEROGENEITY	125	A
CULTURAL HOMOGENEITY	123	A
CULTURAL IMPERIALISM	120	A
CULTURAL PATTERNS	123	A
CULTURAL PLURALISM THEORY	125	A
CULTURAL RELATIVISM	114	A
CULTURAL REVOLUTION, CHINA (PRC)	198	A
CULTURAL TRANSFORMATION	132	A
CULTURAL TRANSMISSION	130	A
CULTURAL VARIATIONS	127	A
CULTURE	117	A
CULTURE PATTERNS	119	A

CUMBERLAND ROAD	793	B		CYNICS	468	B
CUMMINGS VS. MISSOURI (1867)	677	B		CYPRUS	275	A
CUMMINGS, E. E.	707	B		CYPRUS CONVENTION	578	B
CUMONT, FRANZ	738	B		CYPRUS QUESTION	244	A
CUMULATIVE RECORD	577	B		CYRANKIEWICZ, J.	738	B
CUMULATIVE SCALE	130	A		CYRUS THE GREAT	707	B
CUMULATIVE VOTING	212	A		CZAR	182	A
CURACAO	282	A		CZAR RED	548	B
CURATIVE STATUTE	577	B		CZARDOM	189	A
CURE	650	B		CZARINA	187	A
CURFEW	243	A		CZARISM	127	A
CURIOSITY	455	B		CZECH CRISIS	234	A
CURMUDGEON	707	B		CZECHOSLOVAK-FRENCH TREATY	626	B
CURRENCY	287	A		CZECHOSLOVAK-U.S.S.R. TREATY	600	B
CURRENCY AREA	468	B		CZECHOSLOVAKIA	274	A
CURRENCY DECLARATION, THREE POWER	577	B		D-BANKS	843	B
				D-DAY	207	A
CURRENCY DEVALUATION	200	A		D'ALEMBERT	738	B
CURRENCY RESERVE RATIO	600	B		D'ANNUNZIO, GABRIELE	692	B
CURRENCY, VARIETIES USED IN THE U.S.	288	A		D'ARCY, M. C.	738	B
				D'ENTREVES, PROF. A. P.	738	B
CURRENT TAX PAYMENT ACT OF 1943	626	B		D'ORCO, RAMIRO	738	B
				DA VINCI, LEONARDO	264	A
CURRICULUM	434	B		DACHAU	275	A
CURSE OF BIGNESS	835	B		DACOITS	518	B
CURTAIL	626	B		DADE	793	B
CURTAILMENTS OF BUDGET APPROPRIATIONS	577	B		DAG HAMMARSKJOLD LIBRARY (UN)	468	B
				DAHL, ROBERT A.	263	A
CURTAIN	822	B		DAHLGREN, HAROLD E.	738	B
CURTIN, JOHN	738	B		DAHOMAN	518	B
CURTIS, CARL THOMAS	738	B		DAHOMEY	278	A
CURZON LINE	787	B		DAI	518	B
CUSANUS	738	B		DAIL EIRANN (IRISH HOUSE OF REPRESENTATIVES)	482	B
CUSHMAN, ROBERT C.	692	B				
CUSHMAN, ROBERT E.	738	B		DAILY	811	B
CUSTODY	253	A		DAILY BULLETIN	808	B
CUSTOM	219	A		DAILY WORKER	283	A
CUSTOM AND USAGE	212	A		DAIRY INDUSTRY, BUREAU OF	518	B
CUSTOMARY LAW	212	A		DAIS	819	B
CUSTOMHOUSE	289	A		DALADIER, EDOUARD	271	A
CUSTOMS	171	A		DALAI LAMA	187	A
CUSTOMS COOPERATION COUNCIL	518	B		DALAND, R. T.	738	B
CUSTOMS COURT	176	A		DALEY, MAYOR RICHARD	264	A
CUSTOMS DUTY	207	A		DALTON, HUGH	707	B
CUSTOMS SERVICE	171	A		DAMAGES	578	B
CUSTOMS TARIFFS UNION	162	A		DAMIANI, PETER	738	B
CUSTOMS UNION	158	A		DANBURY HATTERS CASE (1908)	674	B
CUTRIGHT, PHILLIPS	738	B		DANE	518	B
CUTTING OF BUDGET APPROPRIATIONS	226	A		DANGER	626	B
				DANIEL BALL, THE	650	B
CUTTLE FISH	843	B		DANIEL, YULI	738	B
CYBERNATION	132	A		DANIELS, JOSEPHUS	738	B
CYBERNETICS	115	A		DANIELSON, JEAN	738	B
CYERT, RICHARD	738	B		DANITE (HEBREW TRIBE)	518	B
CYNEWULF (ANGLO-SAXON POET)	738	B		DANQUAH, DR.	707	B
CYNICISM	135	A		DANTE ALIGHIERI	269	A

DANTON, GEORGES JACQUES	738	B
DANUBE COMMISSION	468	B
DANUBIAN PACT	626	B
DANZIG	277	A
DARK AGES	226	A
DARK CONTINENT OF AMERICAN POLITICS	833	B
DARK LANTERN	826	B
DARK-HORSE CANDIDATE	183	A
DARLAN-CLARK ACCORD	808	B
DARLAN, FRANCOIS-JEAN	707	B
DARNAND, JOSEPH	738	B
DARROW, CLARENCE	269	A
DARTMOUTH COLLEGE VS. WOODWARD (1819)	261	A
DARWIN, CHARLES	264	A
DARWINISM	125	A
DATA	117	A
DATA COLLECTION	117	A
DATE OF APPOINTMENT	244	A
DAUDET, LEON	739	B
DAUGHTERS OF THE AMERICAN REVOLUTION (DAR)	162	A
DAUPHIN	542	B
DAVENPORT, EDUARD	739	B
DAVID, PAUL T.	739	B
DAVIES, A. EMIL	739	B
DAVIES, JAMES C.	707	B
DAVIES, JOSEPH EDWARD	708	B
DAVIS-WADE MANIFESTO	809	B
DAVIS, ANGELA	264	A
DAVIS, JEFFERSON	263	A
DAVIS, KENNETH CULP	739	B
DAVIS, KINGSLEY	692	B
DAWES ACT	601	B
DAWES PLAN	253	A
DAWES, CHARLES	692	B
DAWSON, CHRISTOPHER	708	B
DAWSON, RICHARD	739	B
DAY IN COURT	578	B
DAY OF INFAMY	244	A
DAY-CARE CENTER	289	A
DAYAN, GENERAL MOSHE	269	A
DAYLIGHT SAVING TIME	578	B
DAYS OF GRACE	626	B
DE FACTO	200	A
DE FACTO GOVERNMENT	148	A
DE FACTO RECOGNITION	203	A
DE FACTO SEGREGATION	198	A
DE FACTO WAR	203	A
DE GASPERI, ALCIDE	684	B
DE GAULLE, GENERAL CHARLES ANDRE JOSEPH MARIE	261	A
DE GAULLIST	162	A
DE GRAZIA, ALFRED	269	A
DE GRAZIA, SEBASTIAN	739	B
DE JOUVENEL, BERTRAND	684	B
DE JURE	196	A
DE JURE RECOGNITION	200	A
DE JURE WAR	212	A
DE LEON, DANIEL	739	B
DE MAN, HENDRIK	739	B
DE POMPADOUR, MADAME	684	B
DE ROUVROY, CLAUDE HENRI	739	B
DE UNITATE ECCLESIAE CONSERVANDA	811	B
DE VALERA, EAMONN (EDWARD)	692	B
DEAD	626	B
DEAD BEAT (ADJ. AND NOUN)	555	B
DEAD DUCK	838	B
DEAD END, POLITICAL	291	A
DEAD ISSUE	578	B
DEAD RABBITS	843	B
DEAD-LETTER LAW	626	B
DEAD-LETTER OFFICE	819	B
DEADLINE	601	B
DEADLOCK	234	A
DEADLY	455	B
DEAF--EMPLOYMENT	650	B
DEAL	578	B
DEAN OF THE DIPLOMATIC CORPS	189	A
DEANE, HERBERT A.	739	B
DEAT, MARCEL	739	B
DEATH	626	B
DEATH DUTIES	578	B
DEATH INSTINCT	449	B
DEATH PENALTY	203	A
DEATH SENTENCE CLAUSE	626	B
DEATH-MYTHS	442	B
DEBASEMENT	601	B
DEBATE	212	A
DEBATE PARADIGMS	449	B
DEBATING CLUB (SOCIETY)	482	B
DEBELLATIO	650	B
DEBOLSHEVIZE	601	B
DEBRAY, REGIS	266	A
DEBRE, MICHEL	684	B
DEBS VS. UNITED STATES (1919)	671	B
DEBS, EUGENE VICTOR	263	A
DEBT CEILING	219	A
DEBT DEFAULT ACT OF 1934	626	B
DEBT SERVICE	244	A
DEBT, IMPRISONMENT FOR	226	A
DEBUREAUCRATIZATION	138	A
DECADE	650	B
DECAPITULATION	650	B
DECAY	449	B
DECEIT	449	B
DECEMBRISTS	166	A
DECENCY	626	B
DECENCY PARTY	518	B
DECENTRALIZATION	115	A

DECIDE	234	A
DECIDING VOTE	207	A
DECIPHER	244	A
DECISION	203	A
DECISION MAKERS	181	A
DECISION MAKING	114	A
DECISION THEORY	115	A
DECISION-MAKING ANALYSIS	117	A
DECISION-MAKING APPROACH	115	A
DECISION-MAKING PROCESS	115	A
DECISIONAL ELEMENTS	127	A
DECISIS	253	A
DECLARATION	244	A
DECLARATION OF ELIMINATION OF DISCRIMINATION AGAINST WOMEN	253	A
DECLARATION OF GRANT OF INDEPENDENCE OF COLONIAL TERRITOR. AND PEOPLE	601	B
DECLARATION OF INDEPENDENCE	283	A
DECLARATION OF INTENTION	253	A
DECLARATION OF LIMA, 1938	601	B
DECLARATION OF LONDON	626	B
DECLARATION OF NEUTRALITY	207	A
DECLARATION OF PANAMA	601	B
DECLARATION OF PARIS	601	B
DECLARATION OF RECIPROCITY	226	A
DECLARATION OF RENSE	651	B
DECLARATION OF RIGHTS	284	A
DECLARATION OF WAR	198	A
DECLARATION OF WAR, CONGRESS	207	A
DECLARATION ON OUTER SPACE (1963)	244	A
DECLARATION REGARDING NON-SELF-GOVERNING TERRITORIES	244	A
DECLARATIONS OF HUMAN RIGHTS	283	A
DECLARATORY JUDGMENT	219	A
DECLARE	578	B
DECLARENT ALIEN	542	B
DECLINE	449	B
DECODE	234	A
DECOLONIZATION	207	A
DECONCENTRATION	626	B
DECONTROL	234	A
DECORATION DAY	626	B
DECREE	212	A
DECREE LAW	226	A
DEDICATION	626	B
DEDIJER, VLADIMIR	739	B
DEDUCTION	125	A
DEDUCTION-THEOREM	125	A
DEDUCTIVE REASONING	115	A
DEED	253	A
DEED OF ABDICATION	601	B
DEEDS NOT WORDS	838	B
DEEP FREEZE	833	B
DEFAMATION	234	A
DEFAMATION OF CHARACTER	219	A
DEFAULT	244	A
DEFEASIBILITY	651	B
DEFEAT	244	A
DEFEAT OF THE SPANISH ARMADA	244	A
DEFEATISM	434	B
DEFEATIST	542	B
DEFENDANT	186	A
DEFENDANT'S RIGHTS	200	A
DEFENDER	192	A
DEFENESTRATION OF PRAGUE	651	B
DEFENSE	207	A
DEFENSE AIR TRANSPORTATION ADMINISTRATION	499	B
DEFENSE ASSISTANCE PACT	253	A
DEFENSE COLLEGE (OF NATO)	483	B
DEFENSE COMMUNICATIONS AGENCY (DCA)	483	B
DEFENSE CONTRACT AUDIT AGENCY (DCAA)	483	B
DEFENSE ELECTRIC POWER ADMINISTRATION (DEPA)	518	B
DEFENSE HOMES CORPORATION	518	B
DEFENSE HOUSING	578	B
DEFENSE INDUSTRY	155	A
DEFENSE INTELLIGENCE AGENCY (DIA)	152	A
DEFENSE PLANT CORPORATION	483	B
DEFENSE REORGANIZATION ACT OF 1958	601	B
DEFENSE SPENDING	200	A
DEFENSE SUPPLIES CORPORATION	518	B
DEFENSE SUPPLY AGENCY (DSA)	483	B
DEFENSIVE ALLIANCE	152	A
DEFENSIVE CAMPAIGN	244	A
DEFENSIVE WAR	200	A
DEFENSIVE WEAPONS	286	A
DEFERENCE	132	A
DEFERMENT	234	A
DEFERRED SIGNATURE	651	B
DEFFERRE, GASTON	739	B
DEFIANCE	626	B
DEFICIENCY APPROPRIATION	244	A
DEFICIENCY BILL	234	A
DEFICIT	219	A
DEFICIT BONDS	626	B
DEFICIT FINANCING	207	A
DEFINABILITY	442	B
DEFINITE-DESCRIPTIONS	455	B
DEFINITION	123	A
DEFLATION	219	A
DEFOE, DANIEL	739	B
DEFOLIATE	226	A
DEGAN	739	B
DEGENERATION	442	B

DEGRADATION CEREMONIES	651	B	DEMOCRATIC PARTY	145	A
DEGRESSIVE RATE	651	B	DEMOCRATIC POLICY COMMITTEE	176	A
DEIFICATION OF THE PARTY	651	B	DEMOCRATIC POWER	125	A
DEISM	130	A	DEMOCRATIC REPUBLIC OF VIETNAM	155	A
DEIST, HEINRICH	739	B	(NORTH VIETNAM)		
DELAWARE	278	A	DEMOCRATIC SOCIALISM	115	A
DELEGATE	181	A	DEMOCRATIC SOCIALIST PARTY	158	A
DELEGATION	147	A	DEMOCRATIC SOCIETIES	150	A
DELEGATION OF AUTHORITY	200	A	DEMOCRATIC STUDY GROUP	171	A
DELEGATION OF LEGISLATIVE	200	A	DEMOCRATIC-FARMER LABOR	176	A
POWER			PARTY		
DELEGATION OF POWERS	114	A	DEMOCRATIC-REPUBLICAN PARTY	166	A
DELETION	626	B	DEMOCRATIZATION	195	A
DELHI	787	B	DEMOCRITUS	269	A
DELIBERATE	226	A	DEMOGRAPHIC	125	A
DELIBERATE SPEED	212	A	DEMOGRAPHIC CYCLE	138	A
DELIBERATION	235	A	DEMOGRAPHY	123	A
DELIBERATIVE BODY	147	A	DEMONETIZATION	578	B
DELIMITATION	253	A	DEMONSTRATION	244	A
DELINEATION OF LEGISLATIVE	219	A	DEMONSTRATION CITIES ACT	235	A
DISTRICTS			DEMONSTRATORS	183	A
DELINQUENCY	235	A	DEMOS	192	A
DELINQUENT TAXES	219	A	DEMPSEY, JACK	739	B
DELIVER	601	B	DENATURALIZATION	434	B
DELPHI METHOD	130	A	DENAZIFICATION	212	A
DELUSION	455	B	DENAZIFICATION COURT	468	B
DEMAGOGUE	182	A	DENEUTRALIZATION	578	B
DEMAGOGUERY	212	A	DENIAL	244	A
DEMAND	244	A	DENIAL OF JUSTICE	226	A
DEMAND	203	A	DENIS, JACQUES	739	B
DEMAND AND SUPPLY	117	A	DENK	739	B
DEMAND-PULL	244	A	DENMARK	278	A
DEMARCATION LINE	280	A	DENNEY, REUEL	739	B
DEMARCHE	578	B	DENNIS VS. UNITED STATES (1951)	672	B
DEMARIA,	739	B	DENNIS, JACK	708	B
DEMES (UNIT OF LOCAL	739	B	DENOTATION	130	A
GOVERNMENT) (ATHENS)			DENOTIC-LOGIC	434	B
DEMILITARIZATION	212	A	DENOTING	135	A
DEMILITARIZED ZONE	274	A	DENOUNCE	578	B
DEMIREL, SULEYMAN	708	B	DENSITY	138	A
DEMIURGE	563	B	DENTAL	826	B
DEMOBILIZATION	207	A	DENTON, FRANK	739	B
DEMOCRACY	113	A	DENUCLEARIZATION	207	A
DEMOCRACY IN AMERICA	283	A	DENUNCIATION	235	A
DEMOCRAT	181	A	DENUNCIATION OF TREATIES	244	A
DEMOCRAT WITH A SMALL D	186	A	DENVER, COLORADO	278	A
DEMOCRATIC	195	A	DENY	601	B
DEMOCRATIC CENTRALISM,	121	A	DEONTOLOGY	455	B
COMMUNIST THEORY			DEPART	651	B
DEMOCRATIC CLASSROOM	483	B	DEPART IN PEACE, WAYWARD	838	B
DEMOCRATIC COLLECTIVISM	125	A	SISTERS		
DEMOCRATIC CONFERENCE	212	A	DEPARTEMENT (FRANCE)	162	A
DEMOCRATIC CONVENTION OF 1968	219	A	DEPARTMENT	171	A
DEMOCRATIC DONKEY	835	B	DEPARTMENT OF ADMINISTRATION	468	B
DEMOCRATIC IDEOLOGY	114	A	DEPARTMENT OF AGRICULTURE	150	A
DEMOCRATIC NATIONAL COMMITTEE	162	A	DEPARTMENT OF AIR FORCE	152	A

DEPARTMENT OF COMMERCE	155	A
DEPARTMENT OF COMMERCE AND LABOR	162	A
DEPARTMENT OF DEFENSE (U.S.) (DOD)	147	A
DEPARTMENT OF DIRTY TRICKS	291	A
DEPARTMENT OF FINANCE	158	A
DEPARTMENT OF HEALTH, EDUCATION, AND WELFARE (HEW)	150	A
DEPARTMENT OF HOUSING AND URBAN DEVELOPMENT (HUD)	148	A
DEPARTMENT OF INTERIOR	152	A
DEPARTMENT OF JUSTICE	147	A
DEPARTMENT OF LABOR	150	A
DEPARTMENT OF NATIONAL DEFENSE	166	A
DEPARTMENT OF NATURAL RESOURCES (DNR)	468	B
DEPARTMENT OF OVERSEAS TRADE	483	B
DEPARTMENT OF PUBLIC ECONOMY	483	B
DEPARTMENT OF STATE (U.S.)	146	A
DEPARTMENT OF THE ARMY	152	A
DEPARTMENT OF THE NAVY	150	A
DEPARTMENT OF THE TREASURY	150	A
DEPARTMENT OF TRANSPORTATION (DOT)	152	A
DEPARTMENT OF WAR (ALSO, WAR DEPARTMENT)	150	A
DEPARTMENTAL COMMISSION OF ENQUIRY (GREAT BRITAIN)	468	B
DEPARTMENTAL SERVICE	651	B
DEPENDENCE	125	A
DEPENDENCY	135	A
DEPENDENT	183	A
DEPENDENT STATE	158	A
DEPENDENT TERRITORY	155	A
DEPENDENT VARIABLE	113	A
DEPICTING	651	B
DEPLETION ALLOWANCE	207	A
DEPLOYMENT	244	A
DEPOLITICIZATION	213	A
DEPONENT	563	B
DEPORTATION	203	A
DEPORTATION OF COMMUNISTS	226	A
DEPOSE	213	A
DEPOSIT BANK	176	A
DEPOSIT OF THE INSTRUMENT OF RATIFICATION	244	A
DEPOSITION	226	A
DEPOSITORY	817	B
DEPOSITORY STATE	468	B
DEPRESSED CLASSES	158	A
DEPRESSION	207	A
DEPRESSION PARTY	483	B
DEPRESSION, ECONOMIC	198	A
DEPRESSIONS	244	A
DEPREUX, EDWARD	739	B
DEPRIVATION	125	A
DEPRIVATION OF LIBERTY	219	A
DEPRIVED	192	A
DEPTH INTERVIEW	125	A
DEPTH POLLING	125	A
DEPTH QUESTIONNAIRES	125	A
DEPTH-PSYCHOLOGY	135	A
DEPUTIZE	601	B
DEPUTY	184	A
DEPUTY SHERIFF	189	A
DER STUERMER	285	A
DER STUERMER	805	B
DERELICTION	235	A
DERISI, NICHOLAS	739	B
DERIVATIONS	138	A
DERIVATIVE RIGHT	244	A
DEROGATION	578	B
DEROGATORY CLAUSE	601	B
DERRINGER POLICY	626	B
DES MOINES PLAN	626	B
DESAI, SHRI MORARJI RANCHHODJI	708	B
DESCARTES, RENE	264	A
DESCRIBING	138	A
DESCRIPTION	130	A
DESCRIPTION OF DUTIES	809	B
DESCRIPTIVE STATISTICS	121	A
DESCRIPTIVE THEORIES	132	A
DESCRIPTIVES	434	B
DESCRIPTIVISM	442	B
DESEGREGATION	194	A
DESERET	797	B
DESERTER	187	A
DESERTION	578	B
DESERVING DEMOCRATS	555	B
DESHMUKH, GOPAL HARI	739	B
DESIGN	626	B
DESIGNATE	253	A
DESIRE FOR PEACE	601	B
DESIRE, DESIRING	455	B
DESJARDINS, ARTHUR	740	B
DESPATCH	626	B
DESPOT	182	A
DESPOTIC ABSOLUTISM	130	A
DESPOTISM	117	A
DESTALINIZATION	213	A
DESTINY	442	B
DESTROYER	822	B
DESTROYER-BASE DEAL	253	A
DESTRUCTION	244	A
DETAINING POWER	578	B
DETECTION METHODS	142	A
DETECTION OF UNDERGROUND NUCLEAR EXPLOSIONS	226	A
DETECTIVE	555	B
DETENTE	203	A

DETENTION	235	A
DETENTION HOME	819	B
DETENTION ORDER	578	B
DETERIORATION OF RELATIONS	578	B
DETERMINANTS	130	A
DETERMINATION	626	B
DETERMINATION OF THE AGGRESSOR	235	A
DETERMINISM	121	A
DETERMINIST THEORIES	121	A
DETERRENCE	196	A
DETERRENCE THEORIES	121	A
DETERRENT	200	A
DETROIT, MICHIGAN	275	A
DEUTCHES NACHTRICHTEN BURO (D.N.B)	499	B
DEUTSCH, KARL W.	262	A
DEVALUATION	203	A
DEVELOP	244	A
DEVELOPING NATIONS	147	A
DEVELOPMENT	123	A
DEVELOPMENT ADMINISTRATION	578	B
DEVELOPMENT AID	219	A
DEVELOPMENT ASSISTANCE COMMITTEE (DAC)	499	B
DEVELOPMENT DECADE	235	A
DEVELOPMENT LOAN FUND	162	A
DEVELOPMENT LOANS	235	A
DEVELOPMENT STUDIES	127	A
DEVELOPMENT THEORY	117	A
DEVELOPMENT, SOCIAL AND ECONOMIC	117	A
DEVELOPMENTAL PROFILE	142	A
DEVELOPMENTS	601	B
DEVIANCY	132	A
DEVIANT	183	A
DEVIANT BEHAVIOR	119	A
DEVIATION	203	A
DEVIATIONISM	135	A
DEVICE	289	A
DEVOLUTION	244	A
DEVOTION	455	B
DEWAN NAGARA	518	B
DEWAN RAAYAT	518	B
DEWEY BLITZ	626	B
DEWEY, A. GORDON	740	B
DEWEY, JOHN	263	A
DEWEY, THOMAS EDMUND	267	A
DEWLINE (DEW, DISTANT EARLY WARNING)	280	A
DEY	563	B
DHARMA (HINDUISM)	449	B
DHIMMI	499	B
DHONDT METHOD	601	B
DHONDT, JAN	740	B
DIACHRONIC ANALYSIS	442	B
DIAGNOSIS	132	A
DIALECTIC	196	A
DIALECTICAL MATERIALISM, COMMUNIST THEORY	114	A
DIALECTICAL METHOD	114	A
DIALOGUE	219	A
DIALOGUE OF THE EXCHEQUER	811	B
DIAMANT, ALFRED	692	B
DIAPER IN THE RING	843	B
DIARCHY	483	B
DIARIES	809	B
DIASPORA	578	B
DIAZ ORDAZ, GUSTAVO	269	A
DIAZ, PORFIRIO	269	A
DICAEARCHUS	740	B
DICEY, A. V.	692	B
DICHOTOMIES	135	A
DICHOTOMOUS CLASSIFICAITON	132	A
DICKENS, CHARLES	269	A
DICKINSON, G. LOWES	740	B
DICKINSON, JOHN	740	B
DICTATOR	181	A
DICTATORSHIP	146	A
DICTATORSHIP OF THE PROLETARIAT, COMMUNIST THEORY	144	A
DICTIONARIES	807	B
DICTUM	285	A
DIDEROT, DENIS	692	B
DIE FREIHEIT	805	B
DIE NEUE ZEIT	285	A
DIE-HARD	189	A
DIEFENBAKER, JOHN	267	A
DIEHL, C.	740	B
DIEM, NGO-DINH	264	A
DIEN-BIEN-PHU	275	A
DIES COMMITTEE	468	B
DIET	166	A
DIFFERENCES	626	B
DIFFERENTIAL	442	B
DIFFERENTIATION	142	A
DIFFFERENTIAL DUTY	627	B
DIFFICULTIES	627	B
DIGEST	601	B
DIGEST OF JUSTINIAN	809	B
DIGGERS, THE	483	B
DIGNITARY	548	B
DIGNITY	434	B
DILATORY EFFECT	244	A
DILATORY MOTION	220	A
DILATORY POLICY	235	A
DILEMMA	130	A
DILIGENCE	455	B
DILLON'S RULE	651	B
DILTHEY	708	B
DIMENSION	442	B

DIMENSIONALITY	434	B
DIMITROV, G.M.	708	B
DIMMICRAT	518	B
DIMOUT (WORLD WAR II)	651	B
DINGLEY ACT	627	B
DINNER	651	B
DINOSAUR	556	B
DINOSAUR WING	499	B
DIOCESE	468	B
DIOCLETIAN	708	B
DIOGENES OF SINOPE	708	B
DION CHRYSOSTOMOS	740	B
DION OF SYRACUSE	708	B
DIONYSIAN	548	B
DIONYSIAN PEOPLES	518	B
DIONYSIUS	684	B
DIPLOMACY	121	A
DIPLOMAT	184	A
DIPLOMATIC AGENT	192	A
DIPLOMATIC ASYLUM	207	A
DIPLOMATIC CAREER	192	A
DIPLOMATIC CHANNELS	220	A
DIPLOMATIC CIRCLES	176	A
DIPLOMATIC CORPS	152	A
DIPLOMATIC COURIER	189	A
DIPLOMATIC EXCHANGE	226	A
DIPLOMATIC IMMUNITY	203	A
DIPLOMATIC LAW	253	A
DIPLOMATIC LEVEL	253	A
DIPLOMATIC LIST	805	B
DIPLOMATIC MISSION	220	A
DIPLOMATIC NOTE	284	A
DIPLOMATIC PASSPORT	285	A
DIPLOMATIC POUCH	287	A
DIPLOMATIC PRIVILEGES AND IMMUNITIES	207	A
DIPLOMATIC PROTECTION	213	A
DIPLOMATIC QUARTERS	822	B
DIPLOMATIC RELATIONS	125	A
DIPLOMATIC REPRESENTATION	226	A
DIPLOMATIC SERVICE	155	A
DIPLOMATIC VISA	284	A
DIRECT	627	B
DIRECT ACTION	235	A
DIRECT BURDEN TESTS	627	B
DIRECT DEMOCRACY	119	A
DIRECT ELECTION OF SENATORS	213	A
DIRECT ELECTIONS	200	A
DIRECT EVIDENCE	235	A
DIRECT INITIATIVE	226	A
DIRECT LEARNING	442	B
DIRECT LEGISLATION	203	A
DIRECT NOMINATION	203	A
DIRECT PRIMARY	196	A
DIRECT TAX	207	A
DIRECTED INTERVIEW	135	A
DIRECTED TRADE	578	B
DIRECTIVE	601	B
DIRECTOR GENERAL	548	B
DIRECTOR OF THE BUDGET	182	A
DIRECTORS	548	B
DIRECTORY	805	B
DIRIGISME	578	B
DIRKSEN, EVERETT MCKINLEY	267	A
DIRT EATER	563	B
DIRTY LINEN	835	B
DIRTY POLITICS	290	A
DIRTY SHIRT TICKET	838	B
DISABILITY	244	A
DISABILITY INSURANCE	226	A
DISADVANTAGED	166	A
DISADVANTAGED YOUTH	192	A
DISAGREEMENT	235	A
DISALLOWANCE	244	A
DISAPPROVAL	253	A
DISARMAMENT	203	A
DISARMAMENT AND ARMS CONTROL	200	A
DISARMAMENT AND PEACE CONFERENCES, 1920-1930	220	A
DISARMAMENT COMMISSION, UNITED NATIONS	166	A
DISARMAMENT CONFERENCE OF 1932	601	B
DISARMAMENT INSPECTION	226	A
DISARMAMENT PLANS	235	A
DISASTER LOAN CORPORATION	483	B
DISASTER METAPHORS	843	B
DISASTER UNIT	499	B
DISBARMENT	220	A
DISCHARGE	578	B
DISCHARGE CALENDAR	235	A
DISCHARGE PETITION	220	A
DISCHARGE RULE IN HOUSE OF REPRESENTATIVES	213	A
DISCIPLINARY ACTION	253	A
DISCIPLINARY BOARD	499	B
DISCIPLINARY CAMP	483	B
DISCIPLINARY COUNCIL	499	B
DISCIPLINARY MEASURES	578	B
DISCIPLINARY POWER	235	A
DISCIPLINE	244	A
DISCIPLINE IN THE HOUSE OF REPRESENTATIVES	226	A
DISCIPLINE IN THE SENATE	226	A
DISCLOSURE	235	A
DISCLOSURE OF INFORMATION ACT	235	A
DISCONTENT	235	A
DISCORDANT	627	B
DISCOURSE	253	A
DISCOURSE, LEVELS OF	142	A
DISCOVERY	244	A

DISCRETION	244	A
DISCRETIONARY	226	A
DISCRIMINANT ANALYSIS	434	B
DISCRIMINATION	207	A
DISCRIMINATION, SOCIAL	213	A
DISCRIMINATIVE STIMULUS	434	B
DISCUSSION	235	A
DISEASE	817	B
DISEMBARK	651	B
DISENGAGEMENT	200	A
DISEQUILIBRIUM	123	A
DISESTABLISHMENT	235	A
DISFRANCHISE	203	A
DISFRANCHISEMENT	203	A
DISGRACE	601	B
DISGUISED IMPERIALISM	627	B
DISHONORABLE DISCHARGE	578	B
DISINTEGRATION	220	A
DISLOYAL	187	A
DISMALCRAT	518	B
DISMANTLE	601	B
DISMEMBERMENT	578	B
DISMISSAL FROM OFFICE	226	A
DISOBEDIENCE	213	A
DISORDER	235	A
DISORDERLY CONDUCT	226	A
DISORGANIZATION	213	A
DISPATCH	817	B
DISPENSING POWER	235	A
DISPLACED PERSONS (DPS)	171	A
DISPLACED PERSONS ACT (1948)	627	B
DISPLACEMENT	142	A
DISPLACEMENT AND PROJECTION	138	A
DISPLAY	627	B
DISPOSITIONS	601	B
DISPUTE	253	A
DISPUTE SETTLEMENT (PEACEFUL SETTLEMENT)	235	A
DISPUTED ELECTION	220	A
DISQUALIFICATION	226	A
DISRAELI, BENJAMIN	267	A
DISRUPTIONS	651	B
DISSENT	203	A
DISSENTERS	186	A
DISSENTING OPINION	207	A
DISSOLUTION	220	A
DISSOLUTION OF PRUSSIA	578	B
DISSOLVE	253	A
DISSONANCE	138	A
DISSYMMETRY	449	B
DISTANCE	455	B
DISTINCTION	627	B
DISTINCTIVE EMBLEM	826	B
DISTINGUISHED FLYING CROSS	822	B
DISTINGUISHED GUEST	563	B
DISTINGUISHED SERVICE CROSS	822	B
DISTORTION	579	B
DISTRESS	455	B
DISTRIBUTION	130	A
DISTRIBUTION OF INCOME	127	A
DISTRIBUTION OF POWERS	121	A
DISTRIBUTION OF PROPERTY	130	A
DISTRIBUTION OF RIGHTS AND DUTIES	135	A
DISTRIBUTIVE JUSTICE	123	A
DISTRIBUTIVE SYSTEM	130	A
DISTRICT	274	A
DISTRICT ATTORNEY	182	A
DISTRICT COURT, STATE	155	A
DISTRICT COURTS, FEDERAL	150	A
DISTRICT JUDGE	186	A
DISTRICT LEADER	192	A
DISTRICT OF COLUMBIA	275	A
DISTRICT OF COLUMBIA COMMITTEE	166	A
DISTRICT OF COLUMBIA MANPOWER ADMINISTRATION	499	B
DISTRICT OFFICER	542	B
DISTRICTING	226	A
DISTRUST	135	A
DISTURBANCE	601	B
DISUNITY	235	A
DIVAN	826	B
DIVERGENT	601	B
DIVERSIFICATION OF INDUSTRY	220	A
DIVERSION	579	B
DIVERSION ORDER	627	B
DIVERSIONARY MOVE	253	A
DIVERSITY	244	A
DIVEST	253	A
DIVIDE AND RULE	290	A
DIVIDED COURT	159	A
DIVIDED NATIONS	166	A
DIVIDED SOVEREIGNTY	138	A
DIVINE RIGHT OF KINGS	119	A
DIVINI REDEMPTORIS	627	B
DIVISION	579	B
DIVISION OF BIOLOGICAL STANDARDS	518	B
DIVISION OF CENTRAL ADMINISTRATIVE SERVICES	518	B
DIVISION OF GERMANY	213	A
DIVISION OF LABOR	125	A
DIVISION OF POWERS	196	A
DIVISION OF TERRITORIES AND ISLAND POSESSIONS	518	B
DIVISION VOTE	235	A
DIVISIVE	244	A
DIVORCE	579	B
DIVORCE ISSUE	627	B
DIXIE	787	B
DIXIECRAT	155	A
DIXIECRAT PARTY	166	A

DIXIEGOP	468	B
DIXON, R. D.	740	B
DJIBOUTI (FRENCH SOMALILAND)	787	B
DJILAS, MILOVAN	267	A
DO NOTHING SOVEREIGNTY	651	B
DO-GOODER	189	A
DO-NOTHING EIGHTIETH CONGRESS	468	
DOBRETSBERGER	740	B
DOBRUJA (RUMANIA)	797	B
DOBUANS	518	B
DOCKET	285	A
DOCTORS	556	B
DOCTORS PLOT	601	B
DOCTRINAIRE	138	B
DOCTRINE	235	A
DOCTRINE OF CONTINUOUS VOYAGE	244	A
DOCTRINE OF EQUALITY OF STATES	226	A
DOCTRINE OF HOT PURSUIT	203	A
DOCTRINE OF IMPLIED POWERS	196	A
DOCTRINE OF STATE IMMUNITY	213	A
DOCTRINE OF SUABILITY	253	A
DOCTRINE OF SUPREMACY OF NATIONAL LAW	235	A
DOCTRINE OF VESTED RIGHTS	253	A
DOCUMENT	284	A
DOCUMENT SERVICES (UN)	483	B
DOCUMENTARY	285	A
DOCUMENTARY EVIDENCE	123	A
DOCUMENTATION	115	A
DODD, SENATOR THOMAS J.	684	B
DODD, WALTER F.	708	B
DODDS, ELLIOT	740	B
DODECANESE ISLANDS	798	B
DOENITS, KARL	740	B
DOGGER BANK INCIDENT (1904)	627	B
DOGMATIC METHOD	138	A
DOGMATISM	125	A
DOLE	253	A
DOLE, ROBERT J.	692	B
DOLLAR	287	A
DOLLAR DIPLOMACY	220	A
DOLLAR GAP	253	A
DOLLAR-A-YEAR MAN	192	A
DOLLARD, JOHN	708	B
DOLLFUSS, ENGELBURT	692	B
DOLLY VARDEN	708	B
DOMAIN	434	A
DOMBROWSKI	708	B
DOMEI (JAPANESE NEWS AGENCY)	519	B
DOMESTIC	192	A
DOMESTIC AFFAIRS	220	A
DOMESTIC AND INTERNATIONAL BUSINESS (DIB)	519	B
DOMESTIC CORPORATION	171	A
DOMESTIC JURISDICTION	207	A
DOMESTIC JURISDICTION CLAUSE, UNITED NATIONS	226	A
DOMESTIC POLICY	203	A
DOMESTIC RELATIONS COURT	166	A
DOMESTIC VIOLENCE	213	A
DOMICILE	282	A
DOMINANCE SYSTEM	442	B
DOMINANT	442	B
DOMINATION	142	A
DOMINICAN REPUBLIC	277	A
DOMINICANS	499	B
DOMINICK, PETER HOYT	692	B
DOMINION	280	A
DOMINION COURTS	468	B
DOMINIONS OFFICE	499	B
DOMINO THEORY	121	A
DON'T CHANGE HORSES	833	B
DON'T LET THEM TAKE IT ALL	843	B
DON'T WASTE YOUR VOTE	291	A
DONATION OF CONSTANTINE	627	B
DONATISTS	519	B
DONHAM, WALLACE B.	740	B
DONKEY	838	B
DONKEY, DEMOCRATIC	291	A
DOOB, LEONARD	692	B
DOODLEBUG	843	B
DOOLEY, MR.	684	B
DOOLITTLE, GENERAL JAMES H.	271	A
DOOMSDAY MACHINE	286	A
DOORBELL-RINGING	601	B
DOORKEEPER	563	B
DOPE STORY	843	B
DORR'S REBELLION, RHODE ISLAND	253	A
DORSET, DECLARATION OF THE COUNTY OF	651	B
DORSEY, GEORGE A.	740	B
DOSSIER	285	A
DOSTOEVSKY, FEDOR MIKHAILOVICH	267	A
DOTSON, ARCH	740	B
DOUBLE	563	B
DOUBLE CITIZENSHIP	184	A
DOUBLE JEOPARDY	198	A
DOUBLE NATIONALITY	187	A
DOUBLE STANDARD	579	B
DOUBLE TALK	833	B
DOUBLE TAXATION	213	A
DOUBT	435	A
DOUBTFUL STATES	442	B
DOUGHFACE	499	B
DOUGLAS-HOME, SIR ALEXANDER (ALEC) FREDERICK	269	A
DOUGLAS, PAUL H.	271	A
DOUGLAS, STEPHEN A.	267	A
DOUGLAS, WILLIAM O.	266	A
DOUGLASS, FREDERICK	267	A

DOUVILLE, JEAN-BAPTISTE	740	B	DRUZE REVOLUTION	651	B
DOVES	155	A	DRUZES (AL-DURUZ) (MOSLEM	483	B
DOWAGER	556	B	SECT)		
DOWN TRODDEN	519	B	DRUZHINA	798	B
DOWNING STREET	275	A	DRY	483	B
DOWNS, ANTHONY	271	A	DRYDEN	740	B
DOWNWAY	826	B	DU BOIS, W.E.B.	263	A
DOYEN	548	B	DU PLESSIS-MORNAY, PHILLIPPE	740	B
DOYEN OF THE DIPLOMATIC CORPS	548	B	DUAL ACCESS	790	B
DRAFT	235	A	DUAL ALLIANCE	483	B
DRAFT AGENDA	285	A	DUAL CITIZENNSHIP	182	A
DRAFT BOARD	159	A	DUAL FEDERALISM	132	A
DRAFT CARD BURNING	227	A	DUAL MONARCHY	500	B
DRAFT CLASSIFICATIONS	244	A	DUAL NATIONALITY	182	A
DRAFT CONSTITUTION	285	A	DUAL OFFICEHOLDING	253	A
DRAFT DODGER	186	A	DUAL SYSTEM OF GOVERNMENT	235	A
DRAFT REGISTRATION	227	A	DUALISM	142	A
DRAFT RESOLUTION	284	A	DUBCEK, ALEXANDER	271	A
DRAFT RIOTS	579	B	DUBINSKY, DAVID	708	B
DRAFT TREATY	285	A	DUBLIN REVIEW	811	B
DRAFTED	253	A	DUBOIS, PIERRE	740	B
DRAFTEE	189	A	DUCE	269	A
DRAFTING COMMITTEE	468	B	DUCHESS	548	B
DRAFTSMANSHIP	627	B	DUCHY	790	B
DRAGNET	627	B	DUDES AND PHARISEES	563	B
DRAGO DOCTRINE	244	A	DUE	651	B
DRAINAGE DISTRICT	468	B	DUE DILIGENCE	579	B
DRAMA	579	B	DUE PROCESS	195	A
DRANG NACH OSTEN	244	A	DUE PROCESS CLAUSE	194	A
DRAW	651	B	DUE PROCESS OF LAW	195	A
DRAWBACK	602	B	DUES	602	B
DRAWING	442	B	DUGDALE, R. L.	740	B
DRAWING OF LOTS	253	A	DUGUIT, LEON	740	B
DRAY, WILLIAM	740	B	DUGUIT'S THEORY OF LAW	455	B
DREAD	442	B	DUKE	548	B
DREAM	602	B	DUKE'S LAWS	651	B
DREAM TICKET	483	B	DUKEDOM	563	B
DREAMING	442	B	DULLES, ALLEN WELSH	269	A
DRED SCOTT VS. SANFORD (1857)	260	A	DULLES, JOHM FOSTER	263	A
DREYFUS AFFAIR	227	A	DULY APPOINTED	244	A
DREYFUS, ALFRED	267	A	DULY AUTHORIZED	192	A
DRINK	651	B	REPRESENTATIVE		
DROIT DAUBAINE	651	B	DUMA	166	A
DRONE	556	B	DUMBARTON OAKS CONFERENCE,	227	A
DROOP QUOTA	843	B	UNITED NATIONS		
DROPOUT	542	B	DUMDUM BULLET	819	B
DRUG ABUSE	235	A	DUMP	602	B
DRUG ABUSE PREVENTION	253	A	DUMPING	235	A
DRUG ABUSERS	563	B	DUNBAR, CHARLES F.	740	B
DRUG REGULATION	220	A	DUNCAN VS. KAHANAMOKU (1946)	677	B
DRUG SUPERVISORY BOARD (DSB)	499	B	DUNKIRK	790	B
DRUGS	817	B	DUNKIRK, EVACUATION OF	244	A
DRUM AND FIFE CANDIDACY	651	B	DUNKIRK, TREATY OF	627	B
DRUMHEAD COURT-MARTIAL	602	B	DUNNING, WILLIAM A.	740	B
DRUMONT, EDOUARD	740	B	DUNS, SCOTUS	740	B
DRUNKENNESS	651	B	DUPEUX, GEORGES	740	B

DUPLESSIS-MORNAY, PHILLIPPE	741	B
DURAND LINE	798	B
DURATION	579	B
DURATION OF OFFICE	235	A
DURBIN, EVAN F. M.	692	B
DURESS	135	A
DURHAM (NORTH CAROLINA)	790	B
DURKHEIM, EMILE	264	A
DUROSELL, J.	708	B
DUST BOWL	278	A
DUTIES	227	A
DUTIES OF CITIZENS	207	A
DUTRA, ENRICO	741	B
DUTY	244	A
DUTY STATION	798	B
DUVALIER, FRANCOIS (PAPA DOC)	267	A
DUVERGER, MAURICE	271	A
DYADIC CONFLICTS	579	B
DYARCHY	449	B
DYED-IN-THE-WOOL	835	B
DYKSTRA, CLARENCE A.	741	B
DYNAMIC CONSERVATISM	455	B
DYNAMICS	442	B
DYNAMISM	602	B
DYNAMITE	826	B
DYNAMOS	826	B
DYNASTY	166	A
DYSFUNCTION	119	A
E AWARD	627	B
E PLURIBUS UNUM	290	A
EAGLE	817	B
EAGLETON, THOMAS FRANCIS	266	A
EAKIN VS. RAUB (1825)	672	B
EARL	548	B
EARLDOM	548	B
EARLY SOCIALIZING EXPERIENCES	121	A
EARMARKED REVENUES	227	A
EARMARKED TAX	235	A
EARNED INCOME	253	A
EARTH	288	A
EARTH SATELLITE	288	A
EASEMENT	602	B
EAST	282	A
EAST AFRICA	278	A
EAST AFRICAN COMMON SERVICES ORGANIZATION (EACSO)	519	B
EAST AFRICAN COMMUNITY	166	A
EAST AFRICAN ECONOMIC COMMUNITY	483	B
EAST ASIA	280	A
EAST ASIA CO-PROSPERITY SPHERE	280	A
EAST BENGAL	790	B
EAST BERLIN	274	A
EAST EUROPE	274	A
EAST GERMANY	274	A
EAST INDIA COMPANY	162	A
EAST OF SUEZ	280	A
EAST-WEST RELATIONS	200	A
EAST, EDWARD M.	741	B
EASTERN BLOC	274	A
EASTERN ESTABLISHMENT	155	A
EASTERN EUROPE	274	A
EASTERN EUROPEAN MUTUAL ASSISTANCE TREATY	651	B
EASTERN FRONT	278	A
EASTERN LOCARNO	793	B
EASTERN QUESTION	253	A
EASTLAND, JAMES O.	267	A
EASTMAN, FRED	741	B
EASTON, DAVID	263	A
EASY BOSS	563	B
EATING CROW	833	B
EATON AFFAIR	627	B
EAVESDROPPING	253	A
EAVESDROPPING DEVICES	287	A
EBAN, ABBA S.	269	A
EBENEZER	741	B
EBERT, FRIEDRICH	741	B
EBONY	811	B
ECCLESIA	500	B
ECCLESIASTES	807	B
ECCLESIASTICAL COURTS	176	A
ECHELONS	166	A
ECHEVERRIA, LUIS	265	A
ECKHART	741	B
ECKHOFF, TORSTEIN	741	B
ECKSTEIN, HARRY	692	B
ECLECTIC APPROACH	125	A
ECLECTIC FUNCTIONALISM	135	A
ECLECTICISM	127	A
ECOLE DES HAUTES ETUDES SOCIALES (FRANCE)	483	B
ECOLE LIBRE DES SCIENCES POLITIQUES (FRANCE)	483	B
ECOLE NATIONALE D'ADMINISTRATION (FRANCE)	468	B
ECOLE PRATIQUE DES HAUTES ETUDES (FRANCE)	500	B
ECOLE SUPERIEURE DE JOURNALISME (FRANCE)	519	B
ECOLOGICAL ANALYSIS	130	A
ECOLOGY	125	A
ECOLOGY, POLITICAL	138	A
ECONOMETRICS	142	A
ECONOMIC ADMINISTRATION	253	A
ECONOMIC AID	227	A
ECONOMIC AND FINANCIAL COMMITTEE	519	B
ECONOMIC AND PHILOSOPHIC MANUSCRIPTS	809	B
ECONOMIC ARISTOCRACY	167	A
ECONOMIC ATTACHE	548	B

ECONOMIC BARRIER	602	B
ECONOMIC BLOCKADE	207	A
ECONOMIC CLASS	155	A
ECONOMIC COMMISSION FOR AFRICA (ECA)	483	B
ECONOMIC COMMISSION FOR ASIA AND FAR EAST (ECAFE)	468	B
ECONOMIC COMMISSION FOR EUROPE (ECE)	468	B
ECONOMIC COMMISSION FOR LATIN AMERICA	468	B
ECONOMIC COMMISSIONS, REGIONAL	468	B
ECONOMIC CONFERENCE OF 1933	627	B
ECONOMIC CONFERENCE, WORLD	483	B
ECONOMIC COOPERATION	207	A
ECONOMIC COOPERATION ADMINISTRATION (ECA)	171	A
ECONOMIC DEMAND	208	A
ECONOMIC DEMOCRACY	132	A
ECONOMIC DEPRESSION	208	A
ECONOMIC DETERMINISM	130	A
ECONOMIC DEVELOPMENT	203	A
ECONOMIC DEVELOPMENT ADMINISTRATION	176	A
ECONOMIC DEVELOPMENT INSTITUTE (IBRD)	519	B
ECONOMIC DEVELOPMENT MODELS	121	A
ECONOMIC FACTORS	130	A
ECONOMIC GROWTH	200	A
ECONOMIC IMPERIALISM	121	A
ECONOMIC INTEGRATION	125	A
ECONOMIC INTERDEPENDENCE	125	A
ECONOMIC INTERPRETATION OF HISTORY, COMMUNIST THEORY	125	A
ECONOMIC INTERPRETATION OF THE CONSTITUTION	284	A
ECONOMIC LAW	227	A
ECONOMIC MANAGEMENT	253	A
ECONOMIC MATURITY	142	A
ECONOMIC MEASURES	244	A
ECONOMIC METHOD	135	A
ECONOMIC MIRACLE	253	A
ECONOMIC MODELS	123	A
ECONOMIC NATIONALISM	130	A
ECONOMIC OPPORTUNITY ACT OF 1964	244	A
ECONOMIC ORDER	235	A
ECONOMIC PENETRATION	227	A
ECONOMIC PLANNING	208	A
ECONOMIC POLICY	200	A
ECONOMIC POWER	203	A
ECONOMIC REPORT OF THE PRESIDENT	284	A
ECONOMIC ROYALISTS	435	B
ECONOMIC SANCTIONS	220	A
ECONOMIC SCIENCE	142	A
ECONOMIC STABILIZATION POLICIES	208	A
ECONOMIC STAGES OF MANKIND	244	A
ECONOMIC SYSTEMS	125	A
ECONOMIC THEORY	127	A
ECONOMIC UNION	159	A
ECONOMIC VALUE	244	A
ECONOMIC WAR	220	A
ECONOMICS	123	A
ECONOMISM	442	B
ECONOMISTS	186	A
ECONOMY	150	A
ECONOMY ACT	627	B
ECONOMY OF ABUNDANCE	235	A
ECONOMY OF SCARCITY	244	A
ECUADOR	275	A
ECUMENICAL COUNCIL	159	A
EDELMAN, MURRAY	692	B
EDEN PLAN	602	B
EDEN, SIR ROBERT ANTHONY	271	A
EDES (GREECE)	500	B
EDGE ACT	651	B
EDICT	244	A
EDICT OF CARACALLA	627	B
EDICT OF NANTES	602	B
EDINBURGH GAZETTE	811	B
EDINBURGH REVIEW	811	B
EDINGER, LEWIS	708	B
EDITOR	548	B
EDITORIAL	285	A
EDMUNDS ACT	652	B
EDUCATION	142	A
EDUCATION ACT OF 1965	253	A
EDUCATION AND LABOR COMMITTEE	167	A
EDUCATION GRANT	227	A
EDUCATIONAL INSTITUTIONS	167	A
EDUCATIONAL ORDER	602	B
EDUCATIONAL QUALIFICATION	579	B
EDUCATOR	192	A
EDWARD II	684	B
EDWARD IV	708	B
EDWARD VIII, DUKE OF WINDSOR	684	B
EDWARD, WARD	741	B
EDWARDS VS. SOUTH CAROLINA (1963)	674	B
EDWARDS, THOMAS	741	B
EEL (LONG AND SHORT)	843	B
EEL SKIN	843	B
EFFECT	227	A
EFFECTIVE	135	A
EFFECTIVE BLOCKADE	235	A
EFFECTIVE DATE OF APPOINTMENT	227	A
EFFECTIVENESS	227	A
EFFICACY	119	A
EFFICIENCY	220	A
EFFICIENCY RATING	244	A

EFFORTS	627	B	ELECTION CERTIFICATE	285	A
EGALITARIANISM	115	A	ELECTION DAY	227	A
EGBA, NIGERIA	519	B	ELECTION DISTRICT	273	A
EGGHEAD	542	B	ELECTION MEETING	627	B
EGIDIUS COLONNA	741	B	ELECTION PETITIONS	220	A
EGIDIUS ROMANUS	741	B	ELECTION PLEDGE	235	A
EGO	135	A	ELECTION PRECINCT	274	A
EGO-DEFENSES	135	A	ELECTION PROPAGANDA	198	A
EGO-INVOLVEMENT	132	A	ELECTION RETURNS	200	A
EGOISM	135	A	ELECTIONEER	253	A
EGYPT	277	A	ELECTIONEERING	227	A
EGYPTIAN REVOLUTION OF 1952	235	A	ELECTIONEERING CAMPAIGN	235	A
EGYPTIAN-BRITISH ALLIANCE	176	A	ELECTIONS AT LARGE	208	A
EGYPTIANS	468	B	ELECTIONS, FILING	244	A
EHRENBURG, ILYA	684	B	ELECTIVE MONARCHY	159	A
EICHMANN, ADOLF	264	A	ELECTOR	184	A
EIGHT MILLIONAIRES AND A	519	B	ELECTORAL BEHAVIOR	113	A
PLUMBER			ELECTORAL CHANGE	135	A
EIGHT-HOUR MOVEMENT	627	B	ELECTORAL COLLEGE	150	A
EIGHTEEN NATION DISARMAMENT	469	B	ELECTORAL COMMISSION	171	A
COMMITTEE (ENDC)			ELECTORAL COUNT	213	A
EIGHTEEN YEAR OLD VOTE,	213	A	ELECTORAL COUNT ACT OF 1887	627	B
TWENTY-SIXTH AMENDMENT			ELECTORAL DISTRICT	273	A
EIGHTEENTH AMENDMENT	198	A	ELECTORAL EQUILIBRIUM	142	A
EIGHTH AMENDMENT	213	A	ELECTORAL FRAUD	227	A
EINAUDI, LUIGI	741	B	ELECTORAL LAW (SYSTEM)	203	A
EINHARDT	741	B	ELECTORAL PRIMARIES	220	A
EINHEITSPARTEI	500	B	ELECTORAL PROCEDURE	203	A
EINSTEIN, ALBERT	265	A	ELECTORAL PROCESSES	119	A
EIRE	278	A	ELECTORAL QUOTA	220	A
EISELEN, WERNER	741	B	ELECTORAL REFORM	213	A
EISENHOWER COMMISSION	500	B	ELECTORAL REGISTER	284	A
EISENHOWER DOCTRINE	200	A	ELECTORAL ROLL	283	A
EISENHOWER SYNTAX	835	B	ELECTORAL VOTE	213	A
EISENHOWER, PRESIDENT DWIGHT	262	A	ELECTORATE	146	A
DAVID			ELECTRIC HOME AND FARM	519	B
EISENSTADT, S. N.	271	A	AUTHORITY		
EL SALVADOR	278	A	ELECTRIC POWER COMMITTEE (EPC)	519	B
ELAN	442	B	ELECTRIC VOTING	227	A
ELAN VITA	449	B	ELECTRODYNAMICS	455	B
ELAS (GREECE)	500	B	ELECTRONIC SURVEILLANCE	208	A
ELASTIC CLAUSE (NECESSARY AND	227	A	ELECTRONIC TECHNICIANS	549	B
PROPER CLAUSE)			ELECTRONICS	442	B
ELASTIC CURRENCY	253	A	ELEMENTARY AND SECONDARY	235	A
ELASTIC DEMAND	220	A	EDUCATION ACT OF 1965		
ELAZAR, D.	741	B	ELEMENTS	819	B
ELDER STATESMAN	186	A	ELEPHANT, REPUBLICAN	288	A
ELDERSVELD, SAMUEL J.	708	B	ELEVENTH AMENDMENT	227	A
ELEATIC	455	B	ELEVENTH COMMANDMENT	579	B
ELECT	220	A	ELEVENTH HOUR MEN	563	B
ELECT A LEADER, NOT A LOVER	843	B	ELFBRANDT VS. RUSSELL (1966)	677	B
ELECTION	200	A	ELIGIBILITY	244	A
ELECTION ADDRESS	253	A	ELIGIBLE LIST	285	A
ELECTION BOARD	152	A	ELIJAH	741	B
ELECTION BY ACCLAMATION	244	A	ELIOT, CHARLES	741	B
ELECTION CAMPAIGN	203	A	ELIOT, T. S.	271	A

ELITE GUARD	483	B
ELITES	144	A
ELITES, CIRCULATION OF	130	A
ELITISM	119	A
ELITISM, FASCIST THEORY	121	A
ELITIST THEORY	114	A
ELIZABETH I OF ENGLAND	266	A
ELK HILLS	280	A
ELKIN, A. P.	741	B
ELKIN, FREDERICK	741	B
ELKINS VS. UNITED STATES (1960)	674	B
ELLENDER, ALLEN JOSEPH	692	B
ELLINIKOS DIMOKRATIKOS ETHNIKOS STRATOS (EDES)	519	B
ELLINIKOS LAIKOS APELEUTHERATIKOS STRATOS (ELAS)	519	B
ELLIOT, WILLIAM Y.	741	B
ELLIOT'S DEBATES	811	B
ELLIS, HAVELOCK	741	B
ELLISON, RALPH	692	B
ELLSBERG, DANIEL	266	A
ELLSWORTH, OLIVER	708	B
ELLUL, JACQUES	693	B
ELLWOOD, CHARLES A.	741	B
ELMIRA (NEW YORK) STUDY	285	A
ELPHEGE, SAINT	741	B
ELYSEE PALACE	280	A
EMANATION	652	B
EMANCIPATION	227	A
EMANCIPATION PROCLAMATION	198	A
EMBARGO	203	A
EMBARGO ACT OF 1807	244	A
EMBARGOROON	519	B
EMBASSY	152	A
EMBEZZLEMENT	253	A
EMBLEM	819	B
EMBLEM (UN)	289	A
EMBODIMENT	652	B
EMERGENCE	628	B
EMERGENCY	602	B
EMERGENCY ACTION	579	B
EMERGENCY BANKING RELIEF ACT	579	B
EMERGENCY FUND OF THE STATE DEPARTMENT	483	B
EMERGENCY LAW	227	A
EMERGENCY PEACE FEDERATION	519	B
EMERGENCY PETROLEUM AND GAS ADMINISTRATION (EPGA)	519	B
EMERGENCY POWERS	198	A
EMERGENCY POWERS OF THE PRESIDENT	200	A
EMERGENCY PROCUREMENT SERVICE	500	B
EMERGENCY RELIEF APPROPRIATION ACT	579	B
EMERGENT	442	B
EMERGENT EXPLANATION	449	B
EMERGENT NATIONS	152	A
EMERIGON, BALTHAZARD-MARIE	741	B
EMERSON, RALPH WALDO	266	A
EMIGRANT	182	A
EMIGRANT AID SOCIETIES	483	B
EMIGRATION	227	A
EMIGRE GOVERNMENT	171	A
EMINENCE GRISE	192	A
EMINENT DOMAIN	196	A
EMIR	189	A
EMIRATE	186	A
EMMANUEL, KING	693	B
EMOLUMENTS	227	A
EMOTION	135	A
EMOTIONALLY DISTURBED EMPLOYEES	556	B
EMOTIVISM	435	B
EMPATHY	139	A
EMPEDOCLES	741	B
EMPEROR	187	A
EMPIRE	150	A
EMPIRE, THE	171	A
EMPIRICAL	115	A
EMPIRICAL ARGUMENT	127	A
EMPIRICAL METHOD	113	A
EMPIRICAL STATEMENT	115	A
EMPIRICAL THEORY	113	A
EMPIRICISM	113	A
EMPIRICISM, POSITIVIST	119	A
EMPLOYEE CONDUCT	602	B
EMPLOYEE HEALTH	628	B
EMPLOYEE PUBLICATIONS	807	B
EMPLOYEE--WORKING CONDITION	579	B
EMPLOYEES	189	A
EMPLOYEES COMPENSATION	244	A
EMPLOYEES--PARTICIPATION IN MANAGEMENT	253	A
EMPLOYERS	542	B
EMPLOYERS FEDERATION	519	B
EMPLOYERS LIABILITY LAW	602	B
EMPLOYERS UNION	176	A
EMPLOYMENT ACT OF 1946	244	A
EMPLOYMENT AGENCIES	483	B
EMPLOYMENT SERVICE	171	A
EMPLOYMENT SERVICES AUTOMATED REPORTING SYSTEM (ESARS)	652	B
EMPLOYMENT STANDARDS ADMINISTRATION (ESA)	484	B
EMPLOYMENT TAX (SOCIAL SECURITY ACT)	220	A
EMPOWER	253	A
EMPRESS	189	A
EMPTY CHAIR	843	B

EPONYMY	455	B
EPSTEIN, LEON	693	B
EPURATION	652	B
EQUAL	235	A
EQUAL DISTRIBUTION THEORY	139	A
EQUAL EMPLOYMENT OPPORTUNITIES	227	A
EQUAL EMPLOYMENT OPPORTUNITY COMMISSION	167	A
EQUAL FOOTING	579	B
EQUAL JUSTICE UNDER LAW	203	A
EQUAL OPPORTUNITY IN EMPLOYMENT	208	A
EQUAL PAY ACT OF 1963	602	B
EQUAL PROTECTION CLAUSE	194	A
EQUAL PROTECTION OF THE LAW	200	A
EQUAL RIGHTS AMENDMENT (ERA)	198	A
EQUAL RIGHTS PARTY	500	B
EQUAL TIME	213	A
EQUAL-TIME PROVISION	220	A
EQUALITARIANISM	119	A
EQUALITY	114	A
EQUALITY OF STATES, DOCTRINE OF	125	A
EQUALIZATION	244	A
EQUALIZATION FEE	628	B
EQUALIZATION OF ASSESSMENTS	235	A
EQUILIBRATION	254	A
EQUILIBRIUM	119	A
EQUITABLE	139	A
EQUITY	220	A
EQUITY (EX AEQUO ET BONO)	235	A
EQUIVALENCE	227	A
ERA	579	B
ERA OF GOOD FEELING	235	A
ERASMUS, DESIDERIUS	267	A
ERASTIANISM	435	B
ERCOLE, FRANCESCO	742	B
ERDMAN ACT	652	B
ERFURT PROGRAM	628	B
ERHARD, PROFESSOR LUDWIG	684	B
ERIE BARGE CANAL	793	B
ERIE RAILROAD VS. TOMPKINS (1938)	674	B
ERIKSON, ERIK H.	267	A
ERITREA	275	A
ERIUGENA, JOHNNES SCOTTUS	708	B
ERLANDER, TAGE	708	B
EROBERUNGSTHEORIE	449	B
EROS	267	A
ERRAND-RUNNING	838	B
ERRING BRETHREN	556	B
ERROR	132	A
ERSATZ	288	A
ERVIN, SAMUEL JAMES, JR.	267	A
ERYTHREA	793	B
ESAU	708	B
ESCALATION	203	A
ESCALATOR CLAUSE	227	A
ESCAPE CLAUSE	244	A
ESCHATOLOGY	142	A
ESCHEAT	602	B
ESCOBEDO VS. ILLINOIS (1964)	261	A
ESCROW	254	A
ESHKOL, LEVI	684	B
ESKIMOS	171	A
ESPERANTO	139	A
ESPIONAGE	208	A
ESPIONAGE ACT OF 1917	235	A
ESSAY	805	B
ESSENCE	139	A
ESSENTIALISM	435	B
ESSEX JUNTO	484	B
ESTABLISHED CHURCH	159	A
ESTABLISHED FACT	435	B
ESTABLISHED POST	542	B
ESTABLISHED PRACTICE	442	B
ESTABLISHMENT	159	A
ESTABROOK, A. H.	708	B
ESTATE	288	A
ESTATE TAX	244	A
ESTATES GENERAL (FRANCE)	167	A
ESTIMATES	244	A
ESTONIA	280	A
ESTRADA DOCTRINE	652	B
ESTRANGEMENT	628	B
ETATISM	435	B
ETERNAL OBJECT	826	B
ETERNITY	628	B
ETHICS	121	A
ETHIOPIA	275	A
ETHNIC	183	A
ETHNIC GROUPS	148	A
ETHNIC MINORITIES	155	A
ETHNIC POLITICS	121	A
ETHNICITY	213	A
ETHNIKON APELEUTHEROTIKON METOPON (EAM-GREECE)	500	B
ETHNOCENTRISM	117	A
ETHNOGRAPHICAL PRINCIPLE	442	B
ETHNOGRAPHY	135	A
ETHNOHISTORICAL	142	A
ETHNOLOGY	132	A
ETHOPIA-SOMALI	282	A
ETIQUETTE	602	B
ETRUSCANS	484	B
ETZIONI, AMITAI	267	A
EUCKEN, R.	708	B
EUCKEN, WALTER	708	B
EUCLID	693	B
EUCLID OF MEGARA	709	B
EUDOXUS	709	B
EUFUNCTION	449	B

EUGENIUS	709	B
EULAU, HEINZ	265	A
EUNUCH RULE	628	B
EUPHEMISM, POLITICAL	139	A
EURASIA	278	A
EURIPIDES	693	B
EUROFIMA (EUROPEAN FINANCE COMPANY)	500	B
EUROPE	273	A
EUROPEAN	162	A
EUROPEAN AGRICULTURAL ORIENTATION AND GUARANTEE FUNDS	519	B
EUROPEAN AND MEDITERRANEAN PLANT PROTECTION ORGANIZATION	519	B
EUROPEAN ARMY	469	B
EUROPEAN ATOMIC ENERGY COMMUNITY (EURATOM)	155	A
EUROPEAN CIVIL SERVICE	469	B
EUROPEAN COAL AND STEEL COMMUNITY (ECSC)	167	A
EUROPEAN COMMISSION ON AGRICULTURE	500	B
EUROPEAN COMMISSION ON HUMAN RIGHTS	469	B
EUROPEAN COMMON MARKET	147	A
EUROPEAN COMMUNITY	162	A
EUROPEAN CONFERENCE OF MINISTERS OF TRANSPORT	519	B
EUROPEAN CONFERENCE OF POSTAL AND TELECOMMUNICATIONS ADMIN. (CEPT)	519	B
EUROPEAN CONVENTION ON EXTRADITION	628	B
EUROPEAN CONVENTION ON HUMAN RIGHTS	579	B
EUROPEAN DEFENCE COMMUNITY (EDC)	167	A
EUROPEAN ECONOMIC COMMUNITY (EEC)	146	A
EUROPEAN FEDERALISM	135	A
EUROPEAN FORESTRY COMMISSION	500	B
EUROPEAN FREE TRADE ASSOCIATION (EFTA)	162	A
EUROPEAN FUND FOR MONETARY COOPERATION	519	B
EUROPEAN INTEGRATION	198	A
EUROPEAN INVESTMENT BANK	500	B
EUROPEAN MONETARY AGREEMENT	628	B
EUROPEAN MOVEMENT	171	A
EUROPEAN NUCLEAR ENERGY AGENCY	484	B
EUROPEAN ORGANIZATION FOR NUCLEAR RESEARCH (CERN)	500	B
EUROPEAN PARLIAMENT	162	A
EUROPEAN PAYMENTS UNION	176	A
EUROPEAN PRODUCTIVITY AGENCY	484	B
EUROPEAN RECOVERY PROGRAM (ERP)	152	A
EUROPEAN SOCIALIST AND SOCIAL DEMOCRATIC PARTIES	167	A
EUROPEAN SPACE RESEARCH ORGANIZATION	500	B
EUROPEAN SPACE VEHICLE LAUNCHER DEVELOPMENT (ELDO)	519	B
EUROPEAN UNIFICATION	213	A
EUROPEAN UNION	167	A
EUROPEAN UNION OF FEDERALISTS	500	B
EUROPEAN UNITY	123	A
EUROPEANS	155	A
EUSEBIUS	742	B
EUTHENASIA	244	A
EVACUATION	245	A
EVACUATION OF DUNKIRK	245	A
EVALUATION	135	A
EVANGELICAL CHURCH	484	B
EVANS, F.W.	742	B
EVANS, SIR ARTHUR	742	B
EVENT	254	A
EVER-NORMAL GRANARY PLAN	628	B
EVERS, CHARLES	265	A
EVERS, MEDGAR	266	A
EVERSON VS. BOARD OF EDUCATION OF EWING TOWNSHIP (1947)	672	B
EVERY MAN A KING	839	B
EVERYMAN	192	A
EVIAN AGREEMENT	628	B
EVIDENCE	125	A
EVIL	142	A
EVOLUTION	127	A
EVOLUTIONARY SOCIALISM	283	A
EWING, CORTEZ A. M.	742	B
EX AEQUO ET BONO, DECISION	628	B
EX OFFICIO	182	A
EX PARTE	254	A
EX PARTE GARLAND (1867)	677	B
EX PARTE GROSSMAN (1925)	677	B
EX PARTE MC CARDLE (1869)	674	B
EX PARTE MERRYMAN (1861)	677	B
EX PARTE MILLIGAN (1866)	261	A
EX PARTE SIEBOLD (1880)	674	B
EX POST FACTO LAW	196	A
EXACT SCIENCES	139	A
EXAMINATION	254	A
EXARCHATE (EASTERN BISHOPRIC)	563	B
EXCELLENCE	456	B
EXCEPT	628	B
EXCESS CONDEMNATION	628	B
EXCESS PROFITS TAX	208	A

EXCESSES	579	B	EXECUTIVE WAR	254	A
EXCHANGE	130	A	EXECUTIVE-LEGISLATIVE	117	A
EXCHANGE BEHAVIOR	132	A	RELATIONSHIPS		
EXCHANGE CONTROL	442	B	EXECUTIVES	183	A
EXCHANGE FACILITIES	602	B	EXECUTOR	542	B
EXCHANGE OF INSTRUMENTS OF	254	A	EXEGETIC METHOD	456	B
RATIFICATIONS			EXEMPLIFICATION	435	B
EXCHANGE OF NOTES	235	A	EXEMPT CLASS	176	A
EXCHANGE OF POPULATIONS	602	B	EXEMPTION	254	A
EXCHANGE OF POSTS	628	B	EXEQUATUR	812	B
EXCHANGE OF PRISONERS	213	A	EXERCISE	254	A
EXCHANGE OF TERRITORY	254	A	EXHAUSTION OF LOCAL REMEDIES	235	A
EXCHANGE OF VIEWS	227	A	EXHAUSTIVE BALLOT	628	B
EXCHANGE OFFICE	500	B	EXILE	183	A
EXCHANGE RATE	130	A	EXISTENCE	580	B
EXCHANGE STABILIZATION FUND	602	B	EXISTENTIAL IMPORT	442	B
EXCHANGE STUDENTS	187	A	EXISTENTIALISM	119	A
EXCHANGE THEORY	127	A	EXIT INTERVIEWS	443	B
EXCHEQUER	189	A	EXIT VISA	284	A
EXCISE	227	A	EXODUS	807	B
EXCISE TAX	200	A	EXOGAMY	580	B
EXCLAVE	787	B	EXPANDED PROGRAM OF	602	B
EXCLUDED MIDDLE	139	A	TECHNICAL ASSISTANCE (EPTA)		
EXCLUSION	139	A	EXPANDING BULLET	819	B
EXCLUSIVE JURISDICTION	213	A	EXPANSIONIST POLICY	203	A
EXCLUSIVE POWER	139	A	EXPATRIATE	186	A
EXCUSABILITY	449	B	EXPATRIATION	213	A
EXECUTE	235	A	EXPECTATION	142	A
EXECUTION	220	A	EXPEDIENCY	245	A
EXECUTIONERS	171	A	EXPEDITER	542	B
EXECUTIVE	181	A	EXPEDITIONARY FORCE	159	A
EXECUTIVE AGENCIES	155	A	EXPEL	220	A
EXECUTIVE AGENT	189	A	EXPENSE ALLOWANCE	580	B
EXECUTIVE AGREEMENT	195	A	EXPENSE BUDGET	254	A
EXECUTIVE AND LIASON COMMITTEE	519	B	EXPERIENCE	628	B
(ELC)			EXPERIMENT	121	A
EXECUTIVE BOARD	176	A	EXPERIMENTAL METHOD	117	A
EXECUTIVE BODY	152	A	EXPERIMENTAL STUDY	125	A
EXECUTIVE BRANCH	145	A	EXPERT	189	A
EXECUTIVE BUDGET	200	A	EXPERTISE	139	A
EXECUTIVE CALENDAR	254	A	EXPERTS	542	B
EXECUTIVE CLEMENCY	200	A	EXPERTS REPORT	809	B
EXECUTIVE COMMITTEE	162	A	EXPIRATION	580	B
EXECUTIVE COUNCIL	172	A	EXPLANATION	123	A
EXECUTIVE DEPARTMENT	147	A	EXPLANATION IN SOCIAL SCIENCES	114	A
EXECUTIVE DIRECTORS	549	B	EXPLICATION	130	A
EXECUTIVE DISCRETION	227	A	EXPLICIT RENEWAL	652	B
EXECUTIVE MANSION	817	B	EXPLOITATION OF MAN BY MAN	235	A
EXECUTIVE OFFICE OF THE	145	A	EXPLORATION	254	A
PRESIDENT			EXPLORATORY	254	A
EXECUTIVE ORDER	195	A	EXPLOSIVE	822	B
EXECUTIVE POWER	196	A	EXPORT	286	A
EXECUTIVE PRIVILEGE	196	A	EXPORT BOUNTY (SUBSIDY)	254	A
EXECUTIVE PROCESS	117	A	EXPORT EXPANSION FINANCE ACT	628	B
EXECUTIVE SECRETARY	542	B	OF 1971		
EXECUTIVE SESSION	203	A	EXPORT MARKETING SERVICE (EMS)	520	B

EXPORT TAX	213	A	FACT-FINDING COMMITTEE	155	A
EXPORT-IMPORT BANK OF	155	A	FACT-FINDING TRIP	220	A
WASHINGTON			FACTION	148	A
EXPOSITION	602	B	FACTIONALISM	213	A
EXPRESS POWERS	204	A	FACTOR	130	A
EXPRESS POWERS OF CONGRESS	208	A	FACTOR ANALYSIS	119	A
EXPRESSION	443	B	FACTORY	288	A
EXPRESSIONISM	443	B	FACTORY LAWS	603	B
EXPRESSIVENESS	456	B	FACTORY SYSTEM	235	B
EXPROPRIATION (NATIONALIZATION)	227	A	FACULTADES EXTRAORDINARIAS	500	B
EXPULSION	235	A	(FACULTY EXTRAORDINARY)		
EXPULSION OF MEMBERS	227	A	FACULTATIVE CLAUSE	652	B
EXPUNGE	245	A	FACULTIES OF LAW	500	B
EXTEMPORE	254	A	FACULTY	176	A
EXTENSION	254	A	FAGEN, RICHARD	684	B
EXTENSION OF A CONFLICT	254	A	FAGERNHOLM, KARL-AUGUST	742	B
EXTENSION OF REMARKS	285	A	FAGUET, EMILE	742	B
EXTENSION SERVICE	484	B	FAIL-SAFE	208	A
EXTENSIONAL DEFINITION	135	A	FAINSOD, MERLE	269	A
EXTENSIONALITY	443	B	FAIR DEAL	208	A
EXTENSIVE INTERPRETATION	443	B	FAIR EMPLOYMENT PRACTICES	227	A
EXTERIORITY	456	B	LAWS		
EXTERMINATION CAMP	288	A	FAIR EMPLOYMENT PRACTICES	155	A
EXTERNAL	282	A	COMMISSION (FEPC)		
EXTERNAL LOAN	652	B	FAIR LABOR STANDARDS ACT OF	245	A
EXTERNAL SOVEREIGNTY	254	A	1938		
EXTERNALITY	602	B	FAIR PACKAGING AND LABELING	580	B
EXTINCTION OF STATES	435	B	ACT OF 1966		
EXTORTION	227	A	FAIR SHAKE	603	B
EXTRA CURRICULAR ACTIVITIES	603	B	FAIR TRADE LAWS	227	A
EXTRA SESSION	254	A	FAIR TRIAL	198	A
EXTRA-CONSTITUTIONAL	227	A	FAIR WEATHER POLITICIAN	542	B
EXTRA-LEGAL PARTY	176	A	FAIRBROTHER, W. H.	742	B
EXTRACTIVE INDUSTRY	484	B	FAIRCHILD, FRED R.	742	B
EXTRADITABLE OFFENSES	213	A	FAIRCHILD, HENRY P.	709	B
EXTRADITION	204	A	FAIRLIE, JOHN A.	742	B
EXTRALEGAL	227	A	FAIRMAN, CHARLES	709	B
EXTRALITY	629	B	FAISAL, KING	266	A
EXTRAMURAL	790	B	FAIT ACCOMPLI	208	A
EXTRAMURAL JURISDICTION	603	B	FAITH	443	B
EXTRAORDINARY SESSION	204	A	FAITH AND CREDIT	254	A
EXTRASENSORY	435	B	FAITH AND REASON	443	B
EXTRATERRITORIALITY	200	A	FAITHFUL	443	B
EXTREMISM	117	A	FALA SPEECH	603	B
EXTREMIST PARTY	155	A	FALANGE PARTY	176	A
EYEBALL TO EYEBALL	291	A	FALANGISTS	172	A
EYEWASH	291	A	FALCONRY	629	B
EZEKIEL, MORDECAI	742	B	FALK, R. A.	693	B
FABIAN ESSAYS	805	B	FALKLAND ISLANDS CONTROVERSY	254	A
FABIAN RESEARCH DEPARTMENT	176	A	FALL OF THE THIRD REICH	284	A
FABIAN SOCIALISM	131	A	FALL VACANT	603	B
FABIAN SOCIETY	162	A	FALLACY	135	A
FABIANISM	123	A	FALLBACK POSITION	235	A
FACE-TO-FACE TALK	254	A	FALLIBILISM	443	B
FACT	119	A	FALLIPOLI PENINSULA	793	B
FACT AND VALUE	113	A	FALLOUT	287	A

FALSE	142	A	FASHODA AFFAIR	629	B
FALSE COLORS	839	B	FAT CAT	192	A
FALSE COUNTER	556	B	FAT FRYING	843	B
FALSE IMPRISONMENT	213	A	FAT OFFICE	563	B
FALSIFIABILITY	125	A	FATALISM	139	A
FALSIFICATION	130	A	FATHER ABRAHAM	742	B
FALSIFY	142	A	FATHER OF HIS COUNTRY	271	A
FAMILY	177	A	FATHER OF THE CONSTITUTION	271	A
FAMILY ASSISTANCE PLAN (FAP)	254	A	FATHER OF THE HOUSE	563	B
FAMILY COURT	469	B	FATHER PRINCIPLE	449	B
FAMILY OF NATIONS	177	A	FATHER-ABSENCE	629	B
FAMILY PLANNING	254	A	FATHERLAND	278	A
FAMILY SERVICE BUREAU	484	B	FATHERLAND FRONT	484	B
FAMINE	235	A	FATHERS OF THE CHURCH	192	A
FANATICISM	135	A	FATHERS, THE	500	B
FANFANI, AMINTORE	684	B	FAUBUS, ORVAL E.	693	B
FANNIN, PAUL JONES	709	B	FAULKNER	709	B
FANNY MAY (FANNIE MAE - ALSO,	162	A	FAVORITE SON	192	A
FEDERAL NATIONAL MORTGAGE			FAVORITE, THE	563	B
ASSOCIATION)			FAWKES, GUY	271	A
FANON, FRANTZ	269	A	FAWZI, HUSAYN	709	B
FANTASY	443	B	FAY VS. NEW YORK (1947)	674	B
FAR EAST	274	A	FAY, CHARLES M.	742	B
FAR EASTERN ADVISORY COUNCIL	500	B	FAY, SIDNEY	742	B
FAR EASTERN COMMISSION	520	B	FEAR	139	A
FARM	787	B	FEATHERBEDDING	289	A
FARM BLOC	155	A	FEATHERHEAD	556	B
FARM BUREAU FEDERATION	172	A	FEBRERISTA	500	B
FARM CREDIT ADMINISTRATION	469	B	FEBRUARY REVOLUTION	245	A
(FCA)			FEDAYEEN (ALSO, FIDAIYUN)	167	A
FARM LOAN ASSOCIATION	469	B	FEDER, GOTTFRIED	709	B
FARM MORTGAGE MORATORIUM	603	B	FEDERAL	150	A
ACT			FEDERAL ACT	220	A
FARM PRESSURE GROUPS	152	A	FEDERAL AID	208	A
FARM PRICE SUPPORTS	208	A	FEDERAL AID HIGHWAY ACT	629	B
FARM SECURITY ADMINISTRATION	484	B	FEDERAL AID TO EDUCATION	213	A
FARMER COMMITTEE SYSTEM	603	B	FEDERAL APPOINTMENTS	208	A
FARMER COOPERATIVE SERVICE	484	B	FEDERAL ASSEMBLY	155	A
FARMER FIELDMAN	556	B	FEDERAL AUDIT OFFICE	500	B
FARMER-LABOR PARTY	167	A	FEDERAL AUTHORITY	152	A
FARMERS ALLIANCE	172	A	FEDERAL AVIATION ADMINISTRATION	162	A
FARMERS HOME ADMINISTRATION	484	B	(FAA)		
(FHA)			FEDERAL BOARD OF	520	B
FARMERS PARTY	500	B	HOSPITALIZATION		
FARMERS UNION	162	A	FEDERAL BUDGET	204	A
FAROUK, KING	269	A	FEDERAL BUREAU OF	150	A
FARRIS, CHARLES D.	742	B	INVESTIGATION (FBI)		
FASCES	289	A	FEDERAL CABINET	152	A
FASCISM	113	A	FEDERAL CHANCELLOR	186	A
FASCIST GRAND COUNCIL	500	B	FEDERAL CIVIL DEFENSE	177	A
FASCIST INSTITUTE OF CULTURE	520	B	ADMINISTRATION		
(ITALY)			FEDERAL CIVIL RIGHTS	152	A
FASCIST ORGANIZATIONS, U.S.	167	A	COMMISSION		
FASCIST PARTY	159	A	FEDERAL CLAIMS COURT	155	A
FASCIST THEORY	115	A	FEDERAL CODE ANNOTATED	285	A
FASCIST YOUTH ORGANIZATION	172	A	FEDERAL COMMISSIONERS	469	B

FEDERAL COMMON LAW	254	A
FEDERAL COMMUNICATIONS ACT OF 1934	227	A
FEDERAL COMMUNICATIONS COMMISSION (FCC)	152	A
FEDERAL CONSTITUTIONAL COURT	177	A
FEDERAL CONSUMER ADVOCATE	542	B
FEDERAL CORRUPT PRACTICES ACT	227	A
FEDERAL COUNCIL	167	A
FEDERAL COURT JURISDICTION	213	A
FEDERAL COURTS	147	A
FEDERAL COURTS OF APPEALS	147	A
FEDERAL COURTS, TERRITORIAL	172	A
FEDERAL CROP INSURANCE CORPORATION	501	B
FEDERAL DEBT	220	A
FEDERAL DEPOSIT INSURANCE CORPORATION (FDIC)	172	A
FEDERAL DIET	162	A
FEDERAL DIGEST	285	A
FEDERAL DISTRICT COURTS	146	A
FEDERAL EDUCATION	580	B
FEDERAL ELECTION CAMPAIGN ACT	245	A
FEDERAL ELECTORAL ACT	235	A
FEDERAL EMERGENCY RELIEF ACT	580	B
FEDERAL EMERGENCY RELIEF ADMINISTRATION (FERA)	501	B
FEDERAL EMPLOYEES	167	A
FEDERAL EXECUTIVE BOARDS	177	A
FEDERAL EXECUTIVE DEPARTMENTS	159	A
FEDERAL EXTENSION SERVICE	484	B
FEDERAL FARM BOARD	520	B
FEDERAL FARM LOAN ACT	629	B
FEDERAL FARM LOAN CORPORATION	469	B
FEDERAL FARM MORTGAGE CORPORATION	177	A
FEDERAL GOVERNMENT	147	A
FEDERAL HIGHWAY ADMINISTRATION (FHWA)	172	A
FEDERAL HOME LOAN BANK BOARD (FHLBB)	172	A
FEDERAL HOUSING ADMINISTRATION (FHA)	155	A
FEDERAL INSURANCE ADMINISTRATION (FIA)	484	B
FEDERAL INTERMEDIATE CREDIT BANK	501	B
FEDERAL JUDGES	182	A
FEDERAL JUDICIAL CENTER	520	B
FEDERAL LAND BANK	177	A
FEDERAL LAW	208	A
FEDERAL LAW-ENFORCEMENT AGENCIES	155	A
FEDERAL LEVEL	162	A
FEDERAL MARITIME COMMISSION (FMC)	172	A
FEDERAL MARSHAL	187	A
FEDERAL MEDIATION AND CONCILIATION SERVICE (FMCS)	162	A
FEDERAL MINISTER	189	A
FEDERAL MINISTER FOR ALL-GERMAN QUESTIONS	549	B
FEDERAL NATIONAL MORTGAGE ASSOCIATION (FNMA)	172	A
FEDERAL OFFICE OF EDUCATION	167	A
FEDERAL OPEN MARKET COMMITTEE	501	B
FEDERAL PACT	580	B
FEDERAL POLICE POWER	220	A
FEDERAL POWER ACT OF 1930	629	B
FEDERAL POWER COMM VS. HOPE NATURAL GAS (1944)	677	B
FEDERAL POWER COMMISSION (FPC)	155	A
FEDERAL PRESIDENT	184	A
FEDERAL PUBLIC HOUSING AUTHORITY	167	A
FEDERAL QUESTION	208	A
FEDERAL RADIO COMMISSION	484	B
FEDERAL RAILROAD ADMINISTRATION (FRA)	501	B
FEDERAL REGIONAL COUNCIL	520	B
FEDERAL REGISTER	284	A
FEDERAL REGISTRAR	186	A
FEDERAL REGULATION OF LOBBYING ACT OF 1946 (U.S.)	245	A
FEDERAL RELIEF	254	A
FEDERAL REPORTER	805	B
FEDERAL REPUBLIC OF GERMANY	150	A
FEDERAL RESERVE ACT	213	A
FEDERAL RESERVE BOARD	156	A
FEDERAL RESERVE NOTES	227	A
FEDERAL RESERVE SYSTEM	147	A
FEDERAL SALARIES	629	B
FEDERAL SAVINGS AND LOAN INSURANCE CORPORATION	172	A
FEDERAL SECURITY AGENCY	177	A
FEDERAL SERVICE ENTRANCE EXAMINATION	227	A
FEDERAL STATE	156	A
FEDERAL SUPPLEMENT	254	A
FEDERAL SUPPLY SERVICE	520	B
FEDERAL SYSTEM	145	A
FEDERAL SYSTEM, SOVIET UNION	156	A
FEDERAL TELECOMMUNICATIONS SYSTEM (FTS)	177	A
FEDERAL TRADE COMMISSION (FTC)	152	A
FEDERAL TRADE COMMISSION ACT OF 1914	235	A
FEDERAL TRADE COMMISSION VS. COLGATE-PALMOLIVE (1965)	674	B

FEDERAL UNION	159	A	FERDINAND II OF ARAGON	709	B
FEDERAL WORKS AGENCY	469	B	FERGUSON, ADAM	742	B
FEDERAL-LOCAL COOPERATION IN	254	A	FERGUSON, W.S.	743	B
LAW ENFORCEMENT			FERGUSSON, A.	743	B
FEDERALISM	114	A	FERMENT	603	B
FEDERALIST ,THE	283	A	FERRERO, GUGLIELMO	743	B
FEDERALIST PAPERS, THE	283	A	FERRI, ENRICO	743	B
FEDERALIST PARTY	156	A	FERTILE CRESCENT PLAN	254	A
FEDERALIST PERIOD	213	A	FERTILITY CULT	456	B
FEDERATED CITY	469	B	FERTILIZERS	819	B
FEDERATION	150	A	FESLER, JAMES W.	709	B
FEDERATION DE LA GAUCHE	501	B	FESTINGER, LEON	265	A
DEMOCRATIQUE ET SOCIALISTE			FESTUNG EUROPA (FORTRESS	787	B
FEDERATION OF ARAB EMIRATES	177	A	EUROPE)		
FEDERATION OF ARAB REPUBLICS	177	A	FEUD	580	B
FEDERATION OF MALAYA	172	A	FEUDAL COMMENDATION	652	B
FEDERATION OF NIGERIA	162	A	FEUDAL CONTRACT	220	A
FEDERATION OF RHODESIA AND	159	A	FEUDAL KINGSHIP	192	A
NYASALAND			FEUDAL LORD	184	A
FEDERATION OF SOUTH ARABIA	177	A	FEUDALISM	115	A
FEDERATION OF TAX	520	B	FEUERBACH, LUDWIG	693	B
ADMINISTRATORS (U.S.)			FEW DIE AND NONE RESIGN	839	B
FEDERATION OF THE WEST INDIES	167	A	FIASCO	580	B
FEDERO-AMERICANS	520	B	FIAT	213	A
FEDERZONI, LUIGI	742	B	FIAT MONEY	603	B
FEE	254	A	FICHTE, JOHANN GOTTLIEB	743	B
FEE SYSTEM	629	B	FICINO, MARSILIO	743	B
FEED TROUGH	843	B	FICTION	139	A
FEEDBACK	121	A	FIDAIYUN (ALSO, FEDAYEEN)	501	B
FEEDBACK CHANNEL	132	A	FIDELISMO	132	A
FEEDBACK LOOP	123	A	FIDELITY	435	B
FEEDBACK PHENOMENA	132	A	FIDUCIARY	542	B
FEEDING AT THE PUBLIC TROUGH	291	A	FIEF	274	A
FEELEY, JAMES	742	B	FIELD	278	A
FEELING	443	B	FIELD EXPERIMENT	123	A
FEET TO THE FIRE	839	B	FIELD RESEARCH	119	A
FEHR, KARL	742	B	FIELD SERVICE	172	A
FEINER VS. NEW YORK (1947)	677	B	FIELD STUDY	125	A
FELDMAN, JACOB J.	742	B	FIELD THEORY	121	A
FELIPE, LEON	742	B	FIELD, LOWELL	743	B
FELLMAN, DAVID	709	B	FIELD, OLIVER	743	B
FELLOW COUNTRYMEN	549	B	FIELD, STEPHEN JOHNSON	709	B
FELLOW TRAVELER	187	A	FIEVRE	743	B
FELLOW-SERVANT DOCTRINE	603	B	FIFTEENTH AMENDMENT	200	A
FELLOWSHIPS	192	A	FIFTH AMENDMENT	195	A
FELONY	204	A	FIFTH AMENDMENT COMMUNIST	187	A
FELS, JOSEPH	742	B	FIFTH COLUMN	150	A
FEMALE	542	A	FIFTH COLUMNIST	182	A
FEMALE SUFFRAGE	204	A	FIFTH COMMITTEE	469	B
FENCE MENDING	290	A	FIFTH FREEDOM	580	B
FENCE POLITICIAN	556	B	FIFTH REPUBLIC OF FRANCE	150	A
FENCE STRADDLER	192	A	FIFTIES	603	B
FENCE-VIEWERS	564	B	FIFTY-FOUR FORTY OR FIGHT	291	A
FENCEMAN	564	B	FIGGIS, J. NEVILLE	743	B
FENELON, FRANCOIS	742	B	FIGHT	580	B
FENTON, JOHN H.	742	B	FIGHT THE GOOD FIGHT	835	B

FIGHTER	556	B	FINESSE	629	B
FIGHTING	652	B	FINGER ON THE BUTTON	291	A
FIGHTING FRENCH	469	B	FINITE	133	A
FIGHTING THE PROBLEM	835	B	FINLAND	275	A
FIGL, LEOPOLD	743	B	FINLAYSON, CLARENCE	709	B
FIGLI DELLA LUPA	520	B	FINNISH	484	B
FIGURATIVE LANGUAGE	139	A	FINNISH-RUSSIAN WAR	227	A
FIGURE	652	B	FIRE	652	B
FIGUREHEAD	192	A	FIRE DEPARTMENT	484	B
FIGURERES, JOSE	709	B	FIRE MARSHAL	549	B
FIJI	280	A	FIRE-EATER	556	B
FILE	580	B	FIREBRAND RESOLUTIONS	629	B
FILE LEADER	542	B	FIREMEN	564	B
FILHO, CAFE	743	B	FIRESIDE CHAT	245	A
FILIBUSTER	196	A	FIRM	520	B
FILIBUSTERERS	182	A	FIRM ATTITUDE	443	B
FILIBUSTERING EXPEDITION	603	B	FIRM, THEORY OF	443	B
FILING CLERK	556	B	FIRST AMENDMENT	194	A
FILING FEE	220	A	FIRST BANK OF THE UNITED STATES	167	A
FILING FOR OFFICE	213	A	FIRST CHAMBER	469	B
FILLEBROWNE, C. B.	743	B	FIRST COMMITTEE	484	B
FILLMORE, PRESIDENT MILLARD	267	A	FIRST CONTINENTAL CONGRESS	150	A
FILM	820	B	FIRST CZECH CRISIS	629	B
FILMER, SIR ROBERT	709	B	FIRST EMPIRE (FRANCE)	469	B
FILTRATION	652	B	FIRST GUN	843	B
FINAL ACT	629	B	FIRST IN WAR, FIRST IN PEACE,	835	B
FINAL BALLOT	254	A	FIRST IN THE HEARTS OF HIS		
FINAL COMMUNIQUE	254	A	COUNTRYMEN		
FINAL DISCHARGE	603	B	FIRST INTERNATIONAL	167	A
FINAL HOMAGE	629	B	FIRST LADY	192	A
FINAL PROVISIONS	652	B	FIRST LORD OF THE ADMIRALTY	549	B
FINAL REPORT	285	A	FIRST MOROCCAN CRISIS	629	B
FINAL RESPECTS	629	B	FIRST PAPERS	603	B
FINAL RESTING PLACE	794	B	FIRST PRESIDENT OF THE	542	B
FINAL SOLUTION	227	A	SOUTHERN CONFEDERACY		
FINAL VICTORY	603	B	FIRST READING	208	A
FINALITY	603	B	FIRST REICH	177	A
FINALITY MEN	564	B	FIRST REPUBLIC (FRANCE)	167	A
FINALITY WHIG	520	B	FIRST SECRETARY OF THE PARTY	189	A
FINANCE	245	A	FIRST SOCIALIST INTERNATIONAL	159	A
FINANCE CAPITALISM	130	A	FIRST STRIKE CAPACITY	198	A
FINANCE COMMITTEE	162	A	FIRST VISIT	652	B
FINANCE DEPARTMENT	177	A	FISCAL ADMINISTRATION	227	A
FINANCE, INTERNATIONAL	235	A	FISCAL CORPORATION	484	B
FINANCES (UN)	245	A	FISCAL IMMUNITY	580	B
FINANCIAL ADVISOR	549	B	FISCAL INTEGRITY	227	A
FINANCIAL ATTACHE	549	B	FISCAL LAW	603	B
FINANCIAL INSPECTION	603	B	FISCAL OFFENSES	629	B
FINANCIAL INSTITUTION	469	B	FISCAL PLANNING	208	A
FINANCIAL SOVEREIGNTY	603	B	FISCAL POLICY	213	A
FINDINGS	227	A	FISCAL YEAR	220	A
FINE	580	B	FISCHER, EUGEN	743	B
FINE ARTS	435	B	FISH AND WILDLIFE SERVICE, U.S.	469	B
FINE GAEL	469	B	FISHER, H. A. L.	743	B
FINENESS OF COINS	826	B	FISHER, SIR JOHN	743	B
FINER, HERMAN	684	B	FISHER, SUELLEN	743	B

FISHERIES	822	B
FISHING AGREEMENT	254	A
FISHING EXPEDITION	291	A
FISHING ON THE HIGH SEAS	236	A
FISKE, JOHN	709	B
FISSION	236	A
FISSIONABLE MATERIAL	287	A
FIST LAW	603	B
FITZNEAL, RICHARD	743	B
FIUME INCIDENT	603	B
FIVE FREEDOMS	245	A
FIVE PARTITIONS OF POLAND	580	B
FIVE PERCENTER	192	A
FIVE POWER TREATY	603	B
FIVE PRINCIPLES OF PEACEFUL CO-EXISTENCE	254	A
FIVE YEAR PLANS	236	A
FIVE-FIVE-THREE RATIO	254	A
FIVE-MINUTE RULE	603	B
FIVE-TO-FOUR DECISION	220	A
FIX	603	B
FIXED-TERM APPOINTMENT	227	A
FLAG	287	A
FLAG (UN)	288	A
FLAG DAY	629	B
FLAG OF TRUCE	287	A
FLAG SALUTE CASES	260	A
FLAG, AMERICAN	289	A
FLAK	652	B
FLAMING LIBERAL	189	A
FLAMMABLE FABRICS ACT OF 1953	603	B
FLANIGAN, WILLIAM	743	B
FLANNEL-MOUTHED BOURBON	564	B
FLAP	835	B
FLAPPER VOTE	501	B
FLAST VS. COHEN (1968)	674	B
FLAT-OUT	843	B
FLAUBERT	693	B
FLAX	826	B
FLEMING, DENNA F.	743	B
FLEMINGS	484	B
FLEMISH NATIONALISM	139	A
FLETCHER VS. PECK (1810)	671	B
FLEXIBLE CONSTITUTION	245	A
FLEXIBLE TARIFF	245	A
FLICK, FRIEDRICH KARL	743	B
FLIGHT	629	B
FLINDERS-PETRIE, W. E.	743	B
FLOATER	542	B
FLOATING	603	B
FLOATING DEBT	254	A
FLOATING MINE	822	B
FLOATING VOTE	177	A
FLOO-FLOO BIRD	564	B
FLOOD CONTROL	254	A
FLOOR	820	B
FLOOR DEBATE	220	A
FLOOR FIGHT	236	A
FLOOR LEADER	182	A
FLOOR WAGE	254	A
FLORIDA	282	A
FLORO, GEORGE K.	743	B
FLUX	435	B
FLY THE TRACK	844	B
FLY-UP-THE-CREEK	844	B
FLYER	652	B
FLYING VISIT	629	B
FOCH, FERDINAND	693	B
FOCUS	652	B
FOGELMAN, EDWIN	743	B
FOGGY BOTTOM	280	A
FOLK	167	A
FOLK-MOOT	501	B
FOLK, JOSEPH	743	B
FOLKETING	520	B
FOLKWAYS	245	A
FOLLETT, MARY	693	B
FOLLOWERS	192	A
FOLLOWING	520	B
FONDATION NATIONALE DES SCIENCES POLITIQUES (FRA)	501	B
FONG YUE TING VS. U.S. (1893)	677	B
FONG, HIRAM LEONG	271	A
FONOPOSTAL	520	B
FOOD	288	A
FOOD ADDITIVES AMENDMENT OF 1958	629	B
FOOD AND AGRICULTURE ORGANIZATION (FAO)	162	A
FOOD AND DRUG ADMINISTRATION (FDA)	152	A
FOOD DISTRIBUTION ADMINISTRATION	520	B
FOOD FOR PEACE PROGRAM	213	A
FOOD STAMP PLAN	213	A
FOOD, DRUG AND COSMETIC ACT OF 1938	580	B
FOOT AND MOUTH DISEASE	844	B
FOOT-IN-MOUTH DISEASE	835	B
FOOT, HUGH	743	B
FOOT, MICHAEL	743	B
FOOTBALL, POLITICAL	291	A
FOOTNOTE TO HISTORY	839	B
FOR ROOSEVELT BEFORE CHICAGO	291	A
FORAKER ACT	629	B
FORBIDDEN	652	B
FORCE	204	A
FORCE BILL	604	B
FORCE DE FRAPPE	236	A
FORCE, GOSPEL OF	443	B
FORCED LABOR	227	A
FORCED LABOR CAMPS	159	A

FORCED LOANS	629	B
FORCES OF CHANGE	139	A
FORCING	604	B
FORD CORPORATION	172	A
FORD FOUNDATION	159	A
FORD, PRESIDENT GERALD R.	262	A
FORDNEY-MCCUMBER TARIFF	629	B
FOREBEARANCE	443	B
FORECAST	142	A
FORECLOSURE	580	B
FOREIGN	282	A
FOREIGN AFFAIRS	200	A
FOREIGN AFFAIRS ADMINISTRATION	484	B
FOREIGN AFFAIRS COMMITTEE	159	A
FOREIGN AGENT	192	A
FOREIGN AGENTS REGISTRATION ACT	580	B
FOREIGN AID	220	A
FOREIGN AID PROGRAM	208	A
FOREIGN ASSISTANCE ACT OF 1948	604	B
FOREIGN BONDHOLDERS PROTECTIVE COUNCIL	520	B
FOREIGN COMMERCE	220	A
FOREIGN CORPORATION	484	B
FOREIGN ECONOMIC ADMINISTRATION	520	B
FOREIGN ECONOMIC POLICY	208	A
FOREIGN EXCHANGE	213	A
FOREIGN FUNDS CONTROL	652	B
FOREIGN INVESTMENT	227	A
FOREIGN LEGION	177	A
FOREIGN MESSENGERS SERVICE	520	B
FOREIGN MILITARY ASSISTANCE	227	A
FOREIGN MINISTER	184	A
FOREIGN NATIONALITY	542	B
FOREIGN OFFICE	159	A
FOREIGN OPERATIONS ADMINISTRATION	501	B
FOREIGN POLICY	196	A
FOREIGN POLICY ASSOCIATION (U.S.)	172	A
FOREIGN POSTS	549	B
FOREIGN RELATIONS	121	A
FOREIGN RELATIONS COMMITTEE (U.S. SENATE)	152	A
FOREIGN SECRETARY, BRITAIN	186	A
FOREIGN SERVICE (U.S.)	148	A
FOREIGN SERVICE ACT (1946)	580	B
FOREIGN SERVICE AMBASSADOR	192	A
FOREIGN SERVICE ATTACHE	187	A
FOREIGN SERVICE EXAMINATION	204	A
FOREIGN SERVICE INSTITUTE	469	B
FOREIGN SERVICE LIST	285	A
FOREIGN SERVICE LOCAL EMPLOYEES (FSL)	501	B
FOREIGN SERVICE OFFICER (FSO)	182	A
FOREIGN SERVICE RESERVE OFFICER (FSR)	549	B
FOREIGN SERVICE STAFF (FSS)	484	B
FOREIGN SERVICE, CHARGE D,AFFAIRES	187	A
FOREIGN SERVICE, CONSUL	184	A
FOREIGN TRADE	208	A
FOREIGN VALUATION	254	A
FOREIGN VISITORS	549	B
FOREIGN WARS	236	A
FOREIGN WORKERS	189	A
FOREIGNER	549	B
FOREST PRESERVE DISTRICT	794	B
FOREST RANGERS	542	B
FOREST SERVICE	469	B
FORESTRY	443	B
FORFEITURE	245	A
FORGES-DAVANZATI	744	B
FORGIVE	604	B
FORGOTTEN MAN	556	B
FORM	245	A
FORMAL	254	A
FORMAL LOGIC	127	A
FORMAL MEETING	604	B
FORMAL ORGANIZATION	156	A
FORMAL RECEPTION	604	B
FORMALISM	142	A
FORMALITIES	629	B
FORMALIZATION	135	A
FORMATION	580	B
FORMATION OF PERSONALITY	133	A
FORMATION OF SOCIETY	135	A
FORMER DEPUTY	556	B
FORMOSA (TAIWAN)	275	A
FORMOSA RESOLUTION	254	A
FORMS (PERSONNEL)	289	A
FORMS OF STATE	177	A
FORMULAE	245	A
FORMULATION	604	B
FORRESTAL, JAMES VINCENT	684	B
FORT KNOX	280	A
FORT SUMTER	280	A
FORTAS, JUSTICE ABRAHAM	267	A
FORTENBERRY, CHARLES N.	693	B
FORTESCUE, SIR JOHN	744	B
FORTI	744	B
FORTIFICATION	580	B
FORTUNE BAY OUTRAGES	652	B
FORTUNE MAGAZINE POLL (ROPER)	604	B
FORTY THIEVES	520	B
FORTY-NINER	542	B
FORTY-SHILLING FREEHOLD	822	B
FOSDICK, DOROTHY	744	B
FOSSIL	822	B
FOSTER, W. Z.	709	B
FOUCAULT, M.	744	B

FOUILLEE, ALFRED	744	B	FRANKING PRIVILEGE	213	A
FOUNDATION	469	B	FRANKLIN, BENJAMIN	262	A
FOUNDING FATHERS	159	A	FRANKLIN, JOHN HOPE	744	B
FOUR FREEDOMS	580	B	FRANKS	485	B
FOUR POWER TREATY (PACT)	580	B	FRATERNITY	485	B
FOUR-EIGHTY	629	B	FRATRICIDAL	630	B
FOUR-H CLUBS	484	B	FRAUD	236	A
FOUR-PARTY POLITICS	435	B	FRAUD ORDER	630	B
FOUR-POWER ADMINISTRATION OF BERLIN	159	A	FRAZER, SIR J.	744	B
			FRAZIER-LEMKE ACT OF 1935	630	B
FOUR-YEAR PLAN	604	B	FREAK-OUT	844	B
FOUR-YEAR-TENURE ACT	604	B	FREDEGUNDE, QUEEN	744	B
FOURIER, FRANCOIS CHARLES MARIE	693	B	FREDERICK II	709	B
			FREDERICK THE GREAT	684	B
FOURIERISTS	484	B	FREDERICKSBURG	794	B
FOURTEEN POINTS	236	A	FREDONIAN REPUBLIC	501	B
FOURTEENTH AMENDMENT	194	A	FREE	254	A
FOURTH AMENDMENT	198	A	FREE ACCESS	220	A
FOURTH BRANCH OF GOVERNMENT	152	A	FREE CITY	282	A
FOURTH COMMITTEE	485	B	FREE COINAGE OF SILVER	291	A
FOURTH ESTATE	162	A	FREE COMPETITION	220	A
FOURTH FORCE (FRENCH CONSERVATIVE PARTIES)	501	B	FREE DEMOCRATIC PARTY	485	B
			FREE ECONOMY	127	A
FOURTH INTERNATIONAL	172	A	FREE ELECTIONS	127	A
FOURTH OF JULY SPEECH	580	B	FREE ENTERPRISE	117	A
FOURTH REPUBLIC (FRANCE)	159	A	FREE ENTERPRISE SYSTEM	195	A
FOX, CHARLES JAMES	709	B	FREE FRENCH	172	A
FRACTIONAL CURRENCY	653	B	FREE LIST (FREE GOODS)	809	B
FRACTIONAL ORBITAL BOMB (FOB)	817	B	FREE LOGIC	456	B
FRACTIONALISM	133	A	FREE PORT	277	A
FRAGMENTATION	139	A	FREE RIDE	580	B
FRAME	629	B	FREE SILVER	227	A
FRAME OF REFERENCE	117	A	FREE SOCIETY	167	A
FRAMEWORK	127	A	FREE SOIL	236	A
FRANCE	274	A	FREE SOIL, FREE SPEECH, FREE LABOR, AND FREE MEN	839	B
FRANCE, ANATOLE	744	B	
FRANCE'S SIXTH PLAN	653	B	FREE SPEECH MOVEMENT	227	A
FRANCHISE	227	A	FREE TERRITORY	604	B
FRANCHISE BUSINESS	485	B	FREE TOWN	787	B
FRANCHISE TAX	245	A	FREE TRADE	198	A
FRANCIS OF ASSISI, ST.	693	B	FREE TRADE AREA	159	A
FRANCIS, ROY G.	744	B	FREE WILL	125	A
FRANCIS, SIR PHILIP	744	B	FREE WORLD	147	A
FRANCISCANS	485	B	FREE ZONE	280	A
FRANCO-BRITISH UNION	469	B	FREE-SOIL DEBATE	604	B
FRANCO-GERMAN ARMISTICE	245	A	FREE-SOIL PARTY	469	B
FRANCO-GERMAN FRONTIER	282	A	FREEBOOTER	564	B
FRANCO-PRUSSIAN WAR	236	A	FREEDMAN VS. MARYLAND (1965)	677	B
FRANCO-SOVIET TREATY OF MUTUAL ASSISTANCE	580	B	FREEDMEN	187	A
			FREEDMEN'S BUREAU	172	A
FRANCO, GENERAL FRANCISCO	263	A	FREEDOM	117	A
FRANK, JEROME D.	271	A	FREEDOM AND UNION	833	B
FRANK, PHILIPP	744	B	FREEDOM FIGHTER	187	A
FRANKEL, CHARLES	744	B	FREEDOM FROM ARBITRARY ARREST AND DETENTION	204	A
FRANKEL, JOSEPH	709	B	
FRANKFURTER, FELIX	265	A	FREEDOM FROM ARREST	236	A

FREEDOM FROM DOUBLE JEOPARDY	208	A
FREEDOM FROM FEAR	236	A
FREEDOM FROM HUNGER CAMPAIGN	604	B
FREEDOM FROM SELF-INCRIMINATION	204	A
FREEDOM FROM SLAVERY AND SERVITUDE	236	A
FREEDOM MOVEMENT	227	A
FREEDOM NOW	833	B
FREEDOM OF ASSEMBLY	194	A
FREEDOM OF ASSOCIATION	204	A
FREEDOM OF BELIEF	208	A
FREEDOM OF COMMERCE AND INDUSTRY	581	B
FREEDOM OF COMMERCE AND NAVIGATION	220	A
FREEDOM OF CONSCIENCE	220	A
FREEDOM OF CONTRACT	227	A
FREEDOM OF DEBATE	220	A
FREEDOM OF ENTERPRISE	236	A
FREEDOM OF ENTRY	227	A
FREEDOM OF ESTABLISHMENT	604	B
FREEDOM OF EXPRESSION	208	A
FREEDOM OF INFORMATION	213	A
FREEDOM OF INFORMATION ACT	213	A
FREEDOM OF NAVIGATION ON RIVERS	245	A
FREEDOM OF OPINION	227	A
FREEDOM OF RELIGION	194	A
FREEDOM OF SPEECH	194	A
FREEDOM OF THE AIR	236	A
FREEDOM OF THE PRESS	194	A
FREEDOM OF THE SEAS	208	A
FREEDOM OF THOUGHT	220	A
FREEDOM OF WORSHIP	208	A
FREEDOM RIDERS	167	A
FREEDOM TRAIN	288	A
FREEHOLD	280	A
FREEHOLDERS CHARTER	254	A
FREEMAN	187	A
FREEMASON	167	A
FREEMASONRY	167	A
FREEPORT DOCTRINE	245	A
FREER GALLERY OF ART	520	B
FREGE	744	B
FREI, EDUARDO MONTALVA	684	B
FRENCH	172	A
FRENCH AND INDIAN WAR	213	A
FRENCH ARMISTICE OF 1940	245	A
FRENCH CIVIL SERVICE	172	A
FRENCH COMMITTEE OF NATIONAL LIBERATION	177	A
FRENCH COMMUNIST PARTY	159	A
FRENCH COMMUNITY	172	A
FRENCH COURT SYSTEM	469	B
FRENCH DEMOCRATIC REVOLUTIONARY DOCTRINE	443	B
FRENCH DIRECTOR	556	B
FRENCH ELECTORAL LAW	604	B
FRENCH EMPIRE	172	A
FRENCH FORCES OF THE INTERIOR	469	B
FRENCH LINE	787	B
FRENCH NATIONAL ASSEMBLY	159	A
FRENCH NATIONALIZED INDUSTRIES	172	A
FRENCH PARLIAMENT	162	A
FRENCH RESISTANCE MOVEMENT	177	A
FRENCH REVOLUTION OF 1789	208	A
FRENCH ROYALISTS	172	A
FRENCH SOCIALIST PARTY	177	A
FRENCH SPOILATION CLAIMS	630	B
FRENCH UNION	470	B
FRENKEL-BRUNSWIK, ELSE	693	B
FREQUENCY	228	A
FREUD, SIGMUND	264	A
FREUND, ERNST	744	B
FREUND, LUDWIG	709	B
FRIAR LANDS	794	B
FRICTION	142	A
FRIDAY CONFERENCE	581	B
FRIEDLANDER, FRANK	709	B
FRIEDMAN, HARRY	709	B
FRIEDMAN, MILTON	266	A
FRIEDRICH, CARL J.	267	A
FRIEDSON, ELIOT	709	B
FRIEND OF THE COURT (AMICUS CURIAE)	182	A
FRIENDLY NEUTRALITY	220	A
FRIENDS, AMERICAN	167	A
FRIENDSHIP	435	B
FRIENDSHIP CLIQUES	177	A
FRIES REBELLION	630	B
FRINGE BENEFIT	228	A
FROMM, ERICH	267	A
FRONDE	604	B
FRONDIZI, ARTURO	684	B
FRONT	172	A
FRONT BENCH	278	A
FRONT DE LIBERATION NATIONALE (FLN)	172	A
FRONT FOR THE LIBERATION OF OCCUPIED SOUTH YEMEN (FLOSY)	485	B
FRONT OF NATIONAL UNITY	470	B
FRONT PORCH CAMPAIGN	254	A
FRONT RUNNER	184	A
FRONTIER	274	A
FRONTIER DEMOCRACY	136	A
FRONTIERS	278	A
FRONTLASH	220	A
FROTHINGHAM VS. MELLON (1923)	674	B
FRUNZE, MIKHAIL V.	744	B
FRUSTRATION	139	A

FRUSTRATION-AGGRESSION	117	A
FRY THE FAT	839	B
FUCHS, LAWRENCE H.	709	B
FUCKING	289	A
FUDGE	630	B
FUGITIVE FROM JUSTICE	189	A
FUGITIVE SLAVE LAWS	228	A
FUHRER	262	A
FUHRERPRINZIP	133	A
FULBRIGHT ACT	254	A
FULBRIGHT-CONNALLY RESOLUTION	254	A
FULBRIGHT, J. WILLIAM	265	A
FULFILLMENT	435	B
FULL ASSEMBLY	501	B
FULL DINNER PAIL	817	B
FULL EMPLOYMENT	200	A
FULL EMPLOYMENT ACT	236	A
FULL FAITH AND CREDIT	220	A
FULL FAITH AND CREDIT CLAUSE	228	A
FULL GARAGE	844	B
FULL MEMBER	189	A
FULL POWERS	228	A
FULLER, MELVILLE WESTON	709	B
FULTON SPEECH	245	A
FUN CITY	787	B
FUNCTION	117	A
FUNCTIONAL ANALYSIS	113	A
FUNCTIONAL CONCEPT	117	A
FUNCTIONAL CONSOLIDATION	220	A
FUNCTIONAL CONSOLIDATION, ADMINISTRATIVE	220	A
FUNCTIONAL CONSOLIDATION, LOCAL GOVERNMENT	213	A
FUNCTIONAL ORGANIZATION	119	A
FUNCTIONAL REPRESENTATION	204	A
FUNCTIONAL TITLE	542	B
FUNCTIONALISM	114	A
FUND	254	A
FUND OF UN FOR DEVELOPMENT OF WEST IRIAN (FUNDWI)	501	B
FUNDAMENTAL FREEDOMS	213	A
FUNDAMENTAL LAW	220	A
FUNDAMENTAL RIGHTS	200	A
FUNDED DEBT	236	A
FUNDING	245	A
FUNNEL OF CAUSALITY	136	A
FUR PRODUCTS LABELING ACT OF 1951	630	B
FUR SEAL CONTROVERSY	604	B
FURBINOW, I. M.	710	B
FURTADO, CELSO	693	B
FURTSEVA, YAKETERINA ALEKSEYEVNA	744	B
FURUSETH ACT	653	B
FUSION	236	A
FUSION TICKET	159	A
FUSTEL-DE-COULANGE	744	B
FUTURE	245	A
FUTURE-DESCRIPTIVE STATEMENT	130	A
FUTURISM	133	A
FUTURISTS	189	A
FUTUROLOGY	136	A
FYRD, ANGLO-SAXON	556	B
G.I. BILL OF RIGHTS	236	A
GABON	280	A
GADSDEN PURCHASE	236	A
GAFFE	630	B
GAG RULE	220	A
GAIN	254	A
GAITSKELL, HUGH	693	B
GAIUS	710	B
GAJENDRAGADKAR, PRALHAD BALACHARYA	710	B
GALANSKOV, YURI	710	B
GALBRAITH, JOHN KENNETH	265	A
GALEN	710	B
GALIANI	710	B
GALILEO	266	A
GALLA	794	B
GALLAUDET COLLEGE	501	B
GALLERIES	289	A
GALLIE, W.B.	710	B
GALLOWAY, GEORGE	710	B
GALLUP POLL	196	A
GALLUP, SUOMEN	710	B
GALTON, SIR FRANCIS	685	B
GALTUNG, JOHAN	693	B
GALVAN CASE (MEXICO VS. U.S.) (1927)	672	B
GALVANIZED CORPSE	822	B
GALVESTON PLAN	245	A
GAMBIA	787	B
GAMBRELL, DAVID HENRY	693	B
GAME	236	A
GAME OF CONFLICT	245	A
GAME PRESERVE	282	A
GAME THEORY	117	A
GAME WARDEN	549	B
GANDHI, INDIRA	263	A
GANDHI, MAHATMA	262	A
GANDHISM	133	A
GANG	485	B
GANGSTER	187	A
GANGWAY	822	B
GAOS, JOSE	710	B
GAP	581	B
GARBAGE-DISPOSAL PLANTS	289	A
GARCEAU, OLIVER	710	B
GARCIA-CALDERON, FRANCISCO	710	B
GARDEN CITY MOVEMENT	177	A
GARDEN OF EDEN	788	B
GARDEN-HOSE ANALOGY	835	B

GARDINER, PATRICK	710	B	GENERAL COUNCIL OF THE CHURCH	485	B
GARDINER, PROF. A. G.	710	B	GENERAL COUNCIL OF THE VALLEYS	501	B
GARDNER, JAMES W.	685	B			
GARFIELD, PRESIDENT JAMES A.	266	A	GENERAL COURT	167	A
GARIBALDI, GIUSEPPE	266	A	GENERAL COURT OF THE COLONY	485	B
GARNER VS. BOARD OF PUBLIC WORKS (1951)	674	B	GENERAL DEBATE, UNITED NATIONS	208	A
			GENERAL DELIVERY	604	B
GARNISHMENT	245	A	GENERAL ELECTIONS	200	A
GARRAN, ANDREW	710	B	GENERAL ELECTRIC COMPANY	172	A
GARRISON	167	A	GENERAL FISHERIES COUNCIL FOR THE MEDITERRANEAN	501	B
GARRISON STATE	159	A			
GARRISON VS. LOUISIANA (1964)	671	B	GENERAL FUND	228	A
GARRISON, JIM	269	A	GENERAL GOVERNMENT OF POLAND	485	B
GARRISON, WILLIAM LLOYD	266	A	GENERAL INQUIRER	449	B
GARTER	822	B	GENERAL INTERNATIONAL ORGANIZATION (GIO)	485	B
GARTH, THOMAS	710	B			
GARVEY, MARCUS	271	A	GENERAL LAND OFFICE	172	A
GARY, INDIANA	788	B	GENERAL LAWS	204	A
GAS WARFARE	228	A	GENERAL MANAGER	543	B
GASKELL, ELIZABETH	710	B	GENERAL MOBILIZATION	208	A
GASOLINE TAX	228	A	GENERAL MOTORS CORPORATION	159	A
GASPERI, ALCIDE DE	271	A	GENERAL PAIR	549	B
GASSENDI	710	B	GENERAL POST OFFICE	177	A
GASSET	710	B	GENERAL PROPERTY TAX	220	A
GATEKEEPERS	189	A	GENERAL PROSPERITY AS POLITICAL FACTOR	236	A
GATEWAY AMENDMENT	604	B			
GATLIN, DOUGLAS	710	B	GENERAL SECRETARY, SOVIET UNION	187	A
GAUDET, HAZEL	710	B			
GAULEITER	189	A	GENERAL SERVICES ADMINISTRATION (GSA)	159	A
GAULLISM	128	A			
GAULLIST PARTY IN FRANCE	156	A	GENERAL STAFF	167	A
GAUS, JOHN M.	685	B	GENERAL STRIKE	208	A
GAUTIER, EMILE	693	B	GENERAL SYSTEMS THEORY	115	A
GAVEL RULE	581	B	GENERAL THEORY	121	A
GAZA STRIP	277	A	GENERAL TREATY ON CENTRAL AMERICAN ECONOMIC INTEGRATION (SIECA)	604	B
GAZALI	710	B			
GEE, WILSON	710	B			
GEERTZ, CLIFFORD	710	B	GENERAL WELFARE	208	A
GELASIUS I, POPE	693	B	GENERAL WELFARE CLAUSE	208	A
GENEALOGY	443	B	GENERAL WILL	117	A
GENERAL	192	A	GENERAL ZIONISTS	177	A
GENERAL ACCOUNTING OFFICE (GAO)	152	A	GENERALISSIMO	189	A
			GENERALIST	187	A
GENERAL ACT	236	A	GENERALITY	139	A
GENERAL ACT CHARTER	630	B	GENERALIZATION	119	A
GENERAL AGREEMENT ON TARIFFS AND TRADE (GATT)	208	A	GENERALIZATION METHOD OF POLITICAL LEARNING	133	A
GENERAL ASSEMBLY (UN)	147	A	GENERALIZED OTHER	136	A
GENERAL ASSEMBLY COMMITTEES	167	A	GENERATION	162	A
GENERAL ASSISTANCE	245	A	GENERATIONAL CONFLICT	125	A
GENERAL ASSOCIATION OF GERMAN WORKERS	501	B	GENESIS	285	A
			GENETIC SERIES	142	A
GENERAL CHARTER PLAN	604	B	GENETIC THEORY	136	A
GENERAL COMMITTEE	177	A	GENETICS	139	A
GENERAL CONFERENCE	245	A	GENEVA	275	A
GENERAL CONSCRIPTION	213	A	GENEVA ACCORDS (1954)	198	A

GENEVA ARBITRATION	581	B
GENEVA AWARD	630	B
GENEVA CONFERENCE	236	A
GENEVA CONFERENCE ON NUCLEAR TESTING	236	A
GENEVA CONFERENCES ON THE LAW OF THE SEA (1958,60)	581	B
GENEVA CONVENTION OF 1864	604	B
GENEVA CONVENTION OF 1929	604	B
GENEVA CONVENTION ON THE HIGH SEAS (1958)	581	B
GENEVA CONVENTIONS (1949)	581	B
GENEVA FREE ZONES	282	A
GENEVA NAVAL CONFERENCE	581	B
GENEVA PROTOCOL OF 1925	604	B
GENEVA SPIRIT	245	A
GENEVA SUMMIT CONFERENCE (1955)	220	A
GENIUS	192	A
GENOA CONFERENCE	604	B
GENOCIDE	204	A
GENOCIDE CONVENTION, UNITED NATIONS	208	A
GENRES	435	B
GENRO	520	B
GENTILE	172	A
GENTILE, GIOVANNI	693	B
GENTLEMEN'S AGREEMENT	228	A
GENTZ, F.	710	B
GENTZEN	710	B
GENUFLECTION	581	B
GENY, FRANCOIS	693	B
GEO-POLITICAL METHOD	128	A
GEODESY	443	B
GEOGRAPHIC DETERMINISM	133	A
GEOGRAPHIC DIFFERENTIALS	443	B
GEOGRAPHIC MOBILITY	136	A
GEOGRAPHIC POWER FACTORS	139	A
GEOGRAPHICAL FACTORS	123	A
GEOGRAPHICAL METHOD	435	B
GEOGRAPHICAL REPRESENTATION	208	A
GEOGRAPHY	136	A
GEOLOGICAL SURVEY	245	A
GEOMETRY	142	A
GEOPOLITICS	119	A
GEORGE III OF ENGLAND	264	A
GEORGE, ALEXANDER L.	710	B
GEORGE, DAVID LLOYD	264	A
GEORGE, HENRY	264	A
GEORGE, STEFAN	711	B
GEORGIA	277	A
GEOSOCIAL	449	B
GERBER, KARL FRIEDRICH VON	711	B
GERIATRICS	139	A
GERMAN CHRISTIANS	470	B
GERMAN COLONIES	177	A
GERMAN COMMUNIST PARTY	172	A
GERMAN CONFEDERATION	167	A
GERMAN CUSTOMS UNION	470	B
GERMAN DEMOCRATIC REPUBLIC (GDR) (DDR)	159	A
GERMAN PEACE UNION	501	B
GERMAN PEOPLES CONGRESS FOR UNITY AND JUST PEACE	501	B
GERMAN SOCIAL DEMOCRATS	156	A
GERMAN TRADE UNIONS	172	A
GERMAN-ITALIAN ALLIANCE	159	A
GERMAN-POLISH DECLARATION	581	B
GERMAN-RUSSIAN NON-AGGRESSION PACT	213	A
GERMANIC LAW	245	A
GERMANICUS	711	B
GERMANS	177	A
GERMANY	156	A
GERMANY PARTY	485	B
GERO, ERNOL	711	B
GERONTOLOGY	136	A
GERRYMANDER	195	A
GERSON, JOHN	711	B
GERSONIDES (LEVI BEN GERSON)	711	B
GESTA INNOCENTII	809	B
GESTALT	130	A
GESTALT PSYCHOLOGY	139	A
GESTAPO	156	A
GESTIOLOGY	449	B
GET-OUT-THE-VOTE MOVEMENT	162	A
GETTYSBURG	276	A
GETTYSBURG ADDRESS	213	A
GETULISM	449	B
GEWIRTH, ALAN	711	B
GHANA, REPUBLIC OF	162	A
GHAZALI	693	B
GHAZI	788	B
GHEORGHIEV, K.	711	B
GHEORGHIU-DEJ, GHEORGHE	271	A
GHETTOS	278	A
GHISALBERTI, A. M.	711	B
GHOSTWRITER	187	A
GIANNINI	711	B
GIANTS, ANCESTORS OF GENTILE PEOPLES	485	B
GIAP, VO NGUYEN, GENERAL	264	A
GIBB, CECIL A.	711	B
GIBBON, EDWARD	271	A
GIBBONS VS. OGDEN (1824)	260	A
GIBBS, SIR HUMPHREY VICARY	711	B
GIBRALTAR	278	A
GIDDINGS, G. H.	693	B
GIDE, CHARLES	711	B
GIDEON VS. WAINWRIGHT (1963)	260	A
GIERIK, E.	711	B
GIERKE, OTTO VON	693	B

GIFT	254	A		GO	653	B
GIFT ENTERPRISE	501	B		GO ALONG	581	B
GIFT TAX	236	A		GO FIGHT CITY HALL	291	A
GIL Y ROBLES, E.	693	B		GO FISHING	844	B
GILBERT AND ELLICE ISLANDS	794	B		GO TO THE WELL	839	B
GILBERT DE BALLIOL	711	B		GO-IT-ALONE	291	A
GILES OF ROME	711	B		GOA	788	B
GILLETTE VS. UNITED STATES (1971)	673	B		GOAL	228	A
GILSON	694	B		GOAL ATTAINMENT	123	A
GIMU (JAPANESE - DUTY)	653	B		GOALS, POLITICAL	121	A
GINI, CORRADO	711	B		GOBBLEDYGOOK	839	B
GINSBERG VS. NEW YORK (1968)	671	B		GOBINEAU, COUNT ARTHUR J. DE	711	B
GINSBERG VS. UNITED STATES (1966)	261	A		GOBITIS CASE	671	B
				GOD	136	A
GINSBERG, ASHER	711	B		GOD'S (OWN) COUNTRY	844	B
GINSBERG, MORRIS	711	B		GODDARD, H. H.	712	B
GINZBURG, ALEXANDER	711	B		GODESBERG MEMORANDUM	809	B
GIOLITTI, ANTONIO	711	B		GODFREY OF BOUILLON	712	B
GIOLITTI, GIOVANNI	711	B		GODFREY OF FONTAINES	712	B
GIOVANI FASCISTI	501	B		GODWIN, WILLIAM	712	B
GIRALDUS CAMBRENSIS	744	B		GOEBBELS, DR. JOSEPH	266	A
GIRI, VARAHGIRI	744	B		GOEDEL	712	B
GIRONDISTS	485	B		GOERING, HERMANN	265	A
GIROUARD CITIZENSHIP VS. U.S. (1946)	677	B		GOETHE, JOHANN WOLFGANG VON	269	A
				GOFFE, COL.	712	B
GITLOW VS. NEW YORK (1925)	261	A		GOFFMAN, ERVING	694	B
GIVE 'EM HELL, HARRY	291	A		GOKHALE INSTITUTE OF ECONOMICS AND POLITICS	501	B
GIVE ME LIBERTY OR GIVE ME DEATH	291	A		GOLD	287	A
GIVEAWAY	289	A		GOLD BLOC	172	A
GIZENGA, ANTOINE	744	B		GOLD BUG	470	B
GLABER, RUDOLF	744	B		GOLD CERTIFICATE	581	B
GLADHAND	833	B		GOLD CLAUSE CASES	674	B
GLADHANDER	543	B		GOLD COAST	282	A
GLADSTONE, WILLIAM E.	266	A		GOLD DEMOCRATS	177	A
GLASER, WILLIAM A.	711	B		GOLD EXCHANGE STANDARD	213	A
GLASGOW	788	B		GOLD RESERVE ACT	236	A
GLASIER, J. BRUCE	711	B		GOLD RESERVE SYSTEM	228	A
GLASS-STEAGALL ACT	581	B		GOLD RUSH	236	A
GLASSBORO SUMMIT	254	A		GOLD STANDARD	208	A
GLAUCON	711	B		GOLD, CHARLES W.	744	B
GLAZER, NATHAN	694	B		GOLD, GLORY, AND GOD	839	B
GLEASON, ARTHUR H.	711	B		GOLDBERG, ARTHUR J.	266	A
GLEICHSCHALTUNG	604	B		GOLDEN BULL	822	B
GLOBAL TONNAGE	820	B		GOLDENWEISER, A. A.	744	B
GLOBAL WAR	220	A		GOLDING, WILLIAM	744	B
GLOBALONEY	835	B		GOLDMAN, EMMA	694	B
GLORIOUS REVOLUTION	213	A		GOLDMAN, RALPH M.	269	A
GLOSSARY OF INTERGOVERNMENTAL ORGANIZATIONS (IGO)	807	B		GOLDSCHMIDT, WALTER	744	B
				GOLDSTEIN, MARSHALL	745	B
				GOLDWATER, BARRY M.	262	A
GLOVER	556	B		GOLOID DOLLAR	826	B
GLUBB, LT.-GENERAL JOHN BAGOT	685	B		GOLOMBIEWSKI, ROBERT	694	B
GLUTTONS OF PRIVILEGE	556	B		GOLPE (DE ESTADO)	630	B
GNOSEOLOGY	456	B		GOLTZ, GREIHERR COLMAR VON DER	745	B
GNOSTICS	470	B				

GOMEZ, GENERAL JUAN VICENTE	745	B
GOMILLION VS. LIGHTFOOT (1960)	671	B
GOMPERS, SAMUEL	264	A
GOMULKA, WLADYSLAW	267	A
GOMULKAISM	435	B
GONDRA TREATY	653	B
GOO GOOS	549	B
GOOD	139	A
GOOD ENOUGH MORGAN	844	B
GOOD FAITH	133	A
GOOD FIGHT	581	B
GOOD NEIGHBOR POLICY	208	A
GOOD NEIGHBOR POLICY TOWARD LATIN AMERICA	208	A
GOOD OFFICES	213	A
GOOD SOLDIER	543	B
GOOD-GOVERNMENT ASSOCIATION	177	A
GOOD-TIME LAW	630	B
GOOD-WILL MISSION	245	A
GOODE, WILLIAM J.	712	B
GOODENOUGH, E.R.	745	B
GOODMAN, CHRISTOPHER	745	B
GOODMAN, M. E.	745	B
GOODMAN, PAUL	269	A
GOODNESS	443	B
GOODNOW, FRANK J.	269	A
GOODS	287	A
GOODY GOODY	549	B
GOODYEAR TIRE AND RUBBER COMPANY	485	B
GOOSEY-GANDER REVOLUTION	653	B
GOPHER	826	B
GORBACH, ALFONS	745	B
GORE, WILLIAM	712	B
GOREAU, DR. ANGELINE	745	B
GORER, GEOFFREY	745	B
GORGIAS	712	B
GORI, FERNANDO	745	B
GORKY, M.	685	B
GORTON, JOHN GREY	745	B
GOSLICK (GOSLICIUS), WAWRZYNIEC GRZYMALA	745	B
GOSNELL, HAROLD F.	712	B
GOSPEL OF FORCE	450	B
GOSPEL OF HATE	443	B
GOSPEL OF WEALTH	604	B
GOSPLAN COMMISSION (USSR)	162	A
GOTHA PROGRAM	805	B
GOTTSCHALK, LOUIS	745	B
GOTTWALD, KLEMENT	694	B
GOUGH, G. W.	745	B
GOUGH, J. H.	745	B
GOULART, JOAO	712	B
GOULDNER, ALVIN W.	712	B
GOVERN	123	A
GOVERNANCE	220	A
GOVERNED	186	A
GOVERNING BODY	156	A
GOVERNMENT	146	A
GOVERNMENT AGENCIES	156	A
GOVERNMENT BENCH	277	A
GOVERNMENT BILL	220	A
GOVERNMENT BODIES	167	A
GOVERNMENT BY ALPHABET	291	A
GOVERNMENT BY ASSASSINATION	236	A
GOVERNMENT BY COMMISSION	236	A
GOVERNMENT BY CRONY	245	A
GOVERNMENT BY EXECUTIVE COMMITTEE	228	A
GOVERNMENT BY INJUNCTION	245	A
GOVERNMENT BY PLUNDER	653	B
GOVERNMENT COALITION	150	A
GOVERNMENT CONTRACTS	213	A
GOVERNMENT CORPORATION	152	A
GOVERNMENT CORPORATION CONTROL ACT OF 1945	581	B
GOVERNMENT CRISIS	213	A
GOVERNMENT DEBT	204	A
GOVERNMENT DOCUMENTS	284	A
GOVERNMENT EMPLOYEES	184	A
GOVERNMENT ENTERPRISE	152	A
GOVERNMENT EXPENDITURES	200	A
GOVERNMENT FORCES	172	A
GOVERNMENT INTERVENTION IN BUSINESS	208	A
GOVERNMENT MEMBERS	189	A
GOVERNMENT NATIONAL MORTGAGE ASSOCIATION (GNMA)	485	B
GOVERNMENT OF INDIA ACT	630	B
GOVERNMENT OF LAWS AND NOT OF MEN	289	A
GOVERNMENT OF THE PEOPLE, BY THE PEOPLE, FOR THE PEOPLE	290	A
GOVERNMENT OPERATIONS COMMITTEE	167	A
GOVERNMENT ORGANIZATION	150	A
GOVERNMENT ORGANIZATION MANUAL	284	A
GOVERNMENT OWNERSHIP	208	A
GOVERNMENT PRINTING OFFICE (GPO)	159	A
GOVERNMENT PROGRAMS	204	A
GOVERNMENT REGULATION	204	A
GOVERNMENT REGULATION OF BUSINESS	196	A
GOVERNMENT REPORTS	284	A
GOVERNMENT REVENUE	200	A
GOVERNMENT SERVICE AS A CAREER	187	A
GOVERNMENT SUBSIDY	200	A
GOVERNMENT-IN-EXILE	156	A

GOVERNMENT-OWNED   159   A
  CORPORATION
GOVERNMENTS OF THE LAENDER   501   B
GOVERNOR   181   A
GOVERNOR-GENERAL, BRITAIN   549   B
GOVERNORS CONFERENCE   220   A
GOWN   822   B
GOWON, MAJOR GENERAL YAKUBU   685   B
GRAB BILL   581   B
GRACE   630   B
GRACEFULNESS   630   B
GRADE   605   B
GRADING   581   B
GRADUALISM   119   A
GRADUATE   543   B
GRADUATE SCHOOL   470   B
GRADUATE STUDENTS   549   B
GRADUATED DETERRENCE   236   A
  STRATEGY
GRADUATED INCOME TAX   195   A
GRADUATED TAX   200   A
GRADUATED UNILATERAL   228   A
  DISARMAMENT
GRAFFITI   809   B
GRAFT   204   A
GRAHAM, GEORGE A.   745   B
GRAIN FUTURES ACT OF 1922   653   B
GRAMMAR   142   A
GRAMSCI, ANTONIO   745   B
GRAN CHACO (LATIN AMERICA)   794   B
GRAND ASSEMBLY   501   B
GRAND COUNCIL (ITALY)   470   B
GRAND DESIGN   605   B
GRAND DUCHESS   564   B
GRAND DUCHY   485   B
GRAND DUKE   556   B
GRAND JURY   145   A
GRAND MOGUL   556   B
GRAND MUFTI   192   A
GRAND NATIONAL ASSEMBLY   485   B
GRAND OLD PARTY (GOP)   147   A
GRAND VIZIER   543   B
GRANDFATHER CLAUSE   204   A
GRANDFATHER'S HAT   844   B
GRANDPA'S PANTS WON'T FIT   844   B
  BENNY
GRANDSTANDING   236   A
GRANGE   167   A
GRANGER CASES   261   A
GRANGER LEGISLATION   236   A
GRANGER MOVEMENT   156   A
GRANT   245   A
GRANT, MADISON   712   B
GRANT, PRESIDENT ULYSSES   263   A
  SIMPSON
GRANTS-IN-AID   198   A

GRAPEVINE   289   A
GRAPEVINE (TELEGRAPH)   823   B
GRASS   817   B
GRASS ROOTS   181   A
GRASS WILL GROW IN THE STREETS   836   B
GRASSMUCK, GEORGE L.   712   B
GRATIFICATION   443   B
GRATITUDE, POLITICAL   435   B
GRAVE YARD COMMITTEE   172   A
GRAVE, JEAN   712   B
GRAVEL, MIKE   694   B
GRAVES VS. NEW YORK EX. REL.   677   B
  O'KEEFE (1939)
GRAVESIDE   798   B
GRAVEYARD   798   B
GRAVITATION   630   B
GRAVITY   450   B
GRAY EMINENCE   556   B
GRAY MARKET   630   B
GRAY VS. SANDERS (1963)   677   B
GRAY, JOHN CHIPMAN   745   B
GRAZIANI, RUDOLFO   745   B
GRAZING SERVICE   520   B
GREASE   653   B
GREASY MECHANICS   556   B
GREAT BRITAIN   273   A
GREAT COMPROMISE   220   A
GREAT DEBATES   236   A
GREAT DEPRESSION   208   A
GREAT DESIGN, THE   605   B
GREAT ELECTOR   543   B
GREAT GUN   839   B
GREAT LEAP FORWARD, MAOIST   289   A
GREAT PACIFICATOR   694   B
GREAT POWERS   146   A
GREAT PURGE   213   A
GREAT SCHISM   245   A
GREAT SEAL OF THE U.S.   288   A
GREAT SOCIETY   213   A
GREAT UNKNOWN   844   B
GREAT UNWASHED   291   A
GREAT WALL, CHINESE   287   A
GREAT WHITE FATHER   543   B
GREATER EAST ASIA   280   A
  CO-PROSPERITY SPHERE
GREATEST HAPPINESS PRINCIPLE   128   A
GRECO-TURKISH EXCHANGE OF   630   B
  POPULATIONS
GRECO-TURKISH WAR   245   A
GRECO-YUGOSLAV UNION   485   B
GREECE   274   A
GREEK CATHOLIC CHURCH   470   B
GREEK CITY-STATES   147   A
GREEK CIVILIZATION   125   A
GREEK PATRIOTS   485   B
GREEK-TURKISH AID   236   A

GREEKS	470	B
GREELEY, HORACE	265	A
GREEN BOOK	809	B
GREEN CORN REBELLION	630	B
GREEN POOL	502	B
GREEN REVOLUTION	228	A
GREEN, M.	712	B
GREEN, THOMAS HILL	694	B
GREEN, WILLIAM	694	B
GREENBACK	287	A
GREENBACK PARTY	159	A
GREENBACKISM	254	A
GREENBAUM, STEPHEN	712	B
GREENBELT COMMUNITIES	278	A
GREENE, WILLIAM	745	B
GREENLAND	282	A
GREENSTEIN, FRED I.	685	B
GREER, SCOTT	745	B
GREETING	653	B
GREGOROVIUS	745	B
GREGORY OF NYSSA	745	B
GREGORY OF TOURS	745	B
GREGORY THE GREAT, POPE	712	B
GREGORY VI, POPE	745	B
GREGORY VII, POPE	712	B
GREGORY, DICK	269	A
GREILING, W.	745	B
GREINER, LARRY	745	B
GRESHAM, WALTER QUINTIN	694	B
GRESHAM'S LAW	208	A
GRETTON, R. H.	746	B
GREY, SIR EDWARD	712	B
GRIAULE, MARCEL	746	B
GRIEVANCE	213	A
GRIFFIN, ROBERT P.	694	B
GRIFFITH, ARTHUR	746	B
GRIFFITH, ERNEST S.	712	B
GRIFFUELHES, VICTOR	712	B
GRIGORENKO, PYOTR	712	B
GRIMOND, JOSEPH	712	B
GRISWOLD VS. CONNECTICUT (1965)	671	B
GRIVAS, GENERAL GEORGE	694	B
GROANS	556	B
GROBER RAT	556	B
GRODZINS, MORTON	694	B
GROGSHOP POLITICIAN	557	B
GROMYKO, ANDREI ANDREEVICH	265	A
GRONCHI, GIOVANNI	712	B
GRONOVIUS	746	B
GROOM FOR OFFICE	254	A
GROSS INCOME	220	A
GROSS MISCONDUCT	245	A
GROSS NATIONAL PRODUCT (GNP)	198	A
GROSS SALARY	245	A
GROSS, BERTRAM M.	746	B
GROSS, FELIKS	712	B
GROSSRAUMWIRTSCHAFT	450	B
GROTE, GEORGE	712	B
GROTEWOHL, OTTO	713	B
GROTIUS, HUGO	267	A
GROTTKOPP, W.	713	B
GROUND DETECTION METHODS	581	B
GROUND FORCES	156	A
GROUND INSPECTION	245	A
GROUND NUTS	557	B
GROUND, AIR AND NAVAL FORCES	167	A
GROUNDED THEORY	139	A
GROUNDSWELL	254	A
GROUP	152	A
GROUP BASIS OF POLITICS	117	A
GROUP DYNAMICS	121	A
GROUP IDENTIFICATIONS	121	A
GROUP INFLUENCE	117	A
GROUP INSURANCE	254	A
GROUP LIBEL LAWS	254	A
GROUP MIND	136	A
GROUP NATURALIZATION	581	B
GROUP NORMS	119	A
GROUP OF TEN	502	B
GROUP PERSONALITY	136	A
GROUP PRESSURE	194	A
GROUP RELATIONS	117	A
GROUP REPRESENTATION	196	A
GROUP STANDARDS	136	A
GROUP STATUTES	605	B
GROUP THEORY	123	A
GROUPS	156	A
GROUPS AND ORGANIZATIONS	147	A
GROVE, FREDERICK PHILIP	713	B
GROVEY VS. TOWNSEND (1935)	674	B
GROWTH	130	A
GRUBER, KARL	713	B
GRUENING, ERNEST	271	A
GRUNDY TARIFF	581	B
GUAM	276	A
GUANTANAMO	274	A
GUARABIRA, BRAZIL	794	B
GUARANTEE CLAUSE	254	A
GUARANTEE FUND	605	B
GUARANTEED ANNUAL INCOME	204	A
GUARANTEED ANNUAL WAGE	213	A
GUARANTEES	254	A
GUARD	189	A
GUARD OF HONOR	470	B
GUARDIAN	192	A
GUATEMALA	277	A
GUBERNATORIAL	189	A
GUERRILLA WARFARE	198	A
GUESDE, JULES	713	B
GUETZKOW, HAROLD	271	A
GUEVARA, DR. ERNESTO (CHE)	269	A
GUFFEY COAL ACT	605	B

GUGGENHEIM FOUNDATION	167	A	HACHA, EMIL	713	B
GUICHARDIN	713	B	HACK	192	A
GUIDED DEMOCRACY	159	A	HACKER	713	B
GUIDED MISSILES	286	A	HAD ENOUGH	836	B
GUIDELINES	236	A	HADDON, A. C.	713	B
GUIDEPOSTS	605	B	HADOW COMMITTEE	502	B
GUIDING PRINCIPLES	236	A	HADRIAN, ROMAN EMPEROR	267	A
GUIDING RULES	255	A	HAECKEL, ERNST	713	B
GUIDON DE LA MER	823	B	HAENEL, ALBERT	713	B
GUILD SOCIALISM	142	A	HAGAN, CHARLES B.	713	B
GUILD SYSTEM	136	A	HAGANAH	177	A
GUILLOTINE	289	A	HAGUE ARBITRATION TRIBUNAL	163	A
GUILT	136	A	HAGUE CODE ON LAND WARFARE	581	B
GUILT BY ASSOCIATION	208	A	HAGUE CONFERENCE	245	A
GUINEA-BISSAU	280	A	HAGUE CONVENTIONS	228	A
GUINEA-GHANA UNION	470	B	HAGUE PEACE CONFERENCES	228	A
GUINEA, REPUBLIC OF	162	A	(1899, 1907)		
GUINEAS	794	B	HAGUE TRIBUNAL	167	A
GUINN VS. UNITED STATES (1915)	674	B	HAGUE VS. CIO (1939)	671	B
GUIZOT	713	B	HAIL	630	B
GULAG	470	B	HAIL OF DEAD CATS	839	B
GULICK, LUTHER H.	685	B	HAILE SELASSIE 1, EMPEROR OF	265	A
GUMPLOWICZ, LUDWIG	713	B	ETHIOPIA		
GUMSHOE CAMPAIGN	630	B	HAILSHAM, 2ND VISCOUNT, LORD	685	B
GUN	289	A	HAINES, CHARLES GROVE	694	B
GUN CONTROL LEGISLATION	228	A	HAINES, GEORGE	713	B
GUN-SHOT RANGE	630	B	HAIRBRAINED	836	B
GUNBATSU (A. F. GUNBATSU)	502	B	HAIRSPLITTING	291	A
GUNDEBAD, KING OF THE	713	B	HAITI	276	A
BURGUNDIANS			HAJ AMIN EL HUSSEINI	694	B
GUNG HO	833	B	HALDANE COMMITTEE	485	B
GUNPOWDER PLOT	605	B	HALDANE, PROF. J. B. S.	694	B
GUNS BEFORE BUTTER	290	A	HALF-BREED	190	A
GUNTHER, HANS	713	B	HALF-HORSE, HALF-ALLIGATOR	557	B
GURIN, GERALD	713	B	HALF-MAST	605	B
GURNEY, EDWARD JOHN	713	B	HALF-STAFF	581	B
GURSEL, GENERAL CEMAL	694	B	HALF-TRUTH	136	A
GURVITCH, GEORGES	713	B	HALFWAY HOUSE	485	B
GUT ISSUE	208	A	HALIFAX FISHERY COMMISSION	485	B
GUTFIGHTER	543	B	HALIFAX, EARL OF (EDWARD WOOD)	685	B
GUTTER FLYER	557	B	HALIFAX, FIRST MARQUIS OF,	271	A
GUTTMAN SCALE	119	A	GEORGE SAVILE		
GUYANA	278	A	HALL OF MIRRORS	817	B
GUYER, M. F.	713	B	HALL, ARNOLD H.	713	B
GUYOT, YVES	713	B	HALL, PRESCOTT	713	B
GWIBIT	502	B	HALLECK, CHARLES A.	267	A
H-BOMB	286	A	HALLOWELL, JOHN H.	713	B
HA-HA SPEECH	630	B	HALLSTEIN DOCTRINE	245	A
HAAS, ERNST B.	685	B	HAMILTON, ALEXANDER	262	A
HAAS, MICHAEL	694	B	HAMILTON, ONTARIO, CANADA	794	B
HAASE, HUGO	713	B	HAMILTONIANISM	119	A
HABIT	245	A	HAMLET	267	A
HABITS	142	A	HAMMARSKJOLD, DAG HJALMAR	263	A
HABITUAL OFFENDER	186	A	AGNE CARL		
HABSBURG RESTORATION	245	A	HAMMER AND SICKLE	287	A
HABSBURG, DR. OTTO VON	713	B	HAMMER VS. DAGENHART (1918)	671	B

HAMPTON ROADS CONFERENCE	605	B
HAND-PICKED	190	A
HAND, LEARNED	266	A
HANDBOOK	809	B
HANDICAP	630	B
HANDICAPPED	630	B
HANDKE, PETER	714	B
HANDOUT	818	B
HANDS-OFF POLICY	255	A
HANDSHAKER	192	A
HANGER-ON	543	B
HANKINS, F. H.	714	B
HANNIBAL	685	B
HANSARD	285	A
HANSEN, CLIFFORD PETER	714	B
HANUSCH	714	B
HAPPINESS	142	A
HAPPY DAYS ARE HERE AGAIN	291	A
HAPPY WARRIOR	694	B
HARA-KIRI	236	A
HARA, TAKESHI	714	B
HARARE	790	B
HARD CIDER CAMPAIGN	605	B
HARD CURRENCY	213	A
HARD FISTED	549	B
HARD LINE	290	A
HARD MONEY	214	A
HARD-CORE	167	A
HARDIE, J. KEIR	714	B
HARDIN, CHARLES	714	B
HARDING, PRESIDENT WARREN G.	264	A
HARDS AND SOFTS	470	B
HARDS, OR HARD-SHELLS	485	B
HARDY, THOMAS	694	B
HARE SYSTEM	228	A
HARE, A. P.	714	B
HARE, T.	714	B
HARLAN, JOHN MARSHALL	271	A
HARLEM	276	A
HARM	581	B
HARMEL, PIERRE CHARLES JOSE MARIE	714	B
HARMONY	605	B
HARNESSED VOTE	485	B
HARPER VS. VIRGINIA BOARD OF ELECTIONS (1966)	671	B
HARPERS FERRY	274	A
HARRIMAN, WILLIAM AVERELL	269	A
HARRINGTON, JAMES	694	B
HARRIS VS. NEW YORK (1958)	675	B
HARRIS, FRED ROY	685	B
HARRIS, JOSEPH P.	714	B
HARRISON, PRESIDENT BENJAMIN	266	A
HARRISON, PRESIDENT WILLIAM HENRY	267	A
HARRISON, ROGER	714	B
HART, ALBERT BUSHNELL	694	B
HART, PHILIP ALOYSIUS	271	A
HARTFORD CONVENTION	236	A
HARTKE, VANCE	685	B
HARTLEY, DAVID	714	B
HARTLEY, E. L.	714	B
HARTMANN, EDUARD VON	714	B
HARTZ, LOUIS	685	B
HARVARD GRADUATE SCHOOL OF BUSINESS ADMINISTRATION	177	A
HARVEST	605	B
HARVEY, G. D. N.	714	B
HARYANA, INDIA	714	B
HASBACH, WILHELM	746	B
HASSAN II, KING OF MORROCCO	685	B
HASTINGS, WARREN	714	B
HAT IN THE RING	236	A
HATAY	798	B
HATCH ACTS	204	A
HATCHETMAN	192	A
HATE	139	A
HATFIELD, SENATOR MARK O.	267	A
HATING ALIENS	630	B
HATT, PAUL K.	746	B
HATTENHAUER, HANS	746	B
HAUSA	502	B
HAUSHOFER GEOPOLITIK	435	B
HAUSHOFER, KARL	694	B
HAVANA CHARTER	245	A
HAVANA CONFERENCE	245	A
HAVANA DECLARATION	255	A
HAVE AND HAVE-NOT NATIONS	147	A
HAVE THE TICKETS	844	B
HAVENS, MURRAY L.	714	B
HAVIGHURST, ROBERT J.	685	B
HAWAII	277	A
HAWAIIAN STATEHOOD CONTROVERSY	605	B
HAWES-COOPER ACT	581	B
HAWES-CUTTING ACT	630	B
HAWKES, PROF. CHRISTOPHER	714	B
HAWKS	186	A
HAWLEY-SMOOT ACT OF 1932	245	A
HAWLEY-SMOOT TARIFF OF 1930	245	A
HAWTHORNE EXPERIMENT	204	A
HAY-BUNAU-VARILLA TREATY	581	B
HAY-PAUNCEFOTE TREATY	245	A
HAYA DE LA TORRE, VICTOR RAUL	685	B
HAYDEN, THOMAS	271	A
HAYEK, FRIEDRICH A.	271	A
HAYES, PRESIDENT RUTHERFORD B.	265	A
HAYFORD, FRED KWESI	714	B
HAYMARKET SQUARE RIOTS	236	A
HAYNES, GEORGE	714	B
HAYSEED	557	B
HAYWOOD, WILLIAM	714	B

HAZARDOUS SUBSTANCES LABELING ACT	605	B
HE KEPT US OUT OF WAR	291	A
HEAD	192	A
HEAD TAX	228	A
HEADLANDS THEORY	435	B
HEADMAN	549	B
HEADQUARTERS	177	A
HEADQUARTERS AND FACILITIES (UN)	820	B
HEADQUARTERS DISTRICT	790	B
HEADS OF STATE	182	A
HEADSTART	214	A
HEALEY, DENIS WINSTON	714	B
HEALTH CARE	228	A
HEALTH DEPARTMENT	177	A
HEALTH INSURANCE	220	A
HEALTH INSURANCE PLAN (NATIONAL)	245	A
HEALTH MAINTENANCE ORGANIZATIONS	485	B
HEALTH MANPOWER	502	B
HEALTH SCIENCES	443	B
HEALTH SERVICES AND MENTAL HEALTH ADMINISTRATION .	502	B
HEALTH, EMPLOYEE	543	B
HEAR	255	A
HEARD, ALEXANDER	694	B
HEARING	228	A
HEARING , JUDICIAL	208	A
HEARING EXAMINER	187	A
HEARING, ADMINISTRATIVE	214	A
HEARING, LEGISLATIVE	214	A
HEARINGS	214	A
HEARST, WILLIAM RANDOLPH	264	A
HEART OF ATLANTA MOTELS INC. VS. U.S. (1964)	671	B
HEARTBEAT AWAY FROM THE PRESIDENCY	290	A
HEARTH TAX	605	B
HEARTLAND THEORY, GEOPOLITICS	123	A
HEATH, EDWARD RICHARD GEORGE	271	A
HEBREW	470	B
HECATEUS	746	B
HECKLE	605	B
HECOCK, DONALD	746	B
HEDGE	631	B
HEDONISM	139	A
HEELER	549	B
HEFT, POLITICAL	456	B
HEGEL, GEORG WILHELM FRIEDRICH	262	A
HEGELIANISM	123	A
HEGEMONY	125	A
HEIDEGGER, MARTIN	269	A
HEIKAL, MUHAMMED HASANEIN	746	B
HEIMATLOS	564	B
HEIMATRECHT	653	B
HEIMWEHR	470	B
HEINEMANN, DR. GUSTAV	714	B
HEIR APPARENT	186	A
HEIR PRESUMPTIVE	187	A
HEIRARCHY	119	A
HEISENBERG	271	A
HELD, ADOLF	746	B
HELDERBERG WAR	653	B
HELIOGABALUS	746	B
HELL BENT FOR ELECTION	839	B
HELLENISTIC CULTURE	435	B
HELLENISTIC ERA	255	A
HELLENISTIC UNIVERSAL PHILOSOPHIES	435	B
HELMER, OLAF	746	B
HELMHOLTZ	694	B
HELOU, CHARLES	714	B
HELVERING VS. DAVIS (1937)	677	B
HELVERING VS. GERHARDT (1938)	677	B
HELVETIUS, CLAUDE ADRIEN	694	B
HEMISPHERIC DEFENSE	236	A
HEMISPHERIC SECURITY	214	A
HEMISPHERIC SOLIDARITY	236	A
HEMP	823	B
HEMPEL, CARL G.	746	B
HENCHMAN	557	B
HENDERSON, ARTHUR	746	B
HENLEIN, KONRAD	746	B
HENNESSY, BERNARD	714	B
HENNESSY, C. D.	746	B
HENRY I OF ENGLAND	715	B
HENRY II OF ENGLAND	715	B
HENRY III OF ENGLAND	715	B
HENRY III OF FRANCE	746	B
HENRY IV OF FRANCE	685	B
HENRY LETTERS	812	B
HENRY OF GHENT	715	B
HENRY OF LANGENSTEIN	746	B
HENRY V, EMPEROR	746	B
HENRY VI OF ENGLAND	715	B
HENRY VII OF ENGLAND	695	B
HENRY VIII OF ENGLAND	267	A
HENRY, PATRICK	265	A
HEPBURN ACT	605	B
HEPBURN VS. GRISWOLD (1870)	675	B
HERACLITUS	695	B
HERACLITUS OF EPHESUS	685	B
HERD	470	B
HERDER, JOHANN VON	746	B
HERE	791	B
HEREDITY	255	A
HERETICS	190	A
HERITABILITY	653	B
HERMANN OF METZ	746	B
HERMENEUTICS	456	B

HERMES, ANDREAS	715	B
HERNDON VS. LOWRY (1937)	678	B
HERO	192	A
HERO OF APPOMATTOX	269	A
HERO OF NEW ORLEANS	272	A
HERO-WORSHIP	133	A
HERODOTUS	685	B
HEROINES	549	B
HEROITE	564	B
HERRING, E. PENDLETON	685	B
HERRIOT, EDOUARD	695	B
HERSON, LAWRENCE	746	B
HERTZ	715	B
HERTZOG, JAMES BARRY MUNNIK	715	B
HERUT	520	B
HERVE, GUSTAVE	746	B
HERZ, JOHN J.	715	B
HERZL, THEODOR	695	B
HERZOG, ROMAN	746	B
HESS, MOSES	746	B
HESS, ROBERT	747	B
HESS, RUDOLF	267	A
HESSIANS	167	A
HETEROGENEOUS POLITICAL CULTURE	128	A
HETEROGENOUS SOCIETY	150	A
HETEROTONIC POLITIES	486	B
HETHERINGTON, H. J. W.	715	B
HEURISTIC DEVICE	125	A
HEURISTICS	133	A
HEUSS, PROFESSOR THEODOR	695	B
HEWERS OF WOOD	564	B
HEWGAG	653	B
HEXNER, ERVIN	747	B
HEYDRICH, REINHARD	272	A
HICKEL, W. J.	715	B
HICKENLOOPER, BOURKE BLAKEMORE	272	A
HICKORY (BOY)	747	B
HICKORY CABINET	502	B
HICKORY POLE CANVASS	653	B
HIDE-BOUND	631	B
HIERARCHY	115	A
HIERARCHY AND POLYARCHY	121	A
HIGH AUTHORITY	190	A
HIGH COMMISSIONER	190	A
HIGH COMMISSIONER FOR REFUGEES, UNITED NATIONS	192	A
HIGH CONTRACTING PARTIES	192	A
HIGH COURT OF JUSTICE	177	A
HIGH CRIMES AND MISDEMEANORS	200	A
HIGH DAM	818	B
HIGH FINANCE	581	B
HIGH MINDED (FEDERALIST)	502	B
HIGH PRESSURE SYSTEMS	456	B
HIGH ROAD...LOW ROAD	836	B
HIGH SCHOOL GRADUATES	549	B
HIGH SEAS	278	A
HIGH SEAS, JURISDICTION	220	A
HIGH-LEVEL CONFERENCE	255	A
HIGH-MINDED MEN	564	B
HIGHER EDUCATION	236	A
HIGHER EDUCATION ACT OF 1965	236	A
HIGHER EDUCATION FACILITIES ACT OF 1963	631	B
HIGHER LAW	208	A
HIGHER-LAW DOCTRINE	128	A
HIGHEST AUTHORITY	190	A
HIGHEST GOOD	133	A
HIGHNESS	549	B
HIGHSAW, ROBERT B.	747	B
HIGHWAY	280	A
HIGHWAY BEAUTIFICATION ACT	236	A
HIGHWAY PLANNING AND DEVELOPMENT	605	B
HIJACKING	236	A
HILDEBRAND	715	B
HILFERDING, RUDOLF	747	B
HILGARD, ERNEST R.	747	B
HILL-BURTON ACT (ALSO, HOSPITAL SURVEY AND CONSTRUCTION ACT OF 1946)	631	B
HILL, THE	287	A
HILLQUIT, MORRIS	715	B
HIMALAYAS	282	A
HIMMLER, HEINRICH	266	A
HINCMAR OF RHEIMS	747	B
HINDENBURG, PAUL VON	267	A
HINDUISM	130	A
HINDUS	177	A
HINTERLAND DOCTRINE	443	B
HIPPARCHIA	747	B
HIPPIE	190	A
HIPPOCRATES	269	A
HIPPOGAT	520	B
HIRABAYASHI VS. U.S. (1943)	675	B
HIRELING (-ISM)	549	B
HIROHITO, EMPEROR	265	A
HIROSHIMA	274	A
HIRSCHMAN, ALBERT	715	B
HIS EXCELLENCY	549	B
HIS HOLINESS	550	B
HIS HONOR	192	A
HIS SUPERFLUOUS EXCELLENCY	844	B
HISPANIDAD	520	B
HISS CASE	260	A
HISS, ALGER	265	A
HISTADRUT	470	B
HISTORIAN	543	B
HISTORIC BAY	798	B
HISTORIC COUNTY	794	B
HISTORIC WATERS	788	B

HISTORICAL	443	B
HISTORICAL APPROACH	119	A
HISTORICAL INEVITABILITY, COMMUNIST THEORY	115	A
HISTORICAL JURISPRUDENCE	139	A
HISTORICAL JURISTS	550	B
HISTORICAL MATERIALISM	117	A
HISTORICAL METHOD	117	A
HISTORICISM	125	A
HISTORICISM, CONTEMPORARY	128	A
HISTORICITY	236	A
HISTORICO-JURIDICAL METHOD	139	A
HISTORICO-SOCIOLOGICAL METHOD	125	A
HISTORIOGRAPHY	133	A
HISTORY	128	A
HITLER PUTSCH	221	A
HITLER YOUTH	159	A
HITLER-JUGEND	163	A
HITLER-STALIN PACT	208	A
HITLER, ADOLF	261	A
HITTITES	502	B
HLINKA, MSGR. ADREJ	747	B
HO CHI MINH	262	A
HOARDING	255	A
HOARE-LAVAL AGREEMENT	582	B
HOBBES, THOMAS	261	A
HOBHOUSE, LEONARD	715	B
HOBSON, JOHN A.	685	B
HOBSON, S. G.	715	B
HOBSON'S CHOICE	236	A
HOBSON'S THEORY OF IMPERIALISM	123	A
HOCKING, W. E.	747	B
HOCO POCO	557	B
HODDEN GRAY	502	B
HODGKINS, THOMAS	715	B
HOEBEL, E. ADAMSON	715	B
HOELDERLIN	715	B
HOERNLE, R. F. A.	715	B
HOFFMANN, STANLEY H.	272	A
HOFSTADTER, RICHARD	267	A
HOGBEN, LANCELOT	685	B
HOGG, QUINTIN MCGAREL	695	B
HOLBACH, BARON D, PAUL-HENRI DIETRICH	715	B
HOLCOMBE, ARTHUR N.	715	B
HOLD STILL...GO ALONG	839	B
HOLD-OVER	192	A
HOLD-THE-LINE ORDER	605	B
HOLD-UP BILLS	582	B
HOLDING	582	B
HOLDING APPOINTMENT FOR LIFE	245	A
HOLDING COMPANY	163	A
HOLDING COMPANY ACT OF 1935	582	B
HOLIDAYS	605	B
HOLIER THAN THOU	833	B
HOLISM	139	A
HOLLANDER, JACOB	715	B
HOLLINGS, ERNEST FREDERICK	685	B
HOLLIS, CHRISTOPHER	695	B
HOLLOW MEN	564	B
HOLMAN RULE	653	B
HOLMES, OLIVER WENDELL, JR.	267	A
HOLMES, S. J.	747	B
HOLOCAUST	245	A
HOLT, HAROLD	747	B
HOLT, ROBERT	747	B
HOLTON, LINDWOOD	747	B
HOLY	443	B
HOLY ALLIANCE	172	A
HOLY COMMUNITY	521	B
HOLY FATHER	187	A
HOLY GERMANIC EMPIRE	486	B
HOLY PLACE	788	B
HOLY ROMAN EMPIRE	156	A
HOLY SEE	278	A
HOLY WAR	228	A
HOLY WEDNESDAY	653	B
HOLYOAKE, KEITH	715	B
HOMAGE	255	A
HOMANS, G.C.	695	B
HOME	798	B
HOME AFFAIRS	255	A
HOME BUILDING AND LOAN ASSOC VS. BLAISDELL (1934)	675	B
HOME COMMUNISTS	564	B
HOME LEAVE	631	B
HOME LOAN BANKS	177	A
HOME OFFICE	167	A
HOME OWNERS LOAN CORPORATION (HOLC)	177	A
HOME POLICY	631	B
HOME RULE	198	A
HOME SECRETARY	190	A
HOME STATE	177	A
HOME-SPUN	844	B
HOME, 14TH EARL OF	715	B
HOMEGENEITY	133	A
HOMEOSTATIS	123	A
HOMER	269	A
HOMES DUDDEN, DR.	715	B
HOMESTEAD	276	A
HOMESTEAD ACT OF 1862	204	A
HOMICIDE	236	A
HOMOGENEOUS POLITICAL CULTURE	121	A
HOMONOIA	631	B
HOMOSEXUALS	192	A
HONDURAS	278	A
HONEST BROKER	543	B
HONEST GRAFT	245	A
HONEST MONEY	605	B
HONEYMOON PERIOD	221	A

HONG KONG	276	A
HONKIES	187	A
HONOR	236	A
HONOR COURT	470	B
HONOR GUARD	470	B
HONORABLE	444	B
HONORARY CITIZEN	543	B
HONORIUS AUGUSTODOLENSIS	715	B
HOODLUMS	192	A
HOOKER, J.D.	716	B
HOOKER, RICHARD	695	B
HOOP-LA CAMPAIGN	582	B
HOOPLA	291	A
HOOVER COMMISSION	163	A
HOOVER MORATORIUM	245	A
HOOVER, J. EDGAR	263	A
HOOVER, PRESIDENT HERBERT CLARK	263	A
HOOVERCRAT	486	B
HOOVERIZE	582	B
HOPE	435	B
HOPKINS, ERNEST J.	716	B
HOPKINS, HARRY LLOYD	685	B
HOPPER	788	B
HORIZON	791	B
HORIZONTAL COMBINATION	486	B
HORIZONTAL FEDERALISM	582	B
HORN-STOP CAMPAIGN	582	B
HORNER, HENRY	716	B
HORNEY, KAREN	269	A
HORNY-HANDED	844	B
HOROWITZ, E. L.	747	B
HORSE	818	B
HORSE AND BUGGY	818	B
HORSE-TRADING	228	A
HORSESHOE SEATING ARRANGEMENT	228	A
HORST WESSEL LIED	833	B
HORTHY, ADMIRAL N.	685	B
HOSPITAL	486	B
HOSPITAL SHIP	289	A
HOSPITAL SURVEY AND CONSTRUCTION ACT OF 1946 (ALSO, HILL-BURTON ACT)	605	B
HOSPITAL WORKERS	550	B
HOST	192	A
HOSTAGE	190	A
HOSTESS	543	B
HOSTILE AID	582	B
HOSTILE NEUTRALITY	236	A
HOSTILITIES	214	A
HOT LINE	286	A
HOT OIL	582	B
HOT OIL CASES	671	B
HOT POTATO	291	A
HOT PROPERTY	820	B
HOT PURSUIT	214	A
HOT SPRINGS CONFERENCE	582	B
HOT WAR	236	A
HOT WATER WAR	653	B
HOTMAN, FRANCOIS	747	B
HOTTENTOTS	486	B
HOUPHOUET-BOIGNY, FELIX	716	B
HOURS OF WORK	605	B
HOUSE	287	A
HOUSE ADMINISTRATION COMMITTEE	177	A
HOUSE ARREST	236	A
HOUSE CALENDAR	284	A
HOUSE CONGRESSIONAL RESOLUTION (H CON RES)	208	A
HOUSE FOREIGN AFFAIRS COMMITTEE, CONGRESS	156	A
HOUSE INTERNAL SECURITY COMMITTEE	163	A
HOUSE JOINT RESOLUTION (H J RES)	208	A
HOUSE JOURNAL	284	A
HOUSE OF ASSEMBLY	172	A
HOUSE OF BURGESSES	163	A
HOUSE OF COMMONS, BRITAIN	145	A
HOUSE OF COUNCILLORS	486	B
HOUSE OF DELEGATES	167	A
HOUSE OF DEPUTIES	163	A
HOUSE OF DETENTION	470	B
HOUSE OF HAPSBURG	163	A
HOUSE OF HOHENZOLLERN	167	A
HOUSE OF LORDS, BRITAIN	152	A
HOUSE OF PEERS	163	A
HOUSE OF REPRESENTATIVES (U.S.)	144	A
HOUSE OF REPRESENTATIVES COMMITTEES	150	A
HOUSE OF REPRESENTATIVES SPECIAL POWERS	255	A
HOUSE OF ROMANOV	163	A
HOUSE OF SAVOY	172	A
HOUSE OF WINDSOR	159	A
HOUSE RESOLUTION (H R)	221	A
HOUSE RESOLUTION 1776 (H RES 1776)	582	B
HOUSE RULES	200	A
HOUSE UN-AMERICAN ACTIVITIES COMMITTEE (HUAC; ALSO DIES COMMITTEE)	147	A
HOUSE-DIVIDED SPEECH	228	A
HOUSE, THE	172	A
HOUSEHOLDS	470	B
HOUSING	289	A
HOUSING ACT OF 1949	228	A
HOUSING AGENCIES	167	A
HOUSING AND BUILDING	605	B

HOUSING AND HOME FINANCE AGENCY (HHFA)	177	A	HUMOR	142	A
HOUSING AND URBAN DEVELOPMENT ACT	236	A	HUMOR, SELF-DEPRECATING	142	A
			HUMPHREY, HUBERT HORATIO, JR.	265	A
HOUSING ASSISTANCE ADMINISTRATION	502	B	HUMPHREY, ROBERT L.	716	B
			HUMPHREY'S EXECUTOR (RATHBUN) VS. U.S. (1935)	671	B
HOUSING EXPEDITER	543	B	HUMPTY DUMPTY	543	B
HOUSING LEGISLATION	228	A	HUNDRED DAYS	245	A
HOUSTON	282	A	HUNDRED FLOWERS CAMPAIGN	214	A
HOUZE, E.	716	B	HUNG JURY	152	A
HOVEIDA, AMIR ABBAS	716	B	HUNGARIAN	470	B
HOWARD UNIVERSITY	163	A	HUNGARIAN OPTANTS	502	B
HOWE, FREDERIC C.	695	B	HUNGARIAN REVOLUTION OF 1956	228	A
HOWE, IRVING	695	B	HUNGARY	277	A
HOWELL, G.	695	B	HUNGER BLOCKADE	255	A
HOXHA, ENVER	686	B	HUNTER, FLOYD	695	B
HRUSKA, ROMAN LEE	272	A	HUNTERS' LODGE	486	B
HSIEN	486	B	HUNTING	605	B
HSING	695	B	HUNTINGTON, ELLSWORTH	695	B
HUANG	695	B	HUNTINGTON, SAMUEL	269	A
HUBER, MAX	716	B	HUNTON, P.	695	B
HUBERT OF CANTERBURY	716	B	HURLEY, PATRICK J.	695	B
HUERTA, V.	686	B	HURRAH BOYS	192	A
HUGE PAW	839	B	HURRAH CAMPAIGN	255	A
HUGGINS	716	B	HURTADO VS. CALIFORNIA (1884)	261	A
HUGH OF ST. VICTOR	716	B	HURTING	435	B
HUGHES, CHARLES EVANS	266	A	HUS, JOHN	686	B
HUGHES, EVERETT C.	716	B	HUSAIN IBN ALI	695	B
HUGHES, H. M.	716	B	HUSAK, GUSTAV	695	B
HUGHES, HAROLD EVERETT	695	B	HUSSAIN, ZAKIR	695	B
HUGO, GUSTAV VON	716	B	HUSSEIN I, KING OF JORDAN	266	A
HUGO, VICTOR MARIE	267	A	HUSSEIN-MCMAHON AGREEMENT	606	B
HUGUENOTS	156	A	HUSSERL, EDMUND	272	A
HUIZANGA, J.	716	B	HUSTINGS	280	A
HUKS	163	A	HUTCHINS, ROBERT MAYNARD	267	A
HULA, E.	716	B	HUTCHISON, T.W.	695	B
HULL HOUSE	818	B	HUTTERIANS	486	B
HULL TRADE AGREEMENTS	605	B	HUTTON, VEN. W. H.	695	B
HULL, CORDELL	266	A	HUXLEY, ALDOUS	269	A
HUMAN	192	A	HUXLEY, JULIAN	272	A
HUMAN AND CIVIL RIGHTS	198	A	HUXLEY, THOMAS H.	686	B
HUMAN ELEMENT	136	A	HUYSMANS	695	B
HUMAN ENVIRONMENT	280	A	HYDE PARK DECLARATION	245	A
HUMAN NATURE	125	A	HYDERABAD, INDIA	788	B
HUMAN RELATIONS	133	A	HYDROGEN BOMB	286	A
HUMAN RESOURCES DEVELOPMENT DIVISION OF ECA	177	A	HYDROGRAPHIC OFFICE	486	B
			HYDROLOGY	444	B
HUMAN RIGHTS	194	A	HYKSOS	695	B
HUMAN RIGHTS COMMISSIONS	159	A	HYLOMORPHISM	142	A
HUMAN RIGHTS DAY	236	A	HYLTON VS. U.S. (1796)	673	B
HUMANISM	133	A	HYMAN, HERBERT	716	B
HUMANITARIANISM	130	A	HYMIE'S FERRYBOAT	839	B
HUMANITIES	136	A	HYNDMAN, H.M.	716	B
HUMANITIES, COOPERATION IN	435	B	HYNEMAN, CHARLES S.	716	B
HUMBOLDT, WILHELM VON	716	B	HYPER-ACCOUNTABILITY	631	B
HUME, DAVID	262	A	HYPHENATED AMERICANS	184	A

HYPNOPAEDIA	631	B
HYPNOSIS	142	A
HYPOTHESIS(ES)	113	A
I	543	B
I AM THE LAW	291	A
I DO NOT CHOOSE TO RUN	290	A
I HAVE A DREAM	291	A
I NEED HIM	291	A
I PROPOSE TO FIGHT IT OUT ON THIS LINE IF IT TAKES ALL SUMMER	833	B
I SEE CONSTRUCTION	834	B
I. G. FARBENINDUSTRIE (IGFIG) (GERMAN CHEMICAL TRUST)	172	A
I'D RATHER BE RIGHT THAN BE PRESIDENT	291	A
I'M ALONE, THE	839	B
IAZYKOV, N. M.	716	B
IBANEZ, CARLOS	716	B
IBERO-AMERICAN BUREAU OF EDUCATION	502	B
IBN SAUD, KING ABDUL-AZIZ	267	A
IBN-BAJJAH	716	B
IBN-SINA	716	B
IBO TRIBE	167	A
IBSEN, HENRIK	267	A
ICARIANISM	450	B
ICE-FREE PORT	280	A
ICELAND	277	A
ICELANDIC SAGAS	809	B
ICKES, HAROLD	272	A
ID	133	A
IDEA	133	A
IDEAL	130	A
IDEAL SOCIETY	133	A
IDEAL TYPE ANALYSIS	114	A
IDEALISM	125	A
IDEALIST-REALIST DICHOTOMY	119	A
IDEALITY	436	B
IDENTICAL NOTES	286	A
IDENTICAL PRICING	245	A
IDENTIFIABILITY	139	A
IDENTIFICATION	130	A
IDENTIFICATION METHOD OF POLITICAL LEARNING	139	A
IDENTIFICATION WITH POLITICAL PARTIES	121	A
IDENTITY	133	A
IDEOLOGICAL PSYCHOLOGY	142	A
IDEOLOGICAL WARFARE	200	A
IDEOLOGY	113	A
IDIOGRAPHICAL SCIENCE	436	B
IDIOT ENGINEER	839	B
IDRIS, I.	695	B
IDYLLISM	444	B
IF YOU CAN'T LICK 'EM, JOIN 'EM	290	A
IF YOU CAN'T STAND THE HEAT, GET OUT OF THE KITCHEN	290	A
IF-THEN STATEMENT	119	A
IFFY QUESTION	834	B
IGNORANCE	142	A
IGNORANCE OF LAW	236	A
IHERING, RUDOLF VON	716	B
IKEDA, HAYATO	696	B
IKHNATON	716	B
IL POPOLO D'ITALIA	807	B
ILIN, M.	716	B
ILLEGAL	214	A
ILLEGITIMACY	133	A
ILLEGITIMI NON CARBORUNDUM	839	B
ILLIBERAL	187	A
ILLICH, IVAN	686	B
ILLICIT	255	A
ILLINOIS	277	A
ILLINOIS EX REL. MCCOLLUM VS. BOARD OF EDUCATION (1948)	261	A
ILLITERATES	186	A
ILLOCUTIONARY ACT	606	B
ILLUMINATION	631	B
ILLUSION	142	A
ILLUSIONISM	450	B
IMAGE	130	A
IMAGE STUDIES	136	A
IMAGERY	136	A
IMAGINATION	136	A
IMAGININGS	444	B
IMHOFF TANKS	823	B
IMITATION	245	A
IMMANENCE	582	B
IMMANENTISM	436	B
IMMEDIACY	631	B
IMMEDIATE PURSUIT	582	B
IMMIGRANT	183	A
IMMIGRATION	214	A
IMMIGRATION ACT OF 1924	582	B
IMMIGRATION ACT OF 1965	228	A
IMMIGRATION AND NATIONALITY ACT OF 1952	236	A
IMMIGRATION AND NATURALIZATION SERVICE	163	A
IMMIGRATION LAWS	208	A
IMMIGRATION OF COMMUNISTS	582	B
IMMIGRATION QUOTAS	208	A
IMMIGRATION REFORM ACT	245	A
IMMINENT THREAT	228	A
IMMOBILISM	133	A
IMMORTALITY	246	A
IMMUNITIES OF A DIPLOMAT	221	A
IMMUNITY	198	A
IMMUNITY ACT OF 1954	582	B
IMMUNITY BATH	582	B
IMMUNIZATION	228	A

IMPACT	236	A	INALIENABLE INDIVIDUAL RIGHTS	208	A
IMPACT PANEL	177	A	INAUGURATION	214	A
IMPANEL	236	A	INCAPACITATION	237	A
IMPARTIALITY	128	A	INCARNATION	142	A
IMPEACHMENT	196	A	INCAS	163	A
IMPEDIMENTS	289	A	INCENTIVE AWARDS	246	A
IMPERATIVE LOGIC	436	B	INCENTIVE PAY	237	A
IMPERATIVES	139	A	INCENTIVE SYSTEM	228	A
IMPERFECT RATIFICATION	606	B	INCEST	237	A
IMPERFECT WAR	606	B	INCIDENCE	237	A
IMPERIAL CITY	172	A	INCIDENT	237	A
IMPERIAL CONFERENCE	582	B	INCIDENTAL MOTION	582	B
IMPERIAL CROWN	823	B	INCIDENTAL PROTECTION	631	B
IMPERIAL DIGNITY	444	B	INCITEMENT TO BOYCOTT	582	B
IMPERIAL DYNASTY	159	A	INCITERS OF WAR	192	A
IMPERIAL ELECTORS	543	B	INCLINATION	436	B
IMPERIAL HOUSE LAW	606	B	INCODEL	521	B
IMPERIAL SERVICE ORDER (ISO)	486	B	INCOGNITO	550	B
IMPERIALISM	113	A	INCOME	228	A
IMPERIALISM AND COLONIALISM,	115	A	INCOME DISTRIBUTION	200	A
COMMUNIST THEORY			INCOME LOSS PROTECTION	606	B
IMPERIUM IN IMPERIO (EMPIRE	291	A	INCOME MAINTENANCE	221	A
WITHIN AN EMPIRE)			INCOME TAX	208	A
IMPLEMENTATION	221	A	INCOMPATABILITY	436	B
IMPLEMENTATION AGREEMENT	246	A	INCOMPATIBLE OFFICES	543	B
IMPLICATION	128	A	INCOMPLETE RATIFICATION	246	A
IMPLICATION AND FACT	125	A	INCOMPLETE WAR	582	B
IMPLIED POWERS	194	A	INCONGRUITY	139	A
IMPORT	246	A	INCONSISTENCY	130	A
IMPORT BANK OF WASHINGTON	163	A	INCONTINENCE	653	B
IMPORT DUTY	221	A	INCORPORATED AND	156	A
IMPORT TAXES	221	A	UNINCORPORATED AREAS		
IMPORTANCE	142	A	INCORPORATED TERRITORY	470	B
IMPORTANT QUESTION, UNITED	228	A	INCORPORATED VILLAGE	172	A
NATIONS			INCORPORATION	214	A
IMPORTS	287	A	INCORRIGIBILITY	631	B
IMPOST	246	A	INCRIMINATION	228	A
IMPRESSION	444	B	INCUMBENCY	200	A
IMPRESSMENT	237	A	INCUMBENT	181	A
IMPRISONMENT	214	A	INDEFINITE APPOINTMENT	255	A
IMPRISONMENT FOR DEBT	237	A	INDEMNIFICATION	228	A
IMPROPRIETY	582	B	INDEMNITY	237	A
IMPROVEMENT OF RELATIONS	246	A	INDENTURE	255	A
IMPUGN	246	A	INDENTURED LABOR	183	A
IN ABSENTIA	246	A	INDENTURED SERVANT	186	A
IN FORMA PAUPERIS	255	A	INDEPENDENCE	200	A
IN PLACE	606	B	INDEPENDENCE LEAGUE	521	B
IN RE DEBS (1895)	671	B	INDEPENDENT	184	A
IN RE GAULT (1967)	261	A	INDEPENDENT (NON-PARTY) VOTERS	153	A
IN RE NEAGLE (1890)	675	B	INDEPENDENT AGENCIES AND	153	A
IN THE SADDLE	839•	B	REGULATORY COMMISSIONS		
IN YOUR HANDS	836	B	INDEPENDENT DEPUTY	550	B
IN-BASKET TRAINING	839	B	INDEPENDENT ESTABLISHMENT	177	A
IN-SERVICE TRAINING	221	A	INDEPENDENT EXECUTIVE AGENCIES	156	A
INACTIVE STATUS	246	A	INDEPENDENT LABOR PARTY OF	470	B
INADMISSIBILITY	208	A	GREAT BRITAIN		

INDEPENDENT SOCIALISTS OF	470	B	INDISPENSABLE MAN	192	A
FRANCE			INDIVIDUAL	183	A
INDEPENDENT UNION	470	B	INDIVIDUAL INFLUENCES IN	119	A
INDEPENDENT VARIABLE	113	A	POLITICS		
INDEPENDENT VOTER	182	A	INDIVIDUAL NULLIFICATION	653	B
INDEPENDENT VOTERS	486	B	INDIVIDUAL POLITICAL EFFICACY	119	A
ASSOCIATION			INDIVIDUAL VIOLENCE	582	B
INDEPENDENT WORKERS OF THE	177	A	INDIVIDUALISM	121	A
WORLD			INDIVIDUALISM, ECONOMIC	125	A
INDEPENDENTS	153	A	INDIVIDUALITY	246	A
INDESTRUCTIBLE UNION	167	A	INDIVIDUALS IN INTERNATIONAL	188	A
INDETERMINACY	130	A	ORDER		
INDETERMINATE PERMIT	582	B	INDIVIDUALS, IN GROUPS	183	A
INDETERMINATE SENTENCE	214	A	INDIVIDUATION	139	A
INDETERMINISM	136	A	INDO-CHINESE FEDERATION	502	B
INDEX	805	B	INDO-PACIFIC FISHERIES COUNCIL	521	B
INDEX NUMBERS	133	A	INDOCHINA	274	A
INDEX OF INTERCODER RELIABILITY	130	A	INDOCHINESE	172	A
INDEX OF PROHIBITED BOOKS	285	A	INDOCTRINATION	125	A
INDEXING	246	A	INDOMITABLES	564	B
INDIA	276	A	INDOOR RELIEF	631	B
INDIAN ARTS AND CRAFTS BOARD	502	B	INDUCTEE	192	A
INDIAN CLAIMS COMMISSION	486	B	INDUCTION	128	A
INDIAN COUNCIL OF WORLD	502	B	INDUCTIVE REASONING	113	A
AFFAIRS			INDUCTIVE STATISTICS	117	A
INDIAN HEMP	820	B	INDUS WATERS TREATY	606	B
INDIAN NATIONAL CONGRESS	167	A	INDUSTRIAL CONGRESS	631	B
INDIAN OCEAN	280	A	INDUSTRIAL DEMOCRACY	130	A
INDIAN OFFICE	167	A	INDUSTRIAL DEVELOPMENT	221	A
INDIAN POLITICAL SCIENCE	502	B	INDUSTRIAL DEVELOPMENT BOARD,	486	B
ASSOCIATION			UNIDO		
INDIAN RESERVATION	276	A	INDUSTRIAL PSYCHOLOGY	142	A
INDIAN STUDIES	142	A	INDUSTRIAL RELATIONS	128	A
INDIAN SUB-CONTINENT	278	A	INDUSTRIAL RELATIONS COURT	177	A
INDIAN TERRITORY	277	A	INDUSTRIAL REVOLUTION	194	A
INDIAN WARS	237	A	INDUSTRIAL SOCIETY	148	A
INDIANA	280	A	INDUSTRIAL SYNDICALIST LEAGUE	502	B
INDIANA BALLOT	255	A	INDUSTRIAL UNION	177	A
INDIANA UNIVERSITY	471	B	INDUSTRIAL WORKERS OF THE	153	A
INDIANAPOLIS	282	A	WORLD (IWW)		
INDIANS	167	A	INDUSTRIALISM	130	A
INDIANS IN NATAL	471	B	INDUSTRIALIST	186	A
INDIANS IN SPANISH AMERICA	486	B	INDUSTRIALIZATION	204	A
INDICATIONS	255	A	INDUSTRIALIZATION OF FARMING	255	A
INDICATORS	121	A	INDUSTRY	167	A
INDICTMENT	198	A	INDUSTRY AND NATURAL	521	B
INDIFFERENCE	142	A	RESOURCES, COMM ON(ECAFE)		
INDIGENOUS	274	A	INDUSTRY-WIDE BARGAINING	246	A
INDIRECT APPROACH	582	B	INEFFECTIVE BLOCKADE	255	A
(DISARMAMENT)			INEFFECTUALITY	606	B
INDIRECT ELECTION	214	A	INELIGIBLE ALIEN	557	B
INDIRECT INITIATIVE	221	A	INEQUALITY	125	A
INDIRECT OVERRULING	606	B	INEQUITIES	228	A
INDIRECT RULE	228	A	INERTIA	237	A
INDIRECT TAX	228	A	INEVITABILITY	255	A
INDISCERNIBLES	450	B	INFALLIBILITY	139	A

INSTITUT D'ETHNOLOGIE (PARIS)	521	B
INSTITUT DE GEOGRAPHIE (PARIS)	521	B
INSTITUT DE SCIENCE ECONOMIQUE APPLIQUEE (PARIS)	521	B
INSTITUT DES HAUTES ETUDES INTERNATIONALES (PARIS)	502	B
INSTITUT FRANCAIS DE L'OPINION PUBLIQUE	502	B
INSTITUT NATIONAL D'ETUDES DEMOGRAPHIQUES (PARIS)	502	B
INSTITUT NATIONAL DE LA CONJONCTURE ET DE LA STATISTIQUE (PARIS)	521	B
INSTITUT SCIENTIFIQUE DE RECHERCHES ECONOMIQUES ET SOCIALES (PARIS)	521	B
INSTITUT(S) D'ETUDES POLITIQUES	503	B
INSTITUT(S) DE DROIT COMPARE (FRANCE)	521	B
INSTITUTE FOR FOREIGN CULTURAL RELATIONS (ITALY)	521	B
INSTITUTE OF AGRICULTURAL ECONOMICS (OXFORD)	521	B
INSTITUTE OF COLONIAL STUDIES (OXFORD)	521	B
INSTITUTE OF COMPARATIVE LAW (VIENNA)	503	B
INSTITUTE OF CURRENT WORLD AFFAIRS (U.S.)	521	B
INSTITUTE OF HISTORICAL RESEARCH (LONDON)	521	B
INSTITUTE OF INTERNATIONAL AFFAIRS (WARSAW)	503	B
INSTITUTE OF INTERNATIONAL LAW	486	B
INSTITUTE OF INTERNATIONAL RELATIONS (BELGIUM)	521	B
INSTITUTE OF PACIFIC RELATIONS	521	B
INSTITUTE OF PUBLIC ADMINISTRATION (LONDON)	486	B
INSTITUTE OF PUBLIC ADMINISTRATION (NEW YORK)	486	B
INSTITUTE OF PUBLIC ADMINISTRATION (SYDNEY)	521	B
INSTITUTE OF PUBLIC FINANCE (BELGIUM)	521	B
INSTITUTE OF SOCIAL ANTHROPOLOGY (OXFORD)	521	B
INSTITUTE OF SOCIAL BIOLOGY (BIRMINGHAM)	521	B
INSTITUTE OF SOCIAL ECONOMY (POLAND)	521	B
INSTITUTE OF SOCIAL MEDICINE (OXFORD)	521	B
INSTITUTE OF SOCIAL PROBLEMS (POLAND)	521	B
INSTITUTE OF STATISTICS (OXFORD)	521	B
INSTITUTION	147	A
INSTITUTIONAL ADVERTISING	606	B
INSTITUTIONAL APPROACH	123	A
INSTITUTIONAL GROUP	150	A
INSTITUTIONAL METHOD	133	A
INSTITUTIONALIZATION	121	A
INSTITUTIONALIZED GROUP	153	A
INSTITUTIONALIZED PRESIDENCY	153	A
INSTRUCTED DELEGATE	186	A
INSTRUCTIONS	246	A
INSTRUCTORS	543	B
INSTRUMENT	286	A
INSTRUMENT OF GOVERNMENT	284	A
INSTRUMENTAL	436	B
INSTRUMENTAL INFORMATION	436	B
INSTRUMENTALISM	133	A
INSTRUMENTALIST VIEW OF THE STATE	136	A
INSULAR CASES	444	B
INSULAR POSSESSIONS	280	A
INSULARITY	246	A
INSULATION	255	A
INSULINDIA	798	B
INSURANCE	606	B
INSURANCE POLICY	631	B
INSURANCE SYSTEMS	653	B
INSURGENCY	204	A
INSURGENT	181	A
INSURGENTS REVOLT OF 1910	631	B
INSURRECTION	196	A
INTANGIBLE PROPERTY	823	B
INTANGIBLE PROPERTY TAXATION	583	B
INTEGRAL NATIONALISM	139	A
INTEGRAL SOCIALISM	444	B
INTEGRALISTA (FACTION MEMBER)	503	B
INTEGRATED (INTEGRAL) METHOD	444	B
INTEGRATED GLOBAL OCEAN STATION SYSTEM (IGOSS)	522	B
INTEGRATION	117	A
INTEGRATION, AND CONFLICT	136	A
INTEGRATION, AND GOAL ATTAINMENT	119	A
INTEGRATION, AND INTERNATION RELATIONS	125	A
INTEGRATION, FUNCTION OF SOCIAL SYSTEMS	117	A
INTEGRATIVE	133	A
INTEGRISM	456	B
INTEGRITY	436	B
INTEGRITY, POLITICAL	444	B
INTELLECT	436	B
INTELLECTUAL	188	A
INTELLECTUAL CONSTRUCTS	136	A
INTELLECTUAL COOPERATION ORGANIZATION	503	B
INTELLECTUAL REVOLUTION	255	A

INTELLECTUAL-IN-RESIDENCE	543	B	INTER-GROUP	142	A
INTELLECTUALISM	139	A	INTER-OCEANIC CANAL	280	A
INTELLECTUALS AND POLITICS	192	A	INTER-PARLIAMENTARY UNION (IPU)	471	B
INTELLIGENCE	133	A	INTER-PARTY COMPETITION	128	A
INTELLIGENCE TESTS	246	A	INTER-PERSONAL RELATIONS	130	A
INTELLIGENTSIA	167	A	INTER-STATE COMMERCE	150	A
INTELSAT	818	B	COMMISSION		
INTENDING	653	B	INTERACTION	126	A
INTENSION	456	B	INTERAGENCY	444	B
INTENSIONAL DEFINITION	136	A	INTERCESSION	255	A
INTENSIONAL LOGIC	436	B	INTERCODER RELIABILITY INDEX	142	A
INTENSIONALITY	456	B	INTERCONTINENTAL ROCKETS	287	A
INTENTION	142	A	INTERDEPARTMENTAL AGREEMENT	583	B
INTENTIONALISM	456	B	INTERDEPARTMENTAL COMMITTEE	177	A
INTENTIONALIST FALLACY	450	B	INTERDEPARTMENTAL CONFERENCE	246	A
INTER-AGENCY AGREEMENTS	583	B	INTERDEPENDENCE	123	A
INTER-ALLIED DEBTS	583	B	INTERDISCIPLINARY	123	A
INTER-ALLIED DECLARATIONS	653	B	INTEREST	246	A
INTER-AMERICAN CHILDREN	522	B	INTEREST AGGREGATION	115	A
INSTITUTE			INTEREST ARTICULATION	119	A
INTER-AMERICAN COMMISSION OF	522	B	INTERESTS	146	A
WOMEN			INTERFERENCE	246	A
INTER-AMERICAN CONFERENCE	255	A	INTERGENERATIONAL CONTINUITY	136	A
INTER-AMERICAN CONFERENCE ON	653	B	INTERGOVERNMENTAL AGREEMENT	237	A
SOCIAL SECURITY			INTERGOVERNMENTAL AGREEMENT	237	A
INTER-AMERICAN COOPERATION	255	A	INTERGOVERNMENTAL COMMITTEE	522	B
INTER-AMERICAN COUNCIL OF	522	B	FOR EUROPEAN MIGRATION		
JURISTS			INTERGOVERNMENTAL COPYRIGHT	522	B
INTER-AMERICAN CULTURAL	522	B	COMMITTEE		
COUNCIL			INTERGOVERNMENTAL RELATIONS	123	A
INTER-AMERICAN DEFENSE BOARD	522	B	INTERGOVERNMENTAL TAX	237	A
INTER-AMERICAN DEFENSE TREATY	246	A	IMMUNITY		
INTER-AMERICAN DEVELOPMENT	177	A	INTERGROUP RELATIONS	126	A
BANK (IDB)			INTERIM	255	A
INTER-AMERICAN ECONOMIC AND	522	B	INTERIM AGREEMENT	228	A
SOCIAL COUNCIL			INTERIM COMMISSION	471	B
INTER-AMERICAN HIGHWAY	788	B	INTERIM COMMITTEE	177	A
INTER-AMERICAN INDIAN INSTITUTE	522	B	INTERIM COORDINATING COMM. FOR	538	B
INTER-AMERICAN INSTITUTE OF	522	B	INTERNATIONAL COMMODITY		
AGRICULTURAL SCIENCES			ARRANEMENTS		
INTER-AMERICAN MUTUAL	606	B	INTERIM REPORT	246	A
ASSISTANCE TREATY			INTERIOR AND INSULAR AFFAIRS	486	B
INTER-AMERICAN NUCLEAR ENERGY	486	B	COMMITTEE		
COMMISSION			INTERIORITY	794	B
INTER-AMERICAN PEACE COMMITTEE	522	B	INTERLOCKING DIRECTORATES	153	A
INTER-AMERICAN PEACE FORCE	503	B	INTERLOCUTOR	543	B
INTER-AMERICAN REGIONAL	583	B	INTERLOCUTORY HEARING	246	A
SECURITY			INTERMEDIATE	444	B
INTER-AMERICAN RELATIONS	125	A	INTERMEDIATE COURT	471	B
INTER-AMERICAN TREATY OF	631	B	INTERN	186	A
RECIPROCAL ASSISTANCE			INTERNAL AUDITS	246	A
INTER-GENERATION	139	A	INTERNAL COMMUNICATION	136	A
INTER-GOVERNMENTAL MARITIME	522	B	INTERNAL FACTORS	139	A
CONSULTATIVE ORGANIZATION			INTERNAL IMPROVEMENTS	228	A
(IMCO)					
INTER-GOVERNMENTAL RELATIONS	125	A			

INTERNAL MACEDONIAN REVOLUTIONARY ORGANIZATION (IMRO)	522	B
INTERNAL POLITICAL STRUGGLES	237	A
INTERNAL RELATIONS	126	A
INTERNAL REVENUE	221	A
INTERNAL REVENUE SERVICE	156	A
INTERNAL SECURITY ACT OF 1950	221	A
INTERNAL SECURITY DIVISION	486	B
INTERNAL SECURITY INVESTIGATIONS	246	A
INTERNAL WATERS	275	A
INTERNATIONAL	128	A
INTERNATIONAL ACADEMY	503	B
INTERNATIONAL ADMINISTRATION	228	A
INTERNATIONAL ADMINISTRATIVE LAW	237	A
INTERNATIONAL AGREEMENTS	204	A
INTERNATIONAL AIR TRANSPORT ASSOCIATION	471	B
INTERNATIONAL ALLIANCE OF WOMEN	522	B
INTERNATIONAL ALLIANCES	147	A
INTERNATIONAL ANARCHY	246	A
INTERNATIONAL ASSOC. OF CRAFTS AND SMALL AND MEDIUM-SIZED INDUSTRIES	522	B
INTERNATIONAL ASSOCIATION FOR PROTECTION OF INDUSTRY	522	B
INTERNATIONAL ASSOCIATION OF CONFERENCE INTERPRETERS	522	B
INTERNATIONAL ASSOCIATION OF UNIVERSITIES	522	B
INTERNATIONAL ATOMIC ENERGY AGENCY (IAEA)	156	A
INTERNATIONAL AUTHORITY FOR THE RUHR	471	B
INTERNATIONAL BANK FOR RECONSTRUCTION AND DEVELOPMENT (IBRD,IBRAD)	159	A
INTERNATIONAL BARGAINING	198	A
INTERNATIONAL BEHAVIOR	119	A
INTERNATIONAL BOUNDARY AND WATER COMMISSION	471	B
INTERNATIONAL BOUNDARY COMMISSION, U.S. AND MEXICO	471	B
INTERNATIONAL BRIGADE	471	B
INTERNATIONAL BROTHERHOOD OF AUTO WORKERS (IAW)	177	A
INTERNATIONAL BUREAU FOR THE PUBLICATION OF CUSTOMS AND TARIFFS	522	B
INTERNATIONAL BUREAU OF EDUCATION	522	B
INTERNATIONAL CHAMBER OF COMMERCE	177	A
INTERNATIONAL CHILDREN'S EMERGENCY FUND	486	B
INTERNATIONAL CITY MANAGEMENT ASSOCIATION (ICMA)	471	B
INTERNATIONAL CIVIL AVIATION ORGANIZATION (ICAO)	172	A
INTERNATIONAL CIVIL SERVICE	177	A
INTERNATIONAL CLEARING UNIONS	522	B
INTERNATIONAL COFFEE ORGANIZATION	486	B
INTERNATIONAL COFFEE STUDY GROUP	522	B
INTERNATIONAL COMMERCE BUREAU	522	B
INTERNATIONAL COMMISSION FOR AGRICULTURAL INDUSTRIES	503	B
INTERNATIONAL COMMISSION FOR NORTHWEST ATLANTIC FISHERIES	522	B
INTERNATIONAL COMMISSION OF JURISTS	503	B
INTERNATIONAL COMMISSION ON CIVIL STATUS	503	B
INTERNATIONAL COMMISSIONS	150	A
INTERNATIONAL COMMITTEE OF THE RED CROSS	177	A
INTERNATIONAL COMMUNICATIONS	121	A
INTERNATIONAL COMMUNIST MOVEMENT	147	A
INTERNATIONAL COMMUNITY	147	A
INTERNATIONAL CONCESSION	237	A
INTERNATIONAL CONFEDERATION OF AGRICULTURE	503	B
INTERNATIONAL CONFEDERATION OF EXECUTIVE STAFFS	522	B
INTERNATIONAL CONFEDERATION OF FORMER PRISONERS OF WAR	522	B
INTERNATIONAL CONFEDERATION OF FREE TRADE UNIONS	471	B
INTERNATIONAL CONFEDERATION OF TRADE UNIONS	486	B
INTERNATIONAL CONFLICTS	198	A
INTERNATIONAL CONGRESS ON PHILOSOPHY (PRAGUE,1934)	523	B
INTERNATIONAL CONTROL OF ATOMIC WEAPONS	200	A
INTERNATIONAL COOPERATION	126	A
INTERNATIONAL COOPERATION ADMINISTRATION (ICA)	172	A
INTERNATIONAL COOPERATIVE ALLIANCE	471	B
INTERNATIONAL COPYRIGHT	246	A
INTERNATIONAL COTTON ADVISORY COMMITTEE	523	B
INTERNATIONAL COUNCIL FOR PHILOSOPHY AND HUMAN STUDIES	523	B

INTERNATIONAL COUNCIL OF SCIENTIFIC UNIONS	523	B
INTERNATIONAL COUNCIL OF WOMEN	486	B
INTERNATIONAL COURT OF JUSTICE (ICJ)	153	A
INTERNATIONAL COURTESY	246	A
INTERNATIONAL COVENANT ON CIVIL AND POLITICAL RIGHTS	503	B
INTERNATIONAL COVENANT ON ECONOMIC, SOCIAL AND CULTURAL RIGHTS	631	B
INTERNATIONAL COVENANTS ON HUMAN RIGHTS	237	A
INTERNATIONAL CRIMES	221	A
INTERNATIONAL CRIMINAL JURISDICTION	606	B
INTERNATIONAL CRIMINAL LAW	255	A
INTERNATIONAL CRIMINAL POLICE ORGANIZATION	523	B
INTERNATIONAL CRISES	198	A
INTERNATIONAL CUSTOMARY LAW	237	A
INTERNATIONAL CUSTOMS	246	A
INTERNATIONAL DEVELOPMENT AGENCY	159	A
INTERNATIONAL DEVELOPMENT ASSOCIATION (IDA)	178	A
INTERNATIONAL DIPLOMATIC ACADEMY	503	B
INTERNATIONAL DISARMAMENT ORGANIZATION (IDO)	178	A
INTERNATIONAL ECONOMIC LAW	228	A
INTERNATIONAL ECONOMIC RELATIONS	128	A
INTERNATIONAL ECONOMICS	126	A
INTERNATIONAL EDUCATION	444	B
INTERNATIONAL ETHICS	142	A
INTERNATIONAL EXCHANGE PROGRAM	255	A
INTERNATIONAL EXCHANGE SERVICE	523	B
INTERNATIONAL EXHIBITION BUREAU	523	B
INTERNATIONAL FEDERATION OF CHRISTIAN TRADE UNIONS	178	A
INTERNATIONAL FEDERATION OF JOURNALISTS (IFJ)	503	B
INTERNATIONAL FEDERATION OF RESISTANCE MOVEMENTS	503	B
INTERNATIONAL FEDERATION OF TRANSLATORS	503	B
INTERNATIONAL FINANCE CORPORATION (IFC)	471*	B
INTERNATIONAL FREQUENCY REGISTRATION BOARD	523	B
INTERNATIONAL GEOPHYSICAL YEAR	583	B
INTERNATIONAL HIGHWAY	282	A
INTERNATIONAL HUNTING COUNCIL	487	B
INTERNATIONAL HYDROGRAPHIC BUREAU	503	B
INTERNATIONAL INSTITUTE (VIENNA)	503	B
INTERNATIONAL INSTITUTE OF REFRIGERATION (IIR)	523	B
INTERNATIONAL INSTITUTE OF SOCIAL HISTORY (AMSTERDAM)	523	B
INTERNATIONAL INSTITUTE OF SOCIOLOGY	523	B
INTERNATIONAL INTEGRATION	115	A
INTERNATIONAL INTERGOVERNMENTAL ORGANIZATIONS	156	A
INTERNATIONAL LABOR BUREAU	487	B
INTERNATIONAL LABOR CODE FORMULATED	631	B
INTERNATIONAL LABOR CONFERENCE	255	A
INTERNATIONAL LABOR LAW	255	A
INTERNATIONAL LABOR ORGANIZATION (ILO)	148	A
INTERNATIONAL LAW	194	A
INTERNATIONAL LAW ASSOCIATION	523	B
INTERNATIONAL LAW COMMISSION (ILC)	471	B
INTERNATIONAL LAW OF THE SEA	221	A
INTERNATIONAL LEAGUE FOR THE RIGHTS OF MAN	487	B
INTERNATIONAL LEGISLATION	237	A
INTERNATIONAL LONGSHOREMENS ASSOCIATION (ILA)	178	A
INTERNATIONAL MANAGEMENT	450	B
INTERNATIONAL MILITARY TRIBUNAL	178	A
INTERNATIONAL MISSIONARY COUNCIL	523	B
INTERNATIONAL MONETARY FUND (IMF)	147	A
INTERNATIONAL MONETARY RELATIONS	123	A
INTERNATIONAL MOVEMENT OF CATHOLIC STUDENTS (IMCS)	503	B
INTERNATIONAL NARCOTICS CONTROL BOARD (INCB)	503	B
INTERNATIONAL NON-GOVERNMENTAL ORGANIZATIONS	153	A
INTERNATIONAL NUCLEAR INFORMATION SYSTEM (INIS)	523	B
INTERNATIONAL OFFENSE	221	A
INTERNATIONAL OFFICE OF EPIZOOTICS	523	B
INTERNATIONAL OFFICE OF PUBLIC HEALTH	503	B

INTERNATIONAL OLYMPIC COMMITTEE	178	A
INTERNATIONAL ORDER	198	A
INTERNATIONAL ORGANIZATION	145	A
INTERNATIONAL ORGANIZATION OF EMPLOYERS	523	B
INTERNATIONAL ORGANIZATION OF JOURNALISTS	523	B
INTERNATIONAL PATENT INSTITUTE (IPI)	503	B
INTERNATIONAL PHONETIC ASSOCIATION	523	B
INTERNATIONAL POLICE	159	A
INTERNATIONAL POLICE FORCE, UNITED NATIONS	150	A
INTERNATIONAL POLITICAL PARTY	159	A
INTERNATIONAL POLITICAL SCIENCE ASSOCIATION	163	A
INTERNATIONAL POLITICS	114	A
INTERNATIONAL POPLAR COMMISSION	523	B
INTERNATIONAL POSTAL UNION (IPU)	167	A
INTERNATIONAL PRESS INSTITUTE	523	B
INTERNATIONAL PRIVATE LAW	583	B
INTERNATIONAL PRIZE COURT	487	B
INTERNATIONAL PUBLIC LAW	228	A
INTERNATIONAL RADIO CONSULTATIVE COMMITTEE	523	B
INTERNATIONAL RED CROSS	172	A
INTERNATIONAL REFUGEE ORGANIZATION (IRO)	159	A
INTERNATIONAL REGIONALISM	123	A
INTERNATIONAL RELATIONS	113	A
INTERNATIONAL RELIEF UNION	503	B
INTERNATIONAL RICE COMMISSION	503	B
INTERNATIONAL RICE ORGANIZATION OF FAO	487	B
INTERNATIONAL RIVERS	279	A
INTERNATIONAL ROAD TRANSPORT UNION	503	B
INTERNATIONAL SECURITY	119	A
INTERNATIONAL SERICULTURAL COMMISSION	523	B
INTERNATIONAL SERVITUDES	606	B
INTERNATIONAL SETTLEMENT	221	A
INTERNATIONAL SOCIAL SCIENCE COUNCIL	503	B
INTERNATIONAL SOCIETY	163	A
INTERNATIONAL SOCIETY FOR SOCIAL PROGRESS	523	B
INTERNATIONAL SOCIOLOGY	450	B
INTERNATIONAL STATION	523	B
INTERNATIONAL STATISTICAL INSTITUTE	503	B
INTERNATIONAL STUDY (UNESCO PROGRAM)	654	B
INTERNATIONAL SUGAR AGREEMENT	237	A
INTERNATIONAL SUGAR COUNCIL	487	B
INTERNATIONAL SYSTEM	115	A
INTERNATIONAL TARIFF	204	A
INTERNATIONAL TEA COMMITTEE	523	B
INTERNATIONAL TECHNICAL ASSISTANCE	228	A
INTERNATIONAL TELECOMMUNICATION UNION (ITU)	178	A
INTERNATIONAL TELEGRAPH AND TELEPHONE CONSULTATIVE COMMITTEES	487	B
INTERNATIONAL TENSION	204	A
INTERNATIONAL TERRITORY	275	A
INTERNATIONAL TIN COUNCIL	504	B
INTERNATIONAL TOURING ALLIANCE	654	B
INTERNATIONAL TRADE	200	A
INTERNATIONAL TRADE CENTER OF GATT	167	A
INTERNATIONAL TRADE ORGANIZATION (ITO)	159	A
INTERNATIONAL TRANSIT	631	B
INTERNATIONAL TREATIES AND AGREEMENTS	200	A
INTERNATIONAL TREATY ON PEACEFUL USES OF OUTER SPACE	237	A
INTERNATIONAL TRIBUNAL	153	A
INTERNATIONAL TRUSTEESHIP SYSTEM	228	A
INTERNATIONAL UNION AGAINST ALCOHOLISM	523	B
INTERNATIONAL UNION FOR CHILD WELFARE	523	B
INTERNATIONAL UNION FOR PROTECTION OF INDUSTRIAL PROPERTY	524	B
INTERNATIONAL UNION FOR THE PROTECTION OF LITERARY AND ARTISTIC WORKS	524	B
INTERNATIONAL UNION OF LOCAL AUTHORITIES	524	B
INTERNATIONAL UNION OF PUBLIC TRANSPORT	524	B
INTERNATIONAL UNION OF RAILWAYS	524	B
INTERNATIONAL UNION OF SOCIALIST YOUTH (IUSY)	487	B
INTERNATIONAL UNION OF STUDENTS	504	B
INTERNATIONAL VINE AND WINE OFFICE	524	B
INTERNATIONAL WATERWAYS	279	A

INVISIBLE EMPIRE	504	B
INVISIBLE EXPORTS	255	A
INVISIBLE GOVERNMENT	163	A
INVOKE	255	A
INVOLUNTARY SERVITUDE	221	A
INVOLUTION	631	B
INVOLVEMENT	606	B
IONIAN THINKERS	550	B
IOWA	279	A
IPHICRATES	747	B
IQBAL, M.	747	B
IRAN	275	A
IRAN, ANGLO-SOVIET TREATY WITH	255	A
IRAQ	276	A
IRAQ PETROLEUM COMPANY	504	B
IRELAND, ALLEYNE	747	B
IRELAND, REPUBLIC OF (EIRE)	159	A
IRETON, HENRY	747	B
IRGUN ZVAI LEUMI (ISRAEL)	504	B
IRISH BOUNDARY	282	A
IRISH FREE STATE	163	A
IRISH MAFIA	178	A
IRISH NAVAL STATIONS	826	B
IRISH REPRESENTATIVE PEERS	504	B
IRISH REPUBLICAN ARMY (IRA)	148	A
IRISH-AMERICANS	167	A
IRON	818	B
IRON AND STEEL COMMITTEE (ILO)	504	B
IRON CHANCELLOR	266	A
IRON CURTAIN	273	A
IRON GUARDS	524	B
IRON LAW OF OLIGARCHY	115	A
IRON RING	504	B
IRONCLAD OATH	631	B
IRONY	142	A
IRRATIONAL	133	A
IRRATIONAL FACTORS	128	A
IRRATIONALISM	139	A
IRRATIONALITY	128	A
IRRECEIVABILITY	654	B
IRRECONCILABLE	142	A
IRREDENTISM	126	A
IRREGULAR TROOPS	172	A
IRRELEVANT	142	A
IRREMOVABLE	631	B
IRREPRESSIBLE CONFLICT SPEECH	632	B
IRRIGATION	246	A
IS DODD DEAD	844	B
ISABELLA OF CASTILE	686	B
ISHAQ, ADIB	747	B
ISIDORE OF SEVILLE	748	B
ISKRA	809	B
ISLAM	153	A
ISLAND	788	B
ISM	128	A
ISOCRATES	748	B
ISOLATION	209	A
ISOLATIONISM	115	A
ISOLATIONISTS	183	A
ISOLS	456	B
ISOMORPHISM	139	A
ISRAEL, STATE OF (MENDINAT ISRAEL)	276	A
ISSUES	228	A
ISTIQLAL	524	B
ITALIAN CHRISTIAN DEMOCRATS	167	A
ITALIAN COMMUNISTS	159	A
ITALIAN CONSTITUTION	255	A
ITALIAN FASCIST SECRET POLICE	471	B
ITALIAN LABOR CHARTER OF MUSSOLINI	632	B
ITALIAN LIBERAL PARTY	172	A
ITALIAN MONARCHISTS	178	A
ITALIAN RADICAL PARTY	178	A
ITALIAN REPUBLICAN PARTY	471	B
ITALIAN SOCIAL MOVEMENT	487	B
ITALIAN SOCIALISTS	167	A
ITALIAN SOCIETY FOR THE PROGRESS OF SCIENCE	524	B
ITALIAN-AMERICANS	167	A
ITALIANS	471	B
ITALY	277	A
ITCH TO RUN	836	B
ITEM VETO	195	A
ITEMIZED APPROPRIATIONS	204	A
ITO, HIROBUMI	748	B
IUS	246	A
IUS GENTIUM	214	A
IUS SOLI	228	A
IVAN THE TERRIBLE	267	A
IVES-QUINN ANTI-DISCRIMINATION LAW (1945)	654	B
IVORY COAST	280	A
IVORY TOWER	279	A
IZVESTIA (NEWS)	283	A
JABOTINSKY, VLADIMIR	748	B
JACK MORMON	550	B
JACKPOT	606	B
JACKSON DAY	255	A
JACKSON REPORT	807	B
JACKSON, HENRY (SCOOP)	263	A
JACKSON, PRESIDENT ANDREW	262	A
JACKSON, ROBERT H.	272	A
JACKSONIAN DEMOCRACY	121	A
JACKSONIANISM	128	A
JACOB, HERBERT	717	B
JACOB, PHILLIP E.	717	B
JACOBELLIS VS. OHIO (1964)	678	B
JACOBI	748	B
JACOBIN	182	A
JACOBIN DEMOCRACY	136	A
JACOBINISM	128	A

JAEGER, WERNER	717	B	JEREMAID	812	B
JAGAN, DR. CHEDDI	686	B	JEROME	717	B
JAHODA, GUSTAV	748	B	JERUSALEM	277	A
JAHODA, MARIE	717	B	JESUITS	159	A
JAIL	287	A	JESUS OF NAZARETH	264	A
JAIPUR, INDIA	798	B	JEWELL, MALCOLM	717	B
JAMAICA	280	A	JEWISH	188	A
JAMES	686	B	JEWISH AGENCY FOR ISRAEL	178	A
JAMES I OF ENGLAND	269	A	JEWISH NATIONAL HOME	178	A
JAMES II OF ENGLAND	272	A	JEWISH THOUGHT	444	B
JAMES, WILLIAM	267	A	JEWISHNESS	543	B
JAMESON RAID	606	B	JEWS	159	A
JANET, PAUL	748	B	JHERING, RUDOLF VON	748	B
JANIZARY	524	B	JIHAD (HOLY WAR)	255	A
JANOWITZ, MORRIS	686	B	JIM CROW	204	A
JANSEN, ERNEST GEORGE	748	B	JIM CROW LAWS	221	A
JAPAN	276	A	JINGOISM	123	A
JAPANESE	172	A	JINNAH, MOHAMMED ALI	696	B
JAPANESE CONSTITUTION OF 1946	237	A	JIYU MINSHUTO	524	B
JAPANESE CONSTITUTION, ARTICLE NINE	255	A	JOAN OF ARC	267	A
			JOB	186	A
JAPANESE DIET	167	A	JOB ANALYSIS	228	A
JAPANESE EMPEROR CONCEPT	130	A	JOB CORPS	163	A
JAPANESE IMPERIAL RESCRIPT	654	B	JOB CORPS PERSONNEL	190	A
JAPANESE POLITICAL SCIENCE ASSOCIATION	524	B	JOB DESCRIPTION	221	A
			JOB DESIGN	246	A
JAPANESE WAR CRIMES TRIALS	237	A	JOB ENLARGEMENT	606	B
JAPANESE-AMERICAN SECURITY TREATY	237	A	JOB EVALUATION	221	A
			JOB INFORMATION SERVICES (JIS)	504	B
JAPANESE-AMERICANS	159	A	JOB INSTRUCTION TRAINING	583	B
JARGON	136	A	JOB SATISFACTION	133	A
JARL, OTTO	748	B	JOB SEEKS THE MAN	834	B
JASPERS, KARL	272	A	JOBBER, JOBBERY	550	B
JASZI, O.	748	B	JOBLESS	188	A
JAURES, JEAN	696	B	JODL. ALFRED	696	B
JAVITS, JACOB K.	265	A	JOE SMITH	564	B
JAY TREATY	221	A	JOFFE, ADOLF ABRAMOVITCH	717	B
JAY, JOHN	265	A	JOHN BIRCH SOCIETY	153	A
JAYHAWKERS	524	B	JOHN BROWN REPUBLICANS	504	B
JAZZ	606	B	JOHN BULL	290	A
JEFE MAXIMO (SUPREME LEADER)	550	B	JOHN DOE WARRANT	209	A
JEFFERSON DAY	632	B	JOHN F. KENNEDY CENTER FOR PERFORMING ARTS	818	B
JEFFERSON, PRESIDENT THOMAS	262	A			
JEFFERSON'S MANUAL	286	A	JOHN OF ENGLAND	717	B
JEFFERSONIAN DEMOCRACY	114	A	JOHN OF IBELIN	748	B
JEFFERSONIAN REPUBLICANS	156	A	JOHN OF JANDUN	748	B
JEFFREYS, GEORGE	748	B	JOHN OF PARIS	717	B
JEHOVAH'S WITNESSES CASES	260	A	JOHN OF SALISBURY	717	B
JELLINEK, GEORG	748	B	JOHN OF ST. THOMAS	748	B
JELLY-FISH	564	B	JOHN OF TORQUEMADA	696	B
JENKIN, THOMAS P.	717	B	JOHN Q. PUBLIC	190	A
JENKINS, ROY	717	B	JOHNS HOPKINS UNIVERSITY	178	A
JENKS, JEREMIAH W.	748	B	JOHNS, C. W. H.	748	B
JENNINGS, HERBERT S.	717	B	JOHNSON ACT	654	B
JENNINGS, M. KENT	696	B	JOHNSON TREATMENT	632	B
JEOPARDY	583	B	JOHNSON, DR.	686	B

JOHNSON, HIRAM W.	267	A
JOHNSON, HUGH	696	B
JOHNSON, JACK	717	B
JOHNSON, PRESIDENT ANDREW	263	A
JOHNSON, PRESIDENT LYNDON BAINES	262	A
JOHNSON, R. H.	748	B
JOHNSON, THOMAS L.	748	B
JOINT	820	B
JOINT ANTI-FASCIST REFUGEE COMMITTEE VS. MCGRATH (1951)	678	B
JOINT BALLOT	237	A
JOINT BOARD	471	B
JOINT CHIEFS OF STAFF (JCS)	150	A
JOINT COMMISSION	159	A
JOINT COMMITTEE	150	A
JOINT COMMITTEE ON ATOMIC ENERGY	163	A
JOINT COMMITTEE ON THE ECONOMIC REPORT	168	A
JOINT COMMITTEES, STATE	471	B
JOINT CONGRESSIONAL COMMITTEES	153	A
JOINT CONTROL OF INDUSTRY	606	B
JOINT DISCIPLINARY COMMITTEE	524	B
JOINT ECONOMIC COMMITTEES	159	A
JOINT FAO-WHO EXPERT COMMITTEE ON NUTRITION	504	B
JOINT MARITIME COMMISSION	172	A
JOINT OFFICE OF SCRAP USERS	524	B
JOINT RATE	632	B
JOINT RESOLUTION, CONGRESS	214	A
JOINT RETURN	285	A
JOINT SESSION	214	A
JOINT WAR PRODUCTION COMMITTEE	504	B
JOINT-STOCK ASSOCIATION	178	A
JOKER	564	B
JOLIFFE, J. E. A.	748	B
JOLY, CLAUDE	717	B
JONAH	748	B
JONAS, FRANZ	748	B
JONES ACT	654	B
JONES VS. ALFRED H. MAYER CO. (1968)	675	B
JONES-CONNALLY ACT	654	B
JONES, A. H. M.	748	B
JONES, HENRY ARTHUR	717	B
JONES, JESSE	696	B
JONES, JOSEPH	748	B
JONES, RUFUS	748	B
JONES, SIR HENRY	717	B
JONES, VICTOR	686	B
JORDAN	276	A
JORDAN, BENJAMIN EVERETT	748	B
JORDAN, DAVID STARR	749	B
JORDAN, ELIJAH	749	B
JORDAN, LEONARD BECK	749	B
JORGER, J.	749	B
JOSEPH, H. W. B.	749	B
JOUHAUX, LEON	749	B
JOURNAL	285	A
JOURNAL OF THE FEDERAL CONVENTION	805	B
JOURNAL OF THE HOUSE OF REPRESENTATIVES	284	A
JOURNALISM	436	B
JOURNEYMAN	190	A
JOVANOVIC, SLOBODAN	717	B
JOWETT, B.	717	B
JUARES, JEAN	696	B
JUDAISM	133	A
JUDD, WALTER H.	686	B
JUDGE	186	A
JUDGE ADVOCATE	190	A
JUDGE ADVOCATE GENERAL (JAG)	192	A
JUDGE MADE LAW (COMMON LAW)	228	A
JUDGE OF ELECTIONS	192	A
JUDGE OF PROBATE	192	A
JUDGING	246	A
JUDGMENT	214	A
JUDICIAL ACTIVISM	195	A
JUDICIAL ALLIANCES	487	B
JUDICIAL BEHAVIOR	115	A
JUDICIAL BRANCH	145	A
JUDICIAL COMMITTTEE OF THE PRIVY COUNCIL	487	B
JUDICIAL CONTINENCE	583	B
JUDICIAL COUNCIL	168	A
JUDICIAL DECISIONS	204	A
JUDICIAL DOCTRINE	221	A
JUDICIAL INTERPRETATION	201	A
JUDICIAL LAW MAKING	117	A
JUDICIAL LEGISLATION	201	A
JUDICIAL NOTICE	237	A
JUDICIAL NULLIFICATION	246	A
JUDICIAL POWER	197	A
JUDICIAL PRECEDENT	201	A
JUDICIAL PROCEDURE	198	A
JUDICIAL PROCEEDINGS	246	A
JUDICIAL RECORDS	805	B
JUDICIAL REVIEW	194	A
JUDICIAL SELF-LIMITATION	246	A
JUDICIAL SELF-RESTRAINT	197	A
JUDICIAL SETTLEMENT (ADJUDICATION)	123	A
JUDICIAL SOVEREIGNTY	237	A
JUDICIAL SPOILS	237	A
JUDICIAL SUPREMACY	204	A
JUDICIAL SYSTEM	194	A
JUDICIAL VACATIONS	606	B
JUDICIAL VETO	221	A

JUDICIARY	147	A	JUSTIFICATION	221	A
JUDICIARY ACT OF 1789	228	A	JUSTINIAN	686	B
JUDICIARY ACT OF 1925	583	B	JUVENAL	717	B
JUDICIARY COMMITTEE	153	A	JUVENILE	192	A
JUDSON, FREDERIC N.	717	B	JUVENILE COURT	172	A
JUGGERNAUT	471	A	JUVENILE CRIME	237	A
JUGGLER	564	B	JUVENILE DELINQUENCY	214	A
JUKUN	524	B	JUVENILE DELINQUENT	186	A
JULIAN MARCH	654	B	KAC-JAC	654	B
JULIAN THE APOSTATE	717	B	KACHIN	504	B
JULLIARD VS. GREENMAN (1884)	678	B	KADAR, JANOS	686	B
JULY 14, 1789	237	A	KAFKA, F.	269	A
JULY 20, 1944	606	B	KAGANOVICH, LAZAR	696	B
JULY 4, 1776	221	A	KAHN, H.	268	A
JUNE RISING	654	B	KAHN, OTTO	749	B
JUNG, CARL GUSTAV	265	A	KAHN, R. L.	749	B
JUNIOR COLLEGE	471	B	KAI-SHEK, CHIANG	264	A
JUNIOR HIGH SCHOOL	487	B	KAISER, JAKOB	749	B
JUNKERS	163	A	KALES, ALBERT M.	749	B
JUNKET	214	A	KALISCHER, ZEBI HIRSCH	749	B
JUNKETEERING GUMSHOES	557	B	KALLEN, H. M.	749	B
JUNTA	153	A	KAMAKURA ERA	654	B
JURICYBERNETICS	444	B	KAMARAJ PLAN	654	B
JURIDICAL METHOD	128	A	KAMBATSU	524	B
JURIMETRICS	136	A	KAMENEV, LEV BORISOVICH	717	B
JURISDICTION	195	A	KAMIKAZE	192	A
JURISDICTION CLAUSE	255	A	KANG SHENG	798	B
JURISDICTIONAL DISPUTE	214	A	KANG YEOU WEI	717	B
JURISDICTIONAL STRIKE	237	A	KANGAROO CLOSURE	632	B
JURISPRUDENCE	123	A	KANGAROO COURT	150	A
JURISPRUDENCE CONSTANTE	632	B	KANGAROO TICKET	487	B
JURIST	183	A	KANSAS	279	A
JURY	148	A	KANSAS INDUSTRIAL COURT	524	B
JURY DUTY	221	A	KANSAS PLAN	246	A
JURY SYSTEM	198	A	KANSAS VS. COLORADO (1907)	678	B
JURY TRIAL	201	A	KANSAS-NEBRASKA ACT	237	A
JUS BELLI	214	A	KANT, IMMANUEL	264	A
JUS CIVILE	201	A	KANTIAN IMPERATIVE	126	A
JUS GENTIUM	209	A	KANTOROWICZ, HERMANN	749	B
JUS IN BELLO	246	A	KANU, KENYA	798	B
JUS NATURALE	209	A	KAPLAN, ABRAHAM	686	B
JUS SANGUINIS (LAW OF THE BLOOD)	214	A	KAPLAN, FANYA (DORA)	749	B
			KAPLAN, MORTON A.	686	B
JUS SOLI (LAW OF THE LAND)	204	A	KAPP PUTSCH	607	B
JUST AND LASTING PEACE	291	A	KARAGANDA	524	B
JUST COMPENSATION	214	A	KARAGEORGEVICH	749	B
JUST WAR	204	A	KARAMI, RASHID	749	B
JUSTICE	180	A	KARDELJ, EDUARD	717	B
JUSTICE OF THE PEACE	184	A	KARDINER, A.	749	B
JUSTICE OF THE PEACE COURT	168	A	KARELIA	794	B
JUSTICE SHOP	844	B	KARELIAN REFUGEE PROBLEM	632	B
JUSTICES	184	A	KARIEL, HENRY	696	B
JUSTICIABILITY	221	A	KARLSBAD DEMANDS	654	B
JUSTICIABLE AND NON-JUSTICIABLE DISPUTES	209	A	KARLSSON, GEORG	749	B
			KARMA	237	A
JUSTICIALISMO	444	B	KASAVUBU, JOSEPH	272	A

KASHMIR QUESTION	214	A
KASHMIR, INDIA	279	A
KASRAVI, AHMAD	749	B
KASSEM, GENERAL ABDUL KARIM	749	B
KATANGA	279	A
KATANGAIS (CONGOLESE)	524	B
KATAPHRACTS	524	B
KATAR	524	B
KATHEDER SOZIALIZTER	564	B
KATYN INCIDENT	607	B
KATZ VS. U.S. (1967)	671	B
KATZ, DANIEL	696	B
KATZ, ELIHU	696	B
KATZENBACH	696	B
KATZENBACH VS. MCCLUNG (1964)	675	B
KATZENBACH VS. MORGAN (1966)	673	B
KAUFMAN, ARNOLD S.	749	B
KAUFMAN, HERBERT	717	B
KAUNDA, DR. KENNETH	686	B
KAUTILYA	717	B
KAUTSKY, KARL	272	A
KAVELIN, KONSTANTIN DMITRIEVICH	749	B
KAZAKHSTAN	282	A
KEATING-OWENS ACT OF 1916	654	B
KEEFE, WILLIAM	718	B
KEEZER, DEXTER M.	749	B
KEFAUVER INVESTIGATING COMMITTEE	163	A
KEFAUVER, ESTES	268	A
KEHR, E.	749	B
KEITA, MODIBO	749	B
KEKKONEN, JUHO KALEVA	686	B
KELLER, A. G.	749	B
KELLOGG-BRIAND PACT (TREATY FOR RENUNCIATION OF WAR)	229	A
KELLOGG, VERNON	749	B
KELLY, EDWARD JOSEPH	750	B
KELSEN, HANS	686	B
KELVIN	750	B
KEMAL, MUSTAFA (ATATURK)	269	A
KEMALISM	436	B
KEMPNER, ROBERT M. W.	750	B
KENDALL VS. U.S. (1938)	678	B
KENDALL, WILLMOORE	718	B
KENNAN, C. F.	750	B
KENNAN, GEORGE F.	266	A
KENNEDY ROUND TARIFF NEGOTIATIONS	229	A
KENNEDY, EDWARD MOORE	263	A
KENNEDY, PRESIDENT JOHN F. (JFK)	262	A
KENNEDY, ROBERT F.	264	A
KENNEL PRESS	524	B
KENT STATE UNIVERSITY	168	A
KENT VS. DULLES (1958)	678	B
KENT, FRANK R.	750	B
KENTUCKY	279	A
KENTUCKY AND VIRGINIA RESOLUTIONS	237	A
KENTUCKY VS. DENNISON (1861)	678	B
KENWORTHY, J. M.	750	B
KENYA	276	A
KENYATTA, JOMO	266	A
KENYON, CECILIA M.	750	B
KEPLER	718	B
KER, W. P.	750	B
KERALA	282	A
KERENSKY, ALEXANDER	263	A
KERNER COMMISSION	159	A
KERNER REPORT	283	A
KERR-MILLS ACT	632	B
KESSELMAN, LOUIS L.	750	B
KEY BODY	504	B
KEY POSITION	550	B
KEY, V. O., JR.	263	A
KEYISHIAN VS. BOARD OF REGENTS (1967)	678	B
KEYNES, JOHN MAYNARD	262	A
KEYNESIANISM	117	A
KEYNOTE SPEAKER	192	A
KEYNOTE SPEECH	221	A
KEYNOTER	543	B
KEYSERLING, COUNT HERMAN	696	B
KGB (KOMITET GOSUDARSTEVENNOI BEZOPASNOSTI) (U.S.S.R.)	153	A
KHAMA, SIR SERETSE	750	B
KHAN, FIELD MARSHAL MOHAMMED AYUB	686	B
KHANH, NGUYEN	750	B
KHARIJITES (SECEDERS)	525	B
KHRUSHCHEV, NIKITA SERGEEVICH	262	A
KIBBUTZ	159	A
KICK THE RASCALS OUT	291	A
KICK UPSTAIRS	237	A
KICKBACK	237	A
KICKER	654	B
KID-GLOVE DIPLOMACY	583	B
KID-GLOVE POLITICS	583	B
KIDS	550	B
KIERKEGAARD, SOREN	269	A
KIESINGER, KURT GEORG	269	A
KIICHIRO, HIRANUMA	750	B
KIJAJI	564	B
KIKUYU	794	B
KILL	607	B
KILL IN COMMITTEE	214	A
KILLER	557	B
KILLING	246	A
KILPI, JUHO EINO	750	B
KIM IL-SING	718	B
KIMPAI	525	B
KIND	450	B
KINDLEBERGER, CHARLES P.	718	B

KINETICS	450	B
KING	183	A
KING ALCOHOL	844	B
KING BY THE GRACE OF GOD	291	A
KING CAN DO NO WRONG	290	A
KING CAUCUS	163	A
KING COTTON	229	A
KING-CRANE COMMISSION	525	B
KING, DR. MARTIN LUTHER, JR.	261	A
KING, WILLIAM LYON MACKENZIE	750	B
KING'S COUNCIL	172	A
KING'S PEACE	607	B
KINGDOM	163	A
KINGFISH	192	A
KINGMAKER	190	A
KINGSLEY PICTURES VS. REGENTS OF U.N.Y. (1959)	678	B
KINGSLEY, CHARLES	750	B
KINSHIP	139	A
KIPLING, RUDYARD	686	B
KIPSIGIS	798	B
KIRALY, BELA	750	B
KIRBY, EPHRAIM	750	B
KIRILENKO, A. P.	750	B
KIRK, RUSSELL	686	B
KIROV, SERGEI MIRONOVICH	750	B
KISHI, NOBUSUKE	750	B
KISS JOKE TICKET	525	B
KISS OF DEATH	836	B
KISSINGER, HENRY ALFRED	263	A
KITCHEN CABINET	153	A
KITCHEN DEBATE	583	B
KITCHEN POLICE (KP)	564	B
KITCHENER, HORATIO HERBERT	750	B
KJELLEN, RUDOLF	750	B
KLANDIDATE	564	B
KLAPPER, JOSEPH T.	718	B
KLAUS, JOSEF	750	B
KLEEMOLA, KAUNO ANTERO	750	B
KLEINBURGERTUM	525	B
KLINEBERG, OTTO	718	B
KLOPFER VS. NORTH CAROLINA (1967)	675	B
KLUB 231	525	B
KLUCKHOHN, CLYDE	718	B
KNESSET	159	A
KNICKERBOCKER ICE CO. VS. STEWART (1920)	675	B
KNIFING	632	B
KNIGHT	544	B
KNIGHTHOOD	544	B
KNIGHTS OF LABOR	163	A
KNIGHTS OF THE GOLDEN CIRCLE	525	B
KNOCK ON THE DOOR	834	B
KNOERINGEN, WALDEMAR VON	750	B
KNORR, KLAUS	696	B
KNOW SOMETHING	487	B
KNOW YE MEN	844	B
KNOW-NOTHING PARTY (NATIVE AMERICAN PARTY)	153	A
KNOWING	139	A
KNOWLEDGE	128	A
KNOWLES, HIRAM	750	B
KNOX VS. LEE (1871)	678	B
KNOX, FRANK	750	B
KNOX, JOHN	270	A
KODA HA (IMPERIAL WAY FACTION)	525	B
KODAK	504	B
KOENA	525	B
KOENIG, BISHOP	751	B
KOESTLER, ARTHUR	270	A
KOFF, DAVID	751	B
KOHLER, JOSEPH	751	B
KOHN, HANS	718	B
KOKUIKAI	525	B
KOKUTAI	525	B
KOLAKOWSKI, LESZEK	718	B
KOLKHOZ	791	B
KOLLONTAI, ALEKSANDRA MIKHAILOVNA	718	B
KOLMAN, ARNOST	751	B
KOLYMA	525	B
KOMAROVSKY, MIRRA	751	B
KOMEITO, JAPAN	798	B
KOMMANDATURA (COMMAND)	471	B
KOMSOMOL	163	A
KONIG, RENE	751	B
KOOKS, NUTS AND	844	B
KORAN	284	A
KOREAN	178	A
KOREAN WAR	201	A
KOREMATSU VS. U.S. (1944)	671	B
KORNHAUSER, WILLIAM	272	A
KORNILOV, LAVR G.	718	B
KORSH, KARL	751	B
KORT, FRED	751	B
KOSTOV, T.D.	751	B
KOSYGIN, ALEKSEI NIKOLAEVICH	263	A
KOTA, INDIA	798	B
KOTT	751	B
KOVACS, B.	751	B
KOWEIT	798	B
KOZLOV, FROL	751	B
KPELLE	525	B
KRABBE, HUGO	751	B
KRAFT DURCH FREUDE	487	B
KRAUSISM	456	B
KREDIT-ANSTALT	487	B
KREIS	525	B
KREMLIN	273	A
KREMLINOLOGIST	184	A
KREMLINOLOGY	133	A

KRIEGIE	564	B	LABOR MOVEMENT	150	A
KRISHNA MENON, V. ,	268	A	LABOR PARTY	148	A
KRISTALL NACHT	632	B	LABOR REFORM PARTY	178	A
KROEBER, A. A.	751	B	LABOR REFORMER	192	A
KRONSTADT MUTINY	583	B	LABOR RELATIONS	209	A
KROPOTKIN, PRINCE PETER	272	A	LABOR SERVICE	487	B
KRUGER, STAPHANUS JOHANNESE PAULUS	751	B	LABOR SPIES	192	A
			LABOR STANDARDS ACT OF 1938	229	A
KRUPP	264	A	LABOR THEORY OF VALUE	115	A
KRUPSKAYA, NADEZHDA KONSTANTINOVNA	696	B	LABOR TURNOVER	607	B
			LABOR UNION	146	A
KU KLUX KLAN	150	A	LABOR UNION LEGISLATION	246	A
KUANG, SSU-MA	751	B	LABOR ZIONISM	436	B
KUBITSCHEK DE OLIVEIRA, JUCELINO	718	B	LABOR-MANAGEMENT RELATIONS	229	A
			LABOR-MANAGEMENT RELATIONS ACT OF 1947 (TAFT-HARTLEY LAW)	198	A
KUCHEL, THOMAS H.	696	B			
KUCHUK, FAZIL	751	B	LABOR-MANAGEMENT REPORTING AND DISCLOSURE ACT (1959)	246	A
KULAKS	163	A			
KULSKI, W. W.	718	B	LABOR-MANAGEMENT SERVICES ADMINISTRATION (LMSA)	504	B
KULTUR	142	A			
KULTURKAMPF	142	A	LABOR'S LEAGUE FOR POLITICAL ACTION	504	B
KUN, BELA	696	B			
KUNZ VS. NEW YORK (1951)	675	B	LABOR'S NONPARTISAN LEAGUE	504	B
KUOMINTANG	153	A	LABORATORY APPROACH	136	A
KURDISTAN	280	A	LABORATORY PROGRAM	583	B
KURDS	172	A	LABORATORY TRAINING	139	A
KURLAND, LATVIA	798	B	LABORER	188	A
KURTZMAN, HAROLD	751	B	LABOUR GOVERNMENT	163	A
KUUSINEN, OTTO WILHEMOVITCH	718	B	LABOUR PARTY, BRITAIN	153	A
KUWAIT	276	A	LABRIOLA, ARTURO	751	B
KWIAKUTL INDIANS	471	B	LACK OF CONFIDENCE	214	A
KY, NGUYEN CAO	265	A	LACKEY	190	A
KYOTO	282	A	LACTANTIUS	751	B
K1C2	844	B	LADAKH	794	B
L'ETAT C'EST MOI	290	A	LADDER OF VALUES	142	A
LA CRITICA	812	B	LADIES COMMITTEE	525	B
LA FOLLETTE PROGRESSIVE MOVEMENT	153	A	LADIES PROGRAMME	654	B
			LAENDERRAT	504	B
LA FOLLETTE SEAMEN'S ACT	607	B	LAFAYETTE, MARQUIS DE	265	A
LA FOLLETTE, ROBERT M.	265	A	LAG	237	A
LA GUARDIA, FIORELLO HENRY	268	A	LAGARDELLE, HUBERT	751	B
LA ROCHEFOUCALD	696	B	LAGTING	504	B
LA VOCE	812	B	LAGU, JOSEPH	751	B
LABAND, PAUL	751	B	LAICISM	456	B
LABARUM	826	B	LAIDLER, HARRY W.	696	B
LABELS	289	A	LAIRD, MELVIN R.	266	A
LABOR	156	A	LAISSEZ FAIRE	114	A
LABOR AND PUBLIC WELFARE COMMITTEE	487	B	LAKEPORT	798	B
			LAKEWOOD PLAN	237	A
LABOR DISPUTES	209	A	LAMARCK, JEAN BAPTISTE	686	B
LABOR DISPUTES, MEDIATION OF	214	A	LAMBARENE	798	B
LABOR FORCE	159	A	LAMBERT OF AUXERRE	751	B
LABOR FRONT	178	A	LAMBERT, WALLACE E.	751	B
LABOR LEADER	192	A	LAMBOULAYE, E. DE	751	B
LABOR LEGISLATION	214	A	LAME DUCK	182	A
LABOR MARKET	204	A	LAME DUCK AMENDMENT	201	A

LAME DUCK CONGRESS	198	A		LANHAM TRADEMARK ACT OF 1946	654	B
LAME DUCK SESSION	198	A		LANSBURY, GEORGE	752	B
LAMENNAIS, ROBERT D.	718	B		LANSING-ISHII AGREEMENT	632	B
LAMONT VS. POSTMASTER	675	B		LAO TSZE	272	A
GENERAL (1965)				LAO TZU	272	A
LAMONT, CORLISS	751	B		LAOS	276	A
LAMPRECHT, KARL	752	B		LAPALOMBARA, JOSEPH	696	B
LANCELOT	718	B		LAPLACE	718	B
LAND	287	A		LAPSE	607	B
LAND BANK	163	A		LAPUA MOVEMENT	525	B
LAND DEVELOPMENT	237	A		LARCENY	229	A
LAND DIET	471	B		LASKI, HAROLD J.	268	A
LAND DOMAIN	279	A		LASSALLE, FERDINAND	718	B
LAND FORCES	159	A		LASSWELL, HAROLD D.	264	A
LAND FRONTIER	280	A		LAST DITCH (TO DIE IN THE)	844	B
LAND GRANT	214	A		LAST HURRAH	290	A
LAND GRANT COLLEGES	163	A		LAST SPEAKER	550	B
LAND POLICIES	255	A		LASTING PEACE	583	B
LAND POOR	246	A		LATE UNPLEASANTNESS	839	B
LAND POWER	172	A		LATENT FUNCTION	117	A
LAND REFORM	214	A		LATENT OPINION	136	A
LAND RETIREMENT	255	A		LATENT THEORY, ERA OF	142	A
LAND TENURE	229	A		LATERAN ACCORD	246	A
LAND TENURE REFORM	487	B		LATERAN SYNOD	487	B
ASSOCIATION				LATERANENSI, PATTI	752	B
LAND USE	237	A		LATHAM, EARL	718	B
LAND VALUE TAX	229	A		LATIFUNDIA SYSTEM	229	A
LAND WARFARE	214	A		(LATIFUNDISMO)		
LAND-GRABBER	193	A		LATIN	178	A
LAND-RICH	583	B		LATIN AMERICA	273	A
LAND, AIR AND SEA FORCES	156	A		LATIN AMERICAN FREE TRADE	163	A
LANDA, BISHOP	752	B		ASSOCIATION (LAFTA)		
LANDAUER, G.	752	B		LATIN AMERICAN SOLIDARITY	525	B
LANDE, CARL H.	752	B		ORGANIZATION		
LANDED GENTRY	159	A		LATIN AVERROISM	456	B
LANDER	178	A		LATTICE THEORY	444	B
LANDING FORCES	172	A		LATVIA	279	A
LANDIS, JAMES	718	B		LAUGHLIN, J. LAWRENCE	752	B
LANDLOCKED BAY	282	A		LAUGHTER	583	B
LANDLOCKED COUNTRY	275	A		LAUNDRY TICKET	178	A
LANDLOCKED SEA	277	A		LAUPULA	525	B
LANDLORD	186	A		LAURO, ACHILLE	752	B
LANDMARK	288	A		LAUSANNE CONFERENCE	255	A
LANDRUM-GRIFFIN ACT 1959	246	A		LAUSANNE REPARATION	654	B
LANDSHUT, SIEGFRIED	752	B		AGREEMENTS		
LANDSLIDE	209	A		LAVAL, PIERRE	270	A
LANDTMAN, GUNNAR	752	B		LAVOISIER	696	B
LANE POOLE, SIR R.	752	B		LAW	195	A
LANE, ROBERT E.	265	A		LAW (SCIENTIFIC LAW)	123	A
LANESSAN, J. M. DE	752	B		LAW (STIPULATIVE LAW)	583	B
LANGTON, KENNETH P.	752	B		LAW AND ORDER	221	A
LANGUAGE	133	A		LAW AND ORDER PARTY	471	B
LANGUAGE ACTS	654	B		LAW ENFORCEMENT	201	A
LANGUAGE ALLOWANCE	607	B		LAW ENFORCEMENT ASSISTANCE	173	A
LANGUAGE GAMES	632	B		ADMINISTRATION		
LANGUET, HUBERT	752	B		LAW ENFORCEMENT PERSONNEL	188	A

LAW FIRMS	472	B	LEAD	288	A
LAW LORDS	550	B	LEADER	186	A
LAW OF AIR WARFARE	583	B	LEADER OF THE OPPOSITION	182	A
LAW OF CHRYSIPPUS	654	B	LEADER OF THE PARLIAMENTARY	186	A
LAW OF CONTRADICTION	143	A	GROUP		
LAW OF DIMINISHING	143	A	LEADERSHIP	181	A
ADMINISTRATIVE RETURNS			LEAFLETS	286	A
LAW OF ENFORCEMENT	654	B	LEAGUE	173	A
LAW OF HUMANITY	584	B	LEAGUE OF ARAB STATES	156	A
LAW OF INTERNATIONAL RIVERS	237	A	LEAGUE OF FREE NATIONS	525	B
LAW OF LAND WARFARE	255	A	ASSOCIATION		
LAW OF MARITIME WARFARE	584	B	LEAGUE OF NATIONS (LN)	145	A
LAW OF NATIONS (JUS GENTIUM)	214	A	LEAGUE OF NATIONS SOCIETY	487	B
LAW OF NATURE	201	A	LEAGUE OF RED CROSS SOCIETIES	487	B
LAW OF NAVAL WARFARE	255	A	LEAGUE OF WOMEN VOTERS	153	A
LAW OF OCCUPATION	237	A	LEAGUE TO ENFORCE PEACE	525	B
LAW OF OUTER SPACE	209	A	LEAK	229	A
LAW OF PAPAL GUARANTEES	607	B	LEAP	607	B
LAW OF PEACE	255	A	LEARNING	130	A
LAW OF RECIPROCITY	237	A	LEARNING THEORY	117	A
LAW OF THE JUNGLE	246	A	LEASE AGREEMENT	255	A
LAW OF THE LAND	229	A	LEASE SYSTEM	607	B
LAW OF THE SEA	209	A	LEASED TERRITORY	794	B
LAW OF THE SEA CONFERENCE	246	A	LEASEHOLD	791	B
LAW OF TORTS	229	A	LEASEHOLD AREA	794	B
LAW OF TREATIES	584	B	LEATHERMAN, DANIEL R.	752	B
LAW OF WAGES	255	A	LEAVE	584	B
LAW REFORM	237	A	LEAVE TO PRINT	632	B
LAW SPEAKER, SCANDINAVIAN	564	B	LEAVE WITHOUT PAY	246	A
LAW-MAKING POWER	198	A	LEAVE-TAKING AUDIENCE	655	B
LAW-MAKING TREATY	229	A	LEBANON	276	A
LAW, BONAR	752	B	LEBENSRAUM	276	A
LAW, NATURAL	197	A	LECANUET, JEAN FRANCOIS	718	B
LAW, T. H. GREEN	752	B	LECKY, WILLIAM H.	752	B
LAWLESSNESS	255	A	LECOMPTON COMMISSION	504	B
LAWMAKERS	184	A	LECTURE	255	A
LAWMAKING, CONGRESSIONAL	204	A	LECTURER	193	A
LAWRENCE, T. E.	272	A	LEDO ROAD	791	B
LAWS OF AETHELBERT	654	B	LEE KUAN YEW	718	B
LAWS OF ATHELSTAN	654	B	LEE, GENERAL ROBERT E.	264	A
LAWS OF INE OF WESSEX	654	B	LEFT	156	A
LAWS OF WAR (RULES OF	214	A	LEFT AND RIGHT	148	A
WARFARE)			LEFT DEVIATIONISM	139	A
LAWS WITHOUT RETROSPECTIVE	655	B	LEFT WING	148	A
EFFECT			LEFT-WING GOVERNMENT	159	A
LAWYER	544	B	LEFT-WING OPPOSITION	156	A
LAY ON THE TABLE	237	A	LEFT-WING PARTIES	156	A
LAYING PIPES	655	B	LEFT-WING SOCIALIST	156	A
LAYOFF	237	A	LEFT, THE	147	A
LAZARSFELD, PAUL F.	266	A	LEFTIST	184	A
LE BON, GUSTAVE	718	B	LEG TREASURER	564	B
LE CORBUSIER, CHARLES	696	B	LEGACY	607	B
LE PLAY, FREDERICK	718	B	LEGAL	221	A
LE VINE, ROBERT A.	752	B	LEGAL ACTION	229	A
LEA, HOMER	752	B	LEGAL ADVISOR	190	A
LEACOCK, STEPHEN	752	B	LEGAL AID	214	A

LEGAL AUTHORITY	201	A	LEGISLATIVE REFORM	221	A
LEGAL COMMITTEE	525	B	LEGISLATIVE REORGANIZATION ACT	214	A
LEGAL DEPARTMENT	504	B	OF 1946		
LEGAL DIVISION	487	B	LEGISLATIVE STUDY	284	A
LEGAL FICTION	229	A	LEGISLATIVE SUPREMACY	214	A
LEGAL FORCE OF JUDGMENT	255	A	LEGISLATIVE YUAN	487	B
LEGAL GOVERNMENTS	156	A	LEGISLATOR	182	A
LEGAL HISTORY	133	A	LEGISLATURE	147	A
LEGAL NEUTRALITY	221	A	LEGITIMACY	116	A
LEGAL PERSONALITY	188	A	LEGITIMATION	123	A
LEGAL PROPAGANDA	444	B	LEGITIMATION CARD	812	B
LEGAL REALISM	126	A	LEGITIMIST	456	B
LEGAL SOVEREIGN	182	A	LEIBNIZ, G.W.	686	B
LEGAL SYSTEMS	121	A	LEICHTER, OTTO	752	B
LEGAL TENDER	287	A	LEIPSIC TRIALS	632	B
LEGAL TENDER CASES	675	B	LEISERSON, AVERY	718	B
LEGAL-AID BUREAUS	178	A	LEISURE	246	A
LEGALISTS	184	A	LEISY VS. HARDIN (1890)	678	B
LEGALITY	214	A	LEITES, NATHAN	696	B
LEGALITY, SOCIALIST	246	A	LEMMER, ERNST	752	B
LEGATE	544	B	LEND-LEASE ACT, MARCH 11, 1941	246	A
LEGATE A LATERE	565	B	LEND-LEASE PROGRAM	237	A
LEGATION	173	A	LENGTH OF SERVICE	246	A
LEGATION ASYLUM	788	B	LENIN, NIKOLAI	261	A
LEGEND OF THE STAB IN THE BACK	836	B	LENIN, VLADIMIR ILICH ULYANOV	261	A
LEGION OF HONOR	504	B	LENIN'S TESTAMENT	805	B
LEGISLATE	204	A	LENINE	752	B
LEGISLATION	197	A	LENINGRAD AFFAIR	607	B
LEGISLATIVE APPORTIONMENT	198	A	LENINISM, COMMUNIST DOCTRINE	113	A
LEGISLATIVE ASSEMBLY	156	A	LENINIST NORMS	143	A
LEGISLATIVE AUTHORITY	204	A	LENNES, N. J.	752	B
LEGISLATIVE BEHAVIOR	117	A	LENTZ, FRITZ	752	B
LEGISLATIVE BLACKMAIL	584	B	LENZ, J.	752	B
LEGISLATIVE BODY	150	A	LEONE, ENRICO	753	B
LEGISLATIVE BRANCH	148	A	LEONI, BRUNO	753	B
LEGISLATIVE CAUCUS	204	A	LEONI, RAUL	718	B
LEGISLATIVE COMMITTEE	148	A	LEPAWSKY, ALBERT	696	B
LEGISLATIVE COUNCIL	163	A	LEPER, LEPROSY	753	B
LEGISLATIVE COUNSEL	184	A	LERNER VS. CASEY (1958)	678	B
LEGISLATIVE COURT	168	A	LERNER, DANIEL	753	B
LEGISLATIVE DAY	584	B	LEROUX, PIERRE	719	B
LEGISLATIVE DRAFTING BUREAU	487	B	LEROY, MAXIME	753	B
LEGISLATIVE INVESTIGATION	201	A	LESOTHO, AFRICA	791	B
LEGISLATIVE JUNKETS	214	A	LESSENING OF TENSION	584	B
LEGISLATIVE LEADERSHIP	182	A	LESSEPS, FERDINAND DE	719	B
LEGISLATIVE LIAISON OFFICER	186	A	LESSING, G.E.	753	B
LEGISLATIVE OVERSIGHT	204	A	LESSON	584	B
LEGISLATIVE PERIOD	255	A	LET A HUNDRED FLOWERS BLOOM	221	A
LEGISLATIVE POWER	198	A	LET ASIANS FIGHT ASIANS	834	B
LEGISLATIVE POWERS, CONGRESS	197	A	LET THE DUST SETTLE	844	B
LEGISLATIVE PROCEDURE	204	A	LET THE UNION SLIDE	844	B
LEGISLATIVE PROCESS	117	A	LET US ALONE	844	B
LEGISLATIVE REAPPORTIONMENT	198	A	LET US CONTINUE	836	B
LEGISLATIVE RECIPROCITY	237	A	LET'S TAKE A LOOK AT THE	291	A
LEGISLATIVE REFERENCE BUREAU	173	A	RECORD		
LEGISLATIVE REFERENCE SERVICE	168	A	LET'S TALK SENSE	839	B

LETICIA DISPUTE	655	B		LIAISON OFFICE	178	A
LETOURNEAU, ROGER	753	B		LIAISON OFFICER	190	A
LETT	525	B		LIANG SSU-CHENG	719	B
LETTENS, DIRK	753	B		LIAO	525	B
LETTER	805	B		LIB-LAB LOBBY	488	B
LETTER AND SPIRIT OF THE TREATY	237	A		LIBEL	214	A
LETTER OF ACCEPTANCE	807	B		LIBEL AND SLANDER	201	A
LETTER OF APPOINTMENT	285	A		LIBER GOMORRHIANUS	812	B
LETTER OF CONDOLENCE	812	B		LIBER MAIOLICHINUS	812	B
LETTER OF CONVOCATION	809	B		LIBER'S CODE	812	B
LETTER OF CREDENCE	809	B		LIBERAL	181	A
LETTER OF MARQUE AND REPRISAL	285	A		LIBERAL ACTION PARTY	504	B
LETTER OF RESIGNATION	284	A		LIBERAL ARTS	136	A
LETTER OF THANKS	812	B		LIBERAL CONSERVATISM	136	A
LETTERHEAD	809	B		LIBERAL DEMOCRAT	147	A
LETTERS OF COMMENDATION	807	B		LIBERAL DEMOCRATIC PARTY	178	A
LETTERS OF MARQUE AND REPRISAL	286	A		LIBERAL EDUCATION	133	A
				LIBERAL INTERNATIONAL	504	B
LETTERS OF NATURALIZATION	285	A		LIBERAL NATIONAL PARTY	505	B
LETTERS OF RECALL	807	B		LIBERAL NATIONALISM	436	B
LETTERS ROGATORY	809	B		LIBERAL PARTY	163	A
LETTISH	487	B		LIBERAL PARTY, BRITAIN	163	A
LETTRE DE RECREANCE	809	B		LIBERAL REPUBLICAN PARTY	472	B
LEVANT FEDERATION	488	B		LIBERAL-LEFT	156	A
LEVANT STATES	472	B		LIBERAL-REPUBLICANS	160	A
LEVEE	607	B		LIBERALISM	113	A
LEVEE EN MASSE	247	A		LIBERATION	209	A
LEVEL	788	B		LIBERATION MOVEMENTS	204	A
LEVEL OF ANALYSIS	123	A		LIBERATION OF CAPTIVE PEOPLES	247	A
LEVEL OF EDUCATION	584	B		LIBERIA	280	A
LEVELLER MANIFESTO, AGREEMENT OF THE PEOPLE	809	B		LIBERMANISM	436	B
				LIBERTARIANISM	133	A
LEVELLERS	168	A		LIBERTE, EGALITE, FRATERNITE	289	A
LEVERAGE	237	A		LIBERTIES	209	A
LEVI-STRAUSS, CLAUDE	719	B		LIBERTY	195	A
LEVI, PAUL	753	B		LIBERTY AND UNION, NOW AND FOREVER, ONE AND INSEPARABLE	839	B
LEVI, WERNER	719	B				
LEVIATHAN	284	A		LIBERTY BELL	289	A
LEVIN, MURRAY B.	719	B		LIBERTY LEAGUE, AMERICAN	505	B
LEVINE, DONALD N.	753	B		LIBERTY LOANS	632	B
LEVY	247	A		LIBERTY PARTY	472	B
LEVY BRUHL	719	B		LIBERTY POLE	823	B
LEVY, MARION J.	753	B		LIBERUM VETO	632	B
LEWIN, KURT	719	B		LIBIDO	143	A
LEWIS AND CLARK EXPEDITION	221	A		LIBRARIANS	550	B
LEWIS III OF FRANCE	753	B		LIBRARY DISTRICT	794	B
LEWIS THE BAVARIAN	753	B		LIBRARY OF CONGRESS	168	A
LEWIS, G. CORNEWALL	753	B		LIBYA	276	A
LEWIS, HELEN SONNENBURG	753	B		LICENSE	221	A
LEWIS, JOHN L.	272	A		LICENSING	229	A
LEWIS, OSCAR	719	B		LIDICE MASSACRE	237	A
LEWIS, VERNE	753	B		LIE, TRYGVE	270	A
LEWIS, WYNDHAM	753	B		LIEBKNECHT, KARL	686	B
LEXICOGRAPHY	450	B		LIEBKNECHT, WILHELM	686	B
LEXICONS	805	B		LIECHTENSTEIN	282	A
LIAISON COMMITTEE	178	A		LIEN	221	A

LIEUTENANT GOVERNOR	182	A	LINKLETTER VS. WALKER (1965)	678	B
LIFE	247	A	LINKS	436	B
LIFE CYCLE	229	A	LINTON, RALPH	719	B
LIFE EXPECTANCY	436	B	LION	839	B
LIFE INSURANCE	607	B	LIPPMANN, WALTER	264	A
LIFE SCIENCE	450	B	LIPSET, SEYMOUR MARTIN	262	A
LIFE SPAN	584	B	LIPSKY, GEORGE R.	719	B
LIFE TENURE	214	A	LIQUIDATE	256	A
LIFE, LIBERTY AND THE PURSUIT OF HAPPINESS	290	A	LIQUIDATION	237	A
			LIQUIDATION OF THE RUMP CZECH STATE	607	B
LIFE, LIBERTY OR PROPERTY	289	A	LIQUOR REGULATION	256	A
LIFESAVING SERVICE	655	B	LIQUOR TRAFFIC	256	A
LIGHT	820	B	LISKA, GEORGE	696	B
LIGHT POLL	632	B	LIST OF SPEAKERS	805	B
LIGHTNING MAY STRIKE	839	B	LIST SYSTEM OF VOTING	221	A
LIGHTNING WAR	229	A	LISTENING	607	B
LIGHTWEIGHT	557	B	LITERACY	247	A
LIKERT, RENSIS	686	B	LITERACY TEST	221	A
LILBURNE, JOHN	753	B	LITERARY	456	B
LILIENTHAL, DAVID E.	272	A	LITERARY METHOD	450	B
LILLY, WILLIAM S.	753	B	LITERATURE	286	A
LILY WHITE	291	A	LITERATURE AND POLITICS	283	A
LIMA CONFERENCE	607	B	LITHUANIA	279	A
LIMA, ALCEU AMOROSO	753	B	LITIGANTS	186	A
LIMIT	237	A	LITIGATION	209	A
LIMITATION OF ARMAMENTS	214	A	LITT, EDGAR	687	B
LIMITATIONS	584	B	LITTAUER SCHOOL (HARVARD)	525	B
LIMITED GOVERNMENT	145	A	LITTLE ASSEMBLY OF THE UNITED NATIONS	472	B
LIMITED MONARCHY	148	A			
LIMITED VOTING	209	A	LITTLE BAND	505	B
LIMITED WAR	195	A	LITTLE ENTENTE	168	A
LIMITS	255	A	LITTLE EUROPE	282	A
LIN PIAO	264	A	LITTLE GIANT	719	B
LIN PIAO STRATEGY (WARS OF NATIONAL LIBERATION)	204	A	LITTLE GROUP OF WILLFUL MEN	472	B
LINCOLN BRIGADE	173	A	LITTLE HOOVER COMMISSIONS	156	A
LINCOLN-ROOSEVELT LEAGUE	525	B	LITTLE LADIES IN TENNIS SHOES	190	A
LINCOLN, PRESIDENT ABRAHAM	261	A	LITTLE MAC	505	B
LINCOLN'S BIRTHDAY	607	B	LITTLE MAGICIAN	719	B
LINDBERGH LAW	247	A	LITTLE N.R.A.	488	B
LINDBERGH, CHARLES E.	270	A	LITTLE OCTOBRISTS, SOVIET UNION	472	B
LINDBLOM, CHARLES E.	270	A	LITTLE ROCK, ARKANSAS	279	A
LINDSAY, A.D.	270	A	LITTLE RUHR	794	B
LINDSAY, JOHN V.	266	A	LITTLE STEEL	472	B
LINDZEY, GARDNER	719	B	LITTLE STEEL FORMULA	607	B
LINE	282	A	LITVINOV, MAXIM	272	A
LINE AGENCY	163	A	LITVINOV, PAVEL	719	B
LINE AND STAFF	182	A	LIU SHAO-CHI	264	A
LINE DEPARTMENTS IN THE CITY GOVERNMENT	163	A	LIVE PAIR	844	B
			LIVELIHOOD	607	B
LINE OF SUCCESSION	204	A	LIVERMORE, MARY ASHTON RICE	753	B
LINE ORGANIZATION	160	A	LIVING	584	B
LINGUET, S. H. N.	753	B	LIVING SPACE	290	A
LINGUISTIC ANALYSIS	128	A	LIVING WAGE	238	A
LINGUISTICS	128	A	LLERAS RESTREPO, CARLOS	719	B
LINKAGE	126	A	LLOYD GEORGE, DAVID	263	A

LLOYD, JOHN SELWYN BROOKE	753	B
LOAD	632	B
LOADED QUESTION (IN POLLING)	130	A
LOAFER	557	B
LOAN FLOTATION	247	A
LOAVES AND FISHES	836	B
LOBBY	147	A
LOBBY REGULATION	198	A
LOBBYGOG	844	B
LOBBYING	195	A
LOBBYING ACT	214	A
LOBBYISTS	181	A
LOCAL	276	A
LOCAL COUNCIL	178	A
LOCAL CURRENCY	818	B
LOCAL FEDERALISM	133	A
LOCAL FINANCE	221	A
LOCAL GOVERNMENT	145	A
LOCAL LAW	221	A
LOCAL LEGISLATION	201	A
LOCAL LIST	505	B
LOCAL OPTION	214	A
LOCAL POLITICS	117	A
LOCAL POWER	136	A
LOCAL RELIEF	256	A
LOCAL REMEDIES	256	A
LOCAL SOVEREIGNTY (SELF GOVERNMENT)	160	A
LOCAL SOVIETS	156	A
LOCAL STAFF	472	B
LOCALES	791	B
LOCALISM	130	A
LOCALIZATION OF A CONFLICT	214	A
LOCALIZATION OF LABOR	632	B
LOCARNO CONFERENCE, 1924	584	B
LOCARNO TREATIES	256	A
LOCATION	788	B
LOCATION, GEOGRAPHIC POWER FACTOR	279	A
LOCHNER VS. NEW YORK (1905)	671	B
LOCKARD, DUANE	719	B
LOCKE, JOHN	261	A
LOCKOUT	214	A
LOCOFOCOS	505	B
LOCUST CONTROL	632	B
LOCUTIONARY ACTS	632	B
LODGE RESERVATIONS	607	B
LODGE-GOSSETT PROPOSAL	632	B
LODGE, HENRY CABOT	268	A
LODGING ALLOWANCE	607	B
LOEB, ISIDOR	719	B
LOEWE VS. LAWLER (1908)	678	B
LOFTUS, PIERSE	753	B
LOG CABIN	820	B
LOG CABIN AND HARD CIDER CAMPAIGN	607	B
LOG CABIN BILL	632	B
LOGAN, FRANK A.	753	B
LOGIC	123	A
LOGICAL ATOMISM	444	B
LOGICAL EMPIRICISM	114	A
LOGICAL IMPOSSIBILITY	130	A
LOGICAL METHOD	123	A
LOGICAL POSITIVISM	114	A
LOGICAL STATEMENT	121	A
LOGICAL THEORY	128	A
LOGICISM	444	B
LOGROLLING	198	A
LOK SABHA	525	B
LOKAHITAVADI (GAPAL HARI DESHMUKH)	753	B
LOLLARDS	525	B
LOMBROSO, CESARE	753	B
LOMONOSOV	798	B
LONDON	277	A
LONDON AND WESTMINSTER REVIEW	812	B
LONDON CONFERENCE OF 1908-1909	632	B
LONDON COUNTY COUNCIL	472	B
LONDON DAILY HERALD	809	B
LONDON DECLARATION	632	B
LONDON ECONOMIC CONFERENCE 1933	607	B
LONDON GAZETTE	809	B
LONDON NAVAL CONFERENCE OF 1930	607	B
LONDON NAVAL TREATY OF 1936	607	B
LONDON ROUND TABLE CONFERENCE (1930-1932)	608	B
LONDON SCHOOL OF ECONOMICS AND POLITICAL SCIENCE	160	A
LONDON, DECLARATION OF	632	B
LONDON, PACT OF (1915)	633	B
LONDON, SECRET TREATY OF	655	B
LONELIEST JOB IN THE WORLD	193	A
LONER	550	B
LONG BALLOT	197	A
LONG CONVENTION	584	B
LONG FAMILY	719	B
LONG HAIR	193	A
LONG HOT SUMMER	256	A
LONG MARCH	201	A
LONG PARLIAMENT	163	A
LONG PULL	836	B
LONG SESSION	247	A
LONG TOM	823	B
LONG-AND-SHORT HAUL	256	A
LONG-BOW	820	B
LONG-DISTANCE BLOCKADE	256	A
LONG-TERM	247	A
LONG-TERM APPOINTMENT	229	A

LONG-TERM BORROWING	229	A	LOVED FOR THE ENEMIES HE MADE	836	B
LONG, HUEY PIERCE	265	A	LOW COUNTRIES	279	A
LONG, NORTON	719	B	LOW ROAD	836	B
LONG, RUSSELL B.	270	A	LOW-INCOME	214	A
LONGITUDINAL ANALYSIS	123	A	LOW-RENT HOUSING	221	A
LONGITUDINAL STUDIES	126	A	LOW-WATER MARK	836	B
LONGO, LUIGI	697	B	LOW, SETH	754	B
LONGUET, JEAN	754	B	LOWELL, A. LAWRENCE	754	B
LOOPHOLE	238	A	LOWELL, JAMES RUSSELL	754	B
LOOSE BIPOLAR SYSTEM	123	A	LOWER CHAMBER	148	A
LOOSE CONSTRUCTION	229	A	LOWER HOUSE	150	A
LOOSE INTERPRETATION OF THE	209	A	LOWER LAW	655	B
CONSTITUTION			LOWER LAW MAN	565	B
LOOSE MONEY POLICY	238	A	LOWER LEVEL THEORY	123	A
LOOTERS	544	B	LOWER MIDDLE CLASS	148	A
LOOTING	247	A	LOWER-CLASS	147	A
LOPEZ, MATEOS, ADOLF	719	B	LOWIE, ROBERT H.	719	B
LORD	190	A	LOYAL	133	A
LORD CHAMBERLAIN	193	A	LOYAL LEAGUE	505	B
LORD CHANCELLOR	185	A	LOYAL LEGION	488	B
LORD MAYOR OF LONDON	550	B	LOYAL OPPOSITION	150	A
LORD OF APPEAL IN ORDINARY	565	B	LOYALIST	160	A
LORD PRESIDENT OF THE PRIVY	550	B	LOYALTY	128	A
COUNCIL			LOYALTY OATH	199	A
LORD PRIVY SEAL	288	A	LOYALTY PROGRAM	247	A
LORD SPIRITUAL	557	B	LOYALTY REVIEW BOARD	168	A
LORD TEMPORAL	544	B	LOYALTY-SECURITY PROGRAMS	214	A
LORDS OF APPEAL IN ORDINARY	557	B	LOYALTY, PRINCIPLE OF	247	A
LORDS OF THE LASH, LORDS OF	845	B	LOYOLA	719	B
THE LOOM			LU YING	754	B
LORDS, HOUSE OF	150	A	LUBELL, SAMUEL	266	A
LORENZ, KONRAD	268	A	LUBKE, HEINRICH	754	B
LORIMER SCANDAL	655	B	LUBLIN COMMITTEE	178	A
LORIOT, FERNAND	754	B	LUBLIN GOVERNMENT	173	A
LOS ANGLES	279	A	LUCA, V.	754	B
LOSE	238	A	LUCE, R. DUNCAN	754	B
LOSONCZY, GEZA	754	B	LUCE, S. B.	754	B
LOSS OF CITIZENSHIP	238	A	LUCRETIUS	754	B
LOSS OF NATIONALITY	238	A	LUDLOW, J. MAURICE	754	B
LOST CAUSE	290	A	LUDOVICI, A. M.	754	B
LOST-PROPERTY DEPARTMENT	526	B	LUFTHANSA	505	B
LOT	584	B	LUFTWAFFE	163	A
LOTOPHAGI	565	B	LUGBARA	505	B
LOTTERY	238	A	LUHMANN, N.	754	B
LOTUS CASE	675	B	LUKACS, GEORG	687	B
LOUIS III OF FRANCE	754	B	LULCHEV, K.	754	B
LOUIS THE PIOUS	754	B	LULU	845	B
LOUIS XI OF FRANCE	719	B	LUMP-SUM APPROPRIATION	221	A
LOUIS XIV OF FRANCE	266	A	LUMUMBA, PATRICE	264	A
LOUIS XV	697	B	LUNATIC FRINGE	163	A
LOUISIANA	280	A	LUNS, JOSEPH M. A.	754	B
LOUISIANA PURCHASE	199	A	LURIA, A.R.	754	B
LOUVRE	820	B	LUSAKA CONFERENCE	633	B
LOVE	436	B	LUSITANIA, THE	288	A
LOVE FEAST	840	B	LUST	437	B
LOVE OF LIBERTY	139	A	LUTHER VS. BORDEN (1849)	678	B

LUTHER, MARTIN	263	A
LUTHERAN WORLD FEDERATION	505	B
LUTHERANISM	143	A
LUTHULI, CHIEF ALBERT JOHN	719	B
LUVALE	526	B
LUXEMBOURG, GRAND DUCHY OF	279	A
LUXEMBURG, ROSA	265	A
LUXURIA	456	B
LUZON	794	B
LYALIN, N. A.	754	B
LYCANTHROPY	456	B
LYCOPHRON, THE SOPHIST	754	B
LYDE, PROF. L.	754	B
LYING	256	A
LYING-IN-STATE	584	B
LYNCH LAW	214	A
LYNCH, JOHN	754	B
LYNCHING	214	A
LYNCHISM	456	B
LYNCHITE	565	B
LYND, HELEN	687	B
LYND, ROBERT	270	A
LYNN, DAVID B.	754	B
LYSENKOISM	133	A
LYSIAS	754	B
LYTTON COMMISSION, LEAGUE OF NATIONS	526	B
M-DAY	655	B
MA	557	B
MA, MA, WHERE'S PA	840	B
MAAS, ARTHUR	754	B
MABLY, GABRIEL BONNOT DE	755	B
MACAO	282	A
MACARTHUR, GENERAL DOUGLAS	263	A
MACAULAY, T.B.	272	A
MACBETH	272	A
MACCOBY, ELEANOR E.	719	B
MACCULLOCH, J.R.	755	B
MACDONALD, J. RAMSEY	755	B
MACDONALD, NEIL A.	755	B
MACE	287	A
MACGREGOR, SIR WILLIAM	755	B
MACH, ERNST	687	B
MACHETISMO	655	B
MACHIAVELLI, NICCOLO	261	A
MACHIAVELLIAN DIPLOMACY	201	A
MACHIAVELLIANISM	114	A
MACHINE	160	A
MACHINE POLITICS	194	A
MACHINERY OF GOVERNMENT	289	A
MACHTPOLITIK (POWER POLITICS)	139	A
MACHTSTAAT	472	B
MACIVER, ROBERT M.	268	A
MACK, RAYMOND W.	755	B
MACKAY, THOMAS	755	B
MACKENZIE, J. S.	755	B
MACKINAC DECLARATION	633	B
MACKINDER, SIR HALFORD J.	687	B
MACLEISH, ARCHIBALD	697	B
MACLEOD, IAN	755	B
MACMAHON, ARTHUR W.	719	B
MACMAHON, PATRICE MAURICE DE, DUC DE MAGENTA	755	B
MACMILLAN, PRIME MINISTER HAROLD	264	A
MACPHERSON, C. B.	697	B
MACRAE, DUNCAN	720	B
MACRIDIS, ROY C.	270	A
MACRO-MICRO ANALYSIS	116	A
MACRO-POLITICS	116	A
MACROECONOMICS	119	A
MACROTHEORIES	128	A
MACY, JESSE	755	B
MACY, R. H., AND COMPANY	526	B
MADAGASCAR	280	A
MADARIAGA, SALVADOR DE	697	B
MADE-WORK	608	B
MADERO, FRANCISCO I.	697	B
MADISON AVENUE TECHNIQUES	221	A
MADISON, PRESIDENT JAMES	262	A
MADISON'S JOURNAL	285	A
MADRAS	794	B
MADRID	280	A
MAEZTU, R. DE	755	B
MAFIA	150	A
MAFIA INCIDENT	655	B
MAGHREB	794	B
MAGIC	444	B
MAGID, H. M.	755	B
MAGINOT LINE	273	A
MAGISTRACY	544	B
MAGISTRATE	193	A
MAGISTRATE COURTS	178	A
MAGNA CARTA	195	A
MAGNANIMITY	608	B
MAGNETIC STATESMAN	557	B
MAGNOLIA TALK	845	B
MAGNUSON, WARREN GRANT	687	B
MAGSAYSAY, R.	720	B
MAGYAR	178	A
MAHAN, ALFRED THAYER	270	A
MAHARAJAH	544	B
MAHARANEE	550	B
MAHARASHTRA, INDIA	798	B
MAHASABHA	526	B
MAHATMA (REVERED PERSON)	550	B
MAHDI (MUSLIM MESSIAH)	755	B
MAHGOUB, MOHAMMED AHMED	755	B
MAHRATTA CONFEDERACY	526	B
MAIDEN SPEECH	229	A
MAIESTAS	456	B
MAIL	289	A

MAILER, N.	687	B	MALENESS	550	B
MAIMONIDES, MOSES	720	B	MALENKOV, GEORGI M.	268	A
MAIN COMMITTEE	526	B	MALETER, GENERAL P.	755	B
MAIN STREET	791	B	MALFEASANCE	238	A
MAINE LAW PROHIBITION	655	B	MALI, REPUBLIC OF	279	A
MAINE, SIR HENRY SUMNER	697	B	MALICE	437	B
MAINE, THE	287	A	MALIK, CHARLES	697	B
MAINLAND	279	A	MALIKUL-SHUARA	755	B
MAINSTREAM	290	A	MALINOVSKY, RODION	720	B
MAINTAIN	608	B	MALINOWKSI, BRONISLAW	687	B
MAINTENANCE	247	A	MALLOCK, H. W.	755	B
MAINTENANCE OF PEACE	214	A	MALLORY VS. U.S. (1958)	671	B
MAISTRE, JOSEPH DE	755	B	MALLOY VS. HOGAN (1964)	671	B
MAITLAND, FREDERIC W.	755	B	MALNUTRITION	229	A
MAJESTY	550	B	MALON, BENOIT	720	B
MAJLIS	526	B	MALPRACTICE	238	A
MAJOR WAR CRIMINALS	184	A	MALRAUX, ANDRE	270	A
MAJORITARIAN DEMOCRACY	121	A	MALTA	277	A
MAJORITARIANISM	116	A	MALTHUS, THOMAS ROBERT	263	A
MAJORITY	145	A	MALTHUSIANISM	133	A
MAJORITY FLOOR LEADER	181	A	MALVERN, LORD	755	B
MAJORITY GOVERNMENT	145	A	MAN	190	A
MAJORITY LEADER	181	A	MAN AND BROTHER	845	B
MAJORITY OPINION	116	A	MAN FRIDAY	557	B
MAJORITY PARTY	145	A	MAN IN THE STREET	193	A
MAJORITY REPORT	283	A	MAN OF STRAW	550	B
MAJORITY RULE, DEMOCRATIC THEORY	113	A	MAN OF THE PEOPLE	190	A
			MAN ON HORSEBACK	190	A
MAJORITY SOVEREIGNTY	214	A	MAN ON THE WEDDING CAKE	565	B
MAJORITY WHIP	182	A	MAN OWNERS	565	B
MAKARIOS III, ARCHIBISHOP	266	A	MAN STEALER	565	B
MAKE THE WORLD SAFE FOR DEMOCRACY	290	A	MAN-OF-WAR	289	A
			MAN, ECONOMIC	182	A
MAKE-WORK FALLACY	608	B	MAN, SOCIAL	184	A
MAKERERE	720	B	MANAGE	238	A
MAKERS	565	B	MANAGEABLE VOTER	557	B
MAKKAWI, ABDUL	720	B	MANAGED CURRENCY	256	A
MAKONNEN, T.I.	720	B	MANAGED MASSES	178	A
MALA PROHIBITA (PROHIBITED EVIL)	655	B	MANAGED NEWS	221	A
MALAGASY REPUBLIC	280	A	MANAGEMENT	183	A
MALAN, DANIEL FRANCOIS	755	B	MANAGEMENT INTERNSHIP EXAMINATION	608	B
MALAPARTE, C.	755	B			
MALAPPORTIONMENT IN LEGISLATURE	204	A	MANAGEMENT ANALYSTS	186	A
			MANAGEMENT COMMITTEE	472	B
MALARIA	608	B	MANAGEMENT CONTROL	238	A
MALATESTA, ENRICO	697	B	MANAGEMENT IMPROVEMENT	584	B
MALAWI	279	A	MANAGEMENT OF PUBLIC AFFAIRS	133	A
MALAYA	276	A	MANAGEMENT SCIENCE	130	A
MALAYSIA	276	A	MANAGEMENT THEORY	130	A
MALCOLM X	262	A	MANAGER	190	A
MALCONTENT	190	A	MANAGERIAL ECONOMICS	136	A
MALDON, SONG OF	812	B	MANAGERIAL OBSOLESCENCE	247	A
MALE SEX	550	B	MANAGERIAL REVOLUTION	214	A
MALE SUFFRAGE	238	A	MANCHESTER	794	B
MALEBRANCHE	755	B	MANCHESTER SCHOOL	472	B
MALEFACTORS OF GREAT WEALTH	550	B	MANCHILD	565	B

MANCHU DYNASTY	268	A
MANCHURIA	277	A
MANCHURIA INDUSTRIAL DEVELOPMENT CORPORATION	526	B
MANDARIN	186	A
MANDATE	214	A
MANDATED AREA	275	A
MANDATES SYSTEM, LEAGUE OF NATIONS	221	A
MANDATORY	247	A
MANDATORY LAW	584	B
MANDATORY POWER	247	A
MANDATORY REFERENDUM	256	A
MANDEL, ERNEST	697	B
MANDEL, G.	755	B
MANDELA, NELSON	755	B
MANDEVILLE, BERNARD DE	755	B
MANEGOLD OF LAUTENBACH	756	B
MANGLA DAM	798	B
MANHANDLING	633	B
MANHATTAN CLUB	526	B
MANHATTAN PROJECT	156	A
MANHOOD SUFFRAGE	201	A
MANICHEANS	472	B
MANICHEES	505	B
MANIFEST	633	B
MANIFEST DESTINY	197	A
MANIFEST FUNCTION	128	A
MANIFEST THEORY	437	B
MANIFESTO	284	A
MANIPULATION	238	A
MANIPULATION OF ELECTIONS	229	A
MANLEY, NORMAN WASHINGTON	720	B
MANN ACT	238	A
MANN, HEINRICH	756	B
MANN, TOM	720	B
MANNED ORBITING LABORATORY (MOL)	818	B
MANNERHEIM, CARL GUSTAV EMIL	756	B
MANNHEIM, KARL	265	A
MANPOWER	163	A
MANPOWER ADMINISTRATION	178	A
MANPOWER DEVELOPMENT AND TRAINING ACT	256	A
MANPOWER FORECASTING	608	B
MANPOWER PLANNING	256	A
MANSFIELD, HARVEY C.	756	B
MANSFIELD, MICHAEL JOSEPH	687	B
MANSLAUGHTER	229	A
MANTLE	826	B
MANUAL FOR COURTS-MARTIAL	805	B
MANUFACTURING	229	A
MANUFACTURING INDUSTRIES	173	A
MANY-VALUED LOGICS	444	B
MAO TSE-TUNG	261	A
MAOISM, COMMUNIST DOCTRINE	116	A
MAPAI (ISRAEL WORKERS' PARTY)	488	B
MAPAM	526	B
MAPHILINDO	655	B
MAPP VS. OHIO (1961)	671	B
MAPS AND ATLASES	285	A
MAQUIS	178	A
MARA	456	B
MARAT, JEAN PAUL	687	B
MARAVIGLIA, LUIGI	756	B
MARBURY VS. MADISON (1803)	260	A
MARCEL, GABRIEL	756	B
MARCH	633	B
MARCH ON ROME	584	B
MARCH ON WASHINGTON	247	A
MARCH REVOLUTION OF 1917	209	A
MARCH, JAMES G.	697	B
MARCHANT, P.D.	756	B
MARCHERS	565	B
MARCHES	655	B
MARCHIONESS	565	B
MARCO POLO BRIDGE INCIDENT	633	B
MARCOS, FERDINAND E.	272	A
MARCUS AURELIUS	687	B
MARCUSE, HERBERT	263	A
MARE CLAUSUM (CLOSED SEA)	633	B
MARE LIBERUM (OPEN SEA)	608	B
MARE NOSTRUM (OUR SEA)	256	A
MARECHAL, SYLVAN	756	B
MARGIN OF PREFERENCE (TARIFF)	633	B
MARGINAL	229	A
MARGINAL MAN	190	A
MARGINAL SEA	791	B
MARGINALITY	229	A
MARGRAVATE	565	B
MARGRAVE	756	B
MARIANA, JUAN DE	756	B
MARIATEGUI, J.	756	B
MARIJUANA	288	A
MARINE CORPS (U.S.)	168	A
MARINE HOSPITAL SERVICE	526	B
MARINES	178	A
MARINETTI, F. T.	756	B
MARITAIN, JACQUES	697	B
MARITIME ADMINISTRATION	505	B
MARITIME BELT	798	B
MARITIME CONSULTATIVE ORGANIZATION	505	B
MARITIME DOMAIN	794	B
MARITIME JURISDICTION	584	B
MARITIME LAW	229	A
MARITIME PROVINCES	282	A
MARITIME SAFETY COMMITTEE OF IMCO	526	B
MARITIME WARFARE	256	A
MARK	655	B
MARK-UP	256	A

MARKELIUS, SVEN	756 B	MARY OF REGELSBURG	757 B
MARKET	274 A	MARYLAND	282 A
MARKETING SYSTEM	123 A	MARZ, ROGER H.	757 B
MARKETPLACE	275 A	MASANOBU, TSUJI	757 B
MARKING OUT	655 B	MASARYK, JAN	268 A
MARKING-UP SESSION	584 B	MASARYK, THOMAS G.	720 B
MARLBOROUGH, DUKE OF	756 B	MASOCHISM	139 A
MARLOWE	756 B	MASON-DIXON LINE	274 A
MARQUESS	557 B	MASONS	505 B
MARQUESSATE	565 B	MASS	163 A
MARQUESSE	557 B	MASS COMMUNICATIONS	119 A
MARQUIS	550 B	MASS DESTRUCTION WEAPONS	286 A
MARQUISATE	565 B	MASS EXECUTIONS	221 A
MARQUISE	565 B	MASS MEDIA	145 A
MARRIAGE	256 A	MASS MEDIA, TWO-STEP FLOW	126 A
MARRIAGE AND DIVORCE LAWS	238 A	MASS MEETING	229 A
MARRIOTT, J. A. R.	756 B	MASS OBSERVATION	450 B
MARROW FAT FRAUD	655 B	MASS PARTICIPATION	119 A
MARSANICH, AUGUSTO DE	756 B	MASS PRODUCTION	229 A
MARSEILLAISE	788 B	MASS PUBLIC, PUBLIC OPINION	145 A
MARSEILLES ASSASSINATIONS	655 B	MASS SOCIETY	145 A
MARSHAL	544 B	MASSACHUSETTS	280 A
MARSHALL MISSION TO CHINA	163 A	MASSACHUSETTS BALLOT	238 A
MARSHALL PLAN (EUROPEAN	195 A	MASSACHUSETTS BAY COLONY	277 A
RECOVERY PROGRAM)		MASSACHUSETTS VS. MELLON	675 B
MARSHALL, CHARLES B.	756 B	(1923)	
MARSHALL, GENERAL GEORGE C.,	264 A	MASSACRE	238 A
MARSHALL, JOHN	262 A	MASSES	150 A
MARSHALL, THURGOOD	265 A	MASSIVE RESISTANCE	256 A
MARSILIO OF PADUA	720 B	MASSIVE RETALIATION	204 A
MARTI Y PEREZ, JOSE JULIAN	720 B	MASTER RACE DOCTRINE	214 A
MARTIAL	584 B	MASTERLY INACTIVITY	655 B
MARTIAL LAW	204 A	MASTERMAN, C. F. G.	757 B
MARTIN VS. HUNTERS LESSEE	675 B	MASTERS	550 B
(1816)		MASTERY	450 B
MARTIN VS. STRUTHERS (1943)	678 B	MASTERY OF THE AIR	608 B
MARTIN, BARTON AND FISH	756 B	MATCHING FUNDS	229 A
MARTIN, E. D.	756 B	MATEOS, ADOLFO LOPEZ	720 B
MARTIN, H.	756 B	MATERIAL	823 B
MARTIN, JOSEPH WILLIAM, JR.	720 B	MATERIAL BASIS (OF SOCIAL LIFE)	437 B
MARTIN, ROSCOE C.	756 B	MATERIAL CO-ORDINATING	526 B
MARTINIQUE	282 A	COMMITTEE	
MARTLING MEN	526 B	MATERIAL EVIDENCE	608 B
MARTOV, JULIUS	756 B	MATERIAL IMPLICATION	608 B
MARTOV, L.	756 B	MATERIAL WITNESS	193 A
MARTYR	193 A	MATERIALISM	117 A
MARUYAMA, MASAO	756 B	MATERIALISTIC INTERPRETATION OF	114 A
MARVICK, DWAINE	756 B	HISTORY	
MARX, KARL	261 A	MATERIEL ELEMENTS	823 B
MARX, MELVIN	756 B	MATERNAL AND CHILD WELFARE	608 B
MARXIAN SOCIALISM	113 A	PROGRAM	
MARXISM-LENINISM	113 A	MATERNITY LEAVE	608 B
MARXISM, COMMUNIST DOCTRINE	114 A	MATHEMATICAL ANALYSIS	133 A
MARXIST METHOD	119 A	MATHEMATICAL ECONOMICS	450 B
MARXISTS	146 A	MATHEMATICAL METHODS	139 A
MARY II OF ENGLAND	697 B	MATHEMATICAL MODELS	128 A

MATHIAS, CHARLES MCCURDY, JR.	720	B	MCCARTHY-ARMY HEARINGS	229	A
MATRIARCHATE	437	B	MCCARTHY, EUGENE J.	264	A
MATRIARCHY	160	A	MCCARTHY, JOSEPH RAYMOND	266	A
MATRICIDE	633	B	MCCARTHYISM	121	A
MATRIMONY	608	B	MCCLELLAN, GENERAL GEORGE C.	272	A
MATRIX	121	A	MCCLELLAN, JOHN L.	720	B
MATSON, FLOYD W.	757	B	MCCLELLAND, CHARLES	720	B
MATSU	794	B	MCCLOSKEY, PAUL	270	A
MATTEOTTI, GIACOMO	757	B	MCCLOSKEY, ROBERT G.	720	B
MATTEOTTI, MATTEO	757	B	MCCLOSKY, HERBERT	687	B
MATTER	820	B	MCCOLLUM VS. BOARD OF	261	A
MATTER OF PRESTIGE	608	B	EDUCATION (1948)		
MATTERS AFFECTING BOTH	256	A	MCCONE	697	B
COUNTRIES			MCCORMICK, THOMAS C.	757	B
MATTHEW OF PARIS	757	B	MCCULLOCH VS. MARYLAND (1819)	260	A
MATTHEWS, DONALD R.	697	B	MCDOUGAL, M. S.	720	B
MATTHEWS, RICHARD E.	757	B	MCDOUGALL, WILLIAM	720	B
MATURING	143	A	MCDUFFIE-TYDINGS BILL	633	B
MATURISM	457	B	MCGAUPHY, J. R.	757	B
MAU MAU	156	A	MCGEE, GALE W.	720	B
MAUDE, COLONEL F. N.	757	B	MCGOVERN, GEORGE S.	263	A
MAUDLING, REGINALD	757	B	MCGOWAN VS. MARYLAND (1819)	678	B
MAUPERITUS	757	B	MCGRAIN VS. DAUGHERTY (1927)	678	B
MAURER, ION GHEORGHE	757	B	MCGREGOR, CLARK	720	B
MAURICE, F. D.	757	B	MCGUFFERY, WILLIAM HOLMES	757	B
MAURITANIA	279	A	MCILWAIN, CHARLES H.	757	B
MAURITIUS	788	B	MCINTYRE, THOMAS JAMES	757	B
MAURRAS, CHARLES	720	B	MCKINLEY TARIFF ACT	256	A
MAVERICK	188	A	MCKINLEY, CHARLES	720	B
MAXENTIUS	757	B	MCKINLEY, PRESIDENT WILLIAM	263	A
MAXIM, HUDSON	757	B	MCLEOD CASE	678	B
MAXIMIAN GALERIUS	757	B	MCLUHAN, MARSHALL	265	A
MAXIMIZATION	133	A	MCMAHON CORRESPONDENCE	809	B
MAXTON, JAMES	757	B	MCMAHON LINE	791	B
MAY CRISIS	655	B	MCNABB VS. U.S. (1943)	678	B
MAY FIRST	247	A	MCNAMARA, ROBERT STRANGE	263	A
MAY FOURTH MOVEMENT	526	B	MCNARY-HAUGEN BILL	633	B
MAY 13 INSURRECTION (FRANCE)	633	B	MCNEIL, ELTON B.	758	B
MAY, STACY	757	B	MCPHEE, WILLIAM N.	720	B
MAYFLOWER COMPACT	221	A	ME TOO	834	B
MAYO, ELTON	272	A	MEAD	826	B
MAYOR	181	A	MEAD, GEORGE HERBERT	720	B
MAYOR-ADMINISTRATOR PLAN	201	A	MEAD, MARGARET	268	A
MAYOR-COUNCIL FORM OF	147	A	MEADOWS, PAUL	758	B
GOVERNMENT			MEAN	123	A
MAYOR-MANAGER FORM	201	A	MEANING	136	A
MAYORALITY	183	A	MEANS	287	A
MAZARIN, CARDINAL	757	B	MEANS TO END ANALYSIS	119	A
MAZHAR, ISMA'IL	757	B	MEANS, GARDINER C.	758	B
MAZRUI, ALI A.	757	B	MEANWHILE, BACK AT THE RANCH	845	B
MAZZINI, GIUSEPPE	266	A	MEANY, GEORGE	264	A
MBOYA, TOM	687	B	MEANY, WILLIAM GEORGE	265	A
MCCARRAN INTERNAL SECURITY	214	A	MEASURE	136	A
ACT OF 1950			MEASURED RESPONSE	238	A
MCCARRAN-WALTER IMMIGRATION	247	A	MEASUREMENT	123	A
AND NATIONALITY ACT			MEASURES NOT MEN	840	B

MEASURES OF ASSOCIATION	128	A
MEASURES SHORT OF WAR	215	A
MEAT INSPECTION ACT OF 1901	584	B
MECCA	277	A
MECHANICS	450	B
MECHANISM	288	A
MECHANISTIC CONCEPTION	130	A
MECKLENBERG DECLARATION OF INDEPENDENCE	633	B
MEDES	505	B
MEDIA	145	A
MEDIAEVAL COMMUNES	488	B
MEDIAN	117	A
MEDIATE	204	A
MEDIATION	201	A
MEDIATION AND CONCILIATION, LABOR	221	A
MEDIATION COMMISSION	472	B
MEDIATORS	186	A
MEDICAID	209	A
MEDICAL CARE	221	A
MEDICAL DEVICES	826	B
MEDICAL EDUCATION ACT	608	B
MEDICAL EXAMINER	551	B
MEDICAL INSURACE	221	A
MEDICAL SERVICES ADMINISTRATION	526	B
MEDICAL TRAINING	608	B
MEDICARE	204	A
MEDICARE LAW	221	A
MEDICI, CATHERINE DE	697	B
MEDICI, LORENZO DE	687	B
MEDICINE	437	B
MEDICINE BALL CABINET	526	B
MEDICINE SHOW	845	B
MEDIEVAL	130	A
MEDIEVAL SOCIETY	160	A
MEDITERRANEAN COUNTRIES	173	A
MEDIUM	168	A
MEDLARS	826	B
MEDVEDEV, ROY	721	B
MEEHAN, EUGENE J.	272	A
MEETING	633	B
MEETINGS AND CONFERENCES, REPORTS OF	807	B
MEGALOPOLIS	274	A
MEGALOPOLITAN	282	A
MEGARICS	526	B
MEHRING, FRANZ	721	B
MEIJI CONSTITUTION	238	A
MEIJI, THE REIGN OF EMPEROR MUTSUHITO OF JAPAN	229	A
MEINICKE, FRIEDRICH	721	B
MEINONG, ALEXIUS	758	B
MEIR, MRS. GOLDA	268	A
MEJLIS	758	B
MEKONG RIVER PROJECT	247	A
MELANESIA	280	A
MELBOURNE, AUSTRALIA	281	A
MELLER, NORMAN	758	B
MELLOR, W.	758	B
MELTING POT	275	A
MELVILLE, HERMAN	721	B
MEMBER	188	A
MEMBER BANK	178	A
MEMBER OF CONGRESS (MC)	181	A
MEMBER OF PARLIAMENT (M.P.)	182	A
MEMBER STATE	163	A
MEMBERS BILL	238	A
MEMBERSHIP	163	A
MEMBERSHIP (UN)	188	A
MEMEL TERRITORY	798	B
MEMOIRS	807	B
MEMORANDUM	284	A
MEMORANDUM DECISION	633	B
MEMORANDUM OF DISAPPROVAL	807	B
MEMORIAL DAY	608	B
MEMORIALS	820	B
MEMORY	136	A
MEN	551	B
MEN OF THOUGHT	557	B
MENACE	557	B
MENCIUS	758	B
MENCKEN, HENRY L.	268	A
MENDEL	687	B
MENDELISM	450	B
MENDELSON, WALLACE	758	B
MENDELSSOHN, MOSES	758	B
MENDERES, ADNAN	758	B
MENDES-FRANCE, PIERRE	272	A
MENDING FENCES	834	B
MENES, KING OF UPPER EGYPT	758	B
MENO	812	B
MENON, VENGALIL KRISHNAN KRISHNA	687	B
MENSHEVIKS	148	A
MENTAL HEALTH	140	A
MENTAL HEALTH ACT OF 1949	633	B
MENTAL STATES	445	B
MENTAL TESTS	256	A
MENTALLY RESTORED EMPLOYEES	565	B
MENTALLY RETARDED	557	B
MENTON, ANTON	758	B
MENZIES, SIR ROBERT	687	B
MERCANTILISM	117	A
MERCENARIES	183	A
MERCENARIES, GEPID	505	B
MERCHANT	188	A
MERCHANT MARINE AND FISHERIES COMMITTEE	488	B
MERCHANT PRINCE	557	B
MERCHANT SHIP	820	B

MERCHANT VESSEL	820	B	METHOD OF VOTING	121	A
MERCHANTMAN	823	B	METHODISTS	472	B
MERCHANTS OF DEATH	544	B	METHODOLOGICAL CONCEPTS	126	A
MERCIER, CARDINAL	758	B	METHODOLOGY	114	A
MERCY	256	A	METHODS IN POLITICAL SCIENCE	114	A
MEREDITH, JAMES	270	A	METHODS OF STUDY	128	A
MERGE	256	A	METHODS OF VOTING IN CONGRESS	204	A
MERGER	247	A	METICS (GREEK)	565	B
MERGER OF POWERS	247	A	METRO FUNCTIONAL	256	A
MERIT	221	A	CONSOLIDATION		
MERIT SYSTEM	197	A	METROPOLIS	273	A
MERITOCRACY	148	A	METROPOLITAN	273	A
MERKEL, ADOLF	721	B	METROPOLITAN ANNEXATION	209	A
MERLEAU PONTY	758	B	METROPOLITAN AREA	273	A
MERMAID TICKET	845	B	METROPOLITAN CITY-COUNTY	209	A
MEROVINGIANS	505	B	CONSOLIDATION		
MERRHEIM, A.	758	B	METROPOLITAN CITY-COUNTY	221	A
MERRIAM, CHARLES E.	264	A	SEPARATION		
MERRITT, RICHARD	758	B	METROPOLITAN DEVELOPMENT ACT	633	B
MERRY-GO-ROUND	840	B	METROPOLITAN DISTRICT	277	A
MERTON, ROBERT K.	262	A	METROPOLITAN FEDERATION	472	B
MESCAMERICAN	526	B	METROPOLITAN GOVERNMENT	147	A
MESLIER, JEAN	758	B	METROPOLITAN REGION	277	A
MESOPOTAMIA	279	A	METROPOLITAN SYSTEMS, AND	156	A
MESS IN WASHINGTON	834	B	SUBURBIA		
MESSAGE	136	A	METROPOLITAN URBAN COUNTY	178	A
MESSAGE FLOWS	133	A	METROPOLITICS	130	A
MESSAGE ON THE STATE OF THE	209	A	MEXICAN	160	A
UNION			MEXICAN CESSION	238	A
MESSAGE TO CONGRESS	283	A	MEXICAN FARM LABOR	163	A
MESSENGER	565	B	MEXICAN WAR	215	A
MESSIANISM	126	A	MEXICAN WHIG	526	B
MESTIZO	193	A	MEXICAN-AMERICANS	153	A
META-CONCEPTS	140	A	MEXICANIZE	633	B
METABLETICS	457	B	MEXICO	276	A
METAETHICS	140	A	MEXICO PETROLEUM	289	A
METAJURIDICAL FACTORS	450	B	MEYER, ALFRED G.	721	B
METAL TRADES COMMITTEE OF ILO	526	B	MGB	526	B
METALOGIC	143	A	MI-SOUVERAIN	526	B
METALS RESERVE COMPANY	526	B	MICHAEL OF CESENA	758	B
METAPHILOSOPHY	143	A	MICHAEL, KING	758	B
METAPHOR	128	A	MICHEL, HENRI	758	B
METAPHYSICS	133	A	MICHELET	758	B
METAPOLICY	633	B	MICHELS, ROBERTO	270	A
METAPSYCHOLOGY	457	B	MICHIGAN	282	A
METASCIENCE	437	B	MICHIGAN STATE UNIVERSITY	472	B
METATASKS	445	B	MICHIGAN, UNIVERSITY OF	178	A
METATHEORIES, AND PARADIGMS	119	A	MICHURIN, IVAN VLADIMIROVICH	758	B
METATHEORIES, IN INTERNATIONAL	136	A	MICRO ANALYSIS	116	A
RELATIONS			MICRO STATES	173	A
METAXAS, JOANNIS	758	B	MICRO-POLITICS	123	A
METCALF, LEE	758	B	MICROECONOMICS	123	A
METEOROLOGY	457	B	MICRONESIA	275	A
METER VERSUS FLAT RATES FOR	655	B	MID-TERM	238	A
WATER FEES			MIDDLE	788	B
METHOD	140	A	MIDDLE AGES	221	A

MIDDLE CLASS	145	A
MIDDLE COLONIES	282	A
MIDDLE EAST	274	A
MIDDLE EAST CONFLICT	201	A
MIDDLE EAST PACT	256	A
MIDDLE MANAGEMENT	153	A
MIDDLE RANGE THEORY	119	A
MIDDLE-GAUGE THEORIES	123	A
MIDDLE-INCOME	183	A
MIDDLE-OF-THE-ROAD	183	A
MIDDLE-OF-THE-ROAD POPULISTS	178	A
MIDDLE-SIZED	457	B
MIDDLETON, RUSSELL	758	B
MIDDLETOWN STUDIES	284	A
MIDNIGHT JUDGES	190	A
MIDWAY, BATTLE OF	256	A
MIDWEST	281	A
MIEVILLE, ROBERTO	758	B
MIGRANT WORKERS	182	A
MIGRANTS	186	A
MIGRATION	221	A
MIGRATORY BIRD ACT	633	B
MIHAILOVICH, DRAZA	687	B
MIKADO	826	B
MIKOLAJCZYK, STANISLAW	721	B
MIKOYAN, ANASTAS	272	A
MILAN DECREE	655	B
MILBRATH, LESTER W.	721	B
MILEAGE	584	B
MILIEU	238	A
MILITANCY	126	A
MILITANT	182	A
MILITARISM	121	A
MILITARISM, FASCIST THEORY	123	A
MILITARY	153	A
MILITARY ACADEMIES	168	A
MILITARY AGENCY FOR STANDARDIZATION	505	B
MILITARY AID	204	A
MILITARY AIRLIFT COMMAND (MAC)	505	B
MILITARY ALLIANCES	150	A
MILITARY AND STRATEGIC POLICIES	229	A
MILITARY AREA	282	A
MILITARY ATTACHE	186	A
MILITARY AUTHORITIES	168	A
MILITARY COMMITTEE	488	B
MILITARY CONSCRIPTION	209	A
MILITARY COURTS	160	A
MILITARY DICTATORSHIP	145	A
MILITARY ESTABLISHMENT	153	A
MILITARY ESTABLISHMENT, RESTRICTIONS OF	238	A
MILITARY GOVERNMENT	147	A
MILITARY GOVERNOR	190	A
MILITARY HISTORY	437	B
MILITARY HOSPITAL SHIP	823	B
MILITARY IN LATIN AMERICAN POLITICS	146	A
MILITARY INDEMNITY	256	A
MILITARY INFLUENCES IN POLITICS	123	A
MILITARY INTEGRATION OF WESTERN EUROPE	221	A
MILITARY INTELLIGENCE	184	A
MILITARY INTERN	557	B
MILITARY INTERNMENT	584	B
MILITARY JUNTA	148	A
MILITARY JUSTICE	215	A
MILITARY LAW	221	A
MILITARY METAPHORS	834	B
MILITARY MISSION	584	B
MILITARY NECESSITY	221	A
MILITARY OCCUPATION	215	A
MILITARY OFFICES	551	B
MILITARY PACT	221	A
MILITARY PERSONNEL	472	B
MILITARY POLICY	229	A
MILITARY REGIMES	153	A
MILITARY RESERVES	178	A
MILITARY RESOURCES	286	A
MILITARY RETIREES	551	B
MILITARY SANCTIONS	209	A
MILITARY SERVICE	238	A
MILITARY SERVICE ACT	584	B
MILITARY SOCIOLOGY	450	B
MILITARY SOVEREIGNTY	633	B
MILITARY SPENDING	215	A
MILITARY STAFF COMMITTEE (MSC), UNITED NATIONS	488	B
MILITARY TRAINING	585	B
MILITARY TREATY	222	A
MILITARY-INDUSTRIAL COMPLEX	145	A
MILITARY-INDUSTRIAL RELATIONS	121	A
MILITIA	168	A
MILITIA (NATIONAL GUARD)	168	A
MILK CONTROL	585	B
MILK FOR HOTTENTOTS	840	B
MILL	823	B
MILL, JAMES	697	B
MILL, JOHN STUART	262	A
MILLAGE	585	B
MILLAH (MILLET)	826	B
MILLENIUM	256	A
MILLER-FORM	450	B
MILLER-TYDINGS LAW, 1937 (FAIR TRADES ACT)	585	B
MILLER, ARTHUR	697	B
MILLER, HENRY	721	B
MILLER, JACK RICHARD	759	B
MILLER, JAMES G.	759	B
MILLER, NEAL M.	759	B
MILLER, WARREN E.	721	B
MILLERAND, ETIENNE ALEXANDRE	721	B

MILLETT, JOHN	721	B
MILLIARD, PETER	759	B
MILLIGAN CASE	673	B
MILLIONAIRE'S CLUB	488	B
MILLIONS	437	B
MILLIONS FOR DEFENSE BUT NOT A CENT FOR TRIBUTE	836	B
MILLS, C. WRIGHT	263	A
MILLSPAUGH, ARTHUR C.	759	B
MILNER, VISCOUNT	759	B
MILTON, JOHN	268	A
MILYUKOV, PAUL	759	B
MIND	143	A
MINDSZENTY, CARDINAL J.	266	A
MINE LAYING	608	B
MINERAL RESOURCES	289	A
MINERAL RESOURCES DEVELOPMENT	608	B
MINERSVILLE SCHOOL DISTRICT VS. GOBITIS (1940)	672	B
MINIATURE	826	B
MINIFUNDISMO	633	B
MINIMUM RATES	585	B
MINIMUM WAGE LAW	215	A
MINIMUM WAGE LAW OF NEW YORK STATE (1937)	608	B
MINIMUM WAGE LEGISLATION	215	A
MINION	558	B
MINISTER	185	A
MINISTER (DIPLOMAT)	190	A
MINISTER FOR CULTURAL AFFAIRS (MCA)	551	B
MINISTER OF FOREIGN AFFAIRS, FRANCE	193	A
MINISTER PLENIPOTENTIARY	185	A
MINISTER POWERS	229	A
MINISTER RESIDENT	551	B
MINISTER WITHOUT PORTFOLIO	182	A
MINISTER-PRESIDENT	190	A
MINISTERIAL ACT	256	A
MINISTERIAL DEPARTMENTS	178	A
MINISTERIAL RESPONSIBILITY	222	A
MINISTERS-PARLIAMENT MEMBERS	184	A
MINISTRABLE	655	B
MINISTRY	160	A
MINISTRY OF INTERIOR (USSR) (M.V.D.)	505	B
MINISTRY OF JUSTICE	156	A
MINK COATS	823	B
MINNESOTA	282	A
MINNESOTA MORTGAGE MORATORIUM	633	B
MINNESOTA RATE CASES	673	B
MINOAN CIVILIZATION	488	B
MINOR	193	A
MINOR PARTIES	153	A
MINORITIES, NATIONAL AND RACIAL	147	A
MINORITY	146	A
MINORITY FLOOR LEADER	182	A
MINORITY GOVERNMENT	147	A
MINORITY GROUPS	150	A
MINORITY LEADER	182	A
MINORITY OPINION	119	A
MINORITY PARTY	146	A
MINORITY PRESIDENT	183	A
MINORITY REPORT	283	A
MINORITY REPRESENTATION	197	A
MINORITY RIGHTS	195	A
MINORITY TREATY	655	B
MINORITY WHIP	182	A
MINSEITO PARTY	526	B
MINT	289	A
MINUTEMAN	184	A
MINUTES	286	A
MIRABEAU, HONORE GABRIEL RIQUETTI, COMTE DE	759	B
MIRACLE	633	B
MIRANDA VS. ARIZONA (1966)	260	A
MIRV (MULTIPLE INDEPENDENT REENTRY VEHICLE)	286	A
MIS-EDUCATION	633	B
MIS-IDENTIFICATION, PROBLEM OF	585	B
MISCALCULATION	143	A
MISCEGENATION	229	A
MISCONDUCT	585	B
MISCONDUCT IN OFFICE	215	A
MISDEMEANOR	201	A
MISES, L.	697	B
MISFEASANCE	229	A
MISHMASH	845	B
MISINFORM	585	B
MISSILE GAP	204	A
MISSILES	287	A
MISSING PERSONS	558	B
MISSION	472	B
MISSIONARIES	188	A
MISSISSIPPI VS. JOHNSON (1867)	678	B
MISSOURI	281	A
MISSOURI COMPROMISE	201	A
MISSOURI COURT PLAN	238	A
MISSOURI VS. HOLLAND (1920)	261	A
MISTAKE	437	B
MISUNDERSTANDINGS	437	B
MISUSE OF A FLAG	633	B
MISUSE OF POWER	209	A
MITCHELL VS. U.S. (1941)	675	B
MITCHELL, GENERAL BILLY	721	B
MITCHELL, JOHN N.	265	A
MITHRAISM	457	B
MITSUBISHI	266	A
MITSUI	697	B
MITTELEUROPA	281	A

MITTERAND, FRANCOIS	270	A
MIXED ARBITRAL TRIBUNAL	472	B
MIXED CAUCUS	163	A
MIXED COMMISSION	168	A
MIXED CONSTITUTION	238	A
MIXED COURTS	488	B
MIXED ECONOMY	148	A
MIXED ENTERPRISE	160	A
MIXED GOVERNMENT	163	A
MIXED STATE	488	B
MIXED TRIBUNAL	472	B
MIZRACHI (ISRAELI PARTY)	526	B
MLAMJE	799	B
MOAT FILLING	655	B
MOB	153	A
MOB BEHAVIOR	119	A
MOB VIOLENCE	222	A
MOB-LYNCHING	209	A
MOBERG, WILHELM	759	B
MOBILE WARFARE	256	A
MOBILITY	124	A
MOBILITY, OCCUPATIONAL	133	A
MOBILIZATION	201	A
MOBUTU, GENERAL JOSEPH	268	A
MOCH, JULES	721	B
MOCZAR, GENERAL M.	759	B
MODAL LOGIC	143	A
MODAL PERSONALITY	126	A
MODALITY	143	A
MODE	121	A
MODE OF ANALYSIS	117	A
MODEL	114	A
MODEL CITIES	148	A
MODEL METHOD	136	A
MODEL METROPOLITAN CHARTER	247	A
MODEL SECONDARY SCHOOL FOR THE DEAF (MSSD)	527	B
MODEL STATE CONSTITUTION	238	A
MODEL STUDIES	140	A
MODELS AND MODELING	117	A
MODELS, CAUSAL	116	A
MODELS, REFERENCE	124	A
MODERATE	184	A
MODERATE PARTY	163	A
MODERATE POLICY	238	A
MODERATION	238	A
MODERATOR	193	A
MODERN	143	A
MODERN POLITICAL PARTIES	148	A
MODERN REPUBLICANISM	133	A
MODERN SOCIETY	147	A
MODERN TOTALITARIANISM	121	A
MODERNISM	143	A
MODERNITY	140	A
MODERNIZATION	116	A
MODERNIZATION, AND STRUCTURAL-FUNCTIONALISM	116	A
MODERNIZING SOCIETIES	145	A
MODIFICATION OF THE CONSTITUTION	222	A
MODOC	505	B
MODUS VIVENDI	247	A
MOGUL	551	B
MOHAMMED	270	A
MOHAMMEDAN	168	A
MOHAMMEDANISM	133	A
MOHAWK	527	B
MOHIEDDIN, ZAKARIA	759	B
MOILLIET, LOUIS	759	B
MOLECULE	289	A
MOLLET, GUY	697	B
MOLLY MCGUIRES	472	B
MOLLYCODDLE	840	B
MOLOTOV-RIBBENTROP PACT	229	A
MOLOTOV, VYACHESLAV M.	272	A
MOLTKE, FIELD MARSHAL VON	759	B
MOLYBDENUM	826	B
MOMENTUM	256	A
MOMMSEN	565	B
MONACO	282	A
MONARCH	183	A
MONARCH BY DIVINE RIGHT	186	A
MONARCHIA	505	B
MONARCHISM	133	A
MONARCHIST	185	A
MONARCHOMACHS	565	B
MONARCHY	146	A
MONASTERIES	823	B
MONCKTON REPORT	812	B
MOND	812	B
MONDLANE, EDUARDO CHIVAMBO	759	B
MONEGASQUE	527	B
MONETARY	287	A
MONETARY AGREEMENT	238	A
MONETARY CONFERENCE	247	A
MONETARY POLICY	201	A
MONETARY REFORM	215	A
MONETARY SOVEREIGNTY	585	B
MONETARY SYSTEM	128	A
MONEY	286	A
MONEY BILL	215	A
MONEY, COINAGE OF	238	A
MONEY, SIR LEO CHIOZZA	759	B
MONGOLIA	277	A
MONGOLS	472	B
MONGREL	565	B
MONGREL CAUCUS	527	B
MONIMA, MADAGASCAR	799	B
MONISM	140	A
MONNET PLAN	247	A
MONNET, JEAN	697	B

MONOCRACY	488	B	MORAL TURPITUDE	133	A
MONOLITH	140	A	MORALE	133	A
MONOLITHIC STATE	163	A	MORALE BUILDING	585	B
MONOLOGUE	585	B	MORALITY	136	A
MONOPOLY	145	A	MORALS COURT	505	B
MONOPOLY CAPITALISM	116	A	MORATORIUM	209	A
MONOPOLY LEGISLATION	229	A	MORBID	143	A
MONOPOLY OF POLITICAL POWER	229	A	MORBIDITY	445	B
MONOTHEISM	133	A	MORE, PAUL ELMER	759	B
MONROE DOCTRINE	194	A	MORE, SIR THOMAS	264	A
MONROE DOCTRINE	195	A	MORELLY	759	B
MONROE, PRESIDENT JAMES	262	A	MORENO, GABRIEL GARCIA	759	B
MONROVIA POWERS	634	B	MORES	128	A
MONROVIAN BLOC	472	B	MOREY LETTER	809	B
MONSTER	823	B	MORGAN LINE	799	B
MONTAGU-CHELMSFORD REPORT	812	B	MORGAN, ARTHUR	759	B
MONTAGUE, C. E.	759	B	MORGAN, LEWIS	759	B
MONTAIGNE, MICHEL DE	272	A	MORGAN, PIERPONT	272	A
MONTALEMBERT, C. DE	759	B	MORGAN, THOMAS HUNT	760	B
MONTANA	788	B	MORGENTHAU PLAN	215	A
MONTEIL,	759	B	MORGENTHAU, HANS J.	261	A
CHARLES-FRANCOIS-LOUIS-EDGAR			MORGLEY, JOHN	760	B
MONTENEGRINS	488	B	MORLEY-MONTO CONSTITUTION	656	B
MONTES, ISMAEL	759	B	MORMON WAR	656	B
MONTESQUIEU, BARON	262	A	MORMONS	168	A
CHARLES-LOUIS DE LA BREDE ET			MORNAY	760	B
DE			MORNING HOUR	656	B
MONTEVIDEO CONFERENCE	247	A	MOROCCO	276	A
MONTGOMERY, RICHARD	721	B	MORPHOLOGY	437	B
MONTHLY LABOR REVIEW	812	B	MORRILL ACT OF 1862	247	A
MONTHLY REPORT	809	B	MORRILL TARIFF	608	B
MONTINI	759	B	MORRIS, GOUVENEUR	265	A
MONTOIRE AGREEMENT	655	B	MORRIS, WILLIAM	687	B
MONTOYA, JOSEPH M.	721	B	MORRIS, WILLY	760	B
MONTREUX CONVENTION, 1936	634	B	MORRISON, HERBERT S.	721	B
MONTREUX STRAITS CONVENTION	634	B	MORSE, WAYNE	270	A
MOOD	143	A	MORSTEIN MARX, FRITZ	760	B
MOONEY CASE	675	B	MORTAL REMAINS	823	B
MOONLIGHTING	238	A	MORTGAGE MORATORIUM	256	A
MOORE	721	B	MORTON, ANTON S.	760	B
MOORE VS. DEMPSEY (1923)	678	B	MOSAIC	823	B
MOORE, BARRINGTON, JR.	687	B	MOSCA GAETANAO	268	A
MOORE, G. E.	721	B	MOSCOW DECLARATIONS	634	B
MOORE, JOHN BASSETT	721	B	MOSCOW TRIALS OF 1936	215	A
MOORE, SAMUEL T.	759	B	MOSCOW-PEKING AXIS	153	A
MOORE, WILBERT E.	759	B	MOSES	268	A
MOORE'S DIGEST	812	B	MOSHAVA	527	B
MOOS, MALCOLM	687	B	MOSLEM	160	A
MOOSE LODGE 107 VS. IVIS (1972)	675	B	MOSLEM BROTHERHOOD	173	A
MORAL	133	A	MOSLEM LEAGUE	163	A
MORAL EQUIVALENT OF WAR	238	A	MOSLEY, SIR OSWALD	697	B
MORAL LAW	204	A	MOSQUE	823	B
MORAL PHILOSOPHY	126	A	MOSQUITO ABATEMENT	634	B
MORAL REARMAMENT	229	A	DISTRICTION		
MORAL RELATIONS	450	B	MOSS, FRANK EDWARD	760	B
MORAL RELATIVISM	126	A	MOSSADEGH, MOHAMMED	270	A

MOSSBACK	193	A	MUD MACHINE	845	B
MOST-FAVORED-NATION CLAUSE	201	A	MUDANIA ARMISTICE	656	B
MOST, JOHANN	760	B	MUDROS ARMISTICE	656	B
MOTEL	826	B	MUDSLINGING	238	A
MOTHER	544	B	MUFFLED	656	B
MOTHER COUNTRY	163	A	MUFTI	818	B
MOTHER PRINCIPLE	445	B	MUGWUMP	173	A
MOTHERLAND	163	A	MUGWUMPERY	256	A
MOTHERS PENSION	634	B	MUHAMMED - ABDUH	760	B
MOTION	215	A	MUHS, KARL	760	B
MOTION FOR ADJOURNMENT	215	A	MUIR, RAMSEY	760	B
MOTION HAVING PRIORITY	238	A	MUJIBUR, SHEIK, RAHMAN	270	A
MOTION OF CENSURE	201	A	MUKDEN INCIDENT	634	B
MOTION OF CONFIDENCE	222	A	MULATTO CANDIDATE	565	B
MOTION OF NO-CONFIDENCE	204	A	MULATTO DEMOCRACY	845	B
MOTION PICTURES	818	B	MULE RIDING	845	B
MOTION TO DISMISS	256	A	MULFORD VS. SMITH (1939)	678	B
MOTION TO LAY UPON THE TABLE	238	A	MULLAH	826	B
MOTION TO POSTPONE	585	B	MULLER VS. OREGON (1908)	678	B
CONSIDERATION OF A QUESTION			MULLIGAN LETTERS	809	B
MOTION TO RECONSIDER	238	A	MULTI-NATIONAL STATE	146	A
MOTION-PICTURE CENSORSHIP	215	A	MULTI-NUCLEAR FORCE	156	A
MOTIVATION	118	A	MULTI-PARTITE	160	A
MOTIVATION RESEARCH	124	A	MULTI-PARTY SYSTEM	194	A
MOTIVATION, MOTIVES	140	A	MULTI-RACIAL SOCIETY	150	A
MOTIVE	130	A	MULTICENTERED SOCIETIES	178	A
MOTOR CARRIER ACT	608	B	MULTIDIMENSIONALITY	124	A
MOTOR VEHICLE OPERATORS	544	B	MULTILATERAL	147	A
MOTOR VEHICLE TAXATION	585	B	MULTILATERAL FORCE (MLF)	204	A
MOTOR VEHICLE THEFT ACT	656	B	PROPOSAL		
MOTT, RODNEY	760	B	MULTILATERAL TRADE	201	A
MOUND	799	B	MULTILATERAL TREATY	199	A
MOUNIER, E.	760	B	MULTILINGUAL	140	A
MOURIR POUR DANZIG	845	B	MULTIMETHODOLOGISM	445	B
MOUVEMENT REPUBLICAIN	173	A	MULTINATIONAL CORPORATIONS	145	A
POPULAIRE (MRP)			(MNC)		
MOVEMENT	156	A	MULTIPARTY SYSTEM	194	A
MOVER	565	A	MULTIPLE	143	A
MOVERS AND SHAKERS	544	B	MULTIPLE CORRELATION	116	A
MOVIMENTO NACIONAL	505	B	MULTIPLE ELECTION	247	A
REVOLUCIONARIO (MNR), BOLIVIA			MULTIPLEX SOCIETY	505	B
MOVING EXPENSES	656	B	MULTIPOLARITY	209	A
MOYNIHAN, DANIEL PATRICK	268	A	MULTIVARIATE ANALYSIS	115	A
MOZAMBIQUE	277	A	MUM CANDIDATE	565	B
MOZAMBIQUE CONVENTION	634	B	MUMFORD, LEWIS	270	A
MR. CLEAN	551	B	MUNDT-COUDERT PROPOSAL	634	B
MR. DOOLEY	697	B	MUNDT, KARL E.	687	B
MR. REPUBLICAN	272	A	MUNICH ACCORD	229	A
MR. X	836	B	MUNICH AGREEMENT	215	A
MUCK-A-MUCKS	845	B	MUNICH CONFERENCE	209	A
MUCKER	565	B	MUNICH CONFERENCE (1938)	215	A
MUCKEY-MUCKS	845	B	MUNICH, ANOTHER	290	A
MUCKRAKERS	182	A	MUNICIPAL	275	A
MUD	845	B	MUNICIPAL ADMINISTRATION	215	A
MUD BATTERIES	845	B	MUNICIPAL APPRENTICESHIPS	565	B
MUD HUNT	845	B	MUNICIPAL CORPORATION	160	A

MUNICIPAL COUNCIL	163	A
MUNICIPAL COURTS	153	A
MUNICIPAL ELECTIONS	201	A
MUNICIPAL FINANCE OFFICERS' ASSOCIATION (U.S.)	505	B
MUNICIPAL GOVERNMENT	146	A
MUNICIPAL HOME RULE	204	A
MUNICIPAL INDEBTEDNESS MORATORIUM LEGISLATION	608	B
MUNICIPAL LAW	209	A
MUNICIPAL LIABILITY	238	A
MUNICIPAL LIST	488	B
MUNICIPAL OFFICER	188	A
MUNICIPAL OWNERSHIP	229	A
MUNICIPAL SOCIALISM	140	A
MUNICIPALITY	150	A
MUNITIONS	287	A
MUNITIONS ACT, GREAT BRITAIN	656	B
MUNITIONS ASSIGNMENT BOARD	527	B
MUNITIONS INDUSTRY	156	A
MUNN VS. ILLINOIS (1877)	672	B
MUNNICH, FERENC	760	B
MUNOZ MARIN, LUIS	721	B
MUNRO, WILLIAM B.	760	B
MUNROE, RUTH L.	760	B
MURCHISON LETTER	812	B
MURDER	229	A
MURDERER	544	B
MURDICK VS. PENNSYLVANIA (1943)	678	B
MURMANSK ROUTE	282	A
MURPHY VS. WATERFRONT COMMISSION	678	B
MURRAY VS. CURLETT	675	B
MURRAY, A.R.M.	760	B
MURRAY, ROBERT	760	B
MUSCAT AND OMAN	281	A
MUSCLE SHOALS	791	B
MUSCOVITES	173	A
MUSE	558	B
MUSEE DE L'HOMME	826	B
MUSHROOM (POLITICIAN, ARISTOCRAT)	566	B
MUSIC	450	B
MUSIC IN INDUSTRY	634	B
MUSICAL METAPHORS	840	B
MUSKIE, EDMUND SIXTUS	266	A
MUSKRAT VS. U.S. (1911)	675	B
MUSLIM	163	A
MUSLIM BROTHERHOOD (IKHWAN AL-MUSLIMIN)	488	B
MUSLIM PEOPLE AND RELIGION	160	A
MUSSOLINI, BENITO	262	A
MUSSOLINI, VITTORIO	697	B
MUTATIS MUTANDIS	608	B
MUTAWAKKILITE KINGDOM OF YEMEN	527	B
MUTINEER	190	A
MUTINY	238	A
MUTUAL AID	222	A
MUTUAL SECURITY AGENCY	178	A
MUZZLE	585	B
MY FRIENDS	840	B
MY LAI INCIDENT	209	A
MYCENAEAN CULTURE	445	B
MYERS VS. U.S. (1926)	679	B
MYNORS, PROF. R. A. B.	760	B
MYRDAL, GUNNAR	262	A
MYRMIDON	527	B
MYSORE, INDIA	794	B
MYSTERY	608	B
MYSTERY RELIGIONS	445	B
MYSTIC RED	527	B
MYSTICISM	136	A
MYSTIQUE	437	B
MYTH	126	A
MYTH IN POLITICAL THEORY	121	A
MYTHOLOGICAL METHOD	143	A
MYTHOLOGY	131	A
MYTHS AND SYMBOLS	121	A
NAACP VS. ALABAMA (1958)	675	B
NAACP VS. BUTTON (1963)	679	B
NADARS	505	B
NADER, RALPH	262	A
NAGAI	760	B
NAGALAND, INDIA	799	B
NAGARJUNA	457	B
NAGASAKI	282	A
NAGEL, ERNEST	760	B
NAGUIB, GENERAL MOHAMMED	272	A
NAGY, IMRE	268	A
NAHAS PASHA	721	B
NAME	247	A
NAME OF THE GAME	836	B
NAMIBIA	788	B
NAMING	450	B
NANSEN PASSPORT	812	B
NAOROJI	760	B
NAPLES	788	B
NAPOLEON BONAPARTE	262	A
NAPOLEON I, EMPEROR	262	A
NAPOLEON III	263	A
NAPOLEON'S GRAND ARMY	178	A
NAPOLEONIC CODE	197	A
NAPOLEONIC EMPIRE	153	A
NAPOLEONIC WARS	209	A
NARCISSISM	437	B
NARCOTIC DRUGS CONTROL	256	A
NARCOTICS	288	A
NARDONE VS. U.S. (1939)	679	B
NARODNAYA VOLYA	506	B
NARRATIVE	451	B
NARROW MAJORITY	160	A

NARROW SEAS	794	B
NARROW-GAUGE THEORY	128	A
NASHVILLE CONVENTION	634	B
NASSAU AGREEMENT, 1962	256	A
NASSER, GAMAL ABDUL	263	A
NAT TURNER'S INSURRECTION	229	A
NATAL, INDIANS IN	488	B
NATION	145	A
NATION OF SHOPKEEPERS	178	A
NATION-BUILDING	197	A
NATION-STATE SYSTEM	113	A
NATIONAL	183	A
NATIONAL ACADEMY OF SCIENCE (NAS)	168	A
NATIONAL ADVISORY COMMISSION ON CIVIL DISORDER	153	A
NATIONAL ADVISORY COMMITTEE FOR AERONAUTICS	506	B
NATIONAL AERONAUTICS AND SPACE ADMINISTRATION (NASA)	156	A
NATIONAL AERONAUTICS AND SPACE COUNCIL (NASC)	527	B
NATIONAL AIR AND SPACE MUSEUM	527	B
NATIONAL AND STATE RELATIONS	124	A
NATIONAL ANTHEM	284	A
NATIONAL ARCHIVES	163	A
NATIONAL ARCHIVES AND RECORD SERVICE (NARS)	506	B
NATIONAL ASSEMBLY, FRANCE	156	A
NATIONAL ASSOCIATION FOR THE ADVANCEMENT OF COLORED PEOPLE (NAACP)	150	A
NATIONAL ASSOCIATION OF ASSESSING OFFICERS (U.S.)	527	B
NATIONAL ASSOCIATION OF BROADCASTERS (NAB)	178	A
NATIONAL ASSOCIATION OF HOUSING OFFICIALS (U.S.)	488	B
NATIONAL ASSOCIATION OF LOCAL GOVERNMENT OFFICERS	488	B
NATIONAL ASSOCIATION OF MANUFACTURERS (NAM)	156	A
NATIONAL ASSOCIATION OF SOIL CONSERVATION DISTRICTS	527	B
NATIONAL BANK	153	A
NATIONAL BEHAVIOR	121	A
NATIONAL BUDGET	195	A
NATIONAL BUILDING GUILD	527	B
NATIONAL BUREAU OF STANDARDS	173	A
NATIONAL CHAIRMAN- POLITICAL PARTY	182	A
NATIONAL CHARACTER	119	A
NATIONAL CHURCH	163	A
NATIONAL CIVIL SERVICE REFORM LEAGUE	506	B
NATIONAL CIVIL SERVICE REFORM LEAGUE	506	B
NATIONAL COLLECTION OF FINE ARTS	506	B
NATIONAL COLORS	818	B
NATIONAL COMMISSION ON CAUSES AND PREVENTION OF VIOLENCE	163	A
NATIONAL COMMISSION ON CONSUMER FINANCE	527	B
NATIONAL COMMITTEE	168	A
NATIONAL COMMITTEE FOR AN EFFECTIVE CONGRESS	488	B
NATIONAL COMMITTEE OF LIBERATION	488	B
NATIONAL COMMITTEE ON THE CAUSES AND PREVENTION OF VIOLENCE	173	A
NATIONAL COMMUNISM (TITOISM)	116	A
NATIONAL COMPLIANCE BOARD	527	B
NATIONAL CONFERENCE OF COMMISSIONERS ON UNIFORM STATE LAWS	472	B
NATIONAL CONGRESS	163	A
NATIONAL CONSCIOUSNESS	133	A
NATIONAL CONVENTION (OF PARTIES IN U.S.A.)	222	A
NATIONAL COOPERATIVE SOIL SURVEY	527	B
NATIONAL COUNCIL OF CHURCHES	163	A
NATIONAL COUNCIL OF CORPORATIONS	506	B
NATIONAL COUNCIL OF FARMER COOPERATIVES	488	B
NATIONAL COUNCIL OF RESEARCH	488	B
NATIONAL COUNCIL OF THE RESISTANCE (CNR)	506	B
NATIONAL COUNCIL ON INDIAN OPPORTUNITY	527	B
NATIONAL COUNCILLOR	566	B
NATIONAL COUNCILS (POLAND)	506	B
NATIONAL COURT OF APPEALS	168	A
NATIONAL CURRENCY	287	A
NATIONAL DEBT	197	A
NATIONAL DECISIONS	133	A
NATIONAL DEFENSE	199	A
NATIONAL DEFENSE (PROTECTIONISM)	229	A
NATIONAL DEFENSE EDUCATION ACT OF 1958 (NDEA)	247	A
NATIONAL DEFENSE RESERVE FLEET	488	B
NATIONAL DEMOCRACY	128	A
NATIONAL DEMOCRATIC PARTY (NPD), GERMANY	168	A
NATIONAL DEVICE	609	B
NATIONAL ECONOMIC COUNCIL	173	A

NATIONAL EDUCATION ASSOCIATION	164	A
NATIONAL FARMERS UNION	160	A
NATIONAL FEDERATION OF BUSINESS AND PROFESSIONAL WOMENS CLUBS	488	B
NATIONAL FEDERATION OF FEDERAL EMPLOYEES	472	B
NATIONAL FLAG	288	A
NATIONAL FOREST SERVICE	473	B
NATIONAL FOREST SYSTEM	473	B
NATIONAL FOUNDATION ON ARTS AND HUMANITIES	506	B
NATIONAL FRONT (OF GERMAN DEMOCRATIC REPUBLIC)	473	B
NATIONAL GALLERY OF ART	527	B
NATIONAL GENERAL MOBILIZATION ACT	585	B
NATIONAL GOVERNMENT	156	A
NATIONAL GRANGE	178	A
NATIONAL GUARD	168	A
NATIONAL GUILDS LEAGUE	527	B
NATIONAL HEALTH INSURANCE	209	A
NATIONAL HEALTH SERVICE ACT (BRITAIN)	247	A
NATIONAL HIGHWAY TRANSPORTATION SAFETY ADMINISTRATION (NHTSA)	527	B
NATIONAL HOLIDAY	247	A
NATIONAL HOME	795	B
NATIONAL HONOR	229	A
NATIONAL HOUSING AGENCY	473	B
NATIONAL IDENTIFICATION	238	A
NATIONAL INCOME	209	A
NATIONAL INDEPENDENCE	205	A
NATIONAL INDUSTRIAL RECOVERY ACT (NIRA)	229	A
NATIONAL INSTITUTES OF HEALTH (NIH)	164	A
NATIONAL INSURANCE	247	A
NATIONAL INTEREST	194	A
NATIONAL JOINT COUNCIL FOR LOCAL AUTHORITIES (GREAT BRITAIN)	527	B
NATIONAL LABOR PARTY	173	A
NATIONAL LABOR RELATIONS ACT (WAGNER ACT) OF 1935	215	A
NATIONAL LABOR RELATIONS BOARD (NLRB)	150	A
NATIONAL LABOR RELATIONS BOARD VS. J«L STEEL (1937)	261	A
NATIONAL LAW	222	A
NATIONAL LEAGUE OF CITIES (NLC)	164	A
NATIONAL LEAGUE OF WOMEN VOTERS	156	A
NATIONAL LEGAL SERVICE CORPORATION	527	B
NATIONAL LEPROSARIUM	527	B
NATIONAL LIBERATION FRONT (NLF)	160	A
NATIONAL LIBERATION WARS	199	A
NATIONAL LIBRARY OF MEDICINE	527	B
NATIONAL LIST	473	B
NATIONAL LOYALTY	134	A
NATIONAL MEDIATION BOARD	178	A
NATIONAL MENTAL HEALTH ACT OF 1946	656	B
NATIONAL MILITARY ESTABLISHMENT	164	A
NATIONAL MUNICIPAL LEAGUE (U.S.)	173	A
NATIONAL MUSEUM OF NATURAL HISTORY	527	B
NATIONAL NON-PARTISAN LEAGUE, THE	488	B
NATIONAL OCEANIC, ATMOSPHERIC ADMINISTRATION	527	B
NATIONAL OPINION RESEARCH CENTER (U.S.)	164	A
NATIONAL ORIGINS	185	A
NATIONAL ORIGINS ACT	238	A
NATIONAL ORIGINS QUOTA SYSTEM	215	A
NATIONAL PARK SERVICE	178	A
NATIONAL PARKS	282	A
NATIONAL PARTY	156	A
NATIONAL PEOPLE'S CONGRESS (NPC), CHINA (PRC)	178	A
NATIONAL PLANNING ASSOCIATION (WASHINGTON)	473	B
NATIONAL POLITICAL SYSTEMS	118	A
NATIONAL POWER, ELEMENTS OF	116	A
NATIONAL PRIMARY	201	A
NATIONAL PUBLIC WORKS BOARD	506	B
NATIONAL RAILROAD ADJUSTMENT BOARD	506	B
NATIONAL RECLAMATION ACT	634	B
NATIONAL RECOVERY ADMINISTRATION (NRA)	156	A
NATIONAL REFORMER	566	B
NATIONAL REGIONALISM	140	A
NATIONAL REPORTER SYSTEM	807	B
NATIONAL REPUBLICAN PARTY	160	A
NATIONAL RESEARCH COUNCIL	506	B
NATIONAL RESOURCES	286	A
NATIONAL RESOURCES BOARD	473	B
NATIONAL RESOURCES PLANNING BOARD (U.S.)	178	A
NATIONAL REVIEW	284	A
NATIONAL SCHOOL OF JURISPRUDENCE (MEXICO)	528	B
NATIONAL SCIENCE FOUNDATION (NSF)	164	A
NATIONAL SECURITY	201	A
NATIONAL SECURITY ACTS, 1947 AND 1949	247	A

NATIONAL SECURITY AGENCY (NSA)	168	A
NATIONAL SECURITY COUNCIL (NSC)	150	A
NATIONAL SECURITY RESOURCES BOARD	528	B
NATIONAL SELF-DETERMINATION	195	A
NATIONAL SILVER PARTY	473	B
NATIONAL SOCIALISM	114	A
NATIONAL SOCIALIST GERMAN WORKERS PARTY	160	A
NATIONAL SOCIALIST PARTY	164	A
NATIONAL STYLE	247	A
NATIONAL SUPREMACY	222	A
NATIONAL SYNDICALISM	143	A
NATIONAL TEACHER CORPS	473	B
NATIONAL TECHNICAL INFORMATION SERVICE (NTIS)	528	B
NATIONAL TERRITORY	276	A
NATIONAL TRAFFIC AND MOTOR VEHICLE SAFETY ACT OF 1968	634	B
NATIONAL TRANSPORTATION SAFETY BOARD	489	B
NATIONAL TREATMENT	634	B
NATIONAL UNION PARTY	506	B
NATIONAL UNIVERSITY (AUSTRALIA)	528	B
NATIONAL UNIVERSITY OF POLITICAL SCIENCE (CHINA)	528	B
NATIONAL URBAN LEAGUE	164	A
NATIONAL WAR LABOR BOARD	473	B
NATIONAL WATERS	275	A
NATIONAL WILDERNESS PRESERVATION SYSTEM	506	B
NATIONAL WILDLIFE FEDERATION	528	B
NATIONAL YOUTH ADMINISTRATION (NYA)	473	B
NATIONAL ZOOLOGICAL PARK	528	B
NATIONAL-REPUBLICANS	168	A
NATIONALISM	113	A
NATIONALIST CHINA (TAIWAN)	274	A
NATIONALISTIC FACTORS	128	A
NATIONALISTIC UNIVERSALISM	437	B
NATIONALITIES	153	A
NATIONALITY	181	A
NATIONALIZATION	195	A
NATIONALIZATION OF GOLD	585	B
NATIONALIZATION OF THE SUEZ CANAL COMPANY	256	A
NATIONALIZATION, OF PARTIES	585	B
NATIONALIZED ENTERPRISE	164	A
NATIONALIZED INDUSTRIES OF FRANCE	178	A
NATIONALS	186	A
NATIONS	146	A
NATIVE	190	A
NATIVE AMERICAN STUDIES	134	A
NATIVE COUNTRY	178	A
NATIVE PRINCE	558	B
NATIVE STATES	282	A
NATIVISM	131	A
NATO COUNTRIES	274	A
NATO PARLIAMENTARIANS CONFERENCE	506	B
NATOLIN GROUP	528	B
NATURAL BOUNDARY	279	A
NATURAL DEDUCTION	451	B
NATURAL ECONOMY	506	B
NATURAL EXPERIMENT	143	A
NATURAL FRONTIER	276	A
NATURAL LANGUAGE	451	B
NATURAL LAW (JUS NATURALE)	194	A
NATURAL LAW, DEMOCRATIC THEORY	197	A
NATURAL MONOPOLY	134	A
NATURAL RELIGION	451	B
NATURAL RESOURCES	286	A
NATURAL RESOURCES, CONSERVATION OF	201	A
NATURAL RIGHTS	199	A
NATURAL SCIENCE	136	A
NATURAL SELECTION	128	A
NATURAL THEOLOGY	451	B
NATURAL-BORN CITIZEN	186	A
NATURALISM	445	B
NATURALIST CONCEPTION OF LAW	143	A
NATURALISTIC FALLACY	143	A
NATURALIZATION	201	A
NATURALIZATION OF COMMUNISTS	634	B
NATURALIZED CITIZEN	183	A
NATURE	140	A
NATURE, STATE OF	201	A
NAVAL AGREEMENT	585	B
NAVAL ATTACHE	551	B
NAVAL BASE	281	A
NAVAL BASES, AMERICAN	282	A
NAVAL BLOCKADE	229	A
NAVAL CRUISE MISSILES	807	B
NAVAL DISARMAMENT	585	B
NAVAL DISARMAMENT CONFERENCES	256	A
NAVAL FORCES	160	A
NAVAL MATERIAL COMMAND (NMC)	528	B
NAVAL OPERATIONS	247	A
NAVAL POWER	238	A
NAVAL RATIOS	609	B
NAVAL SUPREMACY	229	A
NAVAL TREATY	256	A
NAVAL WAR COLLEGE	178	A
NAVAL WARFARE	247	A
NAVICERT	827	B
NAVIGABLE WATERS	281	A
NAVIGATION ACTS	256	A
NAVY	164	A

NAVY SECOND TO NONE	836	B
NAVY YARD	795	B
NAXALITES	528	B
NAYARS	528	B
NAYLORIZING	656	B
NAZI	181	A
NAZI MOVEMENT	148	A
NAZI NEOPAGANISM	445	B
NAZI-SOVIET PACT OF 1939	209	A
NAZIFICATION OF GERMANY	229	A
NAZISM	118	A
NE WIN, GENERAL	697	B
NEANDERTHAL WING	489	B
NEAR VS. MINNESOTA (1931)	672	B
NEBBIA VS. NEW YORK (1934)	675	B
NEBRASCAL	528	B
NEBRASKA	282	A
NECESSARY AND PROPER CLAUSE OF THE CONSTITUTION	199	A
NECESSITY	247	A
NECROPHILIA	457	B
NEEDS	128	A
NEGATION	585	B
NEGATIVE	143	A
NEGATIVE - EVENTS	609	B
NEGATIVE (NOUN AND VERB)	437	B
NEGATIVE INCOME TAX	201	A
NEGATIVE REFERENCE GROUPS	168	A
NEGATIVE VOTE	222	A
NEGATIVISM	445	B
NEGLECT	256	A
NEGLIGENCE	229	A
NEGOTIATE	215	A
NEGOTIATED CONTRACT	247	A
NEGOTIATED DISENGAGEMENT	238	A
NEGOTIATED PEACE	222	A
NEGOTIATED SAFEGUARDS	247	A
NEGOTIATION	195	A
NEGOTIATOR	182	A
NEGRITUDE	551	B
NEGRO	164	A
NEGRO SUFFRAGE	209	A
NEGRO SUPREMACY	247	A
NEGRO THIEVES	558	B
NEGRO-AMERICANS	178	A
NEGROANA	827	B
NEGROPHILIST	558	B
NEGUIB, GENERAL MOHAMED	697	B
NEHRU, JAWAHARLAL	263	A
NEHRU, PUNDIT MOTILAL	266	A
NEHRUISM	134	A
NEIGHBORHOOD	791	B
NEIGHBORHOOD ASSOCIATIONS	178	A
NEIGHBORHOOD YOUTH CORPS (NYC)	168	A
NEIGHBORING STATE	164	A
NEIGHBORS	566	B
NELSON VS. COUNTY OF LOS ANGELES (1960)	679	B
NELSON, GAYLORD ANTON	698	B
NEMESIS	544	B
NENNI, PIETRO	687	B
NEO-COLONIALISM	116	A
NEO-DESTOUR, TUNISIA	656	B
NEO-FASCISM	126	A
NEO-FREUDIANS	190	A
NEO-FUNCTIONALISM	126	A
NEO-HEGELIANISM	136	A
NEO-HUMBOLTIANISM	457	B
NEO-KANTIANISM	437	B
NEO-LIBERALISM	134	A
NEO-MALTHUSIANISM	134	A
NEO-MERCANTILISM	140	A
NEO-MILITARISM	140	A
NEO-NAZI	188	A
NEO-ORTHODOXY	143	A
NEO-PLATONISM	136	A
NEO-POSITIVISM	134	A
NEO-PYTHAGOREANISM	457	B
NEO-THOMISM	143	A
NEOPHYTE	558	B
NEOPOSITIVISM	136	A
NEPAL	281	A
NEPMEN	551	B
NEPOTISM	205	A
NERO, ROMAN EMPEROR	687	B
NERVOUS NELLIES	558	B
NEST EGG	845	B
NET INCOME	209	A
NET SALARY	247	A
NETHERAVON	799	B
NETHERLANDS ANTILLES	788	B
NETHERLANDS, KINGDOM OF THE	173	A
NETSCHAIEV, SERGEI	698	B
NETWORK	437	B
NETWORK THEORY	437	B
NEUBERGER, MAURINE BROWN	760	B
NEUBERGER, RICHARD LEWIS	698	B
NEUGARTEN, BERNICE L.	760	B
NEUMANN, JOHN VON	760	B
NEUMANN, SIGMUND	698	B
NEURATH, BARON CONSTANTINE VON	721	B
NEURATH, OTTO	721	B
NEUROPHYSIOLOGY	457	B
NEUROSES	143	A
NEUROTIC	551	B
NEUTRAL	126	A
NEUTRAL ASYLUM	281	A
NEUTRAL HOSPITALITY	585	B
NEUTRAL STATE	153	A
NEUTRAL WATERS	277	A

NEUTRAL ZONE	275	A
NEUTRALISM	119	A
NEUTRALIST	188	A
NEUTRALITY	195	A
NEUTRALITY ACTS	229	A
NEUTRALITY PROCLAMATION OF 1793	609	B
NEUTRALITY ZONE	282	A
NEUTRALIZATION	215	A
NEUTRALIZED ZONE	279	A
NEVER LOST A WAR OR WON A PEACE	834	B
NEW AGE	656	B
NEW BROOM	840	B
NEW BRUNSWICK, CANADA	795	B
NEW CALEDONIA	795	B
NEW CHINESE MAN (MAOISM)	136	A
NEW COMMERCE	609	B
NEW CONSERVATISM	131	A
NEW DEAL	197	A
NEW DEAL LEGISLATION	199	A
NEW DELHI	281	A
NEW DEPARTURE	634	B
NEW ECONOMIC POLICY OF THE U.S.S.R.	229	A
NEW ECONOMICS	238	A
NEW ENGLAND CONFEDERATION	489	B
NEW ENGLAND TOWN MEETING	153	A
NEW EXPANSIONISM	437	B
NEW FACE	558	B
NEW FEDERALISM	119	A
NEW FREEDOM	291	A
NEW FRONTIER	215	A
NEW GUINEA	282	A
NEW HAMPSHIRE GRANTS	656	B
NEW HAVEN	282	A
NEW IDEA REPUBLICAN	528	B
NEW IDEALISM	445	B
NEW JERSEY PLAN	229	A
NEW LEFT	145	A
NEW LIBERALISM	136	A
NEW LIGHT (DEMOCRAT)	528	B
NEW LOOK	840	B
NEW MODEL ARMY	489	B
NEW NATIONALISM	437	B
NEW NATIONS	274	A
NEW ORDER	256	A
NEW ORDER IN EUROPE	256	A
NEW ORDER OF EAST ASIA	609	B
NEW ORDER, NAZI	238	A
NEW ORLEANS	788	B
NEW REALISM	457	B
NEW REPUBLIC	285	A
NEW RIGHT	164	A
NEW ROMANTICISM	457	B
NEW ROOF	845	B
NEW SOUTH	160	A
NEW SOVIET MAN	190	A
NEW STATES	178	A
NEW TESTAMENT	805	B
NEW TOWN	179	A
NEW WORLD	282	A
NEW YEAR'S ADDRESS	656	B
NEW YEAR'S MESSAGE	634	B
NEW YORK CITY (NYC)	277	A
NEW YORK SCHOOL PRAYER CASE (1962)	260	A
NEW YORK STATE	279	A
NEW YORK STATE COMMISSION	489	B
NEW YORK TIMES	284	A
NEW YORK TIMES VS. SULLIVAN (1964)	673	B
NEW YORK WORLD	506	B
NEW ZEALAND	282	A
NEW, POLITICAL USE OF	457	B
NEWBERRY VS. U.S. (1921)	675	B
NEWCOMB, THEODORE M.	760	B
NEWELL, ALLEN	760	B
NEWLANDS ACT OF 1902	634	B
NEWLY CREATED TOWNS	506	B
NEWMAN, CARDINAL	698	B
NEWS	238	A
NEWS BAN	222	A
NEWS BLACKOUT	222	A
NEWSPAPER	284	A
NEWTON, SIR ISAAC	268	A
NEWTONIANISM	143	A
NEXUS	445	B
NGUYEN AI QUOC	761	B
NICARAGUA	281	A
NICHOLAS I, CZAR	270	A
NICHOLAS OF CUSA	761	B
NICHOLSON, J. S.	761	B
NICKEL	827	B
NICKNAMES	457	B
NIEBUHR, REINHOLD	266	A
NIEMEYER, GERHART	761	B
NIEMEYER, OSCAR	761	B
NIEMOTKO VS. MARYLAND (1951)	679	B
NIETZSCHE, FRIEDRICH	262	A
NIEUWENHUIS, FERDINAND	761	B
NIGER	281	A
NIGERIA, FEDERATION OF	173	A
NIGGER BROKER	566	B
NIGGER IN THE WOODPILE	840	B
NIGGER WORSHIPPER	558	B
NIGHT COURT	473	B
NIGHT MAYOR	566	B
NIGHTMARE	457	B
NIGHTRIDERS	544	B
NIHILISM	128	A
NILOTIC FEDERATION	506	B

NIMROD	761	B	NON-AMERICAN	551	B
NINE OLD MEN	160	A	NON-ARYAN	544	B
NINE-POWER PACT	634	B	NON-AUTONOMOUS TERRITORIES,	609	B
NINETEENTH AMENDMENT	222	A	ADMINISTRATION OF		
NINTH AMENDMENT	238	A	NON-BELLIGERENCY	222	A
NINUS, KING OF THE ASSYRIANS	761	B	NON-BELLIGERENT	184	A
NIPPON	788	B	NON-COMBATANT	186	A
NISEI	179	A	NON-COMMITTED COUNTRIES	164	A
NISI PRIUS COURT	528	B	NON-COMMUNIST LEFT	153	A
NITTO, FRANCESCO	761	B	NON-COMPLIANCE	215	A
NITTY-GRITTY	845	B	NON-CONFORMING USES	634	B
NIXON DOCTRINE	215	A	NON-CONTRACTING STATES	473	B
NIXON VS. CONDON (1932)	679	B	NON-COOPERATION	585	B
NIXON VS. HERNDON (1927)	679	B	NON-DISCRIMINATION	238	A
NIXON, CHARLES R.	761	B	NON-EXTRADITION	229	A
NIXON, PRESIDENT RICHARD M.	261	A	NON-FICTION	807	B
NKOMO, JOSHUA	761	B	NON-FORTIFICATION	609	B
NKRUMAH, DR. KWAME	268	A	NON-GOVERNMENTAL	168	A
NO COMMENT	609	B	NON-GOVERNMENTAL ENTITIES	168	A
NO CONFIDENCE	205	A	NON-GOVERNMENTAL	153	A
NO FACE	845	B	ORGANIZATION (NGO)		
NO KNOCK SEARCH PROVISION	215	A	NON-HIERARCHIC PRIMARY GROUP	164	A
NO SUBSTITUTE FOR VICTORY	836	B	NON-IMMIGRANT VISITORS	558	B
NO TAXATION WITHOUT	289	A	NON-INTERFERENCE	222	A
REPRESENTATION			NON-INTERVENTION	201	A
NO-DEAL	609	B	NON-INTERVENTION COMMITTEE	506	B
NO-MAN'S-LAND	282	A	NON-LAWMAKING TREATY	609	B
NO-WIN POLICY	229	A	NON-MEMBER	188	A
NOBEL LAUREATES	544	B	NON-MEMBER GOVERNMENT	173	A
NOBEL PEACE PRIZE	287	B	NON-MEMBER STATE	164	A
NOBILITY	160	A	NON-PARTICIPATING GOVERNMENTS	179	A
NOBILITY, TITLES OF	285	A	NON-PARTICIPATING STATES	473	B
NOBLE	544	B	NON-PHYSICAL INSPECTION	634	B
NOBLE BIRTH	256	A	METHODS		
NOBLE EXPERIMENT	256	A	NON-PROLIFERATION TREATY	205	A
NOBODY SHOOTS AT SANTA CLAUS	845	B	NON-QUOTA IMMIGRANT	185	A
NOCTURNAL COUNCIL	489	B	NON-RECOGNITION	121	A
NOETHER	721	B	NON-RECOGNITION DOCTRINE	238	A
NOGEE, PHILIP	761	B	NON-RESIDENT	190	A
NOGUCHI, YONE	761	B	NON-RETROACTIVE LAWS	229	A
NOISE	609	B	NON-RETROACTIVITY	256	A
NOLTE, E.	721	B	NON-RULE	609	B
NOMENCLATURE	143	A	NON-SELF-GOVERNING TERRITORIES	151	A
NOMINAL CANDIDATE	188	A	NON-SIGNATORY GOVERNMENTS	168	A
NOMINAL SCALE	119	A	NON-SIGNATORY PARTIES	473	B
NOMINALISM	136	A	NON-STANDARD SYSTEMS	457	B
NOMINATE	209	A	NON-TAX REVENUE	238	A
NOMINATING CONVENTION	197	A	NON-VIOLENCE	199	A
NOMINATION	197	A	NON-VIOLENCE, THEORIES OF	121	A
NOMINATIONS COMMITTEE	164	A	NON-VOTERS	182	A
NOMOCRACY	457	B	NON-VOTING	209	A
NOMOLOGICAL EXPLANATION	451	B	NON-WESTERN	279	A
NOMOTHETIC EXPLANATION	143	A	NON-WHITE	190	A
NON-AGGRESSION PACT	222	A	NON-ZERO-SUM GAME	118	A
NON-ALIGNED NATIONS	150	A	NONALIGNMENT (NEUTRALISM)	121	A
NON-ALIGNMENT	201	A	NONASSOCIATIONAL GROUP	160	A

NONCOMBATANT	185	A
NONCOMISSIONED OFFICERS	193	A
NONCONFORMTIY	247	A
NONDIRECTED INTERVIEW	134	A
NONFEASANCE	609	B
NONGOVERNMENTAL INTERNATIONAL SCIENTIFIC COOPERATION	609	B
NONIMPORTATION ACT	656	B
NONIMPORTATION AGREEMENT	634	B
NONINTERCOURSE ACT	634	B
NONPARAMETRIC STATISTICS	131	A
NONPARTISAN	181	A
NONPARTISAN BALLOT	205	A
NONPARTISAN BOARD (OR COMMISSION OR COMMITTEE)	179	A
NONPARTISAN ELECTION	205	A
NONPARTISAN LEAGUE (NPL)	506	B
NONPARTISAN PRIMARY	201	A
NONPARTISANSHIP	197	A
NONPOLITICAL PARTICIPATION	136	A
NONPOLITICAL TRIP	609	B
NONPROFESSIONALS	193	A
NONSENSE	451	B
NONSTUDENT	551	B
NONTONIC POLITY	528	B
NORAD	506	B
NORDIC COUNCIL	473	B
NORDIC COUNTRIES	282	A
NORDIC DOCTRINE OF RACE SUPERIORITY	585	B
NORDIC ECONOMIC UNION	473	B
NORDIC RACE	473	B
NORDICISM	143	A
NORFOLK SOUTH WEST	799	B
NORM	115	A
NORMAL DISTRIBUTION	119	A
NORMALCY	222	A
NORMANDY, INVASION OF	247	A
NORMATIVE	116	A
NORMATIVE ARGUMENT	114	A
NORMATIVE CONCEPTION	128	A
NORMATIVE DOCTRINE	128	A
NORMATIVE ETHICS	128	A
NORMATIVE METHOD	124	A
NORMATIVE STATEMENT	113	A
NORMATIVE THEORY	113	A
NORMATIVE-JURIDICAL METHOD	134	A
NORMS	119	A
NORRIS AMENDMENT	634	B
NORRIS VS. ALABAMA (1935)	679	B
NORRIS-LAGUARDIA (ANTI-INJUNCTION) ACT OF 1932	256	A
NORRIS, FRANK	698	B
NORRIS, GEORGE W.	698	B
NORTH	791	B
NORTH AFRICA	281	A
NORTH AFRICAN CAMPAIGNS	256	A
NORTH AMERICA	275	A
NORTH AMERICANS	473	B
NORTH ATLANTIC ALLIANCE	164	A
NORTH ATLANTIC COUNCIL	173	A
NORTH ATLANTIC FISHERIES	473	B
NORTH ATLANTIC FREE TRADE AREA	179	A
NORTH ATLANTIC PACT	222	A
NORTH ATLANTIC TREATY ORGANIZATION (NATO)	145	A
NORTH CAROLINA	281	A
NORTH EAST INDIA	795	B
NORTH GERMAN CONFEDERATION	506	B
NORTH KOREA	276	A
NORTH SEA	279	A
NORTH VIETNAM	273	A
NORTH-EAST FRONTIER AGENCY	506	B
NORTHEAST BOUNDARY DISPUTE	609	B
NORTHERN CAP	799	B
NORTHERN IRELAND	274	A
NORTHERN MAN WITH SOUTHERN PRINCIPLES	840	B
NORTHERN SECURITIES COMPANY VS. U.S. (1904)	679	B
NORTHERN TIER	791	B
NORTHERNER	558	B
NORTHRUP, F. S. L.	721	B
NORTHWEST CONSPIRACY	656	B
NORTHWEST ORDINANCE (1787)	222	A
NORTHWEST TERRITORY	276	A
NORTON, CHARLES DYER	698	B
NORTON, JOHN	761	B
NORWAY	283	A
NORWAY CAMPAIGN	609	B
NOSE OF WAX	845	B
NOT FOR ATTRIBUTION	806	B
NOTARY PUBLIC	193	A
NOTE	806	B
NOTESTEIN, FRANK W.	722	B
NOTHING TO FEAR BUT FEAR ITSELF	291	A
NOTHINGNESS	634	B
NOTICE AND HEARING	238	A
NOTICE BOARD	528	B
NOTICE OF TERMINATION OF SERVICE	634	B
NOTICE OF WITHDRAWAL	656	B
NOTIFICATION	609	B
NOTION	445	B
NOUVELLE SOCIETE HELVETIQUE (SWITZERLAND)	506	B
NOVALIS	761	B
NOVELS, POLITICAL	286	A
NOVELTY	634	B
NOVOTNY, A.	761	B
NOVUS ORDO SECLORUM	840	B

NOW IS THE TIME FOR ALL GOOD MEN TO COME TO THE AID OF THEIR COUNTRY	845	B	NUTS AND KOOKS	836	B
			NYAYA	457	B
			NYE COMMITTEE	489	B
NOW, POLITICAL USE OF	445	B	NYERERE, JULIUS KAMBARAGE	270	A
NSITS (NIGERIA)	528	B	NYON AGREEMENT	656	B
NTH NATION PROBLEM	238	A	O.G.P.U. (U.S.S.R.)	473	B
NTRE FOR STUDIES IN STATE REFORM (CERE, BELGIUM)	528	B	O.K.	840	B
			O'NEAL, JAMES	761	B
NU, U.	722	B	O'NEIL, ROBERT P.	722	B
NUCLEAR	287	A	O'NEILL, CAPTAIN TERENCE	761	B
NUCLEAR ARMAMENTS	286	A	OAKESHOTT, MICHAEL	722	B
NUCLEAR ARMS RACE	197	A	OAKLAND, CALIFORNIA	788	B
NUCLEAR CONFLICT	201	A	OATH	247	A
NUCLEAR DETERRENT	195	A	OATH OF ALLEGIANCE	230	A
NUCLEAR DISARMAMENT	197	A	OATH OF INAUGURATION	247	A
NUCLEAR ENERGY	287	A	OATH OF OFFICE	230	A
NUCLEAR PAUSE	635	B	OBEDIENCE	134	A
NUCLEAR POWER	151	A	OBITER DICTUM (INCIDENTAL OPINION)	230	A
NUCLEAR PROLIFERATION	201	A			
NUCLEAR STOCKPILE	286	A	OBITUARIES	812	B
NUCLEAR STRIKING FORCE	153	A	OBJECT	288	A
NUCLEAR SUBMARINE	287	A	OBJECTIFICATION	437	B
NUCLEAR TEST BAN	205	A	OBJECTION	247	A
NUCLEAR TEST BAN TREATY (1963)	205	A	OBJECTIVE	136	A
NUCLEAR TESTING	209	A	OBJECTIVE CORRELATIVE	585	B
NUCLEAR TRIGGER	215	A	OBJECTIVE POLITICAL EVALUATION	136	A
NUCLEAR WARFARE	195	A	OBJECTIVISM	143	A
NUCLEAR WEAPONS	286	A	OBJECTIVITY	116	A
NUCLEAR WEAPONS BAN	205	A	OBKOM	506	B
NUCLEAR WEAPONS BAN ON OCEAN FLOOR	247	A	OBLIGATION	230	A
			OBLIGATION OF CONTRACTS	238	A
NUCLEAR-FREE ZONE	274	A	OBLIGATION TO EXTRADITE	247	A
NUFFIELD COLLEGE (OXFORD)	506	B	OBLIGATION TO VOTE	222	A
NUISANCE	609	B	OBLIGATORY	585	B
NUISANCE TAX	256	A	OBLIGATORY ARBITRATION	209	A
NULL AND VOID	238	A	OBOTE, DR. MILTON	272	A
NULL HYPOTHESIS	115	A	OBREGON, ALVARO	722	B
NULL SET	136	A	OBSCENITY	222	A
NULLIFICATION	199	A	OBSERVABLES	445	B
NULLIFICATION	215	A	OBSERVANCE OF THE RULES OF PROCEDURE	585	B
NUMBER	143	A			
NUMBER THEORY	437	B	OBSERVANCE OF TREATIES	230	A
NUMBER 10	558	B	OBSERVATION	247	A
NUMBERS GAME	247	A	OBSERVATORIES	827	B
NUMERICAL DECISION RULE	143	A	OBSERVER	551	B
NUMERICAL INDICES AND INDICATORS	136	A	OBSERVER-MODEL	140	A
			OBSESSIONS	457	B
NUNCIATURE	566	B	OBSOLESCENCE, MANAGERIAL	586	B
NUREMBERG LAWS	215	A	OBSOLETE POLITICAL TERMS	457	B
NUREMBERG PRINCIPLES	230	A	OBSTACLES	656	B
NUREMBERG WAR CRIMES TRIALS	199	A	OBSTRUCTION	609	B
NUREMBURG CONGRESS	585	B	OBSTRUCTIONIST	185	A
NURSES	566	B	OCCASION	609	B
NURSING	451	B	OCCASIONALISM	457	B
NUT-CUTTING	845	B	OCCIDENT	791	B
NUTRITION	238	A	OCCIDENTAL	551	B

OCCITAN, FRANCE	799	B	OFFICE OF ALIEN PROPERTY	173	A
OCCUPANCY	635	B	OFFICE OF AUTOMATION AND	507	B
OCCUPATION	186	A	MANPOWER		
OCCUPATION AUTHORITIES	551	B	OFFICE OF BUSINESS ECONOMICS	489	B
OCCUPATION COSTS	609	B	OFFICE OF CENSORSHIP	179	A
OCCUPATION FORCES	168	A	OFFICE OF CIVIL AND DEFENSE	160	A
OCCUPATION IN TIME OF WAR	238	A	MOBILIZATION (OCDM)		
OCCUPATION MONEY	823	B	OFFICE OF CIVILIAN DEFENSE (OCD)	489	B
OCCUPATION OUTLOOK HANDBOOK	812	B	OFFICE OF CO-ORDINATOR OF	507	B
OCCUPATION POWER	179	A	INTER-AMERICAN AFFAIRS		
OCCUPATION REPRESENTATION	609	B	OFFICE OF COMPTROLLER OF THE	489	B
OCCUPATION STATUTE	635	B	CURRENCY		
OCCUPATION TAX	609	B	OFFICE OF CONSUMER AFFAIRS	164	A
OCCUPATIONAL CHOICE	586	B	OFFICE OF DEFENSE MOBILIZATION	160	A
OCCUPATIONAL DISEASE	289	A	OFFICE OF DEFENSE	489	B
OCCUPATIONAL GROUP AUTONOMY	609	B	TRANSPORTATION (U.S.) (ODT)		
OCCUPATIONAL GROUPS	153	A	OFFICE OF ECONOMIC	151	A
OCCUPATIONAL MOBILITY	131	A	OPPORTUNITY (OEO)		
OCCUPATIONAL ORGANIZATIONS	473	B	OFFICE OF ECONOMIC	473	B
OCCUPATIONAL REPRESENTATION	256	A	STABILIZATION (OES)		
OCCUPIED TERRITORY	279	A	OFFICE OF EDUCATION (OE)	168	A
OCEANIA	791	B	OFFICE OF EMERGENCY	473	B
OCEANOGRAPHY	445	B	MANAGEMENT (OEM)		
OCEANS	276	A	OFFICE OF EMERGENCY PLANNING	168	A
OCHAB, E.	761	B	(OEP)		
OCHLOCRACY	451	B	OFFICE OF FEDERAL CONTRACT	489	B
OCKHAM, WILLIAM OF	272	A	COMPLIANCE (OFCC)		
OCTAVIAN	722	B	OFFICE OF FOREIGN COMMERCIAL	528	B
OCTOBER REVOLUTION	215	A	SERVICES (OFCS)		
OCTOBER STATES	528	B	OFFICE OF FOREIGN DIRECT	507	B
OCTOBRISTS	173	A	INVESTMENTS (OFDI)		
OCTOPUS	823	B	OFFICE OF INDIAN AFFAIRS	179	A
OCTROI	656	B	OFFICE OF LAND UTILIZATION	507	B
ODDS	437	B	OFFICE OF LEND-LEASE	507	B
ODEGARD, PETER H.	722	B	ADMINISTRATION		
ODELSTING	528	B	OFFICE OF MANAGEMENT AND	151	A
ODER-NIESSE LINE	276	A	BUDGET (OMB)		
ODINGA, AJUMA OGINGA	698	B	OFFICE OF MINORITY BUSINESS	507	B
ODUM, HOWARD W.	761	B	ENTERPRISE		
OEDIPUS COMPLEX	140	A	OFFICE OF NAVAL INTELLIGENCE	179	A
OF THE PEOPLE, BY THE PEOPLE,	289	A	(ONI)		
AND FOR THE PEOPLE			OFFICE OF NAVAL RESEARCH (ONR)	179	A
OFF THE RECORD	290	A	OFFICE OF PRICE ADMINISTRATION	173	A
OFF THE RESERVATION	840	B	(OPA)		
OFF-SHORE PROCUREMENT	586	B	OFFICE OF PRICE STABILIZATION	173	A
OFF-YEAR ELECTION	201	A	OFFICE OF PRODUCTION	179	A
OFFENDER	188	A	MANAGEMENT (OPM)		
OFFENSE	256	A	OFFICE OF SALINE WATER	528	B
OFFENSIVE	256	A	OFFICE OF SCIENTIFIC RESEARCH	528	B
OFFENSIVE WAR	205	A	AND DEVELOPMENT		
OFFENSIVE WEAPONS	286	A	OFFICE OF STRATEGIC SERVICES	164	A
OFFER OF ANGLO-FRENCH UNION	635	B	(OSS)		
OFFICE	190	A	OFFICE OF TEMPORARY CONTROLS	528	B
OFFICE FOR PRODUCTION	489	B	OFFICE OF TERRITORIES	507	B
MANAGEMENT (OPM)			OFFICE OF THE DIRECTOR-GENERAL	179	A
OFFICE LAYOUT	795	B			

OFFICE OF THE HIGH COMMISSIONER	489	B
OFFICE OF THE HIGH COMMISSIONER FOR REFUGEES	489	B
OFFICE OF THE TREASURER OF THE U.S.	168	A
OFFICE OF UNITED NATIONS POLITICAL AFFAIRS	179	A
OFFICE OF WAR INFORMATION (OWI)	473	B
OFFICE OF WAR MOBILIZATION (OWM)	489	B
OFFICE OF WAR MOBILIZATION AND RECONVERSION (OWMR)	473	B
OFFICE OF WATER RESOURCES RESEARCH (OWRR)	528	B
OFFICE SEEKS THE MAN	834	B
OFFICE WORKERS	551	B
OFFICE-BLOCK BALLOT	230	A
OFFICE-COLUMN BALLOT	247	A
OFFICE-HOLDERS	185	A
OFFICER	190	A
OFFICIAL	193	A
OFFICIAL BULLETIN	807	B
OFFICIAL CAPACITY	238	A
OFFICIAL CEREMONY	586	B
OFFICIAL CHANNELS	143	A
OFFICIAL FAMILY	507	B
OFFICIAL GAZETTE	806	B
OFFICIAL JOURNAL OF THE EUROPEAN COMMUNITIES	810	B
OFFICIAL JOURNEY	656	B
OFFICIAL RECEPTION	635	B
OFFICIAL RELIGION	136	A
OFFICIAL REPORT	286	A
OFFICIAL RESIDENCES	791	B
OFFICIAL SUITE	799	B
OFFICIAL VISIT	586	B
OFFICIALESE	836	B
OFFSHORE ISLANDS	281	A
OFFSHORE OIL CONTROVERSY	215	A
OGADEN	799	B
OGBURN, WILLIAM F.	761	B
OGDEN, GLADYS	761	B
OGDENSBURG AGREEMENT	656	B
OGG, FREDERICK A.	761	B
OGLE, MARBURY B.	761	B
OHIO COMPANY	489	B
OHIO GANG	489	B
OHIO IDEA	451	B
OHIO RIVER VALLEY COMPACT	635	B
OHLIN, B.	761	B
OIL	286	A
OIL CORPORATIONS	160	A
OIL SCANDAL	586	B
OIL-DEPLETION ALLOWANCE	215	A
OIL, MIDDLE EAST	287	A
OJUKWU, LT.-COL. CHUKWUEMEKA ODUMEGWA	722	B
OKELLO-OCULI, JOSEPH	761	B
OKIES	179	A
OKINAWA	281	A
OKLAHOMA	281	A
OKLAHOMA VS. U.S. CIVIL SERVICE COMM. (1947)	679	B
OKUMA, COUNT	761	B
OLD ABE	272	A
OLD AGE AND SECURITY INSURANCE	238	A
OLD AGE AND SECURITY TRUST FUND	489	B
OLD AGE AND SURVIVORS INSURANCE (OASI)	230	A
OLD AGE ASSISTANCE	247	A
OLD BAILEY	818	B
OLD BULLION	762	B
OLD CHINA HANDS	193	A
OLD FOGY	566	B
OLD FUSS AND FEATHERS	722	B
OLD GLORY	291	A
OLD GUARD	173	A
OLD HICKORY	687	B
OLD LADY OF THREADNEEDLE STREET	762	B
OLD LAW TENEMENT	656	B
OLD LIBERAL	190	A
OLD LINE WHIG	528	B
OLD MAN ELOQUENT	762	B
OLD PEOPLE	558	B
OLD PRO	193	A
OLD PUBLIC FUNCTIONARY	566	B
OLD ROUGH-AND-READY	698	B
OLD SOLDIERS NEVER DIE	836	B
OLD TESTAMENT	286	A
OLD WHITE HAT	845	B
OLD WORLD	788	B
OLD-AGE, SURVIVORS, DISABILITY INSURANCE (OASDI)	164	A
OLDER AMERICANS ACT	609	B
OLDER NATIONS	489	B
OLDER WORKER	558	B
OLEOMARGARINE TAX	586	B
OLIGARCHIC	131	A
OLIGARCHY	144	A
OLIGOPOLY	147	A
OLIVE OIL	827	B
OLIVIER, N. J. J.	762	B
OLIVIER, SYDNEY	762	B
OLLENHAUER, ERICH	762	B
OLMSTEAD VS. U.S. (1928)	672	B
OLYMPIC	635	B
OMAN QUESTION	656	B
OMBUDSMAN	181	A

OMNIBUS BILL	230	A
OMNIBUS CRIME CONTROL ACT OF 1970	222	A
OMNIPOTENCE	445	B
ON LIBERTY	283	A
ON THE FENCE	290	A
ON THE FRONT	840	B
ON THE POINT	845	B
ON-THE-JOB TRAINING (OJT)	256	A
ONE AND INSEPARABLE	836	B
ONE GLASS OF WATER DOCTRINE	656	B
ONE HUNDRED PERCENT AMERICAN	836	B
ONE IDEA	457	B
ONE MAN POWER	635	B
ONE MAN, ONE VOTE	195	A
ONE THIRD OF A NATION	834	B
ONE WORLD	247	A
ONE-CHAMBER	168	A
ONE-MAN COMMAND	656	B
ONE-PARENT	566	B
ONE-PARTY PRESS	168	A
ONE-PARTY RULE	145	A
ONE-PARTY STATE	145	A
ONE-PARTY SYSTEM	113	A
ONGANIA, GENERAL JUAN CARLOS	762	B
ONTOLOGICAL PROOF	140	A
ONTOLOGY	126	A
OPEN BALLOT	222	A
OPEN CITY	788	B
OPEN CONVENTION	209	A
OPEN COVENANTS OPENLY ARRIVED AT	290	A
OPEN DIPLOMACY	222	A
OPEN DOOR POLICY	205	A
OPEN HOUSING	215	A
OPEN MARKET COMMITTEE	507	B
OPEN MARKET OPERATIONS	586	B
OPEN PERSONNEL SYSTEM	586	B
OPEN PRIMARY	196	A
OPEN SEA	281	A
OPEN SHOP	215	A
OPEN SKIES PROPOSAL	256	A
OPEN SOCIETY	149	A
OPEN SYSTEM	205	A
OPEN TOWN	791	B
OPEN TREATY	586	B
OPENING ADDRESS	247	A
OPENING CEREMONY	586	B
OPENING REMARKS	610	B
OPENING SITTING	635	B
OPERATION MAINSTREAM	657	B
OPERATIONAL DEFINITION	118	A
OPERATIONAL TEST IN POLITICS	140	A
OPERATIONALIZATION	119	A
OPERATIONS COORDINATING BOARD	529	B
OPERATIONS RESEARCH	128	A
OPERATIVE	544	B
OPERATIVE IDEALS	134	A
OPINION	119	A
OPINION ELITES, PUBLIC OPINION	146	A
OPINION LEADER	181	A
OPINION OF MANKIND	445	B
OPINION RESEARCH	118	A
OPINION, AS EVIDENCE	247	A
OPINIONS AND PERSONALITY	121	A
OPINIONS OF THE ATTORNEY GENERAL	286	A
OPIUM	820	B
OPIUM CONFERENCE	635	B
OPIUM PROTOCOL	635	B
OPIUM WARS	230	A
OPP COTTON MILLS VS. WAGE AND HOUR DIV (1941)	679	B
OPPENHEIM, FELIX E.	762	B
OPPENHEIM, PAUL	722	B
OPPENHEIMER, FRANZ	762	B
OPPONENT	185	A
OPPORTUNISM	143	A
OPPORTUNIST	544	B
OPPORTUNITY	137	A
OPPORTUNITY TO BE HEARD	256	A
OPPOSITES	445	B
OPPOSITION	151	A
OPPOSITION BENCH	275	A
OPPOSITION, ROLE OF (BRITAIN)	197	A
OPPRESSION	126	A
OPT	610	B
OPTANT	566	B
OPTATUS MILEVITANUS	762	B
OPTIMALITY	238	A
OPTIMISM	143	A
OPTION	238	A
OPTIONAL CHARTER PLAN	635	B
OPTIONAL CLAUSE	230	A
OPTIONAL PRIMARY	610	B
OPTIONAL REFERENDUM	247	A
OPUS DEI (WORK OF GOD)	256	A
ORAGE, A. R.	762	B
ORAL AGREEMENT	215	A
ORB	657	B
ORBITS	657	B
ORDAZ, DIAZ	762	B
ORDEAL	586	B
ORDER	209	A
ORDER IN COUNCIL	610	B
ORDER OF BRITISH EMPIRE (OBE)	489	B
ORDER OF BUSINESS	256	A
ORDER OF KNIGHTHOOD	489	B
ORDER OF KNIGHTS	529	B
ORDER OF MALTA (O.M.)	529	B
ORDER OF MERIT	507	B

ORDER OF PRECEDENCE	256	A	ORGANIZATION OF CENTRAL	168	A
ORDER OF ST. MICHAEL AND ST.	529	B	AMERICAN STATES (ODECA)		
GEORGE			ORGANIZATION OF INTER-AFRICAN	507	B
ORDER OF ST. PATRICK	529	B	AND MALAGASY STATES		
ORDER OF THE BATH	507	B	ORGANIZATION OF LATIN AMERICAN	507	B
ORDER OF THE GARTER	507	B	SOLIDARITY (OLAS)		
ORDER OF THE INDIAN EMPIRE	529	B	ORGANIZATION OF PETROLEUM	151	A
ORDER OF THE STAR OF INDIA	529	B	EXPORTING COUNTRIES (OPEC)		
ORDER OF THE THISTLE	529	B	ORGANIZATION THEORY	115	A
ORDER-GIVING	610	B	ORGANIZATIONAL CHANGE	121	A
ORDER-IN-COUNCIL	807	B	ORGANIZATIONAL CHARTS	284	A
ORDER, THEORY OF	140	A	ORGANIZATIONAL CONFLICT	121	A
ORDERING	140	A	ORGANIZATIONAL GOAL	116	A
ORDINAL	126	A	ORGANIZATIONAL PROBLEMS	222	A
ORDINAL SCALE	120	A	ORGANIZATIONAL STYLES	128	A
ORDINANCE	222	A	ORGANIZATIONAL TECHNOLOGY	437	B
ORDINANCE POWER	610	B	ORGANIZED INTEREST	149	A
ORDINARY BUDGET	256	A	ORGANIZED LABOR	149	A
ORDINARY DIPLOMATIC CHANNELS	222	A	ORGANIZED RESERVES	473	B
ORDINARY LANGUAGE	437	B	ORGANIZED TERRITORY	281	A
ORDINARY SESSION	230	A	ORGANIZING COMMITTEE	179	A
ORDINARY TREATY	635	B	ORGBUREAU (U.S.S.R.)	474	B
ORDONEZ, JOSE BATTLE Y	722	B	ORIENTAL	544	A
OREGON	283	A	ORIENTAL DESPOTISM	186	A
ORGAN	489	B	ORIENTAL IMMIGRATION	238	A
ORGAN-GRINDER (-EDITOR)	566	B	ORIENTAL SOCIETY	507	B
ORGANIC ACT	256	A	ORIENTALS , EXCLUSION OF	215	A
ORGANIC CONCEPTION OF THE	126	A	ORIENTATION	143	A
STATE			ORIGIN	586	B
ORGANIC DOCUMENT	806	B	ORIGINAL COST THEORY OF RATE	610	B
ORGANIC LAW	222	A	MAKING		
ORGANIC THEORY OF THE STATE	116	A	ORIGINAL JURISDICTION OF COURTS	209	A
ORGANISATION COMMUNE	529	B	ORIGINAL MEMBERSHIP, UNITED	179	A
AFRICAINE ET MALGACHE (OCAM)			NATIONS		
ORGANISM	288	A	ORIGINAL PACKAGE DOCTRINE	635	B
ORGANIZATION	151	A	ORIGINAL SIN	137	A
ORGANIZATION AND	134	A	ORIGINAL STATES	474	B
ADMINISTRATIVE RELATIONSHIPS			ORIGINALITY	657	B
ORGANIZATION AND METHODS	160	A	ORISSA, INDIA	799	B
ORGANIZATION ARMEE SECRETE	529	B	ORLANDO, VITTORIO EMANUELE	698	B
ORGANIZATION BEHAVIOR	120	A	ORPHANS	558	B
ORGANIZATION DEVELOPMENT	230	A	ORPHIC CULT	529	B
ORGANIZATION FOR ECONOMIC	173	A	ORPHISM	457	B
COOPERATION AND			ORTEGA	762	B
DEVELOPMENT (OECD)			ORTEGA Y GASSET, JOSE	272	A
ORGANIZATION FOR EUROPEAN	160	A	ORTHOCEPHALY	657	B
ECONOMIC COOPERATION (OEEC)			ORTHODOX CHURCH	474	B
ORGANIZATION FOR THE	529	B	ORTHODOX SOCIALISTS	168	A
COLLABORATION OF RAILWAYS			ORTHODOXY	131	A
ORGANIZATION FOR TRADE	529	B	ORTHOTONIC POLITIES	529	B
COOPERATION			ORWELL, GEORGE	265	A
ORGANIZATION OF AFRICAN UNITY	160	A	OSBORN, HENRY FAIRFIELD	762	B
(OAU)			OSGOOD, ROBERT E.	722	B
ORGANIZATION OF AMERICAN	151	A	OSHRY, BARRY	762	B
STATES (OAS)			OSLO BLOCK	529	B
			OSLO CONVENTION	657	B

OSSEWABRANDWAG	529	B
OSTEND MANIFESTO	806	B
OSTENTIVE DEFINITIONS	437	B
OSTERHOLM, JOHN EMIL	762	B
OSTRACISM	610	B
OSTRICH POLICY	635	B
OSTROGORSKI, M.	687	B
OSWALD, LEE HARVEY	268	A
OTHER	451	B
OTHER BODY	489	B
OTHER WAR	635	B
OTHER-DIRECTED TYPES	188	A
OTIS, JAMES	762	B
OTTAWA AGREEMENTS	635	B
OTTO I, EMPEROR	762	B
OTTOMAN EMPIRE	164	A
OTTOMANISM	451	B
OUAGADOUGOU, UPPER VOLTA	799	B
OUBANGUI-CHARI	529	B
OUGHT	137	A
OUR FEDERAL UNION , IT MUST BE PRESERVED	836	B
OUT OF CONTEXT	137	A
OUT PARTY	168	A
OUT-OF-COURT SETTLEMENT	222	A
OUTBREAK	610	B
OUTBURST	657	B
OUTCASTS	558	B
OUTCOME	230	A
OUTDOOR RELIEF	635	B
OUTER CONTINENTAL SHELF ACT	610	B
OUTER SEVEN (EFTA)	173	A
OUTER SPACE AND INTERNATIONAL LAW	230	A
OUTER SPACE TREATY	247	A
OUTER SPACE, JURISDICTION	239	A
OUTER-DEPARTMENTAL	529	B
OUTGOING MEMBERS	551	B
OUTLAW	544	B
OUTLAWING OF THE ATOMIC BOMB	239	A
OUTLAWRY OF WAR	230	A
OUTLET TO THE SEA	276	A
OUTPUTS	124	A
OUTRAGE BUSINESS (OUTRAGE MILL)	840	B
OUTSIDE VOTER	566	B
OUTSIDERS	566	B
OUTSTATE	791	B
OUTVOTE	610	B
OVAL OFFICE	275	A
OVER-FULL EMPLOYMENT	635	B
OVERCENTRALIZATION	239	A
OVERCOME	840	B
OVEREXPOSURE	635	B
OVERHEAD ORGANIZATION	474	B
OVERHEATED ECONOMY	209	A
OVERKILL	215	A
OVERLAPPING WITH OTHER MEETINGS	635	B
OVERLOAD	610	B
OVERPOPULATION	205	A
OVERREACT	248	A
OVERRIDE	248	A
OVERRULING	222	A
OVERRULING, INDIRECT	248	A
OVERSEAS	788	B
OVERSEAS CHINESE	164	A
OVERSEAS COUNTRIES	507	B
OVERSEAS DEPARTMENT	529	B
OVERSEAS FOOD CORPORATION (BRITAIN)	507	B
OVERSEAS MANAGEMENT	489	B
OVERSEAS PERSONNEL	551	B
OVERSEAS POSSESSIONS	281	A
OVERSEAS PRIVATE INVESTMENT CORPORATION (OPIC)	489	B
OVERSEAS TERRITORIES	281	A
OVERSEERS	558	B
OVERSIGHT	230	A
OVERT ACT	257	A
OVERTHROW OF A GOVERNMENT	205	A
OVERTHROW OF A REGIME	201	A
OVERTIME PAY	586	B
OVERTIME WORK	586	B
OVERTON, RICHARD	762	B
OVERVIEW	610	B
OVERWHELMING MAJORITY	239	A
OWEN, ROBERT	698	B
OWENITES	489	B
OWING	635	B
OWNERSHIP	248	A
OX-WAGONS, MEROVINGIAN	827	B
OXFORD IDEALISTS	507	B
OXFORD MOVEMENT	507	B
OXFORD SCHOOL OF MODERN HISTORY	529	B
OXYMORON	566	B
OYER AND TERMINER	529	B
PAASIKIVI, JUHO KUSTI	762	B
PACELLI, CARDINAL	762	B
PACIFIC	789	B
PACIFIC AREA TRAVEL ASSOCIATION (PATA)	529	B
PACIFIC BLOCKADE	239	A
PACIFIC ISLAND TRUST TERRITORY	283	A
PACIFIC ISLANDS	283	A
PACIFIC SECURITY PACT	257	A
PACIFIC SETTLEMENT OF INTERNATIONAL DISPUTES	230	A
PACIFIC STATES TELEPHONE AND TELEGRAPH CO. VS. OREGON (1912)	679	B

PACIFIC WAR COUNCIL	507	B
PACIFICATION	209	A
PACIFISM	116	A
PACIFY	239	A
PACK	657	B
PACKAGE DEAL	248	A
PACKED CAUCUS	168	A
PACKENHAM, ROBERT	762	B
PACKING OF THE U.S. SUPREME COURT	209	A
PACKING THE GALLERIES	291	A
PACKWOOD, ROBERT W.	762	B
PACT	222	A
PACT DE CONTRAHENDO	657	B
PACT OF CORFU	257	A
PACT OF LONDON (1915)	635	B
PACT OF PARIS (KELLOGG-BRIAND PACT)	239	A
PACT OF ROME	586	B
PACT OF SAAD-ABAD	657	B
PACT OF WASHINGTON	635	B
PACTA SUNT SERVANDA	586	B
PADEREWSKI, IGNACY JAN	762	B
PADMORE, GEORGE	762	B
PAEPE, CESAR DE	762	B
PAGE BOYS	551	B
PAHLAVI, MOHAMMED REZA SHAH	272	A
PAIN	438	B
PAINE, THOMAS	262	A
PAINI, GIOVANNI	762	B
PAINS AND PENALTIES, BILL OF	657	B
PAINTING	827	B
PAIR	179	A
PAIRING	222	A
PAISLEY, REV. IAN	698	B
PAKHTUNISTAN	799	B
PAKISTAN	281	A
PAKO VS. CONNECTICUT (1937)	675	B
PALACE	823	B
PALACE GUARD	168	A
PALACE REVOLUTION	205	A
PALACKY, FRANTISEK	763	B
PALAZZO VENEZIA	827	B
PALESTINE	274	A
PALESTINE LIBERATION ORGANIZATION (PLO)	149	A
PALESTINE MANDATE	230	A
PALESTINE REFUGEES	153	A
PALESTINIANS	151	A
PALEY	698	B
PALLBEARER	566	B
PALM OIL	827	B
PALMACH	529	B
PALME, OLAF	687	B
PALMERSTON, LORD	722	B
PAN AFRICAN FREEDOM MOVEMENT	507	B
PAN-AFRICAN CONGRESS	164	A
PAN-AFRICANDERDOM	529	B
PAN-AFRICANISM	131	A
PAN-AFRICANIST CONGRESS	490	B
PAN-AMERICAN CONFERENCES	610	B
PAN-AMERICAN DEFENSE BOARD	507	B
PAN-AMERICAN HEALTH ORGANIZATION (PAHO)	507	B
PAN-AMERICAN HIGHWAY	279	A
PAN-AMERICAN INSTITUTE OF GEOGRAPHY AND HISTORY (PAIGH)	529	B
PAN-AMERICAN SANITARY ORGANIZATION	529	B
PAN-AMERICAN UNION	156	A
PAN-AMERICANISM	128	A
PAN-ARABIC MOVEMENT	164	A
PAN-ARABISM	131	A
PAN-ASIATISM	438	B
PAN-ETHICISM	457	B
PAN-EUROPA UNION	490	B
PAN-EUROPEAN	248	A
PAN-GERMANISM	140	A
PAN-IBERIANISM	438	B
PAN-ISLAMISM	134	A
PAN-SLAVISM	134	A
PANACEA	230	A
PANAETIUS OF RHODES	722	B
PANAMA	281	A
PANAMA CANAL	275	A
PANAMA CANAL COMPANY	474	B
PANAMA CANAL ZONE	274	A
PANAMA CANAL ZONE AGREEMENT	248	A
PANAMA CONGRESS	635	B
PANAMA REFINING CO. VS. RYAN (1935)	679	B
PANAY INCIDENT	635	B
PANCH SHILA	635	B
PANCHAYAT	179	A
PANCHEN LAMA	698	B
PANDIT, VIJAYA LAKSHMI	763	B
PANEL	179	A
PANEL MEETING	610	B
PANEL STUDY	137	A
PANHELLENIC LEAGUE	474	B
PANIC	586	B
PANIC OF 1819	586	B
PANIC SESSION	636	B
PANMUNJON TRUCE	248	A
PANTHEISM	140	A
PANTHER	474	B
PANUNZIO, S.	763	B
PAP	846	B
PAPACY	186	A
PAPACY, MEDIAEVAL	474	B
PAPADOPOULOS, GEORGE	272	A

PAPAL LEGATE AND NUNCIO	190	A
PAPAL STATES	279	A
PAPANDREOU, ANDREAS	688	B
PAPANDREOU, GEORGE	272	A
PAPEN, FRANZ VON	698	B
PAPER BLOCKADE	586	B
PAPER MONEY	288	A
PAPER TIGER	290	A
PAPUA-NEW GUINEA	789	B
PARADE	610	B
PARADIGM	114	A
PARADIGMS, AND CONCEPTUAL SCHEMES	113	A
PARADOX	137	A
PARAGUAY	283	A
PARALYZED	657	B
PARAMETERS	124	A
PARAMETRIC STUDIES	445	B
PARAMOUNT ISSUE	636	B
PARAPOLITICAL	451	B
PARAPROFESSIONALS	188	A
PARAPSYCHOLOGY	143	A
PARASCIENCE	451	B
PARCEL POST	636	B
PARDO, JOSE	763	B
PARDON	230	A
PARDONING POWER	201	A
PARDONS AND REPRIEVES	205	A
PARENTS	544	B
PARETO OPTIMUM	438	B
PARETO, VILFREDO	266	A
PARIAH	193	A
PARIS	283	A
PARIS COMMUNE	164	A
PARIS PEACE CONFERENCE	222	A
PARIS PEACE TALKS, 1968-1971	222	A
PARIS PROTOCOL	636	B
PARIS TREATY, ECSC (1952)	586	B
PARISH	795	B
PARITY	205	A
PARITY CLAUSE	586	B
PARITY PRICE	239	A
PARK CHUNG HEE, GENERAL	266	A
PARK-BENCH ORATOR	566	B
PARK, ROBERT E.	763	B
PARKER, GEORGE H.	763	B
PARKING LOT	799	B
PARKINSON, C. NORTHCOTE	270	A
PARKINSON, R.	722	B
PARKS AND RECREATION	795	B
PARLAMENTAIRE	566	B
PARLEMENT OF PARIS	507	B
PARLIAMENT	145	A
PARLIAMENT ACTS, 1911 AND 1949	257	A
PARLIAMENT, BRITISH	147	A
PARLIAMENTARIAN	183	A
PARLIAMENTARIANISM	118	A
PARLIAMENTARY COMMISSIONER FOR THE ADMINISTRATION	566	B
PARLIAMENTARY COMMITTEE	164	A
PARLIAMENTARY CONTROL	209	A
PARLIAMENTARY COUNCIL	474	B
PARLIAMENTARY DEBATE	205	A
PARLIAMENTARY DEPUTY	193	A
PARLIAMENTARY DIPLOMACY	230	A
PARLIAMENTARY ELECTIONS	197	A
PARLIAMENTARY FLAG	827	B
PARLIAMENTARY GOVERNMENT	145	A
PARLIAMENTARY GROUP	164	A
PARLIAMENTARY INVESTIGATIONS	248	A
PARLIAMENTARY LABOUR PARTY (PLP - BRITAIN)	490	B
PARLIAMENTARY LAW	215	A
PARLIAMENTARY LEADER OF A PARTY	185	A
PARLIAMENTARY PARTY, BRITAIN	156	A
PARLIAMENTARY PRIVILEGE	239	A
PARLIAMENTARY PROCEDURE	199	A
PARLIAMENTARY PROCESSES	115	A
PARLIAMENTARY RECESS	257	A
PARLIAMENTARY REGIME	147	A
PARLIAMENTARY SYSTEM	113	A
PARLIAMENTARY UNDERSECRETARY	544	B
PARLIAMENTS, LATE MEDIAEVAL	474	B
PARLOR BOLSHEVIST	551	B
PARLOR CAUCUS	657	B
PARLOR PINK	544	B
PARLOR SOCIALIST	551	B
PARMONIDES	763	B
PAROCHIAL SCHOOL	179	A
PAROLE	248	A
PARRI	763	B
PARSONS, FRANK	722	B
PARSONS, TALCOTT	264	A
PART	289	A
PART-TIME WORK	257	A
PARTEITAG	636	B
PARTI REPUBLICAIN DE LA LIBERTE (PRL)	529	B
PARTI REPUBLICAIN RADICAL ET RADICAL SOCIALISTE	530	B
PARTI SOCIALISTE UNIFIE	530	B
PARTIAL AGREEMENT	610	B
PARTIAL CORRELATION	124	A
PARTIAL MOBILIZATION	239	A
PARTIAL SUCCESSION	610	B
PARTIAL TEST BAN TREATY (1963)	239	A
PARTIAL THEORY	137	A
PARTIAL VETO	586	B
PARTIAL WAR	586	B
PARTIAL-SYSTEM ANALYSIS	438	B
PARTICIPANT	188	A

PARTICIPANT OBSERVATION	124	A	PARTY TRUCE	636	B
PARTICIPATING GOVERNMENTS	168	A	PARTY UNITY	199	A
PARTICIPATING STATES	168	A	PARTY WHIP	181	A
PARTICIPATION (OF CITIZENS IN GOVERNMENT)	120	A	PARTY-COLUMN BALLOT	215	A
			PARTY-LIST SYSTEM	209	A
PARTICIPATORY DEMOCRACY	144	A	PARTYISM	451	B
PARTICULARISM	134	A	PASCAL, BLAISE	698	B
PARTICULARS	810	B	PASCHAL II, POPE	763	B
PARTIES TO A DISPUTE	190	A	PASHA	558	B
PARTISAN	181	A	PASS	636	B
PARTISAN LOYALTIES	131	A	PASS EXAMINATION	610	B
PARTISAN MOVEMENT	168	A	PASSAGE OF A BILL INTO LAW	196	A
PARTISANSHIP	197	A	PASSIN, HERBERT	763	B
PARTITION	215	A	PASSING	657	B
PARTITION OF PALESTINE	222	A	PASSING A DIVIDEND	657	B
PARTITIONS OF POLAND	257	A	PASSION	451	B
PARTNER AT TABLE	566	B	PASSION FOR ANONYMITY	257	A
PARTNER IN A NEGOTIATION	566	B	PASSIVE AIR DEFENSE	657	B
PARTNERSHIP	507	B	PASSIVE OBEDIENCE	239	A
PARTY	145	A	PASSIVE RESISTANCE	205	A
PARTY AFFILIATION TESTS	215	A	PASSPORT	285	A
PARTY BADGE	827	B	PASSPORTS AND VISAS	284	A
PARTY BOSS	183	A	PAST	137	A
PARTY CELL	153	A	PASTER	827	B
PARTY CHIEFS	190	A	PASTERNAK, BORIS	688	B
PARTY CIRCLE	179	A	PASTEUR	722	B
PARTY COMMITTEE	168	A	PASTON LETTERS	812	B
PARTY COMPETITION	131	A	PASTORE, JOHN O.	698	B
PARTY CONFERENCE	215	A	PATANJALI	763	B
PARTY CONGRESS	215	A	PATENT	586	A
PARTY CONVENTION	147	A	PATENT OF NOBILITY	657	B
PARTY DESIGNATION	288	A	PATENT OFFICE	173	A
PARTY DISCIPLINE	115	A	PATERNALISM	445	B
PARTY ELDERS	190	A	PATHET-LAO	160	A
PARTY EMBLEM	288	A	PATHFINDER	810	B
PARTY FAITHFUL	186	A	PATHOLOGY	451	B
PARTY FINANCE	230	A	PATHOS	438	B
PARTY GOVERNMENT, BRITAIN	151	A	PATON, GEORGE,	688	B
PARTY IDENTIFIERS	126	A	PATRASCANU, L.	763	B
PARTY IN POWER	164	A	PATRIARCH	188	A
PARTY LEADERSHIP	181	A	PATRIARCHATE	530	B
PARTY LINE	124	A	PATRIARCHY	149	A
PARTY LOYALTY	120	A	PATRIMONIAL	551	B
PARTY OF PRIVILEGE	474	B	PATRIMONIALISM	438	B
PARTY OF THE PEOPLE	173	A	PATRIOT	190	A
PARTY OFFICIALS	184	A	PATRIOTISM	120	A
PARTY ORGAN	168	A	PATRISTIC OUTLOOK	457	B
PARTY ORGANIZATION	149	A	PATROLMAN	193	A
PARTY ORTHODOXY	128	A	PATRON	551	B
PARTY PLATFORM	209	A	PATRONAGE	201	A
PARTY PRIMARY	199	A	PATRONAGE SYSTEM	196	A
PARTY RALLY	230	A	PATRONAGE, COMMITTEE ON	490	B
PARTY SQUARE	566	B	PATRONS OF HUSBANDRY	507	B
PARTY SYSTEM	116	A	PATTERN	134	A
PARTY SYSTEMS AND VOTER ALIGNMENTS	118	A	PATTERN MAINTENANCE	126	A
			PATTERNS OF CULTURE	121	A

PATTERNS OF POWER	121	A
PATTERSON PLAN	636	B
PATTERSON, CALEB PERRY	763	B
PATTISON, MARK	763	B
PATUAD, EMILE	763	B
PAUKER, ANA	763	B
PAUL	722	B
PAUL-BONCOUR, JOSEPH	763	B
PAUL, APOSTLE	688	B
PAUL, WILLIAM	763	B
PAULINUS	763	B
PAULUS, FRIEDRICH VON	763	B
PAUPER	544	B
PAUPER'S OATH	610	B
PAVELIC, ANTE	763	B
PAVLOV, IVAN	270	A
PAX	248	A
PAX AMERICANA	222	A
PAX BRITANNICA	209	A
PAX CHRISTI	257	A
PAX ROMANA	209	A
PAX SOVIETICA	586	B
PAY	636	B
PAY AFTER STOPPAGES	657	B
PAY AS YOU GO	257	A
PAY BEFORE STOPPAGES	657	B
PAY ROLL TAX (SOCIAL SECURITY ACT)	239	A
PAY SCALE	248	A
PAY-AS-YOU-GO TAXATION	222	A
PAY-ROLL PATRIOT	551	B
PAYMENTS AGREEMENT	636	B
PAYNE-ALDRICH TARIFF	636	B
PAYOFF	239	A
PAYOFF FUNCTION	140	A
PAYROLL PROCEDURE	636	B
PAZ ESTENSSORO, VICTOR	722	B
PEACE	201	A
PEACE AT ANY PRICE	290	A
PEACE BALLOT	586	B
PEACE BLOC	168	A
PEACE CONFERENCE	222	A
PEACE CONFERENCE OF 1919	257	A
PEACE CORPS (U.S.)	147	A
PEACE CORPS EMPLOYEES	193	A
PEACE DEMOCRAT	179	A
PEACE GROUPS	164	A
PEACE IN OUR TIME	290	A
PEACE MOVEMENT	151	A
PEACE NEGOTIATIONS	209	A
PEACE OBSERVATION COMMITTEE	168	A
PEACE OF AUGSBERG	636	B
PEACE OF THE PORT	657	B
PEACE OF THE PYRENEES	636	B
PEACE OF WESTPHALIA	230	A
PEACE OFFENSIVE	239	A
PEACE OFFER	248	A
PEACE OVERTURE	230	A
PEACE PALACE	795	B
PEACE PRELIMINARIES	636	B
PEACE RESEARCH	126	A
PEACE SCARE	657	B
PEACE TREATY	205	A
PEACE WITH HONOR	290	A
PEACE WITHOUT VICTORY	834	B
PEACE-FEELERS	209	A
PEACE-KEEPING	201	A
PEACE-KEEPING OPERATIONS OF THE UN	205	A
PEACE-LOVING PEOPLES	179	A
PEACE, ORDER, AND GOOD GOVERNMENT	840	B
PEACEFUL CHANGE	121	A
PEACEFUL CO-EXISTENCE	197	A
PEACEFUL COMMUNICATION	587	B
PEACEFUL OCCUPATION	248	A
PEACEFUL PENETRATION	587	B
PEACEFUL RELATIONS	230	A
PEACEFUL SPACE EXPLORATION	248	A
PEACEFUL USES OF ATOMIC ENERGY	222	A
PEACEFUL USES OF OUTER SPACE	222	A
PEACENIK	190	A
PEACETIME BLOCKADE	222	A
PEAKING	587	B
PEANUT POLITICIAN	566	B
PEANUT POLITICS	846	B
PEAR, T.H.	763	B
PEARL HARBOR	273	A
PEARL, RAYMOND	763	B
PEARL, STANLEY	763	B
PEARSON, JAMES BLACKWOOD	763	B
PEARSON, KARL	722	B
PEARSON, LESTER	698	B
PEASANT	185	A
PEASANT REVOLTS	222	A
PEASANTRY	160	A
PECCANCY	657	B
PECKING ORDER	134	A
PECOCK, BISHOP	763	B
PECULATION	657	B
PECULIAR INSTITUTION	490	B
PEDAGOGY	438	B
PEDDLERS	566	B
PEDICIDE	657	B
PEDRO II, DOM (BRAGANCA DUCHY)	763	B
PEEL, ROY	722	B
PEELED STICK CONVENTION	657	B
PEER	183	A
PEER GROUP	145	A
PEERAGE	185	A
PEERLESS LEADER	722	B

PEGUY, C.	764	B
PEICK, WILHELM	764	B
PEIPING	283	A
PEIPLE'S COMMISSAR	551	B
PEIRCE	764	B
PEKINGOLOGIST	190	A
PELL, CLAIBORNE	722	B
PELLA, GIUSEPPE	764	B
PELLOUTIER	764	B
PELOPONNESIAN WAR	239	A
PELTASON, JACK W.	698	B
PENAL	248	A
PENAL ADMINISTRATION	168	A
PENAL COLONY	490	B
PENAL LAW	248	A
PENALTY	239	A
PENALTY WAGE RATES	657	B
PENDENCY	657	B
PENDING APPLICATIONS	636	B
PENDING PROBLEMS	658	B
PENDING PROCEEDINGS	610	B
PENDLETON	722	B
PENDLETON CIVIL SERVICE ACT OF 1883	222	A
PENINSULARES	566	B
PENN, WILLIAM	268	A
PENNANT	827	B
PENNIMAN, HOWARD	764	B
PENNOCK, J. ROLAND	722	B
PENNSYLVANIA SYSTEM	610	B
PENNSYLVANIA VS. NELSON (1956)	675	B
PENOLOGY	140	A
PENSION	257	A
PENTAGON	286	A
PENTAGON PAPERS	283	A
PENTAGONESE	836	B
PENTATEUCH	810	B
PENTY, A. J.	764	B
PEON	186	A
PEONAGE	257	A
PEOPLE	179	A
PEOPLE'S ACTION PARTY OF SINGAPORE	530	B
PEOPLE'S ASSEMBLY	179	A
PEOPLE'S CAPITALISM	143	A
PEOPLE'S CHAMBER	507	B
PEOPLE'S COMMISSARIAT OF INTERNAL AFFAIRS (USSR) (N.K.V.D.)	153	A
PEOPLE'S COMMISSARIAT OF STATE SECURITY (USSR) (N.K.G.B.)	173	A
PEOPLE'S COMMUNES	173	A
PEOPLE'S COUNCIL	179	A
PEOPLE'S COURT	160	A
PEOPLE'S DEMOCRACIES	149	A
PEOPLE'S DEMOCRACY	149	A
PEOPLE'S LIBERATION ARMY (PLA)	156	A
PEOPLE'S LOBBY	164	A
PEOPLE'S PARTY	164	A
PEOPLE'S PARTY OF ITALY	530	B
PEOPLE'S POWER LEAGUE	530	B
PEOPLE'S REPUBLIC OF CHINA (PRC)	149	A
PEOPLE'S REVOLUTION	215	A
PEOPLE'S TICKET	508	B
PEOPLE'S UNION	530	B
PEOPLE'S WAR	239	A
PEPIN	764	B
PEPPER AND SALT	827	B
PER CAPITA	137	A
PER CURIAM OPINION	239	A
PERCEIVE	137	A
PERCEIVED ALTERNATIVES	128	A
PERCEIVING	140	A
PERCENTAGE	140	A
PERCEPTION	124	A
PERCEPTUAL	438	B
PERCIPITANTS	445	B
PERCY, CHARLES HARTING	272	A
PERDITION	799	B
PEREMPTORY CHALLENGE	215	A
PERENNIAL CANDIDATE	188	A
PEREZ JIMINEZ, COLONEL MARCOS	722	B
PEREZ VS. BROWNELL (1958)	679	B
PERFECTION	451	B
PERFORM	587	B
PERFORMANCE	248	A
PERFORMANCE BUDGET	239	A
PERFORMANCE CONTRACTING	257	A
PERFORMANCE EVALUATION	215	A
PERFORMANCE TEST	257	A
PERFORMING ARTS	457	B
PERICLES	270	A
PERIL POINT (U.S. TARIFF)	658	B
PERIODIC REGISTRATION	222	A
PERIODICAL DIRECTORIES	807	B
PERIODICAL INDEXES	806	B
PERIODICALS	806	B
PERIPHERAL STATE	283	A
PERISHING	658	B
PERJURY	209	A
PERMANENT APPOINTMENT	230	A
PERMANENT APPROPRIATION	239	A
PERMANENT CENTRAL NARCOTICS BOARD	508	B
PERMANENT CENTRAL OPIUM BOARD	530	B
PERMANENT COMMITTEE	156	A
PERMANENT COUNCIL	179	A
PERMANENT COURT OF ARBITRATION	474	B

PERMANENT COURT OF INTERNATIONAL JUSTICE (HAGUE)	164	A	PERSONAL PREFERENCE	451	B
			PERSONAL PROPERTY	288	A
PERMANENT CUMULATIVE RECORD	810	B	PERSONAL PROPERTY TAX	239	A
PERMANENT DELEGATE	186	A	PERSONAL SOVEREIGNTY	451	B
PERMANENT DIPLOMACY	636	B	PERSONAL STATEMENT	143	A
PERMANENT JOINT BOARD ON DEFENSE	508	B	PERSONAL UNION	658	B
			PERSONALISMO	140	A
PERMANENT MANDATES COMMISSION (LEAGUE OF NATIONS)	474	B	PERSONALITY	134	A
			PERSONALITY CULT	153	A
			PERSONALITY DEVELOPMENT	222	A
PERMANENT MEMBER	184	A	PERSONALITY TESTS	239	A
PERMANENT MISSION	168	A	PERSONALITY TRAITS	137	A
PERMANENT NEUTRALITY	230	A	PERSONALIZATION OF POWER	128	A
PERMANENT OFFICE	552	B	PERSONALLY OBNOXIOUS	445	B
PERMANENT REGISTRATION	209	A	PERSONATION	508	B
PERMANENT REPRESENTATIVE	186	A	PERSONNEL	186	A
PERMANENT REVOLUTION	209	A	PERSONNEL ADMINISTRATION	156	A
PERMANENT SECRETARIAT	173	A	PERSONNEL DEPARTMENTS	179	A
PERMANENT STAFF	188	A	PERSONNEL DIRECTORS	545	B
PERMANENT UNDER-SECRETARY OF STATE, BRITAIN	545	B	PERSONNEL DIVISION	490	B
			PERSONNEL INTERCHANGE	451	B
PERMANENT VISA	284	A	PERSONNEL OFFICE	474	B
PERMISSION	257	A	PERSONNEL OFFICERS	545	B
PERMISSIVE POWERS OF CONGRESS	222	A	PERSONNEL RECORDS	285	A
			PERSONNEL RESEARCH	140	A
PERMISSIVENESS	143	A	PERSONNEL UTILIZATION	636	B
PERMIT	289	A	PERSPECTIVE	438	B
PERON, JUAN DOMINGO	264	A	PERSUASION	128	A
PERONISM	126	A	PERSUASION DEFINITION	438	B
PERORATION	636	B	PERSUASIVE AUTHORITY	190	A
PERPETUAL NEUTRALITY	610	B	PERTAINING TO A COUNT	658	B
PERQUISITES	239	A	PERTICONE, G.	764	B
PERROT	764	B	PERU	277	A
PERRY VS. U.S. (1935)	673	B	PESSIMISM	445	B
PERRY, MATTHEW GALBRAITH	722	B	PESTALOZEI	764	B
PERSIAN GULF	277	A	PESTICIDES AMENDMENT OF 1954	658	B
PERSIAN GULF STATES	277	A	PETAIN, HENRI PHILIPPE	272	A
PERSIMMON	827	B	PETER CRASSUS	764	B
PERSISTENCE	610	B	PETER FUNK	566	B
PERSON	190	A	PETER I, THE GREAT	272	A
PERSON OPTING	636	B	PETER, KING	764	B
PERSONA	552	B	PETERS, R.S.	764	B
PERSONA GRATA	190	A	PETIT JURY	164	A
PERSONA NON GRATA	185	A	PETITION	222	A
PERSONAL COMPETENCE	445	B	PETITION JOBBING	636	B
PERSONAL DATA AND TESTIMONIALS	610	B	PETITION OF NATURALIZATION	636	B
			PETITION OF RIGHT	239	A
PERSONAL DEVELOPMENT	610	B	PETITIONERS	188	A
PERSONAL FILE	806	B	PETKOV, N.	764	B
PERSONAL GOVERNMENT	490	B	PETOFI CIRCLE	530	B
PERSONAL IMMUNITY	239	A	PETRARCH, FRANCESCO	688	B
PERSONAL INVIOLABILITY	239	A	PETROGRAD SOVIET	179	A
PERSONAL JURISDICTION	636	B	PETROLEUM	288	A
PERSONAL LIBERTY	197	A	PETROLEUM ADMINSITRATION FOR WAR (U.S.)	530	B
PERSONAL POLITICS, PERIOD OF	610	B			
PERSONAL POSITION	552	B	PETROLEUM RESOURCES	287	A

PETROLEUM, OIL AND LUBRICANTS (POL)	823	B
PETRONIUS	764	B
PETTICOAT	827	B
PETTY BOURGEOISIE	156	A
PETTY OFFENSE	248	A
PEWTER MUGGERS	530	B
PFIFFNER, JOHN	723	B
PFLIMLIN, PIERRE	764	B
PHALANX	490	B
PHANTOM COINAGE	658	B
PHARISEE (PHARISAICAL)	490	B
PHARMACEUTICALS	827	B
PHATIC-ACT	658	B
PHENOMENALISM	131	A
PHENOMENOLOGY	121	A
PHENOMENON	126	A
PHILADELPHIA CHARTER	587	B
PHILADELPHIA CONVENTION OF 1787	201	A
PHILANTHROPY	248	A
PHILIP II OF SPAIN	698	B
PHILIP OF MACEDON	698	B
PHILIP THE FAIR OF FRANCE	764	B
PHILIP, ANDRE	764	B
PHILIPPIC	658	B
PHILIPPINE INDEPENDENCE ACT	587	B
PHILIPPINES	281	A
PHILLIPS, WENDELL	698	B
PHILO JUDAEUS	764	B
PHILOLOGY	445	B
PHILONISM	458	B
PHILOSOPHER	185	A
PHILOSOPHER-KING	181	A
PHILOSOPHES	179	A
PHILOSOPHICAL ANTHROPOLOGY	445	B
PHILOSOPHICAL JURISPRUDENCE	446	B
PHILOSOPHICAL METHOD	143	A
PHILOSOPHICAL RADICALISM	137	A
PHILOSOPHICO-LEGAL METHOD	140	A
PHILOSOPHY	126	A
PHILOSOPHY OF HISTORY	134	A
PHILOSOPHY OF LAW	126	A
PHILOSOPHY OF SCIENCE	118	A
PHILOSOPHY OF THE STATE	131	A
PHOBIA	137	A
PHONY WAR	587	B
PHOSPHATES	827	B
PHOSPHORUS MATCH TAX	636	B
PHOTOGRAPHY	658	B
PHOTOSTATIC COPIES	810	B
PHRASEMAKER	552	B
PHYSICAL SCIENCE	438	B
PHYSICALISM	458	B
PHYSICIANS	558	B
PHYSICS	458	B
PHYSIOCRATS	474	B
PHYSIOLOGY	446	B
PIAGET, JEAN	270	A
PIASECKI	764	B
PIBUL SONGGRAM	764	B
PICK (THE) FLINT	846	B
PICKET	239	A
PICKETING	230	A
PICTURE-THEORY	451	B
PICTURING	636	B
PIE	827	B
PIE COUNTER	846	B
PIE FOUNDRY	846	B
PIEBALD TICKET	508	B
PIECE RATE	611	B
PIECK, WILHELM	764	B
PIERCE, CHARLES S.	723	B
PIERCE, PRESIDENT FRANKLIN	268	A
PIERRE, ABBE DE ST.	723	B
PIETISTS	530	B
PIETY	446	B
PIG IRON	827	B
PIGEONHOLE	215	A
PIGEONHOLING A BILL	222	A
PIJADE	723	B
PILATE, PONTIUS	723	B
PILGRIMAGE	611	B
PILGRIMS	153	A
PILLAGE	611	B
PILLAR	567	B
PILOTAGE	658	B
PILSUDSKI, JOZEF	764	B
PIMA INDIANS	530	B
PINCHER	567	B
PINCKNEY TREATY	257	A
PINDAR	764	B
PINDLING, LYNDEN OSCAR	764	B
PINEAPPLE PRIMARY	658	B
PINK	558	B
PINKO	545	B
PINSKER, LEON	764	B
PIONEERS	193	A
PIPE-LINE CASES	672	B
PIPPIN	765	B
PIRACY	248	A
PITILESS PUBLICITY	658	B
PITSKINKI, KAARLO VILHELMI	765	B
PITTERMAN	765	B
PIVOTAL STATES	279	A
PLACE CARD	827	B
PLACE IN THE SUN	545	B
PLACE OF COMMISSION	799	B
PLACE OF HONOUR	567	B
PLACE OF PERPETRATION (OF THE CRIME)	791	B
PLACE, FRANCIS	765	B

PLACEMENT	636	B	PLUM	818	B
PLAGUE	658	B	PLUMED KNIGHT	765	B
PLAINS INDIANS	530	B	PLUMMER, C.	723	B
PLAINTIFF	185	A	PLUMP	658	B
PLAINVILLE	799	B	PLUNDER	587	B
PLAN	587	B	PLUNDERBUND	530	B
PLANETS	827	B	PLURAL VOTING	230	A
PLANK	248	A	PLURALISM	115	A
PLANNED ECONOMY	199	A	PLURALISTIC SOCIETY	145	A
PLANNED SOCIETY	151	A	PLURALITY	149	A
PLANNERS	188	A	PLURALITY VOTING	209	A
PLANNING	215	A	PLUTARCH	272	A
PLANNING AND LAND USE	222	A	PLUTOCRACY	151	A
PLANNING BOARD	168	A	POBEDONOSTSEV, KONSTANTIN	765	B
	205	A	POCKET BATTLESHIP	827	B
SYSTEM (PPBS)			POCKET BOROUGH	789	B
PLANT	530	B	POCKET VETO	197	A
PLANTATION	474	B	POCKETBOOK ISSUE	248	A
PLANTATION SYSTEM	248	A	PODGORNY, NIKOLAI VIKTOROVICH	268	A
PLATFORM	209	A	PODHORETZ, NORMAN	765	B
PLATFORM PLANK	205	A	POGROM	210	A
PLATINUM	827	B	POHLE, L.	765	B
PLATO	261	B	POINCARE, HENRI	272	A
PLATONISM	131	A	POINCARE, RAYMOND	698	B
PLATOON SYSTEM	530	B	POINT FOUR PROGRAM	230	A
PLATT AMENDMENT	239	A	POINT OF FACT	611	B
PLATTE PURCHASE	636	B	POINT OF LAW	239	A
PLAUSIBILITY	239	A	POINT OF ORDER	215	A
PLAY	446	B	POINT WITH PRIDE	840	B
PLAYERS	567	B	POINT WITH PRIDE...VIEW WITH	840	B
PLAYING POLITICS	611	B	ALARM		
PLAYS	658	B	POINTER VS. TEXAS (1965)	675	B
PLAZA, GALO	765	B	POISON GAS	289	A
PLEADINGS	611	B	POISON WEAPONS	818	B
PLEASURE	143	A	POLAND	277	A
PLEBISCITARIAN	552	B	POLAR AREAS	791	B
PLEBISCITE	201	A	POLARIS SUBMARINE	287	A
PLEDGE OF ALLEGIANCE	257	A	POLARIZATION	124	A
PLEKHANOV, GEORGY	698	B	POLARIZE	205	A
VALENTINOVICH			POLEMICS	230	A
PLENARY ASSEMBLY	168	A	POLICE	160	A
PLENARY MEETING	222	A	POLICE ACTION	210	A
PLENARY SESSION	230	A	POLICE BRUTALITY	222	A
PLENIPOTENTIARY	188	A	POLICE COURT	474	B
PLENIPOTENTIARY CONFERENCE	587	B	POLICE ESCORT	474	B
PLENITUDO POTESTATIS	451	B	POLICE GUARD	508	B
PLENTITUDE	637	B	POLICE JURY	490	B
PLENUM	474	B	POLICE OF PORTS	530	B
PLESSY VS. FERGUSON (1896)	260	A	POLICE OPERATION	637	B
PLEVEN PLAN	587	B	POLICE POWER	201	A
PLEVEN, RENE JEAN	698	B	POLICE REGIME	173	A
PLINY THE YOUNGER	765	B	POLICE STATE	149	A
PLOT	257	A	POLICE STRIKE 1919	637	B
PLOTINUS	765	B	POLICEMAN	186	A
PLOUGHSHARES	823	B	POLICEMAN OF THE WORLD	188	A
PLOY	257	A	POLICY	197	A

POLICY ANALYSIS	116	A	POLITICAL APATHY	118	A
POLICY APPROACH	134	A	POLITICAL ARRANGEMENTS	611	B
POLICY COMMITTEE	164	A	POLITICAL ASSASSINATION	210	A
POLICY FORMATION	121	A	POLITICAL ASSESSMENT IN U.S.A.	438	B
POLICY FORMULATION	199	A	POLITICAL ASSOCIATION	151	A
POLICY OF ALLIANCES	611	B	POLITICAL ASYLUM	274	A
POLICY OF APPEASEMENT	215	A	POLITICAL ATTACHMENTS	257	A
POLICY OF CONTAINMENT	197	A	POLITICAL ATTITUDES	116	A
POLICY OF ENCIRCLEMENT	215	A	POLITICAL AUTHORITY	118	A
POLICY OF EXPANSION	215	A	POLITICAL AWARENESS	124	A
POLICY OF EXPEDIENCY	248	A	POLITICAL AXIOMS	289	A
POLICY OF FAIT ACCOMPLI	230	A	POLITICAL BARGAIN	239	A
POLICY OF MUTUAL	587	B	POLITICAL BARGAINING POSITION	239	A
UNDERSTANDING			POLITICAL BEHAVIOR	113	A
POLICY OF PIS ALLER	658	B	POLITICAL BUILD-UP	248	A
POLICY OF RAPPROCHMENT	201	A	POLITICAL CAMPAIGN	205	A
POLICY PLANNING STAFF	153	A	POLITICAL CAPITAL	281	A
POLICY PROCESSES	118	A	POLITICAL CHANGE	113	A
POLICY SCIENCES	121	A	POLITICAL CHARACTER	134	A
POLICY-MAKER	181	A	POLITICAL CLEARANCE	611	B
POLICY-MAKING	197	A	POLITICAL CLEAVAGES	131	A
POLIS	153	A	POLITICAL CLUB	173	A
POLISH CAMPAIGN	637	B	POLITICAL COERCION	126	A
POLISH CORRIDOR	277	A	POLITICAL COMMENTARY	285	A
POLISH FRONT OF NATIONAL UNITY	530	B	POLITICAL COMMUNICATION	116	A
(FJN)			POLITICAL COMMUNITY	145	A
POLISH FRONTIERS	789	B	POLITICAL COMPLIANCE	239	A
POLISH LEGION	530	B	POLITICAL CONFLICT	116	A
POLISH OCTOBER	658	B	POLITICAL CONSEQUENCES	230	A
POLISH REVOLUTION OF 1956	587	B	POLITICAL CONTROL	210	A
POLISH ROAD TO SOCIALISM	587	B	POLITICAL CONVENTION	205	A
POLISH SOCIALIST PARTY (PPS)	530	B	POLITICAL CRIME	239	A
POLISH UNITED WORKERS PARTY	508	B	POLITICAL CRITERIA	134	A
POLISH-CZECH DECLARATION	658	B	POLITICAL CRITICISM	126	A
POLITBURO, CHINA (PRC)	164	A	POLITICAL CULTURE	115	A
POLITBURO, SOVIET UNION	153	A	POLITICAL CURRENCIES	137	A
POLITICAL	194	A	POLITICAL DEAD END	611	B
POLITICAL ACRONYMS	140	A	POLITICAL DEADLOCK	239	A
POLITICAL ACTION	197	A	POLITICAL DECISION	197	A
POLITICAL ACTION COMMITTEE	508	B	POLITICAL DEPARTMENTS	490	B
(PAC)			POLITICAL DEVELOPMENT	118	A
POLITICAL ACTIVISTS	182		POLITICAL DIFFERENCES	239	A
POLITICAL ACTIVITIES ACTS OF	611	B	POLITICAL DISABILITY	587	B
1939, 1940			POLITICAL DISCOURSE	248	A
POLITICAL ACTIVITY	230	A	POLITICAL DISOBEDIENCE	205	A
POLITICAL ACTOR	180	A	POLITICAL DISPUTE	210	A
POLITICAL AGITATOR	182	A	POLITICAL ECOLOGY	116	A
POLITICAL ALIENATION	113	A	POLITICAL ECONOMY	118	A
POLITICAL ALTERNATIVES	126	A	POLITICAL ECONOMY SOCIETY	530	B
POLITICAL ANALYSIS	116	A	(BELGIUM)		
POLITICAL AND ECONOMIC	587	B	POLITICAL EDUCATION	120	A
PLANNING (PEP)			POLITICAL EFFICACY	118	A
POLITICAL AND SECURITY	490	B	POLITICAL ELITE	145	A
COMMITTEE			POLITICAL ETHICS	120	A
POLITICAL ANIMAL	190	A	POLITICAL EUPHEMISMS	290	A
POLITICAL ANTHROPOLOGY	128	A	POLITICAL EXECUTIVES	183	A

POLITICAL EXPLANATION	131	A	POLITICAL PARTIES, COMPARATIVE ANALYSIS	116	A
POLITICAL FACTORS	124	A			
POLITICAL FOOTBALL	291	A	POLITICAL PATRONAGE	201	A
POLITICAL FORCES	160	A	POLITICAL PERIODICAL	807	B
POLITICAL FORECASTING	124	A	POLITICAL PERSONALITY	124	A
POLITICAL GENERAL	193	A	POLITICAL PHILOSOPHY	114	A
POLITICAL GENERATIONS	173	A	POLITICAL PLUM	288	A
POLITICAL GEOGRAPHY	124	A	POLITICAL POWER	115	A
POLITICAL GRATITUDE	611	B	POLITICAL PRACTICES	230	A
POLITICAL GROUPS	145	A	POLITICAL PREDISPOSITIONS	134	A
POLITICAL HEFT	658	B	POLITICAL PRESSURE	118	A
POLITICAL HISTORY	124	A	POLITICAL PRINCIPLES	124	A
POLITICAL HONEYMOON	230	A	POLITICAL PRISONER	183	A
POLITICAL IDEAS	128	A	POLITICAL PROCESSES	113	A
POLITICAL IDEOLOGY	115	A	POLITICAL PROTEST	199	A
POLITICAL IMPACT	257	A	POLITICAL PROVERBS	446	B
POLITICAL INDOCTRINATION	124	A	POLITICAL PSYCHOLOGY	122	A
POLITICAL INFLUENCE	114	A	POLITICAL QUESTION	210	A
POLITICAL INFORMATION	121	A	POLITICAL RECRUITMENT	115	A
POLITICAL INSTABILITY	197	A	POLITICAL REFERENCE GROUP	149	A
POLITICAL INSTITUTIONS	145	A	POLITICAL REFERENCE POINT	438	B
POLITICAL INTEGRATION	115	A	POLITICAL REFUGEE	188	A
POLITICAL INTEREST	153	A	POLITICAL REGIME	164	A
POLITICAL INVECTIVE	140	A	POLITICAL RELATIONS	239	A
POLITICAL INVOLVEMENT	120	A	POLITICAL REPRESENTATION	194	A
POLITICAL JURISPRUDENCE	222	A	POLITICAL RESOURCES	286	A
POLITICAL JUSTICE	124	A	POLITICAL REWARDS	215	A
POLITICAL KNOWLEDGE	124	A	POLITICAL RIGHTS	210	A
POLITICAL LABORATORIES	791	B	POLITICAL ROLE OF THE SECRETARY-GENERAL	185	A
POLITICAL LANGUAGE	128	A			
POLITICAL LAW	230	A	POLITICAL ROLES	180	A
POLITICAL LEADERSHIP	181	A	POLITICAL SCIENCE	113	A
POLITICAL LEARNING	122	A	POLITICAL SCIENCE RESEARCH INSTITUTES (CHINA)	530	B
POLITICAL LEGITIMACY	116	A			
POLITICAL LIFE	222	A	POLITICAL SCIENCE, DEVELOPMENT OF	194	A
POLITICAL LITERATURE	284	A			
POLITICAL LOYALTY	128	A	POLITICAL SCIENCE, SUBFIELDS OF	115	A
POLITICAL MACHINE	149	A	POLITICAL SCIENCE, THE PROFESSION	145	A
POLITICAL MATURATION	126	A			
POLITICAL MEMORY	140	A	POLITICAL SCIENTISTS	181	A
POLITICAL METHOD	131	A	POLITICAL SELF	131	A
POLITICAL MILITANCY	126	A	POLITICAL SKILLS	126	A
POLITICAL MIRACLE	658	B	POLITICAL SOCIALIZATION THEORY	116	A
POLITICAL MOBILIZATION	197	A	POLITICAL SOCIOLOGY	122	A
POLITICAL MORALITY	116	A	POLITICAL STABILITY, THEORY	128	A
POLITICAL MOVEMENTS	147	A	POLITICAL STATISTICS	128	A
POLITICAL NECESSITY	215	A	POLITICAL STRATA	185	A
POLITICAL OBLIGATION	197	A	POLITICAL STRATIFICATION	115	A
POLITICAL OFFENSES	222	A	POLITICAL STRUCTURES	118	A
POLITICAL OPINION POLL	160	A	POLITICAL STYLE	120	A
POLITICAL OPPOSITION	149	A	POLITICAL SUBCULTURES	145	A
POLITICAL ORDER	147	A	POLITICAL SUICIDE	257	A
POLITICAL ORGANIZATIONS	145	A	POLITICAL SYMBOLISM	122	A
POLITICAL ORTHODOXY	122	A	POLITICAL SYSTEMS	113	A
POLITICAL PARTICIPATION	194	A	POLITICAL THEOLOGY	143	A
POLITICAL PARTIES	144	A	POLITICAL THEORY	113	A

POLITICAL THEORY, CLASSICAL	113	A	PONY CONVENTION	658	B
POLITICAL THOUGHT	122	A	POOL	658	B
POLITICAL TRAINING	239	A	POOL, ITHIEL DE SOLA	272	A
POLITICAL VALUES	113	A	POOLING	637	B
POLITICIAN	181	A	POOR	168	A
POLITICIZATION	113	A	POOR FARM	490	B
POLITICKING	131	A	POOR LAW TAX	611	B
POLITICO-HISTORICAL METHOD IN SWEDEN	451	B	POOR LAWS	587	B
			POOR MAN'S CANDIDATE	558	B
POLITICO-JURIDICAL METHOD IN POLAND	458	B	POOR MAN'S DOLLAR	658	B
			POOR RELIEF	257	A
POLITICO-JURIDICAL THEORY	140	A	POOR RICHARD	723	B
POLITICO-LEGAL RESEARCH INSTITUTE (ARGENTINA)	530	B	POORHOUSE	490	B
			POPE	190	A
POLITICO-SOCIOLOGICAL METHOD IN ARGENTINA	458	B	POPE ALEXANDER VI	765	B
			POPE BONIFACE VII	765	B
POLITICS	194	A	POPE BONIFACE VIII	723	B
POLITICS OF PREVENTION	248	A	POPE JOHN XXIII	272	A
POLITIES	149	A	POPE JOHN XXIII	268	A
POLITIES, NON-WESTERN	173	A	POPE LEO III	765	B
POLITIES, TONICITY	530	B	POPE LEO XIII	688	B
POLITIQUES	508	B	POPE PAUL VI	272	A
POLITY	144	A	POPE PAUL VI	272	A
POLK STALK (AND OTHER POLK PUNS)	846	B	POPE PIUS IX	765	B
			POPE PIUS XI	699	B
POLK, PRESIDENT JAMES K.	265	A	POPE PIUS XII	699	B
POLL	201	A	POPENOE, P.	765	B
POLL BOOK	806	B	POPLARI	530	B
POLL PROCEDURE	239	A	POPOCRAT	490	B
POLL TAX	201	A	POPPER, KARL R.	268	A
POLL WATCHER	181	A	POPULAR	193	A
POLLING BOOTH	287	A	POPULAR ASSEMBLY	153	A
POLLING DAY	587	B	POPULAR CHAMBER	168	A
POLLING PLACE	277	A	POPULAR CONSENT	199	A
POLLOCK VS. FARMERS LOAN AND TRUST COMPANY (1895)	679	B	POPULAR DEMOCRACY	114	A
			POPULAR ELECTION OF SENATORS	210	A
POLLOCK VS. WILLIAMS (1944)	679	B	POPULAR FRONT	164	A
POLLOCK, JAMES K.	765	B	POPULAR FRONT GOVERNMENT	160	A
POLLOCK, SIR FREDERICK	765	B	POPULAR GOVERNMENT	149	A
POLLS (OF PUBLIC OPINION)	205	A	POPULAR INITIATIVE	210	A
POLLSTER	181	A	POPULAR REFERENDUM	199	A
POLLUTION	230	A	POPULAR REPUBLICAN MOVEMENT	179	A
POLLUTION, ENVIRONMENTAL	199	A	POPULAR SOVEREIGNTY, DEMOCRATIC THEORY	118	A
POLO, MARCO	698	B			
POLSBY, NELSON	272	A	POPULATION	164	A
POLYARCHAL DEMOCRACY	134	A	POPULATION COMMISSION	474	B
POLYARCHY	156	A	POPULATION CONTROL	215	A
POLYBIUS	765	B	POPULATION EXPLOSION	205	A
POLYCENTRISM	120	A	POPULATION GROWTH	215	A
POLYGAMY	587	B	POPULATION POLICY	230	A
POLYGRAPHS	287	A	POPULATION PRESSURE	239	A
POMEROY CIRCULAR	812	B	POPULATION PROGRAM CENTER (ECA)	530	B
POMPIDOU, GEORGES JEAN RAYMOND	270	A			
			POPULATIONS AND FOOD	508	B
PONTIFICAL	567	B	POPULISM	122	A
PONTIFICATE	552	B	POPULIST MOVEMENT	149	A

POUND, EZRA	699	B
POUND, ROSCOE	272	A
POURPARLER	659	B
POUVOIRS	458	B
POVERTY	230	A
POVERTY PROGRAM	210	A
POW WOW	659	B
POWELL VS. ALABAMA (1932)	675	B
POWELL, ADAM CLAYTON	688	B
POWELL, ENOCH	699	B
POWELL, G. BINGHAM	765	B
POWELL, JOHN ENOCH	699	B
POWELL, THOMAS REED	723	B
POWER	113	A
POWER BASE	201	A
POWER BEHIND THE THRONE	290	A
POWER BROKERS	184	A
POWER CORRUPTS	289	A
POWER ECONOMY	179	A
POWER ELITE	145	A
POWER GRAB	248	A
POWER OF APPOINTMENT	205	A
POWER OF DECISION	215	A
POWER OF THE PURSE, CONGRESS	205	A
POWER PATTERNS	126	A
POWER POLITICS	114	A
POWER PROCESS	137	A
POWER STRUCTURE	115	A
POWER THEORY	120	A
POWER TO TAX	205	A
POWER-SEEKERS AND LEADERS	182	A
POWERHOUSE	558	B
POWERLESSNESS	126	A
POWERS (FRANCIS GARY) CASE	260	A
POWERS OF CONGRESS	195	A
POWERS OF THE PRESIDENT	197	A
POZNAN RIOTS	659	B
PRACTICAL POLITICS	201	A
PRACTICES	659	B
PRAESIDIUM OF THE SUPREME SOVIET (USSR)	151	A
PRAGMATIC	215	A
PRAGMATIC SANCTION	611	B
PRAGMATISM	114	A
PRAGUE COUP D'ETAT OF 1948	248	A
PRAIRIE FIRE	659	B
PRAISE	659	B
PRASAD, RAJENDRA	766	B
PRATT, R. C.	766	B
PRAVDA (THE TRUTH)	284	A
PRAXEOLOGY	458	B
PRAXIS	438	B
PRAYER	248	A
PRAYER MEETING	659	B
PRAYER OF TWENTY MILLIONS	846	B
PRE-AUDIT	248	A
PRE-BELLIGERENT	659	B
PRE-EMPTION	239	A
PRE-SCHOOL	567	B
PRE-SOCRATIC PHILOSOPHY	140	A
PRE-TRIAL DETENTION	215	A
PREAMBLE	248	A
PREAMBLE TO THE CONSTITUTION	199	A
PREBISH, R.	723	B
PRECEDENT	205	A
PRECINCT	274	A
PRECINCT CAPTAIN	184	A
PRECINCT CAUCUS	168	A
PRECIPITANTS	451	B
PRECIS WRITER	552	B
PRECONDITIONS	239	A
PREDATORY	567	B
PREDATORY WEALTH	558	B
PREDECESSOR	193	A
PREDESTINATION	134	A
PREDICAMENT	611	B
PREDICATE	257	A
PREDICATE-LOGIC	143	A
PREDICATION	140	A
PREDICTABILITY OF LAW	137	A
PREDICTION	131	A
PREDICTIVE POLITICAL KNOWLEDGE	122	A
PREEMPTIVE STRIKE	201	A
PREFABRICATED HOUSES	828	B
PREFECT (FRANCE)	545	B
PREFECTORAL SYSTEM	257	A
PREFECTURE	490	B
PREFERABLE	458	B
PREFERENCE	137	A
PREFERENCE MORAL	451	B
PREFERENCE POLL	201	A
PREFERENTIAL PRIMARIES	205	A
PREFERENTIAL RIGHT	637	B
PREFERENTIAL TRADE AGREEMENTS	230	A
PREFERENTIAL VOTING	222	A
PREFERMENT	637	B
PREFERRED POSITION CONCEPT	190	A
PREFERRED POSITION TEST	248	A
PREHENCIN	458	B
PREHISTORIC SOCIETY	173	A
PREJUDICE	126	A
PRELATE	552	B
PRELIMINARY AGREEMENT	587	B
PRELIMINARY CANVASS	257	A
PRELIMINARY CONFERENCE	637	B
PRELIMINARY DRAFT	807	B
PRELIMINARY EXAMINATION	637	B
PRELIMINARY HEARING	248	A
PRELIMINARY NEGOTIATIONS	587	B
PRELIMINARY REPORT	286	A
PRELIMINARY TREATY	611	B
PRELUDE	659	B

PREMIER	183	A	PRESIDENT'S RE-EMPLOYMENT	637	B
PREMIERSHIP	184	A	AGREEMENT		
PREMISE	122	A	PRESIDENTIAL APPOINTMENT	183	A
PREPARATIONS FOR WAR	230	A	PRESIDENTIAL ASSASSINATION	222	A
PREPARATORY COMMITTEE	490	B	PRESIDENTIAL BEE	659	B
PREPARATORY WORK	637	B	PRESIDENTIAL BUG	140	A
PREPAREDNESS	611	B	PRESIDENTIAL CANDIDATE	184	A
PREPOSITION	446	B	PRESIDENTIAL DISABILITY	230	A
PREPRIMARY CONVENTION	248	A	PRESIDENTIAL DRAFT	284	A
PREROGATIVE	257	A	PRESIDENTIAL ELECTION OF 1876	587	B
PRESBYTERIANS	508	B	PRESIDENTIAL ELECTIONS	197	A
PRESCRIPTION-PRESCRIPTIVE	126	A	PRESIDENTIAL ELECTORS	185	A
PRESCRIPTIVE THEORY	118	A	PRESIDENTIAL FEVER	143	A
PRESCRIPTIVISM	446	B	PRESIDENTIAL GOVERNMENT	145	A
PRESENCE	552	B	PRESIDENTIAL IMMUNITY	215	A
PRESENT	637	B	PRESIDENTIAL INAUGURATION DAY	257	A
PRESENTATION	637	B	PRESIDENTIAL INITIALS	824	B
PRESENTATION AT COURT	637	B	PRESIDENTIAL LOBBY	168	A
PRESENTMENT	637	B	PRESIDENTIAL MESSAGE	230	A
PRESERVATION OF PEACE	239	A	PRESIDENTIAL OATH	239	A
PRESIDE OVER	611	B	PRESIDENTIAL POWERS	196	A
PRESIDENCY	145	A	PRESIDENTIAL PREFERENTIAL	239	A
PRESIDENT	181	A	SYSTEM		
PRESIDENT « CONGRESS	146	A	PRESIDENTIAL PRESS CONFERENCE	222	A
PRESIDENT OF ALL THE PEOPLE	545	B	PRESIDENTIAL PRIMARY	199	A
PRESIDENT OF THE BOARD OF	558	B	PRESIDENTIAL PROCLAMATIONS	223	A
TRADE			PRESIDENTIAL SHORT BALLOT	257	A
PRESIDENT OF THE BUNDESTAG	545	B	PRESIDENTIAL SUCCESSION	205	A
PRESIDENT OF THE	552	B	PRESIDENTIAL SUCCESSION ACT OF	257	A
CONFEDERATION			1947		
PRESIDENT OF THE COUNCIL OF	558	B	PRESIDENTIAL SYNTAX	637	B
MINISTERS, ITALY			PRESIDENTIAL SYSTEM	118	A
PRESIDENT OF THE REPUBLIC,	185	A	PRESIDENTIAL TERM	223	A
FRANCE			PRESIDENTIAL TIMBER	186	A
PRESIDENT OF THE REPUBLIC, ITALY	193	A	PRESIDENTIAL TRANSITIONS	239	A
PRESIDENT OF THE SENATE	188	A	PRESIDENTIAL VETO	197	A
PRESIDENT OF THE UNITED STATES	181	A	PRESIDIUM OF THE COUNCIL OF	157	A
PRESIDENT PRO TEMPORE	182	A	MINISTERS, U.S.S.R.		
PRESIDENT TRUMAN'S TWELVE	239	A	PRESIDIUM OF THE SUPREME	157	A
POINTS			SOVIET, SOVIET UNION		
PRESIDENT-DESIGNATE	193	A	PRESOCRATICS	545	B
PRESIDENT-ELECT	185	A	PRESS	153	A
PRESIDENT-MAKER	193	A	PRESS ATTACHE	545	B
PRESIDENT'S ANNUAL MESSAGE	222	A	PRESS CAMPAIGN	588	B
PRESIDENT'S COMMISSION ON	179	A	PRESS CONFERENCE	248	A
CAMPUS UNREST			PRESS DEPARTMENT	508	B
PRESIDENT'S COMMISSION ON	179	A	PRESS GALLERY	283	A
INTERGOVERNMENTAL RELATIONS			PRESS SECRETARY	188	A
PRESIDENT'S COMMITTEE ON CIVIL	164	A	PRESSING THE FLESH	588	B
RIGHTS			PRESSURE	230	A
PRESIDENT'S COUNCIL ON AGING	474	B	PRESSURE GROUP	145	A
PRESIDENT'S ECONOMIC MESSAGE	230	A	PRESSURE POLITICS	122	A
PRESIDENT'S ECONOMIC REPORT	215	A	PRESSURE, SOCIAL	128	A
PRESIDENT'S OATH OF OFFICE	230	A	PRESTIGE	129	A
PRESIDENT'S PRESS SECRETARY	190	A	PRESUMPTION OF INNOCENCE	223	A
			PRESUPPOSITION	143	A

PRETENDER TO THE THRONE	193	A
PRETORIAN BAND	531	B
PRETRIAL CONFERENCE	257	A
PRETRIAL DISCOVERY	588	B
PRETRIAL SETTLEMENT	215	A
PREVENT	257	A
PREVENTION	248	A
PREVENTION OF SPREAD OF NUCLEAR WEAPONS	230	A
PREVENTION OF SURPRISE ATTACKS	257	A
PREVENTION OF WAR	216	A
PREVENTIVE DIPLOMACY	230	A
PREVENTIVE JUSTICE	257	A
PREVENTIVE MEASURES	230	A
PREVENTIVE PRE-TRIAL DETENTION	239	A
PREVENTIVE WAR	210	A
PREVIOUS QUESTION	239	A
PREVITE-ORTON, C.W.	766	B
PREWITT, KENNETH	723	B
PREY	567	B
PREZZOLINI, GIUSEPPE	766	B
PRICE	239	A
PRICE CEILING	239	A
PRICE CONTROL ACT	248	A
PRICE CONTROLS	210	A
PRICE FIXING	216	A
PRICE FIXING MONOPOLY	179	A
PRICE STABILIZATION	210	A
PRICE SUPPORT	230	A
PRICE SUPPORT PROGRAM	216	A
PRICE SYSTEM	216	A
PRICE WAR	230	A
PRICE-FIXING	216	A
PRICE-RATE SYSTEM	637	B
PRICE, DON K.	766	B
PRICE, DR. RICHARD	766	B
PRICE, HUGH DOUGLAS	723	B
PRICES AND INCOMES POLICY	248	A
PRIDE	438	B
PRIEST	545	B
PRIESTHOOD	193	A
PRIMA FACIE EVIDENCE	230	A
PRIMACY	588	B
PRIMARY	210	A
PRIMARY BOYCOTT	223	A
PRIMARY COMMODITY	588	B
PRIMARY ELECTIONS	205	A
PRIMARY GROUP	145	A
PRIMARY POLITICAL LOYALTIES	140	A
PRIMARY RELATIONSHIPS	122	A
PRIMARY SOURCE OF LAW	143	A
PRIME MINISTER	181	A
PRIME-MOVER	193	A
PRIMITIVE	438	B
PRIMITIVE POLITICAL SYSTEMS	120	A
PRIMITIVE SOCIETIES	149	A
PRIMITIVISM	438	B
PRIMOGENITURE	239	A
PRIMROSE LEAGUE	531	B
PRINCE	545	B
PRINCE ABBOT	567	B
PRINCE BISHOP	567	B
PRINCE CONSORT	559	B
PRINCE OF THE BLOOD	567	B
PRINCE OF THE CHURCH	545	B
PRINCE OF WALES	193	A
PRINCE REGENT	552	B
PRINCE VS. MASSACHUSETTS (1944)	679	B
PRINCEDOM	567	B
PRINCELY STATES, INDIA	490	B
PRINCESS	552	B
PRINCESS ROYAL	567	B
PRINCETON SCHOOL OF PUBLIC AFFAIRS	508	B
PRINCIPLE OF PEOPLE'S LIVELIHOOD	846	B
PRINCIPLE OF RECIPROCITY	230	A
PRINCIPLE(S)	126	A
PRINCIPLES NOT MEN	840	B
PRINS, ADOLPHE	766	B
PRINTING	611	B
PRIOR RESTRAINT	231	A
PRIORITIES	231	A
PRISMATIC	143	A
PRISON	288	A
PRISON LABOR	637	B
PRISONER	545	B
PRISONER OF WAR	185	A
PRISONER-OF-WAR CAMP	168	A
PRISONER'S REPRESENTATIVE	559	B
PRISONERS DILEMMA	131	A
PRISONS AND PENOLOGY	179	A
PRITCHETT, C. HERMAN	699	B
PRIVACY	216	A
PRIVATE AUDIENCE	248	A
PRIVATE BILL	216	A
PRIVATE CALENDAR	216	A
PRIVATE ENTERPRISE	201	A
PRIVATE EYE	552	B
PRIVATE INDIVIDUALS	193	A
PRIVATE INTERNATIONAL LAW	248	A
PRIVATE INTERNATIONAL UNIONS	474	B
PRIVATE INVESTMENT COMPANY FOR ASIA	531	B
PRIVATE LAW	231	A
PRIVATE MEETING	588	B
PRIVATE MEMBER'S BILL	231	A
PRIVATE ORGANIZATION	173	A
PRIVATE PROPERTY	205	A
PRIVATE SUITE	799	B
PRIVATEER	188	A
PRIVILEGE	231	A

PRIVILEGE TAX	611	B
PRIVILEGED QUESTION	216	A
PRIVILEGED SANCTUARY	279	A
PRIVILEGES AND IMMUNITIES	201	A
PRIVY COUNCIL	173	A
PRIVY COUNCIL APPEALS	637	B
PRIZE	611	B
PRIZE CASES	261	A
PRIZE COURT	474	B
PRIZE CREW	474	B
PRIZE LAW	611	B
PRO BONO	836	B
PRO FORMA AGREEMENT	239	A
PRO TEM	184	A
PRO TEMPORE	184	A
PROBABILISM	134	A
PROBABILITY	115	A
PROBABILITY STATEMENT	116	A
PROBATE	248	A
PROBATE COURT	160	A
PROBATE JUDGE	190	A
PROBATION	248	A
PROBATION AND PAROLE	223	A
PROBATIONARY APPOINTMENT	257	A
PROBATIONARY PERIOD	248	A
PROBE	588	B
PROBLEM	248	A
PROBLEM SOLVING	122	A
PROBLEM-ANALYSIS QUESTIONNAIRE	137	A
PROBLEMS OF CEREMONIAL PRECEDENCE	659	B
PROCEDURAL COMMITTEE	179	A
PROCEDURAL DECISIONS, SECURITY COUNCIL	239	A
PROCEDURAL DUE PROCESS OF LAW	201	A
PROCEDURAL LAW	210	A
PROCEDURAL MATTERS	239	A
PROCEDURAL MOTION	231	A
PROCEDURAL RIGHTS	223	A
PROCEDURAL RULES	210	A
PROCEDURAL SYSTEMS	231	A
PROCEDURALISTS	545	B
PROCEDURE	223	A
PROCEDURE OF COMMISSIONS OF INQUIRY	637	B
PROCEDURE OF CONCILIATION	588	B
PROCEDURE OF GOOD OFFICES	612	B
PROCEPHALY	531	B
PROCES VERBAL	446	B
PROCESS	120	A
PROCESS ANALYSIS	131	A
PROCESSING INDUSTRIES	531	B
PROCESSING TAX	588	B
PROCLAIM	612	B
PROCLAMATION	257	A
PROCLAMATION OF A STATE OF EMERGENCY	231	A
PROCLAMATION OF THE REPUBLIC	637	B
PROCLUS	766	B
PROCURACY	508	B
PROCURATOR (PROSECUTOR)	552	B
PRODUCERS COOPERATIVE	179	A
PRODUCT MOMENT	137	A
PRODUCTION	239	A
PRODUCTION AND MARKETING ADMINISTRATION	508	B
PRODUCTION TAX	257	A
PRODUCTIVE MECHANISMS	818	B
PRODUCTIVE-LOGIC	446	B
PRODUCTIVITY	210	A
PROFESSIONAL	190	A
PROFESSIONAL CAREER INFORMATION SERVICE (PCIS)	508	B
PROFESSIONAL CONSUL	559	B
PROFESSIONAL DIPLOMAT	188	A
PROFESSIONAL EMPLOYEES	552	B
PROFESSIONAL ORGANIZATIONS	169	A
PROFESSIONAL REVOLUTIONARIES	190	A
PROFESSIONALISM	131	A
PROFESSIONALIZATION	140	A
PROFESSIONS	474	B
PROFESSOR	190	A
PROFILE	438	B
PROFILES IN COURAGE	807	B
PROFIT	216	A
PROFIT-SHARING	223	A
PROFUMO AFFAIR	637	B
PROGRAM	239	A
PROGRAM COMMITTEE	490	B
PROGRAM OF THE GOVERNMENT	248	A
PROGRAM OF TWENTY-FIVE POINTS	659	B
PROGRAMMED INSTRUCTION	223	A
PROGRAMMERS	188	A
PROGRESS	129	A
PROGRESSIVE	131	A
PROGRESSIVE CITIZENS OF AMERICA	531	B
PROGRESSIVE EDUCATION	239	A
PROGRESSIVE MODERATION	612	B
PROGRESSIVE MODERATION	612	B
PROGRESSIVE MOVEMENT	147	A
PROGRESSIVE PARTY	157	A
PROGRESSIVE TAX	205	A
PROGRESSIVISM	126	A
PROHIBITED AERIAL SPACE	789	B
PROHIBITION	223	A
PROHIBITION OF ATOMIC WEAPONS	223	A
PROHIBITION OF CRUEL PUNISHMENT, EIGHTH AMENDMENT	210	A

PROHIBITION OF EX-POST-FACTO LAWS	216	A
PROHIBITION OF LIQUOR, EIGHTEENTH AMENDMENT	231	A
PROHIBITION PARTY	169	A
PROJECT	588	B
PROJECT CAMELOT	475	B
PROJECT HEAD START	231	A
PROJECT MANAGEMENT	588	B
PROJECTIBILITY	612	B
PROJECTION OF HISTORICAL TRENDS	124	A
PROJECTION ROOM	799	B
PROJECTION-RULE	659	B
PROJECTION, AND SIMULATION	140	A
PROJECTIVE METHODS	140	A
PROJET DE LOI	659	B
PROLEGOMENA	810	B
PROLETARIAN	183	A
PROLETARIAN INTERNATIONALISM	124	A
PROLETARIAN MILITARY SCIENCE	452	B
PROLETARIAN REVOLUTION	195	A
PROLETARIAT	147	A
PROLIX	659	B
PROMETHEUS	272	A
PROMISE	588	B
PROMOTION	612	B
PROMULGATE	239	A
PROMULGATION	257	A
PRONUNCIO	552	B
PROOF	122	A
PROOF-THEORY	140	A
PROPAGANDA	118	A
PROPAGANDA BY DEED	588	B
PROPAGANDA FOR WAR	248	A
PROPAGANDA MACHINE	160	A
PROPELLER STOP	846	B
PROPENSITIES	143	A
PROPER CHANNELS	239	A
PROPER-NAME	699	B
PROPERTIED CLASSES	160	A
PROPERTY	286	A
PROPERTY OWNERS	552	B
PROPERTY QUALIFICATIONS	231	A
PROPERTY RIGHTS	205	A
PROPERTY TAX	210	A
PROPHECY	446	B
PROPHETS	559	B
PROPHETS OF GLOOM AND DOOM	193	A
PROPORTION	143	A
PROPORTIONAL REPRESENTATION (PR)	195	A
PROPORTIONAL TAXATION	216	A
PROPOSAL	248	A
PROPOSED AMENDMENTS	248	A
PROPOSED BUDGET	223	A
PROPOSITION	126	A
PROPOSITIONAL LOGIC	140	A
PROPRIETARY COLONY	179	A
PROPRIETARY FUNCTION	257	A
PROPRIETARY FUNCTIONS OF CITIES	248	A
PROPRIETOR	559	B
PROROGATION	588	B
PROSECUTED PERSONS	193	A
PROSECUTING ATTORNEY	184	A
PROSECUTION	223	A
PROSECUTOR	186	A
PROSECUTOR, PUBLIC	186	A
PROSPECTIVE OVERRULING	588	B
PROSPECTS	438	B
PROSPECTUS	806	B
PROTAGORAS	699	B
PROTECTED STATE	169	A
PROTECTING POWER	257	A
PROTECTING STATE	490	B
PROTECTION	240	A
PROTECTION OF NATIONALS ABROAD	248	A
PROTECTION OF THE CIVILIAN POPULATION	612	B
PROTECTIONISM	122	A
PROTECTIVE CLAUSE	588	B
PROTECTIVE CUSTODY	231	A
PROTECTIVE TARIFF	216	A
PROTECTOR	552	B
PROTECTOR OF BOHEMIA AND MORAVIA	567	B
PROTECTORATE	151	A
PROTECTORATE, DEPENDENT TERRITORY	283	A
PROTEST	201	A
PROTEST DEMONSTRATION	240	A
PROTEST VOTE	201	A
PROTESTANT	185	A
PROTESTANT POLITICAL PARTIES	173	A
PROTESTANT REVOLUTION	210	A
PROTESTANT UNION	531	B
PROTESTANTISM	126	A
PROTHONOTARY	567	B
PROTHRO, JAMES W.	270	A
PROTOCOL	216	A
PROTOCOL OF AMENDMENT	637	B
PROTOCOL OF EXTENSION	637	B
PROTOCOL OF INTERPRETATION	637	B
PROTOCOL OF MODIFICATION	638	B
PROTOCOL OF RATIFICATIONS	612	B
PROTOCOL OF SIGNATURE	612	B
PROTOCOL SERVICE	490	B
PROTOCOLS OF THE ELDERS OF ZION	285	A
PROTOTYPE	140	A
PROTRACTED DEBATE	588	B

PROUDHON, PIERRE JOSEPH	270	A	PSYCHOLOGY OF LEARNING	129	A
PROUST	272	A	PSYCHOLOGY, AND	118	A
PROUTY, WINSTON LEWIS	766	B	DECISION-MAKING		
PROVIDENCE	452	B	PSYCHOLOGY, INDUSTRIAL	446	B
PROVINCE	283	A	PSYCHOLOGY, OF PERSONALITY	129	A
PROVINCIAL DIET	475	B	PSYCHOLOGY, THE PROFESSION	475	B
PROVINCIAL GOVERNMENT	157	A	PSYCHOMETRIC	131	A
PROVISIONAL AGENDA	286	A	PSYCHONEUROLOGY	452	B
PROVISIONAL ARREST PRIOR TO	659	B	PSYCHOPATHIC	446	B
EXTRADITION			PSYCHOPATHOLOGY	137	A
PROVISIONAL GOVERNMENT	160	A	PSYCHOPATHY	140	A
PROVISIONAL INTERNATIONAL CIVIL	531	B	PSYCHOPHYSICS	458	B
AVIATION ORGANIZAT			PSYCHOSIS	134	A
PROVISIONAL ORDERS	612	B	PSYCHOSOCIAL	143	A
PROVISIONS	638	B	PSYCHOTHERAPY	143	A
PROVISO	231	A	PUBERTY RITES	612	B
PROXIMITY	789	B	PUBLIC	146	A
PROXMIRE, WILLIAM	266	A	PUBLIC ACCOMMODATIONS	279	A
PROXY	183	A	PUBLIC ACTS	223	A
PROXY VOTING	210	A	PUBLIC ADMINISTRATION	120	A
PRUDENCE	438	B	PUBLIC ADMINISTRATION	490	B
PRUDENT INVESTMENT THEORY	458	B	CLEARINGHOUSE (CHICAGO)		
PRUITT-IGOE	766	B	PUBLIC ADMINISTRATION SERVICE	490	B
PRUSSIA	276	A	(U.S.)		
PSEPHOLOGY	452	B	PUBLIC AFFAIRS, SCHOOLS OF	173	A
PSEUDO DIONYSIUS	813	B	PUBLIC ASSISTANCE	223	A
PSEUDO SCOTUS	813	B	PUBLIC AUDIENCE	160	A
PSEUDO-EVENT	612	B	PUBLIC AUTHORITIES	184	A
PSEUDO-ISIDORIAN DECRETALS	813	B	PUBLIC BILL	205	A
PSEUDO-XENOPHON	813	B	PUBLIC BROADCASTING SYSTEM	160	A
PSEUDONYMS	840	B	(PBS)		
PSYCHE	438	B	PUBLIC BUILDINGS ADMINISTRATION	531	B
PSYCHIATRY	134	A	PUBLIC BUILDINGS SERVICE	531	B
PSYCHICAL DISTANCE	446	B	PUBLIC CHARACTER	137	A
PSYCHO-BIOLOGY	458	B	PUBLIC CHARACTER OF DEBATES	638	B
PSYCHO-SOCIOLOGICAL METHOD	143	A	PUBLIC CORPORATIONS AND	153	A
PSYCHOANALYSIS	131	A	ENTERPRISES		
PSYCHOANALYSIS OF INSTITUTIONS	446	B	PUBLIC CRIB	846	B
PSYCHOANALYTIC METHOD	131	A	PUBLIC DEBT	202	A
PSYCHOCULTURAL	559	B	PUBLIC DEFENDER	183	A
ANTHROPOLOGISTS			PUBLIC DOMAIN	231	A
PSYCHOCULTURAL THEORY OF	137	A	PUBLIC EDUCATION ASSOCIATION	531	B
SOCIALIZATION			PUBLIC EMPLOYEE	188	A
PSYCHODYNAMICS	143	A	PUBLIC EMPLOYEE ASSOCIATION	179	A
PSYCHOLOGICAL	446	B	PUBLIC ENTERPRISE	154	A
PSYCHOLOGICAL DOCTRINES	143	A	PUBLIC ENTERPRISE AND PLANNING	231	A
PSYCHOLOGICAL FACTORS	131	A	PUBLIC ESTABLISHMENTS	475	B
PSYCHOLOGICAL MASS COERCION	137	A	PUBLIC EXPENDITURE	216	A
PSYCHOLOGICAL METHOD	134	A	PUBLIC FINANCE	205	A
PSYCHOLOGICAL OPERATIONS	452	B	PUBLIC GALLERY	840	B
PSYCHOLOGICAL PROCESSES	137	A	PUBLIC GOODS	140	A
PSYCHOLOGICAL TESTING	134	A	PUBLIC HEALTH	588	B
PSYCHOLOGICAL WARFARE	210	A	PUBLIC HEALTH LABORATORY	828	B
PSYCHOLOGISM	438	B	PUBLIC HEALTH SERVICE (PHS)	169	A
PSYCHOLOGISTS	190	A	PUBLIC HEALTH, SAFETY, AND	240	A
PSYCHOLOGY	131	A	MORALS		

PUBLIC HOUSING	223	A	PUBLIC UTILITIES	164	A
PUBLIC HOUSING ADMINISTRATION	475	B	PUBLIC UTILITIES COMMISSION	169	A
(PHA)			PUBLIC UTILITY COMMISSIONS	160	A
PUBLIC INDUSTRY	173	A	PUBLIC UTILITY HOLDING COMPANY	612	B
PUBLIC INFORMATION OFFICE (UN)	508	B	ACT		
PUBLIC INFORMATION SERVICES	531	B	PUBLIC UTILITY REGULATION	205	A
(UN)			PUBLIC WEAL	140	A
PUBLIC INSTITUTION	157	A	PUBLIC WELFARE	205	A
PUBLIC INTEGRITY	240	A	PUBLIC WORKS	240	A
PUBLIC INTEREST	202	A	PUBLIC WORKS ADMINISTRATION	179	A
PUBLIC INTEREST, CONVENIENCE	248	A	(PWA)		
AND NECESSITY			PUBLIC WORKS AND ECONOMIC	638	B
PUBLIC INTERNATIONAL LAW	231	A	DEVELOPMENT ACT		
PUBLIC LAND	279	A	PUBLIC WORKS COMMITTEE	169	A
PUBLIC LAW	199	A	PUBLIC-INTEREST LAW	240	A
PUBLIC LAW OF ROMANS	612	B	PUBLICATIONS	806	B
PUBLIC LAW 16	612	B	PUBLICISTS	190	A
PUBLIC LAW 480	257	A	PUBLICITY	216	A
PUBLIC OFFICE	185	A	PUBLICITY LAWS	257	A
PUBLIC OFFICE IS A PUBLIC TRUST	837	B	PUBLICITY PAMPHLET	286	A
PUBLIC OPINION	115	A	PUBLICITY STUNT	588	B
PUBLIC OPINION POLLS	197	A	PUBLIUS	688	B
PUBLIC OPINION QUARTERLY	284	A	PUCHALA, DONALD	688	B
PUBLIC OPINION RESEARCH	118	A	PUEBLO INCIDENT	248	A
PUBLIC OPINION SURVEYS	197	A	PUEBLO INDIANS	490	B
PUBLIC ORDER	205	A	PUERTO RICANS	173	A
PUBLIC OWNERSHIP	210	A	PUERTO RICO	275	A
PUBLIC PERSONNEL	248	A	PUFENDORF, SAMUEL	766	B
ADMINISTRATION			PUFFING	659	B
PUBLIC PHILOSOPHY	126	A	PUJO COMMITTEE	531	B
PUBLIC POLICY	120	A	PULL	638	B
PUBLIC POLICY STUDIES	124	A	PULLMAN STRIKE	612	B
PUBLIC POWER	210	A	PUMP PRIMING	216	A
PUBLIC PRINTER OF THE UNITED	552	B	PUNDIT	552	B
STATES			PUNISHABLE BY DEATH	248	A
PUBLIC PROSECUTOR	186	A	PUNISHMENT	131	A
PUBLIC PURPOSE	131	A	PUNJAB, INDIA	789	B
PUBLIC RELATIONS (P.R.)	202	A	PUNT AND PRAY	659	B
PUBLIC RELIEF	248	A	PUPILS	567	B
PUBLIC REVENUE	231	A	PUPPET	191	A
PUBLIC ROADS ADMINISTRATION	475	B	PUPPET GOVERNMENT	151	A
PUBLIC SAFETY	216	A	PUPPET STATE	157	A
PUBLIC SCHOOL	173	A	PURCHASING AGENTS	567	B
PUBLIC SCHOOL SYSTEM	164	A	PURE FOOD AND DRUG ACTS	231	A
PUBLIC SERVICE	223	A	PURE FOOD, DRUG AND COSMETIC	248	A
PUBLIC SERVICE CAREERS	508	B	ACT		
PROGRAM (PSC)			PURE THEORY	134	A
PUBLIC SERVICE COMMISSION	179	A	PURE THEORY OF LAW	143	A
PUBLIC SERVICE FRANCHISE	588	B	PURGATION	659	B
PUBLIC SERVICE PERSONNEL	545	B	PURGE	216	A
PUBLIC SERVICE TRAINING	248	A	PURIFICATION	638	B
PUBLIC SPEAKING	240	A	PURITAN	185	A
PUBLIC TASKS	638	B	PURITAN REVOLUTION	223	A
PUBLIC TRANSPORTATION	240	A	PURITANISM	126	A
PUBLIC TRIAL	231	A	PURITANS	154	A
PUBLIC USE	248	A	PURITY	638	B

PURPLE	828	B	QUARANTINE SPEECH	257	A
PURPOSE	137	A	QUART OF MILK FOR EVERY	840	B
PURSE STRINGS	216	A	HOTTENTOT		
PURSE-PROUD	659	B	QUARTER-SPHERE DEFENSE	659	B
PUSHER	559	B	QUARTERING OF SOLDIERS	612	B
PUSHTUNISTAN	799	B	QUARTERMASTER CORPS	508	B
PUSSYFOOT	846	B	QUARTORZE JUILLET	659	B
PUTNEY, SNELL	766	B	QUASI-CORPORATION	475	B
PUTSCH	223	A	QUASI-JUDICIAL	231	A
PUTTING INTO FORCE	638	B	QUASI-JUDICIAL AGENCY	157	A
PUTTING-OUT SYSTEM	588	B	QUASI-JUDICIAL POWERS	216	A
PYATAKOV, G. L.	766	B	QUASI-LEGISLATIVE	223	A
PYE, LUCIAN	270	A	QUASI-LEGISLATIVE POWERS	210	A
PYONGYANG	789	B	QUASI-NONPARTISAN	559	B
PYRAMIDS	828	B	QUASI-PARTY SYSTEM	588	B
PYRITES	828	B	QUASI-PUBLIC CORPORATION	173	A
PYRRHIC VICTORY	231	A	QUASI-SOVEREIGN	588	B
PYTHAGORAS	699	B	QUEBEC ACT	638	B
PYTHAGOREANISM	446	B	QUEEN	545	B
Q-SORT	137	A	QUEEN CONSORT	552	B
QABBANI, NIZAR TAWFIQ	766	B	QUEEN DOWAGER	559	B
QADDAFI, MOAMAR AL	268	A	QUEEN MOTHER	559	B
QATAR	283	A	QUELL	612	B
QUACKS	567	B	QUEMOY	791	B
QUADRAGESIMO ANNO	813	B	QUEMOY (KINMEN) AND MATSU	281	A
QUADRILATERAL	531	B	QUERETARO	723	B
QUADRIPARTITE ADMINISTRATION	169	A	QUESNAY, FRANCOIS	766	B
OF BERLIN			QUEST	612	B
QUADRIPARTITE AGREEMENT	612	B	QUESTION	257	A
QUADRIPARTITE CONFERENCE	638	B	QUESTION HOUR, BRITAIN	223	A
QUADROON	567	B	QUESTION OF ALTO ADIGE	660	B
QUADROS, JANIO DA SILVA	766	B	QUESTION OF CONFIDENCE	249	A
QUADRUPLE ALLIANCE	179	A	QUESTION OF PRIVILEGE	588	B
QUAI D'ORSAY	799	B	QUESTIONNAIRE	126	A
QUAKERS	173	A	QUESTIONS AFFECTING BOTH	612	B
QUALIFICATION	257	A	COUNTRIES		
QUALIFIED STATUS	659	B	QUICK AND THE DEAD, THE	846	B
QUALIFIED TO VOTE	231	A	QUICKSILVER	828	B
QUALITY	134	A	QUID PRO QUO	290	A
QUALITY CONTROL	257	A	QUIDS	531	B
QUANDARY	458	B	QUIET DIPLOMACY	257	A
QUANTIFICATION	118	A	QUINE	766	B
QUANTIFIER	188	A	QUINTUPLE ALLIANCE	491	B
QUANTITATIVE ANALYSIS OF	122	A	QUINTUPLE CONSTITUTIONAL	458	B
JUDICIAL BEHAVIOR			THEORY		
QUANTITATIVE APPROACHES	114	A	QUIRINAL	531	B
QUANTITATIVE DATA	118	A	QUISLING (FIFTH COLUMN)	191	A
QUANTITATIVE METHODS	113	A	QUISLING, VIDKUN	270	A
QUANTITATIVE SEMANTICS	143	A	QUIXOTE, DON	272	A
QUANTITY	137	A	QUORUM	154	A
QUANTITY DISCOUNT	659	B	QUOTA	223	A
QUANTUM MECHANICS	446	B	QUOTA SYSTEM	210	A
QUANTUM PHYSICS	446	B	QUOTATION	638	B
QUANTUM THEORY	143	A	QUOTATION MARKS	452	B
QUARANTINABLE DISEASES	828	B	QUOTED OUT OF CONTEXT	223	A
QUARANTINE	223	A	QUWATLI - SHUKRI AL	766	B

R. H. MACY AND COMPANY	531	B	RAILROAD COMMISSION OF TEXAS	679	B
RAAB, ING	766	B	VS. ROWAN«NICHOLS OIL (1940)		
RAAB, JULIUS	766	B	RAILROAD LABOR DISPUTES ACT	612	B
RABBLE ROUSER	545	B	RAILROAD LAND GRANTS	249	A
RACE	151	A	RAILROAD RETIREMENT ACT	638	B
RACE AND POLITICS	154	A	RAILROAD RETIREMENT BOARD	531	B
RACE RELATIONS	223	A	RAILWAY LABOR ACT OF 1926	660	B
RACE RELATIONS ACTS	257	A	RAIN-MAKER	567	B
RACE RIOTS	223	A	RAINBOROUGH, THOMAS	766	B
RACE-TRACK LEGISLATION	660	B	RAINBOW CHASER	567	B
RACIAL DISCRIMINATION	231	A	RAINOLDS, WILLIAM	767	B
RACIAL FACTORS	143	A	RAISON D'ETAT	205	A
RACIAL GROUPINGS	173	A	RAJ, PANCHAYATI	767	B
RACIAL PERSECUTION	216	A	RAJAH	559	B
RACIAL PREJUDICE	126	A	RAJASTHAN, INDIA	799	B
RACIAL PROBLEM	231	A	RAJK, LASZLO	767	B
RACIAL QUESTION	249	A	RAKOSI, JENO	767	B
RACISM	131	A	RAKOSI, MATYAS	723	B
RACIST	193	A	RALEIGH, SIR WALTER	723	B
RACKET	612	B	RALLY	257	A
RACKET-BUSTER	552	B	RALPH, JAMES	767	B
RACKETEER	552	B	RAMADIER, PAUL	767	B
RACKETVILLE	799	B	RAMANUJA	767	B
RADAR	820	B	RAMDAS	767	B
RADAR BASE	795	B	RAMPARTS	810	B
RADEK (SOBELSOHN), KARL B.	766	B	RAMSPECK ACT OF 1940	638	B
RADIATION EFFECTS	289	A	RAND CORPORATION (U.S.)	157	A
RADICAL	183	A	RANDALL, JOHN HERMAN	767	B
RADICAL (REFORM)	231	A	RANDOLPH PLAN	612	B
RADICAL DEMOCRACY	164	A	RANDOLPH, ASA PHILIP	767	B
RADICAL HISTORICISM	439	B	RANDOLPH, JENNINGS	767	B
RADICAL PARTY	164	A	RANDOLPH, JOHN	699	B
RADICAL REPUBLICANS	157	A	RANDOLPH, PHILLIP	767	B
RADICAL RIGHT	149	A	RANDOM	129	A
RADICAL-SOCIALISTS	173	A	RANDOM SAMPLE	114	A
RADICALISM	116	A	RANGER	559	B
RADIO	824	B	RANK	191	A
RADIO ADDRESS	588	B	RANK ORDER	116	A
RADIO FREE EUROPE	164	A	RANK-AND-FILE	157	A
RADIO LIBERATION	508	B	RANKE, LEOPOLD VON	767	B
RADIUM	828	B	RANKING MEMBER	184	A
RADOVITCH VS. NATL FOOTBALL	679	B	RANKING MINORITY MEMBER	183	A
LEAGUE (NFL)(1957)			RANKOVIC, ALEKSANDAR	723	B
RADWAY, LAWRENCE	766	B	RANNEY, AUSTIN	272	A
RAE, DOUGLAS	766	B	RAP IN THE NIGHT	638	B
RAEDER, ERICH	766	B	RAPACKI PLAN	249	A
RAG BABY	846	B	RAPOPORT, ANATOL	688	B
RAHMAN, TUNKU ABDUL	723	B	RAPPARD, WILLIAM	767	B
RAI, L.L.	766	B	RAPPOPORT, CHARLES	767	B
RAID	612	B	RAPPORTEUR	185	A
RAID ON THE TREASURY	257	A	RAPPROCHEMENT	202	A
RAIL SPLITTER	766	B	RAS AL KHAMAH	767	B
RAILROAD	257	A	RASCAL	567	B
RAILROAD AND WAREHOUSE	508	B	RASCALOCRACY	531	B
COMMISSION			RASHTRIYA SWAYAMSEVAK SANGH	531	B
RAILROAD BROTHERHOODS	491	B	(RSS) (INDIA)		

RECIDIVISM	240	A
RECIDIVISTS	545	B
RECIPROCAL LEGISLATION	257	A
RECIPROCAL TARIFF	223	A
RECIPROCAL TARIFF ACT	249	A
RECIPROCAL TRADE	216	A
RECIPROCAL TRADE ACT	249	A
RECIPROCAL TRADE AGREEMENTS	231	A
RECIPROCAL TRADE AGREEMENTS ACT OF 1934	257	A
RECIPROCITY	210	A
RECIPROCITY CLAUSE	240	A
RECIPROCITY TREATY	249	A
RECISION	638	B
RECKITT, M.B.	767	B
RECLAMATION	240	A
RECLUS, ELISEE	767	B
RECOGNITION	223	A
RECOGNITION AS INSURGENTS	257	A
RECOGNITION OF A GOVERNMENT	205	A
RECOGNITION OF A NEW SITUATION	638	B
RECOGNITION OF A RULE OF LAW	613	B
RECOGNITION OF A STATE	216	A
RECOGNITION OF BELLIGERENCY	231	A
RECOGNITION OF FOREIGN GOVERNMENTS	216	A
RECOGNITION OF STATES	216	A
RECOGNITION, DIPLOMATIC, OF THE PEOPLE'S REPUBLIC OF CHINA	257	A
RECOGNIZANCE	240	A
RECOLLECTION	638	B
RECOMMENDATIONS FOR POSITIONS	638	B
RECOMMIT	257	A
RECOMMITTAL	257	A
RECONCILIATION	249	A
RECONSIDER	258	A
RECONSIDERATION	258	A
RECONSTRUCTION	216	A
RECONSTRUCTION ACTS	223	A
RECONSTRUCTION FINANCE CORPORATION (RFC)	173	A
RECONSTRUCTION PERIOD	223	A
RECONSTRUCTION, 'TEN PERCENT PLAN'	613	B
RECONSTRUCTION, RADICAL	223	A
RECONVERSION	638	B
RECONVERSION OF ARMAMENTS	258	A
RECORD	807	B
RECORD VOTE	249	A
RECORDER	552	B
RECORDER OF DEEDS	559	B
RECORDING OF DIRECT OBSERVATIONS	144	A
RECORDING OF INTERVIEWS	144	A
RECOUNT	231	A
RECOURSE (AGAINST GOVERNMENT ACTION)	216	A
RECREATION	613	B
RECRUITING	223	A
RECRUITMENT	205	A
RECTIFICATION	452	B
RECTIFICATION OF BOUNDARIES	660	B
RECTIFICATION OF THE MINUTES	613	B
RECTITUDE	140	A
RECURRENCE	613	B
RECURSION THEORY	452	B
RED	552	B
RED ARMY	157	A
RED BOOK	808	B
RED CHINESE COMMUNES	164	A
RED CHINESE COMMUNIST YOUTH LEAGUE	475	B
RED CHINESE FIVE YEAR PLANS	240	A
RED CHINESE NATIONAL PEOPLES CONGRESS	475	B
RED CHINESE PEOPLES REPUBLIC	164	A
RED CRESCENT	818	B
RED CROSS	164	A
RED CROSS FLAG	820	B
RED GUARD, CHINA (PRC)	151	A
RED HERRING	290	A
RED HUNT (MENACE, SCARE)	223	A
RED MOUTH AND SPECKLED BACK PARTY	532	B
RED PATCH	532	B
RED POINTS	828	B
RED REPUBLICAN	532	B
RED REVOLUTION	223	A
RED SCARE	249	A
RED STAR	288	A
RED SUN	828	B
RED TAPE	231	A
RED TERROR	292	A
RED-BAITING	216	A
RED-HANDED	840	B
REDEEM	660	B
REDEMPTION	639	B
REDFORD, EMMETTE S.	767	B
REDISCOUNT	249	A
REDISCOUNTING	589	B
REDISTRIBUTION	140	A
REDISTRIBUTION (OF ELECTORAL DISTRICTS)	249	A
REDISTRICTING	205	A
REDNECK	191	A
REDRAFTING	639	B
REDRESS OF GRIEVANCES	223	A
REDUCTIO AD ABSURDUM	137	A
REDUCTION	639	B
REDUCTION OF ARMAMENTS	258	A
REDUCTION OF MILITARY FORCES	240	A

REGULARITY OF NOMINATIONS	660	B	RELATIVE ADVANTAGE INDEX	458	B
REGULARLY APPOINTED	258	A	RELATIVE MAJORITY	179	A
REGULATION	210	A	RELATIVE PRONOUN	452	B
REGULATION (CONTROL)	216	A	RELATIVISM	124	A
REGULATION (RULE)	231	A	RELATIVITY	137	A
REGULATION OF BUSINESS	231	A	RELAXATION	660	B
REGULATION OF LOBBYING ACT OF 1946	240	A	RELAXATION OF TENSION	240	A
			RELEASE	639	B
REGULATION OF UNFAIR TRADE PRACTICES	240	A	RELEASE FROM NATIONALITY	639	B
			RELEASED TIME CASES	261	A
REGULATION OF VIOLENCE AND FORCE	589	B	RELEASED-TIME PLAN	258	A
			RELEASEMENT	639	B
REGULATOR	553	B	RELEVANCE	144	A
REGULATORY	258	A	RELEVANT EVIDENCE	131	A
REGULATORY AGENCIES	149	A	RELEVANT LOGIC	439	B
REGULATORY COMMISSIONS	151	A	RELEVANT OTHERS	439	B
REGULATORY IMMUNITY	589	B	RELIABILITY	116	A
REGULATORY TAX	231	A	RELIABLE SOURCE	188	A
REHABILITATION	144	A	RELIEF	589	B
REHABILITATION COUNSELORS	559	B	RELIEF AGENCY	475	B
REHABILITATION SERVICES ADMINISTRATION	532	B	RELIEF COMMITTEE	509	B
			RELIEF FUND	589	B
REHEARING	589	B	RELIGION	140	A
REHNQUIST, WILLIAM H.	268	A	RELIGIOUS FACTORS	129	A
REICH	169	A	RELIGIOUS FREEDOM	124	A
REICH CITIZENSHIP LAW	639	B	RELIGIOUS GROUPS	169	A
REICH, WILLIAM	699	B	RELIGIOUS INTOLERANCE	137	A
REICHENBACH, HANS	767	B	RELIGIOUS ISSUE	589	B
REICHSBANK	509	B	RELIGIOUS LEADERS	559	B
REICHSRAT	179	A	RELIGIOUS METAPHORS	446	B
REICHSTAG	169	A	RELIGIOUS ORGANIZATIONS	173	A
REICHSTAG FIRE	231	A	RELIGIOUS TEST	231	A
REICHSWEHR	491	B	RELIGIOUS TOLERATION	131	A
REID VS. COVERT (1956)	679	B	RELIGIOUS WAR	231	A
REIFICATION	124	A	RELIGOUS WARS IN FRANCE	589	B
REIGN	589	B	RELOCATION	589	B
REIGN OF TERROR	231	A	RELOCATION AUTHORITY	491	B
REIGNING DYNASTY	173	A	RELOCATION CENTERS	157	A
REINFORCEMENT	137	A	REMAINDER	613	B
REINSCH, PAUL S.	768	B	REMAND	589	B
REINSTATEMENTS	639	B	REMARK	639	B
REINSURANCE TREATY	660	B	REMBRANDT VAN RIJN	699	B
REISSMAN, LEONARD	768	B	REMEDIAL LEGISLATION	231	A
REITMAN VS. MULKEY (1967)	676	B	REMEDY	660	B
REJECT	249	A	REMEMBER PEARL HARBOR	292	A
REJECTION	258	A	REMEMBER THE ALAMO	292	A
RELATED DISCIPLINES	137	A	REMEMBER THE MAINE	292	A
RELATIONS	452	B	REMEMBER THE RIVER RAISIN	846	B
RELATIONS AMONG GROUPS	439	B	REMILITARIZATION	589	B
RELATIONS AMONG THREE BRANCHES OF U.S. GOVERNMENT	124	A	REMISSION	660	B
			REMIT	589	B
RELATIONS BETWEEN GOVERNMENTS	137	A	REMNANT	509	B
			REMONSTRANCE	613	B
RELATIONS BETWEEN PERSONS	458	B	REMOVABLE EXPENSES	660	B
RELATIONSHIP	137	A	REMOVABLE FROM OFFICE	240	A
RELATIVE	137	A	REMOVAL	249	A

REMOVAL FROM OFFICE	240	A
REMOVAL OF CASES	639	B
REMOVAL POWER	240	A
REMOVE	258	A
RENAISSANCE	205	A
RENAN, ERNEST	768	B
RENAUDEL	768	B
RENDER	639	B
RENDEZVOUS WITH DESTINY	258	A
RENDITION	589	B
RENEGADE	567	B
RENEWAL	613	B
RENEWAL PROJECTS ADMINISTRATION	532	B
RENNER, KARL	768	B
RENOUNCE	613	B
RENOUVIER, CHARLES	768	B
RENT	639	B
RENT CONTROL	240	A
RENT, CLASSIC THEORY OF	140	A
RENTAL ALLOWANCE	589	B
RENTENMARK	828	B
RENTIERS	475	B
RENUCIATION OF ATOMIC WEAPONS	249	A
RENUNCIATION	589	B
RENUNCIATION OF CITIZENSHIP	231	A
REOCCUPATION OF THE RHINELAND	249	A
REORGANIZATION	589	B
REORGANIZATION ACTS, 1939,1949	589	B
REPARATIONS	240	A
REPARATIONS COMMISSION	173	A
REPARATIONS IN KIND	258	A
REPATRIATION	223	A
REPATRIATION OF PRISONERS OF WAR	240	A
REPEAL	223	A
REPEAL AMENDMENT	240	A
REPEAL OF LAWS	216	A
REPEATER	553	B
REPLACEMENT	559	B
REPLACEMENT COST	639	B
REPLICATION	122	A
REPORT	286	A
REPORT WRITING	589	B
REPORTED OUT	258	A
REPORTER	193	A
REPRESENT	249	A
REPRESENTATION	197	A
REPRESENTATION ALLOWANCE	613	B
REPRESENTATIVE	182	A
REPRESENTATIVE ACTION	613	B
REPRESENTATIVE AT LARGE	184	A
REPRESENTATIVE DEMOCRACY	145	A
REPRESENTATIVE GOVERNMENT	146	A
REPRESENTATIVE REGIME	169	A
REPRESSION	210	A
REPRIEVE	231	A
REPRIMAND	249	A
REPRISALS	249	A
REPRODUCTION COST	639	B
REPRODUCTION COST THEORY	458	B
REPUBLIC	149	A
REPUBLIC ORGANIZING COMMITTEE (R.O.C.)	532	B
REPUBLIC, THE	283	A
REPUBLICAINS INDEPENDANTS	532	B
REPUBLICAN	149	A
REPUBLICAN CONFERENCE	164	A
REPUBLICAN ELEPHANT	289	A
REPUBLICAN FORM OF GOVERNMENT	145	A
REPUBLICAN PARTY	145	A
REPUBLICAN PARTY, JEFFERSONIAN	160	A
REPUBLICAN POLICY COMMITTEE	164	A
REPUBLICAN-SOUTHERN DEMOCRATIC COALITION	157	A
REPUBLICANISM	126	A
REPUBLIQUE PARTIE FRANCAIS (RPF) (FIFTH REPUBLIC)	509	B
REPUDIATION	258	A
REPUDIATION OF OBLIGATIONS	258	A
REPUTATION	144	A
REPUTATIONAL	446	B
REQUA, MARK L.	768	B
REQUEST	589	B
REQUEST FOR EXTRADITION	231	A
REQUEST FOR INCLUSION OF QUESTION IN AGENDA	590	B
REQUESTED PARTY	532	B
REQUESTING PARTY	532	B
REQUIEM MASS	639	B
REQUIREMENTS	639	B
REQUISITION	810	B
RERUM NOVARUM (NEW MATTERS)	590	B
RES ADJUDICATA	590	B
RES COMMUNIS (COMMUNITY MATTERS)	639	B
RES JUDICATA	258	A
RES NULLIUS	791	B
RESCHER, NICHOLAS	768	B
RESCIND	590	B
RESEARCH	129	A
RESEARCH -- ADMINISTRATION	590	B
RESEARCH AND DEVELOPMENT (R AND D)	216	A
RESEARCH CENTER	475	B
RESEARCH DESIGN	115	A
RESENTMENT	458	B
RESERVATION	795	B
RESERVE	491	B
RESERVE OFFICERS TRAINING CORPS (ROTC)	169	A

RESERVE RATIO	639	B	RESULTING POWERS	660	B
RESERVED POWERS	202	A	RESULTS OF THE ELECTIONS	613	B
RESETTLEMENT	590	B	RESUME	813	B
RESETTLEMENT ADMINISTRATION	491	B	RESUMPTION ACT	640	B
RESETTLEMENT FUND-COUNCIL OF EUROPE	509	B	RESURGENCE	640	B
			RESURRECTION	590	B
RESHUFFLING OF THE GOVERNMENT	613	B	RETAILING	613	B
			RETALIATION	249	A
RESIDENCE	791	B	RETENTION	258	A
RESIDENCE REQUIREMENT	210	A	RETIRE	590	B
RESIDENT ALIEN	188	A	RETIRED	640	B
RESIDENT COMMISSIONER	553	B	RETIRED LIST	813	B
RESIDENT GENERAL	559	B	RETIREES	553	B
RESIDENTIAL	800	B	RETIREMENT	590	B
RESIDUAL POWERS	210	A	RETIREMENT PLANS, CIVIL SERVICE	613	B
RESIDUARY POWERS	249	A	RETIRING FROM OFFICE	613	B
RESIDUES	458	B	RETORTION	613	B
RESIGNATION	590	B	RETRAINING	640	B
RESISTANCE	179	A	RETREAT	590	B
RESISTANCE GROUP	475	B	RETRENCHMENT	258	A
RESISTANCE MOVEMENT	169	A	RETRIBUTION	590	B
RESISTANCE TO CHANGE	129	A	RETRIBUTIVISM	458	B
RESISTANCE TO TYRANNY	240	A	RETRIEVAL	640	B
RESOCIALIZATION	137	A	RETROACTIVE	137	A
RESOLUTION	249	A	RETROACTIVE LAW	240	A
RESOURCES	287	A	RETROACTIVE LEGISLATION	249	A
RESPECT	446	B	RETROSPECT	439	B
RESPECT FOR HUMAN RIGHTS	258	A	RETURN	640	B
RESPONSE	613	B	RETURN JOURNEY	661	B
RESPONSIBILITY	129	A	RETURN TO NORMALCY	590	B
RESPONSIBILITY OF STATES	258	A	RETURNING BOARD	509	B
RESPONSIBILITY, LEGAL	131	A	RETURNING OFFICER	559	B
RESPONSIBILITY, POLITICAL	118	A	RETURNS	240	A
RESPONSIBLE GOVERNMENT	151	A	REUNIFICATION OF GERMANY	210	A
RESPONSIBLE PARTY SYSTEM	223	A	REUNION	613	B
RESSENTIMENT	452	B	REUTER, ERNST	723	B
REST PERIODS	613	B	REUTHER, WALTER PHILIP	270	A
RESTATEMENT	660	B	REVANCHISM	137	A
RESTORATION	590	B	REVELATION	614	B
RESTORE	660	B	REVENUE	216	A
RESTRAINING ORDER	249	A	REVENUE CUTTER	828	B
RESTRAINT	258	A	REVENUE REFORMER	559	B
RESTRAINT OF TRADE	223	A	REVENUE-SHARING	202	A
RESTRICTED AREA	795	B	REVERENCE FOR LIFE	140	A
RESTRICTED COMMITTEE	532	B	REVERSAL	614	B
RESTRICTED COMMUNITY	532	B	REVERSE BIGOTRY	249	A
RESTRICTED DISTRICT	795	B	REVERSE IMITATION	458	B
RESTRICTED SUFFRAGE	231	A	REVERSE LEND-LEASE	614	B
RESTRICTION	613	B	REVERSE VETO	614	B
RESTRICTIONIST	458	B	REVES, EMERY	768	B
RESTRICTIONS OF MILITARY ESTABLISHMENT	613	B	REVIEW	249	A
			REVISE AND EXTEND	258	A
RESTRICTIVE COVENANT	231	A	REVISED STATUTES	249	A
RESTRICTIVE INTERPRETATION	258	A	REVISION OF A TREATY	249	A
RESTRICTIVE PROVISIONS	258	A	REVISIONISM	120	A
RESTRUCTURING	639	B	REVISIONIST SOCIALISTS	164	A

REVISIONISTS	183	A		RICHES AND REFORM	846	B
REVOCABLE	590	B		RIDER	284	A
REVOCATION OF THE EDICT OF	640	B		RIDGWAY, MATTHEW BUNKER	699	B
NANTES				RIEMER, NEAL	768	B
REVOLT	240	A		RIESELBACH, LEROY	768	B
REVOLT OF THE NETHERLANDS	661	B		RIESMAN, DAVID	265	A
REVOLT OF THE PALACE GUARD	258	A		RIFT	640	B
REVOLUTION	194	A		RIGGED CONVENTION	231	A
REVOLUTION BY CONSENT	590	B		RIGGED MARKET	179	A
REVOLUTION OF INSTITUTIONS	640	B		RIGGS, FRED W.	265	A
REVOLUTION OF RISING	202	A		RIGHT	131	A
EXPECTATIONS				RIGHT DEVIATIONISM	134	A
REVOLUTION OF 1688	216	A		RIGHT OF ACCESS	223	A
REVOLUTION, NEOLITHIC	661	B		RIGHT OF ACCUSED PERSON TO	197	A
REVOLUTIONARY	183	A		COUNSEL		
REVOLUTIONARY DEFEATISM	459	B		RIGHT OF AMENDMENT	590	B
REVOLUTIONARY GOVERNMENT	154	A		RIGHT OF ANGARY	640	B
REVOLUTIONARY IDEOLOGY	120	A		RIGHT OF APPEAL	216	A
REVOLUTIONARY MOVEMENT	149	A		RIGHT OF ASSEMBLY	216	A
REVOLUTIONARY PURPOSE	131	A		RIGHT OF ASSEMBLY AND PETITION	216	A
REVOLUTIONARY SYNDICALISM	131	A		RIGHT OF ASSOCIATION	199	A
REVOLUTIONARY WAR	199	A		RIGHT OF ASYLUM	216	A
REVOLVING FUND	249	A		RIGHT OF AUBAINE	661	B
REVUELTAS, JOSE	768	B		RIGHT OF CAPTURE	614	B
REX PACIFICUS	813	B		RIGHT OF CHAPEL	661	B
REYNAUD, PAUL	723	A		RIGHT OF CONQUEST	258	A
REYNOLDS VS. SIMS (1964)	672	B		RIGHT OF DISCOVERY	258	A
REYNOLDS VS. U.S. (1879)	679	B		RIGHT OF DISSOLUTION	258	A
REZA PAHLEVI	688	B		RIGHT OF DOMICILE	258	A
RHAPSODY	661	B		RIGHT OF ENTRY	231	A
RHEE, DR. SYNGMAN	266	A		RIGHT OF ESTABLISHMENT	640	B
RHEIMS SURRENDER	640	B		RIGHT OF EXPULSION	249	A
RHENISH-BAVARIAN CATHOLIC	532	B		RIGHT OF GRANTING REPRIEVE	590	B
CENTRE				RIGHT OF INTERPELLATION	614	B
RHETIC ACT	661	B		RIGHT OF LEGATION	640	B
RHETONIC	459	B		RIGHT OF NEUTRALITY	216	A
RHINE	281	A		RIGHT OF OPTION	661	B
RHINELAND REMILITARIZATION	231	A		RIGHT OF PARDON	216	A
RHODES, CECIL	272	A		RIGHT OF PASSAGE	240	A
RHODESIA	275	A		RIGHT OF PETITION	199	A
RHODESIA AND NYASALAND	277	A		RIGHT OF PRE-EMPTION	614	B
RHODESIAN FRONT	800	B		RIGHT OF PRIMOGENITURE	216	A
RHYTHM	446	B		RIGHT OF PROPOSING LAWS	614	B
RIBBENTROP, JOACHIM VON	270	A		RIGHT OF RESISTANCE	258	A
RIBICOFF, ABRAHAM ALEXANDER	270	A		RIGHT OF SELF-DEFENSE	231	A
RICARDO, DAVID	266	A		RIGHT OF SELF-DETERMINATION OF	199	A
RICE	824	B		NATIONS		
RICE, STUART	723	B		RIGHT OF SELF-PRESERVATION	249	A
RICH MAN'S CLUB	509	B		RIGHT OF SETTLEMENT	590	B
RICH MAN'S DOLLAR	846	B		RIGHT OF STOPPAGE	614	B
RICH MAN'S WAR, POOR MAN'S	840	B		RIGHT OF VETO	231	A
FIGHT				RIGHT OF VISIT AND SEARCH	240	A
RICH RICHER, POOR POORER	292	A		RIGHT OF WAR PREVENTION	614	B
RICHARDS, ALLEN	768	B		RIGHT OF WAY	258	A
RICHELIEU, CARDINAL DE (ARMAND	265	A		RIGHT OF WITHDRAWAL	590	B
JEAN DUPLESSIS)				RIGHT OF WOMEN TO VOTE	205	A

RIGHT TO A FAIR TRIAL BY INDEPENDENT AND IMPARTIAL JURY	240	A	RIOT	231	A
			RIOT-PRONE	452	B
			RIPARIAN	283	A
RIGHT TO A NATIONALITY	590	B	RIPARIAN STATE	475	B
RIGHT TO ADDRESS THE MEETING	640	B	RIPPER ACT	640	B
RIGHT TO AN ADEQUATE STANDARD OF LIVING	249	A	RIPPER BILL	640	B
			RISE	661	B
RIGHT TO BE PRESUMED INNOCENT UNTIL PROVEN GUILTY	231	A	RISING SUN	289	A
			RISK	240	A
RIGHT TO BEAR ARMS	216	A	RISORGIMENTO (POLITICAL MOVEMENT)	258	A
RIGHT TO BENEFIT OF COUNSEL	205	A			
RIGHT TO BENEFIT OF COUNSEL	223	A	RITCHIE, D. G.	768	B
RIGHT TO COUNSEL	205	A	RITTER, CONSTANTIN	768	B
RIGHT TO DECLARE WAR	258	A	RITUAL	231	A
RIGHT TO EDUCATION	614	B	RIVAL CANDIDATE	545	B
RIGHT TO KNOW	249	A	RIVALRY	446	B
RIGHT TO LIFE	210	A	RIVER AND HARBOR BILLS	258	A
RIGHT TO MARRY AND TO FOUND A FAMILY	640	B	RIVER BASIN PROGRAMS	661	B
			RIVER PLATE BASIN	795	B
RIGHT TO OPT	640	B	RIVERAIN	800	B
RIGHT TO OWN PROPERTY	210	A	RIVERS, W. H. R.	768	B
RIGHT TO PEACEABLE ASSEMBLY	223	A	RIVONIA TRIAL	661	B
RIGHT TO PENSION	258	A	ROAD COMMISSIONER	559	B
RIGHT TO SOCIAL SECURITY	590	B	ROAD TO DEFEAT	841	B
RIGHT TO SPEAK	249	A	ROADS	800	B
RIGHT TO STRIKE	223	A	ROARING TWENTIES	590	B
RIGHT TO WORK	210	A	ROBERTS, C.	768	B
RIGHT TO WORK LAWS	231	A	ROBERTS, WALTER ORR	768	B
RIGHT WING	151	A	ROBERTSON, HOWARD	768	B
RIGHT-LEFT	160	A	ROBERTSON, J. M.	768	B
RIGHT-TO-KNOW LAWS	258	A	ROBERTSON, SIR DENNIS	768	B
RIGHT-WING COALITION	164	A	ROBESPIERRE, MAXIMILEIN FRANCOIS MARIE ISADORE DE	266	A
RIGHT-WING DEVIATIONIST	188	A			
RIGHT-WING GOVERNMENT	173	A	ROBINSON VS. CALIFORNIA (1962)	679	B
RIGHT-WING MOVEMENTS	151	A	ROBINSON-PATMAN ACT OF 1926	640	B
RIGHT-WING OPPOSITION	169	A	ROBINSON, JAMES	723	B
RIGHT-WING PARTIES	154	A	ROBINSON, RICHARD	768	B
RIGHT-WING RADICALISM	126	A	ROBLES, OSWALDO,	768	B
RIGHTEOUS	567	B	ROBOT	824	B
RIGHTIST	188	A	ROBSON, WILLIAM A.	768	B
RIGHTNESS	459	B	ROCCO, ALFREDO	768	B
RIGHTS OF ACCUSED PERSONS	202	A	ROCHET, WALDECK	723	B
RIGHTS OF CHILDREN	223	A	ROCK ROOTED	846	B
RIGHTS OF MAN	205	A	ROCK-RIBBED	837	B
RIGID CONSTITUTION	258	A	ROCKEFELLER FOUNDATION	169	A
RIGID CONSTRUCTION	258	A	ROCKEFELLER, JOHN D.	263	A
RIKER, WILLIAM H.	270	A	ROCKEFELLER, NELSON A.	264	A
RIKSDAG (SWEDEN)	179	A	ROCKER, RUDOLF	768	B
RIMLAND THEORY, GEOPOLITICS	134	A	ROCKET LAUNCHING BASE	792	B
RINDERPEST	828	B	ROCKETS	287	A
RING	491	B	ROCKETS CARRYING NUCLEAR WARHEADS	288	A
RING-TAILED ROARER	568	B			
RINGLEADER	553	B	ROCKINGHAM WHIGS	532	B
RIO GRANDE COMPACT	640	B	ROCKWELL, LANDON	768	B
RIO TREATY OF 1947	249	A	ROCKY	699	B
RIOM TRIALS	661	B	RODO, JOSE	723	B

ROE, GILBERT	769	B
ROEBUCK, J.A.	769	B
ROEPKE, WILHELM	769	B
ROGERS-FOREIGN SERVICE ACT OF 1924	661	B
ROGERS, LINDSAY	769	B
ROGERS, WILLIAM PIERCE	699	B
ROGOW, ARNOLD A.	723	B
ROHM, ERNST	724	B
ROI SOLEIL	272	A
ROKKAN, STEIN	769	B
ROKOSSOVSKY, KONSTANTIN KONSTANTINOVICH	769	B
ROLE	118	A
ROLE PLAYING	129	A
ROLE THEORY	118	A
ROLL CALL	210	A
ROLL-CALL ANALYSIS	126	A
ROLL-CALL VOTE	199	A
ROLLBACK	614	B
ROMAN	532	B
ROMAN CATHOLIC CHURCH	157	A
ROMAN CATHOLICISM	131	A
ROMAN EMPIRE	154	A
ROMAN LAW	202	A
ROMAN REPUBLIC	160	A
ROMANCE OF THE ROSE	661	B
ROMANTIC IDEALISTS	475	B
ROMANTICISM	134	A
ROME	277	A
ROME PROTOCOLS	661	B
ROME TREATIES	614	B
ROME TREATY, EEC (1957)	231	A
ROME TREATY, EURATOM (1957)	258	A
ROME-BERLIN AXIS	164	A
ROME, BERLIN, TOKYO TRIANGLE	173	A
ROMILLY, SAMUEL	769	B
ROMULO, CARLOS PENA	699	B
ROORBACK	846	B
ROOSEVELT COROLLARY OF THE MONROE DOCTRINE	216	A
ROOSEVELT COURT, THE	157	A
ROOSEVELT DOCTRINE	240	A
ROOSEVELT, ANNA ELEANOR	264	A
ROOSEVELT, PRESIDENT FRANKLIN D.	261	A
ROOSEVELT, PRESIDENT THEODORE	262	A
ROOSTER	828	B
ROOSTER PARTY	532	B
ROOT AND BRANCH	841	B
ROOT FORMULA	661	B
ROOT-TAKAHIRA AGREEMENT	590	B
ROOT, HOG, OR DIE	846	B
ROOTS	459	B
ROPER POLL	154	A
RORSCHACH, HERMANN	270	A
ROSBERG, CARL	769	B
ROSE, ARNOLD M.	724	B
ROSECRANCE, RICHARD	699	B
ROSENAU, JAMES	270	A
ROSENBERG, ALFRED	272	A
ROSENBERG, ARTHUR	769	B
ROSENBERG, NATHAN	769	B
ROSENBLUETH, ARTURO	724	B
ROSENWALD FOUNDATION	532	B
ROSS, W.D.	769	B
ROSSI, PETER H.	699	B
ROSSITER, CLINTON	270	A
ROSSONI	769	B
ROSTOVTZEFF, M.	769	B
ROSTOW, EUGENE	272	A
ROSTRUM	820	B
ROTATING CHAIRMANSHIP	590	B
ROTATION	640	B
ROTATION-IN-OFFICE	258	A
ROTH VS. U.S. (1957)	261	A
ROTH, PHILIP	769	B
ROTH, WILLIAM V.	769	B
ROTHMAN, STANLEY	769	B
ROTHROCK, JOSEPH T.	769	B
ROTHWELL, C. EASTON	769	B
ROTTEN BOROUGH	277	A
ROUGHRIDER	475	B
ROUND ROBIN	640	B
ROUNDER	568	B
ROUNDHEADS	491	B
ROUNDTABLE CONFERENCES	258	A
ROUSSEAU, JEAN JACQUES	262	A
ROUTES	795	B
ROUTINIZATION	144	A
ROUVROY, CLAUDE HENRI DE	769	B
ROVING AMBASSADOR	191	A
ROW	614	B
ROWAN, CARL	699	B
ROWAT, PROFESSOR	769	B
ROWE, LEO S.	769	B
ROWNTREE, B. SEEBOHM	699	B
ROY, M.N.	769	B
ROYAL	545	B
ROYAL ACADEMY OF BELGIUM	532	B
ROYAL COLONY	281	A
ROYAL COMMISSION OF ENQUIRY (BRITAIN)	179	A
ROYAL COMMISSION OF POPULATION	532	B
ROYAL COMMISSION ON LOCAL GOVERNMENT	491	B
ROYAL COMMISSION ON THE CIVIL SERVICE	532	B
ROYAL COMMISSION ON THE COAL INDUSTRY	532	B

ROYAL COMMISSION ON THE POOR LAWS	509	B
ROYAL COMMISSION ON THE PRESS	532	B
ROYAL COMMISSION ON UNEMPLOYMENT INSURANCE	532	B
ROYAL COMMISSION, BRITAIN	179	A
ROYAL DYNASTY	174	A
ROYAL GOVERNOR	191	A
ROYAL HONORS	614	B
ROYAL INSTITUTE OF INTERNATIONAL AFFAIRS (BRITAIN)	174	A
ROYAL INSTITUTE OF PUBLIC ADMINISTRATION	509	B
ROYAL PREROGATIVE	258	A
ROYAL SUCCESSION	240	A
ROYAL VICTORIAN ORDER	532	B
RUANDA URUNDI	279	A
RUBAKIN, NIKOLAI ALEKSANDROVICH	769	B
RUBBER	824	B
RUBBER CHICKEN CIRCUIT	795	B
RUBBER DOLLAR	828	B
RUBBER RESERVE COMPANY	532	B
RUBBER STAMP	590	B
RUBBER STAMP, TO BE A	292	A
RUBY, JACK	699	B
RUFFLE(D) SHIRT	568	B
RUGE, ARNOLD	769	B
RUGGED INDIVIDUALISM	131	A
RUHR OCCUPATION	249	A
RULE	216	A
RULE CONCERNING THE LANGUAGES	661	B
RULE OF FOUR	590	B
RULE OF LAW, DEMOCRATIC THEORY	120	A
RULE OF ORDER	591	B
RULE OF PROCEDURE	231	A
RULE OF REASON	216	A
RULE OF SPECIALTY	661	B
RULE OF TERROR	240	A
RULE OF THE MAJORITY	197	A
RULE OF THREE	258	A
RULE OF TWENTY-FOUR HOURS INTERVAL	661	B
RULE OF UNANIMITY	231	A
RULE OF WAR	591	B
RULE ON INTERNATIONAL NEIGHBORSHIP	661	B
RULE OR RUIN	834	B
RULE UTILITARIANISM	452	B
RULE 22 OF THE SENATE	231	A
RULE-MAKING POWER	202	A
RULED	188	A
RULER	186	A
RULES	205	A
RULES AND ADMINISTRATION COMMITTEE	491	B
RULES OF THE GAME	223	A
RULES OF WARFARE	216	A
RULING	614	B
RULING CASE LAW	249	A
RULING CLASS	147	A
RUM FLEET	828	B
RUM, ROMANISM, AND REBELLION	292	A
RUMANIA (ROUMANIA)	277	A
RUMANIANS	491	B
RUMOR	249	A
RUMOR, MARIANO	699	B
RUMP (CONGRESS)	491	B
RUMP PARLIAMENT	174	A
RUMP SESSION	249	A
RUN	614	B
RUN (ON BANKS)	249	A
RUN AHEAD OF THE TICKET	240	A
RUN SCARED	249	A
RUN WITHOUT WEIGHTS	846	B
RUN-OFF BALLOT	216	A
RUN-OFF PRIMARY	205	A
RUNCIMAN MISSION	640	B
RUNCIMAN, W. G.	769	B
RUNNING FOR THE EXERCISE	846	B
RUNNING LIKE A DRY CREEK	846	B
RUNNING MATE	184	A
RUNOFF	249	A
RUNOFF PRIMARY	216	A
RURAL	281	A
RURAL AREAS	792	B
RURAL COMMUNE	174	A
RURAL DISTRICT	274	A
RURAL ELECTRIFICATION	231	A
RURAL ELECTRIFICATION ADMINISTRATION (REA)	169	A
RURAL ELECTRIFICATION AUTHORITY	475	B
RURAL FREE DELIVERY (RFD)	258	A
RURAL GOVERNMENT	169	A
RURAL LOCAL GOVERNMENT	174	A
RURAL PARISH	792	B
RURAL PARTY	179	A
RURAL SLUMS	283	A
RURAL-URBAN MIGRATION	129	A
RURBAN CENTERS	800	B
RUS, DAVID DEAN	769	B
RUSE OF WAR	640	B
RUSH-BAGOT AGREEMENT (1817)	614	B
RUSH, BENJAMIN	724	B
RUSK VS. CORT (1963)	679	B
RUSK, DAVID DEAN	270	A
RUSKIN COLLEGE	533	B
RUSKIN, JOHN	769	B
RUSS-JAPANESE WAR	232	A

RUSSELL	770	B	SAFETY	258	A
RUSSELL SAGE FOUNDATION	509	B	SAFETY APPLIANCE ACTS	661	B
RUSSELL, BERTRAND	263	A	SAFETY BELT	820	B
RUSSELL, LORD JOHN	724	B	SAFETY COMMISSIONER	559	B
RUSSETT, BRUCE M.	699	B	SAFETY EDUCATION	661	B
RUSSIA	274	A	SAG (USSR - CORPORATIONS)	533	B
RUSSIAN AUTOCRACY UNDER TSARDOM	169	A	SAG NICHTS	533	B
			SAGE OF GREYSTONE	770	B
RUSSIAN CAMPAIGN	640	B	SAGE OF MONTICELLO	272	A
RUSSIAN COMMUNISTS	157	A	SAGE-BRUSH STATES	800	B
RUSSIAN CONSTITUTION	258	A	SAHEL-BENIN UNION	533	B
RUSSIAN REVOLUTION OF 1917	195	A	SAINT	559	B
RUSSIAN SATELLITES	287	A	SAINT ALBANS, NEW ZEALAND	800	B
RUSSIAN SOCIALIST FEDERAL SOVIET REPUBLIC (RSFSR)	169	A	SAINT AUGUSTINE	263	A
			SAINT BARTHOLOMEW'S NIGHT	640	B
RUSSIANS	179	A	SAINT JOHN, VINCENT	724	B
RUSSO-FINNISH WAR	232	A	SAINT LAWRENCE SEAWAY DEVELOPMENT CORPORATION	475	B
RUSSO-GERMAN ALLIANCE OF 1828	533	B			
RUSSO-JAPANESE AGREEMENTS	258	A	SAINT LAWRENCE SEAWAY PROJECT	179	A
RUSSO-JAPANESE PACT	232	A			
RUSSO-JAPANESE WAR	223	A	SAINT LAWRENCE WATERWAY	279	A
RUSTIN	770	B	SAINT LOUIS BISTATE AGENCY	509	B
RUSTLING BEHIND THE JALOUSIES	661	B	SAINT PATRICK	699	B
RUTLEDGE, JOHN	770	B	SAINT PAUL	688	B
RWANDA	279	A	SAINT-JUST, ANTOINE	770	B
RYAN, JOHN A.	770	B	SAINT-MANDE PROGRAMME	661	B
RYE	828	B	SAINT-SIMON, COUNT HENRI DE	273	A
RYE HOUSE PLOT	661	B	SAIT, EDWARD M.	770	B
RYKOV, A. I.	770	B	SAKHALIN	792	B
RYUKU ISLANDS	281	A	SAKHAROV, ANDREI	688	B
S.O.B.	559	B	SALA	459	B
SAAR	277	A	SALADIN	770	B
SAAR AGREEMENT (SA)	258	A	SALAN, RAOUL, GENERAL	724	B
SAAR PLEBISCITE	258	A	SALARY GRAB	614	B
SABAH, SHEIKH SABAH AS-SALIM AS-	770	B	SALAZAR, DR. ANTONIO DE OLIVEIRA	270	A
SABINE, GEORGE H.	724	B	SALES AND USE TAX	216	A
SABOTAGE	249	A	SALES TAX	205	A
SABOTEUR	545	B	SALESMEN	568	B
SACCO-VANZETTI CASE	260	A	SALIC LAW	641	B
SACERDOTIUM AND IMPERIUM	491	A	SALIENCY	140	A
SACHEM	553	B	SALISBURY, MARQUIS DE	699	B
SACHENSPIEGEL	813	B	SALLAL, ABDULLAH	770	B
SACRED	137	A	SALMASIUS, CLAUDIUS	770	B
SACRED COLLEGE OF CARDINALS	174	A	SALOON PARTY	533	B
SACRED COW	292	A	SALT MARCH	641	B
SACRIFICE	640	B	SALT TAX	258	A
SADAT, ANWAR	264	A	SALTER, F. R.	770	B
SADDLE BAG RESOLUTIONS	661	B	SALTER, SIR ARTHUR	770	B
SADISM	140	A	SALTONSTALL, LEVERETT	699	B
SADLER, WILLIAM S.	770	B	SALUTATIONS	614	B
SAFE	661	B	SALUTE	258	A
SAFE DISTRICTS	274	A	SALUTE AT SEA	662	B
SAFE STREETS ACT	249	A	SALVADOR(EL)-HONDURAS	283	A
SAFE-CONDUCT	258	A	SALVADORI	770	B
SAFEGUARD	614	B	SALVATION	249	A

SALVATION ARMY	491	B	SATELLITE	288	A
SALVEMINI, GAETANO	770	B	SATELLITE CITY	283	A
SAMARITANS	509	B	SATELLITE NATION	273	A
SAMOA	279	A	SATELLITE STATE	275	A
SAMOA, AMERICAN	279	A	SATHAGRAHA	446	B
SAMPLE	134	A	SATISFACTION	439	B
SAMPLE BALLOT	283	A	SATO, EISAKU	688	B
SAMPLE SURVEY	122	A	SATRAP	545	B
SAMPLING TECHNIQUES	113	A	SATSUMA-HAN	800	B
SAMUEL, VISCOUNT	770	B	SATYAGRAHA (GHANDIAN POLICY)	258	A
SAMUELSON, PAUL	265	A	SAUD, KING	273	A
SAMURAI	174	A	SAUDI ARABIA	275	A
SAN FRANCISCO CONFERENCE	174	A	SAUERKRAUT MONEY	846	B
(UNCIO)			SAVIGNY, FRIEDRICH KARL VON	724	B
SAN FRANCISCO VIGILANCE	509	B	SAVILE, SIR GEORGE	770	B
COMMITTEE OF 1856			SAVINGS BANK	533	B
SAN MARTIN, JOSE DE	273	A	SAVINGS BONDS AND STAMPS	249	A
SANCHEZ-VILELLA, ROBERTO	770	B	SAVONAROLA, GIROLAMO	724	B
SANCTION OF LAW	240	A	SAWREY, WILLIAM L.	770	B
SANCTIONS	205	A	SAXBE, WILLIAM B.	268	A
SANCTIONS (COLLECTIVE SECURITY)	197	A	SAXO GRAMMATICUS	813	B
SANCTIONS (DISARMAMENT	232	A	SAXONS	179	A
ENFORCEMENT)			SAYING	846	B
SANCTIONS (INTERNATIONAL LAW)	199	A	SAYRE, WALLACE	688	B
SANCTITY OF TREATIES	240	A	SCAB	188	A
SAND LOT (IN VARIOUS	800	B	SCALAWAG	193	A
COMPOUNDS)			SCALE	287	A
SAND-LOT PARTY	533	B	SCALE ANALYSIS	124	A
SANDBAG	641	B	SCALES VS. U.S. (1957)	679	B
SANDHURST	475	B	SCALOGRAM ANALYSIS	126	A
SANDYS, DUNCAN	724	B	SCANDALS	258	A
SANE	452	B	SCANDINAVIA	277	A
SANITARY CODE	591	B	SCANDINAVIAN LAW SPEAKER	559	B
SANITARY CORDON	279	A	SCANDINAVIANS	188	A
SANITARY DISTRICT	792	B	SCAPE-GOATING	240	A
SANJAK OF ALEXANDRETTA	770	B	SCARCITY	232	A
SANKARA	770	B	SCARECROW	553	B
SANKHYA (HINDU PHILOSOPHY)	459	B	SCENARIO	249	A
SANS-CULOTTE	509	B	SCENE	800	B
SANSKRIT	452	B	SCEPTIC	191	A
SANSOM, GEORGE	770	B	SCEPTICISM	134	A
SANTA ANNA, ANTONIO LOPEZ DE	700	B	SCEPTRE	820	B
SANTANDER, FRANCISCO DE PAULA	770	B	SCHACHT, HJALMAR HORACE	771	B
SANTAYANA, GEORGE	265	A	GREELEY		
SANTIAGO, CHILE	281	A	SCHACHTER, STANLEY	771	B
SAPIN, BURTON	770	B	SCHAEFFLE, ALBERT	771	B
SAPIR, EDWARD	724	B	SCHAEFR, ADOLF	771	B
SARAGAT, GIUSEPPE	724	B	SCHAFFNER, JAKOB	771	B
SARAJEVO ASSASSINATIONS	240	A	SCHARF, EDWIN	771	B
SARAWALK	795	B	SCHATTSCHNEIDER, ELMER E.	273	A
SARDINIA, ITALY	789	B	SCHECTER POULTRY CORP VS. U.S.	261	A
SARGON OF AKKAD	770	B	(1935)		
SARIT THANARAT, FIELD MARSHALL	724	B	SCHEDULE	808	B
SARTORI, GIOVANNI	724	B	SCHEDULED CLASSES	491	B
SARTRE, JEAN-PAUL	264	A	SCHEDULES A B AND C	813	B
SARVODAYA	533	B	SCHEDULING	614	B

SCHELER, MAX	771	B
SCHELLING, FRIEDRICH WILHELM VON	771	B
SCHELLING, THOMAS C.	270	A
SCHEMANN, L.	771	B
SCHEME	662	B
SCHENCK VS. U.S. (1919)	261	A
SCHIEL	771	B
SCHILLER, J.C.F.	771	B
SCHISM	240	A
SCHISMOGENESIS	828	B
SCHIZOPHRENIA	140	A
SCHLEIERMACHER, F.D.E.	771	B
SCHLESINGER, JOSEPH	700	B
SCHLIEFFEN PLAN	614	B
SCHLIEMANN	771	B
SCHMERHORN, R. A.	771	B
SCHMIDHAUSER, JOHN R.	688	B
SCHMIDT, JOHANN KASPER	771	B
SCHMIDT, RICHARD	771	B
SCHMITT, CARL	771	B
SCHMITTER, P.	771	B
SCHMOLLER, GUSTAV	771	B
SCHNEIDER VS. RUSK (1964)	679	B
SCHNEIDER-CURESOT	771	B
SCHNEIDER, LOUIS	771	B
SCHOLASTICISM	137	A
SCHOLEM, GERSHOM	700	B
SCHOOL	169	A
SCHOOL BOARDS	154	A
SCHOOL DESEGREGATION	202	A
SCHOOL DISTRICTS	276	A
SCHOOL LUNCH PROGRAM	232	A
SCHOOL OF ORIENTAL STUDIES (LONDON)	533	B
SCHOOL RITUALS	662	B
SCHOOLHOUSE CAMPAIGN	662	B
SCHOOLING	614	B
SCHOOLS OF PHILOSOPHY	160	A
SCHOPENHAUER, ARTHUR	273	A
SCHRECKLICHKEIT	662	B
SCHRODER, GERHARD	700	B
SCHUBERT, GLENDON	688	B
SCHUMACHER, KURT	700	B
SCHUMAN	724	B
SCHUMAN PLAN	249	A
SCHUMAN, ROBERT	688	B
SCHUMPETER, JOSEPH A.	268	A
SCHUSCHNIGG, KURT VON	724	B
SCHUTZ, ALFRED	771	B
SCHUTZSTAFFEL	509	B
SCHWARZE KORPS	533	B
SCHWEIKER, RICHARD SCHULTZ	724	B
SCHWEITZER, ALBERT	268	A
SCHWERING	771	B
SCIENCE	134	A
SCIENCE ADVISORY COMMISSION	491	B
SCIENCE AND ASTRONAUTICS COMMITTEE	509	B
SCIENCE AND GOVERNMENT	129	A
SCIENCE, PURE	134	A
SCIENOMICS	459	B
SCIENTIFIC ADVISORY COMMITTEE OF IAEA	533	B
SCIENTIFIC ATTACHE	553	B
SCIENTIFIC EVIDENCE	122	A
SCIENTIFIC FREEDOM	137	A
SCIENTIFIC MANAGEMENT MOVEMENT	164	A
SCIENTIFIC METHOD	113	A
SCIENTIFIC RESEARCH	122	A
SCIENTIFIC REVOLUTION	205	A
SCIENTISM	134	A
SCIENTIST	185	A
SCIPIO AEMILIANUS	771	B
SCIPIONIC CIRCLE	533	B
SCISSION	662	B
SCOOT	846	B
SCOPE	446	B
SCOPES EVOLUTION TRIAL	232	A
SCORCHED-EARTH POLICY	232	A
SCORE	258	A
SCOTLAND	279	A
SCOTT, HUGH D., JR.	268	A
SCOTT, JOHN W.	771	B
SCOTTISH COMMITTEE	533	B
SCOTTISH NATIONAL PARTY	180	A
SCOTTISH REPRESENTATIVE PEERS	509	B
SCOTTSBORO CASES	261	A
SCRANTON COMMISSION	475	B
SCRAP OF PAPER	808	B
SCRATCH	662	B
SCREENING	591	B
SCREWS VS. U.S. (1945)	679	B
SCRIP	820	B
SCRIPTURES	808	B
SCRUTIN D'ARRONDISSEMENT	641	B
SCRUTIN DE LISTE	641	B
SCRUTIN PUBLIQUE	662	B
SCRUTINEER	568	B
SCULPTURE	824	B
SEA	792	B
SEA FLOOR	283	A
SEA FRONTIERS	789	B
SEA POWER THEORY, GEOPOLITICS	134	A
SEABED	283	A
SEABURY COMMISSION	533	B
SEAGLE, WILLIAM	771	B
SEAL	824	B
SEAL OF THE UNITED STATES	818	B
SEALER	568	B

SEANAD EIREANN (IRISH UPPER HOUSE) 509 B
SEARCH AND SEIZURE 205 A
SEARCH WARRANT 216 A
SEARS, ROEBUCK AND COMPANY 491 B
SEASONAL EMPLOYMENT 258 A
SEAT 249 A
SEATING ARRANGEMENT 591 B
SECESH 533 B
SECESSION 202 A
SECOND 614 B
SECOND AMENDMENT 232 A
SECOND BALLOT SYSTEM 240 A
SECOND BANDUNG CONFERENCE 259 A
SECOND CHAMBER 180 A
SECOND CIVIL RIGHTS ACT 249 A
SECOND CLASS CITIZEN 186 A
SECOND CONTINENTAL CONGRESS 151 A
SECOND DEVELOPMENT DECADE 614 B
SECOND EMPIRE OF FRANCE 174 A
SECOND INTERNATIONAL 164 A
SECOND NATIONAL BANK OF THE U.S. 174 A
SECOND PAPERS 808 B
SECOND READING 259 A
SECOND REICH 174 A
SECOND REPUBLIC OF FRANCE 174 A
SECOND WAR FOR INDEPENDENCE 641 B
SECOND-CLASS MAIL PRIVILEGE 591 B
SECONDARY BOYCOTT 232 A
SECONDARY GROUP 146 A
SECONDARY INSTITUTIONS 174 A
SECONDARY PICKETING 249 A
SECONDARY RELATIONSHIPS 140 A
SECONDARY SOURCE OF LAW 591 B
SECONDARY STRUCTURES 452 B
SECONDARY THEATRE OF WAR 792 B
SECONDAT, CHARLES DE 771 B
SECRECY 240 A
SECRECY IN GOVERNMENT 223 A
SECRECY OF CORRESPONDENCE 641 B
SECRET AGREEMENTS 240 A
SECRET BALLOT 202 A
SECRET CLAUSE 250 A
SECRET DIPLOMACY 223 A
SECRET ORGANIZATION 475 B
SECRET PROTOCOL 250 A
SECRET SERVICE 157 A
SECRET SESSION 250 A
SECRET SOCIETIES 180 A
SECRET TREATIES 216 A
SECRET TREATY OF LONDON 662 B
SECRETARIAT (INTERNATIONAL ORGANIZATION) 160 A
SECRETARIAT BUILDING 818 B
SECRETARIAT OF THE CENTRAL COMMITTEE, U.S.S.R. 157 A
SECRETARIAT OF THE UNITED NATIONS 149 A
SECRETARY 193 A
SECRETARY COUNCIL 475 B
SECRETARY OF AGRICULTURE 186 A
SECRETARY OF AN EMBASSY 559 B
SECRETARY OF COMMERCE 185 A
SECRETARY OF DEFENSE 181 A
SECRETARY OF HEALTH, EDUCATION AND WELFARE 184 A
SECRETARY OF HOUSING AND URBAN DEVELOPMENT 183 A
SECRETARY OF LABOR 185 A
SECRETARY OF STATE 183 A
SECRETARY OF STATE IN STATES 188 A
SECRETARY OF THE AIR FORCE 188 A
SECRETARY OF THE ARMY 187 A
SECRETARY OF THE COMMONWEALTH 568 B
SECRETARY OF THE INTERIOR 183 A
SECRETARY OF THE NAVY 187 A
SECRETARY OF THE TREASURY 185 A
SECRETARY OF TRANSPORTATION 188 A
SECRETARY OF WAR 187 A
SECRETARY-GENERAL 183 A
SECT 174 A
SECTARIANISM 140 A
SECTION 795 B
SECTION 7A 641 B
SECTIONAL TRADING 662 B
SECTIONALISM 124 A
SECTOR BOUNDARY 795 B
SECTOR PRINCIPLE 662 B
SECULAR 140 A
SECULARISM 134 A
SECULARIZATION 210 A
SECURE 641 B
SECURITIES 289 A
SECURITIES ACT OF 1933 232 A
SECURITIES AND EXCHANGE COMMISSION (SEC) 169 A
SECURITIES EXCHANGE ACT OF 1934 232 A
SECURITY 240 A
SECURITY COUNCIL OF THE UNITED NATIONS 146 A
SECURITY GUARANTEE 591 B
SECURITY PACT 240 A
SECURITY PROGRAM 259 A
SECURITY RISK 188 A
SEDITION 210 A
SEDITION ACT OF 1918 250 A
SEDITIOUS LIBEL 240 A
SEED IMPROVEMENT 662 B

SEEGER, HEINZ	700	B
SEEKERS	568	B
SEESAW BILL	662	B
SEGMENTATION	452	B
SEGNI, ANTONIO	772	B
SEGREGATION	196	A
SEGREGATIONIST	185	A
SEIGNIORAGE (MINTING TAX)	614	B
SEISMOLOGICAL UNION	533	B
SEIYUKAI PARTY	533	B
SEIZE	240	A
SEIZURE OF A VESSEL	591	B
SEIZURE OF POWER	223	A
SEKOU TOURE, AHMED	270	A
SELASSIE, HAILE	265	A
SELDEN, JOHN	772	B
SELDES, GILBERT	772	B
SELECT	615	B
SELECT COMMITTEE	164	A
SELECT COMMITTEE ON NATIONAL EXPENDITURE (BRITAIN)	533	B
SELECTION	615	B
SELECTION OF JUDGES	223	A
SELECTIVE DRAFT LAW CASES	676	B
SELECTIVE SERVICE	216	A
SELECTIVE SERVICE ACT	232	A
SELECTIVE SERVICE ADMINISTRATION	174	A
SELECTIVE SERVICE SYSTEM	169	A
SELECTIVE TRAINING AND SERVICE ACT	250	A
SELECTMEN	545	B
SELF	446	B
SELF-APPOINTED	615	B
SELF-AWARENESS	439	B
SELF-CONSCIOUSNESS	452	B
SELF-CRITICISM IN THE U.S.S.R.	250	A
SELF-DECEPTION	140	A
SELF-DEFENSE	210	A
SELF-DEPRECATING HUMOR	615	B
SELF-DETERMINATION	202	A
SELF-DETERMINATION OF NATIONS	210	A
SELF-GOVERNMENT	118	A
SELF-HELP	240	A
SELF-IDENTITY	439	B
SELF-IMAGE	137	A
SELF-INCRIMINATION	206	A
SELF-INTEREST	131	A
SELF-KNOWLEDGE	144	A
SELF-LIQUIDATING DEBT	240	A
SELF-LIQUIDATING PROJECT	259	A
SELF-MANAGEMENT	452	B
SELF-OBSERVATION	447	B
SELF-PERPETUATING BOARD	491	B
SELF-PRESERVATION	250	A
SELF-REALIZATION	439	B
SELF-REFERENCE	459	B
SELF-VERIFICATION	439	B
SELLERS, CHARLES	772	B
SELLING CANDIDATES LIKE SOAP	291	A
SELLING OUT	615	B
SELLOUT	591	B
SELZNICK, PHILIP	724	B
SEMANTIC DIFFERENTIAL	144	A
SEMANTICS	131	A
SEMBAT, MARCEL	772	B
SEMI-OFFICIAL ORGANIZATION	476	B
SEMI-OFFICIAL SOURCE	193	A
SEMI-SOVEREIGN	439	B
SEMILEGAL PRIVATE ASSOCIATIONS	509	B
SEMINAR	641	B
SEMIOFFICIAL	174	A
SEMIOLOGY	459	B
SEMIOTICS	452	B
SEMITES	174	A
SENACA	724	B
SENANAYAKE, DUDLEY	772	B
SENATE	149	A
SENATE COMMITTEES	151	A
SENATE CONGRESSIONAL RESOLUTION (S CON RES)	240	A
SENATE JOINT RESOLUTION (S J RES)	216	A
SENATE JOURNAL	284	A
SENATE OF THE UNITED STATES	148	A
SENATE RESOLUTION (S RES)	223	A
SENATE RULES	223	A
SENATE SPECIAL POWERS	250	A
SENATE-VICE PRESIDENT	188	A
SENATE, FRANCE	174	A
SENATE, ITALY	180	A
SENATOR	184	A
SENATOR FROM FORMOSA	724	B
SENATORIAL CAMPAIGN COMMITTEE	169	A
SENATORIAL COURTESY	216	A
SENATORS FOR LIFE	546	B
SENDING STATE	533	B
SENECA, LUCIUS ANNAEUS	772	B
SENEGAL	277	A
SENEGAL RIVER STATES ORGANIZATION	509	B
SENGHOR, LEOPOLD-SEDAR	724	B
SENIOR CITIZEN	188	A
SENIOR OFFICIALS	193	A
SENIOR SENATOR	188	A
SENIORITY	202	A
SENIORITY RULE	202	A
SENSATION	591	B
SENSE	144	A
SENSE DATA	144	A
SENSES	439	B
SENSIBILITY	459	B

SENSITIVITY TRAINING	137	A
SENSITIVTY-TRAINING DESIGN	452	B
SENTENCE	240	A
SENTENCING	250	A
SENTENTIAL CALCULUS	459	B
SENTIMENTS	447	B
SENUSSI	533	B
SEPARATE BUT EQUAL DOCTRINE	202	A
SEPARATE PEACE	591	B
SEPARATE TREATY	591	B
SEPARATION	439	B
SEPARATION ALLOWANCE	615	B
SEPARATION FROM SERVICE	615	B
SEPARATION OF CHURCH AND STATE	199	A
SEPARATION OF COLONIES FROM MOTHER COUNTRY	591	B
SEPARATION OF POWERS	195	A
SEPARATISM	140	A
SEPOY MUTINY (1857-58)	662	B
SEPTENNATE	662	B
SEQUELS	662	B
SEQUENTIAL DEVELOPMENT	144	A
SEQUESTRATION	615	B
SERBIANS	174	A
SERFDOM	216	A
SERGEANT-AT-ARMS	188	A
SERIAL BONDS	641	B
SERIATIM	447	B
SERMON ON THE MOUNT	250	A
SERRAJ, ABD AL-HAMID	772	B
SERVICE	641	B
SERVICE CONTRACT	662	B
SERVICE DE SONDAGE ET DE STATISTIQUE	533	B
SERVICE INDUSTRY	174	A
SERVICE OF WRITS AND RECORDS OF JUDICIAL VERDICTS	591	B
SERVICE RATING	662	B
SERVICEMEN	546	B
SERVICEMEN'S READJUSTMENT ACT	662	B
SERVICES	641	B
SERVITUDE	241	A
SESSION	259	A
SESSION LAWS	615	B
SESSIONS OF CONGRESS	210	A
SET	180	A
SET THEORY	129	A
SETTING	615	B
SETTING-UP	662	B
SETTING, AND SYSTEMS THEORY	137	A
SETTLEMENT	615	B
SETTLEMENT BY COMPROMISE	241	A
SETTLEMENT HOUSES	174	A
SETTLER	553	B
SEVEN YEARS WAR	259	A
SEVEN-YEAR PLAN	641	B
SEVEN-YEAR TERM OF OFFICE	662	B
SEVENTEENTH AMENDMENT	217	A
SEVENTH AMENDMENT	217	A
SEVENTH-OF-MARCH SPEECH	662	B
SEVERANCE OF DIPLOMATIC RELATIONS	223	A
SEVERANCE PAY	250	A
SEVERANCE TAX	615	B
SEX	591	B
SEX DISCRIMINATION	223	A
SEXBY, COL.	772	B
SEXTUS EMPIRICUS	772	B
SEXUAL BEHAVIOR	144	A
SEXUALITY	447	B
SEYM (POLAND)	509	B
SEYSS-INQUART, ARTHUR	724	B
SFORZA, COUNT CARLO	772	B
SHABBI, ABU AL-QASIM AL-	772	B
SHADOW CABINET	164	A
SHAFTSBURY	724	B
SHAH	191	A
SHAKAITO	533	B
SHAKEDOWN	641	B
SHAKESPEARE, WILLIAM	270	A
SHAKING THE PEAR TREE	841	B
SHAM DEMOCRACY	491	B
SHAMANS	553	B
SHAMBAUGH, BENJAMIN F.	772	B
SHAME	615	B
SHAMOUN, CAMILLE	772	B
SHANGRI-LA	792	B
SHAPER	568	B
SHARE CROPPER	193	A
SHARE-THE-WEALTH MOVEMENT	169	A
SHARECROPPING	241	A
SHARED ATTITUDE	134	A
SHARED PURPOSE	447	B
SHARED TAXES	591	B
SHARES	459	B
SHARIA (SACRED LAW OF ISLAM)	615	B
SHARJAH	533	B
SHARKANSKY, K.	772	B
SHARP, WALTER	772	B
SHASTRI, LAL BAHADUR	724	B
SHAW, ALBERT	772	B
SHAW, ANNA HOWARD	772	B
SHAW, GEORGE BERNARD	266	A
SHAYS' REBELLION	217	A
SHEATSLEY, PAUL B.	772	B
SHEEP IN SHEEP'S CLOTHING	847	B
SHEHAB, FUAD	772	B
SHEIK	193	A
SHELL GAME	292	A
SHELLEY VS. KRAMER (1948)	673	B
SHELLEY, PERCY BYSSHE	724	B

SHELVE (PUT ON THE SHELF)	591	B	SHOWING THE FLAG	591	B
SHEPARD, MAX	772	B	SHREVEPORT RATE CASE	261	A
SHEPARD, WALTER J.	772	B	SHRIEK (-ER)	568	B
SHEPARD'S CITATIONS	285	A	SHRIMPS WHISTLE	847	B
SHEPILOV, DMITRI	724	B	SHRIVER, SARGENT	270	A
SHEPPARD-TOWNER ACT	662	B	SHUBIK, MARTIN	725	B
SHERIA	662	B	SHVERNIK, NIKOLAI	725	B
SHERIDAN	725	B	SHYSTER LAWYER	553	B
SHERIFF	185	A	SI OMNES CLAUSE	663	B
SHERMAN ANTITRUST ACT OF 1890	210	A	SIAMESE TWIN	568	B
SHERMAN SILVER PURCHASE ACT	641	B	SIBLEY, MULFORD	700	B
SHERMAN STATEMENT	615	B	SICK LEAVE	591	B
SHERWOOD, FOSTER H.	772	B	SICK MAN OF EUROPE	688	B
SHIELDS, CURRIN V.	772	B	SIDE PAYMENTS	259	A
SHIFT DIFFERENTIALS	662	B	SIDESHOW	663	B
SHIFT WORK	641	B	SIDETRACK	591	B
SHIFTS	662	B	SIDNEY, ALGERNON	725	B
SHIITE	509	B	SIEGE	259	A
SHILS, EDWARD A.	688	B	SIEGFRIED LINE	283	A
SHINGLE CLAPPER	828	B	SIERRA LEONE	276	A
SHINPLASTERS	828	B	SIEYES	772	B
SHINTOISM	137	A	SIFFIN, WILLIAM	700	B
SHINY HAT BRIGADE	533	B	SIFTING COMMITTEE	533	B
SHIP	828	B	SIGEL, ROBERTA	725	B
SHIP OF STATE	837	B	SIGER OF BRABANT	773	B
SHIP'S PAPERS	808	B	SIGHELE, SCIPIO	773	B
SHIPPING	662	B	SIGISTANI	773	B
SHIPPING BOARD	509	B	SIGN	641	B
SHIPPING SUBSIDY	591	B	SIGNATORY GOVERNMENTS	169	A
SHIRE	789	B	SIGNATORY STATES	174	A
SHIRTSLEEVE DIPLOMACY	615	B	SIGNATURE	285	A
SHOESTRING DISTRICT	795	B	SIGNATURE AD REFERENDUM	641	B
SHOGUNATE	476	B	SIGNIFICANCE	129	A
SHOO-IN	291	A	SIGNIFICANT OTHER	141	A
SHOOT FROM THE HIP	291	A	SIGNIFICATION	447	B
SHOOTING WAR	591	B	SIGNIFY	591	B
SHOPPERS	568	B	SIGNS OF THE TIMES	841	B
SHOREY, PAUL	772	B	SIHANOUK, PRINCE NORODOM	268	A
SHORT BALLOT	202	A	SIKORSKI, GENERAL WLADYSLAW	700	B
SHORT BOYS	568	B	SILENCE	663	B
SHORT HAIRS	560	B	SILENT VOTE	615	B
SHORT HORNS	847	B	SILESIAN WARS	663	B
SHORT SESSION	250	A	SILK-STOCKING DISTRICT	281	A
SHORT-LIVED	663	B	SILVER	818	B
SHORT-TERM BORROWING	224	A	SILVER CERTIFICATE	591	B
SHORT-TERM STAFF	509	B	SILVER GRAYS	534	B
SHORTCHANGE	641	B	SILVER PURCHASE ACT	615	B
SHORTER WORKWEEK	250	A	SILVER SHIRTS	509	B
SHORTHAND SERVICE	533	B	SILVERT, K. H.	773	B
SHOT-GUN	828	B	SILVESTER, POPE	773	B
SHOTWELL, JAMES T.	772	B	SIMILARITY	447	B
SHOULDER HITTER	568	B	SIMKOVITCH, V. Y.	773	B
SHOW TRIALS	241	A	SIMMEL, GEORG	700	B
SHOW-OF-HANDS VOTE	232	A	SIMON OF MONTFORT	725	B
SHOWDOWN	591	B	SIMON-BLALOCK ANALYSIS	459	B
SHOWING	663	B	SIMON, HERBERT A.	266	A

SIMONS, A. M.	725	B	SIX-YEAR PLAN	259	A
SIMPLE MAJORITY	149	A	SIXTEEN-TO-ONE	615	B
SIMPLE RESOLUTION	591	B	SIXTEENTH AMENDMENT	202	A
SIMPLICITY	144	A	SIXTH AMENDMENT	217	A
SIMPLIFIED AGREEMENT	663	B	SIXTH COLUMNISTS	174	A
SIMPSON, GEORGE	725	B	SIXTH COMMITTEE	534	B
SIMULATION	120	A	SIXTY MILLION JOBS	663	B
SIMULATION AND GAMES	120	A	SIZE, GEOGRAPHIC POWER FACTOR	137	A
SIMULATION STUDIES	122	A	SJOBERG, GIDEON	725	B
SIMULATION TECHNIQUES	122	A	SKELETON LAW	663	B
SIMULTANEOUS INTERPRETATION	592	B	SKELTON, O. D.	773	B
SIN	259	A	SKEPTICISM	141	A
SINAI CAMPAIGN	259	A	SKETCH	663	B
SINCERITY	439	B	SKIDDONIANS	534	B
SINCLAIR, UPTON	263	A	SKILL	144	A
SINE DIE (WITHOUT A DAY - INDEFINITELY)	259	A	SKILLET (TOTE ONE'S OWN)	847	B
			SKILLS INVENTORY	447	B
SINECURE	188	A	SKINNER, B. F.	262	A
SINGAPORE	279	A	SKODA MUNITIONS WORKS	773	B
SINGER, J. DAVID	270	A	SKUPSHTINA	534	B
SINGLE CHAMBER	174	A	SKY SKIMMING	663	B
SINGLE CONVENTION ON NARCOTICS DRUGS	663	B	SLACKWATER POLITICS	847	B
			SLAMBANGER	847	B
SINGLE ELECTION	592	B	SLANDER	217	A
SINGLE LIST	180	A	SLANSKY, RUDOLPH	773	B
SINGLE STANDARD	592	B	SLATE	160	A
SINGLE TAX	217	A	SLAUGHTERHOUSE CASES	261	A
SINGLE TRANSFERABLE VOTE SYSTEM	241	A	SLAVE	188	A
			SLAVE CODES	615	B
SINGLE-CENTERED SOCIETIES	534	B	SLAVE REVOLTS	259	A
SINGLE-MEMBER CONSTITUENCIES	164	A	SLAVE TRADE	217	A
SINGLE-MEMBER DISTRICT	276	A	SLAVERY	206	A
SINGLEHEADED	509	B	SLAVERY COMPROMISE	232	A
SINGLETON, PAP	773	B	SLAVERY QUESTION	206	A
SINGULAR	459	B	SLAVS	165	A
SINIAVSKY, ANDREI	773	B	SLAYER	560	B
SINKING FUND	615	B	SLEEP	615	B
SINN FEIN	169	A	SLEEPER	568	B
SINO-INDIAN BORDER	277	A	SLICHTER, SUMNER H.	773	B
SINO-JAPANESE WAR	232	A	SLIP LAWS	641	B
SINO-SOVIET CONFLICT	202	A	SLOCHOWER VS. BOARD OF HIGHER EDUCATION (1956)	679	B
SINO-SOVIET RELATIONSHIPS	129	A			
SISTER CITY MOVEMENT	259	A	SLOGAN	141	A
SIT-DOWN STRIKE	210	A	SLOGANEER	568	B
SIT-IN	217	A	SLOVAK REPUBLIC	795	B
SITHOLE, REV. NDABANINGI	773	B	SLOW BELL CAMPAIGN	663	B
SITTING	615	B	SLOW DOWN STRIKE	241	A
SITTING ON THE FENCE	292	A	SLUM AREA	279	A
SITTING PRESIDENT	546	B	SLUM CLEARANCE	232	A
SITUATION	641	B	SLUMLORD	185	A
SITUATION OF CHOICE	459	B	SLUMP	259	A
SITUATIONAL ANALYSIS	124	A	SLUMS	277	A
SITZKRIEG	592	B	SLUSH FUND	259	A
SIVAI	534	B	SLY, JOHN F.	773	B
SIX DAY WAR	217	A	SMALL BUSINESS ADMINISTRATION (SBA)	160	A
SIX LIVRES DE LA REPUBLIQUE	810	B			

SMALL CLAIMS COURT	157	A
SMALL GROUP POLITICS	131	A
SMALL GROUP THEORY	116	A
SMALL LOAN LAW	663	B
SMALL POTATO	560	B
SMALL, MELVIN	773	B
SMALLER WAR PLANTS CORPORATION	534	B
SMART POLITICS	641	B
SMART SET	534	B
SMEAR	241	A
SMELL OF MAGNOLIAS	847	B
SMELLING COMMITTEE	534	B
SMEND, R.	773	B
SMERSCH	813	B
SMETHWICK	800	B
SMITH ACT	250	A
SMITH ACT -ALIEN REGISTRATION ACT OF 1940	259	A
SMITH VS. ALLWRIGHT (1944)	261	A
SMITH-HUGHES ACT	663	B
SMITH-LEVER ACT OF 1914	663	B
SMITH-MUNDT ACT (1948)	641	B
SMITH, ADAM	263	A
SMITH, ALFRED E.	268	A
SMITH, DAVID G.	773	B
SMITH, IAN DOUGLAS	273	A
SMITH, JAMES ALLEN	773	B
SMITH, M. BREWSTER	773	B
SMITH, M. G.	773	B
SMITH, MARGARET CHASE	700	B
SMITH, MONROE	773	B
SMITH, SIR THOMAS	773	B
SMITH, T. V.	773	B
SMITHBURG, DONALD W.	773	B
SMITHSONIAN INSTITUTION	169	A
SMOKE-FILLED ROOM	277	A
SMOKESCREEN	834	B
SMOOT-HAWLEY TARIFF ACT OF 1930	241	A
SMRKOVSKY, J.	773	B
SMUCKLER, RALPH H.	773	B
SMUGGLING	250	A
SMUTS, JAN CHRISTIAN	268	A
SMYTH VS. AMES (1898)	680	B
SNAP CAUCUS	641	B
SNAP CONVENTION	641	B
SNAPPER	534	B
SNEER WORDS	847	B
SNEH, MOSHE	773	B
SNIPE	841	B
SNOLLYGOSTER	847	B
SNOW UNDER	847	B
SNOWDEN, PHILIP	774	B
SNOY ET D'OPPUERS, JEAN-CHARLES	774	B
SNYDER, RICHARD C.	273	A
SO-CALLED	841	B
SOAK THE RICH	250	A
SOAP BOX	818	B
SOARES, CLAUDIO A. D.	774	B
SOBER SECOND THOUGHT	459	B
SOBLEN CASE	680	B
SOBRANJE	534	B
SOCIABILITY	452	B
SOCIAL	144	A
SOCIAL ACCOUNTING	592	B
SOCIAL ACTION	241	A
SOCIAL ADAPTATION	131	A
SOCIAL ADJUSTMENT	141	A
SOCIAL AGENCIES	174	A
SOCIAL AND BEHAVIORAL SCIENCES	120	A
SOCIAL AND REHABILITATION SERVICE (SRS)	534	B
SOCIAL ANTHROPOLOGY	144	A
SOCIAL ATTITUDES	122	A
SOCIAL CHANGE	115	A
SOCIAL CLASS	148	A
SOCIAL COHESION	126	A
SOCIAL COMMISSION	534	B
SOCIAL COMMITTEE	534	B
SOCIAL CONFLICT	120	A
SOCIAL CONSERVATION AND DOMESTIC ALLOTMENT ACT	663	B
SOCIAL CONTRACT, THEORY OF	115	A
SOCIAL CONTROL	131	A
SOCIAL CONVENTION	141	A
SOCIAL CREDIT	592	B
SOCIAL DARWINISM	129	A
SOCIAL DEMOCRACY	149	A
SOCIAL DEMOCRATIC FEDERATION	476	B
SOCIAL DEMOCRATIC PARTY OF GERMANY (SPD)	157	A
SOCIAL DEMOCRATIC PARTY OF RUSSIA	180	A
SOCIAL DEMOCRATS	149	A
SOCIAL DEVELOPMENT	137	A
SOCIAL ECONOMY	141	A
SOCIAL ENGINEERING	124	A
SOCIAL FACTORS	134	A
SOCIAL GOSPEL	452	B
SOCIAL GROUPS	157	A
SOCIAL HISTORY	131	A
SOCIAL INDICATORS	122	A
SOCIAL INNOVATION	137	A
SOCIAL INSTITUTIONS	151	A
SOCIAL INSURANCE	615	B
SOCIAL INTEGRATION	122	A
SOCIAL JUSTICE	129	A
SOCIAL LAW	592	B
SOCIAL LEARNING	141	A
SOCIAL LEGISLATION	250	A

SOCIAL LIFE	459	B
SOCIAL MATRIX	126	A
SOCIAL MOBILITY	122	A
SOCIAL MOVEMENTS	160	A
SOCIAL ORDER	154	A
SOCIAL PHILOSOPHY	144	A
SOCIAL PHYSICS	452	B
SOCIAL PLURALISM	126	A
SOCIAL POLICY	250	A
SOCIAL PROBLEMS	127	A
SOCIAL PROCESSES	129	A
SOCIAL PROGRESS	134	A
SOCIAL PSYCHOLOGY	127	A
SOCIAL RESPONSIBILITY	134	A
SOCIAL REVOLUTIONARIES OF RUSSIA	491	B
SOCIAL ROLES	184	A
SOCIAL SCIENCE	118	A
SOCIAL SCIENCE RESEARCH COUNCIL (SWEDEN)	509	B
SOCIAL SCIENCE RESEARCH COUNCIL (U.S.)	169	A
SOCIAL SCIENCE, UNIFIED	134	A
SOCIAL SCIENCES	116	A
SOCIAL SCIENTISTS	154	A
SOCIAL SECURITY	206	A
SOCIAL SECURITY ACT	210	A
SOCIAL SECURITY ACT OF 1935	210	A
SOCIAL SECURITY ACT, AMENDED TO 1956	615	B
SOCIAL SECURITY ADMINISTRATION (SSA)	165	A
SOCIAL SECURITY BOARD	491	B
SOCIAL SECURITY CASES	676	B
SOCIAL SELF	452	B
SOCIAL SERVICE ORGANIZATION	510	B
SOCIAL STABILITY	127	A
SOCIAL STATE	180	A
SOCIAL STATUS	127	A
SOCIAL STRATIFICATION	122	A
SOCIAL STRUCTURE	122	A
SOCIAL SYSTEMS	120	A
SOCIAL SYSTEMS, AND STRUCTURAL-FUNCTIONALISM	124	A
SOCIAL THEORY	131	A
SOCIAL TRENDS	137	A
SOCIAL WELFARE	210	A
SOCIAL WELFARE LEGISLATION	232	A
SOCIAL WORK	241	A
SOCIALISM	113	A
SOCIALISM AND NATIONALISM	120	A
SOCIALIST COMPETITION	592	B
SOCIALIST DEMOCRACY	124	A
SOCIALIST INTERNATIONAL	165	A
SOCIALIST LABOR PARTY	169	A
SOCIALIST LEAGUE	492	B
SOCIALIST LEGALITY	615	B
SOCIALIST MOVEMENT FOR THE UNITED STATES OF EUROPE (SMUSE)	510	B
SOCIALIST PARTY	148	A
SOCIALIST PARTY OF FRANCE (SFIO)	510	B
SOCIALIST POLITICAL PARTIES	157	A
SOCIALIST REALISM	134	A
SOCIALIST REVOLUTIONARIES	165	A
SOCIALIST UNITY PARTY	510	B
SOCIALIST WORKERS PARTY	160	A
SOCIALIZATION	116	A
SOCIALIZED MEDICINE	217	A
SOCIALIZING AGENTS	118	A
SOCIETY	151	A
SOCIETY OF JESUS	476	B
SOCIO-ECONOMIC STATUS (SES)	127	A
SOCIO-POLITICAL	129	A
SOCIO-PSYCHOLOGICAL	134	A
SOCIOCULTURAL	134	A
SOCIOECONOMIC	134	A
SOCIOLOGICAL JURISPRUDENCE	134	A
SOCIOLOGICAL METHOD	131	A
SOCIOLOGICO-JURIDICAL METHOD	141	A
SOCIOLOGISM	447	B
SOCIOLOGISTS	546	B
SOCIOLOGY AND POLITICAL THEORY	120	A
SOCIOLOGY OF KNOWLEDGE	131	A
SOCIOLOGY OF LAW	439	B
SOCIOLOGY OF POLITICS	124	A
SOCIOLOGY OF SCIENCE	439	B
SOCIOLOGY, HISTORICAL	141	A
SOCIOLOGY, THE PROFESSION	174	A
SOCIOMETRIC RELATIONS	439	B
SOCIOMETRY	144	A
SOCRATES	261	A
SODALITY	510	B
SOFT CURRENCY	259	A
SOFT LOANS (IDA)	592	B
SOFT ON COMMUNISM	834	B
SOFT-PEDAL	837	B
SOFTS OR SOFT-SHELLS	510	B
SOIL BANK PLAN	259	A
SOIL CONSERVATION - U.S.A.	615	B
SOIL CONSERVATION AND DOMESTIC ALLOTMENT ACT	641	B
SOIL CONSERVATION SERVICE (SCS)	492	B
SOILEUX, G.A.	774	B
SOKA GAKKAI	510	B
SOKOLOVSKY, VASILI DANILOVICH	774	B
SOLDIER	546	B
SOLDIER KING	546	B
SOLDIERS AND WORKMENS COUNCIL	492	B
SOLEMN CEREMONY	663	B
SOLEMN DECLARATION	642	B

SOLICITOR	193	A	SOUTH PACIFIC COMMISSION	510	B
SOLICITOR GENERAL	187	A	SOUTH PACIFIC CONFERENCE	642	B
SOLID FUELS ADMINISTRATION FOR WAR	534	B	SOUTH TIROL QUESTION	592	B
			SOUTH VIETNAM	273	A
SOLID SOUTH	151	A	SOUTHEAST ASIA	276	A
SOLID-WASTE DISPOSAL	250	A	SOUTHEAST ASIA TREATY ORGANIZATION (SEATO)	149	A
SOLIDARITY	259	A			
SOLIDARY	452	B	SOUTHEAST EUROPE	283	A
SOLIMAN I	774	B	SOUTHERN CHRISTIAN LEADERSHIP CONFERENCE (SCLC)	154	A
SOLIPISM	144	A			
SOLOMON	725	B	SOUTHERN DEMOCRAT	182	A
SOLOMON, RICHARD A.	774	B	SOUTHERN PACIFIC RAILROAD	165	A
SOLON	546	B	SOUTHERN REGIONAL COUNCIL	534	B
SOLUTION	592	B	SOUTHERN RHODESIA	277	A
SOLVAY INSTITUTE OF SOCIOLOGY	534	B	SOUTHERN RHODESIA QUESTION	250	A
SOLZHENITSYN, ALEXANDER I.	265	A	SOUTHERNER	553	B
SOMALIA	281	A	SOUTHWEST	792	B
SOMBART, WERNER	774	B	SOUTHWEST AFRICA (NAMABIA)	281	A
SOMNIUM SCIPIONIS	810	B	SOUTHWEST AFRICA QUESTION	232	A
SON	568	B	SOUTHWEST POWER ADMINISTRATION	534	B
SONG OF MALDON	813	B			
SONS OF LIBERTY	492	B	SOVEREIGN	185	A
SONS OF TAMMANY	510	B	SOVEREIGN EQUALITY	224	A
SONS OF THE SOUTH	534	B	SOVEREIGN RIGHT	210	A
SONS OF THE WILD JACKASS	510	B	SOVEREIGN STATE	148	A
SOPHISTS	169	A	SOVEREIGNTY	116	A
SOPHOCLES	270	A	SOVIET	154	A
SOPLONES	568	B	SOVIET BLOC	148	A
SORAUF, FRANK	700	B	SOVIET COMMUNISM	118	A
SOREHEAD	568	B	SOVIET CONSTITUTION	283	A
SOREL, GEORGES	270	A	SOVIET MILITARY ADMINISTRATION IN GERMANY (SMAD)	534	B
SORELLIAN MYTH	439	B			
SORITES	459	B	SOVIET MILITARY REFORMS	663	B
SOROKIN, PITRIM A.	270	A	SOVIET OF NATIONALITIES	174	A
SOUL	447	B	SOVIET OF THE UNION	476	B
SOULE, GEORGE	774	B	SOVIET PEOPLES COURTS	165	A
SOUND	663	B	SOVIET REPARATIONS IN GERMANY	250	A
SOUND MONEY	259	A	SOVIET REPUBLICS	157	A
SOURCES OF INTERNATIONAL LAW	137	A	SOVIET SATELLITES	273	A
SOURCES OF THE LAW	224	A	SOVIET UNION	273	A
SOUSTELLE, JACQUES	774	B	SOVIET-NAZI PACT OF NON-AGGRESSION	210	A
SOUTH	281	A			
SOUTH AFRICA, REPUBLIC OF	157	A	SOVIET-POLISH PACT	592	B
SOUTH ARABIAN FEDERATION	180	A	SOVIETIZATION	241	A
SOUTH ASIA	277	A	SOVKHOZ	476	B
SOUTH CAROLINA PLAN	592	B	SOVMIN (SOVIET MINISTERY)	510	B
SOUTH CAROLINA VS. KATZENBACH (1966)	676	B	SOVNARKHOZ	510	B
			SOVNARKOM (SOVIET NARADNYKH KOMISSAROV, SNR)	534	B
SOUTH CAROLINA VS. U.S. (1905)	680	B			
SOUTH DAKOTA	281	A	SPA CONFERENCE	663	B
SOUTH EAST AFRICA	283	A	SPAAK, PAUL-HENRI	268	A
SOUTH EAST ASIA	276	A	SPACE	789	B
SOUTH EAST EUROPE	789	B	SPACE EXPLORATION AND USE	232	A
SOUTH KOREA	274	A	SPACE JURISDICTION	250	A
SOUTH MANCHURIAN RAILWAY	492	B	SPACE LAW	224	A
SOUTH MOLUCCAS, INDONESIA	800	B	SPACE PLATFORM	824	B

SPACE PROGRAM	259	A	SPECIAL REPRESENTATIVE	553	B
SPACE SATELLITES	789	B	SPECIAL SESSION	232	A
SPAIN	277	A	SPECIAL TRAIN	828	B
SPAIN, AUGUST	774	B	SPECIAL UN FUND FOR ECONOMIC	169	A
SPAN OF CONTROL	141	A	DEVELOPMENT (SUNFED)		
SPANIARDS	492	B	SPECIAL WELFARE	642	B
SPANISH	534	B	SPECIAL-POST ALLOWANCE	663	B
SPANISH CIVIL WAR	206	A	SPECIALIZATION	141	A
SPANISH SAHARA	789	B	SPECIALIZATION OF FUNCTION	129	A
SPANISH TERRITORIES IN AFRICA	789	B	SPECIALIZED AGENCIES	161	A
(IFNI)			SPECIALIZED AGENCY, UNITED	157	A
SPANISH-AMERICAN CULTURE	134	A	NATIONS		
SPANISH-AMERICAN WAR	206	A	SPECIE CIRCULAR	824	B
SPANISH-SPEAKING	592	B	SPECIES	439	B
SPAR	663	B	SPECIFIC POWERS-DELEGATED	210	A
SPARKMAN, JOHN JACKSON	688	B	POWERS		
SPARTA	277	A	SPECIFIC RATE	642	B
SPARTACIST INSURRECTION	259	A	SPECTRE	820	B
SPARTACUS REBELLION	616	B	SPECULATION	439	B
SPARTAN BAND	510	B	SPECULATIVE	144	A
SPAVENTA, S.	774	B	SPEECH	616	B
SPEAKER	184	A	SPEECH FROM THE THRONE	592	B
SPEAKER OF THE HOUSE	181	A	SPEECH OF ACCEPTANCE	241	A
SPEARHEADS	510	B	SPEECH-ACTS	663	B
SPECIAL ACT	642	B	SPEECHWRITER	191	A
SPECIAL ACT CHARTER	642	B	SPEED	828	B
SPECIAL ACTION OFFICE FOR DRUG	534	B	SPEEDING	616	B
ABUSE PREVENTION			SPEISER VS. RANDALL (1958)	680	B
SPECIAL AGREEMENT	663	B	SPELLBINDER	560	B
SPECIAL ASSESSMENT	250	A	SPELLMAN FUND	534	B
SPECIAL AUTHORIZATION	642	B	SPENCER, HERBERT	266	A
SPECIAL COMMITTEE	476	B	SPEND AND SPEND	841	B
SPECIAL COUNCIL OF MINISTERS	510	B	SPENGLER, OSWALD	273	A
SPECIAL DISTRICT	276	A	SPHERE OF INFLUENCE	224	A
SPECIAL DRAWING RIGHTS (SDR)	217	A	SPHERE OF INTEREST	131	A
(INTERNATIONAL MONETARY			SPIETHOFF, ARTHUR	774	B
UNITS)			SPIKED HELMET DEMOCRACY	459	B
SPECIAL ELECTION	224	A	SPILLOVER	616	B
SPECIAL FUND, UNITED NATIONS	241	A	SPINOZA, BARUCH (BENEDICT DE)	270	A
SPECIAL INDUSTRIAL SERVICES	534	B	SPIRAL	663	B
(SIS)			SPIRIT	664	B
SPECIAL INTERESTS	151	A	SPIRIT OF SEVENTY-SIX	847	B
SPECIAL JURY	476	B	SPIRIT OF THE LAWS	285	A
SPECIAL LEAVE	663	B	SPIRITUAL	439	B
SPECIAL LEGISLATION	250	A	SPIRITUAL SOVEREIGNTY	453	B
SPECIAL MAJORITY	180	A	SPIRO, MELFORD E.	774	B
SPECIAL MESSAGE	284	A	SPIT ON THE PLATFORM	841	B
SPECIAL MISSION	476	B	SPITE LEGISLATION	616	B
SPECIAL MUNICIPAL CORPORATION	492	B	SPITSBERGEN ARCHIPELAGO	800	B
SPECIAL ORDER	642	B	SPITZ, DAVID	774	B
SPECIAL PERMIT	616	B	SPLENDID ISOLATION	259	A
SPECIAL PLANE	459	B	SPLINTER GROUP	161	A
SPECIAL POLITICAL COMMITTEE	476	B	SPLINTER PARTIES	154	A
SPECIAL POST OFFICE	534	B	SPLIT	642	B
SPECIAL POWERS	592	B	SPLIT DECISION	224	A
SPECIAL PROTOCOL	616	B	SPLIT DECISIONS, JUDICIAL	217	A

SPLIT PRIMARY	592	B	STAFF COSTS	664	B
SPLIT SESSION	259	A	STAFF DEPARTMENT	510	B
SPLIT SHIFT	664	B	STAFF MEMBER	193	A
SPLIT TICKET	217	A	STAFF PLAN	616	B
SPLIT-TICKET VOTING	206	A	STAFF REGULATIONS	592	B
SPOILER	553	B	STAFF RELATIONS	642	B
SPOILS (-MEN, PARTY, SYSTEM)	193	A	STAGE	664	B
SPOILS SYSTEM	197	A	STAGGERED TERM	232	A
SPOILT VOTING-PAPER	820	B	STAHLHELM	535	B
SPOKESMAN	553	B	STAKHANOVITE	546	B
SPONG, WILLIAM BELSER, JR.	774	B	STALIN, ALLILUEVA SVETLANA	268	A
SPONSION	664	B	STALIN, JOSEPH	261	A
SPONTANEITY	453	B	STALINISM, COMMUNIST DOCTRINE	118	A
SPONTANEOUS DEMONSTRATION	592	B	STALKING HORSE	553	A
SPOOK	568	B	STALLARD, CHARLES FRAMPTON	774	B
SPOONER, LYSANDER	774	B	STALWART	560	B
SPORTS	664	B	STAMMER, OTTO	774	B
SPORTS METAPHORS	439	B	STAMMLER, RUDOLF	774	B
SPOT RESOLUTIONS	616	B	STAMP ACT (1765)	232	A
SPOTTED PIG PARTY	534	B	STAMP ACT CONGRESS	616	B
SPREAD-EAGLE	824	B	STAMPEDE	642	B
SPRING	664	B	STAMPS (UN)	828	B
SPROUT, HAROLD AND MARGARET	270	A	STAND	642	B
SPUTNIK	287	A	STAND IN THE DOORWAY	664	B
SPY	191	A	STAND PAT	642	B
SPY BALLOT	828	B	STANDARD BEARER	193	A
SPYCHALSKI, MARSHAL M.	725	B	STANDARD METROPOLITAN	281	A
SPYKMAN, NICHOLAS J.	270	A	STATISTICAL AREAS (U.S.A.)		
SQUAD	535	B	STANDARD OF LIVING	241	A
SQUADRISM	664	B	STANDARD OIL CO. VS. U.S. (1911)	676	B
SQUADRISTI	568	B	STANDARDIZED EXAMINATION	250	A
SQUALOR	642	B	STANDARDIZED INTERVIEW	250	A
SQUARE DEAL	241	A	STANDARDS	250	A
SQUATTER	193	A	STANDARDS OF PERFORMANCE	259	A
SQUATTER SOVEREIGNTY	259	A	STANDING ARMAMENTS COMMITTEE	510	B
SRI LANKA	279	A	STANDING ARMY	174	A
SRIJDOM, J. G.	774	B	STANDING BODY	510	B
SRINIVAS, M. N.	725	B	STANDING COMMITTEE	157	A
ST. BARTHOLOMEW'S DAY	592	B	STANDING DIVISION	259	A
MASSACRE			STANDING GROUP	510	B
ST. CYR-LECOLE	774	B	STANDING JOINT COMMITTEES	161	A
ST. GEORGE'S HILL, WEYBRIDGE	800	B	STANDING ORDERS OF THE HOUSE	259	A
ST. LAWRENCE SEAWAY	281	A	OF COMMONS		
STAATENBUND	535	B	STANDING TO SUE	592	B
STAATSLEHRE	459	B	STANDING VOTE	259	A
STAB IN THE BACK SPEECH	616	B	STANDPATTER	553	B
STABILITY	131	A	STANFORD UNIVERSITY	510	B
STABILIZATION FUND	616	B	STANFORD, LELAND	700	B
STABILIZED WARFARE	642	B	STANLEY VS. GEORGIA (1969)	680	B
STACKING	592	B	STAR CHAMBER	180	A
STAFF	174	A	STAR ROUTE FRAUDS	642	B
STAFF (UN)	510	B	STAR SPANGLED BANNER, THE	286	A
STAFF AGENCY	476	B	STAR-CHAMBER PROCEEDING	250	A
STAFF AND LINE	157	A	STAR, S. A.	774	B
STAFF COLLEGES	492	B	STARE DECISIS	210	A
STAFF COMMITTEE	476	B	STARKEY, THOMAS	774	B

STARR, JOSEPH R.	774	B	STATE SUCCESSION	250	A
STARS AND BARS	824	B	STATE SUPREME COURT	154	A
STARS AND STRIPES	288	A	STATE TRADE BARRIERS	259	A
STARVATION WAGES	592	B	STATE TREASURER	188	A
STARVING	592	B	STATE UNDER SUZERAINTY	476	B
STASON, E. BLYTHE	774	B	STATE UNIFIED COURT SYSTEM	241	A
STATE	146	A	STATE USE SYSTEM	616	B
STATE AID	232	A	STATE VISIT	592	B
STATE AND LOCAL GOVERNMENT	148	A	STATE-ISM	141	A
STATE AND LOCAL RELATIONS	129	A	STATE-TRADING COUNTRIES	492	B
STATE AND REVOLUTION	210	A	STATE'S ATTORNEY	193	A
STATE ATTORNEY GENERAL	188	A	STATE'S EVIDENCE	187	A
STATE AUDITOR	553	B	STATELESS PERSONS	191	A
STATE BANKS	174	A	STATELESS SOCIETIES	180	A
STATE BOARD OF EXAMINERS	492	B	STATELESSNESS	250	A
STATE CAPITALISM	122	A	STATEMENT	137	A
STATE CENTRAL COMMITTEE	161	A	STATES GENERAL	476	B
STATE CENTRALIZATION	134	A	STATES OF THE CHURCH	664	B
STATE CEREMONY	616	B	STATES, RIGHTS AND DUTIES OF	206	A
STATE CHURCH	165	A	STATES' RIGHTS	196	A
STATE CIRCUIT COURT	174	A	STATES' RIGHTS DEMOCRAT	184	A
STATE CIVIL SERVICE COMMISSION	492	B	STATES' RIGHTS DOCTRINE	206	A
STATE COMPTROLLER	188	A	STATES' RIGHTS PARTY	165	A
STATE CONSTITUTION	224	A	STATESMANSHIP	185	A
STATE CONSTITUTIONAL	241	A	STATESMEN	191	A
CONVENTIONS			STATIC POLICY	664	B
STATE CONTROL	232	A	STATIONARY WARFARE	642	B
STATE COUNCIL, CHINA (PRC)	492	B	STATIONERY	664	B
STATE COURT OF APPEALS	161	A	STATIONING COST	664	B
STATE COURTS	157	A	STATIONING OF TROOPS	616	B
STATE DEPARTMENT	165	A	STATISM, FASCIST THEORY	127	A
STATE DISTRICT COURT	174	A	STATISTIC	131	A
STATE EXECUTIVE DEPARTMENTS	165	A	STATISTICAL ANALYSIS	116	A
STATE GOVERNMENTS	157	A	STATISTICAL COMMISSION	535	B
STATE GUARD	492	B	(ECOSOC)		
STATE INSTRUMENTALITIES	476	B	STATISTICAL CORRELATIONS	118	A
STATE INTERVENTION	241	A	STATISTICAL DATA	122	A
STATE JOINT COMMITTEES	492	B	STATISTICAL METHODS	120	A
STATE LAW	592	B	STATISTICAL OFFICE (UN	510	B
STATE LEGISLATURE	157	A	SECRETARIAT)		
STATE LIABILITY	241	A	STATISTICAL SIGNIFICANCE	127	A
STATE MILITIA	161	A	STATISTICAL YEARBOOK	285	A
STATE OF BLOCKADE	250	A	STATISTICS	124	A
STATE OF EMERGENCY	217	A	STATUARY HALL	800	B
STATE OF HOSTILITIES	232	A	STATUE OF LIBERTY	288	A
STATE OF NATURE	217	A	STATUS	120	A
STATE OF PEACE	224	A	STATUS INCONSISTENCY	144	A
STATE OF SIEGE	232	A	STATUS OF FORCES TREATIES	616	B
STATE OF THE LAW	592	B	STATUS OF INDIANS	250	A
STATE OF THE UNION MESSAGE	206	A	STATUS OF WOMEN	224	A
STATE OF WAR	210	A	STATUS QUO	217	A
STATE POLICE	174	A	STATUS QUO ANTE	250	A
STATE RELIGION	137	A	STATUS QUO ANTE BELLUM	241	A
STATE SERVITUDE	616	B	STATUS QUO POLICY	232	A
STATE SOCIALISM	124	A	STATUTE	232	A
STATE SOVEREIGNTY	131	A	STATUTE LAW	224	A

STATUTE OF LIMITATIONS	210	A	STEVENSON, ADLAI EWING	263	A
STATUTE OF WESTMINSTER, 1931	616	B	STEVENSON, ADLAI EWING, III	265	A
STATUTE-MAKING POWER	217	A	STEVENSON, HAROLD W.	775	B
STATUTES	224	A	STEWARD MACHINE CO. VS. DAVIS	680	B
STATUTES AT LARGE	259	A	(1937)		
STATUTES AT LARGE OF THE	285	A	STEWARDSHIP THEORY	129	A
UNITED STATES			STEWART, EDWARD C.	775	B
STATUTES OF THE PARTY	642	B	STEWART, MICHAEL	725	B
STATUTO OF 1848	642	B	STIFFENING OF ATTITUDE	616	B
STATUTORY CONSTRUCTION	241	A	STIKKER, DIRK	775	B
STATUTORY CORPORATION UNDER	510	B	STILL HUNT	664	B
PUBLIC LAW			STILWELL, G.	775	B
STATUTORY LAW	210	A	STIMSON DOCTRINE	593	B
STATUTORY ORDERS	616	B	STIMSON, HENRY L.	273	A
STAVISKY AFFAIRE	616	B	STIMULUS	439	B
STAY LAW	664	B	STIMULUS-RESPONSE	118	A
STAY OF BELLIGERENT WARSHIPS	616	B	STIPENDIARY MAGISTRATE	568	B
IN NEUTRAL PORTS			STIPULATE	642	B
STAY-AT-HOME VOTER	188	A	STIPULATION	642	B
STAYING BOUGHT	841	B	STIR UP	664	B
STEADY STATE	137	A	STIR UP THE ANIMALS	841	B
STEAL ONE'S THUNDER	837	B	STIRNER, MAX	775	B
STEAMBOAT ELECTION (VOTE)	664	B	STIRRING UP TO BOYCOTT	642	B
STEAMBOAT INSPECTION	642	B	STOCKER, ADOLPH	775	B
STEAMROLLER	476	B	STOCKHOLM CONVENTION, EFTA	476	B
STEEL	829	B	(1959)		
STEEL COMMITTEE OF ECE	535	B	STOCKPILES	288	A
STEEL PACT	642	B	STOCKPILING OF ATOMIC WEAPONS	241	A
STEERING COMMITTEE	161	A	STOCKPILING OF STRATEGIC	241	A
STEFFENS, LINCOLN	273	A	MATERIALS		
STEIN, HAROLD	774	B	STOCKS	818	B
STEIN, LOREZ VON	775	B	STODDARD, LOTHROP	775	B
STEINER, GARY A.	775	B	STOICISM	129	A
STEINER, JURG	775	B	STOICS	154	A
STEINMETZ, S. R.	775	B	STOJANOVIC, S.	775	B
STEMMED	664	B	STOKELY	775	B
STEMWINDER	642	B	STOKER, DONALD	775	B
STENE, HAROLD	775	B	STOKES, C.	725	B
STENNIS, JOHN CORNELIUS	273	A	STOKES, DONALD E.	688	B
STENOGRAPHIC SERVICE	492	B	STOLYPIN, PETER ARKADIEVICH	775	B
STEP	664	B	STONE, DONALD C.	775	B
STEP ACROSS THE PLATFORM	664	B	STONE, HARLAN FISKE	688	B
STEPPINGSTONE	820	B	STONE, HAROLD A.	775	B
STEREOTYPE	120	A	STONE, KATHRYN H.	775	B
STERILIZATION	250	A	STOOL PIGEON	553	B
STERILIZATION LAW	593	B	STOP AND FRISK PROVISION	250	A
STERLING	818	B	STOP-GO	664	B
STERLING AREA	281	A	STOPIAN SOCIALISM	453	B
STERLING BLOC	165	A	STOPPAGE	664	B
STERLING, JOHN	775	B	STOPPING THE CLOCK	292	A
STERN GANG	476	B	STORIES	808	B
STERNBERGER, DOLF	775	B	STORM TROOPERS	169	A
STEROID	829	B	STORMING OF THE BASTILLE	259	A
STETTINIUS, EDWARD REILLY, JR.	700	B	STORTING	510	B
STEVENS, THADDEUS	700	B	STRACHEY, JOHN	775	B
STEVENS, THEODORE FULTON	775	B	STRACHEY, LYTTON	775	B

STRADDLE	642	B
STRADDLE BUG	568	B
STRAIGHT-OUT DEMOCRATS	510	B
STRAIGHT-TICKET VOTING	217	A
STRAIN TOWARD SYMMETRY	453	B
STRAINS	453	B
STRAITS	283	A
STRAITS CLOSED TO WARSHIPS	281	A
STRANGE BEDFELLOWS	560	B
STRANGERS	568	B
STRANGLER	568	B
STRASBOURG	283	A
STRASBOURG PARLIAMENT	476	B
STRASSER, GREGORY	700	B
STRASSER, OTTO	725	B
STRATA	141	A
STRATEGIC AIR COMMAND (SAC)	157	A
STRATEGIC AIR FORCE	169	A
STRATEGIC ARMS	287	A
STRATEGIC ARMS LIMITATION TALKS (SALT)	197	A
STRATEGIC BOMBING	217	A
STRATEGIC INTELLIGENCE	224	A
STRATEGIC METALS	820	B
STRATEGIC TRUSTEESHIP TERRITORY	279	A
STRATEGY	131	A
STRATEGY THEORY	137	A
STRATIFICATION	127	A
STRATIFIED RANDOM SAMPLE	118	A
STRAUSS, DAVID FRIEDRICH	725	B
STRAUSS, FRANZ JOSEPH	268	A
STRAUSS, LEO	268	A
STRAW MAN	188	A
STRAW POLL	232	A
STRAW VOTE	217	A
STRAWSLIDE	664	B
STRAWSON	775	B
STREETCORNER SOCIETY	492	B
STREICHER, JULIUS	688	B
STREIT, CLARENCE	725	B
STRENGTH THROUGH JOY	593	B
STRENGTHENING OF A REGIME	593	B
STRENGTHENING OF PEACE	593	B
STRESA CONFERENCE (I)	616	B
STRESA CONFERENCE (II)	616	B
STRESA FRONT	795	B
STRESEMANN, GUSTAV	700	B
STRESS	144	A
STRICT CONSTRUCTION	206	A
STRICT INTERPRETATION OF THE CONSTITUTION	196	A
STRICT LIABILITY	616	B
STRICT MARXISTS	174	A
STRIFE	616	B
STRIJDOM, JOHANNES GERHARDUS	775	B
STRIKE	217	A
STRIKE A BLOW FOR FREEDOM	841	B
STRIKE BILL	664	B
STRIKEBREAKER	546	B
STRIKES	217	A
STRIPED PANTS DIPLOMACY	642	B
STROEBEL, HEINRICH	775	B
STROESSNER, GENERAL ALFREDO	725	B
STROKE OF A PEN	616	B
STRONG-MAYOR PLAN	206	A
STRONG, MAURICE F.	725	B
STRUCTURAL ANALYSIS	122	A
STRUCTURAL ANALYSIS, SYSTEMS THEORY	116	A
STRUCTURAL-FUNCTIONAL THEORY	116	A
STRUCTURAL-FUNCTIONALISM	115	A
STRUCTURALISM	127	A
STRUCTURE	134	A
STRUCTURES, CONCEPT OF	134	A
STRUCTURES, INFLUENCE OF FORMAL	131	A
STRUCTURES, TRUNCATED INTERACTION	453	B
STRUGGLE	593	B
STRUGGLE FOR POWER	232	A
STRUNSKY, SIMEON	776	B
STRUVE, PETER	776	B
STRUZO, DON LUIGI	776	B
STUART DYNASTY	688	B
STUART RESTORATION	643	B
STUDENT	193	A
STUDENT GOVERNMENT	169	A
STUDENT MOVEMENT	161	A
STUDENT NONVIOLENT COORDINATING COMMITTEE (SNCC)	157	A
STUDENT POWER	232	A
STUDENT PROTESTS	217	A
STUDENTS FOR A DEMOCRATIC SOCIETY (SDS)	154	A
STUDY CENTER	535	B
STUDY GROUP	492	B
STUDY LEAVE	664	B
STUFF	829	B
STUMP	643	B
STUMP CANDIDATE	553	B
STUMP TAIL	847	B
STUMPING	250	A
STURMABTEILUNG	535	B
STURZO, DON LUIGI	776	B
STYLE	241	A
SUAREZ, FRANCISCO	725	B
SUB-SAHARA	277	A
SUBCOMMITTEE	154	A
SUBCOMMUNITY	492	B
SUBCONSCIOUS MIND	131	A

SUBCULTURE	151	A	SUBURBIA	275	A
SUBGROUPS	157	A	SUBURBS	281	A
SUBGROUPS, LEGISLATIVE	174	A	SUBVENTION	617	B
SUBHAS	776	B	SUBVERSION	210	A
SUBJECT	593	B	SUBVERSIVE	184	A
SUBJECT MATTER OF A DISPUTE	259	A	SUBVERSIVE ACTIVITIES CONTROL	250	A
SUBJECT TO DENUNCIATION	643	B	ACT, 1950		
SUBJECT TO LOCAL JURISDICTION	250	A	SUBVERSIVE ACTIVITIES CONTROL	180	A
SUBJECT TO RATIFICATION	241	A	BOARD		
SUBJECTIVE	137	A	SUBVERSIVE ACTIVITY	217	A
SUBJECTIVISM	144	A	SUBVERSIVE LITERATURE	806	B
SUBJECTIVITY	127	A	SUBVERSIVE ORGANIZATIONS	174	A
SUBJUGATION	250	A	SUCCESS	617	B
SUBLIME	459	B	SUCCESSION	232	A
SUBLIME PORTE	800	B	SUCCESSION OF STATES	593	B
SUBMARINE	818	B	SUCCESSION STATES	174	A
SUBMARINE BASE	792	B	SUCCESSION STATES OF THE	476	B
SUBMARINE WARFARE	259	A	AUSTRO-HUNGARIAN EMPIRE		
SUBMERGED LANDS ACT	617	B	SUCCESSION TO THE THRONE	250	A
SUBMISSION MAN	568	B	SUCCESSOR	546	B
SUBMISSION(IST)	560	B	SUCCOTASH PARTY	535	B
SUBOPTIMIZATION	459	B	SUDA	800	B
SUBORDINATE	553	B	SUDAN, REPUBLIC OF (JAMHURYAT	165	A
SUBORDINATE LEGISLATION	593	B	EL-SUDAN)		
SUBORDINATION	439	B	SUDETEN GERMANS	169	A
SUBPOENA	217	A	SUEZ CANAL	275	A
SUBSCRIPTIONS	664	B	SUEZ CANAL USERS ASSOCIATION	492	B
SUBSET	127	A	SUEZ CRISIS OF 1956	232	A
SUBSIDIARY BODY	180	A	SUFFERING	643	B
SUBSIDIARY COINAGE	664	B	SUFFICIENT	447	B
SUBSIDIARY COMMITTEE	492	B	SUFFRAGE	199	A
SUBSIDIARY MOTION	593	B	SUFFRAGE, UNIVERSAL	206	A
SUBSIDIARY ORGAN	510	B	SUFFRAGETTE	188	A
SUBSIDIARY SOURCE	643	B	SUFI (ISLAM)	492	B
SUBSIDIZE	241	A	SUGAR ACT	617	B
SUBSIDY	217	A	SUGAR FRAUDS	617	B
SUBSISTENCE ECONOMY	127	A	SUGGESTIONS	665	B
SUBSISTENCE FARMING	232	A	SUHARTO, GENERAL T. N. J.	273	A
SUBSISTENCE HOMESTEAD	821	B	SUHONEN, PERTTI	776	B
SUBSISTENCE LEVEL	224	A	SUICIDE	617	B
SUBSOIL	829	B	SUING	259	A
SUBSOIL JURISDICTION	593	B	SUIT	593	B
SUBSTANCE	439	B	SUKARNO, ACHMED	273	A
SUBSTANTIVE DECISION, SECURITY	224	A	SULEIMAN THE MAGNIFICENT	776	B
COUNCIL			SULLIVAN, HARRY STACK	725	B
SUBSTANTIVE DUE PROCESS	217	A	SULPHUR	829	B
SUBSTANTIVE LAW	217	A	SULPHURCRAT	535	B
SUBSTANTIVE RIGHTS	224	A	SULTAN	553	B
SUBSTITUTE	560	B	SULTANATE	553	B
SUBSTITUTION	617	B	SUMERIANS	492	B
SUBSTITUTIVITY	459	B	SUMMA ASONIS	813	B
SUBSUMPTION	453	B	SUMMA POTESTAS	453	B
SUBSYSTEM	122	A	SUMMA THEOLOGICA	286	A
SUBTERRANEAN DEMOCRACY	459	B	SUMMARIZE	643	B
SUBTREASURY SYSTEM	643	B	SUMMARY	617	B
SUBURBAN	281	A	SUMMARY ACTION	617	B

SUMMARY OF THE FACTS	617	B
SUMMARY PROCEDURE	617	B
SUMMARY PROCESS	617	B
SUMMARY RECORD	813	B
SUMMER EMPLOYEMNT	665	B
SUMMER RESIDENCE	795	B
SUMMI PONTIFICATUS	810	B
SUMMIT	232	A
SUMMIT CONFERENCE	210	A
SUMMIT DIPLOMACY	206	A
SUMMITRY AS AN INSTRUMENT OF DIPLOMACY	206	A
SUMMONING	617	B
SUMMONS	250	A
SUMNER, B. H.	776	B
SUMNER, WILLIAM GRAHAM	700	B
SUMPTUARY LAWS	643	B
SUMPTUARY TAX	643	B
SUN KING	270	A
SUN TZU	776	B
SUN YAT-SEN	265	A
SUN YEH-FANG	776	B
SUNAKAWA CASE	680	B
SUNAY, CEVDET	776	B
SUNDAY SCHOOL	535	B
SUNFED PROPOSAL (UNITED NATIONS)	617	B
SUNISM	453	B
SUNNIS (SUNNITES)	492	B
SUPER-WATTS	800	B
SUPERANNUATION	617	B
SUPERCITY	800	B
SUPEREGO	129	A
SUPERINTENDENT	553	B
SUPERINTENDENT OF PUBLIC INSTRUCTION	193	A
SUPERINTENDENT OF SCHOOLS	193	A
SUPERIOR	560	B
SUPERIOR COURT-CIRCUIT COURT	165	A
SUPERMEN	188	A
SUPERNUMERARIES	553	B
SUPERPATRIOTS	191	A
SUPERPOWER	148	A
SUPERSERVICEABLE	847	B
SUPERSONIC TRANSPORTS	288	A
SUPERSTATE	180	A
SUPERVISION	593	B
SUPERVISOR	546	B
SUPERVISORY BODY	180	A
SUPPLEMENTARY AGREEMENT	617	B
SUPPLEMENTARY APPROPRIATION	224	A
SUPPLEMENTARY PROTOCOL	643	B
SUPPLEMENTARY REPORT	810	B
SUPPLEMENTS	643	B
SUPPLY	665	B
SUPPORT	259	A
SUPPORT COSTS	665	B
SUPPORTER	560	B
SUPPORTING DOCUMENTS	808	B
SUPRANATIONAL ORGANIZATION	157	A
SUPRANATIONALISM	124	A
SUPREMACY	593	B
SUPREMACY CLAUSE	224	A
SUPREME ALLIED COMMANDER ATLANTIC (SACLANT)	191	A
SUPREME AUTHORITY	188	A
SUPREME COMMAND	174	A
SUPREME COMMANDER FOR THE ALLIED POWERS (SCAP)	169	A
SUPREME COUNCIL	492	B
SUPREME COURT APPEAL	217	A
SUPREME COURT FOLLOWS THE ELECTION RETURNS	290	A
SUPREME COURT OF JUDICATURE	492	B
SUPREME COURT OF JUSTICE	180	A
SUPREME COURT OF NORTHERN IRELAND	535	B
SUPREME COURT OF THE UNITED STATES	146	A
SUPREME COURT PACKING PLAN	217	A
SUPREME COURT REORGANIZATION BILL	593	B
SUPREME COURT REPORTER	193	A
SUPREME HEADQUARTERS ALLIED POWERS EUROPE (SHAPE)	165	A
SUPREME LAW	217	A
SUPREME PONTIFF	546	B
SUPREME SOVIET OF THE USSR	157	A
SUPREME WAR COUNCIL	510	B
SURFACE	665	B
SURFACE TO AIR MISSILES (SAM)	286	A
SURFACE VESSELS	818	B
SURGEON GENERAL	191	A
SURGERY	459	B
SURPLUS	241	A
SURPLUS COMMODITIES CORPORATION	476	B
SURPLUS MARKETING ADMINISTRATION	535	B
SURPLUS VALUE, COMMUNIST THEORY	120	A
SURPRISE ATTACK	593	B
SURPRISE ATTACK ON PEARL HARBOR	232	A
SURREALISM	447	B
SURRENDER	241	A
SURRENDER OF THE PERSON TO BE EXTRADITED	617	B
SURRENDER ON MORNINGSIDE HEIGHTS	643	B
SURROGATE	193	A
SURROGATES COURT	476	B

TAFT, DONALD	776	B
TAFT, PRESIDENT WILLIAM HOWARD	264	A
TAFT, ROBERT ALPHONSO	270	A
TAFT, ROBERT, JR.	688	B
TAI CHI-TAO	776	B
TAI PING REBELLION	593	B
TAIWAN	274	A
TAKE A WALK	837	B
TAKE HER BY THE HAND	847	B
TAKE HIM TO THE MOUNTAIN TOP	841	B
TAKE OVER	593	B
TAKE UP	665	B
TAKING EFFECT	665	B
TAKING OF HOSTAGES	617	B
TAKING POSSESSION	643	B
TAKING THE FIFTH AMENDMENT	202	A
TALENT	439	B
TALESMAN	560	B
TALHOUNI, BAHJAT	776	B
TALK	643	B
TALKATHON	643	B
TALLEYRAND-PERIGORD, CHARLES MAURICE DE	273	A
TALMADGE, HERMAN EUGENE	273	A
TAMIL, SRI LANKA	535	B
TAMILNAC, INDIA	800	B
TAMILNADU	800	B
TAMMANY HALL	157	A
TAMMANY TIGER	819	B
TANAKA MEMORIAL	795	B
TANEY, ROGER BROOKE	273	A
TANGANYIKA	277	A
TANGANYIKA-ZANZIBAR	277	A
TANGIBLE PROPERTY	819	B
TANNER, J. R.	776	B
TANNU TUVA	511	B
TANTAMOUNT TO ELECTION	834	B
TANTRISM	460	B
TANZANIA	277	A
TAOISM	131	A
TAPES	808	B
TAPEWORM TICKET	535	B
TAPLINE	511	B
TARGET	824	B
TARIFF	202	A
TARIFF AGREEMENT	224	A
TARIFF COMMISSION (UNITED STATES)	180	A
TARIFF FOR REVENUE ONLY	259	A
TARIFF NEGOTIATIONS	250	A
TARIFF OF 1816	665	B
TARIFF PROTECTION	224	A
TARIFF WAR	232	A
TARIFFS OF 1828	617	B
TARN, W.W.	776	B
TARSKI	776	B
TARTAR	535	B
TASK	453	B
TASK EXPECTATION	439	B
TASK FORCE	169	A
TASMANIAN DODGE	837	B
TASS	169	A
TASSARA. GARCIA	776	B
TASTE	440	B
TAUBER, KURT P.	776	B
TAUSSIG	776	B
TAUTOLOGY	124	A
TAWNEY, RICHARD HENRY	700	B
TAX	217	A
TAX ABATEMENT	593	B
TAX AND TAX	665	B
TAX AVOIDANCE	250	A
TAX BASE	217	A
TAX COLONY	796	B
TAX COMMISSION	511	B
TAX COURT	476	B
TAX COURT OF THE UNITED STATES	174	A
TAX DODGER	546	B
TAX DUPLICATE	813	B
TAX EVASION	250	A
TAX EXEMPTION	217	A
TAX FARMING	617	B
TAX IMMUNITY	250	A
TAX IMMUNITY-INTERGOVERNMENTAL	259	A
TAX INCENTIVES	224	A
TAX INCIDENCE	259	A
TAX LOOPHOLE	217	A
TAX OFFSET	617	B
TAX PAYING QUALIFICATION	617	B
TAX POWER OF THE STATES	224	A
TAX REFORM	224	A
TAX SHARING	232	A
TAX SHELTER	241	A
TAX THEORIES	127	A
TAX-DEDUCTIBLE EXPENSE	617	B
TAXATION	210	A
TAXATION AND REVENUE	206	A
TAXATION WITHOUT REPRESENTATION	290	A
TAXES	210	A
TAXING POWER	206	A
TAXONOMY	131	A
TAXPAYER'S SUIT	241	A
TAYLOR, FREDERICK	700	B
TAYLOR, HELEN	776	B
TAYLOR, JOHN	777	B
TAYLOR, PRESIDENT ZACHARY	266	A
TAYLOR, PROF. A. E.	777	B
TAYLOR, STIRLING	777	B
TCHAD	796	B
TCHEKA	511	B

TEACH-IN	593	B		TEMPLES	829	B
TEACHER'S CERTIFICATION	618	B		TEMPORAL POWER	593	B
TEACHER'S OATH	259	A		TEMPORALITY	643	B
TEACHERS	554	B		TEMPORARY CHAIRMAN	554	B
TEACHING	259	A		TEMPORARY EMPLOYEES	492	B
TEACHING OF MOST HIGHLY	665	B		TEMPORARY NATIONAL ECONOMIC	511	B
QUALIFIED PUBLICISTS				COMMITTEE (TNEC, U.S.)		
TEAM	511	B		TEMPORARY STAFF	476	B
TEAMSTER UNION	161	A		TEMPS (LE)	808	B
TEAPOT DOME SCANDAL	232	A		TEN BROEK, JACOBUS	777	B
TECHNICAL ADVISER	191	A		TEN-NATION DISARMAMENT	492	B
TECHNICAL ASSISTANCE	210	A		COMMITTEE		
TECHNICAL ASSISTANCE	476	B		TEN-TEN-SEVEN RATIO	618	B
ADMINISTRATION				TENANT FARMING	250	A
TECHNICAL ASSISTANCE BOARD	476	B		TENDENCY	144	A
(TAB)				TENDENCY STATEMENT	132	A
TECHNICAL COMMITTEE	535	B		TENDER	593	B
TECHNICAL ORGANIZATION	535	B		TENDER OF GOOD OFFICES	250	A
TECHNICIAN	560	B		TENEMENT	821	B
TECHNIQUES	447	B		TENNESSEE	283	A
TECHNOCRACY	132	A		TENNESSEE PLAN	643	B
TECHNOCRAT	165	A		TENNESSEE VALLEY AUTHORITY	151	A
TECHNOLOGICAL CHANGE AND	217	A		(TVA)		
POLITICS				TENNIS CABINET	511	B
TECHNOLOGICAL DEVELOPMENTS	232	A		TENNO	568	B
TECHNOLOGICAL UNEMPLOYMENT	241	A		TENOR	665	B
TECHNOLOGICAL, ECONOMIC,	643	B		TENSE LOGIC	460	B
MILITARY, POLITICAL EVALUATION				TENSION	440	B
ROUTINE				TENSION REDUCTION	135	A
TECHNOLOGY	129	A		TENTATIVE PEACE APPROACH	665	B
TECHNOLOGY TRANSFERS	241	A		TENTH AMENDMENT	211	A
TECHNOLOGY, SOCIAL	447	B		TENURE	217	A
TECHNOSTRUCTURE	144	A		TENURE OF OFFICE ACT	241	A
TEEN AGE CENTERS	800	B		TEPEE	829	B
TEEN-AGE	453	B		TERENA	535	B
TEHERAN CONFERENCE	232	A		TERENTISMO	460	B
TELE-TRAGEDY	665	B		TERM	593	B
TELECOMMUNICATIONS SYSTEM	593	B		TERM OF OFFICE	250	A
(UN)				TERMAN, L. M.	700	B
TELECOMMUNICATIONS UNION	180	A		TERMINATE	643	B
TELEGRAM OF CONDOLENCE	810	B		TERMINATION OF THE STATE OF	241	A
TELEGRAM OF CONGRATULATION	810	B		WAR		
TELEOLOGICAL EXPLANATION	129	A		TERMINIELLO VS. CHICAGO (1949)	680	B
TELEOLOGICAL METHODS	440	B		TERMINOLOGY, DEFINITIONS	138	A
TELEOLOGY	132	A		TERMS	259	A
TELEPOLITICS	618	B		TERMS AND CONDITIONS OF	224	A
TELESIO, BERNARDINO	777	B		APPOINTMENT		
TELEVISION	288	A		TERMS OF CONGRESS	232	A
TELL IT LIKE IT IS	834	B		TERMS OF TRADE	241	A
TELLER	560	B		TERRA NULLIUS	792	B
TELLER VOTE	259	A		TERRAPIN (SYSTEM)	643	B
TEMPER	665	B		TERRITORIAL AIR	283	A
TEMPERAMENT	453	B		TERRITORIAL APPLICATION	618	B
TEMPERANCE	259	A		TERRITORIAL ASYLUM	232	A
TEMPERANCE MOVEMENT	154	A		TERRITORIAL CESSION	241	A
TEMPLARS	511	B		TERRITORIAL CHANGE	259	A

TERRITORIAL CLAIM	250	A	THE SPEECH	810	B
TERRITORIAL COURTS	493	B	THE WORLD MUST BE MADE SAFE	290	A
TERRITORIAL INTEGRITY	232	A	FOR DEMOCRACY		
TERRITORIAL JURISDICTION	276	A	THEARCHY	511	B
TERRITORIAL SEA	278	A	THEATRE OF WAR	281	A
TERRITORIAL SOVEREIGNTY	224	A	THEATRE, AND POLITICS	594	B
TERRITORIAL SUPREMACY	232	A	THEISM	138	A
TERRITORIAL WATERS	278	A	THEME	141	A
TERRITORIUM NULLIUS	789	B	THEOCRACY	157	A
TERRITORY	275	A	THEODICY	535	B
TERRITORY OF THE REQUESTING	796	B	THEODORA, EMPRESS	777	B
PARTY			THEODORIC	726	B
TERRITORY SUBJECT TO PLEBISCITE	792	B	THEODOSIUS, EMPEROR	726	B
TERROR RAID	594	B	THEOLOGIAN	191	A
TERRORISM	217	A	THEOLOGY	138	A
TERRORIST	185	A	THEOLOGY OF CRISIS	460	B
TERTULLIAN	777	B	THEOREM	440	B
TERTZ, ABRAM	777	B	THEORETICAL ANALYSIS	132	A
TESCHEN	800	B	THEORETICAL STATISTICS	440	B
TEST	250	A	THEORIES OF NON-VIOLENCE	120	A
TEST ACT	643	B	THEORIES OF PASSIVE RESISTANCE	122	A
TEST BAN	232	A	THEORY	118	A
TEST BAN TREATY	217	A	THEORY OF CONTRACT	122	A
TEST OATH	259	A	THEORY OF DIALECTICAL	116	A
TESTABILITY	135	A	MATERIALISM		
TESTIMONIAL DINNERS	259	A	THEORY OF GAMES	118	A
TESTIMONIALS	618	B	THEORY OF PROGRESS	132	A
TESTIMONY	138	A	THEORY OF SOCIALIST EVOLUTION	135	A
TESTS	665	B	THEORY OF STATE, GENERAL	129	A
TESTS FOR FACTUAL KNOWLEDGE	141	A	THEORY OF THE FIVE-POWER	453	B
TET OFFENSIVE IN 1968	232	A	CONSTITUTION		
TEUTONIC KNIGHTS	535	B	THERAPY	141	A
TEUTONISM	460	B	THERMONUCLEAR WAR	199	A
TEUTONS	511	B	THERMONUCLEAR WEAPONS	286	A
TEXAS	281	A	THESIS, THETICAL	453	B
TEXAS PRIMARY CASES	673	B	THEY SHALL NOT PASS	841	B
TEXAS VS. WHITE (1869)	676	B	THIERRY, AUGUSTIN	777	B
TEXT	285	A	THIEU, GENERAL NGUYEN VAN	265	A
TEXTBOOKS	808	B	THIMBLERIGGING	665	B
TEXTILE PRODUCTS IDENTIFICATION	665	B	THINK PIECE	447	B
ACT			THINK TANK	169	A
TEXTILE TRADE	665	B	THINKING	132	A
TEXTILES	824	B	THINKING COMMITTEE	536	B
TEXTILES COMMITTEE OF ILO	535	B	THIRD AMENDMENT	224	A
TEXTURE	460	B	THIRD COMMITTEE	180	A
THADDEN, ADOLF VON	725	B	THIRD DEGREE	241	A
THAILAND	276	A	THIRD ESTATE	169	A
THALWEG	493	B	THIRD FORCE OF FRANCE (REFORM	477	B
THALWEG, JURISDICTION	618	B	PARTIES)		
THANKSGIVING DAY	643	B	THIRD HOUSE OF CONGRESS	174	A
THANOM KITTIKACHORN, FIELD	726	B	THIRD HOUSE OF LEGISLATURE	174	A
MARSHAL			THIRD INTERNATIONAL	165	A
THAT MAN IN THE WHITE HOUSE	837	B	THIRD PARTIES	146	A
THAW	618	B	THIRD PARTY ARBITRATION	224	A
THE MAN WHO...	841	B	THIRD PARTY CONCILIATION	241	A
THE PASSENGER CASES	676	B	THIRD READING	259	A

THIRD REICH	148	A
THIRD REPUBLIC (FRANCE)	180	A
THIRD WORLD	273	A
THIRD-PARTY MOVEMENT	154	A
THIRD-TERM TRADITION	217	A
THIRTEENTH AMENDMENT	197	A
THIRTY TYRANTS AT ATHENS	536	B
THIRTY YEARS WAR	250	A
THIRTY-EIGHT WITNESSES	813	B
THOMAS AQUINAS	262	A
THOMAS JEFFERSON PROVISO	618	B
THOMAS, ALBERT	777	B
THOMAS, J. H.	777	B
THOMAS, NORMAN	273	A
THOMAS, WILLIAM I.	777	B
THOMASON COLLECTION OF	810	B
TRACTS		
THOMAZ, ADMIRAL AMERICO	726	B
THOMISM	138	A
THOMPSON, CARL D.	777	B
THOMPSON, G. W.	777	B
THOMPSON, J.	777	B
THOMPSON, LEONARD M.	777	B
THOMPSON, VICTOR A.	726	B
THOMPSON, WILLIAM	777	B
THOREAU, HENRY DAVID	266	A
THOREZ, MAURICE	700	B
THORNDIKE, EDWARD L.	689	B
THORNE, WILL	777	B
THORNHILL VS. ALABAMA (1940)	676	B
THORPE, JOHN JEREMY	777	B
THORTONS	777	B
THOU SHALT NOT STEAL	841	B
THOU, MONSIEUR DE	777	B
THOUGHT	447	B
THOUGHT CONTROL	232	A
THOUSAND DAYS	594	B
THRASYMACHUS	273	A
THREAT	241	A
THREAT OF WAR	224	A
THREAT THEORY	132	A
THREAT TO PEACE	241	A
THREAT TO SECURITY	241	A
THREATENING ATTITUDE	453	B
THREE HUNDRED AND SIX (306)	536	B
THREE HUNDRED AND TWENTY-NINE	847	B
(329)		
THREE POWER CURRENCY	618	B
DECLARATION		
THREE PRINCIPLES OF THE PEOPLE	644	B
THREE-ANTI	665	B
THREE-DIMENSIONAL IMAGES	829	B
THREE-FIFTHS COMPROMISE,	232	A
CONSTITUTIONAL CONVENTION		
THREE-FOURTHS RULE	594	B
THREE-MILE LIMIT	224	A
THREE-PARTY SYSTEM	224	A
THREE-POWER AGREEMENT	594	B
THREE-QUARTERS VOTE	644	B
THREE-YEAR PLAN	644	B
THRESHOLD	141	A
THRONE	819	B
THROTTLEBOTTOM	560	B
THROW AWAY YOUR VOTE	292	A
THUCYDIDES	265	A
THUG TICKET	536	B
THUNEN, J. H. VON	777	B
THURMOND, JAMES STROM	270	A
TIBERIUS GRACCHUS	777	B
TIBET	278	A
TIBETAN REFUGEES	560	B
TICKET	259	A
TICKET OF ADMISSION	460	B
TICKET SPLITTING	211	A
TIDELANDS OIL ACT	259	A
TIDELANDS OIL CONTROVERSY	259	A
TIE	618	B
TIE-BREAK	259	A
TIGHT MONEY POLICY	206	A
TIGRIS-EUPHRATES VALLEY	281	A
TILDEN AND REFORM	841	B
TILLETT, BEN	777	B
TILLICH	689	B
TIMBER COMMITTEE OF ECE	511	B
TIMBER-GRABBING	665	B
TIME	594	B
TIME AND MOTION STUDY	138	A
TIME FACTOR	144	A
TIME FOR A CHANGE	834	B
TIME MANAGEMENT	259	A
TIME SERIES ANALYSIS	138	A
TIME SERVING	618	B
TIME TO UNLOAD	665	B
TIMES FILM CORP. VS. CHICAGO	680	B
(1957)		
TIMES MIRROR CO. VS. SUPERIOR	676	B
COURT (1941)		
TIMETABLE	644	B
TIMOCRACY	440	B
TIN	829	B
TIN BOX	824	B
TIN PAN	829	B
TINGSTEN, H.	777	B
TINHORN POLITICIAN	546	B
TINKER VS. DES MOINES SCHOOL	676	B
DISTRICT (1969)		
TIPPECANOE AND TYLER TOO	837	B
TIPPIT, J.	777	B
TISO, MSGR. JOZEF	777	B
TISSUE BALLOT	829	B
TITLE	447	B
TITLE OF NOBILITY	193	A

TITO, JOSIP BROZ	263	A	TORCHLIGHT PROCESSION	644	B
TITOISM, COMMUNIST DOCTRINE	132	A	TORCUATO	778	B
TITULAR LEADER	191	A	TORIES	151	A
TITUS, CHARLES	778	B	TORIES (LOYALISTS)	157	A
TIV	536	B	TORNADO	665	B
TIYOYUTAI ISLANDS	800	B	TORNEY, JUDITH	778	B
TO ERR IS TRUMAN	847	B	TORONTO	283	A
TO MAKE POLITICAL CAPITAL	291	A	TORPEDO	821	B
TO MAKE POLITICAL MILEAGE	834	B	TORQUEMADA	792	B
TO THE VICTORS BELONG THE SPOILS	291	A	TORRENS SYSTEM	665	B
			TORT	232	A
TOAST	644	B	TORT LAW	250	A
TOCQUEVILLE, (CHARLES) ALEXIS (HENRI CLEREL) DE	262	A	TORTURE	594	B
			TORY	154	A
TODAY	618	B	TORY DEMOCRACY	440	B
TODD, GARFIELD	778	B	TORY PARTY	157	A
TOGETHER	536	B	TOSCANO, MARIO	778	B
TOGETHERNESS	644	B	TOTAL ENVIRONMENT	789	B
TOGLIATTI, PALMIRO	689	B	TOTAL VICTORY	250	A
TOGO REPUBLIC	174	A	TOTAL WAR	232	A
TOJO, GENERAL HIDEKI	700	B	TOTALISM	460	B
TOKEN COIN	829	B	TOTALITARIAN	181	A
TOKENISM	232	A	TOTALITARIAN GOVERNMENT	148	A
TOKUGAWA PERIOD OF JAPANESE HISTORY	618	B	TOTALITARIAN STATE	148	A
			TOTALITARIANISM	115	A
TOKYO	281	A	TOTALITARIANISM, FASCIST THEORY	118	A
TOKYO WAR CRIMES TRIALS	217	A	TOTALITY	447	B
TOLBERT, WILLIAM R.	778	B	TOTEMISM	447	B
TOLEDO WAR	665	B	TOTH VS. QUARLES (1955)	676	B
TOLERANCE	135	A	TOUGH-MINDED AND TENDER-MINDED	837	B
TOLERATION	138	A			
TOLERATION ACT	618	B	TOUR	666	B
TOLSTOI, COUNT LEO	689	B	TOURE, SEKOU	273	A
TOM TINKER'S MEN	536	B	TOURISM	594	B
TOM-TOM	847	B	TOWER, JOHN GOODWIN	689	B
TOMAHAWK	829	B	TOWN	281	A
TOMB OF THE UNKNOWN WARRIOR	796	B	TOWN (U.S.A.)	281	A
TOMLINSON, F.R.	778	B	TOWN AND COUNTRY PLANNING ASSOCIATION (BRITAIN)	511	B
TOMMING	618	B			
TONIC POLITIES	536	B	TOWN BOARD	180	A
TONKIN GULF RESOLUTION	211	A	TOWN CLERK	193	A
TONNAGE	460	B	TOWN COUNCIL	165	A
TONNAGE DUTY	618	B	TOWN GOVERNMENT	169	A
TONNIES, FERDINAND	726	B	TOWN HALL	288	A
TOO LITTLE AND TOO LATE	837	B	TOWN MEETING	224	A
TOO OLD TO CRY	847	B	TOWN MEETING	211	A
TOO PROUD TO FIGHT	841	B	TOWN PLANNING	250	A
TOOL	821	B	TOWNSEND PLAN	259	A
TOP EXECUTIVES	546	B	TOWNSHEND DUTY ACT (1766)	644	B
TOP-LEVEL CONFERENCE	618	B	TOWNSHIP	278	A
TOPIC A	453	B	TOWNSHIP BOARD	180	A
TOPINARD, PAUL	778	B	TOYNBEE, ARNOLD J.	265	A
TOPOGRAPHY, GEOGRAPHIC POWER FACTOR	138	A	TOZZER, A. M.	778	B
			TRACHOMA	829	B
TORCASO VS. WATKINS (1961)	680	B	TRACK	666	B
TORCH HAS BEEN PASSED	841	B	TRADE	241	A

TRADE AGREEMENTS ACT OF 1934	644	B
TRADE AND DEVELOPMENT BOARD (UNCTAD)	493	B
TRADE ASSOCIATION	477	B
TRADE BARRIERS, STATE	224	A
TRADE DELEGATION	180	A
TRADE DISPUTES AND TRADE UNION ACT	644	B
TRADE DOLLAR	644	B
TRADE EXPANSION ACT OF 1962 (TEA)	618	B
TRADE FOLLOWS THE FLAG	834	B
TRADE MISSION	477	B
TRADE NAMES, POLITICAL	453	B
TRADE NEGOTIATIONS	241	A
TRADE OFF	241	A
TRADE PRACTICE CONFERENCES	644	B
TRADE PROMOTION CENTER (ECAFE)	511	B
TRADE UNION	154	A
TRADE UNION CONGRESS (TUC)	180	A
TRADE UNIONISM	127	A
TRADE UNIONS FEDERATION	493	B
TRADEMARK	819	B
TRADES DISPUTES ACT	618	B
TRADING-WITH-THE-ENEMY ACT	259	A
TRADITION	132	A
TRADITIONAL APPROACH	129	A
TRADITIONAL ENEMY	493	B
TRADITIONAL LOGIC	440	B
TRADITIONAL ORDER	232	A
TRADITIONAL ORGANIZATIONS	493	B
TRADITIONAL SOCIETY	149	A
TRADITIONALISM	124	A
TRAFFIC COURT	180	A
TRAGEDY	594	B
TRAIL	644	B
TRAINED SEALS	569	B
TRAINEES	569	B
TRAINING	618	B
TRAINING DIRECTORS	569	B
TRAINING OFFICERS	569	B
TRAINS RAN ON TIME	834	B
TRAITOR TO HIS CLASS	292	A
TRAITS	453	B
TRAMP (PARTY, VOTE)	536	B
TRANQUILIZERS	829	B
TRANS-ARABIAN PIPELINE COMPANY	477	B
TRANS-EMPIRICAL THEORISTS	193	A
TRANSACTION	241	A
TRANSCENDENCE	447	B
TRANSCENDENTAL	141	A
TRANSCENDENTAL DEDUCTION	460	B
TRANSCENDENTAL REDUCTION	460	B
TRANSCONTINENTAL RAILROAD	169	A
TRANSCRIPT	806	B
TRANSFER	644	B
TRANSFER BY WAY OF DISCIPLINARY PUNISHMENT	666	B
TRANSFER OF FLAG	644	B
TRANSFER OF POPULATIONS	594	B
TRANSFERENCE	453	B
TRANSFORMATION	447	B
TRANSFORMATION RULES	440	B
TRANSGENERATIONAL TRANSMISSION	644	B
TRANSIT	644	B
TRANSIT DUTIES	644	B
TRANSIT VISA	806	B
TRANSITION	138	A
TRANSITIONAL SOCIETY	151	A
TRANSITIVITY	453	B
TRANSITORY PROVISIONS	644	B
TRANSKEIAN	536	B
TRANSLATION	644	B
TRANSMISSION BELTS	477	B
TRANSMUTATION	460	B
TRANSNATIONAL POLITICS	122	A
TRANSNATIONAL SOCIETY	161	A
TRANSOCEAN NEWS AGENCY	536	B
TRANSPORT HOUSE	829	B
TRANSPORTATION	241	A
TRANSPORTATION ACT	666	B
TRANSPORTATION ACT OF 1920	644	B
TRANSPORTATION ACT OF 1940	618	B
TRAUTMAN, W. E.	778	B
TRAVEL AGENCY	536	B
TRAVEL ALLOWANCES	618	B
TRAVEL DOCUMENTS	810	B
TRAVEL ON OFFICIAL BUSINESS	618	B
TRAVEL, INTERNATIONAL	644	B
TREACHEROUS RUSE	644	B
TREADMILL	644	B
TREASON	206	A
TREASURER	194	A
TREASURER OF THE UNITED STATES	189	A
TREASURY	174	A
TREASURY BENCH	796	B
TREASURY CERTIFICATE	806	B
TREASURY DEPARTMENT	161	A
TREASURY LEECHES	569	B
TREASURY NOTE	285	A
TREASURY RAT	569	B
TREATIES IN FAVOUR OF A THIRD PARTY	644	B
TREATIES OF LAUSANNE	594	B
TREATIES OF WESTPHALIA	232	A
TREATIES PRO TERTIO	644	B
TREATISE	810	B
TREATMENT OF ALIENS	618	B
TREATMENT OF FOREIGNERS	594	B
TREATMENT OF PRISONERS OF WAR	241	A
TREATY	199	A

TREATY COLLECTION	666	B
TREATY COMMITMENTS	250	A
TREATY DENUNCIATION	232	A
TREATY LAW	224	A
TREATY NOT OPEN FOR ACCESSION	644	B
TREATY OF ALLIANCE	232	A
TREATY OF ANTALCIDAS (387 B.C.)	666	B
TREATY OF ARBITRATION	250	A
TREATY OF ASSISTANCE	259	A
TREATY OF BERLIN	594	B
TREATY OF BREST-LITOVSK	232	A
TREATY OF BUCHAREST	618	B
TREATY OF BUCHAREST	594	B
TREATY OF CESSION	618	B
TREATY OF DUNKIRK	618	B
TREATY OF ESTABLISHMENT	666	B
TREATY OF EXTRADITION	224	A
TREATY OF FRANKFORT	645	B
TREATY OF FRIENDSHIP	259	A
TREATY OF GHENT	224	A
TREATY OF GUADALUPE-HIDALGO	241	A
TREATY OF INDEPENDENCE	260	A
TREATY OF LAUSANNE, JULY 24, 1923	594	B
TREATY OF LOCARNO	619	B
TREATY OF MANILA	619	B
TREATY OF MUTUAL ASSISTANCE	232	A
TREATY OF MUTUAL GUARANTEE	594	B
TREATY OF NAVIGATION	594	B
TREATY OF NEUILLY	645	B
TREATY OF NEUTRALITY	241	A
TREATY OF OPTION	645	B
TREATY OF PARIS	232	A
TREATY OF PARIS (1783)	260	A
TREATY OF PARIS (1898)	619	B
TREATY OF PORTSMOUTH	645	B
TREATY OF PROTECTORATE	645	B
TREATY OF RAPALLO	260	A
TREATY OF RIGA	619	B
TREATY OF SAINT-GERMAIN	645	B
TREATY OF SALONICA	645	B
TREATY OF SAN STEFANO	645	B
TREATY OF SEVRES, 10 AUGUST 1920	645	B
TREATY OF SHIMONOSEKI	645	B
TREATY OF SIB	666	B
TREATY OF ST. GERMAIN	645	B
TREATY OF ST. JEAN DE MAURIENNE	645	B
TREATY OF THE PYRANEES	645	B
TREATY OF TLATELOLCO	619	B
TREATY OF TRIANON (1920)	645	B
TREATY OF VERSAILLES	217	A
TREATY OF VERSAILLES (1919)	199	A
TREATY OF VIENNA	260	A
TREATY ON THE NONPROLIFERATION OF NUCLEAR WEAPONS	217	A
TREATY OPEN FOR ACCESSION	645	B
TREATY PORTS	792	B
TREATY POWER OF THE PRESIDENT	206	A
TREATY POWER, CONGRESS	211	A
TREATY RATIFICATION	211	A
TREATY REGISTRATION	594	B
TREATY-BREAKING STATE	180	A
TREBONIAN	536	B
TREE	821	B
TREITSCHKE, HEINRICH VON	689	B
TRENCH WARFARE	645	B
TREND	138	A
TRENT AFFAIR	645	B
TRENTIN, SILVIO	778	B
TRENTINO-SOUTH TYROL, ITALY	800	B
TRIAL	217	A
TRIAL BALLOON	224	A
TRIAL BY JURY	197	A
TRIAL COURT	169	A
TRIAL HEAT	594	B
TRIBAL GROUP	477	B
TRIBAL IDENTIFICATION	144	A
TRIBAL WARFARE	260	A
TRIBALISM	132	A
TRIBES	493	B
TRIBUNAL	174	A
TRIBUNE	493	B
TRIBUNE OF HONOR	511	B
TRIBUTARY STATE	169	A
TRIBUTE	260	A
TRICKLE-DOWN THEORY	129	A
TRICOLOR	289	A
TRIESTE	279	A
TRIGGER-HAPPY	837	B
TRIMMER	560	B
TRINIDAD	279	A
TRINITY	440	B
TRIP	666	B
TRIPARTITE DECLARATION OF MAY 25, 1950	619	B
TRIPARTITE PACT	260	A
TRIPLE ALLIANCE	477	B
TRIPLE DAMAGE ACTION	619	B
TRIPLE ENTENTE	477	B
TRIUMVIRATE	180	A
TROBRIAND ISLANDS	796	B
TROIKA PROPOSAL, UNITED NATIONS	250	A
TROJAN HORSE	288	A
TROLLOPE PLOY	847	B
TROOPS	180	A
TROP VS. DULLES (1958)	676	B
TROPISM	453	B

TROT OUT THE GHOSTS	847	B
TROTSKY, LEON	262	A
TROTSKYISM, COMMUNIST DOCTRINE	122	A
TROTSKYITE	154	A
TROTTER, WILLIAM	778	B
TROUBLE	666	B
TROUBLE SPOT	796	B
TROUBLEMAKER	569	B
TROUGHSMAN	569	B
TROW, MARTIN	778	B
TRUANT OFFICER	560	B
TRUAX VS. CORRIGAN (1921)	676	B
TRUAX VS. RAICH (1915)	676	B
TRUCE	241	A
TRUCE (ARMISTICE)	232	A
TRUCE AGREEMENT	251	A
TRUCE COMMISSION	180	A
TRUCE DELEGATION	477	B
TRUCE FLAT	801	B
TRUCE NEGOTIATIONS	251	A
TRUCE OFFER	260	A
TRUCIAL OMAN	801	B
TRUCIAL STATES	180	A
TRUD (LABOR)	808	B
TRUDEAU, PIERRE	264	A
TRUE	440	B
TRUE BILL	251	A
TRUJILLO, RAFAEL	268	A
TRUMAN DOCTRINE	202	A
TRUMAN, DAVID B.	270	A
TRUMAN, PRESIDENT HARRY S.	262	A
TRUMBALL	778	B
TRUMPET	829	B
TRUST	144	A
TRUST BUSTING	211	A
TRUST TERRITORY OF THE PACIFIC ISLANDS	278	A
TRUST TERRITORY, UNITED NATIONS	276	A
TRUSTEE STATE	174	A
TRUSTEE, TOWNSHIP	554	B
TRUSTEESHIP	233	A
TRUSTEESHIP AGREEMENT	251	A
TRUSTEESHIP COUNCIL	161	A
TRUSTEESHIP COUNCIL, UNITED NATIONS	157	A
TRUSTEESHIP TERRITORIES	276	A
TRUSTIFICATION	645	B
TRUSTS	157	A
TRUTH	135	A
TRUTH FUNCTION	440	B
TRUTH IN PACKAGING LAW	241	A
TRUTH TABLE	144	A
TRUTH VALUE	447	B
TRUTH-IN CONSTRUCTION	460	B
TRUTH-IN-LENDING ACT	241	A
TRUTH, SOJOURNER	460	B
TSAR	187	A
TSAREVITCH	554	B
TSARINA	546	B
TSARISM	141	A
TSHOMBE, MOISE KAPENDE	270	A
TSU	778	B
TSUNGLI	536	B
TUBERCULOSIS	824	B
TUBMAN, HARRIET	270	A
TUBMAN, WILLIAM V. S.	273	A
TUCKER, BENJAMIN R.	778	B
TUCKER, JOSIAH	778	B
TUDOR ABSOLUTISM	144	A
TUDORS	493	B
TUESDAY	645	B
TUESDAY LUNCH	645	B
TUGAN-BARNOWKY, M.	778	B
TUGWELL, REXFORD G.	700	B
TUITION-AID PLANS	619	B
TUKHACHEVSKY TRIAL	666	B
TUKHACHEVSKY, MIKHAIL N.	726	B
TUMIN, MELVIN	778	B
TUNGSTEN	824	B
TUNISIA	278	A
TUNNEY, JOHN VARICK	700	B
TUPAMAROS	165	A
TURCO-ITALIAN WAR	645	B
TURENNE	801	B
TURGENEV, IVAN SERGEEVICH	701	B
TURGOT, ANNE ROBERT, BARON DE LAULNE	778	B
TURGOT, JACQUES	726	B
TURKEY	278	A
TURMOIL	619	B
TURN BACK	666	B
TURNAROUNDS	619	B
TURNER, JULIUS	726	B
TURNER, NAT	689	B
TURNING BACK AT BORDER	619	B
TURNING-POINT	645	B
TURNIP DAY	666	B
TURNOUT	233	A
TURNOVER	594	B
TURNOVER TAX	619	B
TURNPIKE	789	B
TUTELAGE	251	A
TUTHILL, CYNTHIA	778	B
TUTHILL, JOHN	778	B
TUTORING	666	B
TV DEBATES	241	A
TWAIN, MARK	273	A
TWEED RING	493	B
TWEEDLEDUM AND TWEEDLEDEE	841	B
TWELFTH AMENDMENT	217	A
TWELVE-MILE LIMIT	278	A

TWENTIETH AMENDMENT	211	A
TWENTIETH CENTURY FUND	536	B
TWENTIETH JULY 1944	594	B
TWENTIETH PARTY CONGRESS	174	A
TWENTY YEARS OF TREASON	841	B
TWENTY-FIFTH AMENDMENT	224	A
TWENTY-FIRST AMENDMENT	202	A
TWENTY-FIVE POINTS	645	B
TWENTY-FOUR-HOUR RULE	619	B
TWENTY-FOURTH AMENDMENT	211	A
TWENTY-ONE DEMANDS	619	B
TWENTY-SECOND AMENDMENT	202	A
TWENTY-SIXTH AMENDMENT	224	A
TWENTY-THIRD AMENDMENT	199	A
TWILIGHT ZONE	796	B
TWINING VS. NEW JERSEY (1908)	673	B
TWISTING THE LION'S TAIL	841	B
TWO CHINAS PROPOSAL, UNITED NATIONS	233	A
TWO DOLLARS A DAY AND ROAST BEEF	847	B
TWO SWORDS, DOCTRINE OF	594	B
TWO TREATISES OF GOVERNMENT	286	A
TWO-BIT POLITICIAN	569	B
TWO-OCEAN NAVY	180	A
TWO-PARTY SYSTEM	196	A
TWO-POWER NAVY	493	B
TWO-STEP FLOW, MASS MEDIA	120	A
TWO-TERM TRADITION	211	A
TWO-THIRDS RULE	217	A
TWO-THIRDS VOTE	211	A
TWO-YEAR PLAN	619	B
TYCHISM	460	B
TYING CONTRACT	813	B
TYING LEASES	813	B
TYLER, PRESIDENT JOHN	265	A
TYLER, WAT	778	B
TYLERIZE	666	B
TYLOR, E.B.	778	B
TYPE THEORY	440	B
TYPES	447	B
TYPIFICATION	440	B
TYPISTS	569	B
TYPOLOGY	116	A
TYRANNICIDE	233	A
TYRANNUS	726	B
TYRANNY	120	A
TYRANNY OF THE MAJORITY	197	A
TYRANT	185	B
U THANT	262	A
U.N. ADMINISTRATIVE TRIBUNAL	477	B
U.N. ATOMIC ENERGY COMMISSION	154	A
U.N. CAPITAL DEVELOPMENT FUND (UNCDF)	169	A
U.N. CHARTER	283	A
U.N. CHARTER REVISION	217	A
U.N. CHILDRENS INTERNATIONAL EMERGENCY FUND (UNICEF)	161	A
U.N. COMMAND	477	B
U.N. CONFERENCE ON FREEDOM OF INFORMATION	619	B
U.N. CONFERENCE ON INTERNATIONAL ORGANIZATION	594	B
U.N. DECLARATION	594	B
U.N. DEVELOPMENT DECADE	594	B
U.N. DEVELOPMENT ORGANIZATION (UNIDO)	180	A
U.N. DEVELOPMENT PROGRAM (UNDP)	169	A
U.N. DISARMAMENT COMMISSION	161	A
U.N. ECONOMIC AND SOCIAL COUNCIL (ECOSOC)	165	A
U.N. EDUCATIONAL, SCIENTIFIC, AND CULTURAL ORGANIZATION (UNESCO)	151	A
U.N. EMERGENCY FORCE (UNEF)	157	A
U.N. FINANCING	241	A
U.N. FOOD AND AGRICULTURAL ORGANIZATION	157	A
U.N. FORCE IN CYPRUS (UNFICYP)	161	A
U.N. GENERAL ASSEMBLY	146	A
U.N. HIGH COMMISSIONER FOR REFUGEES (UNH)	546	B
U.N. HUMAN RIGHTS COMMISSION	154	A
U.N. INDUSTRIAL DEVELOPMENT ORGANIZATION (UNIDO)	477	B
U.N. INSTITUTE FOR TRAINING AND RESEARCH	511	B
U.N. INTERNATIONAL COURT OF JUSTICE	151	A
U.N. INTERNATIONAL LAW COMMISSION	180	A
U.N. LIBRARY (GENEVA)	493	B
U.N. MONTHLY CHRONICLE	286	A
U.N. OPERATION IN THE CONGO (ONYC)	169	A
U.N. ORGANIZATION (UNO)	161	A
U.N. PARTICIPATION ACT	666	B
U.N. POLITICAL AFFAIRS, OFFICE OF	511	B
U.N. PREPARATORY COMMISSION	180	A
U.N. REGIONAL COMMISSIONS	169	A
U.N. RELIEF AND REHABILITATION ADMINISTRATION (UNRRA)	165	A
U.N. SECRETARIAT	146	A
U.N. SECRETARY-GENERAL	181	A
U.N. SECURITY COUNCIL	146	A
U.N. SPECIAL COMMITTEE ON PALESTINE	493	B
U.N. SPECIAL FUND	165	A
U.N. SPECIALIZED AGENCIES	157	A
U.N. STAFF PENSION COMMITTEE	536	B
U.N. STRATEGIC TRUST TERRITORIES	281	A

U.N. TECHNICAL ASSISTANCE BOARD	180	A
U.N. TRUCE SUPERVISION ORGANIZATION	165	A
U.N. TRUST TERRITORY	274	A
U.N. TRUSTEESHIP COUNCIL	157	A
U.S. AGENCY FOR INTERNATIONAL DEVELOPMENT (AID)	149	A
U.S. AIR FORCE ACADEMY	174	A
U.S. ARMS CONTROL AND DISARMAMENT AGENCY (ACDA)	169	A
U.S. ARMY SPECIAL FORCES	174	A
U.S. ATTORNEY GENERAL	181	A
U.S. BOARD OF TAX APPEALS	477	B
U.S. BOTANIC GARDEN	824	B
U.S. CAPITAL	792	B
U.S. CAPITOL	288	A
U.S. CENSUS	233	A
U.S. CENSUS BUREAU	165	A
U.S. CIVIL SERVICE COMMISSION (CSC)	165	A
U.S. COAST AND GEODETIC SURVEY	174	A
U.S. COAST GUARD ACADEMY	477	B
U.S. CODE ANNOTATED	233	A
U.S. COMMISSION ON FINE ARTS	493	B
U.S. CONCILIATION SERVICE	174	A
U.S. CONSTITUTION	195	A
U.S. COURT FOR CHINA	536	B
U.S. COURT OF MILITARY APPEALS	174	A
U.S. EMPLOYEES COMPENSATION COMMISSION	536	B
U.S. EMPLOYMENT SERVICE	477	B
U.S. FASCIST ORGANIZATIONS	477	B
U.S. FEDERAL AID HIGHWAY ACT OF 1956	260	A
U.S. FEDERAL BUREAU OF INVESTIGATION	157	A
U.S. FEDERAL COMMUNICATIONS COMMISSION	169	A
U.S. FEDERAL HOUSING ADMINISTRATION	165	A
U.S. FEDERAL POWER COMMISSION	169	A
U.S. FEDERAL RESERVE SYSTEM	154	A
U.S. FISH AND WILDLIFE SERVICE	493	B
U.S. GOVERNMENT MANUAL	285	A
U.S. GOVERNMENT ORGANIZATION MANUAL	285	A
U.S. HOUSING AUTHORITY	169	A
U.S. INFORMATION AGENCY (USIA)	154	A
U.S. INTELLIGENCE BOARD	477	B
U.S. MARITIME BOARD	493	B
U.S. MARITIME COMMISSION	180	A
U.S. MARSHAL	187	A
U.S. MERCHANT MARINE	477	B
U.S. MERCHANT MARINE ACADEMY	493	B
U.S. MILITARY ACADEMY	174	A
U.S. NATIONAL MUSEUM	824	B
U.S. NAVAL ACADEMY	169	A
U.S. NAVAL OBSERVATORY	821	B
U.S. OF AMERICA	275	A
U.S. OF EUROPE	161	A
U.S. OF INDONESIA	169	A
U.S. OF MEXICO	165	A
U.S. OFFICE OF EDUCATION (USOE)	169	A
U.S. POSTAL SERVICE	161	A
U.S. REGULATORY COMMISSIONS	151	A
U.S. REPORTS	286	A
U.S. REPRESENTATIVE TO THE UNITED NATIONS	189	A
U.S. SHIPPING BOARD	477	B
U.S. SUPREME COURT	146	A
U.S. TRAINING AND EMPLOYMENT SERVICE (USTES)	511	B
U.S. TRAVEL SERVICE (USTS)	536	B
U.S. VETERANS ADMINISTRATION (VA)	161	A
U.S. VS. AMERICAN TOBACCO CO. (1911)	676	B
U.S. VS. BROWN (1965)	676	B
U.S. VS. BUTLER (1936)	673	B
U.S. VS. CLASSIC (1941)	672	B
U.S. VS. CURTISS-WRIGHT CORPORATION (1936)	260	A
U.S. VS. DARBY LUMBER CO. (1941)	672	B
U.S. VS. E.C. KNIGHT CO. (1895)	672	B
U.S. VS. GUEST (1966)	676	B
U.S. VS. JOHNSON (1966)	676	B
U.S. VS. LANZA (1922)	673	B
U.S. VS. LOVETT (1946)	676	B
U.S. VS. O'BRIEN (1968)	680	B
U.S. VS. PINK (1942)	676	B
U.S. VS. SCHWIMMER (1929)	676	B
U.S. VS. SEEGER (1965)	673	B
U.S. VS. WONG KIM ARK (1898)	676	B
U-ARRANGEMENT	801	B
U-2 INCIDENT	217	A
UD-VE REPUBLIQUE	511	B
UDAIPUR, INDIA	801	B
UGANDA	275	A
UGLY AMERICANS	191	A
UKASE	806	B
UL-ISLAM	511	B
ULAM, ADAM B.	726	B
ULBRECHT, WALTER	270	A
ULIANOV, ALEXANDER	726	B
ULLMAN VS. U.S. (1956)	676	B
ULMER, SIDNEY	726	B
ULPIAN	796	B
ULSTER	276	A
ULTIMATE DISTINATION	796	B
ULTIMATUM	217	A
ULTRA VIRES	279	A

ULTRA VIRES ACTION	251	A		UNEMPLOYMENT	217	A
ULTRAFILTERS	829	B		UNEMPLOYMENT COMPENSATION	233	A
ULTRAMONTANE	796	B		UNEMPLOYMENT INSURANCE	224	A
ULTRAMONTANISM	453	B		UNENFORCED LAW	241	A
UMBERTO, KING	701	B		UNEQUAL TREATIES	233	A
UMBRELLA AGENCY	477	B		UNFAIR COMPETITION	241	A
UMBRELLA SYMBOL	829	B		UNFAIR LABOR PRACTICE	233	A
UMION DES DEMOCRATES POUR LA	493	B		UNFINISHED BUSINESS	594	B
REPUBLIQUE				UNFLAPPABLE	554	B
UMM AL QUWAIN	536	B		UNGS, THOMAS	778	B
UMMAH - ISLAMIC COMMUNITY	511	B		UNHOLY ALLIANCE	169	A
UN-AMERICAN	138	A		UNICAMERAL LEGISLATURE	146	A
UNAM SANCTAM	810	B		UNICAMERAL SYSTEM	196	A
UNAMUNO	726	B		UNIDIMENSIONALISM	144	A
UNANIMITY RULE	211	A		UNIFICATION	224	A
UNANIMOUS	233	A		UNIFIED COURT SYSTEM	165	A
UNANIMOUS CONSENT	224	A		UNIFORM CODE OF MILITARY	251	A
UNANIMOUS DECISION	224	A		JUSTICE		
UNANIMOUS OPINION	217	A		UNIFORM LEGISLATION	241	A
UNATTACHED M.P.	554	B		UNIFORM STATE LAWS	233	A
UNBOSSED	560	B		UNIFORMITY	595	B
UNCERTAINTY PRINCIPLE	141	A		UNIFORMITY ACT	666	B
UNCLE SAM	288	A		UNIFORMITY OF LAW	242	A
UNCLE TOM	184	A		UNIFUNCTIONALISM	141	A
UNCOMMITTED NATIONS	154	A		UNILATERAL ACT	242	A
UNCONDITIONAL NEUTRALITY	251	A		UNILATERAL DECLARATION	242	A
UNCONDITIONAL SURRENDER	202	A		UNILATERAL DECLARATION OF	251	A
UNCONSCIOUS	144	A		INDEPENDENCE (U.D.I.)		
UNCONSTITUTIONAL	196	A		UNILATERAL DISARMAMENT	217	A
UNCONSTITUTIONAL CONDITIONS	241	A		UNIMPEDED ACCESS	789	B
UNCONSTITUTIONALITY	195	A		UNINCORPORATED AREAS	278	A
UNCONVENTIONAL WARFARE	199	A		UNINCORPORATED TERRITORY	281	A
UNDECIDABILITY	645	B		UNINCORPORATED VILLAGE	283	A
UNDECLARED WAR	211	A		UNINOMINAL VOTING	645	B
UNDEMOCRATIC	124	A		UNION	165	A
UNDERDEVELOPED COUNTRIES	148	A		UNION AFRICAINE ET MALGACHE	477	B
UNDERDEVELOPMENT	196	A		(U.A.M.)		
UNDERDOG EFFECT	224	A		UNION AS IT WAS AND THE	292	A
UNDERGROUND DETECTION	241	A		CONSTITUTION AS IT IS		
METHODS				UNION CALENDAR	284	A
UNDERGROUND MOVEMENT	151	A		UNION CENTRAL EXECUTIVE	511	B
UNDERGROUND RAILWAY	157	A		COMMITTEE		
UNDERSECRETARY OF STATE	187	A		UNION COUNCIL OF COMMISSARS	536	B
UNDERSTANDING	440	B		UNION DEMOCRATIQUE ET SOCIALE	511	B
UNDERSTUDIES	560	B		DE RESISTANCE		
UNDERWATER DEMOLITION TEAM	511	B		UNION ECONOMIQUE BENELUX	477	B
(UDT)				UNION HATER	560	B
UNDERWOOD TARIFF	594	B		UNION JACK	287	A
UNDESIRABLE ALIEN	187	A		UNION LABEL	287	A
UNDISPUTED FACT	440	B		UNION LABOR PARTY	536	B
UNDISTRIBUTED PROFITS	233	A		UNION LEAGUE	511	B
UNDISTRIBUTED PROFITS TAX	251	A		UNION LOVER	560	B
UNEARNED INCOME	241	A		UNION MAINTENANCE CLAUSE	619	B
UNEARNED INCREMENT	440	B		UNION MOVEMENT	161	A
UNEMPLOYABLES	194	A		UNION NOW	837	B
UNEMPLOYED	191	A		UNION OF AFRICAN STATES	180	A

UNION OF ARAB REPUBLICS	276	A
UNION OF ASIATIC PARLIAMENTS	511	B
UNION OF CENTRAL AFRICAN STATES (UEAC)	170	A
UNION OF ECONOMIC INTERESTS	512	B
UNION OF INTERNATIONAL ASSOCIATIONS	493	B
UNION OF INTERNATIONAL FAIRS	536	B
UNION OF SOUTH AFRICA	276	A
UNION OF SOVIET SOCIALIST REPUBLICS (USSR)	273	A
UNION OF THE AMERICAN REPUBLICS	493	B
UNION OF TOWNS AND COMMUNES	536	B
UNION PARTY	493	B
UNION POUR LA DEFENSE DE LA REPUBLIQUE (FRANCE)	512	B
UNION POUR LA NOUVELLE REPUBLIQUE	512	B
UNION SAVER (UNION SAVING)	847	B
UNION SHOP	165	A
UNION SHRIEKER	569	B
UNION WITH BRITAIN NOW	834	B
UNION-MAINTENANCE CLAUSE	619	B
UNIONISM	138	A
UNIONIST PARTY	512	B
UNIONS IN THE PUBLIC SERVICE	512	B
UNIT COSTS	595	B
UNIT INSTRUCTION	645	B
UNIT OF ACCOUNT	645	B
UNIT RULE	217	A
UNIT VETO SYSTEM	217	A
UNITARISM	447	B
UNITARY DEMOCRACIES	144	A
UNITARY GOVERNMENT	148	A
UNITARY STATE	146	A
UNITAS	493	B
UNITED ARAB REPUBLIC (UAR)	161	A
UNITED ARAB STATES (U.A.S.)	170	A
UNITED AUTO WORKERS (UAW)	157	A
UNITED FRONT	165	A
UNITED KINGDOM (UK)	273	A
UNITED LABOR PARTY	512	B
UNITED MEXICAN STATES	493	B
UNITED MOTHERS OF AMERICA	536	B
UNITED NATIONS (UN)	144	A
UNITED PARTY	493	B
UNITED PUBLIC WORKERS VS. MITCHELL (1947)	676	B
UNITED SERVICE ORGANIZATION (USO)	493	B
UNITED STATES (U.S.)	274	A
UNITED WE STAND, DIVIDED WE FALL	292	A
UNITED WORLD FEDERALISTS	154	A
UNITING FOR PEACE RESOLUTION, UNITED NATIONS	211	A
UNITS	447	B
UNITY	260	A
UNITY OF COMMAND	595	B
UNIVERSABILITY	460	B
UNIVERSAL	144	A
UNIVERSAL COPYRIGHT CONVENTION	260	A
UNIVERSAL DECLARATION OF HUMAN RIGHTS	211	A
UNIVERSAL DISARMAMENT	206	A
UNIVERSAL MEMBERSHIP	251	A
UNIVERSAL MILITARY SERVICE	242	A
UNIVERSAL MILITARY TRAINING	224	A
UNIVERSAL MILITARY TRAINING AND SERVICE ACT	595	B
UNIVERSAL PHILOSOPHIES, HELLENISTIC	440	B
UNIVERSAL POSTAL CONVENTION	595	B
UNIVERSAL POSTAL UNION (UPU)	165	A
UNIVERSAL POSTAL UNION CONGRESS	174	A
UNIVERSAL SET	144	A
UNIVERSAL SUCCESSION	619	B
UNIVERSAL SUFFRAGE	202	A
UNIVERSAL, EQUAL, DIRECT, AND SECRET SUFFRAGE	242	A
UNIVERSALISM	135	A
UNIVERSALITY	242	A
UNIVERSALITY OF PHENOMENA	138	A
UNIVERSE	129	A
UNIVERSE OF DISCOURSE	447	B
UNIVERSITIES	477	B
UNIVERSITY OF CALIFORNIA	174	A
UNIVERSITY OF CHICAGO	174	A
UNIVERSITY OF MICHIGAN	477	B
UNIVERSITY SUFFRAGE	260	A
UNIVERSITY TRAINING	619	B
UNKNOWN	144	A
UNLAWFUL	251	A
UNLEASH CHIANG	619	B
UNLIMITED	460	B
UNNEUTRAL SERVICE	666	B
UNOBLIGATED TIME EXPENDITURES	666	B
UNOCCUPIED ZONE OF FRANCE	789	B
UNOFFICIAL OBSERVER	546	B
UNPACK	666	B
UNPOLLED ELECTORS	546	B
UNPROVOKED AGGRESSION	242	A
UNREASONABLE	440	B
UNREASONABLE DEADLOCK	666	B
UNREASONABLE SEARCHES AND SEIZURES	217	A
UNRECOGNIZED STATES	170	A
UNRECONSTRUCTED	546	B

UNREGENERATED SLUM	801	B	USURY	224	A
UNREST	619	B	USUS	536	B
UNRESTRICTED SUBMARINE WARFARE	242	A	UTHWATT COMMITTEE	537	B
			UTI POSSEDITIS	646	B
UNSOLVABILITY	619	B	UTILITARIANISM	116	A
UNSTABLE	595	B	UTILITY	132	A
UNSTANDARDIZED INTERVIEW	144	A	UTILITY MAXIMIZATION	453	B
UNTERRIFIED, THE	536	B	UTMOST SECRECY	595	B
UNTOUCHABLES	165	A	UTOPIA AND POLITICS	138	A
UNWASHED (GREAT UNWASHED, UNWASHED DEMOCRACY)	477	B	UTOPIAN	127	A
			UTOPIAN EXPERIMENTS	224	A
UNWRITTEN CONSTITUTION	211	A	UTOPIAN SOCIALISTS	148	A
UNWRITTEN LAW	217	A	UTOPIANISM	122	A
UPAS TREE	847	B	UTTAR PRADESH, INDIA	796	B
UPHEAVAL	619	B	UTTERANCE	666	B
UPPER CHAMBER	165	A	UULGARIS	829	B
UPPER HOUSE	165	A	UXORICIDE	666	B
UPPER VOLTA	279	A	UYOKU	537	B
UPPER-COURT MYTH	453	B	UZBEKISTAN	801	B
UPPITY	569	B	V FOR VICTORY	837	B
UPRISING	251	A	V-E DAY	260	A
UPSALA	792	B	V-J DAY	251	A
UPSET	251	A	V-MAIL	646	B
UPTOWN	801	B	VACANCY	595	B
UPWARD	792	B	VACATIONS	666	B
UPWARD BOUND	260	A	VACCARO, M. A.	778	B
URBAN	275	A	VACHER DE LA POUGE, G.	779	B
URBAN AFFAIRS	211	A	VADERVELDE, EMILE	779	B
URBAN AFFAIRS WORKERS	560	B	VAGRANCY	595	B
URBAN AGENT	569	B	VAGRANT	194	A
URBAN COUNTY	281	A	VAIHINGER, HANS	779	B
URBAN DISTRICT	279	A	VAILLANT, EDOUARD	779	B
URBAN MASS TRANSPORTATION ADMINISTRATION	180	A	VAIZEY, JOHN	726	B
			VALEN, HENRY	779	B
URBAN MUNICIPALITY	174	A	VALENTINIAN, EMPEROR	726	B
URBAN PLANNING	202	A	VALID	138	A
URBAN POLITICS	118	A	VALIDATING ACT	619	B
URBAN RENEWAL	224	A	VALIDATION	129	A
URBAN RENEWAL ADMINISTRATION	170	A	VALIDITY	118	A
URBAN SYSTEM	138	A	VALIDITY OF THE APPOINTMENT	646	B
URBAN-RURAL REPRESENTATION	233	A	VALLA, LAURENTIUS	779	B
URBANISM	124	A	VALLES, J.	779	B
URBANISM, IN EMERGENT NATIONS	132	A	VALLET DE GOYTISOLO	779	B
URBANIZATION	120	A	VALLETTA, VITTORIO	779	B
URGENT DEFICIENCY BILL	646	B	VALUATION	144	A
URREN, W. S.	778	B	VALUATIONAL STATEMENT	135	A
URUGUAY	276	A	VALUE	135	A
USAGE	595	B	VALUE ADDED TAX	217	A
USE	619	B	VALUE CONSENSUS	132	A
USE TAX	242	A	VALUE JUDGMENT	116	A
USEFUL	448	B	VALUE SYSTEM	127	A
USHERS	569	B	VALUE THEORY	116	A
USUCAPION	666	B	VALUES	114	A
USUFRUCT	666	B	VAN BUREN, PRESIDENT MARTIN	265	A
USURP	224	A	VAN HISE, CHARLES	779	B
USURPATION	224	A	VAN ZEELAND REPORT	813	B

VANADIUM	829	B
VANDENBERG TRADITION OF	224	A
BIPARTISAN FOREIGN POLICY		
VANDENBERG, ARTHUR H.	268	A
VANDERLIP, FRANK A.	779	B
VANDERVELDE, EMILE	779	B
VANGUARD	180	A
VANOCRAT	537	B
VANSITTARTISM	453	B
VARANGIANS	537	B
VARGAS, GETULIO DORNELLES	701	B
VARIABLE	114	A
VARIABLE ANALYSIS	127	A
VARIANCE	129	A
VARIANCE ANALYSIS	127	A
VARIATIONS	454	B
VARIETIES OF CURRENCY USED IN	821	B
THE U.S.		
VASCONCELOS, JOSE	726	B
VASSAL	187	A
VASSAL STATE	174	A
VASSALAGE	260	A
VAST WASTELAND	801	B
VASUBANDHU	779	B
VATICAN	154	A
VATICAN CITY	279	A
VATTEL, E. DE	779	B
VAUBAN, SEBASTIEN DE	779	B
VAUGHAN, C. E.	779	B
VEAZIE BANK VS. FENNO (1869)	673	B
VEBLEN, THORSTEIN	263	A
VECHEKA	537	B
VECTOR	440	B
VEDANTA	460	B
VEDEL, G.	779	B
VEEP (VICE PRESIDENT)	554	B
VELASCO IBARRA, JOSE MARIA	701	B
VELASQUISMO, ECUADOR	460	B
VELCHEV, GENERAL D.	779	B
VENAL	646	B
VENERABILEM	810	B
VENEZIA GIULIA	801	B
VENEZUELA	275	A
VENEZUELA BOUNDARY DISPUTE	260	A
VENEZUELA DEBT CONTROVERSY	595	B
VENIRE	646	B
VENIZELOS, ELEUTHERIOS	779	B
VENUE	278	A
VERA CRUZ INCIDENT	619	A
VERB	144	A
VERBA, SIDNEY	270	A
VERBAL DECISION RULE	448	B
VERBAL NOTE	646	B
VERBAL REALISM	460	B
VERBATIM RECORD	285	A
VERDICT	242	A
VERDUN	796	B
VEREADOR (ALDERMAN)	560	B
VERIFIABILITY	118	A
VERIFICATION	118	A
VERIFICATION OF CREDENTIALS	595	B
VERMONT	281	A
VERSION	460	B
VERTICAL FEDERALISM	138	A
VERTICAL INTEGRATION	124	A
VERWALTUNGSLEHRE	460	B
VERWOERD, DR. HENDRIK FRENSCH	270	A
VERY IMPORTANT PERSON (VIP)	554	B
VERY IMPORTANT PERSON INDEED	569	B
(VIPI)		
VEST POCKET VOTE	218	A
VESTED INTERESTS	154	A
VESTED WITH FULL POWERS	595	B
VETERANS	185	A
VETERANS ADMINISTRATION (VA)	154	A
VETERANS AFFAIRS COMMITTEE	477	B
VETERANS BONUS	260	A
VETERANS OF FOREIGN WARS OF	170	A
THE U.S. (VFW)		
VETERANS ORGANIZATIONS	174	A
VETERANS PREFERENCE	242	A
VETO	196	A
VETO (U.S. PRESIDENTIAL)	196	A
VETO GROUPS	174	A
VETO ITEM	224	A
VETO MAYOR	194	A
VETO POWER	197	A
VETO, SECURITY COUNCIL	196	A
VIANNA, O.	779	B
VICE	260	A
VICE CONSUL	546	B
VICE PRESIDENCY	182	A
VICE PRESIDENT	185	A
VICE-CHANCELLOR	554	B
VICE-KING	560	B
VICE-QUEEN	560	B
VICE-REINE	560	B
VICEROY	546	B
VICHY GOVERNMENT	161	A
VICHYITE	477	B
VICO, G	726	B
VICTIM	554	B
VICTORIA, QUEEN	265	A
VICTORIAN	194	A
VICTORIAN ORDER	646	B
VICTORIOUS POWER	180	A
VICTORY	251	A
VICTORY HAS A THOUSAND	841	B
FATHERS		
VICTORY TAX	646	B
VICUNA COAT	819	B
VIDELA, GABRIEL GONZALEZ	779	B

VIENNA AWARD	666	B	VIRGINIA PLAN	224	A
VIENNA CIRCLE	478	B	VIRGINIA RESOLUTIONS	251	A
VIENNA CONGRESS (1814-15)	206	A	VIRGINIA VS. TENNESSEE (1893)	680	B
VIENNA CONVENTION ON	620	B	VIRGINIUS, THE	824	B
CONSULAR RELATIONS			VIRTU	454	B
VIENNA CONVENTION ON TREATY	620	B	VIRTUAL REPRESENTATION	260	A
LAW			VIRTUALITY	460	B
VIENNA JURISTS' SOCIETY	537	B	VIRTUES	454	B
VIERECK, PETER	779	B	VISA	224	A
VIET CONG	148	A	VISCOUNT	554	B
VIET MINH	149	A	VISCOUNTESS	561	B
VIET NAM, WAR IN	196	A	VISIBILITY	646	B
VIET-NAM CONFLICT	199	A	VISIBLE ADMIXTURE	667	B
VIETNAM	273	A	VISIGOTHS	512	B
VIETNAM, DEMOCRATIC REPUBLIC	151	A	VISION	646	B
OF, (NORTH VIETNAM)			VISIT	667	B
VIETNAM, REPUBLIC OF (SOUTH	149	A	VISIT AND SEARCH	251	A
VIETNAM)			VISIT OF CONDOLENCE	667	B
VIETNAMIZATION	199	A	VISITORS BOOK	810	B
VIETNIK	560	B	VISUAL AIDS	829	B
VIEW	460	B	VITA	810	B
VIEWPOINT	440	B	VITAL	454	B
VIGFUSSON, G.	779	B	VITAL CENTER	493	B
VIGILANCE COMMITTEE	478	B	VITAL INTERESTS	138	A
VIGILANTES	189	A	VITAL STATISTICS	141	A
VIGILANTISM	144	A	VITALISM	460	B
VIKING WAR-DOGS	537	B	VITALITY	461	B
VIKINGS	478	B	VIVA VOCE VOTE	595	B
VIKINGS AT WAREHAM	667	B	VIZIER	561	B
VILAMAJO, JULIO	779	B	VLASOV, ANDREI A.	780	B
VILLAGE	792	B	VOCATIONAL COUNSELING	620	B
VILLAGERS	569	B	VOCATIONAL EDUCATION	260	A
VILLARI, L	779	B	VOCATIONAL EDUCATION ACT	646	B
VILLARI, P.	779	B	VOCATIONAL GUIDANCE	620	B
VILLAS RAID	595	B	VOCATIONAL REHABILITATION	620	B
VILNA INCIDENT	595	B	VOCATIONAL REHABILITATION	493	B
VINCIGUERRA, MARIA	779	B	ADMINISTRATION		
VINDICATION	595	B	VOCATIONAL TRAINING	595	B
VINDICIAE CONTRA TYRANNOS	810	B	VOEGELIN, E.	780	B
(1579)			VOELKISCHER BEOBACHTER	806	B
VINES, KENNETH N.	726	B	VOICE FROM THE SEWER	841	B
VINOGRADOFF, P.	780	B	VOICE OF AMERICA	161	A
VINSON, FRED L.	701	B	VOICE OF THE PEOPLE	834	B
VINSON, FREDERICK MOORE	701	B	VOICE VOTE	218	A
VIOLATION	260	A	VOID	595	B
VIOLATION OF INTERNATIONAL LAW	224	A	VOID FOR VAGUENESS DOCTRINE	260	A
VIOLATION OF NEUTRALITY	218	A	VOIDABLE	646	B
VIOLENCE	202	A	VOIVODE	801	B
VIOLENT DECISION RULES	448	B	VOLGA BASIN	283	A
VIRGIL	689	B	VOLGA GERMANS	494	B
VIRGIN ISLANDS	281	A	VOLITION	454	B
VIRGIN LAND CAMPAIGN	620	B	VOLK	180	A
VIRGIN MARY	701	B	VOLKSKONGRESS	667	B
VIRGINIA AND KENTUCKY	242	A	VOLKSRAT	537	B
RESOLUTIONS			VOLKSTURM	512	B
VIRGINIA DYNASTY	180	A	VOLLMAR, GEORG VON	780	B

VOLONTE GENERALE	454	B	VOTING MACHINE	286	A
VOLSTEAD ACT	242	A	VOTING METHODS	202	A
VOLTAIRE, FRANCOIS MARIE	264	A	VOTING PAIR	224	A
AROUET DE			VOTING PROCEDURE	199	A
VOLUNTARINESS	454	B	VOTING RIGHTS ACT OF 1965	211	A
VOLUNTARISM	141	A	VOTING TURNOUT	199	A
VOLUNTARY	595	B	VOTING-PAPER LEFT BLANK	620	B
VOLUNTARY ASSOCIATION	154	A	VOX POPULI (VOICE OF THE PEOPLE)	289	A
VOLUNTARY CONTRIBUTIONS	251	A	VUKMANOVIC-TEMPO	780	B
VOLUNTARY OFFICE	561	B	VULNERABILITY	251	A
VOLUNTARY SERVICE	260	A	VYSHINSKY, ANDREI	689	B
VOLUNTARY STAFF	561	B	WADIES	829	B
VOLUNTEER	546	B	WAFD (EGYPT)	537	B
VOLUNTEER CORPS	180	A	WAFFLE	620	B
VOLUNTEERS IN SERVICE TO	157	A	WAGE AND HOUR DIVISION	494	B
AMERICA (VISTA)			WAGE AND HOUR LAW OF 1938	595	B
VON BERTALANFFY, LUDWIG	689	B	WAGE AND HOUR LAW OF 1949	620	B
VON DER MUHLL	780	B	WAGE AND HOUR LAW OF 1955	620	B
VON FRIEDEBURG	726	B	WAGE AND HOUR PUBLIC	537	B
VON NEUMANN, JOHN	726	B	CONTRACTS DIVISION (WHPC)		
VON OPPENHEIM, MAX FREIHERR	780	B	WAGE AND HOUR REGULATIONS	224	A
VONRANKE, LEOPOLD	780	B	WAGE CONTROLS	211	A
VOODOO	461	B	WAGE FLOOR	233	A
VORKUTA	537	B	WAGER, PAUL W.	780	B
VOROSHILOV, MARSHAL K. E.	689	B	WAGES AND HOURS ACT	260	A
VORSTER, BALTHAZAR JOHANNES	271	A	WAGING PEACE	251	A
VOSK, M.	726	B	WAGNER ACT	242	A
VOTE	196	A	WAGNER-CONNERY LABOR	242	A
VOTE BY A SHOW OF HANDS	233	A	RELATIONS ACT OF 1935		
VOTE BY ACCLAMATION	224	A	WAGNER-PEYSER ACT	646	B
VOTE BY CORRESPONDENCE	595	B	WAGNER, ADOLF	780	B
VOTE BY PROXY	224	A	WAGNER, RICHARD	701	B
VOTE BY SECRET BALLOT	218	A	WAGNERIAN CIRCLE	813	B
VOTE BY SITTING AND STANDING	251	A	WAHHABISM	512	B
VOTE CATCHING	667	B	WAILING WALL	283	A
VOTE FRAUD	224	A	WAIT-AND-SEE POLICY	595	B
VOTE INDICATOR	135	A	WAITE, MORRISON REMICK	780	B
VOTE OF CENSURE	197	A	WAIVE	251	A
VOTE OF CONFIDENCE	197	A	WAIVER	251	A
VOTE OF NO-CONFIDENCE	199	A	WAKEFIELD, EDWARD GIBBON	780	B
VOTE OF THANKS	620	B	WAL-WAL (UAL UAL) DISPUTE	646	B
VOTE YOURSELF A FARM	847	B	WALDECK-ROUSSEAU	780	B
VOTE-GETT(ER, -ING)	191	A	WALDHEIM, KURT	264	A
VOTE-INS	561	B	WALDO, DWIGHT	273	A
VOTELESS	620	B	WALES	281	A
VOTER	181	A	WALK	667	B
VOTER PARTICIPATION	124	A	WALK OVER (VERB AND NOUN)	646	B
VOTER QUALIFICATIONS	211	A	WALKATHON	667	B
VOTER REGISTRATION	199	A	WALKER TARIFF	646	B
VOTER'S APATHY	12Q	A	WALKER, EDWIN A.	780	B
VOTES CAST	242	A	WALKER, ERIC	780	B
VOTING	197	A	WALKING CORPSE	569	B
VOTING BEHAVIOR	114	A	WALKING DELEGATE	561	B
VOTING CATTLE	561	B	WALL OF SHAME	829	B
VOTING FOR A LIST BY SIMPLE	242	A	WALL STREET	278	A
MAJORITY			WALLACE, ALFRED RUSSEL	780	B

WALLACE, GEORGE C.	264	A	WAR OF RELIGION	595	B
WALLACE, HENRY AGARD	273	A	WAR OF ROSES	251	A
WALLACE, SCHULERY	780	B	WAR OF SECESSION	218	A
WALLACE'S FARMER	813	B	WAR OF THE AUSTRIAN	620	B
WALLAS, GRAHAM	701	B	SUCCESSION		
WALLOON NATIONALISM	144	A	WAR OF THE SPANISH SUCCESSION	596	B
WALLOONS	170	A	WAR OF 1812	218	A
WALSH-HEALEY ACT OF 1936	620	B	WAR OFFICE	180	A
(PUBLIC CONTRACTS ACT)			WAR ON POVERTY	211	A
WALSH, WILLIAM H.	780	B	WAR ON TWO FRONTS	233	A
WALTER, H. E.	780	B	WAR PARTY	180	A
WALTZ, KENNETH N.	726	B	WAR POTENTIAL	288	A
WALWYN, WILLIAM	780	B	WAR POWERS OF THE PRESIDENT	195	A
WALZER, M.	780	B	WAR POWERS, CONGRESS	206	A
WANT	260	A	WAR PREVENTION	218	A
WANTED PERSON	561	B	WAR PRODUCTION BOARD (U.S.)	175	A
WAR	206	A	WAR PROFITS TAX	242	A
WAR AIMS	251	A	WAR PROPAGANDA	218	A
WAR ASSETS ADMINISTRATION	494	B	WAR REBELS	194	A
WAR ATROCITIES	218	A	WAR RELOCATION AUTHORITY	175	A
WAR BETWEEN THE STATES	206	A	WAR RESISTERS INTERNATIONAL	494	B
WAR BONDS	242	A	(WRI)		
WAR CABINET	180	A	WAR RISK INSURANCE	620	B
WAR CLOUDS	646	B	WAR SHIPPING ADMINISTRATION	512	B
WAR CONTRIBUTION	620	B	WAR STRATEGEM	251	A
WAR CRIME TRIALS	206	A	WAR TO END WARS	289	A
WAR CRIMES	202	A	WAR TO THE KNIFE	667	B
WAR DAMAGE CORPORATION	537	B	WAR WITHOUT MERCY	667	B
WAR DEBTS	218	A	WAR ZONE	281	A
WAR DEMOCRATS	174	A	WAR-GAMING WORDS	440	B
WAR DEPARTMENT (ALSO,	175	A	WAR-WEARINESS	440	B
DEPARTMENT OF WAR)			WARD	278	A
WAR FINANCE CORPORATION	494	B	WARD HEELER	187	A
WAR FOOD ADMINISTRATION	494	B	WARD, LESTER FRANK	780	B
WAR FOR THE UNIFICATION OF	251	A	WARD, ROBERT E.	726	B
ITALY			WARE PLAN	667	B
WAR GUILT	242	A	WARFARE	206	A
WAR HAWK	161	A	WARFARE AT SEA	260	A
WAR HORSE	554	B	WARFARE ON LAND	251	A
WAR INDEMNIFICATION	595	B	WARLORDS	187	A
WAR LABOR BOARD	512	B	WARM SPRING INDIANS	569	B
WAR LAW	646	B	WARMONGERS	191	A
WAR LOAN	595	B	WARNING-SHOT	620	B
WAR MAKING	595	B	WARRANT	224	A
WAR MANPOWER COMMISSION	494	B	WARRANT, ARREST	233	A
(U.S.)			WARRANTY	667	B
WAR MATERIAL	821	B	WARREN COMMISSION REPORT	283	A
WAR MOBILIZATION DIRECTOR	569	B	WARREN, EARL	262	A
WAR OF AGGRESSION	206	A	WARREN, JOSIAH	780	B
WAR OF ATTRITION	206	A	WARREN, ROBERT PENN	780	B
WAR OF CONQUEST	242	A	WARRIOR	554	B
WAR OF EXTERMINATION	233	A	WARSAW PACT TREATY	154	A
WAR OF INDEPENDENCE	202	A	ORGANIZATION (WTO)		
WAR OF LIBERATION	202	A	WARSAW RISING	260	A
WAR OF NATIONAL LIBERATION	202	A	WARSAW TREATY OF DECEMBER,	596	B
WAR OF NERVES	260	A	1970		

WARSHIP	289	A	WAZYK	781	B
WARTIME TREATMENT OF JAPANESE-AMERICANS	225	A	WE HAVE MET THE ENEMY AND THEY ARE OURS	834	B
WASHINGTON BRIGADE	512	B	WE POLKED YOU IN 1844, WE'LL PIERCE YOU IN 1852	841	B
WASHINGTON CONFERENCE OF 1921-1922	251	A	WE SHALL OVERCOME	289	A
WASHINGTON NAVAL TREATY	260	A	WE WILL BURY YOU	290	A
WASHINGTON STATE	281	A	WEAK-MAYOR PLAN	202	A
WASHINGTON, BOOKER T.	264	A	WEALTH	218	A
WASHINGTON, D.C.	274	A	WEAPONS	286	A
WASHINGTON, D.C. COURTS	165	A	WEAPONS CONTROL	206	A
WASHINGTON, PRESIDENT GEORGE	262	A	WEAPONS TECHNOLOGY	225	A
WASHINGTON'S FAREWELL ADDRESS	211	A	WEASEL WORD (PHRASE)	841	B
WASP	183	A	WEATHER	646	B
WASSERMAN, PAUL	726	B	WEATHER BUREAU	478	B
WASSERSTEIN, B.	780	B	WEATHERMAN	157	A
WASTELAND	801	B	WEBB EXPORT ACT	646	B
WATCH AND WARD SOCIETY	537	B	WEBB-KENYON ACT	646	B
WATCHDOG COMMITTEE	170	A	WEBB-POMERENE EXPORT TRADE ACT OF 1918	646	B
WATCHDOG OF THE TREASURY	191	A	WEBB, BEATRICE	273	A
WATCHER	561	B	WEBB, SIDNEY	268	A
WATCHFUL WAITING	646	B	WEBER, E.	781	B
WATER APPORTIONMENT, UNITED STATES-MEXICO	646	B	WEBER, MAX	261	A
			WEBERIAN	141	A
WATER CONSERVATION, U.S.A.	251	A	WEBSTER-HAYNE DEBATE	620	B
WATER DETECTION METHODS	646	B	WEBSTER, DANIEL	263	A
WATER POLLUTION CONTROL ACT OF 1948	596	B	WEDEMEYER, ALBERT COADY	726	B
			WEDNESDAY CLUB	180	A
WATER POWER	288	A	WEEKEND-EVENING	667	B
WATER QUALITY IMPROVEMENT ACT	620	B	WEEKS VS. U.S. (1914)	672	B
WATER RESOURCES	288	A	WEHLER	781	B
WATER RESOURCES AND MANAGEMENT	596	B	WEHRMACHT	170	A
			WEI YUAN	727	B
WATER SUPPLY	596	B	WEIGHTED VOTING	218	A
WATER'S EDGE	620	B	WEIKER, LOWELL PALMER	701	B
WATERGATE	196	A	WEIL, A. M.	781	B
WATERMAN, ZURIEL	780	B	WEIL, E.	781	B
WATERSHED	596	B	WEILENMANN, HERMANN	781	B
WATERSHED ELECTION	260	A	WEIMAR CONSTITUTION	202	A
WATERWAYS	789	B	WEIMAR REPUBLIC	151	A
WATKINS VS. U.S. (1957)	673	B	WEINER, MYRON	781	B
WATKINS, FREDERICK M.	780	B	WEIR, ERNEST T.	781	B
WATKINS, J.W.M.	726	B	WEIZMANN, CHAIM	689	B
WATSON, JAMES	781	B	WELCOME ADDRESS	620	B
WATSON, JOHN B.	781	B	WELDON MANUFACTURING COMPANY	537	B
WATTS, CALIFORNIA	278	A			
WAUCHOPE, SIR ARTHUR	781	B	WELDON, T.D.	781	B
WAVE OF THE FUTURE	841	B	WELENSKY, SIR ROY	701	B
WAVES	512	B	WELFARE	218	A
WAVING THE BLOODY SHIRT	837	B	WELFARE ADMINISTRATION	170	A
WAXFACE	569	B	WELFARE AND PUBLIC ASSISTANCE	233	A
WAXWORKS	829	B	WELFARE BENEFITS	242	A
WAY OF LIFE	144	A	WELFARE CAPITALISM	129	A
WAYS AND MEANS COMMITTEE	146	A	WELFARE FUND	596	B
WAZIR (VIZIER)	561	B	WELFARE LEGISLATION	206	A

WELFARE PROGRAMS IN THE UNITED STATES	211	A	WHALING COMMISSION	478	B
			WHAMPAO ACADEMY	537	B
WELFARE STATE	148	A	WHAT IS TO BE DONE	806	B
WELL-BEING, BODILY	646	B	WHAT'S GOOD FOR GENERAL MOTORS IS GOOD FOR THE COUNTRY	290	A
WELL-BORN, THE	561	B			
WELL-INFORMED SOURCE	191	A			
WELLES, SUMNER	273	A	WHEAT CONVENTION	647	B
WELLS VS. ROCKEFELLER (1969)	676	B	WHEEL HORSE	554	B
WELLS, DAVID A.	781	B	WHEELBARROW GOVERNMENT	537	B
WELLS, HERBERT GEORGE	727	B	WHEELER-LEA ACT OF 1938	647	B
WELS, O.	781	B	WHEELER-RAYBURN ACT	647	B
WELSH LAWS	647	B	WHEELS WITHIN WHEELS	647	B
WELTENSCHAUUNG	129	A	WHIG	151	A
WENG T'UNG-HO	781	B	WHIG PARTY	149	A
WESBERRY VS. SANDERS (1964)	261	A	WHIG THEORY OF GOVERNMENT	135	A
WESLEY, JOHN	689	B	WHIGGISM	129	A
WEST	789	B	WHIP	181	A
WEST AFRICA	279	A	WHIPPING BOY	189	A
WEST BENGAL, INDIA	281	A	WHIPPLE, LEON	781	B
WEST BERLIN	275	A	WHIPSAW	647	B
WEST COAST HOTEL CO. VS. PARRISH (1937)	673	B	WHIRLWIND CAMPAIGN	596	B
			WHISKEY DEMOCRATS	478	B
WEST COUNTRY WRITERS	569	B	WHISKEY INSURRECTION (1794)	251	A
WEST EUROPE	275	A	WHISKEY MEN	512	B
WEST GERMANY	273	A	WHISKEY REBELLION	225	A
WEST INDIES ASSOCIATED STATES	478	B	WHISKY RING	478	B
WEST INDIES, AMERICAN NAVAL STATIONS IN	801	B	WHISPERING CAMPAIGN	620	B
			WHISTLE STOP	792	B
WEST IRIAN CONFLICT	260	A	WHITE	569	B
WEST MIDLANDS, UNITED KINGDOM	801	B	WHITE ARMY	512	B
WEST NEW GUINEA QUESTION	596	B	WHITE BACKLASH	211	A
WEST POINT	165	A	WHITE BOOK	810	B
WEST VIRGINIA STATE BD. OF ED. VS. BARNETTE (1943)	673	B	WHITE CHARLEY	554	B
			WHITE CITIZENS COUNCILS	170	A
WEST WALL	792	B	WHITE COLLAR WORKER	187	A
WEST-AFRICAN MONETARIAN UNION	512	B	WHITE FEATHER PARTY	537	B
WEST-EAST RELATIONS	122	A	WHITE FLAG	819	B
WESTERN	801	B	WHITE HOUSE	286	A
WESTERN ALLIES	157	A	WHITE HOUSE OFFICE	286	A
WESTERN BLOC	157	A	WHITE HOUSE STAFF	154	A
WESTERN CIVILIZATION	129	A	WHITE LEAGUE	512	B
WESTERN ELECTRIC CORPORATION	494	B	WHITE LEGS	537	B
WESTERN EUROPE	274	A	WHITE LINE (LINER)	561	B
WESTERN EUROPEAN UNION (WEU)	165	A	WHITE MAN'S GOVERNMENT	175	A
WESTERN FRONT	279	A	WHITE MAN'S PARTY	478	B
WESTERN HEMISPHERE	276	A	WHITE MAN'S WAR	251	A
WESTERN POWERS	151	A	WHITE MANS BURDEN	289	A
WESTERN RESERVE	792	B	WHITE NECKTIE FACTION	537	B
WESTERN SOCIETY	165	A	WHITE NIGGER	546	B
WESTWARD MOVEMENT	233	A	WHITE PAPER	284	A
WET	494	B	WHITE PHOSPHOROUS MATCH ACT	620	B
WET BLANKET	561	B	WHITE PLAN	667	B
WETBACKS	184	A	WHITE POWER STRUCTURE	161	A
WETLANDS	796	B	WHITE PRIMARY	233	A
WEYL, WALTER E.	781	B	WHITE RUSSIA	275	A
WHALES	821	B	WHITE SLAVE ACT	260	A

WHITE SUPREMACY	202	A	WILL AND CAPACITY	454	B
WHITE TILE PARTY	537	B	WILL FOR PEACE	448	B
WHITE, BYRON	268	A	WILLARD, FRANCES ELIZABETH	782	B
WHITE, EDWARD DOUGLASS	781	B	WILLIAM III OF ENGLAND	727	B
WHITE, HOWARD B.	781	B	WILLIAM OF MOERBEKE	782	B
WHITE, LEONARD D.	701	B	WILLIAM OF OCCAM	701	B
WHITE, ROBERT	781	B	WILLIAM OF ORANGE, PRINCE	268	A
WHITE, WALTER FRANCIS	781	B	WILLIAM OF SHERWOOD	782	B
WHITE, WILLIAM ALANSON	727	B	WILLIAM THE CONQUEROR	266	A
WHITE, WILLIAM ALLEN	727	B	WILLIAMS VS. NORTH CAROLINA	680	B
WHITEHALL	789	B	(1945)		
WHITEHEAD, PROF. A. N.	271	A	WILLIAMS, H. MURRAY	782	B
WHITEHEAD, SIR EDGAR	727	B	WILLIAMS, HARRISON ARLINGTON,	782	B
WHITEHILL VS. ELKINS (1967)	676	B	JR.		
WHITEWASH	260	A	WILLIAMS, J.D.	782	B
WHITEY	194	A	WILLIAMS, ROGER	273	A
WHITING, ALLEN S.	727	B	WILLIAMS, RT. HON. DR. ERIC	782	B
WHITING, JOHN W. M.	781	B	EUSTACE		
WHITLAM, EDWARD GOUGH	781	B	WILLING	461	B
WHITLEY COUNCILS	478	B	WILLKIE, WENDELL L.	273	A
WHITLOCK, BRAND	781	B	WILLOUGHBY, W. W.	782	B
WHITMAN, WALT	689	B	WILLOUGHBY, WILLIAM F.	782	B
WHITNEY VS. CALIFORNIA (1927)	680	B	WILMOT PROVISO	596	B
WHITNEY, L. F.	781	B	WILOPO (INDONESIA)	537	B
WHIZ KIDS	554	B	WILSON LINE	667	B
WHO GETS WHAT, WHEN, AND HOW	290	A	WILSON-GORMAN TARIFF	620	B
WHO'S POLK	847	B	WILSON, FRANCIS G.	782	B
WHO'S WHO BALLOT	667	B	WILSON, H. H.	727	B
WHOLE HOG, TO GO THE	847	B	WILSON, HAROLD W.	266	A
WHOLESALE MEAT ACT	667	B	WILSON, JAMES HAROLD	727	B
WHOLESALE PRICE INDEX	138	A	WILSON, PRESIDENT WOODROW	262	A
WHORF HYPOTHESIS	454	B	WILSON, ROLAND K.	782	B
WHYTE, W. F.	727	B	WILSON, WOODROW, ON	284	A
WICKARD VS. FILBURN (1942)	672	B	CONGRESS		
WICKERSHAM COMMISSION	494	B	WILSONIAN DEMOCRACY	129	A
WICKSELL, KNUT	781	B	WILT, DANIEL	782	B
WICKWAR, W. HARDY	781	B	WILTSE, CHARLES M.	782	B
WIDE AWAKE	512	B	WIN	620	B
WIDOWS, ANGLO-SAXON	569	B	WINCH, PETER	782	B
WIELDERS	569	B	WINCH, ROBERT F.	782	B
WIEMAN VS. UPDEGRAFF (1952)	680	B	WINDHAM, WILLIAM	782	B
WIENER, NORBERT	266	A	WINDS OF CHANGE	286	A
WIGGAM, ALBERT E.	782	B	WINDSOR, DUKE OF	194	A
WIGWAM	824	B	WINDYPENDENT	537	B
WILBERFORCE	782	B	WING	494	B
WILD-EYED	647	B	WING, CLIFF W.	782	B
WILDCAT BANKS	494	B	WINNERS	561	B
WILDCAT STRIKE	233	A	WINSLOW, E M	782	B
WILDE, NORMAN	782	B	WINSTANLEY, GERRARD	782	B
WILDERNESS ACT	260	A	WINTHROP, JOHN	727	B
WILDMAN, J.	782	B	WIRE WORKER	569	B
WILEY, J.W.	782	B	WIRE-PULLER	554	B
WILHELM II	273	A	WIRETAP COMMISSION	494	B
WILHELMSTRASSE	796	B	WIRETAPPING	218	A
WILKES	727	B	WISCONSIN	279	A
WILL	440	B	WISCONSIN IDEA	647	B

WISCONSIN RATE CASE	673	B	WOOLLY WHIG	537	B
WISDOM	144	A	WOOLSEY, THEODORE DWIGHT	783	B
WISE, JOHN	782	B	WORDS	448	B
WISKINSKI	569	B	WORDSWORTH, WILLIAM	783	B
WISSLER, CLARK	782	B	WORK	620	B
WITCH HUNT	260	A	WORK GROUPS	512	B
WITCHCRAFT	454	B	WORK PROJECTS ADMINISTRATION	165	A
WITENAGEMOT	512	B	(WPA)		
WITH ALL DELIBERATE SPEED	218	A	WORK RELIEF	251	A
WITHDRAWAL	596	B	WORK STUDY PROGRAMS	596	B
WITHDRAWAL (INTERNATIONAL	596	B	WORKER CONTROL	260	A
ORGANIZATION)			WORKERS	194	A
WITHERING AWAY OF THE STATE	197	A	WORKERS ORGANIZATION	494	B
WITHERS, HARLEY	782	B	WORKERS PARTICIPATION	260	A
WITHHOLDING TAX	225	A	WORKERS PARTY	494	B
WITHINPUTS	218	A	WORKERS PARTY OF AMERICA	478	B
WITNESS	194	A	WORKERS' EDUCATIONAL	537	B
WITTE, SERGEI YULIEVICH	727	B	ASSOCIATION (BRITAIN)		
WITTELSBACH	783	B	WORKHOUSE	792	B
WITTGENSTEIN, LUDWIG JOSEF	266	A	WORKIES	569	B
JOHANN			WORKING CLASS	154	A
WIZARD OF KINDERHOOK	727	B	WORKING CONDITIONS	260	A
WOEFF	783	B	WORKING LANGUAGE	808	B
WOHLSTETTER, ROBERTA	783	B	WORKING LUNCHEON	667	B
WOLCOTT, LEON	783	B	WORKING MEETING	620	B
WOLF VS. COLORADO (1949)	680	B	WORKING PAPER	285	A
WOLF, A.	783	B	WORKING PARTY	512	B
WOLFF, ROBERT PAUL	783	B	WORKING PARTY ON THE CHEMICAL	537	B
WOLIN, SHELDON S.	689	B	INDUSTRY		
WOLTMANN, LUDWIG	727	B	WORKING SESSION	596	B
WOMAN	561	B	WORKINGMEN'S PARTY	180	A
WOMEN	554	B	WORKMEN, COMPENSATION	225	A
WOMEN IN POLITICS	182	A	WORKMENS COMPENSATION	478	B
WOMEN, EQUALITY OF	199	A	COMMISSION		
WOMEN'S AIR FORCE (WAFS)	180	A	WORKS PROGRESS	175	A
WOMEN'S ARMY CORPS (WACS)	180	A	ADMINISTRATION (WPA)		
WOMEN'S BUREAU	478	B	WORLD	283	A
WOMEN'S LIBERATION MOVEMENT	148	A	WORLD ALLIANCE OF YMCA	538	B
WOMEN'S RIGHTS	225	A	WORLD ASSEMBLY	478	B
WOMEN'S SUFFRAGE, NINETEENTH	202	A	WORLD ASSOCIATION OF WORLD	170	A
AMENDMENT			FEDERALISTS		
WOOD PRODUCTS LABELING ACT	647	B	WORLD BANK	151	A
OF 1939			WORLD BANK AND INTERNATIONAL	154	A
WOODBINE, PROF.	783	B	MONETARY FUND		
WOODBURY, COLEMAN	783	B	WORLD BANK GROUP (IRBD,IDA,IFC)	170	A
WOODCOCK, GEORGE	727	B	WORLD COMMUNISM	118	A
WOODPECKER TICKET	537	B	WORLD COMMUNITY	149	A
WOODROW WILSON INTERNATIONAL	537	B	WORLD CONFEDERATION OF	170	A
CENTER FOR SCHOLARS			LABOUR		
WOODSON, CARTER G.	783	B	WORLD CONGRESS OF FAITHS	538	B
WOODWORTH, ROBERT S.	783	B	(WCF)		
WOOL HAT	512	B	WORLD COUNCIL OF CHURCHES	165	A
WOOLEY, SIR LEONARD	783	B	(WCC)		
WOOLF, LEONARD	783	B	WORLD COUNCIL OF PEACE	512	B
WOOLLY HEADS	512	B	WORLD COURT (INTERNATIONAL	154	A
WOOLLY HORSE	848	B	COURT OF JUSTICE)		

WORLD DATA	141	A	WRETCHED	570	B
WORLD DEPRESSION	218	A	WRIGHT, BENJAMIN F.	783	B
WORLD DISARMAMENT CONFERENCE	211	A	WRIGHT, HENRY W.	783	B
			WRIGHT, QUINCY	268	A
WORLD DOMINATION	233	A	WRISTON COMMISSION	513	B
WORLD ECONOMIC CONFERENCE	260	A	WRIT	211	A
WORLD ECONOMIC SURVEY	260	A	WRIT OF ASSISTANCE	285	A
WORLD FEDERAL REPUBLIC	478	B	WRIT OF CERTIORARI	199	A
WORLD FEDERALISM	122	A	WRIT OF ERROR	242	A
WORLD FEDERATION FOR PROTECTION OF ANIMALS (WFPA)	538	B	WRIT OF EXECUTION	596	B
			WRIT OF HABEAS CORPUS	195	A
WORLD FEDERATION OF TRADE UNIONS (WFTU)	161	A	WRIT OF MANDAMUS	202	A
			WRIT OF PROHIBITION	621	B
WORLD FESTIVAL OF YOUTH	667	B	WRIT OF QUO WARRANTO	242	A
WORLD FOOD PROGRAM	251	A	WRITE-IN	218	A
WORLD GOVERNMENT	149	A	WRITE-IN CANDIDATES	183	A
WORLD HEALTH ASSEMBLY	538	B	WRITTEN CONSTITUTION	199	A
WORLD HEALTH ORGANIZATION (WHO)	161	A	WRONG	260	A
			WRONG WAR	667	B
WORLD JEWISH CONGRESS	478	B	WYCLIFFE, JOHN	689	B
WORLD LIBERAL UNION	494	B	WYLIE, LAURENCE	783	B
WORLD METEOROLOGICAL ASSOCIATION	512	B	WYNCH, PETER	783	B
WORLD METEOROLOGICAL CONGRESS	647	B	WYSZYNSKI, CARDINAL STEFAN	701	B
			X-Y-Z AFFAIR	596	B
WORLD METEOROLOGICAL ORGANIZATION (WMO)	494	B	XENOPHOBIA	132	A
			XENOPHON	701	B
WORLD MUSLIM CONGRESS	494	B	XERXES	727	B
WORLD OPINION	132	A	XYZ PAPERS	285	A
WORLD ORDER	154	A	YAGODA, HENRIKH GRIGOREVICH	783	B
WORLD ORGANIZATION	151	A	YAHWEH	461	B
WORLD PARLIAMENT ASSOCIATION	180	A	YAKHIMOVICH, IVAN	783	B
WORLD PEACE COUNCIL	478	B	YAKO (WEST AFRICA)	538	B
WORLD PEACE FOUNDATION	494	B	YALE ECONOMIC GROWTH CENTER	494	B
WORLD POPULATION, UNITED NATIONS CONFERENCE	242	A	YALE INSTITUTE OF INTERNATIONAL RELATIONS	513	B
			YALE POLICY SCIENCE PROGRAMME	538	B
WORLD POWER	157	A	YALTA	276	A
WORLD REFUGEE YEAR	647	B	YALTA AGREEMENTS	218	A
WORLD REVOLUTION (TROTSKYISM)	124	A	YALTA CONFERENCE	206	A
WORLD STATE	161	A	YAMAN	801	B
WORLD TOMORROW	806	B	YANKEE	194	A
WORLD UNITY	233	A	YANKEE IMPERIALISM	132	A
WORLD VETERANS FEDERATION	512	B	YARDSTICK	647	B
WORLD VIEW	129	A	YARMOLINSKY, ADAM	727	B
WORLD WAR I	202	A	YATES VS. U.S. (1957)	261	A
WORLD WAR II	197	A	YAWS	829	B
WORLD WAR III	233	A	YAZOO LAND FRAUD	647	B
WORLD WEATHER WATCH	512	B	YEARBOOK	813	B
WORLD-CITY	796	B	YEARBOOK OF THE UNITED NATIONS	284	A
WORLD-ISLAND	283	A			
WORLD-WIDE ORGANIZATION	478	B	YEAS AND NAYS	251	A
WORNS, RENE	783	B	YELLOW BOOK	813	B
WOROSZYLSKI	783	B	YELLOW DOG CONTRACT	242	A
WRANGEL, BARON PETER N.	783	B	YELLOW DOG DEMOCRAT	561	B
WREATH	829	B	YELLOW FEVER	824	B
WRECKER	561	B	YELLOW JOURNALISM	225	A

YELLOW PERIL	157	A
YELLOW-SEAL DOLLAR	667	B
YELLOWSTONE RIVER COMPACT	667	B
YEMEN	278	A
YEMENITE	494	B
YEN-FOU	783	B
YENAN	283	A
YEOMANRY	513	B
YERKES, R. M.	783	B
YES MAN	191	A
YES, BUT	841	B
YEZHOVSHCHINA	647	B
YIELD	647	B
YISHUV	538	B
YOAKUM, C. S.	783	B
YOGA	667	B
YOGAKUSHAS	538	B
YORK TRACTS	813	B
YORUBA	796	B
YOSHIDA, SHIGERU	701	B
YOU CAN'T BEAT SOMEBODY WITH NOBODY	837	B
YOU CAN'T FIGHT CITY HALL	290	A
YOU NEVER HAD IT SO GOOD	842	B
YOUNG AMERICA	494	B
YOUNG CHINA PARTY	478	B
YOUNG CHRISTIAN WORKERS (YCW)	513	B
YOUNG COMMUNIST LEAGUE, SOVIET UNION	158	A
YOUNG DEMOCRAT	170	A
YOUNG HICKORY	727	B
YOUNG INDIANS	513	B
YOUNG MEN'S CONVENTION	667	B
YOUNG MENS CHRISTIAN ASSOCIATION (YMCA)	478	B
YOUNG OFFICERS	554	B
YOUNG PIONEERS, CHINA (PRC)	175	A
YOUNG PLAN	621	B
YOUNG REPUBLICAN	165	A
YOUNG SCRATCHER	570	B
YOUNG TURKS	184	A
YOUNG, G. M.	783	B
YOUNG, MILTON R.	727	B
YOUNG, ORAN	784	B
YOUNG, ROLAND	784	B
YOUNGSTOWN SHEET AND TUBE CO. VS. SAWYER (1952)	261	A
YOUTH	191	A
YOUTH AND POLITICS	189	A
YOUTH CORPS	175	A
YOUTH GROUPS	175	A
YOUTH INTERNATIONAL PARTY (YIPPIES)	175	A
YOUTH LEAGUE, CHINA (PRC)	180	A
YOUTH MEETING	667	B
YOUTH ORGANIZATIONS	170	A
YRIGOYEN	784	B
YU-SHIH-CHENG	784	B
YUAN (CHINESE ADMINISTRATIVE DIVISION)	513	B
YUAN SHIH-KAI	784	B
YUGOSLAVIA	276	A
YUGOSLAVIANS	513	B
YUGOV, A.	784	B
YVETOT	784	B
YZEHOV, N. I.	784	B
ZABARELLA, FRANCISCO	784	B
ZAFRULLAH KHAN, CHAUDHRI MOHAMMED	784	B
ZAGREUS	784	B
ZAIBATSU	180	A
ZAIDAN, JURJI	784	B
ZAIRE	276	A
ZAISSER, WILHELM	784	B
ZAMBIA	276	A
ZANDE	801	B
ZANDER, A.	784	B
ZANU MOVEMENT	494	B
ZANZIBAR	278	A
ZANZIBAR-TANGANYIKA	276	A
ZAPATA, EMILIANO	266	A
ZAPOTOCKY, A.	784	B
ZAPU MOVEMENT	538	B
ZASULICH, VERA	784	B
ZEAL	461	B
ZEELAND, PAULL VAN	727	B
ZEIGLER, HARMON	727	B
ZEIS, PAUL M.	784	B
ZEITSCHRIFT FUR OFFENTLICHES RECHT	813	B
ZELLER, EDUARD	784	B
ZEMEL VS. RUSK (1965)	677	B
ZEMLYA I VOLYA (LAND AND FREEDOM)	835	B
ZEN-BUDDHISM	135	A
ZENGAKUREN	180	A
ZENO OF CITIUM	701	B
ZENRO KAIGI (ZEN NIHON RODO KIMIAI KAIGI)	538	B
ZENTRUM	494	B
ZERO-SUM GAMES	118	A
ZETKIN, CLARA	727	B
ZHDANOV, ANDREI	727	B
ZHIVKOV, T.	784	B
ZHUKOV, GEORGI	271	A
ZIBLATT, DAVID	784	B
ZIMAND	784	B
ZIMMERMAN NOTE	286	A
ZIMMERN, A. E.	784	B
ZINGER	848	B
ZINOVIEFF LETTER	808	B
ZINOVIEV, GRIGORI EVSEYEVICH	701	B

LIBRARY OF DAVIDSON COLLEGE

Books on regular loan may be checked out for **two weeks.** Books must be presented at the Circulation Desk in order to be renewed.

A fine is charged after date due.

Special books are subject to special regulations at the discretion of the library staff.

Goldman   320.014
AUTHOR   G619p
The political science concept
TITLE
            inventory

Goldman   320.014
                                   G619p
The political science concept
            inventory

Microfiches containing 10,000 Secondary Concepts and Terms are in the envelope on the opposite page.